MW00999950

QUICKBOOKS® 2015: A COMPLETE COURSE

QUICKBOOKS 2015: A COMPLETE COURSE

Janet Horne, M.S.
Los Angeles Pierce College

PEARSON

Boston Columbus Indianapolis New York San Francisco
Amsterdam Cape Town Dubai London Madrid Milan Munich Paris Montreal Toronto
Delhi Mexico City Sao Paulo Sydney Hong Kong Seoul Singapore Taipei Tokyo

Vice President, Business Publishing: Donna Battista
Acquisitions Editor: Ellen Geary
Editorial Project Manager: Melissa Pellerano
Editorial Assistant: Christine Donovan
Vice President, Product Marketing: Maggie Moylan
Senior Product Marketing Manager: Alison Haskins
Executive Field Marketing Manager: Lori DeShazo
Senior Strategic Marketing Manager: Erin Gardner
Team Lead, Program Management: Ashley Santora
Program Manager: Daniel Edward Petrino
Team Lead, Project Management: Jeff Holcomb
Project Manager: Karen Carter
Operations Specialist: Carol Melville
Full-Service Project Management and Composition: Integra Software Services Pvt. Ltd.
Cover Designer: Liz Harasymczuk Design
Cover Art:SeanPavonePhoto/Fotolia
Printer/Binder: LSC Communications/Menasha
Cover Printer: Phoenix Color/Hagerstown

Library of Congress Cataloging-in-Publication Data

Horne, Janet.
Quickbooks 2015 : a complete course / Janet Horne.
pages cm
Includes index.
ISBN 978-0-13-413010-1
1. QuickBooks. 2. Small business--Accounting--Computer programs. 3. Small business--Finance--Computer programs. I. Title.
HF5679.H66383 2016
657'.9042028553--dc23

2015003916

5 16

PEARSON

ISBN 10: 0-13-413010-3
ISBN 13: 978-0-13-413010-1

To my family

BRIEF TABLE OF CONTENTS

TABLE OF CONTENTS

Chapter 2—Sales and Receivables: Service Business

Chapter 3—Payables and Purchases: Service Business

Chapter 4—General Accounting and End-of-Period Procedures: Service Business

Appendix B: QuickBooks Features

Appendix C: QuickBooks Online Features

PREFACE

QuickBooks 2015: A Complete Course is a comprehensive instructional learning resource. The text provides training using the *QuickBooks Premier Accountant 2015* accounting program (for simplicity, the program is referred to as *QuickBooks 2015* throughout the text). Even though the text was written using the 2015 Accountant version of QuickBooks Premier, it may be used with the Pro version of the program as well. (Because of the many differences between the Windows and Mac versions of QuickBooks, this text should not be used for training using QuickBooks for the Mac.)

WHAT'S NEW TO THIS EDITION

Each version of QuickBooks comes with changes, enhancements, and new features. Many of these changes are incorporated into the text; while others may or may not be mentioned. Some of the features are only available on a subscription basis. Since the companies in the text are fictitious, the dates used are not current, and the subscriptions are not free, these features are not explored in the greatest detail.

Some of the new features of QuickBooks and changes in the 2015 text include:

- Use an Access Code Card and instructions for downloading QuickBooks 2015 Educational Trial Version of the program
- QuickBooks onscreen report formatting has been changed to show details more clearly
- Create Custom Reports
- Memorize and use Custom Reports
- Explore and use Commented Reports feature
- Add Logos to company files
- Portable company files
- Insights tab for Home Page
- Customize Payment Methods List
- Statement Writer
- Password Vault
- Add Credit Card information for individual customers
- Select Preferred Delivery and Payment Methods for customers
- Add additional information to Employees including:
    - Marital Status
    - U.S. Citizen
    - Ethnicity
    - Disability
- New Business Checklist
- File Manager
- Send and Import General Journal Entries

DISTINGUISHING FEATURES

Throughout the text, emphasis has been placed on the use of QuickBooks' innovative approach to recording accounting transactions based on a business form rather than using the traditional journal format. This approach, however, has been correlated to traditional accounting through adjusting entries, end-of-period procedures, and use of the "behind the scenes" journal. The text uses a tutorial-style training method to guide the students in the use of QuickBooks in a step-by-step manner and is designed to help students transition from training to using *QuickBooks 2015* in an actual business.

The text provides:

- Comprehensive exploration of QuickBooks
- Reinforcement of accounting concepts
- Exploration of error correction and resulting ramifications
- Introduction to and use of many QuickBooks features
- Experience in recording transactions for service and merchandising businesses
- Transactions ranging from simple to complex that simulate real-world occurrences
- Use of Manual Payroll and comparison of Payroll Subscriptions
- Creation of companies for use in QuickBooks
- Printing of business forms and reports
- Opportunity to learn how to customize QuickBooks:
  - Forms
  - Preferences
  - Reports
- Screen shots used liberally to show:
  - QuickBooks screens
  - Completed transactions
  - Reports
- Extensive assignment material including:
  - Tutorials
  - End-of-chapter questions (true/false, multiple-choice, fill-in, and essay)
  - End-of-chapter reinforcement problem
  - Practice sets

ORGANIZATIONAL FEATURES

QuickBooks 2015: A Complete Course is designed to present accounting concepts and their relationship to *QuickBooks 2015*. While completing each chapter, students:

- Learn underlying accounting concepts
- Receive hands-on training using QuickBooks 2015
- Analyze and record transactions for service and merchandising businesses

Text Organization

- Section 1: Accounting for a Service Business
- Section 2: Accounting for a Merchandising Business
- Section 3: Payroll and Creating a Company

- Practice Sets for Sections 1 and 2
- Comprehensive Practice Set for the entire text
- Three Appendices:
  - QuickBooks Program Integration
  - QuickBooks Features (not covered in chapters)
  - QuickBooks Online Features

Chapter Organization

- A single company is used within the chapters for a full business cycle
- A second company is used for the end of each chapter problem for a full business cycle
- At the end of every chapter, the concepts and applications learned are reinforced by completing:
  - True/False questions
  - Multiple-Choice questions
  - Fill-in questions
  - Essay questions

COURSES

QuickBooks 2015: A Complete Course is designed for a one-term course in microcomputer accounting. This text covers using QuickBooks in a service business, a merchandising business, a sole proprietorship, and a partnership. Preparing payroll and creating a new company are also included. When using the text, students should be familiar with the accounting cycle and how it is related to a business. No prior knowledge of or experience with computers, Windows, or QuickBooks is required; however, an understanding of accounting is essential to successful completion of the coursework.

SUPPLEMENTS FOR THE INSTRUCTOR

Pearson Education maintains a Web site where student and instructor materials may be downloaded for classroom use at www.pearsonhighered.com/horne. The ***Instructor's Resource Center*** contains the following:

- Data & Solution Files that include:
  - Backup company files for each chapter that may be restored to a QuickBooks company file (These will be downloaded in several batches)
  - Master data files for all the companies in the text
    - These are the same as the Student company files and will be downloaded in two groups: Chapters 1-4 and Chapters 5-8
    - Logos for Chapter 9 and the Comprehensive Practice set are included with the Company Files for Chapters 5-8
- Instructor's Resource Manual (IM) materials include:
  - An online appendix with instructions to install and register QuickBooks, download company files, open a company file, backup company files, and restore company files
  - Answers to the end-of-chapter questions
  - Excel files containing all the reports prepared in the text

- Lectures for each chapter designed for a hands-on demonstration lecture
- Instructor's Manual Materials, which include:
  - Assignment Sheets for full- and short-term courses
  - IM Preface for instructors
  - IM Table of Contents listing all the files available for download
  - Teaching suggestions
- Transmittal sheets that include the totals of reports and documents
- Textbook errata, which is posted as errors are discovered

- PowerPoint Presentation containing lectures with notes for each chapter in the text and a separate lecture for installing and registering the QuickBooks Trial Version
- Instructor's Solutions Manual containing Adobe .pdf files for all the printouts prepared in the text (In the chapters of the text, some reports are shown in a partial display due to space limitations. The full copies of the printed reports are included in this folder. While instructors may customize the printing required by students, everything that students are asked to print within the text is included in this folder.)
- Test Bank containing four folders:
  - Written Exams containing exams and keys for each area of study and a written final exam
  - Folder for each practice set that contains a computer exam and an answer key for the practice set exam

> If you need assistance with QuickBooks, go to www.QuickBooks.Com/Support and click on one of the Resource Centers for help. The Resource Centers include: Install Center, Download & Updates, Support Tools, and others. For specific information when installing the trial version of the software, please go to the Intuit Install Center at: http://support.quickbooks.intuit.com/Support/InstallCenter/default.aspx

ERRATA AND INSTRUCTOR COMMENTS

While I strive to write an error-free textbook, it is inevitable that some errors will occur. As I become aware of any errors, they will be added to an errata sheet that is posted in the Instructor's Resource Center on the Pearson Web site at **www.pearsonhighered.com/horne**. Once an errata is posted, instructors should feel free to share that information with their students and to check back periodically to see if any new items have been added. If you or your students discover an error, or have suggestions and/or concerns, I would appreciate it if you would contact me and let me know what they are. My email address for instructors is also shown in the Instructor's Resource Center.

ACKNOWLEDGMENTS

I wish to thank my colleagues for testing and reviewing the manuscript, the professors who use the text and share their thoughts and suggestions with me, and my students for providing me with a special insight into problems encountered in training. All of your comments and suggestions are greatly appreciated. A special thank you goes to Cheryl Bartlett for her proofreading and comments. In addition, I would like to thank Donna Battista, Ellen Geary, Daniel Edward Petrino, Melissa Pellerano, Karen Carter, and the production team at Pearson Education for their editorial support and assistance.

INTRODUCTION TO QUICKBOOKS 2015 AND COMPANY FILES

1

LEARNING OBJECTIVES

At the completion of this chapter, you will be able to:

1. Identify QuickBooks desktop features, be familiar with the QuickBooks Centers, and understand the QuickBooks Home Page.
2. Recognize menu commands and use some keyboard shortcuts.
3. Recognize QuickBooks forms and understand the use of lists and registers in QuickBooks.
4. Access QuickBooks' reports.
5. Open and close QuickBooks.
6. Copy a company file and open a company.
7. Add your name to a company name.
8. Learn how to use QuickZoom.
9. Prepare QuickBooks graphs and use QuickReport within graphs.
10. Use QuickMath and the Windows Calculator.
11. Download a company file.
12. Back up a company.
13. Restore a company from a backup file.
14. Close a company.

MANUAL AND COMPUTERIZED ACCOUNTING

The work performed to keep the books for a business is the same whether you use a manual or a computerized accounting system. Transactions need to be analyzed, recorded in a journal, and posted to a ledger. Business documents such as invoices, checks, bank deposits, and credit/debit memos need to be prepared and distributed. Reports to management and owners for information and decision-making purposes need to be prepared. Records for one business period need to be closed before recording transactions for the next business period.

In a manual system, each transaction that is analyzed must be entered by hand into the appropriate journal (the book of original entry where all transactions are recorded) and posted to the appropriate ledger (the book of final entry that contains records for all of the accounts used in the business). A separate business document such as an invoice or a check must be prepared and distributed. In order to prepare a report, the accountant or bookkeeper must go through the journal or ledger and look for the appropriate amounts to include in the report. Closing the books must be done item by item via closing entries, which are recorded in the journal and posted to the appropriate ledger accounts. After the closing entries are recorded, the ledger accounts must be ruled and balance sheet accounts must be reopened with Brought Forward Balances being entered.

When using a computerized system and a program such as QuickBooks, the transactions must still be analyzed and recorded. QuickBooks operates from a business document point of view. As a transaction occurs, the necessary business document (an invoice or a check, for example) is prepared. Based on the information given on the business document, QuickBooks records the necessary debits and credits behind the scenes in the Journal. If an error is made when entering a transaction, QuickBooks allows the user to return to the business document and make the correction. QuickBooks will automatically record the changes in the debits and credits in the Journal. If you want to see or make a correction using the actual debit/credit entries, QuickBooks allows you to view the transaction register and make corrections directly in the register or use the traditional General Journal. Reports and graphs are prepared by simply clicking "Report" on the menu bar.

VERSIONS OF QUICKBOOKS

While this text focuses on training using QuickBooks Accountant Desktop 2015 (for simplicity in the text, the program is referred to as QuickBooks 2015). QuickBooks Accountant is part of the Premier version of the program. In QuickBooks Premier, you may toggle to QuickBooks Pro, Accountant, General Business, Contractor, Manufacturing & Wholesale, Nonprofit, Professional Services, and Retail. The Accountant version used in the text offers some additional enhancements not available in the Pro version, but the basics are the same.

In addition to QuickBooks Premier, there is also QuickBooks Enterprise, which is designed for larger businesses that want a great deal of customization and have more complex accounting requirements. At the time of writing, QuickBooks Enterprise has three different subscription plans beginning with Silver, and then upgrading to Gold, and finally Platinum. Pricing is set based on the number of users—from one to thirty—and the subscription level.

There are several Online Editions of QuickBooks: However, the functions available are limited and many features of QuickBooks cannot be utilized. For Small Businesses there is Simple Start, Online Essentials, and Online Plus. For Accountants there is Online Accountant. All of the online editions are sold on a monthly subscription basis. There are also QuickBooks Apps available for iPhone, iPad, Mac, and Android.

There is a QuickBooks program for Macs with many of the same functions as QuickBooks for Windows. (Because of the many differences between the Windows and Mac versions of QuickBooks, this text should not be used for training using QuickBooks for the Mac.)

For a comparison of features available among the different versions of the QuickBooks programs, access Intuit's Web site at www.quickbooks.intuit.com.

WINDOWS

All computers use an operating system in conjunction with the software applications. Windows 7 is the operating system used in the text. Various screen shots will show procedures using Windows 7.

BEGIN COMPUTER TRAINING

When you see this arrow, it means you will be performing a computer task. Sometimes the computer task will have several steps. Continue until all steps listed are completed.

INSTALL QUICKBOOKS TRIAL VERSION (OPTIONAL)

If you use your school's computers to complete the training in the text, you may omit this step. However, if you purchased a textbook that contains the trial version of QuickBooks 2015 (an Access Code Card for downloading), you may install the software on your home computer. Since the Trial Version is not for use on a school's computers, your school should have a site license for QuickBooks for classroom use.

If you already have any version of QuickBooks 2015 on your home computer, you may not install the Trial Version for 2015. For example, if you have QuickBooks Pro 2015, you may not install the Trial Version of QuickBooks Accountant 2015 on the same computer. Installing QuickBooks 2015 has no effect on earlier versions of QuickBooks.

The free trial of the QuickBooks 2015 program may be installed on your computer and used for 30 days. However, you must register it within 30 days of installation. When you register the program, your trial period will be extended.

If you run into difficulties with the installation, go to the Intuit Install Center at http://support.quickbooks.intuit.com/Support/InstallCenter/InstallCenter.aspx or www.quickbooks.com/support to find help on how to install QuickBooks.

Depending on your version of windows, your storage location, your Internet security system, and a variety of other variables, your screens may not always match those shown in the text. If you find differences and are not sure if you are proceeding correctly, check with your instructor or go to the Intuit Install Center.

You will install the Trial Version from an Access Code Card that comes with the book. The Access Card enables you to download the Trial Version from http://quickbooks.com/download. Follow the instructions provided for the installation.

Install the Trial Version of QuickBooks 2015 by downloading the program

Open your Internet browser (The text uses Internet Explorer 11)
Use the information provided on your Access Code Card (A sample is shown below)

- The steps for downloading, installing, and registering the software are provided as you work through the chapter. Do not install or register without following the step-by-step instructions provided.

SAMPLE ACCESS CODE CARD

To download go to http://quickbooks.com/download .
Click QuickBooks Accountant 2015.
During the installation, you will be asked to enter the license and product numbers. Use:
License: xxxx-xxxx-xxxx-xxx Product Code: xxx-xxx
When the installation is complete, register the program following the on-screen prompts.

Click **http://quickbooks.com/download**

- If you get a message to complete a survey, click the **No Thanks** button

Click **QuickBooks Accountant 2015** on the Download QuickBooks screen

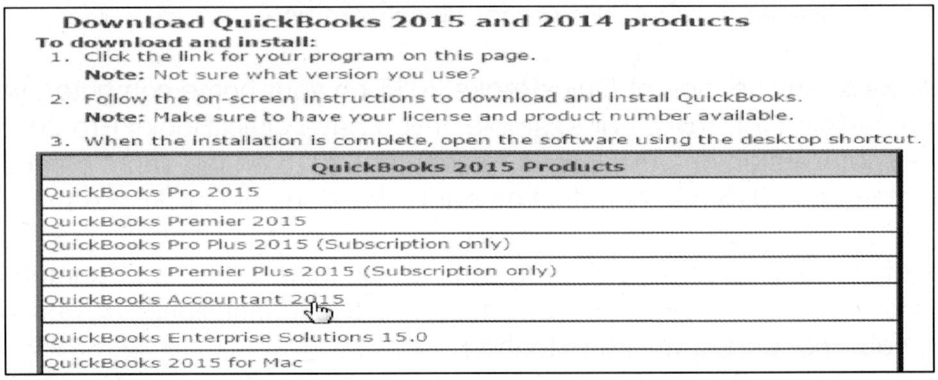

Click **Run**

- You will see a screen for Intuit Download Manager. Just wait while it downloads.

Click **Next** on QuickBooks Financial Software 2015 R5 – InstallShield Wizard

- The R5 may not be the number you see as it changes with QuickBooks updates.
- You may see a screen or two briefly on the screen.
- If you get a message asking if you want to make changes to your computer, click **Yes**.

You should see the QuickBooks 2015 screen briefly

- As QuickBooks is updated by Intuit, the screens you see may change. If they do, simply follow the prompts given by QuickBooks to complete the installation.

- You may see QuickBooks Premier 2015 rather than Accountant. Either screen is fine.
- After the QuickBooks screen, you will see several screens titled Intuit QuickBooks Installer as you complete the program installation.

The first screen shows Welcome to QuickBooks

Click **Next**

Scroll through and read the License Agreement. After reading, click the checkbox for **"I accept the terms of the license agreement"**

Click **Next**

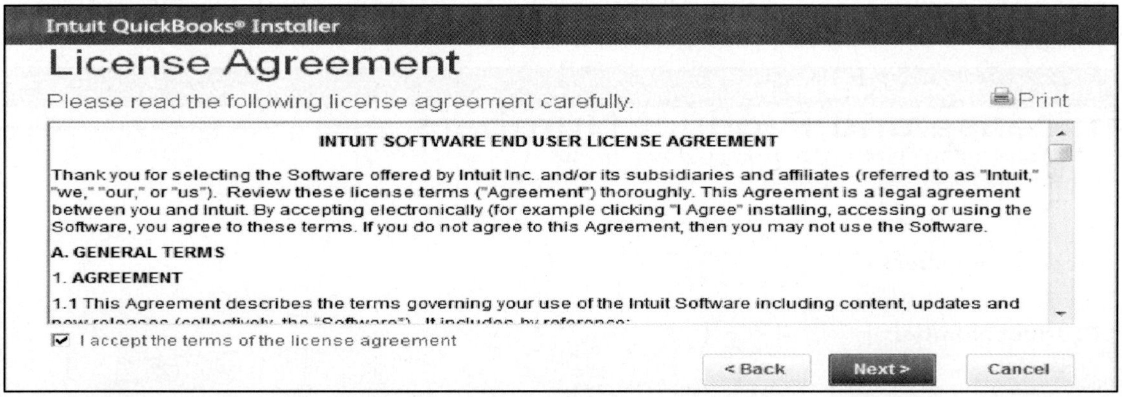

Use the **Custom and Network options** for the installation type; and then, click **Next**

- If you do not have another version of QuickBooks on your computer and do not care where the program is stored, you may use the Express installation type.

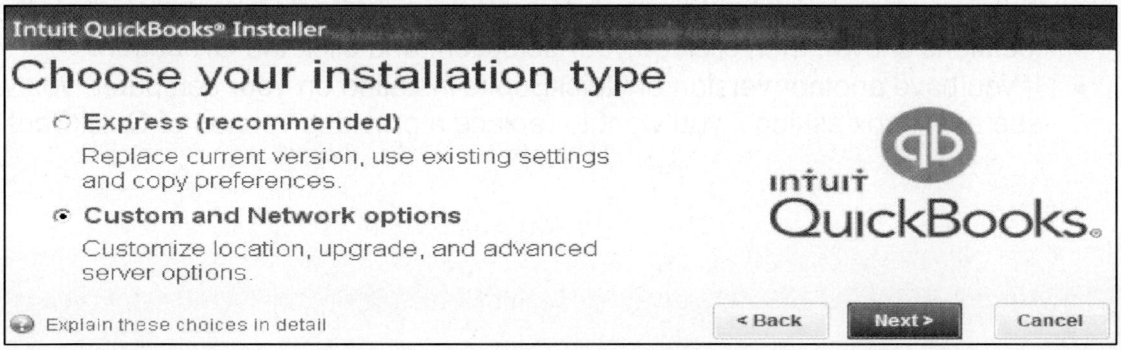

Unless your instructor tells you to select a different answer, click **I'll be using QuickBooks on this computer**; then click **Next**

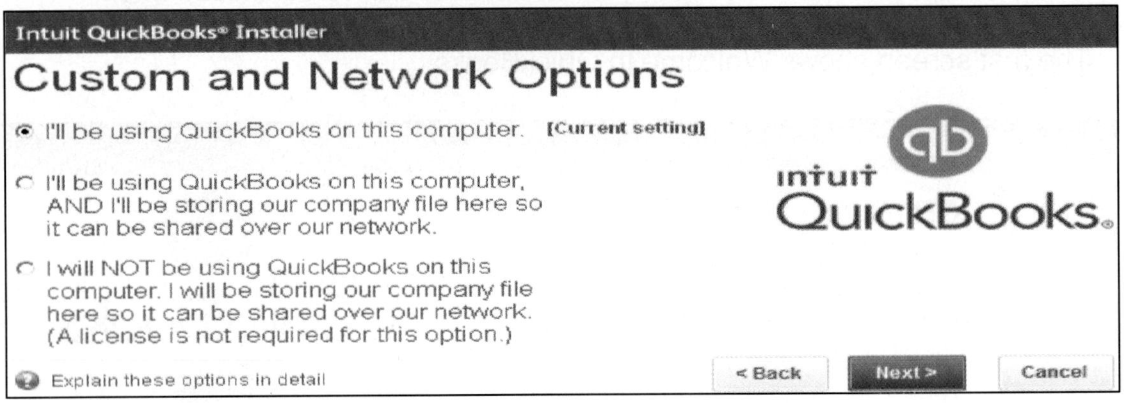

Enter the **License Number** and **Product Number** that appear on the Access Code Card

- You will not need to enter any hyphens or tab between sections. QuickBooks automatically jumps from the License Number to the Product Number as well.
- No license or product numbers are shown below because each copy of the software has a unique number.

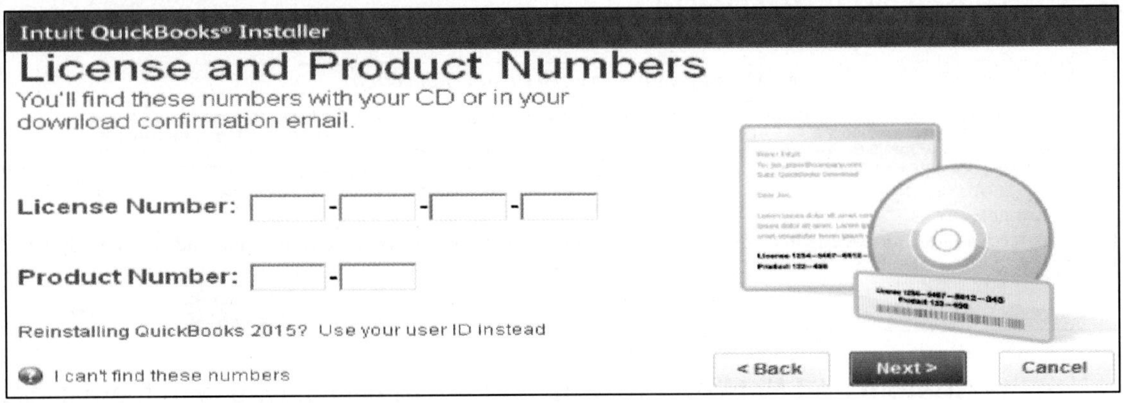

Click **Next**

You will choose installation location for the program

- To change the location shown, click the Browse button and scroll through the locations shown; then click on your selection, and click the OK button.
- If you have another version of QuickBooks installed on your computer, you will see a text box asking if you want to replace a previous version of QuickBooks

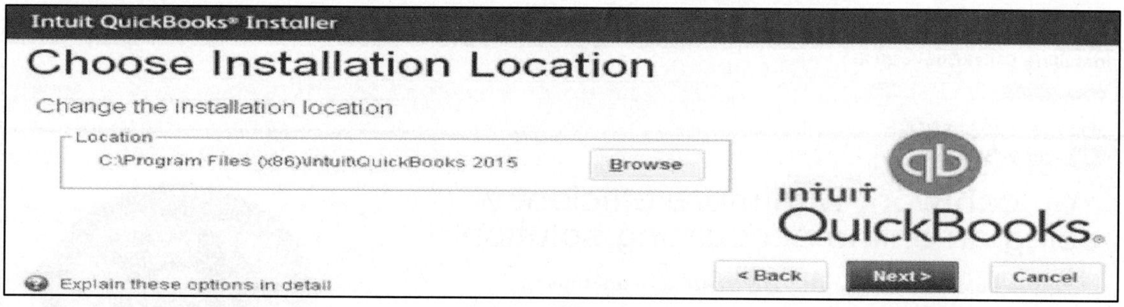

Click **Next**

The screen will show your license number, product number, and program location, click **Install**

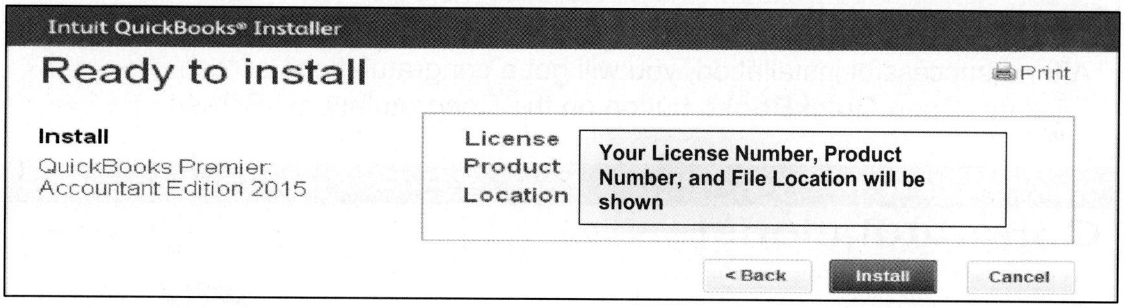

- The next screen enables you to Register QuickBooks during the program installation.

Since you will register QuickBooks later in the chapter, click **Skip this**

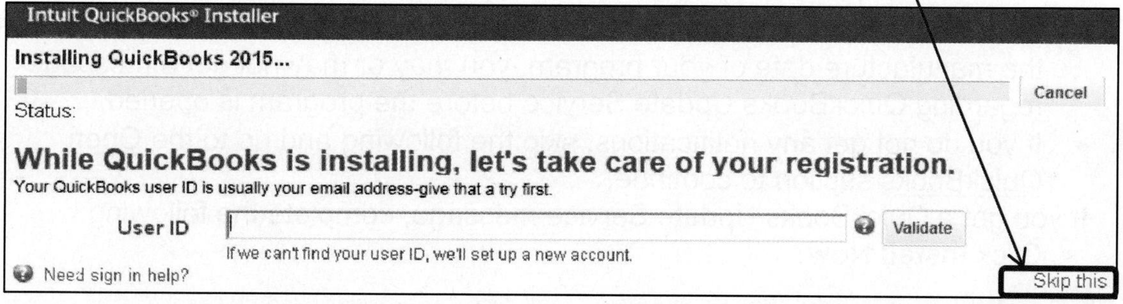

- During the program installation, which may take up to 20 minutes, you will get several more Intuit QuickBooks Installer screens. At the top of the screen, is a status area where you can track the QuickBooks installation.

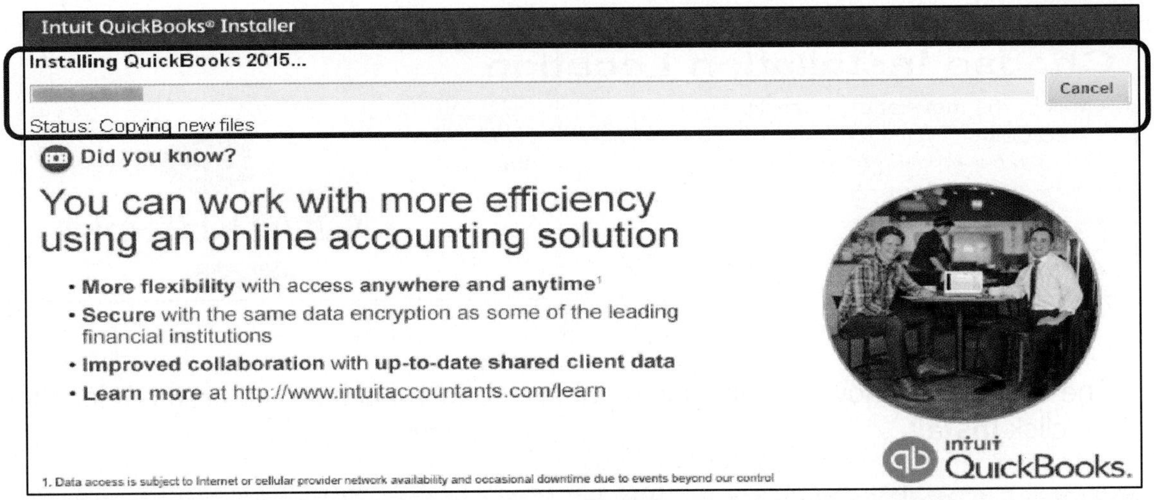

After a successful installation, you will get a congratulations screen
Click the **Open QuickBooks** button on the Congratulations! Screen

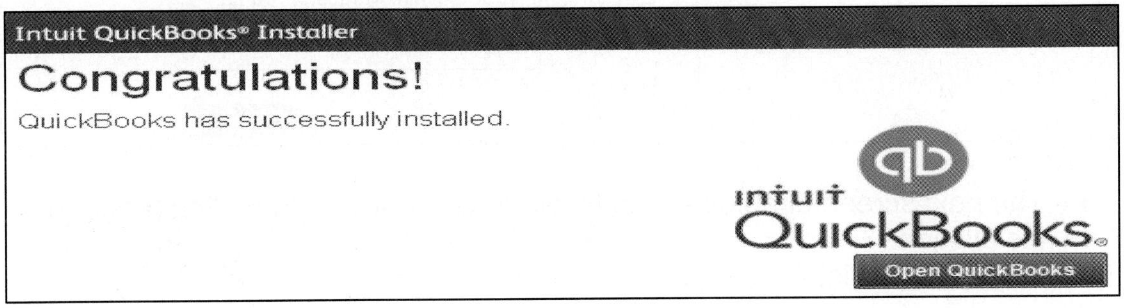

- QuickBooks is frequently updated. When you install your software, depending on the manufacture date of your program, you may or may not get a message regarding QuickBooks Update Service before the program is opened.
- If you do not get any notifications, skip the following and go to the Open QuickBooks section to continue.

If you get a QuickBooks Update Service message, complete the following:
Click **Install Now**

- You may see a QuickBooks Update screen showing you the status of the update.

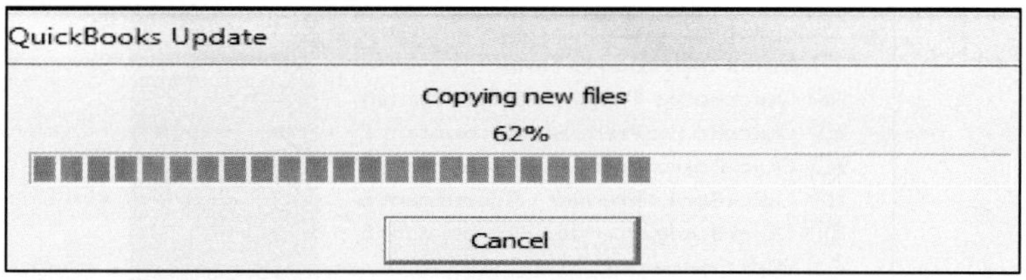

If you get an Update complete screen, click the **OK** button

OR

If you get a QuickBooks Update screen telling you to restart your computer, close any other open programs and then click the **Yes** button

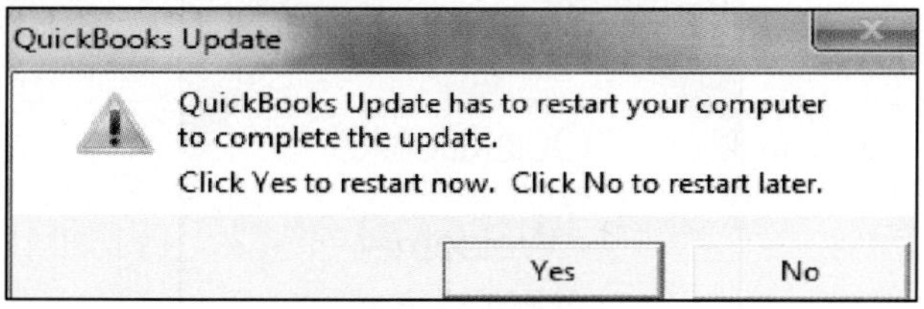

- You might receive a message from Intuit about "How QuickBooks uses your Internet connection;" if so, click the **OK** button.

OPEN QUICKBOOKS

Once you are in Windows, opening QuickBooks is as easy as point and click. Note: instructions illustrate screens using Windows 7.

Open QuickBooks

- QuickBooks should be open and ready to update.
- If QuickBooks is open, resume training after the screen shot that says Opening QuickBooks

If QuickBooks is not open, do the following:

Double-click the **QuickBooks Premier** icon on your desk top

OR

Click the **Start** button in the lower-left of the desktop

Point to **All Programs** and scroll through the list of programs and program folders

Click the **QuickBooks** folder

- You may have to scroll down to see all of the folders on your computer.

Click **QuickBooks Premier-Accountant Edition 2015**

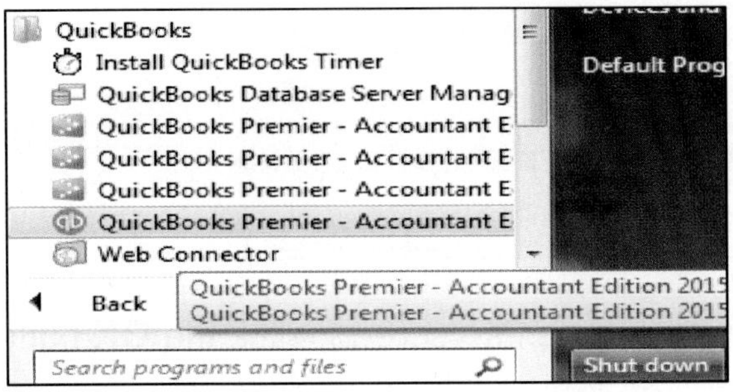

When QuickBooks opens, you will get a screen that says Opening QuickBooks

- When QuickBooks is first opened, you may get an Update Service screen; if so, refer to the previous page for the installation of QuickBooks and follow the steps shown.
- When opening QuickBooks, you may get a Warning screen showing you how many days you have left to use QuickBooks

When QuickBooks is open you will see the title bar

If you run into difficulties with the installation, go to the Intuit Install Center at http://support.quickbooks.intuit.com/Support/InstallCenter/default.aspx or www.quickbooks.com/support to find help on how to install QuickBooks.

You may use QuickBooks for 30 days without registering the program. However, if you register the program, your trial period will be extended. Register QuickBooks is available on the Help menu only if you have not yet registered your copy of QuickBooks.

If you get a screen for Express Start, click the **Close** button on the upper-right corner of the window 

If you get a screen for QuickBooks Usage & Analytics Study, click the **Close** button

REGISTER INSTALLED TRIAL VERSION

Once you have installed QuickBooks Accountant Trial Version, you may use it for 30 days. Because this is an education version of the program, if you register it within the first 30 days of use, the number of days available for use will be extended.

Register QuickBooks

Click **Register** on the Register QuickBooks screen

- If a Register QuickBooks Premier: Accountant Edition 2015 screen does not automatically appear, click the **Help** menu and click **Register QuickBooks**.
- As QuickBooks is updated by Intuit, the screens you see may change. Most of the registration information required is the same. So, if the screens you see are different from the ones displayed in the text, complete the information in the order presented by QuickBooks.

If you are online, you will be instructed to setup an Intuit Account
Click **Don't have an account** on the first screen
You will get a screen to Register QuickBooks and Create your Account
Enter your email address, enter a password, and then re-enter your password again

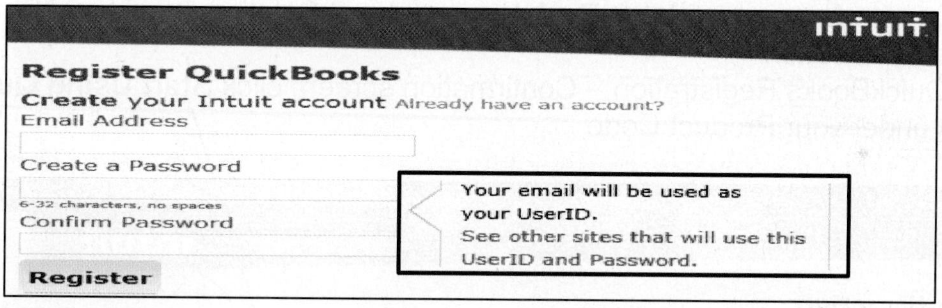

Click **Register**
Complete the information to Review your Customer Account

- If the order sequencing or the questions change from the list below, answer everything that appears with your actual information.

Enter the information for the fields with an asterisk as follows:
Company Information:
Country: **United States** from the drop-down list
Company name: **Student**
Industry: **Other** from the drop-down list
Address 1: Enter your actual street address
City: Enter your city
State: Enter your state
Zip/Postal Code: Enter your Zip or Postal Code
Business Phone: Enter your phone number

Primary Contact:
First Name: Your first name
Last Name: Your last name
Job Title: **Other**
Work Phone: Your phone number
Email Address: Enter your email address again

In the next section, click the drop-down list arrow and then click on the appropriate answer:
Tell us about your company:

1. Is this your company's first version of QuickBooks: **Yes** (unless you own a previous version of the program)
2. Where did you get this copy of QuickBooks?: Since none of the choices are correct, select **A Solution Provider, VAR** or **IT Consultant** from the drop-down list
3. Number of full & part-time employees on your payroll?: **None, just myself**
4. Does your company
    a. Accept credit cards? **No, but want to**
    b. Print checks? **Yes**
    c. Use a payroll service or payroll software? **No**

For Accountants, Intuit ProAdvisors, and Intuit Solution Providers:
Are you an Accountant, Intuit ProAdvisor, or Intuit Solution Provider? **No**

Click the **Next** button

On the QuickBooks Registration – Confirmation screen, click **Start Using QuickBooks Now** under your Product Code

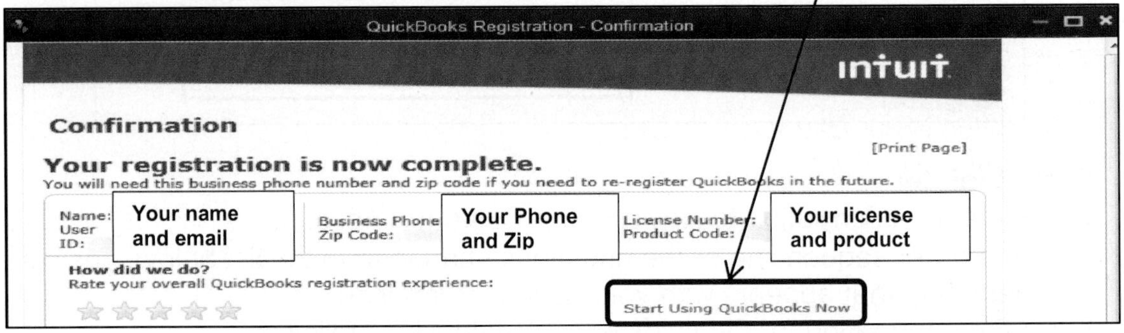

- Once the program has been registered, you will periodically get a Warning message when opening a company file. This message will tell you how many days you have left to use the program

Verify that QuickBooks is registered

Press the **F2** key when QuickBooks is open

- The Product Information window displays either REGISTERED or UNREGISTERED based on the registration status. In addition, this screen tells you which QuickBooks Release you are using, your License Number, Product Number, and other information about the program.

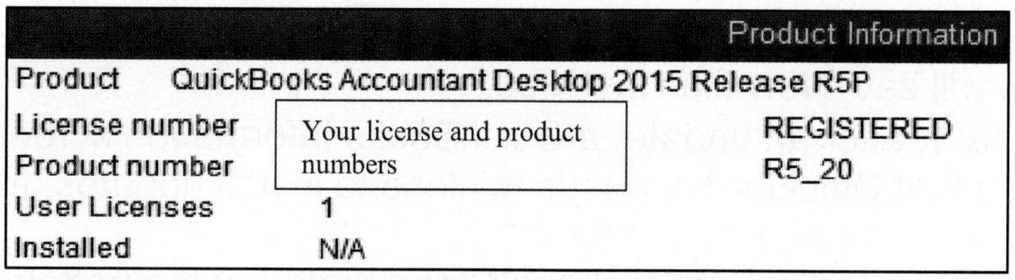

Click **OK** to close the Product Information Window,

UPDATE QUICKBOOKS (OPTIONAL)

QuickBooks is setup to automatically update the program whenever Intuit releases new features, maintenance files, or other enhancements to the program. You may also update the program manually. This is especially important to do if you install a trial version of the software.

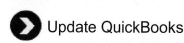

Update QuickBooks

- If you get a dialog box to install a product update, click **Install Now** (This is shown in the Install QuickBooks section earlier in the chapter.) When the update is complete, if you get a message box to restart your computer, click **Yes**. Then, continue with the following instructions

Click the **Help** menu and click **Update QuickBooks…**

- There are three tabs shown on Update QuickBooks: Overview, Options, and Update Now

Read the information shown on the **Overview** tab

- There is a button on the Overview tab that you may also click to Update Now; however, if you click this button, you will not see information about the updates.

Click the **Update Now** tab

Click **Get Updates**

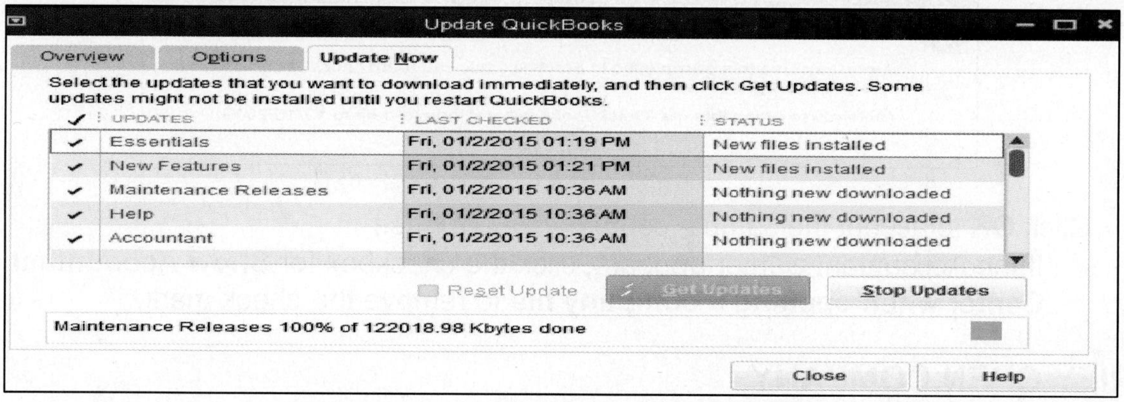

- The dates shown are the computer dates of the author's computer when different updates were performed. The dates will not match your dates.

- After updating is complete, verify the STATUS. If new files have been installed, STATUS will say "New files installed."
- Occasionally, after an update, a QuickBooks Information screen will appear telling you that QuickBooks needs to close to install updates. If this occurs, click **OK**.

When the update is complete, click the **Close** button at the bottom of the Update QuickBooks screen

OPEN COMPANY

To explore some of the features of QuickBooks, you will work with a sample company that comes with the program. The company is Larry's Landscaping & Garden Supply and is stored on the hard disk (C:) inside the computer.

Open a sample company

Click the **Open a sample file** button on the "No Company Open" screen
Click **Sample service-based business**

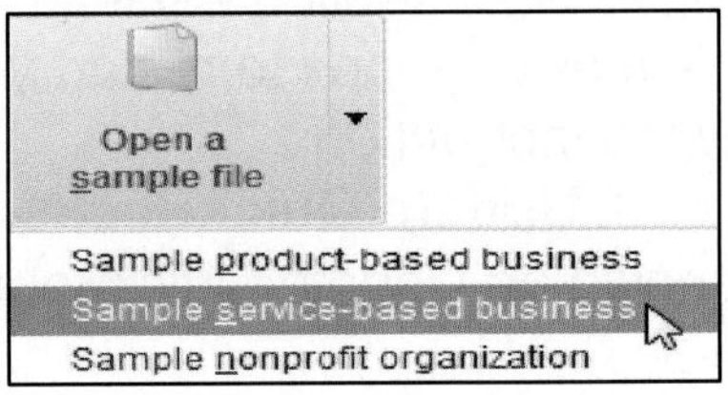

- When using the sample company for training, a warning screen will appear. This is to remind you NOT to enter the transactions for your business in the sample company. It will show a date that is several years into the future.

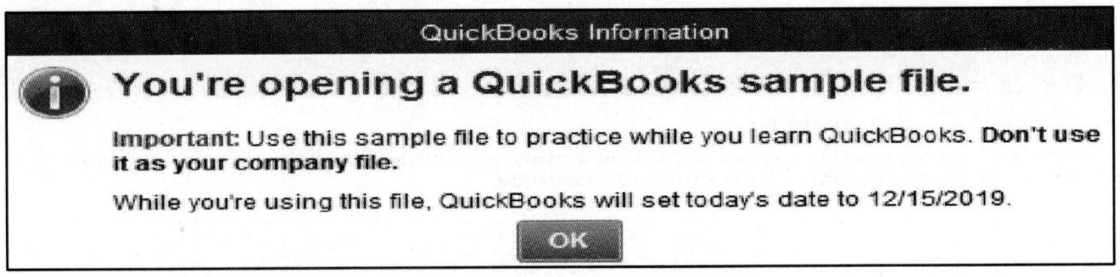

Click **OK** to accept the sample company data for use

- If the Accountant Center appears, click the checkbox for **Show Accountant Center when opening a company file** to remove the check mark.

VERIFY OPEN COMPANY

It is important to make sure you have opened the data for the correct company. Always verify the company name in the title bar. The title bar is located at the top of the screen and will tell you the name of the company and the program.

Verify an open company

Check the **title bar** at the top of the QuickBooks screen to make sure it includes the company name. The title bar should show:

DESKTOP FEATURES

Once you have opened a company, and the title bar displays the **Company Name - QuickBooks 2015.** (The following example shows: Sample Larry's Landscaping & Garden Supply – QuickBooks Accountant Desktop 2015.) Beneath the Title Bar, you will see the Menu Bar. Each menu is for a separate area and is used to give commands to QuickBooks.

Title Bar and Menu Bar

MENU BAR

The first line displayed beneath the title bar is the **Menu Bar**. By pointing and clicking on a menu or using the keyboard shortcut of Alt+ the underlined letter in the menu item you will give QuickBooks the command to display the drop-down menu. For example, the File menu is used to open and close a company and may also be used to exit QuickBooks.

QUICKBOOKS MENUS

Each menu focuses on a different area in QuickBooks. Menus can be the starting point for issuing commands in QuickBooks. Many commands will be the same as the ones you can give when using QuickBooks Home Page (detailed later in the chapter). To use a menu, click the desired menu, then click the command you want to use. Notice that available keyboard shortcuts are listed next to the menu item. Click outside the menu to close it.

Access each of the menus by clicking or pointing to each menu item

File menu is used to access company files and perform several other functions—New Company, New Company from an Existing Company File, Open or Restore Company, Open Previous Company, Open Second Company, Back Up Company, Create Copy, Close Company, Switch to Multi-user Mode, Utilities, Set Up Intuit Sync Manager, Send Company File, Print, Save as PDF, Print Forms, Printer Setup, Send Forms, Shipping, Update Web Services, Toggle to Another Edition, and Exit.

Edit menu is used to make changes such as: Undo, Revert, Cut, Copy, Paste, Copy Line, Paste Line, Use Register, Use Calculator, Find, Search, and Preferences.

View menu is used to select things to view. They include: Open Window List, Top Icon Bar, Left Icon Bar, Hide Icon Bar, Search Box, Customize Icon Bar, Add "Home" to Icon Bar, Favorites Menu, One Window, and Multiple Windows.

Lists menu is used to show lists used by QuickBooks. These lists include: Chart of Accounts (the General Ledger), Item List, Fixed Asset Item List, Price Level List, Billing Rate Level List, Sales Tax Code List, Payroll Item List, Payroll Schedule List, Class List, Workers Comp List, Other Names List, Customer & Vendor Profile Lists, Templates, Memorized Transaction List, and Add/Edit Multiple List Entries.

Favorites menu is used to place your favorite or most frequently used commands on this list. It is customized with your selected commands.

Accountant menu is used to access the Accountant Center, the Chart of Accounts, and the Fixed Asset Item List. It is also used to Batch Enter Transactions, perform a Client Data Review, Make General Journal Entries, Send General Journal Entries, Reconcile (an account), prepare a Working Trial Balance, Set Closing Date, Condense Data, Ask Client about Transaction, View Conversation List, Manage Fixed Assets, QuickBooks File Manager, use the QuickBooks Statement Writer, participate in the ProAdvisor Program, and use the Online Accountant Resources.

Company menu is used to access the Home Page, the Company Snapshot, the Calendar, Documents, and Lead Center. It is also used to access My Company (this contains information about the company), Advanced Service Administration, Set Up Users and Passwords, Customer Credit Card Protection, Set Closing Date, Bulk Enter Business Details, Planning & Budgeting, access the To Do List, access Reminders, use the Alerts Manager, display the Chart of Accounts, Make General Journal Entries, Manage Currency, Enter Vehicle Mileage, Prepare Letters with Envelopes, and Export Company File to QuickBooks Online.

Customers menu is used to access the Customer Center, Create Sales Orders, prepare Sales Order Fulfillment Worksheet, Create Invoices, Create Batch Invoices, Enter Sales Receipts, Enter Statement Charges, Create Statements, Assess Finance Charges, Receive Payments, Create Credit Memos/Refunds, use the Income Tracker, and access the Lead Center. In addition, you may Add Credit Card Processing, Link Payment Service to Company File, and use the Intuit PaymentNetwork. It is also used to access the Item List and to Change Item Prices.

Vendors menu is used to access the Vendor Center. In addition, this menu is used to Enter Bills, Pay Bills, Sales Tax, Create Purchase Orders, Receive Items and Enter Bill, Receive Items, Enter Bill for Received Items, Inventory Activities, Print/E-file 1099s, and access the Item List.

Employees menu is used to access the Employee Center, the Payroll Center, Pay Employees, prepare After-the-Fact Payroll, Add or Edit Payroll Schedules, Edit/Void Paychecks, process Payroll Taxes and Liabilities, access Payroll Tax Forms & W-2s, offer Labor Law Posters, access Workers Compensation, perform My Payroll Service activities, Pay with Direct Deposit, Payroll Setup, Manage Payroll Items, Get Payroll Updates, and access the Billing Rate Level List.

Banking menu is used to Write Checks, Order Checks & Envelopes, Enter Credit Card Charges, Use Register, Make Deposits, Transfer Funds, Reconcile accounts, access Bank Feeds, use the Loan Manager, and access the Other Names List.

Reports menu is used to access the Report Center, Memorized Reports, Commented Reports, Company Snapshot, Process Multiple Reports, and QuickBooks Statement Writer. In addition, it is used to prepare reports in the following categories: Company & Financial; Customers & Receivables; Sales; Jobs, Time & Mileage; Vendors & Payables; Purchases; Inventory; Employees & Payroll; Banking; Accountant & Taxes; Budgets & Forecasts; List; and Industry Specific. You may also create Contributed Reports, Custom Reports, QuickReport, Transaction History, and Transaction Journal.

Window menu is used to Arrange Icons, Close All, Tile Vertically, Tile Horizontally, or Cascade open windows.

Help menu is used to access QuickBooks Help, Ask Intuit, What's New, Find Training, Learning Center Tutorials, Support, Find A Local QuickBooks Expert, and Send Feedback Online. The Help menu includes topics such as: Internet Connection Setup, Year-End Guide, Add QuickBooks Services, App Center: Find More Business Solutions, Update QuickBooks, Manage My License, Manage Data Sync, QuickBooks Privacy Statement, About Automatic Update, QuickBooks Usage & Analytics Study, and About QuickBooks Accountant Desktop 2015. If QuickBooks has not been registered, you will also see Register QuickBooks.

ICON BAR

An icon bar contains small picture symbols called icons that may be clicked to give commands to QuickBooks. By default, QuickBooks 2015 comes with a Left Icon Bar (shown below).

If Insights displays when you open the company, click the tab for **Home Page**

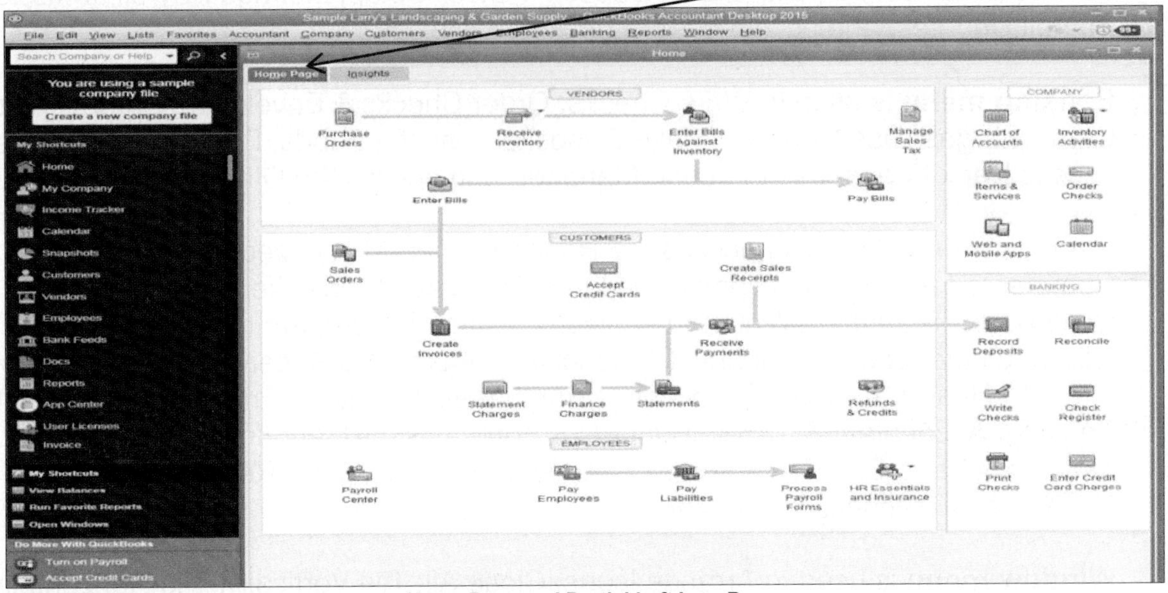

Home Page and Partial Left Icon Bar

You may change the placement of the Icon Bar from the left of the screen to the top of the screen just below the Menu Bar. Throughout the text, the Left Icon bar has been changed to a Top Icon Bar. This is done to save screen space and to focus on tasks rather than shortcuts and Do More With QuickBooks. Once the Top Icon bar is selected, it will appear below the Menu bar and the Left Icon bar will not be seen. The Top Icon bar may be shown in color and it may be customized. The standard icon bar is divided into four specific areas: Home; Snapshots and Command Centers; Command Icons; Services and Search. Depending on the screen size of your computer, not all of the icons may be displayed.

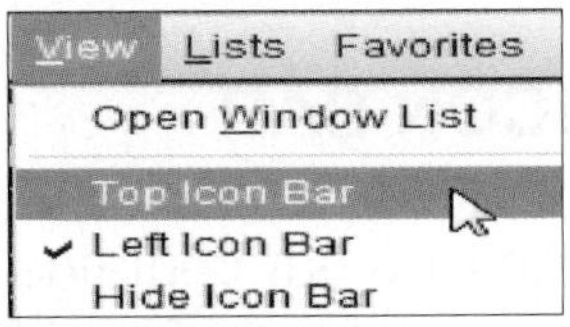

Change to a Top-Icon Bar and display it in color

To change to the top-icon bar, Click the **View Menu**, and click **Top Icon Bar**

- If you already have the Top Icon Bar showing, there is no need to change it.

To change to a colored icon bar, click the **Edit** menu, click **Preferences**, click **Desktop View**, click the **My Preferences** tab, click **Switch to colored icons/light background on the Top Icon Bar**, click **OK**

First Section of the Top Icon Bar:

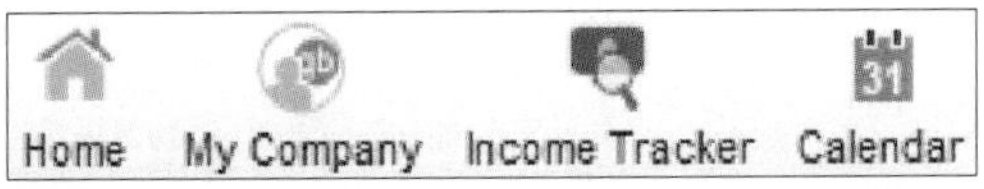

Home is the first icon shown below the Menu bar and is used to go to the Navigator screen, also known as the Home Page.

My Company displays Company Information, which may be edited. It informs you of Product Information; allows you to manage apps, services, and subscriptions; and makes recommendations for you.

Income Tracker allows you to view Unbilled Sales Orders, Unpaid, Overdue, and Paid Invoices. You may view individual customers or all customers. You may perform Batch Actions and Manage Transactions as well.

Calendar is used to maintain a monthly calendar and contains information for the To Do List, Upcoming: Next 7 days, and Due: Past 60 days.

Second Section of the Top Icon Bar:

QuickBooks Snapshots is next to the Calendar icon. When you click this icon, you may click on one of three tabs to get information about the Company, Payments, and Customer. The information displayed on each tab may be customized by selecting a variety of options.

QuickBooks Command Centers Next to the Company Snapshot icon there are icons for Centers. Each center goes to a specific list within the program. The centers are: Customers, Vendors, Employees, Bank Feeds, Docs, Reports, App Center, and User Licenses.

Third Section of the Top Icon Bar:

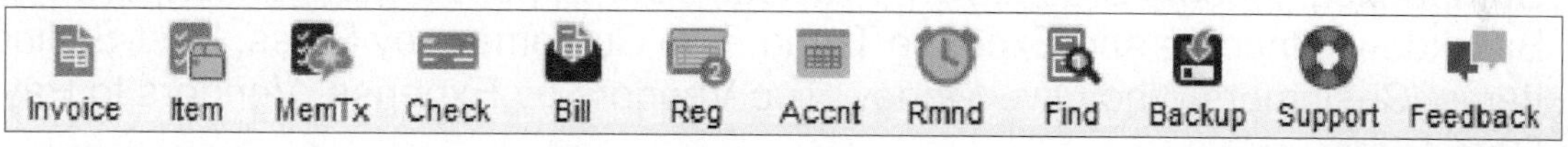

Command Icons are used to give commands to QuickBooks by pointing to a picture and clicking the primary mouse button. Depending on the size of your monitor, you may or may not see the command icons. If they do not appear, click the » to show them.

Fourth Section of the Top Icon Bar:

Services takes you to a QuickBooks Products and Services link where you will be able to add recommended services.

Add Payroll takes you to an Intuit page for Accounting Software for Small Business – Intuit QuickBooks. Once you sign in, you may add services and apps.

Credit Cards allows you to sign up for plans so your company can accept credit card payments and bank transfers using QuickBooks.

QuickBooks Search is used to search through QuickBooks Help for information or through the Company file for various transactions, accounts, items, customers, vendors, employees, etc.

COMPANY SNAPSHOTS

As shown in the screenshot below, QuickBooks 2015 has buttons that allow access to the Company Snapshot and QuickBooks Centers. The snapshot and the centers focus on providing detailed information.

Access the snapshots and each of the centers by clicking the appropriate icon beneath the menu bar and close each Snapshot or Center before opening the next.

Snapshots provides three tabs used to display information about the Company, Payments, and Customers. You may customize the Company Snapshot by clicking Add Content and selecting from among different options.

To see how your business is doing, click the **Company** tab. When you click Add Content, there are 12 different items that may be displayed for the company. These options include listings or graphs for Account Balances, Previous Year Income Comparison, Income Breakdown, Previous Year Expense Comparison, Expense Breakdown, Income and Expense Trend, Top Customers by Sales, Best-Selling Items, Customers Who Owe Money, Top Vendors by Expense, Vendors to Pay, and Reminders.

When you click the **Payments** tab, you get information about the company revenues. You may select from among seven options on Add Content to display information about your company revenue. These include Recent Transactions, Receivables Reports, A/R by Aging Period, Invoice Payment Status, Customers Who Owe Money, QuickLinks, and Payment Reminders.

To view information regarding individual customers, click the **Customer** tab to select from among four items to display on Add Content. These are Recent Invoices, Recent Payments, Sales History, and Best-Selling Items.

CENTERS

The icons for Customers, Vendors, Employees, Bank Feeds, Docs, Reports, App Center, and User Licenses all open different centers. They are:

Customers shows the Customer Center with two tabs: Customers & Jobs and Transactions. In addition to the information displayed on tabs, icons at the top of the Customers Center may be used to perform different tasks.

The **Customers & Jobs** tab is the default tab and displays a list of all your customers and their balances. When you click on an individual customer, Customer Information and Transactions are displayed for that customer. When you click on the icon for New Customer & Job at the top of the Customer Center, you may add a New Customer, a New Job, or Multiple Customer:Jobs. If you click the icon for New Transactions, you may enter Sales Orders, Invoices, Sales Receipts, Statement Charges, Receive Payments, and Credit Memos/Refunds. Clicking the Print icon enables you to print the Customer & Job List, Customer & Job Information, and a Customer & Job Transaction List. Clicking the Excel icon allows you to Export Customer List, Export Transactions, Import from Excel, and Paste from Excel. Clicking the Word icon allows you to Prepare a Letter to the customer whose information is displayed, Prepare Customer Letters, Prepare Collection Letters, and Customize Letter Templates. Click the Income Tracker icon to see which customers have Overdue and Almost Due balances.

Clicking the **Transactions** tab displays transaction categories and allows you to get information about transaction groups. These may include Sales Orders, Invoices, Statement Charges, Sales Receipts, Received Payments, Credit Memos, and Refunds. When the Transactions tab is selected, the icons will allow you to add a New Customer, enter New Transactions, Print transaction reports, display Customer & Job Info, and Export the transaction reports to Excel.

Vendors shows the Vendor Center with two tabs: Vendors and Transactions. In addition to the information displayed on tabs, icons at the top of the Vendors Center may be used to perform different tasks.

The default tab is **Vendors**. It allows you to display a list of vendors and their balances. You may also select a vendor and get Vendor Information and Transactions for that vendor. When the Vendors tab is selected, you may use the New Vendor icon to add New Vendors or Multiple Vendors. When you click the New Transactions icon, you may Enter Bills, Pay Bills, prepare Purchase Orders, Receive Items and Enter Bill, Receive Items, and Enter Bill for Received Items. Clicking the Print icon enables you to print the Vendor List, Vendor Information, and Vendor Transaction List. When the Excel icon is clicked, the Vendor List and Vendor Transactions may be exported to Excel and imported and or pasted from Excel. When the Word icon is clicked, you may Prepare Letter to the vendor whose information is displayed, Prepare Vendor Letters, and Customize Letter Templates.

Clicking the **Transactions** tab displays transaction categories and allows you to get information about transaction groups; such as, Purchase Orders, Item Receipts, Bills, Bill Payments, Checks, Credit Card Activities, and Sales Tax Payments. When the Transactions tab is selected, the icons will allow you to add a New Vendor; enter

New Transactions for Enter Bills, Pay Bills, prepare Purchase Orders, Receive Items and Enter Bill, Receive Items, and Enter Bill for Received Items. Clicking the Print icon allows you to Print transaction reports. The View Vendor Info icon displays the vendor information for a selected transaction, and the Export icon sends a report for All Purchase Orders or Open Purchase Orders to Excel.

Employees displays the Employee Center with three tabs: Employees, Transactions, and Payroll. In addition to the information displayed on the tabs, there are icons that may be used.

The default tab **Employees** allows you to display a list of all employees. You may select an individual employee and see Employee Information and Transactions for that employee. On the Employees tab, you may use the New Employee icon to add an employee. The Manage Employee Information icon allows you to Add/Edit Sales Rep and to Change New Employee Default Settings. The Print icon allows you to print Paychecks, Print/Send Paystubs, Employee List, Employee Information, and the Employee Transaction List. The Excel icon exports the Employee List, Transactions, Client-Ready Payroll Reports and Summarized Payroll Data to Excel. The Word icon may be used to Prepare Letter to the highlighted employee, Prepare Employee Letters, and Customize Letter Templates.

Clicking the **Transactions** tab displays transaction categories and allows you to get information about transaction groups, such as: Paychecks, Liability Checks, Liability Adjustments, Year-To-Date Adjustments, and Non-Payroll Transactions. The Transactions tab has an icon to add a New Employee. The Manage Employee Information icon enables you to Add/Edit Sales Rep and to Change New Employee Default Settings. The Print icon enables you to print a Transaction Report, and the Excel icon is clicked to Export Transactions, Client-Ready Payroll Reports, and Summarize Payroll Data in Excel to Excel.

After clicking the **Payroll** tab, you will see information for Create Paychecks, and Recent Payrolls. There are tabs to Pay Employees, Pay Liabilities, and File Forms. The Payroll tab icons pertain to My Payroll Service and allow you to get Payroll Updates, add Payroll Items, complete the Payroll Setup, change Preferences, get Support, and access Help.

Bank Feeds shows information about your Bank Accounts, allows you to Download Transactions, and Send Items to your bank. By clicking Create New, you may prepare Online Checks, Pay Bills, Transfer Funds, Messages, Inquire About Payments, and Cancel Payments. In addition, you may click icons to Add Account and display Rules.

Docs displays the Document Center that is used to keep track of documents you use with QuickBooks. It allows you to Add a Document to the Doc Center from your computer or scanner. You may attach documents, view and add document details, search for documents, detach documents, and remove documents from the Doc

Center. Documents may be items such as receipts, spreadsheets, bills, invoices, etc.

Reports Center opens the Report Center that allows you to prepare all of the Reports available in QuickBooks. There are several tabs available. The Standard Tab lists reports by category. The categories are: Company & Financial; Customers & Receivables; Sales; Jobs, Time & Mileage; Vendors & Payables; Purchases; Inventory; Employees & Payroll; Banking; Accountant & Taxes; Budgets & Forecasts; List; Contractor; Mfg & Wholesale; Professional Services; Retail; and Nonprofit. The available reports in each category may be displayed in a carousel view, a list view, or a grid view. The Memorized tab allows the use of report formats that have been customized and saved for reports for Accountant, Banking, Company, Customers, Employees, and Vendors. The Favorites tab shows reports that you have marked as favorites. The Recent tab tells you which reports have been viewed recently. The Contributed tab displays customized shared report formats that have been created and are available to be downloaded.

App Center is a link to Intuit apps for Featured, Just Added, Mobile, Billing/Invoicing, Customer Management, Expense Management, eCommerce, and more. You may also access Intuit's App Center to select other Apps. Some Apps are free and others require a subscription service.

User Licenses connects you to a link that will allow you to add multiple users to QuickBooks. You may purchase QuickBooks for a single user (1 individual) or multiple users (5 individuals). Multi-user access to QuickBooks allows up to five individuals to work in a QuickBooks company file at the same time.

COMMAND ICON BAR

In addition to giving commands to QuickBooks via Menus, they may be given by clicking command icons on the icon bar. The command section of the icon bar has a list of buttons (icons) that may be clicked in order to enter transactions. Additional icons to use Find, prepare a Backup, get Support, and give Feedback are shown as well. The icon bar may be turned on or off and it may be customized. If there is a double >> at the edge of the icon bar, that means that there are more icons available for use. The command icons will be discussed in more detail during training.

ACCOUNTANT CENTER

The Accountant Center is accessed by clicking the Accountant menu and then clicking Accountant Center. The Center has Tools that may be customized and used for transactions, reports, and activities completed by accountants. In the Accountant Center you may select an account for reconciliation, select memorized reports, and get accountant updates. You may also select "Show Accountant Center when opening a company file" and the Center will be shown whenever you open QuickBooks.

HOME SCREEN

The QuickBooks Home screen has two tabs: Home Page and Insights.

HOME PAGE

The Home Page allows you to give commands to QuickBooks according to the type of transaction being entered. The Home Page tasks are organized into logical groups (Vendors, Customers, Employees, Company, and Banking). Each of these areas on the Home Page is used to enter different types of transactions. When appropriate, the Home Page shows a flow chart with icons indicating the major activities performed. The icons are arranged in the order in which transactions usually occur. Depending on the type of company in use, the icons on the Home Page may change.

Information regarding Account Balances, Do More with QuickBooks, and Backup Status is displayed on the right side of the Home Page and may be expanded or minimized.

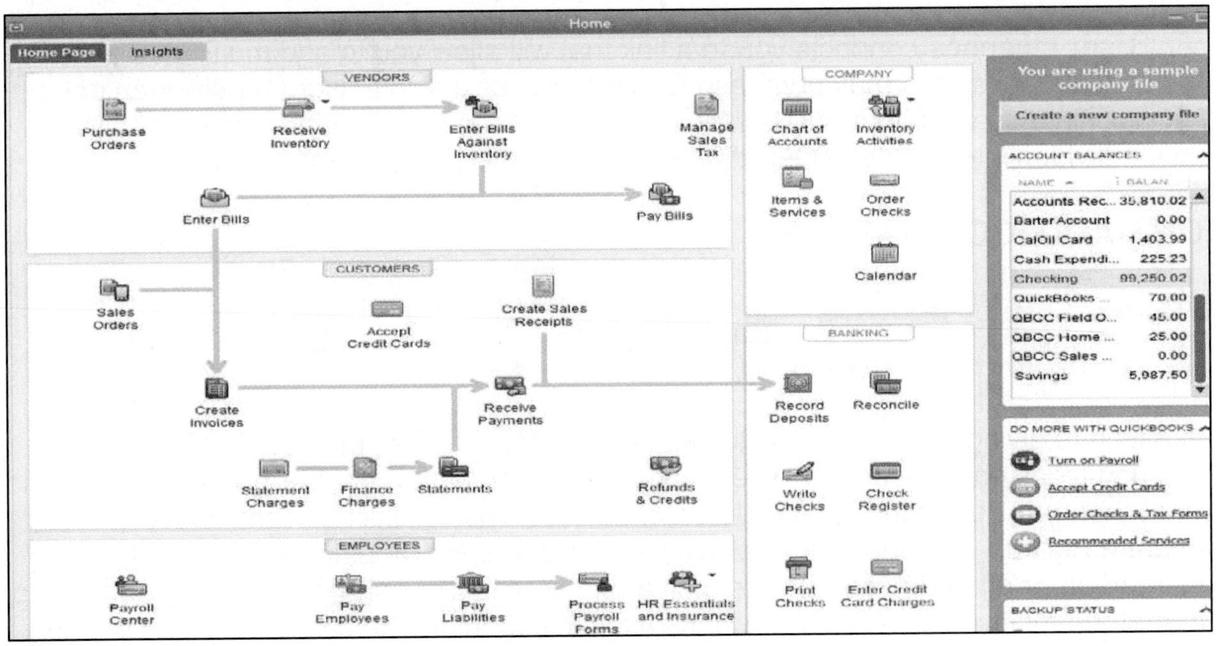

View the five command areas on the Home Page:

Vendors allows service and merchandising businesses to enter bills and to record the payment of bills. Companies with inventory can create purchase orders, receive inventory items, enter bills against inventory, and manage sales tax.

Customers allows you to record transactions associated with Invoices (sales on account or credit sales), Create Sales Receipts (cash sales), Receive Payments (for sales recorded on invoices), Refunds & Credits. Accept Credit Cards enables you to subscribe to Intuit QuickBooks Payments. If you want to use Sales Orders, issue Statement Charges, charge Finance Charges, or prepare Statements, these are entered in this section as well.

Employees allows access to the Payroll Center (if you subscribe to a payroll service), paychecks to be created, payroll liabilities to be paid, payroll forms to be processed, and human resource essentials and insurance information that enables you to produce labor law posters, use Workers' Comp Payment Service, and View My Paycheck (Online Pay Stubs).

Company allows you to display information about your company. There are graphic icons used to display the Chart of Accounts, Inventory Activities, Items & Services, Order Checks, and Calendar.

Banking allows you to Record Deposits, Write Checks, Print Checks, Reconcile (Balance Sheet Accounts), access the Check Register, and Enter Credit Card Charges.

INSIGHTS

The Insights tab on the Home Screen displays information and data about the company. The company name, logo, and date and icons for Print, Refresh, and Customize are shown. The default is to display information about Profit & Loss, Income, and Expenses. There are gray arrows on the right and left sides of the Profit & Loss data that advance you to other selected information; such as, Prev Year Income Comparison and Top Customers by Sales. Clicking the Customize icon allows you to add Income and Expense Trend, Business Growth, Net Profit Margin, and Prev Year Expense Comparison to the information that may be displayed.

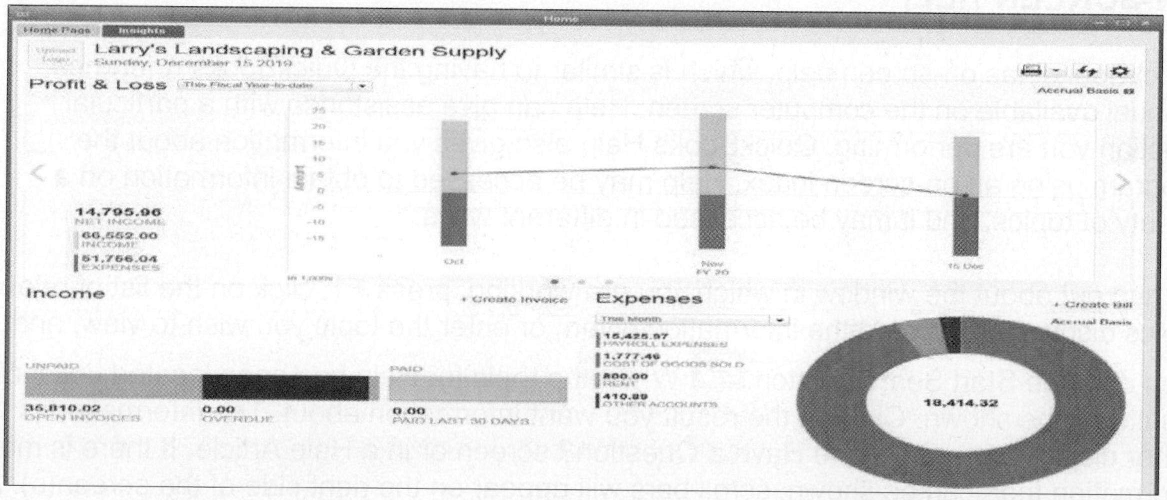

View the Insights tab and click the gray arrows to see the default reports

When finished, click the **Home Page** tab

KEYBOARD CONVENTIONS

When using Windows, there are some standard keyboard conventions for the use of certain keys. These keyboard conventions also apply to QuickBooks and include:

Alt key is used to access the drop-down menus on the menu bar. Rather than click on a menu item, press the Alt key and type the underlined letter in the menu item name. Close the menu by simply pressing the Alt key.

Tab key is used to move to the next field or, if a button is selected, to the next button.

Shift+Tab is used to move back to the previous field.

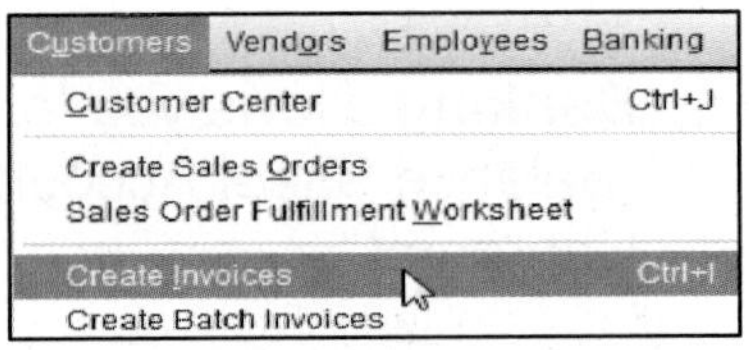

Esc key is used to cancel an active window without saving anything that has been entered. It is equivalent to clicking the Cancel button.

Practice using the keyboard conventions:

Access **Customers** menu: **Alt+U**
Access **Create Invoices**: type **I**

- Note: Ctrl + I is shown on the menu. This is a keyboard shortcut that may be used to open an invoice without using the Customer menu or the Home Page icon.

Press **Tab** key to move forward through the invoice, press **Shift+Tab** to move back through the invoice, press **Esc** to close the invoice

ON-SCREEN HELP

QuickBooks has on-screen help, which is similar to having the QuickBooks reference manual available on the computer screen. Help can give assistance with a particular function you are performing. QuickBooks Help also gives you information about the program using an on-screen index. Help may be accessed to obtain information on a variety of topics, and it may be accessed in different ways:

To find out about the window in which you are working, press F1, click on the list of relevant topics displayed and read the information given; or enter the topic you wish to view, and then click the Start Search button. When the topic for Help has been located, a list of results will be shown. Click on the result you want information about. The information is either displayed on the same Have a Question? screen or in a Help Article. If there is more information than can be shown, scroll bars will appear on the right side of the screen(s). A scroll bar is used to show or go through information. As you scroll through Help, information at the top of the Help screen disappears from view while new information appears at the bottom of the screen.

Sometimes words appear in blue in the QuickBooks Help screen. Clicking on the blue word(s) will give you more information or will take you to other topics. Often, the onscreen help provides links to an external Web site. To visit these links, you must have an Internet connection and be online. The Have a Question? Screen will show Answers in Help and Answers from Community.

If you want to see a different topic, you may type in different key words at the top of the Have a Question? Screen and then click the Search button. Information will be provided on the new topic.

If you want to print a copy of the QuickBooks Have a Question? or Article screen(s), click the Printer icon at the top of the Have a Question? screen. You may close a QuickBooks Help Article or Have a Question? by clicking the Close button ☒ in the upper right corner of the screen.

To get additional information on how to use QuickBooks or to enter a question and get immediate answers drawn from the QuickBooks Help system and the technical support database, click the Help menu and click Support.

USE HELP SEARCH TO FIND KEYBOARD SHORTCUTS

Frequently, it is faster to use a keyboard shortcut to give QuickBooks a command than it is to point and click the mouse through several layers of menus or icons. The list of common keyboard shortcuts may be obtained by using Help.

Use Help

Click **Help** on the Menu bar
Click **QuickBooks Help**
Type **keyboard shortcuts** in the textbox
Click the **Search** button
Look at the list of topics provided

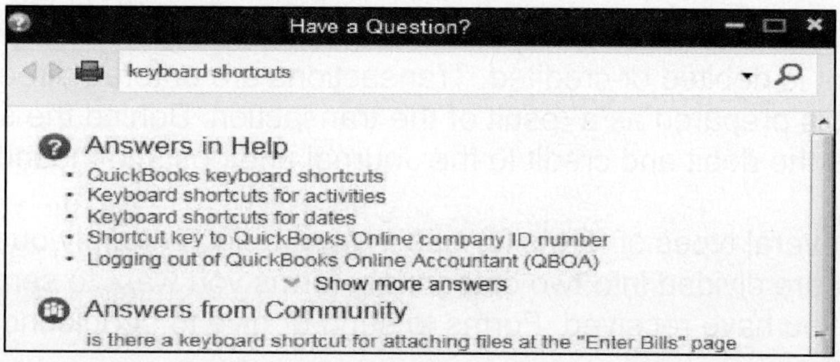

Click **QuickBooks keyboard shortcuts** and view the results

- You may see the results in a Help Article or on the Have a Question? screen.

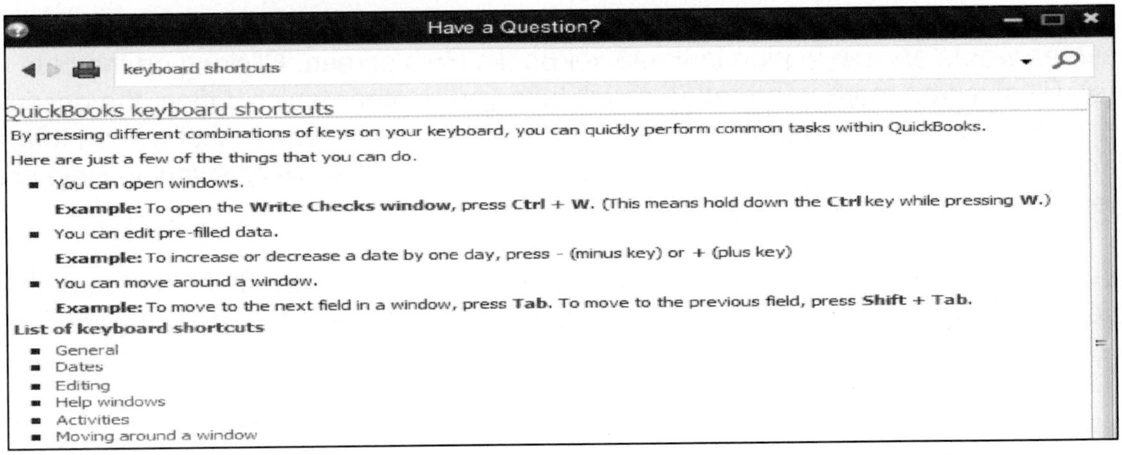

Click **General** in the list of keyboard shortcuts to see the General keyboard shortcuts

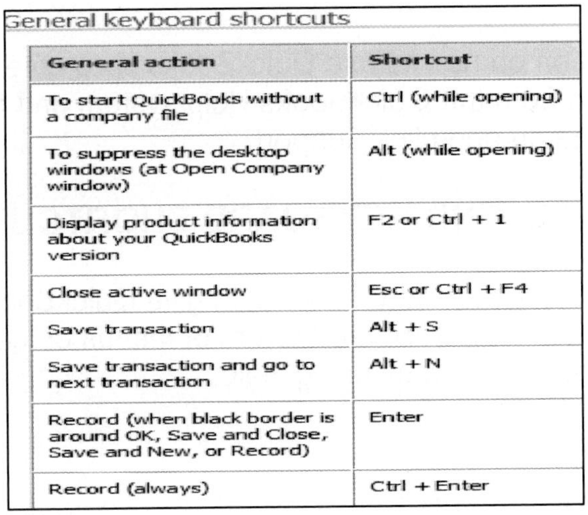

General keyboard shortcuts

General action	Shortcut
To start QuickBooks without a company file	Ctrl (while opening)
To suppress the desktop windows (at Open Company window)	Alt (while opening)
Display product information about your QuickBooks version	F2 or Ctrl + 1
Close active window	Esc or Ctrl + F4
Save transaction	Alt + S
Save transaction and go to next transaction	Alt + N
Record (when black border is around OK, Save and Close, Save and New, or Record)	Enter
Record (always)	Ctrl + Enter

Click the **Close** button in the upper right corner of the Have a Question? screen; and, if shown, the Help Article screen

FORMS

The premise of QuickBooks is to allow you to focus on running the business, not deciding whether an account is debited or credited. Transactions are entered directly onto the business form that is prepared as a result of the transaction. Behind the scenes, QuickBooks enters the debit and credit to the Journal and posts to the individual accounts.

QuickBooks has several types of forms for use in recording your daily business transactions. They are divided into two categories: forms you want to send or give to people and forms you have received. Forms to send or give to people include invoices, sales receipts, credit memos, checks, deposit slips, and purchase orders. Forms you have received include payments from customers, bills, credits for a bill, and credit card charge receipts.

You may use the forms as they come with QuickBooks, you may change or modify them, or you may create your own custom forms for use in the program.

Examine the following invoice and note the terms, icons, and buttons listed as they apply to invoices. These terms will be used throughout the text when giving instructions for entries.

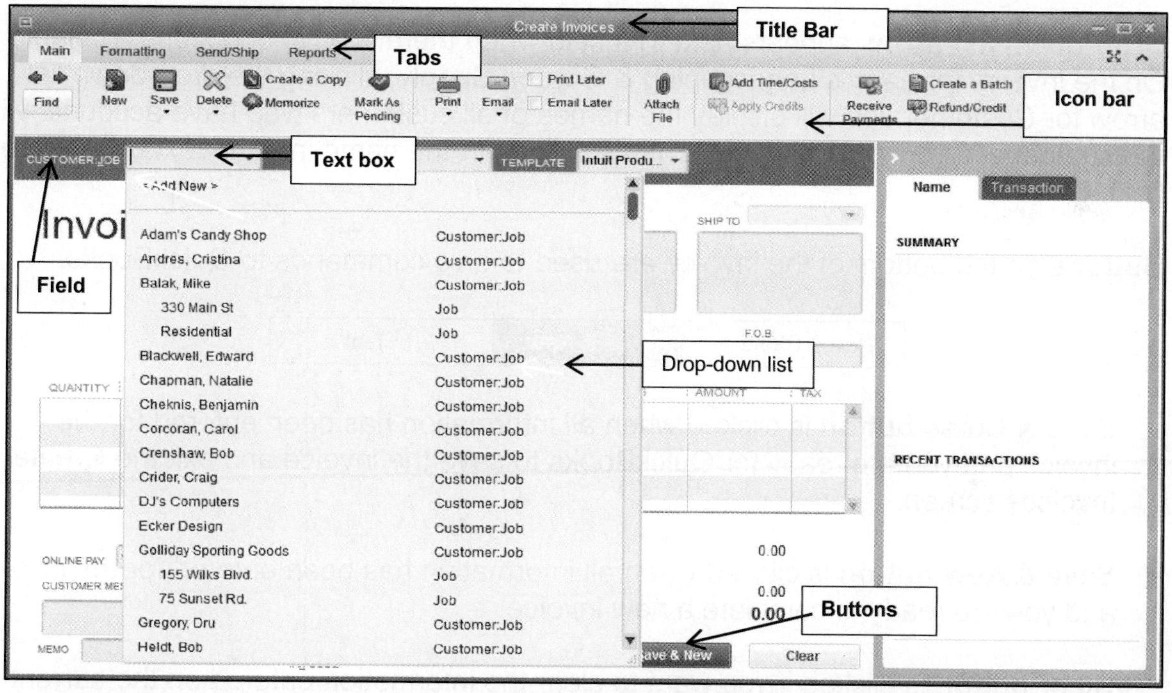

Title bar at the top of the form indicates what you are completing. In this case, it says **Create Invoices**. The title bar also contains some buttons. They include:

Minimize button clicking this will remove the form from the screen but still leave it open. You may click the form on the Taskbar to re-display it.

Maximize **or restore button** enlarges the form to fill the screen or restores the form to its previous size.

Close button closes the current screen.

- Depending on the size of your screen, the task for Create Invoices may be shown on the QuickBooks title bar. (See below) If this happens, the buttons on the title bar are applicable to the program. Clicking on the Close button on the title bar will close QuickBooks, which could result in the loss of data. Clicking on the separate Close button located on the menu bar just below the one for QuickBooks will close the invoice.

Field is an area on a form requiring information. Customer:Job is a field.

Text box is the area within a field where information may be typed or inserted. The area to be filled in to identify the Customer:Job is a text box.

Drop-down list arrow appears next to a field when there is a list of options available. On the invoice for Larry's Landscaping & Garden Supply, clicking the drop-down list arrow for Customer:Job will display the names of all customers who have accounts with the company. Clicking a customer's name will insert the name into the text box for the field.

Buttons on the bottom of the invoice are used to give commands to QuickBooks.

Save & Close button is clicked when all information has been entered for the invoice and you are ready for QuickBooks to save the invoice and exit the Create Invoices screen.

Save & New button is clicked when all information has been entered for the invoice and you are ready to complete a new invoice.

Clear button is clicked if you want to clear the information entered on the current invoice.

Icon Bar a group of commands shown as small pictures (icons) that may be given to QuickBooks. The Icon Bar for an invoice is just below the Create Invoices Title Bar. It has four tabs containing icons that are used to give commands to QuickBooks or to get information regarding linked or related transactions. If an icon has an arrow at the bottom, it means that there is a variety of choices/commands that may be selected.

Tabs show choices of activities. On an Invoice the tabs enable you to select different Icon Bars.

Main Tab Icons include:

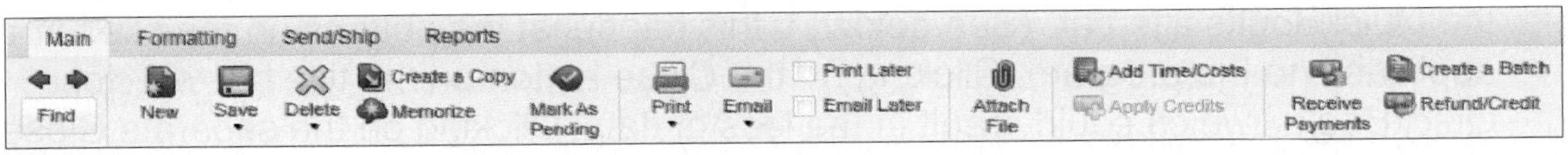

Previous is clicked to go back to the previous invoice. This is used when you want to view, print, or correct the previous invoice. Each time the Previous icon is clicked, you go back one invoice. You may click the Previous icon until you go all the way back to invoices with opening balances.

Next is clicked to go to the next invoice after the one you entered. If the invoice on the screen has not been saved, this saves the invoice and goes to the next one. The next invoice may be one that has already been created and saved or it may be a blank invoice.

Find is used to find invoices previously prepared.

New is clicked to create a new invoice.

Save is clicked to save the invoice and leave it on the screen. The arrow at the bottom of the Save icon means you can save it in more than one way. An invoice may be saved as a QuickBooks invoice or a PDF file.

Delete will delete the invoice. To void the invoice, click the arrow below Delete and then click Void.

Create a Copy allows you to make a copy of the invoice using a new number. This invoice may be edited and saved.

Memorize allows QuickBooks to save an invoice as a template for future use.

Mark As Pending saves the invoice but doesn't record the accounting behind the scenes. Later, the invoice may be marked as Final to record the accounting.

Print is used to print the invoice. The arrow beneath Print may be clicked so you can preview an invoice. Other choices include printing an invoice, a batch of invoices, packing slips, shipping labels, and envelopes. You may also save the invoice as PDF file. There is a checkbox that may be clicked so the invoice may be printed later.

Email is used to e-mail an invoice or a batch of invoices. The arrow below Email allows you to email an invoice, an invoice and its attached files, and to email a batch of invoices. Email also has a checkbox that may be clicked so the invoice is emailed later.

Attach File attaches a file or a scanned document to this invoice.

Add Time/Costs adds any costs you marked as billable to this Customer:Job.

Apply Credits is used to apply an existing credit for this Customer:Job to this invoice. A credit for a return or overpayment is recorded as a Credit Memo.

Receive Payments is used to record the receipt of payment for this invoice.

Create a Batch creates one invoice to send to multiple customers.

Refund/Credit enables you to create a Credit Memo using the items and prices on this invoice. It may be edited and saved and is an alternate method to preparing a Credit Memo in Refunds & Credits.

Formatting Tab Icons include:

Preview allows you to see how the printed invoice will look

Manage Templates allows you to view a list of standard forms available in QuickBooks. These may be copied, edited, and customized.

Download Templates allows you to download preformatted forms that are customized.

Customize Data Layout allows you to customize the information that appears and where it appears on the form your customer sees.

Spelling is used to check the spelling in the item descriptions.

Insert Line will insert a blank line above the selected item so additional text may be added, extra space may be created, or a new line item may be inserted.

Delete Line is used to delete a selected line item.

Copy Line is used to duplicate a selected line item.

Paste Line is used to "paste" the copied line onto a new line.

Customize Design allows online form customization and requires an online Intuit account so you can save your designs.

Send/Ship Tab Icons include:

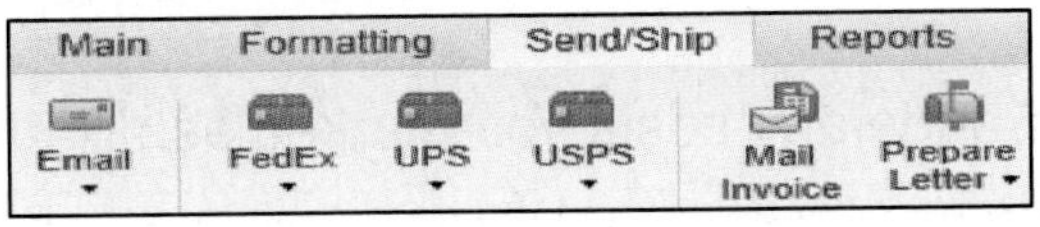

Email is used to email the current invoice, invoices marked to email, and batch invoices.

FedEx, UPS, and **USPS** allow you to send/ship packages, find drop off locations, schedule pickups, and track packages; as well as, setup accounts for shipping.

Mail Invoice uses QuickBooks Billing Solution to mail invoices.

Prepare Letter uses Microsoft® Word to create letters and envelopes for customers using templates provided by QuickBooks. These templates may be edited and/or customized.

Reports Tab Icons include:

QuickReport is used to display transactions for the Customer:Job on this invoice.

Transaction History is a report that lists all transactions that are linked to this invoice.

Transaction Journal displays a report showing the journal entry that QuickBooks makes behind the scenes for this invoice.

View Open Invoices displays a report containing information about unpaid invoices, when they are due, and unapplied refunds/credits.

Sales by Customer Detail displays the sales to each customer and shows the totals of every line item on sales and refunds/credits.

Average Days To Pay Summary analyzes the payment history for each customer and displays the average number of days it takes each customer to pay

LISTS

In order to expedite entering transactions, QuickBooks uses lists as an integral part of the program. Customers, vendors, sales items, and accounts are organized as lists. In fact, the chart of accounts is considered to be a list in QuickBooks. Frequently, information can be entered on a form by clicking on a list item.

Most lists have a maximum. However, it's unlikely that you'll run out of room on your lists. With so many entries available, there is room to add list items "on the fly" as you work. The vendors, customers, and employees lists are all provided in the related Centers. If you open the Customer Center, the Customer List will appear on the left side of the Center.

Examine several lists:

Click the **Customers** icon on the Top Icon Bar. On the left side of the Customer Center, the list of customers is shown; click the **Close** button to exit

- In accounting concepts the Customers list would be referred to as the Accounts Receivable Subsidiary Ledger.

Click the **Lists** menu, click **Chart of Accounts** to view the Chart of Accounts, click the **Close** button to exit

Click the **Vendors** icon on the Top Icon Bar, view the list of vendors on the left side of the Vendor Center; click the **Close** button to exit

- In accounting concepts the Vendors list would be referred to as the Accounts Payable Subsidiary Ledger.

Click the **Items & Services** icon in the Company Section of the Home Page to view the list of items for sale and services performed by the company, click the **Close** button to exit

REGISTERS

QuickBooks prepares a register for every balance sheet account. An account register contains records of all activity for the account. Registers provide an excellent means of looking at transactions within an account. For example, the Accounts Receivable register maintains a record of every invoice, credit memo, and payment that has been recorded for credit customers (in accounting concepts this is the Accounts Receivable account).

Examine the Accounts Receivable Register

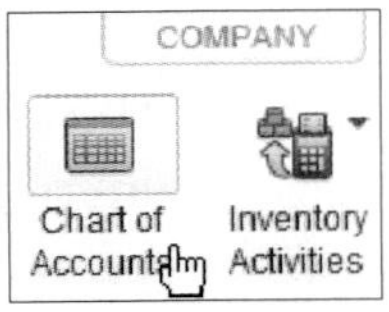

Click **Chart of Accounts** in the Company section of the Home Page
Click **Accounts Receivable**
Click the **Activities** button at the bottom of the screen
Click **Use Register**

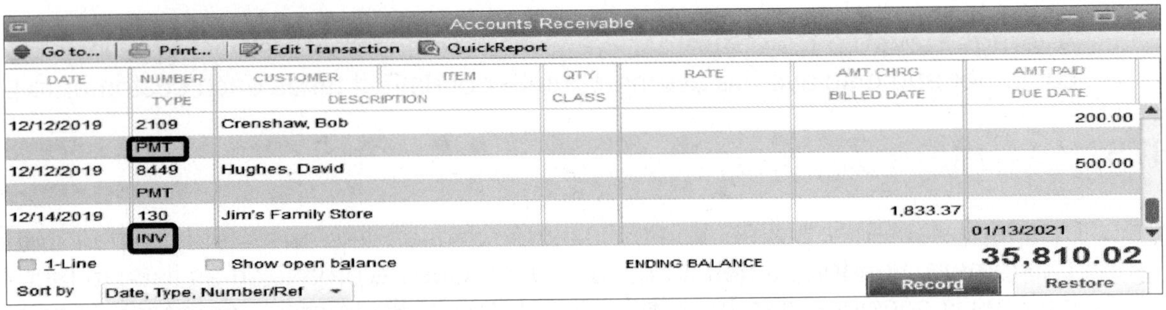

Scroll through the register
Look at the **Number/Type** column
Notice the types of transactions listed:

INV is for an invoice
PMT indicates a payment received from a customer

Click the **Close** button on the Register
Click the **Close** button on the Chart of Accounts

REPORTS

Reports are an integral part of a business. Reports enable owners and managers to determine how the business is doing and to make decisions affecting the future of the company. Reports can be prepared showing the profit and loss for the period, the status of the Balance Sheet (assets equal liabilities plus owner's equity), information regarding accounts receivable and accounts payable, and the amount of sales for each item. QuickBooks has a wide range of reports and reporting options available. Reports may be customized to better reflect the information needs of a company. Reports may be generated in a variety of ways.

Reports menu includes a complete listing of the reports available in QuickBooks and is used to prepare reports including: company and financial reports such as profit and loss (income statement) and balance sheet; accounts receivable reports; sales reports; accounts payable reports; banking reports; transaction detail reports; payroll reports; budget and forecast reports; list reports; industry specific reports; custom reports; graphs showing graphical analysis of business operations; and several other classifications of reports.

Report Center includes a complete listing of the reports available in QuickBooks. Reports may be shown in a Carousel view, a Grid view, and a List view.

Prepare reports from the **Reports** menu

Click **Reports** on the menu bar
Point to **Company & Financial**
Click **Profit & Loss Standard**
Scroll through the Profit and Loss Statement for Larry's Landscaping & Garden Supply

- Notice the Net Income for the period.

Click the **Close** button to exit the report

Prepare reports using the **Report Center**

Click **Reports** on the Icon Bar
Click **Company & Financial** in the list of reports on the left side of the navigator if it is not already highlighted
Explore the report list view options by clicking the following buttons in the upper-right corner of the Report Center:

Click the button for **Carousel View** 

- Sample reports revolve when clicked and are shown in the correct format.

Click the button for **Grid View** 

- Sample reports are shown in a side-by-side grid.

Click the button for **List View**

- Reports and a brief description are listed.

Scroll through the list of reports available until you see Balance Sheet Standard
Click **Balance Sheet Standard**

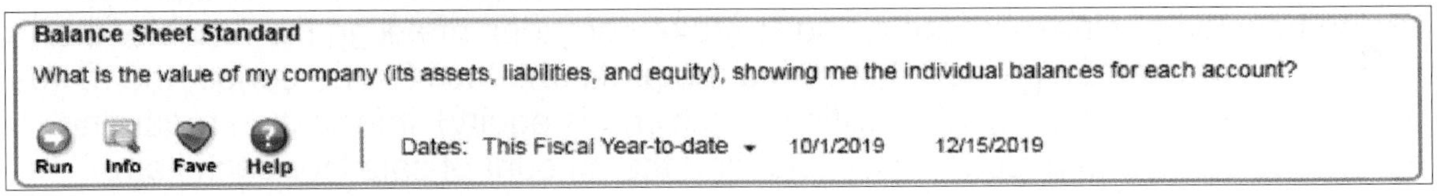

Click the green **Run** button to display the report
Scroll through the report

- Notice that Total Assets equal Total Liabilities & Equity.

Do not close the report

QUICKZOOM

QuickZoom allows you to view transactions that contribute to the data on reports or graphs.

Use QuickZoom

Scroll through the Balance Sheet on the screen until you see the fixed asset **Truck**
Position the mouse pointer over the amount for **Total Truck**

- The mouse pointer turns into .

Double-click the mouse to see the transaction detail for the Total Truck
Click the **Close** button to close the **Transactions by Account** report
Click the **Close** button to close the **Balance Sheet**
Do not close the Report Center

GRAPHS

Using bar charts and pie charts, QuickBooks gives you an instant visual analysis of different elements of your business. You may obtain information in a graphical form for Income & Expenses, Sales, Accounts Receivable, Accounts Payable, Net Worth, and Budget vs. Actual. For example, using the Report Center and Company & Financial as the type of report, double-clicking Net Worth Graph allows you to see an owner's net worth in relationship to assets and liabilities. This is displayed on a bar chart according to the month. To obtain information about liabilities for a given month, you may zoom in on the liabilities portion of the bar, double-click, and see the liabilities for the month displayed in a pie chart.

View a Graph

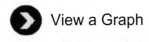

Report Center should be on the screen

Company & Financial is the **Type of Report** 1

Click the **Carousel View** button 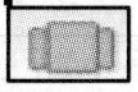

As you use the bottom scroll bar to scroll through the reports, you will see samples displayed

Scroll through the list of reports, click **Net Worth Graph**

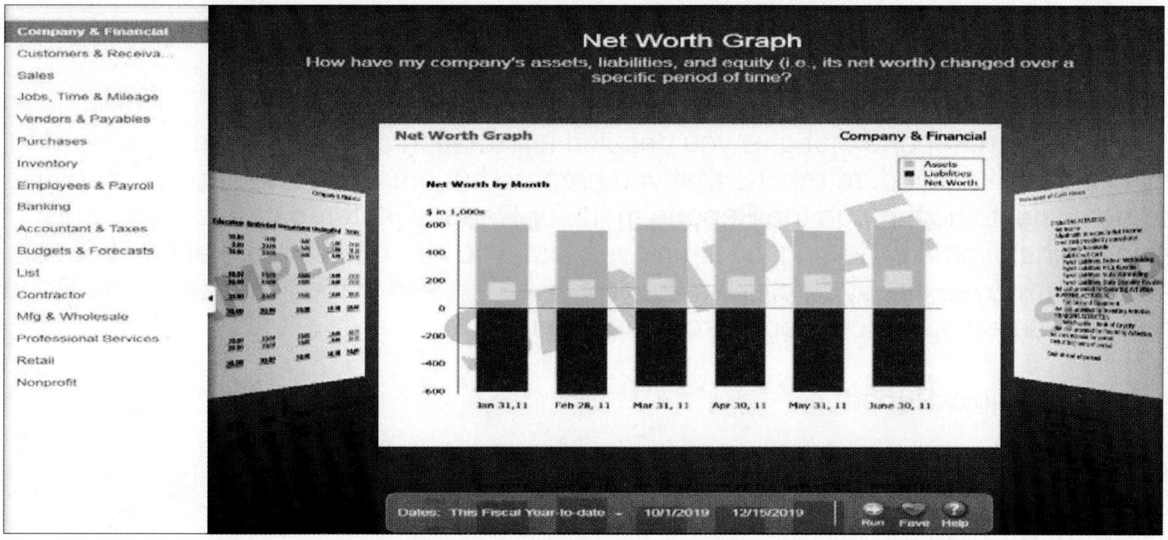

Click **Run** and then view the Net Worth Graph

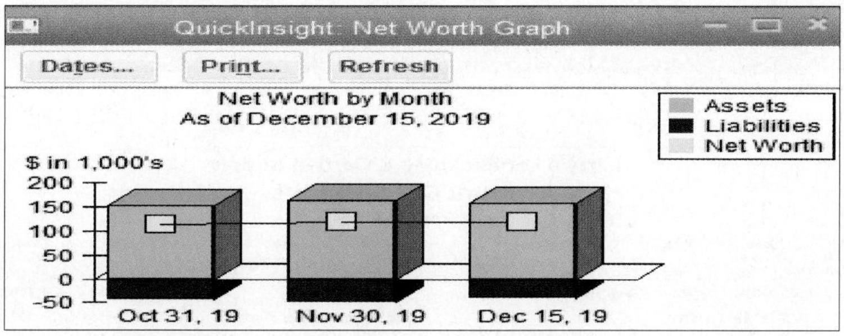

Zoom in on the Liabilities for October by pointing to the liabilities portion of the graph (brown color) and double-clicking

View the pie chart for October's liabilities

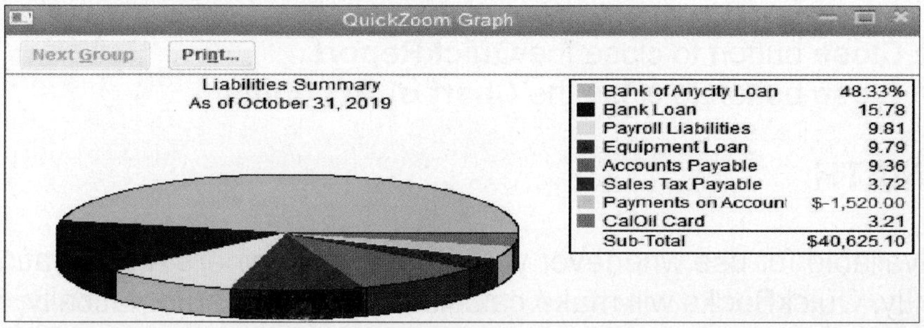

Click the **Close** button to close the pie chart
Zoom in on the **Net Worth** (yellow) for **December** and double-click
View the pie chart for **December's Net Worth Summary**
Use the keyboard shortcut **Ctrl+F4** to close the pie chart
Click the **Close** button to close the Net Worth graph
Close the **Report Center**

QUICKREPORT

QuickReports are reports that give you detailed information about items you are viewing. They look just like standard reports that you prepare but are considered "quick" because you don't have to go through the Reports menu or Report Center to create them. For example, when you are viewing the Employee List, you can obtain information about an individual employee simply by clicking the employee's name in the list, clicking the Reports button, and selecting QuickReports from the menu.

View a QuickReport

Click **Lists** on the menu bar
Click **Chart of Accounts**
Click **Prepaid Insurance**
Click **Reports** button at the bottom of the Chart of Accounts List
Click **QuickReport: Prepaid Insurance**

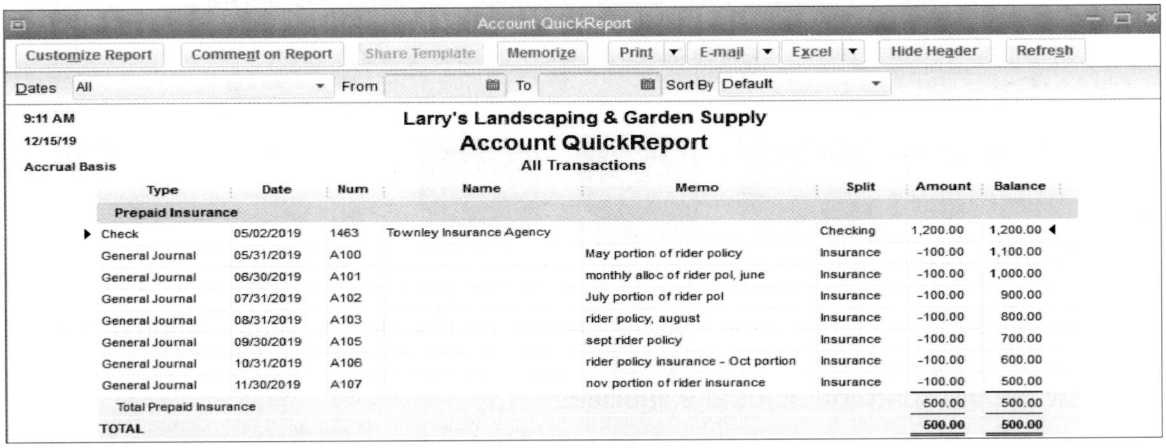
Account QuickReport

Customize Report | Comment on Report | Share Template | Memorize | Print | E-mail | Excel | Hide Header | Refresh

Dates All | From | To | Sort By Default

9:11 AM
12/15/19
Accrual Basis

Larry's Landscaping & Garden Supply
Account QuickReport
All Transactions

Type	Date	Num	Name	Memo	Split	Amount	Balance
Prepaid Insurance							
Check	05/02/2019	1463	Townley Insurance Agency		Checking	1,200.00	1,200.00
General Journal	05/31/2019	A100		May portion of rider policy	Insurance	-100.00	1,100.00
General Journal	06/30/2019	A101		monthly alloc of rider pol, june	Insurance	-100.00	1,000.00
General Journal	07/31/2019	A102		July portion of rider pol	Insurance	-100.00	900.00
General Journal	08/31/2019	A103		rider policy, august	Insurance	-100.00	800.00
General Journal	09/30/2019	A105		sept rider policy	Insurance	-100.00	700.00
General Journal	10/31/2019	A106		rider policy insurance - Oct portion	Insurance	-100.00	600.00
General Journal	11/30/2019	A107		nov portion of rider insurance	Insurance	-100.00	500.00
Total Prepaid Insurance						500.00	500.00
TOTAL						500.00	500.00

Click the **Close** button to close the **QuickReport**
Click the **Close** button to close the **Chart of Accounts**

USE QUICKMATH

QuickMath is available for use whenever you are in a field where a calculation is to be made. Frequently, QuickBooks will make calculations for you automatically; however, there may be instances when you need to perform the calculation. For example, on an invoice,

QuickBooks will calculate an amount based on the quantity and the rate given for a sales item. If for some reason you do not have a rate for a sales item, you may use QuickMath to calculate the amount. To do this, you tab to the amount column, type an **=** or a number and the **+**. QuickBooks will show an adding machine tape on the screen. You may then add, subtract, multiply, or divide to obtain a total or a subtotal. Pressing the enter key inserts the amount into the column.

Use QuickMath

Click the **Create Invoices** icon on the Home Page
Click in the **Amount** column on the Invoice

Enter the numbers: **123+**
456+
789

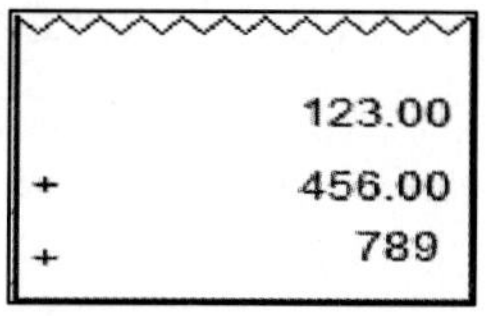

Press **Enter**
The total **1,368** is inserted into the Amount column
Click the **Clear** button to remove the total amount of **1,368**, do not close the invoice

USE WINDOWS CALCULATOR

Windows includes accessory programs that may be used to complete tasks while you are working in QuickBooks. One of these accessory programs is Calculator. Using this program gives you an on-screen calculator. To use the Calculator in Windows, click the Windows Start button, click All Programs, scroll through the list, click the Accessories folder, click Calculator. A calculator appears on your screen. The Windows calculator is also accessible through QuickBooks.

Access Windows Calculator through QuickBooks

Click **Edit** on the menu bar
Click **Use Calculator**
Change from a standard calculator to a scientific calculator: click the **View** menu on the Calculator menu bar, click **Scientific**

- In addition to standard and scientific, you may also select programmer or statistics.

Change back to a standard calculator: click the **View** menu on the Calculator menu bar, click **Standard**
Numbers may be entered by:
Clicking the number on the calculator
Keying the number using the numeric keypad
Typing the keyboard numbers
Enter the numbers: **123+**
456+
789=

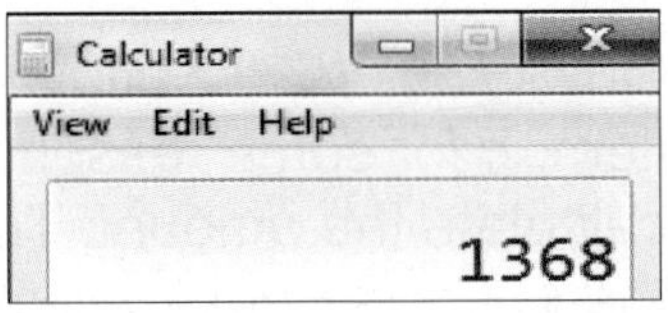

The amount is subtotaled after each entry

After typing 789=, the answer 1368 appears

- Note: Using the Windows Calculator does not insert the amount into a QuickBooks form.

To clear the answer, click the **C** button on the calculator

Enter: **55*6**

Press **Enter** or click **=** to get the answer 330

- Again, note that answer is not inserted into the invoice.

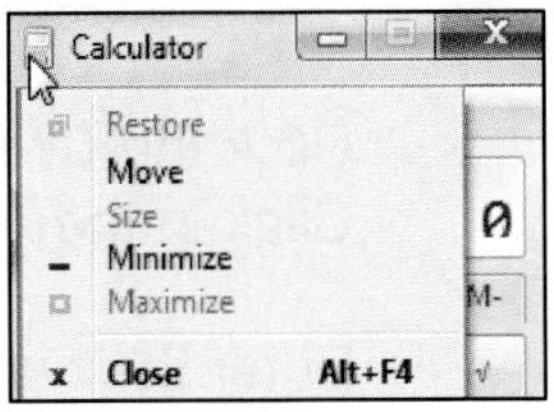

Click the **Control menu icon** (the picture of the Calculator on the left side of the calculator title bar), click **Close** to close the **Calculator**

Click the **Close** button on the Invoice to close the invoice without saving

CLOSE COMPANY

The sample company—Larry's Landscaping & Garden Supply—will appear as the open company whenever you open QuickBooks. In order to discontinue the use of the sample company, you must close the company. In a classroom environment, you should always back up your work and close the company you are using at the end of a work session. If you use different computers when training, not closing a company at the end of each work session may cause your files to become corrupt, your disk to fail, or leave unwanted .qbi (QuickBooks In Use) files on your data disk.

Close a company

Click **File** menu, click **Close Company**

Click the **Close** button to exit and close **QuickBooks**

If you get a message regarding Exiting QuickBooks, click the check box for **"Do not display this message in the future,"** and then click **Yes**

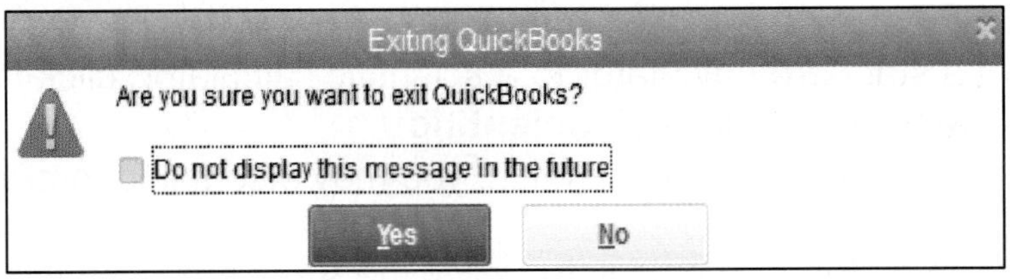

COMPANY FILES

When working in QuickBooks, you will use files that contain data for companies that are in the text. Before beginning to use the program, you need to get a working copy of the company files. This may be done by accessing the Pearson Education Web Site. Instructions follow for downloading and extracting files.

DOWNLOAD COMPANY FILES

The company files for the text are available on the Prentice Hall web site http://www.pearsonhighered.com/horne/. Depending on your internet browser, your version of windows, your storage location, and a variety of other variables, your screens may not always match those shown in the text. If you find differences and are not sure if you are proceeding correctly, check with your instructor.

Download company files

Insert your USB drive into your computer or ask you professor for specific directions to be used at your school

Open **Internet Explorer** or whatever browser you use

Enter the address **http://www.pearsonhighered.com/horne/**

- Sometimes it is difficult to read "horne" so, remember the name is HORNE.
- Note: At the time of writing, a temporary cover image was posted. The actual cover will change when the site is finalized.
- When completing the following steps, be sure to use the section for the QuickBooks 2015 edition of the text.
- Check with your instructor to determine if you will use a different procedure.

Click **Company Master Files Chapters 1-4 (Student Data Files)** next to the QuickBooks 2015 cover image

You will download the files for Chapters 1, 2, 3, 4, and the Service practice set at this time. When you get to Chapter 5, you will download the remaining company files from Company Master Files Chapters 5-8 (Student Data Files)

- **IMPORTANT**: Depending on your version of Windows, Internet Explorer, or browser your screens may be different from the examples shown. If so, complete the download using the prompts from your program. Ask your instructor for assistance if you are not using Internet Explorer

On the Windows Internet Explorer screen, click **Save As**

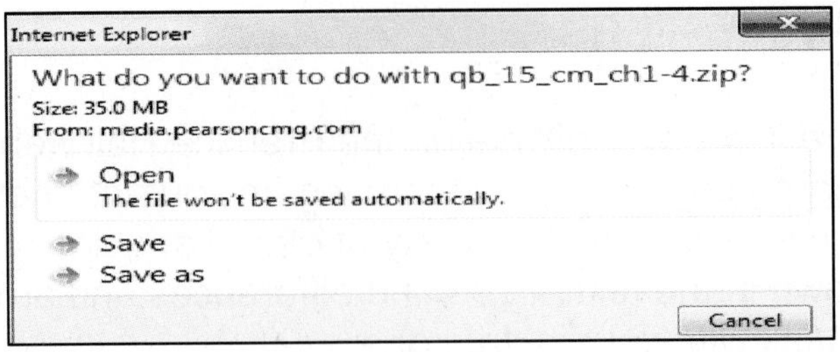

When the **Save As** screen appears, scroll through the listing on the left side of the Save As screen; and then click on the drive location for your USB drive

- In the example, the drive location is G:. Your USB location may show a different letter, accept what you are shown.

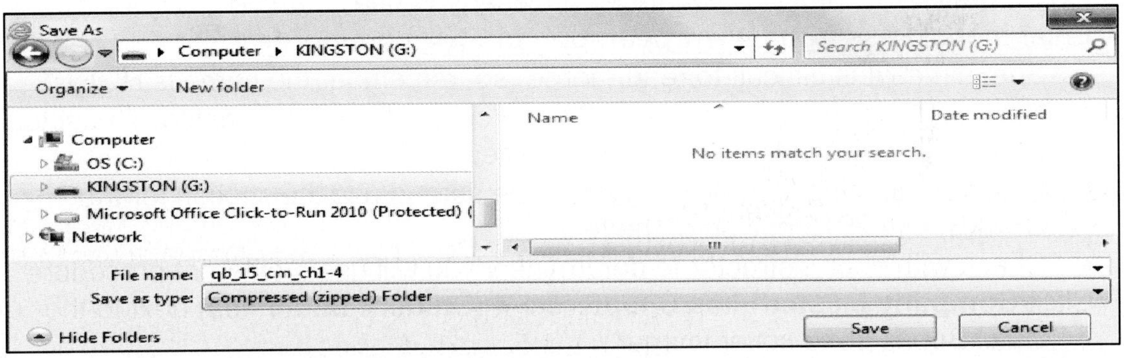

- As you work through these next screens, your file name may or may not show **.zip** at the end. Zip indicates that the file type is compressed or zipped.
- The following screen shots show the file name as it appears when downloading the file using Internet Explorer.

Accept the file name given **qb_15_cm_ch1-4**
Save as type: **Compressed (zipped) Folder**
Click the **Save** button

- It could take several minutes for the download to finish.
- Internet Explorer will show a message at the bottom of the screen while the download is being completed.

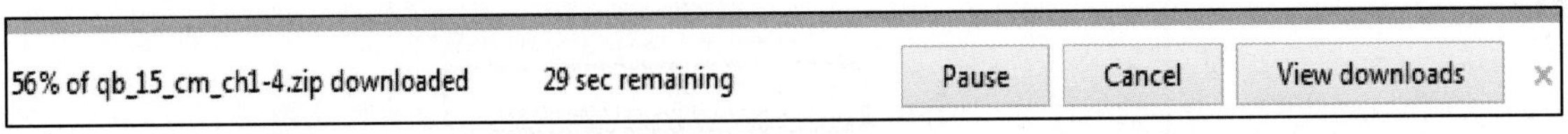

Windows Explorer should be open and the qb_15_cm_ch1-4 folder should show on your USB drive

- You may get a screen from Internet Explorer with a message that the download has completed and will allow you to open the folder. If so, click **Open Folder**.

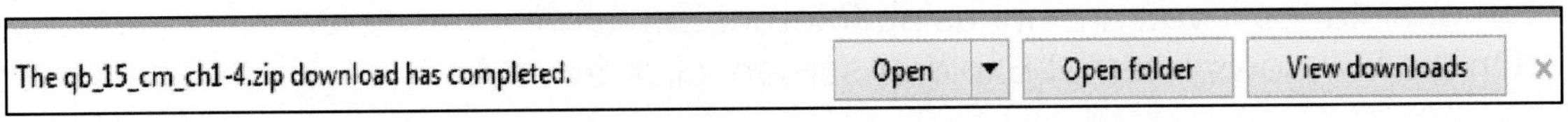

Close **Internet Explorer**

- If you don't see Windows Explorer, click the **Windows Explorer** icon on the Task Bar and click your USB drive location
  OR
- Right-click the **Start** button on the Task Bar in the lower-left corner of your screen, click **Open Windows Explorer** and click your USB drive location
- Notice the zipper folder on the qb_15_cm_ch1-4. This means the compressed folder needs to be unzipped.

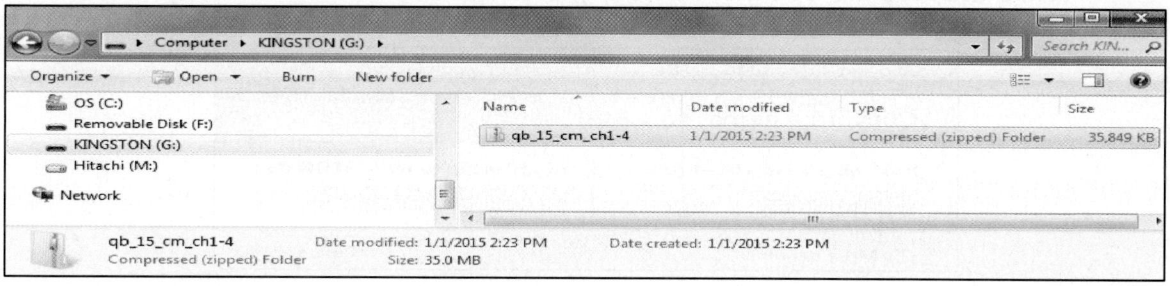

Double-click **qb_15_cm_ch1-4**
Click **Extract all files**

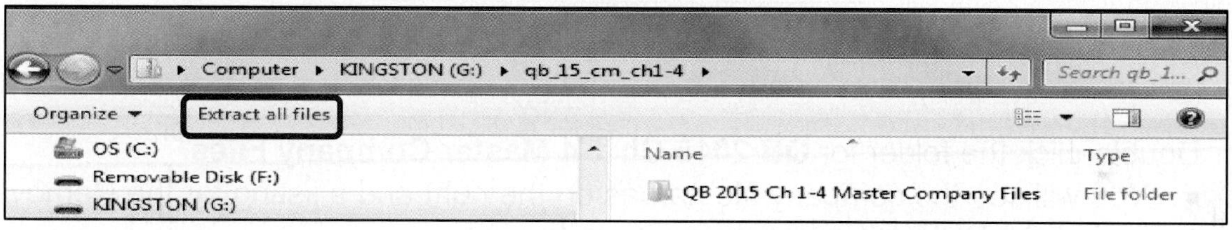

You will get the following screen (your USB may show a different letter):

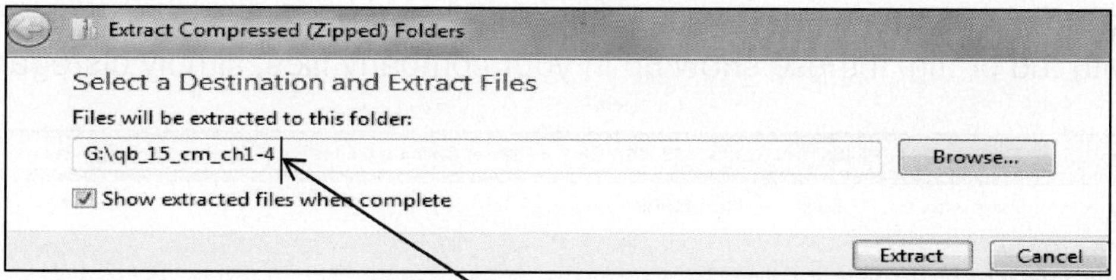

Click at the end of **G:\qb_15_cm_ch1-4**
Backspace until you only see the letter of your USB drive as the folder (**G:** in this example):

- Make sure **Show extracted files when complete** is checked. If it is not marked, click to insert the check mark.

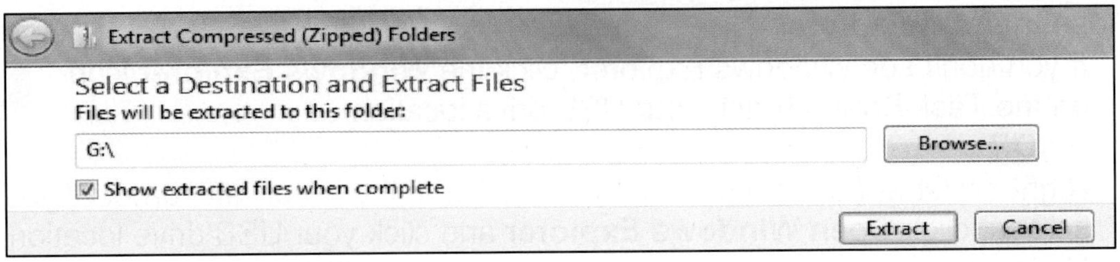

Click the **Extract** button

- While the files are being extracted, you will see:

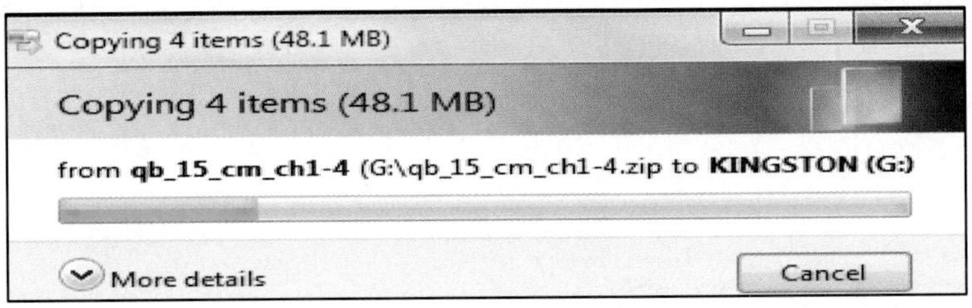

- When the files have been extracted, you will see the zipped folder—qb_15_cm_ch1-4—and a file folder—QB 2015 Ch 1-4 Master Company Files

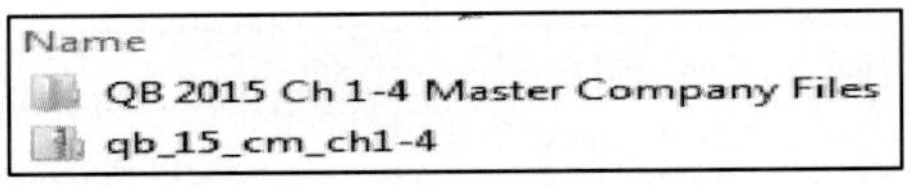

Double-click the folder for **QB 2015 Ch 1-4 Master Company Files**

- You will see the company file names on the right and a listing for the Removable Disk (your USB, the example is G:) on the left.
- Your company files may show the extension **.qbw**, which means the file type is a "QuickBooks Working" file.
- As you work with QuickBooks, you will see files for SearchIndex, and files ending with .nd or .tlg. If these show up in your company files, simply disregard them.

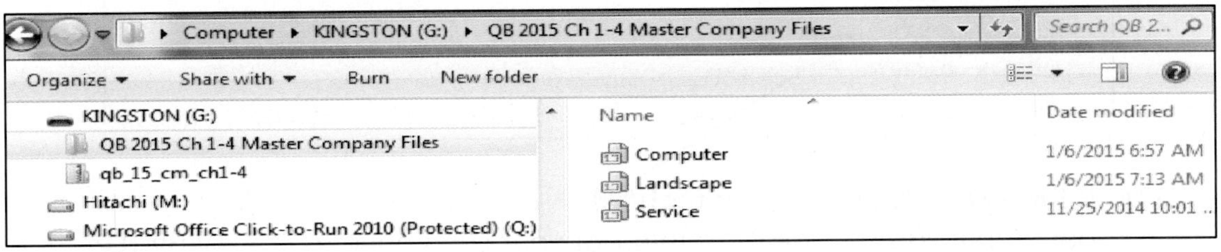

- It is possible that the company file will be marked as "Read Only" and/or "Archive."
- In addition to removing the properties at this point, as you work through the chapters and switch from one company to the next (Computer to Landscape and then back to Computer), QuickBooks might mark your company file as read only. If this happens, refer to the following steps on how to change the file Properties from Read Only.

Right-click the file **Computer**
Click **Properties**

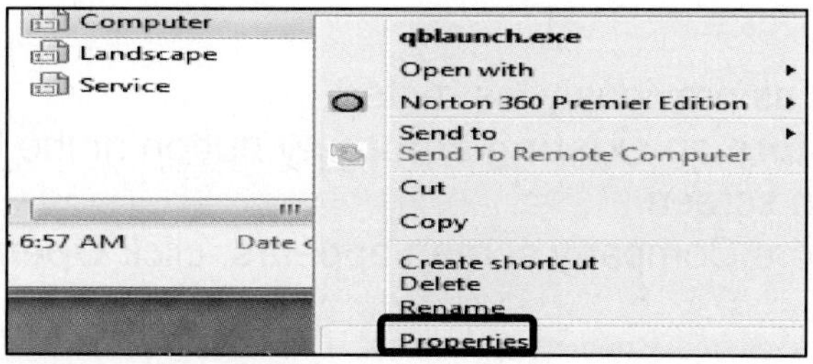

If there is a check mark next to **Read Only** and/or **Archive**, click the check box to remove the mark

- Your Properties for Computer may show a different storage location and different dates. This should not be of any concern.

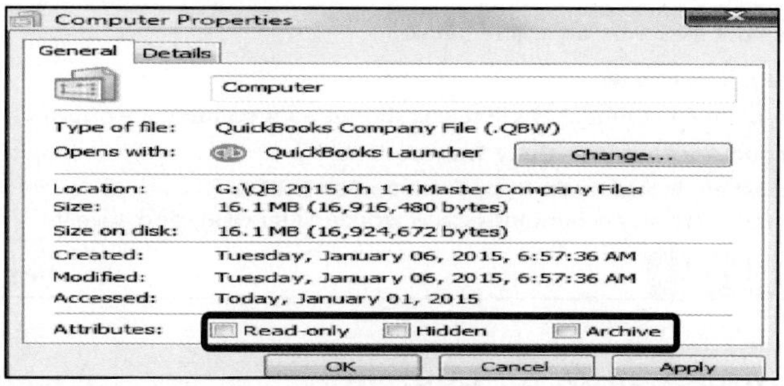

Click the **Apply** button, and then click **OK**

- The file is now ready for use.

Repeat for all of the companies to make those files ready for use
Close all screens

COMPANY DESCRIPTION

In the text you will be recording transactions for a fictional company that specializes in computer consulting. The company provides program installation, training, and technical support for today's business software as well as helping clients learn how to go online and giving instruction in the use of the Internet. In addition, Computer Consulting by Student's Name will set up computer systems and networks for customers and will install basic computer components, such as: memory, modems, sound cards, hard drives, and CD/DVD drives.

This fictitious, small, sole proprietorship company will be owned and run by you. You will be adding your name to the company name and equity accounts. This company will be used for training while completing Chapters 1 through 4.

OPEN AND UPDATE COMPANY FILE

Open a company

Open QuickBooks as previously instructed
Click **Open or restore an existing company** button at the bottom of the No Company Open screen
The Open or Restore Company screen appears, click **Open a company file**, click **Next**

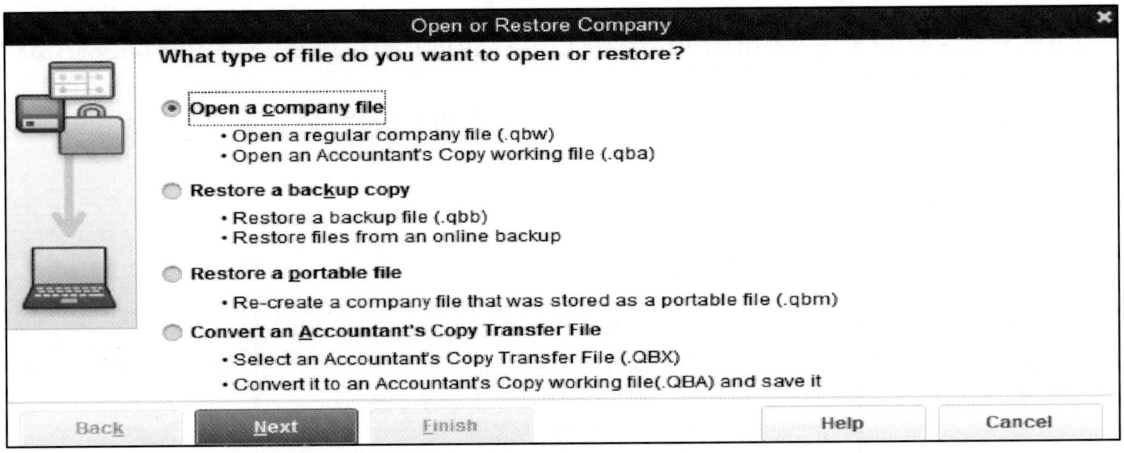

Click the drop-down list arrow for **Look in**
Click **Removable Disk (USB Drive Letter:)**
Double-click the folder **QuickBooks 2015 Ch 1-4 Master Company Files**
Locate and click **Computer** (in the list of file names that appear in the dialog box)

- The File name: textbox now shows **Computer**
- Notice the Files of type: is **QuickBooks Files (*.QBW, *QBA)**
  - **.QBW** stands for QuickBooks Working file and is used to record all transactions for a company
  - **.QBA** is the copy of the company file used by the company's accountant

Click **Open**

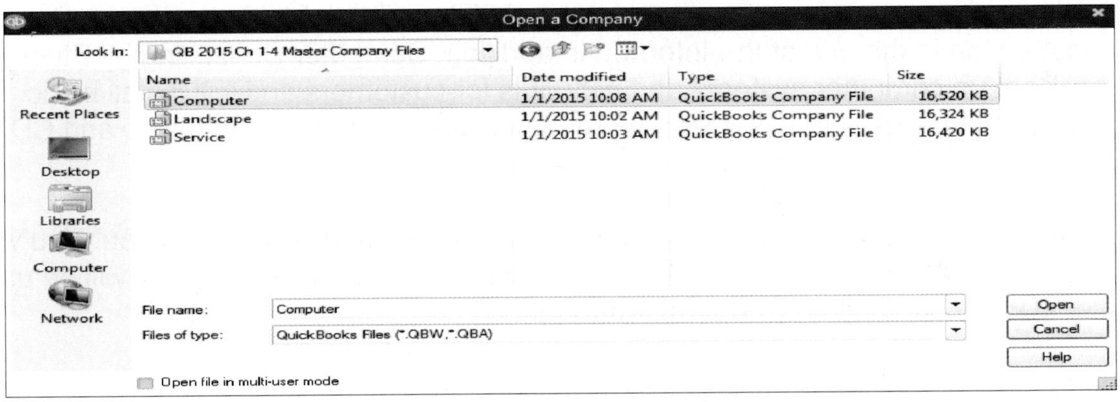

You should get one of two possible update screens.

- If you do not get one of the following screens, continue with the next section: QuickBooks Opening Screens.
- If you get an Update Company File for New Version, skip the instructions below and go to the information shown after **OR**
- If you get the Update Company screen, follow the steps below.

Click **Yes** on the Update Company screen

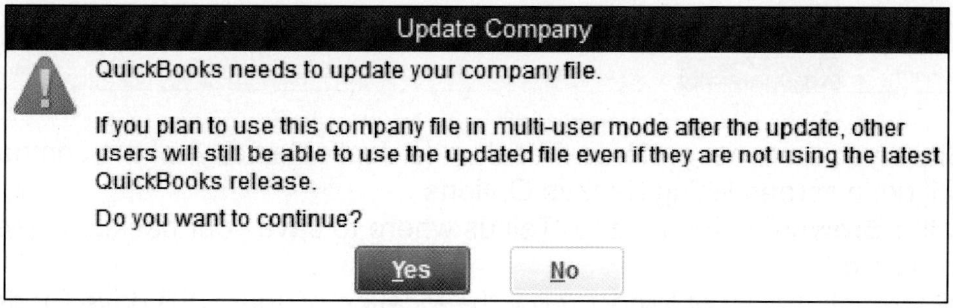

If you get a Set Closing Date Password screen, click **No**

OR

If you get a screen "Update Company File for New Version, click **I understand that my company file will be updated to this new version of QuickBooks**; and then, click the **Update Now** button

Click **OK** on the QuickBooks Information screen to back up your company data

On the Create Backup screen, click **Local backup**; and then, click **Next**

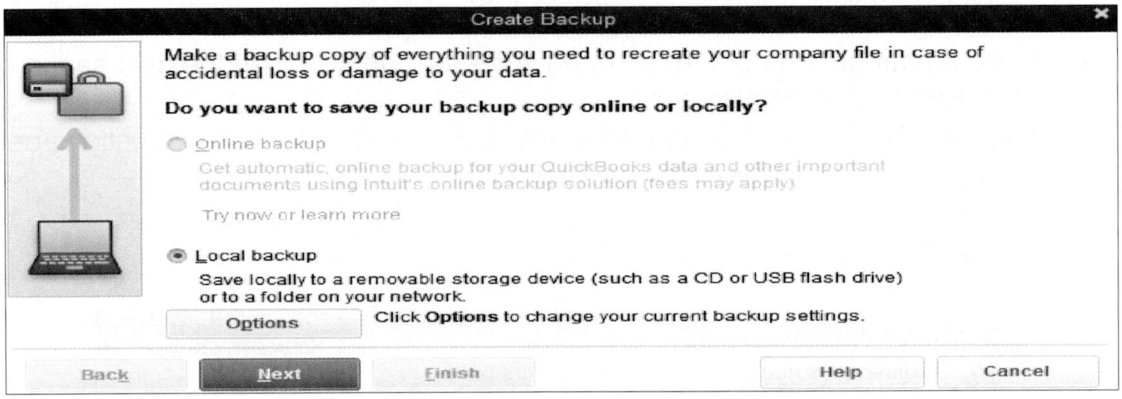

- Since you have never made a backup (a duplicate copy) of the company file, you will get a screen listing Backup Options

Click the **Browse** button next to "Tell us where to save your backup copies (required)"

Scroll through the list of folders, click the location of your USB drive (or designated storage area)

- The text uses (G:\).

Click the checkboxes for **Add the date and time of the backup to the file name** and **Remind me to back up when I close my company file** to remove the check marks

Keep **Complete verification**

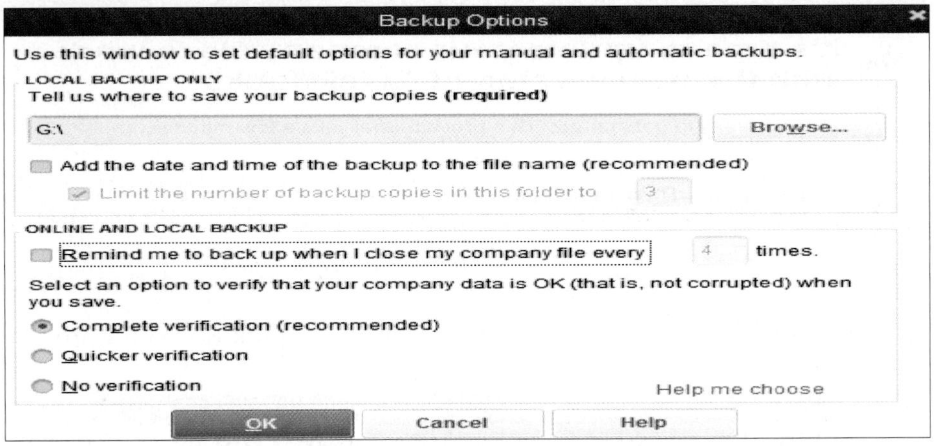

Click **OK**

If you are saving the backup file to the same USB drive that you are using to store the company file, you will get the following screen

Click **Use this Location**
On the Save Backup Copy screen, make sure
  Save in: is your **USB drive**
  File name: is **Computer (Backup)**
  Save as type: is **QBW Backup (*.QBB)**
On the Save Backup Copy, click **Save**
When finished, click **Yes** on the Update Company screen

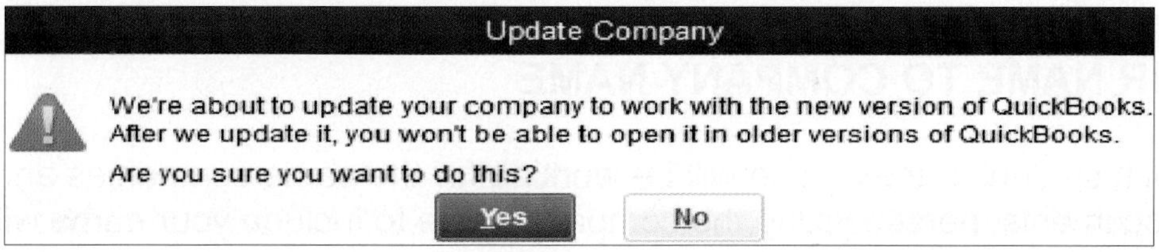

If you get a Set Closing Date Password screen, click **No**

QUICKBOOKS OPENING SCREENS

Sometimes company files open with screens such as Update Company File, QuickBooks Products and Services, QuickBooks Alerts, Set Up an External Accountant User, and others. These screens provide information and/or instructions on how to use QuickBooks, how to subscribe to optional services, or give information regarding reminder alerts. In addition, QuickBooks may open business forms with wizards, questions, or tutorials regarding options, methods of work, and other items. You may see a gold "What's New"

If you receive any opening screens, read them and select an appropriate answer.

- For example, you would always update your company file, but you would not enter passwords or create an external user. If you receive an alert, simply click Mark as Done

If you get the "What's New" message, click the  to close it

- You can turn it back on by using the Help Menu.

VERIFY OPEN COMPANY

Unless you tell QuickBooks to create a new company, open a different company, or close the company, Computer Consulting by Student's Name will appear as the open company whenever you open QuickBooks. However, when you finish a work session, you should always close the company in order to avoid problems with the file in a future work session.

Verify the title bar heading:

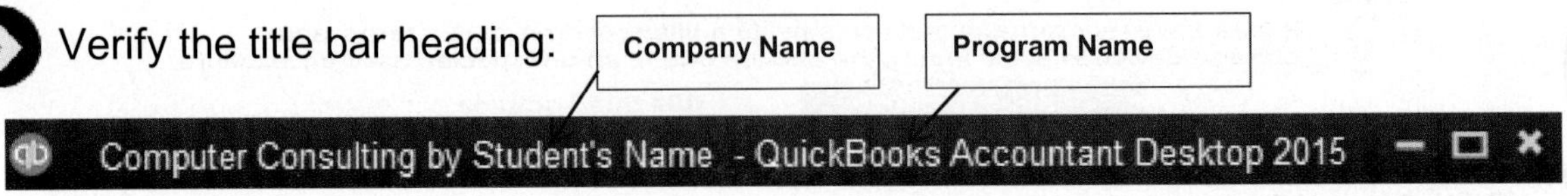

- If your title bar shows QuickBooks Premier Accountant Desktop 2015, that is fine. There is no difference in the program since QuickBooks Accountant Desktop is part of the Premier version of QuickBooks.
- Remember, throughout the text the program is referred to as QuickBooks 2015 rather than QuickBooks Premier or QuickBooks Accountant Desktop, etc. No distinction will be made regarding Premier or Accountant from this point forward in the text.

ADD YOUR NAME TO COMPANY NAME

Because each student in the course will be working for the same companies and printing the same documents, personalizing the company name to include your name will help identify your work.

Add your name to the company name and legal name

Click **Company** on the menu bar
Click **My Company**

Click the **Edit** button in the upper-right corner of My Company
- The Company Information screen will appear with Contact Information highlighted, if not click it

Replace the words **Student's Name** with your real name by holding down the left mouse button and dragging through the "Student's Name" to highlight

OR

Click in front of the S in Student's Name; press the **Delete** key to delete one letter at a time

Type your actual name, *not* the words *Your Name* as is shown in the text. For example, Janet Horne would type **Janet Horne**

Click **Legal Information** on the left side of Company Information
Repeat the steps to change the legal name to **Computer Consulting by Your Name** (Remember to enter your actual name—not the words "Your Name")
Click **OK**

- Note the change on My Company

Click the **Close** button for My Company

- The title bar now shows **Computer Consulting by Your Name – QuickBooks Accountant Desktop 2015**.

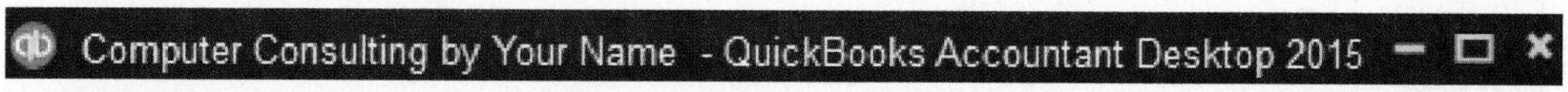

- Remember your actual name is now part of the company name and will be on the title bar. In the text, however, the title bar will show the words **Your Name**.

CREATE COMPANY BACKUP FILE

As you work with a company and record transactions, it is important to back up your work. This allows you to keep the information for a particular period separate from current information. A backup also allows you to restore information in case your data disk becomes damaged. QuickBooks has a feature to make a backup copy of your company file. A condensed file is created by QuickBooks. The file contains the essential transaction and account information. This file has a **.qbb** extension and is not usable unless it is restored to a company file that has a **.qbw** extension. This can be an existing company file or a new company file.

In this text, you will make a backup file at the end of each chapter. It will contain all of the transactions entered up until the time you made the backup. At the end of each chapter, you will be instructed to make a backup file for the chapter. *Future transactions will not be part of the backup file unless you make a new backup file*. For example, Chapter 1 backup will not contain any transactions entered in Chapter 2. However, Chapter 2 backup will contain all the transactions for both Chapters 1 and 2. Chapter 3 backup will contain all the transactions for Chapters 1, 2, and 3, and so on.

In many classroom configurations, you will be storing your backup files onto the same USB drive that you use for the company file. In actual business practice, you should save the backup to a different location. Most likely, you will store your company file on the hard disk of the computer and the backup file will be stored on a USB drive, a network drive, the Cloud, or some other remote location. Check with your instructor to see if there are any other backup file locations you should use in your training.

Make a QuickBooks backup of the company data for Computer Consulting by Your Name.

Click **File** on the Menu Bar
Click **Back Up Company**
Click **Create Local Backup**

- Make sure the Create Backup screen has Local backup selected. If not, click **Local backup** to select.

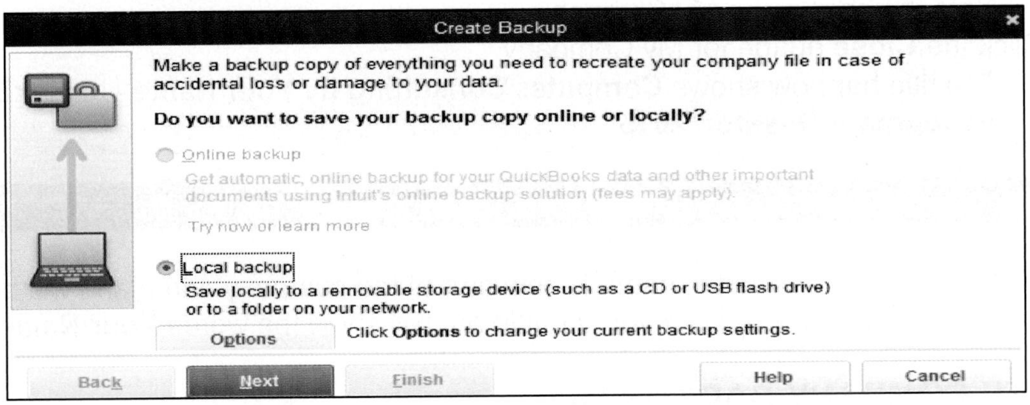

Click the **Next** button

- The first time you backup a file, you will get a screen with Backup Options, complete the following.
- If you created a backup file previously, you will not get the Backup Options screen. Skip the next few lines of instruction and continue with the bullet after "Keep **Complete verification**, click **OK**".

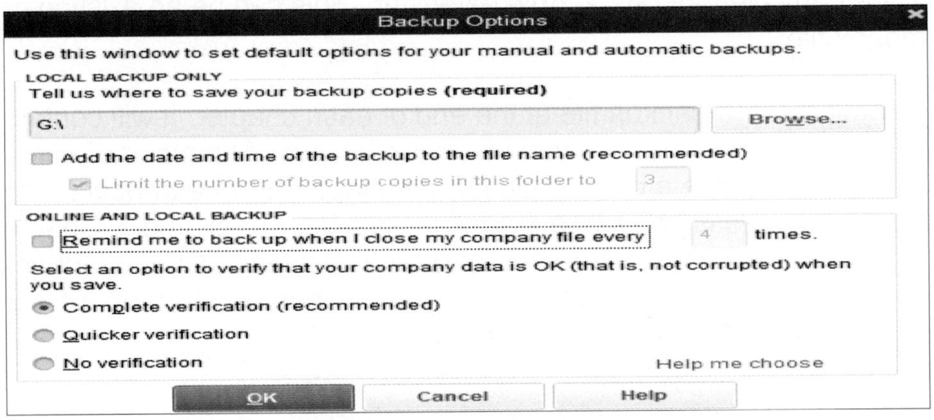

Click the **Browse** button next to "Tell us where to save your backup copies (required)"

Scroll through the list of folders, click the location of your USB drive (or designated storage area)

- The text uses (G:\).

Click **OK**

Click the checkboxes for **Add the date and time of the backup to the file name** and **Remind me to back up when I close my company file** to remove the check marks

Keep **Complete verification**, click **OK**

- If you did not need to select Backup Options, <u>**continue at this point**</u>.

To complete the **Create Backup** screen, make sure **Save it now** is selected, then click the **Next** button

On the Save Backup Copy screen, **Save in:** should be **USB Drive Location**

- If necessary, click the drop-down list arrow next to Save in: and click the USB Drive Location.

Change the File Name to **Computer (Backup Ch. 1)**

Save as type: **QBW Backup (*.QBB)**

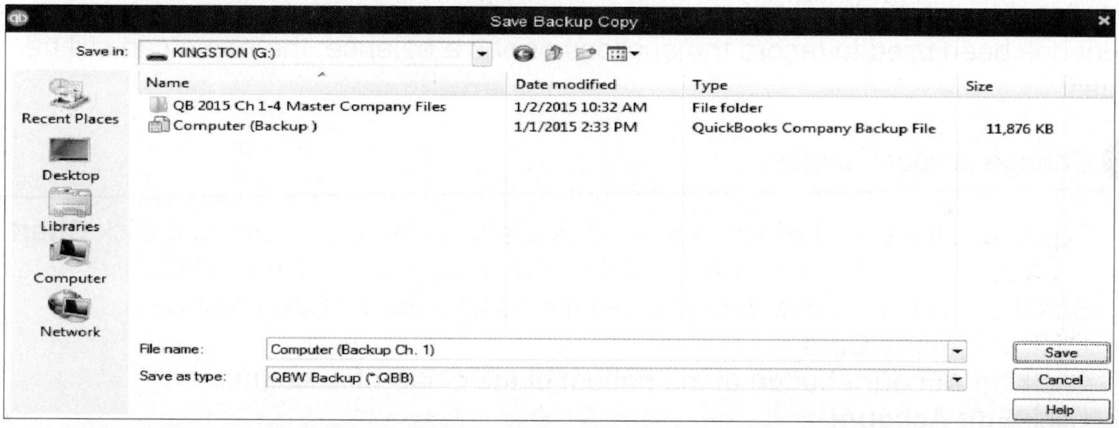

- Do not worry if the Date modified shown above does not match the date of your file. Remember the date modified is the date of your computer when you created the backup file and will be different from the text.

Click the **Save** button

If you are saving the backup file to the same USB drive that you are using to store the company file, you <u>may</u> get the following screen

If you do, click **Use this Location**

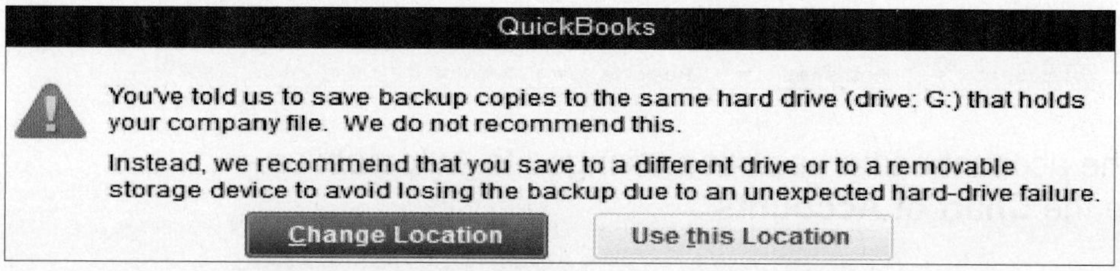

- QuickBooks will back up the information for Computer Consulting by Your Name on the USB disk.

When the backup is complete, you will see

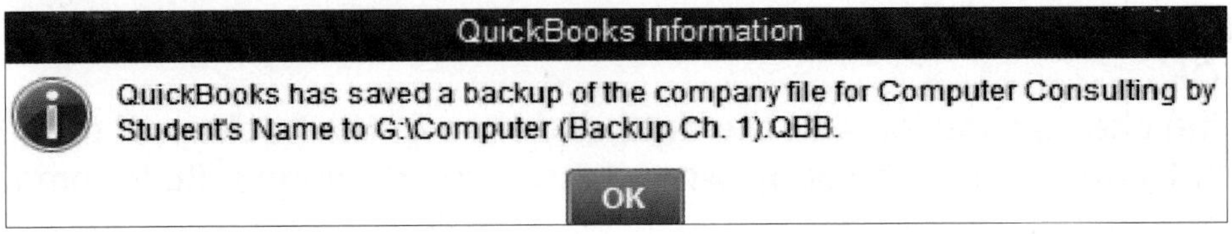

Click **OK**

- Notice that the company name on the title bar still has your name. This change was saved in the backup.

CHANGE ACCOUNT NAME

QuickBooks makes it easy to set up a company using the Easy Step Interview. You will learn how to create a company in Chapter 9 of the text. When creating a company using QuickBooks' EasyStep Interview, account names are assigned automatically. They might need to be changed to names more appropriate to the individual company. Even if an account has been used to record transactions or has a balance, the name can still be changed.

Change account names

To access the **Chart of Accounts**, click **Lists** on the menu bar, and click **Chart of Accounts** or click the **Chart of Accounts** icon on the Home Page
Scroll through accounts until you see the asset account Company Cars
Click **Company Cars**
Click the **Account** button at the bottom of the Chart of Accounts
Click **Edit Account**
On the **Edit Account** screen, highlight **Company Cars**
Enter **Automobiles**
Click the **Save & Close** button

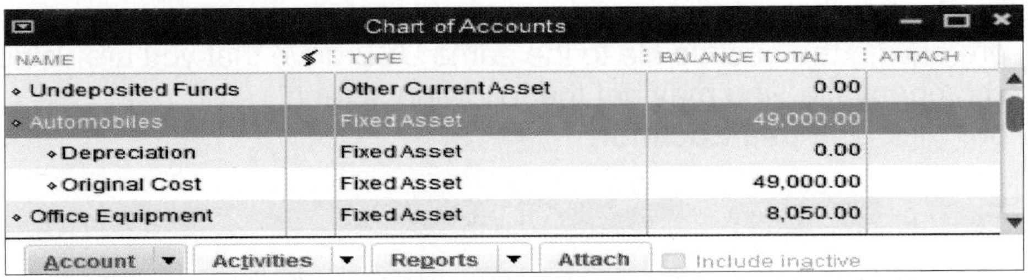

- The account name has been changed to Automobiles.

Close the **Chart of Accounts**

VIEW REPORT

To see the change in the account name in use, you may view a report.

Open the Report Center and view a Trial Balance for January 1, 2015

Click **Reports** on the icon bar to open the Report Center
Click the icon for **List View** 
Click **Accountant & Taxes** on the left side of the screen

Scroll through the reports
Click **Trial Balance** in the Account Activity section
Click **Run**

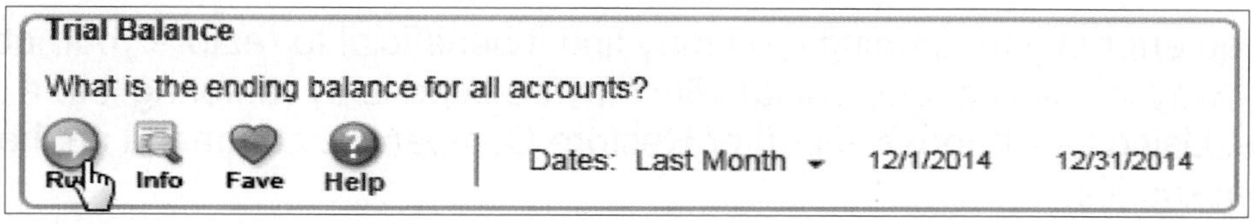

At the top of the screen, Dates should show Last Month

- Since your computer will show a different date than the example in the text you will need to insert the date used for the report.

Press the **Tab** key to highlight the **From** date
Key in the date **01/01/2015**
Press the **Tab** key to highlight the **To** date
When the **To** date is highlighted, enter **01/01/2015**
Press **Tab** two times to generate the Trial Balance for January 1, 2015

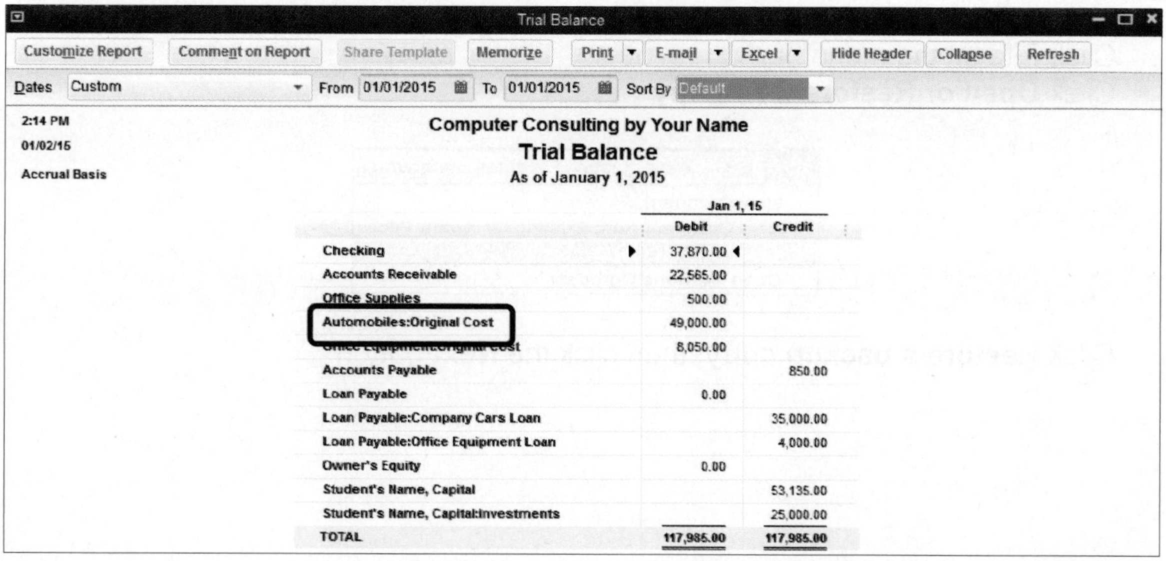

2:14 PM
01/02/15
Accrual Basis

Computer Consulting by Your Name
Trial Balance
As of January 1, 2015

	Jan 1, 15	
	Debit	Credit
Checking	37,870.00	
Accounts Receivable	22,565.00	
Office Supplies	500.00	
Automobiles:Original Cost	49,000.00	
Office Equipment:Original Cost	8,050.00	
Accounts Payable		850.00
Loan Payable	0.00	
Loan Payable:Company Cars Loan		35,000.00
Loan Payable:Office Equipment Loan		4,000.00
Owner's Equity	0.00	
Student's Name, Capital		53,135.00
Student's Name, Capital:Investments		25,000.00
TOTAL	117,985.00	117,985.00

- In the upper-left corner of the report you will see the time and date the report was prepared along with the report basis. Since the date and time of your computer is current, it will not match the dates shown above.
- Notice that the asset account Company Cars now shows as Automobiles: Original Cost. (The subaccount Original Cost is combined with the master account Automobiles.)
- These changes were made when working in Chapter 1 and show in this report.

Click the **Close** button to close the report

- If you get a Memorize Report screen, click **No**.

Click the **Close** button to close the Report Center

RESTORE COMPANY BACKUP FILE

If you make an error in your training, you may find it beneficial to restore your .qbb backup file. The only way in which a .qbb backup file may be used is by restoring it to a .qbw company file. Using QuickBooks' Open or Restore Company… command on the File menu restores a backup file.

IMPORTANT: A restored backup file replaces the current data in your company file with the data in the backup file so any transactions recorded after the backup was made will be erased. In this chapter, the backup was made after you added your name to the company name but before you changed the name of Company Cars to Automobiles. After restoring the Computer (Backup Ch. 1.qbb) backup file to Computer.qbw, the name of the asset account Automobiles will revert back to Company Cars; but the company name will still contain your name.

Practice restoring a backup file after a change has been made in the company file

Click **File** on the menu bar
Click **Open or Restore Company**

Click **Restore a backup copy**, then click the **Next** button

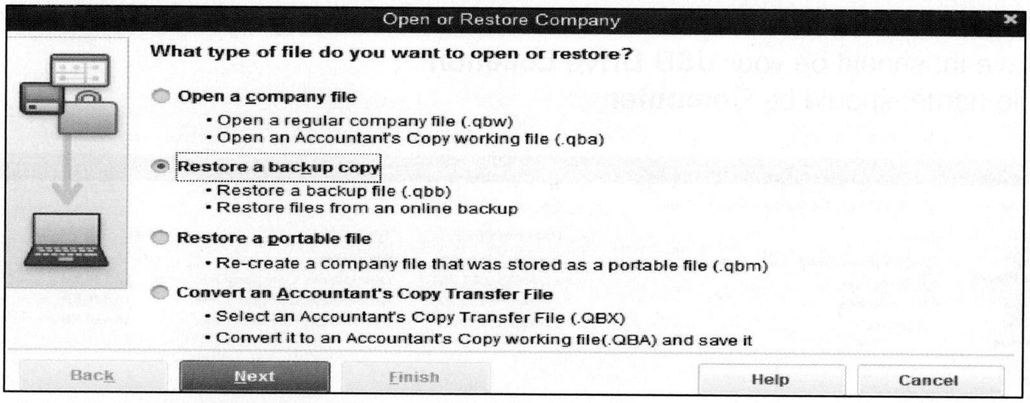

Click **Local backup**, then click the **Next** button

On the Open Backup Copy screen, make sure that Look in: shows the name of your **USB Drive** location

The File name: should be **Computer (Backup Ch. 1)**, if necessary, click the file name to insert it

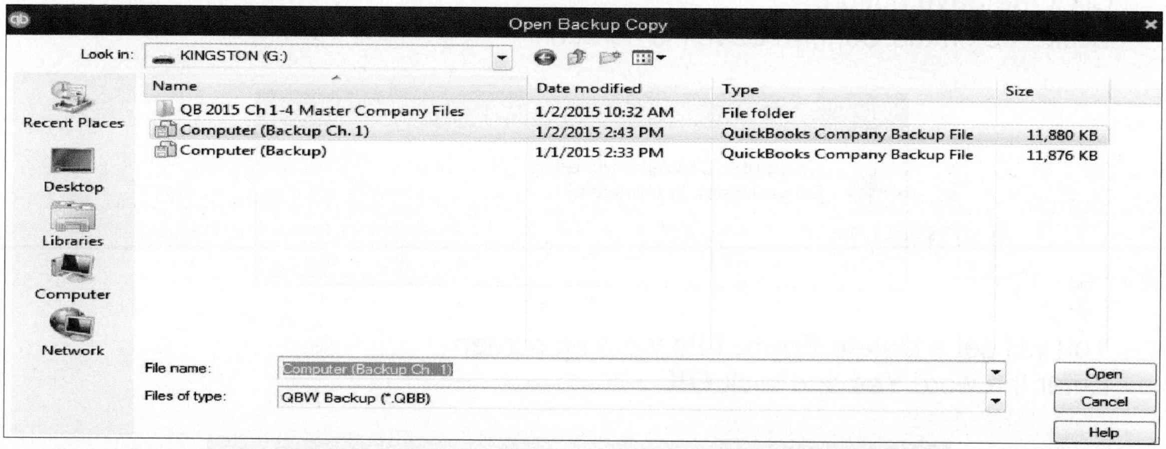

Click the **Open** button

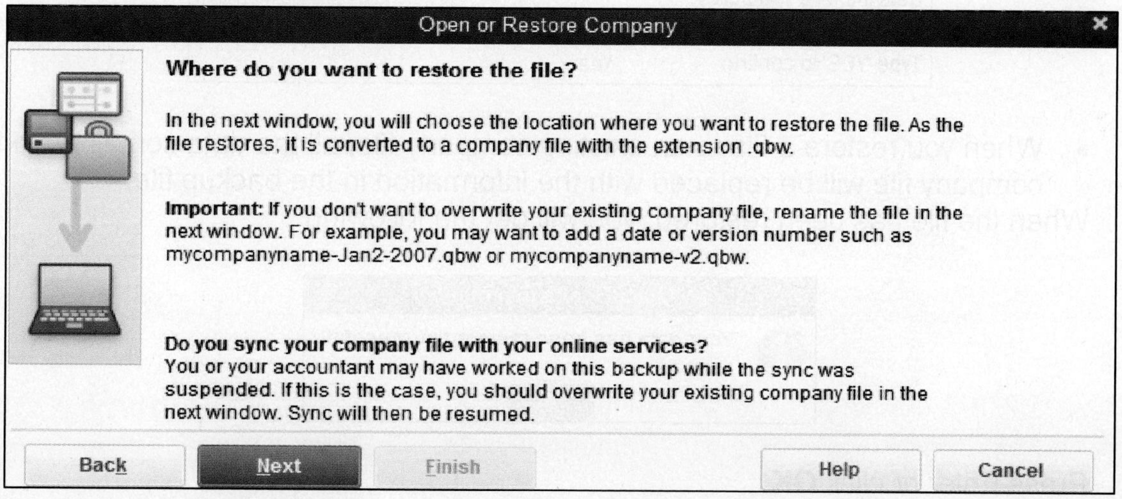

Click the **Next** button
Save in: should be your **USB Drive Location**
File name: should be **Computer**

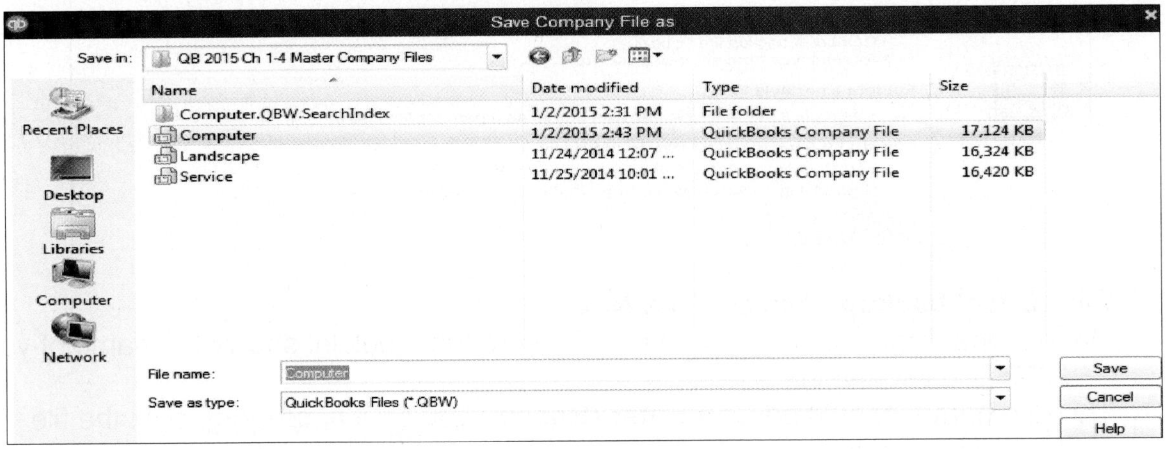

Click the **Save** button
Click **Yes** on the Confirm Save As screen

You will get a **Delete Entire File** warning screen
Enter the word **Yes** and click **OK**

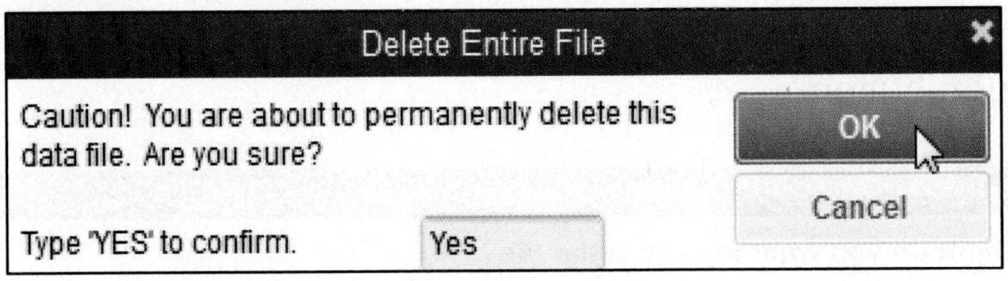

- When you restore a file to an existing company file, all the data contained in the company file will be replaced with the information in the backup file.

When the file has been restored, you will get the following

Press Enter or click **OK**

Verify that Computer Consulting by Your Name is still on the Title bar and that Company Cars rather than Automobiles is the account name

Look at the Title bar to verify the company name

- The company name was changed before you made the backup. Thus, your name remains in the company name.

Open the **Chart of Accounts** as previously instructed

Scroll through the Chart of Accounts until you find the asset account Company Cars

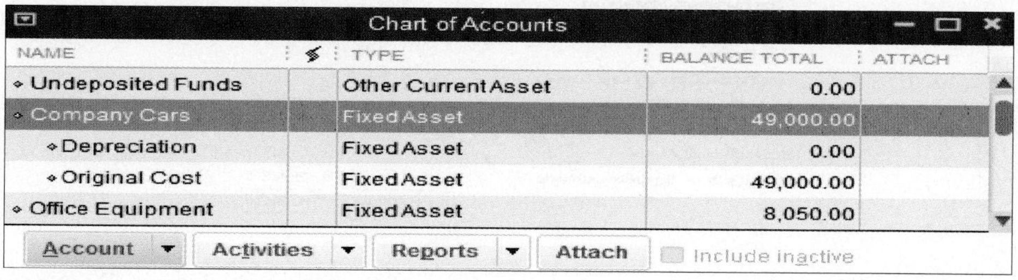

- Automobiles no longer shows as the account name because the company information was restored from the backup file that was made prior to changing the account name.

Close the Chart of Accounts

VIEW REPORT AFTER RESTORING BACKUP FILE

To see the change in the asset account name after the company file was restored, prepare a Trial Balance.

Open the Report Center and view a Trial Balance for January 1, 2015

Click **Reports** on the icon bar to open the Report Center

Click the icon for **List View**

Click **Accountant & Taxes** on the left side of the screen

Scroll through the reports

Click **Trial Balance** in the Account Activity section

Click **Run**

At the top of the screen, **Dates** should show Last Month

- Since your computer will show a different date than the example in the text you will need to insert the date used for the report.

Press the **Tab** key to highlight the **From** date

Key in the date **01/01/15**

Press the **Tab** key to highlight the **To** date

When the **To** date is highlighted, enter **01/01/15**

Press **Tab** two times to generate the Trial Balance for January 1, 2015

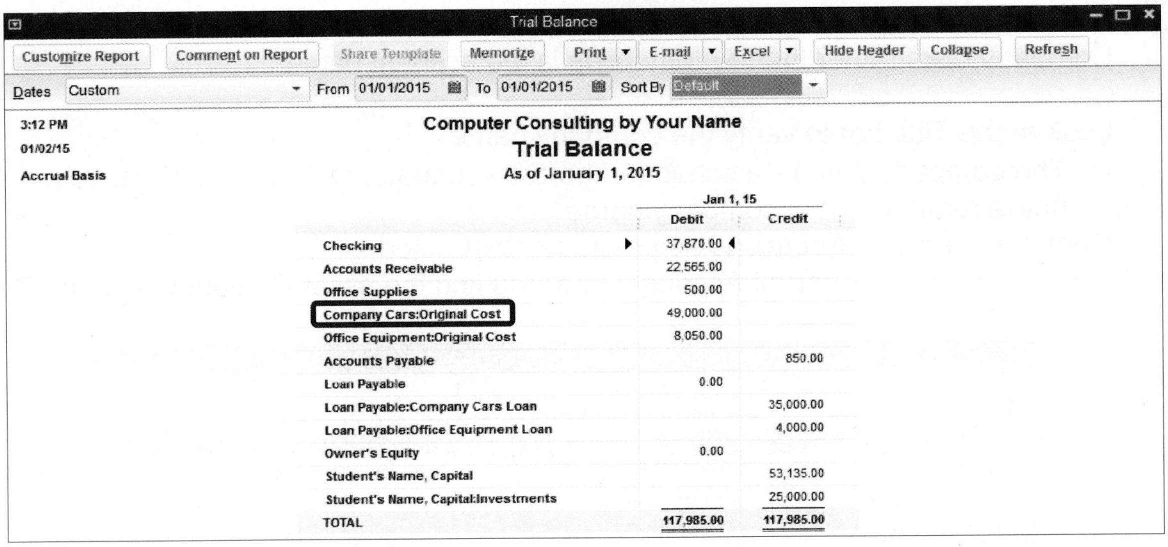
Trial Balance

Customize Report | Comment on Report | Share Template | Memorize | Print | E-mail | Excel | Hide Header | Collapse | Refresh

Dates Custom | From 01/01/2015 | To 01/01/2015 | Sort By Default

3:12 PM
01/02/15
Accrual Basis

Computer Consulting by Your Name
Trial Balance
As of January 1, 2015

	Jan 1, 15 Debit	Credit
Checking	37,870.00	
Accounts Receivable	22,565.00	
Office Supplies	500.00	
Company Cars:Original Cost	49,000.00	
Office Equipment:Original Cost	8,050.00	
Accounts Payable		850.00
Loan Payable	0.00	
Loan Payable:Company Cars Loan		35,000.00
Loan Payable:Office Equipment Loan		4,000.00
Owner's Equity	0.00	
Student's Name, Capital		53,135.00
Student's Name, Capital:Investments		25,000.00
TOTAL	117,985.00	117,985.00

- Notice that the company name in the title of the report shows Computer Consulting by Your Name. This is because the company name was changed before you made your backup file.
- The asset account in the report shows Company Cars: Original Cost. This is because the account name was changed from Company Cars to Automobiles after the backup file was created. When the backup file was restored, it erased all the changes made after the backup was created.

Click the **Close** button to close the report

- If you get a Memorize Reportscreen, click **No**.

Click the **Close** button to close the Report Center

CREATE DUPLICATE USB DRIVE

In addition to making a backup of the company file, you should always have a duplicate of the USB drive you use for your work. Follow the instructions provided by your instructor to copy your files to another USB drive.

EXIT QUICKBOOKS AND REMOVE USB DRIVE (CRITICAL!)

When you complete your work, you need to exit the QuickBooks program. If you are saving work on a separate data disk or USB drive, you must not remove your disk until you exit the program. Once QuickBooks has been closed, your USB drive must be removed properly. Following the appropriate steps to close and exit a program and to remove a USB drive is extremely important. There are program and data files that must be closed in order to leave the program and company data so that they are ready to be used again. If a USB drive is simply removed from the computer, damage to the drive and its files may occur. It is common for a beginning computer user to remove the USB or to turn off the computer without closing the company file and exiting a program. This can cause corrupt program and data files and can make a USB drive or the program unusable.

Close the company file, Computer Consulting by Your Name; close QuickBooks; eject the USB

To close the company file, click **File** on the Menu bar, click **Close Company**

Once you see the No Company Open screen, close QuickBooks by clicking the **Close** button in upper right corner of title bar

If you get a message box for Exiting QuickBooks, If you do not wish to see this screen again, click **Do not display this message in the future**, and then, click **Yes**

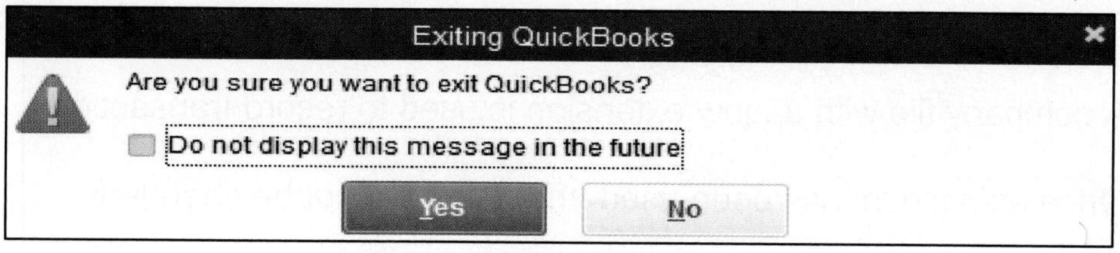

Click the icon for the USB drive in the lower right portion of the Taskbar 

Click on the drive location where you have your USB drive

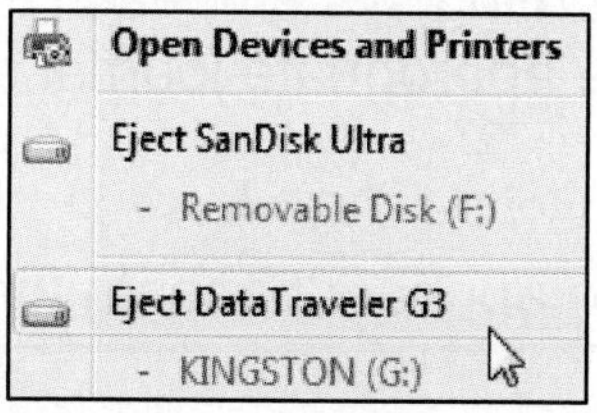

- Your Open Devices and Printers will be different from the example above. Make sure to click on the location for your USB.

When you get the message that it is safe to remove hardware or when the light goes out on your USB drive, remove your USB

SUMMARY

Chapter 1 provides general information regarding QuickBooks. In this chapter, various QuickBooks features were examined. A company file was opened, your name was added to the company name, and an account name was changed. QuickBooks backup files were made and restored. Companies were closed, QuickBooks was closed, and USB drives were removed.

END-OF-CHAPTER QUESTIONS

TRUE/FALSE

ANSWER THE FOLLOWING QUESTIONS IN THE SPACE PROVIDED BEFORE THE QUESTION NUMBER.

_____ 1. There are various methods of giving QuickBooks commands, including use of QuickBooks Home Page, icon bar, menu bar, and keyboard shortcuts.

_____ 2. A company file with a .qbw extension is used to record transactions.

_____ 3. Once an account has been used, the name cannot be changed.

_____ 4. QuickBooks Home Page Insights gives you training in how to complete business documents.

_____ 5. In a computerized accounting system, each transaction that is analyzed must be entered by hand into the appropriate journal and posted to the appropriate ledger.

_____ 6. QuickBooks Home Page appears beneath the title bar and has a list of drop-down menus.

_____ 7. When you use QuickBooks to make a company backup file, you are actually having QuickBooks create a condensed file that contains the essential transaction and account information.

_____ 8. The Alt key + a letter are used to access the drop-down menus on the menu bar.

_____ 9. When you end your work session, you must close your company, close QuickBooks, and remove your USB drive properly.

_____ 10. Transactions entered today will be erased if a backup from an earlier date is restored.

MULTIPLE CHOICE

WRITE THE LETTER OF THE CORRECT ANSWER IN THE SPACE PROVIDED BEFORE THE QUESTION NUMBER.

_____ 1. The extension for a company file that may be used to enter transactions is___.
A. .qbi
B. .qbb
C. .qbw
D. .qbc

_____ 2. A (n) ___ is considered to be a list in QuickBooks.
A. Invoice
B. Chart of Accounts
C. Company
D. none of the above

_____ 3. QuickBooks keyboard conventions ___.
A. are not available
B. use the mouse
C. use certain keys in a manner consistent with Windows
D. incorporate the use of QuickBooks Company Center

_____ 4. Buttons on the invoice icon bar and on the bottom of an invoice are used to ___.
A. give commands to QuickBooks
B. add Customers
C. prepare reports
D. show graphs of invoices prepared

_____ 5. QuickBooks' QuickMath displays ___.
A. a calculator
B. an adding machine tape
C. a calculator with adding machine tape
D. none of the above

_____ 6. QuickBooks Home Page ___.
A. allows you to give commands to QuickBooks according to the type of transaction being entered
B. are icons shown in a row beneath the menu bar
C. appears above the menu bar
D. appears at the bottom of the screen

_____ 7. An icon is ___.
A. a document
B. a picture
C. a chart
D. a type of software

_____ 8. A way to find out the keyboard shortcuts for various commands is to look them up using ___.
A. the Internet
B. Help
C. the File menu
D. a Keyboard icon

_____ 9. A .qbb extension on a file name means that the file is ___.
A. open
B. the working file
C. a restored file
D. a backup file

_____ 10. To verify the name of the open company, look at ___.
A. the icon bar
B. QuickBooks Home Page
C. the menu bar
D. the title bar

FILL-IN

IN THE SPACE PROVIDED, WRITE THE ANSWER THAT MOST APPROPRIATELY COMPLETES THE SENTENCE.

1. Whether you are using a manual or a computerized accounting system, transactions must still be analyzed, recorded, and posted.
2. The File menu is used to open and close a company and may also be used to exit QuickBooks.
3. The Report Center has three different views available to display reports. They are list view, grid view, and Carosel view.
4. In QuickBooks you may change the company name by clicking My Company on the Company menu.
5. The Home Page organizes tasks into logical groups (Vendors, Customers, Employees, Company, and Banking).

SHORT ESSAY

Describe the importance of making a backup of a company file and explain what will happen to transactions entered today if a backup from an earlier date is restored.

____

____

____

____

____

END-OF-CHAPTER PROBLEM

YOUR NAME LANDSCAPE & POOL SERVICE

At the end of each chapter, you will work with a different company and enter transactions that are similar to the ones you competed in the text. Follow the instructions given for transaction entry and printing. You may refer to the chapter for assistance.

Your Name Landscape and Pool Service is owned and operated by you. Melissa Gordon and Zack Vines also work for the company. Melissa manages the office and keeps the books for the business. Zack provides lawn maintenance and supervises the lawn maintenance employees—Wilber Kzoic and Mannie Mendoza. You provide the pool maintenance. The company is located in Santa Barbara, California.

INSTRUCTIONS

- ▶ Open the company file for Student's Name Landscape and Pool Service, **Landscape.qbw**,as instructed in the chapter
  - o You may need to backup and/or update the company file. Follow the instructions provided in Chapter 1.
- ▶ Add your name to the company name and the legal name. The company name will be **Your Name Landscape and Pool Service**. (Type your actual name, *not* the words *Your Name*. Do this whenever you are instructed to add *Your Name*.)
- ▶ Unless your instructor directs you to a different storage location for your backup file, create a Local backup of the Landscape.qbw file to **Landscape (Backup Ch. 1)** on the same USB drive where you have your company file
- ▶ Change the name of the asset account Office Supplies to **Office & Sales Supplies**
- ▶ Use the Report Center to prepare a Trial Balance
- ▶ Verify the asset account name change; then close the report and the Report Center
- ▶ Restore the **Landscape (Backup Ch. 1)** file
  - o The account Office & Sales Supplies reverted to Office Supplies because the company information was restored from the backup file that was made before the account name was changed.
- ▶ Use the Report Center to prepare a Trial Balance
- ▶ Verify that the asset account name is once again Office Supplies; then close the report and the Report Center

SALES AND RECEIVABLES: SERVICE BUSINESS

2

LEARNING OBJECTIVES

At the completion of this chapter, you will be able to:

1. Create invoices and record sales transactions on account.
2. Create sales receipts to record cash sales.
3. Edit, void, and delete invoices/sales receipts.
4. Create credit memos.
5. Add new customers and modify customer records.
6. Record cash receipts.
7. Enter partial cash payments.
8. Display and print invoices, sales receipts, and credit memos.
9. Display and print Quick Reports, Customer Balance Summary Reports, Customer Balance Detail Reports, and Transaction Reports by Customer.
10. Display and print Summary Sales by Item Reports and Itemized Sales by Item Reports.
11. Display and print Deposit Summary, Journal Reports, and Trial Balance.
12. Display Accounts Receivable Graphs and Sales Graphs.

ACCOUNTING FOR SALES AND RECEIVABLES

Rather than use a traditional Sales Journal to record sales on account using debits and credits and special columns, QuickBooks records sales by preparing invoices, cash receipts, or statements.

If your customer doesn't pay you in full at the time you provide your service or sell your product, an invoice is prepared. QuickBooks uses an invoice to record sales transactions for accounts receivable in the Accounts Receivable Register. When a sale is "on account" this means that the customer owes you money and Accounts Receivable is used as the account.

Statements are prepared if you need to track how much your customers owe you and don't want to send an invoice each time you perform a service for a customer. Statements are useful if you want to accumulate charges before requesting payment or if you assess a regular monthly charge. When preparing a statement, you would enter statement charges one by one as you perform services for a customer; and then, once a month send out a statement requesting payment. Statements also use Accounts Receivable to record sales on account.

Because cash sales do not involve accounts receivable and would be recorded in the Cash Receipts Journal in traditional accounting, the transactions are recorded on a Sales Receipt. However, all transactions, regardless of the activity, are placed in the General Journal behind the scenes. Rather than using Accounts Receivable account for the debit part of the transaction, Cash or Checking is used because you received payment at the time the sale was made or the service was performed.

QuickBooks puts the money received from a cash sale and from a customer's payment on account (payment for an existing invoice or statement) into the Undeposited Funds account. When a bank deposit is made the Undeposited Funds are placed in the Checking or Cash account.

A new customer can be added on the fly as transactions are entered. Unlike many computerized accounting programs, in QuickBooks, error correction is easy. A sales form may be edited, voided, or deleted in the same window where it was created. Customer information may be changed by editing the Customer in the Customer Center.

A multitude of reports are available when using QuickBooks. Accounts receivable reports include Customer Balance Summary, Customer Balance Detail, and Transaction Reports by Customer, among others. Sales reports provide information regarding the amount of sales by customer, by sales item, and others are available as well as the traditional accounting reports such as Trial Balance, Profit and Loss, and Balance Sheet. QuickBooks also has graphing capabilities so you can see and evaluate your accounts receivable and sales at the click of a button.

TRAINING TUTORIAL

The following tutorial is a step-by-step guide to recording sales (both cash and credit), customer payments, bank deposits, and other transactions for receivables for a fictitious company with fictional employees. This company was used in Chapter 1 and is called Computer Consulting by Your Name. In addition to recording transactions using QuickBooks, we will prepare several reports and graphs for the company. The tutorial for Computer Consulting by Your Name will continue in Chapters 3 and 4, where accounting for payables, customizing a chart of accounts, bank reconciliations, financial statement preparation, and closing an accounting period will be completed.

TRAINING PROCEDURES

To maximize the training benefits, you should:

1. Read the entire chapter *before* beginning the tutorial within the chapter.
2. Answer the end-of-chapter questions.
3. Be aware that transactions to be entered are given within a **MEMO**.
4. Complete all the steps listed for the Computer Consulting by Your Name tutorial in the chapter. (Indicated by: ❯)

5. When you have completed a section, put a check mark next to the final step.
6. If you do not complete a section, put the date in the margin next to the last step completed. This will make it easier to know where to begin when training is resumed.
7. You may not finish the entire chapter in one computer session. At the end of your work session, make a backup file that will contain all of the work you completed from Chapter 1 through the current day. Name this file **Computer (Daily Backup)**.
8. In addition to the daily backup, always use QuickBooks to back up your work at the end of the chapter as described in Chapter 1. The name of the chapter backup for Chapter 2 is **Computer (Backup Ch. 2)**. Make a duplicate copy of your USB drive as instructed by your professor.
9. As you complete your work, proofread carefully and check for accuracy. Double-check amounts of money and the accounts, items, and dates used.
10. If you find an error while preparing a transaction, correct it. If you find the error after the Invoice, Sales Form, Credit Memo, or Customer:Job List is complete, follow the steps indicated in this chapter to correct, void, or delete transactions.
11. Print as directed within the chapter. (Check with your instructor to see if you should print everything listed or if there is printing that you may omit.)
12. There is a transmittal sheet at the end of the chapter that lists everything that is printed when working through the chapter. There is a blank line next to each document listed so you can mark it when it has been printed and/or completed.
13. When you complete your computer session, always close your company. If you try to use a computer and a previous student did not close the company, QuickBooks may freeze when you start to work. In addition, if you do not close the company as you leave, you may have problems with your company file, your USB drive may be damaged, and you may have unwanted .qbi (QuickBooks In Use) files that cause problems when using the company file.

2

DATES

Throughout the text, the year used for the screen shots is 2015, which is the same year as the version of the program. You may want to check with your instructor to see if you should use 2015 as the year for the transactions.

Always pay special attention to the dates when recording transactions. It is not unusual to forget to enter the date that appears in the text and to use the date of the computer for a transaction. This can cause errors in reports and other entries. There will be times when you can tell QuickBooks which date to use such as, business documents and some reports. There will be other instances when QuickBooks automatically inserts the date of the computer, and it cannot be changed. This will occur later in the chapter when you print the bank deposit summary. When this happens, accept QuickBooks' printed date.

PRINTING

Throughout the text, you will be instructed when to print business documents and reports. Everything that is to be printed within the chapter is listed on a transmittal sheet. The end-of- chapter problem also has everything to be printed listed on a transmittal sheet. In some instances, your instructor may direct you to change what you print. Always verify items to be printed with your instructor.

COMPANY FILE

In Chapter 1, you began using Computer Consulting by Student's Name. You changed the company name from Computer Consulting by Student's Name to Computer Consulting by Your Name (your real name). A backup of the file was made. An account name was changed. The backup file was restored and you learned that the account name change had been replaced with the original account name that was in the backup file. During Chapters 2-4, you will continue to use the Computer.qbw file originally used in Chapter 1 to record transactions. In Chapter 4, you will customize your chart of accounts.

If you did not complete the work in Chapter 1, you will need to download the company file from the Pearson Web site. Refer to Chapter 1 for step-by-step procedures to do this. You will also need to refer to Chapter 1 to add your name to the company name. If you plan to install the trial version of QuickBooks and want to use step-by-step instructions to install and register the program, refer to Chapter 1 or go to www.PearsonHigherEd.com/Horne. You should refer to the Web site periodically for updates, new material, and errata.

COMPANY PROFILE

As you learned in Chapter 1, Computer Consulting by Your Name is a company specializing in computer consulting. The company provides program installation, training, and technical support for today's business software as well as setting up company networks, and giving instruction in the use of the Internet and going online. In addition, Computer Consulting by Your Name will set up computer systems for customers and will install basic computer components, such as memory, modems, sound cards, disk drives, and DVD/CD-ROM drives.

Computer Consulting by Your Name is located in Southern California and is a sole proprietorship owned by you. You are involved in all aspects of the business and have the responsibility of obtaining clients. There are three employees: Jennifer Lockwood, who is responsible for software training; Rom Levy, who handles hardware and network installation and technical support; and Alhandra Cruz, whose duties include being office manager and bookkeeper and providing technical support.

Computer Consulting by Your Name bills by the hour for training, hardware and software installation, and network setup. Each of these items has a minimum charge of $95 for the first hour and $80 per hour thereafter. Clients with contracts for technical support are charged a monthly rate for service.

BEGIN QUICKBOOKS TRAINING

As you continue this chapter, you will be instructed to enter transactions for Computer Consulting by Your Name. As you learned in Chapter 1, in order to work you must boot up or start your computer, open the QuickBooks program, and open the company.

Refer to Chapter 1 to Open QuickBooks

OPEN COMPANY

In Chapter 1, Computer Consulting by Your Name was opened and a backup of the company file was made using QuickBooks. Computer Consulting by Your Name should have been closed in Chapter 1. To open the company for this work session you may click the Open an Existing Company button on the No Company Open screen or by clicking on File menu and Open or Restore Company. Verify this by checking the title bar.

Open **Computer Consulting by Your Name**

Click **Open or Restore an Existing Company** button at the bottom of the No Company Open screen
OR
Click **File** on the Menu bar and click **Open or Restore Company**

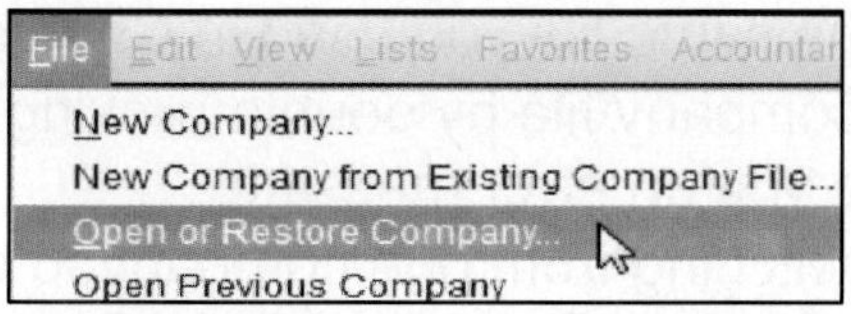

On the Open or Restore Company screen, **Open a Company File** should be selected, click **Next**.
Click the drop-down list arrow for **Look in**
Click **Removable Disk (USB Drive Location:)**
- The screen shot shows (G:) as the USB location. Your location may be different.

Double-click the folder **QB 2015 Ch 1-4 Master Company Files**
Click **Computer** (in the Name section under the Look in text box)
- Your company file may have an extension of **.qbw.** This is the file extension for your "QuickBooks Working" file. This is the company file that may be opened and used. As you learned in Chapter 1, you may not use a .qbb (backup) file for direct entry. A backup file must be restored to a .qbw (company) file.
- The files shown below are the company files for Chapters 1-4. If you downloaded the files for Chapters 5-8 you will have additional company files on the USB drive.

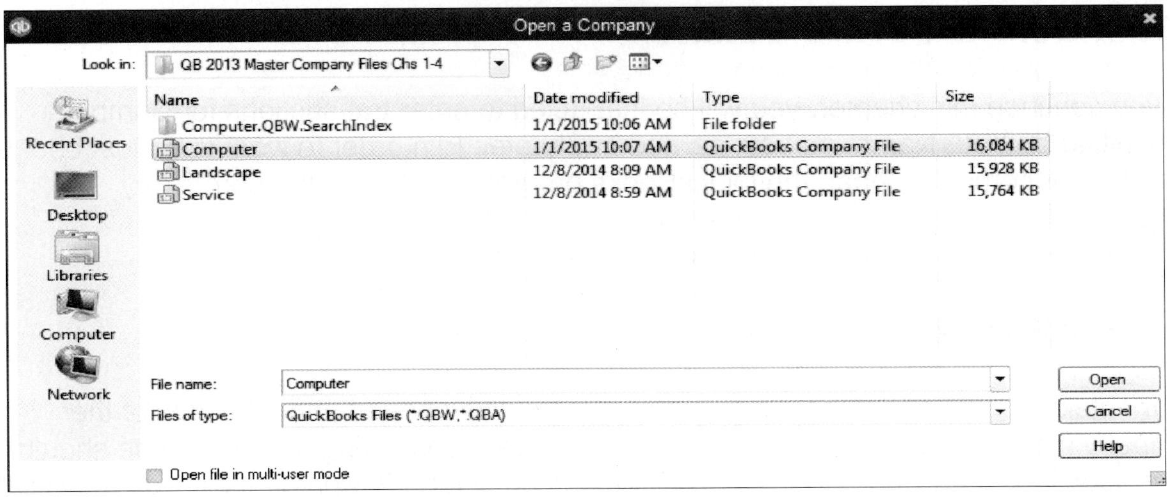

- Since this company was used in Chapter 1, when you see the Open a Company screen, you may see other QuickBooks files and/or folders associated with that company. QuickBooks will create them as you use a company file. Some of these files may have extensions of QBW.ND or .QBW.TLG. Folders that say QuickBooksAutoDataRecovery, Restored, or .QBW.SearchIndex are common. For the most part, you do not use or change any of these files or folders, simply click the company file and click the Open button. (Only the SearchIndex folder is shown above.)

Click **Open**

- Remember, this is the same file you used in Chapter 1.
- If you try to open a company file by double-clicking the company file name, QuickBooks will give you an error message.
- Sometimes, when switching from one company to the next; i.e., Computer to Landscape and then back to Computer, QuickBooks might mark your company file as read only. If this happens, refer to Chapter 1 for steps on how to change the file Properties from Read Only.

If you get a screen to Update Company, click **Yes**

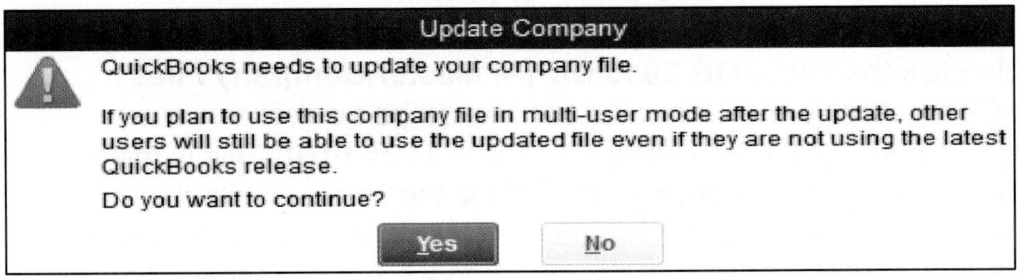

VERIFY OPEN COMPANY

Verify the title bar heading:

- The title bar should show **Computer Consulting by Your Name** as the company name. (Remember you will have your actual name in the title.)
- If your title bar shows QuickBooks Premier Accountant 2015, that is fine. There is no difference in the program since QuickBooks Accountant is part of the Premier version of QuickBooks.
- Remember, throughout the text the program is referred to as QuickBooks 2015 rather than QuickBooks Premier or QuickBooks Accountant, etc.
- Note: Unless you tell QuickBooks to create a new company, open a different company, or close the company, Computer Consulting by Your Name will appear as the open company whenever you open QuickBooks. However, when you finish a work session, you should always close the company in order to avoid problems with the file in a future work session.

QUICKBOOKS HOME PAGE AND TOP ICON BAR

The QuickBooks Home Page allows you to give commands to QuickBooks according to the type of transaction being entered. The Home Page tasks are organized into logical groups (Vendors, Customers, Employees, Company, and Banking). Each of the areas on the Home Page is used to enter different types of transactions. When appropriate, the Home Page shows a flow chart with icons indicating the major activities performed. The icons are arranged in the order in which transactions usually occur and are clicked to access screens in order to enter information or transactions in QuickBooks.

You may also choose to use the menu bar, the icon bar, or the keyboard to give commands to QuickBooks. For more detailed information regarding the QuickBooks Home Page and the Top Icon Bar, refer to Chapter 1. Instructions in this text will be given primarily using the QuickBooks Home Page. However, the menu bar, the Top Icon bar, and/or keyboard methods will be used as well.

➤ If the Top Icon Bar is not showing, click the **View** menu, and then click **Top Icon Bar**; if the Home Page is not showing, click the **Home** icon, and, if necessary, click the **Home Page** tab to display it

BEGIN TUTORIAL

In this chapter you will be entering accounts receivable transactions, cash sales transactions, receipts for payments on account, and bank deposits. Much of the organization of QuickBooks is dependent upon lists. The two primary types of lists you will use in the tutorial for receivables are a Customers & Jobs List and a Sales Item List.

The names, addresses, telephone numbers, credit terms, credit limits, and balances for all established credit customers are contained in the Customer & Jobs List in the Customer Center. To conform with GAAP (Generally Accepted Accounting Principles), the Customer Center may also be referred to as the Accounts Receivable Ledger. QuickBooks does not use this term; however, the Customer Center does function as the Accounts Receivable

Subsidiary Ledger. A transaction entry for an individual customer is posted to the customer's account in the Customer Center just as it would be posted to the customer's individual account in an Accounts Receivable Ledger.

The balance of the Customer & Jobs List in the Customer Center will be equal to the balance of the Accounts Receivable account in the Chart of Accounts. The Chart of Accounts would be referred to as the General Ledger when using GAAP standards. Invoices and accounts receivable transactions can also be related to specific jobs you are completing for customers. To see the balance of all customers, you would click the Transactions tab in the Customer Center.

You will be using the following Customers & Jobs List in the Customer Center for established credit customers.

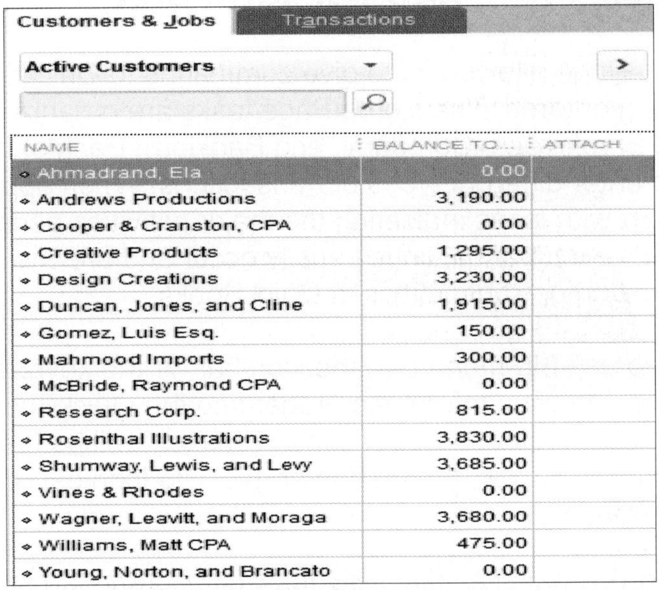

NAME	BALANCE TO...	ATTACH
Ahmadrand, Ela	0.00	
Andrews Productions	3,190.00	
Cooper & Cranston, CPA	0.00	
Creative Products	1,295.00	
Design Creations	3,230.00	
Duncan, Jones, and Cline	1,915.00	
Gomez, Luis Esq.	150.00	
Mahmood Imports	300.00	
McBride, Raymond CPA	0.00	
Research Corp.	815.00	
Rosenthal Illustrations	3,830.00	
Shumway, Lewis, and Levy	3,685.00	
Vines & Rhodes	0.00	
Wagner, Leavitt, and Moraga	3,680.00	
Williams, Matt CPA	475.00	
Young, Norton, and Brancato	0.00	

Note: When you display the Customers & Jobs list in the Customer Center, the customer names may not be displayed in full. The lists shown in the text have been formatted to show the names in full.

Sales are often made up of various types of income. In Computer Consulting by Your Name, there are several income accounts. In order to classify income regarding the type of sale, the sales account may have subaccounts. When recording a transaction for a sale, QuickBooks requires that a Sales Item be used. When the sales item is created, a sales account is required. When the sales item is used in a transaction, the income is credited to the appropriate sales/income account. For example, Training 1 is a sales item and uses the account Training Income, a subaccount of Sales, when a transaction is recorded.

In addition, there are categories within an income account. For example, Computer Consulting by Your Name uses Training Income to represent revenues earned by providing on-site training. The sales items used for Training Income are Training 1 for the first or initial hour of on-site training and Training 2 for all additional hours of on-site training. As you look at the Item List, you will observe that the rates for the two items are different. Using lists for sales items allows for flexibility in billing and a more accurate representation of the way in which income is earned. The following Item List for the various types of sales will be used for the company.

NAME	DESCRIPTION	TYPE	ACCOUNT	PRICE	ATTACH
Tech Sup 1	5 Hours--Monthly Technical Support	Service	Income:Technical Support Income	150.00	
Tech Sup 2	10 Hours--Monthly Technical Support	Service	Income:Technical Support Income	300.00	
Tech Sup 3	15 Hours--Monthly Technical Support	Service	Income:Technical Support Income	450.00	
Training 1	Initial Hour of On-Site Training	Service	Income:Training Income	95.00	
Training 2	Additional Hours of On-Site Training	Service	Income:Training Income	80.00	

In the tutorial all transactions are listed on memos. Unless otherwise specified within the transaction, the transaction date will be the same date as the memo date. Always enter the date of the transaction as specified in the memo. By default, QuickBooks automatically enters the current date of the computer or the last transaction date used. In many instances, this will not be the same date as the transaction in the text. Customer names, when necessary, will be given in the transaction. All terms for customers on account are Net 30 days unless specified otherwise. If a memo contains more than one transaction, there will be a visual separation between transactions.

MEMO

DATE: The transaction date is listed here

Transaction details are given in the body of the memo. Customer names, the type of transaction, amounts of money, and any other details needed are listed here.

Even when you are given instructions on how to enter a transaction step by step, you should always refer to the memo for transaction details. Once a specific type of transaction has been entered in a step-by-step manner, additional transactions will be made without having instructions provided. Of course, you may always refer to instructions given for previous transactions for ideas or for the steps used to enter those transactions. Again, always double-check the date and the year used for the transaction. QuickBooks automatically inserts the computer's current date, which will be different from the date in the text. Using an incorrect date will cause reports to have different totals and contain different transactions than those shown in the text.

ENTER SALE ON ACCOUNT

Because QuickBooks operates on a business form premise, a sale on account is entered via an invoice. You prepare an invoice, and QuickBooks records the transaction in the Journal and automatically posts to the customer's account in the Customer Center.

> **MEMO**
> **DATE:** January 2, 2015
>
> Invoice 1: Luis Gomez has many questions regarding his new computer system. He spoke with you about this and signed up for 10 hours of technical support (Tech Sup 2) for January. Bill him for this and use Thank you for your business. as the message.

Record the sale on account shown in the invoice above. (This invoice is used to bill a customer for a sale using one sales item)

Click the **Create Invoices** icon on the Home Page

- A blank invoice will show on the screen.

Click the drop-down list arrow next to **CUSTOMER:JOB**
Click **Gomez, Luis Esq.**

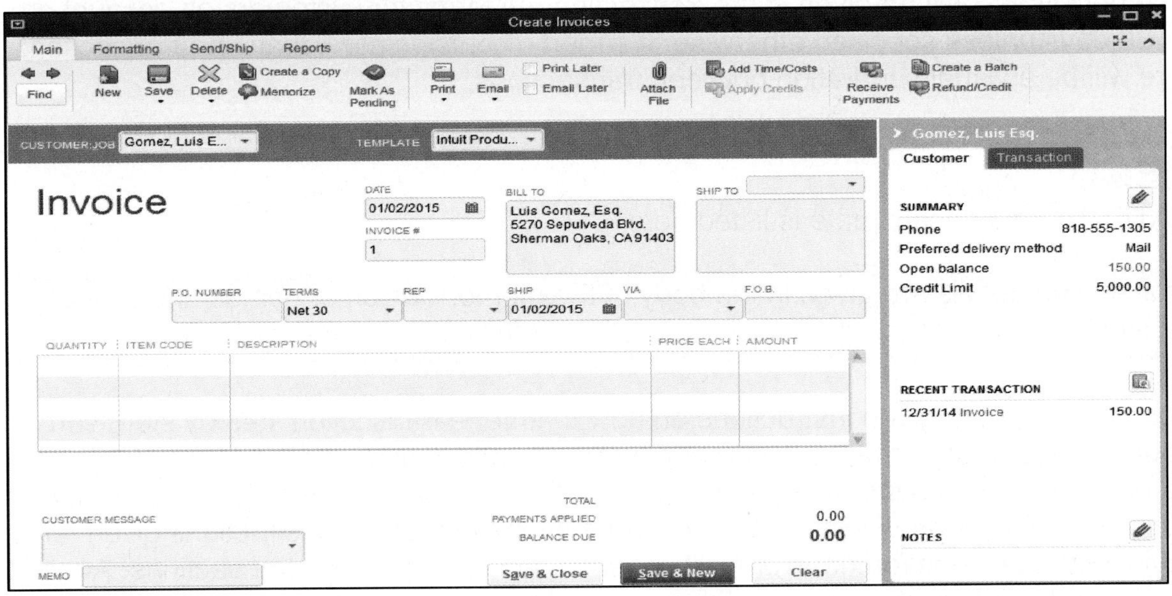

- His name is entered as CUSTOMER:JOB, and Bill To information is completed automatically.

Click the drop-down list arrow for **TEMPLATE**, click **Intuit Service Invoice**

- Intuit Service Invoice is the appropriate invoice to use for this company since only services are sales items. Always check the template. QuickBooks likes to use the Product Invoice and will frequently revert to it rather than use the Service Invoice.

Press the **Tab** to tab to and highlight the date in the **DATE** field

Type **01/02/15** as the date

- This should replace the date shown in the field. If you did not tab to the date, drag through the date to highlight and then type 01/02/15.

Invoice 1 should be showing in the **INVOICE #.** box

- The INVOICE #. should not have to be changed.

There is no PO No. (Purchase Order Number) to record

TERMS should be indicated as **Net 30**

- If not, click the drop-down list arrow next to **TERMS** and click **Net 30**.

Tab to or click in the first line beneath **ITEM**

Click the drop-down list arrow that appears in the first line

- Refer to the memo above and the Item List for appropriate billing information.

Click **Tech Sup 2** to bill for 10 hours of technical support

- Tech Sup 2 is entered as the Item.

Tab to or click **QUANTITY**

Type **1**

- The quantity is one because you are billing for 1 unit of Tech Sup 2. As you can see in the description, Tech Sup 2 is for 10 hours of support. The total for the item and for the invoice is automatically calculated when you tab to the next item or click in a new invoice area. If you forget to tell QuickBooks to use a quantity, it will automatically calculate the quantity as 1.

Click in the textbox for **CUSTOMER MESSAGE**

Click the drop-down list arrow next to **CUSTOMER MESSAGE**

Click **Thank you for your business.**

- Message is inserted in the CUSTOMER MESSAGE box.

Click the **Save** icon on the Main Invoice Icon Bar at the top of the invoice

- Notice the History section on the right side of the invoice. This will give you information about Luis Gomez. Including his Open balance, Credit Limit, and Recent Transactions.

In the Recent Transaction section, you will see 01/02/15 Invoice of 300.00 and the 12/31/14 Invoice for 150.00

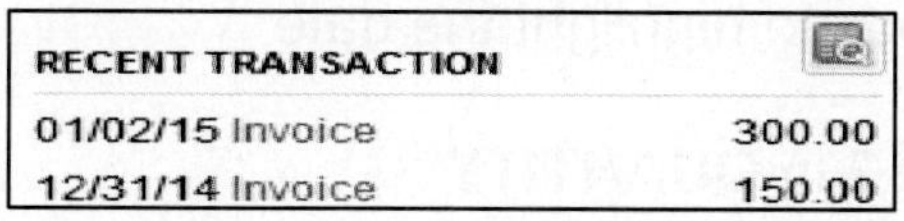

RECENT TRANSACTION
01/02/15 Invoice 300.00
12/31/14 Invoice 150.00

To save space on your screen, click the **Hide history** button to close the History section

- You may wish to resize the invoice to make it smaller, if so, point to the right side of the invoice, when you get a double arrow , hold down the primary mouse button and drag to the left until the invoice is the size you want.

- If the Invoice is maximized, you will not be able to use the sizing handle (double-arrow) to resize the form. If that is the case, click the **Restore** button; and then resize as instructed above.

If you wish to view the history later, simply click the Show History button 

EDIT AND CORRECT ERRORS

If an error is discovered while entering invoice information, it may be corrected by positioning the cursor in the field containing the error. You may return to the field with the error by clicking in the field, tabbing to move forward through each field, or pressing Shift+Tab to move back to the field. If the error is highlighted, type the correction. If the error is not highlighted, you can correct the error by pressing the backspace or the delete key as many times as necessary to remove the error, and then typing the correction. (Alternate method: Point to the error, highlight by dragging the mouse through the error, then type the correction or press the Delete key to remove completely.)

Practice editing and making corrections to Invoice 1

Click the drop-down list arrow next to **CUSTOMER:JOB**
Click **Williams, Matt CPA**
- Name is changed in CUSTOMER:JOB and BILL TO information is also changed.

Click to the left of the first number in the **DATE**—this is **0**
Hold down primary mouse button and drag through the date to highlight.
Type **10/24/15** as the date
- This removes the 01/02/2015 date originally entered.

Click to the right of the **1** in **QUANTITY**
Backspace and type a **2**
Press **Tab** to see how QuickBooks automatically calculates the new total
To eliminate the changes made to Invoice 1, click the drop-down list arrow next to **Customer:Job**
Click **Gomez, Luis, Esq.**
Tab to the **DATE** textbox to highlight the date
Type **01/02/15**
Click to the right of the **2** in **QUANTITY**
Backspace and type a **1**
Press the **Tab** key
- This will cause QuickBooks to calculate the amount and the total for the invoice and will move the cursor to the Description field.
- Verify that Invoice 1 has been returned to the correct customer, date, quantity, and balance due. Compare the information you entered with the information provided in the memo.
- Your invoice may or may not show "Your customer can't pay this invoice online" above the Customer Message textbox. In an actual business you can sign up to receive online payments. Since Computer Consulting by Your Name is not a real business, we are not eligible to sign up and pay for this option so disregard this.

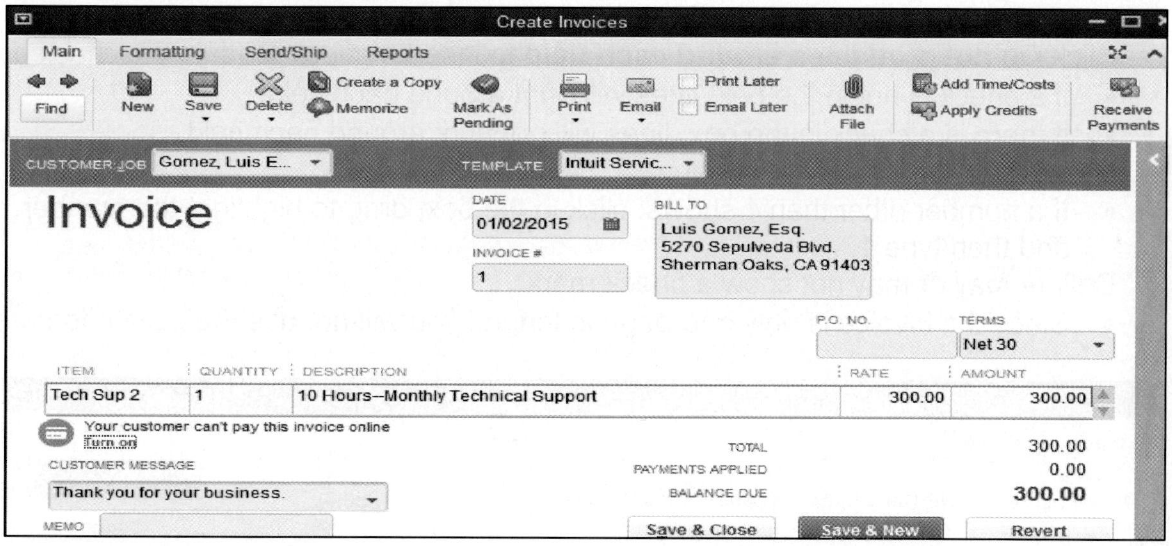

To see how the printed invoice will look, click the **Formatting** tab on the Create Invoices Icon bar

Click the **Preview** icon

- Notice that the column for ITEM (Tech Sup 2) does not show.
- The ITEM column does not appear on a printed Service Invoice.

Click the **Close** button on the Preview to return to Invoice 1

PRINT INVOICE

With Invoice 1 on the screen, print the invoice immediately after entering information

Click the **Main** tab on the Create Invoices Icon bar

Click the **Print** icon (looks like a printer) on the Main icon bar for Create Invoices

- If you click the drop-down list arrow for the Print button, you will get a list of printing options. Click the **Invoice** option.

Because you made changes to the original Invoice 1, click **Yes** on the Recording Transaction message box

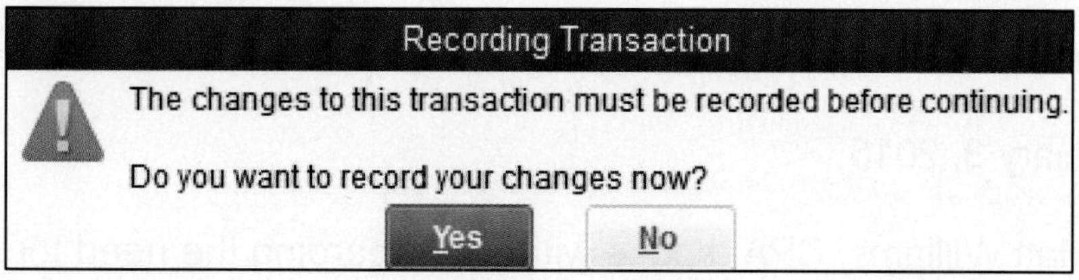

Check the information on the **Print One Invoice Settings** tab:

Printer name: (should identify the type of printer you are using)

- This may be different from the printer identified in this text.

Printer type: Page-oriented (Single sheets)

Print on: Blank paper

- The circle next to this should be filled. If it is not, click the circle to select.

Click **Do not print lines around each field** to insert a check mark in the check box

- If a check is not in the box, lines will print around each field.
- If there is a check in the box, lines will not print around each field.

Number of copies: should be 1

- If a number other than 1 shows: click in the box, drag to highlight the number, and then type **1**.

Collate may or may not show a check mark

- Since the invoice is only one-page in length, you will not use the collate feature.

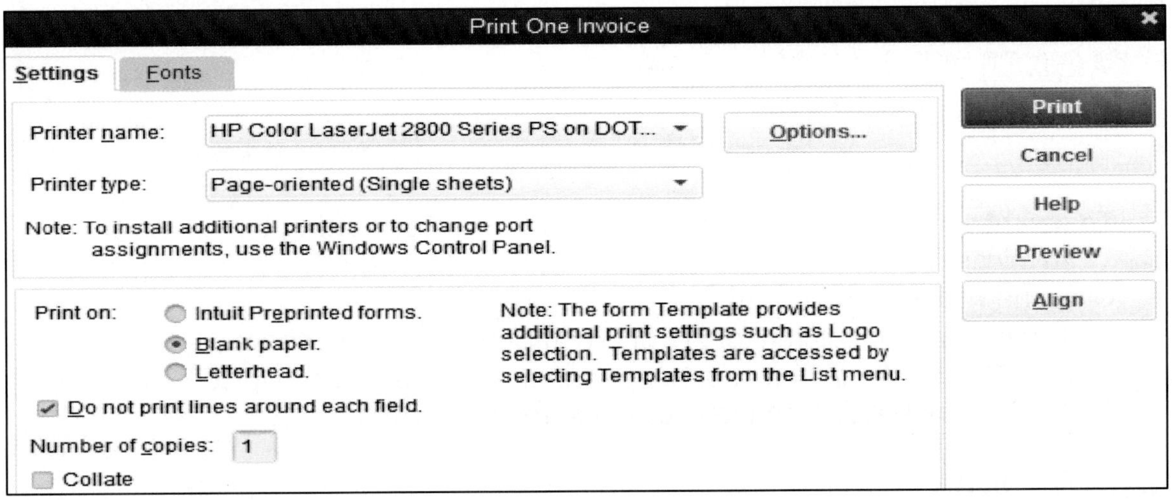

Click the **Print** button

- This initiates the printing of the invoice through QuickBooks. However, because not all classroom configurations are the same, check with your instructor for specific printing instructions.
- If QuickBooks prints your name on two lines, do not be concerned. This will be changed later.

Click the **Save & New** button to save Invoice 1 and go to a new invoice

ENTER TRANSACTION WITH TWO SALES ITEMS

MEMO
DATE: January 3, 2015

Invoice 2: Matt Williams, CPA, spoke with you regarding the need for on-site training to help him get started using the Internet. Bill him for a 5-hour on-site training session with Jennifer Lockwood. Use Thank you for your business. as the message. (Remember to use Training 1 for the first hour of on-site training and Training 2 for the four additional hours of training.)

Record a transaction on account for a sale involving two sales items

On Invoice 2, click the drop-down list arrow next to **CUSTOMER:JOB**
Click **Williams, Matt, CPA**

- Name is entered as CUSTOMER:JOB. Bill To information is completed automatically.
- Make sure that Intuit Service Invoice is shown as the TEMPLATE; if not, click the drop-down list arrow and select it.

Tab to or click **DATE**
Delete the current date

- Refer to instructions for Invoice 1 or to editing practice if necessary.

Type **01/03/15** as the date
Make sure that **2** is showing in the **INVOICE #** text box

- The INVOICE #. should not have to be changed.

There is no PO No. to record
TERMS should be indicated as **Net 30**
Tab to or click the first line beneath **ITEM**

- Refer to the Memo and to the Item List for appropriate billing information.
- *Note:* Services are recorded based on sales items and are not related to the employee who provides the service.

Click the drop-down list arrow next to **ITEM**
Click **Training 1**

- Training 1 is entered as the Item.
- QuickBooks entered the Rate and Amount for Training 1 automatically. This is based on an assumed quantity of 1. Notice the amount of $95.00.

Tab to or click **QUANTITY**
Type **1**

- Even though QuickBooks always assumes a quantity of 1, it is wise to enter the quantity as 1. This gives you better information when preparing reports and other documents.

Tab to or click the second line for **ITEM**
Click the drop-down list arrow next to **ITEM**
Click **Training 2**
Tab to or click **QUANTITY**
Type **4**, press **Tab**

- The total amount of training time is five hours. Because the first hour is billed as Training 1, the remaining four hours are billed as Training 2 hours.
- The total amount due for the Training 2 hours and the total for the invoice were automatically calculated when you pressed the Tab key.

Click **CUSTOMER MESSAGE**
Click the drop-down list arrow next to **CUSTOMER MESSAGE**
Click **Thank you for your business.**

- Message is inserted in the CUSTOMER MESSAGE box.

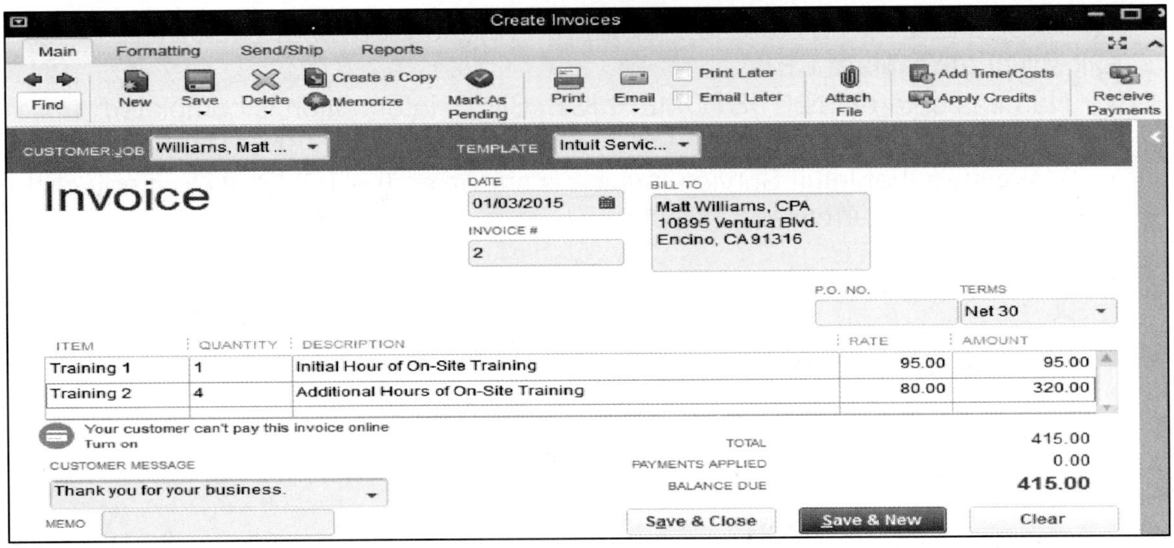

PRINT INVOICE

➔ With Invoice 2 on the screen, print the invoice immediately after entering invoice information

Click the **Print** button on the **Create Invoices** screen

- If you click the drop-down list arrow for the Print button, you will get a list of printing options. Click the **Invoice** option.

Check the information on the **Print One Invoice Settings** tab:

Printer name: (should identify the type of printer you are using)

Printer type: Page-oriented (Single sheets)

Print on: Blank paper

Do not print lines around each field: check box should have a check mark

Click the **Print** button

After the invoice has printed, click the **Save & Close** button at the bottom of the **Create Invoices** screen to record Invoice 2 and exit Create Invoices

ANALYZE TRANSACTIONS IN THE JOURNAL

Whenever a transaction is recorded on an invoice or any other business form, QuickBooks enters the transactions into the Journal in the traditional Debit/Credit format.

➔ View the Journal and verify the transaction entries

Click **Reports** on the Menu bar
Point to **Accountant & Taxes**
Click **Journal**

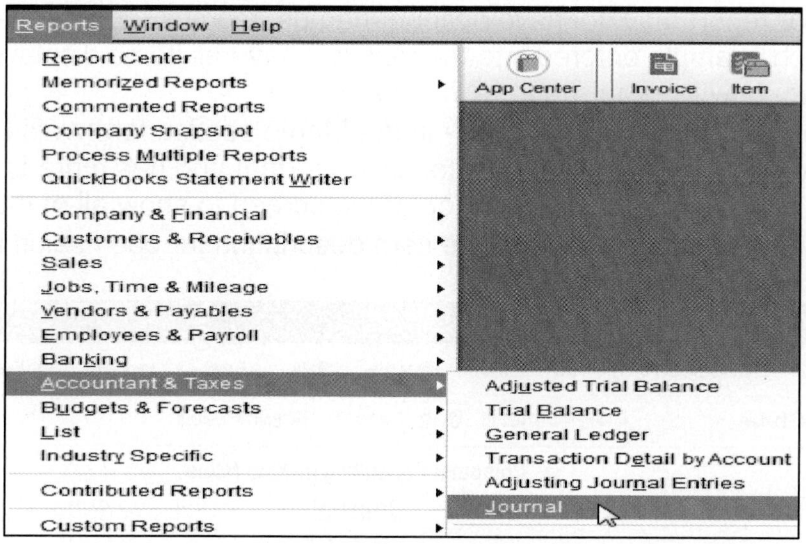

Click **OK** on the Collapsing and Expanding Transactions dialog box

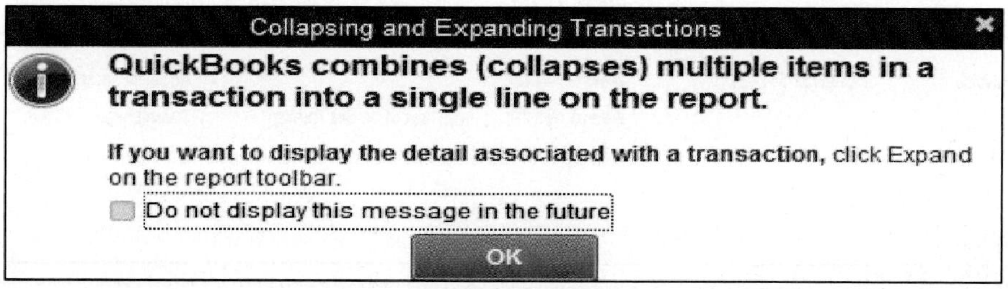

Tab to the **From** textbox
Enter the date **01/01/15**
Tab to the **To** textbox
Enter the date **01/03/15**
Press Tab twice to generate the report

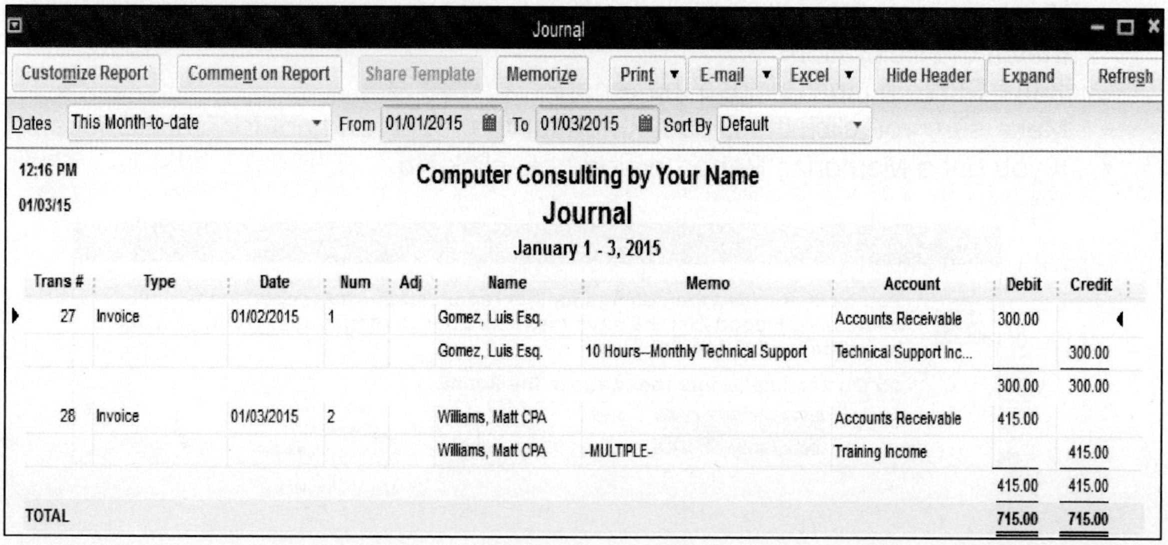

12:16 PM
01/03/15

Computer Consulting by Your Name
Journal
January 1 - 3, 2015

Trans #	Type	Date	Num	Adj	Name	Memo	Account	Debit	Credit
27	Invoice	01/02/2015	1		Gomez, Luis Esq.		Accounts Receivable	300.00	
					Gomez, Luis Esq.	10 Hours--Monthly Technical Support	Technical Support Inc...		300.00
								300.00	300.00
28	Invoice	01/03/2015	2		Williams, Matt CPA		Accounts Receivable	415.00	
					Williams, Matt CPA	-MULTIPLE-	Training Income		415.00
								415.00	415.00
TOTAL								715.00	715.00

- Your report may not have account names, memos, or other items shown in full. Each example entered into the text, will have all items displayed in full. You will learn how to do this later in the chapter.
- Notice the word –MULTIPLE- in the Memo section for Invoice 2. This appears because the report is in the collapsed format and has more than one sales item.

Click the **Expand** button at the top of the screen to show all of the entries

- The Memo column shows the item description for each sales item used.

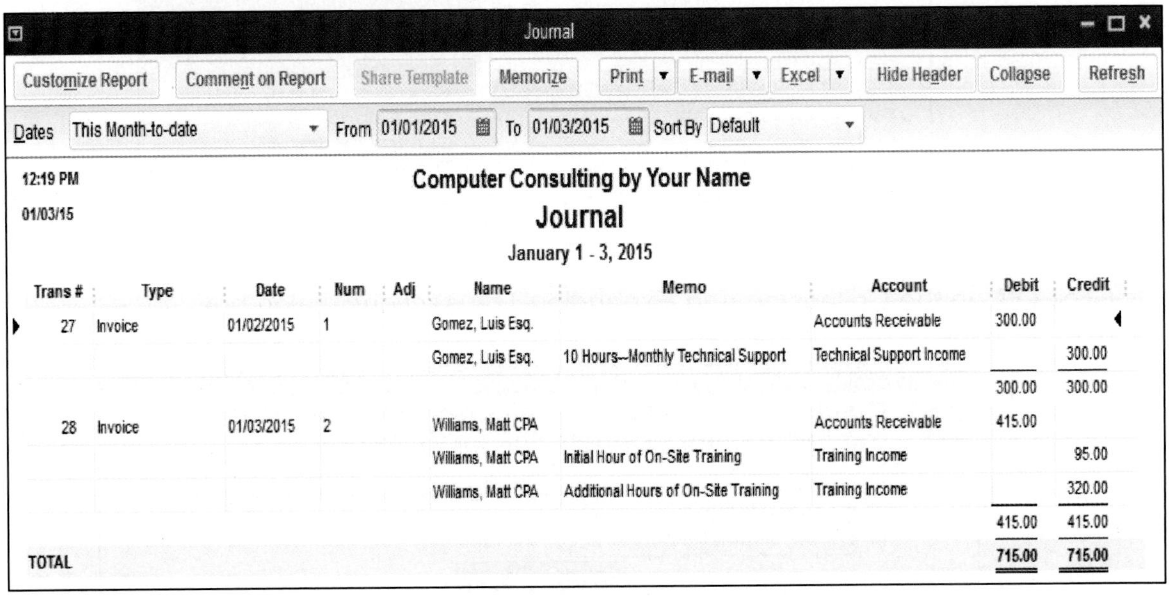

Trans #	Type	Date	Num	Adj	Name	Memo	Account	Debit	Credit
27	Invoice	01/02/2015	1		Gomez, Luis Esq.		Accounts Receivable	300.00	
					Gomez, Luis Esq.	10 Hours--Monthly Technical Support	Technical Support Income		300.00
								300.00	300.00
28	Invoice	01/03/2015	2		Williams, Matt CPA		Accounts Receivable	415.00	
					Williams, Matt CPA	Initial Hour of On-Site Training	Training Income		95.00
					Williams, Matt CPA	Additional Hours of On-Site Training	Training Income		320.00
								415.00	415.00
TOTAL								715.00	715.00

- Notice the debit to Accounts Receivable for both Invoice 1 and 2.
- The credit for each invoice is to an income account. The income accounts are different for each invoice because the sales items are different. Technical Support Income is the account used when any Tech Sup sales item is used. Training Income is the account used when any Training sales item is used.
- In the upper-left corner of the report is the date and time the report was prepared. Your date and time will be the actual date and time of your computer. It will not match the illustration.

Click the **Close** button to close the report

- Make sure you click the Close button for the report and not for QuickBooks.
- If you get a Memorize Report dialog box, click **No**.

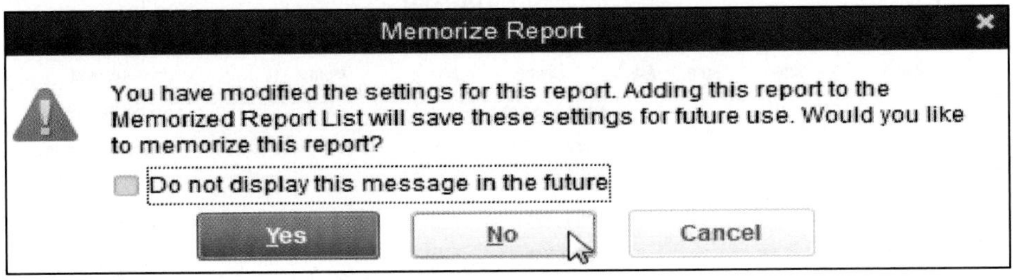

PREPARE ADDITIONAL INVOICES

MEMO

DATE: January 5, 2015

Invoice 3: Ela Ahmadrand needed to have telephone assistance to help her set up her Internet connection. Prepare an invoice as the bill for 10 hours of technical support for January. (Remember customers are listed by last name in the Customers & Jobs List. Refer to Item List to select the correct item for billing.)

Invoice 4: Vines & Rhodes have several new employees that need to be trained in the use of the office computer system. Bill them for 40 hours of on-site training from Jennifer Lockwood. (Computer Consulting by Your Name does not record a transaction based on the employee who performs the service. It simply bills according to the service provided.)

Invoice 5: Cooper & Cranston, CPA, need to learn the basic features of QuickBooks, which is used by many of their customers. Bill them for 10 hours of on-site training and 15 hours of technical support for January so they may call and speak to Rom Levy regarding additional questions. (Note: You will use three sales items in this transaction.)

Invoice 6: Young, Norton, and Brancato have a new assistant office manager. Computer Consulting by Your Name is providing 40 hours of on-site training for Beverly Wilson. To obtain additional assistance, the company has signed up for 5 hours technical support for January.

Enter the four transactions in the memo above. Refer to instructions given for the two previous transactions entered

- Always check the Template to make sure you are using the Intuit Service Invoice.
- Remember, when billing for on-site training, the first hour is billed as Training 1, and the remaining hours are billed as Training 2.
- If you forget to enter the quantity, QuickBooks calculates the amount based on a quantity of 1.
- Always use the Item List to determine the appropriate sales items for billing.
- Use **Thank you for your business.** as the message for these invoices.
- If you make an error, correct it.
- Print each invoice immediately after you enter the information for it.
- To go from one invoice to the next, click the **Save & New** button.
- Click **Save & Close** after Invoice 6 has been entered and printed.

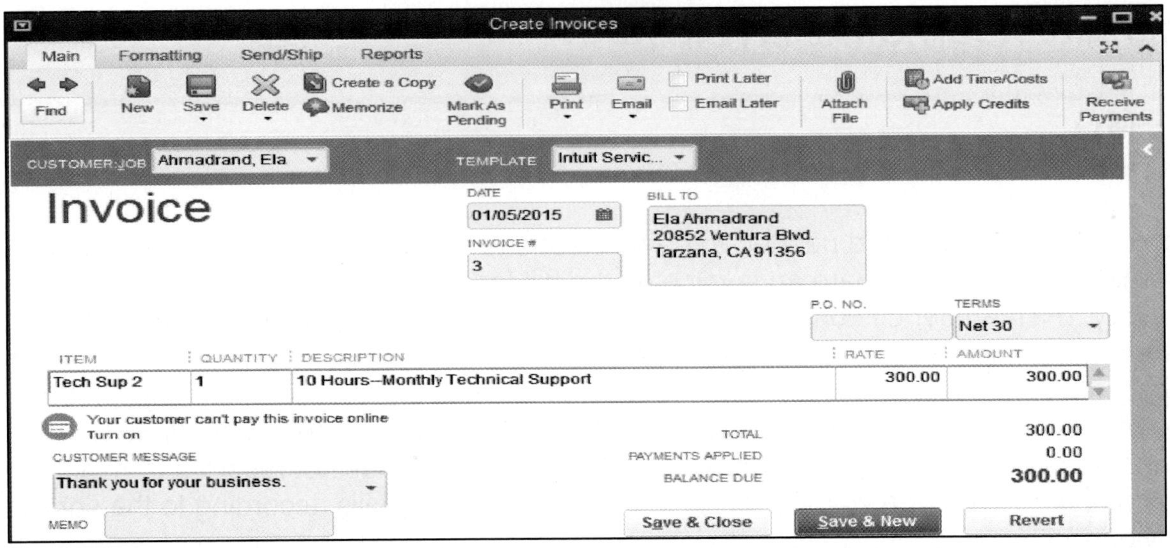
Create Invoices
Main
Formatting
Send/Ship
Reports
Find
New
Save
Delete
Create a Copy
Memorize
Mark As Pending
Print
Email
Print Later
Email Later
Attach File
Add Time/Costs
Apply Credits
Receive Payments
CUSTOMER:JOB Ahmadrand, Ela
TEMPLATE Intuit Servic...
Invoice
DATE 01/05/2015
INVOICE # 3
BILL TO
Ela Ahmadrand
20852 Ventura Blvd.
Tarzana, CA 91356
P.O. NO.
TERMS Net 30
ITEM QUANTITY DESCRIPTION RATE AMOUNT
Tech Sup 2 1 10 Hours--Monthly Technical Support 300.00 300.00
Your customer can't pay this invoice online
Turn on
CUSTOMER MESSAGE
Thank you for your business.
TOTAL 300.00
PAYMENTS APPLIED 0.00
BALANCE DUE 300.00
MEMO
Save & Close
Save & New
Revert

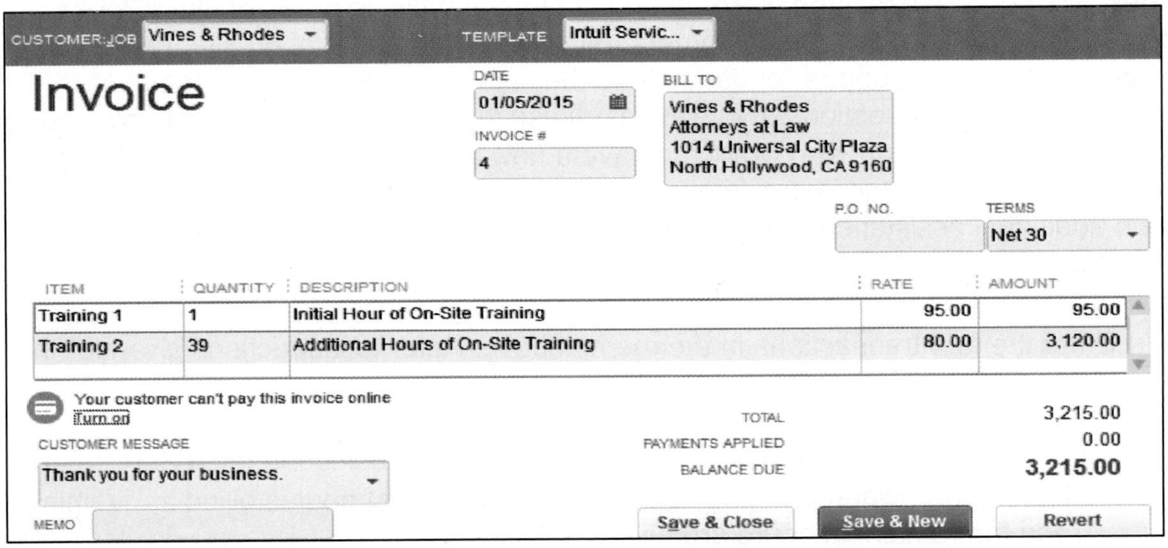
CUSTOMER:JOB Vines & Rhodes
TEMPLATE Intuit Servic...
Invoice
DATE 01/05/2015
INVOICE # 4
BILL TO
Vines & Rhodes
Attorneys at Law
1014 Universal City Plaza
North Hollywood, CA 9160
P.O. NO.
TERMS Net 30
ITEM QUANTITY DESCRIPTION RATE AMOUNT
Training 1 1 Initial Hour of On-Site Training 95.00 95.00
Training 2 39 Additional Hours of On-Site Training 80.00 3,120.00
Your customer can't pay this invoice online
Turn on
CUSTOMER MESSAGE
Thank you for your business.
TOTAL 3,215.00
PAYMENTS APPLIED 0.00
BALANCE DUE 3,215.00
MEMO
Save & Close
Save & New
Revert

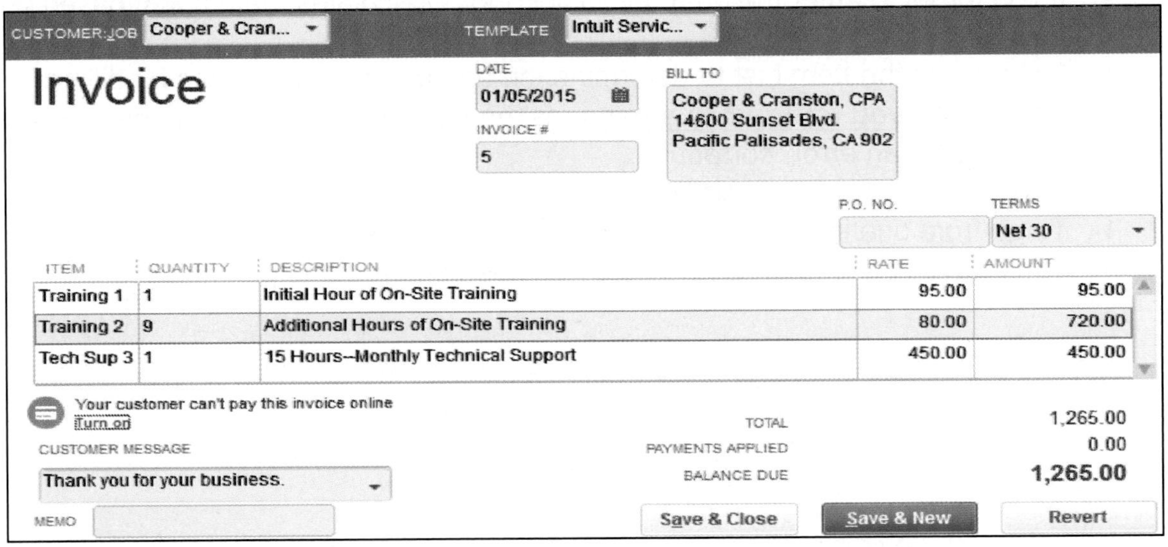
CUSTOMER:JOB Cooper & Cran...
TEMPLATE Intuit Servic...
Invoice
DATE 01/05/2015
INVOICE # 5
BILL TO
Cooper & Cranston, CPA
14600 Sunset Blvd.
Pacific Palisades, CA 902
P.O. NO.
TERMS Net 30
ITEM QUANTITY DESCRIPTION RATE AMOUNT
Training 1 1 Initial Hour of On-Site Training 95.00 95.00
Training 2 9 Additional Hours of On-Site Training 80.00 720.00
Tech Sup 3 1 15 Hours--Monthly Technical Support 450.00 450.00
Your customer can't pay this invoice online
Turn on
CUSTOMER MESSAGE
Thank you for your business.
TOTAL 1,265.00
PAYMENTS APPLIED 0.00
BALANCE DUE 1,265.00
MEMO
Save & Close
Save & New
Revert

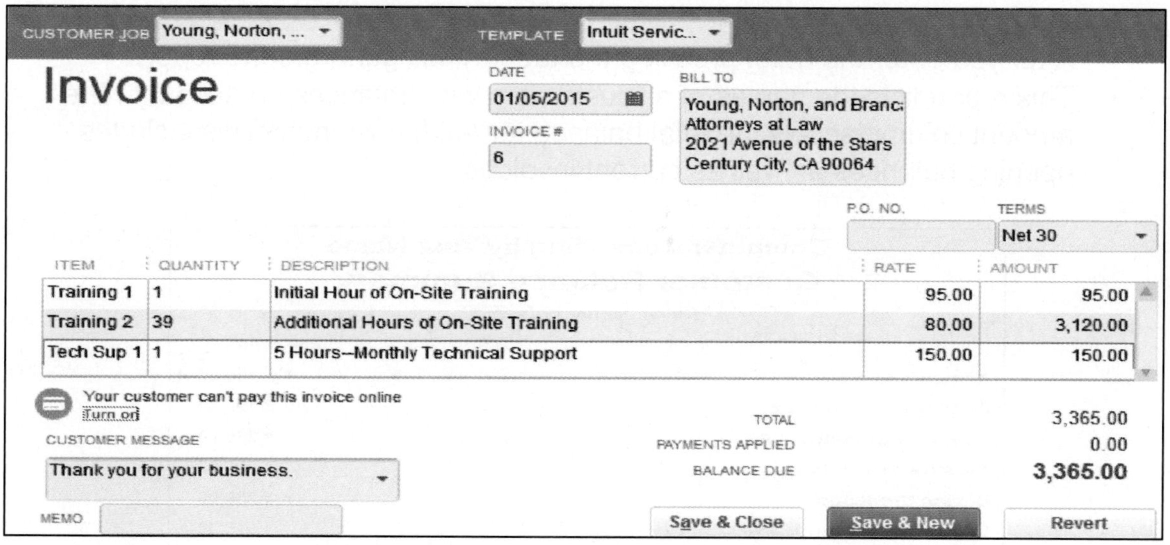

CUSTOMER BALANCE SUMMARY REPORT

QuickBooks has several reports available for accounts receivable. One of the most useful is the Customer Balance Summary Report. It shows you the balances of all the customers on account.

Prepare and print the Customer Balance Summary Report

Click **Reports** on the menu bar
Point to **Customers & Receivables**
Click **Customer Balance Summary**

- The report should appear on the screen.
- The current date and time will appear on the report. Since the dates given in the text will not be the same date as the computer, it may be helpful to remove the date and time prepared from your report.

Remove the date prepared and the time prepared from the report:
Click **Customize Report**
Click the **Header/Footer** tab
Click the check box next to **Date Prepared** to deselect this option
Click the check box next to **Time Prepared** to deselect this option

- *Note:* Some reports will also have a Report Basis—Cash or Accrual. You may turn off the display of the report basis by clicking the check box for this option.

Click **OK** on the **Modify Report** screen

- The Date Prepared and Time Prepared are no longer displayed on the report.
- The modification of the header is only applicable to this report. The next time a report is prepared, the header must once again be modified to deselect the Date Prepared and Time Prepared.

Change the Dates for the report:
Click in or tab to **From**, enter **01/01/15**
Tab to **To**, Enter **01/05/15**

Press the Tab key

- After you enter the date, pressing the tab key will generate the report.
- This report lists the names of all customers with balances on account. The amount column shows the total balance for each customer. This includes opening balances as well as current invoices.

Computer Consulting by Your Name
Customer Balance Summary
As of January 5, 2015

	Jan 5, 15
Ahmadrand, Ela	300.00
Andrews Productions	3,190.00
Cooper & Cranston, CPA	1,265.00
Creative Products	1,295.00
Design Creations	3,230.00
Duncan, Jones, and Cline	1,915.00
Gomez, Luis Esq.	450.00
Mahmood Imports	300.00
Research Corp.	815.00
Rosenthal Illustrations	3,830.00
Shumway, Lewis, and Levy	3,685.00
Vines & Rhodes	3,215.00
Wagner, Leavitt, and Moraga	3,680.00
Williams, Matt CPA	890.00
Young, Norton, and Brancato	3,365.00
TOTAL	31,425.00

Click the **Print** button at the top of the Customer Balance Summary Report
To select between printing a Report or Save as PDF, click **Report**
Complete the information on the **Print Reports Settings** tab:
Printer To: **Printer**: (should identify the type of printer you are using)

- This may be different from the printer identified in this text.

Orientation: Should be Portrait. If it is not, click **Portrait** to select Portrait orientation for this report

- Portrait orientation prints in the traditional 8 ½- by 11-inch paper size.

Page Range: **All** should be selected; if it is not, click **All**
Click **Page Breaks**: **Smart page breaks (widow/orphan control)** to select
Number of copies: should be **1**
Collate is not necessary on a one-page report, it may be left with or without the check mark
If necessary, click on **Fit report to 1 page(s) wide** to deselect this item
If necessary, click on **Fit report to 1 page(s) High** to deselect this item

- When selected, the printer will print the report using a smaller font so it will be one page in width.

Leave **Print in color** without a check mark

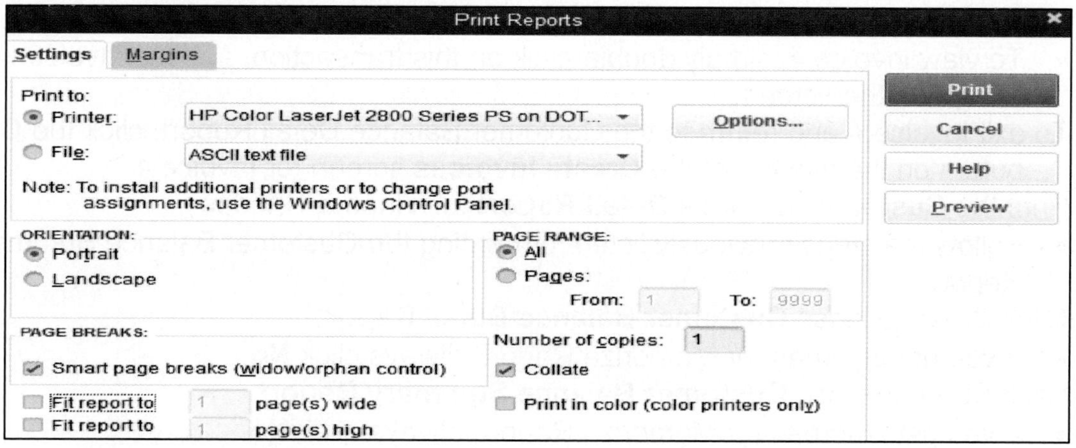

Click **Print** on the **Print Reports** screen
Do not close the **Customer Balance Summary Report**

QUICKZOOM

You ask the office manager, Alhandra Cruz, to obtain information regarding the balance of the Vines & Rhodes account. To get detailed information regarding an individual customer's balance while in the Customer Balance Summary Report, use the QuickZoom feature. With the individual customer's information on the screen, you can print a report for that customer.

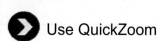

Use QuickZoom

Point to the balance for **Vines & Rhodes**

- Notice that the mouse pointer turns into a magnifying glass with a **Z** in it.

Click once to mark the balance **3,215.00**

- Notice the marks on either side of the amount.

Double-click to **Zoom** in to see the details
The report dates used should be from **01/01/15** to **01/05/15**
Remove the Date Prepared and Time Prepared from the header

- Follow the instructions previously listed for removing the date and time prepared from the header for the Customer Balance Summary Report.

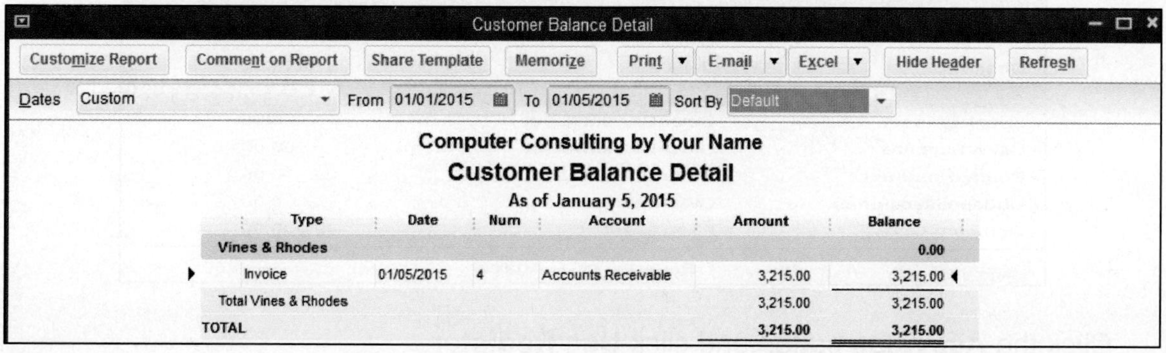

- Notice that Invoice 4 was recorded on 01/05/2015 for $3,215.00.
- To view Invoice 4, simply double-click on this transaction, and the invoice will be shown on the screen.

To exit Invoice 4 and return to the Customer Balance Detail Report, click the **Close** button on the title bar of the **Create Invoices** screen for Invoice 4

Print the **Customer Balance Detail Report** for Vines & Rhodes

- Follow the steps previously listed for printing the Customer Balance Summary Report.

Click **Close** to close **Customer Balance Detail Report**

- If you get a screen for Memorize Report, always click **No**.

Click **Close** to close **Customer Balance Summary Report**

- If you get a screen for Memorize Report, always click **No**.

CORRECT AND PRINT INVOICE

Errors may be corrected very easily with QuickBooks. Because an invoice is prepared for sales on account, corrections may be made directly on the invoice or in the Accounts Receivable account register. We will access the invoice via the register for the Accounts Receivable account. The account register contains detailed information regarding each transaction that used the account. Therefore, anytime an invoice is recorded, it is posted to the Accounts Receivable register.

MEMO
DATE: January 7, 2015

The actual amount of time spent for on-site training at Cooper & Cranston, CPA increased from 10 hours to 12 hours. Change Invoice 5 to correct the actual amount of training hours to show a total of 12 hours.

Correct an error in Invoice 5 using the Accounts Receivable Register and print the corrected invoice

Click the **Chart of Accounts** icon in the Company Section of the Home Page
In the Chart of Accounts, click **Accounts Receivable**

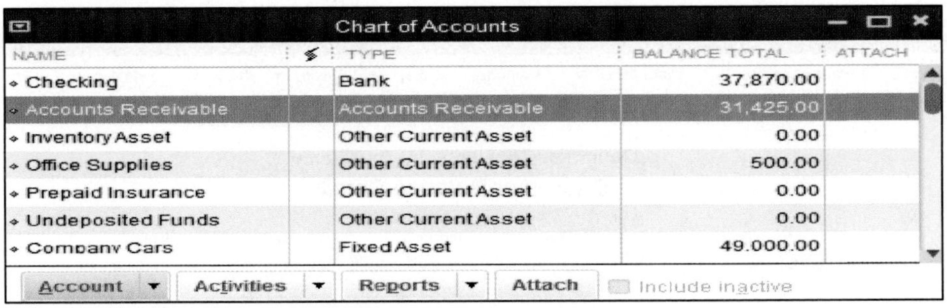

Chart of Accounts
NAME
TYPE
BALANCE TOTAL
ATTACH
Checking
Bank
37,870.00
Accounts Receivable
Accounts Receivable
31,425.00
Inventory Asset
Other Current Asset
0.00
Office Supplies
Other Current Asset
500.00
Prepaid Insurance
Other Current Asset
0.00
Undeposited Funds
Other Current Asset
0.00
Company Cars
Fixed Asset
49,000.00
Account
Activities
Reports
Attach
Include inactive

Click the **Activities** button and click **Use Register**

<u>**OR**</u>

Double-click **Accounts Receivable** in the Chart of Accounts

- The Accounts Receivable Register appears on the screen with information regarding each transaction entered into the account.
- *Note:* This is the same as the Accounts Receivable General Ledger Account.

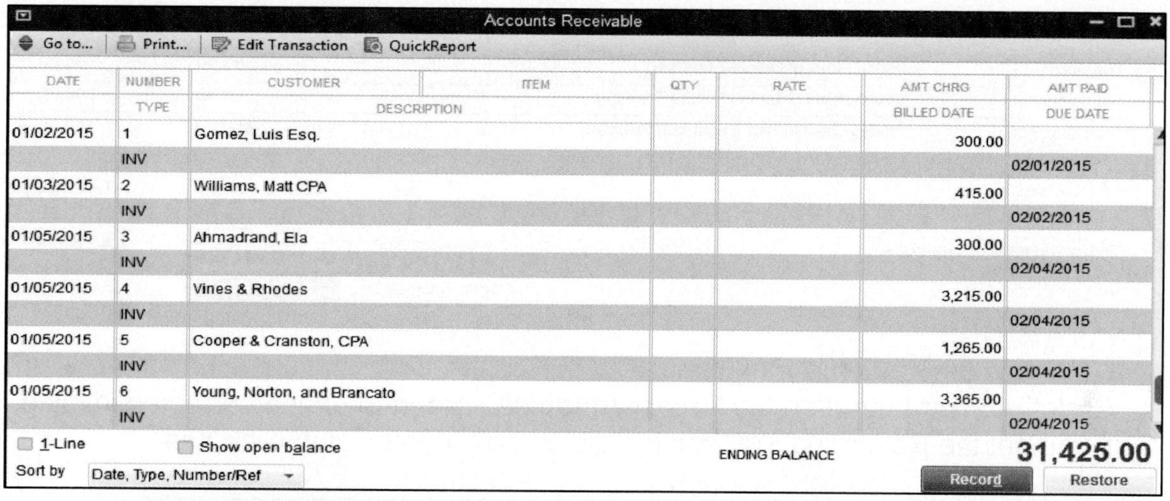
Accounts Receivable
Go to... Print... Edit Transaction QuickReport
DATE NUMBER CUSTOMER ITEM QTY RATE AMT CHRG AMT PAID
TYPE DESCRIPTION BILLED DATE DUE DATE
01/02/2015 1 Gomez, Luis Esq. 300.00
INV 02/01/2015
01/03/2015 2 Williams, Matt CPA 415.00
INV 02/02/2015
01/05/2015 3 Ahmadrand, Ela 300.00
INV 02/04/2015
01/05/2015 4 Vines & Rhodes 3,215.00
INV 02/04/2015
01/05/2015 5 Cooper & Cranston, CPA 1,265.00
INV 02/04/2015
01/05/2015 6 Young, Norton, and Brancato 3,365.00
INV 02/04/2015
1-Line
Show open balance
ENDING BALANCE 31,425.00
Sort by Date, Type, Number/Ref
Record Restore

- Look at the **NUMBER/TYPE** column to identify the number of the invoice and the type of transaction.
- When the <u>NUMBER</u> line shows an <u>invoice number</u>, the <u>TYPE</u> line will show <u>INV</u>.
- If the <u>NUMBER</u> line shows a <u>check number</u>, the <u>TYPE</u> line will show <u>PMT</u>. This indicates that a payment on account was received.

If necessary, scroll through the register until the transaction for **Invoice 5** is on the screen

- When scrolling through the register, you may see some opening balances that are dated 12/31/2014. These amounts are balances from the previous year.

Click anywhere in the transaction for **Invoice 5** to Cooper & Cranston, CPA

Click **Edit Transaction** at the top of the register

- Invoice 5 appears on the screen.

Click the line in the **QUANTITY** field that corresponds to the **Training 2** hours

Change the quantity from 9 hours to 11 hours

Position cursor in front of the 9

Press **Delete**

Type **11**

Press **Tab** to generate a new total

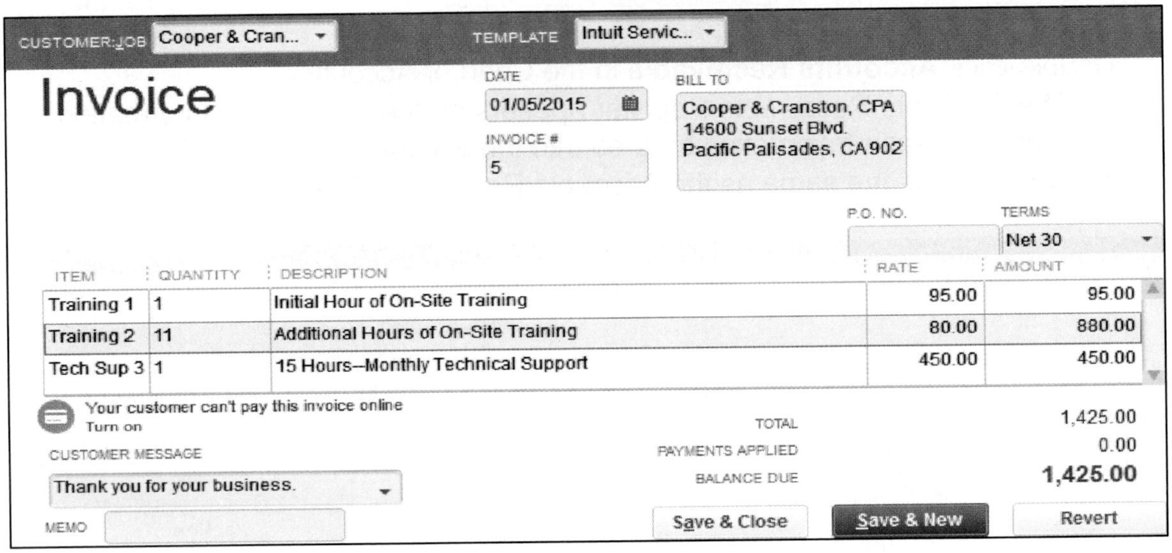

- Notice that the date remains 01/05/2015.

Click the **Print** button on the **Create Invoices** screen to print a corrected invoice

If you get the Recording Transaction dialog box at this point, click **Yes**

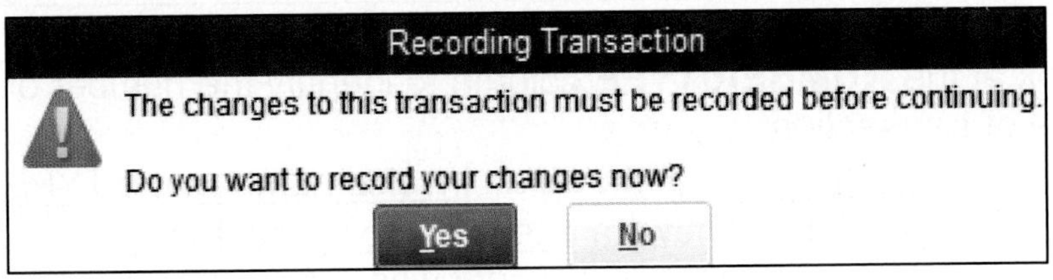

Check the information on the **Print One Invoice Settings** tab

Click **Print**

Click **Save & Close** to record changes and close invoice

- If you did not get the Recording Transaction dialog box before printing and you see it now, click **Yes**.

After closing the invoice, you return to the register

VIEW QUICKREPORT

After editing the invoice and returning to the register, you may get a detailed report regarding the customer's transactions by clicking the QuickReport button.

View a QuickReport for Cooper & Cranston, CPA

Click the **QuickReport** button at the top of the Register to view the **Cooper & Cranston** account

Verify the balance of the account. It should be **$1,425.00**

- *Note:* You will get the date prepared, time prepared, and the report basis in the heading of your QuickReport.

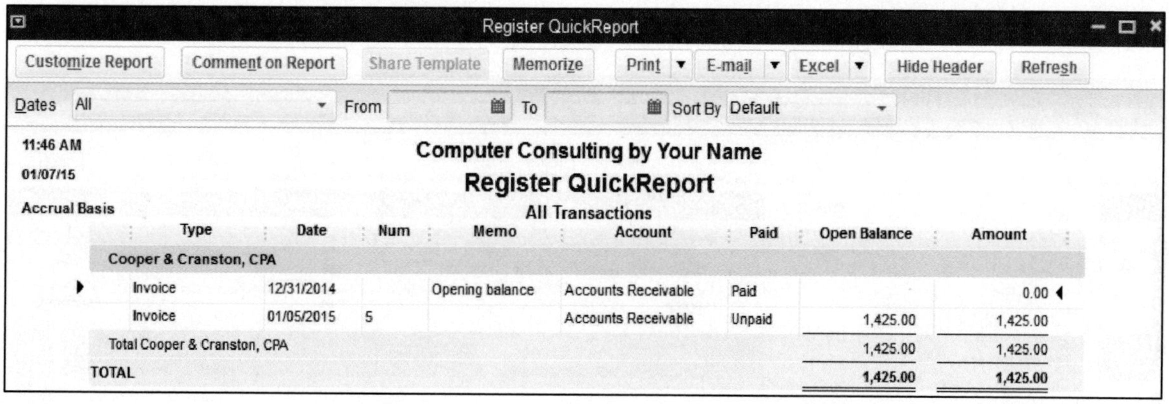

Type	Date	Num	Memo	Account	Paid	Open Balance	Amount
Cooper & Cranston, CPA							
Invoice	12/31/2014		Opening balance	Accounts Receivable	Paid		0.00
Invoice	01/05/2015	5		Accounts Receivable	Unpaid	1,425.00	1,425.00
Total Cooper & Cranston, CPA						1,425.00	1,425.00
TOTAL						1,425.00	1,425.00

ANALYZE QUICKREPORT

Analyze the QuickReport for Cooper & Cranston, CPA

Notice that the total of Invoice 5 is $1,425.00
Close the **QuickReport** without printing
Close the **Accounts Receivable Register**
Close the **Chart of Accounts**

VOID AND DELETE SALES FORMS

Deleting an invoice or sales receipt permanently removes it from QuickBooks without leaving a trace. If you would like to correct your financial records for the invoice that you no longer want, it is more appropriate to void the invoice. When an invoice is voided, it remains in the QuickBooks system with a zero balance.

VOID INVOICE

MEMO
DATE: January 7, 2015

Ela Ahmadrand called to cancel the 10 hours of technical support for January. Since none of the technical support had been used, you decide to void Invoice 3.

Void Invoice 3 by going directly to the original invoice

Use the keyboard shortcut **Ctrl+I** to open the Create Invoices screen
- Remember I stands for Invoice.

Click the **Previous** or **Back** arrow on the Invoice icon bar until you get to **Invoice 3**
With Invoice 3 on the screen, click **Edit** on the QuickBooks Menu bar below the title bar

Click **Void Invoice**

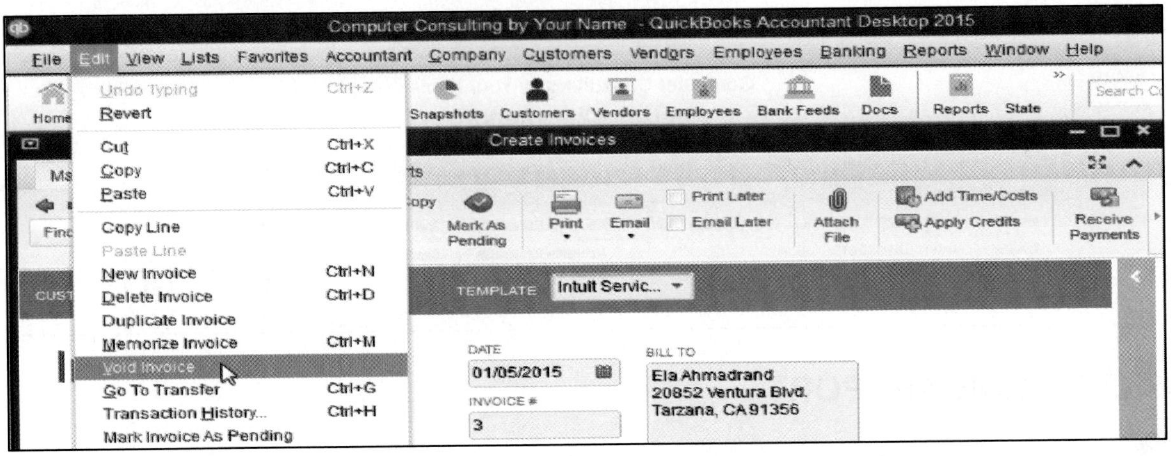

- Notice that the amount and total for the invoice are no longer 300. They are both **0.00**.
- Find the Memo text box at the bottom of the invoice and verify that **VOID:** appears as the memo.

Click **Save & Close** on the **Create Invoices** screen
Click **Yes** on the **Recording Transaction** dialog box
Click the **Reports** button on the Icon bar
Click **Customers & Receivables** as the Type of Report

- The report categories are displayed on the left side of the Report Center. To prepare a report, click the desired type of report.

Click the **List View** button to select the report list 

- Remember there are three ways to view a report list—carousel view, list view, and graph view.

After selecting the List view, scroll through the list of reports, and click **Transaction List by Customer** in the Customer Balance section
Click the **Run** button

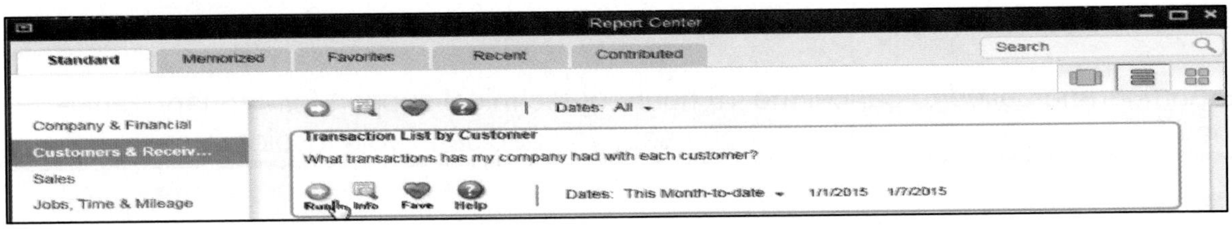

Tab to or Click in **From**
Remove the current date; if it is not highlighted, and enter **010115**

- Using a **/** between the items in a date is optional.

Tab to or click in **To**
Remove the current date; if it is not highlighted, and enter **010715**, press **Tab**
Remove the date prepared and the time prepared from the report heading:
    Click **Customize Report**

Click **Header/Footer** tab

Click the check box next to **Date Prepared** and **Time Prepared** to deselect these options

Click **OK**

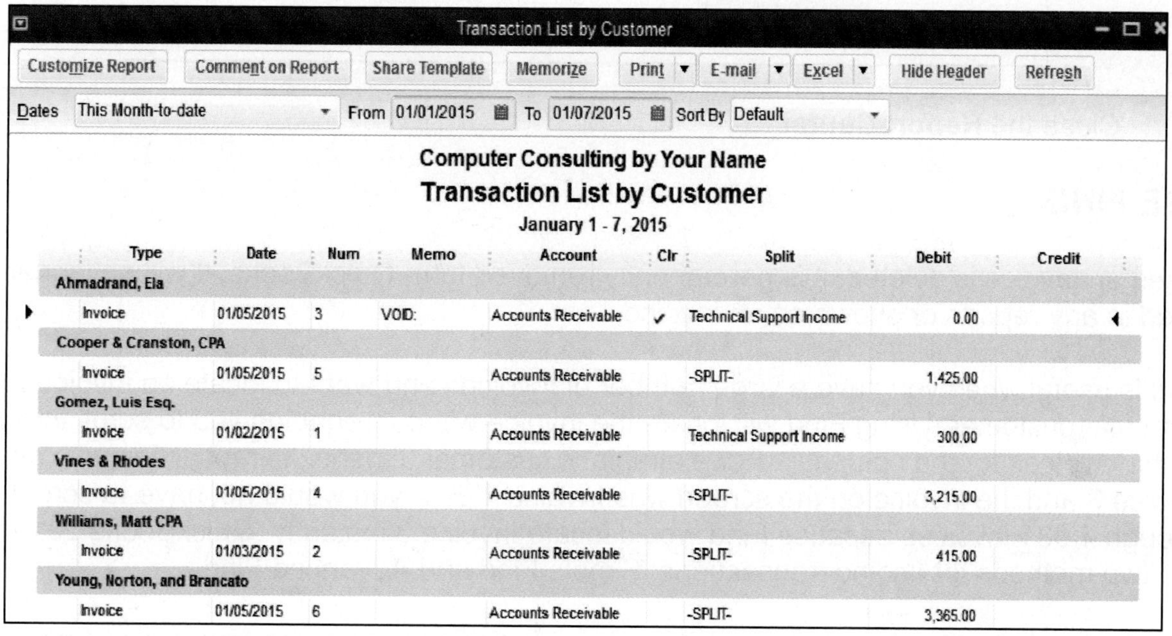

Transaction List by Customer

Customize Report | Comment on Report | Share Template | Memorize | Print | E-mail | Excel | Hide Header | Refresh

Dates This Month-to-date From 01/01/2015 To 01/07/2015 Sort By Default

Computer Consulting by Your Name

Transaction List by Customer

January 1 - 7, 2015

Type	Date	Num	Memo	Account	Clr	Split	Debit	Credit
Ahmadrand, Ela								
Invoice	01/05/2015	3	VOID:	Accounts Receivable	✓	Technical Support Income	0.00	
Cooper & Cranston, CPA								
Invoice	01/05/2015	5		Accounts Receivable		-SPLIT-	1,425.00	
Gomez, Luis Esq.								
Invoice	01/02/2015	1		Accounts Receivable		Technical Support Income	300.00	
Vines & Rhodes								
Invoice	01/05/2015	4		Accounts Receivable		-SPLIT-	3,215.00	
Williams, Matt CPA								
Invoice	01/03/2015	2		Accounts Receivable		-SPLIT-	415.00	
Young, Norton, and Brancato								
Invoice	01/05/2015	6		Accounts Receivable		-SPLIT-	3,365.00	

- This report gives the amount for each transaction with the customer.
- Notice that Invoice 3 is marked VOID in the Memo column and has a √ in the **Clr** (Cleared) column.
- The SPLIT column tells you which account was used to record the income. If the word **-SPLIT-** appears in the column, this means the transaction amount was split or divided among two or more sales items.

Print the **Transactions List by Customer Report** in Landscape orientation following printing instructions provided earlier in the chapter

Click **Landscape** to use Landscape Orientation (11 wide by 8 ½ long)

- Do not use the option to fit the report to one-page wide.

Close the **Transaction List by Customer Report**

- You should get a screen for Memorize Report. When you want to have QuickBooks memorize a report, there are several ways to tell it to do so. At this point, it is better to turn off this message than to have to click No after every report you prepare.

On the Memorize Report message, click **Do not display this message in the future**, then click **No**

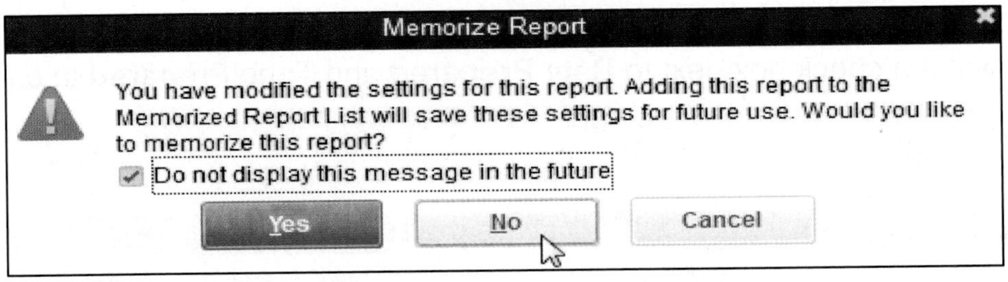

Close the **Report Center**

USE FIND

When an invoice is deleted, it is permanently removed from QuickBooks. It will no longer be listed in any reports or shown as an invoice.

Find is useful when you have a large number of invoices and want to locate an invoice for a particular customer. Using Find will locate the invoice without requiring you to scroll through all the invoices for the company. For example, if customer Jimenez's transaction was on Invoice 3 and the invoice on the screen was Invoice 1,084, you would not have to scroll through 1,081 invoices because Find would locate Invoice 3 instantly. QuickBooks 2015 has two methods for finding transactions: Simple Find and Advanced Find.

Simple Find allows you to do a quick search using the most common transaction types. Transaction Types include Invoice, Sales Receipt, Credit Memo, Check, and others. The search results are displayed in the lower portion of the window. You can view an individual transaction by highlighting it and clicking Go To, you can view a Find Report on the search results by clicking Report, and you can click Export to the export the Find Report to Excel.

Advanced Find is used to do a more detailed search for transactions than you can do using Simple Find. Advanced Find allows you to apply filters to your search criteria. When you apply a filter, you choose how you want QuickBooks to restrict the search results to certain customers, for example. QuickBooks will exclude any transactions that don't meet your criteria. You can apply filters either one at a time or in combination with each other. Each additional filter you apply further restricts the content of the search. The search results are displayed in the lower portion of the window. You can view an individual transaction by highlighting it and clicking Go To, you can view a Find Report on the search results by clicking Report, and you can click Export to export the Find Report to Excel.

MEMO
DATE: January 7, 2015

Because of the upcoming tax season, Matt Williams has had to reschedule his 5-hour training session with Jennifer Lockwood three times. He finally decided to cancel the training session and reschedule it after April 15. Delete Invoice 2.

Use Find to locate Invoice 2 to Matt Williams,

Use Simple Find by clicking **Edit** on the menu bar, clicking **Find** on the Edit menu and clicking the **Simple Find** tab

The Transaction Type should be **Invoice**

- If it is not, click the drop-down list arrow for Transaction Type and click Invoice.

Click the drop-down list arrow for **Customer:Job**

Click **Williams, Matt CPA**

- This allows QuickBooks to find any invoices recorded for Matt Williams.

Click the **Find** button

Click the line for **Invoice 2**

- Make sure you have selected Invoice 2 and not the invoice containing the opening balance.

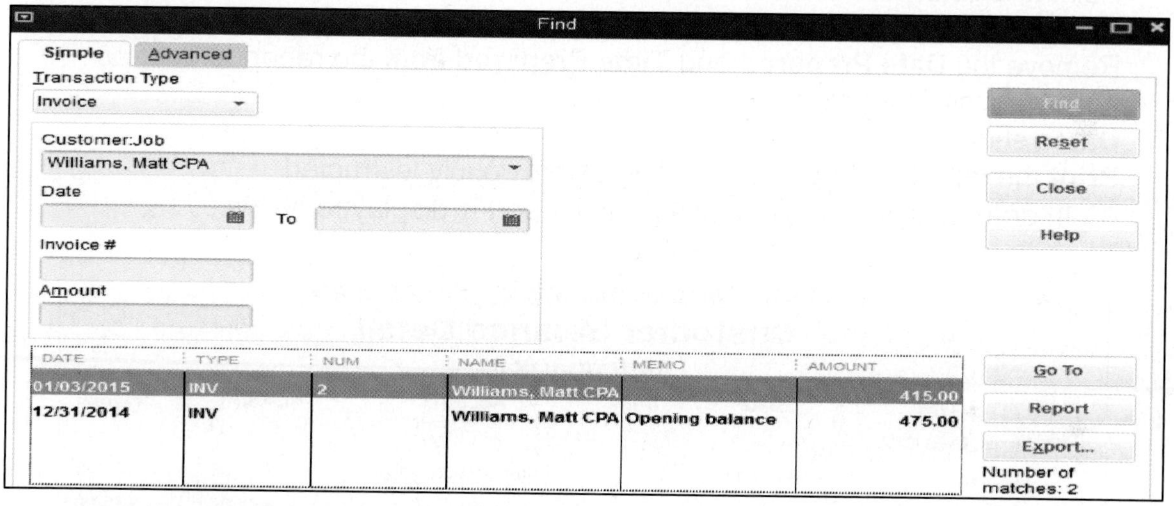

Click the **Go To** button

- Invoice 2 appears on the screen.

DELETE INVOICE

With the Invoice 2 on the screen, click **Edit** on the QuickBooks menu bar

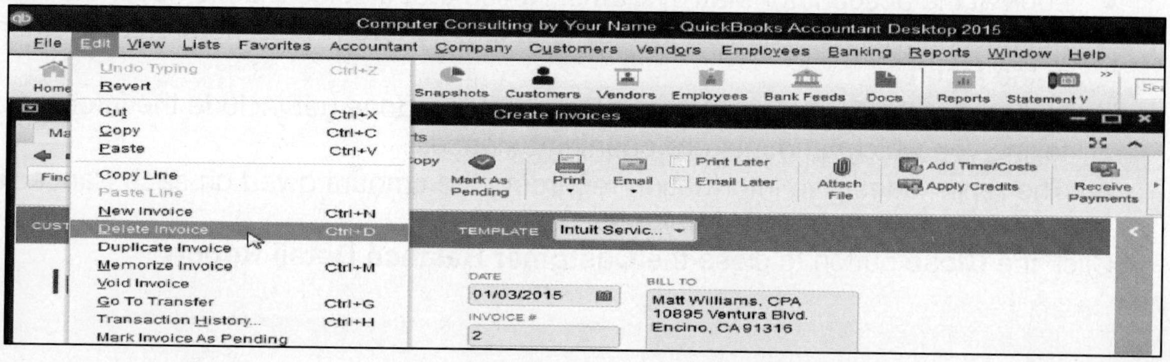

Click **Delete Invoice**
Click **OK** in the **Delete Transaction** dialog box

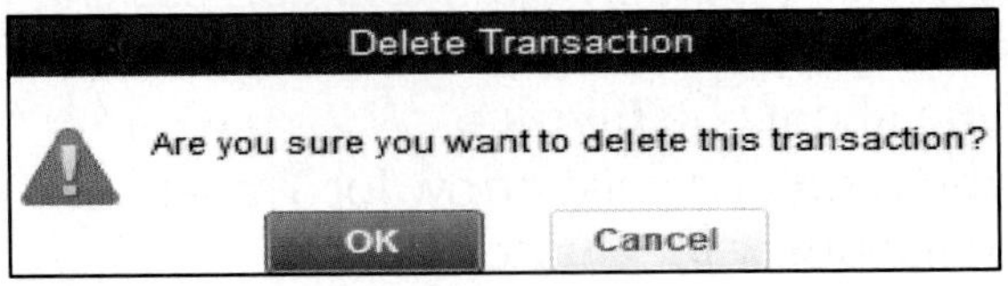

- Notice that the cursor is now positioned on Invoice 3.

Click **Save & Close** button on the **Create Invoices** screen to close the invoice

- Notice that Invoice 2 no longer shows on **Find**.

Click the **Close** button to close **Find**
Click **Reports** on the menu bar
Point to **Customers & Receivables**
Click **Customer Balance Detail**
Remove the **Date Prepared** and **Time Prepared** from the report header as previously instructed
Dates should be **All**
Print the report in Portrait orientation as previously instructed

- In order to save space, only a partial report is displayed below.

Computer Consulting by Your Name
Customer Balance Detail
All Transactions

Type	Date	Num	Account	Amount	Balance
Williams, Matt CPA					
Invoice	12/31/2014		Accounts Receivable	475.00	475.00
Total Williams, Matt CPA				475.00	475.00
Young, Norton, and Brancato					
Invoice	12/31/2014		Accounts Receivable	0.00	0.00
Invoice	01/05/2015	6	Accounts Receivable	3,365.00	3,365.00
Total Young, Norton, and Brancato				3,365.00	3,365.00
TOTAL				30,870.00	30,870.00

Partial Report

- Look at the account for Matt Williams. Notice that Invoice 2 does not show up in the account listing. When an invoice is deleted, there is no record of it anywhere in the report.
- Notice that the Customer Balance Detail Report does not include the information telling you which amounts are opening balances.
- The report does give information regarding the amount owed on each transaction plus the total amount owed by each customer.

Click the **Close** button to close the **Customer Balance Detail Report**

PREPARE CREDIT MEMO

Credit memos are prepared to show a reduction to a transaction. If the invoice has already been sent to the customer, it is more appropriate and less confusing to make a change to a transaction by issuing a credit memo rather than voiding or deleting the invoice and issuing a new one. A credit memo notifies a customer that a change has been made to a transaction.

MEMO
DATE: January 8, 2015

Credit Memo 7: Vines & Rhodes did not need 5 hours of the training billed on Invoice 4. Issue a Credit Memo to reduce Training 2 by 5 hours.

Prepare a Credit Memo

Click the **Refunds and Credits** icon in the Customers area of the Home Page
Click the down arrow for the drop-down list box next to **CUSTOMER:JOB**
Click **Vines & Rhodes**
- Notice that the History for Vines & Rhodes is shown on the right side of the invoice.

The **TEMPLATE** textbox should say **Custom Credit Memo**
- If not, click the drop-down list arrow and click **Custom Credit Memo**.

Tab to or click **DATE**
Type in the date of the credit memo: **01/08/15**
The **Credit No.** field should show the number **7**
- Because credit memos are included in the numbering sequence for invoices, this number matches the number of the next blank invoice.

There is no PO No.
Tab to or click in **ITEM**
Click the drop-down list arrow in the Item column
Click **Training 2**
Tab to or click in **QTY**
Type in **5**
Click the next blank line in the DESCRIPTION column
Type **Deduct 5 hours of unused training. Reduce the amount due for Invoice 4.**
- This will print as a note or explanation to the customer.

Click the drop-down list arrow next to **CUSTOMER MESSAGE**
Click **It's been a pleasure working with you!**

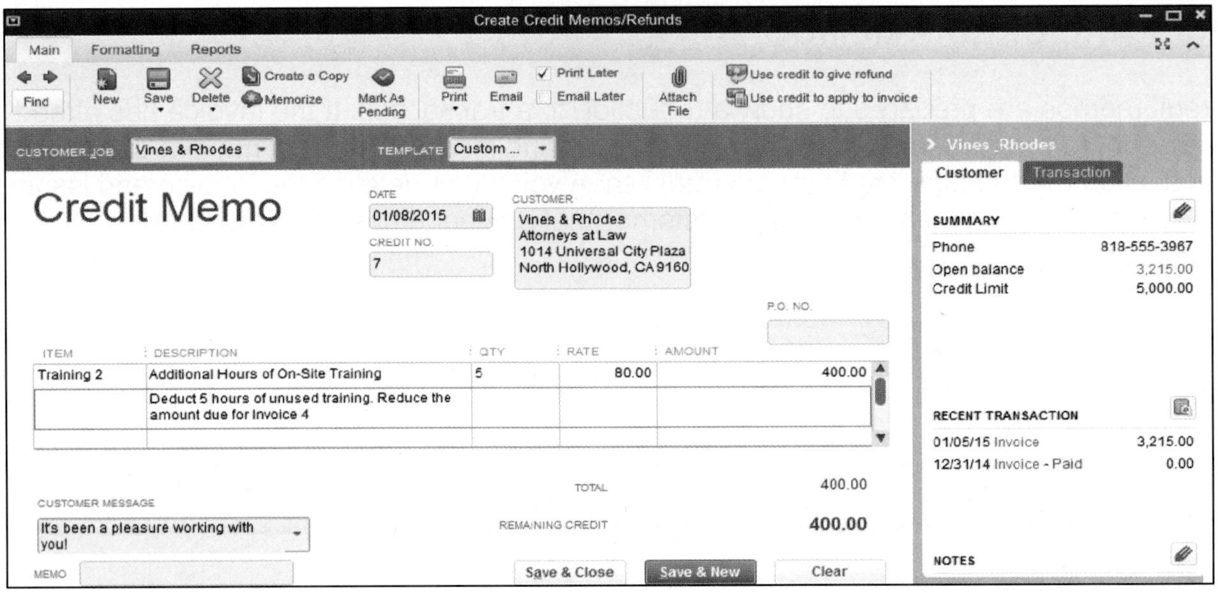

To apply the credit to an invoice, click **Use credit to apply to invoice** on the Create Credit Memos/Refunds Icon bar [Use credit to apply to invoice]

- Make sure there is a check mark for Invoice 4 on the Apply Credit to Invoices screen.

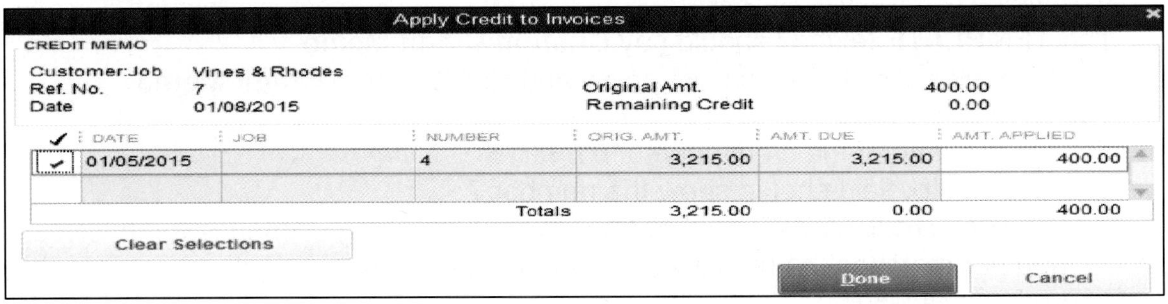

Click **Done**

- Notice the Recent Transactions section in the History pane. It includes the Credit Memo.

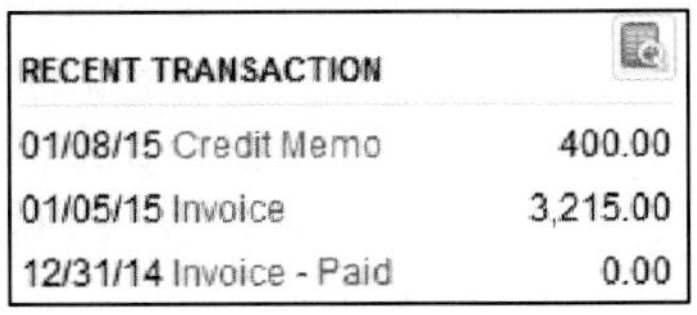

Click the **Print** button on **Create Credit Memos/Refunds**

Click **Print** on the **Print One Credit Memo** screen

- Make sure that there is a check mark for "Do not print lines around each field."

Click the **Save & Close** button

CUSTOMER BALANCE DETAIL REPORT

Periodically viewing reports allows you to verify the changes that have occurred to accounts. The Customer Balance Detail report shows all the transactions for each credit customer. Cash customers must be viewed through sales reports.

View the Customer Balance Detail Report

Click the **Reports** button on the Icon bar
Click **Customers & Receivables** as the report type
In the Customer Balance section, click **Customer Balance Detail** on the list of reports displayed; and then, click the **Run** icon
Scroll through the report

- Notice that the account for Vines & Rhodes shows Credit Memo 7 for $400.00. The total amount owed was reduced by $400 and is $2,815.00.
- In order to save space, only a partial report is displayed below.

2:24 PM
01/08/15

Computer Consulting by Your Name
Customer Balance Detail
All Transactions

Type	Date	Num	Account	Amount	Balance
Vines & Rhodes					
Invoice	12/31/2014		Accounts Receivable	0.00	0.00
Invoice	01/05/2015	4	Accounts Receivable	3,215.00	3,215.00
Credit Memo	01/08/2015	7	Accounts Receivable	-400.00	2,815.00
Total Vines & Rhodes				2,815.00	2,815.00
Wagner, Leavitt, and Moraga					
Invoice	12/31/2014		Accounts Receivable	3,680.00	3,680.00
Total Wagner, Leavitt, and Moraga				3,680.00	3,680.00
Williams, Matt CPA					
Invoice	12/31/2014		Accounts Receivable	475.00	475.00
Total Williams, Matt CPA				475.00	475.00
Young, Norton, and Brancato					
Invoice	12/31/2014		Accounts Receivable	0.00	0.00
Invoice	01/05/2015	6	Accounts Receivable	3,365.00	3,365.00
Total Young, Norton, and Brancato				3,365.00	3,365.00
TOTAL				30,470.00	30,470.00

Partial Report

Click the **Close** button to close the report without printing
Close the **Report Center**

ADD NEW ACCOUNT

Because account needs can change as a business is in operation, QuickBooks allows you to make changes to the chart of accounts at any time. Some changes to the chart of accounts require additional changes to lists.

You have determined that Computer Consulting by Your Name has received a lot of calls from customers for assistance with hardware and network installation. Even though Computer Consulting by Your Name does not record revenue according to the employee performing the service, it does assign primary areas of responsibility to some of the personnel. Rom Levy will be responsible for installing hardware and setting up networks for customers. As a result of this decision, you will be adding a third income account. It will be used when revenue from hardware or network installation is earned. In addition to adding the account, you will also have to add two new sales items to the Item list.

MEMO
DATE: January 8, 2015

Add a new account, Installation Income. It is a subaccount of Income.

Add a new income account for Hardware and Network Installation

Click the **Chart of Accounts** icon in the Company section of the Home Page
- Remember that the Chart of Accounts is also the General Ledger.

Click the **Account** button at the bottom of the Chart of Accounts screen
Click **New**

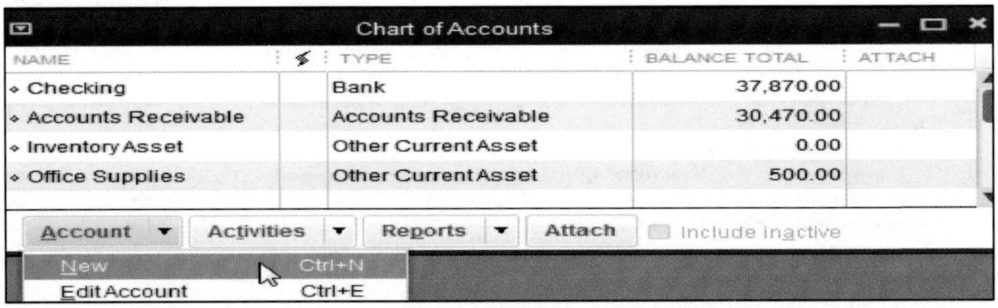

Click **Income** to choose one account type

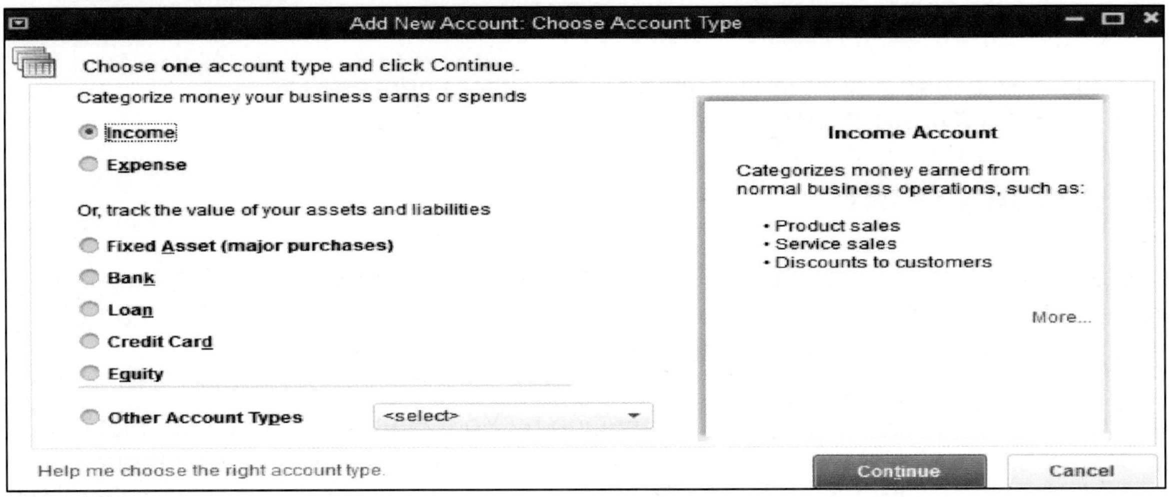

Click the **Continue** button.
If necessary, tab to or click in the text box for **Account Name**
Type **Installation Income**
Click the check box for **Subaccount of**
Click the drop-down list arrow for **Subaccount of**
Click **Income**
Tab to or click **Description**

Type **Hardware and Network Installation Income**

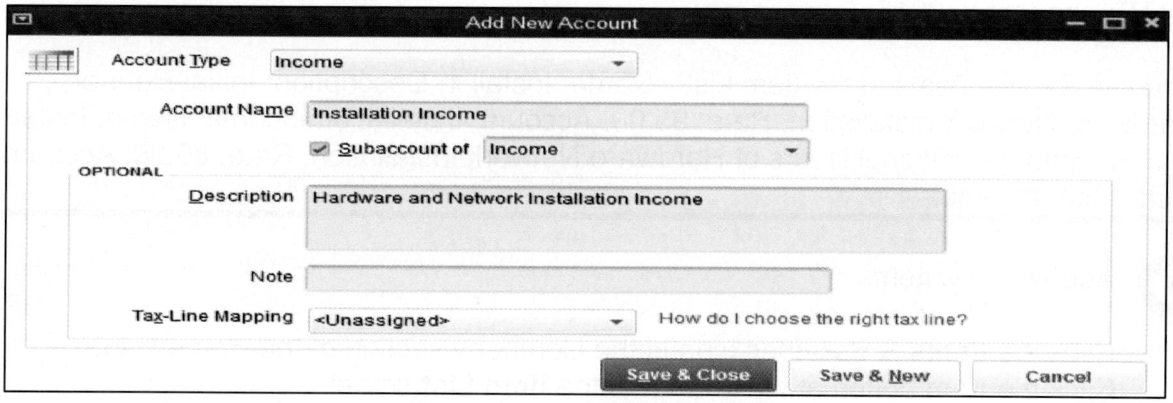

Click the **Save & Close** button
Scroll through the Chart of Accounts
Verify that Installation Income has been added under Income

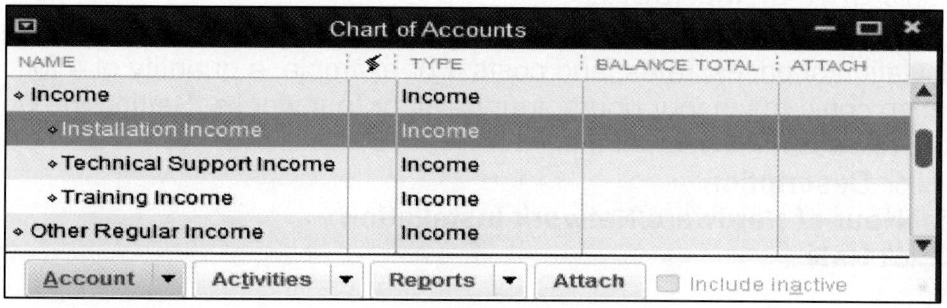

- Notice that the subaccounts are shown below Income and are indented.

Close **Chart of Accounts**

ADD NEW ITEMS

In order to accommodate the changing needs of a business, all QuickBooks lists allow you to make changes at any time. The Item List stores information about the services Computer Consulting by Your Name provides. Items are sometimes called Sales Items because an item is identified when recording a cash or credit sale.

In order to use the new Installation Income account, two new items need to be added to the Item List. When these items are used in a transaction, the amount of revenue earned in the transaction will be posted to the Installation Income account.

MEMO
DATE: January 8, 2015

Add two Service items to the Item List—Name: Install 1, Description: Initial Hour of Hardware/Network Installation, Rate: 95.00, Account: Installation Income. Name: Install 2, Description: Additional Hours of Hardware/Network Installation, Rate: 80.00, Account: Installation Income.

Add two new items

Click the **Items & Services** icon in the Company section of the Home Page
Click the **Item** button at the bottom of the **Item List** screen
Click **New**
TYPE is **Service**
Tab to or click **Item Name/Number**
Type **Install 1**
Do not enable UNIT OF MEASURE

- UNIT OF MEASURE (not available in Pro) is used to indicate the quantities used for calculation of prices, rates, and costs. For example, a quantity of 4 for installation could mean four hours, four days, or four weeks. Setting the unit of measure allows clarification of this.

Tab to or click **Description**
Type **Initial Hour of Hardware/Network Installation**
Tab to or click **Rate**
Type **95**
To indicate the general ledger account to be used to record the sale of this item, click the drop-down list arrow for **Account**
Click **Installation Income**

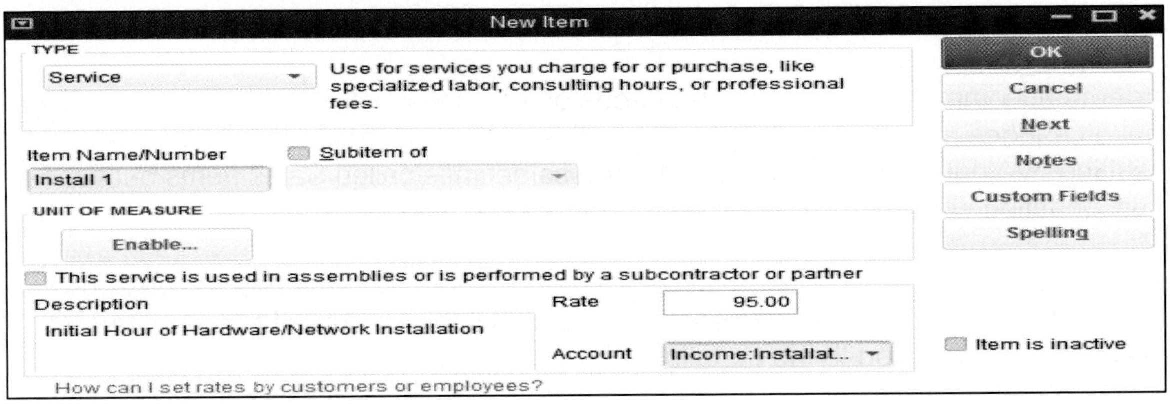

Click **Next** on the New Item dialog box
Repeat the steps above to add **Install 2**
The description is **Additional Hours of Hardware/Network Installation**
The rate is **80.00** per hour

The account is **Installation Income**

When finished adding Install 2, click **OK** to add new items and to close **New Item** screen

- Whenever hardware or network installation is provided for customers, the first hour will be billed as Install 1, and additional hours will be billed as Install 2.

Verify the addition of Install 1 and Install 2 on the Item List

- If you find an error, click on the item with the error, click the **Item** button, click **Edit**, and make corrections as needed.

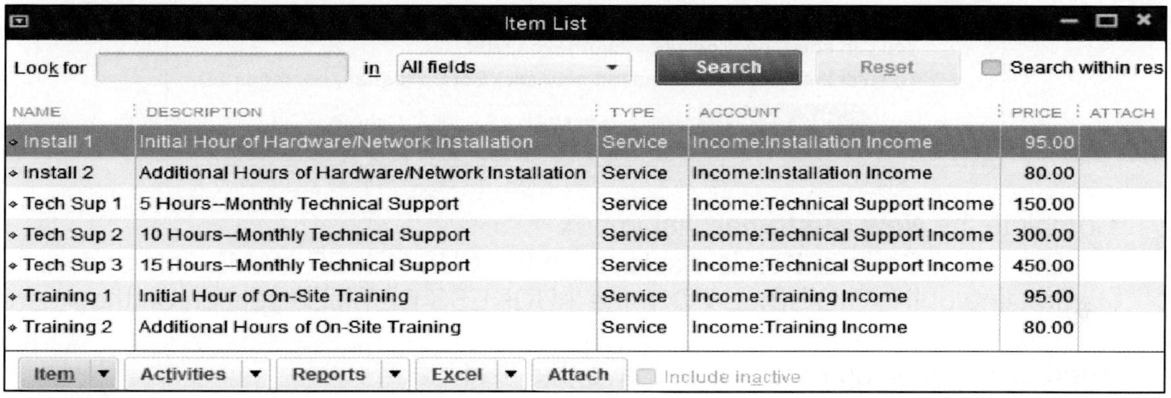
Item List
Look for
in
All fields
Search
Reset
Search within res
NAME | DESCRIPTION | TYPE | ACCOUNT | PRICE | ATTACH
Install 1 | Initial Hour of Hardware/Network Installation | Service | Income:Installation Income | 95.00
Install 2 | Additional Hours of Hardware/Network Installation | Service | Income:Installation Income | 80.00
Tech Sup 1 | 5 Hours--Monthly Technical Support | Service | Income:Technical Support Income | 150.00
Tech Sup 2 | 10 Hours--Monthly Technical Support | Service | Income:Technical Support Income | 300.00
Tech Sup 3 | 15 Hours--Monthly Technical Support | Service | Income:Technical Support Income | 450.00
Training 1 | Initial Hour of On-Site Training | Service | Income:Training Income | 95.00
Training 2 | Additional Hours of On-Site Training | Service | Income:Training Income | 80.00
Item
Activities
Reports
Excel
Attach
Include inactive

Close the **Item List**

ADD NEW CUSTOMER

Because customers are the lifeblood of a business, QuickBooks allows customers to be added "on the fly" as you create an invoice or a sales receipt. You may choose between Quick Add (used to add only a customer's name) and Set Up (used to add complete information for a customer).

> **MEMO**
> **DATE:** January 8, 2015
>
> Invoice 8: A new customer, Ken Collins, has purchased several upgrade items for his personal computer. He needs assistance with the installation. Rom Levy spent two hours installing this hardware. Bill Mr. Collins for 2 hours of hardware installation. His address is: 20985 Ventura Blvd., Woodland Hills, CA 91371. His telephone number is: 818-555-2058. His fax number is 808-555-8502. His E-mail is KCollins@123.com. His credit limit is $1,000; and the terms are Net 30.

Add a new customer and record the above sale on account

Click the **Create Invoices** icon on the Home Page
In the Customer:Job dialog box, type **Collins, Ken**
Press **Tab**

- You will see a message box for **Customer:Job Not Found** with buttons for three choices:
  Quick Add (used to add only a customer's name)
  Set Up (used to add complete information for a customer)
  Cancel (used to cancel the **Customer:Job Not Found** message box)

Click **Set Up**

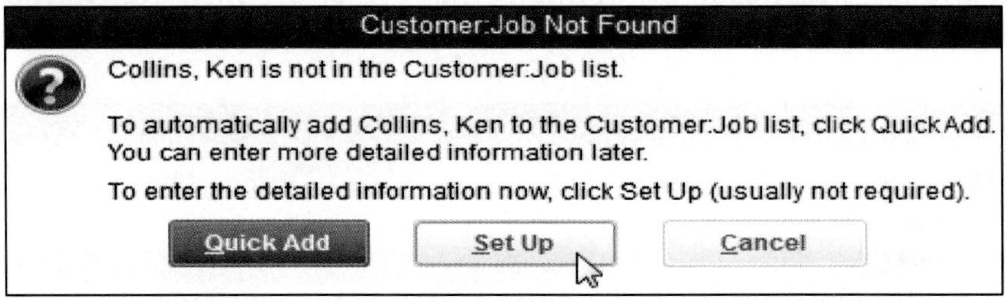

Complete the **New Customer** dialog box

- The name **Collins, Ken** is displayed in the CUSTOMER NAME field and as the first line of INVOICE/BILL TO in the ADDRESS DETAILS section on the Address Info tab.

There is no Opening Balance, so leave this field blank

- An opening balance may be given only when the customer's account is created. It is the amount the customer owes you at the time the account is created. It is not the amount of any transaction not yet recorded.
- Since there is no opening balance, you do not need to change the AS OF date to 01/08/2015.

Complete the information for the **Address Info** tab
Tab to or click in the text box for **First** in the line for Full Name, type **Ken**
Tab to or click in text box for **Last** in the line for Full Name, type **Collins**
Tab to or click in text box for **Main Phone**
Type the phone number **818-555-2058**
Tab to or click in text box for **Main E-mail**, enter **KCollins@123.com**
Tab to or click in text box for **Fax**, enter **818-555-8502**
Tab to or click the first line for **INVOICE/BILL TO**
If necessary, highlight **Collins, Ken**
Type **Ken Collins**

- Entering the customer name in this manner allows for the Customer:Job List to be organized according to the last name, yet the bill will be printed with the first name, then the last name.

Press **Enter** or click the second line of the billing address
Type the address **20985 Ventura Blvd.**
Press **Enter** or click the third line of the billing address
Type **Woodland Hills, CA 91371**

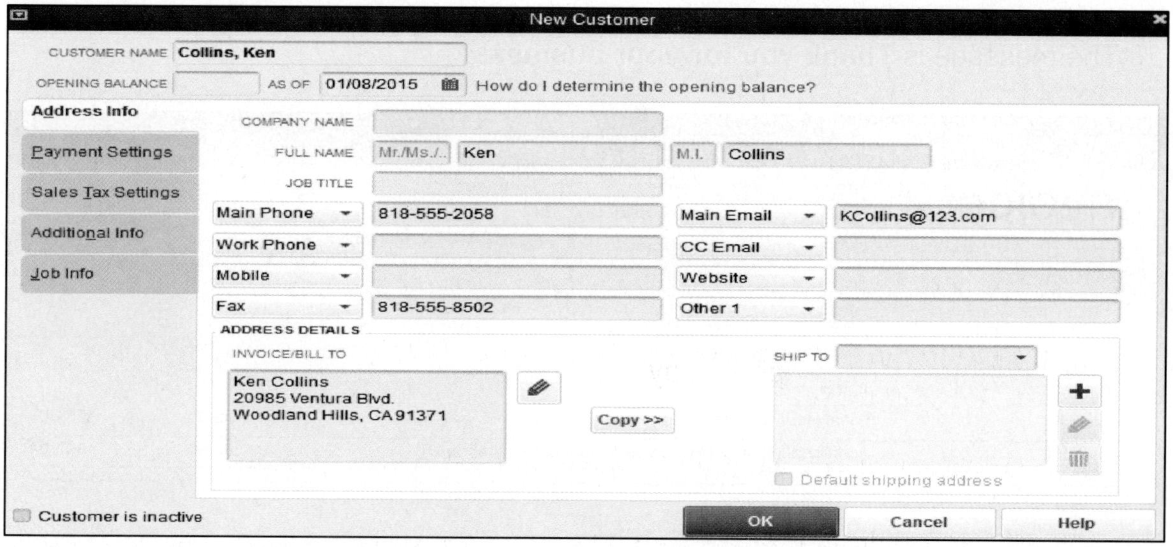

Click the **Payment Settings** tab on the left-side of the New Customer screen
Tab to or click in the **PAYMENT TERMS** text box
Click the drop-down list arrow
Click **Net 30**
Tab to or click in the **CREDIT LIMIT** text box
Type the amount **1000**, press **Tab**

- Do not use a dollar sign. QuickBooks will insert the comma and decimal point.

Click the drop-down list arrow for **PREFERRED DELIVERY METHOD**, click **None**

- You may or may not see the ONLINE PAYMENTS section on the Payment Settings screen.

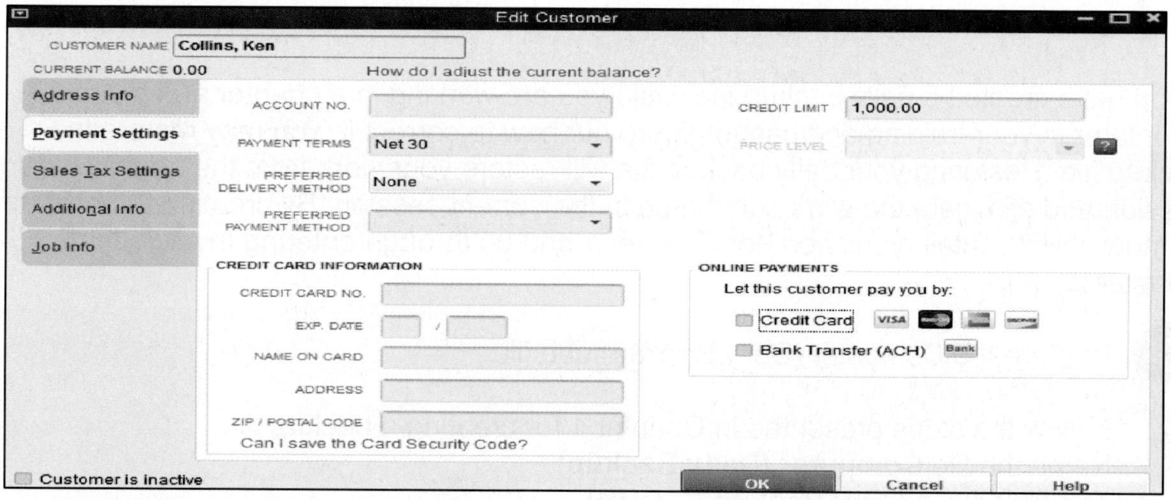

Click **OK** to return to the Invoice
Enter Invoice information as previously instructed
DATE is **01/08/15**
INVOICE # is **8**
The bill is for 2 hours of hardware installation

- Remember to bill for the initial or first hour, then bill the other hour separately. The message is **Thank you for your business.**

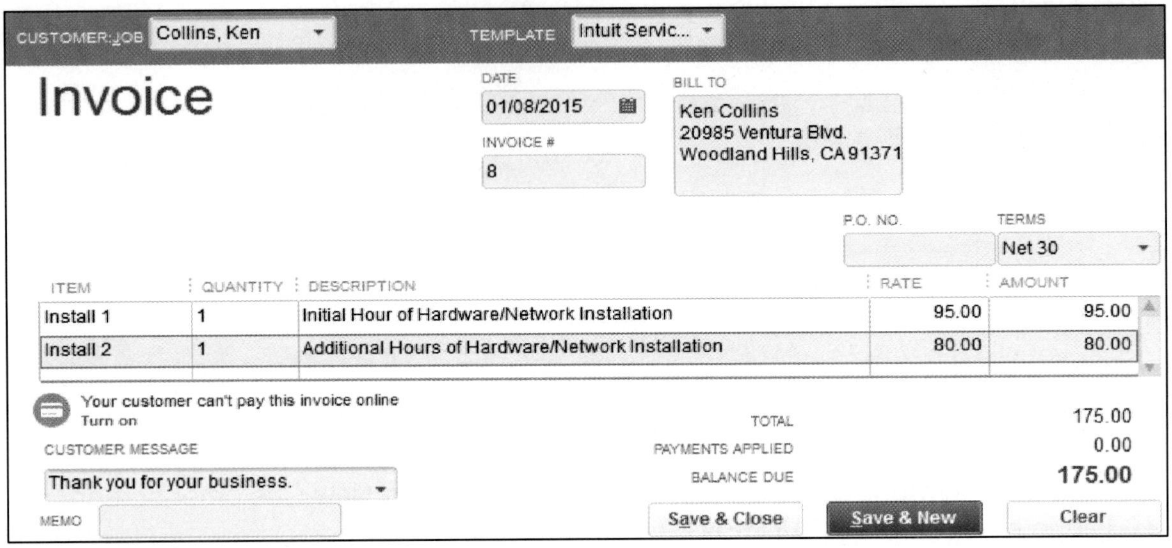

Print the invoice as previously instructed
Click **Save & Close** on the invoice to record and close the transaction

PREPARE DAILY BACKUP

A backup file is prepared as a safeguard in case you make an error. After a number of transactions have been recorded, it is wise to prepare a backup file. In addition, a backup should be made at the end of every work session. The Daily Backup file is an appropriate file to create for saving your work as you progress through a chapter.

If you have created a daily backup file while you are working in a chapter and make an error later in your training and cannot figure out how to correct it, you may restore the backup file. Restoring your daily backup file will restore your work from the previous training session and eliminate the work completed in the current session. By creating the backup file now, it will contain your work for Chapter 1 and up through entering Invoice 8 in Chapter 2.

Prepare the Computer (Daily Backup).qbb file

Follow the steps presented in Chapter 1 for creating a backup file
Name the file **Computer (Daily Backup)**
The file type is **QBW Backup (* .QBB)**

MODIFY CUSTOMER RECORDS

Occasionally, information regarding a customer will change. QuickBooks allows you to modify customer accounts at any time by editing the Customer:Job List.

MEMO

DATE: January 8, 2015

Update the following account: Design Creations has changed its fax number to 310-555-2109, added an e-mail address DesignCreations@abc.com, and a Website www.DesignCreations.

Edit the customer Design Creations:

Access the Customer:Job List using one of the following methods:
Click the **Customers** icon on the icon bar.
Use the keyboard shortcut: **Ctrl+J**
Click the **Customers** icon on the Home Page
Click the **Customers** menu, click **Customer Center**

- When the Customer Center is opened, you may see abbreviated customer names .

Widen the **NAME** column by pointing to the dotted vertical line between **NAME** and **BALANCE TOTAL**

When you get a double arrow, hold down the primary mouse button and drag to the right until the full customer name appears for all the customers

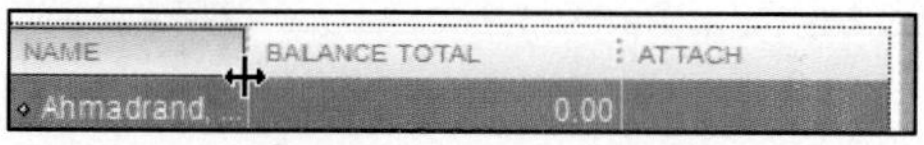

Click **Design Creations** in the Customers & Jobs list in the Customer Center

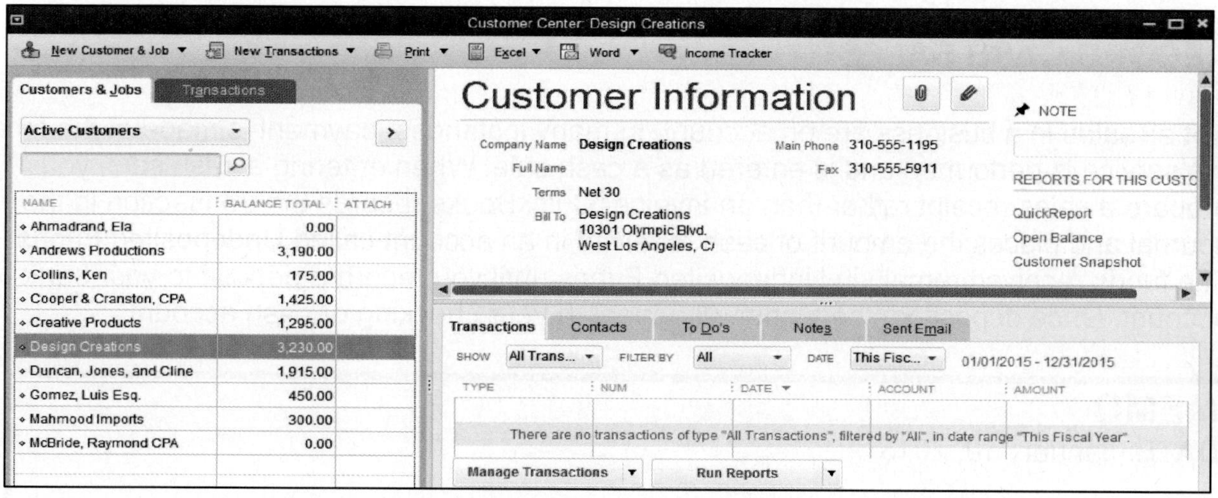

Edit the customer in one of three ways:
Click the **Edit** button 
Use the keyboard shortcut **Ctrl+E**
Double-click **Design Creations** on the **Customer:Job List**

- The Address Info tab should be shown; if not, click it.

To change the fax number to **310-555-2109**: Click at the end of the fax number, backspace to delete **5911**, type **2109**

Tab to or click in the text box for **Main E-mail**, enter the e-mail address <u>**DesignCreations@abc.com**</u>

Tab to or click in the text box for **Website**, enter the Web address <u>**www.DesignCreations**</u>

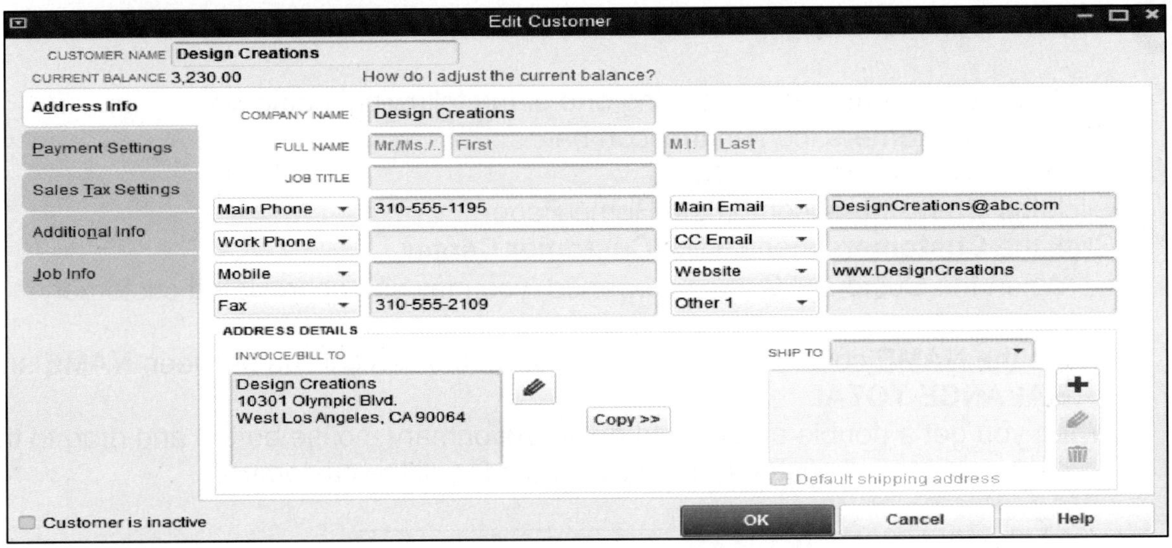

Click **OK**

- Note the change to the Fax, Email, and Website.

Close the **Customer Center**

RECORD CASH SALES

Not all sales in a business are on account. In many instances, payment is made at the time the service is performed and is entered as a cash sale. When entering a cash sale, you prepare a sales receipt rather than an invoice. QuickBooks records the transaction in the Journal and places the amount of cash received in an account called Undeposited Funds. The funds received remain in Undeposited Funds until you record a deposit to your bank account. Once deposited, the funds will appear in your checking or cash account.

MEMO

DATE: January 10, 2015

<u>Sales Receipt 1</u>: You provided 5 hours of on-site training to Raymond McBride, CPA, and received Ray's Check 3287 for the full amount due. Prepare Sales Receipt 1 for this transaction. Use "It's been a pleasure working with you!" as the message.

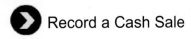

Record a Cash Sale

Click the **Create Sales Receipts** icon in the Customers section of the Home Page

- Since Sales Receipts are used for cash sales, the customer history does not need to be displayed on the right side of the screen each time you create a Sales Receipt.

To remove the History, click the **Hide History** button 

Resize the form by pointing to the right edge of the Sales Receipt

When your cursor turns into a double arrow , hold down the cursor and drag to the left to make the form smaller

- If the Sales Receipt is maximized, you will not be able to using the sizing handle (the double arrow) to resize the form. If that is the case, click the **Restore** button; and then resize as instructed above.

Click the drop-down list arrow next to **CUSTOMER:JOB**

Click **McBride, Raymond, CPA**

Tab to **TEMPLATE**

- This should have **Custom Cash Sale** as the template. If not, click the drop-down list arrow and click **Custom Cash Sale**.

Tab to or click **DATE**

Type **01/10/15**

- You may click on the calendar icon next to the date text box. Make sure the month is January and the year is 2015 then click **10**.

SALE NO. should be **1**

- Below the words Sales Receipt, there are icons showing the different methods of payment

Click the **Check** icon

Tab to or click **CHECK NO.**

Type **3287**

Tab to or click the first line for **ITEM**

Click the drop-down list arrow next to **ITEM**

Click **Training 1**

- If you need to widen the text box, follow the procedures that were used when you were in the Customer Center.

Tab to or click **QTY**

Type **1**

Tab to or click the second line for **ITEM**

Click the drop-down list arrow next to **ITEM**

Click **Training 2**

Tab to or click **QTY**

Type **4**

- The amount and total are automatically calculated when you go to the CUSTOMER MESSAGE or tab past QTY.

Click **CUSTOMER MESSAGE**

Click the drop-down list arrow for **CUSTOMER MESSAGE**

Click **It's been a pleasure working with you!**

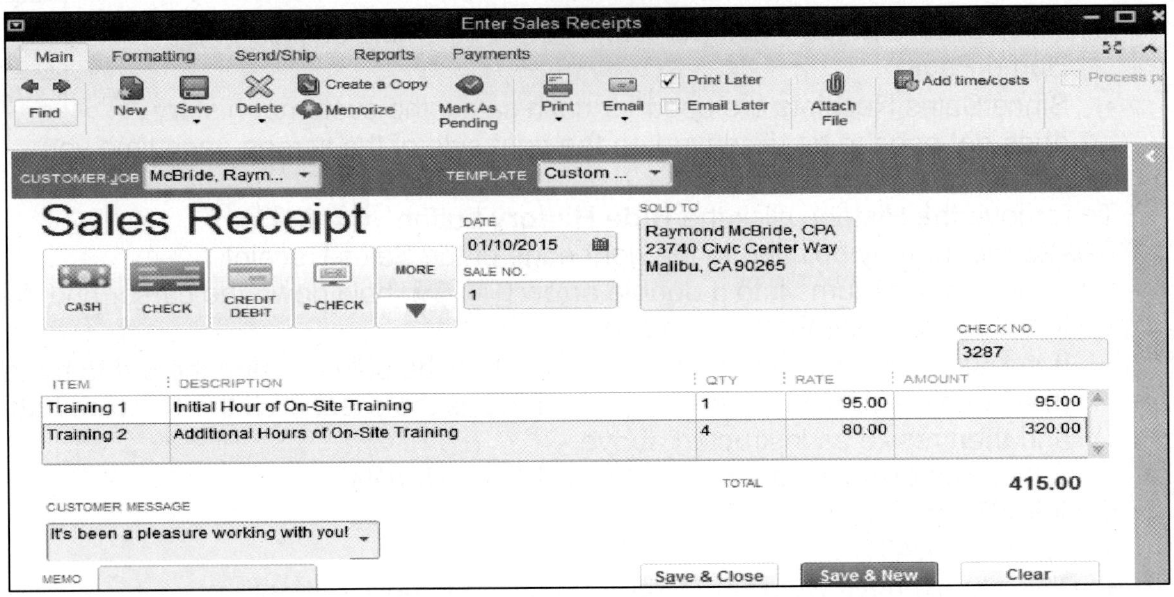

Do not close the Sales Receipt

PRINT SALES RECEIPT

Print the sales receipt

Click the **Print** button on the **Enter Sales Receipts** Icon bar
Check the information on the **Print One Sales Receipt Settings** tab:
Printer name: (should identify the type of printer you are using)
Printer type: Page-oriented (Single sheets)
Print on: Blank paper
Click **Do not print lines around each field** to insert a check mark
Number of copies: should be **1**
Click **Print**

- This initiates the printing of the sales receipt through QuickBooks. However, since not all classroom configurations are the same, check with your instructor for specific printing instructions.

Once the Sales Receipt has been printed, click **Save & New** on the bottom of the **Enter Sales Receipts** screen

- If you get a Recording Transaction message, click **Yes**.

ENTER ADDITIONAL CASH SALES

MEMO

DATE: January 12, 2015

Sales Receipt 2: Raymond McBride needed additional on-site training to correct some error messages he received on his computer. You provided 1 hour of on-site training for Raymond McBride, CPA, and received Check 3306 for the full amount due. (Even though Mr. McBride has had on-site training previously, this is a new sales call and should be billed as Training 1.)

Sales Receipt 3: You provided 4 hours of on-site Internet training for Research Corp. so the company could be online. You received Check 10358 for the full amount due.

Record the two January 12, 2015 transactions listed above

Use the procedures given when you entered Sales Receipt 1:

- Don't forget to use 01/12/2015 for the date.
- Remember, the first hour for on-site training is billed as Training 1 and the remaining hours are billed as Training 2.
- If information from a previous transaction appears, simply replace it with the new information.
- Always use the Item List to determine the appropriate sales items for billing.
- Use **Thank you for your business.** as the message for these sales receipts.
- **Print** each sales receipt immediately after entering the information for it.
- If you make an error, correct it.
- To go from one sales receipt to the next, click the **Save & New** button on the bottom of the **Enter Sales Receipts** screen.
- Click **Save & Close** after you have entered and printed Sales Receipt 3.

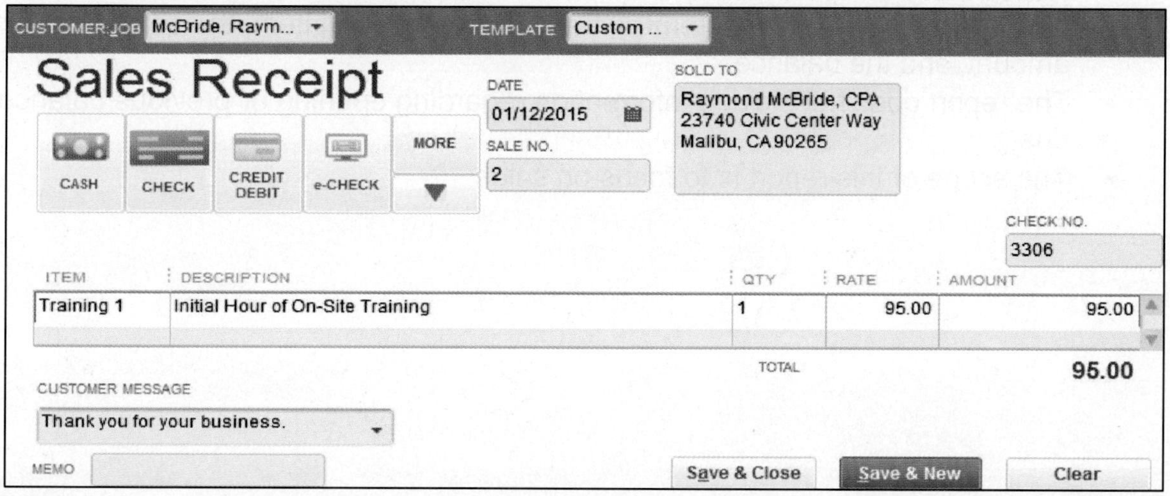

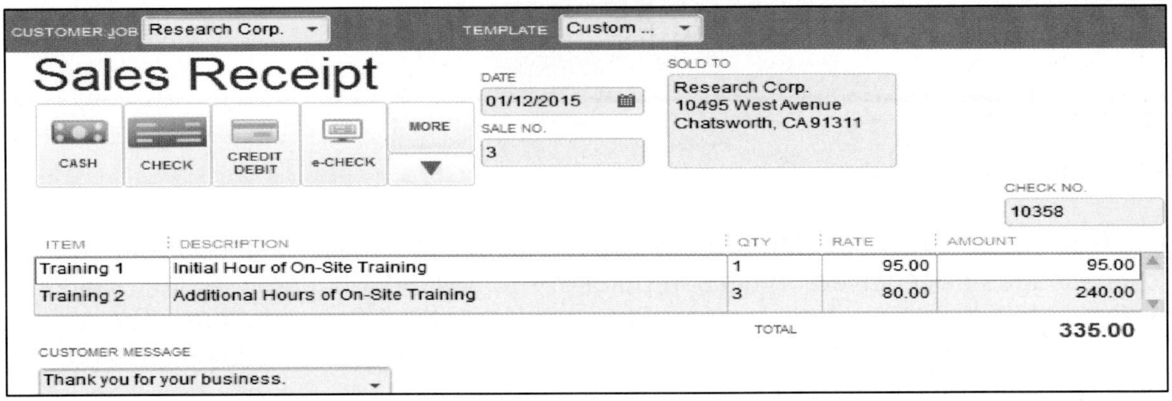

SALES BY CUSTOMER DETAIL REPORT

QuickBooks has reports available that enable you to obtain sales information about sales items or customers. To get information about the total amount of sales to each customer during a specific period, print a Sales by Customer Detail Report. The total shown represents both cash and/or credit sales.

Prepare and print a Sales by Customer Detail Report

Click **Reports** on the menu bar
Point to **Sales**
Click **Sales by Customer Detail**
To remove the **Date Prepared**, **Time Prepared**, and **Report Basis** from the report, click the **Customize Report** button and follow the instructions given previously for deselecting the date prepared, time prepared, and report basis from the Header/Footer
Change the dates to reflect the sales period from **01/01/15** to **01/12/15**
Tab to generate the report

- Notice that the report information includes the type of sales to each customer, the date of the sale, the sales item(s), the quantity for each item, the sales price, the amount, and the balance.
- The report does not include information regarding opening or previous balances due.
- The scope of this report is to focus on sales.

Computer Consulting by Your Name
Sales by Customer Detail
January 1 - 12, 2015

Type	Date	Num	Memo	Name	Item	Qty	Sales Price	Amount	Balance
Ahmadrand, Ela									
Invoice	01/05/2015	3	10 Hours—Monthly Technical Support	Ahmadrand, Ela	Tech Sup 2	0	300.00	0.00	0.00
Total Ahmadrand, Ela						0		0.00	0.00
Collins, Ken									
Invoice	01/08/2015	8	Initial Hour of Hardware/Network Installation	Collins, Ken	Install 1	1	95.00	95.00	95.00
Invoice	01/08/2015	8	Additional Hours of Hardware/Network Installation	Collins, Ken	Install 2	1	80.00	80.00	175.00
Total Collins, Ken						2		175.00	175.00
Cooper & Cranston, CPA									
Invoice	01/05/2015	5	Initial Hour of On-Site Training	Cooper & Cranston, CPA	Training 1	1	95.00	95.00	95.00
Invoice	01/05/2015	5	Additional Hours of On-Site Training	Cooper & Cranston, CPA	Training 2	11	80.00	880.00	975.00
Invoice	01/05/2015	5	15 Hours—Monthly Technical Support	Cooper & Cranston, CPA	Tech Sup 3	1	450.00	450.00	1,425.00
Total Cooper & Cranston, CPA						13		1,425.00	1,425.00
Gomez, Luis Esq.									
Invoice	01/02/2015	1	10 Hours--Monthly Technical Support	Gomez, Luis Esq.	Tech Sup 2	1	300.00	300.00	300.00
Total Gomez, Luis Esq.						1		300.00	300.00
McBride, Raymond CPA									
Sales Receipt	01/10/2015	1	Initial Hour of On-Site Training	McBride, Raymond CPA	Training 1	1	95.00	95.00	95.00
Sales Receipt	01/10/2015	1	Additional Hours of On-Site Training	McBride, Raymond CPA	Training 2	4	80.00	320.00	415.00
Sales Receipt	01/12/2015	2	Initial Hour of On-Site Training	McBride, Raymond CPA	Training 1	1	95.00	95.00	510.00
Total McBride, Raymond CPA						6		510.00	510.00
Research Corp.									
Sales Receipt	01/12/2015	3	Initial Hour of On-Site Training	Research Corp.	Training 1	1	95.00	95.00	95.00
Sales Receipt	01/12/2015	3	Additional Hours of On-Site Training	Research Corp.	Training 2	3	80.00	240.00	335.00
Total Research Corp.						4		335.00	335.00
Vines & Rhodes									
Invoice	01/05/2015	4	Initial Hour of On-Site Training	Vines & Rhodes	Training 1	1	95.00	95.00	95.00
Invoice	01/05/2015	4	Additional Hours of On-Site Training	Vines & Rhodes	Training 2	39	80.00	3,120.00	3,215.00
Credit Memo	01/08/2015	7	Additional Hours of On-Site Training	Vines & Rhodes	Training 2	-5	80.00	-400.00	2,815.00
Total Vines & Rhodes						35		2,815.00	2,815.00
Young, Norton, and Brancato									
Invoice	01/05/2015	6	Initial Hour of On-Site Training	Young, Norton, and Brancato	Training 1	1	95.00	95.00	95.00
Invoice	01/05/2015	6	Additional Hours of On-Site Training	Young, Norton, and Brancato	Training 2	39	80.00	3,120.00	3,215.00
Invoice	01/05/2015	6	5 Hours—Monthly Technical Support	Young, Norton, and Brancato	Tech Sup 1	1	150.00	150.00	3,365.00
Total Young, Norton, and Brancato						41		3,365.00	3,365.00
TOTAL						**102**		**8,925.00**	**8,925.00**

Click the **Print** button on the **Sales by Customer Detail** screen
Click **Report** to select between printing a Report or Save as PDF
On the **Print Report** screen, check the Settings tab to verify that **Print to**: Printer is selected and that the name of your printer is correct
If necessary, click **Landscape** to change the **Orientation** from Portrait

- Landscape changes the orientation of the paper so the report is printed 11-inches wide by 8½-inches long.

Verify that the **Page Range** is **All**
Make sure **Smart page breaks** have been selected
Preview the Report
If necessary, select **Fit report to 1 page(s) wide.**
On the **Print Report** screen, click **Print**
Close the **Sales by Customer Detail Report**

- If you get a Memorize Transaction dialog box, click **No**.

CORRECT AND PRINT SALES RECEIPT

As previously shown on invoices, QuickBooks makes correcting errors user friendly. When an error is discovered in a transaction such as a cash sale, you can simply return to the form where the transaction was recorded and correct the error. Thus, to correct a sales receipt, you would open Sales Receipts, click the Previous button until you found the appropriate sales receipt, and then correct the error. Because cash or checks received for cash sales are held in the Undeposited Funds account until the bank deposit is made, you can access the sales receipt through the Undeposited Funds account in the Chart of Accounts as well. Accessing the receipt in this manner allows you to see all the transactions entered in the account for Undeposited Funds.

When a correction for a sale is made, QuickBooks not only changes the form, it also changes all journal and account entries for the transaction to reflect the correction. QuickBooks then allows a corrected sales receipt to be printed.

MEMO

DATE: January 14, 2015

After reviewing transaction information, you realize the date for the Sales Receipt 1 to Raymond McBride, CPA, was entered incorrectly. Change the date to 1/9/2015.

Correct the error indicated in the memo, then print the corrected sales receipt

Click the **Chart of Accounts** icon on the Home Page
Click **Undeposited Funds**

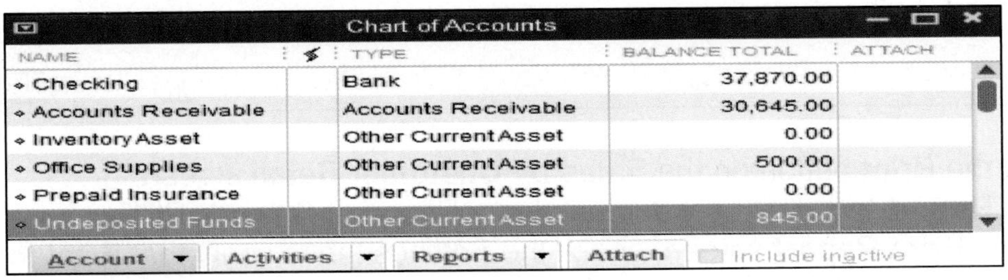

Click the **Activities** button
Click **Use Register**

- The register maintains a record of all the transactions recorded within the Undeposited Funds account.

Click anywhere in the transaction for **Sales Receipt 1** to Raymond McBride, CPA

- Look at the REF/TYPE column to see the type of transaction.
- The number in the REF line indicates the number of the sales receipt or the customer's check number.
- TYPE shows RCPT for a sales receipt.

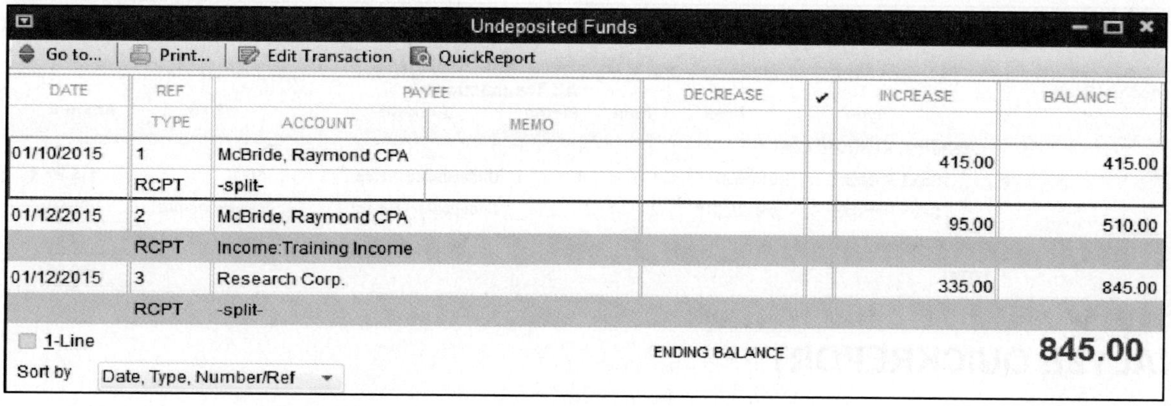

Click the **Edit Transaction** button at the top of the register

- The sales receipt appears on the screen.

Tab to or click **DATE** field

Change the Date to **01/09/15**, press Tab to enter the date

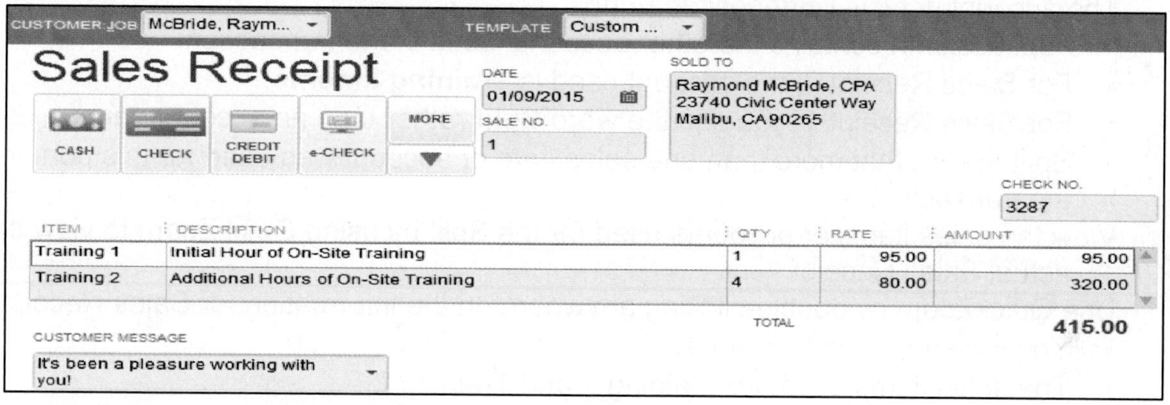

Print the Sales Receipt as previously instructed

Click **Yes** on the **Recording Transaction** dialog box

Click **Save & Close**

- After closing the sales receipt, you are returned to the register for the Undeposited Funds account.

Do not close the register

VIEW QUICKREPORT

After editing the sales receipt and returning to the register, you may get a detailed report regarding the customer's transactions by clicking the QuickReport icon.

Prepare a QuickReport for Raymond McBride

Click the **QuickReport** icon to display the Register QuickReport for Raymond McBride, CPA

10:40 AM
01/14/15
Accrual Basis

Computer Consulting by Your Name
Register QuickReport
All Transactions

Type	Date	Num	Memo	Account	Clr	Split	Amount
McBride, Raymond CPA							
Sales Receipt	01/09/2015	1		Undeposited Funds		-SPLIT-	415.00
Sales Receipt	01/12/2015	2		Undeposited Funds		Training Income	95.00
Total McBride, Raymond CPA							510.00
TOTAL							510.00

ANALYZE QUICKREPORT

Analyze the QuickReport for Raymond McBride

Notice that the date for Sales Receipt 1 has been changed to **01/09/2015**
- You may need to use the horizontal scroll bar to view all the columns in the report.

The account used is Undeposited Funds
The Split column contains the other accounts used in the transaction
- For Sales Receipt 2, the account used is **Training Income**.
- For Sales Receipt 1, you see the word **Split** rather than an account name.
- Split means that more than one sales item or account was used for this portion of the transaction.

View the sales items or accounts used for the Split by using QuickZoom to view the actual Sales Receipt
Use QuickZoom by double-clicking anywhere on the information for Sales Receipt 1
- You will see Sales Receipt 1.
- The sales items used are Training 1 and Training 2.

Close the **Sales Receipt**
Close the **Register QuickReport** without printing
Close the **Register for Undeposited Funds**
Close the **Chart of Accounts**

ANALYZE SALES

To obtain information regarding the amount of sales by item, you can print or view sales reports. Sales reports provide information regarding cash and credit sales. When information regarding the sales according to the Sales Item is needed, a Sales by Item Summary Report is the appropriate report to print or view. This report enables you to see how much revenue is being generated by each sales item. This provides important information for decision making and managing the business. For example, if a sales item is not generating much income, it might be wise to discontinue that sales item.

Print a summarized list of sales by item

Click the **Reports** icon to open the Report Center

Click **Sales** as the type of report
Double-click **Sales by Item Summary** in the Sales by Item report list
The dates of the report are from **01/01/15** to **01/14/15**
Tab to generate the report
Turn off the **Date Prepared**, **Time Prepared**, and **Report Basis** following instructions given previously

Computer Consulting by Your Name
Sales by Item Summary
January 1 - 14, 2015

	Jan 1 - 14, 15			
	Qty	Amount	% of Sales	Avg Price
Service				
Install 1	1	95.00	1.1%	95.00
Install 2	1	80.00	0.9%	80.00
Tech Sup 1	1	150.00	1.7%	150.00
Tech Sup 2	1	300.00	3.4%	300.00
Tech Sup 3	1	450.00	5%	450.00
Training 1	6	570.00	6.4%	95.00
Training 2	91	7,280.00	81.6%	80.00
Total Service	102	8,925.00	100.0%	87.50
TOTAL	102	8,925.00	100.0%	87.50

Click the **Print** button, click **Report**
The Orientation should be **Portrait**
Click **Print** on **Print Reports** dialog box
Close the report, do <u>not</u> close the Report Center

View a Sales by Item Detail report to obtain information regarding which transactions apply to each sales item

Double-click **Sales by Item Detail** on the Sales by Item report list
The dates of the report are from **01/01/15** to **01/14/15**
Tab to generate the report
Scroll through the report to view the types of sales and the transactions that occurred within each category

- Notice how many transactions occurred in each sales item.

10:49 AM
01/14/15
Accrual Basis

Computer Consulting by Your Name
Sales by Item Detail
January 1 - 14, 2015

Type	Date	Num	Memo	Name	Qty	Sales Price	Amount	Balance
Service								
Install 1								
Invoice	01/08/2015	8	Initial Hour of Hardware/Network Installation	Collins, Ken	1	95.00	95.00	95.00
Total Install 1					1		95.00	95.00
Install 2								
Invoice	01/08/2015	8	Additional Hours of Hardware/Network Installation	Collins, Ken	1	80.00	80.00	80.00
Total Install 2					1		80.00	80.00
Tech Sup 1								
Invoice	01/05/2015	6	5 Hours--Monthly Technical Support	Young, Norton, and Brancato	1	150.00	150.00	150.00
Total Tech Sup 1					1		150.00	150.00
Tech Sup 2								
Invoice	01/02/2015	1	10 Hours--Monthly Technical Support	Gomez, Luis Esq.	1	300.00	300.00	300.00
Invoice	01/05/2015	3	10 Hours--Monthly Technical Support	Ahmadrand, Ela	0	300.00	0.00	300.00
Total Tech Sup 2					1		300.00	300.00
Tech Sup 3								
Invoice	01/05/2015	5	15 Hours--Monthly Technical Support	Cooper & Cranston, CPA	1	450.00	450.00	450.00
Total Tech Sup 3					1		450.00	450.00
Training 1								
Invoice	01/05/2015	4	Initial Hour of On-Site Training	Vines & Rhodes	1	95.00	95.00	95.00
Invoice	01/05/2015	5	Initial Hour of On-Site Training	Cooper & Cranston, CPA	1	95.00	95.00	190.00
Invoice	01/05/2015	6	Initial Hour of On-Site Training	Young, Norton, and Brancato	1	95.00	95.00	285.00
Sales Receipt	01/09/2015	1	Initial Hour of On-Site Training	McBride, Raymond CPA	1	95.00	95.00	380.00
Sales Receipt	01/12/2015	2	Initial Hour of On-Site Training	McBride, Raymond CPA	1	95.00	95.00	475.00
Sales Receipt	01/12/2015	3	Initial Hour of On-Site Training	Research Corp.	1	95.00	95.00	570.00
Total Training 1					6		570.00	570.00
Training 2								
Invoice	01/05/2015	4	Additional Hours of On-Site Training	Vines & Rhodes	39	80.00	3,120.00	3,120.00
Invoice	01/05/2015	5	Additional Hours of On-Site Training	Cooper & Cranston, CPA	11	80.00	880.00	4,000.00
Invoice	01/05/2015	6	Additional Hours of On-Site Training	Young, Norton, and Brancato	39	80.00	3,120.00	7,120.00
Credit Memo	01/08/2015	7	Additional Hours of On-Site Training	Vines & Rhodes	-5	80.00	-400.00	6,720.00
Sales Receipt	01/09/2015	1	Additional Hours of On-Site Training	McBride, Raymond CPA	4	80.00	320.00	7,040.00
Sales Receipt	01/12/2015	3	Additional Hours of On-Site Training	Research Corp.	3	80.00	240.00	7,280.00
Total Training 2					91		7,280.00	7,280.00
Total Service					102		8,925.00	8,925.00
TOTAL					**102**		**8,925.00**	**8,925.00**

Close the report without printing
Close the **Report Center**

PREPARE DAILY BACKUP

As you learned earlier in the chapter, creating a backup file saves your work up to that point. The daily backup prepared earlier contains all of Chapter 1 and the portion of Chapter 2 where invoices were entered. By creating the backup file now and using the same file name, it will contain your work for Chapter 1 and all the work completed through entering Sales Receipts in Chapter 2.

Prepare the Computer (Daily Backup).qbb file

Follow the steps presented in Chapter 1 for creating a backup file

Name the file **Computer (Daily Backup)**
The file type is **QBW Backup (* .QBB)**

- This backup is using the same backup file that you prepared earlier in the chapter.
- The daily backup will now contain all of Chapter 1 and Chapter 2 up through entering sales receipts.

RECORD CUSTOMER PAYMENT ON ACCOUNT

Since a sale on account is originally recorded on an invoice, Receive Payments is used when a customer pays you what is owed on an invoice. Frequently, new users of QuickBooks will try to record a payment receipt using a Sales Receipt, which is used only for cash sales not for payments on account.

When you start to record a payment made by a customer who owes you money for an invoice, you see the customer's balance, any credits made to the account, and a complete list of outstanding invoices. QuickBooks automatically places a check in the check mark column for the invoice that has the same amount as the payment. If there isn't an invoice with the same amount, QuickBooks marks the oldest invoice and enters the payment amount in the Payment column for the invoice being paid. When customers make a full or partial payment of the amount they owe, QuickBooks places the money received in the Undeposited Funds account. The money stays in this account until a bank deposit is made.

MEMO
DATE: January 15, 2015

Record the following cash receipt: Received Check 684 for $815 from Research Corp. as payment on account.

Record the receipt of a payment on account

Click the **Receive Payments** icon in the Customers section of the Home Page

- Notice the flow chart line from Create Invoices to Receive Payments. This icon is illustrated in this manner because recording a payment receipt is for a payment made on account. This is not a cash sale.

Click the drop-down list arrow for **RECEIVED FROM**
Click **Research Corp.**

- Notice that the current date or the last transaction date shows in the **DATE** column and the total amount owed appears as the CUSTOMER BALANCE.
- Also note that previous cash sales to Research Corp. are not listed. This is because a payment receipt is used only for payments on account.

Tab to or click **PAYMENT AMOUNT**

- If you click, you will need to delete the 0.00. If you tab, it will be deleted when you type in the amount.

Enter **815**

- QuickBooks will enter the **.00** when you tab to or click **DATE**.
- When you press Tab, QuickBooks automatically places a check in the check mark column for the invoice that has the same amount as the payment. If there isn't an invoice with the same amount, QuickBooks marks the oldest invoice and enters the payment amount in the Payment column for the invoice being paid.

Tab to or click **DATE**

- If you click, you will need to delete the date. If you tab, the date will be replaced when you type 01/15/15.
- You may also click the calendar icon and then click 15 for the month of January.

Type date **01/15/15**

Click the **CHECK** icon to indicate the method of payment

Tab to or click in the text box for **CHECK #**

Enter **684**

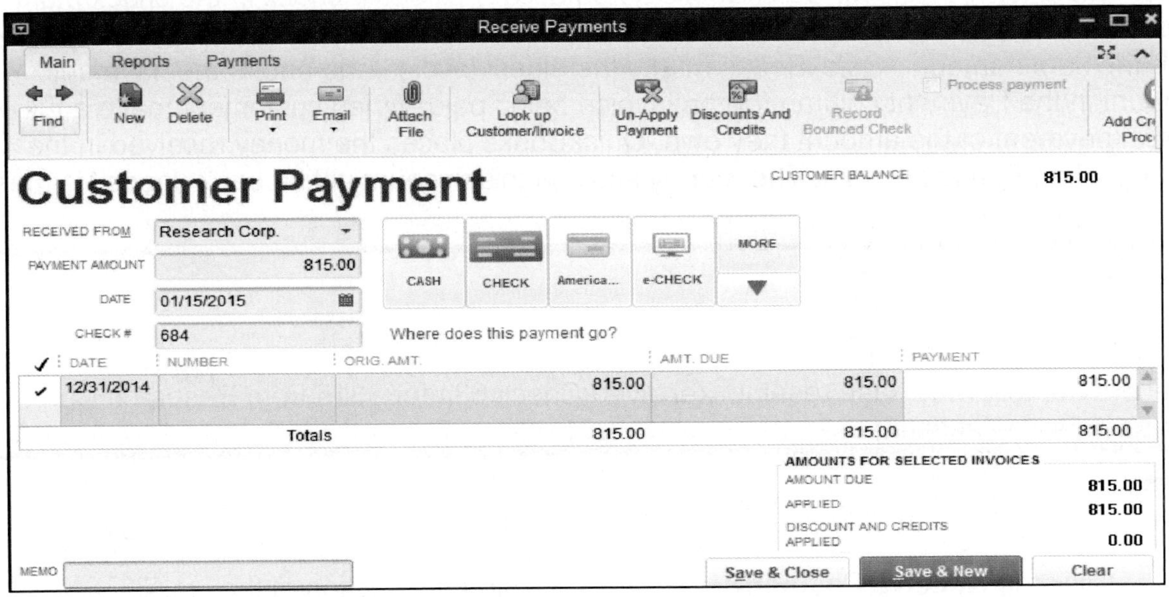

Click the **Print** button and print a copy of the Payment Receipt following steps presented earlier for printing other business forms

When the Payment Receipt has been printed, click **Save & New**

RECORD ADDITIONAL PAYMENTS ON ACCOUNT

MEMO
DATE: January 15, 2015
Received Check 1952 from Wagner, Leavitt, and Moraga for $3,680.
Received Check 8925 for $2,000 from Rosenthal Illustrations in partial payment of account. This receipt requires a Memo notation of Partial Payment. Make sure "Leave as an underpayment" is selected in the lower portion of the Customer Payment.
Received Check 39251 from Matt Williams, CPA for $475.
Received Check 2051 for $2,190 from Andrews Productions as a partial payment. Record a Memo of Partial Payment for this receipt. Leave as an underpayment.
Received Check 5632 from Luis Gomez, Esq. for $150 to pay his opening balance. Since this is payment in full for the opening balance, no memo is required.
Received Check 80195 from Shumway, Lewis, and Levy for $3,685.

Enter the above payments on account; if necessary, refer to the previous steps listed

- If an invoice is not paid in full, enter the amount received, enter a Memo of **Partial Payment**, and make sure **Leave as an underpayment** is selected in the lower portion of the screen.
- Remember, an invoice may be paid in full but an account balance may still remain (refer to the payment for Luis Gomez).
- Print a Payment Receipt for each payment received.
- Click **Save & New** to go from one Receive Payments Screen to the next.
- Click **Save & Close** after all payments received have been recorded.

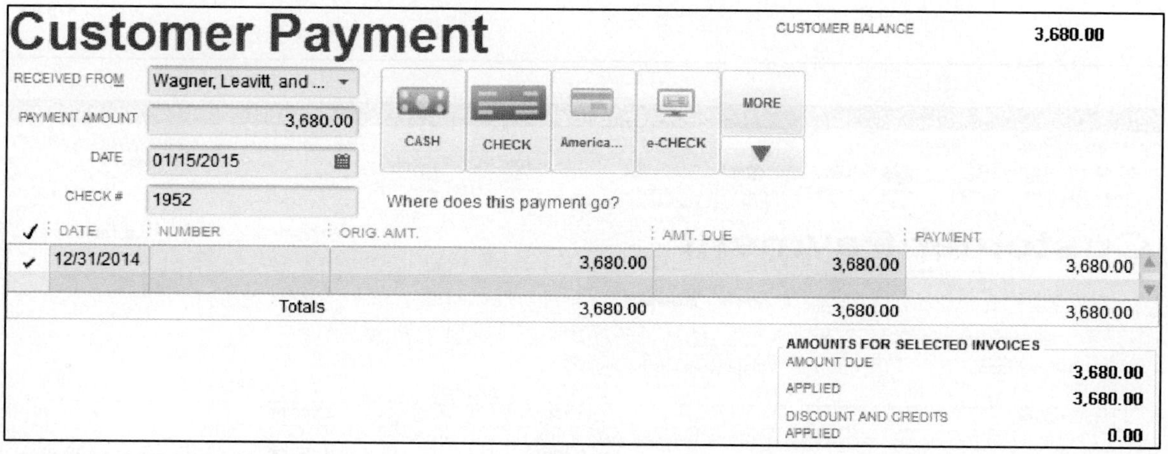

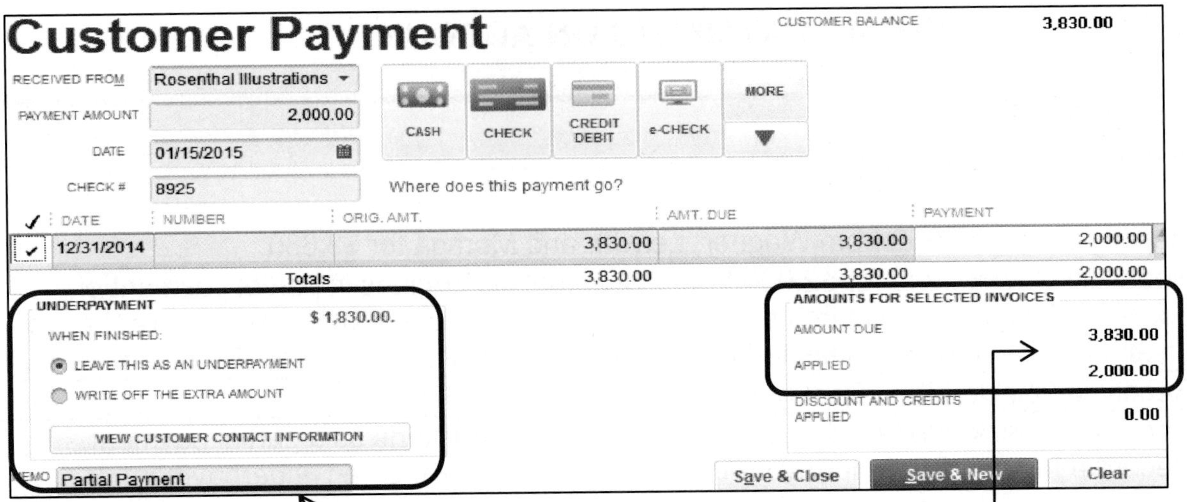

- Note: The UNDERPAYMENT of $1,830.00, the selection of LEAVE THIS AS AN UNDERPAYMENT, and the. MEMO of "Partial Payment."
- Note the AMOUNT DUE of 3,830 and the APPLIED of 2,000

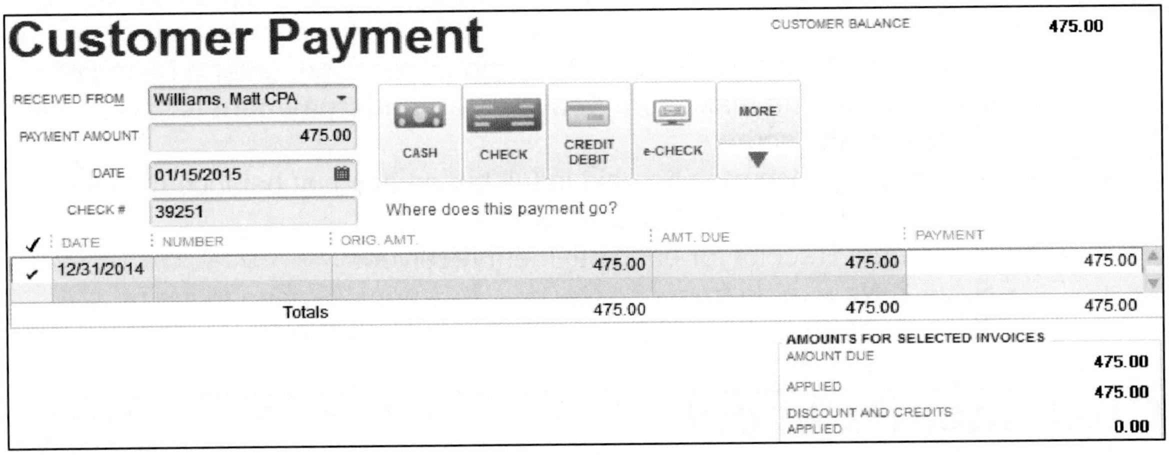

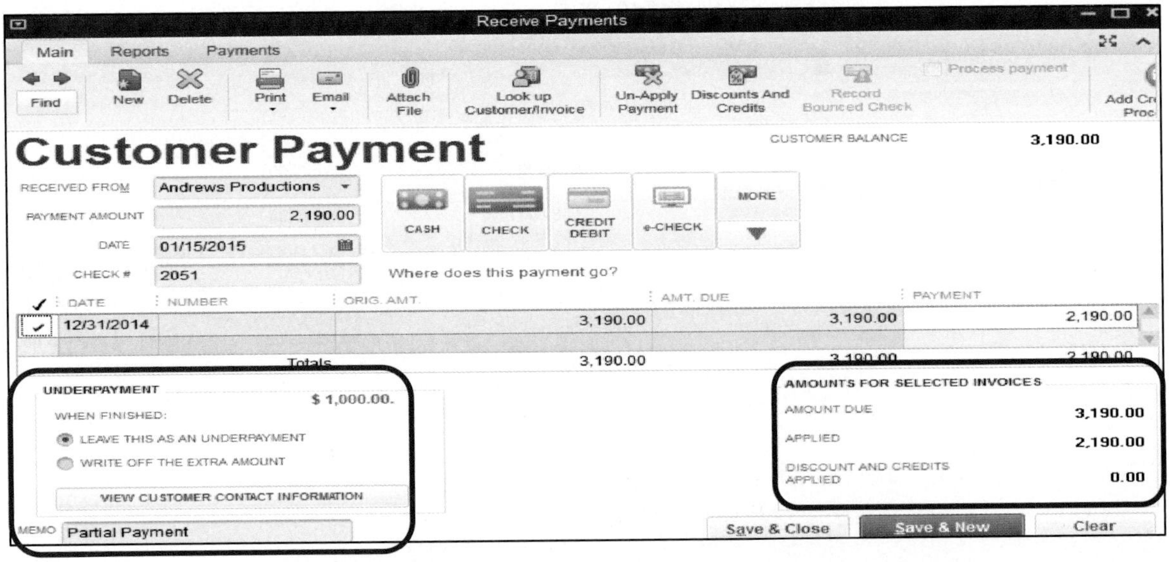

- Verify the underpayment of $1,000 by Andrews Productions
- Note that the AMOUNT DUE shows 3,190.00 and APPLIED shows 2,190.00

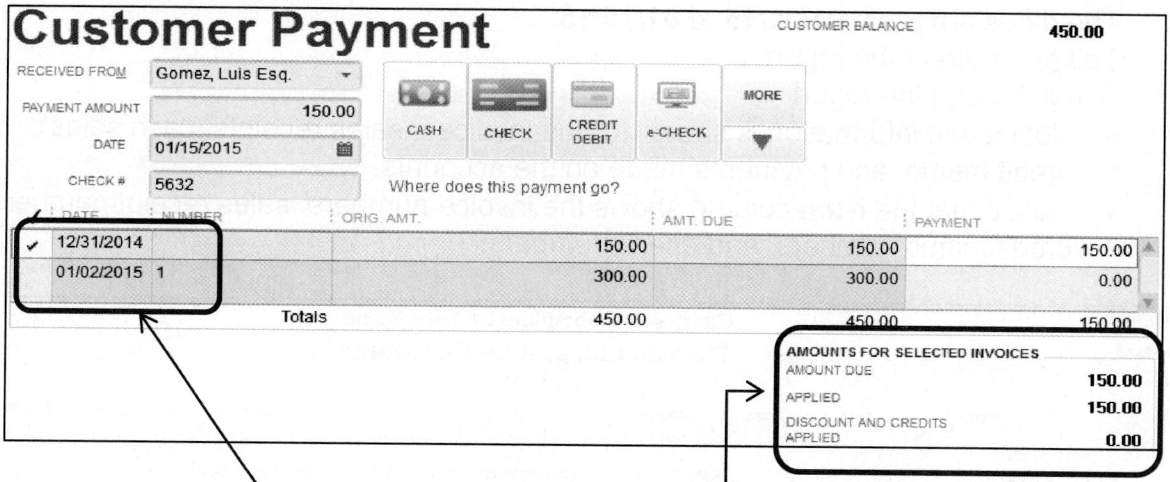

- Note: The 12/31/2014 Opening Balance was marked for the payment—the amount paid is a match to the amount due.
- Note that the marked transaction is the oldest.
- The AMOUNTS FOR SELECTED INVOICES of $150.00 are shown for the 12/31/2014 transaction that is marked.

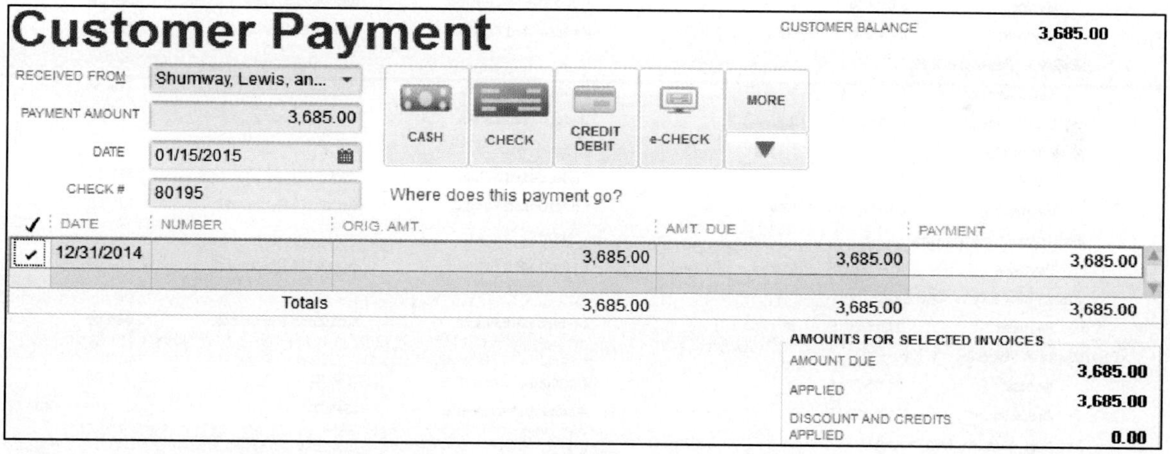

TRANSACTION LIST BY CUSTOMER

In order to see the transactions for credit customers, you need to prepare a transaction report by customer. This report shows all sales, credits, and payments for each customer on account.

Prepare a Transaction List by Customer report

Click **Reports** on the menu bar
Point to **Customers & Receivables**

Click **Transaction List by Customer**

- Since you are only viewing the report, you do not need to remove the Date Prepared and the Time Prepared from the header.

The dates are From **01/01/15** to **01/15/15**

Tab to generate the report

Scroll through the report

- Notice that information is shown for the invoices, sales receipts (cash sales), credit memo, and payments made on the accounts.
- Notice that the **Num** column shows the invoice numbers, sales receipt numbers, credit memo numbers, and check numbers.

2:09 PM

01/15/15

Computer Consulting by Your Name

Transaction List by Customer

January 1 - 15, 2015

Type	Date	Num	Memo	Account	Clr	Split	Debit	Credit
Ahmadrand, Ela								
Invoice	01/05/2015	3	VOID:	Accounts Receivable	✔	Technical Support Income	0.00	
Andrews Productions								
Payment	01/15/2015	2051	Partial Payment	Undeposited Funds		Accounts Receivable	2,190.00	
Collins, Ken								
Invoice	01/08/2015	8		Accounts Receivable		-SPLIT-	175.00	
Cooper & Cranston, CPA								
Invoice	01/05/2015	5		Accounts Receivable		-SPLIT-	1,425.00	
Gomez, Luis Esq.								
Invoice	01/02/2015	1		Accounts Receivable		Technical Support Income	300.00	
Payment	01/15/2015	5632		Undeposited Funds		Accounts Receivable	150.00	
McBride, Raymond CPA								
Sales Receipt	01/09/2015	1		Undeposited Funds		-SPLIT-	415.00	
Sales Receipt	01/12/2015	2		Undeposited Funds		Training Income	95.00	
Research Corp.								
Sales Receipt	01/12/2015	3		Undeposited Funds		-SPLIT-	335.00	
Payment	01/15/2015	684		Undeposited Funds		Accounts Receivable	815.00	
Rosenthal Illustrations								
Payment	01/15/2015	8925	Partial Payment	Undeposited Funds		Accounts Receivable	2,000.00	
Shumway, Lewis, and Levy								
Payment	01/15/2015	80195		Undeposited Funds		Accounts Receivable	3,685.00	
Vines & Rhodes								
Invoice	01/05/2015	4		Accounts Receivable		-SPLIT-	3,215.00	
Credit Memo	01/08/2015	7		Accounts Receivable		-SPLIT-		400.00
Wagner, Leavitt, and Moraga								
Payment	01/15/2015	1952		Undeposited Funds		Accounts Receivable	3,680.00	
Williams, Matt CPA								
Payment	01/15/2015	39251		Undeposited Funds		Accounts Receivable	475.00	
Young, Norton, and Brancato								
Invoice	01/05/2015	6		Accounts Receivable		-SPLIT-	3,365.00	

Click the **Close** button to exit the report without printing

DEPOSIT CHECKS RECEIVED

When you record cash sales and the receipt of payments on accounts, QuickBooks places the money received in the Undeposited Funds account. Once the deposit has been made at the bank, it should be recorded. When the deposit is recorded, the funds are transferred from Undeposited Funds to the account selected when preparing the deposit (usually checking). This is important because, until the money is deposited, it does not show as being available for use.

MEMO
DATE: January 15, 2015

Deposit all checks received for cash sales and payments on account.

Deposit checks received

Click the **Record Deposits** icon in the Banking section of the Home Page

- **Payments to Deposit** window shows all amounts received for cash sales and payments on account that have not been deposited in the bank.
- The column for **TYPE** contains RCPT, which means the amount is for a Sales Receipt (Cash Sale), and PMT, which means the amount received is for a payment on account.
- Notice that the √ column to the left of the DATE column is empty.

Click the **Select All** button

- Notice the check marks in the √ column.

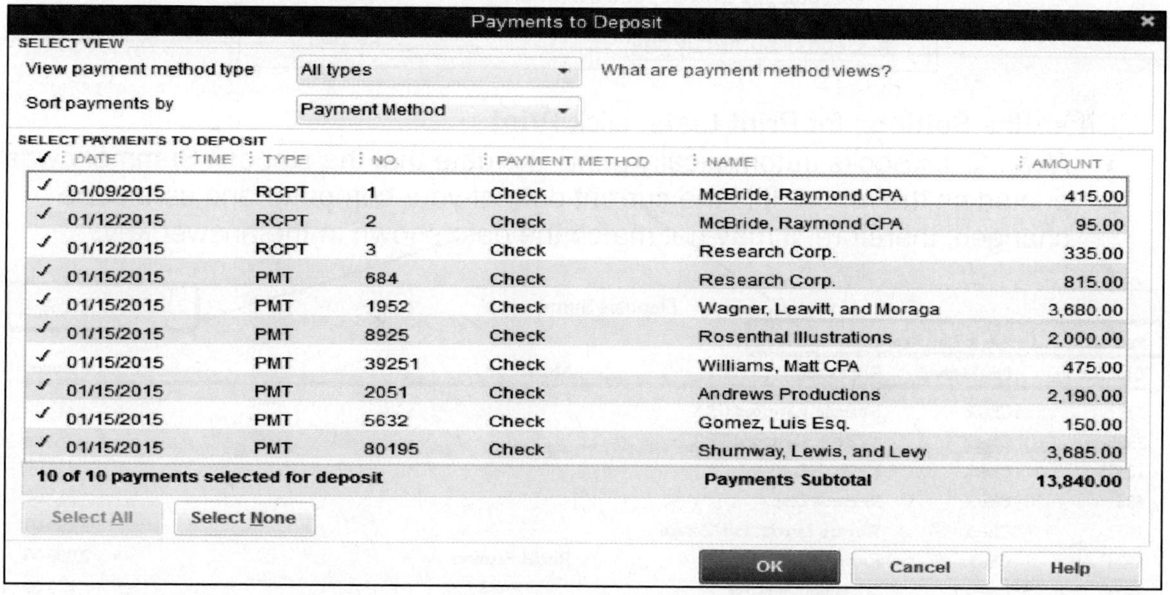

✓	DATE	TIME	TYPE	NO.	PAYMENT METHOD	NAME	AMOUNT
✓	01/09/2015		RCPT	1	Check	McBride, Raymond CPA	415.00
✓	01/12/2015		RCPT	2	Check	McBride, Raymond CPA	95.00
✓	01/12/2015		RCPT	3	Check	Research Corp.	335.00
✓	01/15/2015		PMT	684	Check	Research Corp.	815.00
✓	01/15/2015		PMT	1952	Check	Wagner, Leavitt, and Moraga	3,680.00
✓	01/15/2015		PMT	8925	Check	Rosenthal Illustrations	2,000.00
✓	01/15/2015		PMT	39251	Check	Williams, Matt CPA	475.00
✓	01/15/2015		PMT	2051	Check	Andrews Productions	2,190.00
✓	01/15/2015		PMT	5632	Check	Gomez, Luis Esq.	150.00
✓	01/15/2015		PMT	80195	Check	Shumway, Lewis, and Levy	3,685.00
10 of 10 payments selected for deposit						Payments Subtotal	13,840.00

Click **OK** to close **Payments to Deposit** screen and open **Make Deposits** screen
On the **Make Deposits** screen, **Deposit To** should be **Checking**
Date should be **01/15/2015**

- Tab to date and change if not correct.

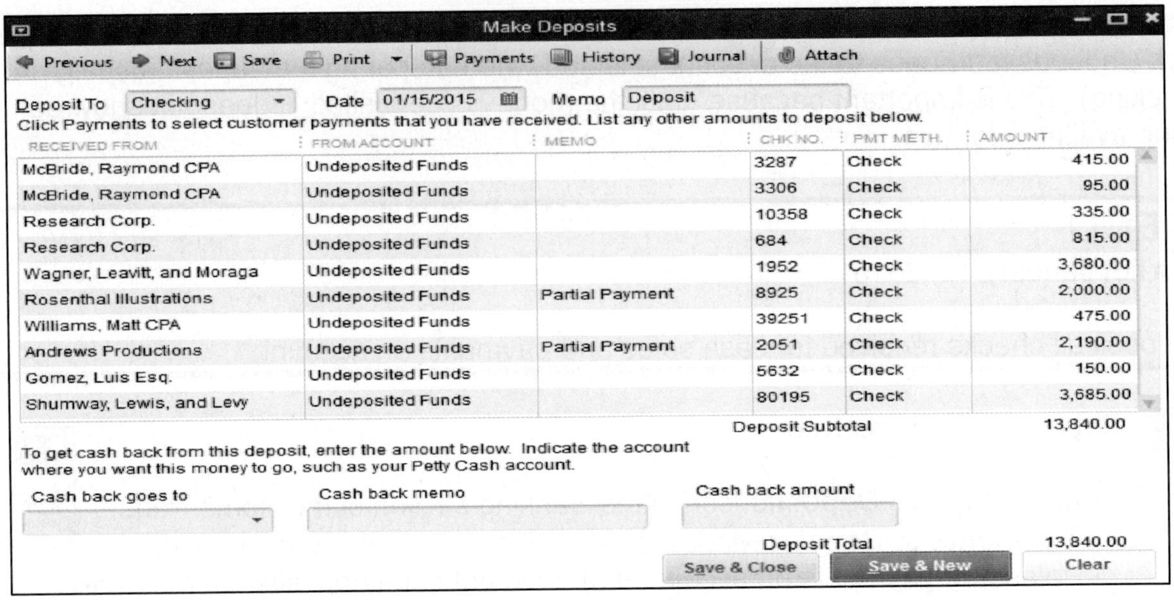

Click the **Print** button to print **Deposit Summary**
Select **Deposit summary only** on the **Print Deposit** dialog box, click **OK**

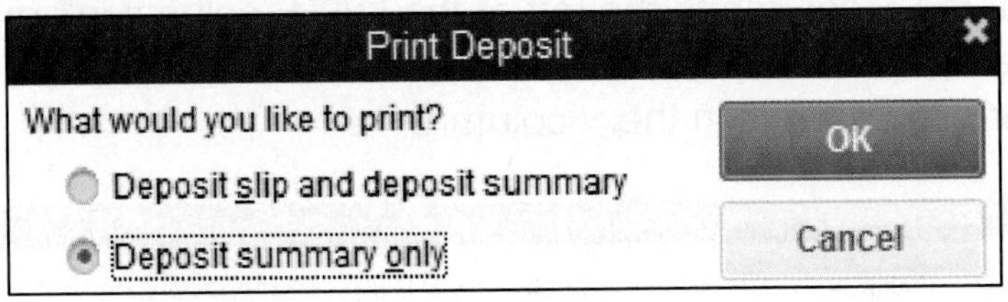

Check the **Settings** for **Print Lists**, click **Print**

- *Note:* QuickBooks automatically prints the date that the Deposit Summary was printed on the report. It is the current date of your computer and cannot be changed; therefore, it may not match the date shown in the answer key.

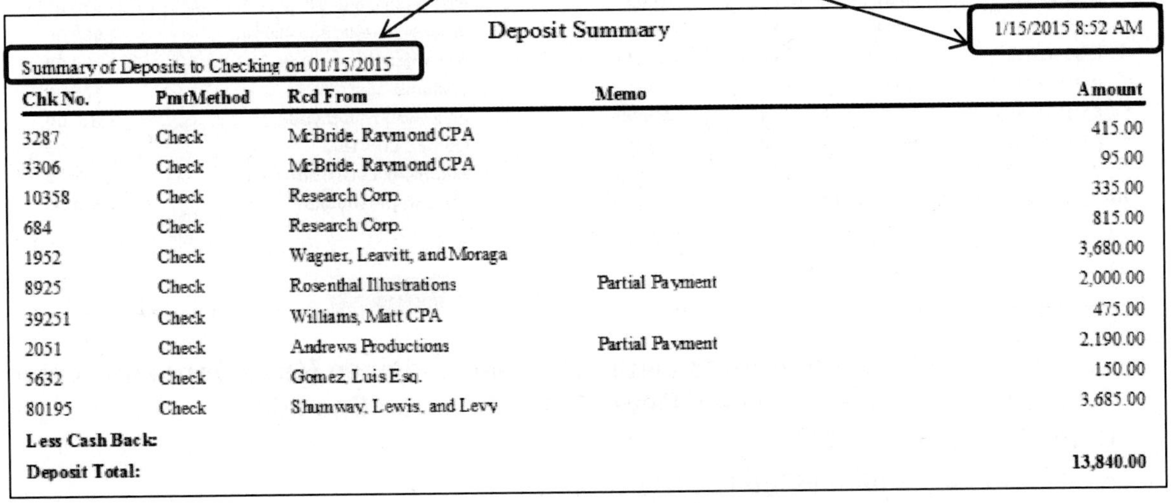
Deposit Summary

1/15/2015 8:52 AM

Summary of Deposits to Checking on 01/15/2015

Chk No.	PmtMethod	Rcd From	Memo	Amount
3287	Check	McBride, Raymond CPA		415.00
3306	Check	McBride, Raymond CPA		95.00
10358	Check	Research Corp.		335.00
684	Check	Research Corp.		815.00
1952	Check	Wagner, Leavitt, and Moraga		3,680.00
8925	Check	Rosenthal Illustrations	Partial Payment	2,000.00
39251	Check	Williams, Matt CPA		475.00
2051	Check	Andrews Productions	Partial Payment	2,190.00
5632	Check	Gomez, Luis Esq.		150.00
80195	Check	Shumway, Lewis, and Levy		3,685.00
Less Cash Back:				
Deposit Total:				**13,840.00**

When printing is finished, click **Save & Close** on **Make Deposits**

PRINT JOURNAL

Even though QuickBooks displays registers and reports in a manner that focuses on the transaction—for example, entering a sale on account via an invoice—it still keeps a Journal. The Journal records each transaction and lists the accounts and the amounts for debit and credit entries. The Journal is very useful; especially, if you are trying to find errors. Always check the transaction dates, the account names, and the items listed in the Memo column. If a transaction does not appear in the Journal, it may be due to using an incorrect date. Remember, only the transactions entered within the report dates will be displayed. In many instances, going through the Journal entries will help you find errors in your transactions.

In your concepts course, you may have learned that the General Journal was where all entries were recorded in debit/credit format. In QuickBooks, you do record some non-recurring debit/credit transactions in the General Journal and then display all debit/credit entries no matter where the transactions were recorded in the Journal. (At times in the text Journal and General Journal are used synonymously to represent the report).

Print the Journal

Open the **Report Center** as previously instructed
Click **Accountant & Taxes** as the Report type
Double-click **Journal**

- If you get the Collapsing and Expanding Transactions dialog box, click **OK**.

When the Journal is displayed, click the **Expand** button
The dates are from **01/01/15** to **01/15/15**
Customize the Report to change the **Header/Footer** so the **Date Prepared** and **Time Prepared** are not selected, click **OK**
Scroll through the report to view the transactions

- You may find that your Trans # is not the same as shown. QuickBooks automatically numbers all transactions recorded. If you have deleted and re-entered transactions more than directed in the text, you may have different transaction numbers. Do not be concerned with this.
- Many of the columns do not display in full. In order to see important information; such as, the account used in the transactions, the columns need to be resized.

Resize the width of the Account column so the account names are displayed in full
Position the cursor on the sizing diamond between **Account** and **Debit**

- The cursor turns into a plus with arrows pointing left and right.

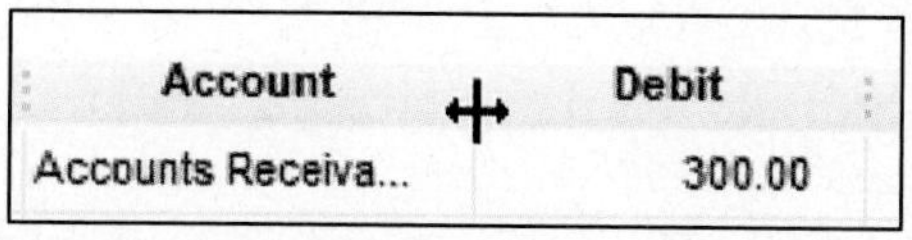

Hold down the primary (left) mouse button

Drag the cursor from the diamond between **Account** and **Debit** to the right until you have the account names displayed in full

- You will see a dotted vertical line while you are dragging the mouse and holding down the primary mouse button.

Look at the other columns, if any have … to represent information not shown, point to the sizing diamond and drag until the information is shown

- You may make columns smaller by pointing to the sizing diamond and dragging to the left.

Point to the sizing diamond between the **Debit** and **Credit** columns

Drag to the left to make the Debit column smaller

- If you make the column too small, the numbers that cannot be displayed will be shown as ******. If this happens, make the column larger.

Resize the remaining columns to eliminate extra space and to display names, memos, and accounts in full

Once the columns have been resized, click the **Print** button, click **Report**

Click **Preview**

- You will be able to see how the report will appear when it is printed. If the report prints two-pages wide, you may want to resize the columns until you can get it to print on one-page wide. If you need to hide a few words in the Memo column in order to do this, that is acceptable. For example, you may need to hide the word Installation for Initial Hour of Hardware/Network Installation in the Memo column.

Click **Close** to close the **Preview**

Once you have the column widths adjusted so the report is one-page wide, click the **Print** button, click **Report**

On the **Print Reports** screen, the settings will be the same used previously except:
Click **Landscape** to select Landscape orientation

- If you cannot get the report to print on one-page even after resizing the columns, click on **Fit report to one page wide** to select this item.
- The printer will print the Journal using a smaller font so the report will fit across the 11-inch width.

Click **Print**

- The Journal will be several pages in length so only a partial report is shown.

2

Computer Consulting by Your Name
Journal
January 1 - 15, 2015

Trans #	Type	Date	Num	Adj	Name	Memo	Account	Debit	Credit
44	Payment	01/15/2015	80195		Shumway, Lewis, and Levy		Undeposited Funds	3,685.00	
					Shumway, Lewis, and Levy		Accounts Receivable		3,685.00
								3,685.00	3,685.00
45	Deposit	01/15/2015				Deposit	Checking	13,840.00	
					McBride, Raymond CPA	Deposit	Undeposited Funds		415.00
					McBride, Raymond CPA	Deposit	Undeposited Funds		95.00
					Research Corp.	Deposit	Undeposited Funds		335.00
					Research Corp.	Deposit	Undeposited Funds		815.00
					Wagner, Leavitt, and Moraga	Deposit	Undeposited Funds		3,680.00
					Rosenthal Illustrations	Partial Payment	Undeposited Funds		2,000.00
					Williams, Matt CPA	Deposit	Undeposited Funds		475.00
					Andrews Productions	Partial Payment	Undeposited Funds		2,190.00
					Gomez, Luis Esq.	Deposit	Undeposited Funds		150.00
					Shumway, Lewis, and Levy	Deposit	Undeposited Funds		3,685.00
								13,840.00	13,840.00
TOTAL								**36,560.00**	**36,560.00**

Partial Report

Close the report, do <u>not</u> close the Report Center

TRIAL BALANCE

When all sales transactions have been entered, it is important to prepare and print the Trial Balance and verify that the total debits equal the total credits.

Print the Trial Balance

Click **Trial Balance** on the Report Center list of Accountant & Taxes reports
Click the **Run** icon
Enter the dates from **010115** to **011515**

- Shortcut: You do not have to use **/** to separate the date into month, day, year.

Click the **Customize Report** button and change **Header/Footer** so **Date Prepared**, **Time Prepared**, and **Report Basis** do not print
Print the report in **Portrait** orientation following instructions presented earlier in the chapter

- If necessary, click on **Fit report to one page wide** to deselect this item.

Computer Consulting by Your Name
Trial Balance
As of January 15, 2015

	Jan 15, 15	
	Debit	**Credit**
Checking	51,710.00	
Accounts Receivable	17,650.00	
Office Supplies	500.00	
Undeposited Funds	0.00	
Company Cars:Original Cost	49,000.00	
Office Equipment:Original Cost	8,050.00	
Accounts Payable		850.00
Loan Payable	0.00	
Loan Payable:Company Cars Loan		35,000.00
Loan Payable:Office Equipment Loan		4,000.00
Owner's Equity	0.00	
Student's Name, Capital		53,135.00
Student's Name, Capital:Investments		25,000.00
Income:Installation Income		175.00
Income:Technical Support Income		900.00
Income:Training Income		7,850.00
TOTAL	126,910.00	126,910.00

Close the report
Do not close the Report Center

GRAPHS

Once transactions have been entered, transaction results can be visually represented in a graphic form. QuickBooks illustrates Accounts Receivable by Aging Period as a bar chart, and it illustrates Accounts Receivable by Customer as a pie chart. For further details, double-click on an individual section of the pie chart or chart legend to create a bar chart analyzing an individual customer. QuickBooks also prepares graphs based on sales and will show the results of sales by item and by customer.

ACCOUNTS RECEIVABLE GRAPHS

Accounts Receivable graphs illustrate account information based on the age of the account and the percentage of accounts receivable owed by each customer.

Create Accounts Receivable Graphs

Click **Customers & Receivables** in the Report Center list to select the type of report
Scroll through the list of reports; and then, double-click **Accounts Receivable Graph** to select the report
Click **Dates** on the QuickInsight: Accounts Receivable Graph screen
On the **Change Graph Dates** change **Show Aging As of** to **01/15/15**
Click **OK**

- QuickBooks generates a bar chart illustrating Accounts Receivable by Aging Period and a pie chart illustrating Accounts Receivable by Customer.

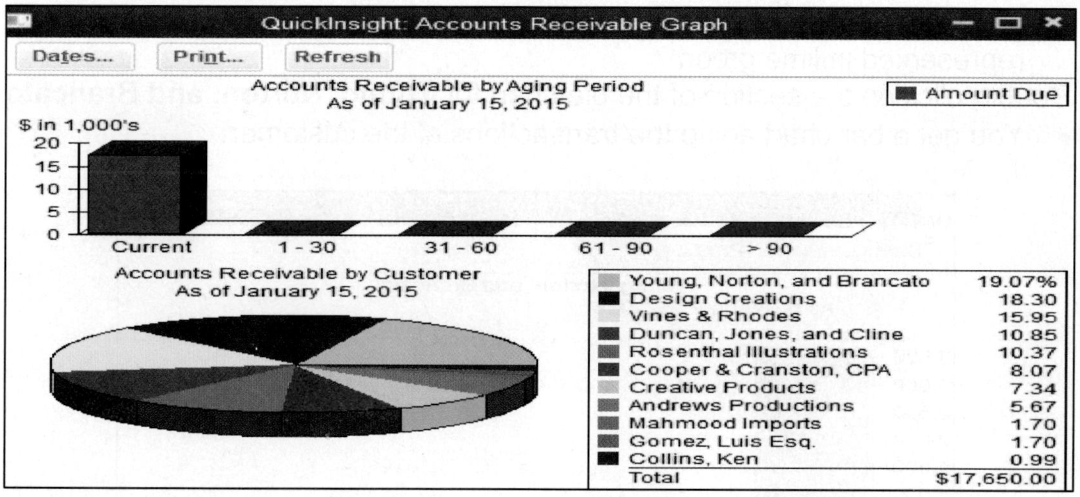

Printing is not required for this graph

- If you want a printed copy, click **Print** and print in Portrait mode.

Click the **Dates** button

Enter **02/15/15** for the **Show Aging As of** date

Click **OK**

- Notice the difference in the aging of accounts.

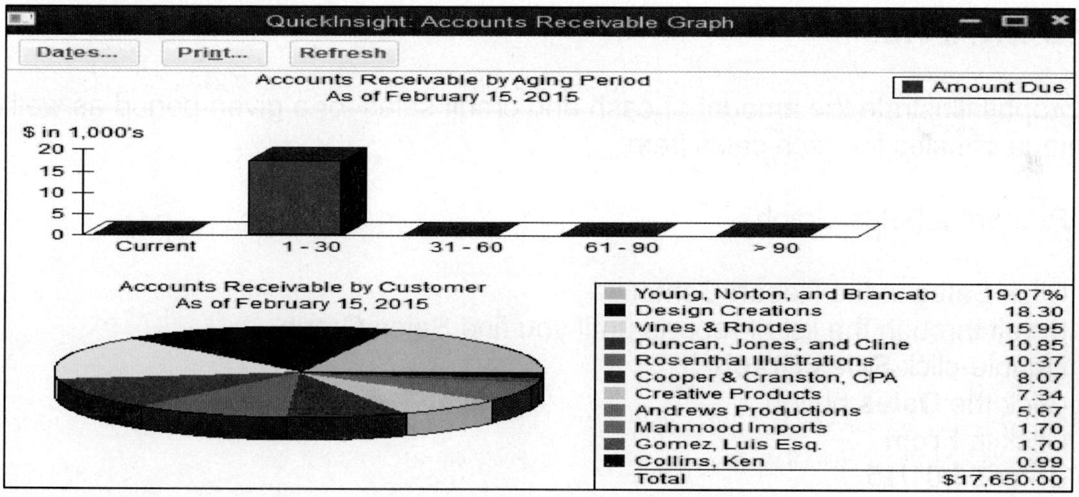

Click **Dates**

Enter **01/15/15**

Do not close the graph

QUICKZOOM FOR INDIVIDUAL CUSTOMER DETAILS

It is possible to get detailed information regarding the aging of transactions for an individual customer by using the QuickZoom feature of QuickBooks.

Use QuickZoom to see information for Young, Norton, and Brancato

- The color in the ledger shows you that Young, Norton, and Brancato is represented in lime green

Double-click on the section of the pie chart for **Young, Norton, and Brancato**

- You get a bar chart aging the transactions of the customer.

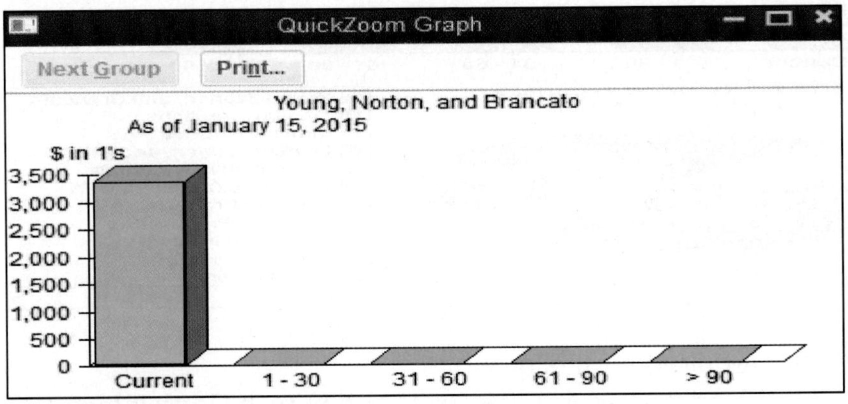

Printing is not required for this graph
Close the **QuickZoom Graph** for Young, Norton, and Brancato
Close the **Accounts Receivable Graph**
Do <u>not</u> close the Report Center

SALES GRAPHS

Sales graphs illustrate the amount of cash and credit sales for a given period as well as the percentage of sales for each sales item.

Prepare a Sales Graph

Click **Sales** in the Report Center
Scroll through the list of reports until you find Sales Graph
Double-click **Sales Graph**
Click the **Dates** button
Click in **From**
Enter **01/01/15**
Tab to **To**
Enter **01/15/15**
Click **OK**
The **By Item** button should be selected

- You will see a bar chart representing Sales by Month and a pie chart displaying a Sales Summary by item.

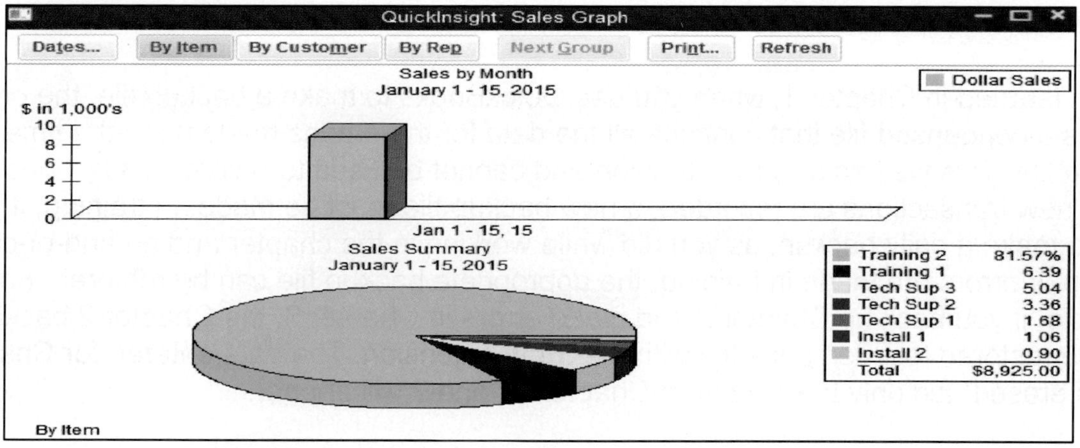

- If the **By Customer** button is indented, you will see the same bar chart but the pie chart and chart legend will display a Sales Summary by customer.
- If the **By Rep** button is indented, you will see the same bar chart but the pie chart and chart legend will display a Sales Summary by sales rep.

Printing is not required for this graph
Do not close the graph

QUICKZOOM TO VIEW ITEM

It is possible to use QuickZoom to view details regarding an individual item's sales by month.

Use QuickZoom to see information for Install 1

Since Install 1 is such a small area in the pie chart, double-click **Install 1** In the chart legend

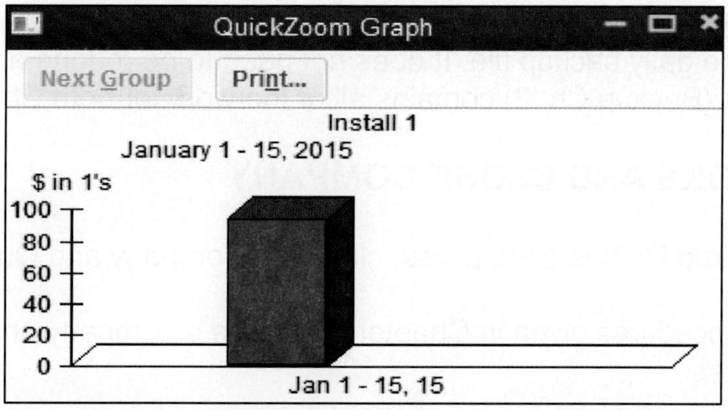

You will see the Sales by Month for Install 1
Close the **QuickZoom Graph** and the **Sales Graph** without printing
Close the **Report Center**

CREATE CHAPTER BACK UP

As you learned in Chapter 1, when you use QuickBooks to make a backup file, the program creates a condensed file that contains all the data for the entries made up to the time of the backup file. This file has a **.qbb** extension and cannot be used to record transactions. When new transactions are recorded, a new backup file must be made. In training, it is wise to make a daily backup, as you did while working in the chapter and an end-of-chapter backup. If errors are made in training, the appropriate backup file can be restored. For example, if you back up Chapter 2 and make errors in Chapter 3, the Chapter 2 backup may be restored to a company file with the **.qbw** extension. The data entered for Chapter 3 will be erased and only the data from Chapters 1 and 2 will appear.

A duplicate copy of the file may be made using Windows. Instructions for this procedure should be provided by your professor. You may hear the duplicate copy referred to as a backup file. This is different from the QuickBooks backup file.

Back up the company

Follow the instructions provided in Chapter 1 to make your backup
The name for the Chapter 2 backup file should be **Computer (Backup Ch. 2)**

- Your Computer (Backup Ch. 1) file contains all of your work from Chapter 1.
- Your Computer (Backup Ch. 2) file contains all your work from Chapters 1 and 2.
- The Computer (Backup Ch. 2) will not contain transactions from the work you do in Chapter 3.
- Keeping a separate backup file for each chapter is helpful for those times when you have made errors and cannot figure out how to correct them. Restoring your Chapter 2 back up file will restore your work from Chapters 1 and 2 and eliminate any work completed in Chapter 3. This will allow you to start over at the beginning of Chapter 3. If you do not have a backup file for Chapter 2, you would need to re-enter all the transactions for Chapter 2 before beginning Chapter 3.
- Your Daily Backup file will contain all of your work up to the point where you created the daily backup file. It does not need to be redone at this point since the Computer (Backup Ch. 2) contains all of the work for both Chapters 1 and 2.

EXIT QUICKBOOKS AND CLOSE COMPANY

After the backup file has been made, close the Company and QuickBooks

Follow the procedures given in Chapter 1 to close a company and to close QuickBooks

SUMMARY

In this chapter, cash and credit sales were prepared for Computer Consulting by Your Name, a service business, using sales receipts and invoices. Credit memos were issued.

Customer accounts were added and revised. Invoices and sales receipts were edited, deleted, and voided. Cash payments were received and bank deposits were made. All the transactions entered reinforced the QuickBooks concept of using the business form to record transactions rather than enter information in journals. However, QuickBooks does not disregard traditional accounting methods. Instead, it performs this function in the background. The Journal was accessed and printed. The fact that the Customer:Job List functions as the Accounts Receivable Ledger and that the Chart of Accounts is the General Ledger in QuickBooks was pointed out. The importance of reports for information and decision-making was illustrated. Exploration of the various sales and accounts receivable reports and graphs allowed information to be viewed from a sales standpoint and from an accounts receivable perspective. Sales reports emphasized both cash and credit sales according to the sales item generating the revenue. Accounts Receivable reports focused on amounts owed by credit customers. The traditional trial balance emphasizing the equality of debits and credits was prepared.

END-OF-CHAPTER QUESTIONS

TRUE/FALSE

ANSWER THE FOLLOWING QUESTIONS IN THE SPACE PROVIDED BEFORE THE QUESTION NUMBER.

___T___ 1. A new customer can be added to a company's records on the fly.

___T___ 2. In QuickBooks, error correction for a sale on account can be accomplished by editing the invoice.

___F___ 3. An Item List stores information about products you purchase.

___F___ 4. Once transactions have been entered, modifications to a customer's account may be made only at the end of the fiscal year.

___F___ 5. In QuickBooks all transactions must be entered using the traditional debit/credit method.

___T___ 6. Checks received for cash sales are held in the Undeposited Funds account until the bank deposit is made.

___T___ 7. When a correction for a transaction is made, QuickBooks not only changes the form used to record the transaction, it also changes all journal and account entries for the transaction to reflect the correction.

___T___ 8. QuickGraphs allow information to be viewed from both a sales standpoint and from an accounts receivable perspective.

___F___ 9. QuickZoom allows you to print a report instantly.

___F___10. A customer's payment on account is immediately recorded in the cash account.

MULTIPLE CHOICE

WRITE THE LETTER OF THE CORRECT ANSWER IN THE SPACE PROVIDED BEFORE THE QUESTION NUMBER.

___B___ 1. To remove an invoice without a trace, it is ___.

A. voided
B. deleted
C. blocked
D. reversed

C 2. To enter a cash sale, ___ is completed.
A. a debit
B. an invoice
C. a sales receipt
D. receive payments

D 3. Two primary types of lists used in this chapter are ___.
A. receivables and payables
B. invoices and checks
C. registers and navigator
D. customers and item

D 4. When you enter an invoice, an error may be corrected by ___.
A. backspacing or deleting
B. tabbing and typing
C. dragging and typing
D. all of the above

B 5. While in the Customer Balance Summary Report, it is possible to get an individual customer's information by using ___.
A. QuickReport
B. QuickZoom
C. QuickGraph
D. QuickSummary

A 6. Undeposited Funds represents ___.
A. cash or checks received from customers but not yet deposited in the bank
B. all cash sales
C. the balance of the accounts receivable account
D. none of the above

B 7. QuickBooks uses graphs to illustrate information about ___.
A. the chart of accounts
B. sales
C. the cash account
D. supplies

C 8. Changes to the chart of accounts may be made ___.
A. at the beginning of a fiscal period
B. before the end of the fiscal year
C. at any time
D. once established, the chart of accounts may not be modified

D 9. To obtain information about sales by item, you can view ___.
A. the income statement
B. the trial balance
C. receivables reports
D. sales reports

A 10. When you add a customer using the Set Up method, you add ___.
A. complete information for a customer
B. only a customer's name
C. the customer's name, address, and telephone number
D. the customer's name and telephone number

FILL-IN

IN THE SPACE PROVIDED, WRITE THE ANSWER THAT MOST APPROPRIATELY COMPLETES THE SENTENCE.

1. The report used to view only the balances on account of each customer is the Customer. Balance Summary Report
2. The form prepared to show a reduction to a sale on account is a(n) CM.
3. The report that proves that debits equal credits is the Trial Balance.
4. QuickBooks shows icons on the Home Page and on the Top Icon Bar that may be clicked to open the business documents used in recording transactions.
5. To verify the company being used in QuickBooks, you check the Title Bar.

SHORT ESSAY

Explain how the method used to enter an Accounts Receivable transaction in QuickBooks is different from the method used to enter a transaction according to an accounting textbook.

NAME_________________________

CHAPTER 2: TRANSMITTAL

COMPUTER CONSULTING BY YOUR NAME

Check the items below as you print them; then attach the documents and reports in the order listed when you submit them to your instructor.

___ Invoice 1: Luis Gomez, Esq.
___ Invoice 2: Matt Williams, CPA
___ Invoice 3: Ela Ahmadrand
___ Invoice 4: Vines & Rhodes
___ Invoice 5: Cooper & Cranston, CPA
___ Invoice 6: Young, Norton, and Brancato
___ Customer Balance Summary, January 5, 2015
___ Customer Balance Detail, Vines & Rhodes
___ Invoice 5 (corrected): Cooper & Cranston, CPA
___ Transaction List by Customer, January 1-7, 2015
___ Customer Balance Detail Report
___ Credit Memo 7: Vines & Rhodes
___ Invoice 8: Ken Collins
___ Sales Receipt 1: Raymond McBride, CPA
___ Sales Receipt 2: Raymond McBride, CPA
___ Sales Receipt 3: Research Corp.
___ Sales by Customer Detail Report, January 1-12, 2015
___ Sales Receipt 1 (corrected): Raymond McBride, CPA
___ Sales by Item Summary, January 1-14, 2015
___ Payment Receipt: Research Corp.
___ Payment Receipt: Wagner, Leavitt, and Moraga
___ Payment Receipt: Rosenthal Illustrations
___ Payment Receipt: Matt Williams, CPA
___ Payment Receipt: Andrews Productions
___ Payment Receipt: Luis Gomez, Esq.
___ Payment Receipt: Shumway, Lewis, and Levy
___ Deposit Summary
___ Journal, January 1-15, 2015
___ Trial Balance, January 15, 2015

END-OF-CHAPTER PROBLEM

YOUR NAME LANDSCAPE AND POOL SERVICE

Chapter 2 continues with the entry of both cash and credit sales, receipt of payment by credit customers, credit memos, and bank deposits. In addition, reports focusing on sales and accounts receivable are prepared.

INSTRUCTIONS

Use the company file **Landscape.qbw** that you used for Chapter 1. The company name should be Your Name Landscape and Pool Service. (You changed the company name to include your real name in Chapter 1.) Since this company was used in Chapter 1, when you see the Open a Company screen, you may see other QuickBooks files and/or folders associated with that company. QuickBooks will create them as you use a company file. Some of these files may have extensions of QBW.ND or .QBW.TLG. Folders that say QuickBooksAutoDataRecovery, SearchIndex, or Restored are common. For the most part, you do not use or change any of these files or folders, simply click the company file and click the Open button. Sometimes, when switching from one company to the next; i.e., Computer to Landscape, QuickBooks might mark your company file as read only. If this happens, refer to Chapter 1 for steps on how to change the file Properties from Read Only.

The invoices and sales receipts are numbered consecutively. Invoice 25 is the first invoice number used in this problem. Sales Receipt 15 is the first sales receipt number used when recording cash sales in this problem. If you wish, you may hide the History for customers on the invoices and sales receipts. Each invoice recorded should be a Service Invoice and contain a message. When selecting a message, choose the one that you feel is most appropriate for the transaction. Print each invoice and sales receipt as it is completed and do not print lines around each field. Remember that payments received on account should be recorded as Receive Payments and not as a Sales Receipt.

When recording transactions, use the following Sales Item chart to determine the item(s) billed. If the transaction does not indicate the size of the pool or property, use the first category for the item; for example, LandCom 1 or LandRes 1 would be used for standard-size landscape service. Remember that SpaCom 1 and SpaRes 1 are services for spas—not pools. The appropriate billing for a standard-size pool would be PoolCom 1 or PoolRes 1. If you get a message regarding the spelling of Lg., click Ignore All.

When printing reports, always remove the Date Prepared, Time Prepared, and Report Basis from the Header/Footer and adjust the column size to display the information in full.

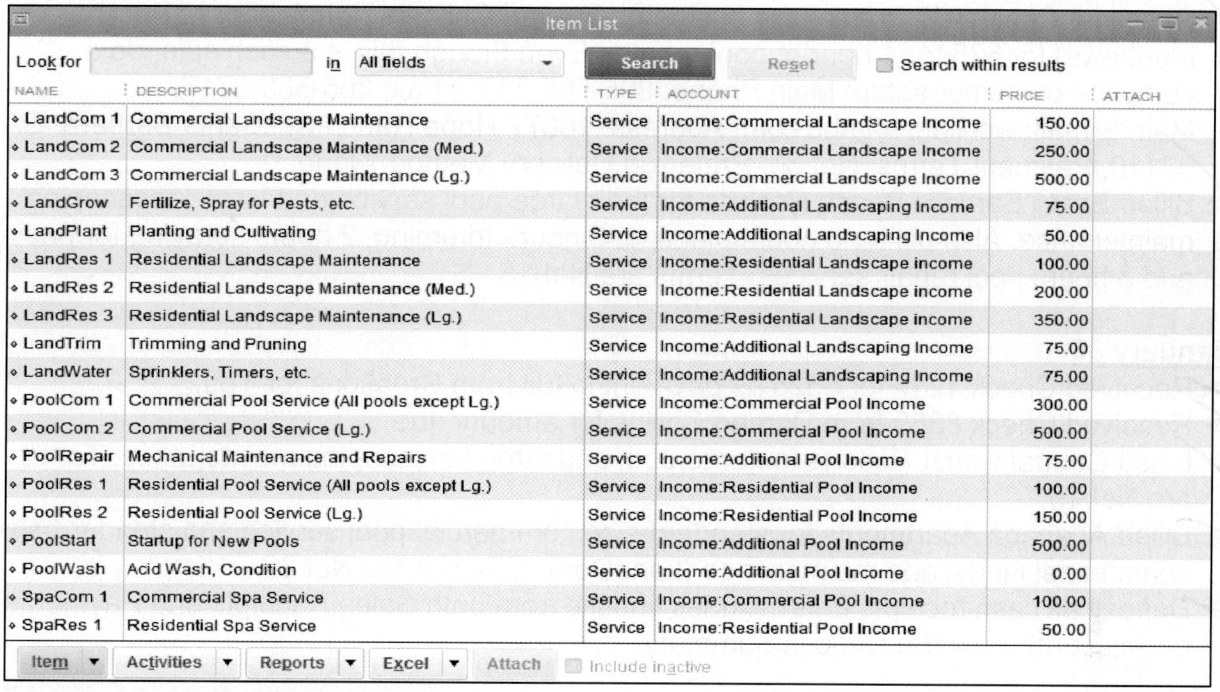

Item List

Look for [ ] in All fields | Search | Reset | Search within results

NAME	DESCRIPTION	TYPE	ACCOUNT	PRICE	ATTACH
LandCom 1	Commercial Landscape Maintenance	Service	Income:Commercial Landscape Income	150.00	
LandCom 2	Commercial Landscape Maintenance (Med.)	Service	Income:Commercial Landscape Income	250.00	
LandCom 3	Commercial Landscape Maintenance (Lg.)	Service	Income:Commercial Landscape Income	500.00	
LandGrow	Fertilize, Spray for Pests, etc.	Service	Income:Additional Landscaping Income	75.00	
LandPlant	Planting and Cultivating	Service	Income:Additional Landscaping Income	50.00	
LandRes 1	Residential Landscape Maintenance	Service	Income:Residential Landscape income	100.00	
LandRes 2	Residential Landscape Maintenance (Med.)	Service	Income:Residential Landscape income	200.00	
LandRes 3	Residential Landscape Maintenance (Lg.)	Service	Income:Residential Landscape income	350.00	
LandTrim	Trimming and Pruning	Service	Income:Additional Landscaping Income	75.00	
LandWater	Sprinklers, Timers, etc.	Service	Income:Additional Landscaping Income	75.00	
PoolCom 1	Commercial Pool Service (All pools except Lg.)	Service	Income:Commercial Pool Income	300.00	
PoolCom 2	Commercial Pool Service (Lg.)	Service	Income:Commercial Pool Income	500.00	
PoolRepair	Mechanical Maintenance and Repairs	Service	Income:Additional Pool Income	75.00	
PoolRes 1	Residential Pool Service (All pools except Lg.)	Service	Income:Residential Pool Income	100.00	
PoolRes 2	Residential Pool Service (Lg.)	Service	Income:Residential Pool Income	150.00	
PoolStart	Startup for New Pools	Service	Income:Additional Pool Income	500.00	
PoolWash	Acid Wash, Condition	Service	Income:Additional Pool Income	0.00	
SpaCom 1	Commercial Spa Service	Service	Income:Commercial Pool Income	100.00	
SpaRes 1	Residential Spa Service	Service	Income:Residential Pool Income	50.00	

Item | Activities | Reports | Excel | Attach | Include inactive

RECORD TRANSACTIONS

January 1

- Billed Ocean View Motel for monthly landscape services and monthly pool maintenance services, Invoice 25. (Use a Service Invoice. Use LandCom 1 to record the monthly landscape service fee and PoolCom 1 to record the monthly pool service fee. The quantity for each item is 1.) Terms are Net 15. If you get a message regarding the spelling of Lg., click Ignore All. (Don't forget to add a Customer Message.)
- Billed Ron Sampson for monthly landscape and pool services at his home. Both the pool and landscaping are standard size. The terms are Net 30. (Did you use an Intuit Service Invoice?)
- Billed Creations for You for 2 hours shrub trimming (Item: LandTrim). Terms: Net 30.
- Received Check 381 for $500 from Annabelle Andrews for pool startup services at her home, Sales Receipt 15.
- Received Check 8642 from Hiroshi Chang for $150 as payment in full on his account. (Don't forget to print the Payment Receipt.)

January 15

- Billed a new customer: Eric Matthews (remember to enter the last name first for the customer name and change the billing name to first name first)— Main Phone: 805-555-9825, Main Email: EMatthews@123.com, Address: 10824 Hope Ranch St., Santa Barbara, CA 93110, Payment Terms: Net 30, Preferred Delivery Method: None—for monthly service on his large pool and large residential landscape maintenance.
- Received Check 6758 from Ocean View Motel in full payment of Invoice 25.

2

- Received Check 987 from a new customer: Wayne Childers (a neighbor of Eric Matthews) for $75 for 1 hour of pool repairs. Even though this is a cash sale, do a complete customer setup: Main Phone: 805-555-7175, Fax: 805-555-5717, Main E-mail: wchilders@abc.com, Address: 10877 Hope Ranch St., Santa Barbara, CA 93110, Payment Terms: Net 30. Preferred Delivery Method: None.
- Billed Santa Barbara Beach Resorts for their large pool service and large landscaping maintenance. Also bill for 5 hours planting, 3 hours trimming, 2 hours spraying for pests, and 3 hours pool repair services. Terms are Net 15.

January 30

- Received Check 1247 for $525 as payment in full from Creations for You.
- Received Check 8865 from Doreen Collins for amount due.
- Billed Central Coast Resorts for large pool and large landscaping maintenance. Terms are Net 15.
- Billed Anacapa Apartments for standard-size commercial pool service and standard-size commercial landscape maintenance (LandCom1). Terms are Net 30.
- Deposit all cash receipts (this includes checks from both Sales Receipts and Payments on Account). Print the Deposit Summary.

PRINT REPORTS AND BACKUP

- Customer Balance Detail Report for all transactions. Remember to remove Date Prepared and Time Prepared from all reports. Use Portrait orientation.
- Sales by Item Summary Report for 1/1/2015 through 1/30/2015. Portrait orientation.
- Journal for 1/1/2015 through 1/30/2015. Remember to Expand the transactions in the report. Print in Landscape orientation, fit to one page wide.
- Trial Balance for 1/1/2015 through 1/30/2015. Portrait orientation.
- Backup your work to **Landscape (Backup Ch. 2)**.

NAME ____________________

CHAPTER 2: TRANSMITTAL

YOUR NAME LANDSCAPE AND POOL SERVICE

Check the items below as you print them; then attach the documents and reports in the order listed when you submit them to your instructor.

___ Invoice 25: Ocean View Motel
___ Invoice 26: Ron Sampson
___ Invoice 27: Creations for You
___ Sales Receipt 15: Annabelle Andrews
___ Payment Receipt: Hiroshi Chiang
___ Invoice 28: Eric Matthews
___ Payment Receipt: Ocean View Motel
___ Sales Receipt 16: Wayne Childers
___ Invoice 29: Santa Barbara Beach Resorts
___ Payment Receipt: Creations for You
___ Payment Receipt: Doreen Collins
___ Invoice 30: Central Coast Resorts
___ Invoice 31: Anacapa Apartments
___ Deposit Summary
___ Customer Balance Detail
___ Sales by Item Summary, January 1-30, 2015
___ Journal, January 1-30, 2015
___ Trial Balance, January 30, 2015

PAYABLES AND PURCHASES: SERVICE BUSINESS

3

LEARNING OBJECTIVES

At the completion of this chapter you will be able to:

1. Understand the concepts for computerized accounting for payables.
2. Enter, edit, correct, delete, and pay bills.
3. Add new vendors and modify vendor records.
4. View Accounts Payable transaction history from the Enter Bills window.
5. View and/or print QuickReports for vendors, Accounts Payable Register, etc.
6. Use the QuickZoom feature.
7. Record and edit transactions in the Accounts Payable Register.
8. Enter vendor credits.
9. Print, edit, void, and delete checks.
10. Pay for expenses using petty cash.
11. Add new accounts.
12. Display and print the Accounts Payable Aging Summary Report, an Unpaid Bills Detail Report, and a Vendor Balance Summary Report.
13. Display an Accounts Payable Graph by Aging Period.

ACCOUNTING FOR PAYABLES AND PURCHASES

In a service business, most of the accounting for purchases and payables is simply paying bills for expenses incurred in the operation of the business. Purchases are for things used in the operation of the business. Some transactions will be in the form of cash purchases, and others will be purchases on account.

Bills can be paid when they are received or when they are due. Rather than use cumbersome journals, QuickBooks continues to focus on recording transactions based on the business document; therefore, you use the Enter Bills and Pay Bills features of the program to record the receipt and payment of bills. QuickBooks can remind you when payments are due and can calculate and apply discounts earned for paying bills early. Payments can be made by recording payments in the Pay Bills window or, if using the cash basis for accounting, by writing a check. A cash purchase can be recorded by writing a check or by using petty cash. Even though QuickBooks focuses on recording transactions on the business forms used, all transactions are recorded behind the scenes in the Journal.

QuickBooks uses a Vendor List for all vendors with which the company has an account. QuickBooks does not refer to the Vendor List as the Accounts Payable Ledger; yet, that is exactly what it is. The total of the Vendor List/Accounts Payable Ledger will match the total of the Accounts Payable account in the Chart of Accounts/General Ledger. The Vendor List may be accessed through the Vendor Center.

As in Chapter 2, corrections can be made directly on the business form or within the account. New accounts and vendors may be added on the fly as transactions are entered. Reports illustrating vendor balances, unpaid bills, accounts payable aging, transaction history, and accounts payable registers may be viewed and printed. Graphs analyzing the amount of accounts payable by aging period provide a visual illustration of the accounts payable.

TRAINING TUTORIAL AND PROCEDURES

The following tutorial will once again work with Computer Consulting by Your Name. As in Chapter 2, transactions will be recorded for this fictitious company. You should enter the transactions for Chapter 3 in the same company file that you used to record the Chapter 2 transactions. The tutorial for Computer Consulting by Your Name will continue in Chapter 4, where accounting for bank reconciliations, financial statement preparation, and closing an accounting period will be completed. To maximize training benefits, you should follow the Training Procedures given in Chapter 2.

DATES

As in the other chapters and throughout the text, the year used for the screen shots is 2015, which is the same year as the version of the program. You may want to check with your instructor to see if you should use 2015 as the year for the transactions. The year you used in Chapters 1 and 2 should be the same year you use in Chapters 3 and 4.

PRINTING

Throughout the text, you will be instructed when to print business documents and reports. Everything that is to be printed within the chapter is listed on a transmittal sheet. The end-of- chapter problem also has everything to be printed listed on a transmittal sheet. In some instances, your instructor may direct you to change what you print. Always verify items to be printed with your instructor.

BEGINNING THE TUTORIAL

In this chapter, you will be entering bills incurred by the company in the operation of the business. You will also be recording the payment of bills, purchases using checks, and purchases/payments using petty cash.

The Vendor List keeps information regarding the vendors with whom you do business and is the Accounts Payable Ledger. Vendor information includes the vendor names, addresses, telephone numbers, payment terms, credit limits, and account numbers. You will be using the following list for vendors with which Computer Consulting by Your Name has an account:

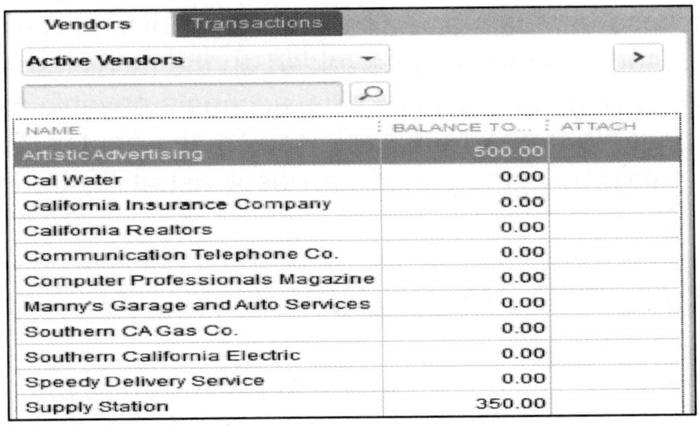

As in the previous chapters, all transactions are listed on memos. The transaction date will be the same as the memo date unless specified otherwise within the transaction. Vendor names, when necessary, will be given in the transaction. Unless other terms are provided, the terms are Net 30. Once a specific type of transaction has been entered in a step-by-step manner, additional transactions of the same or a similar type will be recorded without having instructions provided. Of course, you may always refer to instructions given for previous transactions for ideas or for steps used to enter those transactions. To determine the account used in the transaction, refer to the Chart of Accounts. When you are entering account information on a bill, clicking on the drop-down list arrow will show a copy of the Chart of Accounts.

OPEN QUICKBOOKS AND COMPANY FILE

➤ Open QuickBooks and Computer Consulting by Your Name as instructed in Chapter 1 (the transactions for both Chapters 1 and 2 will be in this company file)

ENTER BILL

QuickBooks provides accounts payable tracking. Entering bills as soon as they are received is an efficient way to record your liabilities. Once bills have been entered, QuickBooks will be able to provide up-to-date cash flow reports. A bill is divided into two sections: a vendor-related section (the upper part of the bill that looks similar to a check and has a memo text box under it) and a detail section (the area that is divided into columns for Account, Amount, and Memo). The vendor-related section of the bill is where information for the actual bill is entered, including a memo with information about the transaction. The detail section is where the expense accounts, expense account amounts, and transaction explanations are indicated.

MEMO
DATE: January 16, 2015

Record the bill: Artistic Advertising prepared and placed advertisements in local business publications announcing our new hardware and network installation service. Received Artistic's Invoice 9875 for $260 as a bill with terms of Net 30.

Record a bill

Click the **Enter Bills** icon in the Vendors section of the Home Page
Verify that Bill and Bill Received are marked at the top of the form
Complete the Vendor-section of the bill:
Click the drop-down list arrow next to **VENDOR**
Click **Artistic Advertising**
- Name is entered as the vendor.

Tab to **DATE**
- As with other business forms, when you tab to the date, it will be highlighted.
- When you type in the new date, the highlighted date will be deleted.

Type **01/16/15** as the date
Tab to **REF. NO.**
Type the vendor's invoice number: **9875**
Tab to **AMOUNT DUE**
Type **260**
- QuickBooks will automatically insert the .00 after the amount.

Tab to **TERMS**
Click the drop-down list arrow next to **TERMS**
Click **Net 15**
- QuickBooks automatically changes the Bill Due date to show 15 days from the transaction date.

Click the drop-down list arrow for **TERMS**, and click **Net 30**
- QuickBooks automatically changes the Bill Due date to show 30 days from the transaction date.

Tab to or click the first line in **MEMO** at the bottom of the Vendor section
Enter the transaction explanation of **Ads for Hardware/Network Installation Services**
- The memo will appear as part of the transaction in the Accounts Payable account as well as all in any report that used the individual transaction information.

Complete the detail section of the bill using the **Expenses** tab
- Notice that the Expenses tab shows $260, the amount of the bill.

Tab to or click in the column for **ACCOUNT**
Click the drop-down list arrow next to **ACCOUNT**
Click **Advertising Expense**

- Based on the accrual method of accounting, Advertising Expense is selected as the account used in this transaction because this expense should be matched against the revenue of the period.

The **AMOUNT** column already shows **260.00**—no entry required

Copy the memo **Ads for Hardware/Network Installation Services** from the Memo text box in the Vendor section of the bill to the Memo column in the Detail section of the bill:

Click to the left of the letter **A** in Ads

Highlight the memo text—**Ads for Hardware/Network Installation Services** by holding down the primary mouse button and dragging through the memo text

Click **Edit** on the menu bar; and then, click **Copy**

- Notice that the keyboard shortcut **Ctrl+C** is listed. This shortcut could be used rather than using the Edit menu and the Copy command.
- This actually copies the text and places it in a temporary storage area of Windows called the Clipboard.

Click in the **MEMO** column on the Expenses tab

Click **Edit** on the menu bar; and then, click **Paste**

- Notice the keyboard shortcut **Ctrl+V**.
- This inserts a copy of the material in the Windows Clipboard into the Memo column.
- This memo prints on all reports that include the transaction.

Click the **Save** icon at the top of the bill to save the transaction, leave it on the screen, and update the History

- If you get an Information Changed box for terms, click **No**.
- The Recent Transaction section of the Vendor History has been updated to include this bill.

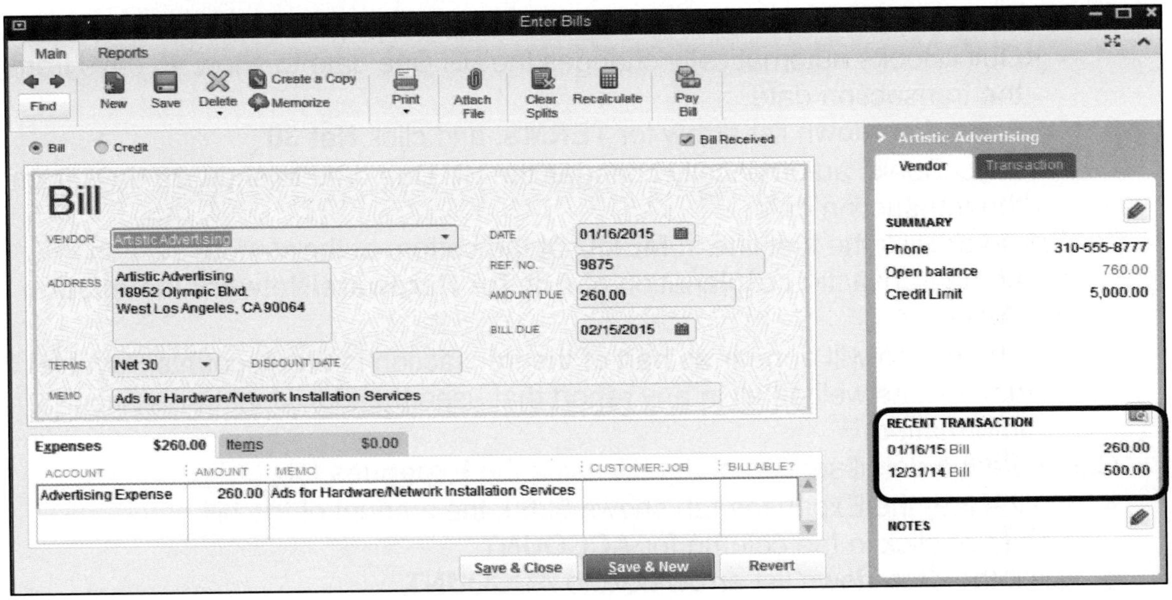

If you want to save screen space, hide the vendor history

Do this by clicking the tab for **Hide history**
Do not click Save & Close

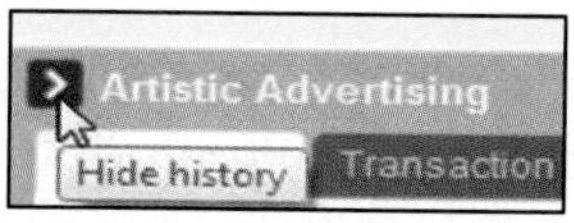

EDIT AND CORRECT ERRORS

If an error is discovered while you are entering information, it may be corrected by positioning the cursor in the field containing the error. You may do this by tabbing to move forward through each field or pressing Shift+Tab to move back to the field containing the error. If the error is highlighted, type the correction. If the error is not highlighted, you can correct the error by pressing the backspace or the delete key as many times as necessary to remove the error, and then type the correction. (*Alternate method:* Point to the error, highlight it by dragging the mouse through the error, and then type the correction.)

Practice editing and making corrections to the bill for Artistic Advertising

Click the drop-down list arrow for **Vendor**
Click **Communication Telephone Co.**
Tab to **DATE**
To increase the date by one day, press **+**
- You may press shift and the **=** key next to the backspace key, or you may press the **+** key on the numerical keypad.

Press **+** two more times
- The date should be **01/19/15**.

To decrease the date by one day, press **-**
- You may type a hyphen (**-**) next to the number **0** or you may press the hyphen (**-**) key on the numerical keypad.

Press **-** two more times
- The date should be **01/16/15**.

Change the date by clicking on the calendar next to the date
Click **19** on the calendar for January 2015
Click the calendar again
Click **16** to change the date back to 01/16/2015
To change the amount, click between the **2** and the **6** in **AMOUNT DUE**
Press the **Delete** key two times to delete the **60**
Key in **99** and press the **Tab** key
- The Amount Due should be **299.00**. The amount of 299.00 should also be shown on the Expenses tab in the detail section of the bill.

Click the drop-down list arrow for **VENDOR**
Click **Artistic Advertising**
Click to the right of the last **9** in **AMOUNT DUE**
Backspace two times to delete the **99**
Key in **60**
- The **AMOUNT DUE** should once again show **260.00**.
- If the terms do not show Net 30, click the **TERMS** drop-down list arrow, and click **Net 30**.

Refer back to the original bill from Artistic Advertising shown before Edit and Correct Errors to verify your entries

- Since you received the bill from the vendor, you do not print this entry unless your professor requests printing. When you print a bill, it automatically prints with lines around each field.

Click **Save & New** button to record the bill and go to the next bill

- If you get the Recording Transaction dialog box, click **Yes**.

PREPARE BILL WITH TWO EXPENSES

MEMO
DATE: January 18, 2015

On the recommendation of the office manager, Alhandra Cruz, the company is trying out several different models of fax machines on a monthly basis. Received a bill from Supply Station for one month's rental of a fax machine, $25, and for fax supplies, which were consumed during January, $20, Invoice 1035A, Terms Net 10.

Record a bill using two expense accounts

Complete the vendor-related section of the bill
Click the drop-down list arrow next to **VENDOR**
Click **Supply Station**
Tab to or click **DATE**

- If you click in Date, you will have to delete the current date.

Enter **01/18/15**
Tab to or click **REF. NO.**
Key in the vendor's invoice number: **1035A**
Tab to or click **AMOUNT DUE**
Enter **45**
Tab to or click on the line for **TERMS**
Type **Net 10** on the line for Terms, press the **Tab** key
You will get a **Terms Not Found** message box

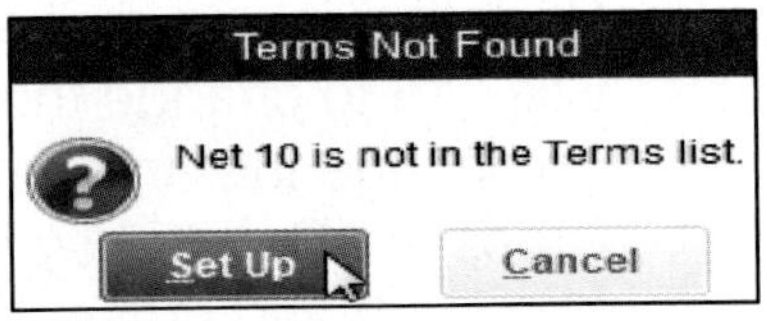

Click the **Set Up** button
Complete the information required in the **New Terms** dialog box:

Net 10 should appear as the Terms
Standard should be selected
Change the **Net due** from 0 to **10** days
Discount percentage should be **0%**
Discount if paid within **0** days

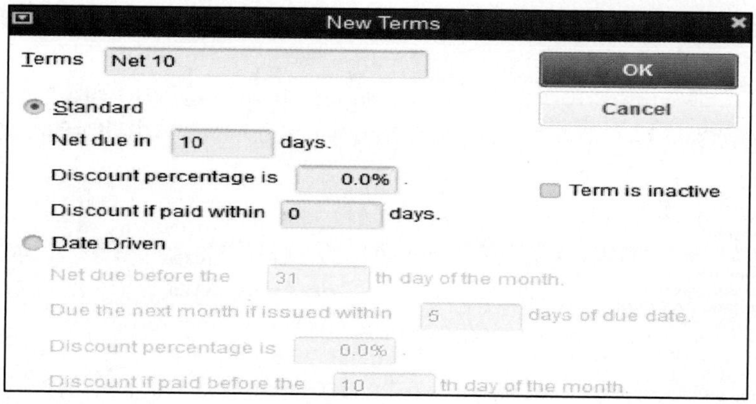

Click **OK**

Tab to or click **MEMO** beneath the Terms

Enter **Fax Rental and Fax Supplies for the Month** as the transaction description

To complete the **DETAIL SECTION** of the bill, use the Expenses tab and click the first line for **ACCOUNT**

Click the drop-down list arrow next to **ACCOUNT**

Click **Equipment Rental**

- Because a portion of this transaction is for equipment that is being rented, Equipment Rental is the appropriate account to use.

AMOUNT column shows **45.00**

Change this to reflect the actual amount of the Equipment Rental

Tab to **AMOUNT** to highlight

Type **25**

Tab to **MEMO**

Enter **Fax Rental for the Month** as the transaction explanation

Tab to **ACCOUNT**

Click the drop-down list arrow next to **ACCOUNT**

Click **Office Supplies Expense**

- The transaction information indicates that the fax supplies will be used within the month of January. Using Office Supplies Expense account correctly charges the supplies expense against the period.
- If the transaction indicated that the fax supplies were purchased to have on hand, the appropriate account to use would be the asset Office Supplies.
- Remember the formula:
  - Used within the month = Expense
  - Have on hand = Asset

The **AMOUNT** column correctly shows **20.00** as the amount

Tab to or click **MEMO**

Enter **Fax Supplies for the Month** as the transaction explanation

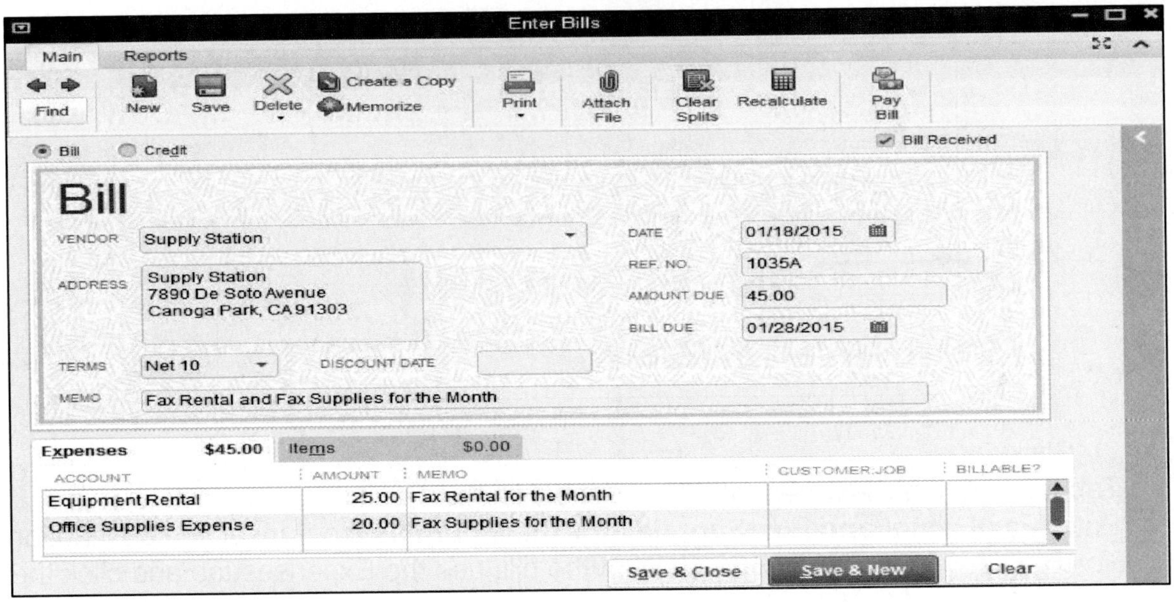

Click **Save & Close** to close the bill

- If you get an Information Changed message regarding the change of Terms for Supply Station, click **Yes**. This will change the Terms to Net 10 for all transactions with Supply Station.

TRANSACTION LIST BY VENDOR REPORT

To obtain information regarding individual transactions grouped by vendor, you prepare a Transaction Report by Vendor. This allows you to view the vendors for which you have recorded transactions. The type of transaction is identified; for example, the word *Bill* appears when you have entered the transaction as a bill. The transaction date, any invoice numbers or memos entered when recording the transaction, the accounts used, and the transaction amount appear in the report.

Prepare a **Transaction List by Vendor Report**

Click **Reports** on the Top Icon Bar to open the Report Center
Click **Vendors & Payables** to select the type of report
Double-click **Transaction List by Vendor** in the Vendor Balances Section
Enter the Dates From **01/01/15** To **01/18/15**, press **Tab**
Once the report is displayed, click the **Customize Report** button
Click the **Header/Footer** tab
Click **Date Prepared** and **Time Prepared** to deselect these features
Click **OK**
Resize the width of the Memo column so the memos are displayed in full:
Position the cursor on the sizing diamond between **Memo** and **Account**

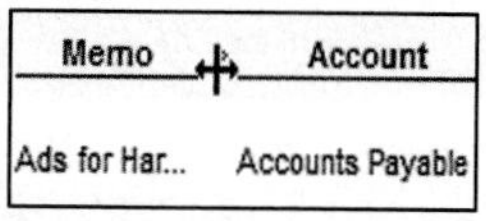

- The cursor turns into a plus with arrows pointing left and right.

Hold down the primary (left) mouse button

Drag the cursor from the diamond between **Memo** and **Account** to the right until you have the memo displayed in full

- You will see a dotted vertical line while you are dragging the mouse and holding down the primary mouse button.

Look at the other columns, if any have … to represent information not shown, point to the sizing diamond and drag until the information is shown

- You may make columns smaller by pointing to the sizing diamond and dragging to the left.

Once the columns have been resized, click the **Print** button

You may choose Report or Save As PDF, click **Report**

Click **Landscape** for the orientation

Click **Preview**

- You will be able to see how the report will appear when it is printed. If the report prints two-pages wide, you may want to resize the columns until you can get it to print on one-page wide.

Click **Close** to close the **Preview**

Click **Cancel** to cancel printing

With the resized report on the screen, look at each vendor account

- Note the type of transaction in the Type column and the invoice numbers in the Num column.
- The Memos shown are the ones entered in the Vendor (upper) section of the bill.
- The **Account** column shows **Accounts Payable** as the account.
- As in any traditional accounting transaction recording a purchase on account, the Accounts Payable account is credited.
- The **Split** column shows the other accounts used in the transaction.
- If the word **-SPLIT-** appears in this column, it indicates that more than one account was used.
- The transaction for Supply Station has -SPLIT- in the Split Column. This is because the transaction used two accounts: Equipment Rental and Office Supplies Expense for the debit portion of the transaction.

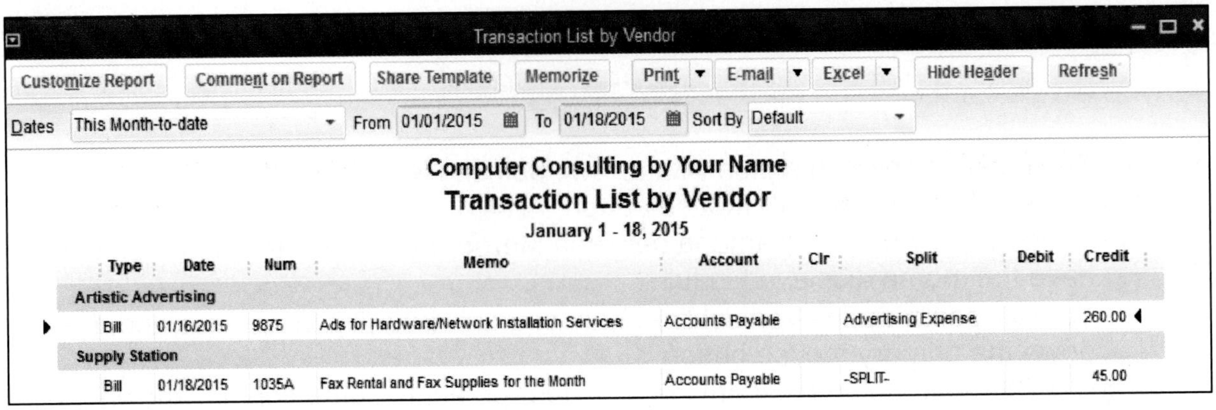

Print the report in Landscape orientation (11-inches wide by 8 ½ inches long) as instructed in Chapter 2, do not close the report

QUICKZOOM

Alhandra Cruz wants more detailed information regarding the accounts used in the Split column of the report. Specifically, she wants to know what accounts were used for the transaction of January 18, 2015 for Supply Station. In order to see the account names, Alhandra will use the QuickZoom feature of QuickBooks.

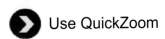

Use QuickZoom

Point to the word **-SPLIT-** in the Split column

- The mouse pointer turns into  .

Double-click to **Zoom** in to see the accounts used in the transaction

- This returns you to the *original bill* entered for Supply Station for the transaction of 01/18/2015.
- The Expense accounts used are Equipment Rental and Office Supplies Expense.

Click the **Close** button on the bill to return to the Transaction List by Vendor Report

To close the report, click the **Close** button

- If you get a Memorize Report dialog box, click **No**.

Close the Report Center

EDIT VENDOR

The Vendor Center contains a list of all the vendors with whom Computer Consulting by Your Name has an account. As information changes or errors in the vendor information are noted, the Vendor Information may be edited.

MEMO
DATE: January 19, 2015

It has been called to your attention that the address for Manny's Garage and Auto Services does not have a space between Manny's and Garage. Please correct this. Also, change the word **and** in the company name to the symbol **&**.

Open the Vendor Center and correct the address for Manny's Garage and Auto Services

Click **Vendors** on the Top Icon Bar
Click **Manny's Garage and Auto Services** in the Vendor List, click the **Edit** icon 
In the VENDOR NAME delete the word **and**; then, enter the symbol **&** (make sure there is a space before and after the symbol)
Repeat to change the COMPANY NAME
In the ADDRESS DETAILS BILLED FROM section, click between **Manny's** and **Garage**, press the **Space** bar
Change the word **and** in the Billed From section to the symbol **&** (make sure there is a space before and after the symbol)
Click the **Payment Settings** tab
Change the PRINT NAME ON CHECK AS to: **Manny's Garage & Auto Services**
Click **OK**
View the corrected information as shown; and, then, close the Vendor Center

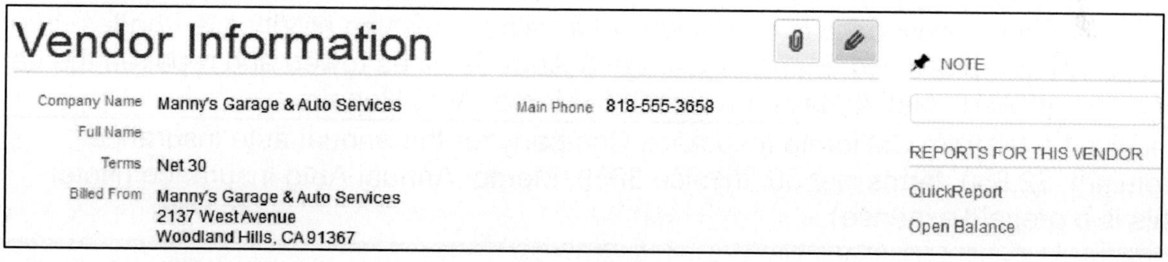

ACCRUAL METHOD OF ACCOUNTING

The accrual method of accounting matches the expenses of a period against the revenue of the period. Frequently, when in training, there may be difficulty in determining whether something is recorded as an expense or as an asset (a prepaid expense). When you buy or pay for something in advance that will eventually be an expense for operating the business, it is recorded as an increase to an asset rather than an increase to an expense.

When you have an expense that is paid for in advance, such as insurance, it is called a prepaid expense. At the time the prepaid asset is used (such as using one month of the six months of insurance shown in the Prepaid Insurance account), an adjusting entry is made to account for the amount used during the period. This adjusting entry will be made in Chapter 4.

Unless otherwise instructed in a transaction, use the accrual basis of accounting when recording the following entries. (Notice the exception in the first transaction.)

PREPARE ADDITIONAL BILLS

MEMO **DATE:** January 19, 2015: Received a bill from Computer Professionals Magazine for a 6-month subscription. Invoice 1579-53, $74, Net 30 days,. (Enter as a Dues and Subscriptions expense.) Memo: Six-Month Subscription
Alhandra Cruz received office supplies from Supply Station, Invoice 8950, $450, terms Net 10 days. (Note: After you enter the vendor's name, the information from the previous bill appears on the screen. As you enter the transaction, simply delete any unnecessary information. This may be done by tabbing to the information and pressing the delete key until the information is deleted. Or you may drag through the information to highlight, and press the Delete key. After the "old" information is deleted, enter the new information. If the amount of $450 doesn't show on the Expenses tab automatically, simply enter $450 in the Amount Column. You will need to delete information on the second line of Expenses.) These supplies will be used over a period of several months so record the entry in the asset account Office Supplies. Memo: Supplies to have on hand
While Jennifer Lockwood was on her way to a training session at Vines & Rhodes, the company car broke down. Manny's Garage & Auto Services towed and repaired the car for a total of $575, Net 30 days, Invoice 630, Memo: Auto Repairs
Received a bill from California Insurance Company for the annual auto insurance premium, $2,850, terms Net 30, Invoice 3659, Memo: Annual Auto Insurance (Note: This is a prepaid expense)

Enter the four transactions in the memo

- Refer to the instructions given for the two previous transactions entered.
- Remember, the Vendor's Invoice Number is entered for the REF. NO.
- When recording bills, you will need to determine the accounts used in the transaction. Refer to the Chart of Accounts/General Ledger for account names.
- If a memo is required for a bill, enter it in the vendor (top) section and in the detail (lower) section of the bill.
- To go from one bill to the next, click the **Save & New** button.
- Do not change terms for any of the vendors.
- After entering the fourth bill, click **Save & Close**.

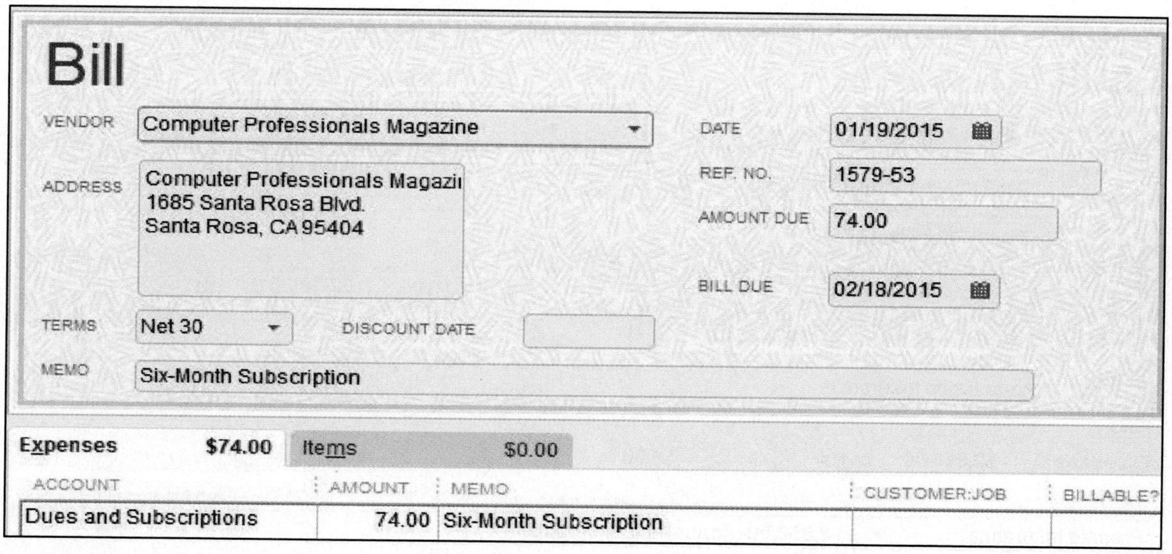

Bill

VENDOR: Computer Professionals Magazine
DATE: 01/19/2015
ADDRESS: Computer Professionals Magazi
1685 Santa Rosa Blvd.
Santa Rosa, CA 95404
REF. NO.: 1579-53
AMOUNT DUE: 74.00
BILL DUE: 02/18/2015
TERMS: Net 30
DISCOUNT DATE:
MEMO: Six-Month Subscription

Expenses $74.00 | Items $0.00

ACCOUNT	AMOUNT	MEMO	CUSTOMER:JOB	BILLABLE?
Dues and Subscriptions	74.00	Six-Month Subscription		

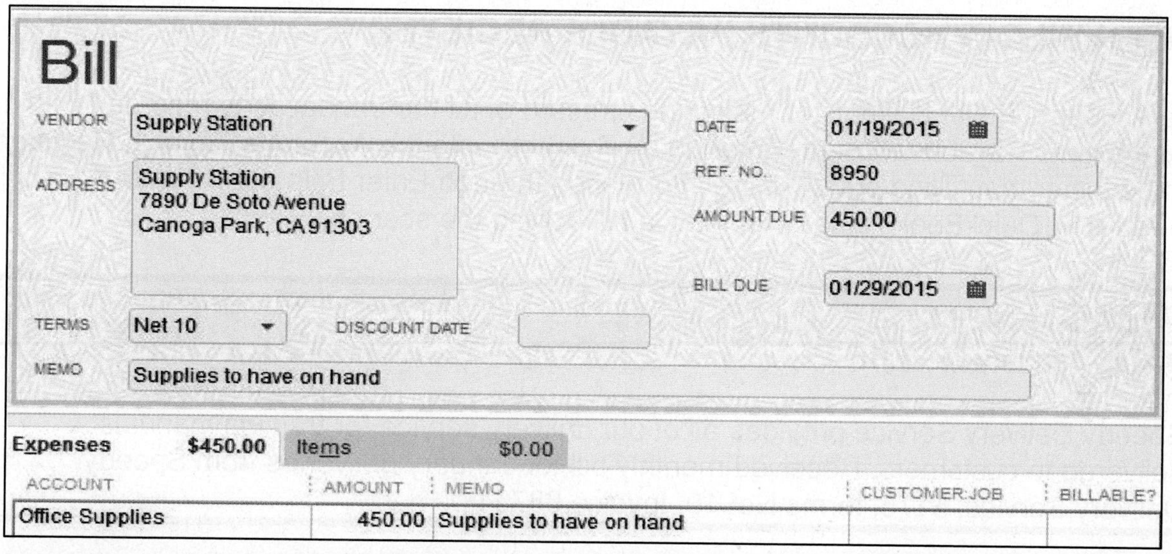

Bill

VENDOR: Supply Station
DATE: 01/19/2015
ADDRESS: Supply Station
7890 De Soto Avenue
Canoga Park, CA 91303
REF. NO.: 8950
AMOUNT DUE: 450.00
BILL DUE: 01/29/2015
TERMS: Net 10
DISCOUNT DATE:
MEMO: Supplies to have on hand

Expenses $450.00 | Items $0.00

ACCOUNT	AMOUNT	MEMO	CUSTOMER:JOB	BILLABLE?
Office Supplies	450.00	Supplies to have on hand		

3

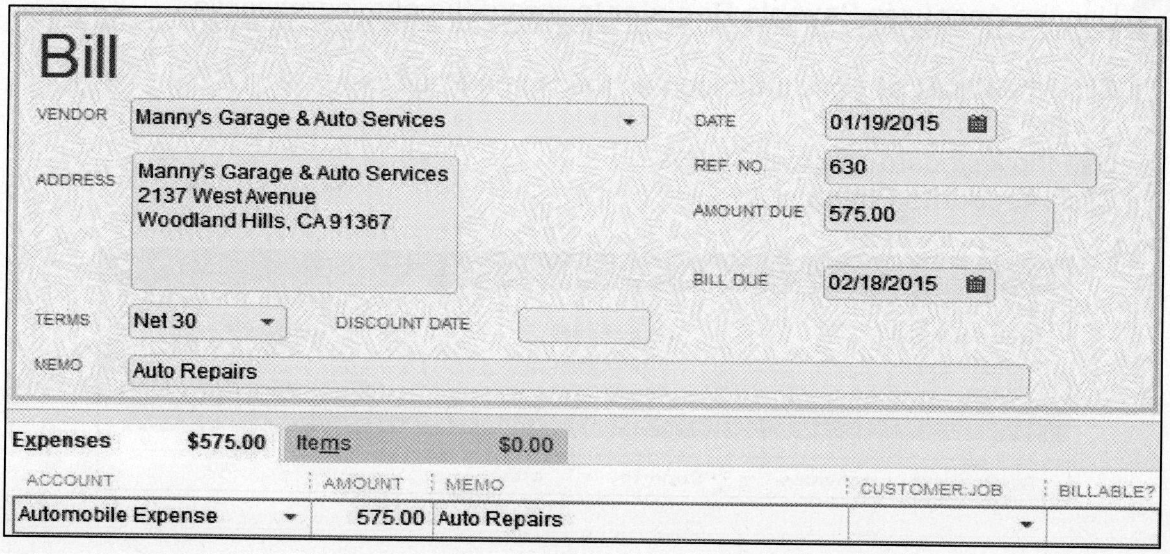

Bill

VENDOR: Manny's Garage & Auto Services
DATE: 01/19/2015
ADDRESS: Manny's Garage & Auto Services
2137 West Avenue
Woodland Hills, CA 91367
REF. NO.: 630
AMOUNT DUE: 575.00
BILL DUE: 02/18/2015
TERMS: Net 30
DISCOUNT DATE:
MEMO: Auto Repairs

Expenses $575.00 | Items $0.00

ACCOUNT	AMOUNT	MEMO	CUSTOMER:JOB	BILLABLE?
Automobile Expense	575.00	Auto Repairs		

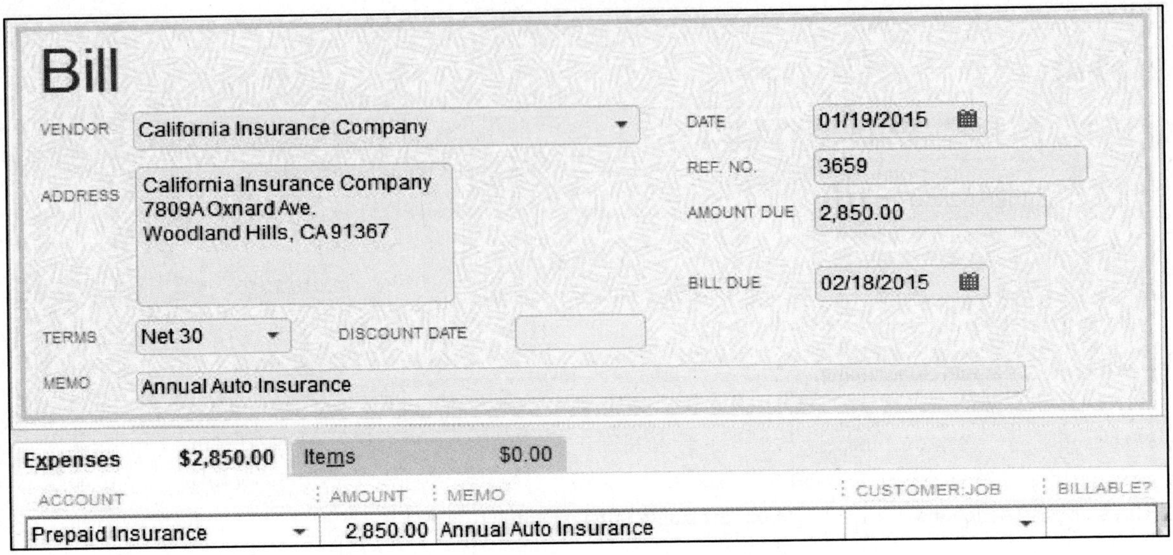

ENTER BILL IN ACCOUNTS PAYABLE REGISTER

The Accounts Payable Register maintains a record of all the transactions recorded within the Accounts Payable account. Entering a bill directly into the Accounts Payable Register can be faster than filling out all of the information through Enter Bills. When entering a bill in the register, QuickBooks also completes a bill behind the scenes.

MEMO
DATE: January 19, 2015

Speedy Delivery Service provides all of our delivery service for training manuals delivered to customers. Received monthly bill for January deliveries from Speedy Delivery Service, $175, terms Net 10, Invoice 88764.

Use the **Accounts Payable Register** to record the above transaction

Click the **Chart of Accounts** icon on the Home Page
OR
Use the keyboard shortcut **Ctrl+A**
Click **Accounts Payable**

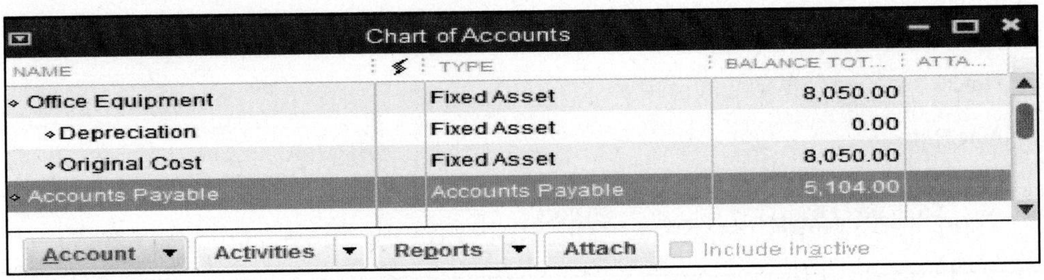

Click the **Activities** button at the bottom of the Chart of Accounts
Click **Use Register**
    OR
Use the keyboard shortcut **Ctrl+R**

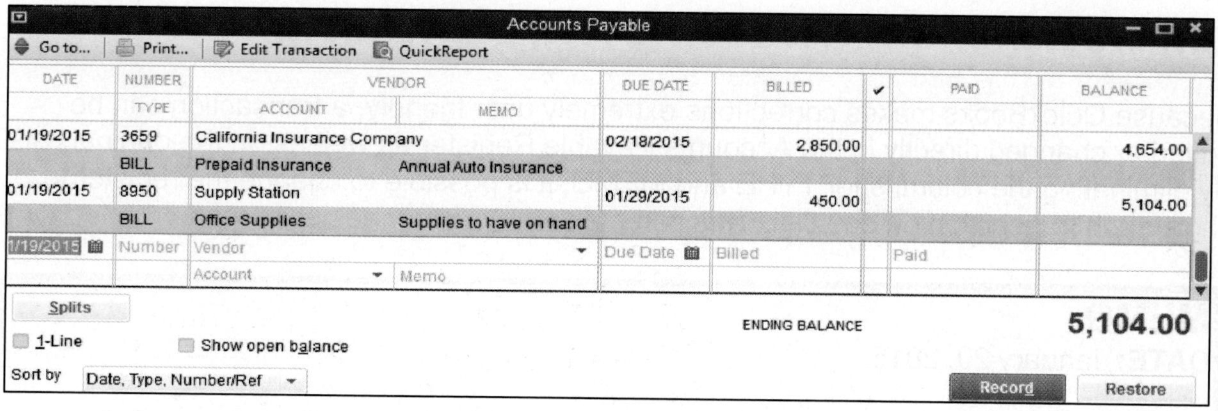

The transaction date of **01/19/2015** is highlighted in the blank entry at the end of the Accounts Payable Register

- If it is not, click in the date column in the blank entry and key in **01/19/15**.

The word *Number* is in the next column
Tab to or click in the **NUMBER** column

- The word *Number* disappears.

Enter the Invoice Number **88764**
Tab to or click in the **VENDOR** column
Click the drop-down list arrow for **VENDOR**
Click **Speedy Delivery Service**
Tab to or click in the **DUE DATE** column
Since the terms are Net 10, the DUE DATE is **01/29/2015**, enter the date if necessary

- There is no place in the register to enter the Terms. If the vendor has 30-day terms and you are using different terms, you may need to enter the Due Date.

Tab to or click in the **BILLED** column
Enter the amount **175**
Tab to or click **ACCOUNT**

- Note that “Bill” is inserted into the Type field.

Click the drop-down list arrow for **ACCOUNT**
Determine the appropriate account to use for the delivery expense

- Scroll through the accounts until you find the one appropriate for this entry.

Click **Postage and Delivery**
Tab to or click **Memo**
For the transaction memo, key **January Delivery Expense**

- If you view the bill that QuickBooks prepares when entering this transaction, you will see the memo in the Vendor (top) section of the bill but not in the Detail (lower) section of the bill.

Click the **Record** button to record the transaction

01/19/2015	88764	Speedy Delivery Service		01/29/2015	175.00		5,279.00
	BILL	Postage and Delivery	January Delivery Expense				

Do <u>not</u> close the register

EDIT TRANSACTION IN ACCOUNTS PAYABLE REGISTER

Because QuickBooks makes corrections extremely user friendly, a transaction can be edited or changed directly in the Accounts Payable Register as well as on the original bill. By eliminating the columns for TYPE and MEMO, it is possible to change the register to show each transaction on one line. This can make the register easier to read.

MEMO
DATE: January 20, 2015

Upon examination of the invoices and the bills entered, Alhandra Cruz discovers two errors: The actual amount of the invoice for Speedy Delivery Services was $195. The amount recorded was $175. The amount of the Invoice for *Computer Professionals Magazine* was $79, not $74. Change the transaction amounts for these transactions.

Correct the above transactions in the Accounts Payable Register

Click the check box for **1-line** to select
- Each Accounts Payable transaction will appear on one line.

Click the transaction for *Speedy Delivery Service*
Click between the **1** and **7** in the BILLED column for the transaction
Press **Delete** to delete the 7, type **9**
- The amount should be **195.00**.

Scroll through the register until the transaction for *Computer Professionals Magazine* is visible
Click the transaction for *Computer Professionals Magazine*
The **Recording Transaction** dialog box appears on the screen

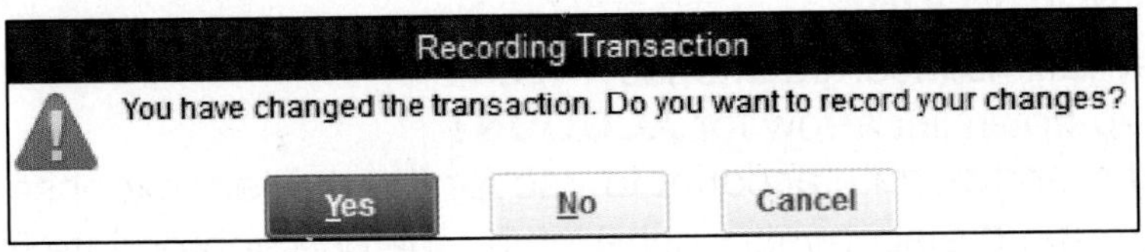

Click **Yes** to record the changes to the Speedy Delivery Service transaction
- The transaction for *Computer Professionals Magazine* will be the active transaction.

Click between the **4** and the **decimal point** in the BILLED column
Press the **Backspace** key one time to delete the 4, type **9**
- The amount for the transaction should be **79.00**.

3

Click the **Record** button at the bottom of the register to record the change in the transaction

Click **Yes** on the Recording Transaction Dialog Box

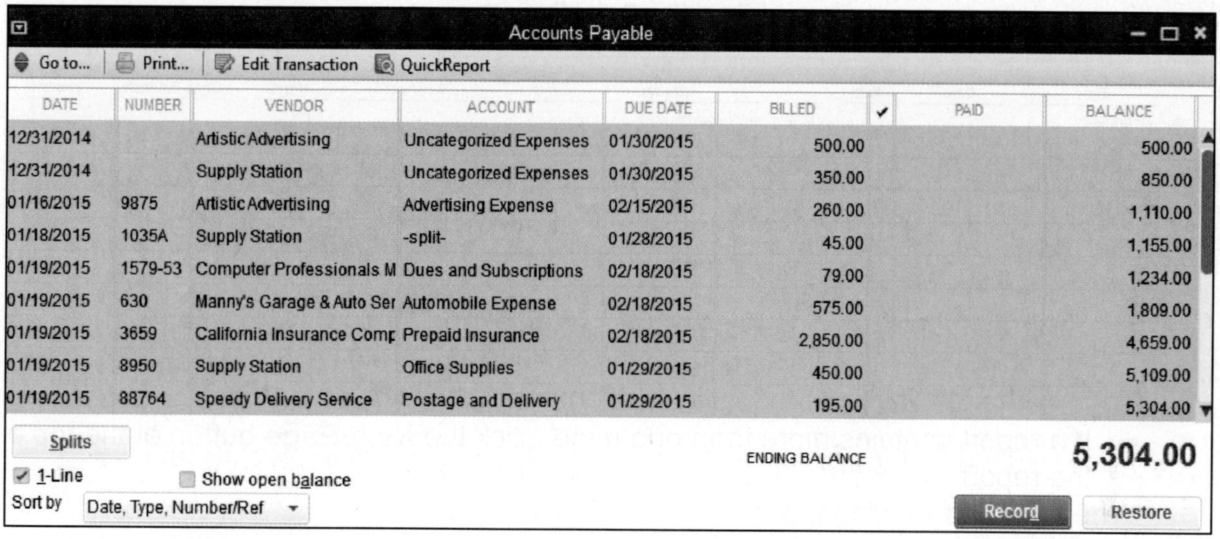

DATE	NUMBER	VENDOR	ACCOUNT	DUE DATE	BILLED	✔	PAID	BALANCE
12/31/2014		Artistic Advertising	Uncategorized Expenses	01/30/2015	500.00			500.00
12/31/2014		Supply Station	Uncategorized Expenses	01/30/2015	350.00			850.00
01/16/2015	9875	Artistic Advertising	Advertising Expense	02/15/2015	260.00			1,110.00
01/18/2015	1035A	Supply Station	-split-	01/28/2015	45.00			1,155.00
01/19/2015	1579-53	Computer Professionals M	Dues and Subscriptions	02/18/2015	79.00			1,234.00
01/19/2015	630	Manny's Garage & Auto Ser	Automobile Expense	02/18/2015	575.00			1,809.00
01/19/2015	3659	California Insurance Comp	Prepaid Insurance	02/18/2015	2,850.00			4,659.00
01/19/2015	8950	Supply Station	Office Supplies	01/29/2015	450.00			5,109.00
01/19/2015	88764	Speedy Delivery Service	Postage and Delivery	01/29/2015	195.00			5,304.00

Do not close the register

PREPARE REGISTER QUICKREPORT

After editing a transaction, you may want to view information about a specific vendor. This can be done quickly and efficiently by clicking the vendor's name within a transaction and then clicking the QuickReport button at the top of the Register.

MEMO
DATE: January 20, 2015

Several transactions have been entered for Supply Station. You like to view transaction information for all vendors that have several transactions within a short period of time.

Prepare a QuickReport for Supply Station

Click any field in any transaction for *Supply Station*

Click the **QuickReport** button at the top of the Register 

- The Register QuickReport for All Transactions for Supply Station appears on the screen.

Remove the **Date Prepared**, **Time Prepared**, and **Report Basis** as previously instructed

Resize any columns that are not fully displayed and make the Amount column smaller

Click the **Print** button, click **Report**

Select **Landscape** orientation

Click **Preview** to view the report before printing

Computer Consulting by Your Name
Register QuickReport
All Transactions

Type	Date	Num	Memo	Account	Paid	Open Balance	Amount
Supply Station							
Bill	12/31/2014		Opening balance	Accounts Payable	Unpaid	350.00	350.00
Bill	01/18/2015	1035A	Fax Rental and Fax Supplies for the Month	Accounts Payable	Unpaid	45.00	45.00
Bill	01/19/2015	8950	Supplies to have on hand	Accounts Payable	Unpaid	450.00	450.00
Total Supply Station						845.00	845.00
TOTAL						845.00	845.00

- The report appears on the screen as a full page.
- Sometimes, a full-page report on the screen cannot be read.

To read the text in the report, click the report page shown

- If a report contains more than one page, click the **Next Page** button at the top of the report.

When finished viewing the report, click **Close**

- You will return to the **Print Reports** screen.

After resizing, the report should fit on one page; if it doesn't keep resizing or click **Fit report to one page wide** to select

Click **Print** button on the **Print Reports** screen

Close the **Register QuickReport**, the **Accounts Payable Register**, and the **Chart of Accounts**

PREPARE UNPAID BILLS DETAIL REPORT

It is possible to get information regarding unpaid bills by simply preparing a report—no more digging through tickler files, recorded invoices, ledgers, or journals. QuickBooks prepares an Unpaid Bills Report listing each unpaid bill grouped and subtotaled by vendor.

MEMO

DATE: January 25, 2015

Alhandra Cruz prepares an Unpaid Bills Report for you each week. Even though Computer Consulting by Your Name is a small business, you like to have a firm control over cash flow so you determine which bills will be paid during the week.

Prepare and print an Unpaid Bills Report

Click **Unpaid Bills Detail** in the **Vendors & Payables** list on the Reports Menu

OR

Click **Reports** on the Top Icon Bar, click **Vendors & Payables**, and double-click **Unpaid Bills Detail** in the Vendor Balances section of the Report Center

Remove the Date Prepared and Time Prepared from the report header
Provide the report date by clicking in the text box for **Dates**, dragging through the date to highlight, and typing **01/25/15**
Tab to generate the report

Computer Consulting by Your Name
Unpaid Bills Detail
As of January 25, 2015

Type	Date	Num	Due Date	Aging	Open Balance
Artistic Advertising					
Bill	12/31/2014		01/30/2015		500.00 ◀
Bill	01/16/2015	9875	02/15/2015		260.00
Total Artistic Advertising					760.00
California Insurance Company					
Bill	01/19/2015	3659	02/18/2015		2,850.00
Total California Insurance Company					2,850.00
Computer Professionals Magazine					
Bill	01/19/2015	1579-53	02/18/2015		79.00
Total Computer Professionals Magazine					79.00
Manny's Garage & Auto Services					
Bill	01/19/2015	630	02/18/2015		575.00
Total Manny's Garage & Auto Services					575.00
Speedy Delivery Service					
Bill	01/19/2015	88764	01/29/2015		195.00
Total Speedy Delivery Service					195.00
Supply Station					
Bill	01/18/2015	1035A	01/28/2015		45.00
Bill	01/19/2015	8950	01/29/2015		450.00
Bill	12/31/2014		01/30/2015		350.00
Total Supply Station					845.00
TOTAL					**5,304.00**

Adjust column widths as necessary and print in **Portrait** orientation

- Notice that the bills for each vendor are organized by Due Date rather than the date of the transaction.

Click **Close** to close the report
Click **No** if you get a Memorize Report dialog box
If necessary, click **Close** to close the **Report Center**

DELETE BILL

QuickBooks makes it possible to delete any bill that has been recorded. No adjusting entries are required in order to do this. Simply access the bill or go to the transaction in the Accounts Payable Register and delete the bill.

> **MEMO**
> **DATE:** January 26, 2015
>
> After reviewing the Unpaid Bills Report, Alhandra realizes that the bill recorded for *Computer Professionals Magazine* should have been recorded for *Computer Technologies Magazine*.

➔ Delete the bill recorded for Computer Professionals Magazine

Access the Chart of Accounts:

Click the **Chart of Accounts** icon on the Home Page

OR

Use the keyboard shortcut **Ctrl+A**

OR

Use the menu bar, click **Lists**, and click **Chart of Accounts**

With the Chart of Accounts showing on the screen, click **Accounts Payable**

Open the Accounts Payable Register:

Use keyboard shortcut **Ctrl+R**

OR

Click **Activities Button**, click **Use Register**

Click on the bill for *Computer Professionals Magazine*

To delete the bill:

Click **Edit** on the QuickBooks menu bar, click **Delete Bill**

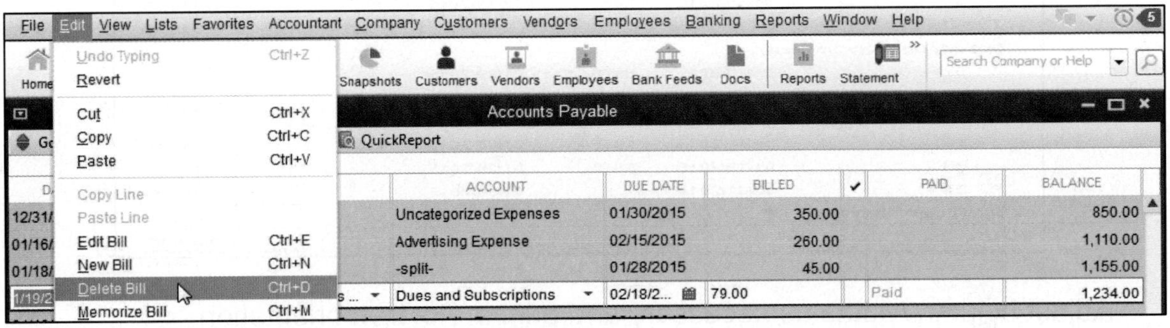

OR

Use the keyboard shortcut **Ctrl+D**

- The **Delete Transaction** dialog box appears on the screen.

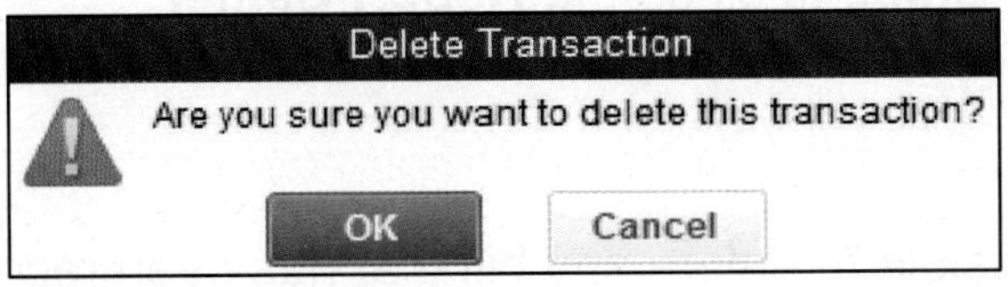

Click **OK** to delete the bill

- Notice that the transaction no longer appears in the Accounts Payable Register and that the Ending Balance of the account is 5,225.00 rather than 5,304.00.

Close the **Accounts Payable Register**

Close the **Chart of Accounts**

ADD VENDOR WHILE RECORDING BILL

When you type the first letter(s) of a vendor name on the Vendor Line, QuickBooks tries to match the name to one in the Vendor List and enter it on the Vendor line. If the vendor is not in the Vendor List, a QuickBooks dialog box for Vendor Not Found appears with choices for a Quick Add—adding just the vendor name—or Set Up—adding the vendor name and all vendor account information. When the new vendor information is complete, QuickBooks fills in the blanks on the bill for the vendor, and you finish entering the rest of the transaction.

MEMO

DATE: January 26, 2015

Record the bill for a six-month subscription to *Computer Technologies Magazine*. The transaction date is 01/19/15, amount $79, Terms Net 30, Invoice 1579-53. This is recorded as an expense. The address and telephone for *Computer Technologies Magazine* is 12405 Menlo Park Drive, Menlo Park, CA 94025, 510-555-3829.

Record the above transaction

Access the **Enter Bills** screen

- Step-by-step instructions will be provided only for entering a new vendor.
- Refer to transactions previously recorded for all other steps used in entering a bill.
- When you key the first few letters of a vendor name, QuickBooks will automatically enter a vendor name.

On the line for VENDOR, type the **C** for *Computer Technologies Magazine*

- The vendor name **Cal Water** appears on the vendor line and is highlighted and the list of Vendor names that start with C is displayed.

Type **omp**

- The vendor name changes to **Computer Professionals Magazine**.

Finish typing **uter Technologies Magazine**

- The entire Vendor List is displayed.

Press **Tab**

The **Vendor Not Found** dialog box appears on the screen with buttons for:

- **Quick Add**—adds only the name to the vendor list.
- **Set Up**—adds the name to the vendor list and allows all account information to be entered.
- **Cancel**—cancels the addition of a new vendor.

Click **Set Up**

- Computer Technologies Magazine is shown in the VENDOR NAME text box.

If necessary, highlight the VENDOR NAME in the VENDOR NAME text box

Copy the name to the Company Name textbox by using the **Ctrl+C** keyboard shortcut for copy

Click in the COMPANY NAME textbox and use **Ctrl+V** to paste the name into the textbox

- Since this is a new vendor, notice that there is no OPENING BALANCE to enter.

Tab to or click in the text box for **Main Phone**

Enter the telephone number **510-555-3829**

Tab to or click the first line for **BILLED FROM** in the **ADDRESS DETAILS** section

- Computer Technologies Magazine appears as the first line in the address.

Position the cursor at the end of the name, press **Enter** or click the line beneath the company name (Do not tab)

Type the address listed in the Memo

Press **Enter** at the end of each line

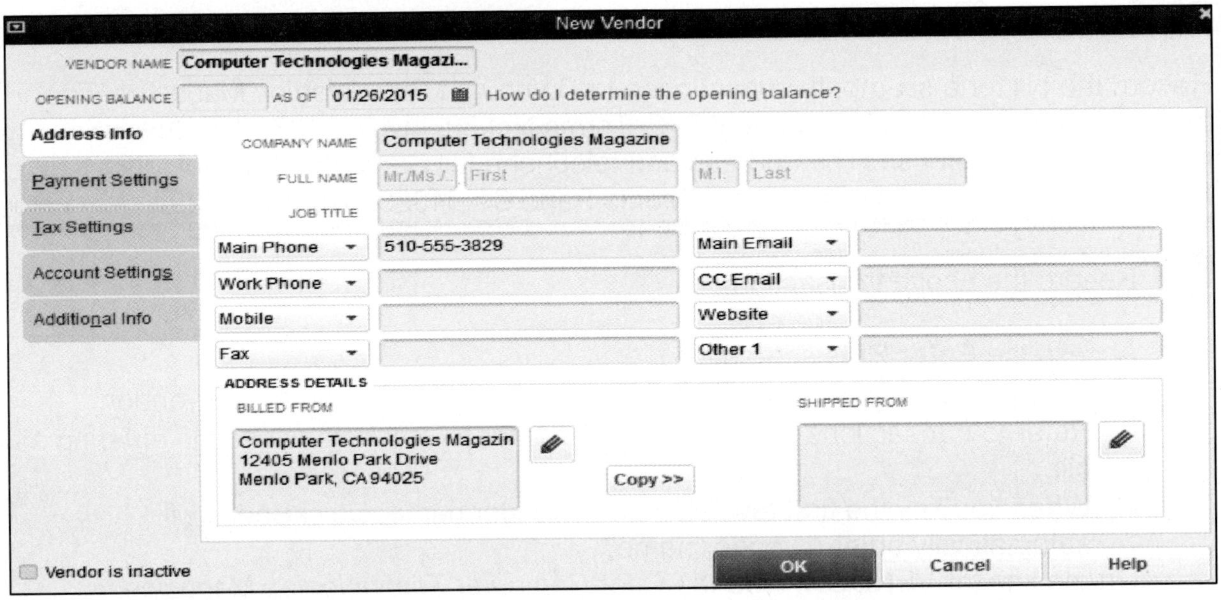

To enter the information for Terms, click the **Payment Settings** tab on the left side of the New Vendor screen

Click drop-down list arrow next to **PAYMENT TERMS**

Click **Net 30**

Make sure **PRINT NAME ON CHECK AS** shows **Computer Technologies Magazine**

- If not enter the name.

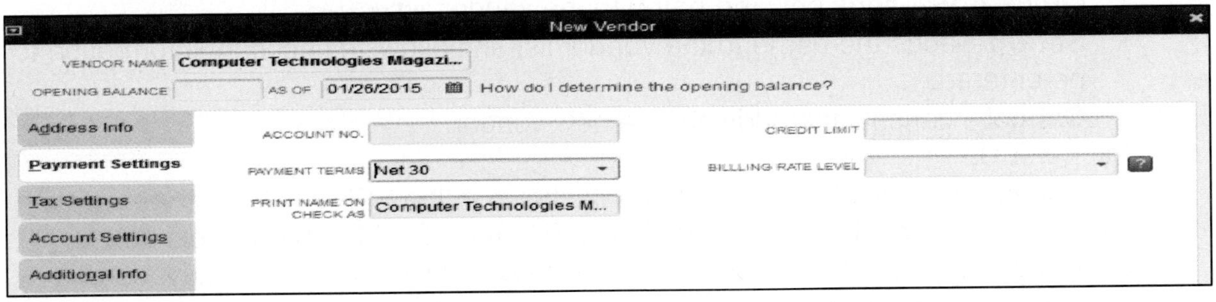

Click the **OK** button for **New Vendor** screen

- The information for Vendor, Terms, and the Dates is filled in on the Enter Bills screen.

If necessary, change the transaction date to **01/19/15**

Complete the bill using the information in the Memo and the instructions previously provided for entering bills

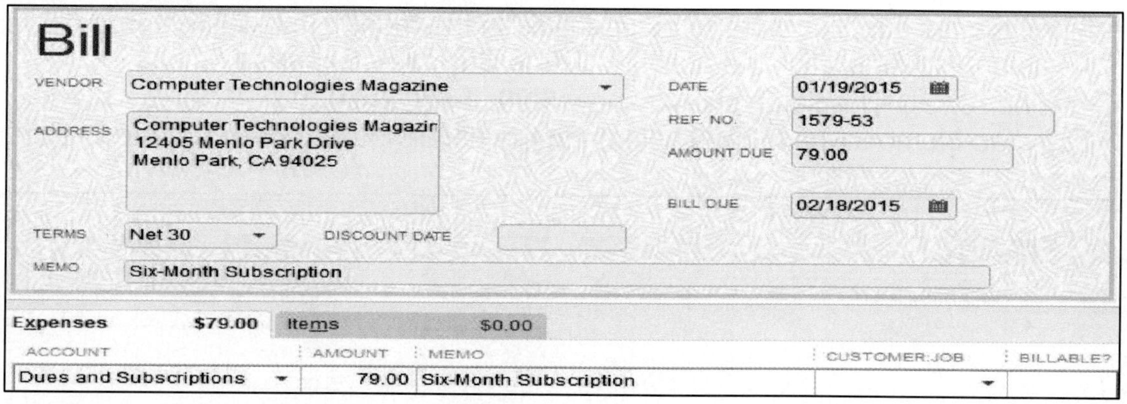

When finished, click **Save & Close** to close the bill and exit

ENTER VENDOR CREDIT

Credit memos are prepared to record a reduction to a transaction. With QuickBooks, you use the Enter Bills window to record credit memos received from vendors acknowledging a return of or an allowance for a previously recorded bill and/or payment. The amount of a credit memo is deducted from the amount owed.

MEMO
DATE: January 26, 2015

Received Credit Memo 789 for $5 from Supply Station for a return of fax paper that was damaged.

Record a credit memo

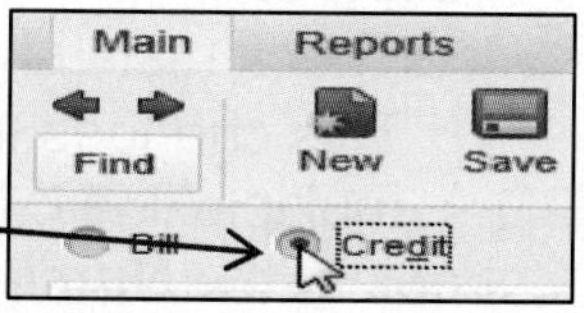

Access the **Enter Bills** window as previously instructed
On the **Enter Bills** screen, click **Credit** to select
- Notice that the word *Bill* changes to *Credit*.

Click the drop-down list arrow next to **VENDOR**
Click **Supply Station**
Tab to or click the **DATE**
Type **01/26/15**
Tab to or click **REF. NO.**
Type **789**
Tab to or click **CREDIT AMOUNT**
Type **5**
Tab to or click in **MEMO** in the vendor (upper) section of the Credit
Enter **Returned Damaged Fax Paper**
Tab to or click the first line of **ACCOUNT**
Click the drop-down list arrow

Since the fax supplies were to be used within the month, this was entered originally as an expense, click the account **Office Supplies Expense**

- The AMOUNT column should show **5.00**; if not, enter **5**.

Copy the Memo to the **MEMO** column in the detail (lower) section of the Credit

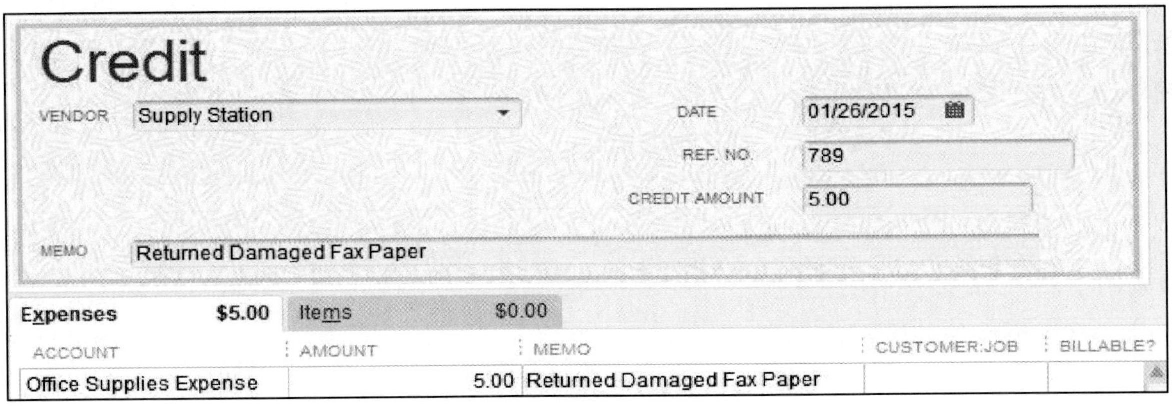

Click **Save & Close** to record the credit and exit **Enter Bills**

- QuickBooks records the credit in the Accounts Payable account and shows the transaction type as BILLCRED in the Accounts Payable Register.

VIEW CREDIT IN ACCOUNTS PAYABLE REGISTER

When recording the credit in the last transaction, QuickBooks listed the transaction type as BILLCRED in the Accounts Payable Register.

Verify the credit from Supply Station

Follow steps previously provided to access the Accounts Payable Register

If a check mark shows in the **1-Line** check box, remove it by clicking the check box

- This changes the display in the Accounts Payable Register from 1-Line to multiple lines.

Look at the **Number/Type** column and verify the type **BILLCRED**

- Notice the balance of 5,299.00. The balance of Accounts Payable after the bill for Computer Technologies Magazine was entered was 5,304.00. The new balance of 5,299.00 is 5.00 less, which is the amount of the credit.

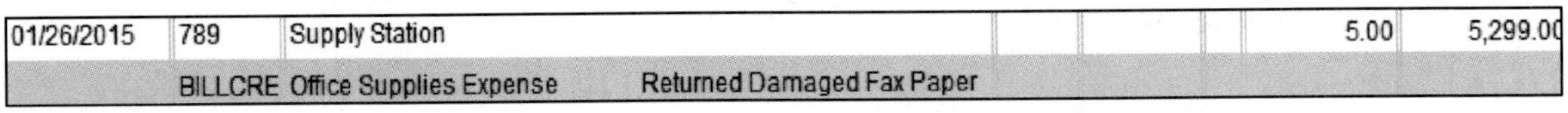

Close the **Accounts Payable Register**

Close the **Chart of Accounts**

PREPARE DAILY BACKUP

A backup file is prepared as a safeguard in case you make an error. After a number of transactions have been recorded, it is wise to prepare a backup file. In addition, a backup should be made at the end of every work session. As you learned in Chapters 1 and 2, the Daily Backup file is an important file to create for saving your work as you progress through a chapter.

If you have created a daily backup file while you are working in a chapter and make an error later in your training and cannot figure out how to correct it, you may restore the backup file. Restoring your daily backup file will restore your work from the previous training session and eliminate the work completed in the current session. By creating the backup file now, it will contain your work for Chapters 1, 2 and up through entering the Credit Memo in Chapter 3.

Prepare the Computer (Daily Backup).qbb file

Follow the steps presented in Chapter 1 for creating a backup file
Name the file **Computer (Daily Backup)**
The file type is **QBW Backup (* .QBB)**

- This uses the same backup file that you prepared in Chapter 2.
- The daily backup file will now contain the work from Chapters 1 and 2 plus Chapter 3 up through entering the credit for a vendor.

PAY BILLS

When using QuickBooks, you should pay any bills entered through "Enter Bills" directly from the pay bills command and let QuickBooks write your checks for you. QuickBooks will mark the bills "Paid." If you have recorded a bill for a transaction and write the check for payment yourself, the bill will not be marked as being paid and will continue to show up as an amount due. If you have not entered a bill for an amount you owe, you will need to write the check yourself

Using the Pay Bills window enables you to determine which bills to pay, the method of payment—check or credit card—and the appropriate account. When determining which bills to pay, QuickBooks allows you to display the bills by due date, discount date, vendor, or amount. All bills may be displayed, or only those bills that are due by a certain date may be displayed.

MEMO
DATE: January 26, 2015

Whenever possible, Alhandra pays the bills on a weekly basis. With the Pay Bills window showing the bills due for payment on or before 01/31/2015, Alhandra compares the bills shown with the Unpaid Bills Report previously prepared. The report has been marked by you to indicate which bills should be paid. Alhandra will select the bills for payment and record the bill payment for the week.

Pay the bills for the week

Click the **Pay Bills** icon in the Vendors section of the Home Page to access the **Pay Bills** window

- The Pay Bills screen is comprised of three sections: SELECT BILLS TO BE PAID, DISCOUNT & CREDIT INFORMATION FOR HIGHLIGHTED BILL, and PAYMENT.

Complete the SELECT BILLS TO BE PAID section:

If necessary, click **Show All Bills** to select

Click the drop-down list arrow for Filter By, click **All vendors**

Sort By should be **Due Date**

- If this is not showing, click the drop-down list arrow next to the **Sort By** text box, click **Due Date**.

Scroll through the list of bills

Click the drop-down list arrow next to the **Sort By** text box

Click **Vendor**

- This shows you how much you owe each vendor.

Again, click the drop-down list arrow next to the **Sort By** text box

Click **Amount Due**

- This shows you your bills from the highest amount owed to the lowest.

Click drop-down list arrow next to the **Sort By** text box, click **Due Date**

- The bills will be shown according to the date due.

Click **Due on or before** in the Select Bills to be Paid section For Show Bills to select this option

Click in the text box for the date

Drag through the date to highlight, enter **01/31/15** as the date, press **Tab**

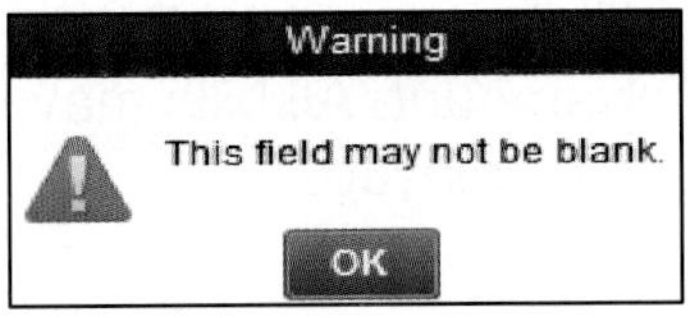

- Since you pressed Tab after making a change to **Show Bills**, you must select **Filter By** or you will get a warning message. If this happens, click **OK**.

Click the drop-down list arrow on **Filter By**. Select **All Vendors**.

Scroll through the list of bills due

Select the bills to be paid

- The bills shown on the screen are an exact match to the bills you marked to be paid when you reviewed the Unpaid Bills Report.

Click the **Select All Bills** button beneath the listing of bills

- The **Select All Bills** button changes to **Clear Selections** so bills can be unmarked and the bills to be paid may be selected again.
- If you do not want to pay all of the bills shown, mark each bill to be paid by clicking on the individual bill or using the down-cursor key to select a bill and then press the space bar.

To apply the **$5** credit from **Supply Station**, click in the **VENDOR** column for the **$45** transaction for Supply Station with a DUE DATE of **01/28/2015**

- This will highlight the bill and leave the check in the check box for selecting the bill. If you click the check box and remove the check mark, you will need to click the check box a second time to mark the bill as being selected.

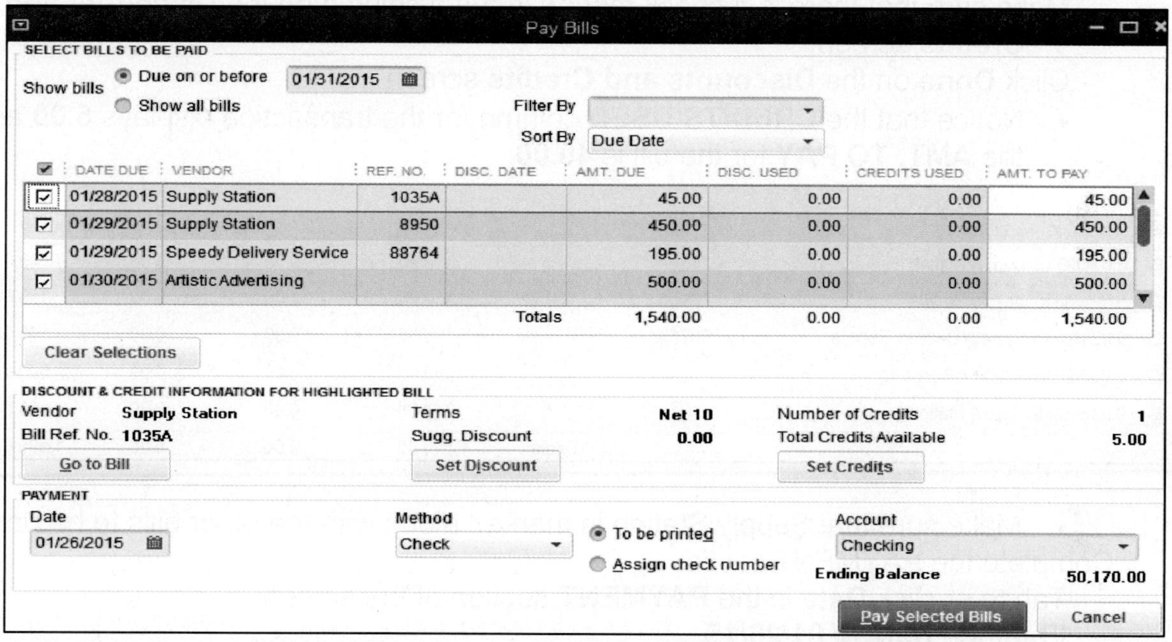

Complete the DISCOUNT & CREDIT INFORMATION FOR HIGHLIGHTED BILL section:

The **Vendor** is **Supply Station**

The Number of **Credits** is **1**

Total Credits Available is **$5.00**

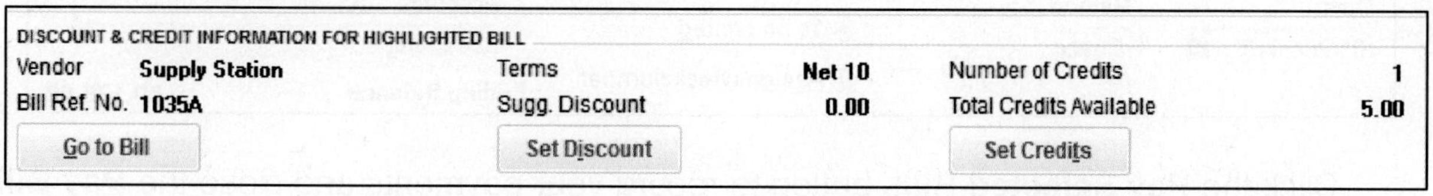

Click the **Set Credits** button

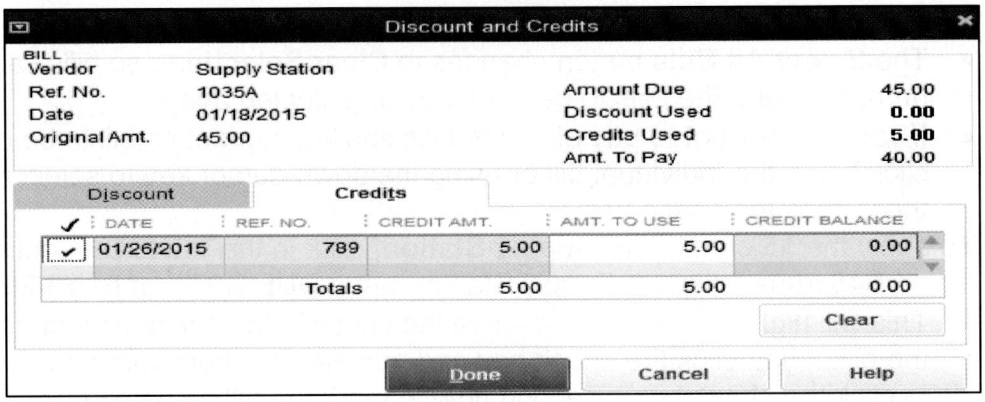

Make sure that there is a check mark √ in the √ column on the **Discounts and Credits** screen

Click **Done** on the **Discounts and Credits** screen

- Notice that the **CREDITS USED** column for the transaction displays **5.00** and the **AMT. TO PAY** for the bill is **40.00**.

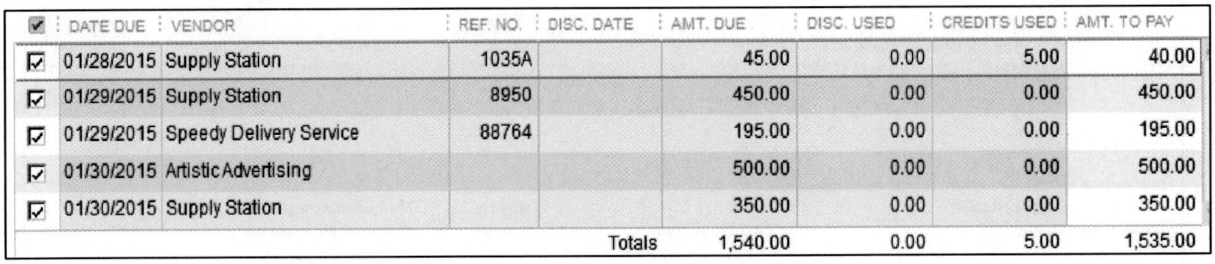

✓	DATE DUE	VENDOR	REF. NO.	DISC. DATE	AMT. DUE	DISC. USED	CREDITS USED	AMT. TO PAY
✓	01/28/2015	Supply Station	1035A		45.00	0.00	5.00	40.00
✓	01/29/2015	Supply Station	8950		450.00	0.00	0.00	450.00
✓	01/29/2015	Speedy Delivery Service	88764		195.00	0.00	0.00	195.00
✓	01/30/2015	Artistic Advertising			500.00	0.00	0.00	500.00
✓	01/30/2015	Supply Station			350.00	0.00	0.00	350.00
				Totals	1,540.00	0.00	5.00	1,535.00

- Make sure that Supply Station is marked along with the other bills to be paid.

Complete the PAYMENT section:

Tab to or click **Date** in the **PAYMENT** section of the screen

Enter the **Date** of **01/26/15**

Check should be selected as the **Method**

Make sure **To be printed** box has been selected

- If it is not selected, click in the circle to select.

The **Account** should be **Checking**

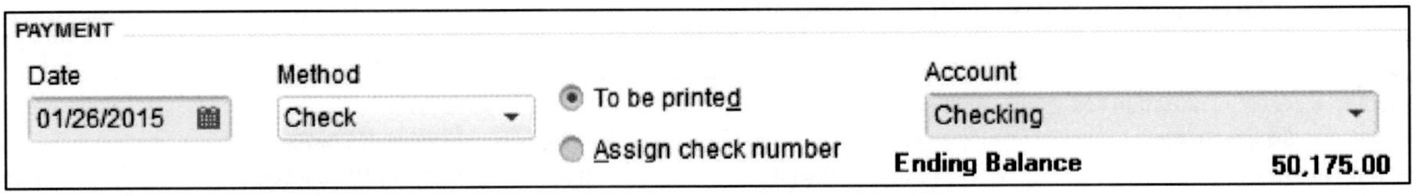

Click the **Pay Selected Bills** button to record your payments and close the **Pay Bills** window

After clicking Pay Selected Bills, you will see a Payment Summary screen

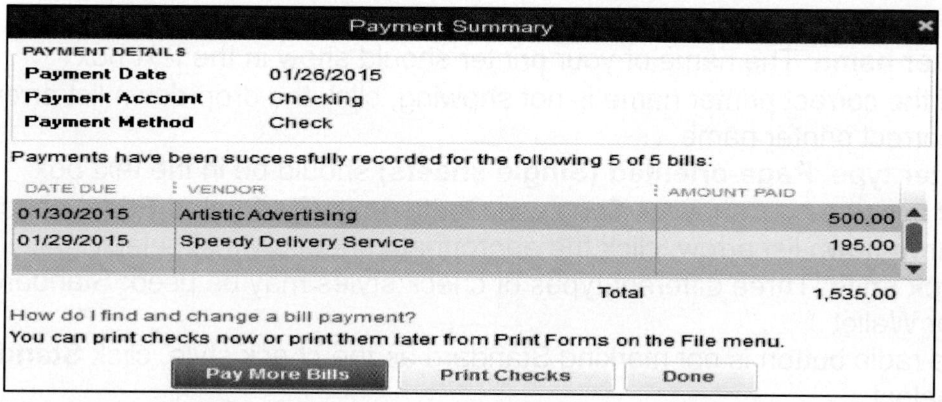

- Scroll through the Payment Summary and review the Vendors and Amounts Paid. Notice the three amounts for Supply Station of $40, $450, and $350.

Continue with the PRINTING CHECKS FOR BILLS section

PRINT CHECKS FOR BILLS

Once bills have been marked and recorded as paid, you may handwrite checks to vendors, or you may have QuickBooks print the checks to vendors. If there is more than one amount due for a vendor, QuickBooks totals the amounts due to the vendor and prints one check to the vendor.

Print the checks for the bills paid

Click **Print Checks** on the Payment Summary screen
Bank Account should be **Checking**

- If this is not showing, click the drop-down list arrow, click **Checking**.

The **First Check Number** should be **1**

- If not, delete the number showing, and key **1**.

In the √ column, the checks selected to be printed are marked with a check mark

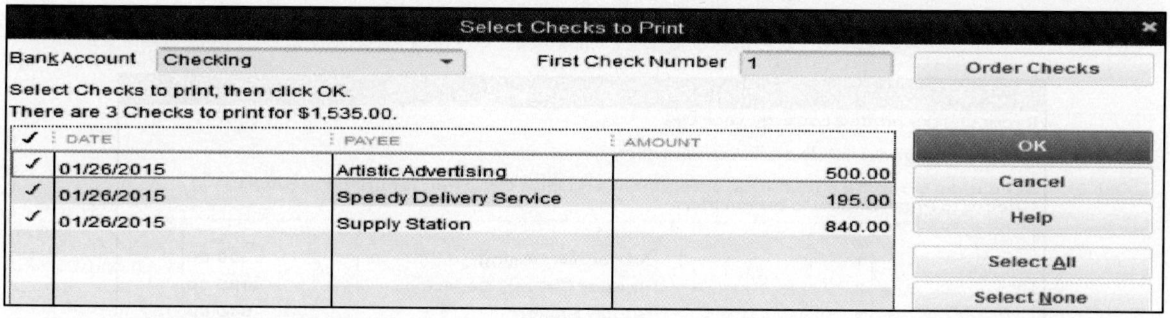

- Notice that the three bills from Supply Station have been combined into one check for payment.

Click **OK** to print the checks

- The **Print Checks** screen appears.

Verify and if necessary change information on the **Settings** tab

Printer name: The name of your printer should show in the text box

- If the correct printer name is not showing, click the drop-down list arrow, click the correct printer name.

Printer type: **Page-oriented (Single sheets)** should be in the text box

- If this does not show or if you use Continuous (Perforated Edge) checks, click the drop-down list arrow, click the appropriate sheet style to select.

Check style: Three different types of check styles may be used: Standard, Voucher, or Wallet

If the radio button is not marking Standard as the check style, click **Standard** to select

Print Company Name and Address: If the box does not have a check mark, click to select

Use Logo should not be selected; if a check mark appears in the check box, click to deselect

Print Signature Image should not have a check mark

- Notice the Number of checks on first page is 3.

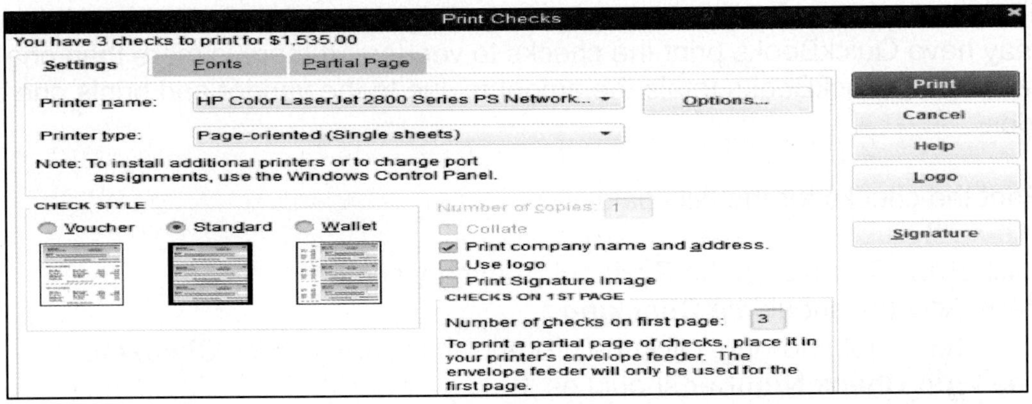

Click **Print** to print the checks

- All three checks will print on one page.

Print Checks - Confirmation dialog box appears

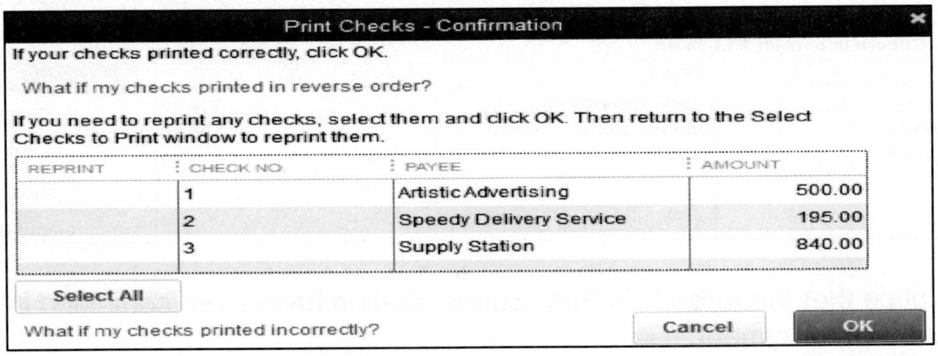

In addition to verifying the correct amount, payee, and payment date, review the checks for the following:

- The checks have the address for Computer Consulting by Your Name, the name and address of the company being paid, and the amount being paid.
- The actual checks will not have a check number printed because QuickBooks is set up to work with preprinted check forms containing check numbers.
- In the memo section of the check, any memo entered on the bill shows.
- If there was no memo entered for the bill, the vendor account number appears as the memo.
- If you cannot get the checks to print on one page, it is perfectly acceptable to access the checks by clicking the **Write Checks** icon in the Banking section of the Home Page, and printing them one at a time. This method is also useful if you need to correct a check and reprint it.

If checks **printed** correctly, click **OK**

- If the checks did not print correctly, click the checks that need to be reprinted to select, and then click **OK**. Return to the Select Checks to print window and reprint them.
- If you get a message box regarding purchasing checks, click **No**

REVIEW PAID BILLS

In order to avoid any confusion about the payment of a bill, QuickBooks marks the paid bills as PAID but does not mark credit memos that have been applied. Scrolling through the recorded bills in the Enter Bills window, you will see the marked bills.

Scroll the **Enter Bills** window to view PAID bills

Click **Enter Bills** in the Vendors section of the Home Page
Click the **Previous** or back arrow on the Bills Icon bar to go back through all of the bills recorded

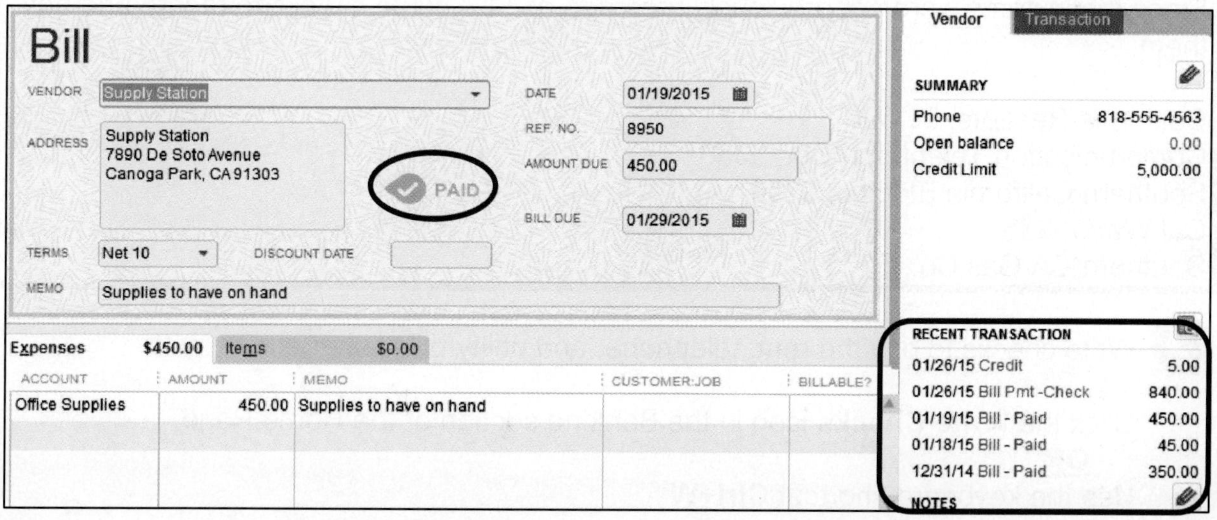

- If the History section does not display, click the History icon 
- Notice that the bills paid for Supply Station, Speedy Delivery Service, and Artistic Advertising are marked **PAID**.
- The Credit from Supply Station remains unmarked even though it has been used.
- If the Detail section columns do not display properly, point to the dotted line between column headings and resize as instructed in reports.

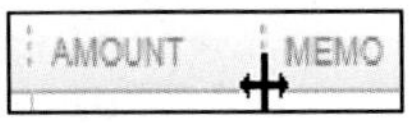

Look at the History for Supply Station

- Notice the Open Balance is 0.00. In the Recent Transaction section, all the bills have been marked paid, the Bill Pmt – Check shows, and the $5 credit shows.

Click the **Close** button

WRITE CHECKS TO PAY BILLS

Although it is more efficient to record all bills in the Enter Bills window and pay all bills through the Pay Bills window, QuickBooks also allows bills to be paid by writing a check to record and pay bills. This may be a more appropriate process for bills that you pay routinely every month. (Remember, though, if you record a bill in Enter Bills, you must use Pay Bills to write the bill payment check.) When you write a check, it is not entered as a bill in Enter Bills.

When writing a check to record a bill and its payment, you will note that the check window is divided into two main areas: the check face and the detail area. The check face includes information such as the date of the check, the payee's name, the check amount, the payee's address, and a line for a memo—just like a paper check. The detail area is used to indicate transaction accounts and amounts.

MEMO

DATE: January 30, 2015

Since these items were not previously recorded as bills, write checks to record and pay them:

California Realtors, $1,500
Communication Telephone Co., $350
Southern California Electric, $250
Cal Water, $35
Southern CA Gas Co., $175

Write checks to pay the rent, telephone, and utility bills listed above

Click the **Write Checks** icon in the Banking section of the Home Page

OR

Use the keyboard shortcut **Ctrl+W**

The BANK ACCOUNT used for the check should be **Checking**.

- The ENDING BALANCE of the Checking account is shown. This lets you know how much money is in the account before your write the check. This will not change until the check is saved.
- NO. is where the check number will be entered

NO. should show **To Print**, which means that the check will be printed later

- If 1 is showing for the check number, click the **Print Later** checkbox on the Write Checks - Checking Icon Bar.

Tab to or click **Date**

Enter **01/30/15**

To complete the check face, click the drop-down list arrow next to **PAY TO THE ORDER OF**

Click **California Realtors**

Tab to or click in the text box for **$**

Enter the amount of the rent, **1500**

Tab to or click **MEMO**

- If you do not provide a memo on the check, QuickBooks will enter an account number, a telephone number, an address, or a description as the memo.
- Since the address for Computer Consulting by Your Name is on West Avenue, leave the memo as shown.
- The memo will print on the check, not on reports.

Use the **Expenses** tab to complete the detail section of the check

Tab to or click the first line of **ACCOUNT**

Click the drop-down list arrow for **ACCOUNT**

Click the Expense account **Rent**

- The total amount of the check is shown in AMOUNT column.
- If you want a transaction description to appear in reports, enter the description in the MEMO column in the detail section of the check. Because these are standard transactions, no memo is entered.

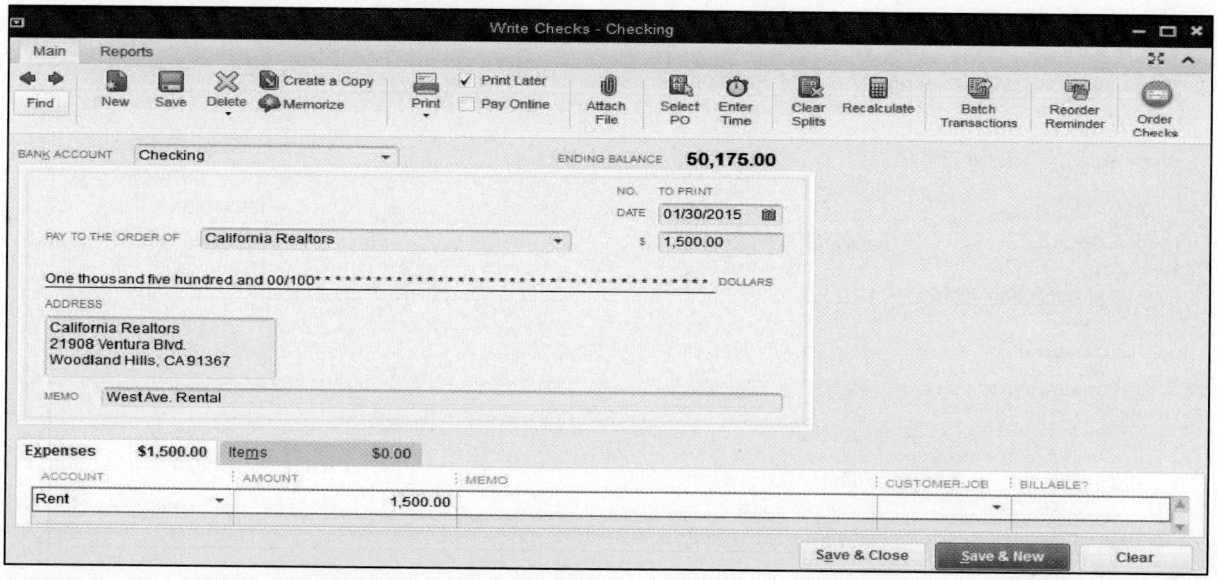

Do not print any of the checks being entered

Click the **Save & New** button or click **New** on the Check Icon bar to record the check and advance to the next check

Repeat the steps indicated above to record payment of the telephone bill and the utility bills for electricity, water, and heating (gas)

- While entering the bills, you may see a dialog box on the screen, indicating that QuickBooks allows you to do online banking. Online banking will not be used at this time. Click **OK** to close the dialog box.

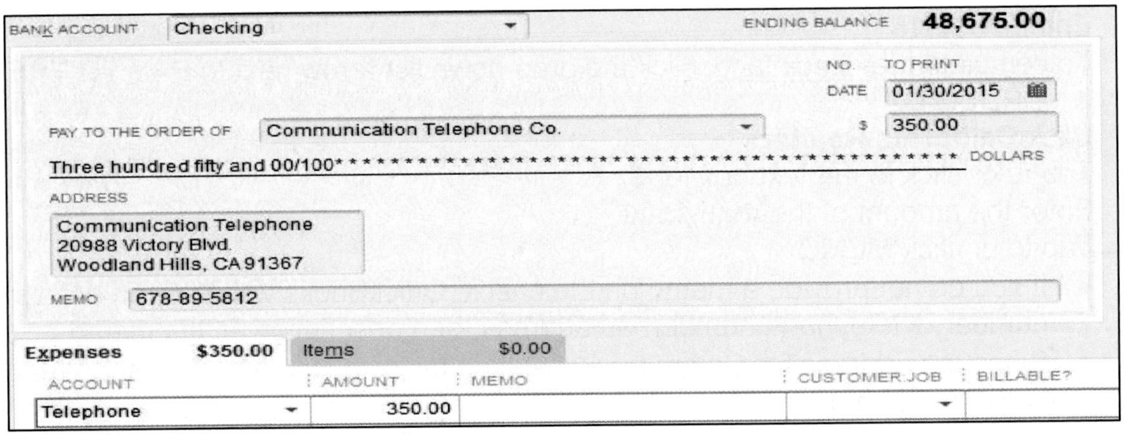

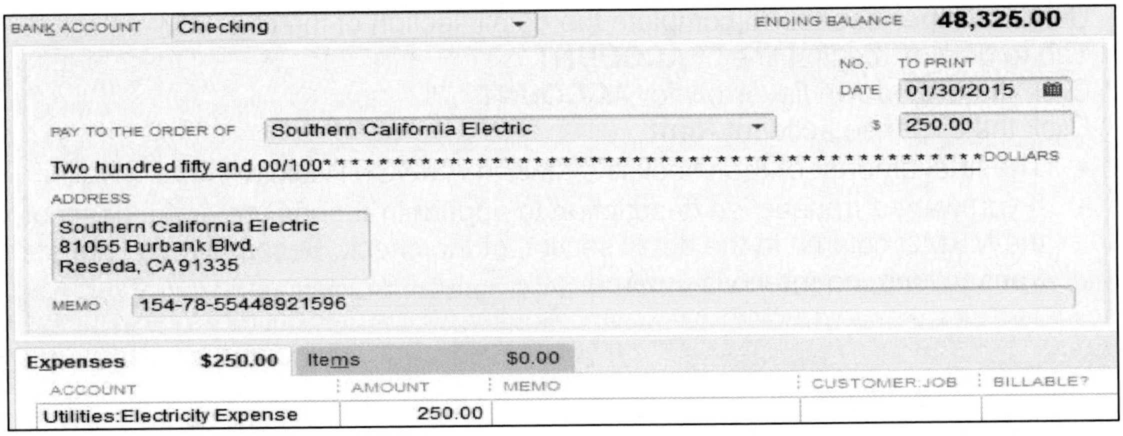

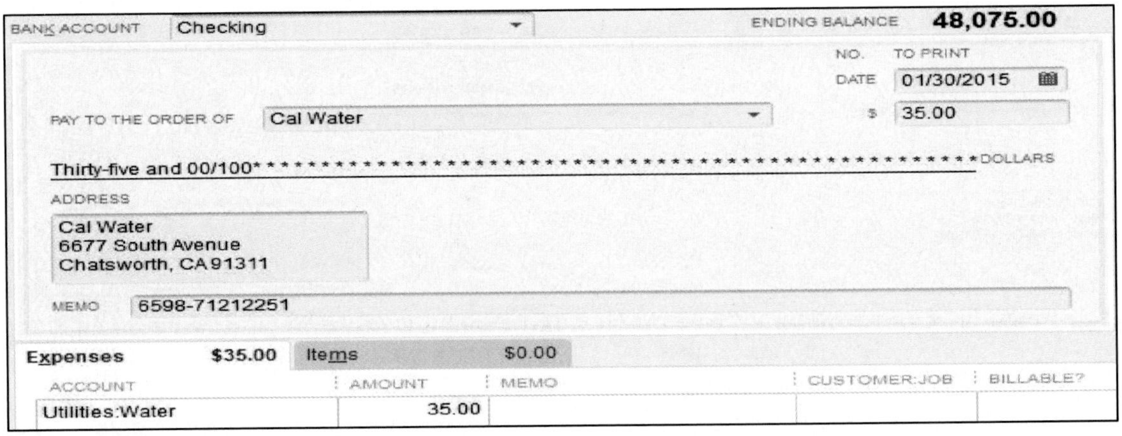

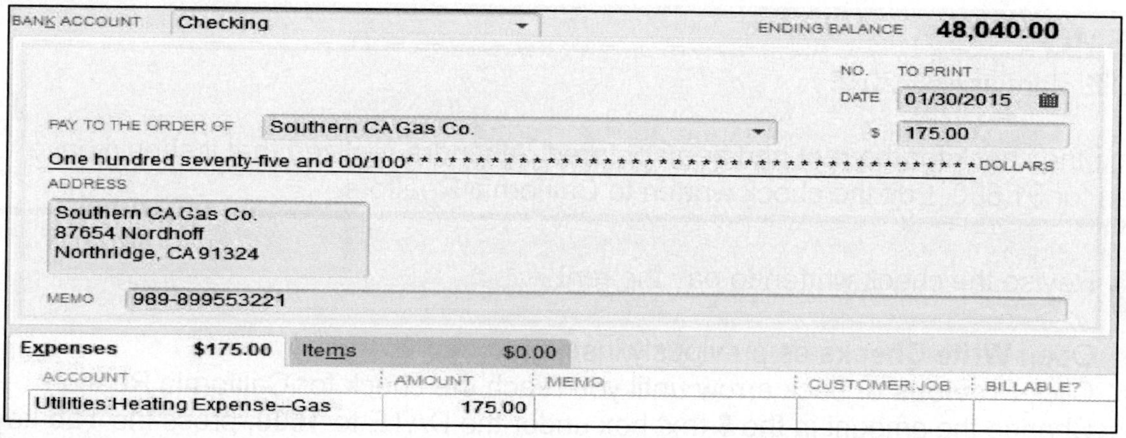

ENTER THE CHECK FOR THE ELECTRIC BILL A SECOND TIME

Click the drop-down list arrow and click **Southern California Electric**

- The first payment entered for the payment of the bill for electricity appears on the screen.
- This is helpful but can cause a duplicate entry to be made.

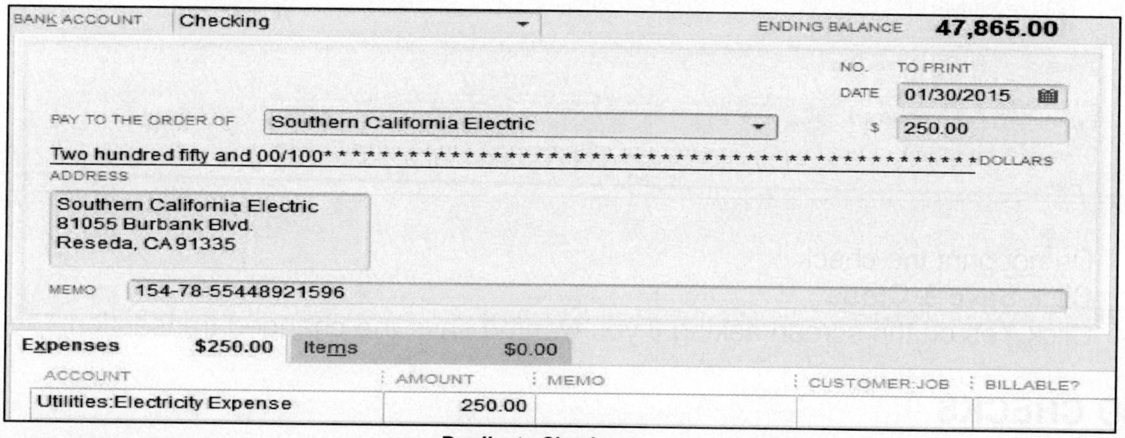

Duplicate Check

Click the **Save & Close** button to record the second payment for the electric bill and exit the **Write Checks** window

EDIT CHECKS

Mistakes can occur in business—even on a check. QuickBooks allows for checks to be edited at any time. You may use either the Check Register or the Write Checks window to edit checks.

MEMO
DATE: January 30, 2015

Once the check for the rent had been entered, Alhandra realized that it should have been for $1,600. Edit the check written to California Realtors.

Revise the check written to pay the rent

Open **Write Checks** as previously instructed
Click **Previous** or back arrow until you reach the check for California Realtors
Change the amount in the **$** text box under the DATE to **1600**, press the **Tab** key

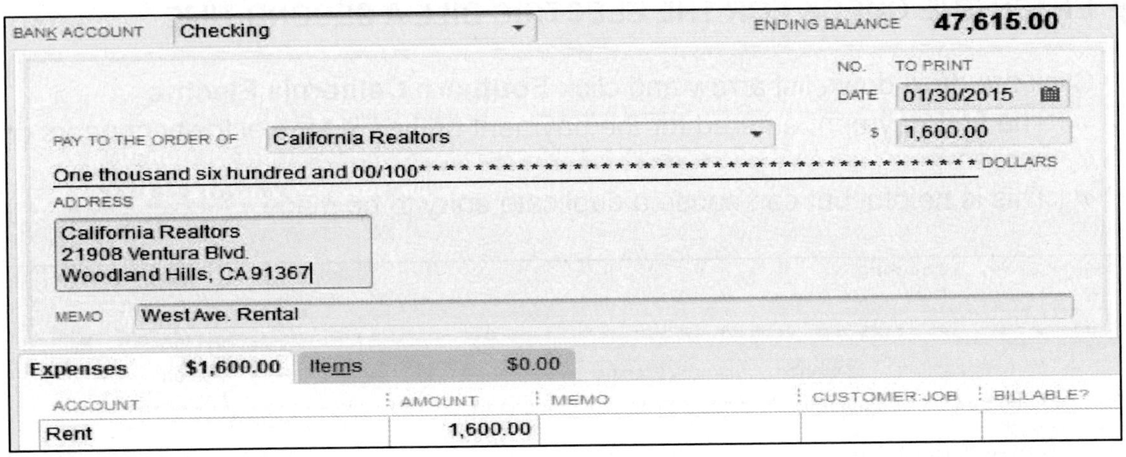

Do not print the check
Click **Save & Close**
Click **Yes** on the screen asking if you want to save the changed transaction

VOID CHECKS

QuickBooks allows checks to be voided. Rather than deleting the transaction, voiding a check changes the amount of the check to zero but keeps a record of the transaction. The check may be voided in the Checking account register or on the check. The following transaction will show you how to void a check in the Checking account register.

MEMO
DATE: January 30, 2015

The telephone bill should not have been paid until the first week of February. Void the check written for the telephone expense.

Void the check written to pay the telephone bill
Click the **Check Register** icon in the BANKING section of the Home Page

- Make sure **Checking** is shown as the Register account

Void the check written for the telephone expense:

Click anywhere in the check to **Communication Telephone Co.**

Click **Edit** on the QuickBooks menu bar at the top of the screen—not the Edit Transaction button

Click **Void Check**

Click the **Record** button in the Checking Register

Click **Yes** on the Recording Transaction dialog box

Click **No, just void the check** on the QuickBooks dialog box

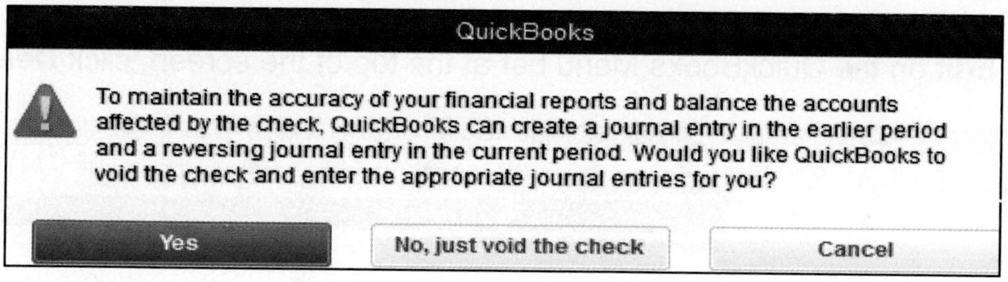

- The amount of the check is now 0.00. The memo shows VOID: Monthly Telephone Bill.

Do not close the register for checking

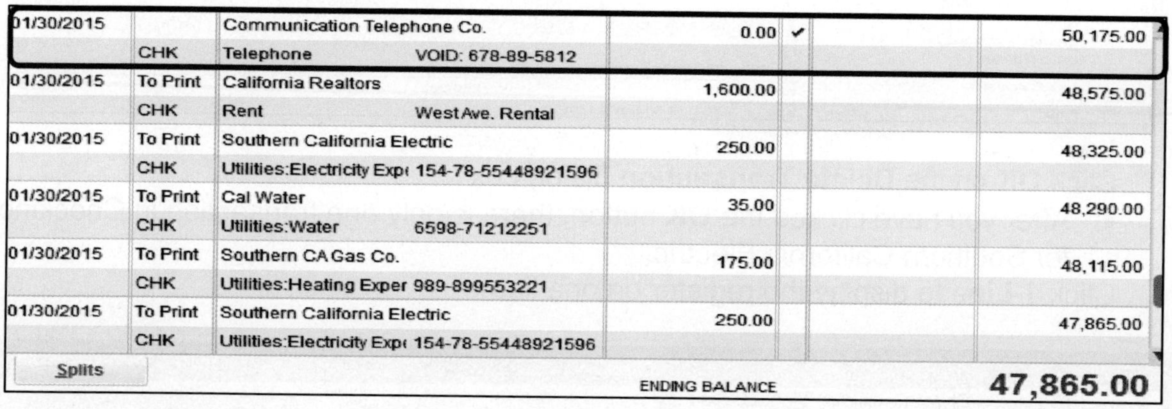

01/30/2015		Communication Telephone Co.	0.00	✔		50,175.00
	CHK	Telephone VOID: 678-89-5812				
01/30/2015	To Print	California Realtors	1,600.00			48,575.00
	CHK	Rent West Ave. Rental				
01/30/2015	To Print	Southern California Electric	250.00			48,325.00
	CHK	Utilities:Electricity Exp(154-78-55448921596				
01/30/2015	To Print	Cal Water	35.00			48,290.00
	CHK	Utilities:Water 6598-71212251				
01/30/2015	To Print	Southern CA Gas Co.	175.00			48,115.00
	CHK	Utilities:Heating Exper 989-899553221				
01/30/2015	To Print	Southern California Electric	250.00			47,865.00
	CHK	Utilities:Electricity Exp(154-78-55448921596				
Splits			ENDING BALANCE			47,865.00

DELETE CHECKS

Deleting a check completely removes it and any transaction information for the check from QuickBooks. Make sure you definitely want to remove the check before deleting it. Once it is deleted, a check cannot be recovered. It is often preferable to void a check than to delete it because a voided check is maintained in the company records; whereas, no record is kept in the active company records of a deleted check.

MEMO
DATE: January 30, 2015

In reviewing the register for the checking account, Alhandra Cruz discovered that two checks were written to pay the electric bill. Delete the second check.

Delete the second entry for the electric bill

- Notice that there are two transactions showing for Southern California Electric.

Click anywhere in the second entry to Southern California Electric

Click **Edit** on the QuickBooks Menu bar at the top of the screen, click **Delete Check**

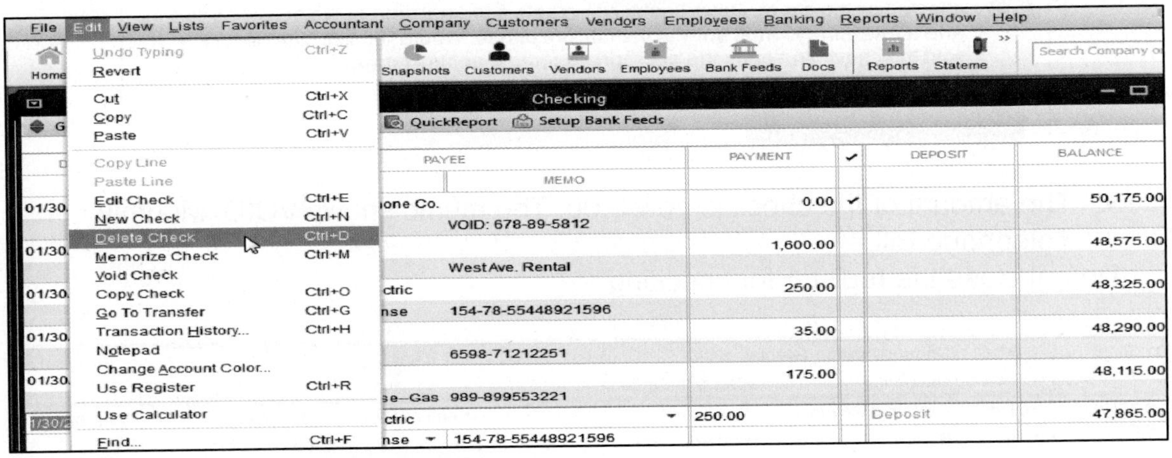

Click **OK** on the **Delete Transaction** dialog box

- After you have clicked the **OK** button, there is only one transaction in Checking for Southern California Electric.

Click **1-Line** to display the register on one line

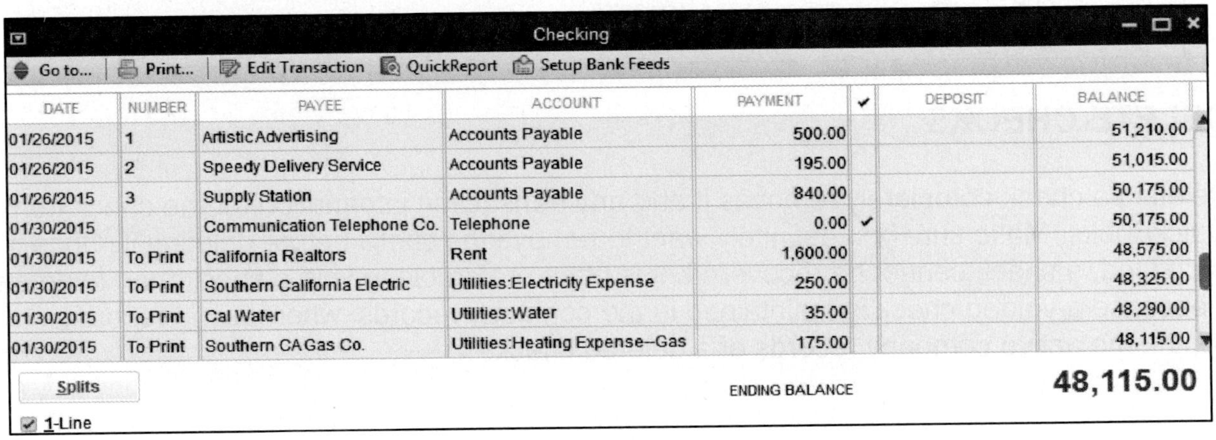

DATE	NUMBER	PAYEE	ACCOUNT	PAYMENT	✔	DEPOSIT	BALANCE
01/26/2015	1	Artistic Advertising	Accounts Payable	500.00			51,210.00
01/26/2015	2	Speedy Delivery Service	Accounts Payable	195.00			51,015.00
01/26/2015	3	Supply Station	Accounts Payable	840.00			50,175.00
01/30/2015		Communication Telephone Co.	Telephone	0.00	✔		50,175.00
01/30/2015	To Print	California Realtors	Rent	1,600.00			48,575.00
01/30/2015	To Print	Southern California Electric	Utilities:Electricity Expense	250.00			48,325.00
01/30/2015	To Print	Cal Water	Utilities:Water	35.00			48,290.00
01/30/2015	To Print	Southern CA Gas Co.	Utilities:Heating Expense--Gas	175.00			48,115.00

Splits ENDING BALANCE **48,115.00**
1-Line

- Notice the change in the Checking account balance.

Close the **Check Register**

PRINT CHECKS

Checks may be printed as they are entered, or they may be printed at a later time. When checks are to be printed, QuickBooks inserts the words *To Print* rather than a check number in the Check Register. The appropriate check number is indicated during printing. Because QuickBooks is so flexible, a company must institute a system for cash control. For example, if the check for rent of $1,500 had been printed, QuickBooks would allow a second check for $1,600 to be printed. In order to avoid any impropriety, more than one person should be designated to review checks. As a matter of practice in a small business, the owner or a person other than the one writing checks should sign the checks. Pre-numbered checks should be used, and any checks printed but not mailed should be submitted along with those for signature.

As a further safeguard, QuickBooks automatically tracks all the additions, deletions, and modifications made to transactions in your data file. This record of tracked changes is called an audit trail. The audit trail ensures that an accurate record of your data is maintained. QuickBooks' Audit Trail Report should be printed and viewed on a regular basis.

MEMO
DATE: January 30, 2015

Alhandra needs to print checks and obtain your signature so they can be mailed.

Print the checks for the rent and the utility bills paid by writing checks

Click the **File** menu, point to **Print Forms**, click **Checks**
On the Select Checks to Print dialog box, the **Bank Account** should be **Checking**
- If Checking does not show, click the drop-down list arrow and click **Checking**.

Because Check Nos. 1, 2, and 3 were printed previously, **4** should be the number in the **First Check Number** text box
- If not, delete the number showing, and key **4**.

In the √ column, the checks selected for printing are marked with a check mark
- If not, click the **Select All** button.

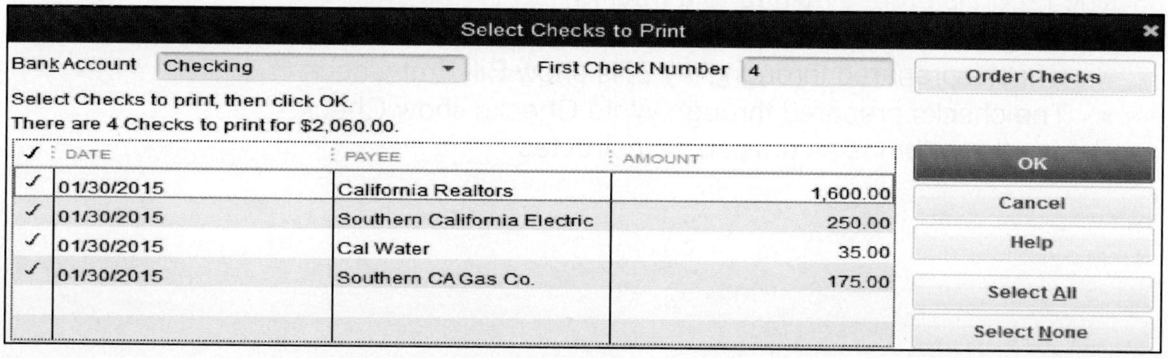

Click **OK** to print the checks

- The **Print Checks** screen appears.

Verify and, if necessary, change information on the **Settings** tab to use **Standard Checks** as previously shown in this chapter

Click **Print** to print the checks

- The checks have the address for Computer Consulting by Your Name, the name and address of the company being paid, and the amount being paid. There is no check number printed on the checks because QuickBooks is set up to use pre-numbered checks.
- If you run into difficulties or find you made an error and want to correct and/or print an individual check, you may do so by printing directly from the check.

Did check(s) print OK? dialog box appears

If the checks printed correctly, click **OK**

CHECK DETAIL REPORT

Once checks have been printed, it is important to review information about checks. The Check Detail Report provides detailed information regarding each check, including the checks for 0.00 amounts. Information indicates the type of transaction, the date, the check number, the payee, the account used, the original amount, and the paid amount of the check.

MEMO
DATE: January 30, 2015

Now that the checks have been printed, Alhandra prints a Check Detail Report. She will give this to you to examine when you sign the printed checks.

Print a Check Detail Report

Open the **Report Center**

The type of report should be **Banking**

Double-click **Check Detail** to select the report

Remove the **Date Prepared** and **Time Prepared** from the report header

The report is From **01/01/15** to **01/30/15**

Tab to **generate** report

- Checks prepared through Pay Bills show Bill Pmt-Check.
- The checks prepared through Write Checks show Check.

Resize the columns as previously instructed

Computer Consulting by Your Name
Check Detail
January 1 - 30, 2015

Type	Num	Date	Name	Item	Account	Paid Amount	Original Amount
Check		01/30/2015	Communication Telephone Co.		Checking		0.00
TOTAL						0.00	0.00
Bill Pmt -Check	1	01/26/2015	Artistic Advertising		Checking		-500.00
Bill		12/31/2014			Uncategorized Expenses	-500.00	500.00
TOTAL						-500.00	500.00
Bill Pmt -Check	2	01/26/2015	Speedy Delivery Service		Checking		-195.00
Bill	88764	01/19/2015			Postage and Delivery	-195.00	195.00
TOTAL						-195.00	195.00

Partial Report

Print the report in **Landscape** Orientation
Click **Close** to close the report
Do <u>not</u> close the Report Center

3

MISSING CHECKS REPORT

A Missing Checks Report lists the checks written for a bank account in order by check number. If there are any gaps between numbers or duplicate check numbers, this information is provided. The report indicates the type of transaction, Check or Bill Payment-Check, check date, check number, payee name, account used for the check, the split or additional accounts used, and the amount of the check. Check means that you wrote the check and Bill Payment-Check means the check was written when you used Pay Bills.

MEMO
DATE: January 30, 2015

To see a listing of all checks printed, view a Missing Checks Report for all dates.

View a Missing Checks Report

Double-click **Missing Checks** in the Banking section to select the report being prepared
- If **Checking** appears as the account on the **Missing Checks Report** dialog box, click **OK**.
- If it does not appear, click the drop-down list arrow, click **Checking**, click **OK**.

Examine the report:

11:49 AM
01/30/15

Computer Consulting by Your Name
Missing Checks
All Transactions

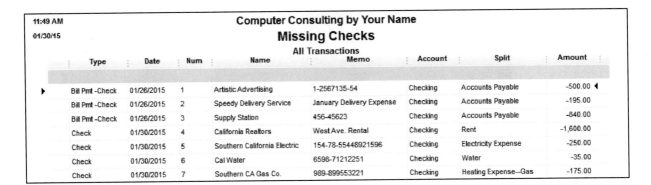

Type	Date	Num	Name	Memo	Account	Split	Amount
Bill Pmt -Check	01/26/2015	1	Artistic Advertising	1-2567135-54	Checking	Accounts Payable	-500.00
Bill Pmt -Check	01/26/2015	2	Speedy Delivery Service	January Delivery Expense	Checking	Accounts Payable	-195.00
Bill Pmt -Check	01/26/2015	3	Supply Station	456-45623	Checking	Accounts Payable	-840.00
Check	01/30/2015	4	California Realtors	West Ave. Rental	Checking	Rent	-1,600.00
Check	01/30/2015	5	Southern California Electric	154-78-55448921596	Checking	Electricity Expense	-250.00
Check	01/30/2015	6	Cal Water	6598-71212251	Checking	Water	-35.00
Check	01/30/2015	7	Southern CA Gas Co.	989-899553221	Checking	Heating Expense--Gas	-175.00

- In a transaction that is decreasing cash, you would credit cash or checking and debit the expense or accounts payable account used in the transaction.
- The **Account** in all cases is **Checking**, which is the account credited.
- The **Split** column indicates which accounts in addition to checking have been used in the transaction. The Split accounts are the accounts debited.

Look at the **Type** column:

- The checks written through Pay Bills indicate the transaction type as **Bill Pmt-Check** and the Split account is **Accounts Payable**.
- The bills paid by actually writing the checks show **Check** as the transaction type and indicates the other accounts used.

Close the report without printing, do not close the Report Center

VOIDED/DELETED TRANSACTION SUMMARY

QuickBooks has a report for all voided/deleted transactions. This report appears in the Accountant & Taxes section for reports. This report may be printed as a summary or in detail. It will show all the transactions that have been voided and/or deleted.

MEMO
DATE: January 30, 2015

In order to be informed more fully about the checks that have been written, you have Alhandra prepare the Voided/Deleted Transaction Summary Report for January.

Prepare the Voided/Deleted Transaction Summary report

Click **Accountant & Taxes** in the Report Center
Double-click **Voided/Deleted Transaction Summary** in the Account Activity section
The report dates are **All**

11:55 AM
01/30/15

Computer Consulting by Your Name
Voided/Deleted Transactions Summary
Entered/Last Modified January 30, 2015

Num	Action	Entered/Last Modified	Date	Name	Memo	Account	Split	Amount
Transactions entered or modified by Admin								
Check								
	Voided Transaction	01/30/2015 09:14:18	01/30/2015	Communication Telephone Co.	VOID: 678-89-5812	Checking	Telephone	0.00 ◀
	Added Transaction	01/30/2015 08:08:15	01/30/2015	Communication Telephone Co.	678-89-5812	Checking	Telephone	-350.00
Check								
	Deleted Transaction	01/30/2015 11:24:50						0.00
	Added Transaction	01/30/2015 08:20:38	01/30/2015	Southern California Electric	154-78-55448921596	Checking	Utilities:Electricity Expense	-250.00

- The Entered Last Modified column shows the actual date and time that the entry was made. The report header shows your computer's current date and time. The dates and times shown will not match your date and time.
- In addition, your report may not match the one illustrated if you have voided or deleted anything else during your work session.

Close the report without printing, and close the Report Center

PETTY CASH

Frequently, a business will need to pay for small expenses with cash. These might include expenses such as postage, office supplies, and miscellaneous expenses. For example, rather than write a check for postage due of 75 cents, you would use money from petty cash. QuickBooks allows you to establish and use a petty cash account to track these small expenditures. Normally, a Petty Cash Voucher or Petty Cash Ticket is prepared; and, if available, the receipt(s) for the transaction is (are) stapled to it. In QuickBooks you can scan a receipt and attach it electronically to the transaction. (This will be discussed in a later chapter.) It is important in a business to keep accurate records of the petty cash expenditures, and procedures for control of the Petty Cash fund need to be established to prohibit access to and unauthorized use of the cash. Periodically, the petty cash expenditures are recorded so that the records of the company accurately reflect all expenses incurred in the operation of the business.

ADD PETTY CASH ACCOUNT

QuickBooks allows accounts to be added to the Chart of Accounts list at any time. Petty Cash is identified as a "Bank" account type so it will be placed at the top of the Chart of Accounts along with other checking and savings accounts.

MEMO
DATE: January 30, 2015

Occasionally, there are small items that should be paid for using cash. Alhandra Cruz needs to establish a petty cash account for $100.

Add Petty Cash to the **Chart of Accounts**

Access **Chart of Accounts** as previously instructed
Click the **Account** button at the bottom of the Chart of Accounts, click **New** or use the keyboard shortcut **Ctrl+N**
Click **Bank** on the Add New Account: Choose Account Type screen
Click the **Continue** button
Enter **Petty Cast** in the **Account Name** text box

- Yes, it should be Cash and will be changed later. So enter Cast.

Leave the other items blank

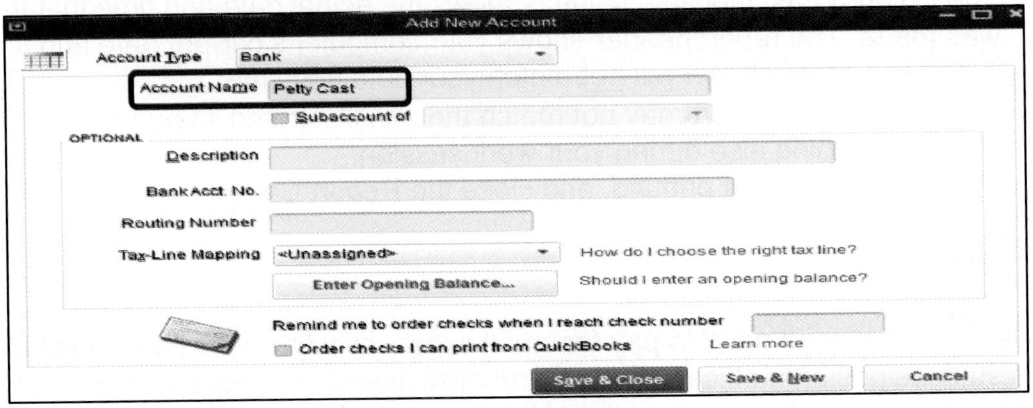

Click **Save & Close** to record the new account

- If you get a message to Set Up Bank Feed, click **No**.

Look at the Chart of Accounts and see that you misspelled the name as Petty Cast
Click **Petty Cast**
Edit the account name by using the keyboard shortcut **Ctrl+E**
Change the account name to **Petty Cash**

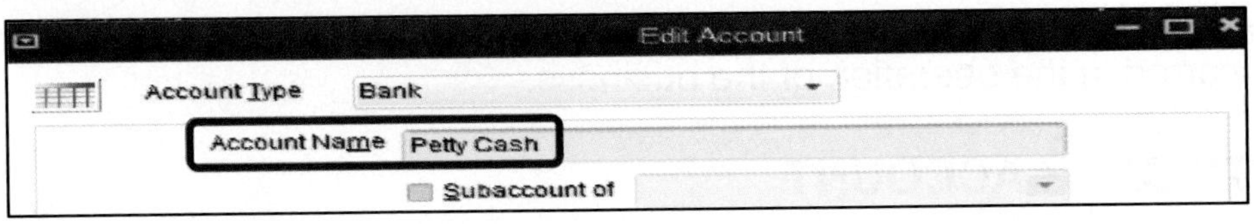

Click **Save & Close**

- If you get a dialog box, to Set up Bank Feed, click **No**.

Do not close the **Chart of Accounts**

ESTABLISH PETTY CASH FUND

Once the account has been established, the petty cash fund must have money in order to pay for small expenses. Two alternate methods for obtaining the funds for Petty Cash are: make a withdrawal from the company checking account at the bank or write a check for cash and then cash it at the bank. If a check is used to obtain cash, the transaction is recorded when writing the check. If a withdrawal is made, it is either recorded directly in the Checking account register or by completing a Transfer Funds Between Accounts. Since you know how to write a check and how to record a transaction in an account register, completing the Transfer of Funds will be illustrated below.

Record the Transfer of Funds from Checking to Petty Cash

Click the **Banking** menu
Click **Transfer Funds**

- As discussed above, this method may be used when a withdrawal is made from the Checking account and the amount is made available for Petty Cash.
- If the cursor is not already in the DATE text box, click in it.
- The date should be highlighted; if it is not, drag through the date to highlight.

If the DATE is not 01/30/2015, enter **01/30/15**
Click the drop-down list arrow for TRANSFER FUNDS FROM
Click **Checking**

- The **ACCOUNT BALANCE** for Checking should show **48,115.00**.

Click the drop-down list arrow for **TRANSFER FUNDS TO**
Click **Petty Cash**

- The **ACCOUNT BALANCE** for Petty Cash should show **0.00**.

Tab to or click in the textbox for **TRANSFER AMOUNT**
Enter **100**
Click after the **MEMO** that says **Funds Transfer**
Add **to Establish Petty Cash Fund**

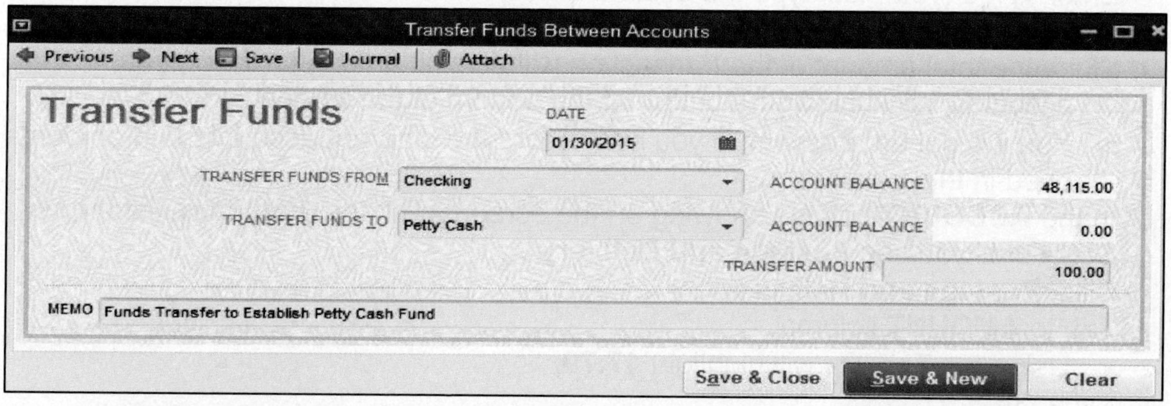

Click **Save & Close** button to record the transfer
View the results in the account balances in the Chart of Accounts

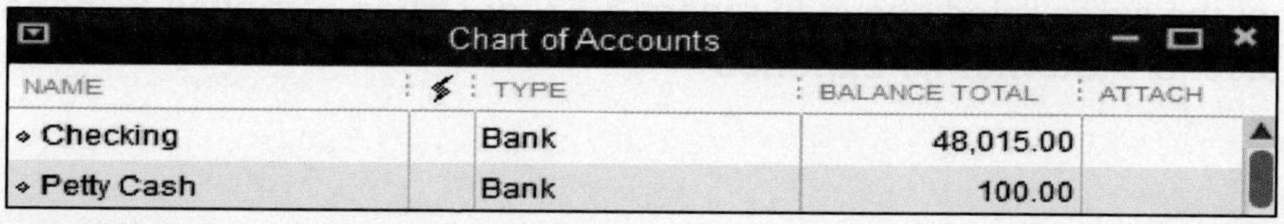

Do not close the **Chart of Accounts**

PAY EXPENSE WITH PETTY CASH

As petty cash is used to pay for small expenses in the business, these payments must be recorded. QuickBooks makes it a simple matter to record petty cash expenditures directly into the Petty Cash Register.

MEMO
DATE: January 30, 2015

Alhandra Cruz needs to record the petty cash expenditures made during the week: postage due, 34 cents; purchased staples and paperclips, $3.57 (this is an expense); reimbursed Jennifer Lockwood for gasoline purchased for company car, $13.88.

In the Petty Cash account, record a compound entry for the above expenditures

In the **Chart of Accounts,** double-click **Petty Cash** to open the **Register**
Click in the **DATE** column, highlight the date if necessary
Type **01/30/15**
Tab to Number, enter **1** for the number

- This would be the number of the Petty Cash Voucher or Petty Cash Ticket that would be filled out and have the receipts stapled to it.
- No entry is required for Payee.

Tab to or click **Payment**
Enter **17.79** (you must type the decimal point)
Tab to or click in **Account** text box
Since the total amount of the transaction will be split among three expense accounts, click the **Splits** button at the bottom of the screen

- You will get an area where you can record the different accounts and amounts used in this transaction.

In the **ACCOUNT** column showing on the screen, click the drop-down list arrow
Scroll until you see **Postage and Delivery**
Click **Postage and Delivery**
Tab to **AMOUNT** column

- Using the Tab key will highlight **17.79**.

Type **.34**

- MEMO notations are not necessary because the transactions are self-explanatory.

Tab to or click the next blank line in **ACCOUNT**
Repeat the steps listed above to record **3.57** for **Office Supplies Expense** and **13.88** for **Automobile Expense**

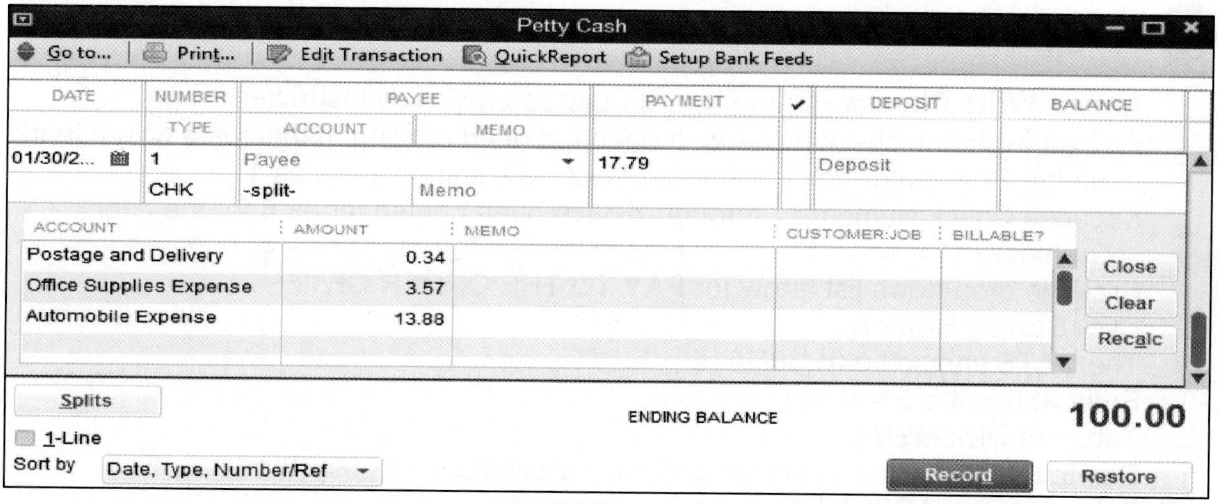

Click the **Close** button for Splits when all expenses have been recorded
Click **Record** to record the transaction

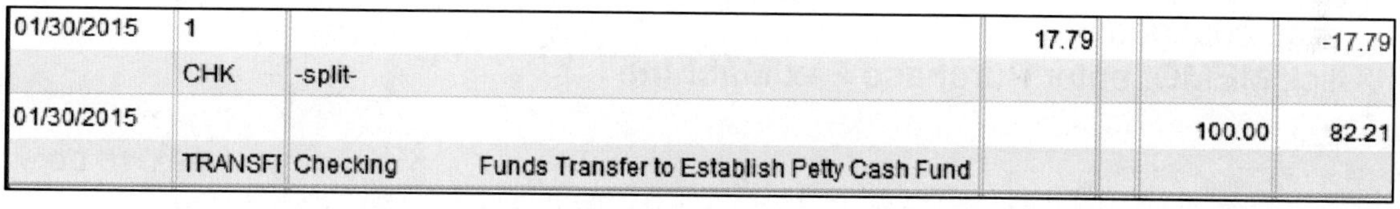

01/30/2015 1 17.79 -17.79
CHK -split-
01/30/2015 100.00 82.21
TRANSFI Checking Funds Transfer to Establish Petty Cash Fund

- Since the transfer of funds and the recording of petty cash expenditures are shown on the same date, the expenditures show first.
- Notice that after the Record button has been clicked, the word "payee," the account name, and memo are removed from the transaction. Instead of showing the accounts used, **-split-** is shown.
- In the Num column, the transaction is marked as a CHK. This actually refers to the number of the Petty Cash Voucher or Ticket, but QuickBooks does not use an identifier of Voucher or Ticket.
- Verify the account Ending Balance of 82.21.

Close the **Petty Cash Register** and the **Chart of Accounts**

PURCHASE ASSET WITH COMPANY CHECK

Not all purchases will be transactions on account. If something is purchased and paid for with a check, a check is written and the purchase is recorded.

> **MEMO**
> **DATE:** January 30, 2015
>
> Having tried out several fax machines from Supply Station on a rental basis, you decide to purchase one from them. Because the fax machine is on sale if it is purchased for cash, you decide to buy it by writing a company check for the asset for $486.

Record the check written for the purchase of a fax machine

Access **Write Checks - Checking** window as previously instructed

- You wrote the check by hand. It does not need printing. If there is a check mark. in the **Print Later** box, click to deselect. **NO.** should show as **1**.

Because Check Numbers 1 through 7 have been printed, enter **8** for the check number

Click the drop-down list arrow for **PAY TO THE ORDER OF**

Click **Supply Station**

The **DATE** should be **01/30/2015**

Enter **486** in the **$** text box

Tab to or click **MEMO**

Delete the Memo that is shown and enter **Purchase Fax Machine**

Tab to or click **ACCOUNT** on the **Expenses** tab

Click the drop-down list arrow, scroll to the top of the **Chart of Accounts**, and click **Original Cost** under **Office Equipment**

- **AMOUNT** column shows the transaction total of **486.00**. This does not need to be changed.

Click **MEMO**, enter **Purchase Fax Machine**

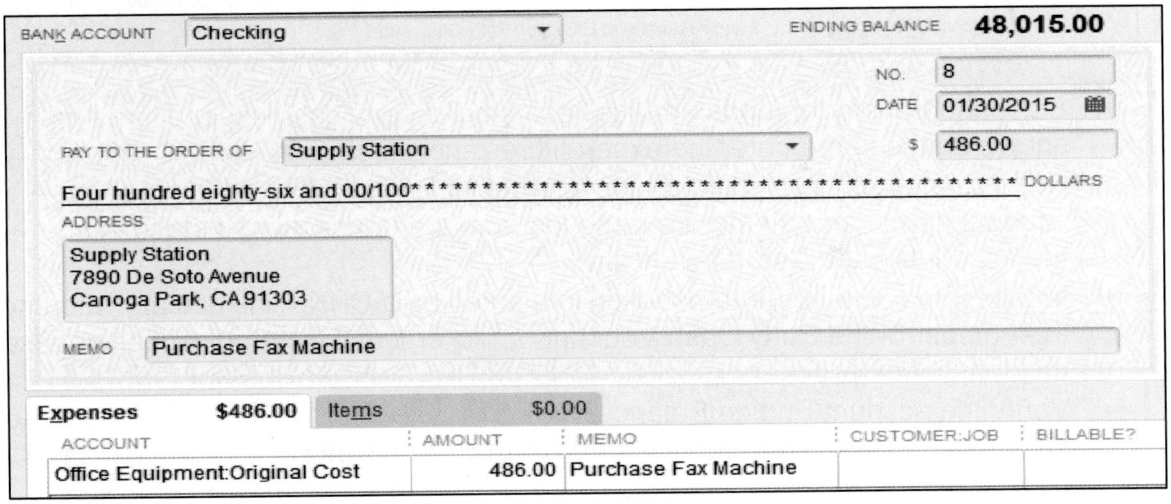

Click **Save & Close** to record the check and exit the **Write Checks - Checking** window without printing

CUSTOMIZE REPORT FORMAT

The report format used in one company may not be appropriate for all companies that use QuickBooks. In order to allow program users the maximum flexibility, QuickBooks makes it very easy to customize many of the user preferences of the program. For example, you may customize menus, reminder screens, as well as reports and graphs.

Customize the report preferences to make permanent changes for all reports so reports are automatically refreshed, and the date prepared, time prepared, and report basis do not print on reports

Click the QuickBooks **Edit** menu, click **Preferences**

Scroll through the items listed on the left side of the screen until you get to Reports and Graphs

Click the **Reports and Graphs** icon 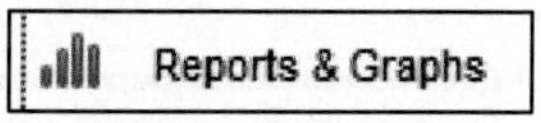

- If not already selected, click the **My Preferences** tab.
- If **Refresh Automatically** on the My Preferences tab has not been selected, click it to select.

Whenever data is changed and a report appears on the screen, QuickBooks will automatically update the report to reflect the changes.

Click the **Company Preferences** tab

Click the **Format** button

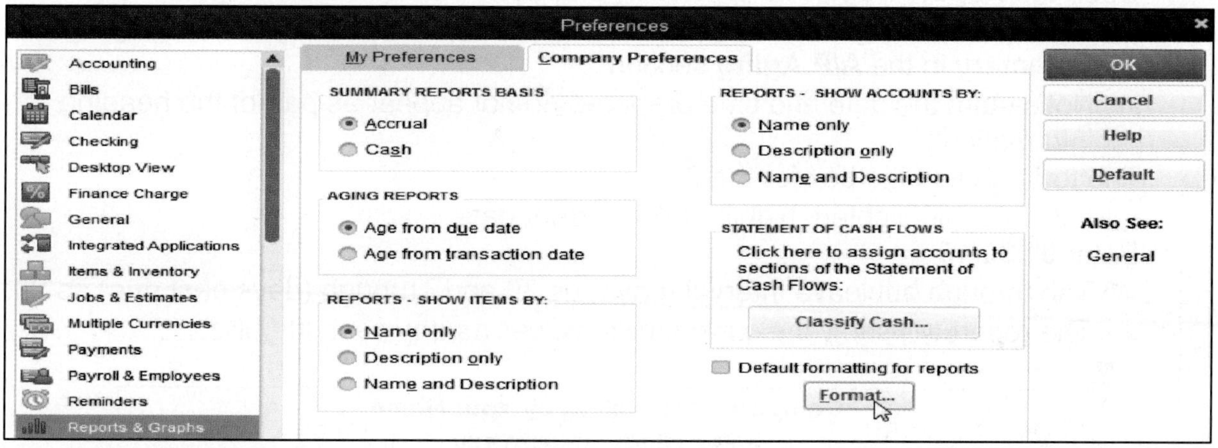

- If necessary, click the **Header/Footer** tab.

Click **Date Prepared**, **Time Prepared**, and **Report Basis** to deselect

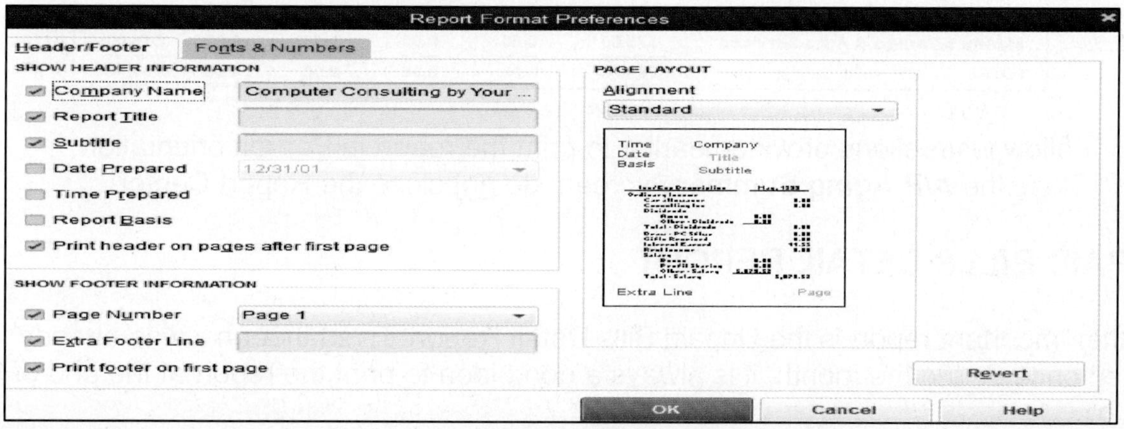

Click **OK** to save the change, click **OK** to close **Preferences**

ACCOUNTS PAYABLE AGING SUMMARY

It is important in a business to maintain a good credit rating and to make sure that payments are made on time. In order to avoid overlooking a payment, the Accounts Payable Aging Summary lists the vendors to which the company owes money and shows how long the money has been owed.

MEMO
DATE: January 30, 2015

Prepare the Accounts Payable Aging Summary

Prepare an **Accounts Payable Aging Summary**

Open the **Report Center** as previously instructed
Click **Vendors & Payables** to select the type of report, double-click **A/P Aging Summary** in the **A/P Aging** section

- Notice that the date and time prepared do not appear as part of the heading information.

Tab to or click in the box for the **Date**

- If it is not highlighted, highlight the current date.

Enter **01/30/15**

- Tab through but leave Interval (days) as 30 and Through (days past due) as 90.
- The report will show the current bills as well as any past due bills.

Computer Consulting by Your Name
A/P Aging Summary
As of January 30, 2015

	Current	1 - 30	31 - 60	61 - 90	> 90	TOTAL
Artistic Advertising	260.00	0.00	0.00	0.00	0.00	260.00
California Insurance Company	2,850.00	0.00	0.00	0.00	0.00	2,850.00
Computer Technologies Magazine	79.00	0.00	0.00	0.00	0.00	79.00
Manny's Garage & Auto Services	575.00	0.00	0.00	0.00	0.00	575.00
TOTAL	3,764.00	0.00	0.00	0.00	0.00	3,764.00

Follow instructions provided earlier to print the report in Portrait orientation
Close the **A/P Aging Summary** screen; do not close the Report Center

UNPAID BILLS DETAIL REPORT

Another important report is the Unpaid Bills Detail Report. Even though it was already printed once during the month, it is always a good idea to print the report at the end of the month.

MEMO
DATE: January 30, 2015

At the end of every month, Alhandra Cruz prepares and prints an Unpaid Bills Detail Report for you.

Prepare and print the report

Follow instructions provided earlier in the chapter to prepare an **Unpaid Bills Detail Report** for **01/30/2015**

Computer Consulting by Your Name
Unpaid Bills Detail
As of January 30, 2015

Type	Date	Num	Due Date	Aging	Open Balance
Artistic Advertising					
Bill	01/16/2015	9875	02/15/2015		260.00
Total Artistic Advertising					260.00
California Insurance Company					
Bill	01/19/2015	3659	02/18/2015		2,850.00
Total California Insurance Company					2,850.00
Computer Technologies Magazine					
Bill	01/19/2015	1579-53	02/18/2015		79.00
Total Computer Technologies Magazine					79.00
Manny's Garage & Auto Services					
Bill	01/19/2015	630	02/18/2015		575.00
Total Manny's Garage & Auto Services					575.00
TOTAL					3,764.00

Print in Portrait orientation; then, close the report

- If you get a Memorize Report dialog box, remember to always click No.

Do not close the Report Center

VENDOR BALANCE SUMMARY

There are two Vendor Balance Reports available in QuickBooks. There is a Summary Report that shows unpaid balances for vendors and a Detail Report that lists each transaction for a vendor. In order to see how much is owed to each vendor, prepare a Vendor Balance Summary report.

MEMO
DATE: January 30, 2015

At the end of each month, Alhandra prepares and prints a Vendor Balance Summary Report to give to you so you can see how much is owed to each vendor. In addition, she will prepare an Accounts Payable Graph and will use QuickZoom to view graph details. Alhandra will also prepare a Journal and Trial Balance.

Prepare and print a **Vendor Balance Summary Report**

Double-click **Vendor Balance Summary** in the Vendor Balances section
The report dates will say **All**

- The report should show only the totals owed to each vendor on January 30, 2015.

Computer Consulting by Your Name
Vendor Balance Summary
All Transactions

	Jan 30, 15
Artistic Advertising	260.00
California Insurance Company	2,850.00
Computer Technologies Magazine	79.00
Manny's Garage & Auto Services	575.00
TOTAL	3,764.00

Follow steps listed previously to print the report in Portrait orientation
Close the report; do not close the **Report Center**

ACCOUNTS PAYABLE GRAPH BY AGING PERIOD

Graphs provide a visual representation of certain aspects of the business. It is sometimes easier to interpret data in a graphical format. For example, to determine if any payments are overdue for accounts payable accounts, use an Accounts Payable Graph to provide that information instantly on a bar chart. In addition, the Accounts Payable Graph feature of QuickBooks also displays a pie chart showing what percentage of the total amount payable is owed to each vendor.

Prepare an Accounts Payable Graph

Double-click **Accounts Payable Graph** in the Vendors & Payables list of reports
Click the **Dates** button at the top of the report
Enter **01/30/15** for **Show Aging as of** in the **Change Graph Dates** text box
Click **OK**

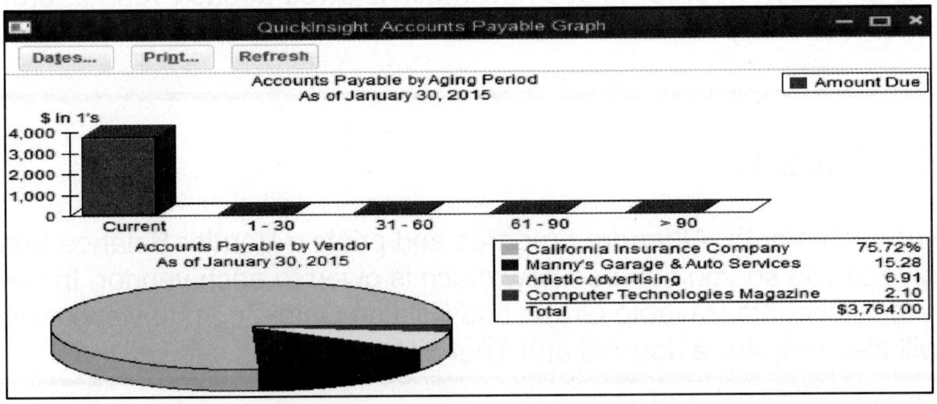

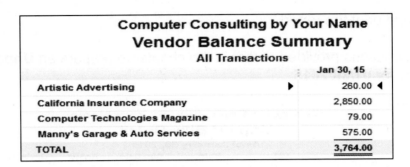

Click the **Dates** button again; enter **02/28/15** for the date
Click **OK**

- Notice that the bar moved from Current to 1-30. This means at the end of February the bills will be between 1 and 30 days overdue.

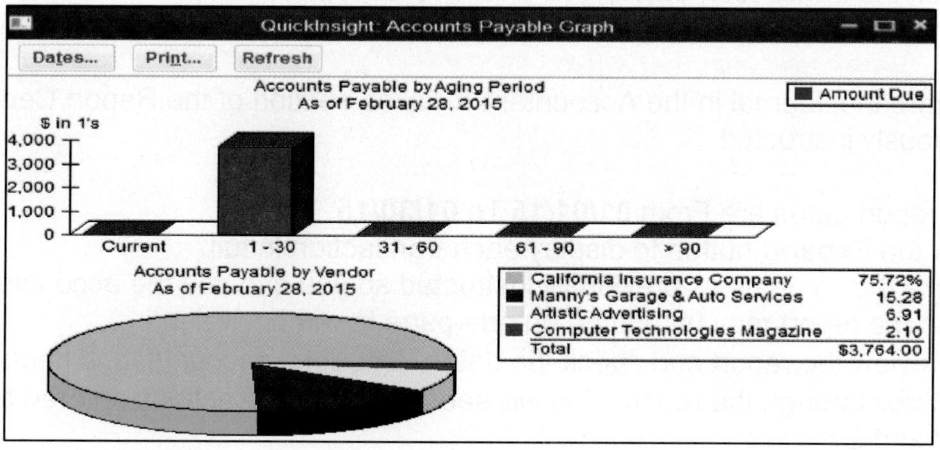

QUICKZOOM TO VIEW GRAPH DETAILS

To obtain detailed information from a graph, use the QuickZoom feature. For example, to see the overdue category of an individual account, double-click on a vendor in the pie chart or in the legend, and this information will appear in a separate bar chart.

Use QuickZoom to see how many days overdue the California Insurance Company's bill will be at the end of February

Point to the section of the pie chart for **California Insurance Company**
Double-click

- The bar chart shows the bill will be in the 1-30 day category at the end of February.

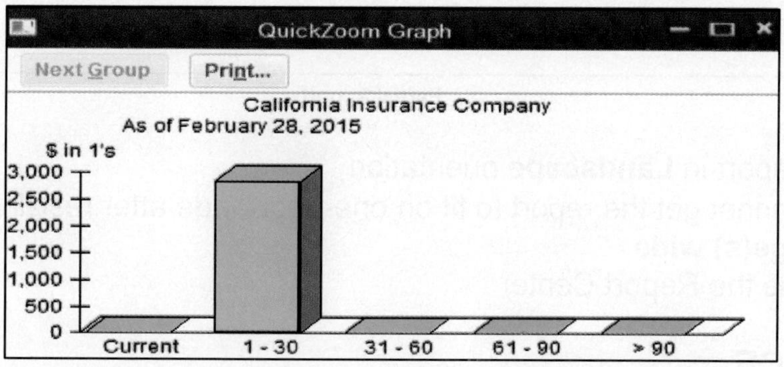

Close the QuickZoom Graph for California Insurance Company
Close the **QuickInsight: Accounts Payable Graph**

JOURNAL

It is always a good idea to review your transactions for appropriate amount, account and item usage. In tracing errors, the Journal is an invaluable tool. If you suspect an error, always check the transaction dates, amounts, accounts used, and items listed in the Memo column to verify the accuracy of your entry.

Prepare the Journal in the Accountant & Taxes section of the Report Center as previously instructed

The report dates are From **01/01/15** To **01/30/15**
Click the **Expand** button to display each transaction in full
Resize the columns as previously instructed so you can see the accounts in full and so the report may be printed on one-page in width

- Review the report and check the dates, amounts, accounts, and items used.
- Scroll through the report. You will see all of the transactions entered for Chapters 2 and 3.

Computer Consulting by Your Name
Journal
January 1 - 30, 2015

Trans #	Type	Date	Num	Adj	Name	Memo	Account	Debit	Credit
								175.00	175.00
64	Transfer	01/30/2015				Funds Transfer to Establish Petty Cash Fund	Checking		100.00
						Funds Transfer to Establish Petty Cash Fund	Petty Cash	100.00	
								100.00	100.00
65	Check	01/30/2015	1				Petty Cash		17.79
							Postage and Delivery	0.34	
							Office Supplies Expense	3.57	
							Automobile Expense	13.88	
								17.79	17.79
66	Check	01/30/2015	8		Supply Station	Purchase Fax Machine	Checking		486.00
					Supply Station	Purchase Fax Machine	Original Cost	486.00	
								486.00	486.00
TOTAL								45,217.79	45,217.79

Partial Report

Print the Report in **Landscape** orientation

- If you cannot get the report to fit on one-page wide after resizing, click **Fit report to 1 page(s) wide**.

Do not close the Report Center

TRIAL BALANCE

It is always helpful to create a trial balance as of a specific date to show the balance of each account in debit and credit format.

Prepare a Trial Balance as previously instructed

The report dates are From **01/01/15** To **01/30/15**
Your account balances should match the following:

Computer Consulting by Your Name
Trial Balance
As of January 30, 2015

	Jan 30, 15	
	Debit	Credit
Checking	47,529.00	
Petty Cash	82.21	
Accounts Receivable	17,650.00	
Office Supplies	950.00	
Prepaid Insurance	2,850.00	
Undeposited Funds	0.00	
Company Cars:Original Cost	49,000.00	
Office Equipment:Original Cost	8,536.00	
Accounts Payable		3,764.00
Loan Payable	0.00	
Loan Payable:Company Cars Loan		35,000.00
Loan Payable:Office Equipment Loan		4,000.00
Owner's Equity	0.00	
Student's Name, Capital		53,135.00
Student's Name, Capital:Investments		25,000.00
Income:Installation Income		175.00
Income:Technical Support Income		900.00
Income:Training Income		7,850.00
Advertising Expense	260.00	
Automobile Expense	588.88	
Dues and Subscriptions	79.00	
Equipment Rental	25.00	
Office Supplies Expense	18.57	
Postage and Delivery	195.34	
Rent	1,600.00	
Telephone	0.00	
Utilities:Electricity Expense	250.00	
Utilities:Heating Expense--Gas	175.00	
Utilities:Water	35.00	
TOTAL	129,824.00	129,824.00

Close the report without printing
Close the Report Center

BACK UP AND CLOSE COMPANY

Whenever an important work session is complete, you should always back up your data. If your data disk or company file is damaged or an error is discovered at a later time, the backup file (.qbb) may be restored to the same or a new company file and the information used for recording transactions. As in previous chapters, you should close the company at the end of each work session.

Follow the instructions given in Chapters 1 and 2 to back up data for Computer Consulting by Your Name and to close the company. Refer to the instructions provided by your professor for making a duplicate disk

Name your back up file **Computer (Backup Ch. 3)**

SUMMARY

In this chapter, bills were recorded and paid, checks were written, and reports were prepared. The petty cash fund was established and used for payments of small expense items. Checks were voided, deleted, and corrected. Accounts were added and modified. QuickReports were accessed in various ways, and QuickZoom was used to obtain transaction detail while in various reports. Reports were prepared for Missing Checks and Check Details. Unpaid Bills and Vendor Balance Summary Reports provided information regarding bills that had not been paid. The graphing feature of QuickBooks allowed you to determine Accounts Payable by aging period and to see the percentage of Accounts Payable for each vendor.

END-OF-CHAPTER QUESTIONS

TRUE/FALSE

ANSWER THE FOLLOWING QUESTIONS IN THE SPACE PROVIDED BEFORE THE QUESTION NUMBER.

_____ 1. Credit Memos are prepared to record a reduction to a transaction.

_____ 2. When using QuickBooks, checks may not be written in a checkbook.

_____ 3. QuickZoom is a QuickBooks feature that allows detailed information to be displayed.

_____ 4. A cash purchase can be recorded by writing a check or by using petty cash.

_____ 5. Once a report format has been customized as a QuickBooks preference for a company, QuickBooks will automatically use the customized format.

_____ 6. In a service business, most of the accounting for purchases and payables is simply paying bills for expenses incurred in the operation of the business.

_____ 7. Report columns may not be resized and report formats may not be customized.

_____ 8. A Missing Check Report lists any duplicate check numbers or gaps between check numbers.

_____ 9. The Accounts Payable Register keeps track of all checks written in the business.

_____ 10. If a check has been edited, it cannot be printed.

MULTIPLE CHOICE

WRITE THE LETTER OF THE CORRECT ANSWER IN THE SPACE PROVIDED BEFORE THE QUESTION NUMBER.

_____ 1. When using QuickBooks' graphs, information regarding the percentage of accounts payable owed to each vendor is displayed as a ___.
A. pie chart
B. bar chart
C. line chart
D. both A and B

D 2. A check may be edited in ___.
   A. the Write Checks window
   B. the Check Register
   C. in the Pay Bills window
   D. both A and B

B 3. When a document prints 11" wide by 8 ½" long, it is in ___ orientation.
   A. portrait
   B. landscape
   C. standard
   D. horizontal

D 4. To erase an incorrect amount in a bill, you may ___, then key the correction.
   A. drag through the amount to highlight
   B. position the cursor in front of the amount and press the delete key until the amount has been erased
   C. position the cursor after the amount and press the backspace key until the amount has been erased
   D. all of the above

C 5. A correction to a bill that has been recorded can be made on the bill or ___.
   A. not at all
   B. on the Accounts Payable Graph
   C. in the Accounts Payable Register
   D. none of the above

D 6. When you enter a bill, typing the first letter(s) of a vendor's name on the Vendor line ___.
   A. enters the vendor's name on the line if the name is in the Vendor List
   B. displays a list of vendor names
   C. displays the Address Info tab for the vendor
   D. both A and B

C 7. When a bill is deleted, ___.
   A. the amount is changed to 0.00
   B. the word *"Deleted"* appears as the Memo
   C. it is removed without a trace
   D. both A and B

A 8. To increase the date on a bill by one day, ___.
   A. press the + key
   B. press the - key
   C. tab
   D. press the # key

__B__ 9. If a bill is recorded in the Enter Bills window, it is important to pay the bill by ___.
A. writing a check
B. using the Pay Bills window
C. using petty cash
D. allowing QuickBooks to generate the check automatically five days before the due date

__B__ 10. When entering several bills at once on the Enter Bills screen, it is most efficient to ___ to go to the next blank screen.
A. click Previous
B. click Save & New
C. click OK
D. click Preview

FILL-IN

IN THE SPACE PROVIDED, WRITE THE ANSWER THAT MOST APPROPRIATELY COMPLETES THE SENTENCE.

1. The __check face__ section of a check is used to record the check date, payee, and amount for the actual check. The __detail__ area of a check is used to record the accounts used for the bill, the amount for each account used, and transaction explanations.

2. An Accounts Payable Graph by Aging Period shows a __bar__ chart detailing the amounts due by aging period and a __pie__ chart showing the percentage of the total amount payable owed to each vendor.

3. Three different check styles may be used in QuickBooks: __Standard__, __Voucher__, or __Wallet__.

4. The keyboard shortcut to edit or modify an account in the Chart of Accounts is __Ctrl+E__.

5. Petty Cash is identified as a __Bank__ account type so it will be placed at the top of the Chart of Accounts along with checking and savings accounts.

SHORT ESSAY

When viewing a Transaction by Vendor Report that shows the entry of a bill for the purchase of office supplies and office equipment, you will see the term **-split-** displayed. Explain what the term **Split** means when used as a column heading and when used within the Split column for the bill indicated.

NAME______________________

CHAPTER 3: TRANSMITTAL

COMPUTER CONSULTING BY YOUR NAME

Check the items below as you complete and/or print them; then attach the documents and reports in the order listed when you submit them to your instructor. Printing is optional for Bills (unless your instructor requires them to be printed); however, they are included on the transmittal sheet so they can be checked as they are completed.

Note: When paying bills and printing a batch of checks, your checks may be in a different order than shown below. As long as you print the checks to the correct vendors and have the correct amounts, do not be concerned if your check numbers are not an exact match.

___ Bill: Artistic Advertising (Optional)
___ Bill: Supply Station (Optional)
___ Transaction List by Vendor, January 1-18, 2015
___ Bill: Computer Professionals Magazine (Optional)
___ Bill: Supply Station (Optional)
___ Bill: Manny's Garage & Auto Services (Optional)
___ Bill: California Insurance Company (Optional)
___ Register QuickReport, Supply Station
___ Unpaid Bills Detail Report, January 25, 2015
___ Bill: Computer Technologies Magazine (Optional)
___ Credit Memo: Supply Station (Optional)
___ Check 1: Artistic Advertising
___ Check 2: Speedy Delivery Service
___ Check 3: Supply Station
___ Check 4: California Realtors
___ Check 5: Southern California Electric
___ Check 6: Cal Water
___ Check 7: Southern CA Gas Co.
___ Check Detail Report, January 1-30, 2015
___ Check 8: Supply Station (Information Only)
___ A/P Aging Summary, Current and Total
___ Unpaid Bills Detail Report, January 30, 2015
___ Vendor Balance Summary, January 30, 2015
___ Journal, January 1-30, 2015

3

END-OF-CHAPTER PROBLEM

YOUR NAME LANDSCAPE AND POOL SERVICE

Chapter 3 continues with the transactions for bills, bill payments, and purchases for Your Name Landscape and Pool Service. Cash control measures have been implemented. Melissa prints the checks and any related reports; and you, the owner, sign the checks.

INSTRUCTIONS

Continue to use the company file that you used in Chapters 1 and 2 **Landscape.qbw**. Record the bills, bill payments, and purchases as instructed within the chapter. Always read the transactions carefully and review the Chart of Accounts when selecting transaction accounts. Print reports and graphs as indicated. Even though bills may be printed, it is not required. Check with your instructor to see if printing bills is assigned. If a bill is recorded on the Enter Bills screen, it should be paid on the Pay Bills screen—not by writing the check.

RECORD TRANSACTIONS

January 1

- Change the vendor information for Richard's Cooler/Heating to Richard's Cooling & Heating. You will need to change the Vendor Name, the Company Name, the Billed From Address, and on the Payment Settings tab the Print Name on Check As.
- Received a bill from Communications Services for cellular phone service, $485, Net 10, Invoice 1109, Memo: January Cell Phone Services.
- Received a bill from the Office Supply Store for the purchase of office supplies to have on hand, $275, Net 30, Invoice 58-9826. (This is a prepaid expense so an asset account is used.) No memo is necessary.
- Received a bill from Wayne's Motors for truck service and repairs, $519, Net 10, Invoice 1-62, Memo: Truck Service and Repairs. (Use Automobile Expense as the account for this transaction. We will change the name to something more appropriate in Chapter 4.)
- Received a bill from State Street Gasoline for gasoline for the month, $375, Net 10, Invoice 853, Memo: Gasoline for the Month.
- Received a bill from Richard's Cooling & Heating for a repair of the office heater, $150, Net 30, Invoice 87626, Memo: Heater Repair. (The heater is part of the building.)

January 15

- Add a new expense account: Disposal Expense, Description: County Dump Charges.
- Received a bill from County Dump for disposing of lawn, tree, and shrub trimmings, $180, Net 30, Invoice 667, no memo necessary.
- Received a bill from Santa Barbara Water Company, $25, Net 10, Invoice 098-1, no memo necessary.

- Change the QuickBooks Company Preferences to customize the report format so that reports refresh automatically, and that the Date Prepared, the Time Prepared, and the Report Basis do not print as part of the header.
- Prepare an Unpaid Bills Detail Report for January 15, 2015; resize columns as needed, print in Portrait orientation.
- Pay all bills *due on or before January 15*, print the checks. (Use Pay Bills to pay bills that have been entered in the Enter Bills window.) Make sure the Payment Date is 01/15/2015. Use standard style for the checks.
- Add Petty Cash to the Chart of Accounts.
- After obtaining $50 as a cash withdrawal from the bank, complete a Transfer Funds form to transfer $50 from Checking to Petty Cash, Memo: Funds Transfer to Establish Petty Cash Fund.
- Record the receipt of a bill from Repairs Plus. Add this new vendor as you record the transaction. Additional information needed to do a complete Set Up is: 7234 State Street, Santa Barbara, CA 93110, Main Phone: 805-555-0770, Main Email: RepairsPlus@sb.com, Website: www.RepairsPlus, Terms: Net 10. The bill was for the repair of the lawn mower (equipment), $75, Invoice 5-1256, Memo: Lawn Mower Repair.
- Change the telephone number for County Dump. The new number is 805-555-3798.
- Prepare, resize columns, and print the Vendor Balance Detail Report for all transactions.

3

January 30

- Received a $10 credit from Repairs Plus. The repair of the lawn mower wasn't as extensive as originally estimated. (Print the Credit Memo.)
- Record the use of Petty Cash to pay for postage due 64 cents, and office supplies, $1.59 (this is a current expense). Memo notations are not necessary.
- Write and print Check 5 to Repairs Plus to buy a lawn fertilizer spreader as a cash purchase of equipment, $349, Check Memo: Purchase Fertilizer Spreader. Print the check. (If you get a dialog box indicating that you currently owe money to Repairs Plus, Click **Continue Writing Check**. Remember, this is a purchase of equipment.)
- Prepare, resize columns and print an Unpaid Bills Detail Report for January 30.
- Pay all bills *due on or before January 30*; print the checks. (Note: There may be some bills that were due after January 15 but before January 30. Be sure to pay these bills now. If any vendor shows a credit and has a bill that is due, apply it to the bill prior to payment. You may need to click on each bill individually in order to determine whether or not there is a credit to be applied.) Print the checks using standard style.
- Prepare an Accounts Payable Graph as of 1/30/2015. Do not print.
- Prepare a QuickZoom Graph for County Dump as of 1/30/2015. Do not print.
- Prepare the Journal for January 1-30, 2015, expand the report, resize the columns, and then print the report in Landscape.
- Print a Trial Balance for January 1-30, 2015.
- Back up your data and close the company.

NAME________________________

CHAPTER 3: TRANSMITTAL

YOUR NAME LANDSCAPE AND POOL SERVICE

Check the items below as you complete and/or print them; then attach the documents and reports in the order listed when you submit them to your instructor. Printing is optional for Bills (unless your instructor requires them to be printed); however, they are included on the transmittal sheet so they can be checked as they are completed.

(Note: When paying bills and printing a batch of checks, your checks may be in a different order than shown below. As long as you print the checks to the correct vendors and have the correct amounts, do not be concerned if your check numbers are not an exact match.)

___ Bill: Communications Services (Optional)
___ Bill: Office Supply Store (Optional)
___ Bill: Wayne's Motors (Optional)
___ Bill: State Street Gasoline (Optional)
___ Bill: Richard's Cooling & Heating (Optional)
___ Bill: County Dump (Optional)
___ Bill: Santa Barbara Water Company (Optional)
___ Unpaid Bills Detail Report, January 15, 2015
___ Check 1: Communications Services
___ Check 2: County Dump
___ Check 3: State Street Gasoline
___ Check 4: Wayne's Motors
___ Bill: Repairs Plus (Optional)
___ Vendor Balance Detail
___ Credit Memo: Repairs Plus
___ Check 5: Repairs Plus
___ Unpaid Bills Detail Report, January 30, 2015
___ Check 6: Repairs Plus
___ Check 7: Santa Barbara Water Co.
___ Journal, January 1-30, 2015
___ Trial Balance, January 1-30, 2015

GENERAL ACCOUNTING AND END-OF-PERIOD PROCEDURES: SERVICE BUSINESS

4

LEARNING OBJECTIVES

At the completion of this chapter, you will be able to:

1. Complete the end-of-period procedures.
2. Change account names, delete accounts, and make accounts inactive.
3. View an account name change and its effect on subaccounts.
4. Record depreciation and enter the adjusting entries required for accrual-basis accounting.
5. Record owner's equity transactions for a sole proprietor including capital investment and owner withdrawals.
6. Reconcile the bank statement, record bank service charges, automatic payments, and mark cleared transactions.
7. Print Trial Balance, Profit & Loss Report, and Balance Sheet.
8. Export a report to Microsoft Excel.
9. Perform end-of-period backup and close the end of a period.

GENERAL ACCOUNTING AND END-OF-PERIOD PROCEDURES

As previously stated, QuickBooks operates from the standpoint of a business document rather than an accounting form, journal, or ledger. While QuickBooks does incorporate all of these items into the program, in many instances they operate behind the scenes. QuickBooks does not require special closing procedures at the end of a period. At the end of the fiscal year, QuickBooks transfers the net income into the Owner's Equity account and allows you to protect the data for the year by assigning a closing date to the period. All of the transaction detail is maintained and viewable, but it will not be changed unless OK is clicked on a warning screen.

Even though a formal closing does not have to be performed within QuickBooks, when you use accrual-basis accounting, several transactions must be recorded to reflect all expenses and income for the period. For example, bank statements must be reconciled and any charges or bank collections need to be recorded. During the business period, the accountant for the company will review things such as account names, adjusting entries, depreciation schedules, owner's equity adjustments, and so on. Sometimes the changes and adjustments will be made by the accountant in a separate file called the Accountant's

Copy of the business files. This file is then imported into the company file that is used to record day-to-day business transactions, and all adjustments made by the accountant are added to the current company file. There are certain restrictions to the types of transactions that may be made on an Accountant's Copy of the business files.

Once necessary adjustments have been made, reports reflecting the end-of-period results of operations should be prepared. For archive purposes at the end of the fiscal year an additional backup disk is prepared and stored.

TRAINING TUTORIAL AND PROCEDURES

The following tutorial will once again work with Computer Consulting by Your Name. As in Chapters 2 and 3, transactions will be recorded for this fictitious company. To maximize training benefits, you should follow the steps illustrated in Chapter 2 and be sure to use the same file that you used to record transactions for Chapters 2 and 3.

OPEN QUICKBOOKS AND COMPANY FILE

Open QuickBooks

Open Computer Consulting by Your Name as previously instructed

- This file should contain all the transactions that you recorded for Chapters 2 and 3.

Check the title bar to verify that Computer Consulting by Your Name is the open company

Prepare a Journal for 01/01/15 – 01/30/15

Verify that all transactions from Chapters 2 and 3 are shown

- Hint: the last transaction should be the Check 8 written to Supply Station for the purchase of a Fax machine and the report total should be $45,217.79.

Close the Journal without printing

DATES

As in the other chapters in the text, the year used for the screen shots is 2015, which is the same year as the version of the program. You may want to check with your instructor to see if you should use 2015 as the year for the transactions. Be sure to use the same year for all the transactions in Chapters 2, 3, and 4.

PRINTING

Throughout the text, you will be instructed when to print business documents and reports. Everything that is to be printed within the chapter is listed on a transmittal sheet. The end-of-chapter problem also has everything to be printed listed on a transmittal sheet. As in the other chapters, check with your instructor for printing requirements.

BEGIN TUTORIAL

In this chapter, you will be recording end-of-period adjustments, reconciling bank statements, changing account names, and preparing traditional end-of-period reports. Because QuickBooks does not perform a traditional "closing" of the books, you will learn how to assign a closing date to protect transactions and data recorded during previous accounting periods.

As in the earlier chapters, all transactions are listed on memos. Unless otherwise specified, the transaction date will be the same as the memo date. Once a specific type of transaction has been entered in a step-by-step manner, additional transactions of the same or a similar type will be made without instructions being provided. Of course, you may always refer to instructions given for previous transactions for ideas or for steps used to enter those transactions. To determine the account used in the transaction, refer to the Chart of Accounts, which is also the General Ledger.

CHANGE ACCOUNT NAME

Even though transactions have been recorded during the month of January, QuickBooks makes it a simple matter to change the name of an existing account. Once the name of an account has been changed, all transactions using the "old" name are updated and show the "new" account name.

MEMO

DATE: January 31, 2015

Upon the recommendation from the company's CPA, you decided to change the names of several accounts: Student's Name, Capital to Your Name, Capital (Use your actual name); Company Cars to Business Vehicles; Company Cars Loan to Business Vehicles Loan; Automobile Expense to Business Vehicles Expense; Auto Insurance Expense to Business Vehicles Insurance; Office Equipment Loan to Office Furniture/Equipment Loan; and Office Equipment to Office Furniture/Equipment.

Change the account names

Access the **Chart of Accounts** using the keyboard shortcut **Ctrl+A**
Scroll through accounts until you see **Student's Name, Capital**, click the account.
Click the **Account** button at the bottom of the Chart of Accounts, click **Edit Account**
OR
Use the keyboard shortcut **Ctrl+E**
On the **Edit Account** screen, highlight **Student's Name**
Enter your name

- The name of the account should be **Your Name, Capital** (your real name!).

Click **Save & Close** to record the name change and close the **Edit Account** screen

- Notice that the name of the account appears as **Your Name, Capital** in the Chart of Accounts and that the balance of $78,135.00 shows.
- The balances of any subaccounts of Your Name, Capital will be reflected in the account total on the Chart of Accounts and in reports.
- While the subaccount names remain unchanged, the name of the account to which they are attached is changed.

Follow the steps above to change the names of:

Company Cars to **Business Vehicles**

- If the subaccount included the name of Company Cars, the subaccount name would need to be changed. Changing the name of the master account does not change the name of a related subaccount.
- Remember the account name was changed in Chapter 1 after the Computer (Backup Ch. 1).qbb file was created. When the backup file was restored, the account name reverted back to the original name Company Cars.

Company Cars Loan to **Business Vehicles Loan**

Automobile Expense to **Business Vehicles Expense**

Delete the Description by highlighting it and then pressing the **Delete** key

Auto Insurance Expense to **Business Vehicles Insurance** (Subaccount of Insurance Expense)

Office Equipment to **Office Furniture/Equipment**

- Due to exceeding the allotted number of characters in an account name, the was used to separate the words Furniture and Equipment.

Office Equipment Loan to **Office Furniture/Equipment Loan**

Do not close the **Chart of Accounts**

EFFECT OF ACCOUNT NAME CHANGE ON SUBACCOUNTS

Any account (even a subaccount) that uses Company Cars (the master account) as part of the account name needs to be changed. When the account name of Company Cars was changed to Business Vehicles, the subaccounts of Company Cars automatically became subaccounts of Business Vehicles. Because the subaccount did not include "Business Vehicles" as part of the account name, the name did not change. If the subaccount included "Business Vehicles" as part of the account name, then the subaccount name would need to be changed.

Examine the Depreciation and Original Cost accounts for Business Vehicles

Click **Depreciation** under Business Vehicles

Use the keyboard shortcut **Ctrl+E**

The text box for **Subaccount of** shows as **Business Vehicles**

- Remember you do not have to change the name of the Depreciation account. You are just verifying that Depreciation is a subaccount of Business Vehicles.

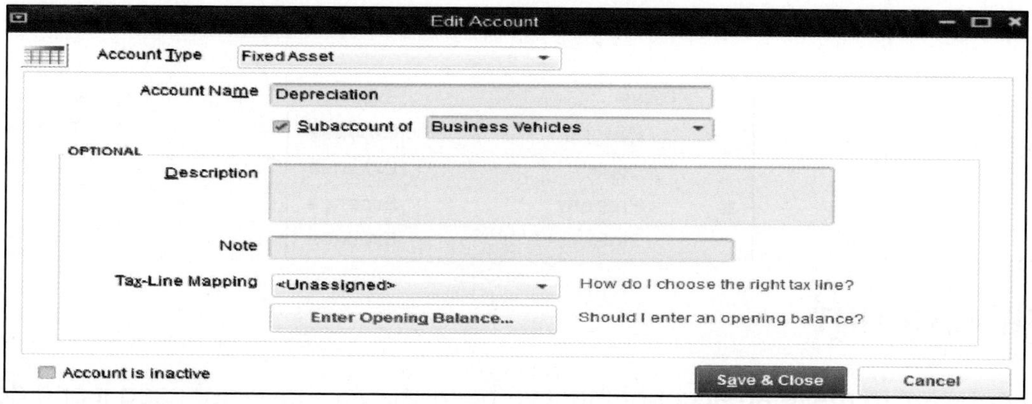

Click **Cancel**

- Repeat the above steps to examine the **Original Cost** account.
- Examine **Your Name, Capital** and **Office Furniture/Equipment** and their subaccounts.

Do not close the **Chart of Accounts**

MAKE ACCOUNT INACTIVE

If you are not using an account and do not have plans to use it in the near future, the account may be made inactive. The account remains available for use, yet it does not appear on your chart of accounts unless you check the Show All check box.

> **MEMO**
> **DATE:** January 31, 2015
>
> At present, the company does not plan to purchase its own building. Make Interest Expense: Mortgage and Taxes: Property inactive.

Make the accounts listed in the memo inactive

Click **Mortgage** under Interest Expense
Click the **Account** button at the bottom of the **Chart of Accounts**
Click **Make Account Inactive**

- The account no longer appears in the Chart of Accounts.

To view all accounts including the inactive ones, click the **Include Inactive** check box at the bottom of the **Chart of Accounts** and all accounts will be displayed

- Notice the icon next to Mortgage. It marks the account as inactive.

	◆Interest Expense	Expense
	◆Finance Charge	Expense
	◆Loan Interest	Expense
✖	◆Mortgage	Expense

Repeat the previous steps to make **Taxes: Property** inactive

	⋄Taxes	Expense
	⋄Federal	Expense
	⋄Local	Expense
✖	⋄Property	Expense
	⋄State	Expense

DELETE ACCOUNT

If you do not want to make an account inactive because you have not used it and do not plan to use it at all, QuickBooks allows an unused account to be deleted at any time. As a safeguard, QuickBooks prevents the deletion of an account once it has been used even if it simply contains an opening balance, an existing balance, or a 0.00 balance.

MEMO
DATE: January 31, 2015

In addition to previous changes to account names, you find that you do not use nor will use the expense account: Cash Discounts. Delete this account from the Chart of Accounts. In addition, delete the accounts: Inventory Asset, Cost of Goods Sold, and Dues and Subscriptions account.

Delete the **Cash Discounts** expense account

Scroll through accounts until you see Cash Discounts, click **Cash Discounts**
Click the **Account** button at the bottom of the Chart of Accounts, click **Delete Account** **OR** use the keyboard shortcut **Ctrl+D**
Click **OK** on the **Delete Account** dialog box

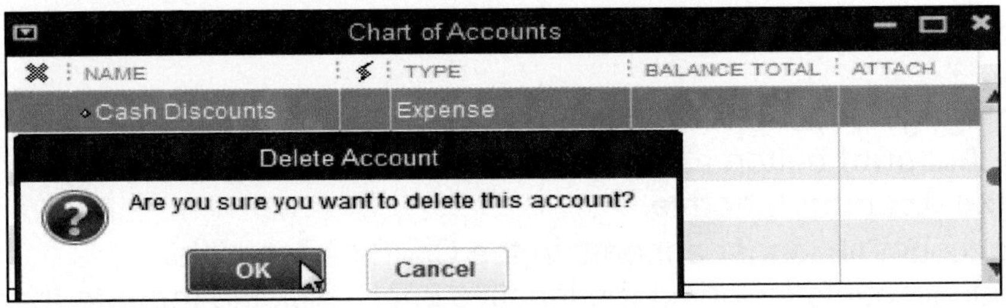

- The account has now been deleted.

Repeat the above steps for the deletion of **Inventory Asset**, **Cost of Goods Sold**, **Dues and Subscriptions**

- Since this Dues and Subscriptions account has been used, QuickBooks will not allow it to be deleted.

- As soon as you try to delete Dues and Subscriptions, a **QuickBooks Message** appears. It describes the problem (account has a balance or has been used) and offers a solution (make account inactive).

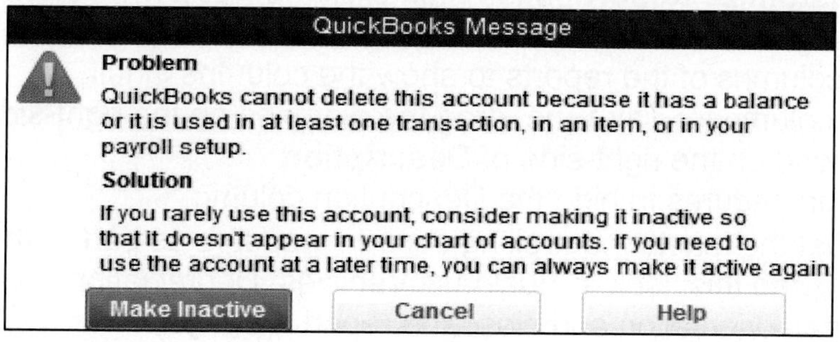

Click **Cancel**

- The account remains in the Chart of Accounts.

Chart of Accounts

NAME	TYPE	BALANCE TOTAL	ATTACH
◆Checking	Bank	47,529.00	
◆Petty Cash	Bank	82.21	
◆Accounts Receivable	Accounts Receivable	17,650.00	
◆Office Supplies	Other Current Asset	950.00	
◆Prepaid Insurance	Other Current Asset	2,850.00	
◆Undeposited Funds	Other Current Asset	0.00	
◆Business Vehicles	Fixed Asset	49,000.00	
◆Depreciation	Fixed Asset	0.00	
◆Original Cost	Fixed Asset	49,000.00	
◆Office Furniture/Equipment	Fixed Asset	8,536.00	
◆Depreciation	Fixed Asset	0.00	
◆Original Cost	Fixed Asset	8,536.00	
◆Accounts Payable	Accounts Payable	3,764.00	
◆Payroll Liabilities	Other Current Liability	0.00	
◆Loan Payable	Long Term Liability	39,000.00	
◆Business Vehicles Loan	Long Term Liability	35,000.00	
◆Office Furniture/Equipment Loan	Long Term Liability	4,000.00	
◆Owner's Equity	Equity		
◆Your Name, Capital	Equity	78,135.00	
◆Draws	Equity	0.00	
◆Investments	Equity	25,000.00	
◆Income	Income		
◆Installation Income	Income		
◆Technical Support Income	Income		
◆Training Income	Income		
◆Other Regular Income	Income		
◆Reimbursed Expenses	Income		
◆Uncategorized Income	Income		
◆Advertising Expense	Expense		
◆Bank Service Charges	Expense		
◆Business Vehicles Expense	Expense		
◆Contributions	Expense		
◆Depreciation Expense	Expense		
◆Dues and Subscriptions	Expense		
◆Equipment Rental	Expense		

Partial Chart of Accounts

Review the changes made, and then close the **Chart of Accounts**

To print the Chart of Accounts, click **Reports** on the menu bar, point to **List**, click **Account Listing** (QuickBooks will insert the date of your computer as the report date)
Click the **Customize Report** button then click the **Header/Footer** tab
Enter **January 31, 2015** as the Subtitle, click the **OK** button
Resize the columns of the reports to show the columns in full
To hide the column for **Tax Line**, drag the diamond on the right-side of **Tax Line** to the diamond on the right-side of **Description**
Repeat the procedures to hide the Description column

- Notice that the master/controlling account appears as part of the subaccount name. To see this, look at Business Vehicles: Depreciation.

Print in Portrait orientation and close the report

ADJUSTMENTS FOR ACCRUAL-BASIS ACCOUNTING

As previously stated, the accrual-basis of accounting matches the income and the expenses of a period in order to arrive at an accurate figure for net income or net loss. Thus, the revenue is earned at the time the service is performed or the sale is made no matter when the actual cash is received. The cash-basis of accounting records income or revenue at the time cash is received no matter when the sale was made or the service performed. The same holds true when a business buys things or pays bills. In accrual-basis accounting, the expense is recorded at the time the bill is received or the purchase is made regardless of the actual payment date. In cash-basis accounting, the expense is not recorded until it is paid. In QuickBooks, the Summary Report Basis for either Accrual or Cash is selected as a Report Preference. The default setting is Accrual.

For example, to record $1,000 of sales on account and one year of insurance for $600 in November: Using the accrual-basis of accounting, you would record $1,000 as income or revenue and $600 as a prepaid expense in an asset account—Prepaid Insurance. Month by month, an adjusting entry for $50 would be made to record the amount of insurance used for the month. In the accrual-basis of accounting, when the $1,000 payment on account is received, it will not affect income. It will be recorded as an increase in cash and a decrease in accounts receivable. When using the cash-basis of accounting, you would have no income and $600 worth of insurance recorded as an expense for November with nothing else recorded for insurance until the following November. The income of $1,000 would not be shown until the cash payment was received. A Statement of Profit & Loss prepared in November would show:

November	Accrual		Cash	
Income		$1,000		$ 0
Insurance Expense	($600/12) =	-50		-600
Net Profit (Loss)	**Profit**	**$950**	**Loss**	**-$600**

When you are using the accrual-basis of accounting, there are several internal transactions that must be recorded. These entries are called adjusting entries. Some items used in a business are purchased and or paid for in advance. When this occurs, they are recorded as an asset. These are called prepaid expenses. As these are used, they become expenses of the business. For example, insurance for the entire year would be used up month by month and should, therefore, be a monthly expense. Commonly, the insurance is billed and paid for the entire year. Until the insurance is used, it is an asset. Each month, the portion of the insurance used becomes an expense for the month. (Refer to the chart above.) Another example for adjusting entries is in regard to equipment. Since it does wear out and will eventually need to be replaced, rather than wait until replacement to record the use of the equipment, an adjusting entry is made to allocate the use of equipment as an expense for a period. This is called depreciation.

ADJUSTING ENTRIES—PREPAID EXPENSES

As previously stated, a prepaid expense is an item that is paid for in advance. Examples of prepaid expenses include: Insurance—policy is usually for six months or one year; Office Supplies—buy to have on hand and use as needed. (This is different from supplies that are purchased for immediate use.) A prepaid expense is an asset until it is used. As the insurance or supplies are used, the amount used becomes an expense for the period. In accrual-basis accounting, an adjusting entry is made in the General Journal at the end of the period to allocate the amount of prepaid expenses (assets) used to expenses.

The transactions for these adjustments may be recorded in the register for the account by clicking on the prepaid expense (asset) in the Chart of Accounts, or they may be made in the General Journal.

MEMO

DATE: January 31, 2015

Alhandra, remember to record the monthly adjustment for Prepaid Insurance. The amount we paid for the year for business vehicles insurance was $2,850. Also, we used $350 worth of office supplies this month. Please adjust accordingly.

Record the adjusting entries for office supplies expense and business vehicles insurance expense in the General Journal

To access the General Journal, click **Company** on the menu bar; and then, click **Make General Journal Entries…**

On the screen regarding Assigning Numbers to Journal Entries, click **Do not display this message in the future** to insert a check mark; and then, click **OK**

The General Journal Entries screen appears

- Note the checkbox for Adjusting Entry.
- A list of entries made Last Month is shown at the bottom of the screen.
  - If the date of your computer does not match the text, you may not have anything shown in the List of Entries.

- If you wish, you can change the time period to be displayed by clicking the drop-down list arrow for **List of Selected General Journal Entries** and selecting a time period or you may hide the list by clicking the **Hide List** icon on the Make General Journal Entries icon bar.

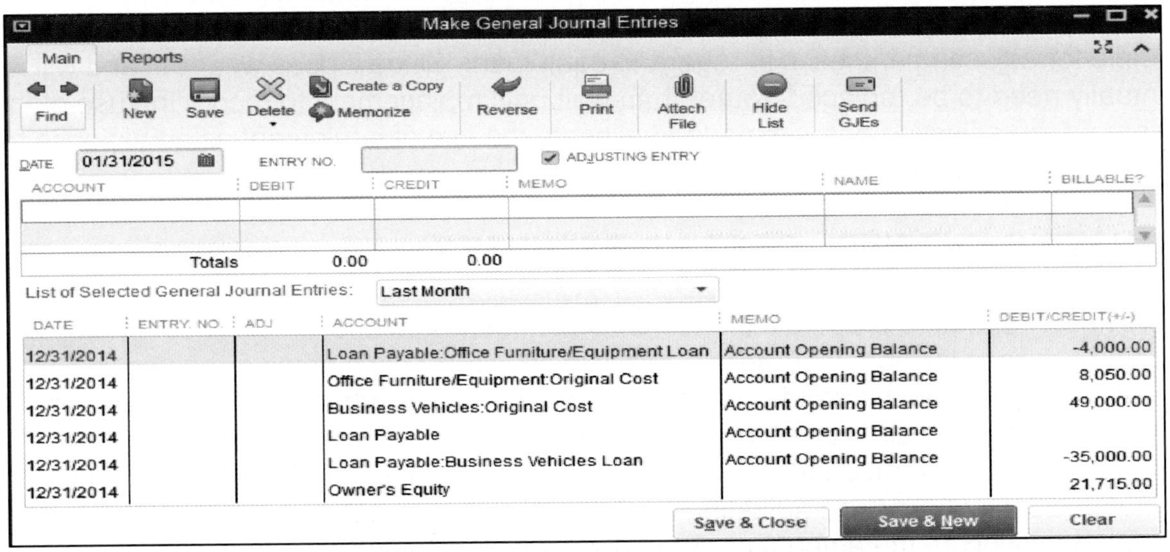

Record the adjusting entry for Prepaid Insurance
Enter **01/31/15** as the **DATE**

- QuickBooks will enter the year as 2015.
- **ENTRY NO.** is left blank unless you wish to record a specific number.
- Because all transactions entered for the month have been entered in the Journal as well as on an invoice or a bill, all transactions automatically have a Journal entry number.
- Notice the check box for **ADJUSTING ENTRY** is marked. The ADJUSTING ENTRY check box allows QuickBooks to indicate whether or not an entry is an adjustment.
- Adjusting journal entries are entered by accountants to make after-the-fact changes to specific accounts.
- Accountants make adjustments for a variety of reasons, including depreciation, prepaid income or expenses; adjusting sales tax payable; and entering bank or credit card fees or interest.
- You can view a list of all adjusting journal entries in the Adjusting Journal Entries report.
- By default, the ADJUSTING ENTRY checkbox is selected for new transactions.

Tab to or click the **ACCOUNT** column

Click the drop-down list arrow for **ACCOUNT**; click the expense account **Business Vehicles Insurance**

Tab to or click **DEBIT**

- The $2,850 given in the memo is the amount for the year; calculate the amount of the adjustment for the month by using QuickBooks QuickMath or the Calculator.

Use QuickBooks QuickMath

Enter **2850** by:

Keying the numbers on the **10-key pad** (preferred)

- Be sure Num Lock is on. If not, press Num Lock to activate.

<u>**OR**</u>

Typing the numbers at the top of the keyboard

Press **/** for division

Key **12**

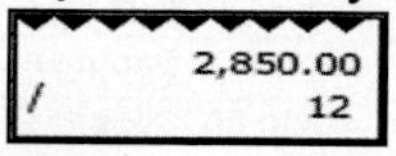

Press **Enter** to close QuickMath and enter the amount in the DEBIT column

Or use the Calculator as instructed in Chapter 1

Enter the amount of the adjustment **237.5** in the **DEBIT** column

- QuickBooks will change 237.5 into 237.50.
- Notice that the amount must be entered by you when using Calculator; QuickBooks Math automatically enters the amount.

Tab to or click the **MEMO** column

Type **Adjusting Entry, Insurance**

Tab to or click **ACCOUNT**

Click the drop-down list arrow for **ACCOUNT**

Click the asset account **Prepaid Insurance**

- The amount for the Credit column should be entered automatically. However, there are several reasons why an amount may not appear in the Credit column. If 237.50 does not appear, type it in the Credit column.
- If the memo does not appear automatically, tab to or click the **MEMO** column, and type **Adjusting Entry, Insurance**.

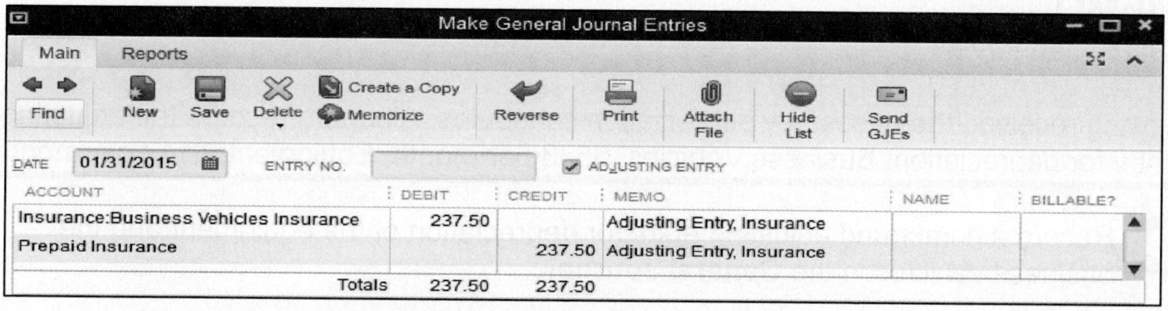

- Note the Totals for the Debit and Credit shown at the bottom of the screen.

Click **Save & New** to record the adjustment and advance to the next **Make General Journal Entries** screen

Repeat the above procedures to record the adjustment for the office supplies used

Use the Memo **Supplies Used**

- The amount given in the memo is the actual amount of the supplies used in January so you will not need to use QuickMath or the calculator.

- Remember, when supplies are purchased to have on hand, the original entry records an increase to the asset Office Supplies. Once the supplies are used, the adjustment correctly records the amount of supplies used as an expense.

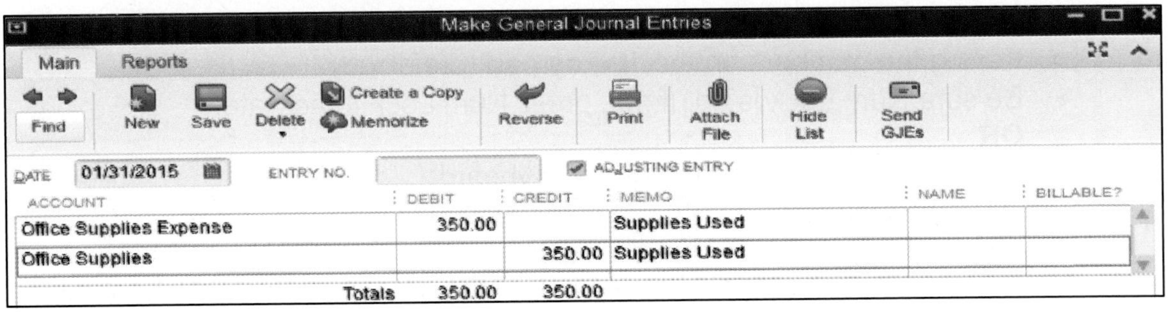

Click **Save & New**

ADJUSTING ENTRIES—DEPRECIATION

Equipment and other long-term assets lose value over their lifetime. Unlike supplies—where you can actually see, for example, the paper supply diminishing—it is very difficult to see how much of a computer has been "used up" during the month. To account for the fact that machines do wear out and need to be replaced, an adjustment is made for depreciation. This adjustment correctly matches the expenses of the period against the revenue of the period.

The adjusting entry for depreciation can be made in the account register for Depreciation, or it can be made in the General Journal.

MEMO
DATE: January 31, 2015

Having received the necessary depreciation schedules, Alhandra records the adjusting entry for depreciation: Business Vehicles, $583 per month; Equipment, $142 per month.

Record a compound adjusting entry for depreciation of the equipment and the business vehicles in the **General Journal**

Continue to use **Make General Journal Entries**

- The **DATE** should show as **01/31/15** and **ADJUSTING ENTRY** should have a check. If not, enter the date and click ADJUSTING ENTRY to select.

ENTRY NO. is left blank

- Normally, the debit portion of a General Journal entry is entered first. However, in order to use the automatic calculation feature of QuickBooks, you will enter the **credit** entries first.

Tab to or click in the **ACCOUNT** column

Click the drop-down list arrow for **ACCOUNT**, click **Depreciation** under **Business Vehicles**

- Make sure that you do <u>not</u> click the controlling account, Business Vehicles.

Tab to or click in the **CREDIT** column, enter **583**

Tab to or click in the **MEMO** column, enter **Adjusting Entry, January**

Tab to or click the **ACCOUNT** column

- The amount of the 583 credit shows in the DEBIT column temporarily.

Click the drop-down list arrow for **ACCOUNT**; click **Depreciation** under **Office Furniture/Equipment**

- Again, make sure that you do <u>not</u> use the controlling account, Office Furniture/Equipment.
- If the DEBIT column shows 583.00, do not worry about it.

Tab to or click in the **CREDIT** column, enter **142**

- The 583 in the DEBIT column is removed when you tab to or click **MEMO**.
- The adjusting entry **Adjusting Entry, January** should have been entered automatically. If not, enter it in the **MEMO** column.

Tab to or click in the **ACCOUNT** column

Click the drop-down list arrow for **ACCOUNT**, click **Depreciation Expense**

<u>DEBIT</u> column should automatically show **725**

- If 725 does not appear, enter it in the DEBIT column. The MEMO **Adjusting Entry, January** should be entered automatically. If not, enter it.

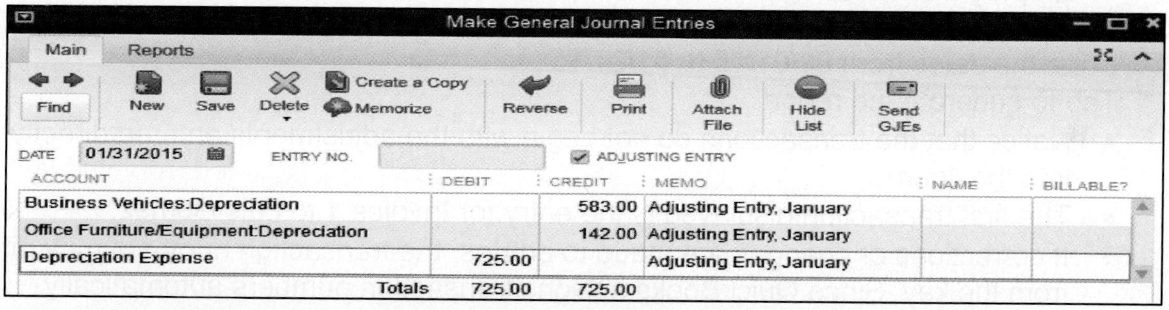

Click the **Save** icon to record the adjustment

- If you get a message regarding Tracking Fixed Assets, click **Do not display this message in the future** and click **OK**.

Click the drop-down list arrow for **List of Selected General Journal Entries** shown below the Totals

Click **This Fiscal Year**

- If your computer does not have 2015 as the year, click **Last Fiscal Year**.

View the entries recorded in 2015

- Note that only the first line/account used in a transaction appears.
- If you click on one of the transactions, it will take to you that transaction in the General Journal.

List of Selected General Journal Entries: This Fiscal Year

DATE	ENTRY NO.	ADJ	ACCOUNT	MEMO	DEBIT/CREDIT(+/-)
01/31/2015		✔	Business Vehicles:Depreciation	Adjusting Entry, January	-583.00
01/31/2015		✔	Insurance:Business Vehicles Insurance	Adjusting Entry, Insurance	237.50
01/31/2015		✔	Office Supplies Expense	Supplies Used	350.00

Close **Make General Journal Entries**

JOURNAL

Once transactions have been entered in the General Journal, it is important to view them. QuickBooks refers to the General Journal as the location of a transaction entry and to the Journal as a report. Even with the special ways in which transactions are entered in QuickBooks through invoices, bills, checks, and account registers, the Journal is still the book of original entry. All transactions recorded for the company may be viewed in the Journal even if they were entered elsewhere. The Journal may be viewed or printed at any time.

View the Journal for January

Click **Reports** on the menu bar, point to **Accountant & Taxes,** and click **Journal**
If you get the Collapsing and Expanding Transactions dialog box, click the **Do not display this message in the future**; and then, click **OK**
Always **Expand** your transactions even if not specifically instructed to do so
Enter the dates from **01/01/15** to **01/31/15**
Tab to generate the report

- Notice that the transactions do not begin with the adjustments entered directly into the Journal.
- The first transaction displayed is the entry for Invoice 1 to Luis Gomez.
- If corrections or changes are made to entries, the transaction numbers may differ from the key. Since QuickBooks assigns transaction numbers automatically, disregard any discrepancies in transaction numbers.

Scroll through the report to view all transactions recorded in the Journal
Verify the total Debit and Credit Columns of $46,530.29

- If your totals do not match, check for errors and make appropriate corrections.
- Since the adjusting entries were marked as adjustments when entered in the General Journal, the Adj column shows checks for these entries.

Computer Consulting by Your Name
Journal
January 2015

Trans #	Type	Date	Num	Adj	Name	Memo	Account	Debit	Credit
67	General Journal	01/31/2015		✔		Adjusting Entry, Insurance	Business Vehicles Insurance	237.50	
				✔		Adjusting Entry, Insurance	Prepaid Insurance		237.50
								237.50	237.50
68	General Journal	01/31/2015		✔		Supplies Used	Office Supplies Expense	350.00	
				✔		Supplies Used	Office Supplies		350.00
								350.00	350.00
69	General Journal	01/31/2015		✔		Adjusting Entry, January	Depreciation		583.00
				✔		Adjusting Entry, January	Depreciation		142.00
				✔		Adjusting Entry, January	Depreciation Expense	725.00	
								725.00	725.00
TOTAL								46,530.29	46,530.29

Partial Report

Close the Journal without printing

OWNER WITHDRAWALS

In a sole proprietorship an owner cannot receive a paycheck because he or she owns the business. An owner withdrawing money from a business—even to pay personal expenses—is similar to withdrawing money from a savings account. A withdrawal simply decreases the owner's capital. QuickBooks allows you to establish a separate account for owner withdrawals. If a separate account is not established, owner withdrawals may be subtracted directly from the owner's capital or investment account.

MEMO
DATE: January 31, 2015

Because you work in the business full time, you do not earn a paycheck. Prepare the check for your monthly withdrawal, $2,500.

Write Check 9 to yourself for $2,500 withdrawal

Open the **Write Checks - Checking** window:
Click **Banking** on the menu bar, click **Write Checks**
OR
Click the **Write Checks** icon in the Banking section of the Home Page
OR
Use the keyboard shortcut **Ctrl+W**
NO. should be **TO PRINT**
- If not, click the check box **Print Later** on the Write Checks - Checking icon bar.

DATE should be **01/31/15**
Enter **Your Name** (type your real name) on the **PAY TO THE ORDER OF** line
Press the **Tab** key
- Because your name was not added to any list when the company was created, the **Name Not Found** dialog box appears on the screen.

Click **Quick Add** to add your name to a list

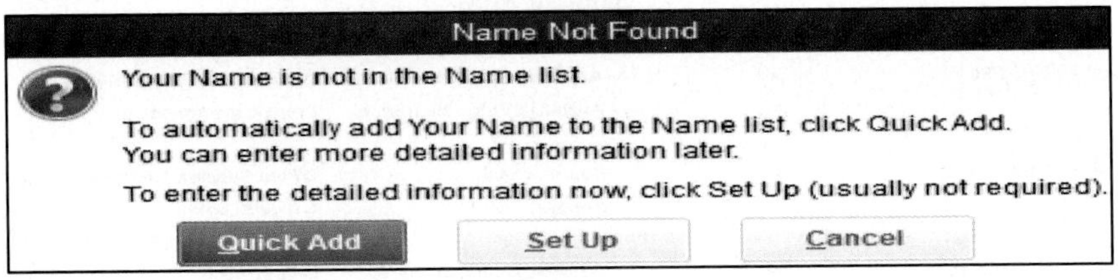

The **Select Name Type** dialog box appears
Click **Other**

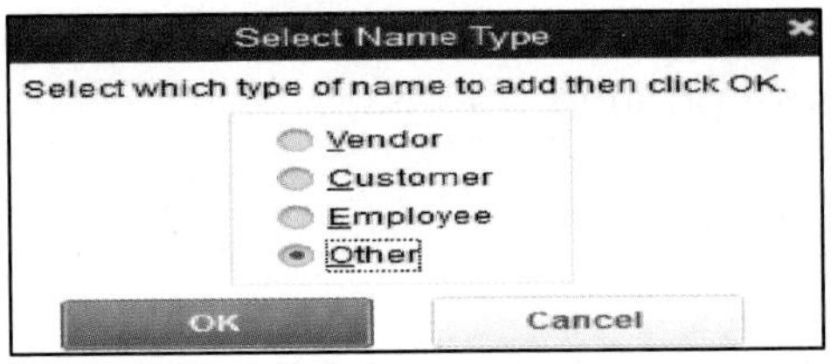

Click **OK**

- Your name is added to a list of "Other" names, which are used for owners, partners, and other miscellaneous names.

Tab to or click in the textbox for **$**

- If necessary, delete any numbers showing for the amount (0.00).

Enter **2500** in the text box for **$**
Tab to or click **MEMO** on the check face and enter **Monthly Withdrawal**
Tab to or click in the **ACCOUNT** column in the detail section at the bottom of the check
Click the drop-down list arrow, click the Equity account **Draws**

- This account is a subaccount of Your Name, Capital.
- The amount 2,500.00 should appear in the **AMOUNT** column.
- If it does not, tab to or click in the **AMOUNT** column and enter 2500.

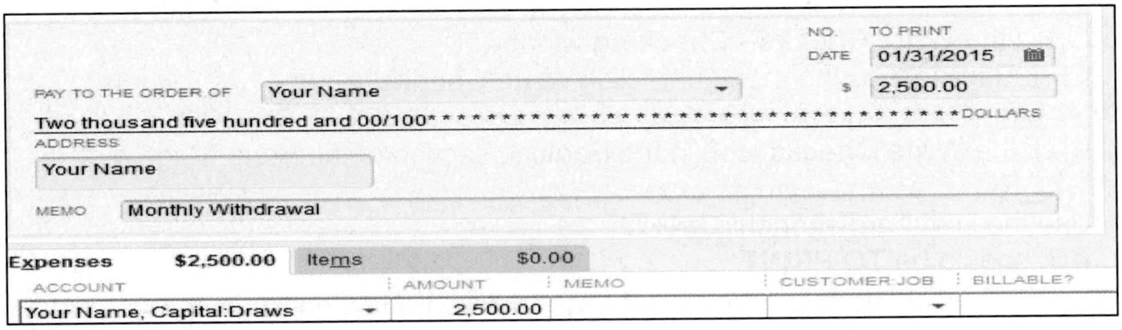

Click **Print** to print the check
The **Print Check** dialog box appears; the **Printed Check Number** should be **9**

- If necessary, change the number to 9.

Click **OK**

Print the standard style check as previously instructed
Once the check has printed successfully, click **OK** on the **Print Checks - Confirmation** dialog box
Click **Save & Close** to record the check, close any reminder screens that may appear

CASH INVESTMENT BY OWNER

An owner may decide to invest more of his or her personal cash in the business at any time. The new investment is entered into the owner's investment account and into cash. The investment may be recorded in the account register for checking or in the register for the owner's investment account. It may also be recorded in the General Journal.

> **MEMO**
> **DATE:** January 31, 2015
>
> You received money from a certificate of deposit. Rather than reinvest in another certificate of deposit, you have decided to invest an additional $5,000 in the company.

Record the owner's additional cash investment in the Journal

Access Make General Journal Entries as previously instructed
The **DATE** should be **01/31/15**

- Nothing is needed for ENTRY No.

This is not an adjusting entry, so click **ADJUSTING ENTRY** to remove the check
DEBIT **Checking, $5,000**
The MEMO for both entries should be **Cash Investment**
CREDIT the Equity account **Investments, $5,000**

- This account is listed as a subaccount of Your Name, Capital.

DATE 01/31/2015 ENTRY NO. ADJUSTING ENTRY

ACCOUNT	DEBIT	CREDIT	MEMO	NAME	BILLABLE?
Checking	5,000.00		Cash Investment		
Your Name, Capital:Investments		5,000.00	Cash Investment		
Totals	5,000.00	5,000.00			

Click **Save & New**

NON-CASH INVESTMENT BY OWNER

An owner may make investments in a business at any time. The investment may be cash; but it may also be something such as reference books, equipment, tools, buildings, and so on. Additional investments by an owner(s) are added to owner's equity. In the case of a sole proprietorship, the investment is added to the Capital account for Investments.

MEMO
DATE: January 31, 2015

Originally, you planned to have an office in your home as well as in the company and purchased new office furniture for your home. Since then, you decided the business environment would appear more professional if the new furniture were in the office rather than your home. You gave the new office furniture to the company as an additional owner investment. The value of the investment is $3,000.

Record the non-cash investment in the Journal

The **DATE** should be **01/31/15, ENTRY NO**. should be blank, **ADJUSTING ENTRY** should not be marked
DEBIT **Original Cost** (the subaccount of **Office Furniture/Equipment**) **$3,000**
The MEMO for both entries should be **Investment of Furniture**
CREDIT **Investments** (the subaccount of **Your Name, Capital**) **$3,000**

- When you select the account and press tab, the Memo should automatically appear. If it does not, copy the memo for the second entry rather than retype it, drag through the memo text to highlight; press Ctrl+C; position the cursor in the memo area for the second entry; press Ctrl+V.

DATE 01/31/2015 ENTRY NO. ADJUSTING ENTRY

ACCOUNT	DEBIT	CREDIT	MEMO	NAME	BILLABLE?
Office Furniture/Equipment:Original Cost	3,000.00		Investment of Furniture		
Your Name, Capital:Investments		3,000.00	Investment of Furniture		
Totals	3,000.00	3,000.00			

Click **Save & Close** to record and exit

- If you get a message regarding Tracking Fixed Assets, click **OK**.

BALANCE SHEET (STANDARD)

Prior to writing the check for the monthly withdrawal, there had been no withdrawals by the owner, and the drawing account balance was zero. Once a withdrawal is made, that amount is carried forward in the owner's drawing account. Subsequent withdrawals are added to this account. When you view the Balance Sheet, notice the balance of the Drawing account after the check for the withdrawal was written. Also notice the Net Income account that appears in the equity section of the Balance Sheet. This account is automatically added by QuickBooks to track the net income for the year.

View a Balance Sheet (Standard)

Click **Reports** on the menu bar, point to **Company & Financial**, and click **Balance Sheet Standard**

- Unless otherwise instructed, all Balance Sheets prepared are Standard.

Tab to or click **As of**
Enter the date **01/31/15**
Tab to generate the report
Scroll through the report

- Notice the Equity section, especially Net Income.
- The ▼ next to Equity and Your Name, Capital show that the report is expanded. If you click it, you will collapse the detail and only the heading **Equity** and the total equity amount of **$88,020.71** will show.

Computer Consulting by Your Name
Balance Sheet
As of January 31, 2015

	Jan 31, 15
▼ Equity	
▼ Your Name, Capital	
Draws	-2,500.00
Investments	33,000.00
Your Name, Capital - Other	53,135.00
Total Your Name, Capital	83,635.00
Net Income	4,385.71
Total Equity	88,020.71
TOTAL LIABILITIES & EQUITY	130,784.71

Partial Report

Close the report without printing

PREPARE DAILY BACKUP

By creating the backup file now, it will contain your work for Chapters 1, 2, 3 and up through the investments made by the owner in Chapter 4.

Prepare the Computer (Daily Backup).qbb file

Follow the steps presented in Chapter 1 for creating a backup file
Name the file **Computer (Daily Backup)**
The file type is **QBW Backup (* .QBB)**
click **Yes** on the Confirm Save As screen

BANK RECONCILIATION

Each month, the checking account should be reconciled with the bank statement to make sure that the balances agree. The bank statement will rarely have an ending balance that matches the balance of the checking account. This is due to several factors: outstanding checks (written by the business but not paid by the bank), deposits in transit (deposits that were made too late to be included on the bank statement), bank service charges, interest earned on checking accounts, collections made by the bank, and errors made in recording checks and/or deposits by the company or by the bank.

In order to have an accurate amount listed as the balance in the checking account, it is important that the differences between the bank statement and the checking account be reconciled. If something such as a service charge or a collection made by the bank appears on the bank statement, it needs to be recorded in the checking account.

Reconciling a bank statement is an appropriate time to find any errors that may have been recorded in the checking account. The reconciliation may be out of balance because a transposition was made (recording $94 rather than $49), a transaction was recorded backwards, a transaction was recorded twice, or a transaction was not recorded at all. If a transposition was made, the error may be found by dividing the difference by 9. For example, if $94 was recorded and the actual transaction amount was $49, you would subtract 49 from 94 to get 45. The number 45 can be divided by 9, so your error was a transposition. If the error can be evenly divided by 2, the transaction may have been entered backwards. For example, if you were out of balance $200, look to see if you had any $100 transactions. Perhaps you recorded a $100 debit, and it should have been a credit (or vice versa).

BEGIN RECONCILIATION

To begin the reconciliation, you need to open the Reconcile - Checking window. Verify the information shown for the checking account. The Opening Balance should match the amount of the final balance on the last reconciliation, or it should match the starting account balance.

> **MEMO**
> **DATE:** January 31, 2015
>
> Received the bank statement from Sunshine Bank. The bank statement is dated January 31, 2015. Alhandra Cruz needs to reconcile the bank statement and to print a Detail Reconciliation Report for you.

Reconcile the bank statement for January

Click the **Reconcile** icon in the Banking section of the Home Page to open the **Begin Reconciliation** window and enter preliminary information

The **Account** should be **Checking**

If not, click the drop-down list arrow, click **Checking**

The **Statement Date** should be **01/31/2015**

- The Statement Date is entered automatically by the computer. If the date is not shown as 01/31/2015, change it.

Beginning Balance should be **12,870**

- This is the same amount as the checking account starting balance.

ENTER BANK STATEMENT INFORMATION

Some information appearing on the bank statement is entered into the Begin Reconciliation window as the next step. This information includes the ending balance, bank service charges, and interest earned.

Use the following bank statement as you follow the written instructions to reconcile the checking account (Do not try to reconcile the bank statement without following the instructions provided.

SUNSHINE BANK
12345 West Colorado Avenue
Woodland Hills, CA 91377
(818-555-3880)

Computer Consulting by Your Name
2895 West Avenue
Woodland Hills, CA 91367

Acct. # 123-456-7890 **January, 2015**

Beginning Balance, 1/1/2015			**$12,870.00**
1/02/15 Deposit	25,000		37,870.00
1/15/15 Deposit	13,840.00		51,750.00
1/26/15 Check 1		500.00	51,210.00
1/29/15 Check 2		195.00	51,015.00
1/29/15 Check 3		840.00	50,175.00
1/30/15 Cash Transfer		110.00	50,065.00
1/31/15 Business Vehicle Loan Pmt.: $467.19 Principal, $255.22 Interest		722.41	49,342.59
1/31/15 Office Furniture/Equipment Loan Pmt.: $29.17 Principal, $53.39 Interest		82.56	49,260.03
1/31/15 Service Charge		8.00	49,252.03
1/31/15 Interest	66.43		49,318.46
1/31/15 Ending Balance			**49,318.46**

Enter the **Ending Balance** from the Bank Statement, **49,318.46**
Tab to or click **Service Charge**
Enter **8**
Tab to or click Service Charge **Date**; if necessary, change to **01/31/2015**

- Don't forget to check the date, especially the year. If you leave an incorrect date, you will have errors in your accounts and in your reports.

Click the drop-down list arrow for **Account**

- Shortcut: If you click the drop-down list arrow, you do not have to Tab to the account text box.

Click **Bank Service Charges**
Tab to or click **Interest Earned**, enter **66.43**
Tab to or click Interest Earned **Date**; if necessary, change to **01/31/2015**
Click the drop-down list arrow for **Account**
Scroll through the list of accounts, click **Interest Income**

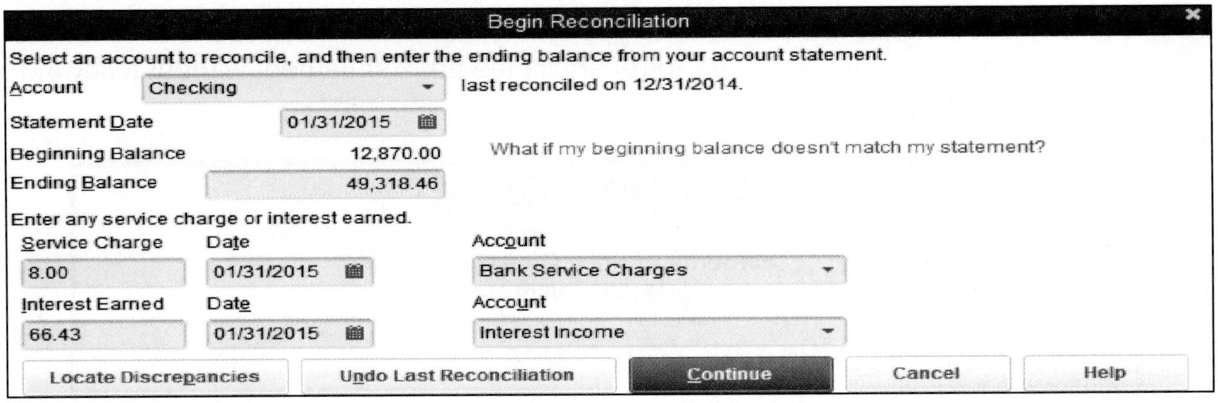

Click the **Continue** button

MARK CLEARED TRANSACTIONS

Once bank statement information for service charges and interest has been entered, compare the checks and deposits listed on the statement with the transactions for the checking account. Remember, the dates shown for the checks on the bank statement are the dates the checks were processed by the bank, not the dates the checks were written. If a deposit or a check is listed correctly on the bank statement and in the Reconcile - Checking window, it has cleared and should be marked. An item may be marked individually by positioning the cursor on the deposit or the check and clicking the primary mouse button. If all deposits and checks match, click the Mark All button. To remove all the checks, click the Unmark All button. To unmark an individual item, click the item to remove the check mark.

Mark cleared checks and deposits

Compare the bank statement with the **Reconcile - Checking** window
Click the items that appear on both statements

- *Note*: The date next to the check or the deposit on the bank statement is the date the check or deposit cleared the bank, not the date the check was written or the deposit was made.
- If you are unable to complete the reconciliation in one session, click the **Leave** button to leave the reconciliation and return to it later.
- Under <u>no</u> circumstances should you click **Reconcile Now** until the reconciliation is complete.

Make sure that the **Highlight Marked** checkbox in the lower-left corner is checked

- This will change the background color of everything that you mark and make it easier to view the selections in the reconciliation.

For Deposits and Other Credits, include the Voided Check for **0.00** on **01/30/2015**

Even though the transaction shows 110.00 on the Bank Statement, select the transaction for **100.00** on **01/30/2015** on the Checks and Payments side of the screen

- This was the transfer from Checking to Petty Cash.

Once you have marked the transactions that appear on the bank statement and in the Reconcile-Checking screen, look at the bottom of screen

In the section labeled "**Items you have marked cleared**" should show the following:

3 Deposits and Other Credits for 38,840.00

- This includes the voided check to Communication Telephone Co.

4 Checks and Payments for 1,635.00

- This includes the $100 for petty cash.

On the right-side of the lower section next to the Modify button, the screen should show:

The Service Charge is -8.00

The Interest Earned is 66.43

The Ending Balance is 49,318.46

The Cleared Balance is 50,133.43

There is a Difference of -814.97

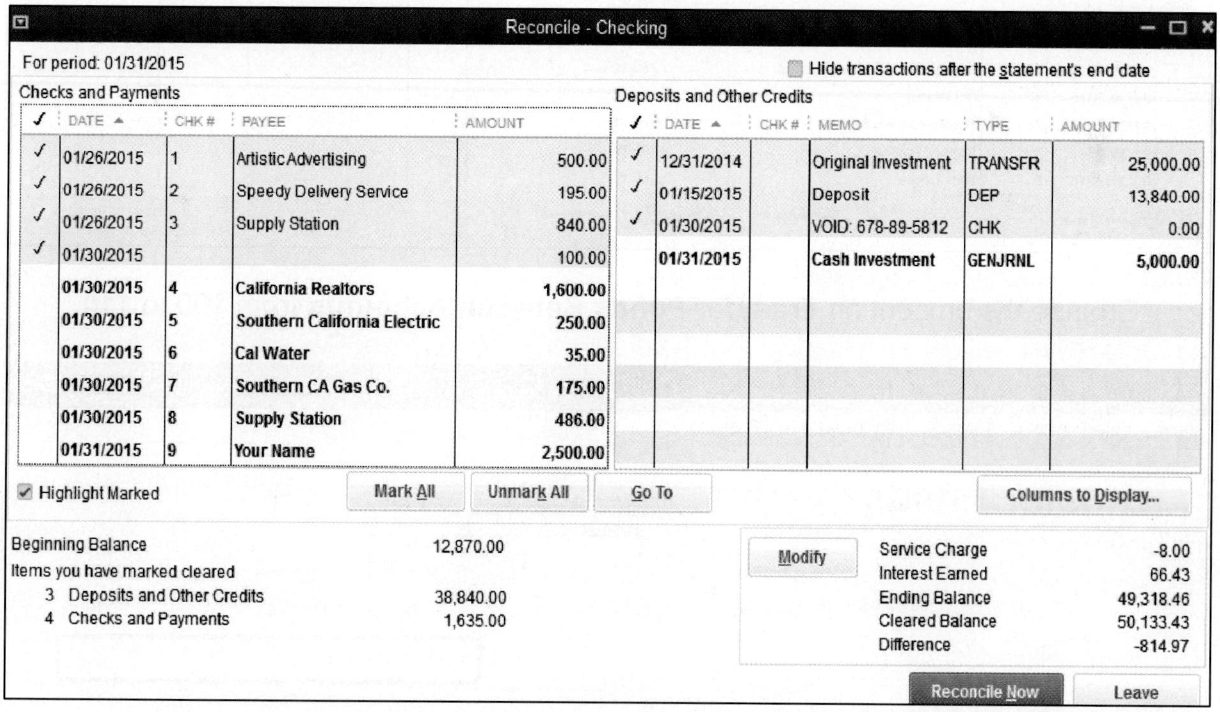

CORRECTING ENTRIES—BANK RECONCILIATION

As you complete the reconciliation, you may find errors that need to be corrected or transactions that need to be recorded. Anything entered as a service charge or interest earned will be entered automatically when the reconciliation is complete and the Reconcile Now button is clicked. To correct an error such as a transposition or an incorrect amount, click on the entry, then click the Go To button. The original entry will appear on the screen. The correction can be made and will show in the Reconcile - Checking window. If there is a transaction, such as an automatic loan payment to the bank, you need to access the register for the account used in the transaction and enter the payment.

Correct the error on the cash transfer into Petty Cash

In the section of the reconciliation for **Checks and Payments**, click the entry for **100.00** dated **01/30/2015**

- This was actually the Cash transfer to Petty Cash from Checking.

Click the **Go To** button

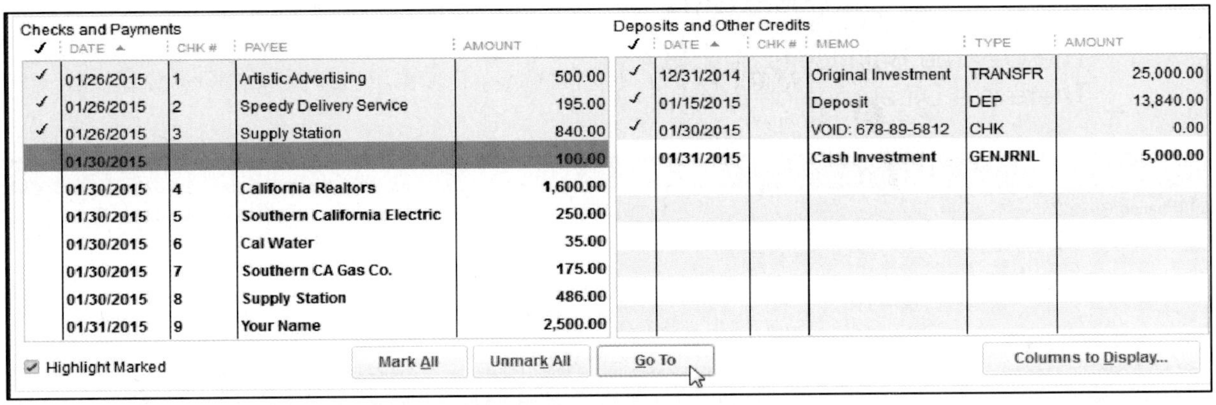

Checks and Payments

✓	DATE	CHK #	PAYEE	AMOUNT
✓	01/26/2015	1	Artistic Advertising	500.00
✓	01/26/2015	2	Speedy Delivery Service	195.00
✓	01/26/2015	3	Supply Station	840.00
	01/30/2015			100.00
	01/30/2015	4	California Realtors	1,600.00
	01/30/2015	5	Southern California Electric	250.00
	01/30/2015	6	Cal Water	35.00
	01/30/2015	7	Southern CA Gas Co.	175.00
	01/30/2015	8	Supply Station	486.00
	01/31/2015	9	Your Name	2,500.00

Deposits and Other Credits

✓	DATE	CHK #	MEMO	TYPE	AMOUNT
✓	12/31/2014		Original Investment	TRANSFR	25,000.00
✓	01/15/2015		Deposit	DEP	13,840.00
✓	01/30/2015		VOID: 678-89-5812	CHK	0.00
	01/31/2015		Cash Investment	GENJRNL	5,000.00

Highlight Marked | Mark All | Unmark All | Go To | Columns to Display...

Change the amount on **Transfer Funds Between Accounts** from 100 to **110**

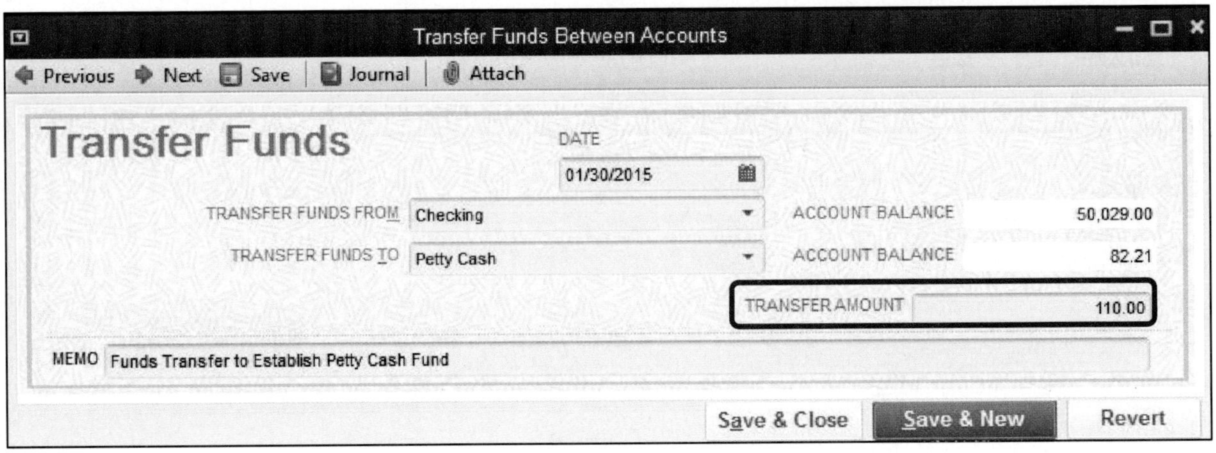

Click **Save & Close**

Click **Yes** on the **Recording Transaction** dialog box

- Notice that the amount for the Petty Cash transaction now shows 110.

Click the cash transfer to Petty Cash transaction to mark it (if not already marked)

- The amount shown at the bottom of the Reconcile window for the 4 Checks and Payments, shows 1,645.00.

ADJUSTING ENTRIES—BANK RECONCILIATION

With the **Reconcile - Checking** window still showing, enter the automatic loan payments

To enter the automatic payments, access the Checking Account Register by using the keyboard shortcut **Ctrl+R**

- If the register is shown on 1-Line, click the deselect

In the blank transaction at the bottom of the Checking register enter the **Date**, **01/31/15**

Tab to or click **Number**

Enter **Transfer**

Tab to or click **Payee**

Enter **Sunshine Bank**

Tab to or click the **Payment** column

- Because Sunshine Bank does not appear on any list, you will get a **Name Not Found** dialog box when you move to another field.

Click the **Quick Add** button to add the name of the bank to the Name list

Click **Other**

Click **OK**

- Once the name of the bank has been added to the Other list, the cursor will be positioned in the **PAYMENT** column.

Enter the amount of the Business Vehicles Loan payment of **722.41** in the **PAYMENT** column

Since more than one account is used, click the **Splits** button at the bottom of the register

Click the drop-down list arrow for **ACCOUNT**

Click **Loan Interest** under Interest Expense

Tab to or click **AMOUNT**, delete the amount 722.41 shown

Enter **255.22** as the amount of interest

Tab to or click **MEMO**

Enter **Business Vehicles Loan, Interest**

Tab to or click **ACCOUNT**

Click the drop-down list arrow for **ACCOUNT**

Click **Business Vehicles Loan** a subaccount of Loan Payable

- The correct amount of principal, 467.19, should be showing for the amount.

Tab to or click **MEMO**

Enter **Business Vehicles Loan, Principal**

4

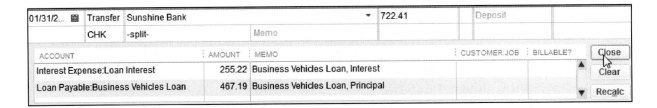

01/31/2...	Transfer	Sunshine Bank	722.41		Deposit
	CHK	-split- Memo			

ACCOUNT	AMOUNT	MEMO	CUSTOMER:JOB	BILLABLE?	Close
Interest Expense:Loan Interest	255.22	Business Vehicles Loan, Interest			Clear
Loan Payable:Business Vehicles Loan	467.19	Business Vehicles Loan, Principal			Recalc

Click the **Close** button in the Splits window

- This closes the window for the information regarding the way the transaction is to be "split" between accounts.

For the **Memo** in the Checking Register, record **Loan Pmt. Business Vehicles**

Click the **Record** button to record the transaction

- Because the **Register** organizes transactions according to date and the transaction type, you will notice that the loan payment will not appear as the last transaction in the Register. You may need to scroll through the Register to see the transaction since transfers are shown before other transactions entered on the same date.

01/31/2015	Transfer	Sunshine Bank	722.41		46,796.59
	CHK	-split- Loan Pmt. Business Vehicles			

Repeat the procedures to record the loan payment for office furniture/equipment

- When you enter the Payee as Sunshine Bank, the amount for the previous transaction (722.41) appears in Amount.

Enter the new amount, **82.56**

Click **Splits** button

Click the appropriate accounts and enter the correct amount for each item

- *Note*: The amounts for the previous loan payment automatically appear. You will need to enter the amounts for both accounts in this transaction.
- Refer to the bank statement for details regarding the amount of the payment for interest and the amount of the payment applied to principal.

ACCOUNT	AMOUNT	MEMO	CUSTOMER:JOB	BILLABLE?	Close
Interest Expense:Loan Interest	53.39	Office Furniture/Equipment Loan, Interest			Clear
Loan Payable:Office Furniture/Equipment Loan	29.17	Office Furniture/Equipment Loan, Principal			Recalc

Click **Close** to close the window for the information regarding the "split" between accounts

Enter the transaction Memo **Loan Pmt. Office Furniture/Equipment**

Click **Record** to record the loan payment

01/31/2015	Transfer	Sunshine Bank	82.56		46,714.03
	CHK	-split- Loan Pmt. Office Furniture/Equipment			

Close the **Checking** Register

- You should return to **Reconcile - Checking**.

Scroll through **Checks and Payments** until you find the two Transfers
Mark the two entries

- At this point, the **Ending Balance** and **Cleared Balance** should be equal—$49,318.46 with a difference of 0.00.

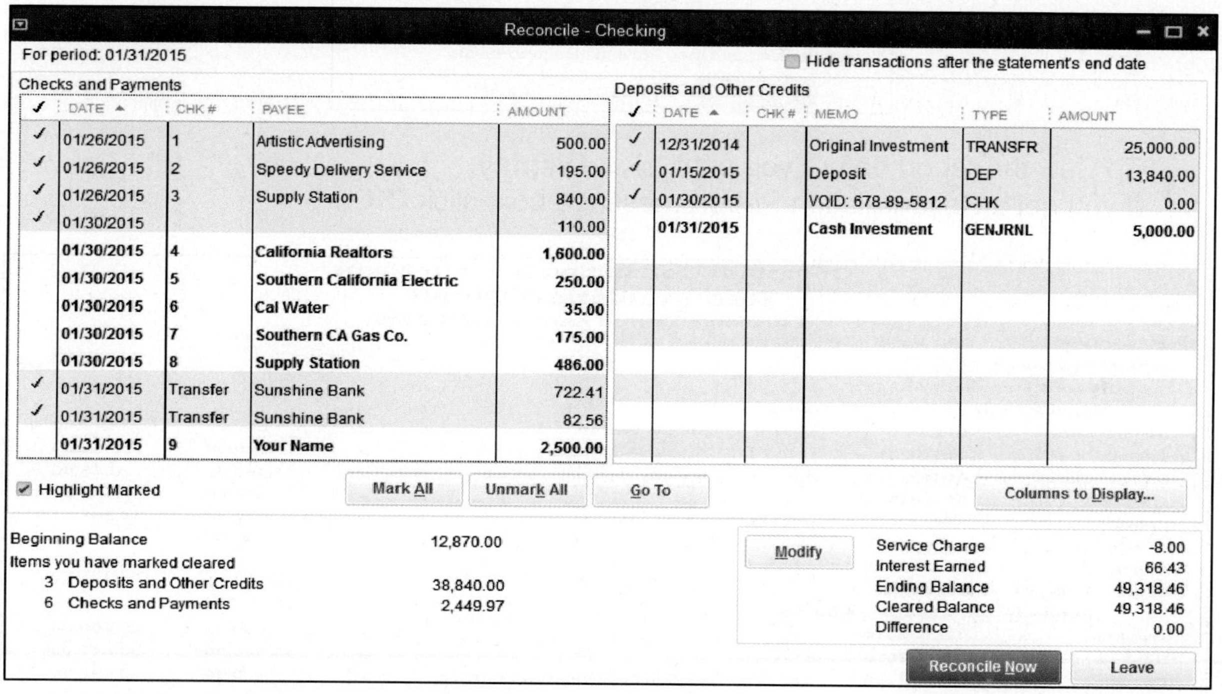

If your entries agree with the above, click **Reconcile Now** to finish the reconciliation

- If your reconciliation is not in agreement, do not click **Reconcile Now** until the errors are corrected.
- Once you click **Reconcile Now**, you may not return to this **Reconciliation - Checking** window.
- If you get an information screen regarding Online Banking, click **OK**.

RECONCILIATION DETAIL REPORT

As soon as the Ending Balance and the Cleared Balance are equal or when you finish marking transactions and click Reconcile Now, a screen appears allowing you to select the level of Reconciliation report you would like to print. You may select Summary and get a report that lists totals only or Detail and get all the transactions that were reconciled on the report. You may print the report at the time you have finished reconciling the account or you may print the report later by returning to the Reconciliation window. If you think you may want to print the report again in the future, print the report to a file to save it permanently.

Print a **Reconciliation Detail Report**

On the **Select Reconciliation Report** screen, click **Detail**

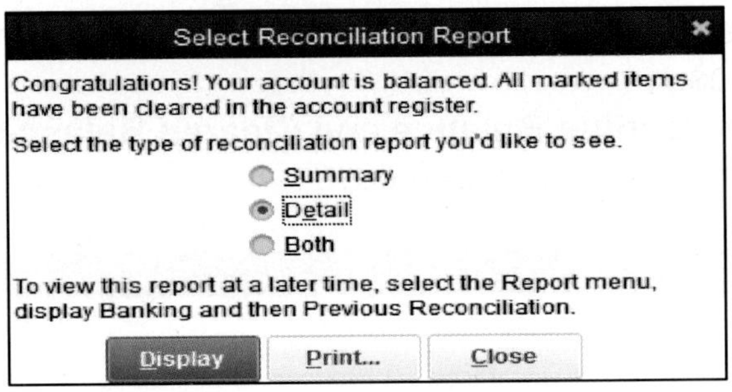

To view the report before you print, click **Display**;
If you get a Reconciliation Report message box, click **OK**

Computer Consulting by Your Name
Reconciliation Detail
Checking, Period Ending 01/31/2015

Type	Date	Num	Name	Clr	Amount	Balance
Beginning Balance						12,870.00
Cleared Transactions						
Checks and Payments - 7 items						
Bill Pmt -Check	01/26/2015	3	Supply Station	✔	-840.00	-840.00
Bill Pmt -Check	01/26/2015	1	Artistic Advertising	✔	-500.00	-1,340.00
Bill Pmt -Check	01/26/2015	2	Speedy Delivery Service	✔	-195.00	-1,535.00
Transfer	01/30/2015			✔	-110.00	-1,645.00
Check	01/31/2015	Transfer	Sunshine Bank	✔	-722.41	-2,367.41
Check	01/31/2015	Transfer	Sunshine Bank	✔	-82.56	-2,449.97
Check	01/31/2015			✔	-8.00	-2,457.97
Total Checks and Payments					-2,457.97	-2,457.97
Deposits and Credits - 4 items						
Transfer	12/31/2014			✔	25,000.00	25,000.00
Deposit	01/15/2015			✔	13,840.00	38,840.00
Check	01/30/2015		Communication Telephone Co.	✔	0.00	38,840.00
Deposit	01/31/2015			✔	66.43	38,906.43
Total Deposits and Credits					38,906.43	38,906.43
Total Cleared Transactions					36,448.46	36,448.46
Cleared Balance					36,448.46	49,318.46
Uncleared Transactions						
Checks and Payments - 6 items						
Check	01/30/2015	4	California Realtors		-1,600.00	-1,600.00
Check	01/30/2015	8	Supply Station		-486.00	-2,086.00
Check	01/30/2015	5	Southern California Electric		-250.00	-2,336.00
Check	01/30/2015	7	Southern CA Gas Co.		-175.00	-2,511.00
Check	01/30/2015	6	Cal Water		-35.00	-2,546.00
Check	01/31/2015	9	Your Name		-2,500.00	-5,046.00
Total Checks and Payments					-5,046.00	-5,046.00
Deposits and Credits - 1 item						
General Journal	01/31/2015				5,000.00	5,000.00
Total Deposits and Credits					5,000.00	5,000.00
Total Uncleared Transactions					-46.00	-46.00
Register Balance as of 01/31/2015					36,402.46	49,272.46
Ending Balance					36,402.46	49,272.46

- The uncleared information may be different from the report above. This is due to the fact that your computer's date may be different than January 31, 2015. As long as the cleared balance is $49,318.46, your report should be considered correct.

Resize the columns in report as previously instructed; and then, print the report in Portrait orientation

If your report printed correctly, close the report

CHECKING ACCOUNT REGISTER

Once the bank reconciliation has been completed, it is wise to scroll through the Checking account register to view the effect of the reconciliation on the account. You will notice that the check column shows a check mark for all items that were marked as cleared during the reconciliation. If at a later date an error is discovered, the transaction may be changed, and the correction will be reflected in the Beginning Balance on the reconciliation.

View the register for the Checking account

Open the Chart of Accounts and access the Checking account register as previously instructed

To display more of the register, click the check box for **1-Line**

Scroll through the register

- Notice that the transactions are listed in chronological order and that cleared transactions have a check mark.

4

Checking

Go to... | Print... | Edit Transaction | QuickReport | Setup Bank Feeds

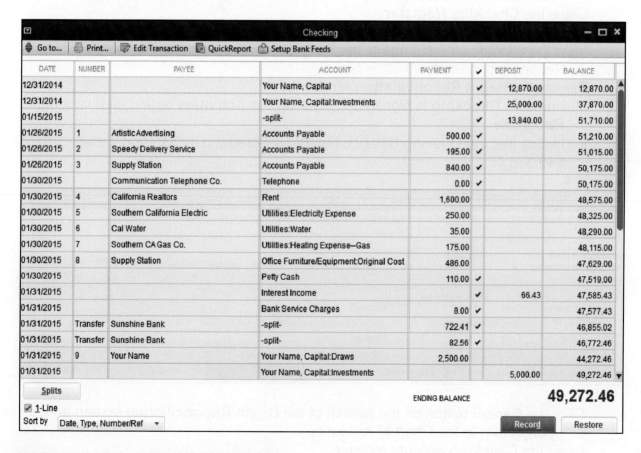

DATE	NUMBER	PAYEE	ACCOUNT	PAYMENT	✔	DEPOSIT	BALANCE
12/31/2014			Your Name, Capital		✔	12,870.00	12,870.00
12/31/2014			Your Name, Capital:Investments		✔	25,000.00	37,870.00
01/15/2015			-split-		✔	13,840.00	51,710.00
01/26/2015	1	Artistic Advertising	Accounts Payable	500.00	✔		51,210.00
01/26/2015	2	Speedy Delivery Service	Accounts Payable	195.00	✔		51,015.00
01/26/2015	3	Supply Station	Accounts Payable	840.00	✔		50,175.00
01/30/2015		Communication Telephone Co.	Telephone	0.00	✔		50,175.00
01/30/2015	4	California Realtors	Rent	1,600.00			48,575.00
01/30/2015	5	Southern California Electric	Utilities:Electricity Expense	250.00			48,325.00
01/30/2015	6	Cal Water	Utilities:Water	35.00			48,290.00
01/30/2015	7	Southern CA Gas Co.	Utilities:Heating Expense--Gas	175.00			48,115.00
01/30/2015	8	Supply Station	Office Furniture/Equipment:Original Cost	486.00			47,629.00
01/30/2015			Petty Cash	110.00	✔		47,519.00
01/31/2015			Interest Income		✔	66.43	47,585.43
01/31/2015			Bank Service Charges	8.00	✔		47,577.43
01/31/2015	Transfer	Sunshine Bank	-split-	722.41	✔		46,855.02
01/31/2015	Transfer	Sunshine Bank	-split-	82.56	✔		46,772.46
01/31/2015	9	Your Name	Your Name, Capital:Draws	2,500.00			44,272.46
01/31/2015			Your Name, Capital:Investments			5,000.00	49,272.46

Splits — ENDING BALANCE **49,272.46**

☑ 1-Line

Sort by: Date, Type, Number/Ref — Record — Restore

EDIT CLEARED TRANSACTIONS

Edit a transaction that was marked and cleared during the bank reconciliation:

Edit the **Petty Cash** transaction:

Click in the entry for the transfer of funds to **Petty Cash** on January 30
Change the **Payment** amount to **100**
Click the **Record** button

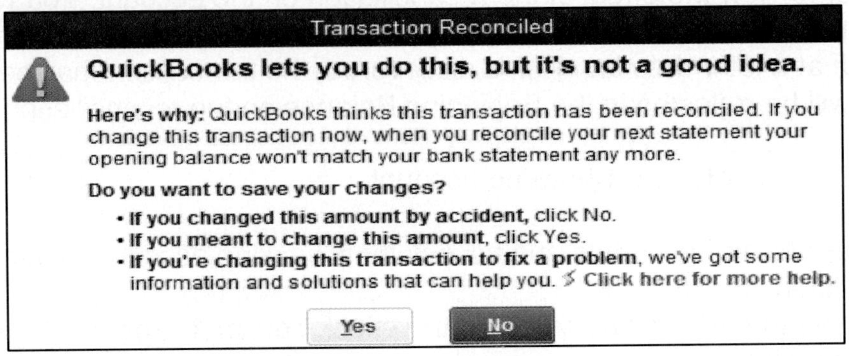

Click **Yes** on the **Transaction Reconciled** dialog box

- The transaction amount has been changed.

Close the **Checking Register**
Do <u>not</u> close the **Chart of Accounts**
View the effects of the change to the Petty Cash transaction in the "Begin Reconciliation window":
Display the **Begin Reconciliation** window by:
Making sure **Checking** is highlighted, clicking the **Activities** button, and clicking **Reconcile**

- Notice that the Opening Balance has been increased by $10 and shows $49,328.46.

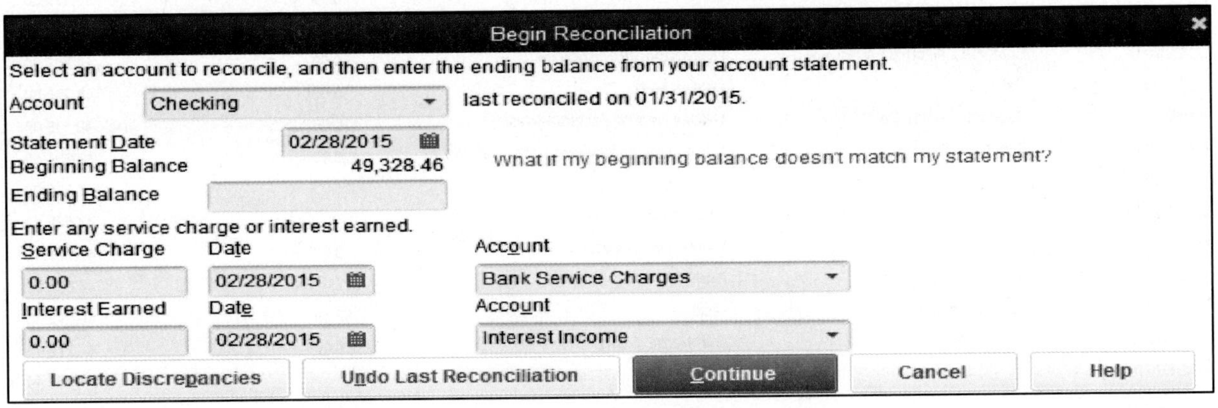

Click the **Cancel** button on the bottom of the **Begin Reconciliation** screen and, if open, return to the Chart of Accounts
Open the **Checking** account register
Change the amount for the **Petty Cash** transaction back to **110**
Click **Record** to record the change
Click **Yes** on the **Transaction Reconciled** dialog box
Reopen the **Begin Reconciliation** following the steps presented earlier

- Make sure the Beginning Balance shows **49,318.46**.

Close the **Checking Register**, and, if open, the **Chart of Accounts**

SELECT ACCRUAL-BASIS REPORTING PREFERENCE

QuickBooks allows a business to customize the program and select certain preferences for reports, displays, graphs, accounts, and so on. There are two report preferences available in QuickBooks: Cash and Accrual. You need to choose the one you prefer. If you select Cash as the report preference, income on reports will be shown as of the date payment is received and expenses will be shown as of the date you pay the bill. If Accrual is selected, QuickBooks shows the income on the report as of the date of the invoice and expenses as of the bill date. Prior to printing end-of-period reports, it is advisable to verify which reporting basis is selected. If cash has been selected and you are using the accrual-basis, it is imperative that you change your report basis.

MEMO
DATE: January 31, 2015

Prior to printing reports, check the report preference selected for the company. If necessary, choose Accrual.

Select **Accrual** as the **Summary Reports Basis**

Click **Edit** on the menu bar, click **Preferences**
Scroll through the Preferences list until you see **Reports & Graphs**
Click **Reports & Graphs**, click the **Company Preferences** tab
If necessary, click **Accrual** to select the **Summary Reports Basis**

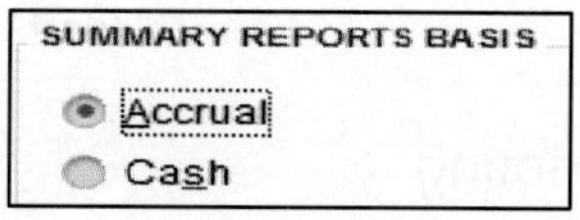

Click **OK** to close the **Preferences** window

JOURNAL

After entering several transactions, it is helpful to view the Journal. In the Journal, all transactions, regardless of the method of entry are shown in traditional debit/credit format. (Remember, you may have learned this as the General Journal in your concepts course.)

View the **Journal** for January

Click the **Reports** icon to open the Report Center, use the view you prefer
Click **Accountant & Taxes** as the type of report, and double-click **Journal**

- If you will be preparing several reports, using the Report Center is much more efficient than using the Reports menu.

Tab to or click **From**

- If necessary, delete existing date.

Enter **01/01/15**
Tab to or click **To**
Enter **01/31/15**
Tab to generate the report
Click the **Expand** button
Scroll through the report
Verify the total of $57,919.69

- If your total does not match, you may have an error in a date used, an amount entered, a transaction not entered, etc.

Computer Consulting by Your Name
Journal
January 2015

Trans #	Type	Date	Num	Adj	Name	Memo	Account	Debit	Credit
73	Check	01/31/2015	Transfer		Sunshine Bank	Loan Pmt. Business Vehicles	Checking		722.41
					Sunshine Bank	Business Vehicles Loan, Interest	Loan Interest	255.22	
					Sunshine Bank	Business Vehicles Loan, Principal	Business Vehicles Loan	467.19	
								722.41	722.41
74	Check	01/31/2015	Transfer		Sunshine Bank	Loan Pmt. Office Furniture/Equipment	Checking		82.56
					Sunshine Bank	Office Furniture/Equipment Loan, Interest	Loan Interest	53.39	
					Sunshine Bank	Office Furniture/Equipment Loan, Principal	Office Furniture/Equipment Loan	29.17	
								82.56	82.56
75	Check	01/31/2015				Service Charge	Checking		8.00
						Service Charge	Bank Service Charges	8.00	
								8.00	8.00
76	Deposit	01/31/2015				Interest	Checking	66.43	
						Interest	Interest Income		66.43
								66.43	66.43
TOTAL								57,919.69	57,919.69

Partial Report

Close the **Journal** without printing
Do not close the Report Center

TRIAL BALANCE

After all adjustments have been recorded and the bank reconciliation has been completed, it is wise to prepare the Trial Balance. As in traditional accounting, the QuickBooks Trial Balance proves that debits equal credits.

MEMO
DATE: January 31, 2015

Because adjustments have been entered, prepare a Trial Balance.

Prepare and print the Trial Balance

Double-click **Trial Balance** in the Accountant & Taxes section of the Report Center
Enter the dates from **01/01/15** to **01/31/15**, and Tab to generate the report
Scroll through the report and study the amounts shown
- Notice that the final totals of debits and credits are equal: $138,119.07.

Computer Consulting by Your Name
Trial Balance
As of January 31, 2015

	Jan 31, 15 Debit	Jan 31, 15 Credit
Owner's Equity	0.00	
Your Name, Capital		53,135.00
Your Name, Capital:Draws	2,500.00	
Your Name, Capital:Investments		33,000.00
Income:Installation Income		175.00
Income:Technical Support Income		900.00
Income:Training Income		7,850.00
Advertising Expense	260.00	
Bank Service Charges	8.00	
Business Vehicles Expense	588.88	
Depreciation Expense	725.00	
Dues and Subscriptions	79.00	
Equipment Rental	25.00	
Insurance:Business Vehicles Insurance	237.50	
Interest Expense:Loan Interest	308.61	
Office Supplies Expense	368.57	
Postage and Delivery	195.34	
Rent	1,600.00	
Telephone	0.00	
Utilities:Electricity Expense	250.00	
Utilities:Heating Expense--Gas	175.00	
Utilities:Water	35.00	
Interest Income		66.43
TOTAL	138,119.07	138,119.07

Partial Report

Resize the columns and **Print** the **Trial Balance** in Portrait orientation as previously instructed
Do not close the **Report Center** or the **Trial Balance**

EXPORT REPORTS TO EXCEL (OPTIONAL)

Many of the reports prepared in QuickBooks can be exported to Microsoft Excel. This allows you to take advantage of extensive filtering options available in Excel, hide detail for some but not all groups of data, combine information from two different reports, change titles of columns, add comments, change the order of columns, and to experiment with "what if" scenarios. In order to use this feature of QuickBooks you must also have Microsoft Excel.

Optional Exercise: Export a report from QuickBooks to Excel

With the **Trial Balance** on the screen, click the Excel ▼ button on the Trial Balance icon bar

Click **Create New Worksheet**

On the Send Report to Excel message screen, make sure **Create new worksheet In a new workbook** are marked

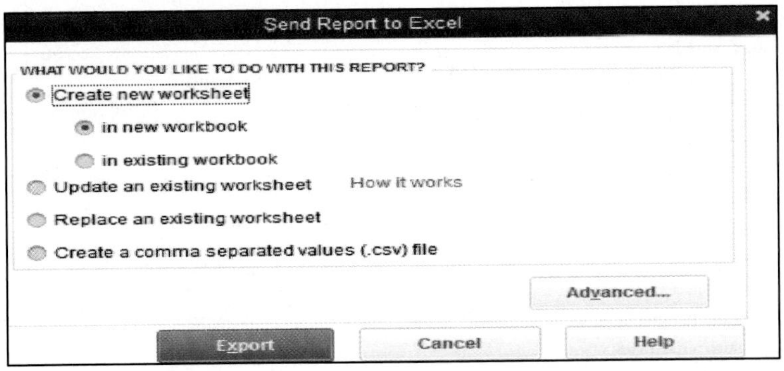

Click the **Export** button

- The **Trial** Balance will be displayed in Excel.
- The Book number may change depending on how many reports have been sent to Excel. The following example shows Book5.

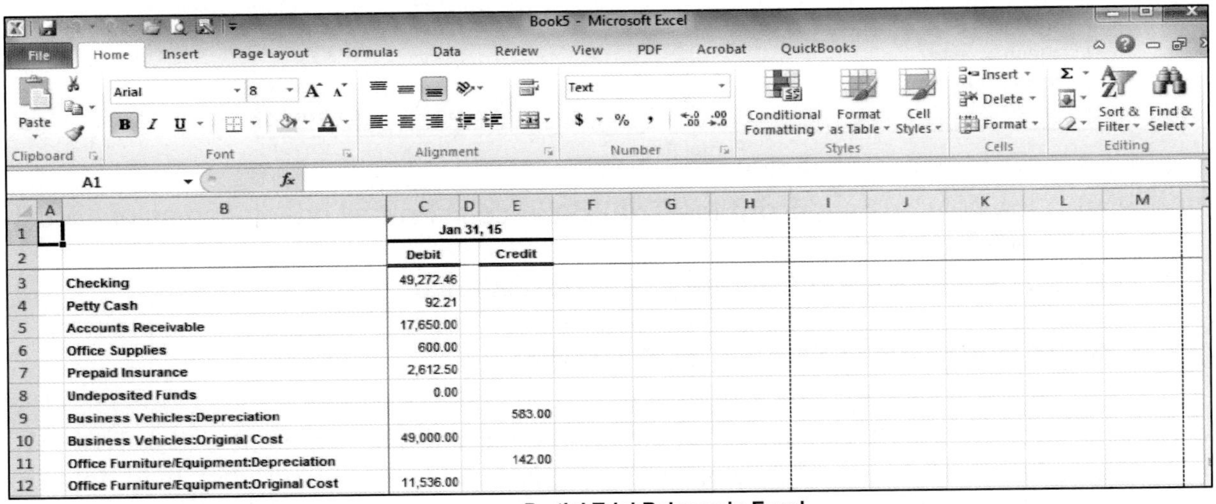

Partial Trial Balance in Excel

Double-click in Cell **C1**, change the heading by typing **JANUARY 31, 2015**

Double-click in Cell **C2**, type **DEBIT** to change Debit to all capitals

Double-click in Cell **E2**, type **CREDIT** to change Credit to all capitals

	A	B	C	D	E
1			JANUARY 31, 2015		
2			DEBIT		CREDIT

Click the **Close** button in the top right corner of the Excel title bar to close Excel
Click **Don't Save** to close Excel without saving the Trial Balance
Close the **Trial Balance**, do <u>not</u> close the **Report Center**

CASH FLOW FORECAST

In planning for the cash needs of a business, QuickBooks can prepare a Cash Flow Forecast. This report is useful when determining the expected income and disbursement of cash. It is important to know if your company will have enough cash on hand to meet its obligations. A company with too little cash on hand may have to borrow money to pay its bills, while another company with excess cash may miss out on investment, expansion, or dividend opportunities. QuickBooks Cash Flow Forecast does not analyze investments. It simply projects the amount you will be receiving if all those who owe you money pay on time and the amounts you will be spending if you pay your accounts payable on time.

MEMO
DATE: January 31, 2015

Since this is the end of January, prepare Cash Flow Forecast for February 1-28, 2015.

Prepare Cash Flow Forecast for February

The Report Center should still be on the screen; if it is not, open it as previously instructed
Click **Company & Financial** in the type of reports section, scroll through the list of reports, double-click **Cash Flow Forecast**
Enter the **From** date of **02/01/15** and the **To** date of **02/28/15**

- This will change **Dates** from Next 4 Weeks to **Custom**.

Tab to generate the report

- Notice that **Periods** show **Week**. Use Week, but click the drop-down list arrow to see the periods available for the report.
- If you are not using 2015 as the year, the individual amounts listed per week may be different from the report shown. As long as the totals are the same, consider the report as being correct.
- Analyze the report for February: The Beginning Balance for Accounts Receivable shows the amounts due from customers as of 1/31/15.
- Depending on whether or not you applied the Credit Memo to Invoice 4 in Chapter 2, you may have a $400 difference in the Accounts Receivable detail and the Projected Balance; however, the Ending Balance for Accounts Receivable and Projected Balance will still be the same.

- The amounts for Accnts Receivable and Accts Payable for the future weeks are for the customer payments you expect to receive and the bills you expect to pay. This information is based on the due dates for invoices and bills and on the credit memos recorded.
- The Bank Accnts amount for future weeks is based on deposits made or deposits that need to be made.
- Net Inflows summarizes the amounts that should be received and the amounts that should be paid to get a net inflow of cash.
- The Proj Balance is the total in all bank accounts if all customer and bill payments are made on time.

Computer Consulting by Your Name
Cash Flow Forecast
February 2015

	Accnts Receivable	Accnts Payable	Bank Accnts	Net Inflows	Proj Balance
Beginning Balance	9,570.00	0.00	49,364.67		58,934.67
Week of Feb 1, 15	8,080.00	0.00	0.00	8,080.00	67,014.67
Week of Feb 8, 15	0.00	0.00	0.00	0.00	67,014.67
Week of Feb 15, 15	0.00	3,764.00	0.00	-3,764.00	63,250.67
Week of Feb 22, 15	0.00	0.00	0.00	0.00	63,250.67
Feb 15	8,080.00	3,764.00	0.00	4,316.00	
Ending Balance	17,650.00	3,764.00	49,364.67		63,250.67

If necessary, adjust the column widths; print the report for February in **Landscape**
Close the report; do not close the Report Center

STATEMENT OF CASH FLOWS

Another report that details the amount of cash flow in a business is the Statement of Cash Flows. This report organizes information regarding cash in three areas of activities: Operating Activities, Investing Activities, and Financing Activities. The report also projects the amount of cash at the end of a period.

MEMO
DATE: January 31, 2015

Prepare Statement of Cash Flows for January 1-31, 2015.

Prepare Statement of Cash Flows for January

Double-click **Statement of Cash Flows** in the **Company & Financial** list of reports
Enter the **From** date of **01/01/15** and the **To** date of **01/31/15**
Tab to generate the report

Computer Consulting by Your Name
Statement of Cash Flows
January 2015

	Jan 15
OPERATING ACTIVITIES	
Net Income	4,135.53
Adjustments to reconcile Net Income	
to net cash provided by operations:	
Accounts Receivable	4,915.00
Office Supplies	-100.00
Prepaid Insurance	-2,612.50
Accounts Payable	2,914.00
Net cash provided by Operating Activities	9,252.03
INVESTING ACTIVITIES	
Business Vehicles:Depreciation	583.00
Office Furniture/Equipment:Depreciation	142.00
Office Furniture/Equipment:Original Cost	-3,486.00
Net cash provided by Investing Activities	-2,761.00
FINANCING ACTIVITIES	
Loan Payable:Business Vehicles Loan	-467.19
Loan Payable:Office Furniture/Equipment Loan	-29.17
Your Name, Capital:Draws	-2,500.00
Your Name, Capital:Investments	8,000.00
Net cash provided by Financing Activities	5,003.64
Net cash increase for period	11,494.67
Cash at beginning of period	37,870.00
Cash at end of period	49,364.67

4

Print the report in **Portrait** mode following previous instructions
Close the report; close the Report Center

PREPARE MULTIPLE REPORTS

When you are preparing a lot of reports at the same time, you have the option of telling QuickBooks to prepare multiple reports. While not every available report may be selected, there are a number of frequently prepared reports available.

Prepare the Standard Profit & Loss Report and the Balance Sheet using Multiple Reports

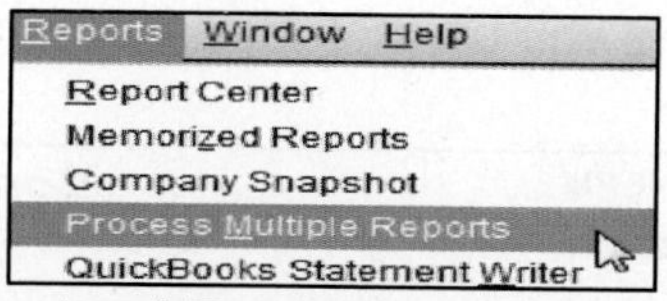

Click **Reports** on the Menu Bar
Click **Process Multiple Reports**
On the Process Multiple Reports screen, Memorized Reports should be selected
The Select Memorized Reports From should be **<All Reports>**

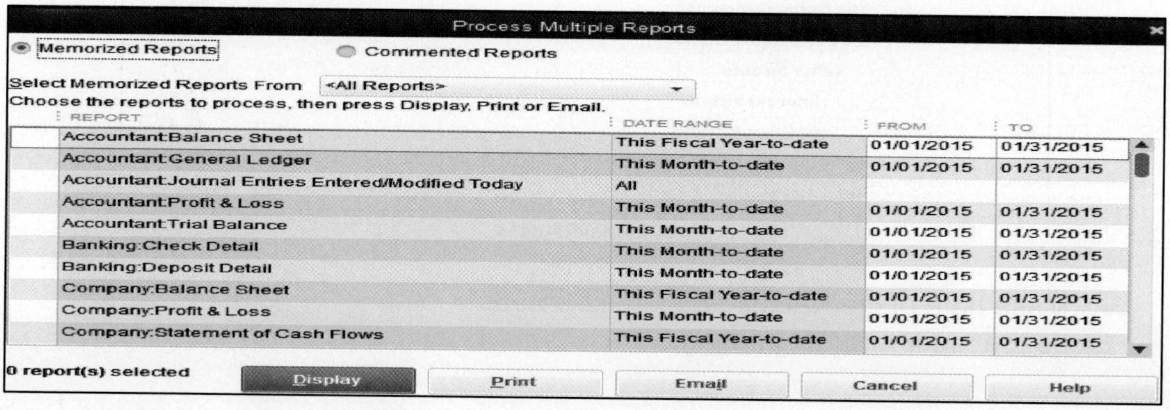

REPORT	DATE RANGE	FROM	TO
Accountant:Balance Sheet	This Fiscal Year-to-date	01/01/2015	01/31/2015
Accountant:General Ledger	This Month-to-date	01/01/2015	01/31/2015
Accountant:Journal Entries Entered/Modified Today	All		
Accountant:Profit & Loss	This Month-to-date	01/01/2015	01/31/2015
Accountant:Trial Balance	This Month-to-date	01/01/2015	01/31/2015
Banking:Check Detail	This Month-to-date	01/01/2015	01/31/2015
Banking:Deposit Detail	This Month-to-date	01/01/2015	01/31/2015
Company:Balance Sheet	This Fiscal Year-to-date	01/01/2015	01/31/2015
Company:Profit & Loss	This Month-to-date	01/01/2015	01/31/2015
Company:Statement of Cash Flows	This Fiscal Year-to-date	01/01/2015	01/31/2015

Click **Accountant: Balance Sheet**
Click in the column for From, enter the date **01/01/2015**
Click in the column for To, enter the date **01/31/2015**
Repeat the procedures for **Accountant: Profit & Loss**, From **01/01/2015** and To **01/31/2015**
Click the **Display button**

ACCOUNTANT: PROFIT &LOSS REPORT

Because all income, expenses, and adjustments have been made for the period, a Profit & Loss Report can be prepared. This statement is also known as the Income Statement and shows the income and the expenses for the period and the net income or the net loss for the period (Income-Expenses=Net Profit or Net Loss).

The Accountant: Profit & Loss Report is prepared from Multiple Reports on the Reports Menu. It gives the same data as a Standard Profit & Loss prepared from the Company & Financial section on the Reports Menu or in the Report Center. This report summarizes income and expenses. When preparing multiple reports, changes made to customize reports in the Report Center or reports prepared from the Reports Menu are not used.

View the **Accountant: Profit & Loss Report**

Scroll through the report prepared using the Multiple Reports feature to view the income and expenses listed

- In Chapter 3 report preferences were change so the Date Prepared, Time Prepared, and Report Basis did not appear in reports prepared in the Report Center or from the Reports Menu
- When using Multiple Reports, the Date Prepared, Time Prepared, and Report Basis will be included in the report.

3:48 PM
01/31/15
Accrual Basis

Computer Consulting by Your Name
Profit & Loss
January 2015

	Jan 15
Total Expense	4,855.90
Net Ordinary Income	4,069.10
Other Income/Expense	
Other Income	
Interest Income	66.43
Total Other Income	66.43
Net Other Income	66.43
Net Income	4,135.53

Partial Report

- Make note of the Net Income of $4,135.53.

Close the report without printing

ACCOUNTANT: BALANCE SHEET

The Balance Sheet proves the fundamental accounting equation: Assets = Liabilities + Owner's Equity. When all transactions and adjustments for the period have been recorded, a balance sheet should be prepared. The Accountant: Balance Sheet provides the same data as a Standard Balance Sheet and shows as of the report dates the balance in each balance sheet account with subtotals provided for assets, liabilities, and equity. As with the Accountant: Profit & Loss Report, customizations made for reports in the Report Center or on the Reports Menu will not be used when preparing multiple reports.

View the **Accountant: Balance Sheet**

Scroll through the report prepared using the Multiple Reports feature to view the assets, liabilities, and equities listed

- As with the Accountant: Profit & Loss Report, the report customization to remove the date prepared, time prepared, and report basis is not used when preparing multiple reports.
- Notice the Net Income listed in the Equity section of the report. This is the same amount of Net Income shown on the Profit & Loss Report.
- Your Name, Capital – Other is the balance of the Your Name, Capital account. The word Other is used by QuickBooks so that it is not confused with the Equity Section heading Your Name, Capital.
- Also note the Total Assets of $130,038.17. Compare that to the Total Liabilities & Equity of $130,038.17. This proves the Fundamental Accounting Equation of Assets=Liabilities + Owner's Equity.

3:47 PM
01/31/15
Accrual Basis

Computer Consulting by Your Name
Balance Sheet
As of January 31, 2015

	Jan 31, 15
TOTAL ASSETS	130,038.17
LIABILITIES & EQUITY	
Total Liabilities	42,267.64
Equity	
Your Name, Capital	
Draws	-2,500.00
Investments	33,000.00
Your Name, Capital - Other	53,135.00
Total Your Name, Capital	83,635.00
Net Income	4,135.53
Total Equity	87,770.53
TOTAL LIABILITIES & EQUITY	130,038.17

Partial Report

Close the report without printing

CLOSING ENTRIES

In accounting, there are four closing entries that need to be made in order to close the books for a period. They include closing all income and expense accounts, closing the drawing account, closing the Income Summary account, and transferring the net income or net loss to the owner's capital account.

In QuickBooks, setting a closing date will replace closing the income and expense accounts. QuickBooks does not close the owner's drawing account. This closing entry will be completed in this chapter. QuickBooks does not use an Income Summary account so net income is automatically transferred into owner's equity. While it is included on the Balance Sheet in the Equity section, QuickBooks categorizes Owner's Equity as a Retained Earnings account. Therefore, the account only contains the amount of Net Income earned and is separate from Your Name, Capital. According to GAAP, a sole proprietorship should have net income included in the owner's capital account. The following section will illustrate the transfer of Net Income into Your Name, Capital.

TRANSFER NET INCOME/OWNER'S EQUITY INTO CAPITAL

Because Computer Consulting by Your Name is a sole proprietorship, the amount of net income should be included in the balance of Your Name, Capital rather than set aside in a separate account—Owner's Equity—as QuickBooks does automatically. In many instances, this is the type of adjustment the CPA makes on the Accountant's Copy of the QuickBooks company files. The adjustment may be made before the closing date for the fiscal year, or it may be made after the closing has been performed. Because QuickBooks automatically transfers Net Income into the Retained Earnings Account named Owner's Equity, the closing entry will transfer the net income into Your Name, Capital account. This adjustment is made in a General Journal entry that debits Owner's Equity and credits Your Name, Capital. After you have entered the adjustment, a Standard Balance Sheet prepared before the end of the year will include an amount in Net Income and the same amount as a negative in Owner's Equity. If you view this report after the end of the year, you will not see any information regarding Owner's Equity or Net Income because the adjustment correctly transferred the amount into Your Name, Capital.

If you prefer to use the power of the program and not make the adjustment, QuickBooks simply carries the amount of Owner's Equity forward. Each year net income is added to Owner's Equity. On the Balance Sheet, Owner's Equity and/or Net Income appears as part of the equity section.

Transfer the net income into Your Name, Capital account

Open the General Journal by clicking on **Company** on the menu bar, and clicking **Make General Journal Entries…**

If you get a screen regarding Assigning Numbers to Journal Entries, click **Do not display this message in the future**, and then click **OK**

Enter the date of **01/31/15**

Since this a closing entry, if necessary, click the checkbox for ADJUSTING ENTRY to remove the check mark

The first account used is **Owner's Equity**

- Remember, Owner's Equity is a Retained Earnings account and contains all of the net income earned by the business.

Debit **Owner's Equity** for the amount of Net Income **4,135.53**

- This is the amount of Net Income shown in the Profit & Loss report.

The Memo is **Transfer Net Income into Capital**

The other account used is **Your Name, Capital**

- **4,135.53** should appear as the credit amount for **Your Name, Capital**.
- If the memo does not appear when pressing tab, enter the same Memo.

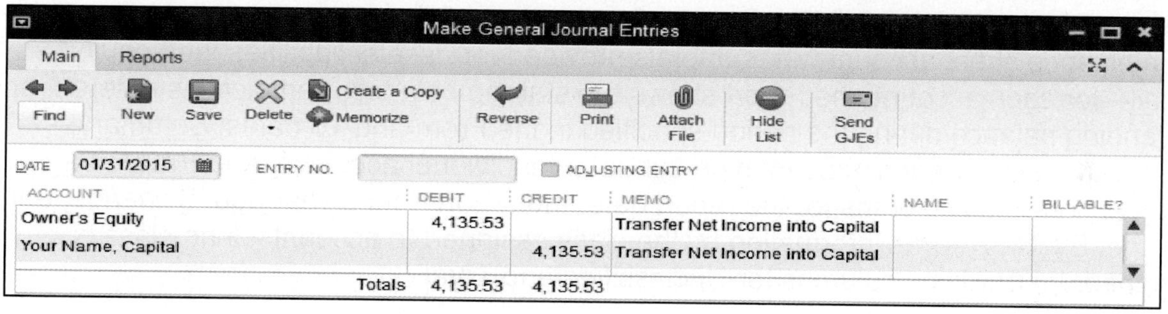

Click **Save & New**

If a Retained Earnings screen appears, click **OK**

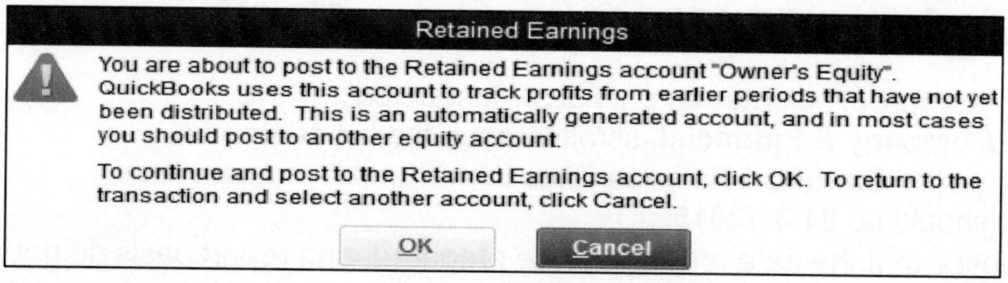

CLOSE DRAWING

The closing entry to transfer the net income into Your Name, Capital has already been made. While this is not the actual end of the fiscal year for Computer Consulting by Your Name, the closing entry for the Drawing account will be entered at this time so that you will have experience in recording this closing entry.

Close Draws into Your Name, Capital

On the new **Make General Journal Entries** screen, make sure the **DATE** is **01/31/15**

Since this a closing entry, the check box for ADJUSTING ENTRY is not marked

Debit **Your Name, Capital**, for the amount of the drawing account **2,500**

The Memo for the transaction is **Close Drawing**
Credit **Draws**, for **2,500**

DATE 01/31/2015 ENTRY NO. ADJUSTING ENTRY

ACCOUNT	DEBIT	CREDIT	MEMO	NAME	BILLABLE?
Your Name, Capital	2,500.00		Close Drawing		
Your Name, Capital:Draws		2,500.00	Close Drawing		
Totals	2,500.00	2,500.00			

Click **Save & Close**

BALANCE SHEET STANDARD

In addition to the Accountant: Balance Sheet, QuickBooks has several different types of Balance Sheet reports available: Standard—shows as of the report dates the balance in each balance sheet account with subtotals provided for assets, liabilities, and equity; Detail—for each account, the report shows the starting balance, transactions entered, and the ending balance during the period specified in the From and To dates; Summary—shows amounts for each account type but not for individual accounts; and Prev. Year Comparison—has columns for the report date, the report date a year ago, $ change, and % change; By Class—has information by the class assigned to accounts, if no class is assigned, there will be columns for Unclassified and Total.

Once the adjustment for Net Income/Owner's Equity has been performed, viewing or printing the Balance Sheet will show you the status of the Equity.

View the **Balance Sheet Standard** as of January 31, 2015

Open the **Report Center** as previously instructed
Click **Company & Financial**, scroll through the list of reports
Double-click **Standard Balance Sheet**
As of should be **01/31/2015**

- Notice that the date prepared, time prepared, and report basis do not appear.
- Look at the Equity section, especially Owner's Equity and Net Income.

Computer Consulting by Your Name
Balance Sheet
As of January 31, 2015

Equity	
Owner's Equity	-4,135.53
Your Name, Capital	
Investments	33,000.00
Your Name, Capital - Other	54,770.53
Total Your Name, Capital	87,770.53
Net Income	4,135.53
Total Equity	87,770.53
TOTAL LIABILITIES & EQUITY	130,038.17

Partial Report

- Remember, Your Name, Capital – Other is the balance of the Your Name, Capital account and is used by QuickBooks to avoid confusion between the actual account and the section heading.
- The amount of Net Income has been added to Your Name, Capital - Other. The Owner's Equity and Net Income amounts shown cancel out each other (notice the positive Net Income and the negative Owner's Equity).
- Draws is no longer shown on the Balance Sheet.
- Verify these two transactions by adding the net income of 4,135.53 to 53,135.00, which was shown as the balance of the Your Name, Capital - Other account on the Balance Sheet prepared before the adjusting entry was made. Then subtract 2,500.00, which is the amount of the owner withdrawals that were subtracted from Capital. The Total Your Name, Capital - Other should be 54,770.53.

Change the **As of** date on the Balance Sheet to **01/31/16**, press **Tab**

- Notice the Equity section. Nothing is shown for Owner's Equity or Net Income.

Computer Consulting by Your Name
Balance Sheet
As of January 31, 2016

	Jan 31, 16
Equity	
Your Name, Capital	
Investments	33,000.00
Your Name, Capital - Other	54,770.53
Total Your Name, Capital	87,770.53
Total Equity	87,770.53
TOTAL LIABILITIES & EQUITY	130,038.17

Partial Report

Close the **Balance Sheet** without printing
Close the Report Center

JOURNAL

Normally, you would prepare a Journal before completing the end-of-period procedures so you have a printed or "hard copy" of the data for January. At this point, we will postpone printing until all of the closing procedures have been completed.

END-OF-PERIOD BACKUP

Once all end-of-period procedures have been completed, a regular backup and a second/archival backup of the company data should be made. Preferably the archive copy will be located someplace other than on the business premises. The archive copy is set aside in case of emergency or in case damage occurs to the original company file and current backup copies of the company data. Normally, a backup and an archive copy would be made before closing the period. Since we will be making changes to transactions for the closed period, the backup will be made at the end of the chapter.

Prepare an archive copy of your company file

For training purposes, use your USB drive
Follow the procedures given previously to make your backup files
Name the file **Computer (Archive 01-31-15)**

- In actual practice, the company (.qbw) file would be on your hard drive and the backup (.qbb) file would be stored on a separate disk, USB drive, online, or in the cloud.
- If you get a QuickBooks screen regarding the files location, click **Use this Location**.

Once the archive copy has been made, click **OK** on the QuickBooks Information dialog box to acknowledge the successful backup

PASSWORDS

Not every employee of a business should have access to all the financial records for the company. In some companies, only the owner will have complete access. In others, one or two key employees will have full access while other employees are provided limited access based on the jobs and tasks they perform. Passwords are secret words used to control access to data. QuickBooks has several options available when assigning passwords.

In order to assign any passwords at all, you must have an administrator. The administrator has unrestricted access to all of QuickBooks functions, sets up users and user passwords for QuickBooks and for Windows, and assigns areas of transaction access for each user. Areas of access can be limited to transaction entry for certain types of transactions or a user may have unrestricted access into all areas of QuickBooks and company data. To obtain more information regarding QuickBooks' passwords, refer to Help.

A password should be kept secret at all times. It should be something that is easy for the individual to remember, yet difficult for someone else to guess. Birthdays, names, initials, and similar devices are not good passwords because the information is too readily available. Never write down your password where it can be easily found or seen by someone else. In QuickBooks passwords are case sensitive. It is wise to use a complex password. The requirements for a password to be accepted as complex are: a minimum of seven characters including at least one number and one uppercase letter. Use of special characters is also helpful. Complex passwords should be changed every 90 days. Make sure your password is something you won't forget. Otherwise, you will not be able to access your Company file.

Since the focus of the text is in training in all aspects of QuickBooks, no passwords will be assigned. Also, if you set a password and then forget it, you will not be able to access QuickBooks; and your instructor will not be able to override your password.

SET PERIOD CLOSING DATE

Instead of closing entries for income and expense accounts, QuickBooks uses a closing date to indicate the end of a period. When a closing date is assigned, income and expenses are effectively closed. When a transaction involving income or expenses is recorded after the closing date, it is considered part of the new period and will not be used in calculating net income (or loss) for the previous period.

A closing date assigned to transactions for a period prevents changing data from the closed period without acknowledging that a transaction has been changed. This is helpful to discourage casual changes or transaction deletions to a period that has been closed. Setting the closing date is done by accessing Preferences in QuickBooks.

MEMO
DATE: January 31, 2015

Alhandra, protect the data by setting the closing date to 1/31/15.

Assign the closing date of **01/31/15** to the transactions for the period

Click **Edit** on the menu bar, click **Preferences**
Click **Accounting** in the list of Preferences
Click **Company Preferences**
OR
Click **Accountant** on the menu bar; and then click **Set Closing Date...**
Click the **Set Date/Password** button

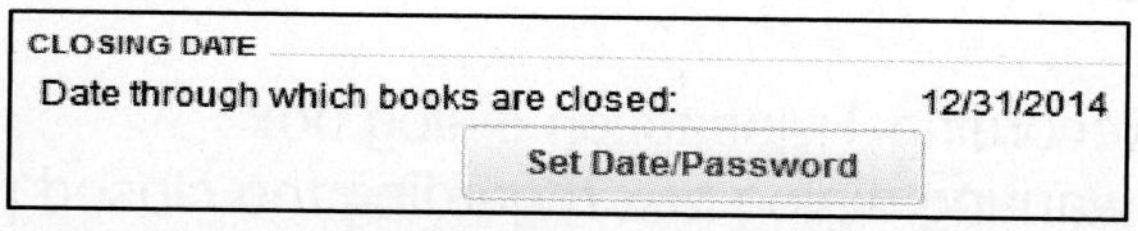
CLOSING DATE
Date through which books are closed:
12/31/2014
Set Date/Password

Enter **01/31/15** as the closing date.

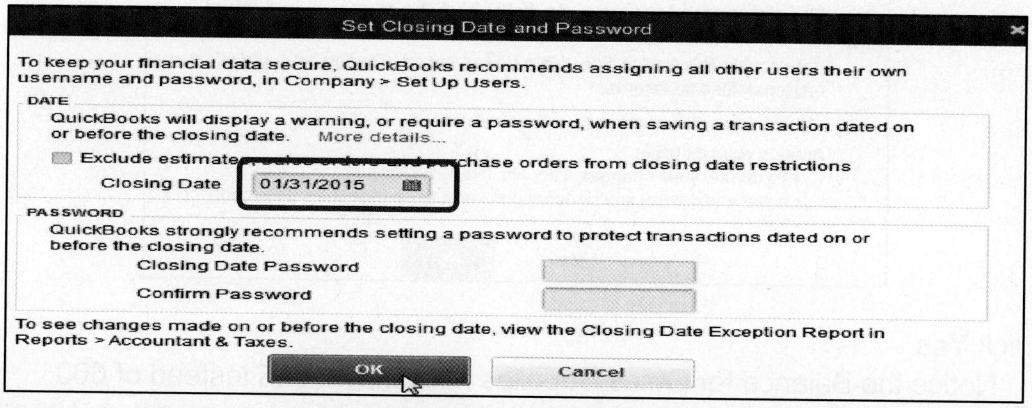
Set Closing Date and Password
To keep your financial data secure, QuickBooks recommends assigning all other users their own username and password, in Company > Set Up Users.
DATE
QuickBooks will display a warning, or require a password, when saving a transaction dated on or before the closing date.
More details...
Exclude estimate
chase orders from closing date restrictions
Closing Date
01/31/2015
PASSWORD
QuickBooks strongly recommends setting a password to protect transactions dated on or before the closing date.
Closing Date Password
Confirm Password
To see changes made on or before the closing date, view the Closing Date Exception Report in Reports > Accountant & Taxes.
OK
Cancel

Do not enter anything in the text boxes for Password, click the **OK** button
If you get a No Password Entered screen, click **Do not display this message in the future**; and then click **No**.
Click **OK** to close the period and to close Preferences

EDIT CLOSED PERIOD TRANSACTION

Even though the month of January has been "closed," transactions still appear in the account registers, the Journal, and so on. If it is determined that an error was made in a previous period, QuickBooks does allow the correction. The edited transactions may not be changed unless you click Yes on the screen warning you that you have changed a transaction to a closed period. Changes to transactions involving income and expenses will also necessitate a change to the transfer of net income into the owner's capital account.

MEMO
DATE: January 31, 2015

After reviewing the journal for January, you determine that the amount of supplies used was $325, not $350. Make the correction to the adjusting entry of January 31. This will also require a change to the closing entry to transfer Net Income.

Change Office Supplies adjusting entry to $325 from $350

Access the **Office Supplies** account register as previously instructed
Click the **DECREASE** column for the GENJRN Entry recorded to the account on 01/31/15
Change 350 to **325**
Click **Record**
Click **Yes** on the Recording Transaction dialog box
The **QuickBooks** warning dialog box regarding the closed period appears

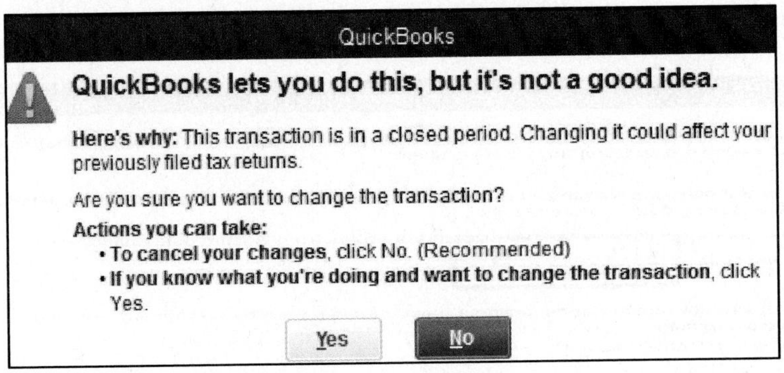

Click **Yes**

- Notice the Balance for Office Supplies now shows 625 instead of 600.

01/31/2015			325.00			625.00
	GENJRN Office Supplies Exp Supplies Used					

Close the Register for **Office Supplies** and close the **Chart of Accounts**

- The adjusting entry used to transfer Owner's Equity/Net Income into the owner's capital account also needs to be adjusted as a result of any changes to transactions.

Change the Adjusting Entry where Net Income was transferred from Owner's Equity into Your Name, Capital

Click **Make General Journal Entries…** on the Accountant or the Company menus

Click on the Make General Journal Entries icon bar until you find the entry adjusting Owner's Equity

- Since the correction to Office Supplies decreased the amount of the expense by $25, there is an increase in net income of $25 (Income – Expenses = Net Income).

Change the Debit to Owner's Equity by 25.00 from 4135.53 to **4160.53**

Change the Credit to Your Name, Capital by 25.00 from 4135.53 to **4160.53**

4

Make General Journal Entries

DATE 01/31/2015 ENTRY NO. ADJUSTING ENTRY

ACCOUNT	DEBIT	CREDIT	MEMO	NAME	BILLABLE?
Owner's Equity	4,160.53		Transfer Net Income into Capital		
Your Name, Capital		4,160.53	Transfer Net Income into Capital		
Totals	4,160.53	4,160.53			

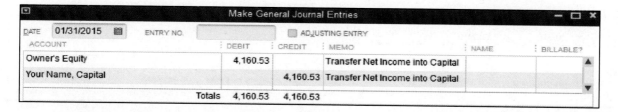

Click **Save & Close**

Click **Yes** on the Recording Transaction dialog box

Click **Yes** on the QuickBooks dialog box regarding transactions in a closed period

Click **OK** on the Retained Earnings dialog box

REDO ARCHIVE COPY OF COMPANY FILE

Since we have made changes to transactions for the closed period, the archive copy of the company file should be redone.

Create an archive copy of the company data

Replace the previous file **Computer (Archive 1-31-15)**

Follow the procedures given previously to make your backup files

JOURNAL

Normally, you would have printed the Journal prior to closing the period. Since changes to the "previous" period have been made, the Journal would need to be reprinted to replace the one printed before closing.

Print the Journal for January

Open the Report Center, click **Accountant & Taxes** as the type of report
Double-click **Journal**
Click the **Expand** button
Enter the dates From **01/01/15** To **01/31/15**

- Notice that the report contains all the transactions from Chapters 2, 3, and 4.

Click the **Expand** button
Resize the columns to display the information in full
Verify that the final total for debits and credits is **$64,555.22**

- If it is not, make the necessary corrections to incorrect transactions. Frequent errors include incorrect dates, incorrect accounts used, incorrect amounts, and incorrect sales items.

Computer Consulting by Your Name
Journal
January 2015

Trans #	Type	Date	Num	Adj	Name	Memo	Account	Debit	Credit
75	Check	01/31/2015				Service Charge	Checking		8.00
						Service Charge	Bank Service Charges	8.00	
								8.00	8.00
76	Deposit	01/31/2015				Interest	Checking	66.43	
						Interest	Interest Income		66.43
								66.43	66.43
77	General Journal	01/31/2015				Transfer Net Income into Capital	Owner's Equity	4,160.53	
						Transfer Net Income into Capital	Your Name, Capital		4,160.53
								4,160.53	4,160.53
78	General Journal	01/31/2015				Close Drawing	Your Name, Capital	2,500.00	
						Close Drawing	Draws		2,500.00
								2,500.00	2,500.00
TOTAL								64,555.22	64,555.22

Partial Report

Adjust column widths to display information in full, print in **Landscape** orientation after selecting **Fit report to one page wide**
Close the **Journal** do not close the **Report Center**

TRIAL BALANCE

After the adjustments have been recorded and the "closing" has been completed, it is helpful to print reports. A Trial Balance is printed to prove that debits still equal credits. Post-closing reports are typically prepared as of the last day of the fiscal year after all closing entries for the year have been recorded. Since our closing was simply for a period, this means that income and expenses will be shown in the Trial Balance and in the Profit & Loss reports for January.

MEMO
DATE: January 31, 2015

Print a Trial Balance, a Profit & Loss Report, and a Balance Sheet for Computer Consulting by Your Name. The dates should be as of or for 01/31/15.

Print a Trial Balance to prove that debits equal credits

Click **Accountant & Taxes** in the **Report Center**, double-click **Trial Balance**
Enter the **From** and **To** dates as **01/31/15**, tab to generate the report
Scroll through the report and study the amounts shown

- Notice that the final totals of debits and credits are equal.
- Notice that Office Supplies has a balance of $625.00 and Office Supplies Expense is $343.57, which is the 25.00 change you made in the register after the period was closed.

4

Computer Consulting by Your Name
Trial Balance
As of January 31, 2015

	Jan 31, 15 Debit	Credit
Advertising Expense	260.00	
Bank Service Charges	8.00	
Business Vehicles Expense	588.88	
Depreciation Expense	725.00	
Dues and Subscriptions	79.00	
Equipment Rental	25.00	
Insurance:Business Vehicles Insurance	237.50	
Interest Expense:Loan Interest	308.61	
Office Supplies Expense	343.57	
Postage and Delivery	195.34	
Rent	1,600.00	
Telephone	0.00	
Utilities:Electricity Expense	250.00	
Utilities:Heating Expense--Gas	175.00	
Utilities:Water	35.00	
Interest Income		66.43
TOTAL	139,779.60	139,779.60

Partial Report

Print the report in **Portrait** orientation

QUICKZOOM

QuickZoom is a QuickBooks feature that allows you to make a closer observation of transactions, amounts, and other entries. With QuickZoom you may zoom in on an item when the mouse pointer turns into a magnifying glass with a Z inside. If you point to an item and you do not get a magnifying glass with a Z inside, you cannot zoom in on the item. For example, if you point to Interest Expense, you will see the magnifying glass with the Z inside. This means that you can see transaction details for Interest Expense.

Use QuickZoom to view the details of Office Supplies Expense

Scroll through the Trial Balance until you see Office Supplies Expense
Position the mouse pointer over the amount of Office Supplies Expense, **343.57**

- Notice that the mouse pointer changes to .

Double-click the primary mouse button

- A Transactions by Account report appears on the screen showing the transactions for Office Supplies Expense as of 01/31/2015.

If necessary, enter the From date **010115** and the To date **013115**

- QuickBooks will enter the / in a date and convert the year to four digits.

Tab to generate the report; then scroll through the report

- Notice the adjusting entry. It is marked by a check in the Adj column.

Computer Consulting by Your Name
Transactions by Account
As of January 31, 2015

Type	Date	Num	Adj	Name	Memo	Clr	Split	Debit	Credit	Balance
Office Supplies Expense										
Bill	01/18/2015	1035A		Supply Station	Fax Supplies for the Month		Accounts Payable	20.00		20.00
Credit	01/26/2015	789		Supply Station	Returned Damaged Fax Paper		Accounts Payable		5.00	15.00
Check	01/30/2015	1					Petty Cash	3.57		18.57
General Journal	01/31/2015		✔		Supplies Used		Office Supplies	325.00		343.57
Total Office Supplies Expense								348.57	5.00	343.57
TOTAL								348.57	5.00	343.57

Close the Transactions by Account report without printing; close the **Trial Balance**

PROFIT & LOSS (STANDARD)

In addition to the Standard Profit & Loss, which summarizes income and expenses, QuickBooks has several different types of Profit & Loss reports available: Detail—shows the year-to-date transactions for each income and expense account. The other Profit & Loss reports are like the Standard Profit & Loss but have additional information displayed as indicated in the following: YTD Comparison—summarizes your income and expenses for this month and compares them to your income and expenses for the current fiscal year; Prev Year Comparison—summarizes your income and expenses for both this month and this month last year; By Job—has columns for each customer and job and amounts for this year to date; By Class—has columns for each class and sub-class with the amounts for this year to date, and Unclassified—shows how much you are making or losing within segments of your business that are not assigned to a QuickBooks class.

Since the closing was done as of January 31, 2015, the Profit & Loss Report for January 31, 2015 will give the same data as a Profit & Loss Report prepared manually on January 31. To verify the closing of income and expense accounts for January, you would prepare a Profit & Loss Report for February 1. Since no income had been earned or expenses incurred in the new period, February, the Net Income will show $0.00.

Print a Profit & Loss Standard report for January and view the report for February

Click **Company & Financial** in the **Report Center**, double-click **Profit & Loss Standard**
The **Dates** are From **01/01/15** To **01/31/15**

Computer Consulting by Your Name Profit & Loss January 2015	Jan 15
Total Expense	4,830.90
Net Ordinary Income	4,094.10
Other Income/Expense	
Other Income	
Interest Income	66.43
Total Other Income	66.43
Net Other Income	66.43
Net Income	4,160.53

Partial Report

- Note the Net Income of **4,160.53**.

Print the report in **Portrait** orientation

To view the effect of closing the period, prepare the Profit & Loss report for February
Change the dates From **02/01/15** to **02/01/15**
Tab to generate the report

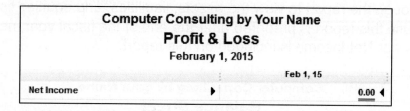

Computer Consulting by Your Name Profit & Loss February 1, 2015	Feb 1, 15
Net Income	0.00

- Note the Net Income of **0.00**.

Close the **Profit & Loss Report**

BALANCE SHEET (STANDARD)

Proof that assets are equal to liabilities and owner's equity needs to be displayed in a Balance Sheet. Because this report is for a month, the adjustment to Owner's Equity and Net Income will result in both accounts being included on the Balance Sheet. If, however, this report were prepared for the year, neither account would appear.

Prepare and print a **Balance Sheet Standard** report for January 31, 2015, and view the report as of January 31, 2016

Prepare a **Balance Sheet Standard** as previously instructed
Tab to or click **As of**, enter **01/31/15**

Tab to generate the report
Scroll through the report to view the assets, liabilities, and equities listed

- Because this report is for a one-month period, both Owner's Equity and Net Income are included on this report.
- Also notice that the amount of Owner's Equity shows -4,160.53 and Net Income shows 4,160.53. This is the amount of the adjusting entry after the change in supplies of $25.00.

Computer Consulting by Your Name
Balance Sheet
As of January 31, 2015

	Jan 31, 15
Total Liabilities	42,267.64
▼ Equity	
Owner's Equity	-4,160.53
▼ Your Name, Capital	
Investments	33,000.00
Your Name, Capital - Other	54,795.53
Total Your Name, Capital	87,795.53
Net Income	4,160.53
Total Equity	87,795.53
TOTAL LIABILITIES & EQUITY	130,063.17

Partial Report

Print the report in **Portrait** orientation
Change the date to **01/31/16**, tab to generate the report
Scroll through the report to view the assets, liabilities, and equities listed

- Because this report is prepared after the end of the fiscal year, neither Owner's Equity nor Net Income is included on this report.

Computer Consulting by Your Name
Balance Sheet
As of January 31, 2016

	Jan 31, 16
Total Liabilities	42,267.64
▼ Equity	
▼ Your Name, Capital	
Investments	33,000.00
Your Name, Capital - Other	54,795.53
Total Your Name, Capital	87,795.53
Total Equity	87,795.53
TOTAL LIABILITIES & EQUITY	130,063.17

Partial Report

Close the **Balance Sheet** for **January 2016** without printing
Close the **Report Center**

END-OF-CHAPTER BACKUP AND CLOSE COMPANY

As in previous chapters, you should back up your company and then close the company. This backup file will contain all of your work for Chapters 1-4.

Follow instructions previously provided to back up company files, close the company, and make a duplicate disk

Name the backup **Computer (Backup Ch. 4)**

SUMMARY

In this chapter, end-of-period adjustments were made, a bank reconciliation was performed, backup and archive copies were prepared, and a period was closed. The use of Net Income and Owner's Equity accounts was explored and interpreted for a sole proprietorship. Account name changes were made, and the effect on subaccounts was examined. Even though QuickBooks focuses on entering transactions on business forms, a Journal recording each transaction is kept by QuickBooks. This chapter presented transaction entry directly into the General Journal in Debit/Credit format, which were then displayed in the Journal. The differences between accrual-basis and cash-basis accounting were discussed. Company preferences were established for reporting preferences. Owner withdrawals and additional owner investments were made. Many of the different report options available in QuickBooks were examined, and the exporting of reports to Excel was explored. A variety of reports were printed. Correction of errors was explored, and changes to transactions in "closed" periods were made. The fact that QuickBooks does not require an actual closing entry at the end of the period was examined.

END-OF-CHAPTER QUESTIONS

TRUE/FALSE

ANSWER THE FOLLOWING QUESTIONS IN THE SPACE PROVIDED BEFORE THE QUESTION NUMBER.

__T__ 1. Accrual-basis accounting matches the income from the period and the expenses for the period in order to determine the net income or net loss for the period.

__F__ 2. In QuickBooks, the Journal is called the book of final entry.

__F__ 3. Adjusting entries are recorded when cash-basis accounting is used.

__F__ 4. In a sole proprietorship, an owner's name is added to the Vendor List for recording withdrawals.

__T__ 5. Additional investments made by an owner may be cash or noncash items.

__T__ 6. QuickBooks records every transaction in the Journal.

_____ 7. A Reconciliation Detail Report prints the last two bank reconciliation reports.

__F__ 8. Once an account has been used in a transaction, no changes may be made to the account name.

__T__ 9. When completing a bank reconciliation, anything entered as a service charge or as interest earned will be entered in the Journal automatically when the reconciliation is complete.

__F__ 10. A Balance Sheet is prepared to prove the equality of debits and credits.

MULTIPLE CHOICE

WRITE THE LETTER OF THE CORRECT ANSWER IN THE SPACE PROVIDED BEFORE THE QUESTION NUMBER.

__B__ 1. To close a period, you must ___.

A. have a closing password
B. enter a closing date in the Company Preferences for Accounting
C. enter a closing date in the Company Preferences for Company
D. enter the traditional closing entries for income and expenses in debit/credit format in the General Journal

__B__ 2. When a master account name such as “cars” is changed to “automobiles,” the subaccount “depreciation” ___.
A. needs to be changed to a subaccount of automobiles
B. automatically becomes a subaccount of automobiles
C. cannot be changed
D. must be deleted and re-entered

__D__ 3. The report that proves Assets = Liabilities + Owner’s Equity is the ___.
A. Trial Balance
B. Income Statement
C. Profit & Loss Report
D. Balance Sheet

______ 4. If the adjusting entry to transfer Net Income/Owner’s Equity into the owner’s capital account is made prior to the end of the year, the Balance Sheet shows ___.
A. Owner’s Equity
B. Net Income
C. both Net Income and Owner’s Equity
D. none of the above because the income/earnings has been transferred into capital

__D__ 5. The type of Profit & Loss report showing year-to-date transactions instead of totals for each income and expense account is a ___ Profit & Loss Report.
A. Standard
B. YTD Comparison
C. Prev Year Comparison
D. Detailed

__D__ 6. A bank statement may ___.
A. show service charges or interest not yet recorded
B. be missing deposits in transit or outstanding checks
C. show automatic payments
D. all of the above

__A__ 7. The Journal shows ___.
A. all transactions no matter where they were recorded
B. only those transactions recorded in the General Journal
C. only transactions recorded in account registers
D. only those transactions that have been edited

D 8. A QuickBooks backup file ___.
A. is a condensed file containing company data
B. is prepared in case of emergencies or errors
C. must be restored before information can be used
D. all of the above

A 9. An error known as a transposition can be found by ___.
A. dividing the amount out of balance by 9
B. dividing the amount out of balance by 2
C. multiplying the difference by 9, then dividing by 2
D. dividing the amount out of balance by 5

C 10. The type of Balance Sheet Report showing information for today and a year ago is a ___ Balance Sheet.
A. Standard
B. Summary
C. Comparison
D. Detailed

FILL-IN

IN THE SPACE PROVIDED, WRITE THE ANSWER THAT MOST APPROPRIATELY COMPLETES THE SENTENCE.

1. Bank reconciliations should be performed on a(n) monthly basis.
2. Exporting report data from QuickBooks to Microsoft Excel can be made in order to perform "what if" scenarios.
3. In a sole proprietorship, an owner's paycheck is considered a(n)U withdrawal.
4. The Summary Report Basis for Cash or Accrual is selected as a Report Preference.
5. The Cash Flow Forecast Projected Balance column shows the total in all bank accounts if all Customer and bill payments are made on time.

SHORT ESSAY

Describe the five types of Balance Sheet Reports available in the Report Center.

NAME________________

CHAPTER 4: TRANSMITTAL

COMPUTER CONSULTING BY YOUR NAME

Check the items below as you print them; then attach the documents and reports in the order listed when you submit them to your instructor.

___ Account Listing
___ Check 9: Your Name
___ Reconciliation Detail Report
___ Trial Balance, January 1-31, 2015
___ Cash Flow Forecast, February 1-28, 2015
___ Statement of Cash Flows, January 2015
___ Journal, January 1-31, 2015
___ Trial Balance, January 31, 2015
___ Profit & Loss Report (Standard), January 31, 2015
___ Balance Sheet (Standard), January 31, 2015

END-OF-CHAPTER PROBLEM

YOUR NAME LANDSCAPE AND POOL SERVICE

Chapter 4 continues with the end-of-period adjustments, bank reconciliation, archive copies, and closing the period for Your Name Landscape and Pool Service. The company does use a certified public accountant for guidance and assistance with appropriate accounting procedures. The CPA has provided information for use in recording adjusting entries and so on.

INSTRUCTIONS

Continue to use the company file **Landscape.qbw** that you used for Chapters 1, 2, and 3. Record the adjustments and other transactions as you were instructed in the chapter. Always read the transaction carefully and review the Chart of Accounts when selecting transaction accounts. Expand reports, adjust columns so they display in full, and print the reports and journals as indicated.

RECORD TRANSACTIONS

<u>January 31</u>

- Change the names of the following accounts:
  - **Student's Name, Capital** to **Your Name, Capital**
    - Remember to use your actual name.
  - **Business Trucks** to **Business Vehicles** (Notice that the names of the subaccounts were not affected by this name change.)
  - **Business Trucks Loan** to **Business Vehicles Loan**
  - **Automobile Expense** to **Business Vehicles Expense** (Delete the description)
  - **Auto Insurance Expense** to **Business Vehicles Insurance**
  - Capitalize the i in income for the account **Residential Landscape income**
- Make the following accounts inactive:
  - **Recruiting**
  - **Travel & Ent** (Notice that the subaccounts are also made inactive.)
- Delete the following accounts:
  - **Sales**
  - **Services**
  - **Amortization Expense**
  - **Interest Expense: Mortgage**
  - **Taxes: Property**
- Print the Chart of Accounts by clicking **Reports** on the menu bar, pointing to **List**, clicking **Account Listing.** Adjust the column widths so that all information is displayed, hide the Tax Line and Description columns. Use Portrait orientation.

January 31

- Enter adjusting entries in the Journal for:
  - Office Supplies Used, $185. Memo: January Supplies Used
  - Business vehicles insurance expense for the month, $250. Memo: January Insurance Expense
  - Depreciation for the month (Use a compound entry), Memo: January Depreciation
    - Business Vehicles, $950
    - Equipment, $206.25
- Enter transactions for Owner's Equity (Any General Journal entries are not adjusting entries):
  - Additional cash investment by you, $2,000. Memo: Investment: Cash
  - Additional noncash investment by owner, $1,500 of lawn equipment. Memo: Investment: Equipment (Note: The value of the lawn equipment is the original cost of the asset.)
  - Write the check for the owner withdrawal of $1,000. Memo: January Withdrawal (Add your name as "Other," include the memo on the check face and in the Memo column in the detail section of the check, print the check.)
- Prepare Bank Reconciliation and Enter Adjustments for the Reconciliation for January 31, 2015. (Be sure to enter automatic payments, service charges, and interest. Pay close attention to the dates—especially for service charges and interest earned.)

SANTA BARBARA BANK
1234 Coast Highway
Santa Barbara, CA 93100 (805) 555-9310

Your Name Landscape and Pool Service
18527 State Street
Santa Barbara, CA 993103

Acct. # 987-352-9152 January 31, 2015

Beginning Balance January 2, 2015			**$23,850.00**
1/18/15 Check 1		485.00	23,365.00
1/18/15 Check 2		180.00	23,185.00
1/18/15 Check 3		375.00	22,810.00
1/18/15		669.00	22,141.00
1/31/15 Service Charge		10.00	22,131.00
1/31/15 Business Vehicles Loan Pmt.: Interest, 795.54; Principal, 160.64		956.18	21,174.82
1/31/15 Interest	59.63		21,234.45
Ending Balance 1/31/15			**$21,234.45**

- Print a Detailed Reconciliation Report in Portrait orientation.
- Change or Verify Reports & Graphs Preferences: Summary Reports Basis to Accrual.

4

- Transfer Net Income/Owner's Equity into Capital Account (Did you prepare a Profit & Loss report to find out the amount of Net Income?) Use the Memo: Transfer Net Income into Capital. (This is not an adjusting entry.)
- Close the Draws account. Use the Memo: Close Drawing. (This is not an adjusting entry.)
- Prepare the archive backup file: **Landscape (Archive 01-31-15)**
- Close the period. The closing date is **01/31/15**. (Do not use a password.)
- Edit a Transaction from a closed period: Discovered an error in the amount of office supplies used. The amount used should be **$175**, not $185. (Don't forget to adjust Owner's Equity and Capital.)
- Replace the archive backup file: **Landscape (Archive 01-31-15)**

January 31, 2015

Use the dates given for each report, expand, resize columns, and print the following in Portrait orientation unless specified as Landscape:

- Cash Flow Forecast for February 1-28, 2015 (Landscape orientation).
- Statement of Cash Flows, January 1-31, 2015.
- Journal for January, 2015. (Expand the report. Use Landscape orientation, and Fit report to one page wide)
- Trial Balance, January 31, 2015.
- Profit & Loss Report (Standard), January 31, 2015
- Balance Sheet (Standard), January 31, 2015
- Backup your work to **Landscape (Backup Ch. 4)**.

NAME______________________

CHAPTER 4: TRANSMITTAL

YOUR NAME LANDSCAPE AND POOL SERVICE

Check the items below as you print them; then attach the documents and reports in the order listed when you submit them to your instructor.

___ Account Listing, January 31, 2015
___ Check 8: Your Name
___ Reconciliation Detail Report
___ Cash Flow Forecast, February 1-28, 2015
___ Statement of Cash Flows, January 2015
___ Journal, January 2015
___ Trial Balance, January 31, 2015
___ Profit and Loss Report (Standard), January 31, 2015
___ Balance Sheet (Standard), January 31, 2015

4

SECTION 1 PRACTICE SET, SERVICE BUSINESS:

YOUR NAME AT YOUR SERVICE

The following is a comprehensive practice set combining all the elements of QuickBooks studied in Chapters 1-4. In this practice set, you will keep the books for a company for one month. Entries will be made to record invoices, receipt of payments on invoices, cash sales, bills and bill payments, credit memos for invoices and bills. Account names will be added, changed, deleted, and made inactive. Customer, vendor, owner names, and items will be added to the appropriate lists. Adjusting entries for depreciation, supplies used, and insurance expense will be recorded. A bank reconciliation will be prepared. Reports will be prepared to analyze sales, bills, and receipts. Formal reports including the Trial Balance, Profit and Loss Statement, and Balance Sheet will be prepared.

YOUR NAME AT YOUR SERVICE

Located in Beverly Hills, California, Your Name At Your Service is a service business providing assistance with errands, shopping, home repairs, and simple household chores. The company is going to start providing transportation for children and others who do not drive. Rates are on a per-hour basis and differ according to the service performed.

Your Name At Your Service is a sole proprietorship owned and operated by you. You have one assistant, Olivia Reynolds, helping you with errands, scheduling of duties, and doing the bookkeeping for Your Name At Your Service. In addition, a part-time employee, Lewis Brown, works weekends for Your Name At Your Service.

INSTRUCTIONS

Use the company file **Service.qbw**. If you get a message to update the file, follow the steps listed in QuickBooks.

The following lists are used for all sales items, customers, and vendors. You will be adding additional customers and vendors as the company is in operation. When entering transactions, you are responsible for any memos or customer messages you wish to include in transactions. Unless otherwise specified, the terms for each sale or bill will be the terms specified on the Customer or Vendor List. (View the terms for the individual customers or vendors in the Customer Center and Vendor Center.)

Customers:

Customers & Jobs | Transactions

Active Customers

NAME	BALANCE TOTAL	ATTACH
Aguilar, Juan Dr.	275.00	
Ashford, Will	750.00	
Bailey, Gloria	150.00	
Blair, Danielle	600.00	
Evans, Drake	50.00	
Jackson, Jeff	1,000.00	
Lim, Keiko	200.00	
Perez, Jorge	250.00	
Peterson, Alex	450.00	
Sanchez, Ricardo	500.00	
Waters, Samantha	0.00	

Vendors:

Vendors | Transactions

Active Vendors

NAME	BALANCE TOTAL	ATTACH
Beverly Hills Flowers	25.00	
Bruin Stationers	350.00	
Employment Development	0.00	
Robertson Realtors	0.00	
Sunshine Gasoline	250.00	
United States Treasury	0.00	
Westside Utilities	0.00	
Westwood Automotive	500.00	

Sales Items:

Item List

Look for [ ] in All fields | Search | Reset

NAME	DESCRIPTION	TYPE	ACCOUNT	PRICE	ATTACH
Errands	Household Errands	Service	Services	35.00	
Household	Household Chores	Service	Services	25.00	
Party	Party Planning and Supervision	Service	Services	50.00	
Pets	Pet Sitting	Service	Services	25.00	
Repairs	Repair Service	Service	Services	65.00	
Shopping	Client Shopping	Service	Services	35.00	

Item | Activities | Reports | Excel | Attach | Include inactive

Each Item is priced per hour. Unless otherwise specified within the transactions, a minimum of one hour is charged for any service provided. As you can see, there is no difference in amount between the first hour of a service and subsequent hours of service.

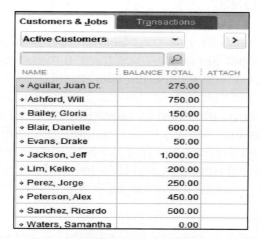

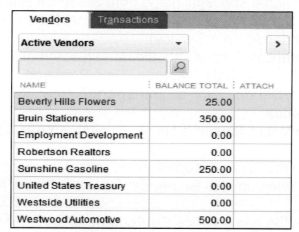

RECORD TRANSACTIONS

Enter the transactions for Your Name At Your Service and print as indicated. When preparing invoices, use an Intuit Service Invoice form, a message of your choosing, and do not e-mail invoices or accept online payments. Start numbering the Invoices with number 35 and Sales Receipts with the number 22. Unless the transaction indicates something different, use the standard terms provided by QuickBooks. Print invoices and sales receipts without lines. Provide transaction memos when needed for clarification. Print invoices, sales receipts, and checks as they are entered. Unless instructed to do so by your professor, do not print Payment Receipts and Bills (even if not printed, they are included on the transmittal sheet). Always resize the columns in reports to display information in full.

Week 1: January 1-6, 2015:

- Change the company name and legal name from Student's Name At Your Service to **Your Name At Your Service**. (Type your actual name. For example, Mark Randall would enter Mark Randall At Your Service).
- Change Report Preferences: Reports should refresh automatically, Report Header/ Footer should *not* include the Date Prepared, Time Prepared, or the Report Basis.
- Add a new Item: Type: **Service**, Name: **Transport**, Description: **Transportation**; Rate: **35.00**, Account: **Services**.
- Change the Capital account Student's Name, Capital to **Your Name, Capital**. (Use your own name.)
- Find all accounts with the name **Automobile** as part of the account name. Change every occurrence of Automobile to **Business Vehicles**. Delete any unwanted descriptions.
- Find all accounts with the name **Office Equipment** as part of the account name. Change every occurrence of Office Equipment to **Office Furniture/Equipment**. Delete any unwanted descriptions.
- Make the following inactive: **Interest Expense: Mortgage**; **Taxes: Property**; **Travel & Ent**.
- Delete the following accounts: **Sales, Amortization Expense, Professional Development,** and **Recruiting**.
- Add **Petty Cash** to the Chart of Accounts. Transfer **$100** from Checking to Petty Cash to fund the account. Use January 1, 2015 as the transaction date.
- Print an Account Listing in Portrait orientation. Hide the columns for Description and Tax Line and resize any columns that are not displayed in full.
- Prior to recording any transactions, print a Trial Balance as of January 1, 2015.

1/1/15

- We were out of paper, toner cartridges for the laser printer, and various other office supplies that we need to have on hand. Received a bill—Invoice 1806-1—from Bruin Stationers for $450 for the office supplies we received today. (Even though the Bills are listed on the transmittal sheet, check with your instructor to see if you should print them. Bills print with lines around each field.)
- Dr. Ricardo Sanchez has arranged for you to take his dogs to the vet for shots and to feed and walk his dogs 1 hour per day every day. Bill Dr. Sanchez for 3 hours transport

and pet sitting for one hour a day for 14 days, terms Net 30. (Refer to the Item List for the appropriate sales items and put this all on Invoice 35. Remember to use an Intuit Service Invoice as the business form.) Use an appropriate customer message and print the invoice without lines. On the Name Information Changed dialog box, click "No" so you do not change the terms for Dr. Sanchez from Net 15 to Net 30.

- Samantha Waters is having a party in two weeks. Bill Samantha Waters for 12 hours of party planning. Invoice 36, terms Net 30.

1/2/15

- Mr. Peterson's mother has several doctor appointments. He has asked Your Name At Your Service to take her to these appointments. Bill Alex Peterson for 8 hours of transportation.

1/3/15

- Gloria Bailey needed to have her shelves relined. You did part of the house this week and will return next week to continue the work. Bill her for 12 hours of household chores for this week.

1/4/15

- Record the bill from Western Insurance, (7654 Western Avenue, Hollywood, CA 90721, Main Phone 310-555-1598, Main Email WesternIns@abc.com, Fax 310-555-8951, terms Net 30) for Business Vehicles Insurance for the year, $2,400, Invoice 2280.
- Received checks for Customer Payments on account for balances dated 12/31/2014 from the following customers: Dr. Juan Aguilar, $275, Check 713; Jorge Perez, $250, Check 36381; Alex Peterson, $450, Check 6179; Jeff Jackson, $1,000, Check 38142. (Even though the Payment Receipts are listed on the transmittal sheet, check with your instructor to see if you should print them.)

1/5/15

- Prepare Sales Receipt 22 to record a cash sale. Received Check 2894 for 2 hours of errands and 1 hour of household chores for a new customer: Fatema Nasseri, 18062 Beverly Drive, Beverly Hills, CA 90210, Main Phone: 310-555-7206, Fax: 310-555-6027, Main E-mail: FNasseri@abc.com, Payment Terms: Net 10, Preferred Delivery Method: None. (*Note:* Remember to key the last name first for the customer name.) Print the sales receipt.

1/6/15

- Prepare Unpaid Bills Detail Report for January 6, 2015. Print the report.
- Pay bills for the amount owed to Beverly Hills Flowers and Sunshine Gasoline on December 31. (Refer to the Vendor List shown on the second page of the practice set or to the Unpaid Bills Detail Report to determine the amounts for the checks. Remember that the due dates will not be 12/31/14 they will be 01/10/15.) Print the checks using a Standard check style—they may be printed on one page or individually.
- Make the bank deposit for the week. Deposit date is 1/6/15. Print a Deposit Summary.
- Print Trial Balance from 01/01/15 to 01/06/15.
- Back up your work for the week. Use **Service (Backup Week 1)** as the file name.

Week 2: January 7-13, 2015

1/9/15

- Received checks for payment on accounts from the following customers: Dr. Sanchez, $500, No. 7891; Ms. Lim, $200, No. 97452; Ms. Blair, $600, No. 925; Mr. Evans, $50, No. 178; and Mr. Ashford, $750, No. 3916.
- Received a bill—Invoice 81085—from Sunshine Gasoline, $325 for the bi-weekly gasoline charge.
- Every week we put fresh flowers in the office in order to provide a welcoming environment for any customers who happen to come to the office. Received a bill—Invoice 9287—from Beverly Hills Flowers for $60 for office flowers for two weeks. (Miscellaneous Expense)

1/10/15

- Danielle Blair really likes the floral arrangements in the office of Your Name At Your Service. She has asked that flowers be brought to her home and arranged throughout the house. When you complete the placement of the flowers in the house, Danielle gives you Check 387 for $180 for 3 hours of errands and 3 hours of household chores. This is payment in full for three weeks of floral arrangements. Prepare the Sales Receipt.
- Jeff Jackson has arranged for Your Name At Your Service to supervise and coordinate the installation of new tile in his master bathroom. Bill Mr. Jackson for 5 hours of repair service for hiring the subcontractor, scheduling the installation for 1/14, 1/15 and 1/16, and contract preparation.

1/11/15

- Returned faulty printer cartridge that we had purchased in December to have on hand. Received Credit Memo 5 from Bruin Stationers, $95. (Did you use the asset account?)

1/13/15

- Pay all bills for the amounts due on or before January 13. (*Hint:* Are there any credits to apply?) There should be two checks. Print the checks–all on one page or individually.
- Correct the invoice issued to Gloria Bailey on 1/03/15. The number of hours billed should be 14 instead of 12. Print the corrected invoice. (Do not change the date.)
- Make the bank deposit for the week. Deposit date is 1/13/15. Print a Deposit Summary.
- Print Trial Balance from 01/01/15 to 01/13/15.
- Back up your work for the week. Use **Service (Backup Week 2)** as the file name.

Week 3: January 14-20, 2015

1/15/15

- Pay postage due 64 cents. Use Petty Cash. Number is 1 for Petty Cash.
- Print Petty Cash Account QuickReport in by clicking the Report button at the bottom of the Chart of Accounts. Print in Landscape orientation.

1/17/15

- Mr. Jackson's bathroom tile was installed on 1/14, 1/15 and 1/16. The installation was completed to his satisfaction. Bill him for 24 hours of repair service.

1/18/15

- Danielle Blair's neighbor, Avi Levin, really liked the flowers in Danielle's house and asked you to bring flowers to his home and office. This week he gave you Check 90-163 for 1 hour of errands and 1 hour of household chores. Add him to the customer list: Avi Levin, Main Phone: 310-555-0918, 236 West Camden Drive, Beverly Hills, CA 90210, Payment Terms: Net 10, Preferred Delivery Method: None.

1/19/15

- Tonight is Samantha's big party. She has arranged for both you and Lewis to supervise the party from 3 p.m. until 1 a.m. Bill Samantha Waters for 20 hours of party planning and supervision.
- Print a Customer Balance Summary Report for all transactions.

1/20/15

- Record the checks received from customers for the week: Mr. Peterson, $280, No. 9165, Ms. Bailey, $150, No. 7-303, Dr. Sanchez, $455, No. 89162, and Mr. Jackson, $325, No. 38197.
- Make the bank deposit for the week. Deposit date is 1/20/15. Print a Deposit Summary.
- Print Trial Balance from 01/01/15 to 01/20/15.
- Back up your work for the week. Use **Service (Backup Week 3)** as the file name.

Week 4: January 21-27, 2015

1/23/15

- Samantha's party went so smoothly on the 19th that you went home at 11 p.m. rather than 1 a.m. Issue a Credit Memo to Samantha Waters for 2 hours of party planning and supervision. Apply the credit to Invoice 41 dated January 19, 2015.
- Drake Evans arranged to have his pets cared for by Your Name At Your Service during the past 7 days. Bill him for 1 hour of pet sitting each day. Drake wants to add a doggie door and a fenced area for his dog. Bill him 24 hours of repair service for the planning and overseeing of the project.
- Use Petty Cash to pay for a box of file folders to be used immediately in reorganizing some of the files in the office, $14.84. (This is an expense and is Check 2 for Petty Cash.)
- Print a Petty Cash Account QuickReport in Landscape. Fit the report to one page wide.

1/24/15

- You arranged for theater tickets, dinner reservations, and an after-theater surprise party for Dr. Aguilar to celebrate his wife's birthday. Bill him for 4 hours of errands, 3 hours shopping for the gift, and 5 hours of party planning.
- Received a bill—Invoice 9802—from Beverly Hills Flowers for $60 for office flowers for two weeks.
- Received a bill—Invoice 81116—from Sunshine Gasoline, $355 for the bi-weekly gasoline charge.
- Write a check to Bruin Stationers for the purchase of a new printer for the office, $500. (*Note:* If you get a warning to use Pay Bills because we owe the company money, click Continue Writing Check.) Print the check using standard-style checks.

1/27/15

- Dr. Sanchez has arranged for Your Name At Your Service to feed and walk his dogs every day. Bill him for pet sitting, 1 hour per day for the past two weeks. In addition, Dr. Sanchez is going to have a party and wants Your Name At Your Service to plan it for him. Bill him for 20 hours party planning. When the dogs were puppies they did some damage to the interior of the house. In order to prepare for the party several areas in the house need to be reorganized and repaired. Bill him for 18 hours of household chores and 20 hours of repairs.
- Write checks to pay for telephone, rent, and utilities. The telephone company will need to be added to the Vendor List. Vendor information is provided in each transaction. Print the checks using standard-style checks. They may be printed as a batch or individually.
    - Monthly telephone bill: $150, Bel Air Telephone. Add the vendor: Bel Air Telephone, Main Phone 310-555-4972, 2015 Beverly Boulevard, Bel Air, CA 90047, Payment Terms Net 30.
    - Monthly rent for office space: $1,500, Robertson Realtors.
    - Monthly utility bill $477 for: water $183 and gas and electric $294, Westside Utilities.
- Prepare and print in Portrait orientation an Unpaid Bills Detail Report for January 27.
- Pay bills for all amounts due on or before January 27. Print check(s).
- Prepare a Check Detail Report from 1/1/15 to 1/27/15. Use Landscape orientation and fit report to one page wide.
- Record payments received from customers: Ms. Waters, $600, No. 4692; Dr. Sanchez, $1,550, No. 7942; Mr. Evans, $735, No. 235; Dr. Aguilar, $495, No. 601; Ms. Bailey, $140, No. 923-10. (If any of the payments are not payments in full, leave as an underpayment. Include the Memo: Partial Payment.)
- Make the bank deposit for the week. Deposit date is 1/27/15. Print a Deposit Summary.
- Print Customer Balance Detail Report in Portrait orientation for All Transactions.
- Print Trial Balance from 01/01/15 to 01/27/15.
- Back up your work for the week. Use **Service (Backup Week 4)** as the file name.

Week 5: January 28-30, 2015

1/30/15

- Write a check for your monthly withdrawal, $1,200.
- Since a fax machine is a business necessity, you decided to give your new fax machine to Your Name At Your Service. Record this additional $350 investment of equipment by you.
- Because they are remodeling the offices, Robertson Realtors decreased the amount of rent to $1,000 per month. Correct and reprint Check 7 for rent payment.
- Record adjusting entries for:
    - Business Vehicles Insurance, $200.
    - Office Supplies Used, $150.
    - Depreciation: Business Vehicles, $500 and Office Furniture/Equipment, $92.
- Print Trial Balance from 01/01/15 to 01/30/15.
- Back up your work for the week. Use **Service (Backup Week 5)** as the file name.

End of the Month: January 31, 2015

- Prepare the bank reconciliation using the following bank statement. Record any adjustments necessary as a result of the bank statement.

Beverly Hills Bank
1234 Rodeo Drive
Beverly Hills, CA 90210

Your Name At Your Service
2789 Robertson Boulevard
Beverly Hills, CA 90210

Beginning Balance, 1/1/15			$25,350.00
1/1/15, Transfer		100.00	25,250.00
1/6/15, Deposit	2,070.00		27,320.00
1/7/15, Check 1		25.00	27,295.00
1/7/15, Check 2		250.00	27,045.00
1/13/15, Deposit	2,280.00		29,325.00
1/15/15, Check 4		500.00	28,825.00
1/16/15, Check 3		255.00	28,570.00
1/20/15, Deposit	1,270.00		29,840.00
1/28/15, Check 5		500.00	29,340.00
1/29/15, Check 7		1,000.00	28,340.00
1/31/15, Payment: Business Vehicles Loan: Interest $551.87; Principal $177.57		729.44	27,610.56
1/31/15, Payment: Office Furniture/ Equipment Loan: Interest $59.45; Principal $15.44		74.89	27,535.67
1/31/15, Service Charge		25.00	27,510.67
1/31/15, Interest	53.00		27,563.67
1/31/15, Ending Balance			$27,563.67

- Print a Reconciliation Detail Report.
- Print the following reports as of 1/31/15:
    - Trial Balance from 1/1/15 through 1/31/15 in Portrait.
    - Cash Flow Forecast from 2/1/15 through 2/28/15 in Landscape.
    - Statement of Cash Flows from 1/1/15 through 1/31/15 in Portrait.
    - Profit & Loss (Standard) from 1/1/15 through 1/31/15 in Portrait.
- Transfer the net income/retained earnings to owner's capital account.
- Close the Drawing account.
- Close the period as of 01/31/15. Do not use any passwords.
- Prepare a Balance Sheet a (Standard) as of 1/31/15. Print in Portrait.
- Prepare the Journal from 1/1/15 through 1/31/15, expand the report, print in Landscape orientation, and Fit to 1 page wide.
- Create an Archive Backup named **Service (Archive 01-31-15)**.
- Back up your work for the week. Use **Service (Backup Complete)** as the file name.

NAME ____________________

SECTION 1 PRACTICE SET: TRANSMITTAL

YOUR NAME AT YOUR SERVICE

Check the items below as you complete and/or print them; then attach the documents and reports in the order listed when you submit them to your instructor. Printing is optional for Payment Receipts and Bills (unless your instructor requires them to be printed); however, they are included on the transmittal sheet so they can be checked as they are completed.

(Note: When paying bills and printing a batch of checks, your checks may be in a different order than shown below. As long as you print the checks to the correct vendors and have the correct amounts, do not be concerned if your check numbers are not an exact match.)

Week 1

___ Account Listing
___ Trial Balance, January 1, 2015
___ Bill: Bruin Stationers (Optional)
___ Invoice 35: Ricardo Sanchez
___ Invoice 36: Samantha Waters
___ Invoice 37: Alex Peterson
___ Invoice 38: Gloria Bailey
___ Bill: Western Insurance (Optional))
___ Payment Receipt: Juan Aguilar (Optional)
___ Payment Receipt: Jorge Perez (Optional)
___ Payment Receipt: Alex Peterson (Optional)
___ Payment Receipt: Jeff Jackson (Optional)
___ Sales Receipt 22: Fatema Nasseri
___ Unpaid Bills Detail, January 6, 2015
___ Check 1: Beverly Hills Flowers
___ Check 2: Sunshine Gasoline
___ Deposit Summary, January 6, 2015
___ Trial Balance, January 6, 2015

Week 2

___ Payment Receipt: Ricardo Sanchez (Optional)
___ Payment Receipt: Keiko Lim (Optional)
___ Payment Receipt: Danielle Blair (Optional)
___ Payment Receipt: Drake Evans (Optional)
___ Payment Receipt: Will Ashford (Optional)
___ Bill: Sunshine Gasoline (Optional)
___ Bill: Beverly Hills Flowers (Optional)
___ Sales Receipt 23: Danielle Blair
___ Invoice 39: Jeff Jackson
___ Credit Memo: Bruin Stationers
___ Check 3: Bruin Stationers
___ Check 4: Westwood Automotive
___ Invoice 38 (Corrected): Gloria Bailey
___Deposit Summary, January 13, 2015
___ Trial Balance, January 13, 2015

Week 3

___ Petty Cash QuickReport, January 15, 2015
___ Invoice 40: Jeff Jackson
___ Sales Receipt 24: Avi Levin
___ Invoice 41: Samantha Waters
___ Customer Balance Summary, January 19, 2015
___ Payment Receipt: Alex Peterson (Optional)
___ Payment Receipt: Gloria Bailey (Optional)
___ Payment Receipt: Ricardo Sanchez (Optional)
___ Payment Receipt: Jeff Jackson (Optional)
___ Deposit Summary, January 20, 2015
___ Trial Balance, January 20, 2015

Week 4

___ Credit Memo 42: Samantha Waters
___ Invoice 43: Drake Evans
___ Petty Cash QuickReport, January 23, 2015
___ Invoice 44: Juan Aguilar
___ Bill: Beverly Hills Flowers (Optional)
___ Bill: Sunshine Gasoline (Optional)
___ Check 5: Bruin Stationers
___ Invoice 45: Ricardo Sanchez
___ Check 6: Bel Air Telephone
___ Check 7: Robertson Realtors
___ Check 8: Westside Utilities
___ Unpaid Bills Detail, January 27, 2015
___ Check 9: Beverly Hills Flowers
___ Check Detail, January 1-27, 2015
___ Payment Receipt: Samantha Waters (Optional)
___ Payment Receipt: Ricardo Sanchez (Optional)
___ Payment Receipt: Drake Evans (Optional)
___ Payment Receipt: Juan Aguilar (Optional)
___ Payment Receipt: Gloria Bailey (Optional)
___ Deposit Summary, January 27, 2015
___ Customer Balance Detail, January 27, 2015
___ Trial Balance, January 27, 2015

Week 5

___ Check 10 Your Name
___ Check 7 (Corrected): Robertson Realtors
___ Trial Balance, January 30, 2015

End of the Month

___ Bank Reconciliation Detail Report
___ Trial Balance, January 31, 2015
___ Cash Flow Forecast, February 1-28, 2015
___ Statement of Cash Flows, January 2015
___ Profit & Loss, January 2015
___ Balance Sheet, January 31, 2015
___ Journal, January 2015

SALES AND RECEIVABLES: MERCHANDISING BUSINESS

5

LEARNING OBJECTIVES

At the completion of this chapter, you will be able to:

1. Enter sales transactions for a retail business.
2. Prepare invoices that use sales tax, have sales discounts, and exceed a customer's credit limit.
3. Prepare sales orders; and then, once fulfilled, use to prepare a Custom S. O. Invoice.
4. Prepare transactions for cash sales with sales tax.
5. Prepare transactions for customers using debit and credit cards.
6. Learn about Credit Card Compliance requirements and protection.
7. Add new accounts to the Chart of Accounts and new sales items to the Item List.
8. Add new customers and modify existing customer records.
9. Delete and void invoices.
10. Prepare credit memos with and without refunds.
11. Record customer payments on account with and without discounts and use the Look Up Invoice feature.
12. Deposit checks, debit card, and credit card receipts for sales and customer payments.
13. Record a transaction for a NSF check and use QuickBooks' Bounced Check feature.
14. Customize report preferences and prepare and print Customer Balance Detail Reports, Open Invoice Reports, Sales Reports, and Inventory Valuation Reports.
15. View a QuickReport and use the QuickZoom feature.
16. Use the Customer Center to obtain information regarding credit customers.
17. Prepare Trial Balance, Profit & Loss, Journal, and other reports.
18. Memorize a report.

ACCOUNTING FOR SALES AND RECEIVABLES

Rather than using a traditional Sales Journal to record transactions using debits and credits and special columns, QuickBooks uses an Invoice to record sales on account. Because cash sales do not involve accounts receivable, a Sales Receipt is prepared and the money is placed into the Undeposited Funds account until a deposit is made. When customers pay their bills, a Payment Receipt is prepared. All transactions, regardless where they are recorded are placed in the Journal. A new account, sales item, or customer can be added as transactions are entered. Customer information may be changed in the Customer List. The Customer List is the same as the Accounts Receivable Subsidiary Ledger.

For a retail business, QuickBooks tracks inventory, maintains information on reorder limits, tracks the quantity of merchandise on hand, maintains information on the value of the inventory, computes the cost of goods sold using the average cost basis, and informs you of the percentage of sales for each inventory item. Early-payment discounts as well as discounts to certain types of customers can be given. Different price levels may be created for sales items and/or customers.

A multitude of reports are available when using QuickBooks. Accounts receivable reports include Customer Balance Summary and Customer Balance Detail reports. Sales reports provide information regarding the amount of sales by item. Transaction Reports by Customer are available as well as the traditional accounting reports such as Trial Balance, Profit and Loss, and Balance Sheet. QuickBooks also has graphing capabilities so that you can see and evaluate your accounts receivable and sales. Reports created in QuickBooks may be exported to Microsoft Excel.

DOWNLOAD COMPANY FILES

Refer to Chapter 1 procedures for downloading company files for Chapters 5-8.

Download **Company Master Files Chapters 5-8 (Student Data Files)**

- Follow the steps provided in Chapter 1 to download the company files and to make sure the company files are not marked as “Read Only” or “Archive.”
- In addition to the five company files in the Company Master Files for Chapters 5-8 there are three logo files that will be used in Chapter 9 and the final practice set.

5

TRAINING TUTORIAL

The following tutorial is a step-by-step guide to recording sales (both cash and credit) for a fictitious company. This company is called Student’s Name Mountain Sports. In addition to recording transactions using QuickBooks, you will prepare several reports and graphs for the company. The tutorial for Student’s Name Mountain Sports will continue in Chapters 6 and 7, when accounting for payables, bank reconciliations, financial statement preparation, and closing an accounting period for a merchandising business will be completed.

Since the company used in training is fictitious, there are transactions that will be entered for illustration but will not be able to be entered in a way that will take full advantage of QuickBooks. For example, in an actual business when a credit card is accepted for payment, the payment would be processed. If there are supplemental or subscription enhancements to QuickBooks, they may be noted but will not be utilized.

DATES

As in Chapters 1-4, the year used for the screen shots is 2015, which is the same year as the version of the program. Verify the year you are to use with your instructor. The year you use in Chapter 5 should be the year you use in Chapters 6 and 7.

PRINTING

As in Chapters 1-4, you will be instructed when to print business documents and reports. Everything that may be printed within the chapter is listed on a transmittal sheet. The end-of- chapter problem includes a transmittal sheet listing everything that may be printed. As you print, check off the document on the transmittal sheet. Always verify items to be printed with your instructor.

BASIC INSTRUCTIONS

In this chapter you will be entering both accounts receivable and cash sale transactions for a retail company that sells merchandise and charges its customers sales tax. As in previous chapters, all transactions are listed on memos. The transaction date will be the same date as the memo date unless otherwise specified within the transaction. Customer names, when necessary, will be given in the transaction. Unless otherwise specified, all terms for customers on account are Net 30 days.

Even when instructions for a transaction are given transaction step-by-step, always refer to the memo for transaction details. Once a specific type of transaction has been entered in a step-by-step manner, additional transactions will be made without having instructions provided. Of course, you may always refer back to previous instructions.

COMPANY PROFILE

Student's Name Mountain Sports is a sporting goods store located in Mammoth Lakes, California. Currently, the company is open only during the winter. As a result, the company specializes in equipment, clothing, and accessories for skiing and snowboarding. The company is a partnership between you and Larry Muir. Each partner has a 50 percent share of the business, and both of you devote all of your efforts to Student's Name Mountain Sports. You have several part-time employees who work during ski season. There is a full-time bookkeeper and manager, Ruth Morgan, who oversees purchases, maintains the inventory, and keeps the books for the company.

OPEN A COMPANY

Use the Sports.qbw file to complete the training in Chapters 5, 6, and 7.

➤ Open **QuickBooks**, and open **Sports.qbw**

- Use the **Sports.qbw** file that you downloaded in the folder for **Company Master Files Chapters 5-8 (Student Data Files)**.
- If QuickBooks has received an update from Intuit, you may get a screen to Update Company. If so, click **Yes**.
- If you see the "What's New" icon on the right-side of the Home Page, click the [X] to close it.

ADD YOUR NAME TO THE COMPANY NAME

As in earlier chapters, each student in the course will be working with the same company and printing the same documents. Personalizing the company name to include your name will help identify many of the documents you print during your training.

Add your name to the company name

Click **Company** on the menu bar, click **My Company,** click the **Edit** icon
In the Company Name textbox, drag through the words **Student's Name** to highlight
Type **your real name**

- Type your real name, *not* the words *Your Real Name*. For example, Pamela Powers would type—**Pamela Powers**.

Repeat for the Legal Name on the Legal Information tab
Click **OK**

- The title bar now shows Your Name Mountain Sports.

Close the My Company screen

ACCOUNT NUMBERS

QuickBooks has a choice to use or not use account numbers for the accounts in the Chart of Accounts. In this section of the text, account numbers will be used.

The account numbering may be four or five digits. The structure is:

ACCOUNT NUMBER	TYPE OF ACCOUNT
1000-1999	Assets
2000-2999	Liabilities
3000-3099	Capital
4000-4999	Income or Revenue
5000-5999	Cost of Goods Sold
6000-6999	Expenses
7000-7999	Other Income
8000-8999	Other Expenses

LISTS

Much of the organization of QuickBooks is dependent on lists. The primary types of lists you will use in the chapter are a Customer List and a Sales Item List. There are also lists for templates, payment methods, terms, customer messages, and so on.

Customers & Jobs List

The names, addresses, telephone numbers, credit terms, credit limits, balances, and tax terms for all established credit customers are contained in the Customers & Jobs List. The Customers & Jobs List is also the Accounts Receivable Ledger. You will be using the following Customers & Jobs List for established credit customers:

Customers & Jobs | Transactions

NAME	BALANCE TOTAL	ATTACH
◆ Cooper, Eileen Dr.	417.00	
◆ Daily, Gail	1,136.00	
◆ Deardorff, Ramona	650.00	
◆ Gardener, Monique	53.57	
◆ Kandahar, Mahmet	1,085.00	
◆ Mountain Schools	0.00	
◆ Perez, Jose Dr.	95.45	
◆ Perkins, Sandra	408.48	
◆ Rhodes, Leslie	455.00	
◆ Taka, Mikko	670.31	
◆ Thomsen, Kevin	911.63	
◆ Villanueva, Oskar	975.00	
◆ Watson, Russ	85.00	

Item List

Sales are often made up of various types of income. In Your Name Mountain Sports there are several income accounts. In order to classify income regarding the type of sale, the sales account may have subaccounts. When recording a transaction for a sale, QuickBooks requires that a Sales Item be used. When the sales item is created, a sales account is required. When the sales item is used in a transaction, the income is credited to the appropriate sales/income account. For example, Ski Boots is a sales item and uses Equipment Income, a subaccount of Sales, when a transaction is recorded.

QuickBooks uses lists to organize sales items. Using lists for sales items allows for flexibility in billing and a more accurate representation of the way in which income is earned. If the company charges a standard price for an item, the price of the item will be included on the list. Your Name Mountain Sports sells all items at different prices, so the price given for each item is listed at 0.00.

In a retail business with an inventory, the number of units on hand can be tracked; and, when the amount on hand gets to a predetermined limit, an order can be placed. By giving an item a Maximum, the quantity to order can be calculated easily. The following Item List for the various types of merchandise and sales categories will be used for Your Name Mountain Sports:

Item List

Look for [ ] in All fields | Search | Reset | Search within results

NAME	DESCRIPTION	TYPE	ACCOUNT	TOTAL QUANTITY ON HAND	ON SALES ORDER	PRICE	ATTACH
Accessories	Sunglasses, Ski Wax, Sunscreen, Ski Holders, Boot Carriers, etc.	Inventory Part	4011 · Clothing & Accessory Sales	800	0	0.00	
Bindings-Skis	Ski Bindings	Inventory Part	4012 · Equipment Sales	50	0	0.00	
Bindings-Snow	Snowboard Bindings	Inventory Part	4012 · Equipment Sales	50	0	0.00	
Boots	After Ski Boots and Shoes	Inventory Part	4011 · Clothing & Accessory Sales	20	0	0.00	
Boots-Ski	Ski Boots	Inventory Part	4012 · Equipment Sales	15	0	0.00	
Boots-Snowbrd	Snowboard Boots	Inventory Part	4012 · Equipment Sales	12	0	0.00	
Gloves	Gloves	Inventory Part	4011 · Clothing & Accessory Sales	22	0	0.00	
Hats	Hats and Scarves	Inventory Part	4011 · Clothing & Accessory Sales	30	0	0.00	
Pants-Ski	Ski Pants	Inventory Part	4011 · Clothing & Accessory Sales	95	0	0.00	
Pants-Snowbrd	Snowboard Pants	Inventory Part	4011 · Clothing & Accessory Sales	50	0	0.00	
Parkas	Parkas and Jackets	Inventory Part	4011 · Clothing & Accessory Sales	75	0	0.00	
Poles-Ski	Ski Poles	Inventory Part	4012 · Equipment Sales	18	0	0.00	
Skis	Snow Skis	Inventory Part	4012 · Equipment Sales	50	0	0.00	
Snowboard	Snowboard	Inventory Part	4012 · Equipment Sales	30	0	0.00	
Socks	Ski and Snowboard Socks	Inventory Part	4011 · Clothing & Accessory Sales	75	0	0.00	
Sweaters	Sweaters & Shirts	Inventory Part	4011 · Clothing & Accessory Sales	75	0	0.00	
Underwear	Long Underwear	Inventory Part	4011 · Clothing & Accessory Sales	33	0	0.00	
CA Sales Tax	CA Sales Tax	Sales Tax Item	2200 · Sales Tax Payable			8.0%	
Out of State	Out-of-state sale, exempt from sales tax	Sales Tax Item	2200 · Sales Tax Payable			0.0%	

CUSTOMIZE THE PAYMENT METHOD LIST

QuickBooks does not automatically include all methods of payment in the list. It allows the list to be customized for an individual company. There is no need to have a list of payment methods that you do not use. By customizing the list, you will avoid errors by listing on the methods of payment you select.

MEMO
DATE: January 1, 2015

After viewing the Payment Method List, you realize that you need to add MasterCard and delete Discover Card.

Add MasterCard and delete Discover from the list
Click **Lists** on the menu bar, point to **Customer & Vendor Profile Lists**
Click **Payment Method List**
Click the **Payment Method** button, click **New**
Enter **MasterCard** in the Payment Method textbox
Click the drop-down list arrow for **Payment Type**, click **MasterCard**, click **OK**
Click **Discover** in the list, use **Ctrl+D** to delete
Click **OK** on the Delete Payment Method message box

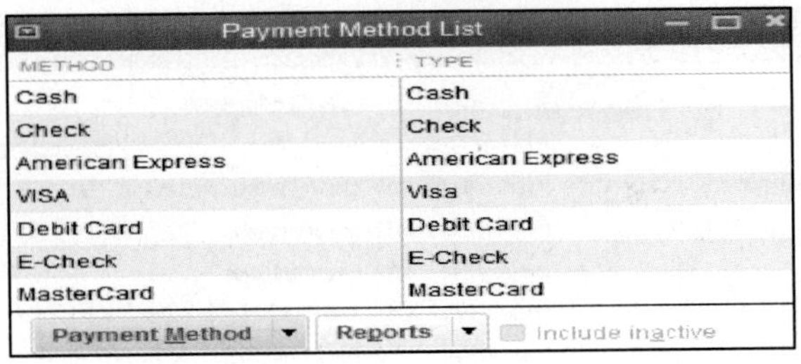

Close the Payment Method List

CUSTOMIZE REPORT PREFERENCES

The report format used in one company may not be appropriate for all companies that use QuickBooks. The preferences selected in QuickBooks are only for the current company. In Section 1 of the text, report preferences were changed for Computer Consulting by Your Name, but those changes have no effect on Your Name Mountain Sports. The header/footer for reports in Your Name Mountain Sports must be customized to eliminate the printing of the date prepared, time prepared, and report basis as part of a report heading.

MEMO

DATE: January 1, 2015

Before recording any transactions or preparing any reports, customize the report format by removing the date prepared, time prepared, and report basis from report headings.

Customize the preferences as indicated in the memo

Click **Edit**, click **Preferences**, click **Reports and Graphs**
Click the **Company Preferences** tab, click the **Format** button
Click the **Header/Footer** tab
Click **Date Prepared**, **Time Prepared**, and **Report Basis** to deselect

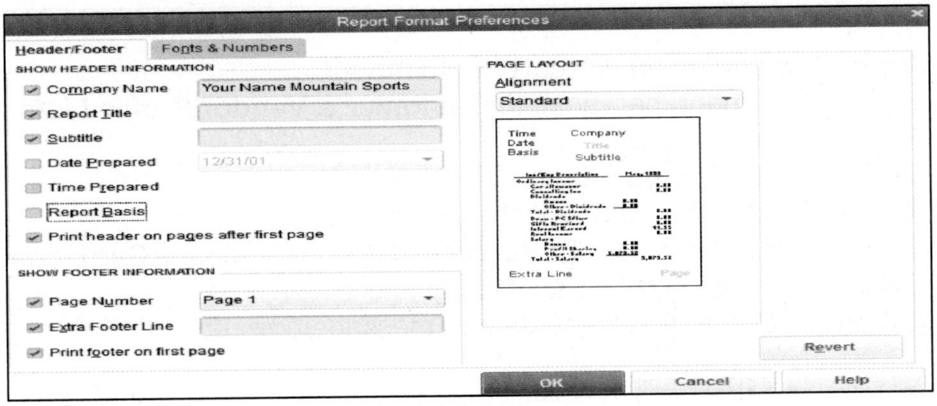

Click **OK** to save the change; click **OK** to close **Preferences**

CUSTOMIZE BUSINESS FORMS

In QuickBooks it is possible to customize the business forms used in recording transactions. Forms that may be customized include Credit Memo, Estimate, Invoice, Purchase Order, Sales Order, Sales Receipt, Statement, and Donation. In addition to customizing the forms within QuickBooks, Intuit allows users to download templates of forms without charge by accessing the Forms/Intuit Community. To do this, click Lists menu, click Templates, click the Templates button, and click Download Templates.

In earlier chapters some student names included as part of the company name may not have printed on the same line as the company name. In order to provide more room for the company title, QuickBooks' Layout Designer must be used. Some business forms may be changed directly within the form, while others need to have the form duplicated. When you access an invoice, for example, QuickBooks uses a ready-made form. This is called a *template*. In order to make changes to an invoice, you must first duplicate the template and then make changes to it.

MEMO
DATE: January 2, 2015

Customize the Sales Receipt form, the Credit Memo form, the Custom Sales Order, and the template used for Product Invoices.

Customize the forms listed in the Memo

Click the **Create Sales Receipts** icon to open a sales receipt
Click the **Formatting** tab in the Sales Receipt Icon bar
Click the **Customize Data Layout** icon

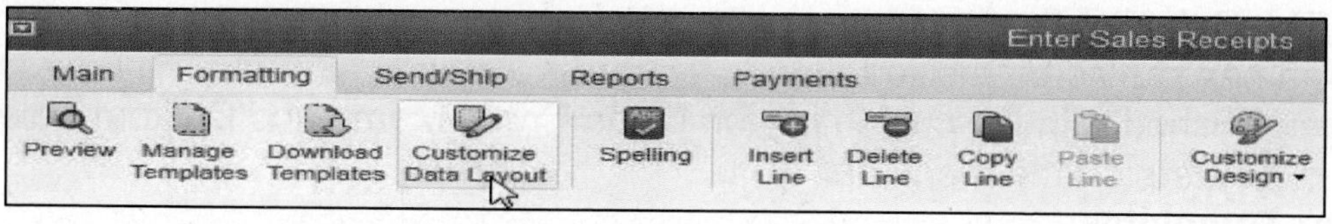

- Look at the tabs for Header, Columns, Footer, and Print. Each tab has selections that you may select to indicate what is shown on the form when it is displayed on the screen or when it is printed.

Click in the Default Title text box for Sales Receipt, highlight and delete the words Sales Receipt, key in **SALES RECEIPT**

Click the **Layout Designer** button at the bottom of the Additional Customization screen

- If you get a Layout Designer Message regarding overlapping fields, click **Do not display this message in the future**, and then click **OK**.

Click the **Layout Designer** button at the bottom of the Additional Customization screen

Point to one of the black squares (sizing handles) on the left border of the frame around the words SALES RECEIPT

When the cursor turns into a double arrow, hold the primary (left) mouse button and drag until the size of the frame begins at **5 ½** on the ruler bar

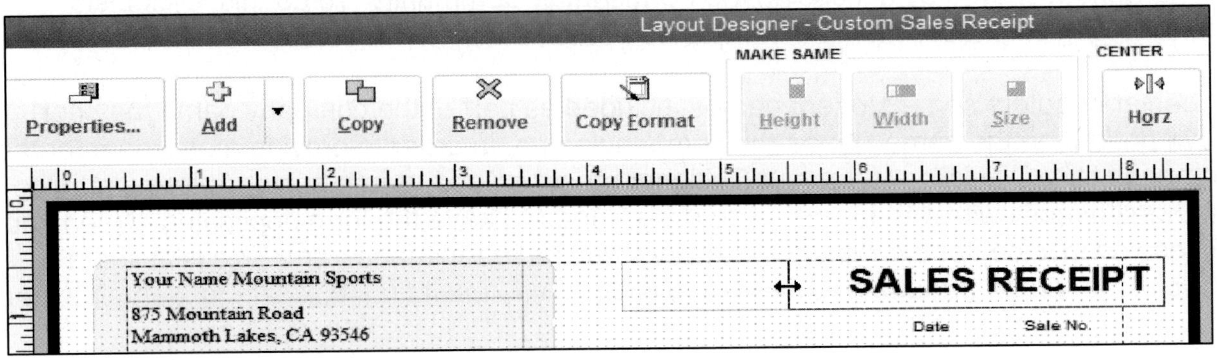

Click in the textbox for **Your Name Mountain Sports**

Drag the right border of the frame until it is a **5 ¼** on the ruler bar

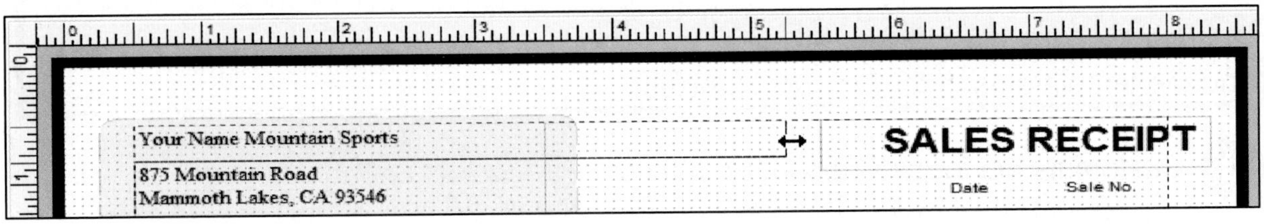

Click **OK** on Layout Designer; click **OK** on the Additional Customization screen

Close the **Enter Sales Receipts** screen

Repeat the steps to customize the **Credit Memo** and the **Custom Sales Order**

- The Default Title should be in all capital letters, and the company name and form names should be resized.

When finished with the customization of the Credit Memo and Custom Sales Order, click **Lists** on the menu bar

Click **Templates**

- A template is a predesigned form and defines what is shown, determines the structure, and contains the visual elements on the form.
- *Note:* As you scroll through the Template list, you will see that the Custom Credit Memo, Custom Sales Receipt, and Custom Sales Order are on the list.

Click **Intuit Product Invoice** on the Templates List

- The Intuit Product Invoice is designed for Intuit preprinted forms. To customize the invoice, a duplicate copy of the Intuit Product Invoice must be made.

Click the **Templates** button

Click **Duplicate**

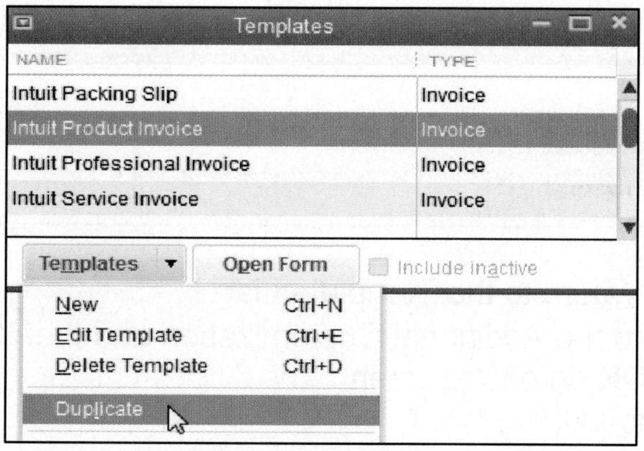

On the Select Template Type make sure Invoice is selected and click **OK**

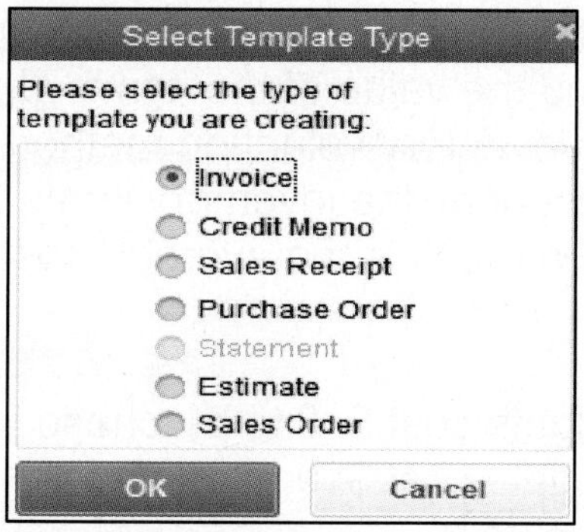

Make sure **Copy of: Intuit Product Invoice** is selected
Click the **Templates** button, click **Edit Template**

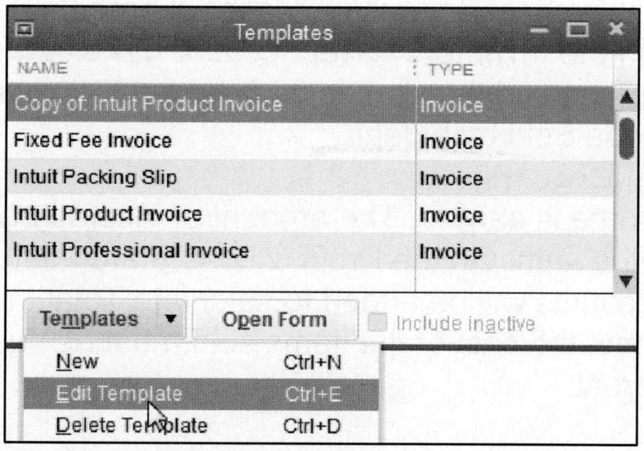

Click the **Additional Customization…** button
Change the Default Title to **INVOICE**
Click the **Layout Designer** button

- If you get the Layout Designer message, click **OK**; and, then, click the Layout Designer button again.

Change the layout as instructed for SALES RECEIPTS

5

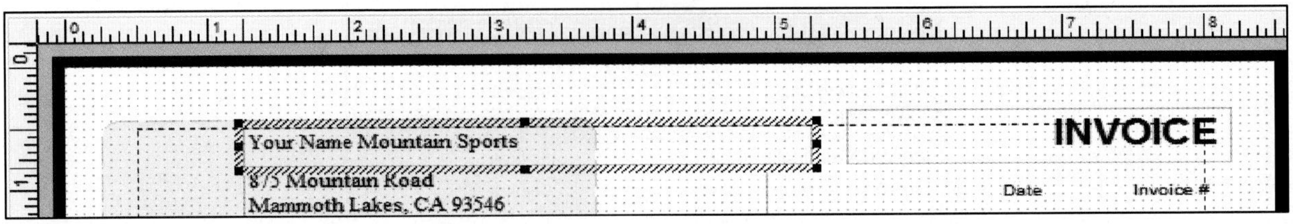

Click **OK** until you return to the Template List

- If you go back to the Additional Customization and then the Basic Customization screens, click **OK** on each screen.

Close the Template List

INVENTORY

When your company sells inventory items, QuickBooks keeps track of each inventory item, the number of items on hand, and the value of the items. Unless you use the Enterprise version of QuickBooks, the only inventory valuation method available for use is Average Cost. Average Cost adds the cost of all the inventory items together, divides by the total number of items on hand, and the result is the average cost. For example, if your company purchased and sold widgets:

50 widgets cost $ 5 to purchase	= $250
50 widgets cost $10 to purchase	= $500
Total value	= $750

$750 total value / 100 widgets = $7.50 average cost

When inventory items are purchased to have on hand for resale, QuickBooks shows the average cost of the item in the Inventory Asset account. When the item is sold, the average cost of the item is removed behind the scenes from Inventory Asset by a credit and transferred to Cost of Goods Sold by a debit.

When an item is sold, income is earned. The amount of income earned will be different from the average cost of the item. On the Profit & Loss Statement all the income earned from different revenue accounts will be added to calculate Total Income. Since the income was earned by selling items, the cost of the items sold must be subtracted from income in order to calculate gross profit.

On the Profit & Loss report, the total of Cost of Goods Sold is calculated as: Cost of Goods Sold – Merchandise Purchases Discounts = Net Cost of Goods Sold. The Net Cost of Goods Sold is subtracted from Total Income to determine the Gross Profit. Expenses are subtracted from Gross Profit to determine the Net Income or Net Loss.

ENTER SALE ON ACCOUNT

Because QuickBooks operates on a business form premise, a sale on account is entered via an invoice. When you sell merchandise on account, you prepare an invoice including sales tax and payment terms and QuickBooks records the transaction in the Journal and updates the customer's account automatically. QuickBooks allows you to set up different price levels for customers. Since our small company has not established sales prices for each item it sells, we will not be using Price Levels in this tutorial. For information on Price Levels, refer to Appendix B.

MEMO

DATE: January 2, 2015

Bill the following: Invoice 1—An established customer, Russ Watson, purchased a pair of after-ski boots for $75.00 on account. Terms are Net 15.

Record the sale on account shown in the transaction above.

Access a blank invoice as previously instructed in Chapter 2

To remove the customer's history on the invoice, click the **Hide history** tab

- If you hide the history and the invoice becomes wider, resize by pointing to the right edge of the invoice until you get a double arrow, and then hold down the primary mouse button and drag to the left.

Click the drop-down list arrow next to **CUSTOMER:JOB**, click **Watson, Russ**

TEMPLATE is **Copy of: Intuit Product Invoice**

- QuickBooks does not allow you to permanently change the default invoice. It should remember to use the same invoice if you enter several invoices at a time, but it may revert back to the default invoice the next time you enter an invoice.
- Notice the change in the format when using a product invoice rather than a service invoice.

Tab to **Date** and enter the date of **01/02/2015**

Invoice **1** should be showing in the **Invoice #** box

There is no PO Number to record, Terms should be indicated as **Net 15**

Tab to or click **QUANTITY**, type **1**

- The quantity is 1 because you are billing for one pair of after-ski boots.

Click the drop-down list arrow next to **ITEM CODE**

- Refer to the memo above and the Item list for appropriate billing information.

Click **Boots** to bill for one pair of after-ski boots

- The Description ***After Ski Boots and Shoes*** is automatically inserted.

Once the ITEM CODE has been entered (Boots), an icon appears in the Quantity column

5

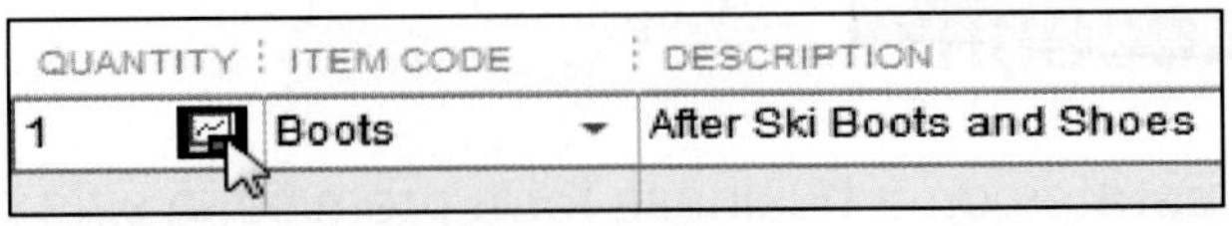

Click on the icon to see the current availability of Boots in stock

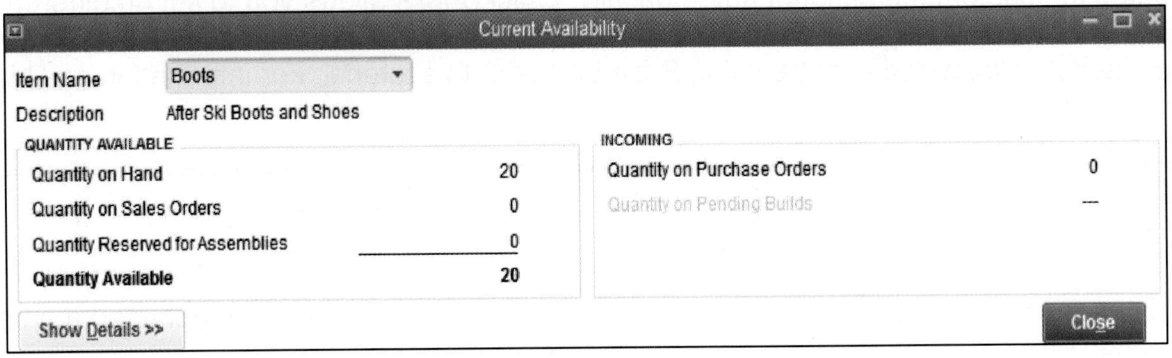

Click **Close** on the Current Availability screen
Tab to or click **PRICE EACH**
Type in the amount of the after-ski boots **75**

- Because the price on ski boots differs with each style, QuickBooks has not been given the price in advance. It must be inserted during the invoice preparation. If you chose to set up separate sales items for each type of ski boot, sales prices could be and should be assigned. In addition, different price levels could be designated for the item.

Click in the drop-down list arrow for **CUSTOMER MESSAGE**

- If you get a dialog box regarding Price Levels, click **Do not display this message in the future**, and click **OK**. (Information about Price Levels is in Appendix B.)

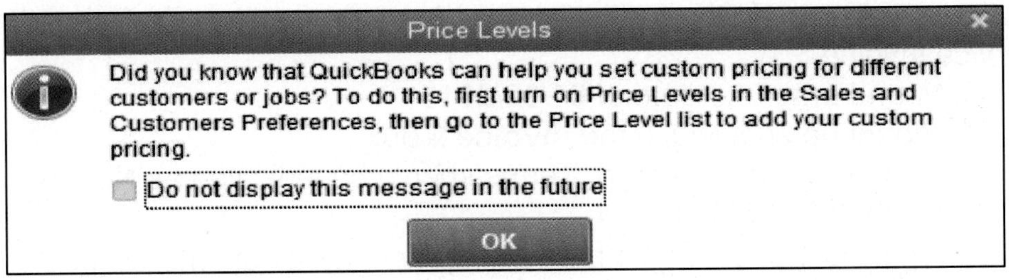

- QuickBooks will automatically calculate the total in the **AMOUNT** column.
- Because this is a taxable item, QuickBooks inserts the word **Tax** in the **TAX** column.

Click the message **Thank you for your business.**

- Notice that QuickBooks automatically calculates the tax for the invoice and adds it to the invoice total.

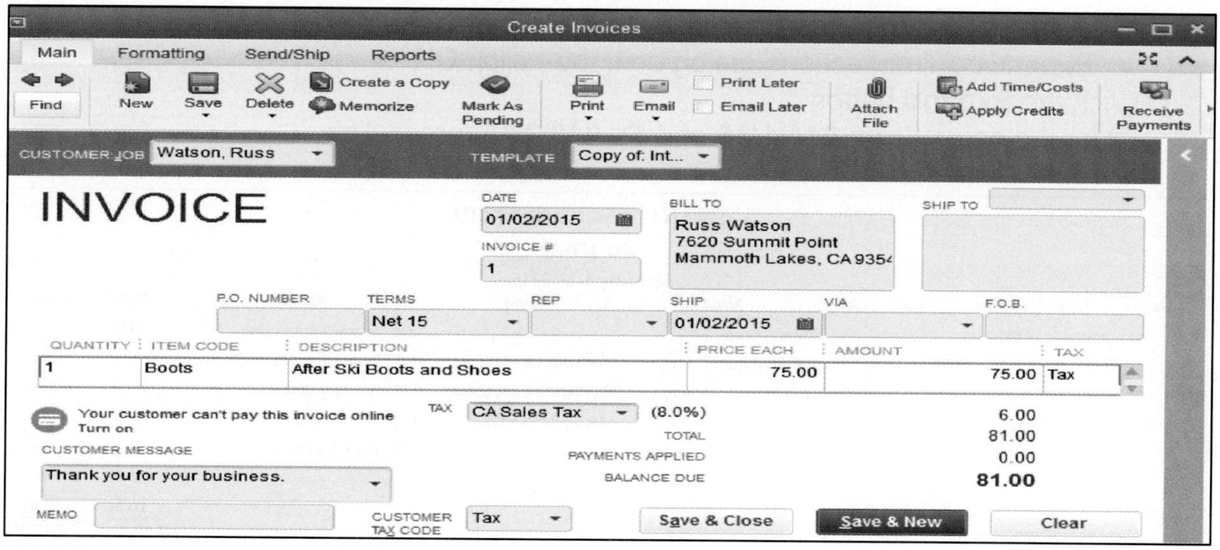

PRINT AN INVOICE

With Invoice 1 on the screen, print the invoice with lines around each field immediately after entering the corrected information

Follow the instructions given previously for printing invoices

- If you get a message regarding printing Shipping Labels, click the **Do not display this message in the future** checkbox, click **OK**.

Make sure that the check box for **Do not print lines around each field** does <u>not</u> have a check mark; if it does, click the box to remove the check mark.

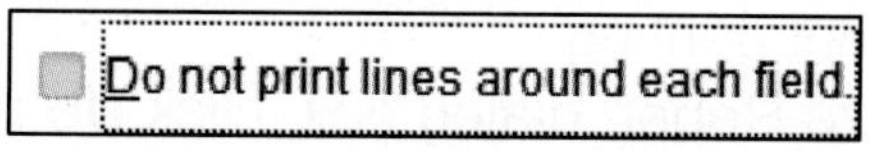

When finished printing, click **Save & Close**

ANALYZE INVOICE IN JOURNAL

As learned previously, QuickBooks records all transactions in the Journal. When recording sales in a merchandising business, QuickBooks will not only debit Accounts Receivable and credit Sales, it will also debit Cost of Goods Sold, credit Inventory Asset, debit Sales Discounts (if a discount was used), and credit Sales Tax Payable. This is important because it allows QuickBooks to keep an accurate record of inventory on hand, to calculate the Cost of Goods Sold, keep track of sales discounts used, and record the liability for sales taxes.

Prepare the Journal for January 1-2, 2015 as previously instructed and analyze the entry for Invoice 1

Click the **Do not display this message in the future** on the Collapsing and Expanding Transactions dialog box, then click **OK**
Click the **Expand** button
Enter the dates **From 01/01/15** and **To 01/02/15**, press **Tab**

Your Name Mountain Sports
Journal
January 1 - 2, 2015

Trans #	Type	Date	Num	Adj	Name	Memo	Account	Debit	Credit
48	Invoice	01/02/2015	1		Watson, Russ		1200 · Accounts Receivable	81.00	
					Watson, Russ	After Ski Boots and Shoes	4011 · Clothing & Accessory Sales		75.00
					Watson, Russ	After Ski Boots and Shoes	1120 · Inventory Asset		30.00
					Watson, Russ	After Ski Boots and Shoes	5000 · Cost of Goods Sold	30.00	
					State Board of Equalization	CA Sales Tax	2200 · Sales Tax Payable		6.00
								111.00	111.00
TOTAL								111.00	111.00

- Note the $81.00 debit to Accounts Receivable is for the total amount of the invoice. This amount is matched with corresponding credits to Clothing & Accessory Sales for $75.00 (the amount of the sale) and to Sales Tax Payable for $6.00 (the sales tax collected).
- There is also a debit to Cost of Goods Sold for $30.00 (the average cost of the item) and credits to Inventory Asset for $30.00 (the average cost of the item). Since you no longer have the item available for sale, this removes it from the inventory on hand and places the value into the cost of goods sold.
- Because QuickBooks removes the average cost of the asset from Inventory Assets and puts it into Cost of Goods Sold, the Total of the transaction recorded for Invoice 1 includes this and becomes $111.00 not $81.00.

Close the Journal without printing
- If you get a Memorize Report dialog box, click **Do not display this message in the future**; and then, click **No**.

INVENTORY ASSETS, COST OF GOODS SOLD, SALES TAX LIABILITY

The following illustrates the types of accounts and calculations used in the Journal for an invoice entered for the sale of a pair of after ski boots:

Sales: The amount for which an inventory item is sold is entered into the revenue account. The pair of after ski boots was sold for $75 and is recorded as a credit to increase income.

Inventory Assets: When a merchandise item is on hand it is an asset. QuickBooks uses Inventory Asset as the account. To reduce an asset, you credit the account for the value of the item. QuickBooks uses the Average Cost method of inventory valuation. As previously illustrated, the average cost of an item is calculated by dividing the total value of the item by the number of items. If, for example, there are 20 pairs of after ski boots in stock, the Average Cost is calculated:

10 pair cost $40 to purchase = $400
10 pair cost $20 to purchase = $200
Total value = $600

$600 total value / 20 pairs of boots = $30 average cost per pair

Cost of Goods Sold: Is used when there is merchandise to keep track of the amount the merchandise cost the company. This amount is deducted from sales to determine the amount of gross profit earned when the merchandise sold. If the pair of after ski boots is sold for $75 and it cost the company $30, the amount of gross profit is $45. (Sales - Cost of Goods Sold = Gross Profit). Since the cost of goods sold will ultimately decrease the revenue, you debit the account.

Sales Tax: When sales tax is collected, it is a liability that is owed to the government. To record the liability, you credit the liability account—Sales Tax Payable

ENTER TRANSACTIONS WITH MORE THAN ONE SALES ITEM

Frequently, sales to customers will be for more than one item. For example, new bindings are usually purchased along with a new pair of skis. Invoices can be prepared to bill a customer for several items at once.

5

MEMO
DATE: January 3, 2015

Bill the following: Invoice 2—Every year Dr. Jose Perez gets new ski equipment. Bill him for his equipment purchase for this year: skis, $425; ski bindings, $175; ski boots, $250; and ski poles, $75.

Record a transaction on account for a sale involving several taxable sales items:

Create an invoice for **Perez, Jose Dr.** as previously instructed
Verify the TEMPLATE as **Copy of: Intuit Product Invoice**

- Since QuickBooks does not let you select a specific invoice as the default, you will need to verify that you are using the Copy of: Intuit Product Invoice.

DATE is **01/03/15**; **INVOICE #** is **2**
There is no PO NUMBER; **TERMS** should be indicated as **2% 10 Net 30**

- The terms mean that if Dr. Perez's payment is received within ten days, he will get a two percent discount. Otherwise, the full amount is due in 30 days.

QUANTITY, type **1**
Click the drop-down list arrow for **ITEM CODE**, click **Skis**
Tab to or click **PRICE EACH,** enter **425**, press **Tab**

- Because Dr. Perez is a taxable customer and Skis are a taxable item, sales tax is indicated by **Tax** in the **TAX** column.

Tab to or click the second line for **QUANTITY**, type **1**
Click the drop-down list arrow next to **ITEM CODE**, click **Bindings-Skis**
Tab to or click **PRICE EACH**, enter **175**

- Notice that sales tax is indicated by **Tax** in the **TAX** column.

Repeat the above steps to enter the information for the ski boots and the ski poles and use a quantity of 1 for each item
Click the drop-down list arrow next to **CUSTOMER MESSAGE**
Click **Thank you for your business.**

- QuickBooks automatically calculated the tax for the invoice and added it to the invoice total.

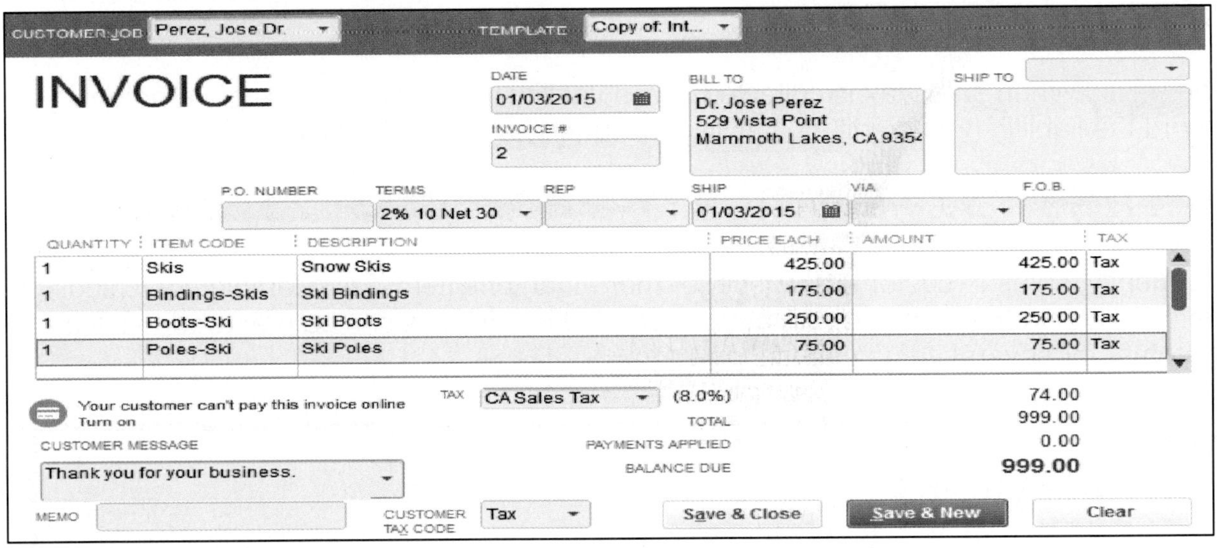

Print the invoice, and click **Save & New**

EMAIL INVOICES (INFORMATION ONLY)

In addition to printing and mailing invoices, QuickBooks 2015 allows invoices to be sent to customers via email. While this text will not actually require sending invoices by email, it is important to be aware of this time-saving feature. In order to use the email feature of QuickBooks, you must subscribe to one of QuickBooks other services. However, QuickBooks now supports different Web Mail providers and can be used without charge or any required QuickBooks subscriptions. Web mail providers include: Gmail, Hotmail, Yahoo Mail, Outlook, Outlook Express, Windows Mail, or your own SMTP email provider.

Information only: To email an invoice, you must activate email by clicking **Edit** on the menu bar, clicking **Preferences**, and clicking **Send Forms**

- If you have an active subscription for QuickBooks Connect, Intuit Data Protect, QuickBooks Attached Documents, Intuit Commissions Manager, or QuickBooks Time and Billing Manager, you may use QuickBooks Email.

Since Your Name Mountain Sports does not have any subscriptions, click **Web Mail**

- If you select Outlook to send email, you do not have to provide more information.

Click the **Add** button to create your Email Id
On the Add Email Info dialog box, enter your Email ID
Click the drop-down list arrow for Email Provider, click the one you use, the information for Server Name and Port should automatically be entered on the form, click **OK**

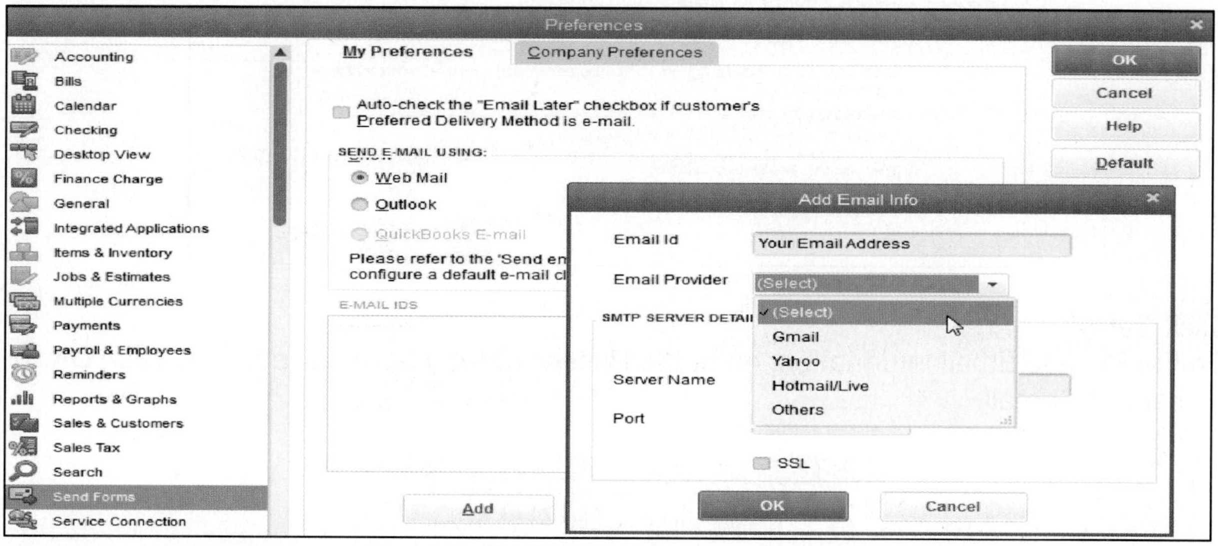

- Your Email ID will show your email address

Click **OK** to close the Preferences screen
With the invoice for Dr. Perez showing on the Create Invoices screen, click the **Email** icon
Since Dr. Perez does not have an email address, enter your Email address, click **OK**

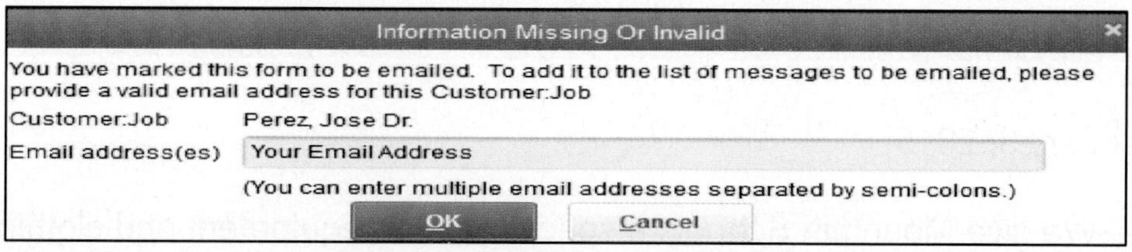

A Send Invoice screen will appear containing information for:
FROM: Your Email address.
TO: The email address of your customer. (Your email is used in the example.)
ATTACH: Shows that Inv. 2 will be attached to the message as a PDF file.
TEMPLATE: Basic Invoice
SUBJECT: Invoice 2 from Your Name Mountain Sports.
The Email Text is prewritten but may be changed.

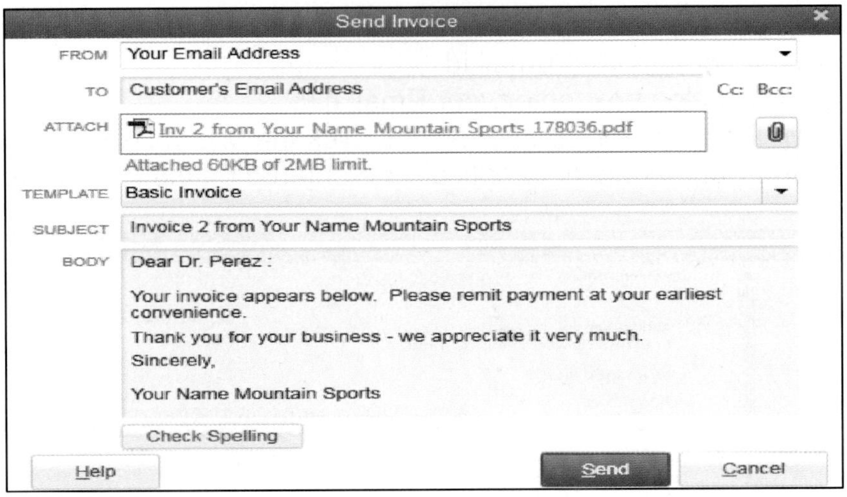

Click **Send**

On the Provide Email Information, enter the Password for your email account, click **OK** to send the email

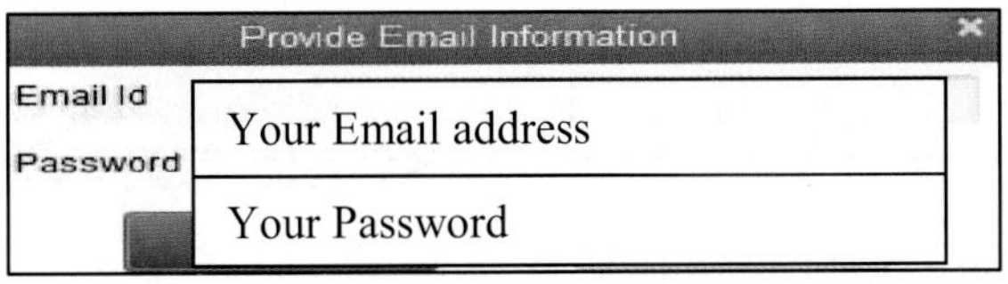

When the email has been sent, you will get a QuickBooks Information box, click **OK**

PREPARE INVOICES WITHOUT INSTRUCTIONS

MEMO

DATE: January 3, 2015

Invoice 3—We give Mountain Schools a special rate on equipment and clothing for the ski team. This year the school purchases 5 pairs of skis, $299 each; 5 pairs of ski bindings, $100 each; and 5 sets of ski poles, $29 each. Terms 2/10 Net 30.

Invoice 4—Sandra Perkins purchased a new ski outfit. Quantity is 1 for all items: parka, $249; hat, $25; sweater, $125; ski pants, $129; long underwear, $68; gloves, $79; ski socks, $15.95; sunglasses, $89.95; and boot carrier, $2.95. Terms Net 15.

Prepare and print invoices without step-by-step instructions.

If Invoice 2 is still on the screen, click the **Next** arrow or **Save & New**

Enter the two transactions in the memo above. Refer to instructions given for the two previous transactions entered.

- Make sure the TEMPLATE that you are using is: Copy of: Intuit Product Invoice.

- Always use the Item List to determine the appropriate sales items for billing.
- Use *"Thank you for your business."* as the message for these invoices.
- If you make an error, correct it.
- Print each invoice immediately after you enter the information for it, and print lines around each field.
- If you get a Check Spelling on Form message for Snowboard, click **Ignore All**.
- Click **Save & Close** after Invoice 4 has been entered and printed.

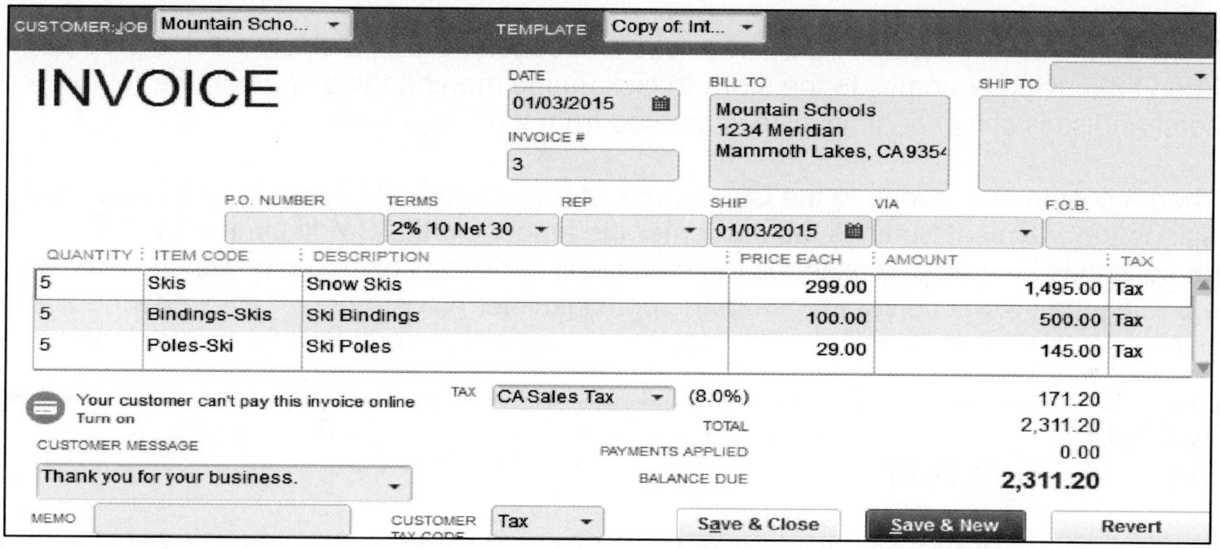

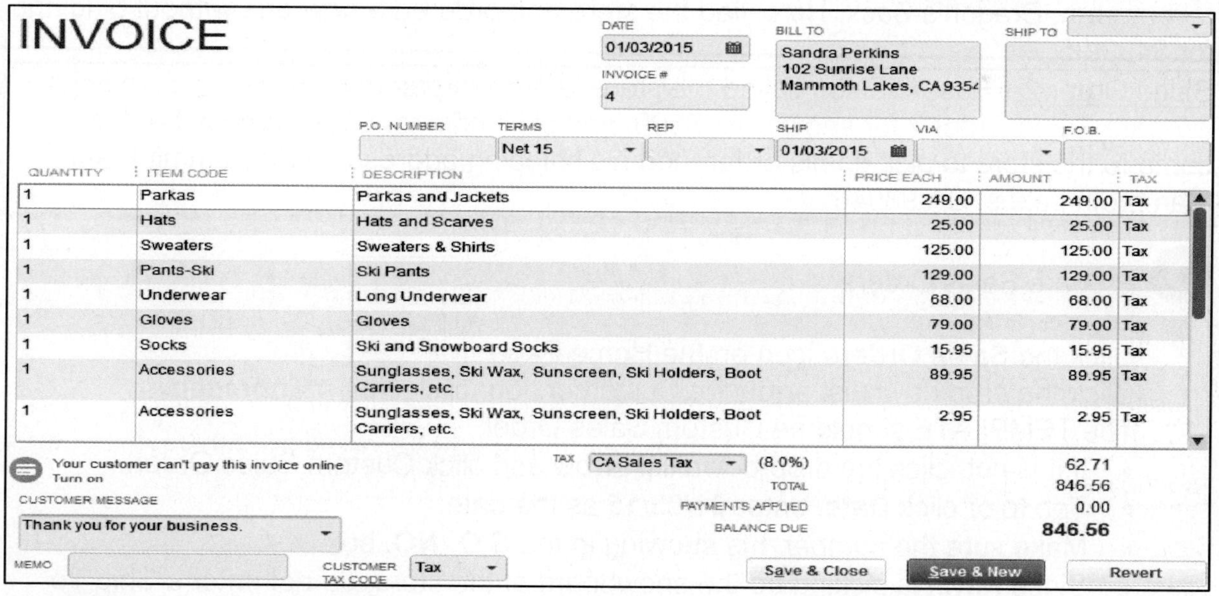

ENTER SALES ORDERS

Sales orders help you manage the sale of the products your customers order. Using sales orders is optional and must be selected as a Preference. Typically, when a customer places an order, a sales order is filled out with the customer information and the items ordered. The sales order is fulfilled when you get the products to your customer. Once the sales order is fulfilled, you create an invoice based on your sales order.

When you create and fill out a sales order, you have not recorded the sale—you've only recorded the information you need to fulfill the order. The sale is recorded only after you create an invoice. For example, items you sell are not deducted from inventory until you create an invoice based on the sales order.

When Your Name Mountain Sports receives a telephone order, a sales order is prepared. When the customer comes to the store to pick up the merchandise or when the merchandise is shipped, an invoice is created from the Sales Order.

When a customer is added to the Customer List and a complete setup is performed, you click on the Payment Settings tab and enter the amount in the Credit Limit field. If a transaction is entered that exceeds the credit limit, a dialog box appears with information regarding the transaction amount and the credit limit for a customer. To override the credit limit, click OK on the dialog box. This does not change the credit limit for the customer.

MEMO
DATE: January 3, 2015

Sales Order 1—Kevin Thomsen broke his snowboard when he was going down his favorite run, Dragon's Back. He called the store and ordered a new one without bindings for $499.95

Sales Order 2—Russ Watson called the store to order a pair of new skis and bindings. Prepare Sales Order 2 for snow skis, $599, and ski bindings, $179. In case he doesn't come to the store to pick up his order, add his shipping address: 7620 Summit Point, Mammoth Lakes, CA 93546.

Prepare Sales Orders

Click the **Sales Orders** icon on the Home Page
Click the drop-down list arrow for Customer:Job, click **Kevin Thomsen**
The TEMPLATE should be Custom Sales Order

- If it is not, click the drop-down list arrow and click Custom Sales Order.
- Tab to or click **Date**, enter **01/03/15** as the date.
- Make sure the number **1** is showing in the **S.O. NO.** box.
- Since Kevin is picking up the snowboard at the store, do not enter a Ship To address.

Click in the drop-down list arrow in the **ITEM** column
Click **Snowboard**, press Tab until you get to the **ORDERED** column
Enter **1** for **ORDERED**, press Tab; enter the **RATE** of **499.95**, press Tab

- If you get a message regarding Price Levels, click **Do not display this message in the future**, then click **OK**.

Click the drop-down list arrow for **CUSTOMER MESSAGE**, and click **Thank you for your business.**

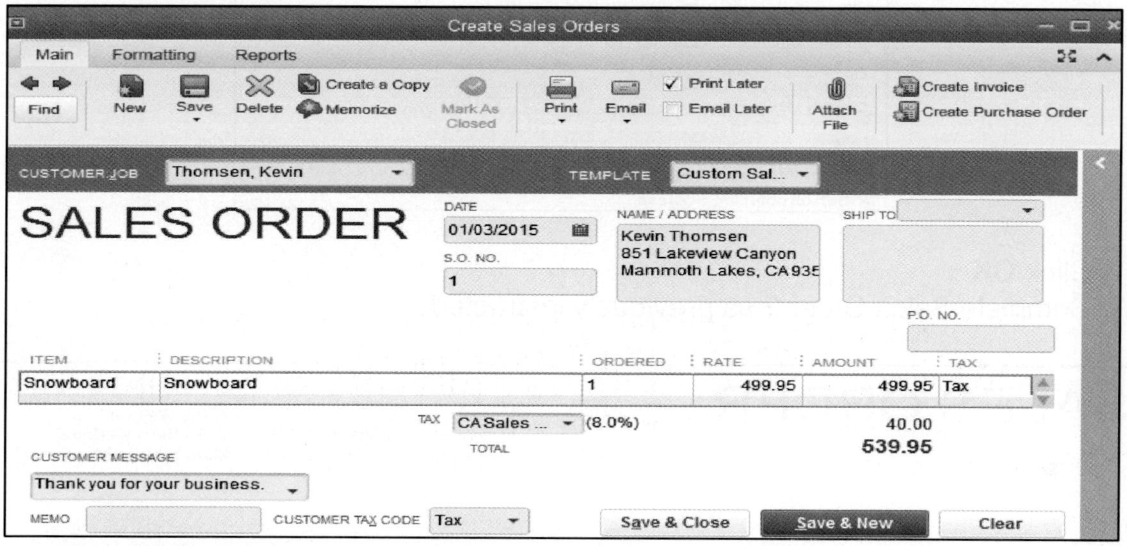

Click **Print** and print the Sales Order

- If you get a Check Spelling on Form message for Snowboard, always click **Ignore All**.
- If you get a message regarding Shipping Labels, click **Do not display this message in the future** and then, click **OK**.
- After printing the Sales Order, notice the addition of the Invoiced and Clsd columns.

Click **Save & New**

- If you get a Recording Transaction message, click **Yes**.

Prepare Sales Order 2 for Russ Watson as previously instructed

Add the Ship To address

Click the drop-down list arrow for **Ship To**

Click **<Add New>**

The Address Name **Ship To 1** should appear automatically

Tab to **Address**

Key **Russ Watson**, press **Enter**; key **7620 Summit Point**, press **Tab**

City is **Mammoth Lakes**, press **Tab**; State is **CA**, press **Tab**; Zip Code is **93546**

- You do not need to include information for Country/Region or Note.
- Leave the check marks in **Show this window again when address is incomplete or unclear** and in **Default shipping address**.

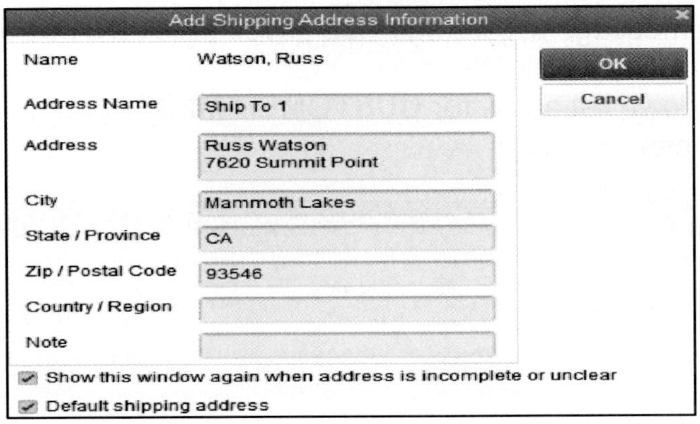

Click **OK**

Complete Sales Order 2 as previously instructed

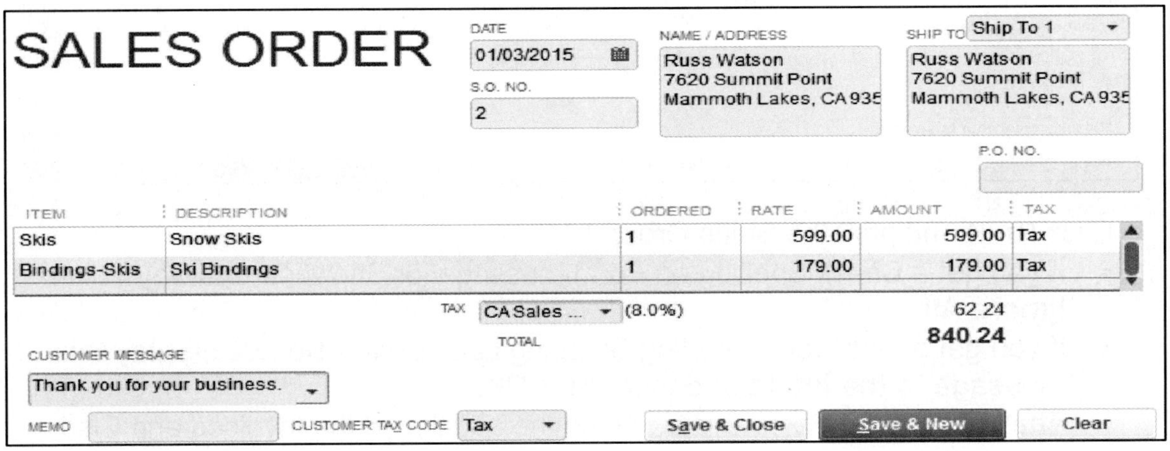

Print the Sales Order

Since this transaction puts Russ over his established credit limit, a Recording Transaction message appears

- If you click **No**, you are returned to the sales in order to make changes.
- If you click **Yes**, the sales order will be printed.

Click **Yes** to exceed the credit limit go to the Print One Sales Order screen

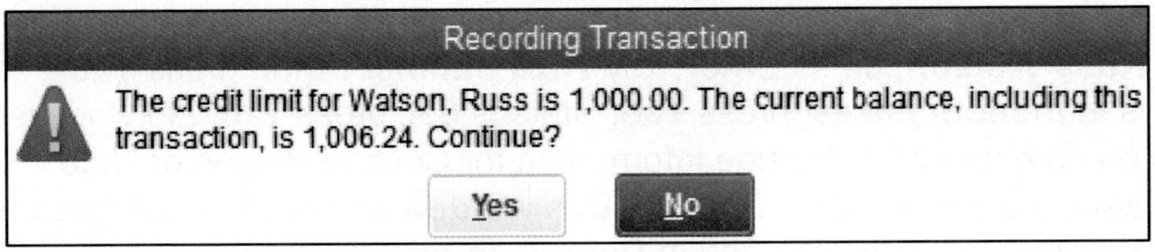

After printing, click **Save & Close**

CREATE INVOICES FOR SALES ORDERS

When a sales order is filled, shipped, or picked up at the store, an invoice is created. Creating an invoice enters the sale in the Journal, decreases inventory on hand, and increases accounts receivable and sales.

> **MEMO**
> **DATE:** January 3, 2015
>
> Create the following invoices from Sales Orders 1 and 2:
> Invoice 5—Kevin Thomsen picked up his new snowboard: Terms 1% 10 Net 30.
> Invoice 6—Russ Watson came into the store to pick up his new skis and bindings. He added a ski carrier for $10.99 to his purchase. Payment Terms 1% 10 Net 30. (Include the additional purchase on Invoice 6.

Create Invoices from Sales Orders 1 and 2

Click the **Sales Orders** icon and click **Previous** until the Sales Order 1 is shown
Click **Create Invoice** on the Create Sales Orders Icon bar

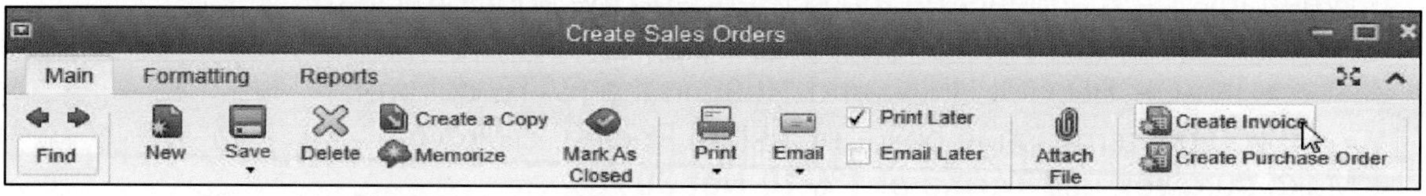

Make sure **Create invoice for all of the sales order(s).** is selected, click **OK**

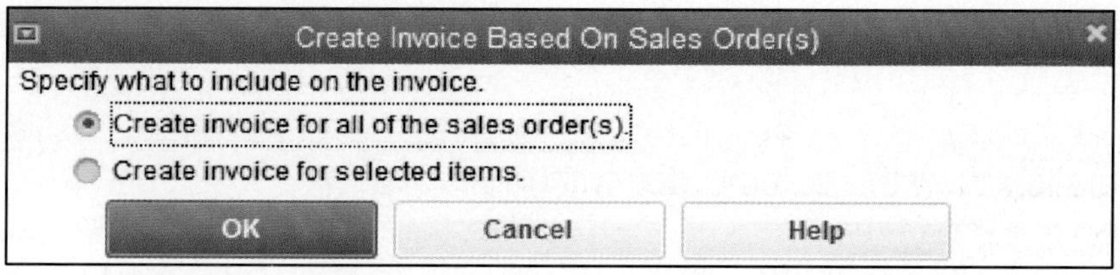

- Invoice 5 appears on the screen. The template used is Custom S. O. Invoice.

Customize the form to allow room for your name and to print the default title as
INVOICE
Click **Formatting** on the Create Invoices Icon bar
Click **Customize Data Layout**
Key in **INVOICE** for the Default Title
Click **Layout Designer**

- If you get the message regarding Layout Designer, click **OK**; click Layout Designer again; and then resize.

Resize INVOICE to begin at **5 ½”** and Your Name Mountain Sports to end at **5 ¼”**

Click **OK** to close Layout Designer, and then click **OK** on Additional Customization

- Notice the columns for Ordered, Prev. Invoiced, Backordered, and Invoiced.
- The Terms of 1% 10 Net 30 automatically appear because they are the standard terms for Kevin Thomsen.

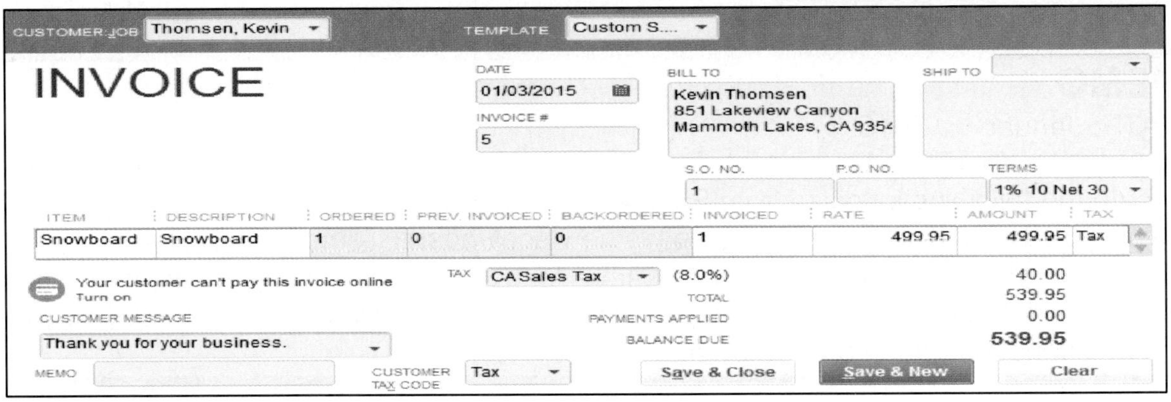

Print the invoice
Click **Ignore All** on the Check Spelling on Form for Snowboard
Close Create Invoices
Repeat the steps listed previously to create the Invoice for Russ Watson
When Invoice 6 appears on the screen, add the additional item:

Click the drop-down list arrow for ITEM, select **Accessories**, and enter **1** in the INVOICED COLUMN**,** and **10.99** in the RATE column

- If you get a message box for Custom Pricing, click **No**.

Make sure you use **Terms** of **1% 10 Net 30**

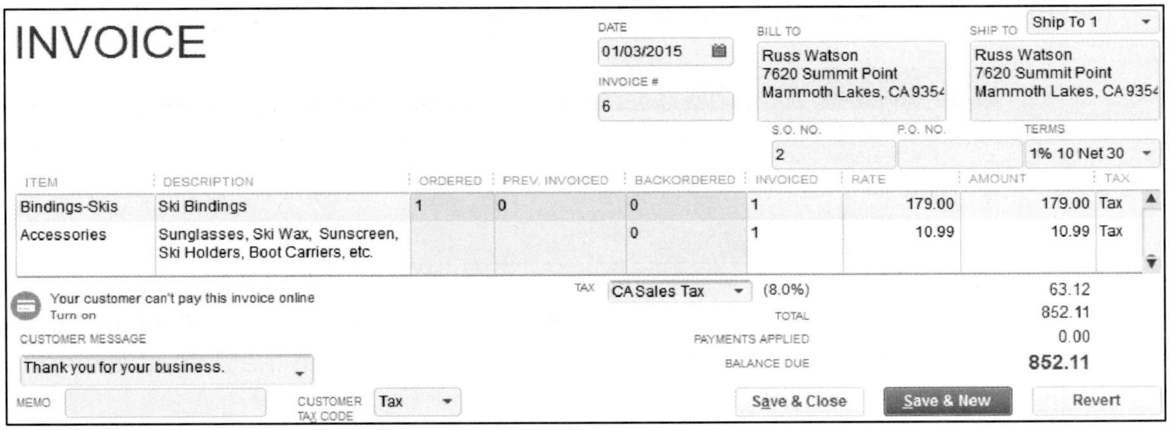

Print the invoice
Click **Yes** on the Recording Transaction message to exceed the credit limit

- If you get a Recording Transaction message about the sales order being linked to the invoice, click **Yes**.

Click **No** on the Information Changed message to change the Terms for Russ
Close Create Invoices

VIEW SALES ORDERS THAT HAVE BEEN INVOICED

Once a sales order has been used to create an invoice, it will be marked "Invoiced in Full"

View Sales Orders 1 and 2

Click the **Sales Orders** icon and **Previous** to view Sales Orders 1 and 2

- Note the stamped "INVOICED IN FULL" on both Sales Orders
- For Kevin, INVOICED should show 1 and the Clsd (Closed) column should have a check mark.

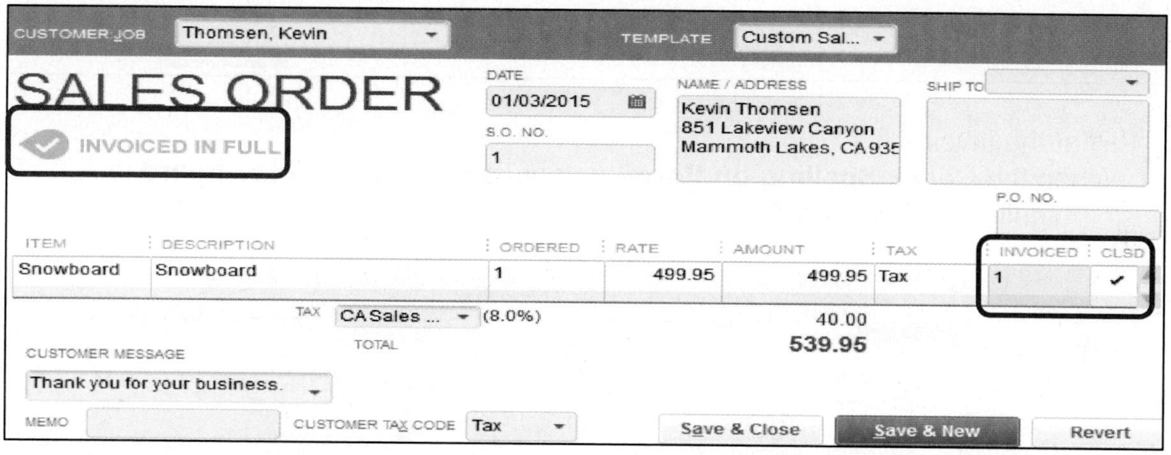

Close Sales Orders

ENTER TRANSACTION AND ADD A WORD TO THE DICTIONARY

As was experienced in the last set of transactions, QuickBooks has a spell check. When the previous invoices were printed, QuickBooks' Spell Check identified snowboard as being misspelled. In fact, the word is spelled correctly. It just needs to be added to the QuickBooks dictionary. This is done by clicking the Add button when the word is highlighted in spell check.

MEMO
DATE: January 4, 2015

Invoice 7—Monique Gardener decided to get a new snowboard, $489.95; snowboard bindings, $159.99; snowboard boots, $249; and a special case to carry her boots, $49.95. Terms are Net 30.

Prepare Invoice 7 as instructed previously

Make sure to use **Copy of: Intuit Product Invoice** for the Template

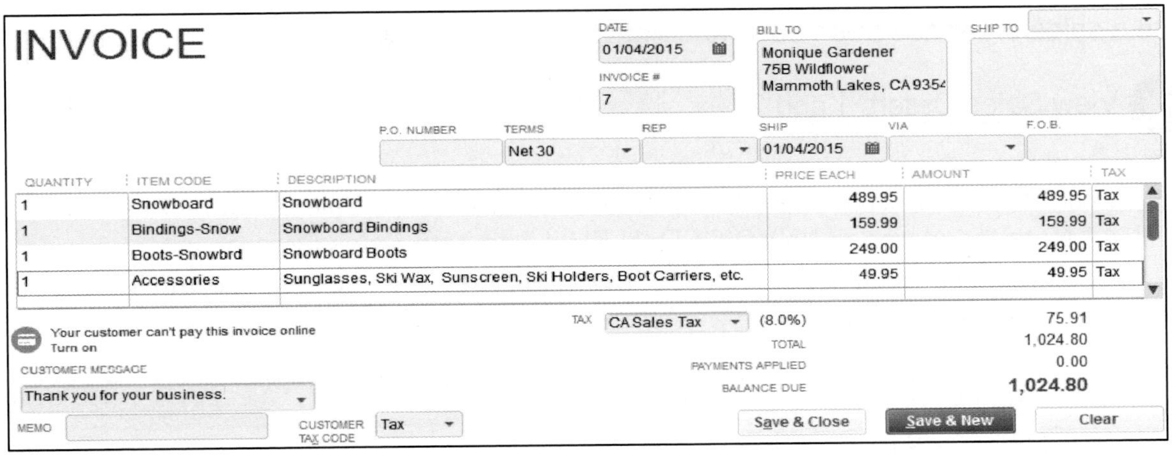

Print the invoice

When the **Check Spelling on Form** appears and the word **Snowboard** is highlighted, click the **Add** button

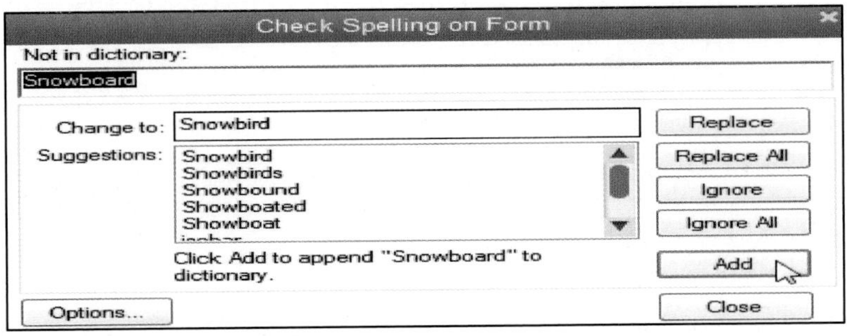

A Recording Transaction message box appears; click **Yes** to exceed the credit limit

After Invoice 7 has been entered and printed click **Save & Close**

ACCOUNTS RECEIVABLE REPORTS

A variety of reports are available regarding accounts receivable. Data regarding customers may be displayed on the basis of account aging, open invoices, collections reports, customer balances; or they may be itemized according to the sales by customer. Many reports may be printed in a summarized form while other reports provide detailed information.

PREPARE CUSTOMER BALANCE DETAIL REPORT

The Customer Balance Detail Report lists information regarding each customer. The information provided includes the customer name, all invoices with a balance, the date of the invoice, the invoice number, the account used to record the invoice, the amount of each invoice, the balance after each invoice, and the total balance due from each customer.

MEMO
DATE: January 5, 2015

Prepare a Customer Balance Detail Report so that the owners can see exactly how much each customer owes to Your Name Mountain Sports.

Prepare a Customer Balance Detail Report for all customers for all transactions:

Click **Reports** on the menu bar, point to **Customers & Receivables**, and click **Customer Balance Detail**

- *Note:* When preparing a single report, it is more convenient to use the Reports menu. When preparing several reports, using the Report Center is more efficient.

Dates should be **All**

- If not, click the drop-down list arrow next to the **Dates** text box, click **All**.
- Scroll through the report. See how much each customer owes for each invoice.
- Notice that the amount owed by Monique Gardener for Invoice 7 is $1,024.80 and that her total balance is $1,078.37.

Do not print or close the **Customer Balance Detail Report** at this time

USE QUICKZOOM

QuickZoom is a feature of QuickBooks that allows you to view additional information within a report. For example, an invoice may be viewed when the Customer Balance Detail Report is on the screen simply by using the QuickZoom feature.

MEMO
DATE: January 5, 2015

The bookkeeper, Ruth Morgan, could not remember if Invoice 7 was for ski equipment or snowboard equipment. With the Customer Balance Detail Report on the screen, use QuickZoom to view Invoice 7.

Use QuickZoom in the Customer Balance Detail Report to view Invoice 7

Position the cursor over any part of the information about Invoice 7

- The cursor will turn into a magnifying glass with a letter **Z** inside. 

Double-click

- Invoice 7 appears on the screen.
- Check to make sure the four items on the invoice are: Snowboard, Bindings-Snow, Boots-Snowbrd, and Accessories.

With Invoice 7 on the screen, proceed to the next section.

CORRECT AND PRINT INVOICE

QuickBooks allows corrections and revisions to an invoice even if the invoice has been printed. The invoice may be corrected by going directly to the original invoice or by accessing the original invoice via the Accounts Receivable Register.

> **MEMO**
> **DATE:** January 5, 2015
>
> While viewing Invoice 7 for Monique Gardener in QuickZoom, the bookkeeper, Ruth Morgan, realizes that the snowboard should be $499.95, not the $489.95 that is on the original invoice. Make the correction and reprint the invoice.

Correct Invoice 7

Click in the **PRICE EACH** column
Change the amount for the snowboard to **499.95**
Press Tab to change the **AMOUNT** calculated for the Snowboard
Print the corrected Invoice 7
Click **Yes** on the Recording Transaction dialog box to record the change to the transaction
A **Recording Transaction** message box appears on the screen regarding the credit limit of $500 for Monique Gardener
Click **Yes** to accept the current balance of $1,089.17
When the invoice has been printed, click **Save & Close**

- This closes the invoice and returns you to the Customer Balance Detail Report.

PRINT CUSTOMER BALANCE DETAIL REPORT

When you return to a report after using QuickZoom, any corrections or changes should show in the report.

Review the correction for Invoice 7, then resize columns, and print the report

- The correction for Invoice 7 should be shown in the report. If it does not show, click the **Refresh** button
- Notice that the total amount for Invoice 7 is $1,035.60 and that Monique Gardener's total balance is $1,089.17.
- As you can see, the Account column does not fully display the account names.

Resize the columns as instructed in Chapter 2 so the Account names are displayed in full as shown below

Your Name Mountain Sports
Customer Balance Detail
All Transactions

Type	Date	Num	Account	Amount	Balance
Gardener, Monique					
Invoice	12/31/2014		1200 · Accounts Receivable	53.57	53.57
Invoice	01/04/2015	7	1200 · Accounts Receivable	1,035.60	1,089.17
Total Gardener, Monique				1,089.17	1,089.17

After the columns have been resized, click **Print**

- Verify that **Fit report to one page wide** is not selected.
- If it is selected, click the check box to remove the check mark.

Click **Preview**

- The report will fit on one page wide and the account names will be shown in full.

Click **Close** to close the **Preview**, then click **Print**

Your Name Mountain Sports
Customer Balance Detail
All Transactions

Type	Date	Num	Account	Amount	Balance
Watson, Russ					
Invoice	12/31/2014		1200 · Accounts Receivable	85.00	85.00
Invoice	01/02/2015	1	1200 · Accounts Receivable	81.00	166.00
Invoice	01/03/2015	6	1200 · Accounts Receivable	852.11	1,018.11
Total Watson, Russ				1,018.11	1,018.11
TOTAL				13,607.86	13,607.86

Partial Report

After the report is printed, close the **Customer Balance Detail Report**

- If you get a Memorize Report dialog box, click **Do not display this message in the future**, and then click **No**.

DISCOUNTS

There are three types of discounts used in QuickBooks: Sales Discount, Purchase Discount, and Merchandise Discount. In Chapter 5, Sales Discounts will be used for customer payments. A Sales Discount is used when you give customers a discount for early payment with terms of 2/10, n/30 or 1/10, n/30. Sales Discount is categorized as an Income account. Using a sales discount results in a decrease in income because it the company will receive less money for a sale.

ADD NEW ITEMS AND ACCOUNTS

In order to accommodate the changing needs of a business, all QuickBooks lists allow you to make changes at any time. New items and accounts may be added in the Item List or Chart of Accounts. They may also be added *"on the fly"* while entering invoice information. The Item List stores information about the items the company sells.

Your Name Mountain Sports does not use price levels, so it is appropriate to have an item allowing for sales discounts. Sales discounts decrease income and function as a contra account to income (similar to accumulated depreciation decreasing the value of an asset). Having a discount item allows discounts to be recorded on the sales form. A discount can be a fixed amount or a percentage. A discount is calculated only on the amount shown in the line above it. To allow the entire amount of the invoice to receive the discount, an item for a subtotal will need to be added. When you complete the sales form, the subtotal item will appear before the discount item.

MEMO
DATE: January 5, 2015

Add an item for Sales Discounts and a Subtotal Item. Add a new income account, 4050 Sales Discount, to the Chart of Accounts. The description for the account should be Discount on Sales.

Add new items and accounts

Click the **Items & Services** icon on the QuickBooks Home Page
Use the keyboard shortcut **Ctrl + N** to add a new item
Item **TYPE** is **Discount**
Tab to or click **Item Name/Number**, type **Nonprofit Discount**
Tab to or click **Description**, type **10% Discount to Nonprofit Agencies**
Tab to or click **Amount or %**, key in **10%**

- The % sign must be included in order to differentiate between a $10 discount and a 10% discount.

Click the drop-down list arrow for **Account**
Scroll to the top of the list, and then, click **<Add New>**
Complete the information for a New Account:
Account Type should be **Income**

- If not, click the drop-down list arrow next to the text box for Type. Click **Income**.
- Giving a sales discount to a customer means that your profit for selling an inventory item is less. This will mean that revenue decreases, and this will ultimately decrease the amount of Net Income.

Tab to or click in the **Number** text box, enter the Account Number **4050**

- Your Name Mountain Sports uses account numbers for all accounts.
- Numbers in the 4000 category are income.

Tab to or click **Account Name**, enter **Sales Discounts**
Tab to or click **Description**, enter **Discount on Sales**

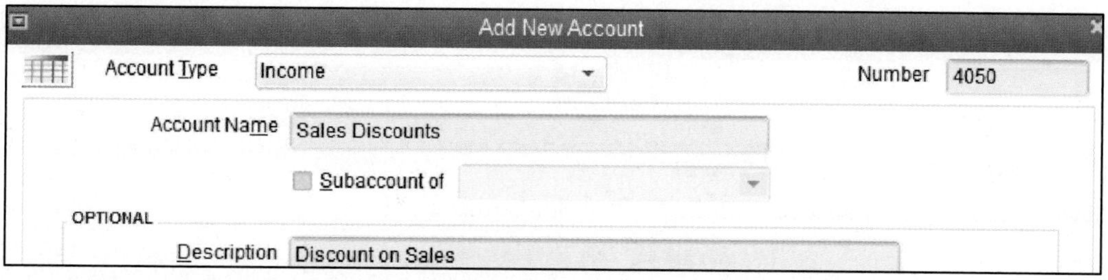

Click **Save & Close** to add the **Sales Discounts** account

Close the **New Account** dialog box, and return to the New Item screen

- At the bottom of the screen you should see the Tax Code as **Tax** and the statement **Discount is applied before sales tax** should be displayed.

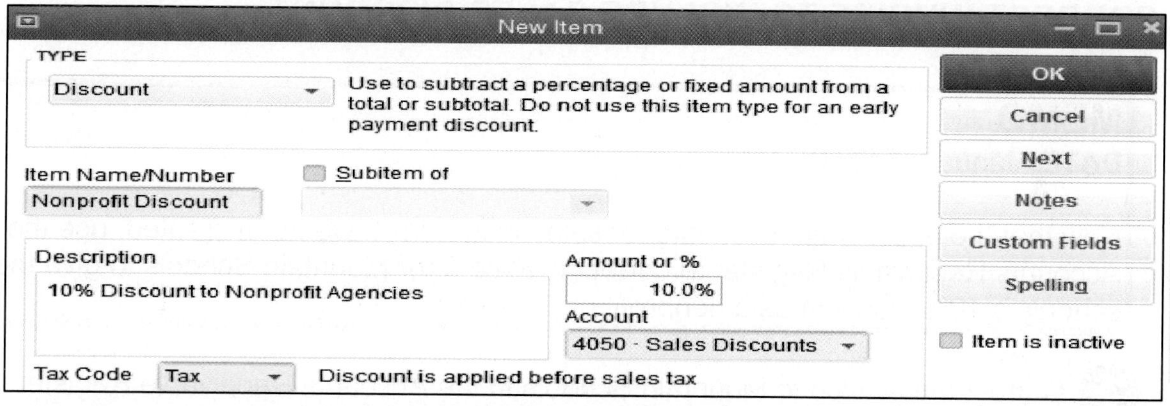

Click **Next** on the **New Item** dialog box

- A discount is calculated only on the line above it on the sales form. To allow the entire amount of the invoice to receive the discount, a subtotal needs to be calculated; so, an item for a subtotal will also need to be added.

Repeat the steps for adding a New Item to add **Subtotal**

TYPE is **Subtotal**, **Item Name/Number** is **Subtotal**, and **Description** is **Subtotal**

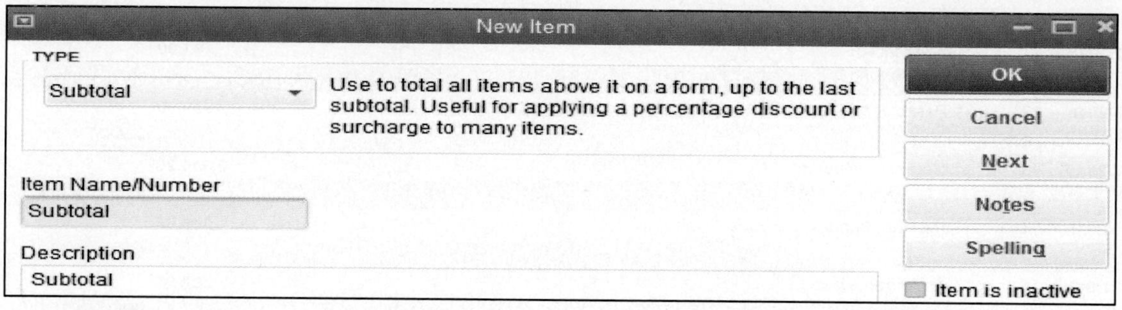

Click **OK** to add the new item and to close the **New Item** screen

- Verify the addition of Nonprofit Discount and Subtotal on the Item List.
- If you find an error, click on the item with the error, use the keyboard shortcut **Ctrl + E**, and make corrections as needed.

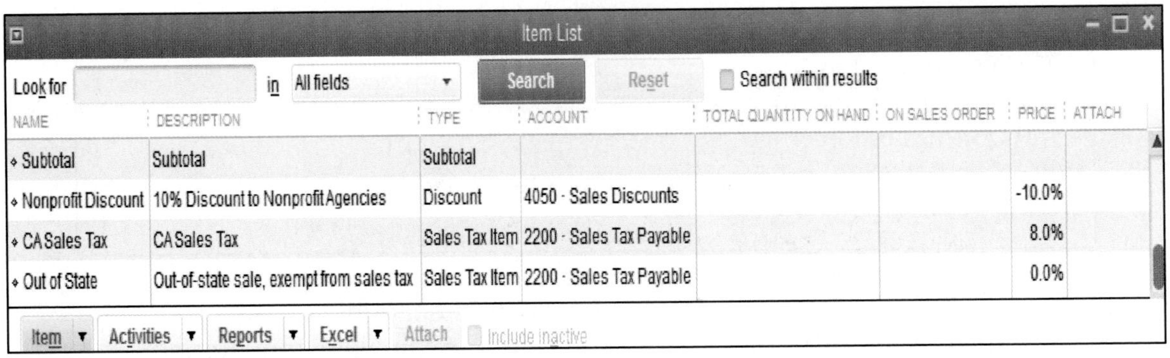

Close the **Item List**

CORRECT INVOICE TO INCLUDE SALES DISCOUNT

MEMO

DATE: January 6, 2015

Now that the appropriate accounts for sales discounts have been created, use the Accounts Receivable Register to correct Invoice 3 for Mountain Schools to give the schools a 10% discount as a nonprofit organization.

Correct the invoice to Mountain Schools in the Accounts Receivable Register

Use the keyboard shortcut, **Ctrl + A** to open the Chart of Accounts
In the Chart of Accounts, double-click **Accounts Receivable**

- Double-clicking opens the register.

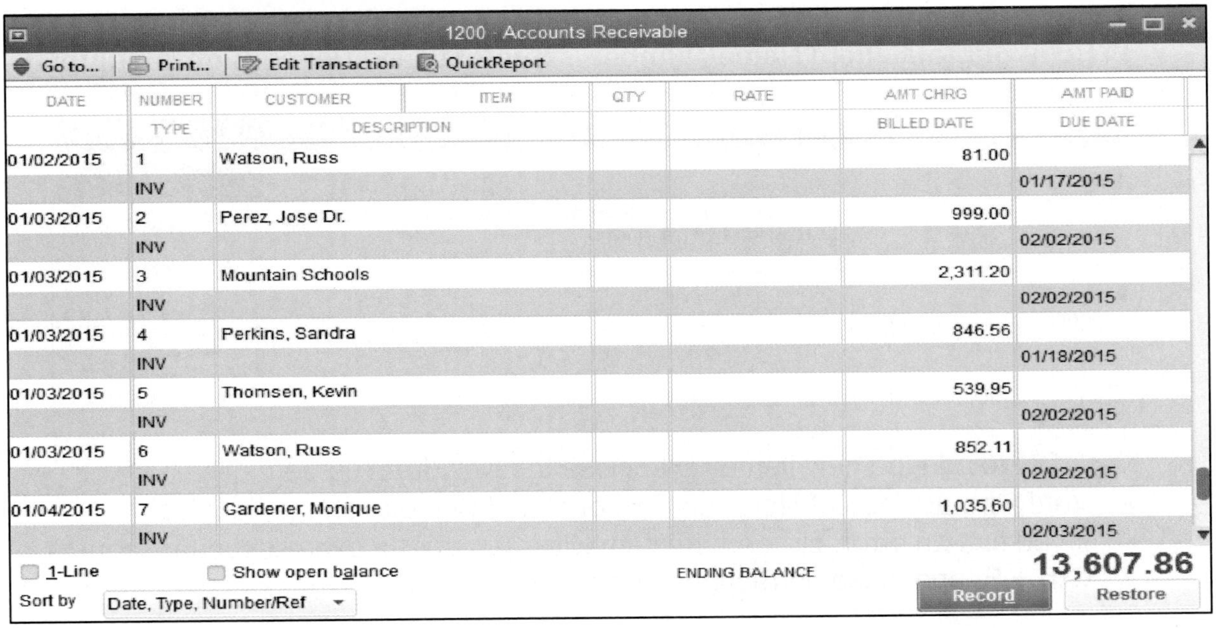

If necessary, scroll through the register until the transaction for **Invoice 3** is on the screen

- **Look** at the **NUMBER/TYPE** column to identify the number of the invoice and the type of transaction.
- On the **NUMBER** line you will see a check number or an invoice number.
- At this time, our Accounts Receivable Register only contains invoices. On the **TYPE** line you will see **INV**. If a payment had been received on account, you would see **PMT** on the Type line

Click anywhere in the transaction for Invoice 3 to Mountain Schools

Click the **Edit Transaction** button at the top of the register or use the shortcut **Ctrl+E**

- Invoice 3 appears on the screen.

Click in **ITEM CODE** beneath the last item, Poles-Ski

Click the drop-down list arrow for **ITEM CODE**, click **Subtotal**

- You may need to scroll through the Item List until you find Subtotal.
- Remember in order to calculate a discount for everything on the invoice, QuickBooks must calculate the subtotal for the items on the invoice.

Tab to or click the next blank line in **ITEM CODE**

Click **Nonprofit Discount**

- You may need to scroll through the Item List until you find Nonprofit Discount.

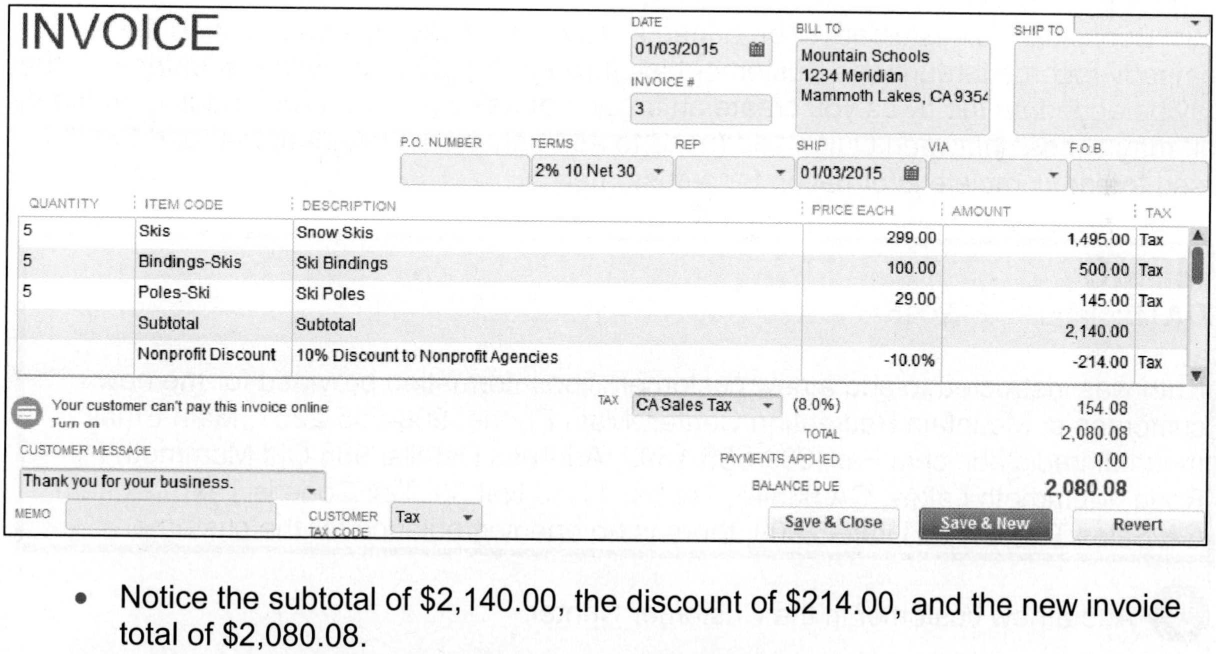
INVOICE

DATE 01/03/2015

INVOICE # 3

BILL TO
Mountain Schools
1234 Meridian
Mammoth Lakes, CA 9354

SHIP TO

P.O. NUMBER | TERMS 2% 10 Net 30 | REP | SHIP 01/03/2015 | VIA | F.O.B.

QUANTITY	ITEM CODE	DESCRIPTION	PRICE EACH	AMOUNT	TAX
5	Skis	Snow Skis	299.00	1,495.00	Tax
5	Bindings-Skis	Ski Bindings	100.00	500.00	Tax
5	Poles-Ski	Ski Poles	29.00	145.00	Tax
	Subtotal	Subtotal		2,140.00	
	Nonprofit Discount	10% Discount to Nonprofit Agencies	-10.0%	-214.00	Tax

Your customer can't pay this invoice online
Turn on

TAX CA Sales Tax (8.0%) 154.08

TOTAL 2,080.08

PAYMENTS APPLIED 0.00

BALANCE DUE 2,080.08

CUSTOMER MESSAGE
Thank you for your business.

MEMO

CUSTOMER TAX CODE Tax

Save & Close | Save & New | Revert

- Notice the subtotal of $2,140.00, the discount of $214.00, and the new invoice total of $2,080.08.

Print the corrected invoice with lines around each field

Click **Yes** on the **Recording Transaction** screen

After printing, click **Save & Close** on the **Create Invoices** screen

- Notice the new AMT CHRG of $2,080.08 for Invoice 3 in the register.

Do not close the **Accounts Receivable Register**

VIEW AND ANALYZE QUICKREPORT

After editing the invoice and returning to the register, you may get a detailed report regarding the customer's transactions by clicking the QuickReport button.

With the cursor in Invoice 3, click the **QuickReport** button QuickReport to view the **Mountain Schools** account

Your Name Mountain Sports
Register QuickReport
All Transactions

Type	Date	Num	Memo	Account	Paid	Open Balance	Amount
Mountain Schools							
Invoice	01/03/2015	3		1200 · Accounts Receivable	Unpaid	2,080.08	2,080.08
Total Mountain Schools						2,080.08	2,080.08
TOTAL						**2,080.08**	**2,080.08**

- Notice that the total of Invoice 3 is $2,080.08

Close the **QuickReport** without printing, the **Accounts Receivable Register**, and the **Chart of Accounts**

ADD NEW CUSTOMER WITH SHIPPING ADDRESS

QuickBooks allows customers to be added at any time. They may be added to the company records through the Customer List, through Add/Edit Multiple List entries, or they may be added *on the fly* as you create an invoice or sales receipt. When adding *on the fly*, you may choose between Quick Add (used to add only a customer's name) and Set Up (used to add complete information for a customer).

MEMO
DATE: January 8, 2015

Ruth was instructed to add a new customer. The information provided for the new customer is: Mountain Recreation Center, Main Phone: 909-555-2951, Main Email: mountainrec@abc.com Fax: 909-555-1592, Address Details: 985 Old Mammoth Road, Mammoth Lakes, CA 93546, Terms: 1%10 Net 30, Tax Code is Tax, Tax Item: CA Sales Tax, Credit Limit: 5,000, there is no opening balance for the customer.

Add a new customer in the Customer Center

Click the **Customers** icon on the icon bar or the **Customers** button in the Customers section of the Home Page

Use the keyboard shortcut **Ctrl + N** to create a new customer

In the **Customer** text box, enter **Mountain Recreation Center**

- QuickBooks will show the current date of your computer as the As Of Date even though there is no Opening Balance.

Tab to or click **COMPANY NAME**

Enter **Mountain Recreation Center** or copy the Customer Name as previously instructed

Tab to or click in the text box for **Main Phone**, enter the telephone number

Tab to or click in the text box for **Main Email**, enter the email address

Tab to or click in the text box for **Fax**, enter the fax number

In the INVOICE/BILL TO section for ADDRESS DETAILS, click at the end of Mountain Recreation Center, press **Enter**

Key in the address

Click the **Copy>>** button to copy the address to SHIP TO

Verify that the same company address information appears on the Add Shipping Address Information screen, and click **OK**

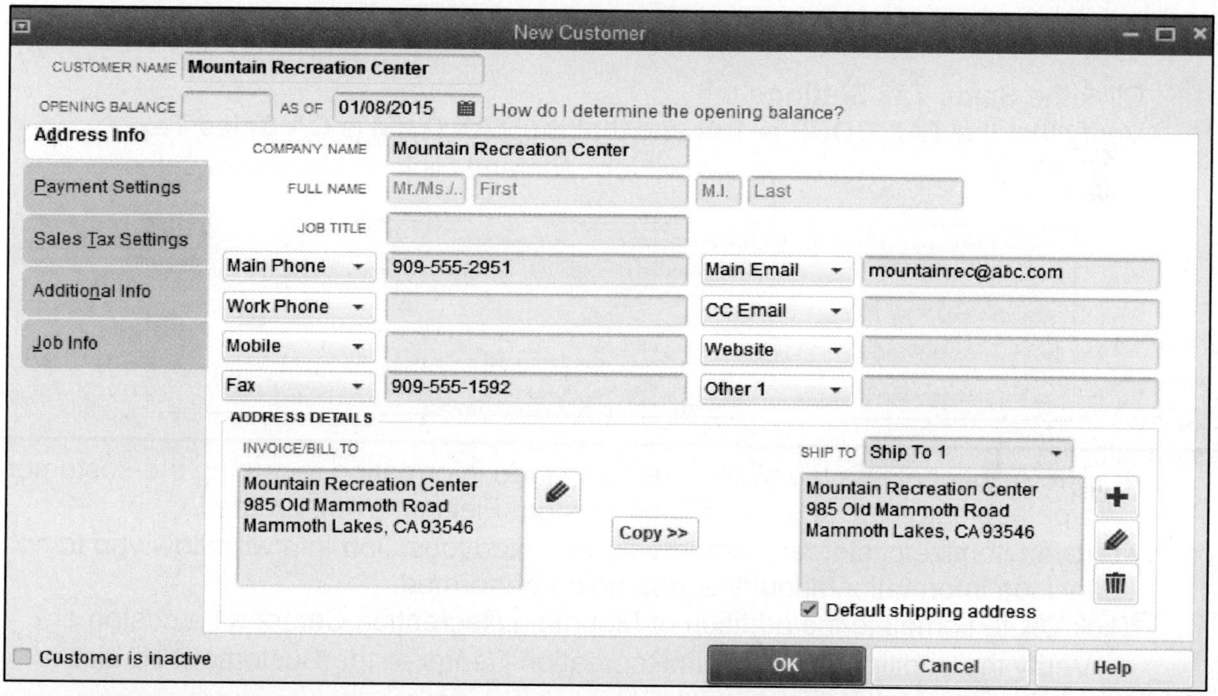

Click the **Payment Settings** tab

Tab to or click in the text box for **CREDIT LIMIT**, enter **5,000**

Click the drop-down list arrow for **PAYMENT TERMS**, click **1% 10 Net 30**

Click the drop-down list arrow for **PREFERRED DELIVERY METHOD**, click **None**

- Note: Your may also add An ACCOUNT NUMBER, a PREFERRED PAYMENT METHOD, and CREDIT CARD INFORMATION.

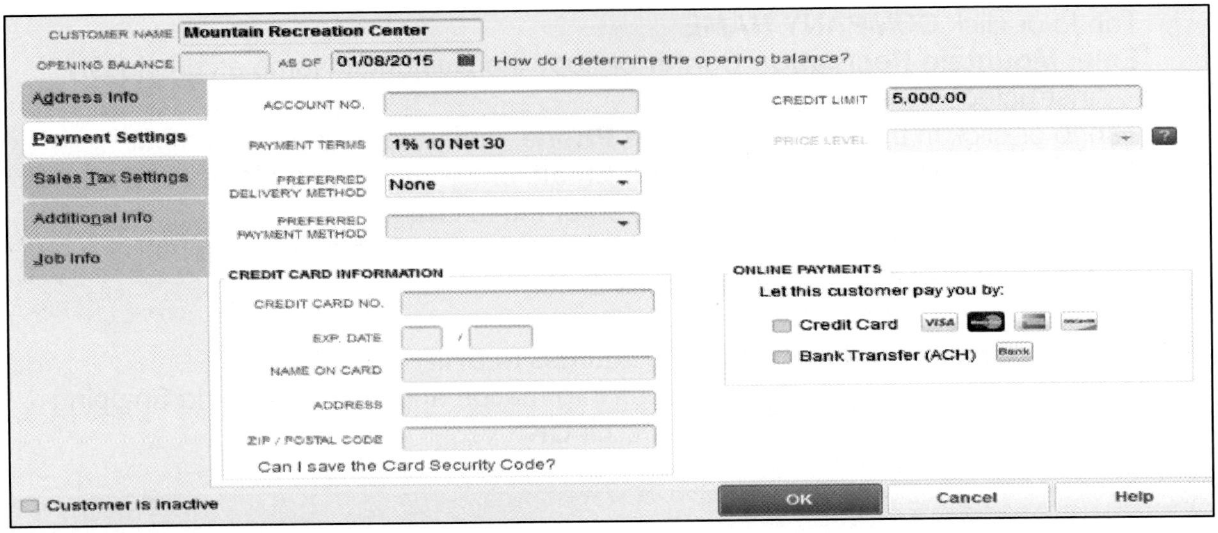

Click the **Sales Tax Settings** tab

Verify that the **TAX CODE** is **Tax** and that the **TAX ITEM** is **CA Sales Tax**

- If not, click the drop-down arrows for each and click on the proper selection.

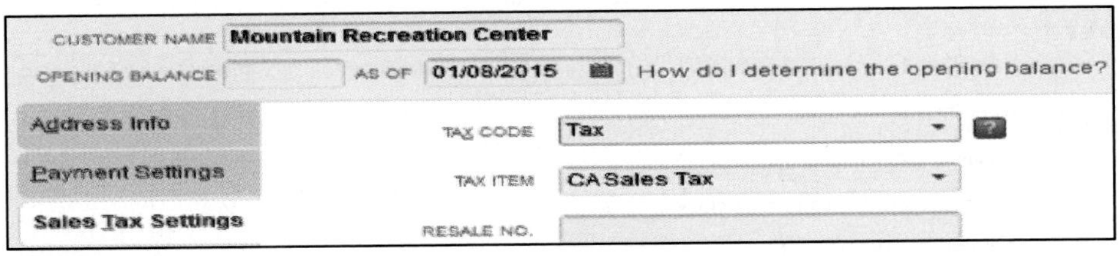

- The Additional Info tab allows you to include information regarding the customer type and sales rep info. In addition Custom Fields may be created.
- If you itemize customers based on contracted jobs, Job Info will allow you to include information about the jobs being performed.

Click **OK** to complete the addition of Mountain Recreation Center as a customer

- Verify the addition of Mountain Recreation Center to the Customer:Job List.

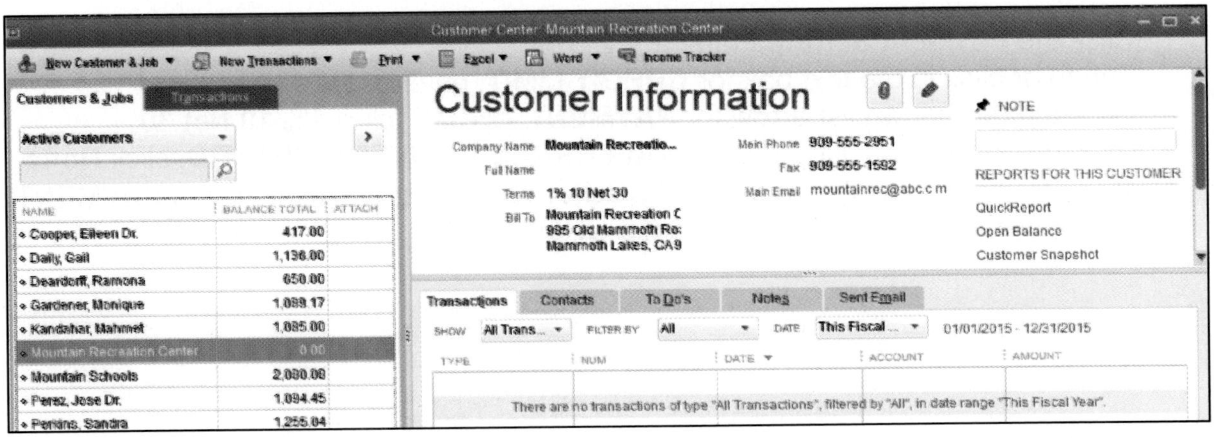

Close the **Customer Center**

RECORD SALE OF NEW ITEM

Once a customer has been added, sales may be recorded for a customer.

> **MEMO**
> **DATE:** January 8, 2015
>
> Record a sale of 5 sleds at $119.99 each, 5 toboggans at $229.95, and 5 helmets at $69.95 each to Mountain Recreation Center. Because the sale is to a nonprofit organization, include a nonprofit discount.

Record the sale on account and add three new sales items as indicated in the Memo

Access a blank invoice by using the keyboard shortcut **Ctrl + I**
Enter invoice information for **Mountain Recreation Center** on the customized invoice copy as previously instructed
Date of the invoice is **01/08/2015**
INVOICE # is **8**
Tab to or click **QUANTITY**, enter **5**
Tab to or click **ITEM CODE**, key in the word **Sleds**, press **Enter**
On the Item Not Found dialog box, click **Yes** to create the new item.

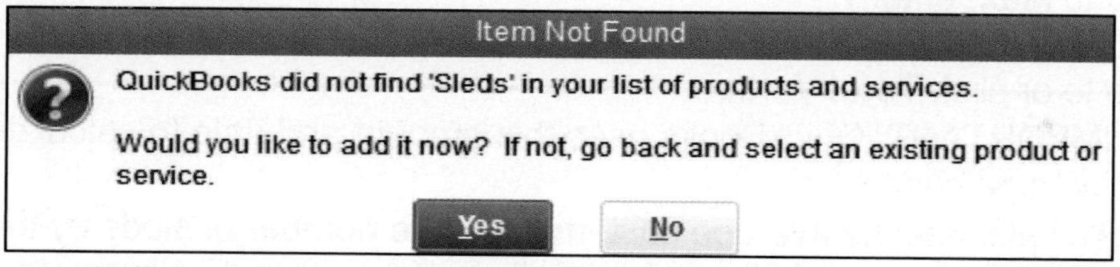

On the **New Item** screen, click **Inventory Part** for **TYPE**

- If necessary, click the drop-down list menu to get a list of choices for **TYPE**.

The Inventory Item is divided into three parts:

- PURCHASE INFORMATION: used when purchasing the inventory item.
- SALES INFORMATION: used when selling the merchandise.
- INVENTORY INFORMATION: used to calculate the value of the item, calculate the average cost of the item, track the amount of inventory on hand, and prompt when inventory needs to be ordered.

The **Item Name/Number** is **Sleds**
Do not enable Unit of Measure

- Unit of Measure is used to indicate what quantities, prices, rates, and costs are based on.

Complete the **PURCHASE INFORMATION**:
Description on Purchase Transactions enter **Sleds**
Cost leave at **0.00**

- Your Name Mountain Sports has elected to keep the item list simple and not use different items for different styles and models of sleds. Thus, sleds are purchased at different prices so the Cost is left at 0.00.

COGS Account is **5000 - Cost of Goods Sold**

- If 5000 – Cost of Goods Sold is not shown, click the drop-down list arrow and click the account to select it.

Preferred Vendor: leave blank because we do not use the same vendor for this item every time we order it

Complete the **SALES INFORMATION**:

Description on Sales Transactions is **Sleds**

- If Sleds was not inserted at the same time as the Purchase Information Description, enter **Sleds** for the description.

Sales Price leave at **0.00**

- As with the Purchase Information, the Sales Price remains as 0.00.

Tax Code is **Tax** because sales tax is collected on this item

Click the drop-down list arrow for **Income Account**, click **4012 Equipment Sales**

Complete the **INVENTORY INFORMATION**:

Asset Account should be **1120 Inventory Asset**

- If this account is not in the **Asset Account** text box, click the drop-down list arrow, click **1120 Inventory Asset**. This asset account keeps track of the value of the inventory we have on hand.

Tab to **Reorder Point (Min)**, enter **5**

Tab to **Max**, enter **7**

Tab to **On hand**, enter **10**

Tab to or click **Total Value**

- IMPORTANT: QuickBooks uses this amount and date to calculate the average cost.
- To calculate the average cost, multiply the number of sleds by their purchase price; and then, add the value of all sleds together. For example, five of the ten sleds were purchased by Your Name Mountain Sports for $75 each (Total $375). The other five sleds were purchased for $60 each (Total $300) Total value: $375 + $300 = $675.

Total Value of the sleds is **$675**

Tab to **As of**

- The date is very important! A common error in training is to use the computer date—not the date in the text. An incorrect date may cause a change in the value of your inventory, and it is very difficult to correct the date later.

Enter the As of date **01/08/15**

Check your entry with the following screen shot:

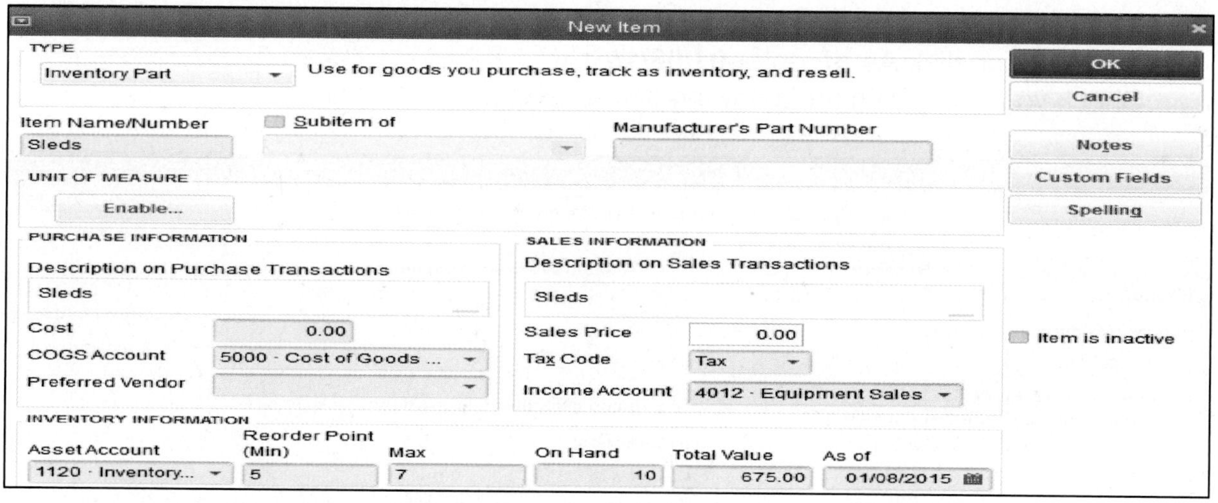

Click **OK** to add Sleds as a sales item and return to Invoice 8
On the invoice, tab to or click **PRICE EACH**, enter **119.99**
Tab to or click the second line in **QUANTITY**, enter **5**
Tab to or click **ITEM CODE**
Click the drop-down list arrow for **ITEM CODE**

- There is no item listed for Toboggans.

Click **<Add New>** at the top of the **Item List**
On the **New Item** screen, click **Inventory Part** for **TYPE**
Tab to or click **Item Name/Number**, enter **Toboggans**
Do <u>not</u> enable Unit of Measure
Complete **PURCHASE INFORMATION**:

Tab to or click **Description on Purchase Transactions** enter **Toboggans**
Cost is **0.00**
COGS Account is **5000 Cost of Goods Sold**

- If 5000 – Cost of Goods Sold is not shown, click the drop-down list arrow and click **5000 Cost of Goods Sold** to select the account.

Preferred Vendor leave blank

Complete **SALES INFORMATION**:

Description on Sales Transactions should be **Toboggans**
Sales Price leave at **0.00**
Tax Code should be **Tax**
Click the drop-down list arrow for **Income Account**
Click **4012 Equipment Sales**

Complete the **INVENTORY INFORMATION**:

Asset Account should be **1120 Inventory Asset**
Tab to or click **Reorder Point (Min)**, enter **5**, tab to or click **Max**, enter **7**
Tab to or click **On Hand**, enter **10**
Tab to or click **Total Value**

- Five of the ten toboggans were purchased by Your Name Mountain Sports for $125 each (Total $625). The other five toboggans were purchased for $150 each ($750). Total Value is $625 + $750 = $1,375.

Enter **1375** for the **Total Value**

Tab to or click **As of**, enter **01/08/15**

Check your entry with the following screen shot:

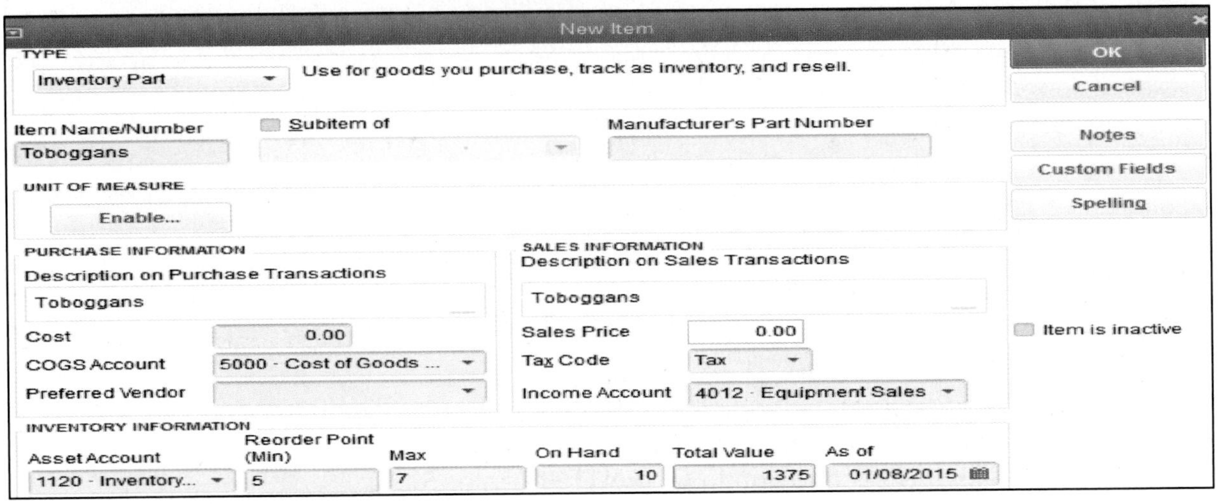

Click **OK** to add Toboggans as a sales item and return to Invoice 8

Enter the Price for the Toboggans of **229.95**

Repeat the steps shown above to add **Helmets** as a sales item

Cost and Sales Price are **0.00**

COGS account is **5000 Cost of Goods Sold**

Income Account is **4011 Clothing & Accessory Sales**

Asset Account is **1120 Inventory Asset**

Enter the **Reorder Point (Min)** of **5**, **Max** of **30**, and **On Hand 25**

Calculate the Total Value: purchased 10 helmets @ $25 each, purchased 15 helmets @ $30 each, enter the amount of **Total Value** as of **01/08/2015**

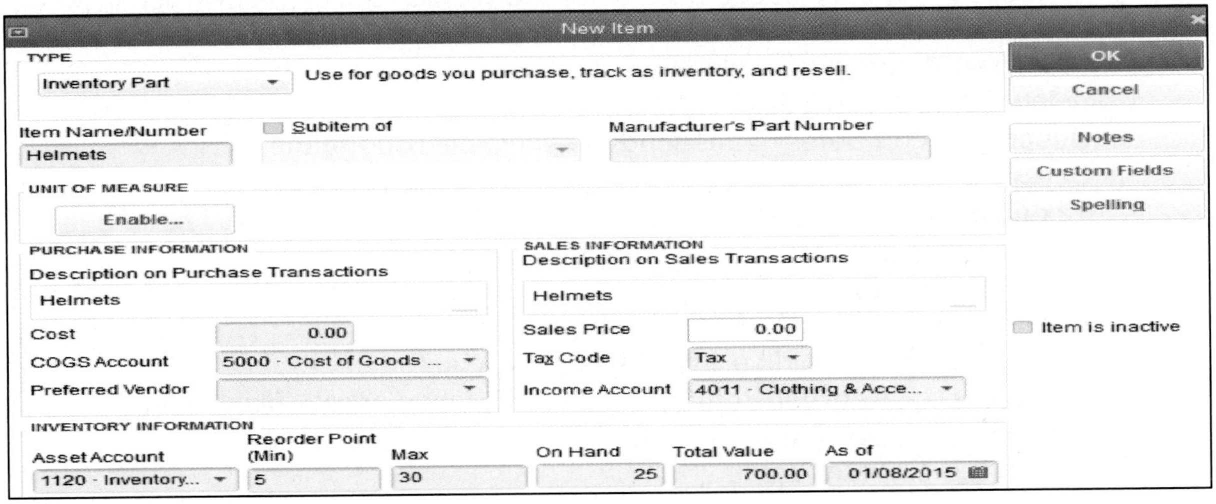

Click **OK**, then, use the information in the Memo to complete the invoice

- Remember that Mountain Recreation Center is a nonprofit organization and is entitled to a Nonprofit Discount.

The **CUSTOMER MESSAGE** is **Thank you for your business.**

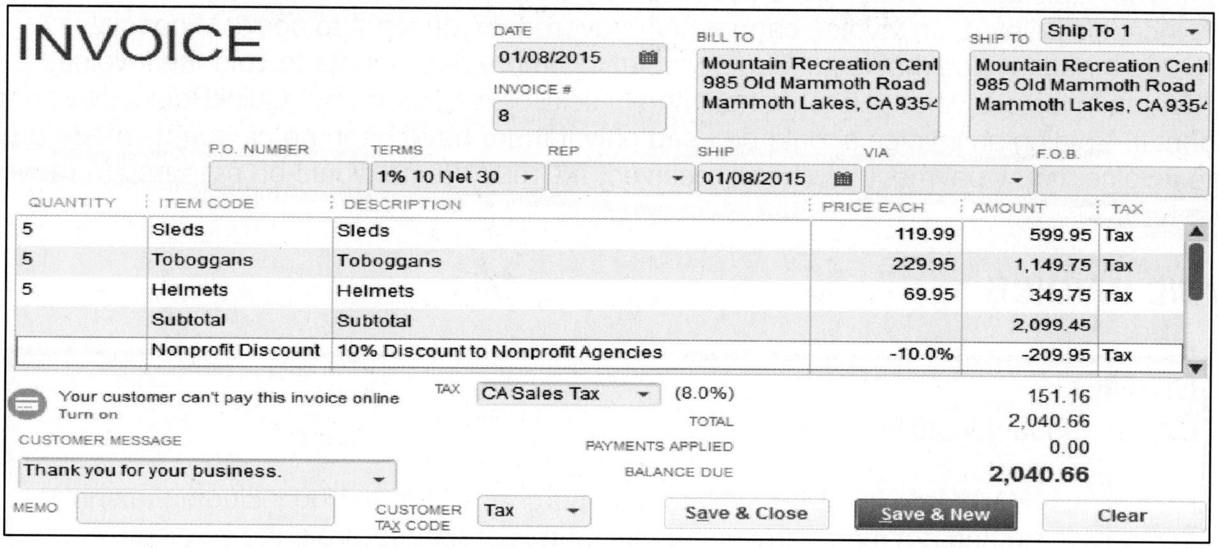

Print the invoice as previously instructed

Click **Save & Close** to record the invoice and close the transaction

5

MODIFY CUSTOMER RECORDS

Occasionally information regarding a customer will change. QuickBooks allows customer accounts to be modified at any time by editing the Customer List.

MEMO
DATE: January 8, 2015

In order to update Monique Gardener's account, change her credit limit to $2,500.00.

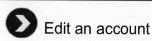

Edit an account

Use **Ctrl + J** to access the **Customer List**

Double-click **Gardener, Monique** on the Customer:Job List.

Click the **Payment Settings** tab

Tab to or click **CREDIT LIMIT**, enter **2500** for the amount

Click **OK** to record the change and exit the information for Monique Gardener

Close the **Customer Center**

VOID AND DELETE SALES FORMS

Deleting an invoice or sales receipt completely removes it and any transaction information for it from QuickBooks. Make sure you definitely want to remove the invoice before deleting it. Once it is deleted, an invoice cannot be recovered. If you want to correct financial records for an invoice that is no longer viable, it is more appropriate to void the invoice. When an invoice is voided, it remains in the QuickBooks system, but QuickBooks does not count it. Voiding an invoice should be used only if there have been no payments made on the invoice. If any payment has been received, a Credit Memo would be prepared to record a return.

VOID INVOICE

> **MEMO**
> **DATE:** January 8, 2015
>
> Russ Watson returned the after-ski boots he purchased for $81.00 including tax on January 2. He had not made any payments on this purchase. Void the invoice.

Void the transaction for Russ Watson using **Advanced Find** to locate the invoice:

Click **Find** on the **Edit** menu, click the **Advanced** tab

- **Advanced Find** is useful when you have a large number of invoices and want to locate an invoice for a particular customer.
- Using **Advanced Find** will locate the invoice without requiring you to scroll through all the invoices for the company. For example, if customer Sanderson's transaction was on Invoice 7 and the invoice on the screen was 784, you would not have to scroll through 777 invoices because Find would locate Invoice 7 instantly.

Scroll through the list displayed under **FILTER**, click **Name**

- A Filter allows you to specify the type of search to be performed.

In the **Name** text box, click the drop-down list arrow, click **Watson, Russ**
Click the **Find** button on the upper-right side of the **Find** dialog box

- QuickBooks will find all transactions recorded for Russ Watson.

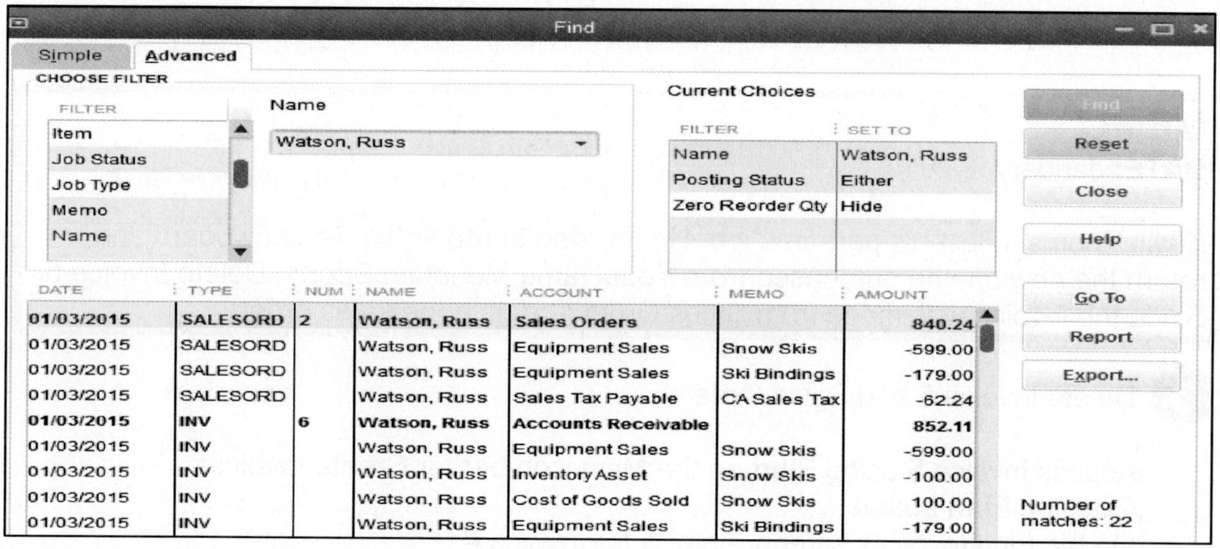

- Because there are several invoices, a second filter would be used to find the exact amount of 81.00.

Click **Amount** under **FILTER**
Click the circle in front of the **=** sign
Key **81.00** in the text box, press the **Tab** key

- The first two lines of the Current Choices Box shows *FILTER: Amount* and *SET TO: 81.00*: followed by *FILTER: Name* and *SET TO: Watson, Russ.*

Click the **Find** button, click the line for **Invoice 1**

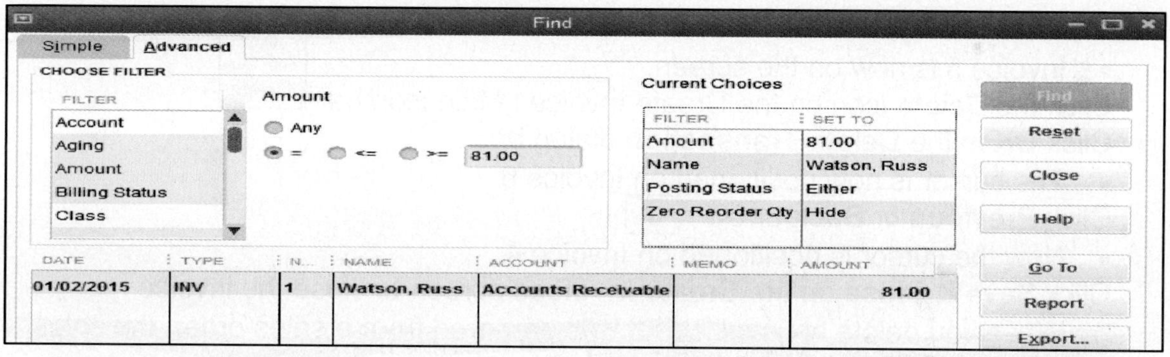

Click the **Go To** button

- Invoice 1 appears on the screen.

With the invoice on the screen, click QuickBooks **Edit** menu, click **Void Invoice**

- Notice that the amount and the total for Invoice 1 are no longer 81.00. Both are **0.00**. Also note that the Memo box contains the word **VOID:**.

Print the invoice
Click **Yes** on the **Recording Transaction** screen
Click **Save & Close** button on the **Create Invoices** screen to close the invoice

- Invoice 1 is no longer displayed on the **Advanced Find** screen.

Click **Close** button to close **Find**

DELETE INVOICE AND SALES ORDER

MEMO
DATE: January 8, 2015

Kevin Thomsen lost his part-time job. He decided to repair his old snowboard and return the new one he purchased from Your Name Mountain Sports. Delete Invoice 5. Since the invoice was made from Sales Order 1, delete the sales order.

Delete Invoice 5 and Sales Order 1

Access Invoice 5 using **Find** on the Main icon bar for Create Invoices
Click the **Find** button
On the Find Invoices screen, enter **5** for Invoice #

- You may enter any or all of the information items shown.

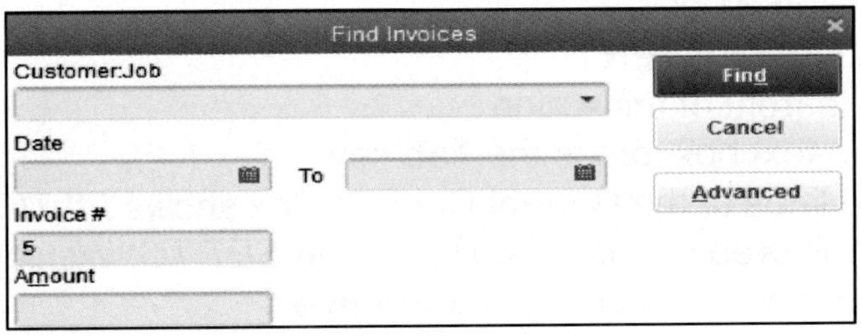

Click the **Find** button

- Invoice 5 is now on the screen.

Click the **Delete** icon on the Create Invoices Main icon bar 

Click **OK** in the **Delete Transaction** dialog box

- The cursor is now positioned on Invoice 6.

Click **Previous** or **Back** arrow 

- Now the cursor is positioned on Invoice 4.

Click **Save & Close** on the **Create Invoices** screen to close the invoice

- When you delete an invoice that was prepared from a sales order, the sales order must be deleted as well.

Access Sale Order 1 as previously instructed

- Notice that the Sales Order is no longer marked INVOICED IN FULL.

Delete the Sales Order following the same procedures used when deleting an invoice
Click **OK** when asked if you want to delete the transaction
Close **Create Sales Orders**

View the **Customer Balance Detail Report**

Prepare the report from the Report Center

Scroll through the report

- Look at Kevin Thomsen's account. Notice that Invoice 5 does not show up in the account listing. When an invoice is deleted, there is no record of it anywhere in the report.
- Look at Russ Watson's account. The amount for Invoice 1 shows as **0.00**. Nothing is shown for the Sales Order because a sales order is not recorded in accounts or journals.

Your Name Mountain Sports
Customer Balance Detail
All Transactions

Type	Date	Num	Account	Amount	Balance
Thomsen, Kevin					
Invoice	12/31/2014		1200 · Accounts Receivable	911.63	911.63
Total Thomsen, Kevin				911.63	911.63
Villanueva, Oskar					
Invoice	12/31/2014		1200 · Accounts Receivable	975.00	975.00
Total Villanueva, Oskar				975.00	975.00
Watson, Russ					
Invoice	12/31/2014		1200 · Accounts Receivable	85.00	85.00
Invoice	01/02/2015	1	1200 · Accounts Receivable	0.00	85.00
Invoice	01/03/2015	6	1200 · Accounts Receivable	852.11	937.11
Total Watson, Russ				937.11	937.11
TOTAL				14,796.45	14,796.45

Partial Report

Close the report without printing, do not close the Report Center

PREPARE VOIDED/DELETED TRANSACTIONS SUMMARY

The report that lists the information regarding voided and deleted transactions is the Voided/Deleted Transaction Detail Report.

View the Voided/Deleted Transactions Detail Report

Click **Accountant & Taxes** in the Report Center
Double-click **Voided/Deleted Transaction Summary**
The dates are **From 01/08/15** and **To 01/08/15**

- IMPORTANT: If the report does not match the text when preparing the report with the dates of 01/08/15, use **All** as the date selection.
- The Entered Last Modified column shows the actual date and time that the entry was made.
- In addition, your report may not match the one illustrated if you have voided or deleted anything else during your work session.

Scroll through the report to see the transactions

- Notice the entries for Invoice 1 include both the original and the voided entries.
- The entries for Invoice 5 show the original entry and the deleted entry.

- Sales Order 1 shows both the original and deleted transactions.

Your Name Mountain Sports
Voided/Deleted Transactions Summary
Entered/Last Modified January 8, 2015

Num	Action	Entered/Last Modified	Date	Name	Memo	Account	Split	Amount
Transactions entered or modified by Admin								
Invoice 1								
1	Voided Transaction	01/08/2015 12:21:25	01/02/2015	Watson, Russ	VOID:	1200 · Accounts Receivable	-SPLIT-	0.00
1	Added Transaction	01/02/2015 13:29:03	01/02/2015	Watson, Russ		1200 · Accounts Receivable	-SPLIT-	81.00
Invoice 5								
5	Deleted Transaction	01/08/2015 12:32:11						0.00
5	Added Transaction	01/03/2015 16:04:06	01/03/2015	Thomsen, Kevin		1200 · Accounts Receivable	-SPLIT-	539.95
Sales Order 1								
1	Deleted Transaction	01/08/2015 12:33:37						0.00
1	Added Transaction	01/03/2015 15:39:52	01/03/2015	Thomsen, Kevin		90200 · Sales Orders	-SPLIT-	539.95

Close the report without printing, and close the Report Center

PREPARE CREDIT MEMOS

A credit memo is prepared to show a reduction to a transaction and to notify a customer that a change has been made to a transaction. If the invoice has already been sent to the customer, it is more appropriate and less confusing to make a change to a transaction by issuing a credit memo rather than voiding an invoice and issuing a new one.

When applying a credit to an invoice, QuickBooks marks either the oldest invoice or the invoice that matches the amount of the credit.

MEMO
DATE: January 10, 2015

Credit Memo 9—Monique Gardener returned the boot carrying case purchased for $49.95 on Invoice 7.

Credit Memo 10—Russ Watson returned the ski carrier purchased for $10.99 on Invoice 6.

Prepare the Credit Memos in the Memo above
Click the **Refunds and Credits** icon on the Home Page
CUSTOMER:JOB is **Gardener, Monique**
Use the **Custom Credit Memo** Template
The **Date** of the Credit Memo is **01/10/15**
The **Credit No.** field should show the number **9**

- Because Credit Memos are included in the numbering sequence for invoices, this number matches the number of the next blank invoice.

There is no PO No.
Click the drop-down list arrow next to **ITEM**, click **Accessories**

Tab to or click in **QTY**, type in **1**
Tab to or click **RATE**, enter **49.95**
Press tab to enter 49.95 in the **AMOUNT** column
Click the drop-down list arrow for CUSTOMER MESSAGE, click **<Add New>**
Key in **We have processed your return.** as the Message, click **OK**

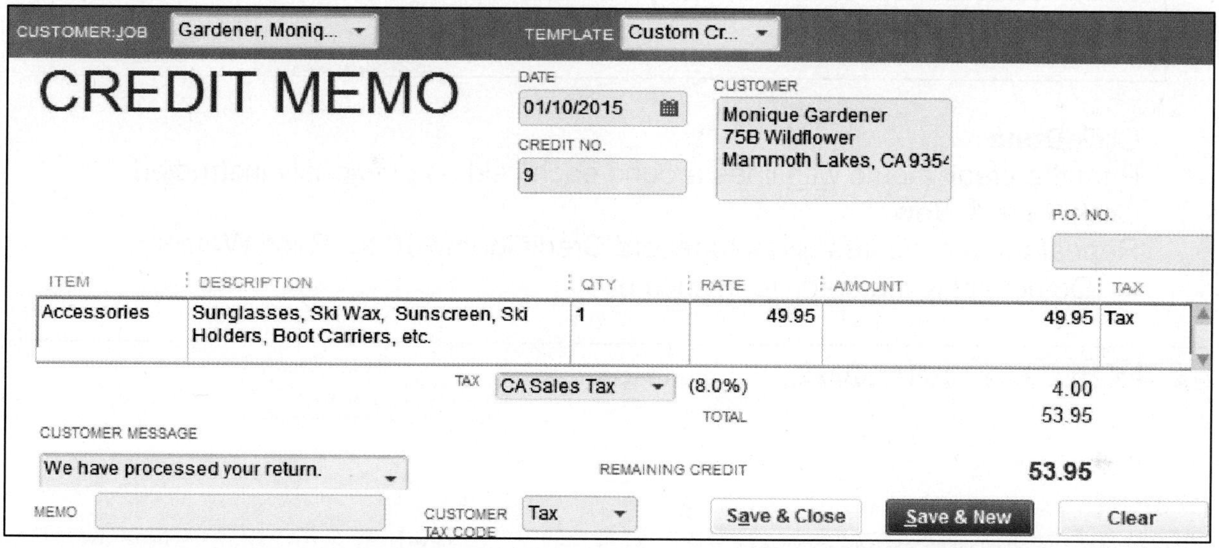

Since the return was for an item purchased on Invoice 7, it is appropriate to apply the credit to Invoice 7

Click the **Use Credit to apply to an invoice** on the Create Credit Memos/Refunds icon bar

Click **Yes** if you get a Recording Transaction message box

The Apply Credit to Invoices screen will appear.

- Unless an exact match in the Amt. Due occurs, QuickBooks applies the credit to the oldest item.
- You will see a checkmark in the column next to the date of 12/31/2014, which is the Opening Balance and the oldest transaction. You will also see a check mark for the Date 01/04/2015. This is because the oldest transaction is selected by QuickBooks and because the amount of the credit is for more than the opening balance.

Since the credit is for a return to the boot carrier purchased on Invoice 7, click the **Clear Selections** button

Click in the check column to mark Invoice 7 on 01/04/2015

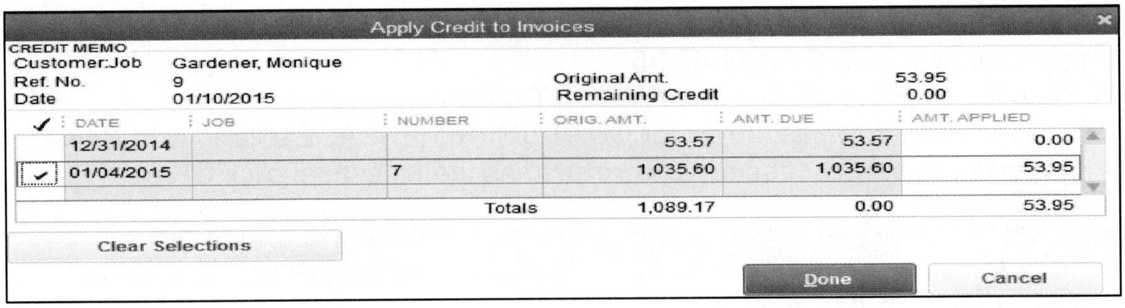

Click **Done**

Print the credit memo <u>with</u> lines around each field as previously instructed

Click **Save & New**

Repeat the procedures given to record Credit Memo 10 for Russ Watson

- Do not apply the credit to Invoice 6

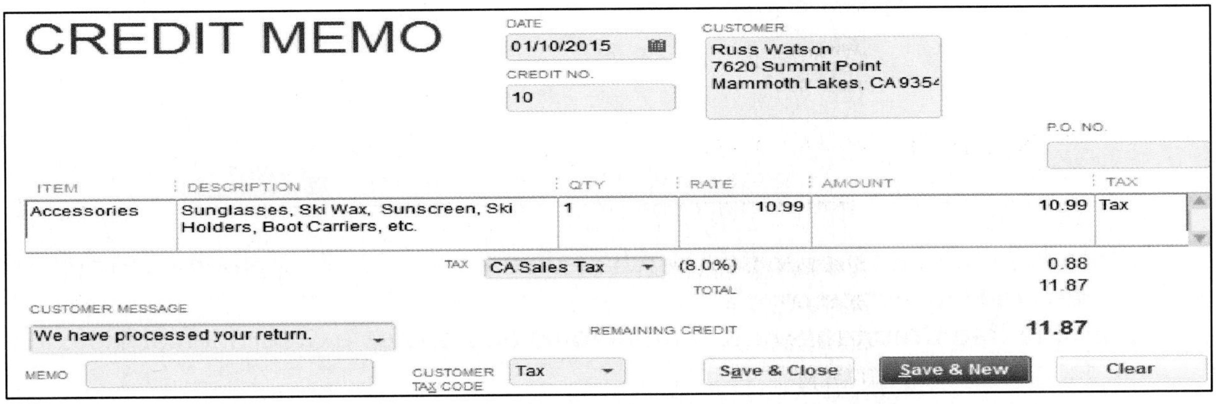

Print the credit memo

Click **Save & Close**

Click **OK** on the Available Credit screen to **Retain as an available credit**

APPLY CREDIT TO INVOICE

When a Credit Memo is recorded, it may be applied to an invoice at the time the credit is recorded. If that is not done, it is possible to go to the invoice and apply the credit directly to the invoice.

➔ Apply Credit Memo 10 to Invoice 6

Click the **Create Invoices** icon on the Home Page

Click the Previous button until you get to Invoice 6 for Russ Watson

Click the **Apply Credits** icon on the Main Create Invoices icon bar

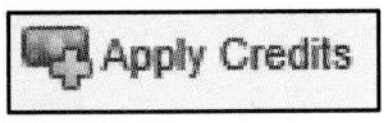

- In the Available Credits section of the Apply Credits screen, look at the information listed and make sure that there is a check mark next to the DATE 01/10/2015, if not click to select.

- The CREDIT NO. should show 10, and the CREDIT AMT. should be 11.87.

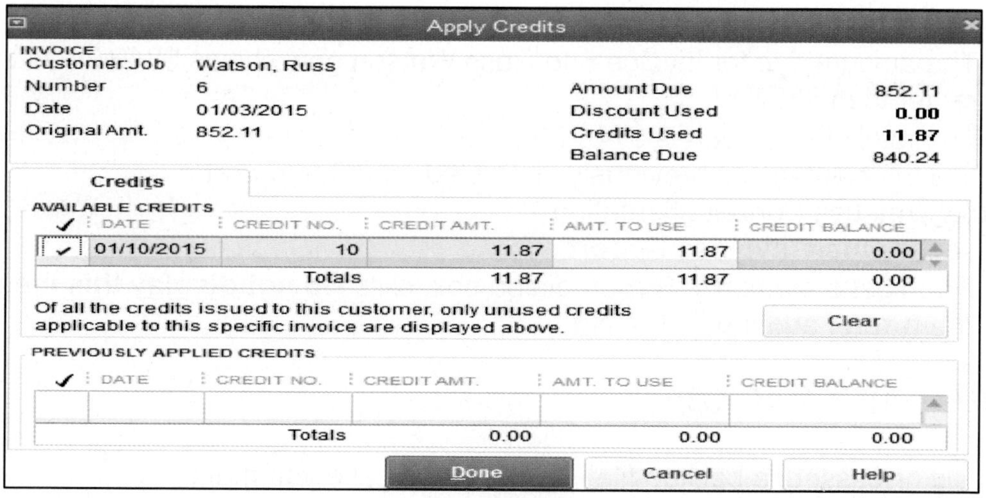

Click **Done** on the Apply Credits screen, click **Save & Close** on Create Invoices

PRINT OPEN INVOICES REPORT

To determine which invoices are still open—they have not been paid—QuickBooks allows you to print an Open Invoices report. This report lists unpaid invoices and statement charges grouped and subtotaled by customer. It also shows the transaction date, the Invoice number, a Purchase Order number (if there is one), terms of the sale, due date, aging, and the amount of the open balance. The total amount due from each customer for all open invoices less credit memos is also listed. If a credit memo has been applied to an invoice, the new total due is reflected in this report and the credit memo is not shown separately.

MEMO
DATE: January 10, 2015

Ruth needs to prepare and print an Open Invoices Report to give to Larry and you, so you can see which invoices are open. When preparing the report, adjust the width of the columns. The report should be one page wide without selecting the print option *Fit report to one page wide.*

Prepare, resize, and print an Open Invoices Report

Click **Reports** on the Menu bar, point to **Customers & Receivables**, and click **Open Invoices**

Enter the date **011015**

- QuickBooks will insert the / between the items in the date.

Press the **Tab** key to generate the report

- Notice the amount due for Invoice 7. It now shows $981.65 as the total rather than $1,035.60. This verifies that the credit memo was applied to Invoice 7.
- The amount due for Invoice 6 to Russ Watson now shows $840.24 as the total rather than $852.11.
- The total of the report is $14,730.63

Resize the columns as previously instructed, print the report
Click **Print**, use Portrait orientation
Close the **Open Invoices Report**

- If you get a Memorize Report dialog box, click **Do not display this message in the future**; and then, click **No**.

PREPARE DAILY BACKUP

As previously discussed, a backup file is prepared in case you make an error. After a number of transactions have been recorded, it is wise to prepare a backup file. In addition, a backup should be made at the end of every work session. The Daily Backup file is an appropriate file to create for saving your work as you progress through a chapter. By creating the backup file now, it will contain your work for Chapter 5 up through the preparation of the credit memos.

Prepare the Sports (Daily Backup).qbb file

Follow the steps presented in Chapter 1 for creating a backup file
Name the file **Sports (Daily Backup)**
The file type is **QBW Backup (* .QBB)**

RECORD CASH SALES WITH SALES TAX

Not all sales in a business are on account. In many instances, payment is made at the time the merchandise is purchased. This is entered as a cash sale. Sales with cash, debit cards, credit cards, or checks as the payment method are entered as cash sales. When entering a cash sale, you prepare a Sales Receipt rather than an Invoice. QuickBooks records the transaction in the Journal and places the amount of cash received in an account called *Undeposited Funds*. The funds received remain in Undeposited Funds until you record a deposit to your bank account.

MEMO
DATE: January 11, 2015

Record Sales Receipt 1—Received cash from a customer who purchased a pair of sunglasses, $29.95; a boot carrier, $2.99; and some lip balm, $1.19. Use the message *Thank you for your business.*

Enter the above transaction as a cash sale to a cash customer

Click the **Create Sales Receipts** icon on the Home Page

- Depending on the size of your computer screen, the History can take up more room than you wish. You may want to hide the history panel.

If any of the columns in the Sales Receipt are not shown in full, resize them by pointing between the column headings and dragging the double arrow until the column is shown in full

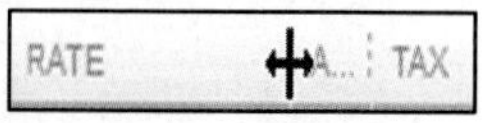

Enter **Cash Customer** in the **CUSTOMER:JOB** text box, press Tab

Because Your Name Mountain Sports does not have a customer named Cash Customer, a **Customer:Job Not Found** dialog box appears on the screen.

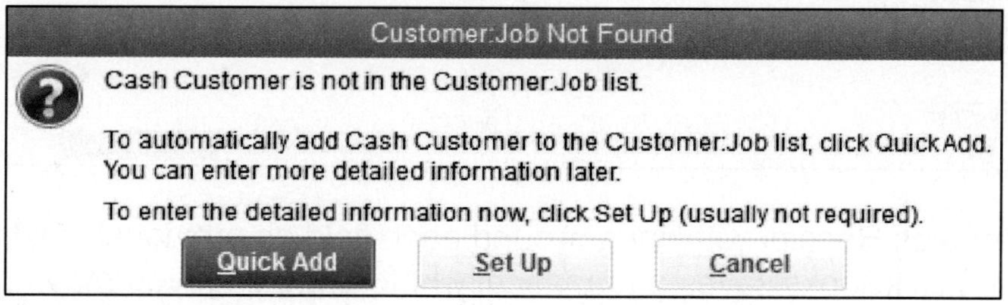

Click **Quick Add** to add the customer name Cash Customer to the Customer List

- Details regarding Cash Customer are not required, so Quick Add is the appropriate method to use to add the name to the list.
- Now that the customer name has been added to the Customer:Job List, the cursor moves to the **Template** field.

Template should be **Custom Sales Receipt**

- If not, click the drop-down list arrow and click Custom Sales Receipt.

Tab to or click **Date**, type **01/11/15**

- As shown in earlier chapters, the date may be entered 01/11/2015; 01/11/15; or 011115; or by clicking on the calendar, clicking the forward or back arrows until you get to the correct month, and then clicking on the date.

Sale No. should be **1**

Click the **Cash** icon on the Sales Receipt

- QuickBooks will allow you to accept cash, checks, credit cards, debit cards, and e-checks.
- Your business must subscribe to the optional QuickBooks Merchant Accounts, to allow credit card, debit card, and e-payment processing to be completed without additional software or hardware.
- If you do not subscribe to QuickBooks Merchant Accounts, you can still accept the different methods of payment by using your merchant account processor.

Use **Accessories** as the **ITEM** for each of the items sold and complete the Sales Receipt as instructed in Chapter 2

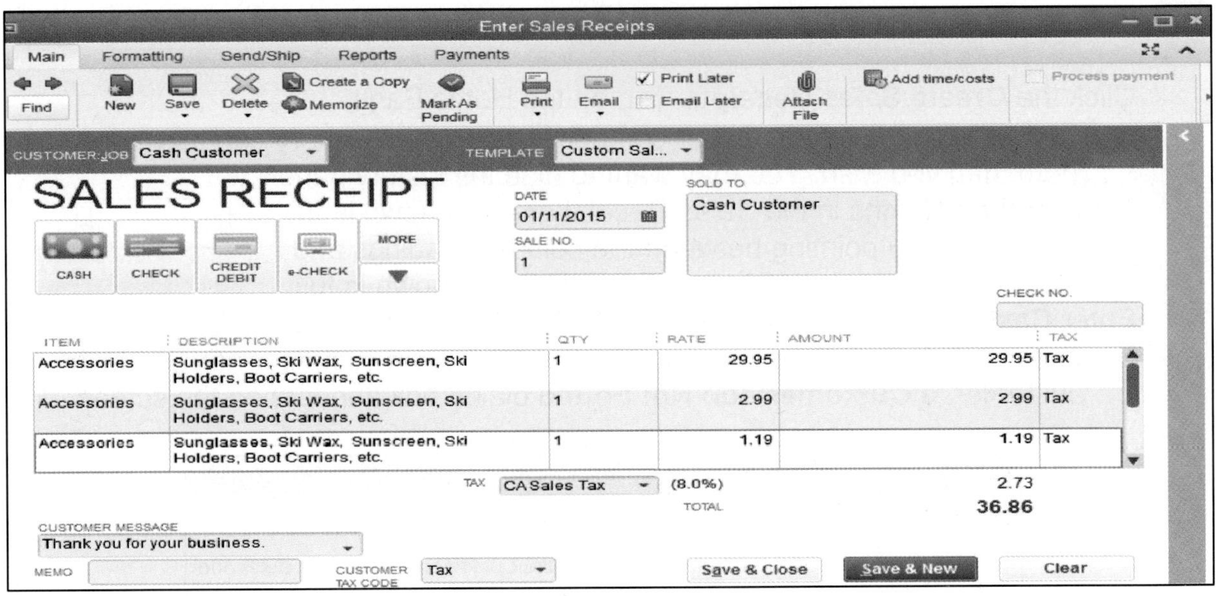

Print the Sales Receipt with lines around each field as previously instructed

Because QuickBooks saves automatically before printing, you may get a Recording Transaction dialog box after printing; if so, always click **Yes**

Click **Save & New**

DEBIT CARDS AND CREDIT CARDS

In QuickBooks, Debit and Credit cards sales are treated the same as a cash sale. When you prepare the Sales Receipt, the payment method is selected by clicking on the Credit/Debit button and the amount of the sale is placed into the Undeposited Funds account. When the actual bank deposit is made, the amount is deposited into the checking or bank account. The bank fees for the cards are deducted directly from the bank account. When a company accepts debit and/or credit cards as payment methods, payments may be processed through the company's merchant account processor, Intuit Payment Solutions, or by enrolling in QuickBooks Merchant Services.

ENTER CREDIT CARD SALE

Complete a Sales Receipt for a customer using a credit card. No matter the brand of credit card, the procedures remain the same.

MEMO

DATE: January 11, 2015

Enter a sale to a Cash Customer using a Visa credit card. The card number is 4123 4567 8901 234 with an expiration date of 01/2018. The sale was for a sled, $199.95. Use the message *Thank you for your business.*

Record the credit card sale

CUSTOMER:JOB is **Cash Customer**
DATE is **01/11/15**
Sale No. should be **2**
Click the **CREDIT/DEBIT** button
In the PAYMENT section of Enter Card Information, click the drop-down list arrow, click **VISA**
Tab to CARD NUMBER and enter **4123 4567 8901 234**
Tab to EXP DATE and enter **01** for the month, press tab, enter **2018** for the year

- On the Enter Card Information screen, notice that the PAYMENT shows VISA; and, depending on the length of the card number, the last three or four digits of the credit card number.

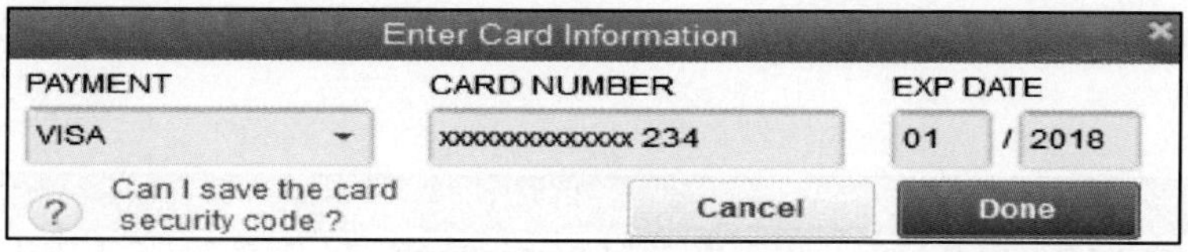

Click **Done** and complete the Sales Receipt as previously instructed

- At the time of writing, QuickBooks had a glitch in the Payment Method screen. Sometimes the CREDIT/DEBIT icon would change to show the Payment Method as VISA and other times the Payment Method would not change from CREDIT/DEBIT. As long as you entered the Payment Method, that is of no concern.

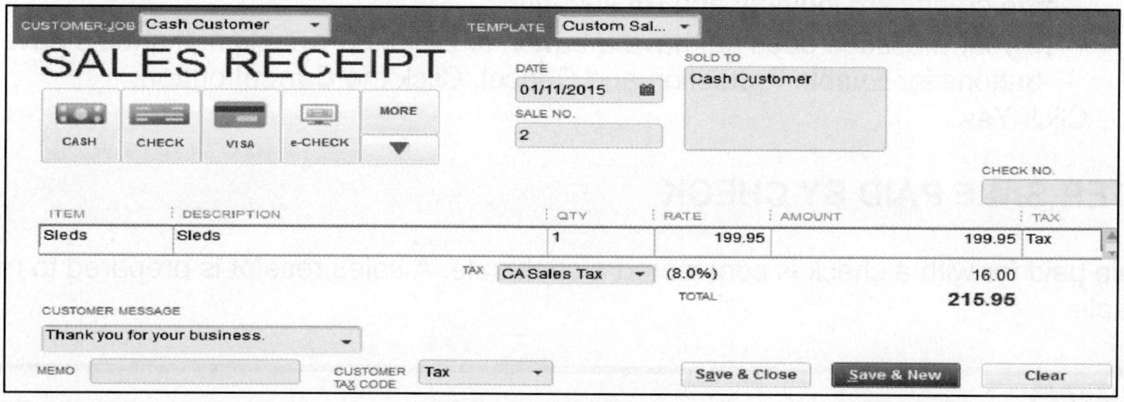

Print the sales receipt with lines around each field
Click **Save & New** to go to Sales Receipt 3

CUSTOMER CREDIT CARD PROTECTION

QuickBooks users who store, process, or transmit customer debit card and/or credit card information in QuickBooks are required to protect that information by complying with the

Payment Card Industry Data Security Standard (PCI DSS). To enable QuickBooks Customer Credit Card Protection, you must create a complex password for you and all others who view complete credit card numbers, which must be changed every 90 days, and the three-digit number near the signature panel must not be stored. If you do not provide protection, your business may be liable for fines and other damages. If you accept credit cards and do not enable protection, you will get a Customer Credit Card Protection dialog box every time you open QuickBooks. The message shown for Customer Credit Card Protection may vary depending on whether or not you have entered credit card information. Since all credit cards used in the text are fictitious and we are not using passwords, click **Disable Protection** once you get the button in the message.

Disable Protection for Credit Cards

Click the **Company** menu, then click **Customer Credit Card Protection**
Since we are not using passwords or actual credit card numbers, click **Disable Protection**

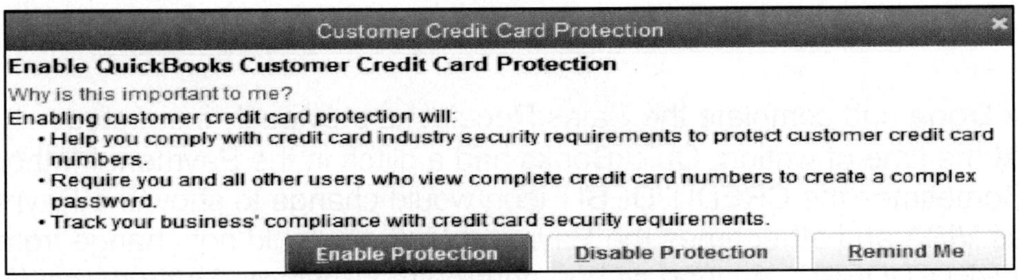

- When you click Disable, you will get a warning screen regarding compliance with the credit card industry and PII security.
- If your message does not have a button to Disable Protection, it should have buttons for Enable Protection and Cancel. Click the **Cancel** button.

Click **Yes**

ENTER SALE PAID BY CHECK

A sale paid for with a check is considered a cash sale. A sales receipt is prepared to record the sale.

MEMO
DATE: January 11, 2015

We do take checks for sales even if a customer is from out of town. Record the sale of 2 pairs of socks at $15.99 each to a Cash Customer using Check 5589. The message for the Sales Receipt is *Thank you for your business.*

With Sales Receipt 3 on the screen, enter the information for the transaction

CUSTOMER:JOB is **Cash Customer**
DATE is **01/11/15**
SALE NO. should be **3**
Click the **CHECK** button on the Sales Receipt
Tab to or click **CHECK NO.**, type **5589**
Complete and print Sales Receipt 3 as previously instructed

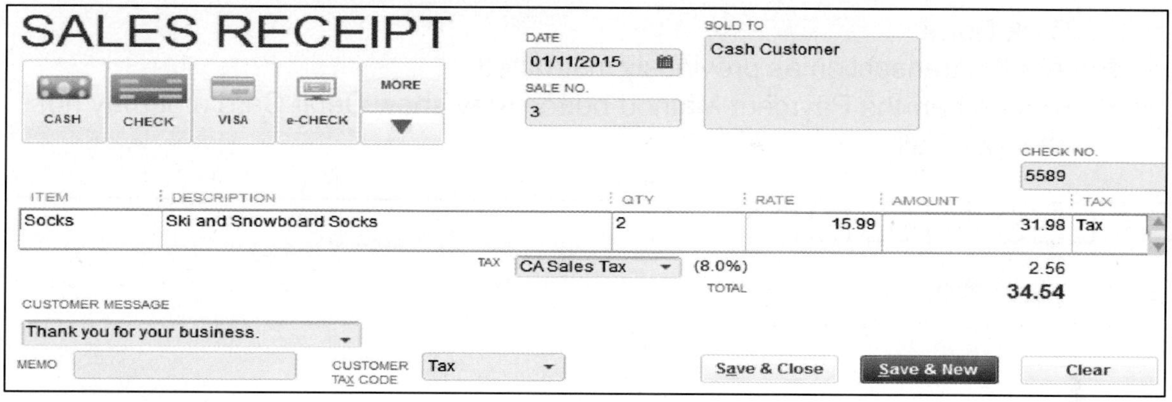

Click **Save & New**

ENTER SALE PAID BY DEBIT CARD

As previously mentioned, when customers use a debit card as payment, it is processed just like a credit card sale.

MEMO

DATE: January 11, 2015

Record Sales Receipt 4 for the sale of a sweater, $89.95, to a Cash Customer using a Debit card. The number is 6789 9123 4567 890 with an expiration date of 02/2018. The message for the Sales Receipt is *Thank you for your business.*

Record the Debit Card purchase by Cash Customer

CUSTOMER:JOB is **Cash Customer**, **DATE** is **01/11/2015**, **SALE NO**. is **4**
Click the button that shows either **CREDIT/DEBIT** or **VISA**

- Sometimes, the previous payment method; such as, VISA, may show on the Payment button other times it stays as CREDIT/DEBIT.

To Complete the Enter Card Information:
For **PAYMENT** click the drop-down list arrow, click **Debit Card**, press Tab
CARD NUMBER is **6789 9123 4567 890**, press Tab
EXP DATE is **02** for the month, tab to the year and enter **2018**

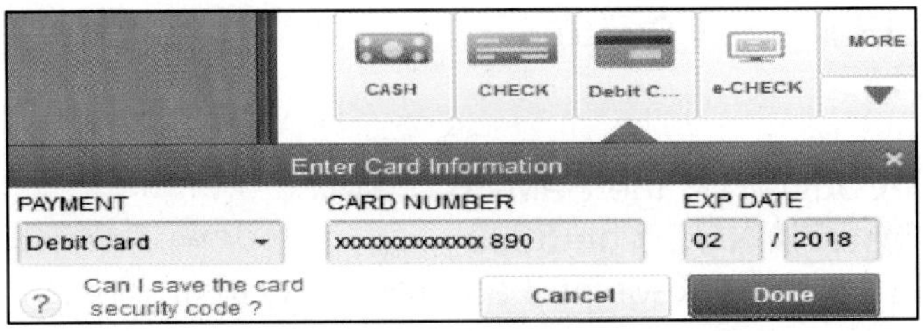

Click **Done**

Record the transaction as previously instructed

- Remember, the Payment Method button may show Debit Card or it may not change at all.

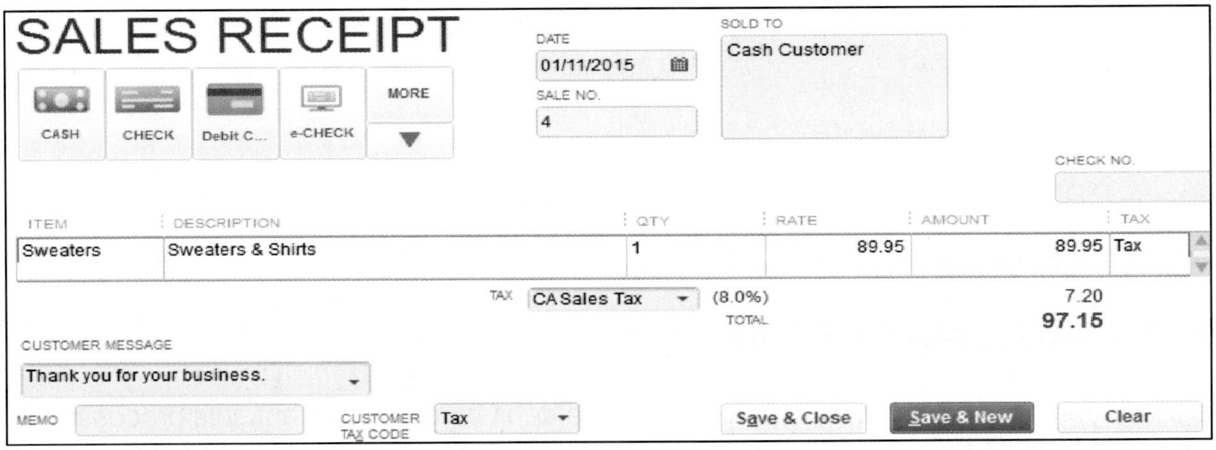

Click **Save & New**

ENTER ADDITIONAL CASH SALES TRANSACTIONS

MEMO

DATE: January 12, 2015

After a record snowfall, the store is really busy. Use Cash Customer as the customer name. Record the following cash, check, credit card, and debit card sales:

Sales Receipt 5—Cash Customer used Check 196 to purchase a ski parka, $249.95, and ski pants, $129.95.

Sales Receipt 6—Cash Customer used a Debit card number 6543 2109 8765 432 with an expiration date of 03/2018 to purchase a snowboard, $389.95, and snowboard bindings, $189.95.

Sales Receipt 7—Cash Customer purchased a pair of gloves for $89.95 and paid cash.

Sales Receipt 8—Cash Customer purchased a pair of snowboard boots for $229.95 using Master Card number 5432 1234 5678 910 with an expiration date of 04/2018.

Repeat the procedures used previously to record the transactions listed above

- Use the date 01/12/2015 (or the year you have used previously).
- For Sales Receipt 8, click the Payment Method button that says either CREDIT/DEBIT or DEBIT Card, click the drop-down list arrow and click MasterCard, enter the card number, and expiration date. Notice that the button next to e-CHECK changes to MasterC…
- Always use the Item List to determine the appropriate sales items for billing.
- Use **Thank you for your business.** as the CUSTOMER MESSAGE for these sales receipts.
- Print each Sales Receipt immediately after entering the information for it.
- If you get a Merchant Service message, click **Not Now**.
- Click **Save & Close** after you have entered and printed Sales Receipt 8.

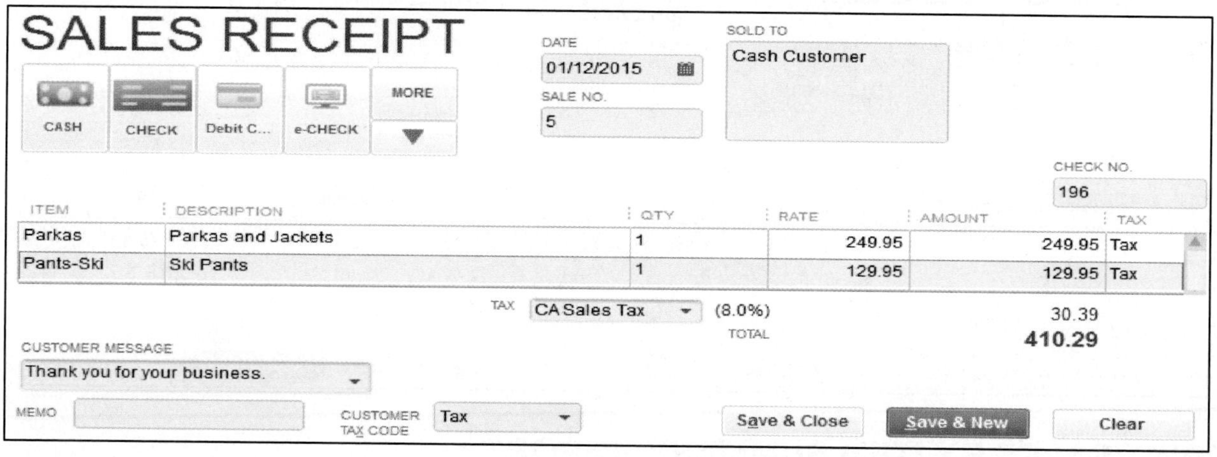

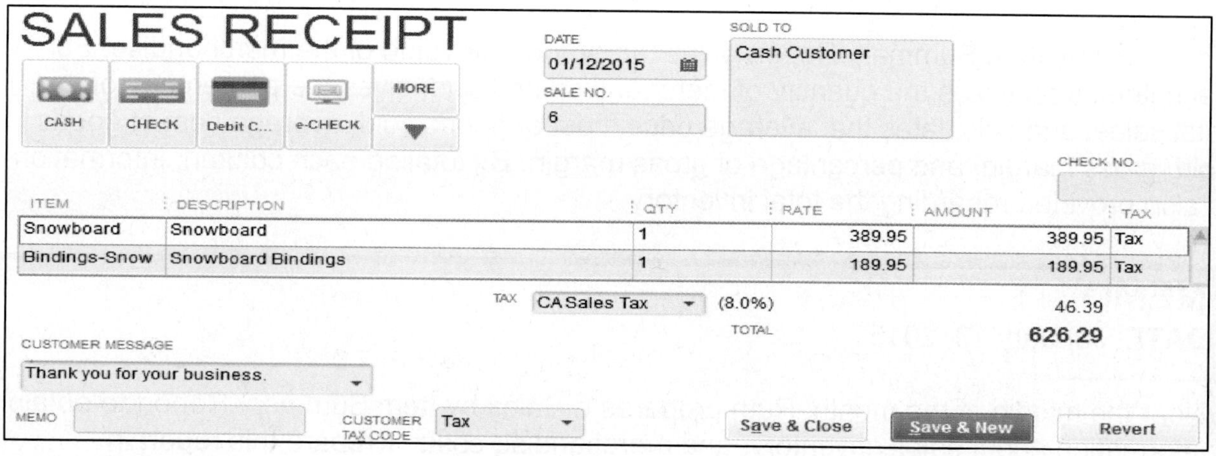

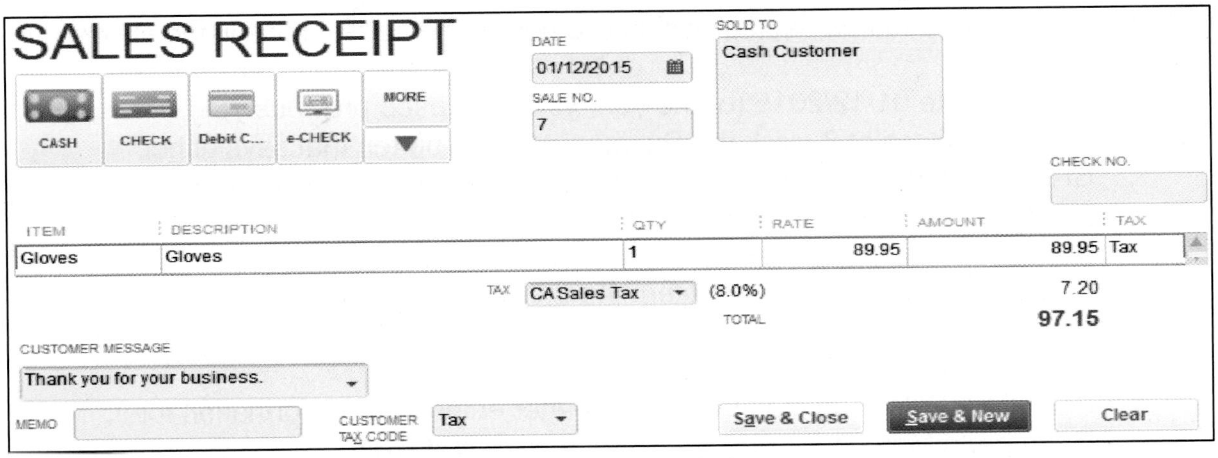

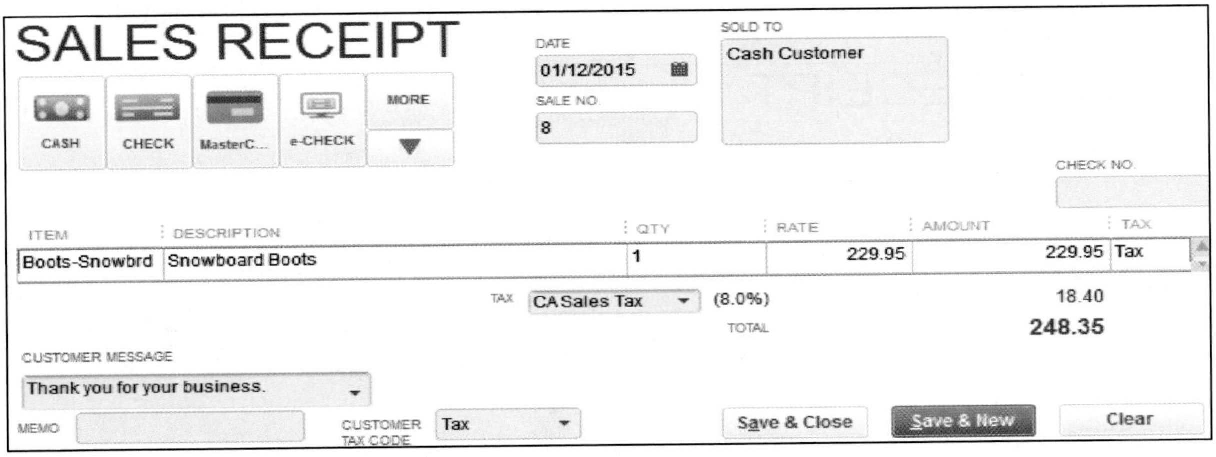

PRINT SALES BY ITEM SUMMARY REPORT

The Sales by Item Summary Report gives the amount or value of the merchandise. For each item, it analyzes the quantity of merchandise on hand, gives the percentage of the total sales, and calculates the: average price, cost of goods sold, average cost of goods sold, gross margin, and percentage of gross margin. By totaling each column, information is also provided regarding the total inventory.

MEMO
DATE: January 13, 2015

Near the middle of the month, Ruth prepares a Sales by Item Summary Report to obtain information about sales, inventory, and merchandise costs. Prepare this report in landscape orientation for 1/1/2015-1/13/2015. Adjust the widths of the columns so the report prints on one page without selecting the print option *Fit report to one page wide.*

Prepare the Sales by Item Summary report

Click **Reports** on the menu bar, point to **Sales**, and click **Sales by Item Summary**
The report dates are From **010115** To **011315**
Tab to generate the report
Scroll through the report
Click **Print**, select **Orientation: Landscape**
Click **Preview**, click **Next Page**

- Notice that the report does not fit on one page wide.

Click **Close** to close the Preview, and click **Cancel** to return to the report
Position the cursor on the diamond between columns

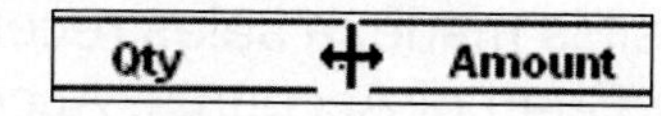

Drag to resize the columns

- The names of the column headings should appear in full and should not have ... as part of the heading.
- If columns are really large, Qty for example, make them smaller.

If you get a **Resize Columns** dialog box wanting to know if all columns should be the same size, click **No**
When the columns have been resized, click **Print** and **Preview**

5

Your Name Mountain Sports
Sales by Item Summary
January 1 - 13, 2015

	Jan 1 - 13, 15							
	Qty	Amount	% of Sales	Avg Price	COGS	Avg COGS	Gross Margin	Gross Margin %
Inventory								
Accessories	5	127.03	1.4%	25.41	18.30	3.66	108.73	85.6%
Bindings-Skis	7	854.00	9.7%	122.00	525.00	75.00	329.00	38.5%
Bindings-Snow	2	349.94	4%	174.97	150.00	75.00	199.94	57.1%
Boots	0	0.00	0.0%	0.00	0.00	0.00	0.00	0.0%
Boots-Ski	1	250.00	2.8%	250.00	75.00	75.00	175.00	70.0%
Boots-Snowbrd	2	478.95	5.4%	239.48	150.00	75.00	328.95	68.7%
Gloves	2	168.95	1.9%	84.48	30.00	15.00	138.95	82.2%
Hats	1	25.00	0.3%	25.00	8.00	8.00	17.00	68.0%
Helmets	5	349.75	4%	69.95	140.00	28.00	209.75	60%
Pants-Ski	2	258.95	2.9%	129.48	60.00	30.00	198.95	76.8%
Parkas	2	498.95	5.6%	249.48	116.66	58.33	382.29	76.6%
Poles-Ski	6	220.00	2.5%	36.67	180.00	30.00	40.00	18.2%
Skis	7	2,519.00	28.5%	359.86	700.00	100.00	1,819.00	72.2%
Sleds	6	799.90	9%	133.32	405.00	67.50	394.90	49.4%
Snowboard	2	889.90	10.1%	444.95	200.00	100.00	689.90	77.5%
Socks	3	47.93	0.5%	15.98	9.00	3.00	38.93	81.2%
Sweaters	2	214.95	2.4%	107.48	50.00	25.00	164.95	76.7%
Toboggans	5	1,149.75	13%	229.95	687.50	137.50	462.25	40.2%
Underwear	1	68.00	0.8%	68.00	8.00	8.00	60.00	88.2%
Total Inventory	61.00	9,270.95	104.8%	151.98	3,512.46	57.58	5,758.49	62.1%
Discounts								
Nonprofit Discount		-423.95	-4.8%					
Total Discounts		-423.95	-4.8%					
TOTAL	61	8,847.00	100.0%	145.03		57.58		

When the report fits on one page wide, print and close the report

CORRECT AND PRINT SALES RECEIPT

QuickBooks makes correcting errors user friendly. When an error is discovered in a transaction such as a cash sale, you can simply return to the form where the transaction was recorded and correct the error. Thus, to correct a sales receipt, you could click Customers on the menu bar, click Enter Sales Receipts, click the Previous or Back arrow until you found the appropriate sales receipt, and then correct the error. Since cash or checks received for cash sales are held in the Undeposited Funds account until the bank deposit is made, a sales receipt can be accessed through the Undeposited Funds account in the Chart of Accounts. Accessing the receipt in this manner allows you to see all the transactions entered in the account for Undeposited Funds.

When a correction for a sale is made, QuickBooks not only changes the form, it also changes all Journal and account entries for the transaction to reflect the correction. QuickBooks then allows a corrected sales receipt to be printed.

MEMO
DATE: January 13, 2015

After reviewing transaction information, you realize that the date for Sales Receipt 1 was entered incorrectly. Change the date to 1/8/2015.

Use the Undeposited Funds account register to correct the error in the memo above, and print a corrected Sales Receipt

Open the **Chart of Accounts**, use the keyboard shortcut **Ctrl+A**
Double-click **Undeposited Funds**

- The register maintains a record of all the transactions recorded within the Undeposited Funds account.

Click anywhere in the transaction for **RCPT 1**

- Look at the **REF/TYPE** column to see the type of transaction.
- The number in the REF column indicates the number of the sales receipt or the customer's check number.
- Type shows **RCPT** for a sales receipt.

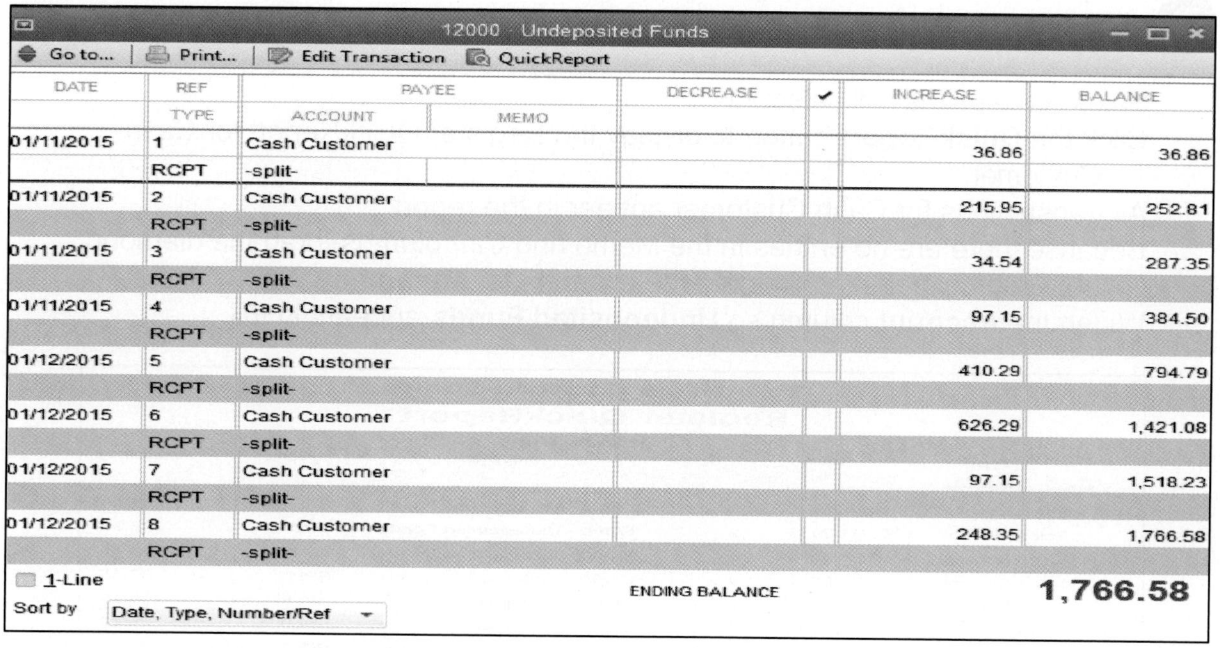
12000 · Undeposited Funds
Go to... | Print... | Edit Transaction | QuickReport
DATE | REF / TYPE | PAYEE / ACCOUNT | MEMO | DECREASE | ✔ | INCREASE | BALANCE
01/11/2015 | 1 RCPT | Cash Customer -split- | 36.86 | 36.86
01/11/2015 | 2 RCPT | Cash Customer -split- | 215.95 | 252.81
01/11/2015 | 3 RCPT | Cash Customer -split- | 34.54 | 287.35
01/11/2015 | 4 RCPT | Cash Customer -split- | 97.15 | 384.50
01/12/2015 | 5 RCPT | Cash Customer -split- | 410.29 | 794.79
01/12/2015 | 6 RCPT | Cash Customer -split- | 626.29 | 1,421.08
01/12/2015 | 7 RCPT | Cash Customer -split- | 97.15 | 1,518.23
01/12/2015 | 8 RCPT | Cash Customer -split- | 248.35 | 1,766.58
1-Line
Sort by Date, Type, Number/Ref
ENDING BALANCE 1,766.58

Click **Edit Transaction** or double-click the transaction

- The sales receipt appears on the screen.

Tab to or click **DATE** field, and change the Date to **01/08/15**

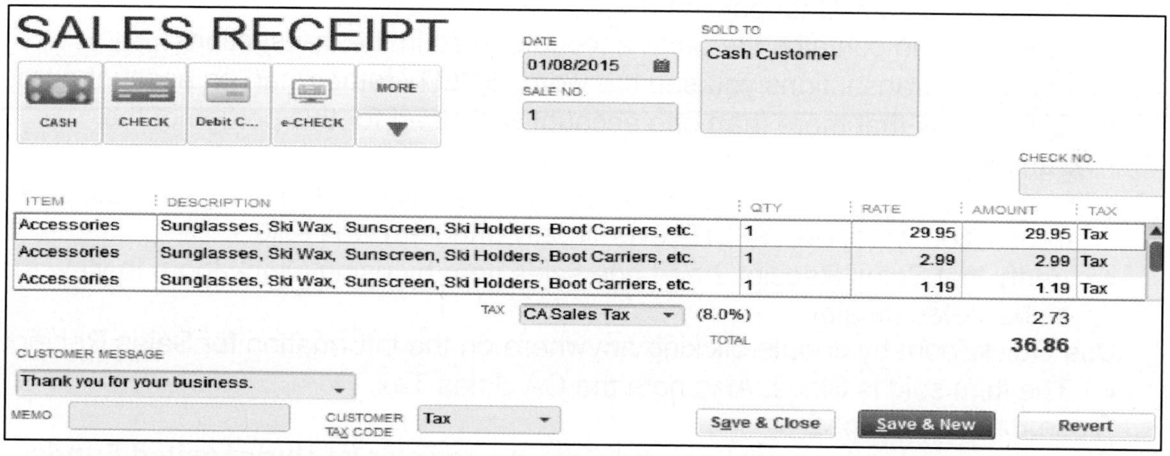

Print the corrected sales receipt as previously instructed
Click **Yes** on the **Recording Transactions** dialog box, click **Save & Close**
Return to the **Register for Undeposited Funds** do not close the register

VIEW AND ANALYZE CASH CUSTOMER QUICKREPORT

After editing the sales receipt and returning to the register, you may get a detailed report regarding the customer's transactions by clicking the QuickReport button. If you use Cash Customer for all cash sales, a QuickReport will be for all the transactions of Cash Customer.

Prepare a QuickReport for Cash Customer

Sales Receipt 1 is still selected
Click the **QuickReport** button to display the Register QuickReport for Cash Customer
All transactions for Cash Customer appear in the report
Because there are no entries in the Memo and Clr columns, drag the diamond between columns to eliminate the columns for **Memo** and **Clr**
Widen the **Account** column so **Undeposited Funds** appears in full

Your Name Mountain Sports
Register QuickReport
All Transactions

Type	Date	Num	Account	Split	Amount
Cash Customer					
Sales Receipt	01/08/2015	1	12000 · Undeposited Funds	-SPLIT-	36.86
Sales Receipt	01/11/2015	2	12000 · Undeposited Funds	-SPLIT-	215.95
Sales Receipt	01/11/2015	3	12000 · Undeposited Funds	-SPLIT-	34.54
Sales Receipt	01/11/2015	4	12000 · Undeposited Funds	-SPLIT-	97.15
Sales Receipt	01/12/2015	5	12000 · Undeposited Funds	-SPLIT-	410.29
Sales Receipt	01/12/2015	6	12000 · Undeposited Funds	-SPLIT-	626.29
Sales Receipt	01/12/2015	7	12000 · Undeposited Funds	-SPLIT-	97.15
Sales Receipt	01/12/2015	8	12000 · Undeposited Funds	-SPLIT-	248.35
Total Cash Customer					1,766.58
TOTAL					1,766.58

- Notice that the date for Sales Receipt 1 has been changed to **01/08/2015**.

The account used is Undeposited Funds
The Split column contains the other accounts used in the transactions

- For all the transactions you see the word **-SPLIT-** rather than an account name.
- Split means that more than one account was used for this portion of the transaction.
- In addition to a variety of sales items, sales tax was charged on all sales, so each transaction will show **-SPLIT-** even if only one item was sold.
- Verify that Sales Receipt 2 had one sales item by using QuickZoom to view the actual sales receipt

Use QuickZoom by double-clicking anywhere on the information for Sales Receipt 2

- The item sold is Sleds. Also note the CA Sales Tax.

Close **Sales Receipt 2**
Close the report without printing, and close the register for **Undeposited Funds**
Do not close the **Chart of Accounts**

VIEW SALES TAX PAYABLE REGISTER

The Sales Tax Payable Register shows a detailed listing of all transactions with sales tax. The option of 1-Line may be selected in order to view each transaction on one line rather than the standard two lines. The account register provides information regarding the vendor and the account used for the transaction.

View the register for the Sales Tax Payable account

Double-click **2200-Sales Tax Payable** in the Chart of Accounts
Once the register is displayed, click **1-Line** to view the transactions

- The amount of sales tax for each sale, whether cash or credit, in which sales tax was collected is displayed.

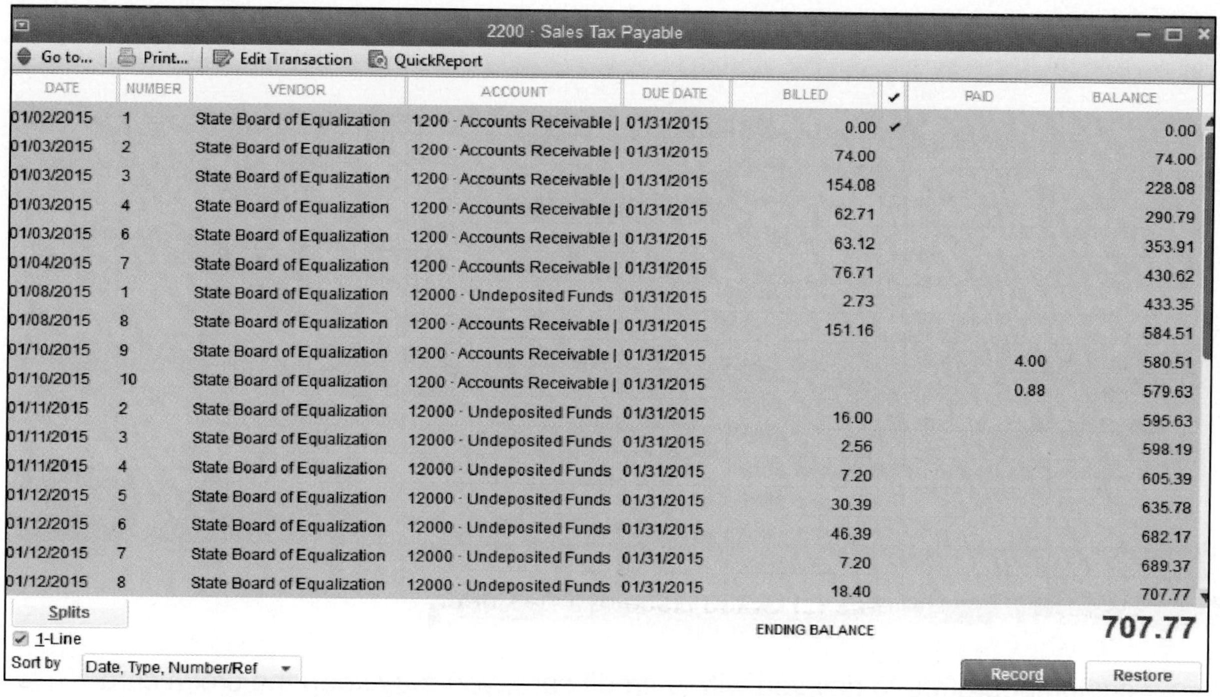

2200 · Sales Tax Payable

Go to... | Print... | Edit Transaction | QuickReport

DATE	NUMBER	VENDOR	ACCOUNT	DUE DATE	BILLED	✓	PAID	BALANCE
01/02/2015	1	State Board of Equalization	1200 · Accounts Receivable	01/31/2015	0.00	✓		0.00
01/03/2015	2	State Board of Equalization	1200 · Accounts Receivable	01/31/2015	74.00			74.00
01/03/2015	3	State Board of Equalization	1200 · Accounts Receivable	01/31/2015	154.08			228.08
01/03/2015	4	State Board of Equalization	1200 · Accounts Receivable	01/31/2015	62.71			290.79
01/03/2015	6	State Board of Equalization	1200 · Accounts Receivable	01/31/2015	63.12			353.91
01/04/2015	7	State Board of Equalization	1200 · Accounts Receivable	01/31/2015	76.71			430.62
01/08/2015	1	State Board of Equalization	12000 · Undeposited Funds	01/31/2015	2.73			433.35
01/08/2015	8	State Board of Equalization	1200 · Accounts Receivable	01/31/2015	151.16			584.51
01/10/2015	9	State Board of Equalization	1200 · Accounts Receivable	01/31/2015			4.00	580.51
01/10/2015	10	State Board of Equalization	1200 · Accounts Receivable	01/31/2015			0.88	579.63
01/11/2015	2	State Board of Equalization	12000 · Undeposited Funds	01/31/2015	16.00			595.63
01/11/2015	3	State Board of Equalization	12000 · Undeposited Funds	01/31/2015	2.56			598.19
01/11/2015	4	State Board of Equalization	12000 · Undeposited Funds	01/31/2015	7.20			605.39
01/12/2015	5	State Board of Equalization	12000 · Undeposited Funds	01/31/2015	30.39			635.78
01/12/2015	6	State Board of Equalization	12000 · Undeposited Funds	01/31/2015	46.39			682.17
01/12/2015	7	State Board of Equalization	12000 · Undeposited Funds	01/31/2015	7.20			689.37
01/12/2015	8	State Board of Equalization	12000 · Undeposited Funds	01/31/2015	18.40			707.77

Splits
1-Line
Sort by Date, Type, Number/Ref
ENDING BALANCE 707.77
Record Restore

Close the register for **Sales Tax Payable**, and the **Chart of Accounts**

CUSTOMER CENTER

The Customer Center provides information about individual customers. The customer list shows all of your customers and their Balance Total. As you click each customer, you will see the customer information and transaction details for the individual customer. You may also view transaction details for specific types of transactions by clicking the drop-down list arrow.

View the Customer Center and the information for Cash Customer

Click the **Customers** icon to open the Customer Center; then click **Cash Customer**
Click the drop-down list arrow next to **Show** to see the list of the types of transactions that may be displayed

5

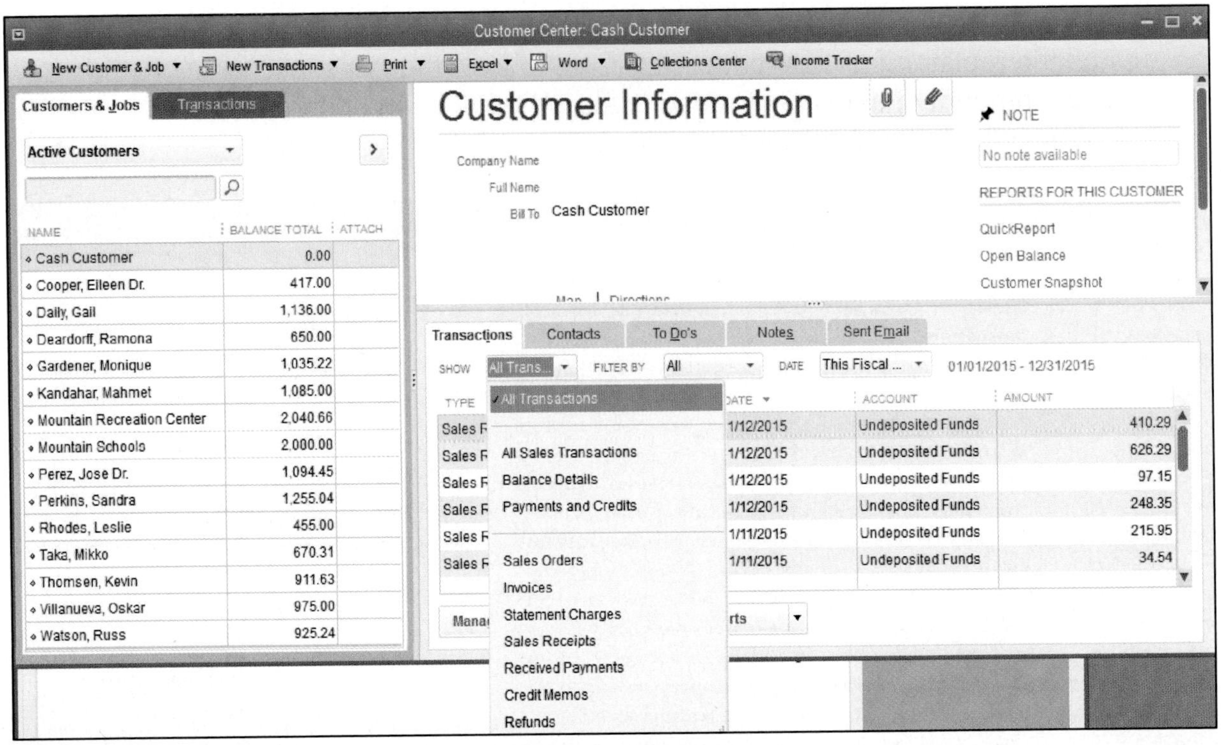

ADD CREDIT CARD TO CUSTOMER RECORD

If your customer prefers to pay you with a credit card, you may keep the credit card information in the Payment Settings section of the customer record. In addition, you may also mark the credit card to be used for online payments (not available for use in training).

Once you add a credit card to a customer's account, you should Enable Protection for credit cards. If you have not done so, every time you close and then reopen QuickBooks, you will get a Customer Credit Card Protection dialog box. As stated in the earlier section regarding Disabling Credit Card Protection, all cards used in the text are fictitious and we are not using passwords so if you get the dialog box, click **Disable Protection**.

Add Credit Card information for Monique Gardener

Double-click **Gardener, Monique** in the Customer Center
Click the **Payment Settings** tab
Since you are entering Monique's credit card information, click the drop-down list arrow for **PREFERRED PAYMENT METHOD**, and click **MasterCard**
Enter CREDIT CARD NO. **5123 9876 4567 123**, the EXP. DATE of **06/2019**
Press the **Tab** key three times to automatically enter the NAME ON CARD, ADDRESS, and ZIP/POSTAL CODE

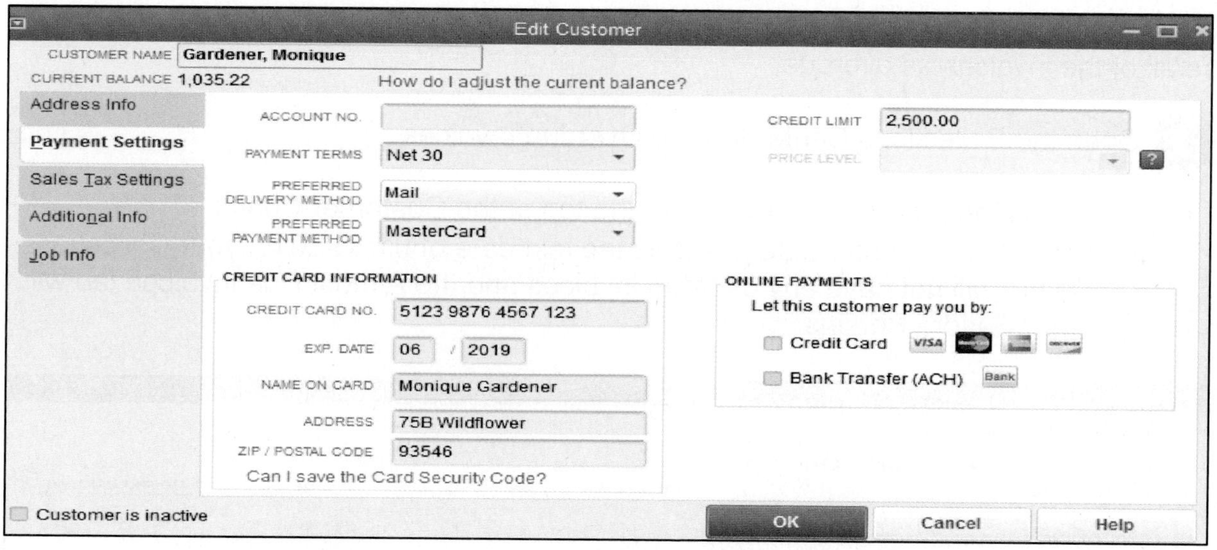

- For security reasons, the Card Security Code (CSC) may not be saved.
- Note the Online Payments section. If you subscribe to Intuit QuickBooks Payments, you may accept credit card and bank transfers (ACH) payments from online customers. You are charged a fee for each payment collected online. This is not available for use in training.

Click **OK** to save the credit card information for Monique

Do not close the Customer Center

5

SELECT COLLECTIONS CENTER PREFERENCES

QuickBooks has a Collection Center that will display Overdue and Almost Due invoices.

Set the Preferences to use the Collection Center

Click **Edit** on the Menu Bar, click **Preferences**, click **Sales & Customers**, click the **Company Preferences** tab

- On the Company Preferences tab, look at the section for COLLECTIONS CENTER; if it is not marked, click **Enable Collections Center** to select the feature. If it is marked, do not click it.

Click **OK** on the Preferences

- If you get a Warning screen to close all its open windows, click **OK**.
- If you got a warning screen, click the **Home** icon to redisplay the Home Page, and click the **Customers** icon to reopen the Customer Center.

VIEW COLLECTIONS CENTER

To use the Collection Center, you must go to the Customer Center and click the Collections Center icon. The Collections Center is date driven based on the date of your computer and the due date of the transactions. Since your computer date will not match the text, you will see all of the invoices as overdue.

Open the Collections Center to view Overdue Invoices

Click the **Collections Center** icon at the top of the Customer Center

- When the computer date matches the text date of 01/13/2015, your Collections Center will not have any overdue invoices and the Almost Due invoices tab will show Sandra Perkins

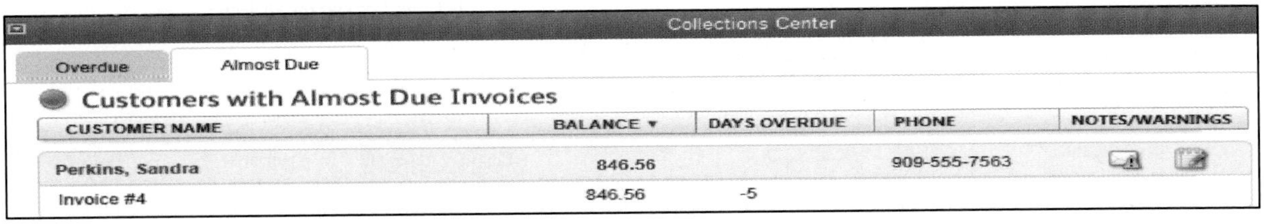

- Since your computer date is not 01/13/2015, you will see all invoices as overdue. The days overdue is determined by subtracting the due date from the actual date of your computer. The following screen shot shows the Collections Center as it would appear on 02/05/2015.

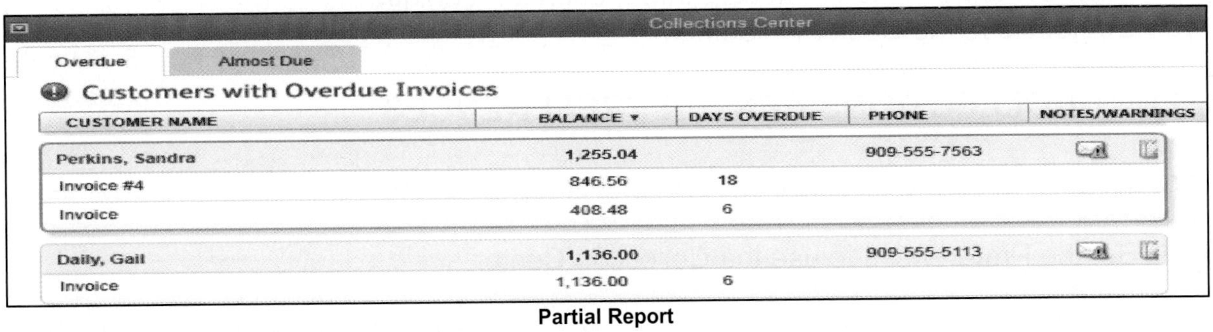

Partial Report

- Note the Invoice for Sandra Perkins

Close the **Collections Center**, do <u>not</u> close the Customer Center

VIEW INCOME TRACKER

QuickBooks has an Income Tracker that provides information about all forms of income. The Income Tracker uses the date of your computer to determine whether an invoice is Open or Overdue. The amounts for Unbilled Sales Orders, Unpaid Invoices, Overdue receipts, and Paid amounts for the past 30 days are displayed in colored blocks at the top of the Income Tracker. You may get information on all Customers or a single customer. You may display all types of income transactions or select an individual type. You may display all income transactions or just the ones that are open, paid, or overdue. You may also select a date range of transactions to display.

For each transaction, information is provided regarding the customer name, type of transaction, the business document number, the transaction date, the due date, the amount, the open balance, the date that you last sent an email, the status of the transaction, and an action column where you can print or email the row of information regarding a transaction.

View the Income Tracker

Click the **Income Tracker** icon at the top of the Customer Center

- May need to adjust column widths to display information in full
- Look at the transaction for Sandra Perkins and note that it is due on January 18, 2015.
- The screen shot was taken with a computer date of 01/13/2015. Since your computer date is not the same, your Income Tracker will show all invoices as Overdue.

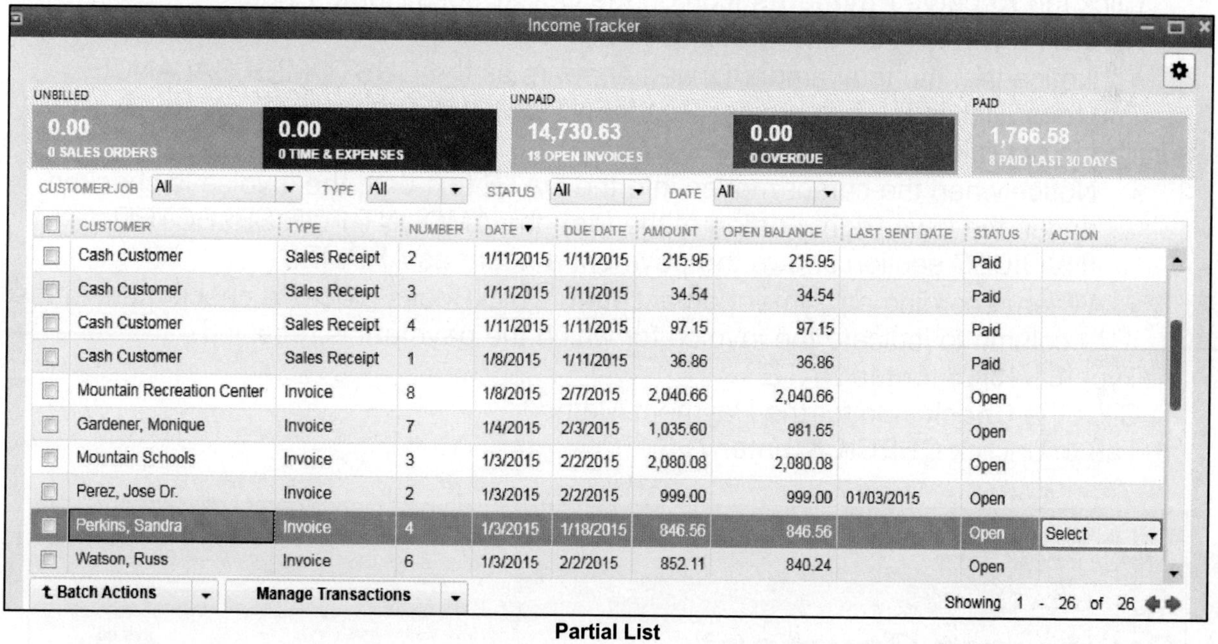

CUSTOMER	TYPE	NUMBER	DATE	DUE DATE	AMOUNT	OPEN BALANCE	LAST SENT DATE	STATUS	ACTION
Cash Customer	Sales Receipt	2	1/11/2015	1/11/2015	215.95	215.95		Paid	
Cash Customer	Sales Receipt	3	1/11/2015	1/11/2015	34.54	34.54		Paid	
Cash Customer	Sales Receipt	4	1/11/2015	1/11/2015	97.15	97.15		Paid	
Cash Customer	Sales Receipt	1	1/8/2015	1/11/2015	36.86	36.86		Paid	
Mountain Recreation Center	Invoice	8	1/8/2015	2/7/2015	2,040.66	2,040.66		Open	
Gardener, Monique	Invoice	7	1/4/2015	2/3/2015	1,035.60	981.65		Open	
Mountain Schools	Invoice	3	1/3/2015	2/2/2015	2,080.08	2,080.08		Open	
Perez, Jose Dr.	Invoice	2	1/3/2015	2/2/2015	999.00	999.00	01/03/2015	Open	
Perkins, Sandra	Invoice	4	1/3/2015	1/18/2015	846.56	846.56		Open	Select
Watson, Russ	Invoice	6	1/3/2015	2/2/2015	852.11	840.24		Open	

Partial List

Close the Income Tracker and the Customer Center

CUSTOMER PAYMENTS ON ACCOUNT

As previously noted, whenever money is received, whether it is for a cash sale or when customers pay the amount they owe on account, QuickBooks uses the account called *Undeposited Funds* to record the receipt of funds. The money stays in the account until a bank deposit is made. The amount is then transferred into Checking. When you start to record a payment on account, you see the customer's balance, any credits or discounts, and a complete list of unpaid invoices. QuickBooks automatically applies the payment received to a matching amount or to the oldest invoice.

If a customer owes you money for a purchase made "on account" (an invoice) you record the payment in Receive Payments. If a customer paid you at the time the purchase was made, a sales receipt was prepared and the amount received was recorded at that time.

RECORD CUSTOMER PAYMENT

MEMO
DATE: January 13, 2015

Record the following receipt of Check 765 for $975 from Oskar Villanueva as payment in full on his account.

Record the payment on account detailed in the Memo

Click the **Receive Payments** icon on the QuickBooks Home Page
RECEIVED FROM is **Villanueva, Oskar**

- Notice that the total amount owed appears as the CUSTOMER BALANCE.

Tab to or click in the text box for **PAYMENT AMOUNT**, enter **975**
Tab to or click in the text box for **DATE**

- Notice when the cursor moves into the **DATE** text box, the invoice is checked, and in the lower-right portion of the form the AMOUNT FOR SELECTED INVOICES section shows the payment amount as APPLIED.
- When recording a payment on account, QuickBooks places a check mark in the √ column to indicate the invoice for which the payment is received.

Type **01/13/15** for the DATE
Click the **Check** icon for the Payment Method
Tab to or click **CHECK #**, enter **765**

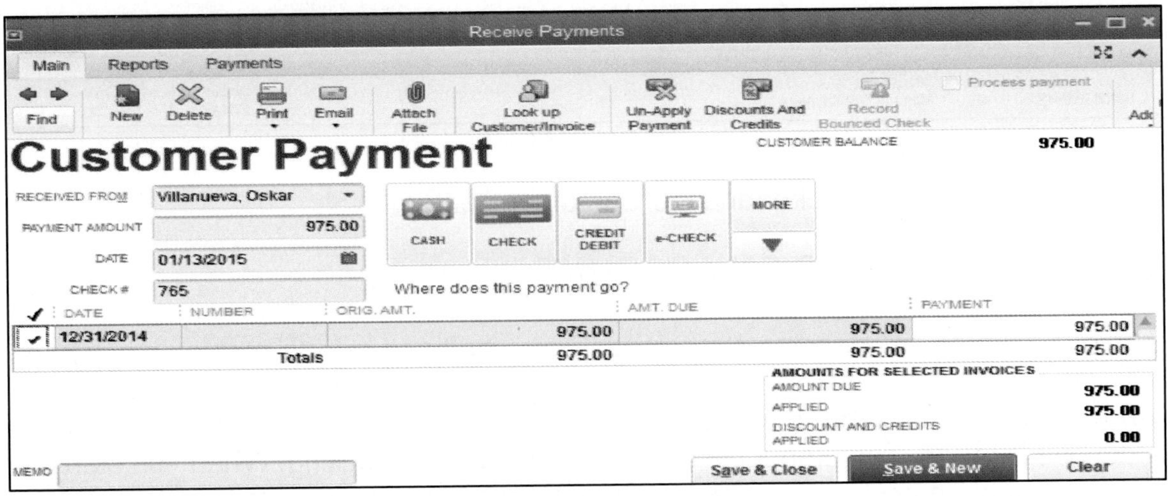

Click the **Print** icon at the top of the Receive Payments screen and print the Payment Receipt

Click the **Next** arrow or **Save & New** to record this payment and advance to the next **Receive Payments** screen

RECORD CREDIT CARD PAYMENT AND USE APPLIED CREDIT

If there are any existing credits (such as a Credit Memo) on an account that have not been applied to the account, they may be applied to a customer's account when a payment is made. If a credit was recorded and applied to an invoice, the total amount due on the invoice will reflect the credit.

> **MEMO**
> **DATE:** January 13, 2015
>
> Monique Gardener used her MasterCard for $1,035.22 to pay her account in full. Apply unused credits when recording her payment on account.

Record the credit card payment by Monique Gardener and apply her unused credits

RECEIVED FROM is **Gardener, Monique**

- Notice the Customer Balance shows the total amount owed by the customer.
- In the center portion of the **Receive Payments** screen, notice the list of unpaid invoices for Monique Gardener.
- Monique has her MasterCard recorded in her account. Notice that the Credit/Debit button automatically changed to show MasterC…

Tab to or click **AMOUNT**, enter **1035.22**

Tab to or click **DATE**, type the date **01/13/15**

Click the **MasterC…** icon for the Payment Method

- Note that the information for Monique's MasterCard was automatically inserted.

Click **Done**

- Notice the ORIG. AMT. of the two transactions, the AMT. DUE, and the PAYMENT amounts. The AMT. DUE for Invoice 7 shows 981.65 this reflects the application of the Credit Memo 9 for $53.95 that was previously recorded.

5

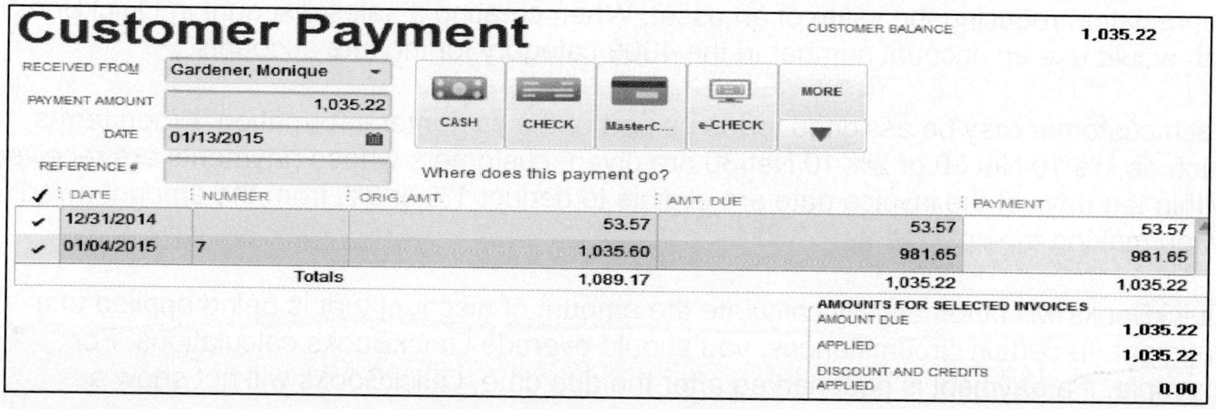

To view Monique's credits, click the line for Invoice 7

Click the **Discounts and Credits** icon on the Receive Payments Icon bar

- The Discounts and Credits screen is shown on the screen.

Click the **Credits** tab

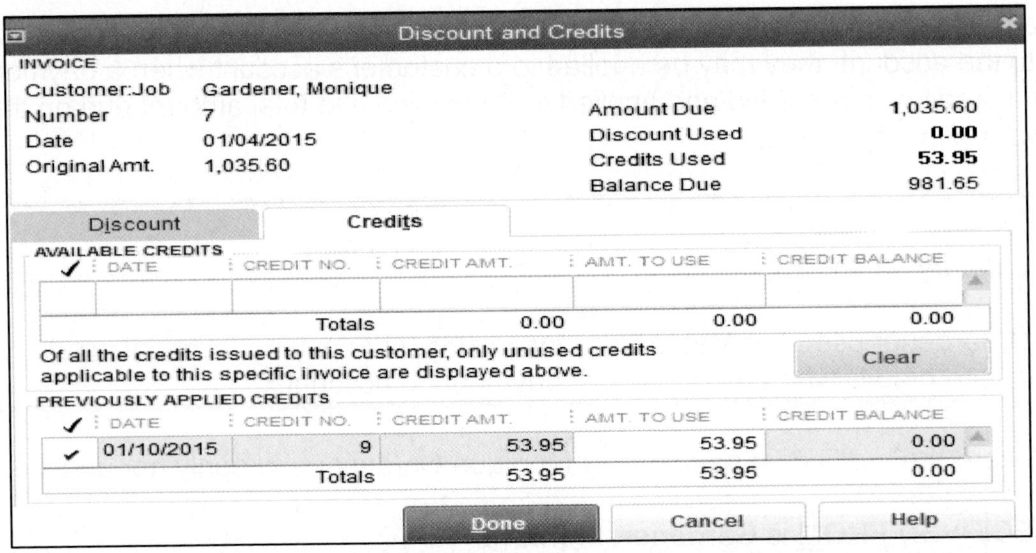

- If you did not apply a credit directly to an invoice, the Available Credits will show the information for CREDIT NO. 9. You may apply the credit now by clicking in the √ column in the AVAILABLE CREDITS section.

Click the **Done** button

Print the Payment Receipt

Click **Next** or **Save & New**

RECORD PAYMENT AND APPLY DISCOUNT

Giving customers a sales discount lowers the income. However, the advantage of making a sales discount available is that it encourages customers to make their payments in a more timely manner and brings in cash to the business. Sales discounts function as a contra revenue account by decreasing total income. This is similar in theory to accumulated depreciation reducing the value of an asset. When creating a sales discount in QuickBooks you would use an account number in the 4000 category for income accounts.

Each customer may be assigned terms as part of the customer information. When terms such as 1% 10 Net 30 or 2% 10 Net 30 are given, customers whose payments are received within ten days of the invoice date are eligible to deduct 1% or 2% from the amount owed when making their payments.

QuickBooks will automatically calculate the amount of discount that is being applied to a payment. In certain circumstances, you should override QuickBooks calculations. For example, if a payment is postmarked after the due date, QuickBooks will not show a discount. You may change this by clicking the Discounts and Credits icon and entering the discount amount yourself. To do this, use QuickMath: key in the total amount owed in the Amount of Discount text box, press * to multiply, key in .02 (the discount percentage), and press Enter. The Balance Due is automatically calculated by QuickBooks.

Another instance in which an override is essential is if a customer has made a return. QuickBooks always calculates the amount of the discount on the original Amount Due. To override this, subtract the amount of the return from the original amount due to determine the actual amount owed. Then, calculate the discount amount by multiplying the corrected amount due by the discount percentage. For example: Using a transaction with an Amount Due of $500, a Credit Used of $50, and Discount Terms of 2%, calculating the 2% discount can have different results. If you allow QuickBooks to calculate the discount, (2% of $500 = $10) The Balance Due would be: $500 - $50 (return) - $10 (discount) = $440 Balance Due. More accurately, the amount due of $500 less a return of $50 equals a corrected amount due of $450. A 2% discount on $450 is $9, which leaves a Balance Due of $441.

MEMO

DATE: January 13, 2015

Received Check 981-13 for $2,020.25 from Mountain Recreation Center as full payment for Invoice 8. Record the payment and the 1% discount for early payment under the invoice terms of 1% 10 Net 30.

Record the receipt of the check and apply the discount to the above transaction

RECEIVED FROM is **Mountain Recreation Center**

- The total amount owed, $2,040.66, appears as the CUSTOMER BALANCE.

Enter the **PAYMENT AMOUNT** of **2020.25**

- Notice that this amount is different from the balance of $2,040.66.
- The PAYMENT AMOUNT is entered in the **PAYMENT** column for Invoice 8.
- You will get a message in the UNDERPAYMENT section, which is in the lower-left portion of Receive Payments

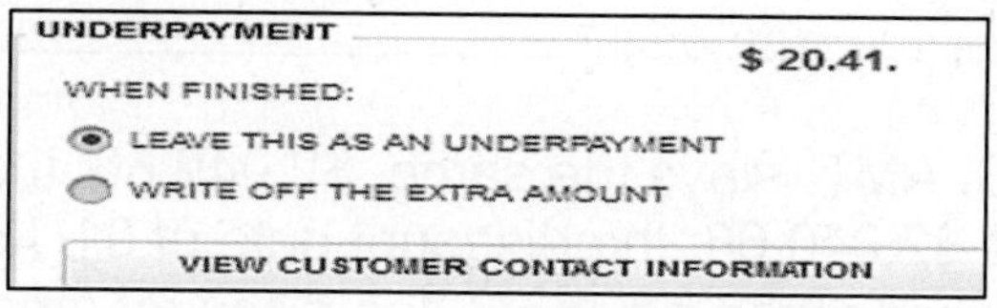

DATE is **011315**

Click the **CHECK** icon for the Payment Method

Tab to or click **CHECK #**, enter **981-13**

Click in the text box for **MEMO** below the UNDERPAYMENT section

Key in **Includes Early Payment Discount**

- Since the column for DISC. DATE is displayed, you will see that the Invoice is being paid within the discount date and is eligible to receive a discount.

Click the **Discounts And Credits** icon on the Receive Payments Icon bar

- Make sure the Discount tab is selected. If not, click the tab.
- QuickBooks displays the 1% discount amount, which was calculated on the total amount due.

Click the drop-down list arrow for **Discount Account**, click **4050 Sales Discounts**

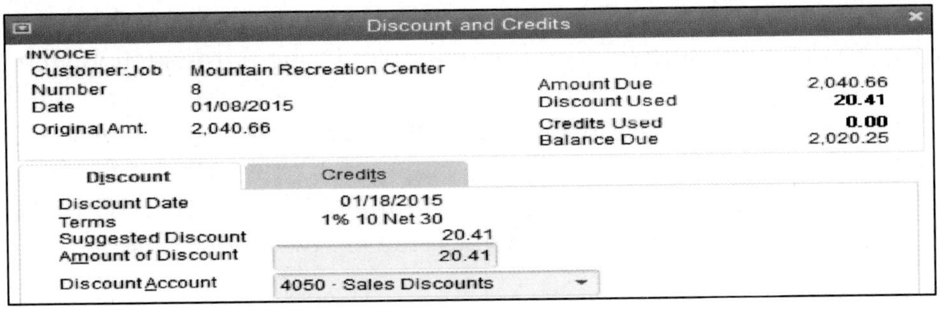

Click the **Done** button at the bottom of the Discounts and Credits screen to apply the discount of $20.41

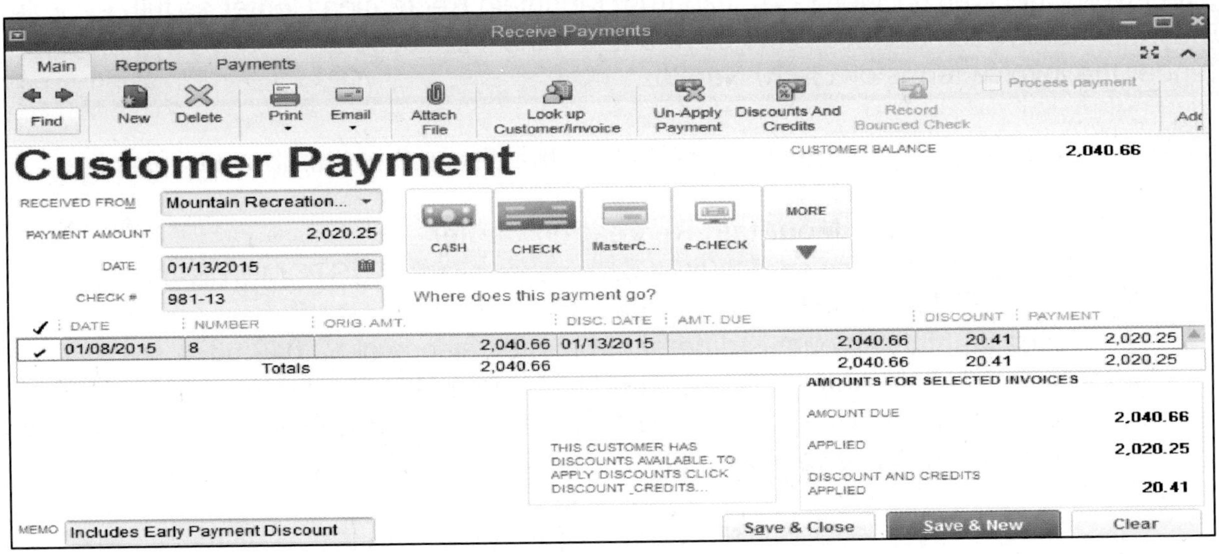

- Notice that ORIG. AMT. stays the same, $2,040.66; the AMT. DUE for Invoice Number 8 shows $2,040.66; the discount date of 01/13/2015 is the date the discount was applied to the payment, the discount amount of $20.41 shows in the DISCOUNT column, and the PAYMENT shows $2,020.25.
- In the area for AMOUNTS FOR SELECTED INVOICES, you will see the AMOUNT DUE, 2,040.66; APPLIED, 2,020.25; and DISCOUNTS AND CREDITS APPLIED, 20.41.
- The Underpayment section no longer appears.

- You may or may not have a message "This Customer has Discounts Available. To Apply Discounts Click Discount_Credits…" Once you save the Customer Payment, the message should disappear.

Print the Payment Receipt
Click the **Next** arrow or **Save & New**

RECORD LATE PAYMENT WITH DISCOUNT

As learned previously, QuickBooks will automatically calculate discounts. If you receive a payment after the due date, QuickBooks will not calculate a discount. The discount must be entered on the Discounts and Credit screen.

> **MEMO**
> **DATE:** January 14, 2015
>
> Received Debit Card Payment dated January 10 and postmarked 1/11 for $2,038.48 from Mountain Schools. Date the payment receipt 01/14/15. Debit Card Number 7658 2358 9854 354, Expiration 09/2016.

5

Record the receipt of the payment and apply the appropriate discounts to the above transactions

Click the **Look up Customer/Invoice** icon on the Receive Payments Icon bar
Click the drop-down list arrow for **Search by** on the Find a Customer/Invoice screen
Click **Customer Name:Job**
Tab to or click in the **Customer** text box, enter **Mountain Schools**
Click the **Search** button
Click the line for **Invoice 3**

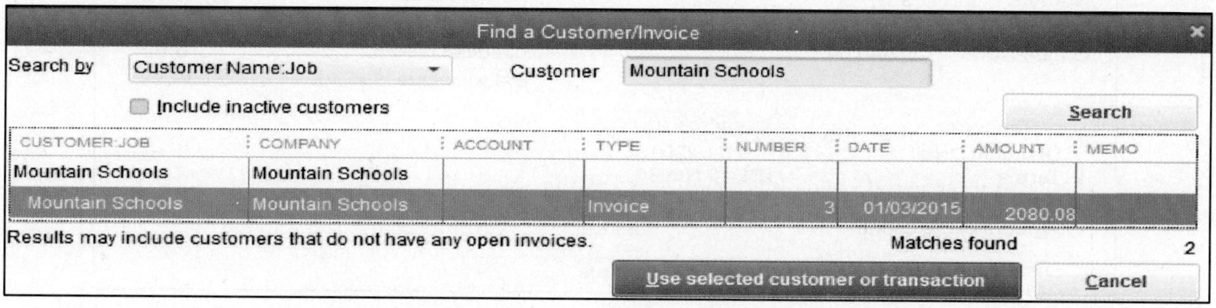

Click the **Use selected customer or transaction** button

- Notice that **Mountain Schools** is shown in RECEIVED FROM and that the PAYMENT AMOUNT shows 2,080.08.

Change the PAYMENT AMOUNT TO **2038.48**
Use the DATE **01/14/2015**

Click the **MasterC...** icon

- The last credit or debit payment received was a MasterCard so QuickBooks shows that on the button.

Click the drop-down list arrow for **PAYMENT**, the click **Debit Card**
Enter the **CARD NUMBER** of **7658 2358 9854 354**, and the **EXP DATE** of **09/2016**
Click **Done**

- Notice that the MasterC... button now shows Debit C...
- Note the UNDERPAYMENT of $41.60.

Click the **Discounts And Credits** icon on the Receive Payments icon bar
Make sure the **Discount** tab is selected

- Note that the Amount Due and the Balance Due are both 2,080.08. The Discount Date shows as 01/13/2015 with Terms of 2% 10 Net 30 and a Suggested Discount is shown as 0.00.
- Even though we are recording the payment after the discount date, the check was postmarked within the discount period. We will apply the discount for early payment to this transaction.
- Since the payment is being recorded after the discount date, you need to calculate and enter the amount of the 2% discount.

Click in the **Amount of Discount** text box, and enter **2080.08,** then press the * (asterisk)

- This opens QuickMath.

Enter **.02**, press **Enter**, press **Tab**

- QuickMath calculates the 2% discount of $41.60, enters it into the text box, and shows the amount as Discount Used at the top of the Discounts and Credits screen.
- Once the Discount Used is applied, the Balance Due shows 2,038.48.

The Discount Account is **4050 Sales Discounts**

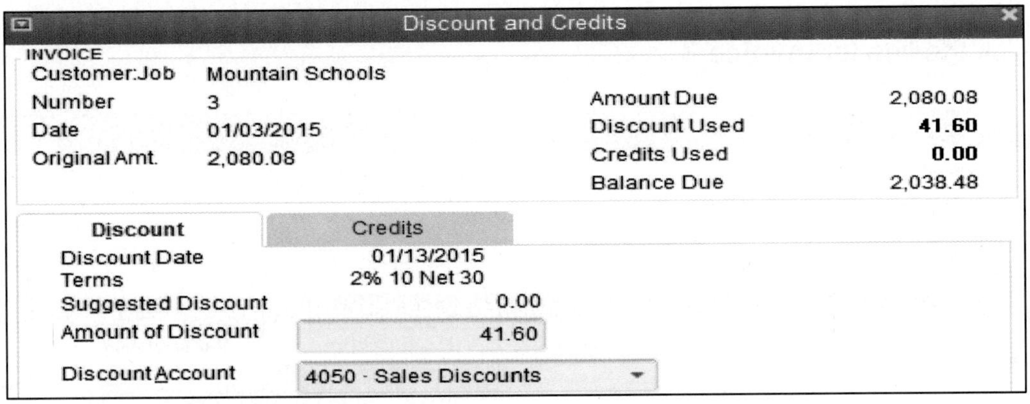

Click **Done** and return to the Customer Payment
Enter the MEMO: **Includes Early Payment Discount**

- Notice that the Customer Payment now shows a DISC. DATE of 01/14/2015 and that the AMOUNTS FOR SELECTED INVOICES includes the DISCOUNT AND CREDITS APPLIED of $41.60.

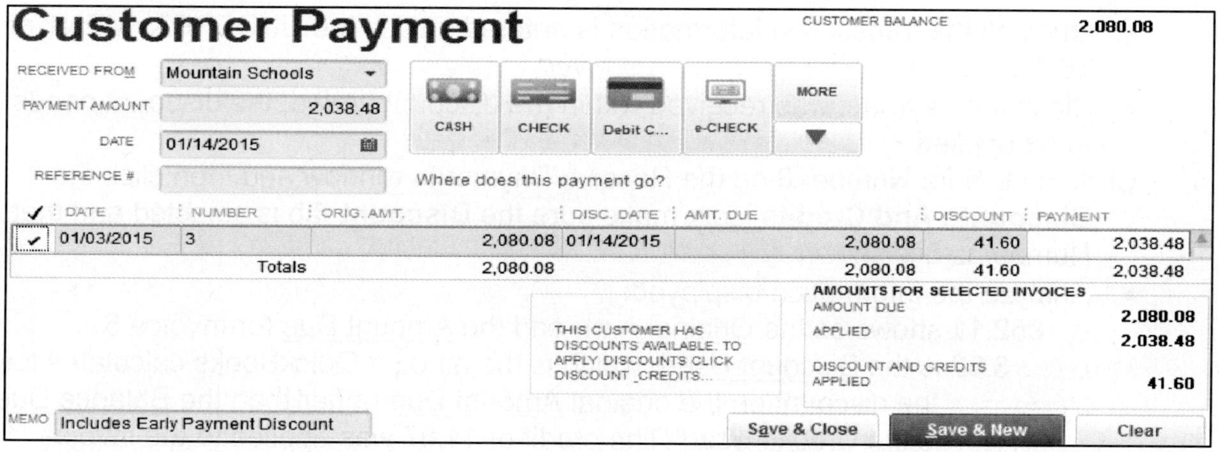

Print the Customer Payment and then click **Save & Close**

RECORD LATE PAYMENT WITH CREDIT AND DISCOUNT

Sometimes, QuickBooks' automatic calculation of a discount is not correct. For example when a payment is received and a return has been made. QuickBooks will apply the discount to the original amount owed, which gives a discount on returned merchandise. In this instance, the discount must be calculated on the amount owed after the credit has been applied.

MEMO

DATE: January 14, 2015

On January 13, we received but did not record Check 152 dated January 11 and postmarked 1/12 from Russ Watson for $916.84 to pay his account in full. Date the payment receipt 01/13/15.

Record the payment described above

Click the Create Invoices icon on the Home Page; click Previous until you get to Invoice 6 for Russ Watson

Click the **Receive Payments** icon on the Create Invoices Main icon bar

- A Receive Payments screen opens for recording the transaction.
- Since we accessed the Receive Payments screen from an invoice, the amount of the invoice was inserted as the PAYMENT AMOUNT.
- Also note that Invoice 6 has a check mark in the check column.

Change the PAYMENT AMOUNT to **916.84** for **Russ Watson**, press Tab

- Now both transactions have been marked.

Use the date the check was received **01/13/15** as the DATE

Enter CHECK # **152**

- Once all the transaction information is entered, notice the UNDERPAYMENT of $8.40.
- Since the payment was received within the discount period, the discount needs to be applied.

Click the line for Number 6 on the Receive Payments window and then click the **Discounts And Credits** icon, make sure the **Discount** tab is selected and that Number is 6 is shown

- Analyze the information displayed:
  - 852.11 shows as the Original Amt. and the Amount Due for Invoice 6.
  - 8.52 is the Discount Used, which is the amount QuickBooks calculates for the discount on the original Amount Due rather than the Balance Due.
  - 11.87 is the Credits Used (The credit of 11.87 was applied to the invoice when the return was recorded.)
  - 831.72 is the Balance Due (This is incorrect because the discount should not be calculated before the Credit Used is subtracted. It should be calculated 852.11 – 11.87 = 840.24 Balance Due.)

The terms are **1% 10 Net 30**

Click in the **Amount of Discount** text box, delete the discount of **8.52**

Use QuickMath to calculate the discount amount:

Amount Due **852.11** – Credits Used **11.87 * .01** (discount percentage) **=** a discount of **8.40**, press **Enter** to enter the discount, press **Tab** to update Discount Used

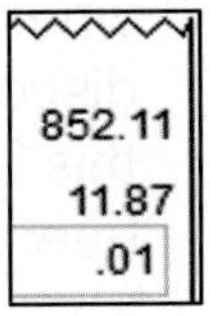

- Note that QuickBooks shows the Suggested Discount of 8.52, which is the discount for the Amount Due before subtracting the Credits Used. The Discount Used is 8.40, the amount calculated by QuickMath.

Use the Discount Account **4050 Sales Discounts**

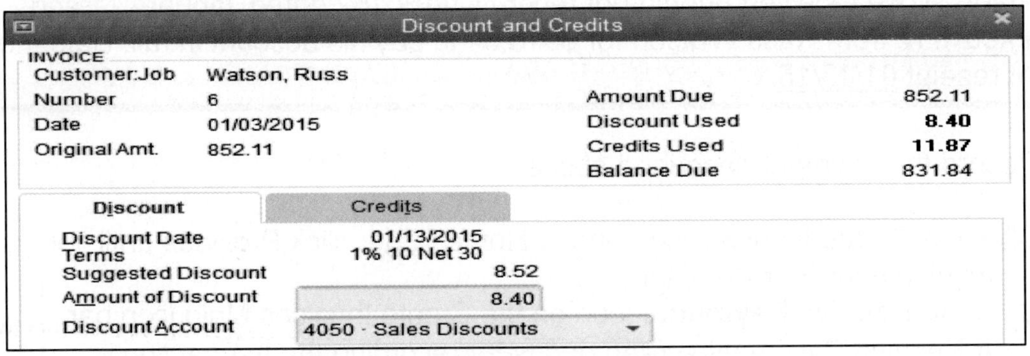

Click **Done**

Enter the MEMO: **Includes Early Payment Discount**

- Notice that AVAILABLE CREDITS shows 0.00 but says "THIS CUSTOMER HAS DISCOUNTS AVAILABLE… This is because QuickBooks calculated that a discount of 8.52 was available. Disregard this message.

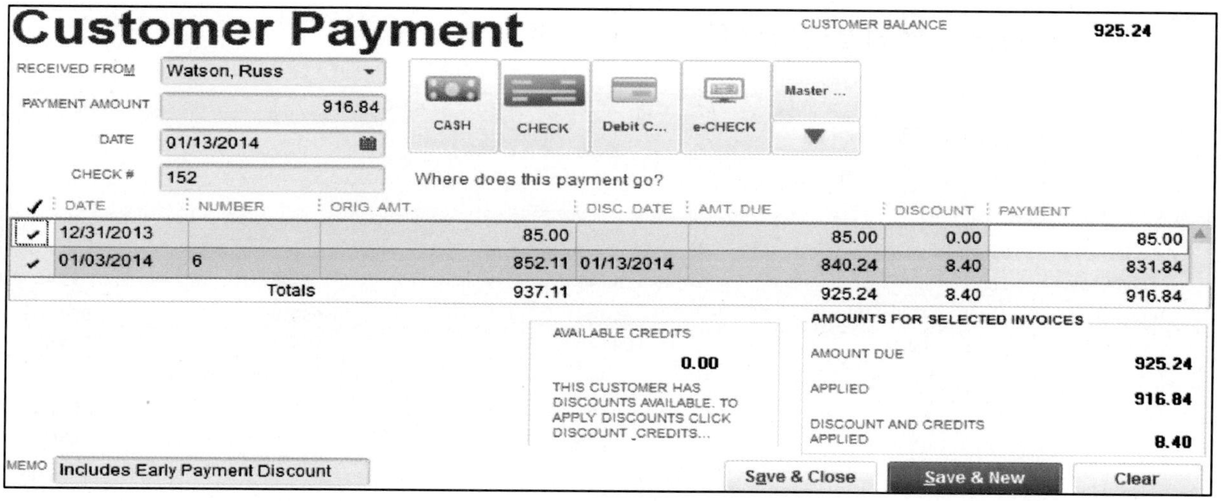

Print the Customer Payment, click **Save & New**

RECORD ADDITIONAL PAYMENTS ON ACCOUNT

MEMO

DATE: January 14, 2015

Received Check 3951 from Dr. Jose Perez for $1,094.45. Since he dropped off his check today, it does not qualify for an early payment discount.

Received Debit Card payment for $500 from Gail Daily in partial payment of account. Debit Card Number 7890 6587 3698 258, Expiration 05/2018. Record the memo: Partial Payment. Leave this as an underpayment.

Received Visa payment from Sandra Perkins for $408.48 in payment of the 12/31/2014 balance. Visa Card Number 4598 2323 7785 126, Expiration 06/2018.

Received Check 819 from Kevin Thomsen for $100 in partial payment of his account. Leave this as an underpayment.

5

Refer to the previous steps listed to enter the above payments:

- Any discounts or partial payments should be noted as a Memo.
- A partial payment should have *LEAVE THIS AS AN UNDERPAYMENT* marked. Refer to Chapter 2 if you do not remember how to record an underpayment.
- Be sure to apply any discounts.

Print a Payment Receipt for each payment recorded

Click the **Save & Close** button after all payments received have been recorded

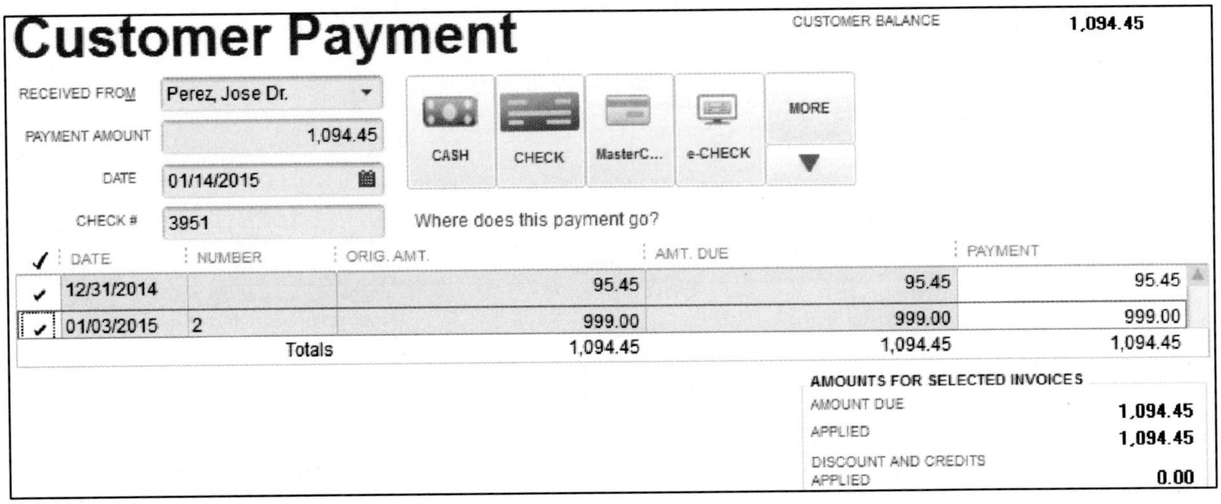

Customer Payment

CUSTOMER BALANCE 1,094.45

RECEIVED FROM: Perez, Jose Dr.
PAYMENT AMOUNT: 1,094.45
DATE: 01/14/2015
CHECK #: 3951

CASH | CHECK | MasterC... | e-CHECK | MORE

Where does this payment go?

✓	DATE	NUMBER	ORIG. AMT.	AMT. DUE	PAYMENT
✓	12/31/2014		95.45	95.45	95.45
✓	01/03/2015	2	999.00	999.00	999.00
		Totals	1,094.45	1,094.45	1,094.45

AMOUNTS FOR SELECTED INVOICES
AMOUNT DUE 1,094.45
APPLIED 1,094.45
DISCOUNT AND CREDITS APPLIED 0.00

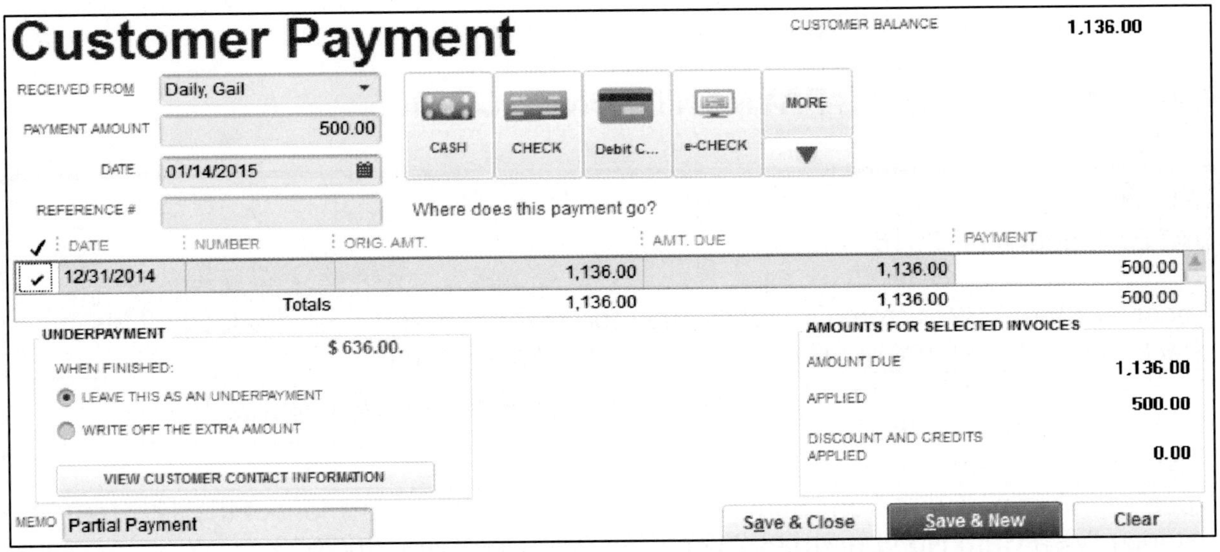

Customer Payment

CUSTOMER BALANCE 1,136.00

RECEIVED FROM: Daily, Gail
PAYMENT AMOUNT: 500.00
DATE: 01/14/2015
REFERENCE #:

CASH | CHECK | Debit C... | e-CHECK | MORE

Where does this payment go?

✓	DATE	NUMBER	ORIG. AMT.	AMT. DUE	PAYMENT
✓	12/31/2014		1,136.00	1,136.00	500.00
		Totals	1,136.00	1,136.00	500.00

UNDERPAYMENT $ 636.00.
WHEN FINISHED:
(•) LEAVE THIS AS AN UNDERPAYMENT
( ) WRITE OFF THE EXTRA AMOUNT
VIEW CUSTOMER CONTACT INFORMATION

AMOUNTS FOR SELECTED INVOICES
AMOUNT DUE 1,136.00
APPLIED 500.00
DISCOUNT AND CREDITS APPLIED 0.00

MEMO: Partial Payment

Save & Close | Save & New | Clear

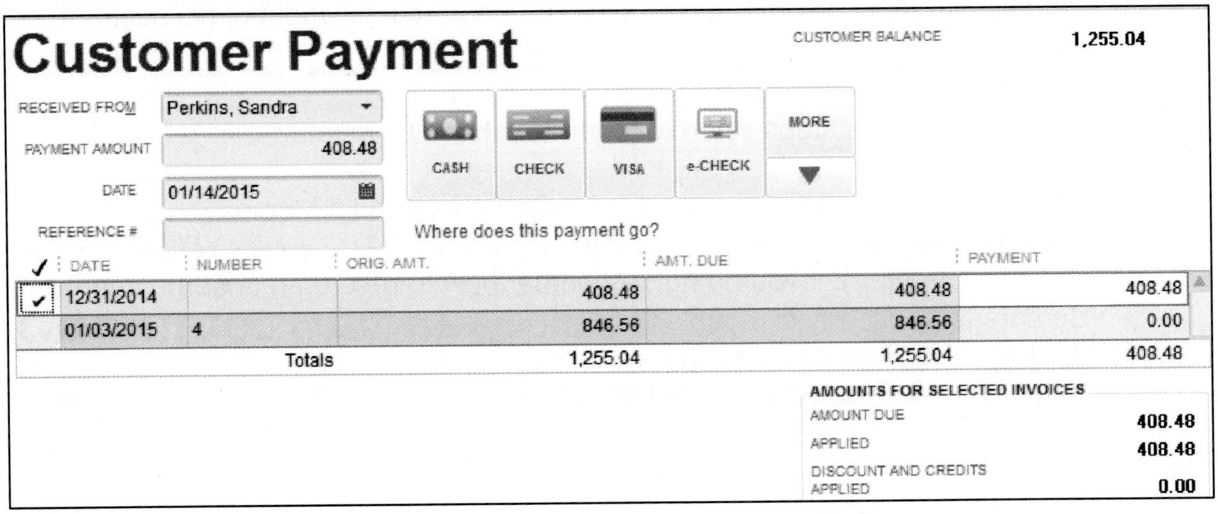

Customer Payment

CUSTOMER BALANCE 1,255.04

RECEIVED FROM: Perkins, Sandra
PAYMENT AMOUNT: 408.48
DATE: 01/14/2015
REFERENCE #:

CASH | CHECK | VISA | e-CHECK | MORE

Where does this payment go?

✓	DATE	NUMBER	ORIG. AMT.	AMT. DUE	PAYMENT
✓	12/31/2014		408.48	408.48	408.48
	01/03/2015	4	846.56	846.56	0.00
		Totals	1,255.04	1,255.04	408.48

AMOUNTS FOR SELECTED INVOICES
AMOUNT DUE 408.48
APPLIED 408.48
DISCOUNT AND CREDITS APPLIED 0.00

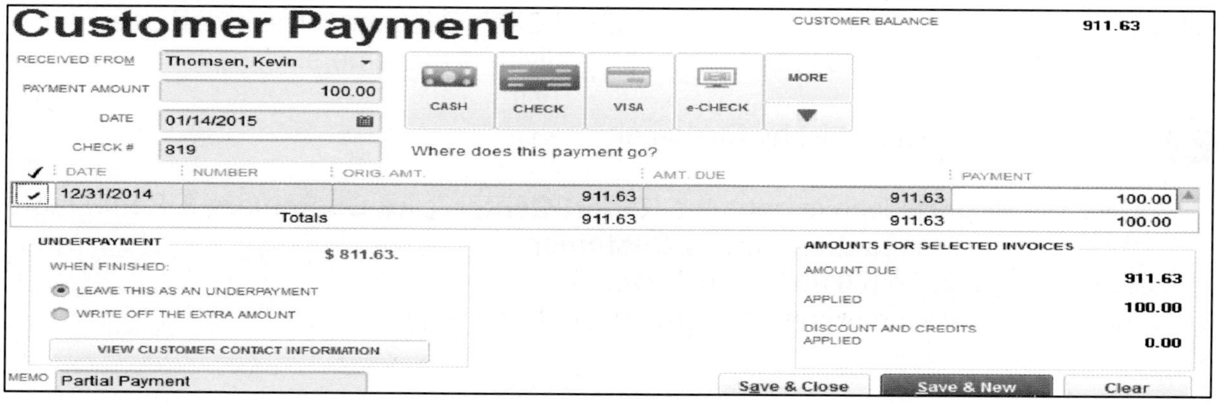

PRINT CUSTOMER BALANCE SUMMARY

A report that will show you the balance owed by each customer is the Customer Balance Summary. The report presents the total balance owed by each customer as of a certain date.

MEMO
DATE: January 14, 2015

Larry and you want to see how much each customer owes to Your Name Mountain Sports. Print a Customer Balance Summary Report for All Transactions.

Prepare and print a **Customer Balance Summary** following the steps given previously for printing the report in Portrait orientation

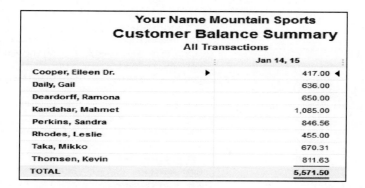

Your Name Mountain Sports
Customer Balance Summary
All Transactions

	Jan 14, 15
Cooper, Eileen Dr.	417.00
Daily, Gail	636.00
Deardorff, Ramona	650.00
Kandahar, Mahmet	1,085.00
Perkins, Sandra	846.56
Rhodes, Leslie	455.00
Taka, Mikko	670.31
Thomsen, Kevin	811.63
TOTAL	5,571.50

Print the report as instructed then close the report

VIEW TRANSACTION LIST BY CUSTOMER

In order to see the transactions for customers, you need to prepare a report called Transaction List by Customer. This report shows all sales, credits, and payments for each customer on account and for the customer named Cash Customer. The report does not show the balance remaining on account for the individual customers.

View the Transaction List by Customer

Click the **Reports** icon to open the **Report Center**, click **Customers & Receivables**
Double-click **Transaction List by Customer**
Enter the dates from **01/01/15** to **01/14/15**
Tab to generate the report and scroll through the report

Your Name Mountain Sports
Transaction List by Customer
January 1 - 14, 2015

Type	Date	Num	Memo	Account	Clr	Split	Debit	Credit
Cash Customer								
Sales Receipt	01/08/2015	1		12000 · Undeposited Funds		-SPLIT-	36.86	
Sales Receipt	01/11/2015	2		12000 · Undeposited Funds		-SPLIT-	215.95	
Sales Receipt	01/11/2015	3		12000 · Undeposited Funds		-SPLIT-	34.54	
Sales Receipt	01/11/2015	4		12000 · Undeposited Funds		-SPLIT-	97.15	
Sales Receipt	01/12/2015	5		12000 · Undeposited Funds		-SPLIT-	410.29	
Sales Receipt	01/12/2015	6		12000 · Undeposited Funds		-SPLIT-	626.29	
Sales Receipt	01/12/2015	7		12000 · Undeposited Funds		-SPLIT-	97.15	
Sales Receipt	01/12/2015	8		12000 · Undeposited Funds		-SPLIT-	248.35	
Daily, Gail								
Payment	01/14/2015		Partial Payment	12000 · Undeposited Funds		1200 · Accounts Receivable	500.00	
Gardener, Monique								
Invoice	01/04/2015	7		1200 · Accounts Receivable		-SPLIT-	1,035.60	
Credit Memo	01/10/2015	9		1200 · Accounts Receivable		-SPLIT-		53.95
Payment	01/13/2015			12000 · Undeposited Funds		1200 · Accounts Receivable	1,035.22	
Mountain Recreation Center								
Invoice	01/08/2015	8		1200 · Accounts Receivable		-SPLIT-	2,040.66	
Payment	01/13/2015	981-13	Includes Early Payment Discount	12000 · Undeposited Funds		1200 · Accounts Receivable	2,020.25	
Mountain Schools								
Invoice	01/03/2015	3		1200 · Accounts Receivable		-SPLIT-	2,080.08	
Payment	01/14/2015		Includes Early Payment Discount	12000 · Undeposited Funds		1200 · Accounts Receivable	2,038.48	
Perez, Jose Dr.								
Invoice	01/03/2015	2		1200 · Accounts Receivable		-SPLIT-	999.00	
Payment	01/14/2015	3951		12000 · Undeposited Funds		1200 · Accounts Receivable	1,094.45	
Perkins, Sandra								
Invoice	01/03/2015	4		1200 · Accounts Receivable		-SPLIT-	846.56	
Payment	01/14/2015			12000 · Undeposited Funds		1200 · Accounts Receivable	408.48	
Thomsen, Kevin								
Payment	01/14/2015	819	Partial Payment	12000 · Undeposited Funds		1200 · Accounts Receivable	100.00	
Villanueva, Oskar								
Payment	01/13/2015	765		12000 · Undeposited Funds		1200 · Accounts Receivable	975.00	
Watson, Russ								
Invoice	01/02/2015	1	VOID:	1200 · Accounts Receivable	✓	-SPLIT-	0.00	
Sales Order	01/03/2015	2		90200 · Sales Orders		-SPLIT-	840.24	
Invoice	01/03/2015	6		1200 · Accounts Receivable		-SPLIT-	852.11	
Credit Memo	01/10/2015	10		1200 · Accounts Receivable		-SPLIT-		11.87
Payment	01/13/2015	152	Includes Early Payment Discount	12000 · Undeposited Funds		1200 · Accounts Receivable	916.84	

- Information is shown for the Invoices, Sales Receipts, Credit Memos, and Payments made on the accounts and the Num column shows the Invoice numbers, Sales Receipt numbers, Credit Memo numbers, and Check numbers. Nothing is shown for beginning balances or for Debit and Credit card numbers.

Close the report without printing and close the Report Center

MAKE DEPOSITS

When cash sales are made and payments on accounts are received, QuickBooks places the money received in the *Undeposited Funds* account. Once the deposit is recorded, the funds are transferred from *Undeposited Funds* to the account selected when preparing the deposit, usually Cash or Checking.

MEMO
DATE: January 14, 2015

Deposit all cash, checks, debit card, and credit card receipts for cash sales and payments on account into the Checking account.

Deposit cash, checks, debit card, and credit card receipts

Click the **Record Deposits** icon on the QuickBooks Home Page
The View payment method type should be **All types**

- The **Payments to Deposit** window shows all amounts received for cash sales (including bank credit cards) and payments on account that have not been deposited in the bank organized by category—Cash, Check, Credit Card, and Debit Card.

Sort is by **Payment Method**

- Notice that the **check** column to the left of the Date column is empty.

Click the **Select All** button

- Notice the check marks in the check column.

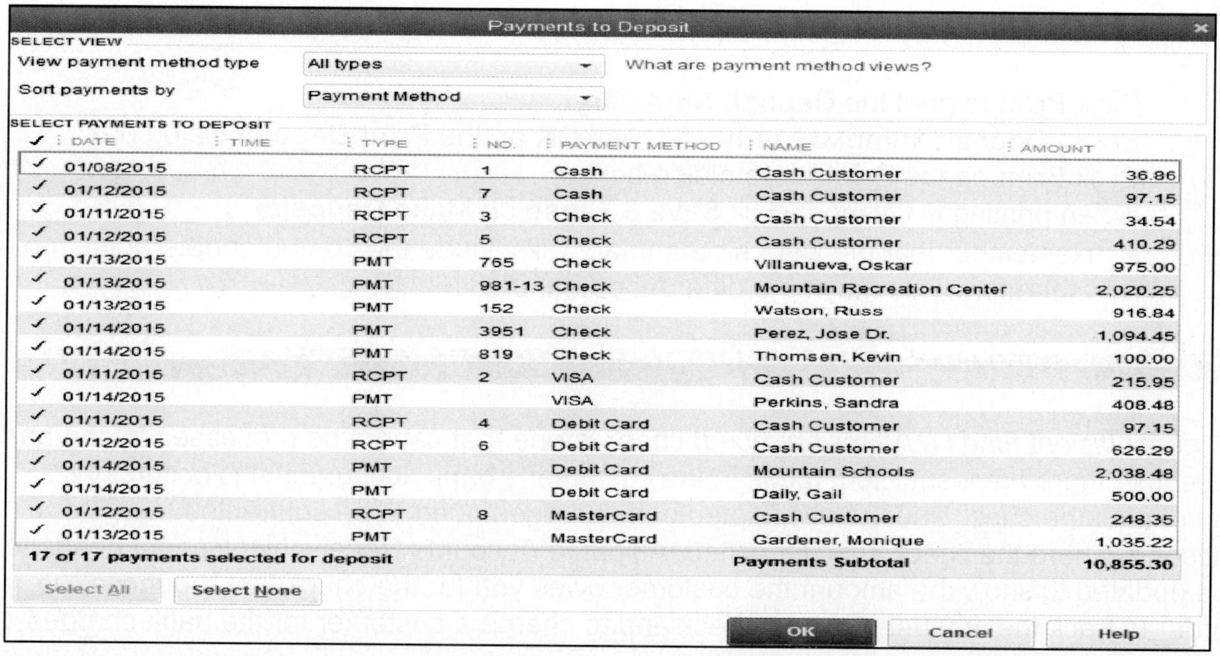
Payments to Deposit

SELECT VIEW
View payment method type: All types — What are payment method views?
Sort payments by: Payment Method

SELECT PAYMENTS TO DEPOSIT

✓	DATE	TIME	TYPE	NO.	PAYMENT METHOD	NAME	AMOUNT
✓	01/08/2015		RCPT	1	Cash	Cash Customer	36.86
✓	01/12/2015		RCPT	7	Cash	Cash Customer	97.15
✓	01/11/2015		RCPT	3	Check	Cash Customer	34.54
✓	01/12/2015		RCPT	5	Check	Cash Customer	410.29
✓	01/13/2015		PMT	765	Check	Villanueva, Oskar	975.00
✓	01/13/2015		PMT	981-13	Check	Mountain Recreation Center	2,020.25
✓	01/13/2015		PMT	152	Check	Watson, Russ	916.84
✓	01/14/2015		PMT	3951	Check	Perez, Jose Dr.	1,094.45
✓	01/14/2015		PMT	819	Check	Thomsen, Kevin	100.00
✓	01/11/2015		RCPT	2	VISA	Cash Customer	215.95
✓	01/14/2015		PMT		VISA	Perkins, Sandra	408.48
✓	01/11/2015		RCPT	4	Debit Card	Cash Customer	97.15
✓	01/12/2015		RCPT	6	Debit Card	Cash Customer	626.29
✓	01/14/2015		PMT		Debit Card	Mountain Schools	2,038.48
✓	01/14/2015		PMT		Debit Card	Daily, Gail	500.00
✓	01/12/2015		RCPT	8	MasterCard	Cash Customer	248.35
✓	01/13/2015		PMT		MasterCard	Gardener, Monique	1,035.22

17 of 17 payments selected for deposit — Payments Subtotal 10,855.30

Select All | Select None | OK | Cancel | Help

Click **OK** to close the **Payments to Deposit** screen and go to the **Make Deposits** screen

On the **Make Deposits** screen, **Deposit To** should be **1100 Checking**

Date should be **01/14/2015**

- Tab to date and change if not correct.

Your Make Deposits screen should look like the following:

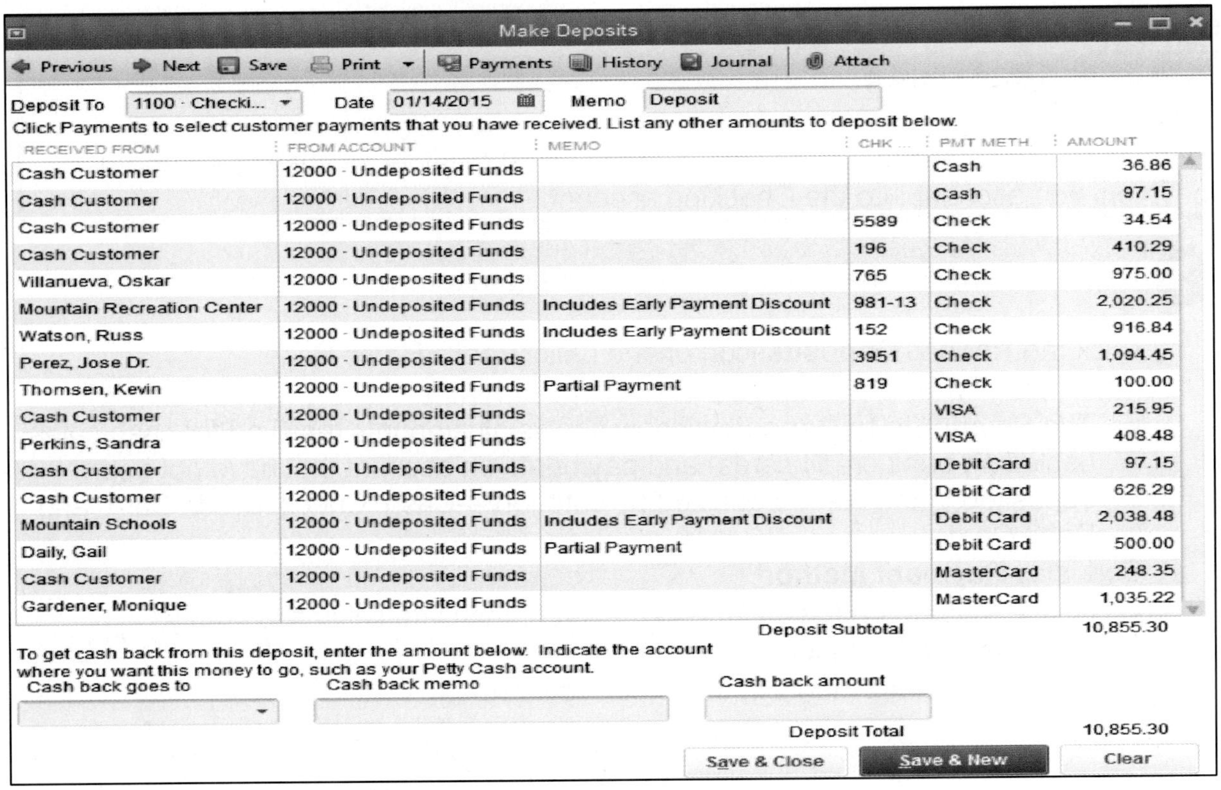
Make Deposits

Previous | Next | Save | Print | Payments | History | Journal | Attach

Deposit To 1100 · Checki... Date 01/14/2015 Memo Deposit

Click Payments to select customer payments that you have received. List any other amounts to deposit below.

RECEIVED FROM	FROM ACCOUNT	MEMO	CHK ...	PMT METH	AMOUNT
Cash Customer	12000 · Undeposited Funds			Cash	36.86
Cash Customer	12000 · Undeposited Funds			Cash	97.15
Cash Customer	12000 · Undeposited Funds		5589	Check	34.54
Cash Customer	12000 · Undeposited Funds		196	Check	410.29
Villanueva, Oskar	12000 · Undeposited Funds		765	Check	975.00
Mountain Recreation Center	12000 · Undeposited Funds	Includes Early Payment Discount	981-13	Check	2,020.25
Watson, Russ	12000 · Undeposited Funds	Includes Early Payment Discount	152	Check	916.84
Perez, Jose Dr.	12000 · Undeposited Funds		3951	Check	1,094.45
Thomsen, Kevin	12000 · Undeposited Funds	Partial Payment	819	Check	100.00
Cash Customer	12000 · Undeposited Funds			VISA	215.95
Perkins, Sandra	12000 · Undeposited Funds			VISA	408.48
Cash Customer	12000 · Undeposited Funds			Debit Card	97.15
Cash Customer	12000 · Undeposited Funds			Debit Card	626.29
Mountain Schools	12000 · Undeposited Funds	Includes Early Payment Discount		Debit Card	2,038.48
Daily, Gail	12000 · Undeposited Funds	Partial Payment		Debit Card	500.00
Cash Customer	12000 · Undeposited Funds			MasterCard	248.35
Gardener, Monique	12000 · Undeposited Funds			MasterCard	1,035.22

Deposit Subtotal 10,855.30

To get cash back from this deposit, enter the amount below. Indicate the account where you want this money to go, such as your Petty Cash account.

Cash back goes to | Cash back memo | Cash back amount

Deposit Total 10,855.30

Save & Close | Save & New | Clear

Click **Print** to print the **Deposit Summary**

Select **Deposit summary only** and click **OK** on the **Print Deposit** dialog box

Click **Print** on the **Print Lists** dialog box

When printing is finished, click **Save & Close** on **Make Deposits**

- Remember that the Deposit Summary will include the computer date at the top of the report. This may be a different date than 01/14/2015.

RECORD RETURN OF NONSUFFICIENT FUNDS CHECK

A *nonsufficient funds* (*NSF* or *bounced)* check is one that cannot be processed by the bank because there are insufficient funds in the customer's bank account. If this occurs, the amount of the check and the associated bank charges need to be subtracted from the account where the check was deposited. Also, the Accounts Receivable account needs to be updated to show the amount the customer owes you for the check that "bounced." In order to track the amount of a bad check and to charge a customer for the bank charges and any penalties you impose, Other Charge items may need to be created and an invoice for the total amount due must be prepared.

Money received for the bad check charges from the bank and for Your Name Mountain Sports is recorded as income. When the bank account is reconciled, the amount of bank charges will offset the income recorded on the invoice.

MEMO
DATE: January 15, 2015

The bank returned Oskar Villanueva's Check 765 marked NSF. The bank imposed a $10 service charge for the NSF check. Your Name Mountain Sports charges a $25 fee for NSF checks. Record the NSF (Bounced) Check

Record the NSF (Bounced) Check from Oskar Villanueva and all the related charges

Go to the Receive Payments screen where Oskar's $975 check was recorded

- If not already selected, click the 12/31/2014 Invoice for the Opening balance of 975.00 to select
- Notice the Customer Payment shows the ORIG. AMT., AMT. DUE, and PAYMENT as 975.00

Click the **Record Bounced Check** icon on the Receive Payments icon bar

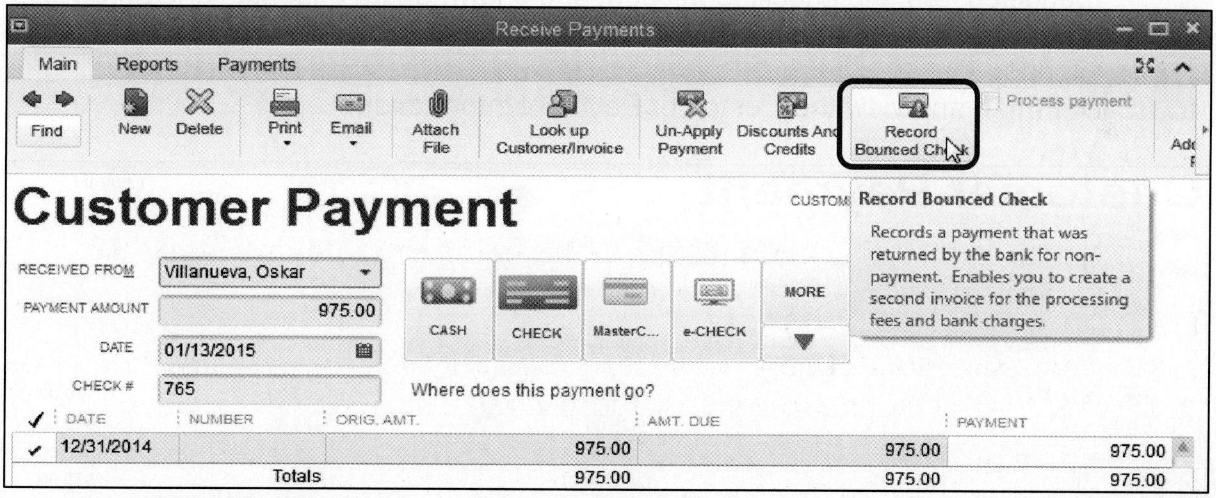

On the Manage Bounced Check screen, enter:

BANK FEE of **10.00**, the DATE is **01/15/2015**, the EXPENSE ACCOUNT IS **6120 Bank Service Charges**

Enter **25.00** for the CUSTOMER FEE

- When the amount of the Bank Fee of $10 is subtracted from the $25 Customer Fee charged by Your Name Mountain Sports, the net result of the Customer Fee will result in an actual other income of $15.00.

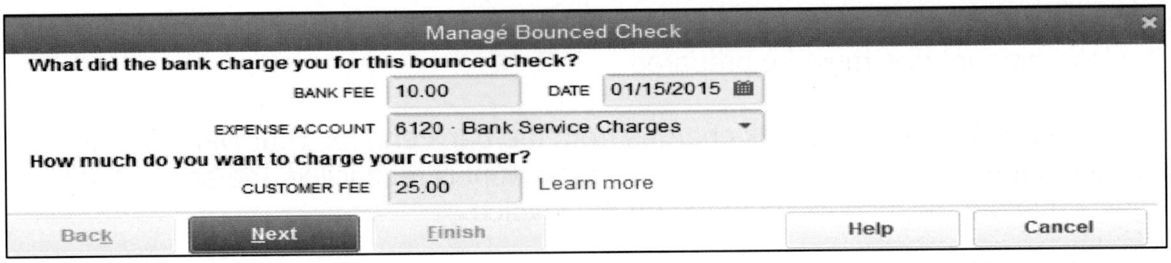

Click **Next**
Read the Bounced Check Summary

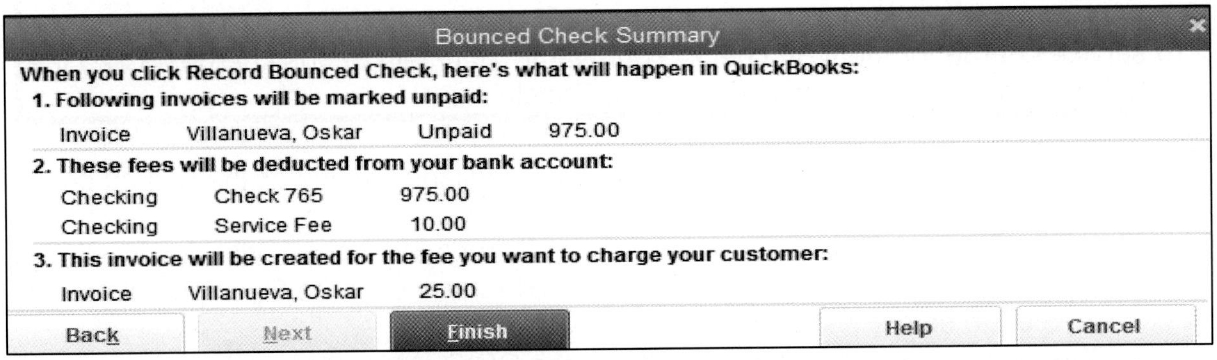

- The Invoice for the Opening Balance will now be marked as unpaid, Check 765 for $975 will be deducted from our checking account, the $10 bank fee will be deducted from the checking account and shown as an expense, and an Invoice will be created for the $25 Customer Fee charged by Your Name Mountain Sports.

Click **Finish** and view the Customer Payment information

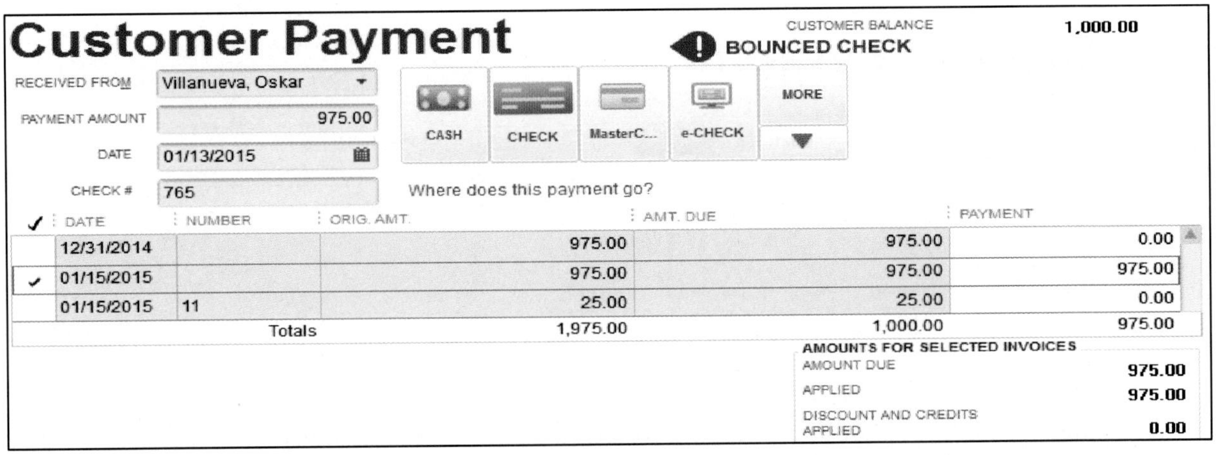

- Notice the CUSTOMER BALANCE of 1,000.00. This is the $975 due from the bounced check and the $25 Customer Fee collected by Your Name Mountain Sports. The transaction for 12/31/2014 now shows as PAYMENT 0.00, the payment made on 01/15/2015 basically cancels out the Payment recorded earlier for the 12/31/2014 balance. Invoice 11 was created for the additional $25 owed for the bad check fee.

- If the date for Invoice 11 shows as 01/14/15 (the last transaction date used), you may leave it as that date.

Click **Save & Close**

Open the Item List to see the Bounced Check Item created by QuickBooks

- Note that the NAME is Bounce Check Charge and the ACCOUNT is 5009 Returned Check Charges
- Notice that the other income accounts are in the 4000 number group for income. While 5009 Returned Check was assigned a 5000 category account.

Open the Chart of Accounts, scroll through until you see Account 5009 Returned Check Charges

Click on the account and use the keyboard shortcut **Ctrl+E** to edit the account

Change the Account Number to **4090** so that it is in the same number category as the other income accounts

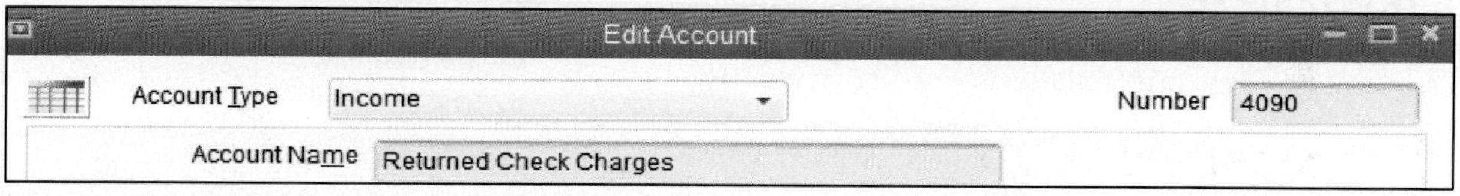

Click **Save & Close** to change the account number

Look at the Income accounts and note how they are organized

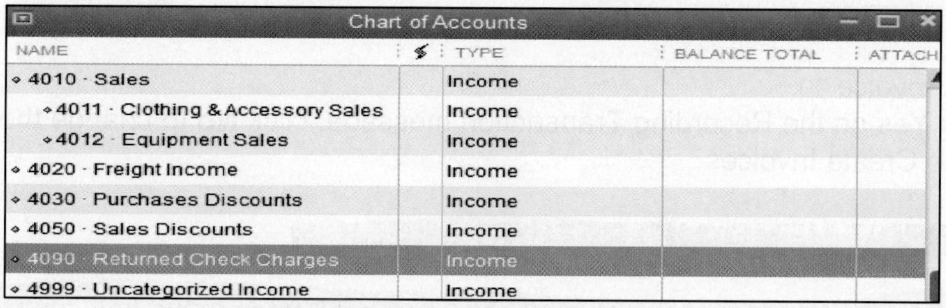

Close the Chart of Accounts, open **Create Invoices**

Go to the Opening balance invoice for Oskar Villanueva and notice that it shows a Balance Due of 975.00

Change the TEMPLATE to Copy of: Intuit Produce Invoice
Click the drop-down list arrow for TERMS, click **Due on receipt**

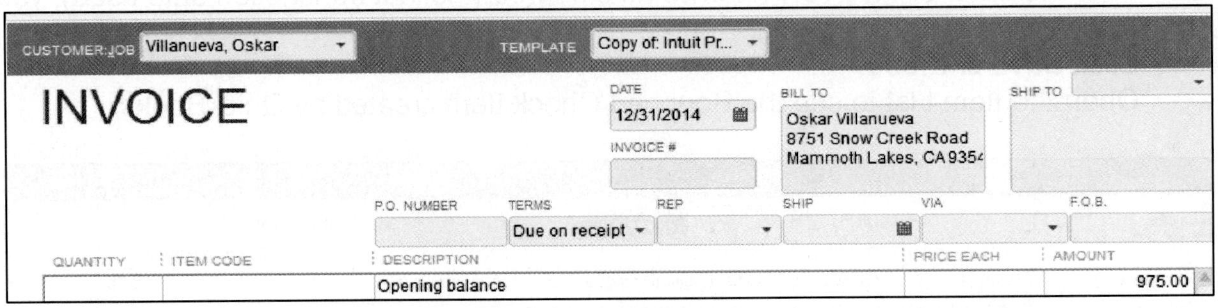

Print the Revised Invoice for the Opening balance, click **Yes** to record the transaction, click **Yes** to change an entry for a closed period, click **No** on the Information Changed dialog box to change the Terms
Go to **Invoice 11**, review the invoice
Change TEMPLATE to **Copy of: Intuit Product Invoice**
Make sure the date of the Invoice is **01/15/2015**; if not, change it
Click the drop-down list arrow for TERMS, click **Due on Receipt**
Insert the CUSTOMER MESSAGE **Please remit to above address.**

- QuickBooks should enter the MEMO for Bounced Check #765 automatically; if not, enter it

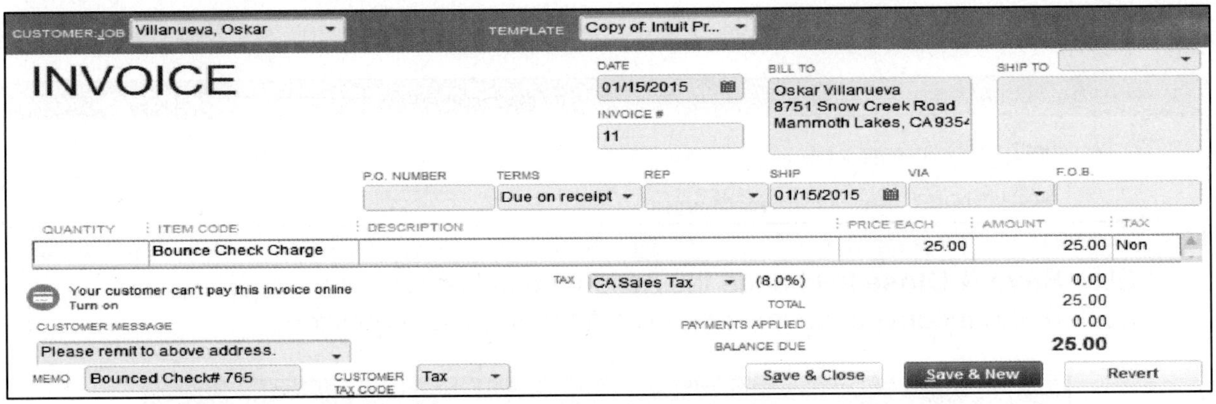

Print Invoice 11
Click **Yes** on the Recording Transaction message, click **No** to change the Terms
Close Create Invoices

ISSUE CREDIT MEMO AND REFUND CHECK

If merchandise is returned and the invoice has been paid in full or the sale was for cash, a refund check may be issued at the same time the credit memo is prepared. Simply clicking the "Use credit to give refund" icon instructs QuickBooks to prepare a refund check for you.

MEMO
DATE: January 15, 2015

Dr. Jose Perez returned the ski poles he purchased January 3 for $75 on Invoice 2. He has already paid his bill in full. Record the return and issue a check refunding the $75 plus tax.

Prepare a Credit Memo to record the return and issue a refund check

Issue a Credit Memo as previously instructed
Use the Customer Message **Thank you for your business.**
At the top of the Credit Memo, click 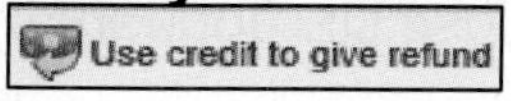

The Issue a Refund dialog box appears.

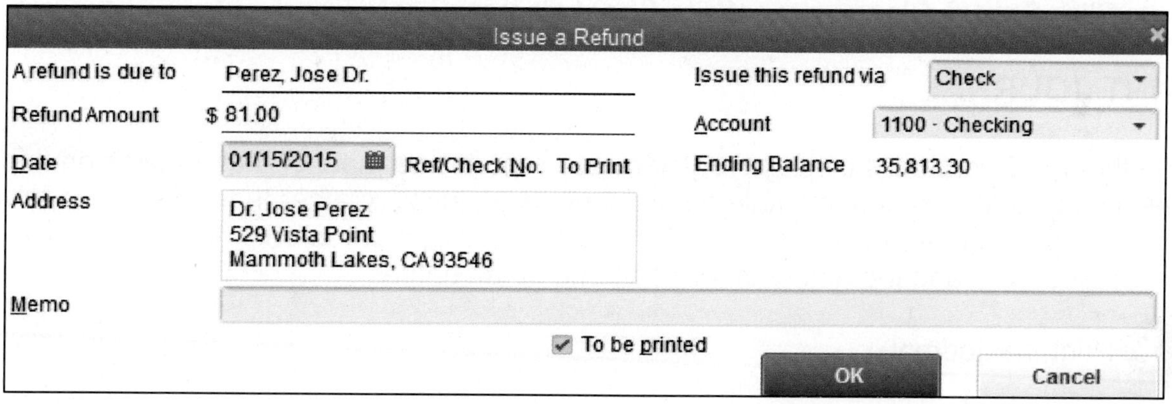

Verify the information and click **OK**.
The Credit Memo will be stamped "REFUNDED."

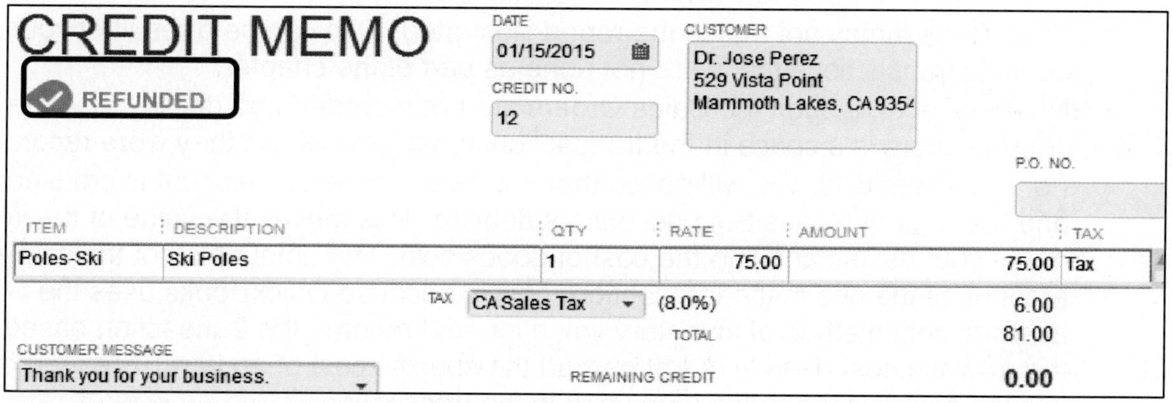

Print the Credit Memo with lines around each field
Click **Save & Close** to record the **Credit Memo** and exit
Click the **Write Checks** icon on the Home Page, click the **Previous** or back arrow until you get to the check for Dr. Perez

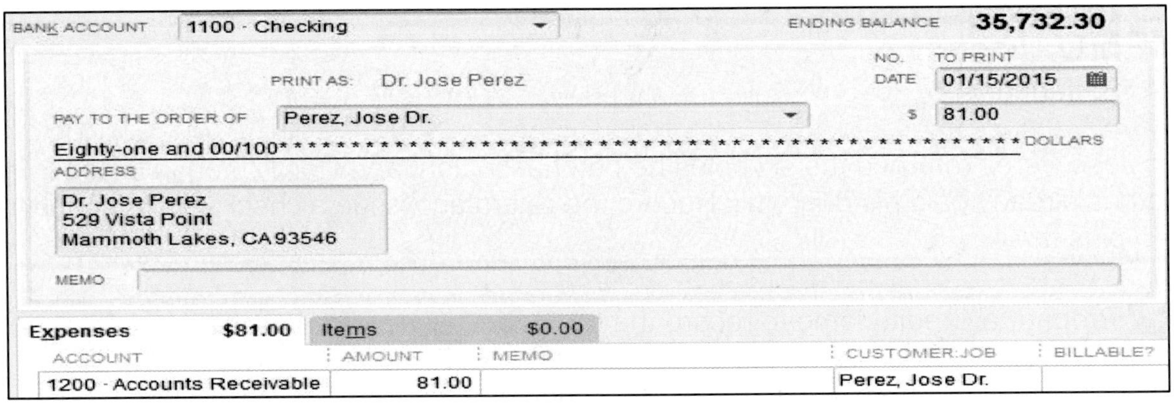

- Note that Perez, Jose Dr. appears in the CUSTOMER:JOB column on the Expenses tab.

Print Check 1 in Standard format as previously instructed
Click **Save & Close** on the **Write Checks** screen

PRINT JOURNAL

Even though QuickBooks displays registers and reports in a manner that focuses on the transaction—that is, entering a sale on account via an invoice rather than a Sales Journal or a General Journal—it still keeps a Journal. The Journal records each transaction and lists the accounts and the amounts for debit and credit entries.

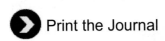

Print the Journal

Open the **Report Center** and prepare the **Journal** as previously instructed
The report date is from **01/01/15** to **01/15/15**
Make sure to **Expand** the report
Scroll through the report to view the transactions

- Your Trans # may not match the report illustrated. This can be a result of your deleting transactions that were not done as part of the chapter.
- Note that even though the Sales Orders are not recorded and displayed in the Journal, there is a space in the transaction numbering where they were recorded.
- For each item sold, you will notice that the Inventory Asset account is credited and the Cost of Goods Sold account is debited. This moves the value of the item out of your assets and into the cost of goods sold. The amount is not the same amount as the one in the transaction. This is because QuickBooks uses the average cost method of inventory valuation and records the transaction based on the average cost of an item rather than the specific cost of an item. The Memo column contains the Sales Item used in the transaction.

Resize the columns by positioning the cursor on the diamond and dragging so that the report columns do not have a lot of blank space
Since it is not used, eliminate the **Adj** column from the report

- Make sure that the account names are displayed in full.

- It is acceptable if the Information in the Memo column is not displayed in full, but make sure enough information is shown so the sales item can be identified.

Print the report in **Landscape** orientation; if need be, click **Fit report to 1 pages(s) wide**

Your Name Mountain Sports
Journal
January 1 - 15, 2015

Trans #	Type	Date	Num	Name	Memo	Account	Debit	Credit
81	General Journal	01/15/2015		Villanueva, Oskar	Bounced Check# 765	1200 · Accounts Receivable	975.00	
				Villanueva, Oskar	Bounced Check# 765	1100 · Checking		975.00
							975.00	975.00
82	General Journal	01/15/2015			Bank service charges for bounced check# 765	6120 · Bank Service Charges	10.00	
				Villanueva, Oskar	Bank service charges for bounced check# 765	1100 · Checking		10.00
							10.00	10.00
83	Invoice	01/15/2015	11	Villanueva, Oskar	Bounced Check# 765	1200 · Accounts Receivable	25.00	
				Villanueva, Oskar	Bounced Check# 765	4090 · Returned Check Charges		25.00
				State Board of Equalization	CA Sales Tax	2200 · Sales Tax Payable	0.00	
							25.00	25.00
84	Credit Memo	01/15/2015	12	Perez, Jose Dr.		1200 · Accounts Receivable		81.00
				Perez, Jose Dr.	Ski Poles	4012 · Equipment Sales	75.00	
				Perez, Jose Dr.	Ski Poles	1120 · Inventory Asset	30.00	
				Perez, Jose Dr.	Ski Poles	5000 · Cost of Goods Sold		30.00
				State Board of Equalization	CA Sales Tax	2200 · Sales Tax Payable	6.00	
							111.00	111.00
85	Check	01/15/2015	1	Perez, Jose Dr.		1100 · Checking		81.00
				Perez, Jose Dr.		1200 · Accounts Receivable	81.00	
							81.00	81.00
TOTAL							37,603.89	37,603.89

Partial Report

When the report is printed, close it.
Do not close the Report Center

PRINT TRIAL BALANCE

When all sales transactions have been entered, it is important to print the trial balance and verify that the total debits equal the total credits.

Prepare and print the Trial Balance

Prepare and print the report from the Report Center as previously instructed
The report dates are from **01/01/2015** to **01/15/2015**

Your Name Mountain Sports
Trial Balance
As of January 15, 2015

	Jan 15, 15	
	Debit	Credit
1100 · Checking	35,732.30	
1200 · Accounts Receivable	6,571.50	
1120 · Inventory Asset	32,766.54	
12000 · Undeposited Funds	0.00	
1311 · Office Supplies	850.00	
1312 · Sales Supplies	575.00	
1340 · Prepaid Insurance	250.00	
1511 · Original Cost	5,000.00	
1521 · Original Cost	4,500.00	
2000 · Accounts Payable		8,500.00
2100 · Visa		150.00
2200 · Sales Tax Payable		701.77
2510 · Office Equipment Loan		3,000.00
2520 · Store Fixtures Loan		2,500.00
3000 · Owners' Equity	0.00	
3010 · Your Name & Muir Capital		26,159.44
3011 · Your Name, Investment		20,000.00
3012 · Larry Muir, Investment		20,000.00
4011 · Clothing & Accessory Sales		1,759.51
4012 · Equipment Sales		7,436.44
4050 · Sales Discounts	494.36	
4090 · Returned Check Charges		25.00
5000 · Cost of Goods Sold	3,482.46	
6120 · Bank Service Charges	10.00	
TOTAL	90,232.16	90,232.16

Print the Trial Balance in **Portrait** orientation
Do not close the Report Center

PREPARE INVENTORY VALUATION DETAIL REPORT

To obtain information regarding the inventory, you may prepare an Inventory Valuation Summary or an Inventory Valuation Detail report. Both reports give you information regarding an item, the number on hand, the average cost, and asset value. The detail report includes information for transactions that affected the value of your inventory during a particular period of time.

The detail report includes the type of transaction, date of transaction, customer name, number, quantity, and cost. If an inventory item was not used within the time period of the report, it will not be included in the detail report. Preparing the Inventory Valuation Detail will allow you to verify the inventory item used and average cost for each transaction. In addition, you will know the number of items on hand.

Prepare and print an Inventory Valuation Detail report in Landscape orientation for January 1-15, 2015

Click **Inventory** in the Report Center
Double-click **Inventory Valuation Detail**
Enter the dates From **01/01/15** To **01/15/15**
Resize the columns to display the information in full
Use Landscape orientation

Your Name Mountain Sports
Inventory Valuation Detail
January 1 - 15, 2015

Type	Date	Name	Num	Qty	Cost	On Hand	Avg Cost	Asset Value
Sweaters								
Invoice	01/03/2015	Perkins, Sandra	4	-1		74	25.00	1,850.00
Sales Receipt	01/11/2015	Cash Customer	4	-1		73	25.00	1,825.00
Total Sweaters						73		1,825.00
Toboggans								
Inventory Adjust	01/08/2015			10		10	137.50	1,375.00
Invoice	01/08/2015	Mountain Recreation Center	8	-5		5	137.50	687.50
Total Toboggans						5		687.50
Underwear								
Invoice	01/03/2015	Perkins, Sandra	4	-1		32	8.00	256.00
Total Underwear						32		256.00
Total Inventory						1,435		31,016.54
TOTAL						**1,435**		**31,016.54**

Partial Report

Print the report, do not close the Report Center

PREPARE AND MEMORIZE INVENTORY VALUATION SUMMARY

Preparing the Inventory Valuation Summary will allow you to verify the number on hand, average cost, asset value, percentage of Total Assets, sales price, retail value, and percentage of Total Retail value for each inventory item whether or not it was used during the report time period.

5

Once a report has been prepared and customized, it may be memorized for future use. Any changes to the report will be saved and will be used automatically the next time the report is prepared.

Prepare the Inventory Valuation Summary report and then memorize it

Double-click **Inventory Valuation Summary** in the Report Center
The date should be **01/15/15**, press **Tab**
Since no information is shown for **Sales Price**, **Retail Value**, **% of Tot Retail**, remove the columns from the report as instructed previously
Click the **Memorize** button
Click **OK** on the Memorize Report dialog box

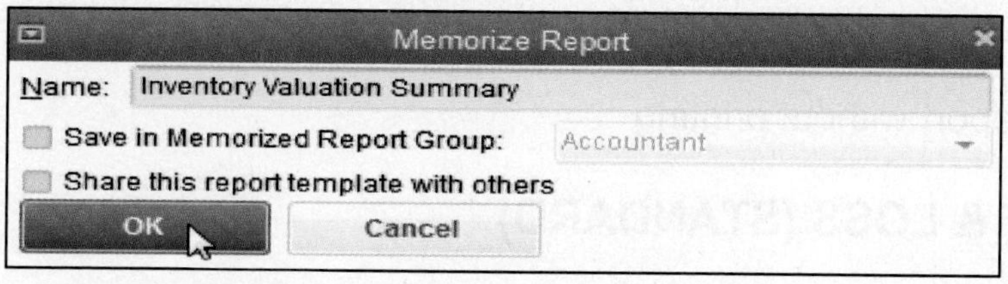

Close the report and the Report Center

PREPARE MEMORIZED REPORT

To illustrate the use of a memorized report, the previous report was closed after memorizing in order to prepare it using the memorized format.

Prepare the Memorized Report, Inventory Valuation Summary

Click **Reports** on the Menu bar, point to **Memorized Reports**, and click **Inventory Valuation Summary**

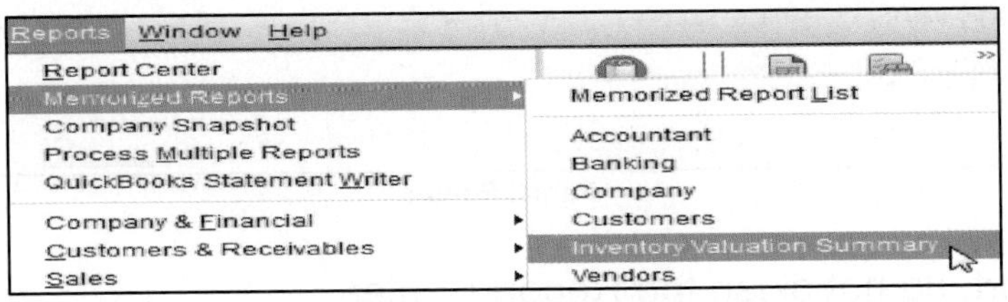

Enter the date As of **01/15/2015**

- The Inventory Valuation Summary is shown without columns for Sales Price, Retail Value, % of Tot Retail.

Your Name Mountain Sports
Inventory Valuation Summary
As of January 15, 2015

	On Hand	Avg Cost	Asset Value	% of Tot Asset
Inventory				
Accessories	795	3.66	2,906.70	8.9%
Bindings-Skis	43	75.00	3,225.00	9.8%
Bindings-Snow	48	75.00	3,600.00	11.0%
Boots	20	30.00	600.00	1.8%
Boots-Ski	14	75.00	1,050.00	3.2%
Boots-Snowbrd	10	75.00	750.00	2.3%
Gloves	20	15.00	300.00	0.9%
Hats	29	8.00	232.00	0.7%
Helmets	20	28.00	560.00	1.7%
Pants-Ski	93	30.00	2,790.00	8.5%
Pants-Snowbrd	50	35.00	1,750.00	5.3%
Parkas	73	58.33	4,258.34	13.0%
Poles-Ski	13	30.00	390.00	1.2%
Skis	43	100.00	4,300.00	13.1%
Sleds	4	67.50	270.00	0.8%
Snowboard	28	100.00	2,800.00	8.5%
Socks	72	3.00	216.00	0.7%
Sweaters	73	25.00	1,825.00	5.6%
Toboggans	5	137.50	687.50	2.1%
Underwear	32	8.00	256.00	0.8%
Total Inventory	1,485		32,766.54	100.0%
TOTAL	1,485		32,766.54	100.0%

Close the report without printing

PRINT PROFIT & LOSS (STANDARD)

Chapter 5 focuses on receivables. In order to see the income earned for the month, you prepare a Profit & Loss (Standard) report. On this statement, you will see the income earned for each sales account. Sales Discounts will be subtracted from Sales and the Returned Check Charges will be added to Sales to calculate the Total Income. The Cost of Goods Sold section will include the total of the average cost for all the items sold. Cost of Goods Sold is subtracted from Total Income to get the Gross Profit. Finally, the Expenses are listed and subtracted from Gross Profit to get the Net Income.

Prepare and print the Profit & Loss (Standard) report for January 1-15, 2015

Follow previous instructions to prepare the report from the Company & Financial section of the Report Center

- Unless instructed otherwise, all Profit & Loss reports will be Standard.

Analyze the Profit & Loss report

- Note: Total Sales is calculated by adding account 4011 and 4012 together.
- 4050 Sales Discounts are subtracted and 4090 Returned Check Charges are added to 4010 Sales to calculate Total Income.
- 5000 Cost of Goods Sold is the total of the average cost of all items sold.
- The Total COGS is subtracted from Total Income to get the Gross Profit.
- The Expenses are listed and totaled and then subtracted from Gross Profit to get the Net Income.

Your Name Mountain Sports
Profit & Loss
January 1 - 15, 2015

	Jan 1 - 15, 15
Ordinary Income/Expense	
Income	
4010 · Sales	
4011 · Clothing & Accessory Sales	1,759.51
4012 · Equipment Sales	7,436.44
Total 4010 · Sales	9,195.95
4050 · Sales Discounts	-494.36
4090 · Returned Check Charges	25.00
Total Income	8,726.59
Cost of Goods Sold	
5000 · Cost of Goods Sold	3,482.46
Total COGS	3,482.46
Gross Profit	5,244.13
Expense	
6120 · Bank Service Charges	10.00
Total Expense	10.00
Net Ordinary Income	5,234.13
Net Income	5,234.13

Print the report

BACK UP YOUR NAME MOUNTAIN SPORTS

Whenever an important work session is complete, you should always back up your data. If your data or storage media is damaged or an error is discovered at a later time, the backup may be restored and the information used for recording transactions. The backup being made will contain all of the transactions entered in Chapter 5. In addition, it is always wise to make a duplicate of your data on a separate storage media just in case the original is damaged

Back up data for Your Name Mountain Sports to **Sports (Backup Ch. 5).qbb**

SUMMARY

In this chapter, cash, bank charge card, and credit sales were prepared for Your Name Mountain Sports, a retail business, using sales receipts, sales orders, and invoices. Credit memos and refund checks were issued, and customer accounts were added and revised. Invoices and sales receipts were edited, deleted, and voided. Sales orders were changed into invoices. Cash payments were received, and bank deposits were made. Methods of payment included cash, checks, credit cards, and debit cards. Nonsufficient funds payments were recorded and penalty charges were made. New accounts were added to the Chart of Accounts, and new items were added to the Item List while entering transactions. Inventory items were added and sold. All the transactions entered reinforced the QuickBooks concept of using the business form to record transactions rather than entering information in journals. The Journal was accessed, analyzed, and printed. The importance of reports for information and decision-making was illustrated. Sales reports emphasized both cash and credit sales according to the customer or according to the sales item generating the revenue. Accounts receivable reports focused on amounts owed by credit customers. The traditional trial balance emphasizing the equality of debits and credits was prepared.

END-OF-CHAPTER QUESTIONS

TRUE/FALSE

ANSWER THE FOLLOWING QUESTIONS IN THE SPACE PROVIDED BEFORE THE QUESTION NUMBER.

T 1. If a return is made after an invoice has been paid in full, a refund check is issued along with a credit memo.

T 2. QuickBooks automatically applies a payment received to the most current invoice.

T 3. Sales tax will be calculated automatically on an invoice if a customer is marked taxable.

F 4. A new sales item may be added only at the beginning of a period.

F 5. Items on a Sales Order are immediately removed from inventory.

F 6. All business forms must be duplicated before they can be customized.

F 7. The Discounts and Credits icon on the Receive Payments window allows discounts to be applied to invoices being paid by clicking Cancel.

F 8. Cash sales are recorded in the Receive Payments window and marked paid.

T 9. If a customer issues a check that is returned marked NSF, you may charge the customer the amount of the bank charges and any penalty charges you impose.

F 10. Sales tax must be calculated manually and added to sales receipts.

MULTIPLE CHOICE

WRITE THE LETTER OF THE CORRECT ANSWER IN THE SPACE PROVIDED BEFORE THE QUESTION NUMBER.

C 1. Information regarding details of a customer's balance may be obtained by viewing ___.
A. the Trial Balance
B. the Customer Balance Summary Report
C. the Customer Balance Detail Report
D. the check detail report

___ 2. Even though transactions are entered via business documents such as invoices and sales receipts, QuickBooks keeps track of all transactions ___.
A. in a chart
B. in the master account register
C. on a graph
D. in the Journal

___ 3. If a transaction is ___, it will not show up in the Customer Balance Detail Report.
A. voided
B. deleted
C. corrected
D. canceled

___ 4. A credit card sale is treated exactly like a ___.
A. cash sale
B. sale on account until reimbursement is received from a bank
C. sale on account
D. bank deposit

___ 5. If the word -Split- appears in the Split column of a report rather than an account name, it means that the transaction is split between two or more ___.
A. accounts or items
B. customers
C. journals
D. reports

___ 6. When adding a customer *on the fly*, you may choose to add just the customer's name by selecting ___.
A. Quick Add
B. Set Up
C. Condensed
D. none of the above—a customer cannot be added *on the fly*

_____ 7. The Item List stores information about ___.
A. each item that is out of stock
B. each item in stock
C. each customer with an account
D. each item a company sells

_____ 8. A report prepared to obtain information about sales, inventory, and merchandise costs is a ___.
A. Stock Report
B. Income Statement
C. Sales by Vendor Summary Report
D. Sales by Item Summary Report

_____ 9. If a customer has a balance for an amount owed and a return is made, a credit memo is prepared and ___.
A. a refund check is issued
B. the amount of the return is applied to an invoice
C. the customer determines whether to apply the amount to an invoice or to get a refund check
D. all of the above

_____ 10. Purchase information regarding an item sold by the company is entered ___.
A. in the Invoice Register
B. when adding a sales item
C. only when creating the company
D. when the last item in stock is sold

FILL-IN

IN THE SPACE PROVIDED, WRITE THE ANSWER THAT MOST APPROPRIATELY COMPLETES THE SENTENCE.

1. A report showing all sales, credits, and payments for each customer on account and the remaining balance on the account is the Customer Balance Detail report.
2. When a customer with a balance due on an account makes a payment, it is recorded in the Receive Payments window.
3. If the Quantity and Price Each are entered on an invoice, pressing the Tab key will cause QuickBooks to calculate and enter the correct information in the Amount column of the invoice.

4. QuickBooks allows you to view additional information within a report by using the__Zoom__ feature.

5. When you receive payments from customers, QuickBooks places the amount received in an account called__undeposited funds__.

SHORT ESSAY

Explain why you would use Find to locate an invoice. Based on chapter information, what is used to instruct Find to limit its search?

____
____
____
____
____

NAME______________________

CHAPTER 5: TRANSMITTAL

YOUR NAME MOUNTAIN SPORTS

Check the items below as you print them; then attach the documents and reports in the order listed when you submit them to your instructor.

___ Invoice 1: Russ Watson
___ Invoice 2: Jose Perez
___ Invoice 3: Mountain Schools
___ Invoice 4: Sandra Perkins
___ Sales Order 1: Kevin Thomsen
___ Sales Order 2: Russ Watson
___ Invoice 5: Kevin Thomsen
___ Invoice 6: Russ Watson
___ Invoice 7: Monique Gardener
___ Invoice 7 (Corrected): Monique Gardener
___ Customer Balance Detail
___ Invoice 3 (Corrected): Mountain Schools
___ Invoice 8: Mountain Recreation Center
___ Invoice 1 (Voided): Russ Watson
___ Credit Memo 9: Monique Gardener
___ Credit Memo 10: Russ Watson
___ Open Invoices Report, January 10, 2015
___ Sales Receipt 1: Cash Customer
___ Sales Receipt 2: Cash Customer
___ Sales Receipt 3: Cash Customer
___ Sales Receipt 4: Cash Customer
___ Sales Receipt 5: Cash Customer
___ Sales Receipt 6: Cash Customer
___ Sales Receipt 7: Cash Customer
___ Sales Receipt 8: Cash Customer
___ Sales by Item Summary, January 1-13, 2015
___ Sales Receipt 1 (Corrected): Cash Customer
___ Payment Receipt: Oskar Villanueva
___ Payment Receipt: Monique Gardener
___ Payment Receipt: Mountain Recreation Center
___ Payment Receipt: Mountain Schools
___ Payment Receipt: Russ Watson
___ Payment Receipt: Jose Perez
___ Payment Receipt: Gail Daily
___ Payment Receipt: Sandra Perkins
___ Payment Receipt: Kevin Thomsen
___ Customer Balance Summary
___ Deposit Summary
___ Opening Balance Invoice: Oskar Villanueva
___ Invoice 11: Oskar Villanueva
___ Credit Memo 12: Jose Perez
___ Check 1: Jose Perez
___ Journal, January 1-15, 2015
___ Trial Balance, January 1-15, 2015
___ Inventory Valuation Detail, January 1-15, 2015
___ Profit & Loss, January 1-15, 2015

5

END-OF-CHAPTER PROBLEM

YOUR NAME RESORT CLOTHING

Your Name Resort Clothing is a men's and women's clothing store located in San Luis Obispo, California, that specializes in resort wear. The store is owned and operated by you and your partner Karen Olsen. Karen keeps the books and runs the office for the store, and you are responsible for buying merchandise and managing the store. Both partners sell merchandise in the store, and they have some college students working part time during the evenings and on the weekends.

INSTRUCTIONS

As in previous chapters, use a copy of **Clothing.qbw** that you downloaded following the directions presented in Chapter 1. If QuickBooks wants to update the program, click Yes. Open the company, and record the following transactions using invoices, sales receipts, and Receive Payments. Your Name Resort Clothing accepts cash, checks, debit cards, and credit cards for *cash* sales. Make bank deposits as instructed. Print the reports as indicated. Add new accounts, items, and customers where appropriate. Pay attention to the dates and note that the year is **2015**. Verify the year to use with your instructor and use the same year for Clothing in Chapters 5, 6, and 7.

When recording transactions, use the Item List to determine the item(s) sold. All transactions are taxable unless otherwise indicated. Terms for sales on account are the standard terms assigned to each customer individually. If a customer exceeds his or her credit limit, accept the transaction. When receiving payment for sales on account, always check to see if a discount should be given. A customer's beginning balance is not eligible for a discount. The date of the sale begins the discount period. A check should be received or postmarked within ten days of the invoice in order to qualify for a discount. If the customer has any credits to the account because of a return, apply the credits to the appropriate invoice. If the customer makes a return and does not have a balance on account, prepare a refund check for the customer.

Invoices begin with number 15, are numbered consecutively, and have lines printed around each field. Sales Receipts begin with number 25, are also numbered consecutively, and have lines printed around each field. Sales Orders are accepted for orders made by telephone, begin with the number 1, and have lines printed around each field. Each invoice, sales order and sales receipt should contain a message. Use the one you feel is most appropriate. If you write any checks, keep track of the check numbers used. QuickBooks does not always display the check number you are expecting to see. Remember that QuickBooks does not print check numbers on checks because most businesses use checks with the check numbers preprinted.

If a transaction can be printed, print the transaction when it is entered unless your instructor specifies the transactions to print.

LISTS

The Item List and Customers & Jobs List are displayed for your use in determining which sales item and customer to use in a transaction.

Item List

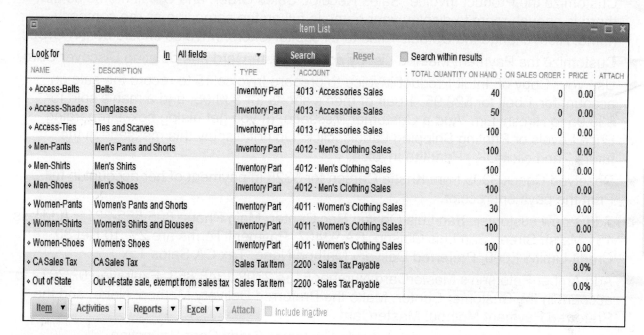

NAME	DESCRIPTION	TYPE	ACCOUNT	TOTAL QUANTITY ON HAND	ON SALES ORDER	PRICE	ATTACH
Access-Belts	Belts	Inventory Part	4013 · Accessories Sales	40	0	0.00	
Access-Shades	Sunglasses	Inventory Part	4013 · Accessories Sales	50	0	0.00	
Access-Ties	Ties and Scarves	Inventory Part	4013 · Accessories Sales	100	0	0.00	
Men-Pants	Men's Pants and Shorts	Inventory Part	4012 · Men's Clothing Sales	100	0	0.00	
Men-Shirts	Men's Shirts	Inventory Part	4012 · Men's Clothing Sales	100	0	0.00	
Men-Shoes	Men's Shoes	Inventory Part	4012 · Men's Clothing Sales	100	0	0.00	
Women-Pants	Women's Pants and Shorts	Inventory Part	4011 · Women's Clothing Sales	30	0	0.00	
Women-Shirts	Women's Shirts and Blouses	Inventory Part	4011 · Women's Clothing Sales	100	0	0.00	
Women-Shoes	Women's Shoes	Inventory Part	4011 · Women's Clothing Sales	100	0	0.00	
CA Sales Tax	CA Sales Tax	Sales Tax Item	2200 · Sales Tax Payable			8.0%	
Out of State	Out-of-state sale, exempt from sales tax	Sales Tax Item	2200 · Sales Tax Payable			0.0%	

Customer & Jobs List

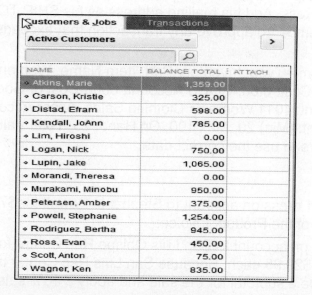

NAME	BALANCE TOTAL	ATTACH
Atkins, Marie	1,359.00	
Carson, Kristie	325.00	
Distad, Efram	598.00	
Kendall, JoAnn	785.00	
Lim, Hiroshi	0.00	
Logan, Nick	750.00	
Lupin, Jake	1,065.00	
Morandi, Theresa	0.00	
Murakami, Minobu	950.00	
Petersen, Amber	375.00	
Powell, Stephanie	1,254.00	
Rodriguez, Bertha	945.00	
Ross, Evan	450.00	
Scott, Anton	75.00	
Wagner, Ken	835.00	

RECORD TRANSACTIONS

January 1, 2015:

- Add your name to the Company Name and the Legal Name. The name will be **Your Name Resort Clothing** (Type your actual name, *not* the words *Your Name*.)
- Change the company preferences so that the date prepared, time prepared, and report basis do not print as part of the heading on reports. Have the reports refresh automatically.
- Customize the Product Invoice, Sales Receipt, Sales Order, and Credit Memo so that there is enough room to display your name in full on the same line as the company name. Also, change the Default Titles to all capital letters. (Invoice should be INVOICE).
- Customize the Payment Method List by adding MasterCard and deleting Discover Card.
- Use your Copy of: Intuit Product Invoice to prepare Invoice 15 to record the sale on account for 1 belt for $29.95, 1 pair of men's shorts for $39.95, and a man's shirt for $39.95 to Hiroshi Lim. Add a Customer Message. (If you get dialog boxes regarding Price Levels or Printing Shipping Labels, click "Do not display this message in the future," and click OK.) Print the invoice.
- Received Check 3305 from Kristie Carson for $325 in payment of her account in full. Print the payment receipt.
- Add a new customer: San Luis Obispo Rec Center, Main Phone 805-555-2241, Address 451 Marsh Street, San Luis Obispo, CA 93407, Payment Terms are 2% 10 Net 30, Credit Limit $1,000, Preferred Delivery Method None, Tax CA Sales Tax.
- Add Amber Petersen's MasterCard Number 5134 2798 1348 858, Expiration 02/2019 to account in the Customer Center. Make the Preferred Delivery Method: None, and the Preferred Payment Method: MasterCard.
- Use the Company Menu to click Disable Customer Credit Card Protection.
- Prepare a Sales Order for 1 pair of sunglasses for $89.95, a belt for $69.95, and a tie for $39.95 to Evan Ross. Add his mailing address as his SHIP TO address. Print the Sales Order. (Remember to approve any transaction that exceeds a customer's credit limit.)
- Add a new sales item—Type: Inventory Part, Item Name: Women-Dress, Description: Women's Dresses, Cost: 0.00, COGS Account: 5000-Cost of Goods Sold, Tax Code: Tax, Income Account: 4011 Women's Clothing Sales, Asset Account: 1120-Inventory Asset; Reorder Point: (Min) 20, Max 100, On Hand: 25, Total Value: $750, as of 01/01/2015—be sure to use the correct date.

January 3, 2015:

- Record the sale of 1 dress on account to Stephanie Powell for $79.95. Make sure you are using the Copy of the Product Invoice.
- Sold 5 men's shirts on account to San Luis Obispo Rec Center for $29.95 each, 5 pair of men's shorts for $29.95 each. Because San Luis Rec Center is a nonprofit organization, include a subtotal for the sale and apply a 10% sales discount for a

nonprofit organization. (Create any new sales items necessary by following the instructions given in the chapter. If you need to add an income account for Sales Discounts to the Chart of Accounts, assign account number 4050. The nonprofit discount is marked Taxable so the discount is applied before adding sales tax.)

- ▶ Sold 1 woman's blouse for $59.95 to a cash customer using Check 378 for the full amount including tax. Record the sale to Cash Customer on Sales Receipt 25. (If necessary, refer to steps provided within the chapter for instructions on creating a cash customer.)
- ▶ Received a belt returned by Ken Wagner. The original price of the belt was $49.95. Prepare a Credit Memo. Add the new message **Your return has been processed.** to the Credit Memo. Apply the credit to his Opening Balance, then print the Credit Memo.
- ▶ Sold a dress to a customer for $99.95. The customer paid with her Visa Number 4012 2345 5678 910, Expiration Date 01/2018. Record the sale. If there is a number in CHECK NO., delete it.
- ▶ Sold a scarf for $19.95 plus tax for cash. Record the sale. (Hint: Look at the description for the Access-Ties item.)
- ▶ Received payments on account from the following customers:
  - o Efram Distad, $598.00, Check 145.
  - o Amber Petersen, $375, paid with MasterCard on file.
  - o Nick Logan, $750, Check 8915-02.
  - o Ken Wagner, $781.05, Debit Card 7652 1267 9824 225, Expiration 03/2019.

5

January 5, 2015:

- ▶ Evan Ross came into the store to pick up his items on order. Create an invoice from the sales order. (Use the date 01/05/15, approve any transaction that exceeds a customer's credit limit, and customize the Sales Order Invoice so that the Default Title is INVOICE. Resize your name and the default title so they do not overlap as you did for other templates earlier.) Print the invoice.
- ▶ Deposit all cash, checks, debit card, and credit card receipts. Print a Deposit Summary.

January 7, 2015

- ▶ Evan Ross returned the tie he purchased on 01/05/15 for $39.95. (Did you apply this to Invoice 19?)

January 15, 2015:

- ▶ Received an NSF notice from the bank for the check for $325 from Kristie Carson. Enter the necessary transaction for this nonsufficient funds (bounced) check to be paid on receipt. The bank's charges are $15, and Your Name Resort Clothing charges $30 for all NSF checks. Print the revised Payment Receipt. (If necessary, refer to steps provided within the chapter for instructions on changing the QuickBooks Account 5009 Returned Check Charges to Account Number 4090.) Access Invoice 21. Make sure the Invoice DATE is 01/15/2015. Make the following changes: TEMPLATE Copy of: Intuit Product Invoice, TERMS "Due on receipt" and CUSTOMER MESSAGE Please remit to above address. Print Invoice 21. Edit her Opening Balance invoice to show terms of Due on receipt. Use the template "Copy of Intuit Product Invoice." Print the invoice. Accept any messages regarding previous periods. Do not change her Terms permanently.

- Nick Logan returned a shirt he had purchased for $54.99 plus tax. Record the return. Check the balance of his account. If there is no balance, issue a refund check. Print the Credit Memo and Check 1.
- Sold 3 men's shirts to a cash customer, for $39.95 each plus tax. He used his MasterCard 5210 5689 2356 134, Expiration 07/2018 for payment.
- Sold on account 1 dress for $99.99, 1 pair of women's sandals for $79.95, and a belt for $39.95 to JoAnn Kendall.
- Sold 1 pair of women's shorts for $34.95 to a cash customer. Accepted Check 8160 for payment.
- Received payments on account from the following customers:
    - Partial payment from Jake Lupin, $250, Debit Card Number 7210 4567 1234 856, Expiration 11/2018. Leave as an underpayment.
    - Payment in full from Anton Scott, Visa Number 4235 8965 4893 225, Expiration 12/2018.
    - Received $1,338.62 from Stephanie Powell as payment in full on account, Check 2311. The payment was postmarked 1/11/2015. (Apply the discount to Invoice 16, click the line for Invoice 16; click the Discounts And Credits icon; calculate the 2 percent discount (be sure to round up to the nearest cent) and enter the amount on the Discounts and Credits screen, select the appropriate account for the sales discount, click Done to apply the discount.
    - Received Check 2805 for $619.24 as payment in full from Evan Ross. (If eligible for a discount on Invoice 19, apply it to the actual amount that is owed after the return rather than accept QuickBooks' discount on the original invoice amount.)
- Sold on account to Bertha Rodiguez: 3 pairs of men's pants for $75.00 each, 3 men's shirts for $50.00 each, 3 belts for $39.99 each, 2 pairs of men's shoes for $90.00 each, 2 ties for $55.00 each, and 1 pair of sunglasses for $75.00. (If the amount of the sale exceeds Bertha's credit limit, accept the sale anyway.)
- Change the Sales Item Access-Shades to Access-Sunglasses.
- Sold on account 1 pair of sunglasses for $95.00, 2 dresses for $99.95 each, and 2 pairs of women's shoes for $65.00 each to Amber Petersen.
- Print Customer Balance Detail Report for All Transactions in Portrait orientation. Adjust column widths so the account names are shown in full and the report is one page wide without selecting Fit report to one page wide. The report length may be longer than one page.
- Print a Sales by Item Summary for 01/01/2015 to 01/15/2015 in Landscape orientation. Adjust column widths so the report fits on one page wide. Do not select Fit report to one page wide.

- Deposit all payments, checks, and charges received from customers. Print the Deposit Summary.
- Print a Journal for 01/01/2015 to 01/15/2015 in Landscape orientation. (Remember to Expand the report, adjust the column widths, and remove any unused columns from display. In order to print the report on one page wide, the information in the memo column may not show in full.)
- Print the Trial Balance for 01/01/2015 to 01/15/2015.
- Print an Inventory Valuation Summary for 01/15/2015. (Remove the columns for Sales Price, Retail Value, and % of Tot Retail). Memorize the report.
- Print Profit & Loss (Standard) for 01/01/2015 to 01/15/2015
- Backup your work to Clothing (Backup Ch. 5).

NAME ______________________

CHAPTER 5: TRANSMITTAL

YOUR NAME RESORT CLOTHING

Check the items below as you print them; then attach the documents and reports in the order listed when you submit them to your instructor.

___ Invoice 15: Hiroshi Lim
___ Payment Receipt: Kristie Carson
___ Sales Order 1: Evan Ross
___ Invoice 16: Stephanie Powell
___ Invoice 17: San Luis Obispo Rec Center
___ Sales Receipt 25: Cash Customer
___ Credit Memo 18: Ken Wagner
___ Sales Receipt 26: Cash Customer
___ Sales Receipt 27: Cash Customer
___ Payment Receipt: Efram Distad
___ Payment Receipt: Amber Petersen
___ Payment Receipt: Nick Logan
___ Payment Receipt: Ken Wagner
___ Invoice 19: Evan Ross
___ Deposit Summary, January 5, 2015
___ Credit Memo 20: Evan Ross
___ Invoice 21: Kristie Carson
___ Opening Balance Invoice (Revised): Kristie Carson
___ Credit Memo 22: Nick Logan
___ Check 1: Nick Logan
___ Sales Receipt 28: Cash Customer
___ Invoice 23: JoAnn Kendall
___ Sales Receipt 29: Cash Customer
___ Payment Receipt: Jake Lupin
___ Payment Receipt: Anton Scott
___ Payment Receipt: Stephanie Powell
___ Payment Receipt: Evan Ross
___ Invoice 24: Bertha Rodriguez
___ Invoice 25: Amber Petersen
___ Customer Balance Detail
___ Sales by Item Summary, January 1-15, 2015
___ Deposit Summary, January 15, 2015
___ Journal, January 1-15-2015
___ Trial Balance, January 1-15, 2015
___ Inventory Valuation Summary, January 1-15, 2015
___ Profit & Loss, January 1-15, 2015

PAYABLES AND PURCHASES: MERCHANDISING BUSINESS

6

LEARNING OBJECTIVES

At the completion of this chapter you will be able to:

1. Understand the concepts for computerized accounting for payables in a merchandising business.
2. Customize a Purchase Order template.
3. Prepare, view, and print purchase orders and checks.
4. Enter items received against purchase orders.
5. Enter bills, enter vendor credits, and pay bills by check or credit card.
6. Edit and correct errors in bills and purchase orders.
7. Add new vendors, add new accounts.
8. Assign preferred vendors to sales items.
9. View accounts payable transaction history from the Enter Bills window.
10. Use the QuickZoom feature to view and/or print QuickReports for vendors, accounts payable register, and so on.
11. Record and edit transactions in the Accounts Payable Register.
12. Use various payment options including writing checks, using Pay Bills to write checks, and company debit and credit cards.
13. Use early payment discounts.
14. Display and print a Sales Tax Liability Report, an Accounts Payable Aging Summary Report, an Unpaid Bills Detail Report, a Vendor Balance Summary Report, an Inventory Stock Status by Item Report, and an Inventory Valuation Detail Report.
15. Use the Vendor Center to obtain or modify vendor information, and to assign accounts to vendors.
16. Use the Inventory Center to view information about individual inventory items and to prepare an Inventory Stock Status report.
17. Add comments to a report.

ACCOUNTING FOR PAYABLES AND PURCHASES

In a merchandising business, much of the accounting for purchases and payables consists of ordering merchandise for resale and paying bills for expenses incurred in the operation of the business. Purchases are for things used in the operation of the business. Some transactions will be in the form of cash purchases; others will be purchases on account. Bills can be paid when they are received or when they are due. Merchandise received must be checked against purchase orders, and completed purchase orders must be closed. Rather than use journals, QuickBooks continues to focus on recording transactions based on the business document; therefore, you use the Enter Bills and Pay Bills features of the program to record the receipt and payment of bills. While QuickBooks does not refer to it as such, the Vendor List is the same as the Accounts Payable Subsidiary Ledger.

QuickBooks can remind you when inventory needs to be ordered and when payments are due. Purchase orders are prepared when ordering merchandise and sent to a vendor who will process the order and send the merchandise to the company. When the merchandise is received, the quantity received is recorded. The program automatically tracks inventory and uses the average cost method to value the inventory.

If the bill accompanies the merchandise, both the bill and the merchandise receipt are recorded together on a bill. If the merchandise is received without a bill, the receipt of items is recorded; and, when the bill arrives, it is recorded. When the inventory receipt is recorded, the purchase order is closed automatically.

QuickBooks can calculate and apply discounts earned for paying bills early. Payments can be made by recording payments in the Pay Bills window; or, if using the cash basis for accounting, by writing a check. Merchandise purchased may be paid for at the same time the items and the bill are received, or it may be paid for at a later date. A cash purchase can be recorded by writing a check, using a credit or debit card, or using petty cash. Even though QuickBooks focuses on recording transactions on the business forms used, all transactions are recorded behind the scenes in the Journal.

As in previous chapters, corrections can be made directly on the bill or within the account register. New accounts and vendors may be added *on the fly* as transactions are entered. Purchase orders, bills, or checks may be voided or deleted. Reports illustrating vendor balances, unpaid bills, accounts payable aging, sales tax liability, transaction history, accounts payable registers, and inventory may be viewed and printed. Once a report is prepared, you may add a comment to it and print and/or save the commented report. A commented report may <u>not</u> be exported to Excel.

TRAINING TUTORIAL AND PROCEDURES

The following tutorial will once again work with the fictitious company, Your Name Mountain Sports. Use the company file for Your Name Mountain Sports that contains the transactions you entered for Chapter 5. Continue using the same year that you used in Chapter 5. The text uses the year 2015. As in previous chapters, you will be instructed when to print business documents and reports. Everything that is to be printed within the chapter and at the end of the chapter is listed on transmittal sheets that contain lines so you can check the items you have printed. Always verify printing requirements with your instructor.

OPEN QUICKBOOKS AND COMPANY FILE

➤ Open QuickBooks and Your Name Mountain Sports as previously instructed

BEGIN TUTORIAL

In this chapter you will be entering purchases of merchandise for resale in the business and entering bills incurred by the company in the operation of the business. You will also be recording the payment of bills and purchases using checks and credit cards.

The Vendor List keeps information regarding the vendors with which you do business. This information includes the vendor names, addresses, telephone number, fax number, e-mail address, payment terms, credit limits, and account numbers. You will be using the following list for vendors:

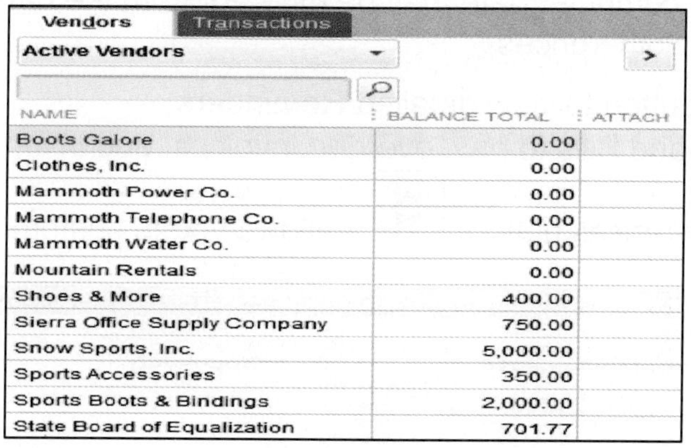
Vendors
Transactions
Active Vendors
NAME
BALANCE TOTAL
ATTACH
Boots Galore 0.00
Clothes, Inc. 0.00
Mammoth Power Co. 0.00
Mammoth Telephone Co. 0.00
Mammoth Water Co. 0.00
Mountain Rentals 0.00
Shoes & More 400.00
Sierra Office Supply Company 750.00
Snow Sports, Inc. 5,000.00
Sports Accessories 350.00
Sports Boots & Bindings 2,000.00
State Board of Equalization 701.77

As in previous chapters, transactions are listed on memos. The transaction date is the same as the memo date unless otherwise specified. Vendor names, when necessary, will be given in the transaction. Unless the memo tells you a different term, use 2% 10 Net 30. To determine the account used in the transaction, refer to the Chart of Accounts.

6

REMINDERS

QuickBooks has a feature for Reminders that is used to remind you of things that need to be completed. The Company menu allows you to display Reminders. Reminders uses a dash board layout to display information in summary (collapsed) form. Click on the arrow for a category to display information in detailed (expanded) form. The information displayed is affected by the date of the computer; so, what you see on your screen will not match the text display.

MEMO
DATE: January 16, 2015

Display Reminders to determine which items need to be ordered.

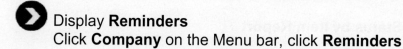

Display **Reminders**
Click **Company** on the Menu bar, click **Reminders**

- Reminders appears on the screen in Summary (Collapsed) form.

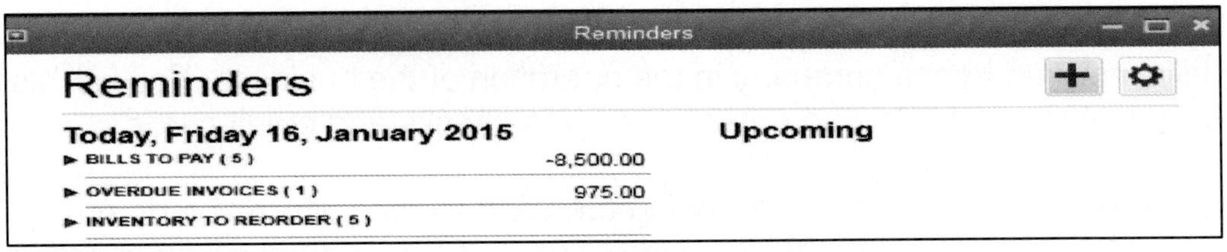

- Note: Your Reminders Summary (Collapsed) form and Reminders Detail (Expanded) form may not match the ones displayed in the text. This is due to the fact that your computer date may be different from the date used in the chapter. Disregard any differences.

Click the ▶ button to view detailed Reminders

- You may expand Bills to pay, overdue invoices, and inventory to reorder.
- The Set Preferences button ⚙ allows you to customize the data shown.

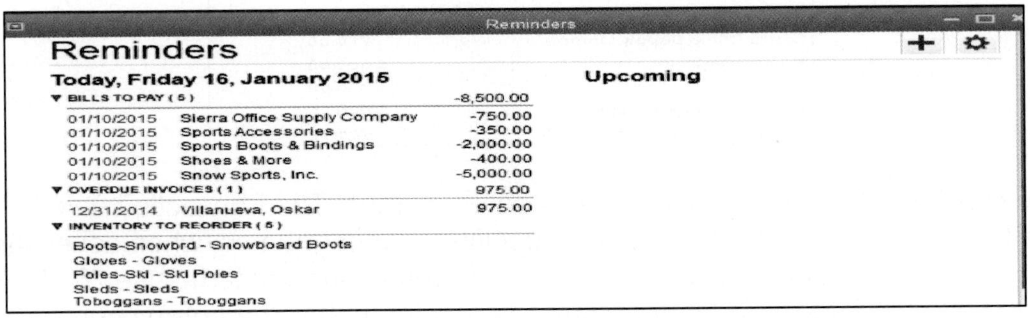

Close Reminders

INVENTORY STOCK STATUS BY ITEM REPORT

In addition to the Inventory Valuation Detail Report prepared in Chapter 5, several Inventory Reports are available for viewing and/or printing. One report is the Inventory Stock Status by Item report. This report provides information regarding the stock on hand, the stock on order, and the stock that needs to be reordered.

MEMO

DATE: January 16, 2015

More detailed information regarding the stock on hand, ordered, and needing to be ordered needs to be provided. View the report for Inventory Stock Status by Item.

View the **Inventory Stock Status by Item Report**

Click **Reports** on the Menu bar, point to **Inventory,** click **Inventory Stock Status by Item**
The dates are From **01/01/15** and To **01/16/15**
Tab to generate the report and view the report

Your Name Mountain Sports
Inventory Stock Status by Item
January 1 - 16, 2015

	Pref Vendor	Reorder Pt (Min)	Max	On Hand	Available	Order	On PO	Reorder Qty	Sales/Week
Inventory									
Accessories	Sports Accessories	100	850	795	795		0	0	2.2
Bindings-Skis	Sports Boots & Bindings	10	65	43	43		0	0	3.1
Bindings-Snow	Sports Boots & Bindings	5	65	48	48		0	0	0.9
Boots	Shoes & More	10	35	20	20		0	0	0
Boots-Ski	Boots Galore	10	35	14	14		0	0	0.4
Boots-Snowbrd	Boots Galore	10	35	10	10	✓	0	25	0.9
Gloves	Clothes, Inc.	20	45	20	20	✓	0	25	0.9
Hats	Sports Accessories	20	40	29	29		0	0	0.4
Helmets		5	30	20	20		0	0	2.2
Pants-Ski	Clothes, Inc.	10	100	93	93		0	0	0.9
Pants-Snowbrd	Clothes, Inc.	10	100	50	50		0	0	0
Parkas	Clothes, Inc.	25	100	73	73		0	0	0.9
Poles-Ski	Snow Sports, Inc.	15	28	13	13	✓	0	15	2.2
Skis	Snow Sports, Inc.	15	60	43	43		0	0	3.1
Sleds		5	7	4	4	✓	0	3	2.6
Snowboard	Snow Sports, Inc.	15	60	28	28		0	0	0.9
Socks	Boots Galore	25	100	72	72		0	0	1.3
Sweaters	Clothes, Inc.	25	100	73	73		0	0	0.9
Toboggans		5	7	5	5	✓	0	2	2.2
Underwear	Clothes, Inc.	30	50	32	32		0	0	0.4

- Since there is no information and for better clarity, the columns for On Sales Order, For Assemblies, and Next Delivery have been removed.
- Notice the items marked in the Order column. This tells you that you need to prepare and send purchase orders.
- If the items on hand are equal to or less than the number of items indicated in the Reorder Pt (Min) so QuickBooks marks the Order column.
- The marked items are the same items that were shown in Reminders.
- To enable you to determine the quantity to order, QuickBooks shows you the Max column so you can see the maximum number to have in stock.
- The column for Reorder Qty calculates the amount to reorder. This is based on the difference between the maximum and the number on hand.

Make note of the items and quantities that need to be ordered, and close the report

PURCHASE ORDERS

Using the QuickBooks Purchase Order feature helps you track your inventory. Information regarding the items on order or the items received may be obtained at any time. Once merchandise has been received, QuickBooks marks the purchase order *Received in full,* which closes the purchase order automatically. The Purchase Order feature must be selected as a Preference when setting up the company, or it may be selected prior to processing your first purchase order. QuickBooks will automatically set up an account called Purchase Orders in the Chart of Accounts. The account does not affect the balance sheet or the profit and loss statement of the company. As with other business forms, QuickBooks allows you to customize your purchase orders to fit the needs of your individual company or to use the purchase order format that comes with the program.

VERIFY PURCHASE ORDERS PREFERENCE

Verify that Purchase Orders are active by checking the Company Preferences for inventory.

> **MEMO**
> **DATE:** January 16, 2015
>
> Prior to completing the first purchase order, verify that Purchase Orders are active.

Verify that Purchase Orders are active

Click **Edit** menu, click **Preferences**
Click **Items & Inventory**, click the **Company Preferences** tab

- Make sure there is a check mark in the check box for **Inventory and purchase orders are active**. If not, click the check box to select.

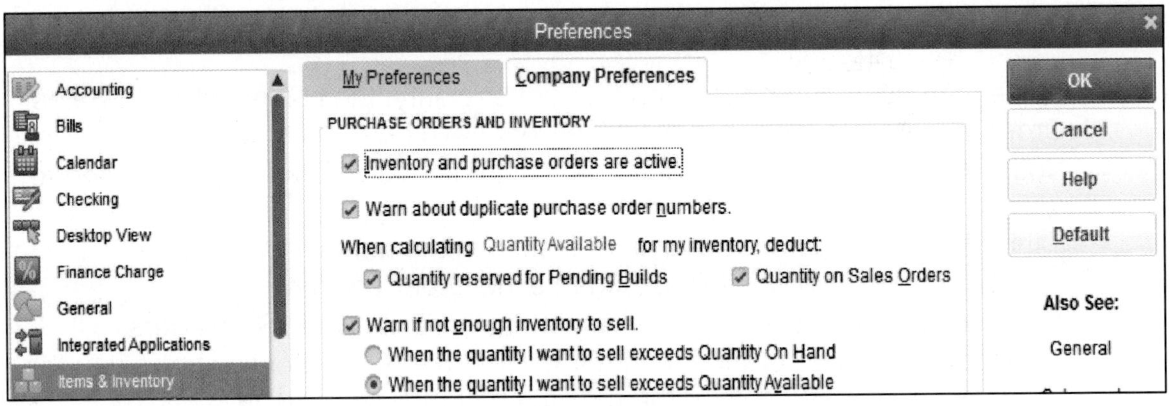

Click **OK** to accept and close the Preferences screen

CUSTOMIZE PURCHASE ORDERS

As instructed in Chapter 5, business forms may be customized. Prior to recording your first purchase order, it should be customized.

Customize a Purchase Order

Click the **Purchase Orders** icon in the **Vendors** section of the Home Page

Click the **Formatting** tab on the Create Purchase Orders Icon bar, click **Customize Data Layout**

Change the Default Title in the Additional Customization screen to **PURCHASE ORDER**

On the Additional Customization screen, click the **Layout Designer...** button

- If you get a message regarding overlapping fields, click **Do not display this message in the future**, and then click **OK**, and then click **Layout Designer**.

Follow the procedures in Chapter 5 to change the size for **PURCHASE ORDER** to begin at **5**:

Expand the area for **Your Name Mountain Sports** to **4 ¾**

Click **OK** to close the Layout Designer

Click **OK** to close the Additional Customization screen

Do <u>not</u> close the Purchase Order

PREPARE PURCHASE ORDER

Once Purchase Orders are active, they may be prepared. Typically, Purchase orders are prepared to order merchandise; but they may also be used to order non-inventory items like supplies or services. The same purchase order may not be sent to several vendors. Each vendor should receive a separate purchase order. A purchase order, however, may have more than one item listed. To determine the quantity to order, you may calculate and order any quantity or you may order the amount suggested in the Reorder Qty column on the Inventory Stock Status by Item report.

MEMO

DATE: January 16, 2015

With only 10 pairs of snowboard boots in stock in the middle of January an additional 25 pairs of boots in assorted sizes need to be ordered from Boots Galore for $75 per pair. Prepare Purchase Order 1.

Prepare Purchase Order 1 for 25 pairs of snowboard boots

Purchase Order 1 should be on the screen

- If not, click the **Purchases Order** icon on the Home Page.

If you wish to save space on the screen, click the Hide History button

To resize the purchase order so it is smaller, point to the edge of the form and drag the sizing handle

Click the drop-down list arrow for **Vendor**, click **Boots Galore**

The Template should be Custom Purchase Order, select if necessary

Tab to or click **Date**, enter **01/16/2015**

- P.O. No. should be 1. If not, enter 1 as the P.O. No.

Tab to or click **Item**, click **Boots-Snowbrd**

Tab to or click **Qty**, enter **25**

- The cost of the item was entered when Boots-Snowbrd was created. The Rate should appear automatically as **75.00**.

Tab to generate Amount

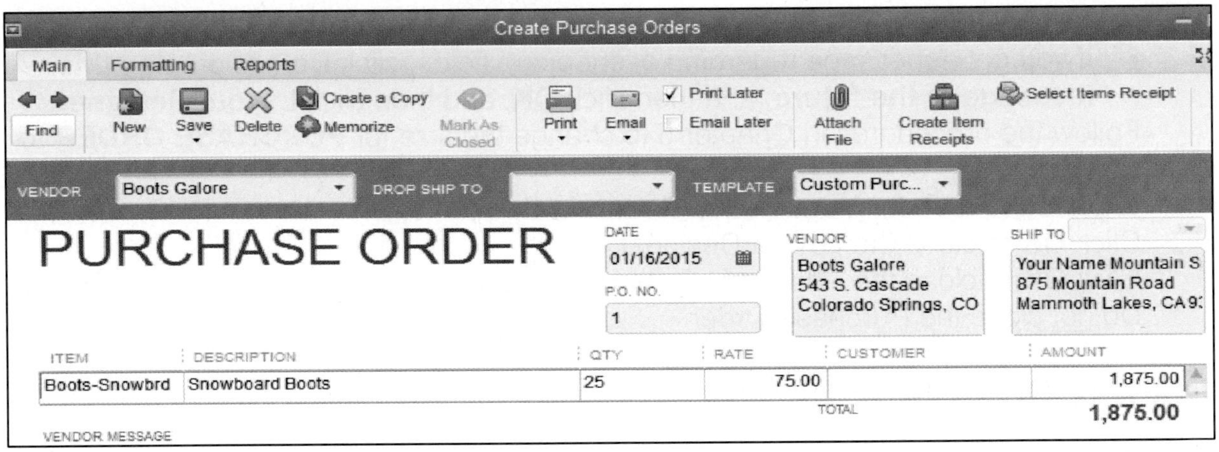

On the Create Purchase Orders **Main** Icon bar, click **Print** to print the **Purchase Order**

Check printer settings

- Be sure to print lines around each field.

Click **Print**

- Sometimes, after printing, you will get a Recording Transaction message, if you have made no changes, click **Yes**.

Click **Save & Close**

ADD NEW VENDOR

MEMO

DATE: January 16, 2015

Add a new vendor: Snow Stuff, Main Phone: 303-555-7765, Fax: 303-555-5677, Main E-mail: SnowStuff@ski.com, 7105 Camino del Rio, Durango, CO 81302, Terms: 2% 10 Net 30, Credit Limit: $2000.

Add a new vendor

Open the **Vendor Center** as previously instructed

Click the **New Vendor…** button at the top of the Vendor Center

Click **New Vendor**

Enter **Snow Stuff** for the **Vendor** name and the **Company** name

There is no Opening Balance

Use the information in the Memo to complete the Address Info tab as previously instructed

Click the **Payment Settings** tab, click the drop-down list arrow for **PAYMENT TERMS**, and click **2% 10 Net 30**
Tab to or click **CREDIT LIMIT**, enter **2000**
Click **OK** to add Vendor, close the Vendor Center

ASSIGN PREFERRED VENDOR AND COST TO ITEM

Most of the items in the Item List have a Preferred Vendor and a Cost entered as Purchase Information. This enables you to prepare a purchase order and have QuickBooks insert the Vendor Name and cost automatically when an Item Code is entered on a Purchase Order.

Assign Snow Stuff as the Preferred Vendor for Sleds and Toboggans. Also assign a Cost of $50 to Sleds and $110 to Toboggans

Open the **Item List** as previously instructed
Double-click **Sleds**
Click in the text box for **Cost**, enter **50**, press **Tab** twice
Click the drop-down list arrow for **Preferred Vendor**
Click **Snow Stuff**, click **OK**

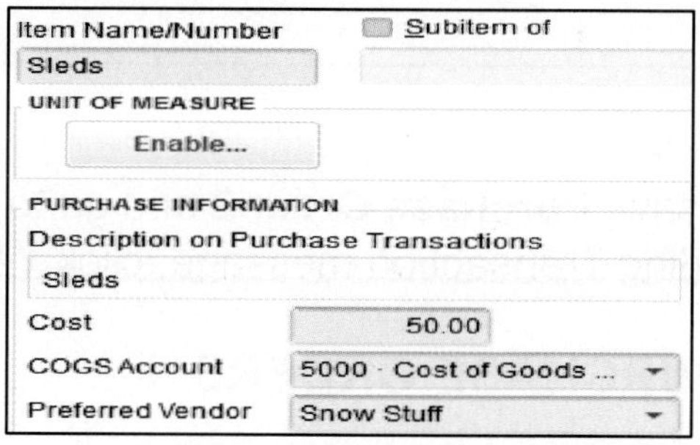

Repeat for Toboggans using **$110** for Cost and **Snow Stuff** as the Preferred Vendor
Close the Item List

PREPARE PURCHASE ORDER FOR MULTIPLE ITEMS

If more than one item is purchased from a vendor, all items purchased can be included on the same purchase order.

MEMO
DATE: January 16, 2015

Prepare a purchase order for 3 sleds @ $50 each, and 2 toboggans @ $110 each from Snow Stuff

Prepare a purchase order using an assigned vendor

Click the **Purchase Orders** icon on the Home Page

- The **Date** should be **01/16/2015**.
- P.O. No. should be **2**. If it is not, enter **2**.

Tab to or click the first line in the column for **Item**

Click the drop-down list arrow for **Item**, click **Sleds**

- Vendor information for Snow Stuff is automatically completed.

Tab to or click **Qty**, enter **3**

- The quantities ordered for sleds and toboggans are the same quantities listed in the Reorder Qty column of the Inventory Stock Status by Item report.
- The purchase cost of $50 is automatically entered.

Tab to generate the total for **Amount**

Repeat steps necessary to enter the information to order 2 toboggans

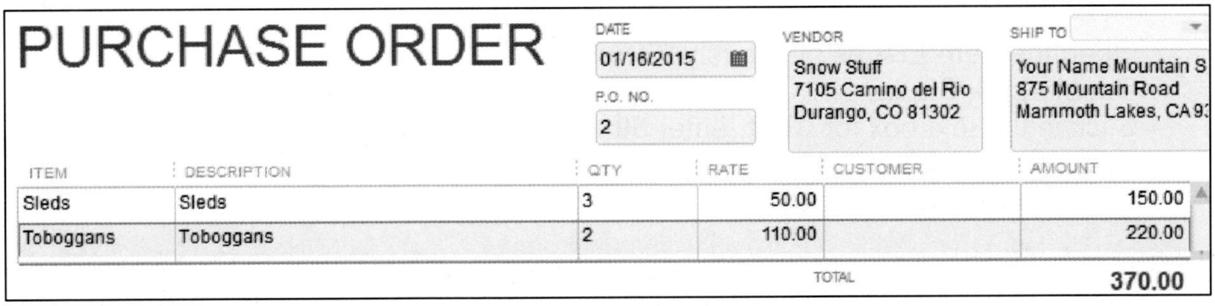

PURCHASE ORDER

DATE: 01/16/2015

P.O. NO.: 2

VENDOR: Snow Stuff, 7105 Camino del Rio, Durango, CO 81302

SHIP TO: Your Name Mountain S, 875 Mountain Road, Mammoth Lakes, CA 9

ITEM	DESCRIPTION	QTY	RATE	CUSTOMER	AMOUNT
Sleds	Sleds	3	50.00		150.00
Toboggans	Toboggans	2	110.00		220.00
				TOTAL	370.00

Print **Purchase Order 2**

Click **Save & New** to save **Purchase Order 2** and go to the next purchase order

- If you get a Recording Transaction message, click **Yes**.

ENTER ADDITIONAL PURCHASE ORDERS

MEMO

DATE: January 16, 2015

After referring to the Inventory Stock Status by Item report, prepare purchase orders:
25 pairs of gloves @ 15.00 each from Preferred Vendor: Clothes, Inc.
12 sets of ski poles @ 30.00 each from Preferred Vendor: Snow Sports, Inc.

Prepare and print the purchase orders indicated above.

Compare your completed purchase orders with the ones following:

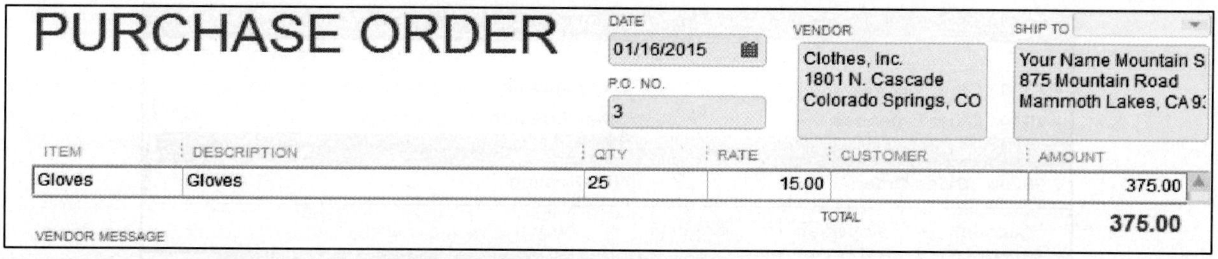

PURCHASE ORDER

DATE 01/16/2015

P.O. NO. 3

VENDOR
Clothes, Inc.
1801 N. Cascade
Colorado Springs, CO

SHIP TO
Your Name Mountain S
875 Mountain Road
Mammoth Lakes, CA 9

ITEM	DESCRIPTION	QTY	RATE	CUSTOMER	AMOUNT
Gloves	Gloves	25	15.00		375.00

TOTAL 375.00

VENDOR MESSAGE

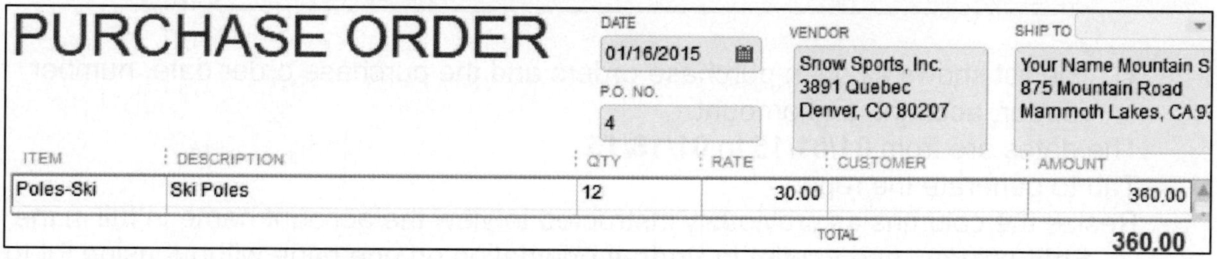

PURCHASE ORDER

DATE 01/16/2015

P.O. NO. 4

VENDOR
Snow Sports, Inc.
3891 Quebec
Denver, CO 80207

SHIP TO
Your Name Mountain S
875 Mountain Road
Mammoth Lakes, CA 9

ITEM	DESCRIPTION	QTY	RATE	CUSTOMER	AMOUNT
Poles-Ski	Ski Poles	12	30.00		360.00

TOTAL 360.00

Save and **Close** after entering and printing Purchase Order 4

PURCHASE ORDERS QUICKREPORT

To see a list of purchase orders that have been prepared, open the Chart of Accounts, select Purchase Orders, click the Reports button, and choose QuickReport from the menu shown.

MEMO
DATE: January 16, 2015

Larry and you need to see which purchase orders are open. Prepare and print the Purchase Orders QuickReport.

View the open purchase orders for Your Name Mountain Sports

Click the **Chart of Accounts** icon on the Home Page
Scroll through the accounts until you get to the end of the accounts
Your will see **2 Purchase Orders** in the Name column and **Non-Posting** in the Type column
Click **2 Purchase Orders**
Click the **Reports** button
Click **QuickReport: 2 Purchase Orders**

6

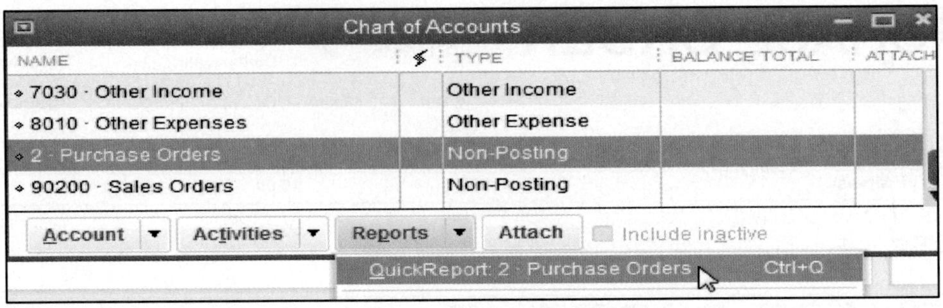

- The list shows all open purchase orders and the purchase order date, number, vendor, account, and amount.

The dates are from **01/01/15** to **01/16/15**

Tab to generate the report

Resize the columns as previously instructed to view the account name in full in the **Split** column, and to print in Portrait orientation on one page without using Fit to one page wide

Click **Print** to print the report

Your Name Mountain Sports
Account QuickReport
As of January 16, 2015

Type	Date	Num	Name	Memo	Split	Amount
2 · Purchase Orders						
Purchase Order	01/16/2015	1	Boots Galore		1120 · Inventory Asset	-1,875.00
Purchase Order	01/16/2015	2	Snow Stuff		-SPLIT-	-370.00
Purchase Order	01/16/2015	3	Clothes, Inc.		1120 · Inventory Asset	-375.00
Purchase Order	01/16/2015	4	Snow Sports, Inc.		1120 · Inventory Asset	-360.00
Total 2 · Purchase Orders						-2,980.00
TOTAL						**-2,980.00**

Close the **Purchase Order QuickReport** and the **Chart of Accounts**

CHANGE REORDER LIMITS

Any time that you determine your reorder limits are too low or too high, you can change the Reorder Point by editing the Item in the Item List.

> **MEMO**
> **DATE:** January 16, 2015
>
> View the Item List to see the amount on hand for each item. In viewing the list, Larry and you determine that there should be a minimum of 35 sets of long underwear on hand at all times. Currently, there are 32 sets of long underwear in stock. Change the Reorder Point (Min) for long underwear to 35.

View the **Item List** as previously instructed

Scroll through Item List, double-click **Underwear**
Click in **Reorder Point (Min)**
Change 30 to **35**

- Notice the Average Cost. For example, 32 on hand * $8 average cost = $256 total value. If 16 pair cost $10, the value would be $160. If the other 16 pair cost $6, the value would be $96. The total value for all 16 would be $160 + $96 = $256. Remember $256 / 32 = $8 average cost.

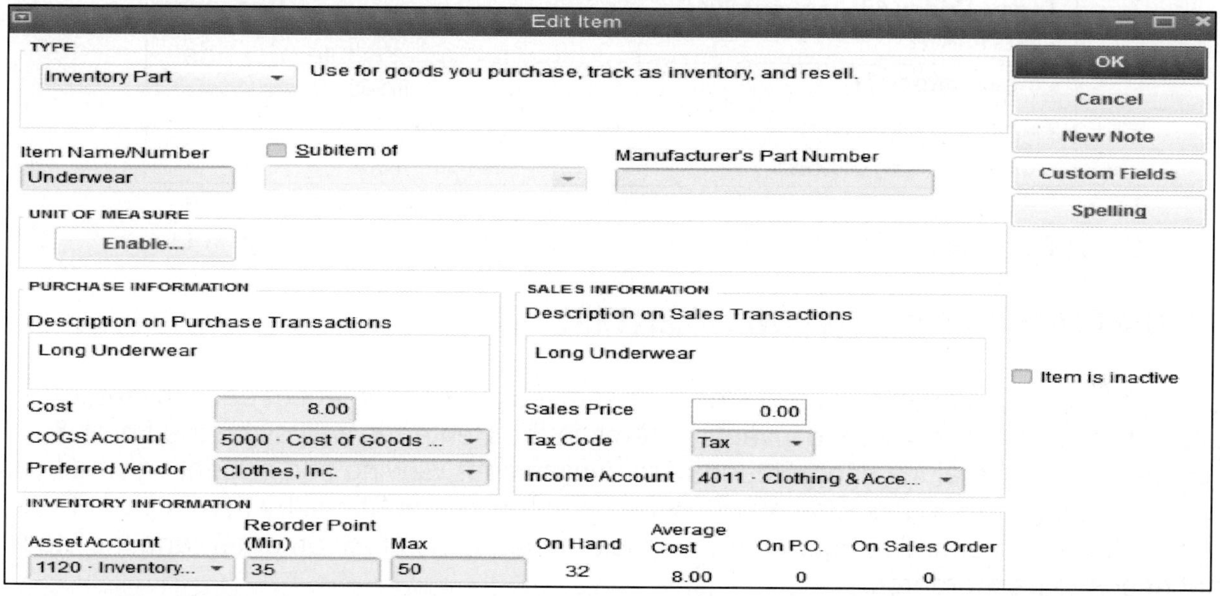

Click **OK** to save and exit, close the **Item List**

VIEW EFFECT OF REORDER POINT ON REMINDERS

Once the reorder point has been changed and the quantity on hand is equal to or falls below the new minimum, the item will be added to Reminders so you will be reminded to order it.

> **MEMO**
> **DATE:** January 16, 2015
>
> Look at Reminders to see what items need to be ordered.

Look at **Reminders**

Open **Reminders** using the Company Menu and expand Inventory to Reorder as previously instructed

- The items shown previously on the Reminders List as Inventory to Reorder (Snowboard Boots, Gloves, Ski Poles, Sleds, and Toboggans) are no longer present because they have been ordered. Underwear appears because the reorder point has been changed.

- If your computer date is not January 16, 2015 your Reminders screen will be different.

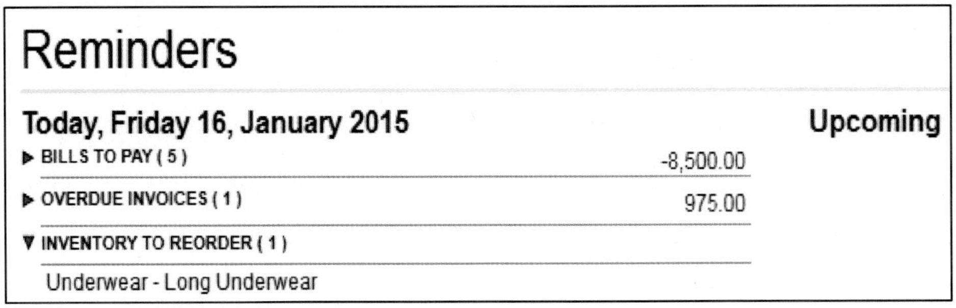

Close **Reminders**

VIEW REPORT IN INVENTORY CENTER

QuickBooks 2015 has an Inventory Center that gives information about each inventory item. Changes may be made to inventory items in the Center as well as on the Items & Services List. Several Inventory Reports are available for viewing and/or printing when you are in the Inventory Center. One report is the Inventory Stock Status by Item report. This report provides information regarding the stock on hand, the stock on order, and the stock that needs to be reordered.

MEMO
DATE: January 16, 2015

More detailed information regarding the stock on hand, stock ordered, and stock needing to be ordered needs to be provided. Open the Inventory Center and prepare the report for Inventory Stock Status by Item.

Open the Inventory Center and view the **Inventory Stock Status by Item Report**

Click the **Vendors** menu, point to **Inventory Activities,** click **Inventory Center**
Click **Underwear**

- Note the Reorder Point of 35 that was changed earlier in the chapter and the Quantity on Hand.
- At the bottom of Inventory Information, you will see that Underwear was sold on Invoice 4.

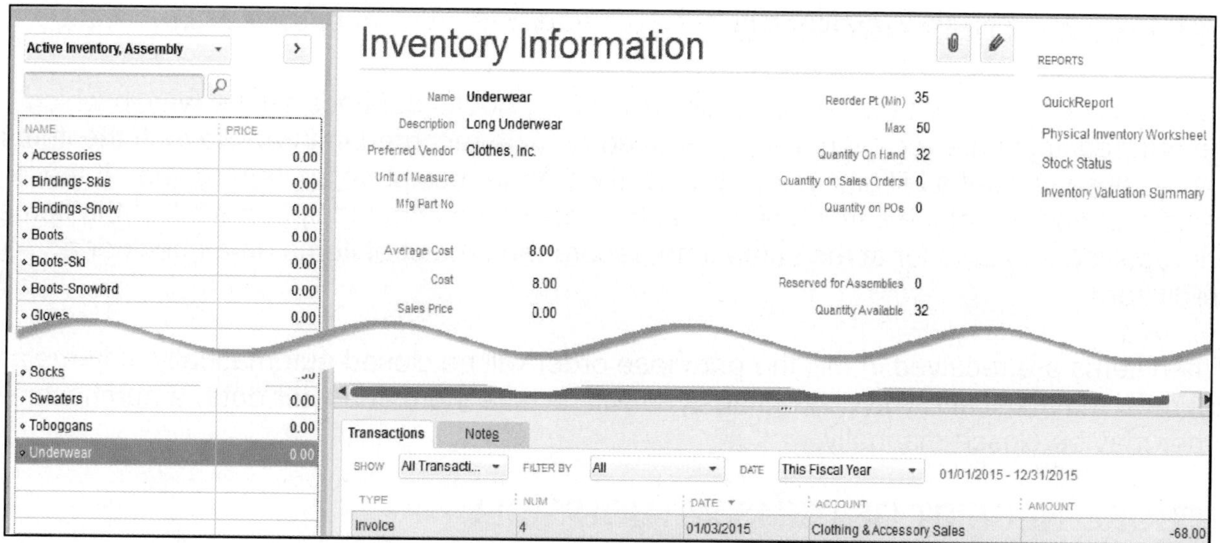

Partial Listing

In the Reports area on the right side of Inventory Information, click **Stock Status**
The dates are From **01/01/15** to **01/16/15**
Tab to generate the report (Columns with zero are removed from the following)

Your Name Mountain Sports
Inventory Stock Status by Item
January 1 - 16, 2015

	Pref Vendor	Reorder Pt (Min)	Max	On Hand	Available	Order	On PO	Reorder Qty	Next Deliv	Sales/Week
Inventory										
Accessories	Sports Accessories	100	850	795	795		0	0		2.2
Bindings-Skis	Sports Boots & Bindings	10	65	43	43		0	0		3.1
Bindings-Snow	Sports Boots & Bindings	5	65	48	48		0	0		0.9
Boots	Shoes & More	10	35	20	20		0	0		0
Boots-Ski	Boots Galore	10	35	14	14		0	0		0.4
Boots-Snowbrd	Boots Galore	10	35	10	10		25	0	01/16/2015	0.9
Gloves	Clothes, Inc.	20	45	20	20		25	0	01/16/2015	0.9
Hats	Sports Accessories	20	40	29	29		0	0		0.4
Helmets		5	30	20	20		0	0		2.2
Pants-Ski	Clothes, Inc.	10	100	93	93		0	0		0.9
Pants-Snowbrd	Clothes, Inc.	10	100	50	50		0	0		0
Parkas	Clothes, Inc.	25	100	73	73		0	0		0.9
Poles-Ski	Snow Sports, Inc.	15	28	13	13		12	0	01/16/2015	2.2
Skis	Snow Sports, Inc.	15	60	43	43		0	0		3.1
Sleds	Snow Stuff	5	7	4	4		3	0	01/16/2015	2.6
Snowboard	Snow Sports, Inc.	15	60	28	28		0	0		0.9
Socks	Boots Galore	25	100	72	72		0	0		1.3
Sweaters	Clothes, Inc.	25	100	73	73		0	0		0.9
Toboggans	Snow Stuff	5	7	5	5		2	0	01/16/2015	2.2
Underwear	Clothes, Inc.	35	50	32	32	✓	0	18		0.4

Scroll through the report

- Notice the items in stock and the reorder point for items.
- Find the items marked as needing to be ordered. They are marked with a √.
- Notice the Next Deliv dates of the items that have been ordered.

Close the report without printing, and close the Inventory Center

6

RECEIVING ITEMS ORDERED

The form used to record the receipt of items in QuickBooks depends on the way in which the ordered items are received. Items received may be recorded in three ways. If the items are received without a bill and you pay later, record the receipt on an item receipt. If the items are received at the same time as the bill, record the item receipt on a bill. If the items are received and paid for at the same time, record the receipt of items on a check or a credit card.

When items are received in full, the purchase order will be closed automatically. If items are not received in full and you do not think you will receive them at a later date, a purchase order may be closed manually.

RECORD RECEIPT OF ITEMS WITHOUT BILL

The ability to record inventory items prior to the arrival of the bill keeps quantities on hand, quantities on order, and inventory up to date. Items ordered on a purchase order that arrive without a bill are recorded on an item receipt. When the bill arrives, it is recorded.

MEMO
DATE: January 18, 2015

The sleds and toboggans ordered from Snow Stuff arrive without a bill. Record the receipt of the 3 sleds and 2 toboggans.

Record the receipt of the items above

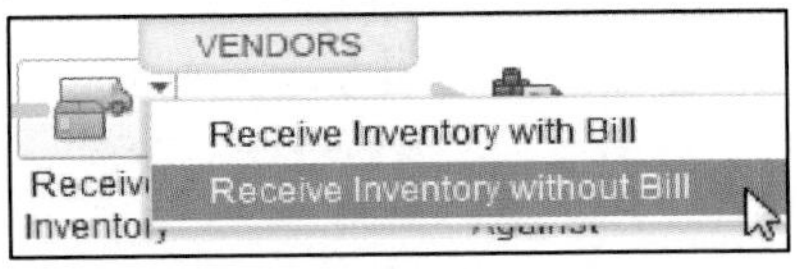

Click the **Receive Inventory** icon on the Home Page
Click **Receive Inventory without Bill**
Click **Hide History** and **resize** the Item Receipt as previously discussed
On the Item Receipt, click the drop-down list arrow for **Vendor**, click **Snow Stuff**
Click **Yes** on the **Open POs Exist** message box

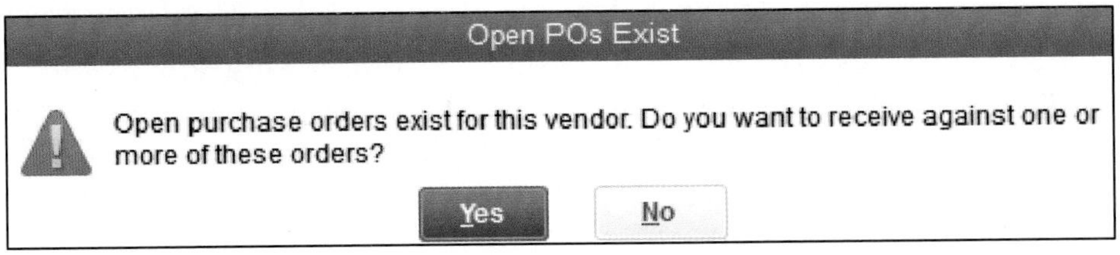

- An **Open Purchase Orders** dialog box appears showing all open purchase orders for the vendor, Snow Stuff.

Point to any part of the line for P.O. NO. 2
Click to select **Purchase Order 2**

- This will place a check mark in the check mark column.

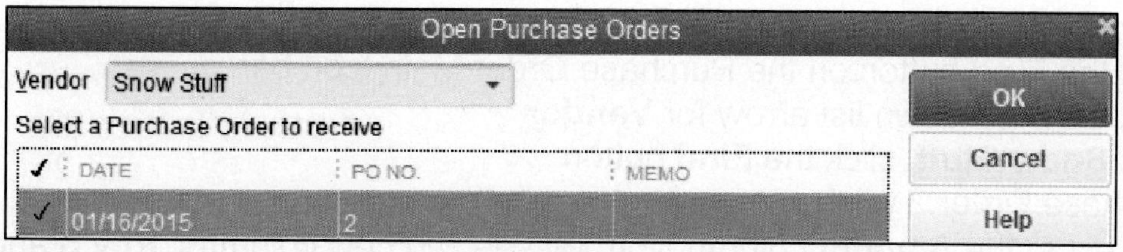

Click **OK**
Change the date to **01/18/2015**.

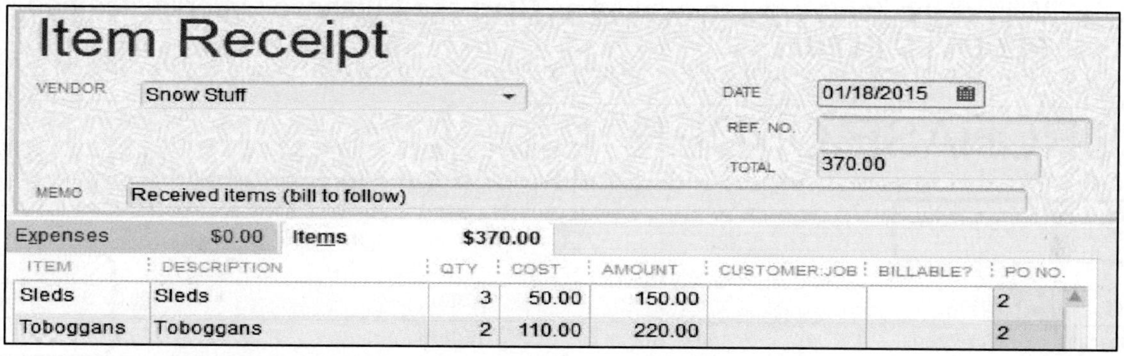

- REF. NO. is blank
- Notice that the **Items** tab displays the Total of $370
- In the columns, information for sleds and toboggans is completed.
- Notice the **Memo** of ***Received items (bill to follow).***
- The Item Receipt may be printed but is not required. Check with your instructor to see if you should print this document.

Click **Save & Close**

VERIFY PURCHASE ORDER RECEIVED IN FULL

As each line on a Purchase Order is received in full, QuickBooks marks it as *Clsd*. When all the items on the Purchase Order are marked *Clsd*, QuickBooks automatically stamps the P.O. as *Received in Full* and closes the purchase order.

On the Create Purchase Orders Main Icon bar, you may use Find in order to locate a specific Purchase Order.

MEMO
DATE: January 18, 2015

View the original Purchase Order 2 to verify that it has been stamped "Received in Full" and each item received is marked "Clsd."

Verify information for Purchase Order 2 by using **Find** within Purchase Orders

Open Create Purchase Orders as previously instructed
Click the **Find** button on the Purchase Order Main Icon bar
Click the drop-down list arrow for **Vendor**
Click **Snow Stuff**, click the **Find** button
Purchase Order 2 will be shown

- Next to the **Amount** column, you will see two new columns: **Rcv'd** and **Clsd**.
  - **Rcv'd** indicates the number of the items received.
  - **Clsd** indicates that the number of items ordered was received in full so the Purchase Order has been closed for that Item.
- With all the items ordered marked as **Clsd**, the Purchase Order is stamped **RECEIVED IN FULL**.

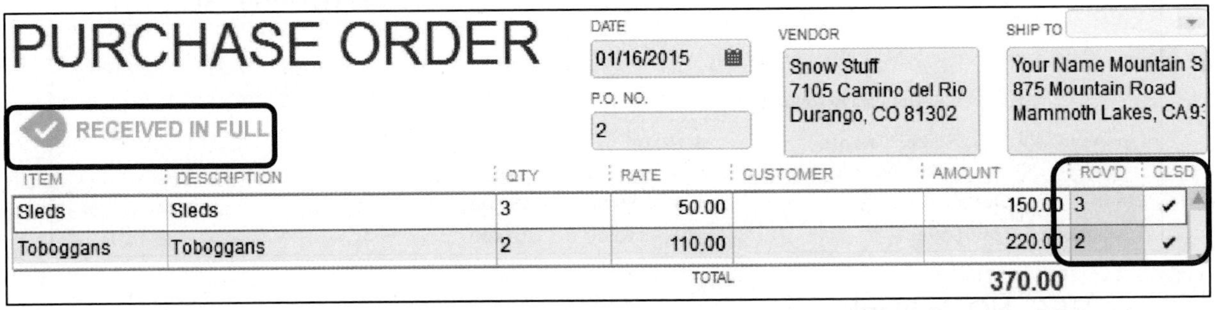

Close **Create Purchase Orders** window

CHANGE SEARCH PREFERENCES

The use of Search on the Icon bar is optional. Your Name Mountain Sports has elected to use the Search feature on the Icon bar. You can choose to search for something within the company or you may access Help. Preferences may be set to automatically search a company file or to go to Help. Even when preferences are set, you have the option to use either search. In addition to setting a preference for Search, you can select to Update your company file information automatically and give QuickBooks an update time interval.

Customize the Icon bar Search Preferences

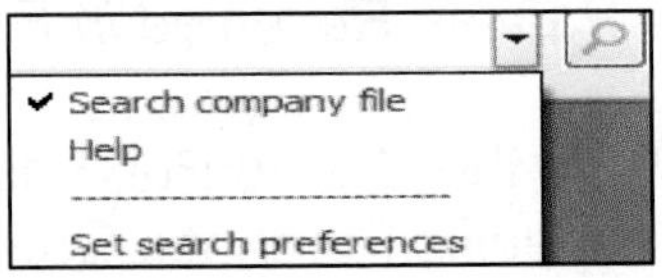

Click the drop-down list arrow for Search on the Icon bar
Click **Set search preferences**
On the **My Preferences** tab, click **Search my company file** to select

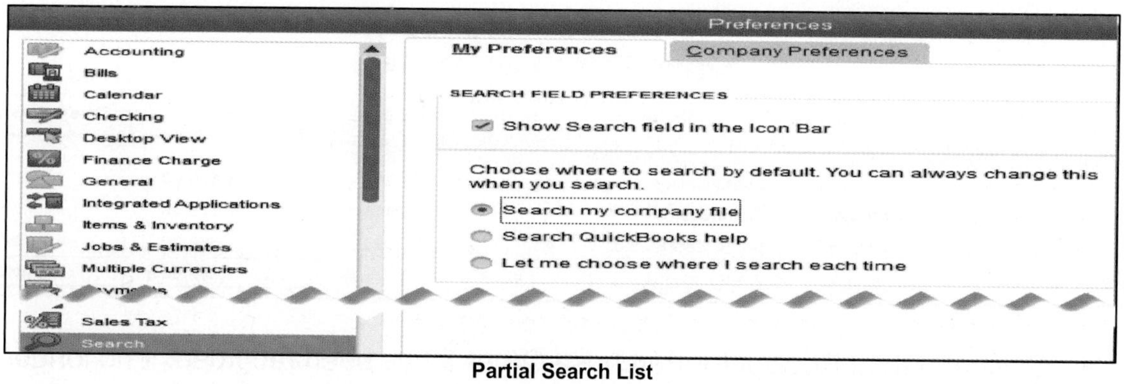

Partial Search List

Click the **Company Preferences** tab
Make sure that **Update automatically** has a check mark
Click the drop-down list arrow for 60 mins – Recommended
Click **15 mins**

- This means that QuickBooks will search through your company file every 15 minutes and update the company information that will be displayed.
- If you want to update your company file immediately, click Update Now.

Click **OK**, if you are prompted that QuickBooks needs to close all windows, click **OK**, you may then need to click the Home icon to display the Home Page

PREPARE REPORT FROM SEARCH

When using search to find purchase orders, reports pertaining to purchase orders were also found. These may be prepared directly from Search. Once the report is selected, you may locate the Menu for the report, launch the report, or add the report to favorites.

6

Prepare the Open Purchase Orders report using **Search**

Type **Purchase Orders** in the Search textbox on the Icon bar

Click **Search** button
In order to make sure all current information is shown, click **Update search information** (on the lower-left side of the Search screen)
Click **OK** on the Search Update message

- Search will find the purchase orders that have been prepared. It will also give you a list of Menu Items that may be used to prepare reports.

Scroll through the Search results until you get to **Menu Item**
Point to the Menu Item **Open Purchase Orders** on the Search screen

- Action items of Locate Menu, Launch, and Add to Favorites should appear.

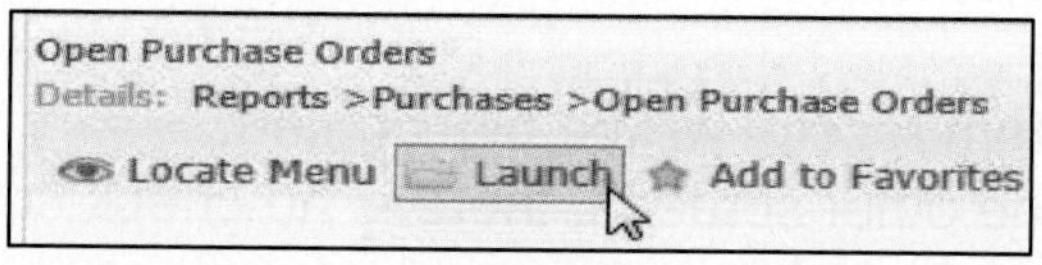

Click the **Launch** icon and the report will be shown on the screen

Your Name Mountain Sports
Open Purchase Orders
All Transactions

	Type	Date	Name	Num	Deliv Date	Amount	Open Balance
	Purchase Order	01/16/2015	Boots Galore	1	01/16/2015	1,875.00	1,875.00
	Purchase Order	01/16/2015	Clothes, Inc.	3	01/16/2015	375.00	375.00
	Purchase Order	01/16/2015	Snow Sports, Inc.	4	01/16/2015	360.00	360.00
Total						2,610.00	2,610.00

- Since the Item Receipt for Purchase Order 2 has been recorded, it no longer shows as an Open Purchase Order.

Close the report without printing and close Search

ENTER BILL FOR ITEMS RECEIVED

For items that are received prior to the bill, the receipt of items is recorded as soon as the items arrive in order to keep the inventory up to date. When the bill is received, it must be recorded. To do this, indicate that the bill is entered against Inventory. When completing a bill for items already received, QuickBooks fills in all essential information on the bill.

A bill is divided into two sections: a vendor-related section (the upper part of the bill that looks similar to a check and has a memo text box under it) and a detail section (the area that has two tabs marked Items and Expenses). The vendor-related section of the bill is where information for the actual bill is entered, including a memo with information about the transaction. The detail section is where the information regarding the items ordered, the quantity ordered and received, and the amounts due for the items received is indicated.

MEMO
DATE: January 19, 2015

Record the bill for the sleds and toboggans already received from Snow Stuff, Vendor's Invoice 97 dated 01/18/2015, Terms 2% 10 Net 30.

Record the above bill for items already received

Click the **Enter Bills Against Inventory** icon on the Home Page

On the **Select Item Receipt** screen, click the drop-down list arrow for **Vendor**, click **Snow Stuff**

Click anywhere on the line **01/18/2015 Received items (bill to follow)** to select the Item Receipt

- The line for the item receipt will be highlighted.
- Unlike many of the other screens, there is no check column so the line must be highlighted to be selected.

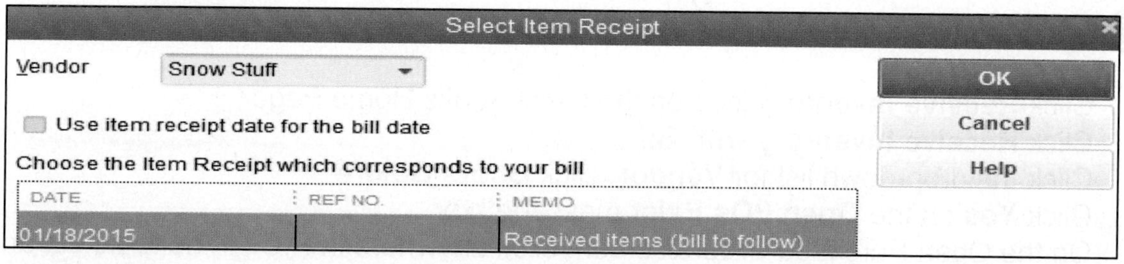

Click **OK**

- QuickBooks displays the **Enter Bills** screen and the completed bill for Snow Stuff.
- The date shown is the date of the Vendor's bill **01/18/2015**.

Tab to or click **Ref No.**, type the vendor's invoice number **97**

- Notice that the **Amount Due** of **370** has been inserted.
- TERMS of **2% 10 Net 30** and dates for DISCOUNT DATE and BILL DUE are shown.

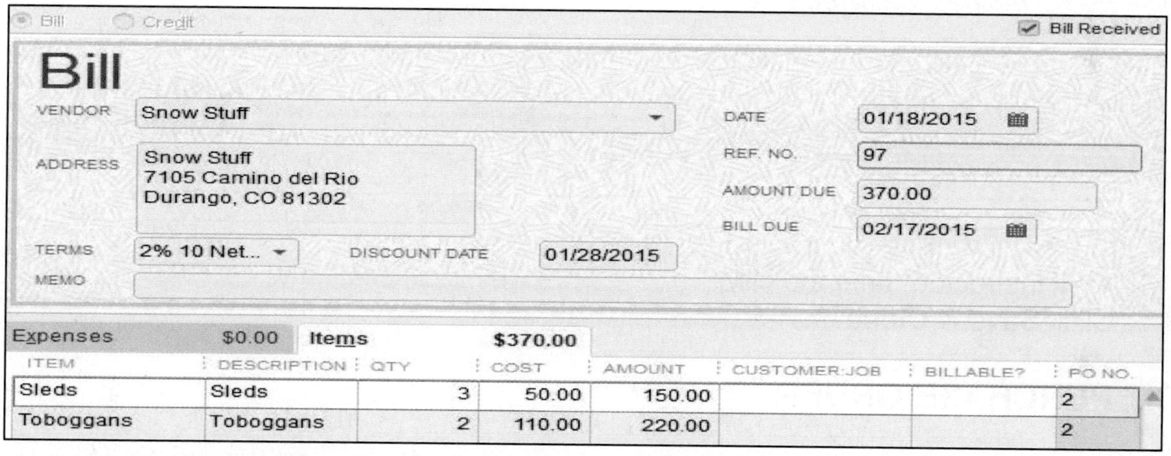

6

- If instructed to do so by your instructor, print the Bill.

Click **Save & Close**

- If you get a Recording Transaction message box regarding the fact that the transaction has been changed, always click **Yes**.

RECORD RECEIPT OF ITEMS AND BILL

When ordered items are received and accompanied by a bill, the receipt of the items is recorded while entering the bill.

MEMO

DATE: January 19, 2015

Received 25 pairs of snowboard boots and a bill from Boots Galore. Record the bill dated 01/18/2015 and the receipt of the items.

Record the receipt of the items and the bill

Click **Receive Inventory** icon on the QuickBooks Home Page
Click **Receive Inventory with Bill**
Click the drop-down list for **Vendor**, click **Boots Galore**
Click **Yes** on the **Open POs Exist** message box
On the Open Purchase Orders screen, click anywhere in P.O. 1 line to select and insert a check mark in the √ column
Click **OK**

- The bill appears on the screen and is complete.
- Because no invoice number was given, leave the **REF. NO.** blank.

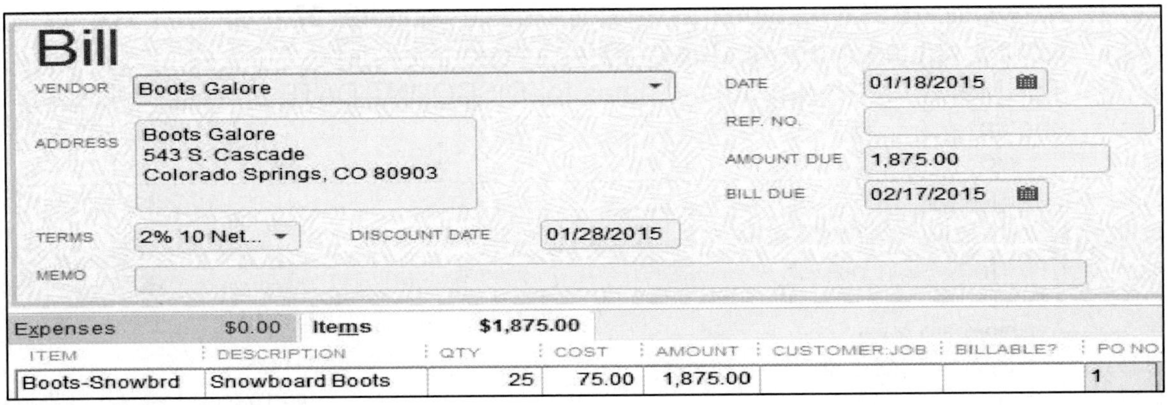

Bill

VENDOR: Boots Galore
ADDRESS: Boots Galore
543 S. Cascade
Colorado Springs, CO 80903
DATE: 01/18/2015
REF. NO.:
AMOUNT DUE: 1,875.00
BILL DUE: 02/17/2015
TERMS: 2% 10 Net...
DISCOUNT DATE: 01/28/2015
MEMO:

Expenses $0.00 Items $1,875.00

ITEM	DESCRIPTION	QTY	COST	AMOUNT	CUSTOMER:JOB	BILLABLE?	PO NO.
Boots-Snowbrd	Snowboard Boots	25	75.00	1,875.00			1

- If instructed, print the bill.

Click **Save & Close**

EDIT PURCHASE ORDER

As with any other form, purchase orders may be edited once they have been prepared. Click on the Purchase Order icon on the QuickBooks Home Page.

MEMO
DATE: January 19, 2015

Ruth realized that Purchase Order 4 should be for 15 pairs of ski poles. Change the purchase order and reprint.

Change Purchase Order 4

Access Purchase Order 4 as previously instructed

- Even though QuickBooks suggested a Reorder Qty of 12, you may choose to order any quantity you wish.

Click in **Qty**; change the number from 12 to **15**
Tab to recalculate the amount due for the purchase order

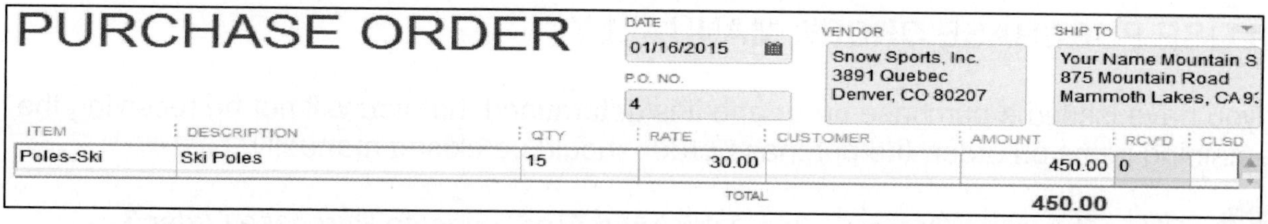

- Notice the columns for Rcv'd and Clsd. Those are included on the Purchase Order once it has been saved.

Print the **Purchase Order** as previously instructed
Click **Save & Close** to record the changes and exit
Click **Yes** on the **Recording Transaction** dialog box to save the changes

RECORD PARTIAL MERCHANDISE RECEIPT

Sometimes when items on order are received, they are not received in full. The remaining items may be delivered as back-ordered items. This will usually occur if an item is out of stock, and you must wait for delivery until more items are manufactured and/or received by the vendor. With QuickBooks you record the number of items you actually receive, and the bill is recorded for that amount.

MEMO
DATE: January 19, 2015

Record the bill and the receipt of 20 pairs of gloves ordered on Purchase Order 3. On the purchase order, 25 pairs of gloves were ordered. Clothes, Inc. will no longer be carrying these gloves, so the remaining 5 pairs of gloves on order will not be shipped. Manually close the purchase order. The date of the bill is 01/18/2015.

6

Record the receipt of and the bill for 20 pairs of gloves from Clothes, Inc.

Access **Receive Inventory with Bill** as previously instructed
If necessary, change the **Date** of the bill to **01/18/2015**
Click the drop-down list arrow for **Vendor**, click **Clothes, Inc.**
Click **Yes** on **Open POs Exist** dialog box
Click anywhere in the line for **P.O. 3** on **Open Purchase Orders** dialog box
Click **OK**
Click the **Qty** column on the Items tab in the middle of the bottom half of the Enter Bills window
Change the quantity to **20**
Tab to change **Amount** to **300**

- Notice the **Amount Due** on the bill also changes.

Print if instructed to do so
Click **Save & Close** to record the items received and the bill

CLOSE PURCHASE ORDER MANUALLY

If you have issued a purchase order and it is determined that you will not be receiving the remaining items on order, the purchase order should be closed manually.

Close Purchase Order 3 using **Advanced Find** to locate Purchase Order 3

Use the keyboard shortcut **Ctrl+F**; and then, click the **Advanced** tab
Scroll through CHOOSE FILTER to the top of the List, click **Transaction Type**
- A filter helps to narrow the search for locating something.

Click the drop-down list arrow for **Transaction Type**, click **Purchase Order**
Click **Find**
- A list of all purchase orders shows on the screen.
- The information shown includes the date of the Purchase Order, type (PURCHORD), purchase order number, vendor name, accounts used, the item(s) ordered, and the amount of the purchase order.
- Unlike Search Company File, no reports are shown.

Click **Purchase Order 3** for **Clothes, Inc.**, then click **Go To**

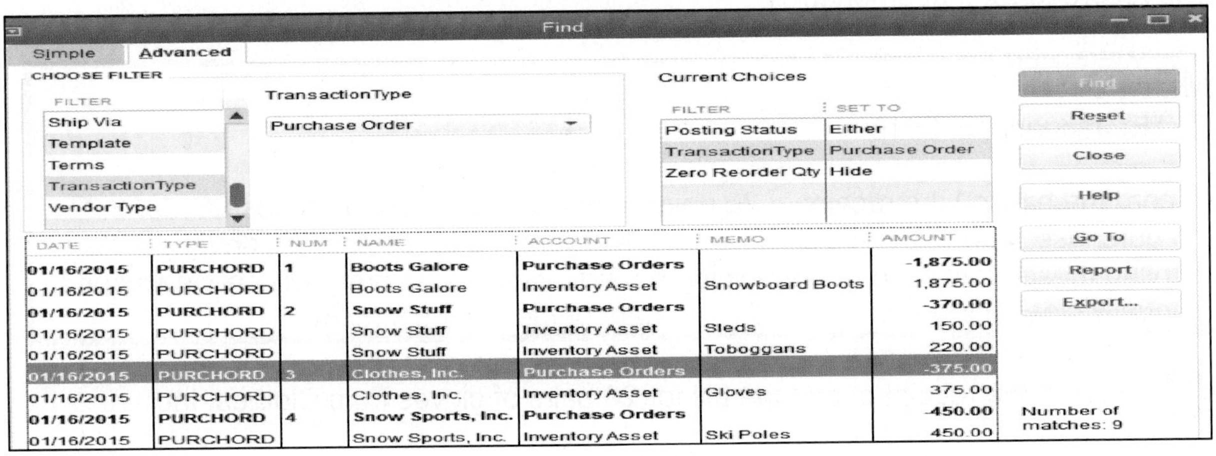

- P.O. 3 will show on the screen.
- Notice that the ordered **Qty** is 25, **Backordered** is 5, and **Rcv'd** is 20.

Click the **Clsd** column for Gloves to mark and close the purchase order
- Notice the check mark in the Clsd column. Backordered is now 0.
- Below PURCHASE ORDER you will see a check mark and the word CLOSED.

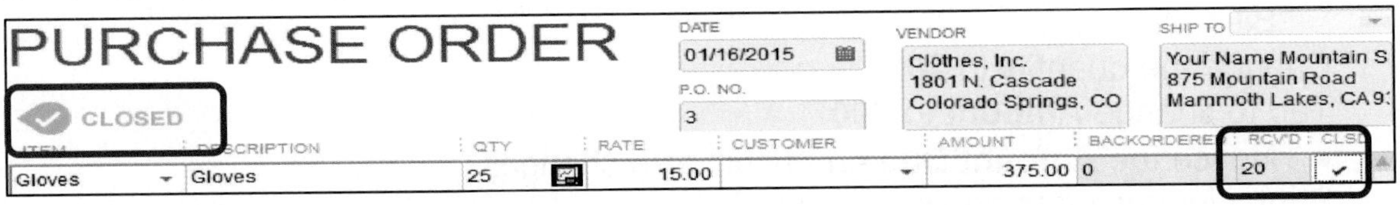

Print the Closed Purchase Order, click **Yes** on Recording Transactions
Click **Save & Close**, close **Find**

ENTER CREDIT FROM VENDOR

Credit memos are prepared to record a reduction to a transaction. With QuickBooks you use the Enter Bills window to record credit memos received from vendors acknowledging a return of items purchased or an allowance for a previously recorded bill and/or payment. The amount of a credit memo can be applied to the amount owed to a vendor when paying bills.

> **MEMO**
> **DATE:** January 21, 2015
>
> Upon further inspection of merchandise received, Ruth Morgan found that one of the sleds received from Snow Stuff, was cracked. The sled was returned. Received Credit Memo 9915 from Snow Stuff for $50 (the full amount on the return of 1 sled).

Check the **Item List** to verify how many sleds are currently on hand

Access **Item List** as previously instructed

- Look at Sleds to verify that there are 7 sleds in stock.

Close the **Item List**

Record the return of one sled

Access the **Enter Bills** window and record the credit memo shown above
On the **Enter Bills** screen, click **Credit** to select

- The word *Bill* changes to *Credit*.

Click the **Items** tab
Tab to or click the first line in the **Item** column, click the drop-down list arrow
Click **Sleds**

- The Vendor **Snow Stuff**, the Amount Due **50**, and the Cost **50** are entered automatically.

Tab to or click **Qty**, enter **1**
Click in the text box for **Date**; enter **01/21/15**
Tab to or click **Ref. No.**, type **9915**
Memo, enter **Returned 1 Sled**

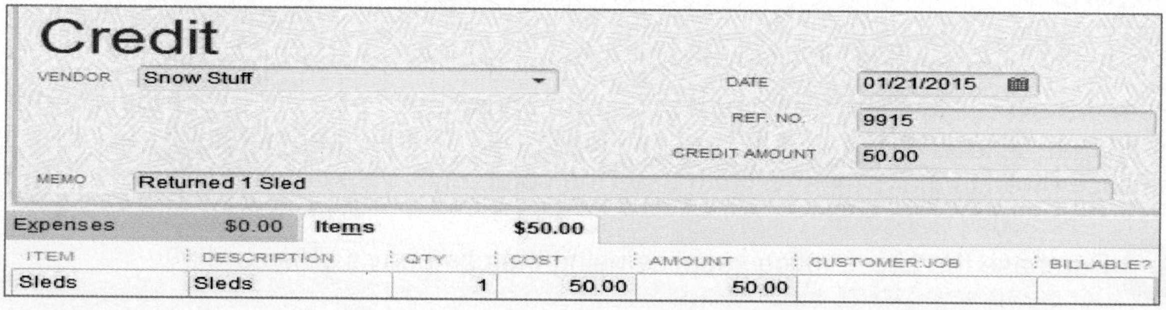

Print the Credit Memo if instructed to do so
Click **Save & Close** to record the credit and exit the **Enter Bills** window

- QuickBooks decreases the quantity of sleds on hand and creates a credit with the vendor that can be applied when paying the bill. The Credit Memo also appears in the Accounts Payable account in the **Paid** column, which decreases the amount owed and shows the transaction type as BILLCRED in the Accounts Payable register.

Verify that there are 6 sleds in stock after the return.

Access the **Item List**
Verify the number of sleds and then close the list

View the return in the Accounts Payable register

Access the **Chart of Accounts** as previously instructed
Double-click **Accounts Payable** to open the Register
Scroll through the register until you see the BILLCRED for Snow Stuff

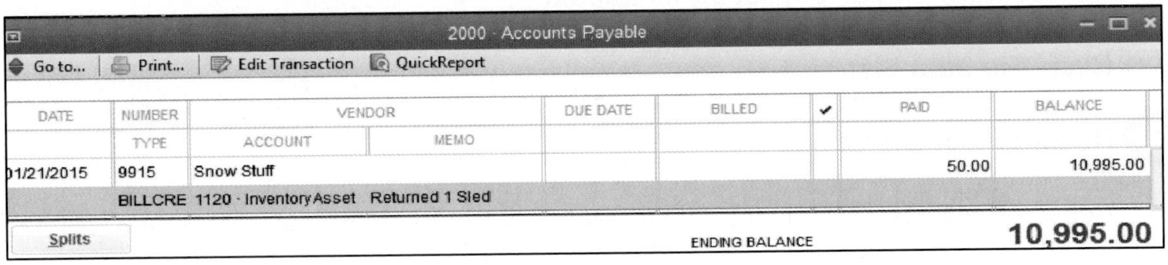

Close the **Accounts Payable Register** and the **Chart of Accounts**

RECORD CREDIT CARD PURCHASE

Some businesses use credit cards as an integral part of their finances. Many companies have a credit card that is used primarily for gasoline purchases for company vehicles. Other companies use credit cards as a means of paying for expenses or purchasing merchandise or other necessary items for use in the business.

> **MEMO**
> **DATE:** January 21, 2015
>
> Ruth discovered that she was out of paper. She purchased a box of paper to have on hand from Sierra Office Supply Company for $21.98. Rather than add to the existing balance owed to the company, Ruth uses the company's Visa card.

Purchase the above office supplies using the company's Visa card

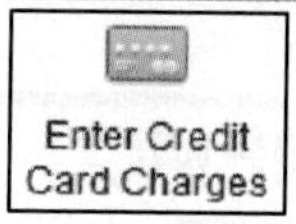

Click the **Enter Credit Card Charges** icon in the **Banking** section of the Home Page

Credit Card should indicate **2100 Visa**

- The radio button for Purchase/Charge should be selected; if not, click to mark.

Click the drop-down list arrow for **Purchased From**, click **Sierra Office Supply Company**

Click **OK** on the **Warning** screen

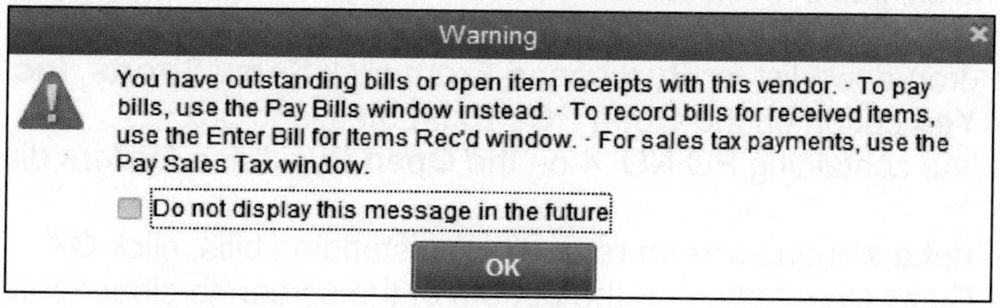

DATE should be **01/21/2015, REF NO.** is blank

Tab to or click **AMOUNT**, enter **21.98**

Tab to or click **MEMO**, enter **Purchase Paper**

Tab to or click the **ACCOUNT** column on the **Expenses** tab, click the drop-down list arrow for **Account**, click **1311 Office Supplies**

- This transaction is for supplies to have on hand, so the Asset Account 1311 Office Supplies is used.

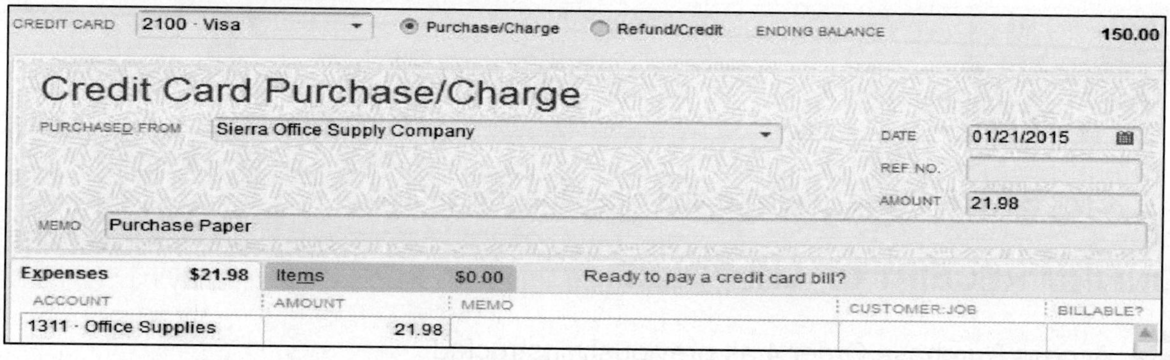

- When entering a Credit Card transaction using Enter Credit Card Charges, QuickBooks does <u>not</u> enable you to print a copy of the transaction.

Click **Save & New** to record the charge and go to the next credit card entry

PAY FOR INVENTORY ITEMS WITH CREDIT CARD

It is possible to pay for inventory items using a credit card. The payment may be made using the Pay Bills window, or it may be made by recording an entry for Credit Card Charges. If you are purchasing something that is on order, you may record the receipt of merchandise on order first, or you may record the receipt of merchandise and the credit card payment at the same time.

MEMO
DATE: January 21, 2015

Note from You: Ruth, record the receipt of 10 ski poles from Snow Sports, Inc... Pay for the ski poles using the company's Visa credit card.

Pay for the ski poles received using the company's Visa credit card

Click the drop-down list for **Purchased From** click **Snow Sports, Inc.**
Click the **Yes** button on the **Open POs Exist** message box
Click the line containing PO NO. 4 on the **Open Purchase Orders** dialog box
Click **OK**

- If you get a warning screen regarding outstanding bills, click **OK**.

Click the **Clear Qtys** button on the bottom of the screen to clear 15 from Qty column
Tab to or click **Qty**, enter **10**
Tab to change the Amount to 300

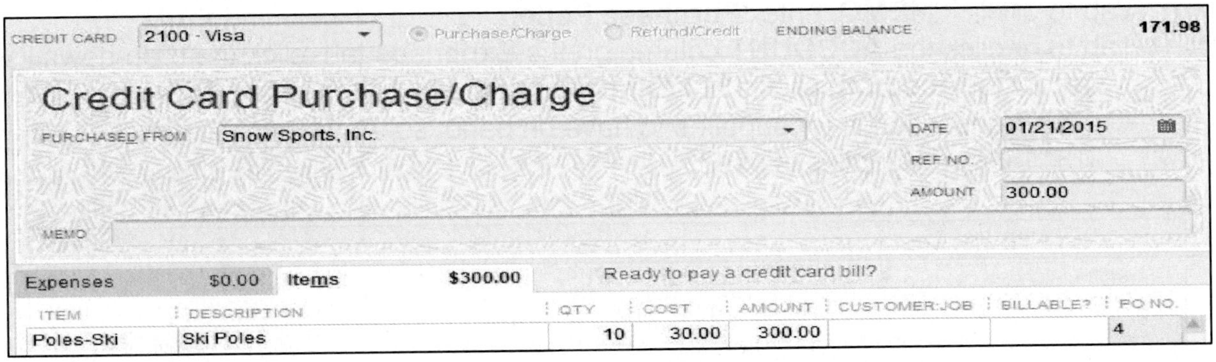

Click **Save & Close** to record and close the transaction

CONFIRM RECEIPT OF SKI POLES

Access Purchase Order 4 as previously instructed

- The **Rcv'd** column should show **10** and **Backordered** shows **5**.
- Notice that the **Qty** column shows **15** and **Clsd** is not marked. This indicates that 5 sets of ski poles are still on order.

Close Purchase Order 4 without changing or printing

ADD/EDIT MULTIPLE LIST ENTRIES

Vendors, customers, and list items may be added through the add/edit multiple list entries on the list menu. This feature is especially useful when importing data from Excel spreadsheets into QuickBooks. In addition, it may be used to quickly add one or more records to a list.

MEMO
DATE: January 23, 2015

Add a new vendor, *Mammoth News*, 1450 Main Street, Mammoth Lakes, CA 93546, Main Phone: 909-555-2525, Fax: 909-555-5252, E-mail: mammothnews@ski.com.

Add the new vendor using Add/Edit Multiple List Entries

Click the **Lists** menu
Click **Add/Edit Multiple List Entries**
Click the drop-down list arrow next to **List**
Click **Vendors**
Click the **Customize Columns** button and remove unwanted columns
Click **Alt. Phone** in the Chosen Columns
Click **Remove**

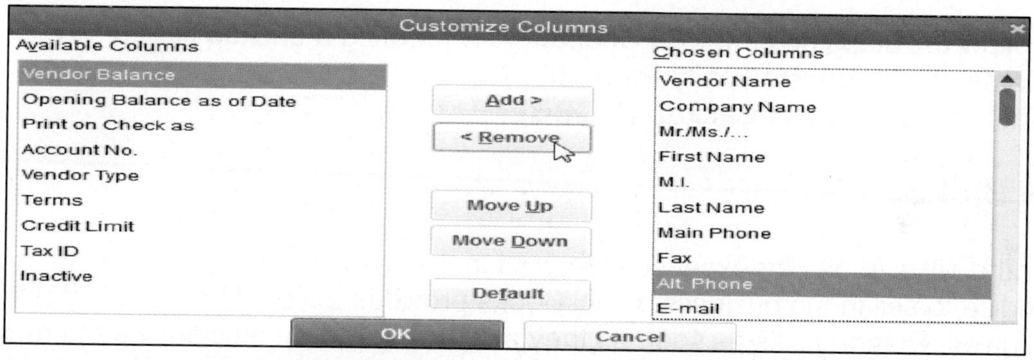

Repeat to remove **Mr./Ms./**, **First Name**, **M.I.**, **Last Name**, and **Address 4 and 5**
When finished removing columns, click **OK**
Click on the Vendor Name, **Mammoth Power Co.**
- If you get a Time Saving tip, click **OK**.

Right-click on Mammoth Power Co., click **Insert Line**
- A blank line is inserted above Mammoth Power Co.

In the Vendor Name column on the blank line, enter **Mammoth News**
Press, **Tab**
Enter the Company Name **Mammoth News**
Tab to or click in the column for **Main Phone**, enter **909-555-2525**
Tab to or click **FAX**, enter **909-555-5252**
Tab to or click **E-mail**, enter **mammothnews@ski.com**
Tab to or click **Address 1**, enter **Mammoth News**
Tab to or click **Address 2**, enter **1450 Main Street**
Tab to or click **Address 3**, enter **Mammoth Lakes, CA 93546**

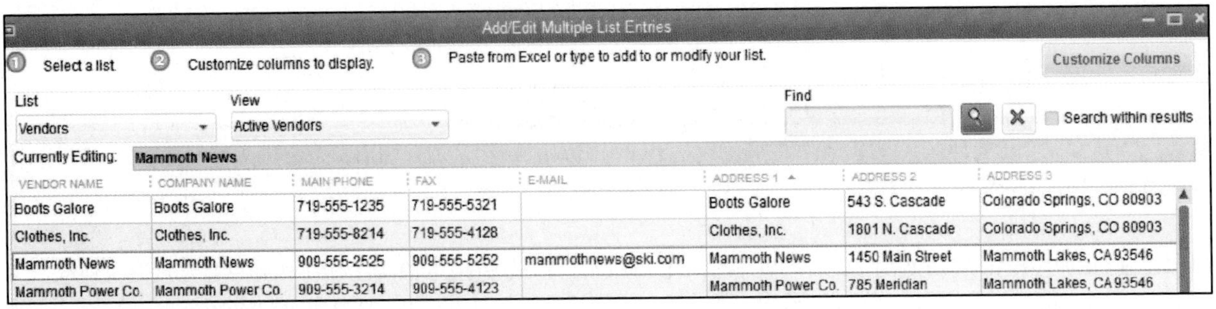

Click **Save Changes**
Click **OK** on the Record(s) Saved dialog box. click **Close**

PREPARE DAILY BACKUP

As previously discussed, a backup file is prepared as a precaution in case you make an error. By creating the backup file now, it will contain your work for Chapters 5 and 6 up through adding the new vendor Mammoth News.

Prepare Sports (Daily Backup).qbb file

Follow the steps presented in Chapter 1 for creating a backup file
Name the file **Sports (Daily Backup)**
The file type is **QBW Backup (* .QBB)**

ENTER BILLS

Whether the bill is to pay for expenses incurred in the operation of a business or to pay for merchandise to sell in the business, QuickBooks provides accounts payable tracking for all vendors owed. Entering bills as soon as they are received is an efficient way to record your liabilities. Once bills have been entered, QuickBooks will be able to provide up-to-date cash flow reports, and will remind you when it's time to pay your bills.

As previously stated, a bill is divided into two sections: a vendor-related section and a detail section. The vendor- related section of the bill is where information for the actual bill is entered. If the bill is for paying an expense, the Expenses tab is used for the detail section. Using this tab allows you to indicate the expense accounts for the transaction, to enter the amounts for the various expense accounts, and to provide transaction explanations. If the bill is for merchandise, the Items tab will be used to record the receipt of the items ordered.

If you use the Document Center, you may scan the bill you receive, store it in the Doc Center, and attach it to the bill electronically. (Refer to Appendix B for more detailed information and examples of using the Document Center and Attaching electronically.)

MEMO
DATE: January 23, 2015

Placed an ad in *Mammoth News* announcing our February sale. Record the receipt of the bill from *Mammoth News* for $95.00, Terms Net 30, Invoice 381-22.

Enter the bill

Click the **Enter Bills** icon on the Home Page
Complete the **Vendor Section** of the bill:
VENDOR: **Mammoth News**
DATE: **01/23/15**
REF NO.: **381-22** (the vendor's invoice number)
AMOUNT DUE: **95**
TERMS: **Net 30**

- QuickBooks automatically changes the Bill Due date to show 30 days from the transaction date.
- Since the terms are Net 30, there is no Discount Date.
- At this time no change will be made to the Bill Due date, and nothing will be inserted as a memo.

Complete the **Detail Section** of the bill:

- If necessary, click the **Expenses** tab.

Click the drop-down list arrow for ACCOUNT, click **<Add New>**

- **Type** of account should show **Expense**. If not, click **Expense**.

Click **Continue**
Enter **6140** as the account number in Number
Account Name: enter **Advertising Expense**

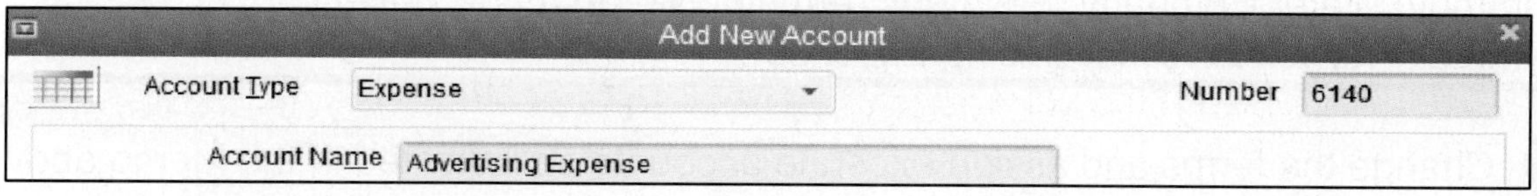

Click **Save & Close**
6140 Advertising Expense shows as the ACCOUNT

- Based on the accrual method of accounting, Advertising Expense is selected as the account for this transaction because this expense should be matched against the revenue of the period.
- The Amount column already shows 95.00—no entry required.
- Tab to or click the first line in the column for **Memo**.

Enter the transaction explanation of **Ad for February Sale**

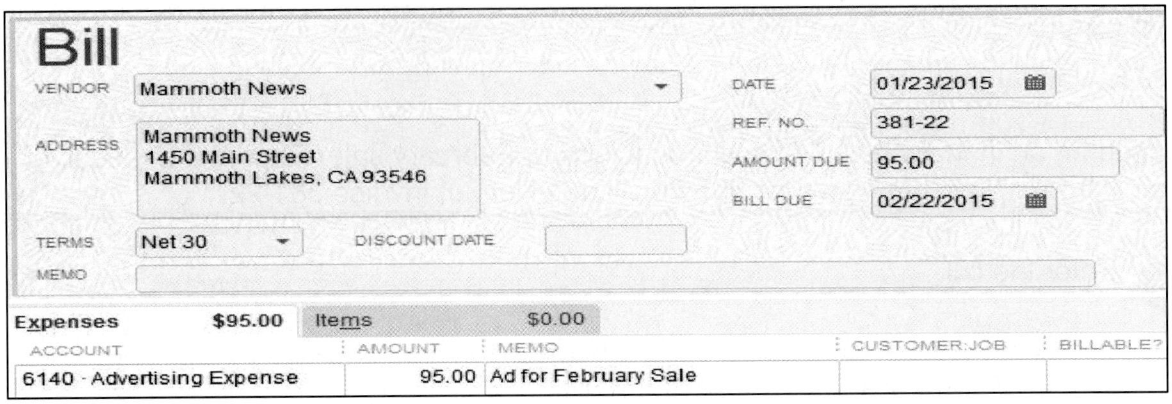

Print if instructed to do so, and then click **Save & Close**
Since no terms were assigned when the company was added to the Vendor List, click **Yes** on the **Name Information Changed** dialog box

ASSIGN TERMS AND ACCOUNTS TO VENDORS

Once a vendor has been established, changes can be made to the vendor's account information. The changes will take effect immediately and will be reflected in any transactions recorded for the vendor.

MEMO
DATE: January 23, 2015

Ruth Morgan wants to add information for the following vendors:
Mammoth Power Company: Payment Terms of Net 30, 6391 Gas and Electric
Mammoth Telephone Company: Payment Terms of Net 30, 6340 Telephone
Mammoth Water Company: Payment Terms of Net 30, 6392 Water
Mammoth News: 6140 Advertising Expense

Change the terms and assign expense accounts as indicated in the Memo above

Access the **Vendor List** in the Vendor Center as previously instructed
Double-click on **Mammoth Power Co.**
Click **Payment Settings** tab
Click the drop-down list arrow for PAYMENT TERMS, click **Net 30**
Click the **Account Settings** tab, click the drop-down list arrow, click the expense account **6391 Gas and Electric**
Click **OK**
Repeat for the other vendors indicated in the memo above
When you enter the information for Mammoth News, check to verify that the terms are Net 30; and then add the expense account **6140 Advertising Expense**
Close the **Vendor Center** when all changes have been made

CREATE MEMORIZED TRANSACTION

Transactions that are entered on a regular basis may be memorized for use. QuickBooks can automatically create the transactions for you. After entering the standard information on a bill to Mammoth Power Co., you can have QuickBooks memorize the transaction. Then, next month you select the transaction in the Memorized Transaction List and QuickBooks prepares the bill.

Memorize the bill for Mammoth Power Co.

Access **Enter Bills** as previously instructed
VENDOR: is **Mammoth Power Company**

- Notice that the terms and account are entered automatically.

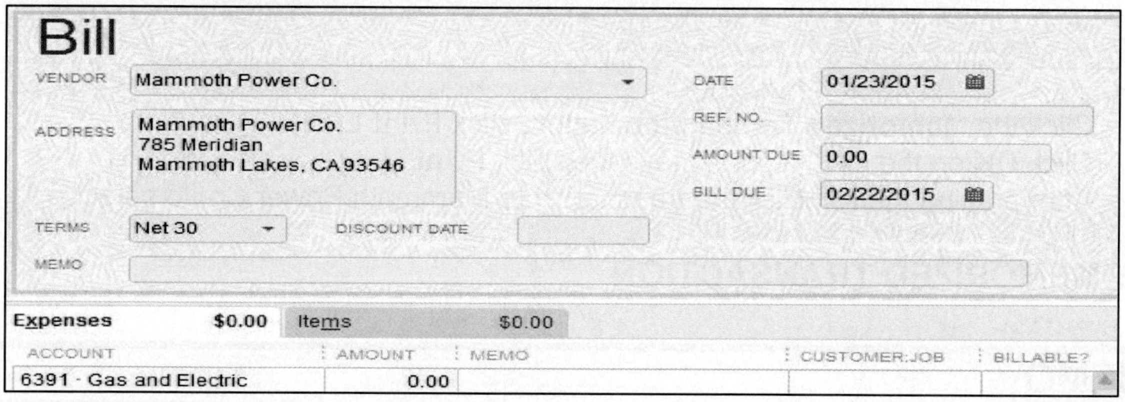

With the bill to Mammoth Power Co. showing on the screen, click the  icon on the Enter Bills Main Icon bar

- On the Memorize Transaction screen, note the Name **Mammoth Power Co.**
- The Transaction is marked to **Add to my Reminders List**
- You have the option to Automate Transaction Entry so QuickBooks can automatically prepare the bill on the frequency you select.
- You may also tell QuickBooks the number of payments remaining. This is great if you are using the transaction to pay a loan.
- You may tell QuickBooks how many Days in Advance to Enter the transaction

Click the drop-down list arrow for **How Often**
Click **Monthly**
Click the Calendar icon for Next Date, click **01/25/2015**

6

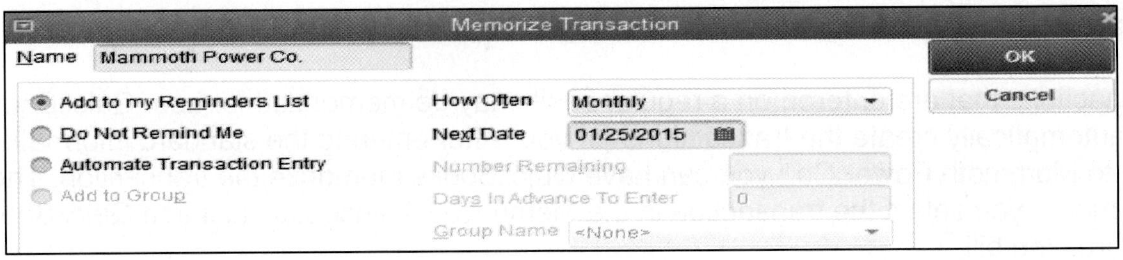

Click **OK**
Close the Enter Bills screen <u>without</u> saving the bill for Mammoth Power Co.
Click the **Lists** menu on the Menu bar, click **Memorized Transaction List**

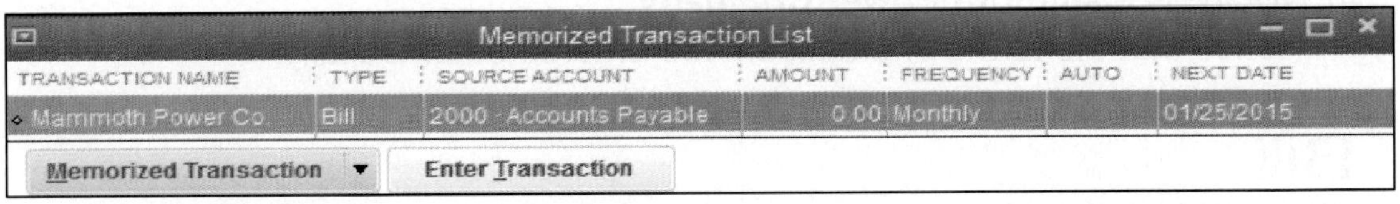

Click the **Memorized Transaction** button, click **Print List**
Click **OK** on the List Reports message, click **Print**
After printing the list, click the transaction to Mammoth Power Co. to select

USE MEMORIZED TRANSACTION

MEMO
DATE: January 25, 2015

Record the bill to Mammoth Power Company electrical power for January:
Invoice 3510-1023, $359.00

Use the Memorized Transaction List to record a bill

With Mammoth Power Co. highlighted, click the **Enter Transaction** button on the Memorized Transaction List
The prepared Bill to Mammoth Power Co. appears on the screen
Make sure the DATE to **01/25/2015**
Enter the REF. NO. **3510-1023**
Enter the AMOUNT DUE **359.00**

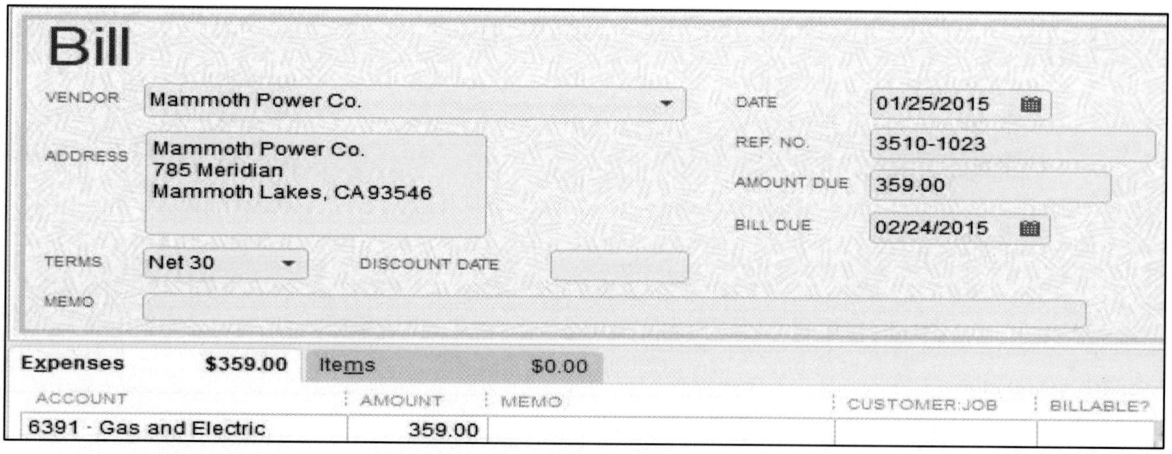

Print if instructed to do so; and then click **Save & New**

PREPARE ADDITIONAL BILLS

It is more efficient to record bills in a group or batch than it is to record them one at a time. If an error is made while preparing the bill, correct it. Your Name Mountain Sports uses the accrual basis of accounting. In the accrual method of accounting the expenses of a period are matched against the revenue of the period. Unless otherwise instructed, use the accrual basis of accounting when recording entries.

MEMO
DATE: January 25, 2015

Record the following bills:
Mammoth Telephone Company telephone service for January: Invoice 7815, $156.40
Mammoth Water Company water for January: Invoice 3105, $35.00

6

Enter the two transactions in the memo above.

- Refer to the instructions given for previous transactions.
- These are standard transactions so no Memo is required.
- Print if instructed to do so.

When finished, click **Save & Close** and close the **Memorize Transaction List**

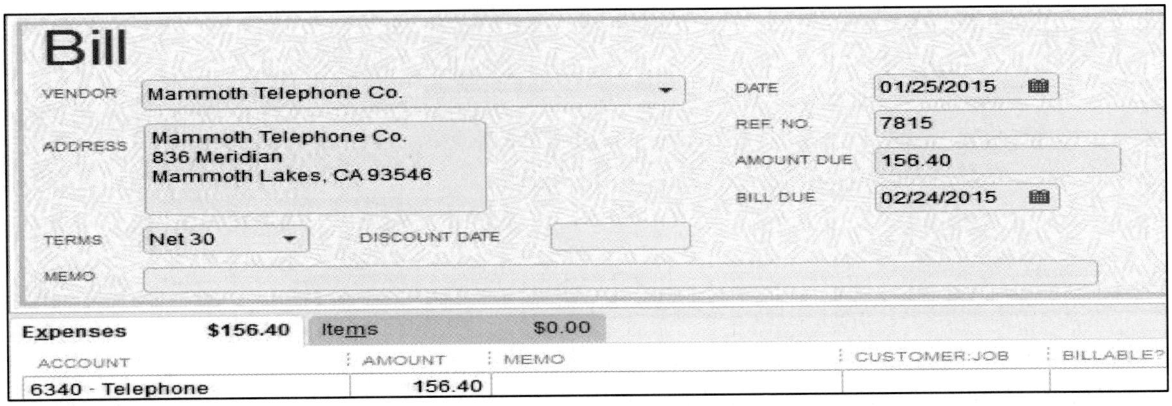

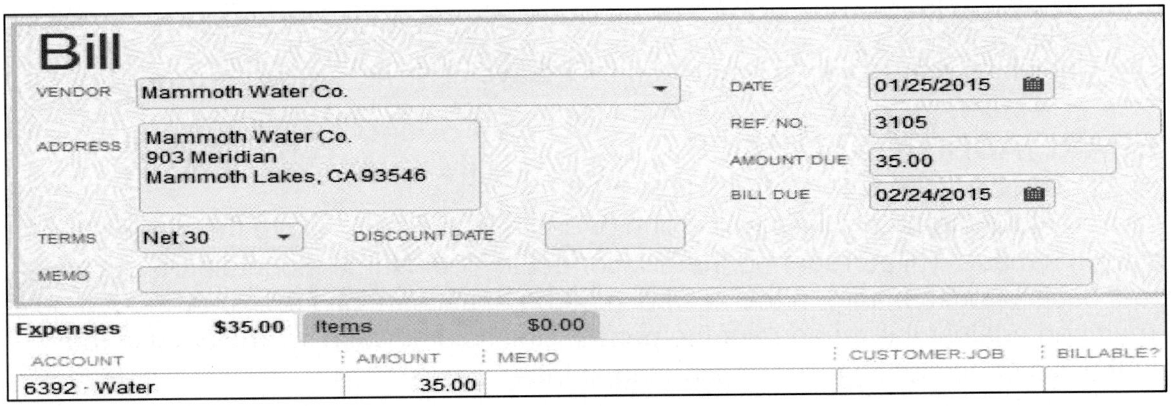

ENTER BILL IN ACCOUNTS PAYABLE REGISTER

The Accounts Payable Register maintains a record of all the transactions recorded within the Accounts Payable account. Not only is it possible to view all of the account activities through the account's register, it is also possible to enter a bill directly into the Accounts Payable register. This can be faster than filling out all of the information through Enter Bills.

MEMO
DATE: January 25, 2015

Received a bill for the rent from Mountain Rentals. Use the Accounts Payable Register and record the bill for rent of $950, Invoice 7164, due February 4, 2015.

Use the Accounts Payable Register to record the above transaction:

Use the keyboard shortcut, **Ctrl+A** to access the Chart of Accounts
Double-click **2000 Accounts Payable** to open the Accounts Payable register
The date is highlighted in the blank entry, key in **01/25/15** for the transaction date
The word *Number* is in the next column
Tab to or click **Number**

- The word *Number* disappears.

Enter the Vendor's Invoice Number **7164**
Click the drop-down list arrow for the VENDOR, click **Mountain Rentals**

- When there is a drop-down list arrow, you do not need to tab or click in the field.

Tab to or click **DUE DATE**; and, if necessary, enter the due date **02/04/15**
Tab to or click **BILLED**, enter the amount **950**
Click the drop-down list arrow for **Account**
Determine the appropriate account to use for rent

- If all of the accounts do not appear in the drop-down list, scroll through the accounts until you find the one appropriate for this entry.

Click **6300 Rent**
Click **Record** to record the transaction

- If the bill for Rent shows before Telephone that is fine. Since they have the same transaction date, QuickBooks alphabetized the Vendor names.

DATE	NUMBER	VENDOR		DUE DATE	BILLED	✓	PAID	BALANCE
	TYPE	ACCOUNT	MEMO					
01/25/2015	7164	Mountain Rentals		02/04/2015	950.00			12,434.00
	BILL	6300 · Rent						
01/25/2015	7815	Mammoth Telephone Co.		02/24/2015	156.40			12,590.40
	BILL	6340 · Telephone						

Do <u>not</u> close the register

EDIT TRANSACTION IN ACCOUNTS PAYABLE REGISTER

Because QuickBooks makes corrections extremely user friendly, a transaction can be edited or changed directly in the Accounts Payable Register as well as on the original bill. By eliminating the columns for Type and Memo, it is possible to change the register to show each transaction on one line. This can make the register easier to read.

MEMO
DATE: January 25, 2015

Upon examination of the invoices and the bills entered, Ruth discovers an error: The actual amount of the bill from the water company was **$85**, not $35. Change the transaction amount for this bill.

Correct the above transaction in the Accounts Payable Register

Click the check box for **1-line** to select

- Each Accounts Payable transaction will appear on one line.

Click the transaction for Mammoth Water Co.
Change the amount of the transaction from $35.00 to **$85.00**

Click the **Record** button at the bottom of the register
Click **Yes** on the Record Transaction dialog box

2000 · Accounts Payable

Go to... | Print... | Edit Transaction | QuickReport

DATE	NUMBER	VENDOR	ACCOUNT	DUE DATE	BILLED	✓	PAID	BALANCE
01/18/2015		Snow Stuff	-split-	02/17/2015	370.00			8,870.00
01/18/2015		Boots Galore	1120 · Inventory Asset	02/17/2015	1,875.00			10,745.00
01/18/2015		Clothes, Inc.	1120 · Inventory Asset	02/17/2015	300.00			11,045.00
01/21/2015	9915	Snow Stuff	1120 · Inventory Asset				50.00	10,995.00
01/23/2015	381-22	Mammoth News	6140 · Advertising Expense	02/22/2015	95.00			11,090.00
01/25/2015	3510-102	Mammoth Power Co.	6391 · Gas and Electric	02/24/2015	359.00			11,449.00
01/25/2015	3105	Mammoth Water Co.	6392 · Water	02/24/2015	85.00			11,534.00
01/25/2015	7164	Mountain Rentals	6300 · Rent	02/04/2015	950.00			12,484.00
01/25/2015	7815	Mammoth Telephone Co.	6340 · Telephone	02/24/2015	156.40			12,640.40

Splits | ENDING BALANCE 12,640.40

1-Line | Show open balance

Sort by Date, Type, Number/Ref | Record | Restore

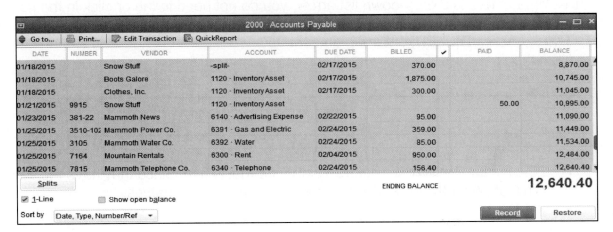

Do not close the register

PREPARE REGISTER QUICKREPORT

After editing the transaction, you may want to view information about a specific vendor. Clicking the vendor's name within a transaction and clicking the QuickReport button at the top of the register can do this quickly and efficiently.

> **MEMO**
> **DATE:** January 25, 2015
>
> More than one transaction has been entered for Snow Stuff. Both Larry and you like to view transaction information for all vendors that have several transactions within a short period of time.

Prepare a QuickReport for Snow Stuff

Click any field in any transaction for Snow Stuff
Click the **QuickReport** button at the top of the Register
- The Register QuickReport for All Transactions for Snow Stuff appears on the screen.

Resize the columns and print in Portrait orientation

Your Name Mountain Sports
Register QuickReport
All Transactions

Type	Date	Num	Memo	Account	Paid	Open Balance	Amount
Snow Stuff							
Bill	01/18/2015			2000 · Accounts Payable	Unpaid	370.00	370.00
Credit	01/21/2015	9915	Returned 1 Sled	2000 · Accounts Payable	Unpaid	-50.00	-50.00
Total Snow Stuff						320.00	320.00
TOTAL						**320.00**	**320.00**

Click the **Close** button to close the report
Close the Accounts Payable register and the Chart of Accounts

If you have been instructed to print bills, print the bills prepared and edited in the Accounts Payable register

Open **Enter Bills**; click **Previous** until you get to the bill for **Mountain Rentals**
Print as previously instructed
Repeat to print the corrected bill for **Mammoth Water Co.**

DISCOUNTS

There are three types of discounts used in QuickBooks: Sales Discount, Purchase Discount, and Merchandise Discount.

A Sales Discount is used when you give customers a discount for early payment with terms of 2/10, n/30 or 1/10, n/30. Sales Discount is categorized as an Income account. Using a sales discount results in a decrease in income because the company will receive less money for a sale. In Chapter 5, Sales Discounts were used for customer payments.

A Purchase Discount is a discount for early payment for purchases made to run the business. Example, a discount on office supplies purchased. A purchase discount is categorized as an Income account because it results in an increase in income since it costs you less to run the business.

A Merchandise Discount is a discount on sales items purchased for resale This is categorized as a Cost of Goods Sold account because the use of this discount results in a decrease in the amount you pay for the goods (merchandise) you sell. This is used in Chapter 6 for payments for sales items purchased.

PREPARE UNPAID BILLS DETAIL REPORT

It is possible to get information regarding unpaid bills by simply preparing a report. No more digging through tickler files, recorded invoices, ledgers, or journals. QuickBooks prepares an Unpaid Bills Detail Report listing each unpaid bill grouped and subtotaled by vendor.

Comments may be added to lines in a report. On an Unpaid Bills report, it could be helpful to add comments to the bills that should be paid.

MEMO
DATE: January 25, 2015

Ruth Morgan prepares an Unpaid Bills Report each week. Because Your Name Mountain Sports is a small business, you like to have a firm control over cash flow so you can determine which bills will be paid during the week. Add the comment "Pay this Bill" to each bill eligible for a discount.

Prepare an **Unpaid Bills Detail Report**

Click **Reports** on the menu bar, point to **Vendors & Payables**, click **Unpaid Bills Detail**
Enter the date of **01/25/15** as the report date
Tab to generate report
Adjust column size as necessary to display all data in the columns in full

- Notice the Due Dates for the bills. Bills from the end of the previous year are due on January 10.
- The days shown for Aging will be different from the report shown because the aging is based on the date of your computer.
- Note: The Unpaid Bills report does not give you information regarding discount eligibility.
- If a column showing Terms was in the report, you could determine which bills would be eligible for a discount.

Your Name Mountain Sports
Unpaid Bills Detail
As of January 25, 2015

Type	Date	Num	Due Date	Aging	Open Balance
Snow Stuff					
Credit	01/21/2015	9915			-50.00
Bill	01/18/2015	97	02/17/2015		370.00
Total Snow Stuff					320.00
Sports Accessories					
Bill	12/31/2014		01/10/2015	15	350.00
Total Sports Accessories					350.00
Sports Boots & Bindings					
Bill	12/31/2014		01/10/2015	15	2,000.00
Total Sports Boots & Bindings					2,000.00
TOTAL					12,640.40

Partial Report

CUSTOMIZE AND MEMORIZE REPORT

While many reports come with QuickBooks, sometimes you do not have all the information that you want displayed in the report. Just as you can customize the header/footer for a report, you can also customize the information shown within a report.

Customize the Unpaid Bills Detail report to show Terms

With the Unpaid Bills report showing on the screen, click the **Customize Report** button

The REPORT DATE RANGE should be From **01/25/2015** and To **01/25/2015**

Scroll through the COLUMNS until you see the word **Terms**, and click to mark

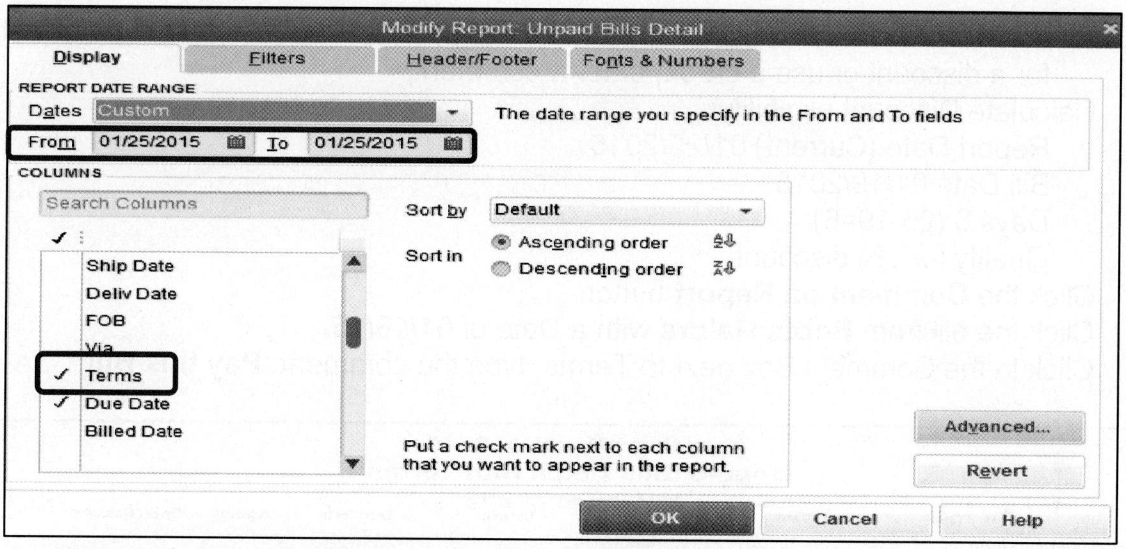

Click **OK**, Terms are now displayed in the report

Adjust the column widths to displayed everything in full; yet, print one-page wide

Click the **Memorize** button

The Name of the report is: **Unpaid Bills Detail with Terms**

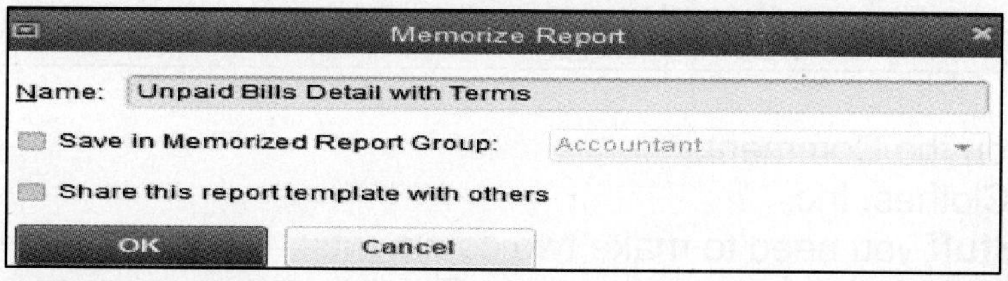

Click **OK**

Close the Unpaid Bills Report

USE MEMORIZED REPORT

To use the report in the future, click Reports on the Menu Bar, click Memorized Reports, and click Unpaid Bills Detail with Terms

Use the Memorized Report Unpaid Bills with Terms

Click **Reports** on the Menu bar, click **Memorized Reports**, and click **Unpaid Bills with Terms**

- Make sure the date is **01/25/2015**, press **Tab**

ADD COMMENTS TO REPORT

With the Unpaid Bills with Terms for 01/25/2015 on the screen, comment on the report

- Look at the vendors who show Terms of 2% 10 Net 30. If any of the bills qualify for a discount or use a credit, enter a comment.

Calculate Discount eligibility:

Report Date (Current) 01/25/2015
Bill Date 01/19/2015
Days 6 (25-19=6)
Qualify for 2% discount

Click the **Comment on Report** button
Click the bill from **Boots Galore** with a Date of **01/18/15**
Click in the Comment Box next to Terms, type the comment: **Pay this Bill**

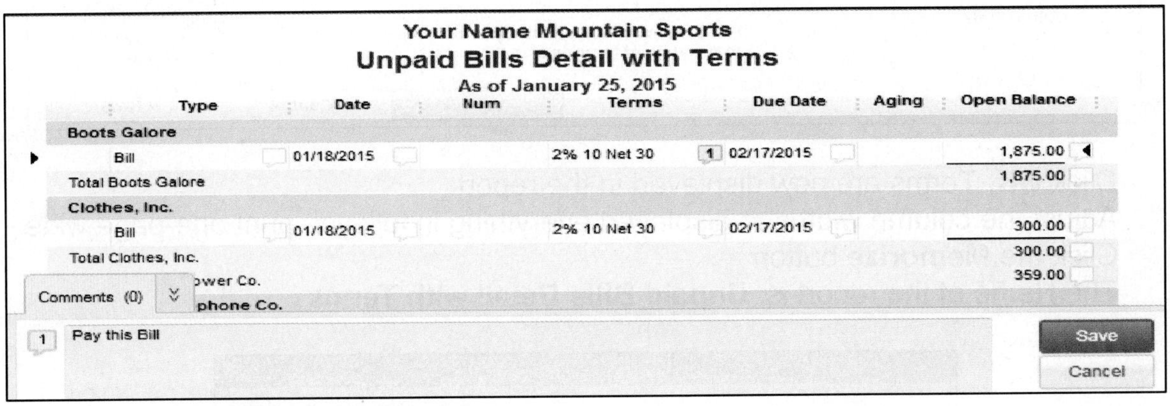

Click **Save** on the Comments
Repeat for Clothes, Inc.
For **Snow Stuff** you need to make two comments:

On the Credit, click in the box next to Credit, enter comment **Use this credit**
For the bill, comment **Pay this Bill** as you did for Boots Galore and Clothes, Inc.

Print in Portrait orientation

- The Commented report can also be saved with the comments. It can also be emailed. It cannot be exported to Excel.

Close the report without saving, click **No** on Save Your Commented Report?
Close the Unpaid Bills Detail with Terms

PAY BILLS

When using QuickBooks, you may choose to pay your bills directly from the Pay Bills command and let QuickBooks write your checks for you, or you may choose to write the checks yourself. If you recorded a bill, you should use the Pay Bills feature of QuickBooks to pay the bill. If no bill was recorded, you should pay the bill by writing a check in

QuickBooks. Using the Pay Bills window enables you to determine which bills to pay, the method of payment—check or credit card—and the appropriate account. When you are determining which bills to pay, QuickBooks allows you to display the bills by due date, discount date, vendor, or amount. All bills may be displayed, or only those bills that are due by a certain date may be displayed. In addition, when a bill has been recorded and is paid using the Pay Bills feature of QuickBooks, the bill will be marked *Paid in Full* and the amount paid will no longer be shown as a liability. If you record a bill and pay it by writing a check and *not* using the Pay Bills feature of QuickBooks, the bill won't be marked as paid and it will show up as a liability.

MEMO

DATE: January 25, 2015

Whenever possible, Ruth Morgan pays the bills on a weekly basis. Show all the bills in the Pay Bills window. As indicated in the comments on the Unpaid Bills report, select the bills for Boots Galore and Clothes, Inc. with discounts dates of 1/28/2015.

Pay the bills that are eligible for a discount

Click **Pay Bills** on the QuickBooks Home Page
Click **Show All Bills** to select
Filter By **All vendors**
Sort By **Due Date**
In the PAYMENT section at the bottom of the **Pay Bills** window, verify and/or select the following items:
Date is **01/25/15**
Method is **Check**
To be printed should be selected
Account is **1100 Checking**
Scroll through the list of bills

- The bills will be shown according to the date due.

6

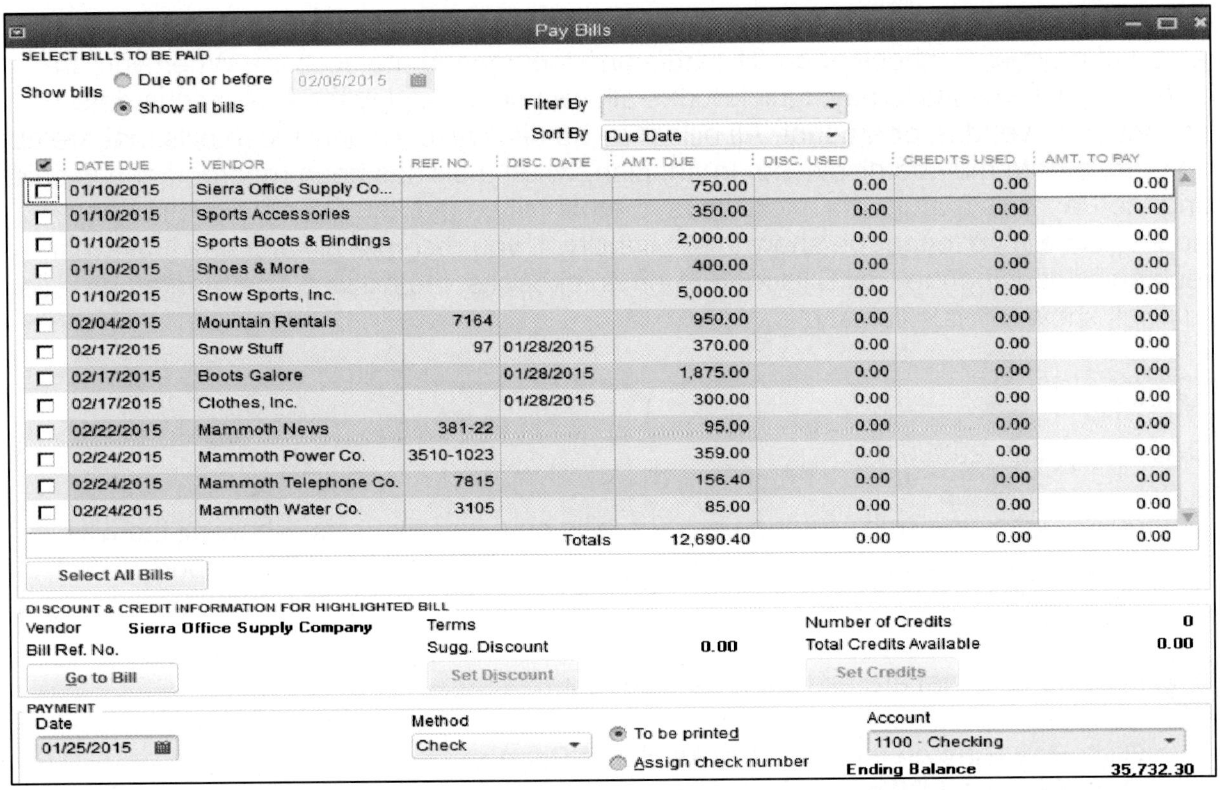

Select the bills to be paid and apply the discounts:

Click in the check mark column for the transaction for **Boots Galore** with a DUE DATE of 2/17/2015 and a DISC Date of 01/28/2015

Click the **Set Discount** button

- Verify the Suggested Discount of **37.50**.

Click the drop-down list arrow for the Discount Account

- Scroll through the list of accounts.
- There is account 4030 Purchases Discounts but it is not appropriate for this transaction. This income account is used for purchases of things used by the business not for merchandise.
- There is 4050 Sales Discounts. This income account is used when we give discounts to customers.
- The bill payment is for merchandise purchased to sell in the business. A cost of goods sold discount account needs to be created for merchandise discounts.

Click **<Add New>**

Click the drop-down list arrow for **Account Type**, click **Cost of Goods Sold**

- Remember the Cost of Goods sold is the average cost you pay for an item you sell and is calculated on the Profit & Loss Statement using the formula: Total Income – Cost of Goods Sold = Gross Profit; Gross Profit – Expenses = Net Profit.

- Using Merchandise Discounts for early payment will decrease the overall Cost of Goods Sold and increase Profit or Net Income. Example: Cost of Goods Sold – Merchandise Discounts = Net Cost of Goods Sold.
- If Cost of Goods Sold is $1,000 and you subtract Merchandise Discounts of $100 the Net Cost of Goods Sold is $900. Without the discount, Cost of Goods Sold is $1,000.

Enter **5200** as the account number
Enter the account name **Merchandise Discounts**
Click **Subaccount** and select **5000 Cost of Goods Sold** as the account

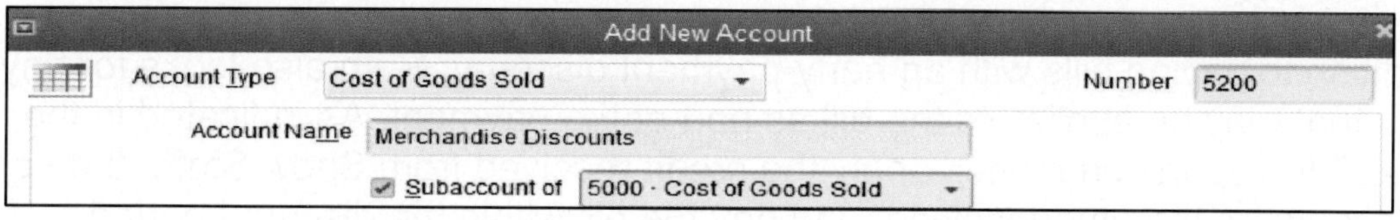

Click **Save & Close**

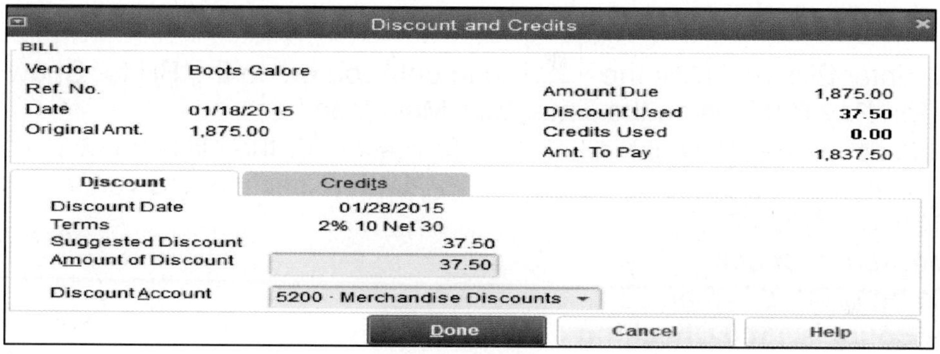

Click **Done** to record the discount
Repeat the steps for the bill from Clothes, Inc. that is eligible for a discount

☑	DATE DUE	VENDOR	REF. NO.	DISC. DATE	AMT. DUE	DISC. USED	CREDITS USED	AMT. TO PAY
☑	02/17/2015	Boots Galore		01/28/2015	1,875.00	37.50	0.00	1,837.50
☑	02/17/2015	Clothes, Inc.		01/28/2015	300.00	6.00	0.00	294.00
				Totals	12,690.40	43.50	0.00	2,131.50

- Once you click **Done** to accept the discount, the DISC. USED and AMT. TO PAY amounts change to reflect the amount of the discount taken.
- Notice the totals provided indicating the DISC. USED and the AMT. TO PAY for the two selected bills.

Click the **Pay Selected Bills** button,

- Notice the two payments shown.

Click the **Done** button on the **Payment Summary** screen

6

PAY BILL WITH CREDIT AND DISCOUNT

When paying bills, it is a good idea to apply credits received for returned or damaged merchandise to the accounts as payment is made. If you want to pay a specific bill, you may access it in Enter Bills and then click the Pay Bills icon. Information for the bill will show in the Pay Bills window.

MEMO

DATE: January 25, 2015

In addition to paying bills with an early-payment discount, Ruth also looks for any credits that may be applied to the bill as part of the payment. As indicated in the Unpaid Bills report comments, apply the credit received from Snow Stuff, then apply the discount on the amount owed, and pay the bill within the discount period.

Apply the credit received from Snow Stuff, as part of the payment for the bill and pay bill within the discount period

Open Enter Bills and click the  icon until you get to the Bill for Snow Stuff

Click the **Pay Bill** icon on the Enter Bills Main Icon bar

- This opens Pay Bills and all of the information for the bill is shown.

Look at the bottom of the screen in the PAYMENT section and verify:

Date of **01/25/2015**

Method is **Check**

To be printed is marked

Account is **1100 Checking**

- Notice that both the Set Credits and Set Discount buttons are now active and that information regarding credits and discounts is displayed.

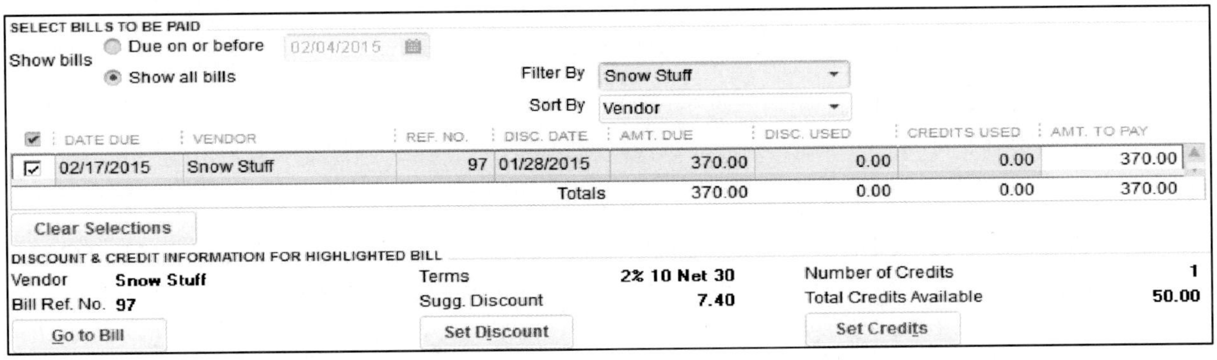

Click the **Set Credits** button

Make sure there is a check in the Check Mark column for the credit amount of **50.00**

Click the **Discount** tab

- On the Discounts and Credits screen, verify the Amount Due of **370**, the Discount Used of **7.40**, and the Credits Used of **50.00**, leaving an Amt. To Pay of **312.60**.

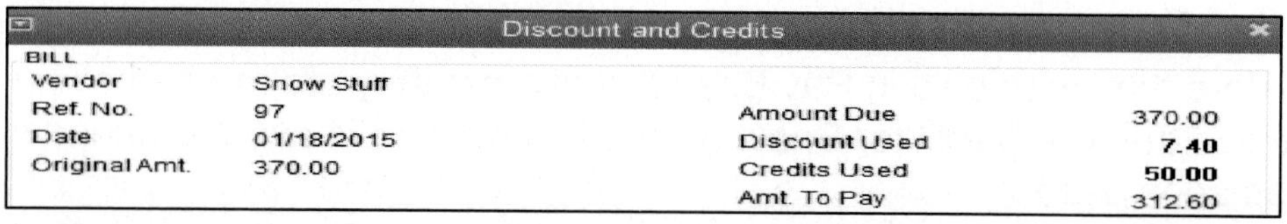

- QuickBooks calculates the discount on the original amount of the invoice rather than the amount due after subtracting the credit. You need to recalculate the discount on the amount due after the credit.

Click in the Amount of Discount column and use QuickMath to calculate the correct discount:
Remove the 7.40 shown
Enter the Amount Due **370** – Credits Used **50** * Discount Percentage **.02**

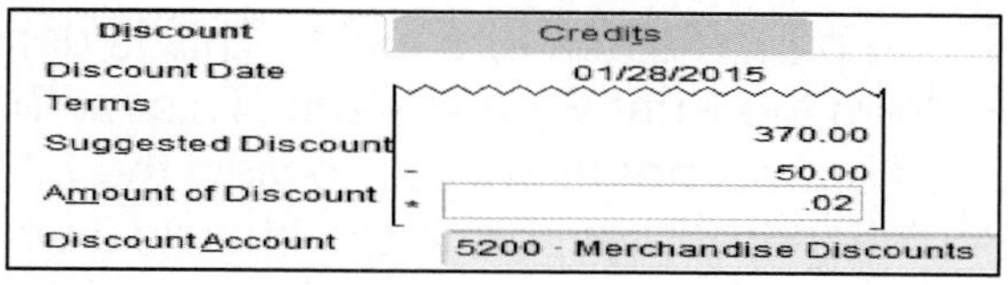

Press **Enter** to enter the discount amount of **6.40**, press **Tab** to update Discount Used
Make sure the Discount Account is **5200 Merchandise Discounts**

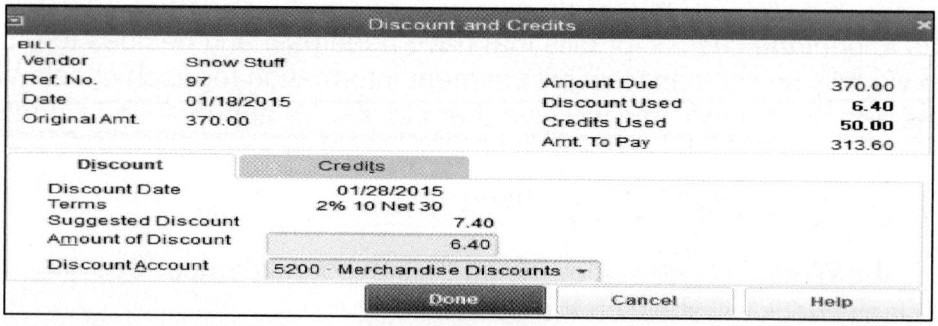

Click the **Done** button
Review the information for DISC USED **6.40** and AMT. TO PAY **313.60**

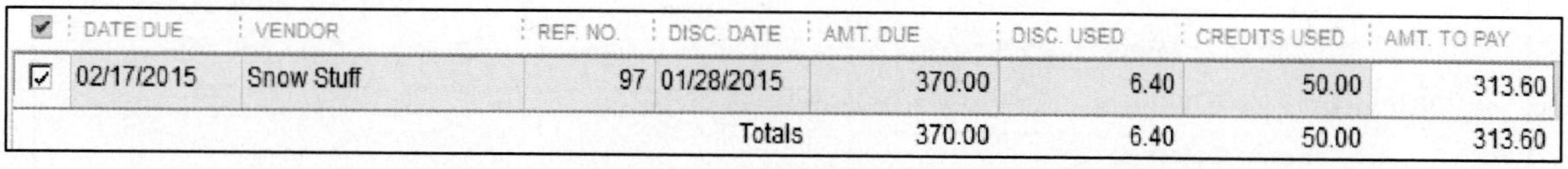
DATE DUE
VENDOR
REF. NO.
DISC. DATE
AMT. DUE
DISC. USED
CREDITS USED
AMT. TO PAY
02/17/2015 Snow Stuff 97 01/28/2015 370.00 6.40 50.00 313.60
Totals 370.00 6.40 50.00 313.60

Click **Pay Selected Bills**, click **Done** on the Payment Summary
- Note that the bill for Snow Stuff appears and is marked PAID.

VERIFY BILLS MARKED PAID

View Paid Bills

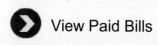

Click **Previous** (Back arrow icon) and view all the bills for Clothes, Inc. and Boots Galore that were paid in Pay Bills to verify that they are marked as paid

- Notice that the Credit for Snow Stuff is *not* marked in any way to indicate that it has been used.

Close the Enter Bills screen

PRINT CHECKS TO PAY BILLS

Once bills have been selected for payment and any discounts taken or credits applied, the checks should be printed, signed, and mailed. QuickBooks has three methods that may be used to print checks. Checks may be printed immediately after a bill has been paid, which is the most efficient method. Secondly, checks may be accessed and printed one at a time using the Write Checks window. This allows you to view the Bill Payment Information for each check. The third way is to print a batch of checks. This is done by clicking the File menu and selecting checks from the Print Forms menu. This method will print all checks that are marked *To be printed* but will not allow you to view the bill payment information for any of the checks. QuickBooks does not separate the checks it writes in Pay Bills from the checks that are written when using the Write Checks feature of the program.

MEMO

DATE: January 25, 2015

Ruth needs to print the checks for bills that have been paid and decides to print checks individually so she can view bill payment information for each check. When she finishes with the checks, she will give them to you for approval and signature.

Print the checks for bills that have been paid

Access the Write Checks window using the keyboard shortcut **Ctrl+W**

- A blank check will show on the screen.

Click **Previous** (Back arrow icon) until you get to the check for **Boots Galore**

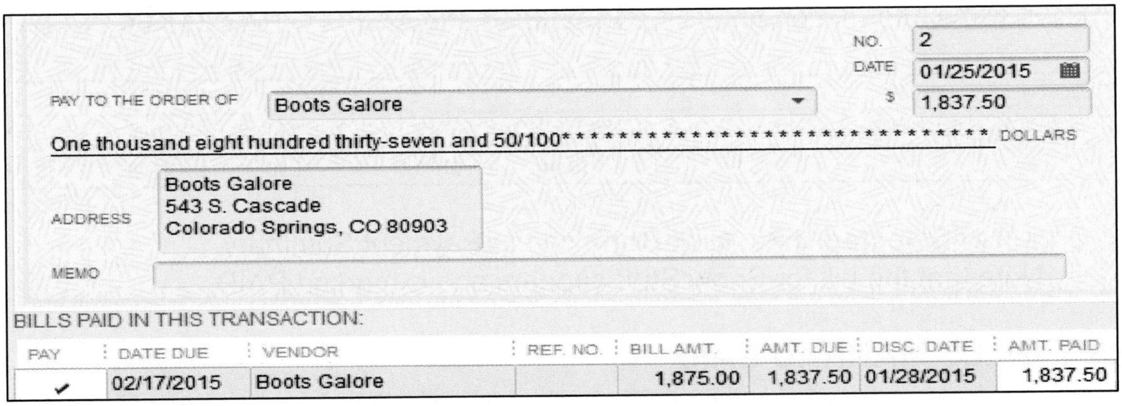

NO. 2
DATE 01/25/2015
PAY TO THE ORDER OF Boots Galore $ 1,837.50
One thousand eight hundred thirty-seven and 50/100****************************** DOLLARS
ADDRESS Boots Galore
543 S. Cascade
Colorado Springs, CO 80903
MEMO

BILLS PAID IN THIS TRANSACTION:

PAY	DATE DUE	VENDOR	REF. NO.	BILL AMT.	AMT. DUE	DISC. DATE	AMT. PAID
✔	02/17/2015	Boots Galore		1,875.00	1,837.50	01/28/2015	1,837.50

Click **Print** at the top of the window to print the check

Click **OK** on the Print Check screen to select Check 2

- Check 1 was issued in Chapter 5 to Dr. Jose Perez for a return. If Check 2 is not on the Print Check screen, change the check number to 2.

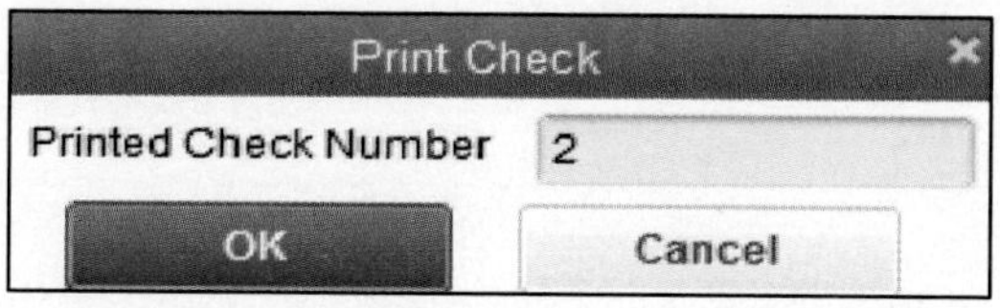

- On the **Print Checks** screen, verify the printer name, printer type.

Select **Standard** check style.

Print Company Name and Address should be selected

- If is not marked with a check, click the check box to select.

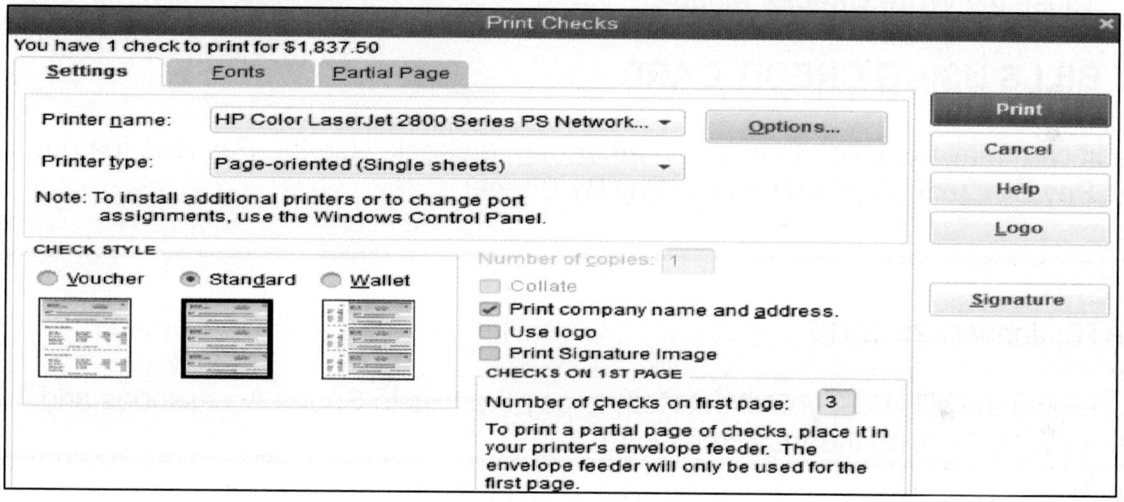

Click **Print** to print the check

Click **OK** on the **Print Checks – Confirmation** screen

Click **Previous** or **Next** arrow icons and repeat the steps to print Check 3 for Clothes, Inc., and Check 4 for Snow Stuff

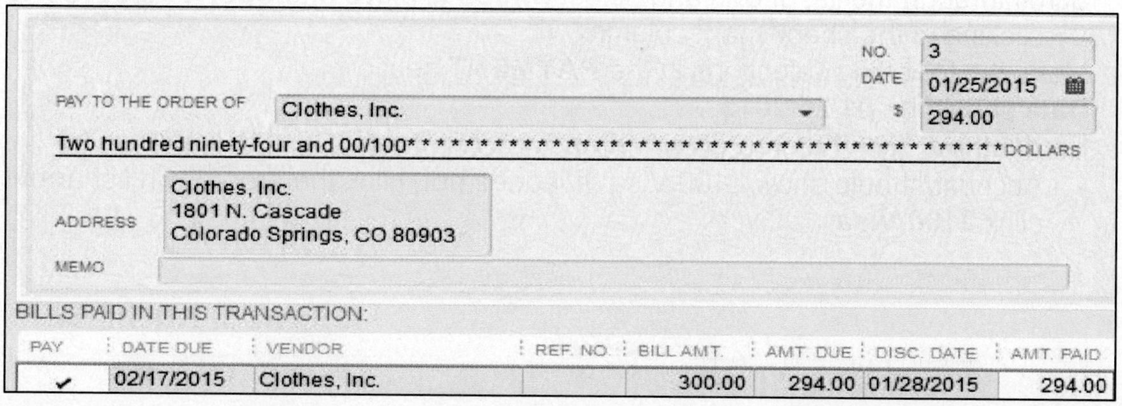

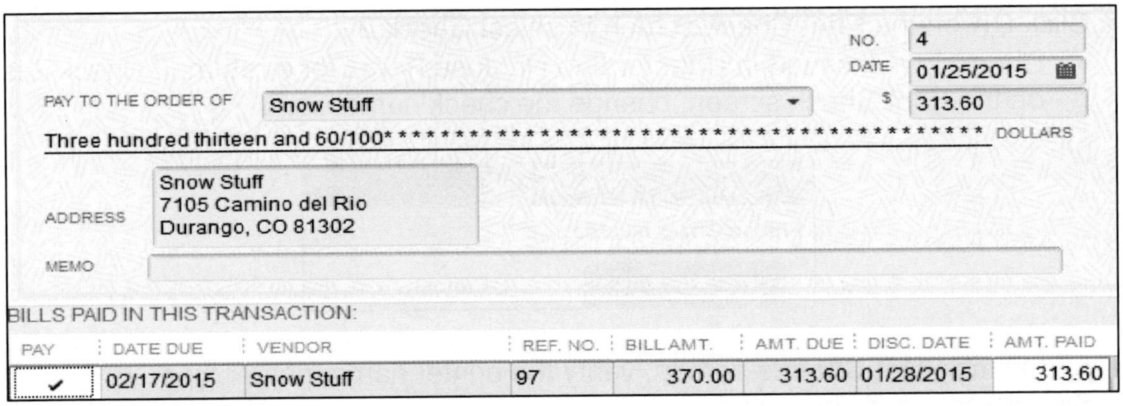

- Notice that the amount of the check to Snow Stuff is $313.60. This allows for the original bill of $370 less the return of $50 and the discount of $6.40.

Close the **Write Checks** window.

PAY BILLS USING CREDIT CARD

A credit card may be used to pay a bill rather than a check. Use the Pay Bills feature, but select Pay By Credit Card rather than Pay By Check.

MEMO
DATE: January 25, 2015

In viewing the bills due, you direct Ruth to pay the bills to Sports Accessories and Shoes & More using the Visa credit card.

Pay the above bills with a credit card

Access **Pay Bills** as previously instructed
Select **Show all bills**
Filter By **All vendors** and Sort By **Vendor**
Scroll through the list of bills and select **Shoes & More** and **Sports Accessories** by clicking in the check mark column
Make the following selections in the **PAYMENT** section:
Date should be **01/25/2015**
For **Method** click the drop-down list arrow, click **Credit Card** to select

- Account should show 2100 Visa. If it does not, click the drop-down list arrow and click **2100 Visa**.

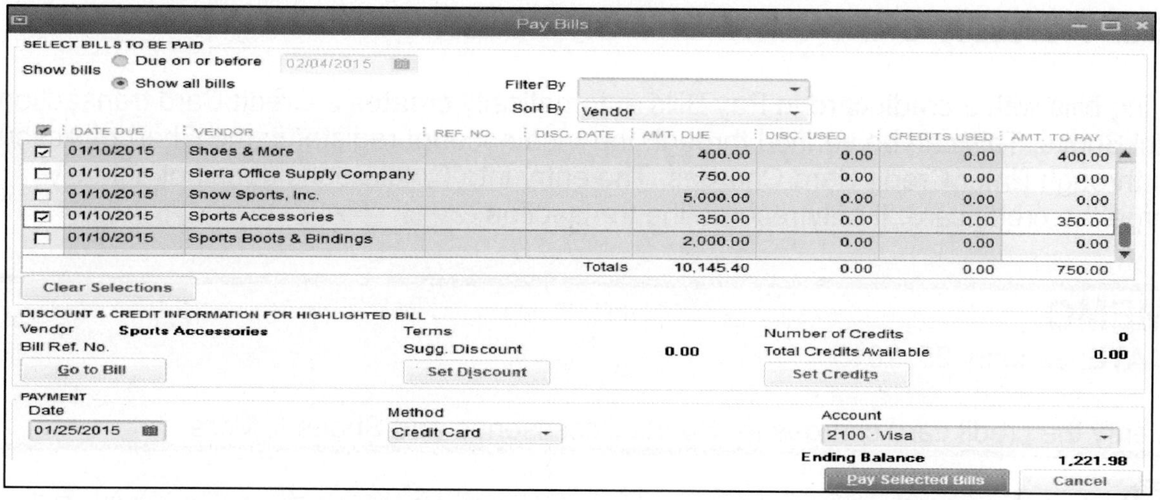

Click **Pay Selected Bills** to record the payment

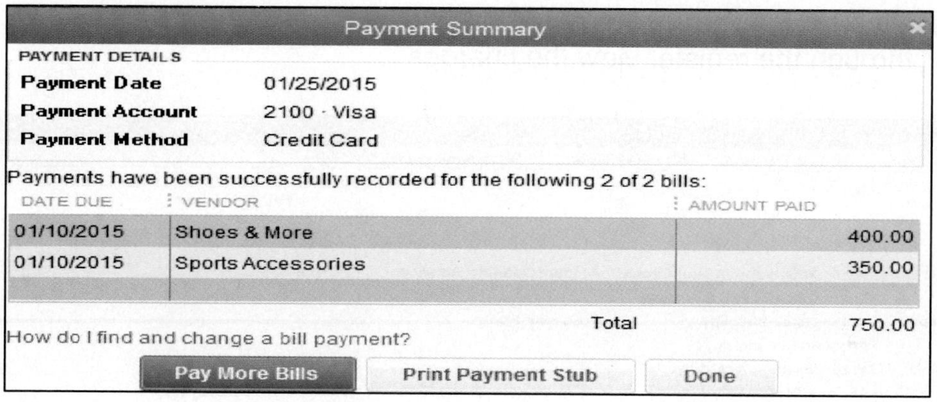

In order to have a printed record of your payment, click **Print Payment Stub**

- Using a credit card in Pay Bills is the only place you can print a Payment Stub for a credit card transaction. You must be logged in to QuickBooks as an administrator or assigned permission to do this.

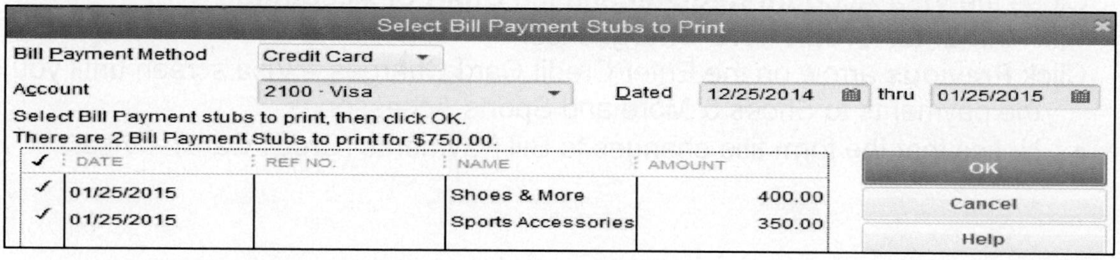

Click **OK**, click **Print** on the Print Bill Payment Stubs

VERIFY CREDIT CARD PAYMENT OF BILLS

Paying bills with a credit card in Pay Bills automatically creates a Credit Card transaction in QuickBooks. This can be verified through the Visa account register in the Chart of Accounts and through Enter Credit Card Charges. The entry into QuickBooks does not actually charge the credit card. It only records the transaction.

MEMO
DATE: January 25, 2015

Verify the credit card charges for Sports Accessories and Shoes & More.

Verify the credit card charges by viewing the Visa Account Register and the Bill Payments (Credit Card) - Visa

Access the **Visa Account Register** in the **Chart of Accounts**
Scroll through the register view the charges

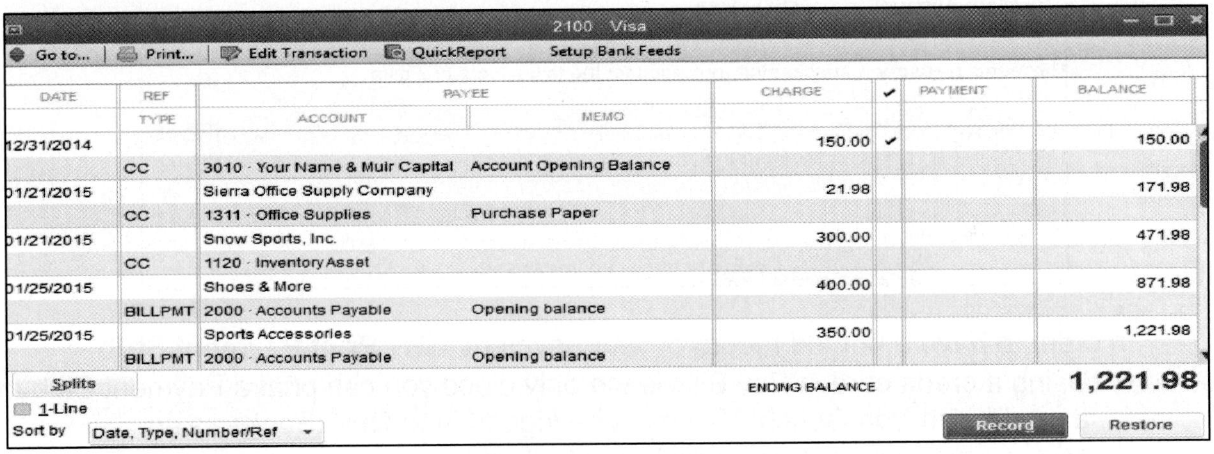

Close the **Visa Account Register** and the **Chart of Accounts**
Click the **Enter Credit Card Charges** icon
Click **Previous** arrow on the Enter Credit Card Charges – Visa screen until you see the payments to Shoes & More and Sports Accessories

- Notice that the form title changes to Bill Payments (Credit Card) – Visa.

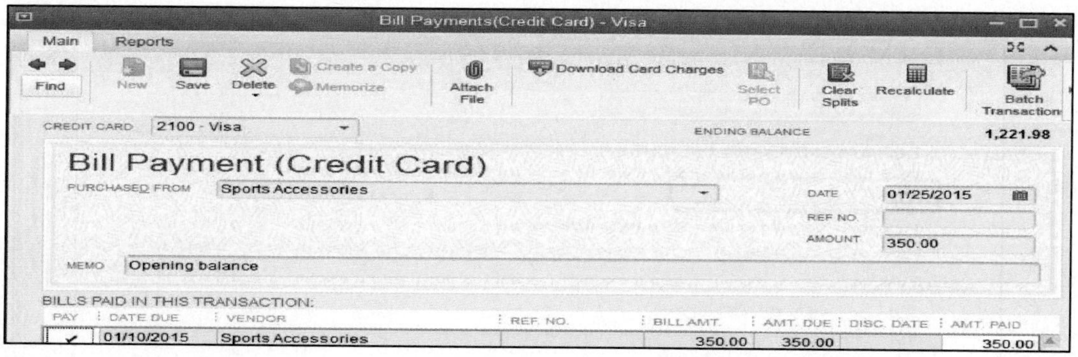

Close Bill Payments

SALES TAX

When a company is set up in QuickBooks, a Sales Tax Payable liability account is automatically created if the company charges sales tax. The Sales Tax Payable account keeps track of as many tax agencies as the company needs. As invoices are written, QuickBooks records the tax liability in the Sales Tax Payable account. To determine the sales tax owed, a Sales Tax Liability Report is prepared.

SALES TAX LIABILITY REPORT

The Sales Tax Liability Report shows your total taxable sales, the total nontaxable sales, and the amount of sales tax owed to each tax agency.

MEMO

DATE: January 25, 2015

Prior to paying the sales tax, Ruth prepares the Sales Tax Liability Report.

Prepare the Sales Tax Liability Report

Click the **Manage Sales Tax** icon in the Vendors section of the Home Page
Click the **Sales Tax Liability** report

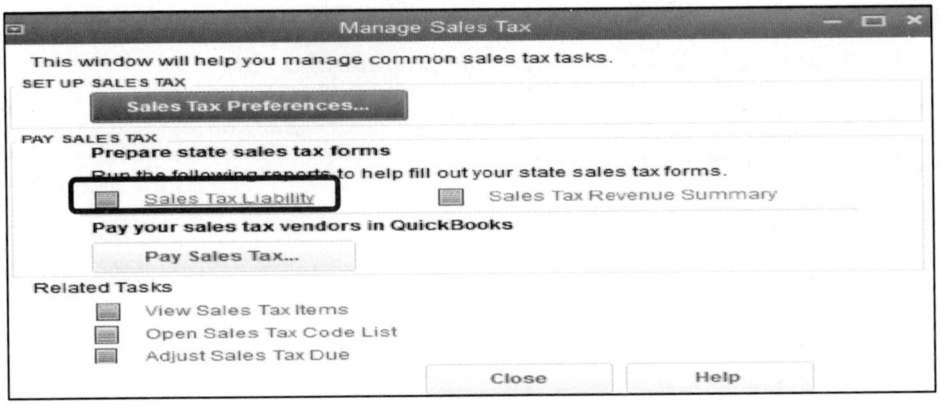

The Report Dates are **From 01/01/2015 To 01/25/2015**

- If necessary, adjust the column widths so the report will fit on one page.
- If you get a message box asking if all columns should be the same size as the one being adjusted, click **No**.

Your Name Mountain Sports
Sales Tax Liability
January 1 - 25, 2015

	Total Sales	Non-Taxable Sales	Taxable Sales	Tax Rate	Tax Collected	Sales Tax Payable As of Jan 25, 15
State Board of Equalization						
CA Sales Tax	8,797.00	25.00	8,772.00	8.0%	701.77	701.77
Total State Board of Equalization	8,797.00	25.00	8,772.00		701.77	701.77
TOTAL	8,797.00	25.00	8,772.00		701.77	701.77

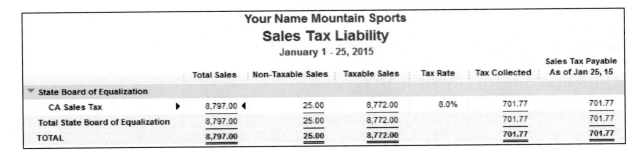

Print in Landscape orientation and close the report after printing

PAY SALES TAX

Use the Manage Sales Tax window to determine how much sales tax you owe and to write a check to the tax agency. QuickBooks will update the sales tax account with payment information.

MEMO
DATE: January 25, 2015

Note from Larry: Ruth, pay the sales taxes owed.

Pay the sales taxes owed

The Manage Sales Tax screen should be showing
Click the **Pay Sales Tax** button
Pay From Account is **1100 Checking**
Check Date is **01/25/2015**

Show sales tax due through is **01/25/2015**
Starting Check No. should be **To Print**
Click the **Pay All Tax** button or click in the Pay column to mark the transaction

- Once the transaction is marked, the Pay All Tax button changes to Clear Selections.

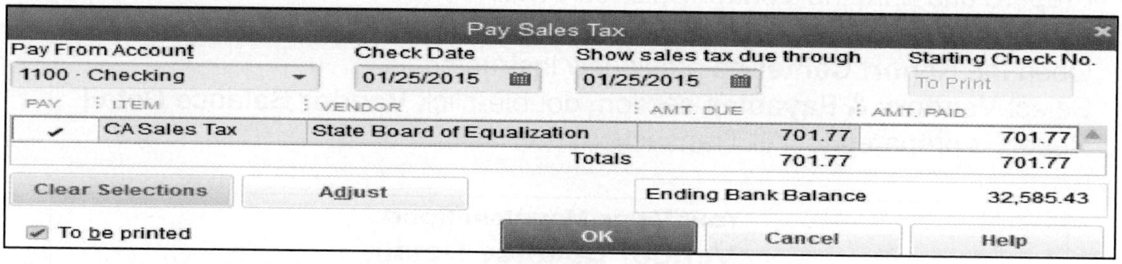

- Once **Pay All Tax** has been clicked and the Sales Tax item is selected, the **Ending Bank Balance** changes to reflect the amount in checking

Click **OK**, and then click **Close** on the Manage Sales Tax screen

Use Print Forms to print Check 5 for the payment of the Sales Tax

Click **File** on the Menu bar, point to **Print Forms**, click **Checks**

- Verify the Bank Account 1100 Checking, the First Check 5, and the check mark in front of State Board of Equalization. If your screen does not match the following, make the appropriate changes.

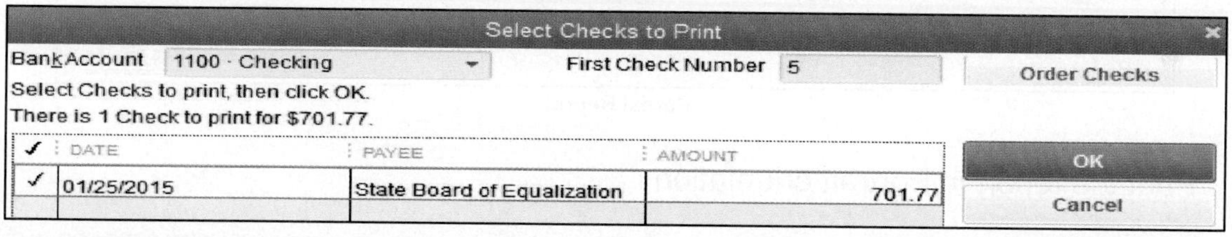

Click **OK**, click **Print**, Check Style is **Standard**, click **OK** on the **Print Checks – Confirmation** screen

VIEW TAX PAYMENT CHECK IN CHECK REGISTER

Whenever a check is prepared, it will show in the Register for the Checking account.

View the payment made for sales tax

Click the **Check Register** icon on the Banking section of the Home Page

- The register for 1100-Checking is shown.

Scroll through the register to view the information for Check 5, and then close it

VENDOR BALANCE DETAIL

When dealing with payables, it is important to be able to see the details of all the transactions made with each vendor during the period.

Prepare and print the Vendor Balance Detail

Open the **Report Center** as previously instructed
Select **Vendors & Payables** section, double-click **Vendor Balance Detail**
Report is prepared for All Transactions

Your Name Mountain Sports
Vendor Balance Detail
All Transactions

Type	Date	Num	Account	Amount	Balance
Snow Stuff					
Bill	01/18/2015	97	2000 · Accounts Payable	370.00	370.00
Credit	01/21/2015	9915	2000 · Accounts Payable	-50.00	320.00
Bill Pmt -Check	01/25/2015	4	2000 · Accounts Payable	-313.60	6.40
Discount	01/25/2015	4	2000 · Accounts Payable	-6.40	0.00
Total Snow Stuff				0.00	0.00
Sports Accessories					
Bill	12/31/2014		2000 · Accounts Payable	350.00	350.00
Bill Pmt -CCard	01/25/2015		2000 · Accounts Payable	-350.00	0.00
Total Sports Accessories				0.00	0.00
Sports Boots & Bindings					
Bill	12/31/2014		2000 · Accounts Payable	2,000.00	2,000.00
Total Sports Boots & Bindings				2,000.00	2,000.00
TOTAL				9,395.40	9,395.40

Partial Report

Print the report in Portrait orientation

TRIAL BALANCE

When all sales transactions have been entered, it is important to print the trial balance and verify that the total debits equal the total credits.

Prepare and print the Trial Balance

Select **Accountant & Taxes** section, double-click **Trial Balance**
The report dates are from **01/01/2015** to **01/25/2015**

Your Name Mountain Sports
Trial Balance
As of January 25, 2015

	Jan 25, 15	
	Debit	Credit
1100 · Checking	32,585.43	
1200 · Accounts Receivable	6,571.50	
1120 · Inventory Asset	35,551.54	
12000 · Undeposited Funds	0.00	
1311 · Office Supplies	871.98	
1312 · Sales Supplies	575.00	
1340 · Prepaid Insurance	250.00	
1511 · Original Cost	5,000.00	
1521 · Original Cost	4,500.00	
2000 · Accounts Payable		9,395.40
2100 · Visa		1,221.98
2200 · Sales Tax Payable	0.00	
2510 · Office Equipment Loan		3,000.00
2520 · Store Fixtures Loan		2,500.00
3000 · Owners' Equity	0.00	
3010 · Your Name & Muir Capital		26,159.44
3011 · Your Name, Investment		20,000.00
3012 · Larry Muir, Investment		20,000.00
4011 · Clothing & Accessory Sales		1,759.51
4012 · Equipment Sales		7,436.44
4050 · Sales Discounts	494.36	
4090 · Returned Check Charges		25.00
5000 · Cost of Goods Sold	3,492.46	
5200 · Merchandise Discounts		49.90
6120 · Bank Service Charges	10.00	
6140 · Advertising Expense	95.00	
6300 · Rent	950.00	
6340 · Telephone	156.40	
6391 · Gas and Electric	359.00	
6392 · Water	85.00	
TOTAL	91,547.67	91,547.67

Print the Trial Balance in **Portrait** orientation
Close the report, do not close the Report Center

JOURNAL

The Journal records each transaction and lists the accounts and the amounts for debit and credit entries. The Journal is very useful; especially if you are trying to find errors. Always check the transaction dates, the account names, and the items listed in the Memo column. If a transaction does not appear in the Journal, it may be due to using an incorrect date. Remember, only the transactions entered within the report dates will be displayed.

Print the Journal for Chapter 6 transactions
In the **Accountant & Taxes** section of the Report Center double-click **Journal**
Click the **Expand** button to show all information
Enter the dates for Chapter 6 transactions: From **01/18/15** and To **01/25/15**

- Using the chapter transaction dates means that the Journal will not show the transactions for Chapter 5. If you wish to see the transactions for Chapters 5 and 6, the From date should be 01/01/15.

Resize the columns so information shows in full

Your Name Mountain Sports
Journal
January 18 - 25, 2015

Trans #	Type	Date	Num	Adj	Name	Memo	Account	Debit	Credit
103	Bill Pmt -Check	01/25/2015	4		Snow Stuff		1100 · Checking		313.60
					Snow Stuff		2000 · Accounts Payable	313.60	
					Snow Stuff		2000 · Accounts Payable	6.40	
					Snow Stuff		5200 · Merchandise Discounts		6.40
								320.00	320.00
104	Bill Pmt -CCard	01/25/2015			Shoes & More	Opening balance	2100 · Visa		400.00
					Shoes & More	Opening balance	2000 · Accounts Payable	400.00	
								400.00	400.00
105	Bill Pmt -CCard	01/25/2015			Sports Accessories	Opening balance	2100 · Visa		350.00
					Sports Accessories	Opening balance	2000 · Accounts Payable	350.00	
								350.00	350.00
106	Sales Tax Paym...	01/25/2015	5		State Board of Equalization		1100 · Checking		701.77
					State Board of Equalization		2200 · Sales Tax Payable	701.77	
								701.77	701.77
TOTAL								8,519.15	8,519.15

Partial Report

Print the Journal in Landscape orientation
Close the **Journal** and the **Report Center**

PREPARE MEMORIZED REPORT

To obtain information regarding the inventory, you may prepare an Inventory Valuation Summary or an Inventory Valuation Detail report. Both reports give you information regarding an item, the number on hand, the average cost, and asset value. The summary report also gives information regarding an item's percentage of total assets, sales price, retail value, and percentage of total retail. The detail report includes information for transactions using inventory items. In addition to the information shown in both reports, the detail report includes type of transaction, date of transaction, customer name, number, quantity, and cost.

Preparing the Inventory Valuation Summary will allow you to verify the number on hand, average cost, asset value, percentage of Total Assets, sales price, retail value, and percentage of Total Retail value for each inventory item.

Prepare and print an Inventory Valuation Summary report in Landscape orientation as of January 25, 2015

To use the Memorized Report, click **Reports** on the Menu bar, point to Memorized Reports, click **Inventory Valuation Summary**

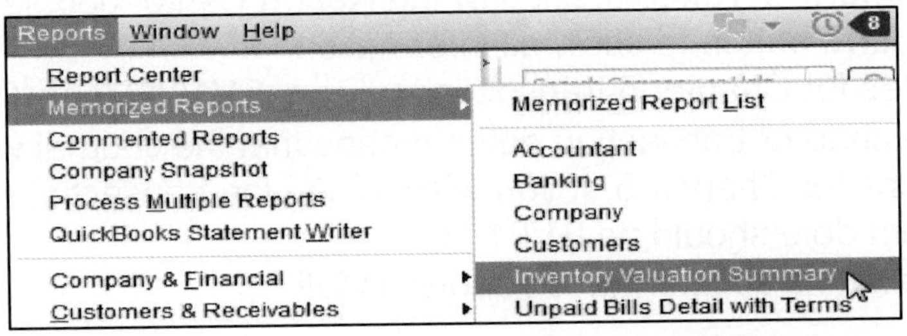

Enter the date **01/25/15**, press **Tab**

- Because we customized the report in Chapter 5 and then memorized it, all the changes we made were saved as part of the memorized report. This means that the columns we removed are not shown
- If you prepare the report from the Reports menu or Report Center, the columns for Sales Price, Retail Value, % of Tot Retail will be shown.

Your Name Mountain Sports
Inventory Valuation Summary
As of January 25, 2015

	On Hand	Avg Cost	Asset Value	% of Tot Asset
Inventory				
Accessories	795	3.66	2,906.70	8.2%
Bindings-Skis	43	75.00	3,225.00	9.1%
Bindings-Snow	48	75.00	3,600.00	10.1%
Boots	20	30.00	600.00	1.7%
Boots-Ski	14	75.00	1,050.00	3.0%
Boots-Snowbrd	35	75.00	2,625.00	7.4%
Gloves	40	15.00	600.00	1.7%
Hats	29	8.00	232.00	0.7%
Helmets	20	28.00	560.00	1.6%
Pants-Ski	93	30.00	2,790.00	7.8%
Pants-Snowbrd	50	35.00	1,750.00	4.9%
Parkas	73	58.33	4,258.34	12.0%
Poles-Ski	23	30.00	690.00	1.9%
Skis	43	100.00	4,300.00	12.1%
Sleds	6	60.00	360.00	1.0%
Snowboard	28	100.00	2,800.00	7.9%
Socks	72	3.00	216.00	0.6%
Sweaters	73	25.00	1,825.00	5.1%
Toboggans	7	129.64	907.50	2.6%
Underwear	32	8.00	256.00	0.7%
Total Inventory	1,544		35,551.54	100.0%
TOTAL	1,544		35,551.54	100.0%

Print in Landscape orientation, and then close the report

6

BACK UP COMPANY

Follow the instructions given in previous chapters to back up data for Your Name Mountain Sports, use the file name **Sports (Backup Ch. 6)**.

SUMMARY

In this chapter, purchase orders were completed, inventory items were received, and bills were recorded. Payments for purchases and bills were made by cash and by credit card and early payment discounts were applied. Sales taxes were paid. Vendors, inventory items, and accounts were added while transactions were being recorded. Accounts were assigned to vendors and preferred vendors were added to sales items. Various reports were prepared to determine unpaid bills, account and vendor QuickReports, and sales tax liability. Reports were customized, contained comments, and memorized.

END-OF-CHAPTER QUESTIONS

TRUE/FALSE

ANSWER THE FOLLOWING QUESTIONS IN THE SPACE PROVIDED BEFORE THE QUESTION NUMBER.

F 1. Receipt of purchase order items is never recorded before the bill arrives.

T 2. A bill can be paid by check or credit card.

F 3. The Cost of Goods Sold account Merchandise Discounts is used to record discounts to customers.

F 4. In QuickBooks, reports are not able to be customized to add a new column.

T 5. The Vendor Center displays the vendor list and information about individual vendors.

F 6. A single purchase order can be prepared and sent to several vendors.

T 7. A Sales Tax account is automatically created if a company indicates that it charges sales tax on sales.

T 8. When a credit is received from a vendor for the return of merchandise, it may be applied to a payment to the same vendor.

F 9. A new vendor cannot be added while recording a transaction.

F 10. A purchase order is closed automatically when a partial receipt of merchandise is recorded.

MULTIPLE CHOICE

WRITE THE LETTER OF THE CORRECT ANSWER IN THE SPACE PROVIDED BEFORE THE QUESTION NUMBER.

A 1. If you change the reorder point for an item, it becomes effective ___.
   A. immediately
   B. the beginning of next month
   C. as soon as outstanding purchase orders are received
   D. the beginning of the next fiscal year

B 2. If an order is received with a bill but is incomplete, QuickBooks will ___.
A. record the bill for the full amount ordered
B. record the bill only for the amount received
C. not allow the bill to be prepared until all the merchandise is received
D. close the purchase order

D 3. The Purchase Order feature must be selected as a preference ___.
A. when setting up the company
B. prior to recording the first purchase order
C. is automatically set when the first purchase order is prepared
D. either A or B

C 4. A faster method of entering bills can be entering the bills ___.
A. while writing the checks for payment
B. in the Pay Bills window
C. in the Accounts Payable Register
D. none of the above

B 5. A Preferred Vendor is selected for an existing Item ___.
A. in the Vendor Center
B. on the Edit Item screen
C. on the Purchase Order
D. when entering the Bill

B 6. Sales tax is paid by using the ___ window.
A. Pay Bills
B. Manage Sales Tax
C. Write Check
D. Credit Card

A 7. A Purchase Order may be customized using the ___.
A. Layout Designer
B. Drawing menu
C. Customize Form button on the Home Page
D. a form may not be changed

C 8. To Comment on a report, you must ___.
A. write your comments on a printed report
B. create a custom report that includes a column for Comments
C. add comments by clicking the Comment on Report button in a report
D. prepare a report from the Comments section in the Report Center

B 9. When items ordered are received with a bill, you record the receipt ___.
A. on an item receipt form
B. on the bill
C. on the original purchase order
D. in the Journal

D 10. Expense accounts for individual vendors may be assigned in the _____.
A. Check Register
B. General Journal
C. Expense Account Register
D. Vendor Center

FILL-IN

IN THE SPACE PROVIDED, WRITE THE ANSWER THAT MOST APPROPRIATELY COMPLETES THE SENTENCE.

1. In the Vendor Center, expense accounts for vendors are assigned using the Acct settings tab when editing or adding a vendor.

2. Information on Reminders may be displayed in Summary or detailed form.

3. The Sales Tax Liability Report shows the total taxable sales and the amount of sales tax owed.

4. A purchase order can be closed automatically or Manually.

5. To see the bill payment information, checks must be printed using the Write Checks window.

SHORT ESSAY

Describe the cycle of obtaining merchandise. Include the process from ordering the merchandise through paying for it. Include information regarding the QuickBooks forms prepared for each phase of the cycle, the possible ways in which an item may be received, and the ways in which payment may be made.

____
____
____
____
____
____

NAME________________________

CHAPTER 6: TRANSMITTAL

YOUR NAME MOUNTAIN SPORTS

Check the items below as you print them; then attach the documents and reports in the order listed when you submit them to your instructor.

___ Purchase Order 1: Boots Galore
___ Purchase Order 2: Snow Stuff
___ Purchase Order 3: Clothes, Inc.
___ Purchase Order 4: Snow Sports, Inc.
___ Account QuickReport, Purchase Orders, January 16, 2015
___ Item Receipt: Snow Stuff (Optional)
___ Bill: Snow Stuff (Optional)
___ Bill: Boots Galore (Optional)
___ Purchase Order 4 (Corrected): Snow Sports, Inc.
___ Bill: Clothes, Inc. (Optional)
___ Purchase Order 3 (Closed): Clothes, Inc.
___ Bill Credit: Snow Stuff (Optional)
___ Bill: Mammoth News (Optional)
___ Memorized Transaction List
___ Bill: Mammoth Power (Optional)
___ Bill: Mammoth Telephone (Optional)
___ Bill: Mammoth Water (Optional)
___ Register QuickReport, Snow Stuff
___ Bill: Mountain Rentals (Optional)
___ Corrected Bill: Mammoth Water Co. (Optional)
___ Unpaid Bills Detail with Terms, January 25, 2015
___ Check 2: Boots Galore
___ Check 3: Clothes, Inc.
___ Check 4: Snow Stuff
___ Bill Payment Stub: Shoes & More
___ Bill Payment Stub: Sports Accessories
___ Sales Tax Liability Report, January 1-25, 2015
___ Check 5: State Board of Equalization
___ Vendor Balance Detail
___ Trial Balance, January 25, 2015
___ Journal, January 18-25, 2015
___ Inventory Valuation Summary, January 25, 2015

6

END-OF-CHAPTER PROBLEM

YOUR NAME RESORT CLOTHING

Chapter 6 continues with the transactions for purchase orders, merchandise receipts, bills, bill payments, and sales tax payments. Your partner, Karen Olsen, prints the checks, purchase orders, and related reports; you sign the checks. This procedure establishes cash control procedures and lets both owners know about the checks being processed.

INSTRUCTIONS

Continue to use the copy of Your Name Resort Clothing you used in Chapter 5. Open the company—the file used is **Clothing.qbw**. Record the purchase orders, bills, payments, and other transactions as instructed within the chapter. Always read the transactions carefully and review the Chart of Accounts when selecting transaction accounts. Add new vendors and minimum quantities where indicated. Verify with your instructor the required printing and whether or not to print Bills. Otherwise, print all purchase orders, bills, and checks. Print reports as indicated making sure to resize columns so all information is displayed in full. The first purchase order used is Purchase Order 1. When paying bills, always check for credits that may be applied to the bill, and always check for discounts.

In addition to the Item List and the Chart of Accounts, you will need to use the Vendor List when ordering merchandise and paying bills.

Active Vendors

NAME	BALANCE TOTAL	ATTACH
Accessories, Inc.	0.00	
Casual Fashion	3,053.00	
Resort Clothing, Inc.	2,598.00	
Sensational Shoes	450.00	
Shades, Inc.	500.00	
State Board of Equalization	188.31	

RECORD TRANSACTIONS

<u>**January 5, 2015**</u>:

- Customize a Purchase Order template so the Default Title is **PURCHASE ORDER**, Company Name is expanded to **4 ¾**, and PURCHASE ORDER begins at **5**.
- Hide the History and resize the Purchase Order to make it smaller on the screen.
- Change Reorder Point (Min) for Women-Dress from 20 to 25 and Max from 100 to 40
- Change Reorder Point (Min) for Women-Pants from 25 to 30 and Max from 39 to 40.
- Prepare and print an Inventory Stock Status by Item Report for <u>January 1-5, 2015</u> in Landscape orientation. Remove the unused columns for On Sales Order, On PO, and Next Deliv. Manually adjust column widths so vendors' names are shown in full. (Note:

In Chapter 5, transactions were entered through January 15. If you prepare the report based on January 15, it will be different from this one.)

- Prepare Purchase Orders for all items marked Order on the Stock Status by Item Inventory Report. Use the vendor Casual Fashion. for the dresses. Since a vendor has been assigned for Women-Pants, VENDOR information will be completed when the Item is entered. The quantity for each item ordered is 10. The rate is $35 for dresses and $20 for pants. Print purchase orders with lines around each field.
  - If you get an Item's Cost Changed dialog box asking if you want to update the item with the new cost, click **Do not display this message in the future**, and click **No**.
- Change the Vendor Name Resort Clothing, Inc. to Trendy Clothing, Inc. Make sure to change Vendor Name, Company Name, and Billed From as well. Change the Main Email to TrendyClothing@abc.com. Finally, on the Payment Settings tab change the Print Name on Check As.
- Reprint Purchase Order 2.
- Add a new vendor: Contempo Clothing, Main Phone 805-555-5512, Main Email Contempo@slo.com, Fax 805-555-2155, 9382 Grand Avenue, San Luis Obispo, CA 93407, Payment terms 2% 10 Net 30, Credit limit $2000.
- Assign Contempo Clothing as the Preferred Vendor for dresses.
- Order an additional 10 dresses from Contempo Clothing. The rate for the dresses is $25. Print the Purchase Order.
- Prepare and print a Purchase Order QuickReport for January 1-5.

January 8, 2015:

- Received pants that were ordered on Purchase Order 2 from Trendy Clothing, Inc. without the bill. Enter the receipt of merchandise. The transaction date is 01/08/2015.Print the Item Receipt if instructed to do so.
- Received dresses ordered on Purchase Order 1 from Casual Fashion with Bill. Use date of 01/08/2015. Enter the receipt of the merchandise and the bill. Print the Bill.
- Received 8 dresses and the bill from Contempo Clothing ordered on Purchase Order 3. Enter the receipt of the merchandise and the bill. Print the bill. This dress style has been discontinued so close the Purchase Order manually, and print it.
- After recording the receipt of merchandise, view the three purchase orders. Notice which ones are marked *Received in Full* and *Closed*.

January 9, 2015:

- Received the bill from Trendy Clothing, Inc. for the pants received on 01/08/15. The bill was dated 01/08/2015 (use this date for the bill). Print the bill if instructed to do so.

January 10, 2015:

- Discovered unstitched seams in two pairs of women's pants ordered on PO 2. Return the pants for credit. Use 2340 as the Reference number. Print the Credit.

January 12, 2015

- Pay for the dresses from Contempo Clothing with the company's Visa credit card. (Take a purchase discount if the transaction qualifies for one. Use the Cost of Goods Sold

6

Subaccount 5200 Merchandise Discounts for the discount. Create any necessary accounts.) Print the Bill Payment Stub.

January 15, 2015:

- Add new vendors:
  - SLO Rental Co., Main Phone 805-555-4100, Fax 805-555-0014, 301 Marsh Street, San Luis Obispo, CA 93407, Payment Terms Net 30. Assign Account 6280 Rent.
  - SLO Telephone, Main Phone 805-555-1029, 8851 Hwy. 58, San Luis Obispo, CA 93407. Payment Terms Net 30. Assign Account 6340 Telephone.
- Create a Memorized Transaction for rent. How Often: Monthly, Next Date: 01/15/2015. When you finish the transaction for rent, clear the Bill without saving.
- Create a Memorized Transaction for telephone. How Often: Monthly, Next Date: 01/15/2015. Clear the Bill. Close Bills. Print the Memorize Transaction List.
- Use the Memorized Transaction List to record and print the bills for rent of $1,150.00 and telephone service of $79.85. Use the date 01/15/15.

January 18, 2015:

- Prepare an Unpaid Bills Detail report. Customize the report by adding a column for Terms. Memorize the report. Name is Unpaid Bills Detail with Terms. If there are any bills that qualify for a discount or have a credit, add the comment "Pay this Bill" or "Use This Credit." Print the Commented Report. Do not save the Commented Report.
- Pay the bills indicated in the Commented Unpaid Bills Detail report. Take any discounts for which you are eligible. If there are any credits, apply the credit and calculate the appropriate discount (if eligible) prior to paying the bill. Pay the bill(s) by check.
- Print Check Nos. 2 and 3 for the bills that were paid.

January 25, 2015:

- Purchase office supplies to have on hand for $250 with the company's Visa credit card from a new vendor (Office Masters, Main Phone 805-555-9915, Main Email OfficeMasters@slo.com, Fax 805-555-5199, 8330 Grand Avenue, Arroyo Grande, CA 93420, Payment Terms Net 30, Credit limit $500).
- Pay bills for rent and telephone. Print the checks prepared for these bills. (They may be printed individually or as a batch.)

January 30, 2015:

- Prepare Sales Tax Liability Report from 01/01/2015 to 01/30/2015. Print the report in Landscape orientation. Change columns widths, if necessary.
- Pay Sales Tax for the amount due through 01/30/15, and print the check.
- Prepare a Vendor Balance Detail Report for All Transactions. Print in Portrait orientation.
- Print a Trial Balance for 01/01/2015 to 01/30/2015.
- Print the Journal for 01/01/2015 to 01/30/2015 (Size columns to display all information.)
- Use the memorized report to prepare an Inventory Valuation Summary Report for 01/30/2015. Print in Portrait.
- Back up data to **Clothing (Backup Ch. 6)**

NAME________________________

CHAPTER 6: TRANSMITTAL

YOUR NAME RESORT CLOTHING

Check the items below as you print them; then attach the documents and reports in the order listed when you submit them to your instructor.

___ Inventory Stock Status by Item, January 1-5, 2015
___ Purchase Order 1: Casual Fashion
___ Purchase Order 2: Resort Clothing, Inc.
___ Purchase Order 2: Reprint: Trendy Clothing, Inc.
___ Purchase Order 3: Contempo Clothing
___ Account QuickReport, Purchase Orders
___ Item Receipt: Trendy Clothing, Inc.
___ Bill: Casual Fashion
___ Bill: Contempo Clothing
___ Purchase Order 3 Closed: Contempo Clothing
___ Bill: Trendy Clothing, Inc.
___ Credit: Trendy Clothing, Inc.
___ Bill Payment Stub: Contempo Clothing
___ Memorized Transaction List
___ Bill: SLO Rental, Inc.
___ Bill: SLO Telephone Co.
___ Unpaid Bills Detail with Terms, January 18, 2015
___ Check 2: Casual Fashion
___ Check 3: Trendy Clothing, Inc.
___ Check 4: SLO Rental Company
___ Check 5: SLO Telephone Company
___ Sales Tax Liability Report
___ Check 6: State Board of Equalization
___ Vendor Balance Detail, January 30, 2015
___ Trial Balance, January 1-30, 2015
___ Journal, January 1-30, 2015
___ Inventory Valuation Summary, January 30, 2015

6

GENERAL ACCOUNTING AND END-OF-PERIOD PROCEDURES: MERCHANDISING BUSINESS

7

LEARNING OBJECTIVES

At the completion of this chapter, you will be able to:

1. Complete the end-of-period procedures.
2. Change the name of existing accounts in the Chart of Accounts, view the account name change, and view the effect of an account name change on subaccounts.
3. Delete an existing account from the Chart of Accounts.
4. Enter the adjusting entries required for accrual-basis accounting.
5. Make an adjustment to inventory.
6. Understand how to record owners' equity transactions for a partnership.
7. Transfer Capital – Other to the individual partners.
8. Enter transactions for owner withdrawals, close the owners' drawing accounts, and transfer net income to the owners' capital accounts.
9. Reconcile the bank statement, record bank service charges, and mark cleared transactions.
10. Reconcile a credit card statement and Undo a reconciliation.
11. Enter a correcting entry after a period has been closed.
12. Prepare and print the Journal and other reports; such as, Trial Balance, Profit & Loss, and Balance Sheet.
13. Memorize a Report.
14. Prepare multiple reports.
15. Export a report to Microsoft Excel and import data from Excel.
16. Perform end-of-period backup, close a period, record transactions in a closed period, and adjust inventory quantities.

GENERAL ACCOUNTING AND END-OF-PERIOD PROCEDURES

As stated in previous chapters, QuickBooks operates from the standpoint of the business document rather than an accounting form, journal, or ledger. While QuickBooks does incorporate all of these items into the program, in many instances they operate behind the scenes. Instead of performing a traditional closing at the end of the fiscal year, QuickBooks transfers the net income into the Owners' Equity account and allows you to protect the data for the year by assigning a closing date to the period. All of the transaction detail is maintained and viewable, but it will not be changed unless approved.

Even though a formal closing does not have to be performed within QuickBooks, when using accrual-basis accounting, several transactions must be recorded in order to reflect all expenses and income for the period accurately. For example, bank statements and credit cards must be reconciled; and any charges or bank collections need to be recorded. Adjusting entries such as depreciation, office supplies used, and so on will also need to be made. These adjustments may be recorded by the CPA or by the company's accounting personnel. At the end of the year, net income for the year and the owner withdrawals for the year should be transferred to the owners' capital accounts.

As in a service business, the CPA for the company will review things such as account names, adjusting entries, depreciation schedules, owner's equity adjustments, and so on. If the CPA makes the changes and adjustments, they may be made on the Accountant's Copy of the business files. An Accountant's Copy is a version of your company file that your accountant can use to make changes. You record the day-to-day business transactions; and, at the same time, your accountant works using the Accountant's Copy. The changes made by the CPA are imported into your company file. There are certain restrictions to the types of transactions that may be made on an Accountant's Copy of the company file. There are also restrictions regarding the types of entries that may be made in the company file that you are using.

Once necessary adjustments have been made, reports reflecting the end-of-period results of operations should be prepared. For archive purposes, at the end of the fiscal year, an additional backup is prepared and stored.

OPEN QUICKBOOKS AND COMPANY

Open **QuickBooks** and **Your Name Mountain Sports** as previously instructed

BEGIN TUTORIAL

The following tutorial will once again work with Your Name Mountain Sports. Continue to use the same year that you used in Chapters 5 and 6. While everything that may be printed is listed on the transmittal sheet, check with your instructor for exact printing assignments and instructions.

CHANGE ACCOUNT NAME

Even though transactions have been recorded during the month of January, QuickBooks makes it a simple matter to change the name of an existing account. Once the name of an account has been changed, all transactions using the old name are updated and show the new account name.

MEMO
DATE: January 31, 2015

On the recommendation of the company's CPA, change the account named Freight Income to Delivery Income.

Change the account name of Freight Income

Access the Chart of Accounts using the keyboard shortcut **Ctrl+A**
Select account **4020 Freight Income**, use the keyboard shortcut **Ctrl+E**
On the **Edit Account** screen, enter the new name **Delivery Income**
Since the account name is self-explanatory, delete the description
Click **Save & Close** on the **Edit Account** screen

- Notice that the name of the account appears as Delivery Income.

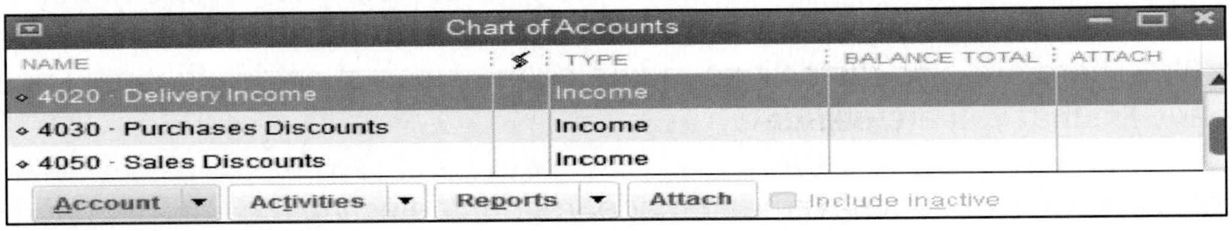

Do not close the **Chart of Accounts**

MAKE ACCOUNTS INACTIVE

If you are not using an account and do not have plans to do so in the near future, the account may be made inactive. The account remains available for use, yet it does not appear on your Chart of Accounts unless you check the Show All check box.

MEMO
DATE: January 31, 2015

At this time, Your Name Mountain Sports does not plan to rent any equipment and does not incur Franchise Fees. Make: 6170 - Equipment Rental and 6290 - Franchise Fees inactive

Make the accounts listed above inactive

Click **6170 - Equipment Rental**
Click the **Account** button at the bottom of the Chart of Accounts, click **Make Account Inactive**

- The account no longer appears in the Chart of Accounts.

To view all accounts, including the inactive ones, click the **Include Inactive** check box at the bottom of the Chart of Accounts

Click account **6290 - Franchise Fees**, use **Ctrl+E** to edit the account
On the Edit Account screen, click the **Account is inactive** check box in the lower-left portion of the screen
Click **Save & Close**

- Notice the icons that mark Equipment Rental and Franchise Fees as inactive accounts.

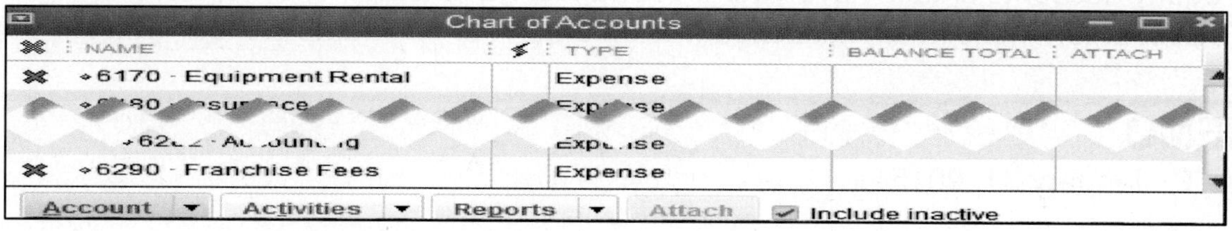

Do not close the **Chart of Accounts**

DELETE EXISTING ACCOUNTS

If you do not want to make an account inactive because you have not used it and do not plan to use it at all, QuickBooks allows the account to be deleted at any time. However, as a safeguard, QuickBooks does prevent the deletion of an account once it has been used at any time or contains an opening or an existing balance.

MEMO
DATE: January 31, 2015

You do not, have not, and will not use: Account 6213 Interest Expense: Mortgage, Account 6523 Taxes: Property, and Account 6350 Travel & Ent. and its subaccounts. Delete these accounts from the Chart of Accounts.

Delete the accounts listed in the memo

Select **6213 - Mortgage**, a subaccount of 6210 Interest Expense
Click the **Account** button at the bottom of the Chart of Accounts, click **Delete Account**, and click **OK** on the **Delete Account** dialog box

- The account has now been deleted.

Click **6523 – Property**, a subaccount of 6520 Taxes, to select the account
Use the keyboard shortcut **Ctrl+D** to delete and then click **OK** on the **Delete Account** dialog box
Follow the same procedures to delete the subaccounts of 6350 Travel & Ent.: **6351 - Entertainment**, **6352 - Meals**, and **6353 - Travel**

- *Note:* Whenever an account has subaccounts, the subaccounts must be deleted before the main account can be deleted.

When the subaccounts have been deleted; delete **6350 - Travel & Ent.**
Do not close the Chart of Accounts

CREATE INDIVIDUAL CAPITAL ACCOUNTS

Currently, all of the owners' accounts are grouped together. A better display of owners' equity would be to show all equity accounts for each owner grouped by owner. In addition, each owner should have an individual capital account.

Your equity accounts should have your first and last name as part of the title, just like Larry Muir's accounts. The joint capital account should be your last name & Muir, Capital.

> **MEMO**
> **DATE:** January 31, 2015
>
> Edit Your Name & Muir, Capital to change the account number to 3100 and add your Last Name to the account name. Create separate Capital accounts for (Your) First and Last Name and Larry Muir. Name the accounts 3110 First and Last Name, Capital, and 3120 Larry Muir, Capital. In addition, change your Investment account to 3111 First and Last Name, Investment and your Drawing account to 3112 First and Last Name, Drawing. Make these subaccounts of 3110 First and Last Name, Capital. Do the same for Larry's accounts: 3121 Investment and 3122 Drawing.

Create separate Capital accounts and change subaccounts for existing owners' equity accounts

Click **3010 - Your Name & Muir, Capital**

- In the controlling account 3010 you will just use your last name. However, in the individual capital accounts, such as, Your Name, Investment, you will use both your first and last names.

Click **Account** at the bottom of the **Chart of Accounts**, click **Edit Account**
Change the account number to **3100**
Tab to or click **Account Name**
Highlight the words Your Name and replace them with your last name to name the account and add a comma between Muir and Capital

- In the textbook **3100 - Your Last Name & Muir, Capital** is shown as the account name, but your work will show your own last name. For example, the author's account name would be 3100 Horne & Muir, Capital.

Click **Save & Close**
Click **Account** at the bottom of the **Chart of Accounts**, click **New**
Click **Equity** as the account type, click **Continue**
Tab to or click **Number**, enter **3120**
Tab to or click **Account Name**, enter **Larry Muir, Capital**
Click **Subaccount**; click the drop-down list arrow next to **Subaccount**, click **3100 - Your Last Name & Muir, Capital**
Click **Save & Close**

Edit the account **3012 - Larry Muir, Investment** and change the Account number to **3121**. It is a **Subaccount of: 3120**

Edit **3014 - Larry Muir, Drawing**, Account number is **3122**, **Subaccount of: 3120**

Chart of Accounts

NAME	⚡	TYPE	BALANCE TOTAL	ATTACH
◆3120 · Larry Muir, Capital		Equity	20,000.00	
◆3121 · Larry Muir, Investment		Equity	20,000.00	
◆3122 · Larry Muir, Drawing		Equity	0.00	

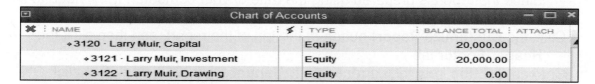

Use the keyboard shortcut **Ctrl+N** to create a new account

Click **Equity** as the account type, click **Continue**

Tab to or click **Number**, enter **3110**

Tab to or click **Account Name**, enter **First and Last Name, Capital**

- Remember to use your real first and last name.
- In the textbook **3110 - First and Last Name, Capital** is shown as the account name, but your work will show your own name. For example, the author's account name would be 3110 - Janet Horne, Capital.
- In QuickBooks, there is not enough room for the words "Your First and Last Name, Capital" so the account name is First and Last Name, Capital, which is used to indicate that the account name contains your actual first and last names.

Click **Subaccount**; click the drop-down list arrow next to **Subaccount**, click **3100 - Your Last Name & Muir, Capital**

Click **Save & Close**

Edit the account **3011 - Your Name, Investment** to change the **Number** to **3111**

Change the **Account Name** to **First and Last Name, Investment**

- Remember to use your actual first and last names. For example, the author's account name would be Janet Horne, Investment.

Make this a **Subaccount of: 3110 - First and Last Name, Capital**

Click **Save & Close** when the changes have been made

Edit **3013 Your Name, Drawing** to change the Number to **3112**; Account Name is **First and Last Name, Drawing**; the account is a **Subaccount of: 3110**

- Remember to use your actual first and last names.

The capital accounts appear as follows:

Chart of Accounts

NAME	⚡	TYPE	BALANCE TOTAL	ATTACH
3100 · Your Last Name & Muir, Capital		Equity	66,159.44	
◆3110 · First and Last Name, Capital		Equity	20,000.00	
◆3111 · First and Last Name, Investment		Equity	20,000.00	
◆3112 · First and Last Name, Drawing		Equity	0.00	
◆3120 · Larry Muir, Capital		Equity	20,000.00	
◆3121 · Larry Muir, Investment		Equity	20,000.00	
◆3122 · Larry Muir, Drawing		Equity	0.00	

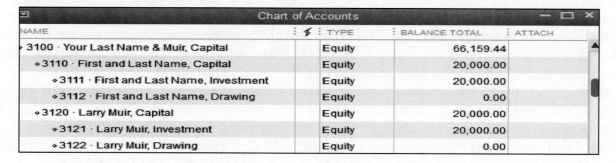

Close the **Chart of Accounts**

Use the **Reports** menu **List** category to print the **Account Listing** in Portrait orientation

Use the date **01/31/15** for the report

- Since the report is prepared using the date of your computer, it will need to be changed to 01/31/15.

Click the **Customize Report** button at the top of the report, and then click the **Header/Footer** tab

Change **Subtitle** from the current date to **January 31, 2015**, and then, click **OK**

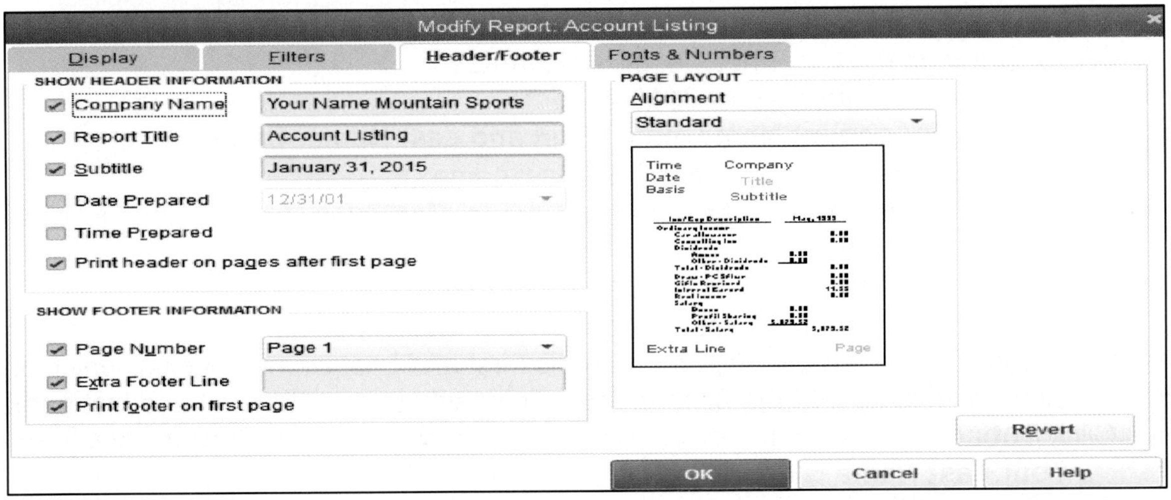

Resize the columns to display the Account Names in full—including subaccounts

Hide the columns for **Description**, **Accnt. #**, and **Tax Line**

Print in **Portrait** orientation; then close the Report

FIXED ASSETS AND FIXED ASSET MANAGER

Fixed assets are the long-term assets that are used in in the business for longer than one year. If the company owns fixed assets, it is helpful to create a fixed asset item list.

In addition to allowing you to keep a list of fixed asset items, QuickBooks Accountant and Enterprise versions include a Fixed Asset Manager that is more comprehensive than the list of fixed assets. When used, the Fixed Asset Manager pulls information about the fixed assets from an open company file. The Fixed Asset Manager allows you to use six depreciation bases—Federal, AMT, ACE, Book, State, and Other. The accountant can use the Fixed Asset Manager to determine the depreciation for the assets and then post a journal entry back to the company file. The Fixed Asset Manager also integrates with Intuit's ProSeries Tax products and must have tax forms identified prior to use. It provides a wide variety of built-in depreciation reports, forms, and multiple ways to import and export data. The Fixed Asset Manager is synchronized with QuickBooks and has its own data files that allow for more detailed asset information than a company file. The Fixed Asset Manager will not be used at this time since it is designed to be used by the company's accountant to calculate depreciation schedules based on the taxation information entered.

FIXED ASSET ITEM LIST

As with other QuickBooks lists, you may keep a record of your company's fixed assets in the Fixed Asset Item List. In the list, you record information about your company's fixed assets including the purchase date and cost, whether the item was new or used when purchased, and the sales price if the item is sold. Note that Depreciation and Book Value are not calculated or stored in the Fixed Asset Item List.

The Fixed Asset List provides a way to keep important information about your assets in one place. This is useful to do whether or not your accountant uses the Fixed Asset Manager. You can create an item to track a fixed asset at several points during the asset's life cycle; however, it is recommended that you create the item when you buy the asset or create the company. You can create a fixed asset item from the Fixed Asset List or a Transaction.

MEMO

DATE: January 31, 2015

When Your Name Mountain Sports was setup in QuickBooks, the Fixed Item Asset List was not created. Create the Fixed Asset Item List:
<u>Store Fixtures</u>: Asset Name/Number, Purchase Description, and Asset Description: Store Fixtures; Item is New; Date: 12/31/14; Cost: $4,500; Asset Account: 1520.
<u>Office Equipment</u>: Asset Name/Number, Purchase Description, and Asset Description: Office Equipment; Item is New; Date: 12/31/14; Cost: $5,000; Asset Account: 1510.

Create a Fixed Asset Item List

Click **Lists** on the menu bar; click **Fixed Asset Item List**
Use the keyboard shortcut **Ctrl+N** to create a new item
Complete the information for the new item:
The **Asset Name/Number** is **Store Fixtures**
The **Asset Account** is **1520**
Complete the PURCHASE INFORMATION:
The Item is **new**
The **Purchase Description** should be **Store Fixtures**
The **Date** is **12/31/14**
The **Cost** is **4500**

- There is no SALES INFORMATION to record.

To complete the ASSET INFORMATION, enter **Store Fixtures** as the **Asset Description**

- Look at the bottom of the screen. Fields are provided to add information for the location, PO Number, Serial Number, and Warranty. There is also room to add Notes about the item.

7

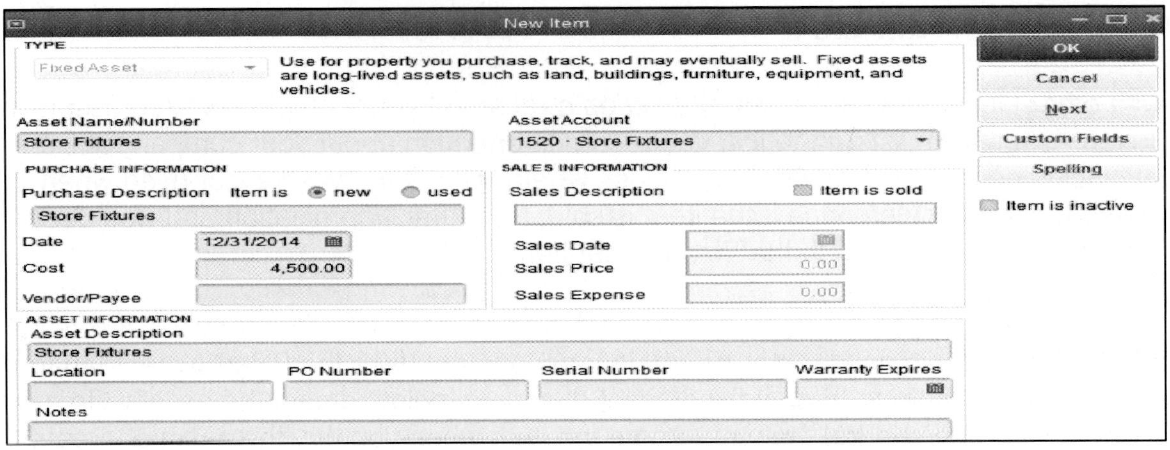

When the information is entered for Store Fixtures, click **Next**

Repeat to add Asset: **Office Equipment**, Asset Account **1510 – Office Equipment**, Date **12/31/14**, and Cost **$5,000.00** to the list

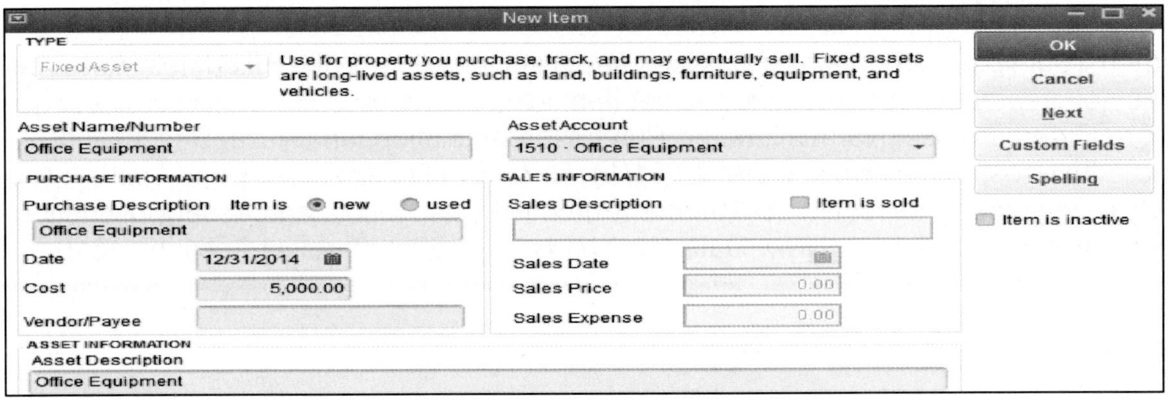

Click **OK**

Fixed Asset Item List

NAME	FAM NUMBER	PURCHASE DATE	PURCHASE DESCRIPTION	ACCOUNT	COST	ATTACH
Office Equipment		12/31/2014	Office Equipment	1510 · Office Equipment	5,000.00	
Store Fixtures		12/31/2014	Store Fixtures	1520 · Store Fixtures	4,500.00	

Item ▾ Activities ▾ Reports ▾ Attach Include inactive

Close the Fixed Asset Item List

ADJUSTMENTS FOR ACCRUAL-BASIS ACCOUNTING

As previously stated, accrual-basis accounting matches the income and the expenses of a period in order to arrive at an accurate figure for net income or net loss. Thus, the revenue is earned at the time the service is performed or the sale is made no matter when the actual cash is received. The cash basis of accounting records income or revenue at the time cash is received no matter when the sale was made or the service performed. The same holds true when a business buys things or pays bills. In accrual-basis accounting, the expense is recorded at the time the bill is received or the purchase is made regardless of the actual payment date. In cash-basis accounting, the expense is not recorded until it is paid. In QuickBooks, the Summary Report Basis for either Accrual or Cash is selected as a Report Preference. The default setting is Accrual.

For example, if $1,000 sales on account and one year of insurance for $600 were recorded in November: Accrual basis would record $1,000 as income or revenue and $600 as a prepaid expense in an asset account—Prepaid Insurance. Month by month, an adjusting entry for $50 would be made to record the amount of insurance used for the month. Using the same figures, Cash basis would have no income and $600 worth of insurance recorded as an expense for November and nothing the rest of the year or during the early portion of the next year for insurance. A Profit & Loss report prepared in November would show: Accrual method—income of $1,000 and insurance expense of $50. Profit of $950. Cash method—no income and insurance expense of $600. Loss of $600.

There are several internal transactions that must be recorded when using accrual-basis accounting. These entries are called adjusting entries. Typically, adjusting entries are entered in the General Journal by accountants to make after-the-fact changes to specific accounts. For example, equipment does wear out and will eventually need to be replaced. Rather than waiting until replacement to record the use of the equipment, an adjusting entry is made to allocate the use of equipment as an expense for a period. This is called *depreciation*. Certain items that will eventually become expenses for the business may be purchased or paid for in advance. When things such as insurance or supplies are purchased or paid for, they are recorded as an asset, and are referred to as prepaid expenses. As these are used, they become expenses of the business.

ADJUSTING ENTRIES—PREPAID EXPENSES

A prepaid expense is an item that is paid for in advance. Examples of prepaid expenses include: Insurance—policy is usually for six months or one year; Office Supplies—buy to have on hand and use as needed. (This is different from supplies that are purchased for immediate use.) A prepaid expense is an asset until it is used. As the insurance or supplies are used, the amount used becomes an expense for the period. In accrual basis accounting, an adjusting entry is made in the General Journal at the end of the period to allocate the amount of prepaid expenses (assets) used to expenses.

7

The transactions for these adjustments may be recorded in the asset account register or they may be entered in the General Journal.

MEMO

DATE: January 31, 2015

The monthly adjustments need to be recorded. The $250 in Prepaid Insurance is the amount for two months of liability insurance. Also, we have a balance of $521.98 in office supplies and a balance of $400 in sales supplies. Please adjust accordingly.

Record the adjusting entries for insurance expense, office supplies expense, and sales supplies expense in the General Journal

Access the **General Journal** and record the adjusting entry for Prepaid Insurance

- If you get a screen regarding Assigning Numbers to Journal Entries, click **Do not display this message in the future**; and then, click **OK**

The General Journal Entries screen appears

- Note the checkbox for Adjusting Entry and the List of Selected General Journal Entries for Last Month
  - If the date of your computer does not match the text, you may not have anything showing in the List of Selected General Journal Entries.

To remove the list of entries, click the **Hide List** icon on the Make General Journal Entries Icon bar

Enter **01/31/15** as the **Date**

- **Entry No.** is left blank unless you wish to record a specific number.
- Because all transactions entered for the month have been entered in the Journal as well as on an invoice or a bill, they automatically have a Journal entry number. When the Journal is printed, your transaction number may be different from the answer key. Disregard the transaction number because it can change based on how many times you delete transactions, etc.

Notice the checkbox for **Adjusting Entry** is marked

- Frequently, adjusting entries are entered by accountants in the General Journal to make after-the-fact changes to specific accounts. Common adjustments include, depreciation, prepaid income or expenses; adjusting sales tax payable; and entering bank or credit card fees or interest.
- If checked, the Adjusting Entry checkbox indicates that an entry is an adjustment.
- By default, this checkbox is selected for General Journal entries in the Accountant version.
- A report showing all adjustments is the Adjusting Journal Entries report.

Tab to or click the **Account** column, click the drop-down list arrow for **Account**, click **6181 Liability Insurance**

Tab to or click **Debit**

- The $250 given in the memo is the amount for two months.

Use the QuickBooks Calculator to determine the amount of the entry:

Enter **250** in the Debit column
Press **/** for division
Key **2**, and press **Enter**

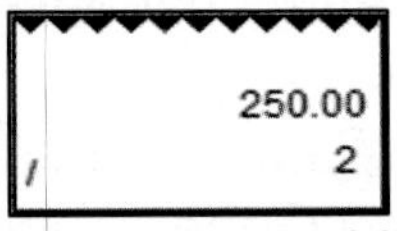

- The calculation is performed and the amount is entered in the Debit column.

Tab to or click the **Memo** column, type **Adjusting Entry, Insurance**

Tab to or click **Account**, click the drop-down list arrow for Account, click **1340 Prepaid Insurance**

- The amount for the **Credit** column should have been entered automatically; if not, enter **125**.

The Memo should have been entered automatically

- If not, enter the Memo information by using the copy command: Click the **Memo** column for the Debit entry, drag through the memo **Adjusting Entry, Insurance**, when the memo is highlighted, use the keyboard command **Ctrl+C** to copy the memo. Click in the **Memo** column for the Credit entry and use the keyboard command **Ctrl+V** to paste the memo into the column

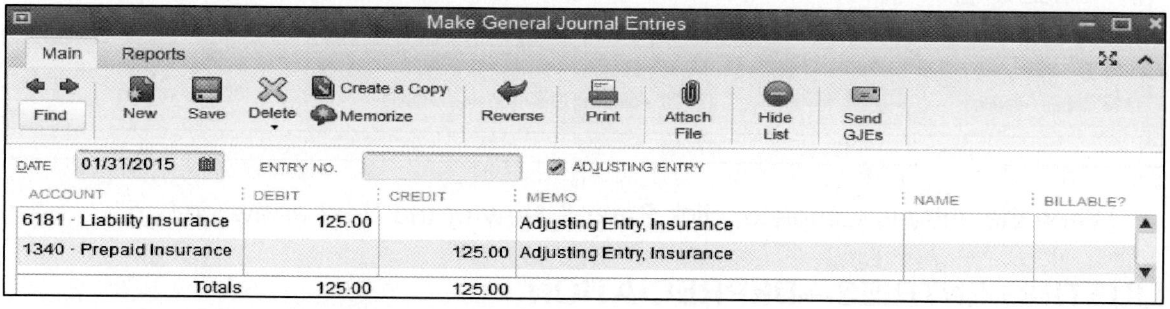

Click **Save & New** or **NEXT** (forward arrow icon)
Record the adjustment for the office supplies used
The DATE is **01/31/2015**
Click the drop-down list arrow for ACCOUNT, and then click the expense account **6472 – Office**, a subaccount of 6470 Supplies Expense

- The amount given in the memo is the balance of the account after the supplies have been used.
- The actual amount of the supplies used in January must be calculated.

Tab to the **DEBIT** column
Determine the current balance of asset account 1311 Office Supplies by using the keyboard shortcut **Ctrl+A** to access the Chart of Accounts
Make note of the balance and then close the Chart of Accounts
Use QuickMath to determine the amount:
In the Debit column, enter the balance of the asset account, press **-**, enter the amount of supplies on hand listed the in memo

Press **Enter** for QuickBooks to enter the amount of the adjustment
Enter an appropriate description and complete the adjustment for office supplies
Click the drop-down list arrow for ACCOUNT on the next line, and click **1311 Office Supplies** as the account to be credited

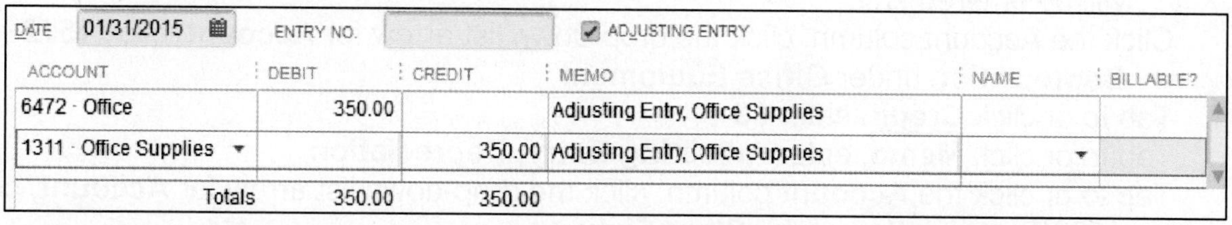

When the entry is complete, click the **Next** arrow icon or **Save & New**
Repeat the procedures to record the adjustment for the sales supplies used

- The amount given in the memo is the balance of the account after the supplies have been used. Remember to subtract the $400 balance in the memo from the asset account total in order to get the amount of sales supplies used.
- If you opened the Chart of Accounts to get an account balance, close it.

DATE 01/31/2015 ENTRY NO. ☑ ADJUSTING ENTRY

ACCOUNT	DEBIT	CREDIT	MEMO	NAME	BILLABLE?
6471 · Sales	175.00		Adjusting Entries, Sales Supplies		
1312 · Sales Supplies		175.00	Adjusting Entries, Sales Supplies		
Totals	175.00	175.00			

When the entry is complete, click **Save & New** or the **Next** arrow icon

ADJUSTING ENTRIES—DEPRECIATION

Using accrual-basis accounting requires companies to record an expense for the decrease in the value of equipment used in the operation of the business. Unlike supplies, where you can actually see the paper supply diminishing, it is very difficult to see how much of a computer has been "used up" during the month. To account for the fact that machines wear out and will need to be replaced, an adjustment is made for depreciation. This adjustment correctly matches the expenses of the period against the revenue of the period.

MEMO
DATE: January 31, 2015

Having received the necessary depreciation schedules from the accountant, Ruth records the adjusting entry for depreciation: Office Equipment, $85 per month and Store Fixtures, $75 per month.

Record a compound adjusting entry for depreciation of the office equipment and the store fixtures in the General Journal

The Date is **01/31/15**, **Entry No.** is left blank

- In order to use the automatic calculation feature of QuickBooks, the credit entries will be entered first.

Click the Account column, click the drop-down list arrow for **Account**, click **1512 Depreciation** under **Office Equipment**

Tab to or click **Credit**, enter **85**

Tab to or click **Memo**, enter **Adjusting Entry, Depreciation**

Tab to or click the **Account** column, click the drop-down list arrow for **Account**, click **1522 Depreciation** under **Store Fixtures**

- Disregard the 85 that shows as a debit. Entering an amount in the credit column and pressing the tab key will eliminate the debit.

Tab to or click **Credit**, enter **75**

- **Memo** column should show **Adjusting Entry, Depreciation**, if not enter it.

Tab to or click the **Account** column, click the drop-down list arrow for **Account**, click **6150 Depreciation Expense**

<u>Debit</u> column should automatically show **160**

- **Memo** column should show **Adjusting Entry, Depreciation**, if not enter it.

DATE 01/31/2015 ENTRY NO. ☑ ADJUSTING ENTRY

ACCOUNT	DEBIT	CREDIT	MEMO	NAME	BILLABLE?
1512 · Depreciation		85.00	Adjusting Entry, Depreciation		
1522 · Depreciation		75.00	Adjusting Entry, Depreciation		
6150 · Depreciation Expense	160.00		Adjusting Entry, Depreciation		
Totals	160.00	160.00			

Verify that you entered <u>Credits</u> to accounts 1512 and 1522 and a <u>Debit</u> to account 6150

Click **Save & Close** to record the adjustment and close the General Journal

- If you get a message regarding Tracking Fixed Assets on Journal Entries, click **Do not display this message in the future** and click **OK**.

JOURNAL

Once transactions have been entered in the General Journal, it is important to view them. QuickBooks refers to the General Journal as the location of a transaction entry. To differentiate between the location of an entry and a report, QuickBooks refers to the report as the Journal. Even with the special ways in which transactions are entered in QuickBooks through invoices, bills, checks, and account registers, the Journal is still considered the book of original entry. All transactions recorded for the company may be viewed in the Journal even if they were entered elsewhere. The Journal may be viewed or printed at any time.

View the Journal for January

Click **Reports** on the menu bar, point to **Accountant & Taxes**, and click **Journal**

Click the **Expand** button.

The Dates are from **01/01/15** to **01/31/15**

Tab to generate the report

Scroll through the report to view all transactions recorded in the Journal

- Only the transactions made from January 1 through January 31, 2015 are displayed. Since opening balances were entered during the creation of the company, note that the first transaction shown is 48—Invoice 1.
- If corrections or changes are made to entries, the transaction numbers may differ from the key. Since QuickBooks assigns transaction numbers automatically, disregard any discrepancies in transaction numbers.
- Viewing the Journal and checking the accounts used in transactions, the dates entered for transactions, the sales items used, and the amounts recorded for the

transactions is an excellent way to discover errors and determine corrections that need to be made.

Verify the total Debit and Credit Columns of **$46,933.04**

- If your totals do not match, check for errors and make appropriate corrections.
- Since the adjusting entries were marked as adjustments when entered in the General Journal, the Adj column shows checks for these entries.

Your Name Mountain Sports
Journal
January 2015

Trans #	Type	Date	Num	Adj	Name	Memo	Account	Debit	Credit
107	General Journal	01/31/2015		✔		Adjusting Entry, Insurance	6181 · Liability Insurance	125.00	
				✔		Adjusting Entry, Insurance	1340 · Prepaid Insurance		125.00
								125.00	125.00
108	General Journal	01/31/2015		✔		Adjusting Entry, Office Supplies	6472 · Office	350.00	
				✔		Adjusting Entry, Office Supplies	1311 · Office Supplies		350.00
								350.00	350.00
109	General Journal	01/31/2015		✔		Adjusting Entries, Sales Supplies	6471 · Sales	175.00	
				✔		Adjusting Entries, Sales Supplies	1312 · Sales Supplies		175.00
								175.00	175.00
110	General Journal	01/31/2015		✔		Adjusting Entry, Depreciation	1512 · Depreciation		85.00
				✔		Adjusting Entry, Depreciation	1522 · Depreciation		75.00
				✔		Adjusting Entry, Depreciation	6150 · Depreciation Expense	160.00	
								160.00	160.00
TOTAL								46,933.04	46,933.04

Partial Report

Close the report without printing

WORKING TRIAL BALANCE

A Working Trial Balance is a window that gathers information in one place. It is available from the Accountant's Menu. In this window, an accountant may see the net income, review and edit transactions, enter adjusting journal entries, and obtain a variety of informational reports using QuickZoom.

Prepare a Working Trial Balance from the Accountant menu

Click **Accountant** on the Menu bar, click **Working Trial Balance**
Change the dates **From 01/01/2015** and **To 01/31/2015**, press Tab

- To analyze the report, look at Office Supplies Beginning Balance of **850** add the Transactions of **21.98**, then subtract the Adjustments of **350** to arrive at the Ending Balance of **521.98**.
- To obtain further details about Office Supplies, you could point to the Ending Balance column and use QuickZoom to prepare a Transactions by Account report (not shown).

Working Trial Balance

Selected Period: Custom | From 01/01/2015 | To 01/31/2015 | Basis: Accrual

ACCOUNT	BEGINNING BALANCE	TRANSACTIONS	ADJUSTMENTS	ENDING BALANCE	WORKPAPER REFERENCE
1100 · Checking	25,943.00	6,642.43		32,585.43	
1200 · Accounts Receivable	6,942.44	-370.94		6,571.50	
1120 · Inventory Asset	33,499.00	2,052.54		35,551.54	
12000 · Undeposited Funds		0.00		0.00	
1311 · Office Supplies	850.00	21.98	-350.00	521.98	
1312 · Sales Supplies	575.00		-175.00	400.00	
1340 · Prepaid Insurance	250.00		-125.00	125.00	
1511 · Original Cost	5,000.00			5,000.00	
1512 · Depreciation			-85.00	-85.00	
1521 · Original Cost	4,500.00			4,500.00	
1522 · Depreciation			-75.00	-75.00	
2000 · Accounts Payable	-8,500.00	-895.40		-9,395.40	
Totals	0.00	0.00	0.00	0.00	

Net Income 2,818.63

Only show accounts with transaction activity | Make Adjustments... | Print...

Partial Report

Close the Working Trial Balance without printing

DEFINITION OF A PARTNERSHIP

A partnership is a business owned by two or more individuals. Because it is unincorporated, each partner owns a share of all the assets and liabilities based on the percentage of his or her investment in the business or according to any partnership agreement drawn up at the time the business was created. In addition, each partner receives a portion of the profits or losses of the business. Because the business is owned by the partners, they do not receive a salary. Any funds obtained by the partners are in the form of withdrawals against their share of the profits.

OWNER WITHDRAWALS

In a partnership, owners cannot receive a paycheck because they own the business. An owner withdrawing money from a business—even to pay personal expenses—is similar to an individual withdrawing money from a savings account. A withdrawal simply decreases the owners' capital. QuickBooks allows you to establish a separate account for owner withdrawals for each owner. If a separate account is not established, owner withdrawals may be subtracted directly from each owner's capital or investment account.

MEMO

DATE: January 31, 2015

Because both partners work in the business full time, they do not earn a paycheck. Prepare separate checks for monthly withdrawals of $1,000 for both Larry and you.

Write the checks for the owner withdrawals

Use the keyboard shortcut **Ctrl+W** to open the **Write Checks - Checking** window
- Make sure there is a check in the check box **Print Later**, and the NO. shows **TO PRINT**. If it is not checked, click **Print Later**.

BANK ACCOUNT should be **1100 – Checking**, if not click the drop-down arrow and select

DATE should be **01/31/15**

Enter **Your First and Last Name** on the **PAY TO THE ORDER OF** line, press **Tab**
- Since QuickBooks allows enough room, “Your First and Last Name” is shown to indicate you should use both your real first and last names. For example, the author’s withdrawal would show Pay to the Order of Janet Horne.

Because your name was not added to any list when the company was created, the **Name Not Found** dialog box appears on the screen

Click **Quick Add** to add your name to a list

The **Select Name Type** dialog box appears

Click **Other** and click **OK**
- Your name is added to a list of *Other* names, which is used for owners, partners, and other miscellaneous names.

Tab to or click in the area for the amount of the check
- If necessary, delete any numbers showing for the amount (0.00).

Enter **1000**

Tab to or click **Memo**, enter **Owner Withdrawal, January**

Use the **Expenses** tab at the bottom of the check

Tab to or click in the Account column, click the drop-down list arrow, click the Equity account **3112 - First and Last Name, Drawing**
- The amount 1,000.00 should appear in the Amount column.
- If it does not, tab to or click in the Amount column and enter 1000.

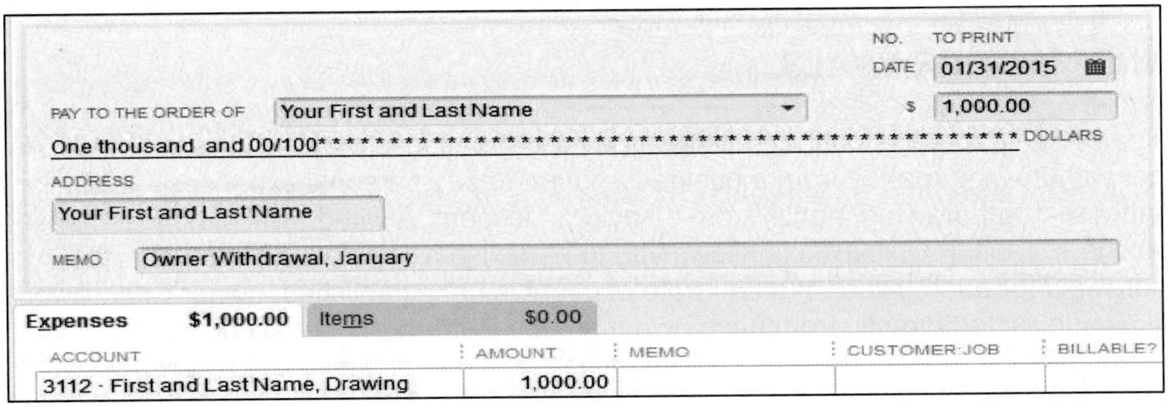

Click the **Next** arrow icon or **Save & New** and repeat the above procedures to prepare the check to Larry Muir for his $1,000 withdrawal
- Use his drawing account **3122 – Larry Muir, Drawing**.

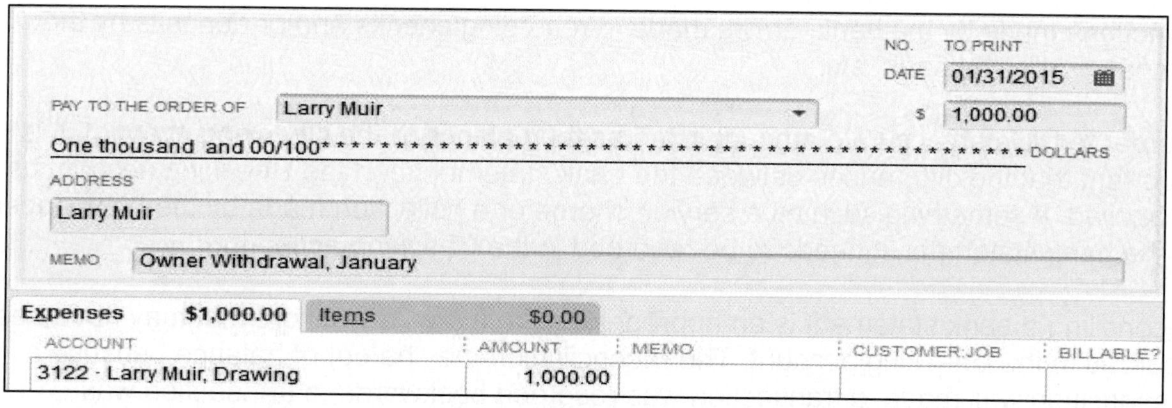

Click the **Next** arrow icon or **Save & New**

On the blank check, click the drop-down list arrow for **Print**, click **Batch**

The **Select Checks to Print** dialog box appears

Bank Account is **1100- Checking**, the **First Check Number** should be **6**

- If necessary, change the number to **6**.

If both checks have a check mark, click **OK**, if not, click **Select All** and then click **OK**

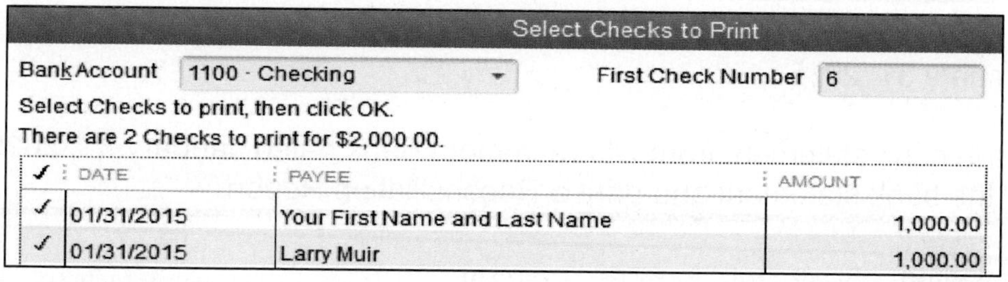

The Check style should be Standard

Once the check has printed successfully, click **OK** on the **Print Checks – Confirmation** dialog box

Close **Write Checks - Checking**

7

PREPARE DAILY BACKUP

A backup file is prepared as a safeguard in case you make an error. By creating the backup file now, it will contain your work for Chapters 5, 6, and up through the owners withdrawals in Chapter 7.

Prepare the Sports (Daily Backup).qbb file as instructed previously

BANK RECONCILIATION

Each month the Checking account should be reconciled with the bank statement to make sure both balances agree. The bank statement will rarely have an ending balance that matches the balance of the Checking account. This is due to several factors: outstanding checks, deposits in transit, bank service charges, interest earned on checking accounts, collections made by the bank, errors made in recording checks and/or deposits by the company or by the bank, etc.

In order to have an accurate amount listed as the balance in the Checking account, it is important that the differences between the bank statement and the Checking account be reconciled. If something such as a service charge or a collection made by the bank appears on the bank statement, it needs to be recorded in the Checking account.

Reconciling a bank statement is an appropriate time to find any errors that may have been recorded in the Checking account. The reconciliation may be out of balance because a transposition was made, a transaction was recorded backwards, a transaction was recorded twice, or a transaction was not recorded at all.

BEGIN BANK RECONCILIATION

The Begin Reconciliation screen initiates the account reconciliation. On this screen, information regarding the ending balance, service charges, and interest earned is entered.

MEMO
DATE: January 31, 2015

Received the bank statement from Old Mammoth Bank dated January 31, 2015. Reconcile the bank statement and print a Reconciliation Report.

Reconcile the bank statement for January

Use the bank statement on the following page to complete the reconciliation
Click the **Reconcile** icon on the QuickBooks Home Page
Enter preliminary information on the **Begin Reconciliation** screen

- *Note:* If you need to exit the Begin Reconciliation screen before it is complete, click **Cancel**.

The **Account To Reconcile** should be **1100 Checking**

- If not, click the drop-down list arrow, click **Checking**.
- The **Statement Date** should be **01/31/15**.
- **Beginning Balance** should be **25,943.00**. This is the same amount as the Checking account starting balance and is shown on the bank statement.

OLD MAMMOTH BANK
12345 Old Mammoth Road
Mammoth Lakes, CA 93546
(909) 555-3880

Your Name Mountain Sports
875 Mountain Road
Mammoth Lakes, CA 93546

Acct. # 123-456-7890 **January, 2015**

Beginning Balance 1/1/15	25,943.00		$25,943.00
1/18/15 Deposit	10,855.30		36,798.30
1/20/15 NSF Returned Check Oskar Villanueva		975.00	35,823.30
1/20/2015 NSF Bank Charge		10.00	35,813.30
1/20/15 Check 1		81.00	35,732.30
1/25/15 Check 2		1,837.50	33,894.80
1/25/15 Check 3		294.00	33,600.80
1/25/15 Check 4		313.60	33,287.20
1/25/15 Check 5		701.77	32,585.43
1/31/15 Office Equip. Loan Pmt.: $10.33 Principal, $53.42 Interest		63.75	32,521.68
1/31/15 Store Fixtures Loan Pmt.: $8.61 Principal, $44.51 Interest		53.12	32,468.56
1/31/15 Service Chg.		8.00	32,460.56
1/31/15 Interest	54.05		32,514.61
Ending Balance 1/31/15			32,514.61

Enter the **Ending Balance** from the bank statement, **32,514.61**
Tab to or click **Service Charge**, enter the **Service Charge, 8.00**
Tab to or click Service Charge **Date**, the date should be **01/31/15**

- Since the date of your computer may appear, double-check the date to avoid errors.

Click the drop-down list arrow for **Account**, click **6120 Bank Service Charges**
Tab to or click **Interest Earned**, enter **54.05**
Date is **01/31/15**
The **Account** is **7010** for **Interest Income**

7

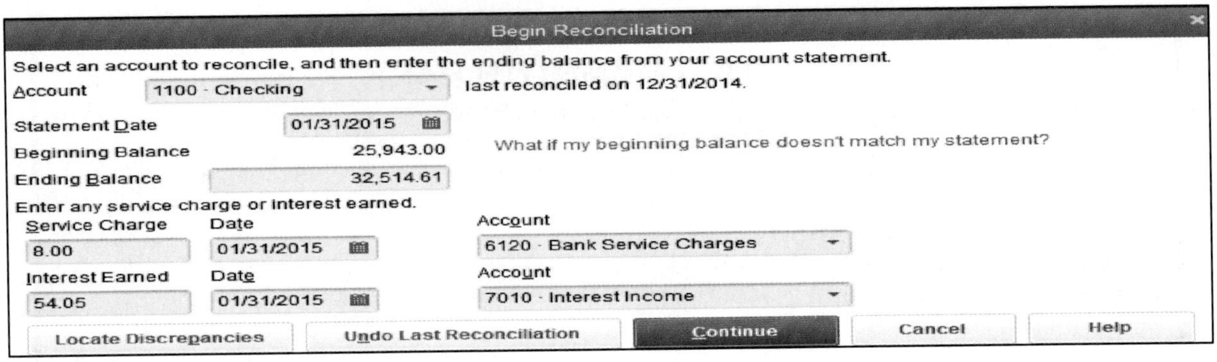

Click **Continue**

MARK CLEARED TRANSACTIONS

Once bank statement information for the ending balance, service charges, and interest earned has been entered, compare the checks and deposits listed on the statement with the transactions for the Checking account. If a deposit or a check is listed correctly on the bank statement and in the Reconcile - Checking window, it has cleared and should be marked. An item may be marked individually by positioning the cursor on the deposit or the check and clicking the primary mouse button. If all deposits and checks match, click the Mark All button to mark all the deposits and checks at once. To remove all the checks, click the Unmark All button. To unmark an individual item, click the item.

Mark cleared checks and deposits

- *Note:* If you need to exit the Reconcile - Checking screen before it is complete, click **Leave**. If you click **Reconcile Now**, you must Undo the reconciliation and start over.
- If you need to return to the Begin Reconciliation window, click the **Modify** button.
- Notice that the **Highlight Marked** is selected. When an item has been selected or marked, the background color changes.

Compare the bank statement with the **Reconcile - Checking** window

- On the bank statement, dates may not be the same as the actual check or deposit dates.

Click the items that appear on both statements

- Make sure to mark the $10.00 amount from Oskar Villanueva, which is the bank charge for his NSF check. (The NSF check and charges were entered in Ch. 5.)

When finished, look at the bottom of the **Reconcile - Checking** window

You have marked cleared:

1 Deposits and Other Credits for 10,855.30

7 Checks and Payments for 4,212.87

The Service Charge of -8.00 and Interest Earned of 54.05 are shown

The Ending Balance is 32,514.61

The Cleared Balance is 32,631.48

There is a Difference of -116.87

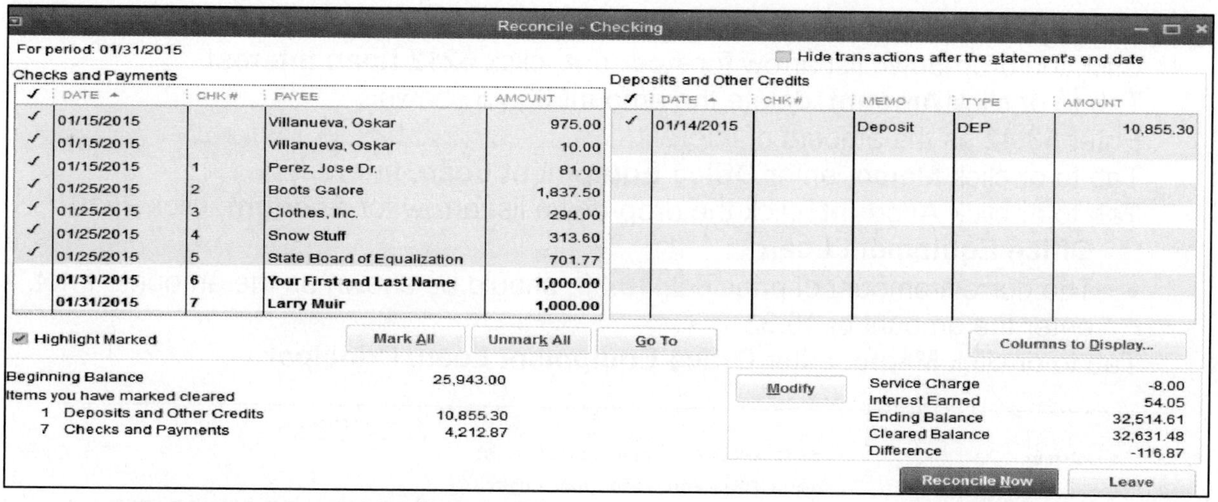

The bank statement should remain on the screen while you complete the next section

COMPLETE BANK RECONCILIATION

As you complete the reconciliation, you may find errors that need to be corrected or transactions that need to be recorded. Anything entered as a service charge or interest earned will be entered automatically when the reconciliation is complete and the Reconcile Now button is clicked. To correct an error such as a transposition, click on the entry then click the Go To button. The original entry will appear on the screen. The correction can be made and will show in the Reconcile - Checking window. If there is a transaction, such as an automatic loan payment to the bank, access the register for the balance sheet account used in the transaction and enter the payment.

Enter the automatic loan payments shown on the bank statement

Use the keyboard shortcut **Ctrl+R** to open the register for the **1100 Checking** account

- Notice that the checks and the deposit marked in the reconciliation now have an * in the √ column.

In the blank transaction at the bottom of the register, enter the **Date**, **01/31/15**
Tab to or click **Number**, enter **Transfer**
Tab to or click **Payee**, enter **Old Mammoth Bank**
Tab to or click the **Payment** column

- Because Old Mammoth Bank does not appear on any list, you will get a **Name Not Found** dialog box when you move to another field.

Click the **Quick Add** button to add the name of the bank to the Other Name List
Click **Other**, and click **OK**

- Once the name of the bank has been added to the Other List, the cursor will be positioned in the **Payment** column.

Enter **63.75** in the **Payment** column

Click **Splits** at the bottom of the register
Click the drop-down list arrow for **Account**, click **6212 Loan Interest**
Tab to or click **Amount**, delete the amount 63.75 shown
Enter **53.42** as the amount of interest
Tab to or click **Memo**, enter **Office Equipment Loan, Interest**
Tab to or click **Account**, click the drop-down list arrow for **Account**, click **2510 Office Equipment Loan**

- The correct amount of principal, 10.33, should be shown as the amount. If not, enter the amount of 10.33

Tab to or click **Memo**, enter **Office Equipment Loan, Principal**

ACCOUNT	AMOUNT	MEMO	CUSTOMER:JOB	BILLABLE?	
6212 · Loan Interest	53.42	Office Equipment Loan, Interest			Close
2510 · Office Equipment Loan	10.33	Office Equipment Loan, Principal			Clear

Click **Close** on the Splits window

- This closes the window for the information regarding the way the transaction is to be "split" between accounts. Notice the word –split- in the ACCOUNT column.

For the **Memo** in the Checking Register, record **Office Equipment Loan, Payment**
Click the **Record** button to record the transaction

- Transfers are shown before checks prepared on the same date; thus, the loan payment does not appear as the last transaction in the register.

1100 · Checking

Go to... | Print... | Edit Transaction | QuickReport | Setup Bank Feeds

DATE	NUMBER / TYPE	PAYEE / ACCOUNT	MEMO	PAYMENT	✔	DEPOSIT	BALANCE
01/31/2015	Transfer	Old Mammoth Bank		63.75			32,521.68
	CHK	-split-	Office Equipment Loan, Payment				

Repeat the procedures to record the loan payment for store fixtures

- When you enter the Payee as Old Mammoth Bank, the amount for the previous transaction (63.75) appears in amount.

Enter the new amount **53.12**
Click **Splits**
Click the appropriate accounts and enter the correct amount for each item

- The accounts and amounts for the office equipment loan payment may appear. Click the drop-down list arrow and select the appropriate accounts for the store fixture loan payment. Be sure to use the information for Store Fixtures <u>not</u> the information for Office Equipment.
- Refer to the bank statement for details regarding the amount of the payment for interest and the amount of the payment applied to principal.

ACCOUNT	AMOUNT	MEMO	CUSTOMER:JOB	BILLABLE?	
6212 · Loan Interest	44.51	Store Fixtures Loan, Interest			Close
2520 · Store Fixtures Loan	8.61	Store Fixtures Loan, Principal			Clear

Click **Close** to close the window for the information regarding the "split" between accounts

Enter the transaction **Memo**: **Store Fixtures Loan, Payment**

Click **Record** to record the loan payment

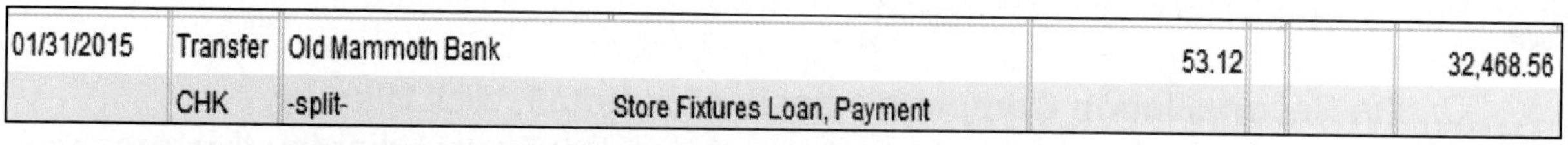

01/31/2015
Transfer
Old Mammoth Bank
53.12
32,468.56
CHK
-split-
Store Fixtures Loan, Payment

Close the **Checking Register**

- You should return to the **Reconcile – Checking** screen.

Scroll to the bottom of **Checks and Payments**

- Notice the two entries for the loan payments in Checks and Payments.

Mark the two entries

- At this point the Ending Balance and Cleared Balance should be equal—$32,514.61 with a difference of 0.00.

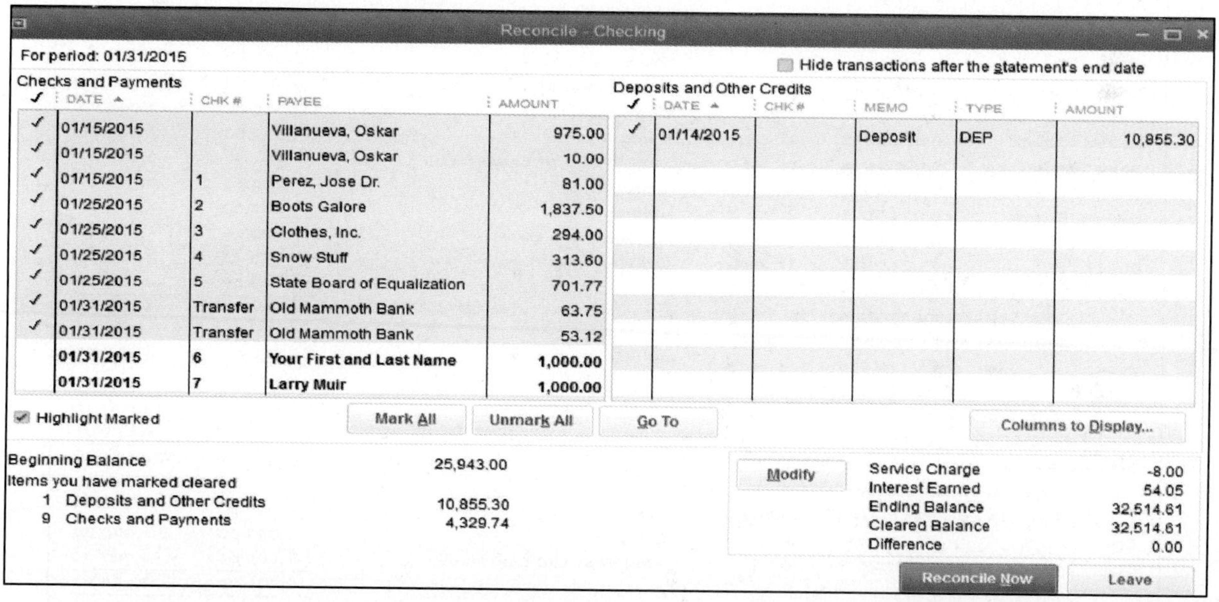

If your entries agree with the above, click **Reconcile Now** to finish the reconciliation

- If your reconciliation is not in agreement, do not click **Reconcile Now** until the errors are corrected.
- Once you click **Reconcile Now**, you may not return to this **Reconcile - Checking** window. You would have to Undo the reconciliation and start over.

PRINT RECONCILIATION REPORT

As soon as the Ending Balance and the Cleared Balance are equal or when you finish marking transactions and click Reconcile Now, a screen appears allowing you to select the level of Reconciliation Report you would like to print. You may select Summary and get a report that lists totals only or Detail and get all the transactions that were reconciled on the report. You may print the report at the time you have finished reconciling the account or you may print the report later by clicking the Reports menu, clicking Banking, and then clicking Previous Reconciliation. If you think you may want to print the report again in the future, print the report to a file to save it permanently.

Print a Detail Reconciliation report

On the **Reconciliation Complete** screen, click **Detail**, click **Display**

- If you get a Reconciliation Report message, click **Do not display this message in the future**, and click **OK**.

Adjust the column widths so the report will print on one page and all information is displayed in full

Your Name Mountain Sports
Reconciliation Detail
1100 · Checking, Period Ending 01/31/2015

Type	Date	Num	Name	Clr	Amount	Balance
Beginning Balance						**25,943.00**
Cleared Transactions						
Checks and Payments - 10 items						
General Journal	01/15/2015		Villanueva, Oskar	✔	-975.00	-975.00
Check	01/15/2015	1	Perez, Jose Dr.	✔	-81.00	-1,056.00
General Journal	01/15/2015		Villanueva, Oskar	✔	-10.00	-1,066.00
Bill Pmt -Check	01/25/2015	2	Boots Galore	✔	-1,837.50	-2,903.50
Sales Tax Paym...	01/25/2015	5	State Board of Equalization	✔	-701.77	-3,605.27
Bill Pmt -Check	01/25/2015	4	Snow Stuff	✔	-313.60	-3,918.87
Bill Pmt -Check	01/25/2015	3	Clothes, Inc.	✔	-294.00	-4,212.87
Check	01/31/2015	Transfer	Old Mammoth Bank	✔	-63.75	-4,276.62
Check	01/31/2015	Transfer	Old Mammoth Bank	✔	-53.12	-4,329.74
Check	01/31/2015			✔	-8.00	-4,337.74
Total Checks and Payments					-4,337.74	-4,337.74
Deposits and Credits - 2 items						
Deposit	01/14/2015			✔	10,855.30	10,855.30
Deposit	01/31/2015			✔	54.05	10,909.35
Total Deposits and Credits					10,909.35	10,909.35
Total Cleared Transactions					6,571.61	6,571.61
Cleared Balance					6,571.61	32,514.61
Uncleared Transactions						
Checks and Payments - 2 items						
Check	01/31/2015	7	Larry Muir		-1,000.00	-1,000.00
Check	01/31/2015	6	Your First and Last Name		-1,000.00	-2,000.00
Total Checks and Payments					-2,000.00	-2,000.00
Total Uncleared Transactions					-2,000.00	-2,000.00
Register Balance as of 01/31/2015					4,571.61	30,514.61
Ending Balance					**4,571.61**	**30,514.61**

Print as previously instructed in Portrait orientation then close the report

VIEW CHECK REGISTER

Once the bank reconciliation has been completed, it is wise to scroll through the Check Register to view the effect of the reconciliation on the account. You will notice that the check column shows a check mark for all items that were marked as cleared during the reconciliation. If at a later date an error is discovered, the transaction may be changed, and the correction will be reflected in the Beginning Balance on the reconciliation.

View the register for the Checking account

Click the **Check Register** icon in the Banking section of the Home Page
To display more of the register, click the check box for **1-Line**
Scroll through the register

- Notice that the transactions are listed in chronological order and that each item marked in the Bank Reconciliation now has a check mark in the check column.
- The interest earned and bank service charges appear in the register.
- Even though the bank reconciliation transactions for loan payments were recorded after the checks written on January 31, the bank reconciliation transactions appear before the checks because they were recorded as a Transfer.

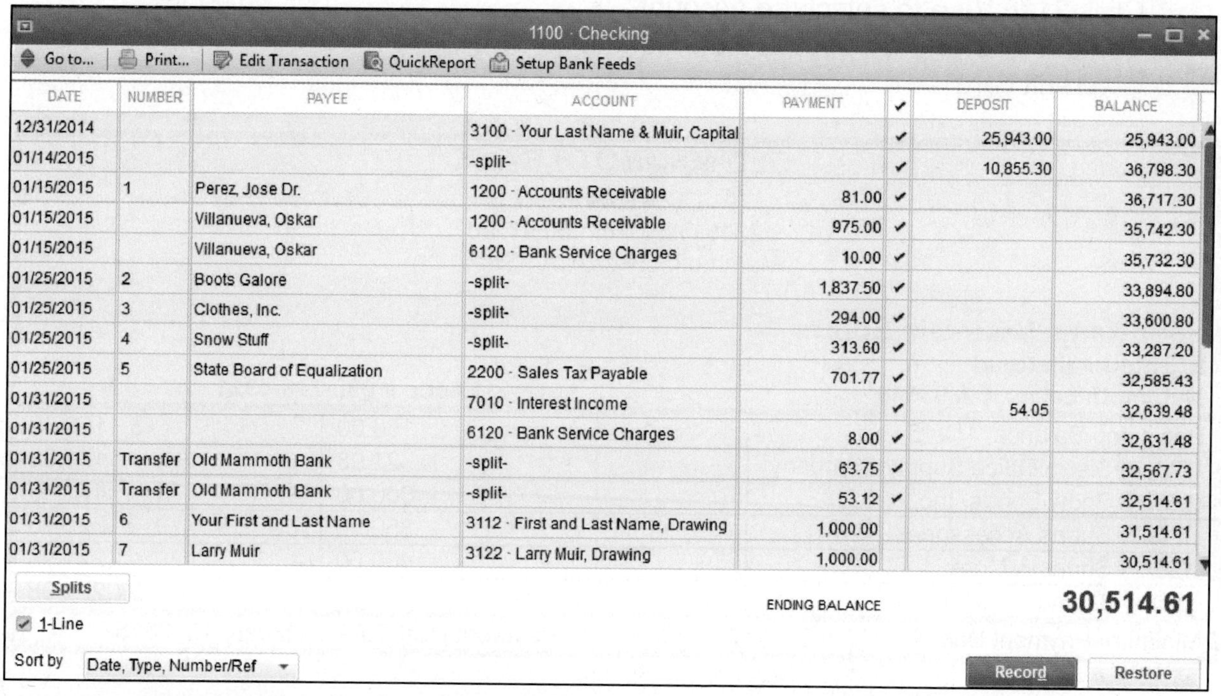

1100 · Checking

Go to... | Print... | Edit Transaction | QuickReport | Setup Bank Feeds

DATE	NUMBER	PAYEE	ACCOUNT	PAYMENT	✔	DEPOSIT	BALANCE
12/31/2014			3100 · Your Last Name & Muir, Capital		✔	25,943.00	25,943.00
01/14/2015			-split-		✔	10,855.30	36,798.30
01/15/2015	1	Perez, Jose Dr.	1200 · Accounts Receivable	81.00	✔		36,717.30
01/15/2015		Villanueva, Oskar	1200 · Accounts Receivable	975.00	✔		35,742.30
01/15/2015		Villanueva, Oskar	6120 · Bank Service Charges	10.00	✔		35,732.30
01/25/2015	2	Boots Galore	-split-	1,837.50	✔		33,894.80
01/25/2015	3	Clothes, Inc.	-split-	294.00	✔		33,600.80
01/25/2015	4	Snow Stuff	-split-	313.60	✔		33,287.20
01/25/2015	5	State Board of Equalization	2200 · Sales Tax Payable	701.77	✔		32,585.43
01/31/2015			7010 · Interest Income		✔	54.05	32,639.48
01/31/2015			6120 · Bank Service Charges	8.00	✔		32,631.48
01/31/2015	Transfer	Old Mammoth Bank	-split-	63.75	✔		32,567.73
01/31/2015	Transfer	Old Mammoth Bank	-split-	53.12	✔		32,514.61
01/31/2015	6	Your First and Last Name	3112 · First and Last Name, Drawing	1,000.00			31,514.61
01/31/2015	7	Larry Muir	3122 · Larry Muir, Drawing	1,000.00			30,514.61

Splits | ENDING BALANCE 30,514.61

1-Line

Sort by Date, Type, Number/Ref | Record | Restore

- Notice that the final balance of the account is $30,514.61.

Close the register

CREDIT CARD RECONCILIATION

Any balance sheet account used in QuickBooks may be reconciled. These include assets, liabilities, and owner's equity accounts. Income, expense, and cost of goods sold accounts are not balance sheet accounts and may not be reconciled.

As with a checking account, it is a good practice to reconcile the Credit Card account each month. When the credit card statement is received, the transactions entered in QuickBooks should agree with the transactions shown on the credit card statement. A reconciliation of the credit card should be completed on a monthly basis.

MEMO

DATE: January 31, 2015

The monthly bill for the Visa has arrived and is to be paid. Prior to paying the monthly credit card bill, reconcile the Credit Card account.

Reconcile and pay the credit card bill

Click the **Reconcile** icon on the Home Page
Click the drop-down list arrow for Account
Click **2100 Visa** to select the account
Use the following credit card statement to complete the reconciliation of the Visa credit card

OLD MAMMOTH BANK
VISA
12345 Old Mammoth Road
Mammoth Lakes, CA 93546

Your Name Mountain Sports
875 Mountain Road
Mammoth Lakes, CA 93546 **Acct. # 098-776-4321**

Beginning Balance, 1/1/15		150.00	$ 150.00
1/23/15 Sierra Office Supply Company		21.98	171.98
1/23/15 Snow Sports, Inc.		300.00	471.98
1/25/15 Sports Accessories		350.00	821.98
1/25/15 Shoes & More		400.00	1,221.98
Ending Balance, 1/31/15			$1,221.98

Minimum Payment Due: $50.00 Payment Due Date: February 15, 2015

Enter the **Statement Date** of **01/31/15**
Enter the **Ending Balance** of **1,221.98** in the **Begin Reconciliation** window

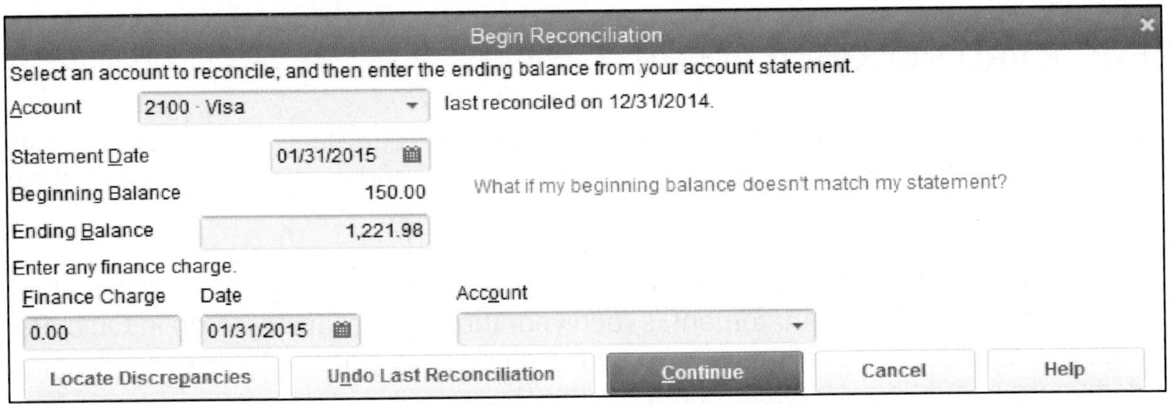

Click the **Continue** button

Mark each item that appears on both the statement and in the reconciliation **EXCEPT** for the **$400** transaction for Shoes & More

ADJUSTMENT—CREDIT CARD RECONCILIATION

In QuickBooks 2015, adjustments to reconciliations may be made during the reconciliation process.

Verify that all items are marked **EXCEPT** the charge for **$400** for Shoes & More

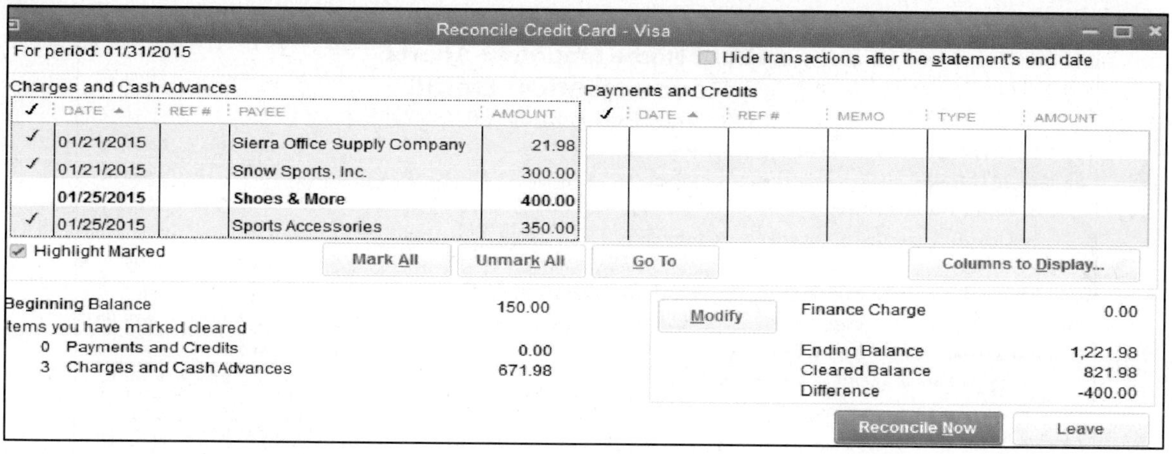

Click **Reconcile Now**

- The Reconcile Adjustment screen appears because there was a $400 Difference shown at the bottom of the reconciliation.
- Even though the error on the demonstration reconciliation is known, an adjustment will be entered and then deleted at a later time.

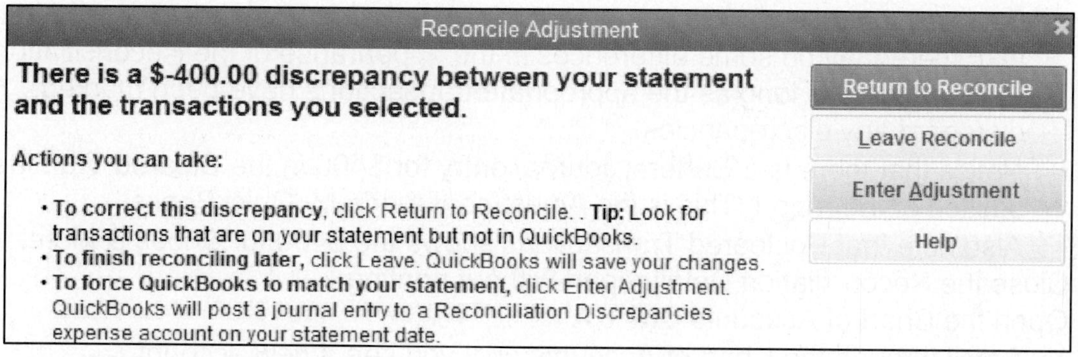

Click **Enter Adjustment**
Click **Cancel** on the Make Payment screen

7

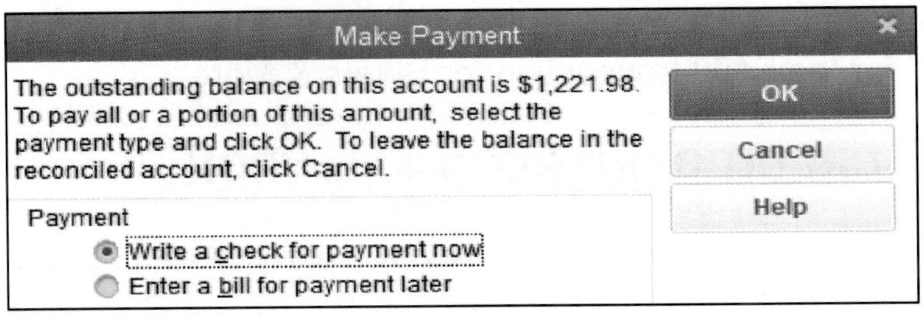

- The Reconciliation report is generated.

Click **Detail** and then click **Display**

Your Name Mountain Sports
Reconciliation Detail
2100 · Visa, Period Ending 01/31/2015

Type	Date	Num	Name	Clr	Amount	Balance
Beginning Balance						**150.00**
Cleared Transactions						
Charges and Cash Advances - 4 items						
Credit Card Charge	01/21/2015		Snow Sports, Inc.	✔	-300.00	-300.00
Credit Card Charge	01/21/2015		Sierra Office Supply Company	✔	-21.98	-321.98
Bill Pmt -CCard	01/25/2015		Sports Accessories	✔	-350.00	-671.98
General Journal	01/31/2015			✔	-400.00	-1,071.98
Total Charges and Cash Advances					-1,071.98	-1,071.98
Total Cleared Transactions					-1,071.98	-1,071.98
Cleared Balance					1,071.98	1,221.98
Uncleared Transactions						
Charges and Cash Advances - 1 item						
Bill Pmt -CCard	01/25/2015		Shoes & More		-400.00	-400.00
Total Charges and Cash Advances					-400.00	-400.00
Total Uncleared Transactions					-400.00	-400.00
Register Balance as of 01/31/2015					1,471.98	1,621.98
Ending Balance					**1,471.98**	**1,621.98**

- Because the date of your computer may be different from the date used in the text, there may be some differences in the appearance of the Reconciliation Detail report. As long as the appropriate transactions have been marked, disregard any discrepancies.
- Notice that there is a General Journal entry for $400 in the Cleared Transactions section of the report. This is the Adjustment made by QuickBooks.
- Also note that Uncleared Transactions shows the $400 for Shoes & More.

Close the Reconciliation Detail report without printing

Open the Chart of Accounts **Ctrl + A**

- Scroll through the Chart of Accounts until you see a new account, **66900 - Reconciliation Discrepancies**.

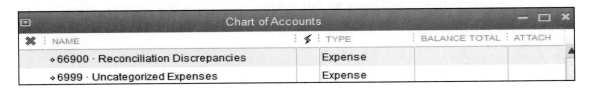

Chart of Accounts

NAME	⚡	TYPE	BALANCE TOTAL	ATTACH
◆66900 · Reconciliation Discrepancies		Expense		
◆6999 · Uncategorized Expenses		Expense		

Double-click **66900 – Reconciliation Discrepancies** to view a QuickReport

Your Name Mountain Sports
Account QuickReport
January 2015

Type	Date	Num	Name	Memo	Split	Amount
66900 · Reconciliation Discrepancies						
General Journal	01/31/2015			Balance Adjustment	2100 · Visa	400.00
Total 66900 · Reconciliation Discrepancies						400.00
TOTAL						400.00

- Note the General Journal entry for Balance Adjustment.

Close the QuickReport without printing; close the Chart of Accounts

REDO RECONCILIATION

If an error is discovered after an account reconciliation has been completed, the reconciliation may be removed by using the Undo Last Reconciliation feature located on the Begin Reconciliation screen. If an adjusting entry for a reconciliation has been made, it may be deleted. This is useful if you had a discrepancy when making the reconciliation and found the error at a later date.

Undo the credit card reconciliation and delete the adjusting entry made by QuickBooks

Click the **Reconcile** icon on the Home Page
Click the drop-down list arrow for Account, select **2100 - Visa**
Click **Undo Last Reconciliation** on the Begin Reconciliation screen

Undo Previous Reconciliation

Intuit recommends that you back up your company file before undoing a previous reconciliation. Click Cancel on this window, then from the "File" menu choose "Save Copy or Backup...".

What to expect...

When you have finished undoing the previous reconciliation, your beginning balance will revert back to the previous beginning balance shown below:

Current Beginning Balance: -1,221.98

Previous Beginning Balance: -150.00

Undoing a previous reconciliation also removes the cleared status of all its transactions, service charges, interest and balance adjustments. You will need to reconcile your previous statement again.

Continue | Cancel

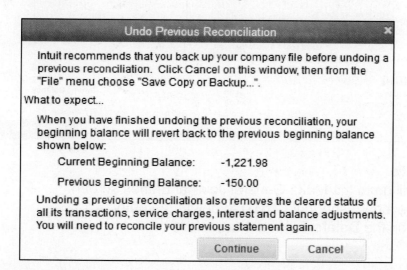

Click the **Continue** button

Click **OK** on the **Undo Previous Reconcile** dialog box

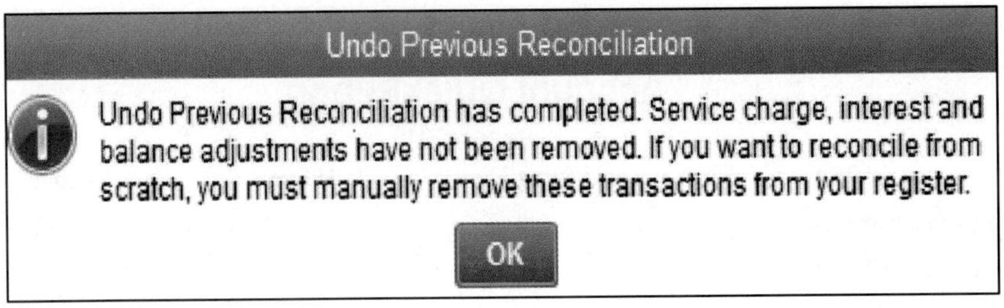

- Remember that service charges, interest, and balance adjustments are <u>not</u> removed. If you have entered any of these items on the previous reconciliation, they will need to be deleted from the Journal manually. None of the items were entered on the previous reconciliation so there is nothing to be deleted.
- You will return to the Begin Reconciliation screen.

Make sure the **Account** is **2100 – Visa** and the **Statement Date** is **01/31/15**
The **Beginning Balance** is once again **$150.00**
Enter the **Ending Balance** of **1221.98**
Click **Continue**
Click **Mark All**

- All of the items listed on the Credit Card Statement **<u>INCLUDING</u>** the **$400** for Shoes & More will be marked.

Click the **400.00 Adjusting Entry** for **01/31/15**

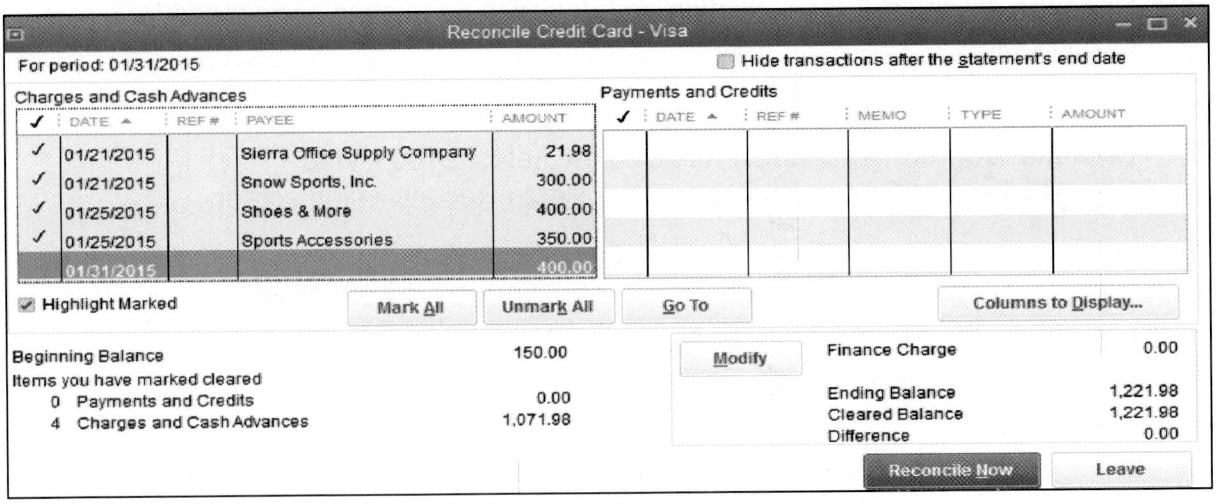

Click **Go To**

- You will go to the Make General Journal Entries screen.

Use the keyboard shortcut **Ctrl+D** to delete the entry
Click **OK** on the **Delete Transaction** screen

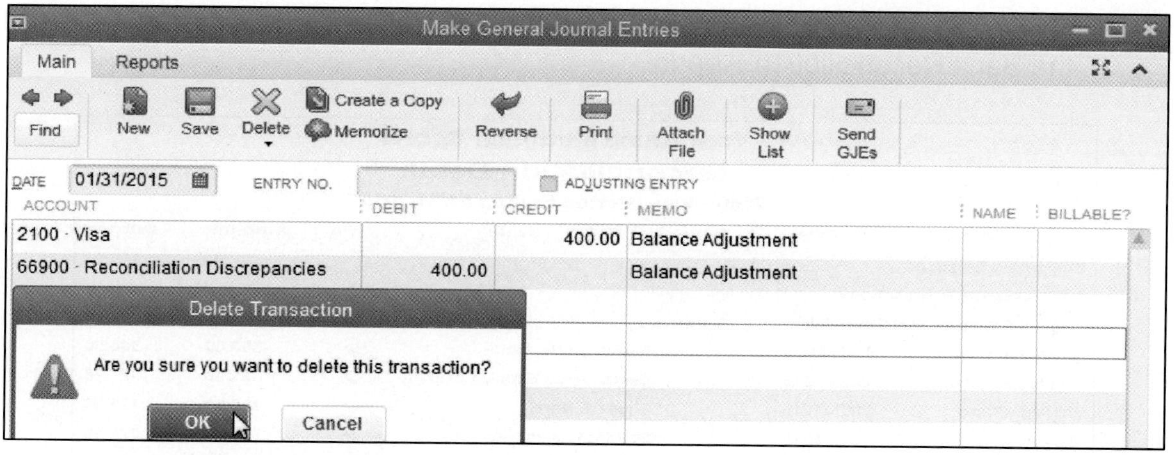

Close the **Make General Journal Entries** screen

Verify that the adjusting entry has been deleted and that the **Ending** and **Cleared Balances** are **1,221.98** and the **Difference** is **0.00**

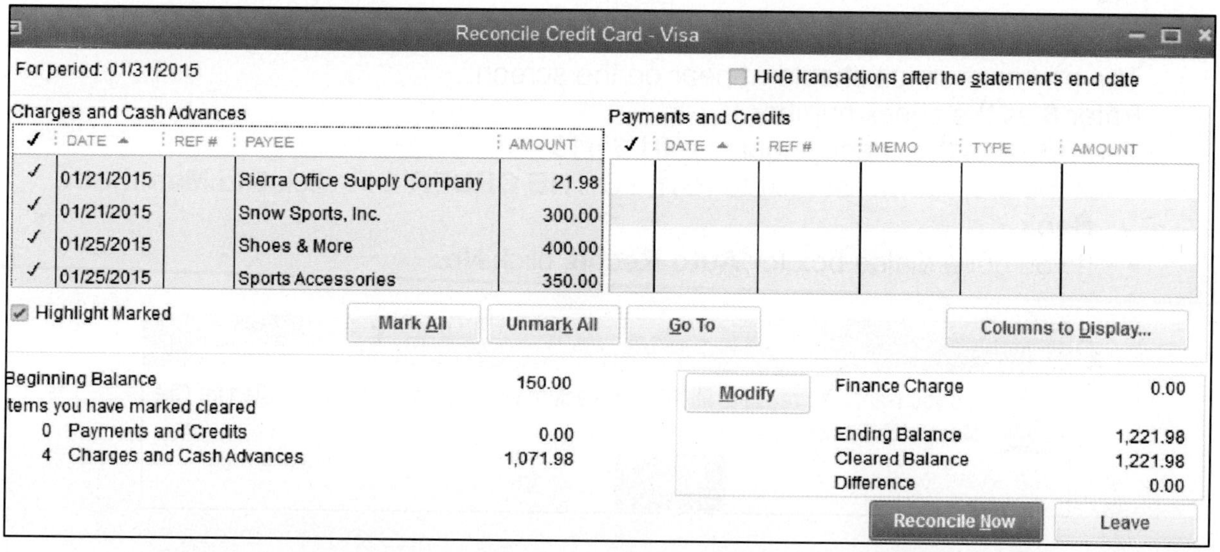

Click **Reconcile Now**

When the **Make Payment** dialog box appears on the screen

Make sure **Write a check for payment now** is selected, click **OK**

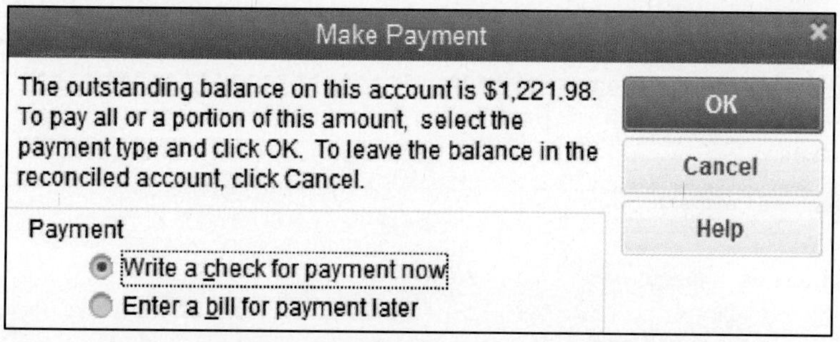

Display and print a **Reconciliation Detail Report** following the procedures given for the Bank Reconciliation Report

Your Name Mountain Sports
Reconciliation Detail
2100 · Visa, Period Ending 01/31/2015

Type	Date	Num	Name	Clr	Amount	Balance
Beginning Balance						**150.00**
Cleared Transactions						
Charges and Cash Advances - 4 items						
Credit Card Charge	01/21/2015		Snow Sports, Inc.	✔	-300.00	-300.00
Credit Card Charge	01/21/2015		Sierra Office Supply Company	✔	-21.98	-321.98
Bill Pmt -CCard	01/25/2015		Shoes & More	✔	-400.00	-721.98
Bill Pmt -CCard	01/25/2015		Sports Accessories	✔	-350.00	-1,071.98
Total Charges and Cash Advances					-1,071.98	-1,071.98
Total Cleared Transactions					-1,071.98	-1,071.98
Cleared Balance					1,071.98	1,221.98
Register Balance as of 01/31/2015					1,071.98	1,221.98
Ending Balance					**1,071.98**	**1,221.98**

Close the Reconciliation Detail report
The payment check should appear on the screen
Enter **8** as the check number
The **DATE** of the check should be **01/31/15**
Click the drop-down list next to **PAY TO THE ORDER OF**, click **Old Mammoth Bank**

- If you get a dialog box for **Auto Recall**, click **No**.

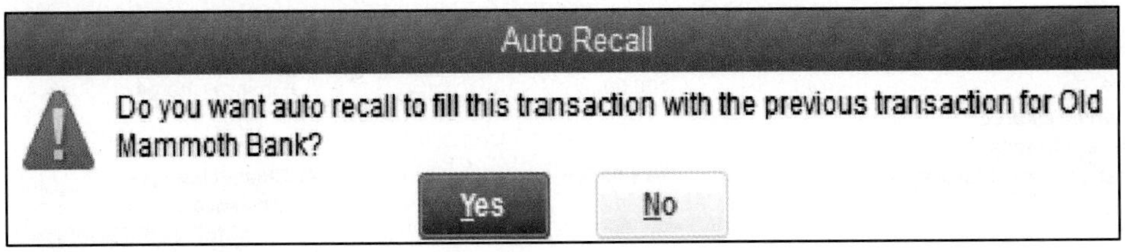

Tab to or click **Memo** on the bottom of the check
Enter **January Visa Payment** as the memo

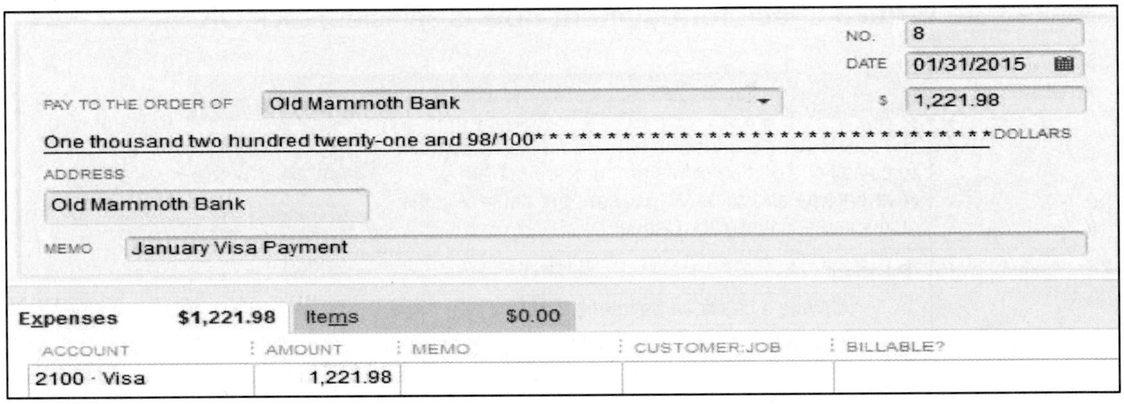

Print the standard-style check, then click **OK** on the Print Checks – Confirmation
Click **Save & Close** to record, and exit **Write Checks**

VIEW JOURNAL

After entering several transactions, it is helpful to view the Journal. In the Journal all transactions regardless of the method of entry are shown in traditional debit/credit format.

View the **Journal** for January

Since you will be preparing several reports, open the Report Center
Click **Accountant & Taxes** as the type of report, double-click **Journal**
The dates are from **01/01/15** to **01/31/15**, press **Tab**
Expand the Journal
Scroll through the report and view all the transactions that have been made

Your Name Mountain Sports
Journal
January 2015

Trans #	Type	Date	Num	Adj	Name	Memo	Account	Debit	Credit
113	Check	01/31/2015	Transfer		Old Mammoth Bank	Office Equipment Loan, Payment	1100 · Checking		63.75
					Old Mammoth Bank	Office Equipment Loan, Interest	6212 · Loan Interest	53.42	
					Old Mammoth Bank	Office Equipment Loan, Principal	2510 · Office Equipment Loan	10.33	
								63.75	63.75
114	Check	01/31/2015	Transfer		Old Mammoth Bank	Store Fixtures Loan, Payment	1100 · Checking		53.12
					Old Mammoth Bank	Store Fixtures Loan, Interest	6212 · Loan Interest	44.51	
					Old Mammoth Bank	Store Fixtures Loan, Principal	2520 · Store Fixtures Loan	8.61	
								53.12	53.12
115	Check	01/31/2015				Service Charge	1100 · Checking		8.00
						Service Charge	6120 · Bank Service Charges	8.00	
								8.00	8.00
116	Deposit	01/31/2015				Interest	1100 · Checking	54.05	
						Interest	7010 · Interest Income		54.05
								54.05	54.05
118	Check	01/31/2015	8		Old Mammoth Bank	January Visa Payment	1100 · Checking		1,221.98
					Old Mammoth Bank	January Visa Payment	2100 · Visa	1,221.98	
								1,221.98	1,221.98
TOTAL								50,333.94	50,333.94

Partial Report

Close the **Journal** without printing
The **Report Center** should remain on the screen

PREPARE ADJUSTED TRIAL BALANCE

After all adjustments have been recorded and the bank reconciliation has been completed, it is wise to prepare an Adjusted Trial Balance. This report has columns for Unadjusted Balance, Adjustments, and Adjusted Balance. If adjusting entries have been made, the amount in the Adjustments column is subtracted from Unadjusted Balance to obtain the Adjusted Balance. The Adjusted Trial Balance proves that debits equal credits.

MEMO
DATE: January 31, 2015

Because adjustments have been entered, prepare an Adjusted Trial Balance.

Use Accountant & Taxes in Report Center to prepare an adjusted trial balance

Report Dates are From **01/01/15** To **01/31/15**

- Scroll through the report and study the amounts shown

Your Name Mountain Sports
Adjusted Trial Balance
January 2015

	Unadjusted Balance		Adjustments		Adjusted Balance	
	Debit	Credit	Debit	Credit	Debit	Credit
1100 · Checking	29,292.63				29,292.63	
1200 · Accounts Receivable	6,571.50				6,571.50	
1120 · Inventory Asset	35,551.54				35,551.54	
12000 · Undeposited Funds	0.00				0.00	
1311 · Office Supplies	871.98			350.00	521.98	
1312 · Sales Supplies	575.00			175.00	400.00	
1340 · Prepaid Insurance	250.00			125.00	125.00	
1511 · Original Cost	5,000.00				5,000.00	
1512 · Depreciation				85.00		85.00
1521 · Original Cost	4,500.00				4,500.00	
1522 · Depreciation				75.00		75.00
2000 · Accounts Payable		9,395.40				9,395.40
2100 · Visa	0.00				0.00	
2200 · Sales Tax Payable	0.00				0.00	
2510 · Office Equipment Loan		2,989.67				2,989.67
2520 · Store Fixtures Loan		2,491.39				2,491.39
3000 · Owners' Equity	0.00				0.00	
3100 · Your Last Name & Muir, Capital		26,159.44				26,159.44
3111 · First and Last Name, Investment		20,000.00				20,000.00
3112 · First and Last Name, Drawing	1,000.00				1,000.00	
3121 · Larry Muir, Investment		20,000.00				20,000.00
3122 · Larry Muir, Drawing	1,000.00				1,000.00	
4011 · Clothing & Accessory Sales		1,759.51				1,759.51
4012 · Equipment Sales		7,436.44				7,436.44
4050 · Sales Discounts	494.36				494.36	
4090 · Returned Check Charges		25.00				25.00
5000 · Cost of Goods Sold	3,492.46				3,492.46	
5200 · Merchandise Discounts		49.90				49.90
6120 · Bank Service Charges	18.00				18.00	
6140 · Advertising Expense	95.00				95.00	
6150 · Depreciation Expense			160.00		160.00	
6181 · Liability Insurance			125.00		125.00	
6212 · Loan Interest	97.93				97.93	
6300 · Rent	950.00				950.00	
6340 · Telephone	156.40				156.40	
6391 · Gas and Electric	359.00				359.00	
6392 · Water	85.00				85.00	
6471 · Sales			175.00		175.00	
6472 · Office			350.00		350.00	
7010 · Interest Income		54.05				54.05
TOTAL	90,360.80	90,360.80	810.00	810.00	90,520.80	90,520.80

- If you look at the Unadjusted Balance and add or subtract the Adjustments, you will obtain the Adjusted Balance.
- Notice that the final totals of debits and credits of the Adjusted Balance columns are equal: $90,520.80.

Do not close the report

USE QUICKZOOM

Use QuickZoom to view the details of Office Supplies:
Scroll through the Trial Balance until you see **1311 Office Supplies**
Position the mouse pointer over the amount of Office Supplies, **521.98**
- Notice that the mouse pointer changes to a magnifying glass with a Z. 

Double-click the primary mouse button
- A **Transactions by Account Report** appears on the screen showing the two transactions entered for office supplies.

Your Name Mountain Sports
Transactions by Account
As of January 31, 2015

Type	Date	Num	Adj	Name	Memo	Clr	Split	Debit	Credit	Balance
1310 · Supplies										850.00
1311 · Office Supplies										850.00
Credit Card Charge	01/21/2015			Sierra Office Supply Company	Purchase Paper		2100 · Visa	21.98		871.98
General Journal	01/31/2015		✓		Adjusting Entry, Office Supplies		6472 · Office		350.00	521.98
Total 1311 · Office Supplies								21.98	350.00	521.98
Total 1310 · Supplies								21.98	350.00	521.98
TOTAL								21.98	350.00	521.98

Close Transactions by Account and Adjusted Trial Balance reports without printing

PROFIT & LOSS (STANDARD)

Because all income, expenses, and adjustments have been made for the period, a Profit & Loss Report can be prepared. This report is also known as the Income Statement and shows the income, expenses, and net income or net loss for the period (Income – Expenses = Net Profit or Net Loss).

QuickBooks has several different types of Profit & Loss Reports available: Standard—summarizes income and expenses; Detail—shows the year-to-date transactions for each income and expense account. The other Profit & Loss reports are like the Profit & Loss Standard but have additional information displayed as indicated in the following: YTD Comparison—summarizes your income and expenses for this month and compares them to your income and expenses for the current fiscal year; Prev Year Comparison—summarizes your income and expenses for both this month and this month last year; By Job—has columns for each customer and job and amounts for this year to date; By Class—has columns for each class and sub-class with the amounts for this year to date, and Unclassified—shows how much you are making or losing within segments of your business that are not assigned to a QuickBooks class

View a **Profit & Loss (Standard) Report**

Use the Company & Financial section of the Report Center and prepare the report
- Unless instructed otherwise, all Profit & Loss reports prepared will be Standard.

If necessary, enter the dates **From 01/01/15** and **To 01/31/15**

Your Name Mountain Sports Profit & Loss January 2015	Jan 15
▼ Ordinary Income/Expense	
▶ Income	8,726.59
▶ Cost of Goods Sold	3,442.56
Gross Profit	5,284.03
▶ Expense	2,571.33
Net Ordinary Income	2,712.70
▼ Other Income/Expense	
▶ Other Income	54.05
Net Other Income	54.05
Net Income	2,766.75

Partial Report

Scroll through the report to view the income and expenses listed

- Remember, accrual basis accounting calculates the net income based on income earned at the time the service was performed or the sale was made and the expenses incurred at the time the bill was received or incurred whether or not they have been paid.
- The calculations shown below may not have all the subtotals shown in the report; but the example is given to help with understanding the calculations made.
- Total Income is calculated:
  - Sales:
    - Clothing & Accessory Sales $1,759.51
    - Equipment Sales 7,436.44
    - Equals Total Sales 9,195.95
    - Less: Sales Discounts -494.36
    - Plus: Returned Check Service Charges 25.00
  - Equals Total Income $8,726.59
- Cost of Goods Sold is calculated:
  - Less: Merchandise Discounts -49.90
  - Plus: Cost of Goods Sold-Other 3,492.46
    (The amount for the merchandise purchased)
  - Equals Total COGS 3,442.56
- Note the calculation to obtain the Net Income:
  - Total Income $8,726.59
  - Less: Total COGS -3,442.56
  - Equals Gross Profit 5,284.03
  - Less: Total Expenses -2,571.33
  - Plus: Interest Income 54.05
  - Equals Net Income $2,766.75

Close the **Profit & Loss Report**, do not close the Report Center

BALANCE SHEET (STANDARD)

The Balance Sheet proves the fundamental accounting equation: Assets = Liabilities + Owner's Equity. When all transactions and adjustments for the period have been recorded, a balance sheet should be prepared. QuickBooks has several different types of Balance Sheet statements available: Standard—shows as of the report dates the balance in each balance sheet account with subtotals provided for assets, liabilities, and equity; Detail—for each account the report shows the starting balance, transactions entered, and the ending balance during the period specified in the From and To dates; Summary—shows amounts for each account type but not for individual accounts; Prev. Year Comparison—has columns for the report date, the report date a year ago, $ change, and % change; and By Class—shows the value of your company or organization by class.

Since Your Name Mountain Sports is a partnership, separate equity accounts for each partner were established earlier in the chapter. You may explore the owner information in the Balance Sheet.

View a **Standard Balance Sheet Report**

Double-click **Balance Sheet Standard**
- Unless instructed otherwise, all Balance Sheets prepared will be Standard.

Tab to or click **As of,** enter **01/31/15**, tab to generate the report
Scroll through the report to view the assets, liabilities, and equities listed
- Notice the Equity section, especially the Investment and Drawing accounts for each owner.
- You will see that your investment and drawing accounts are separate from Larry's.
- Total 3100 Your Last Name & Muir, Capital shows a total of the capital for both owners.
- Notice that there is an amount shown for 3100 - Your Last Name & Muir, Capital – Other of $26,159.44. This balance shows how much "other" capital the owners share. Other capital can include things such as opening balances that represent value belonging to the owners. Originally, the capital for both owners was combined into one account. The report does not indicate how much of the "other" capital is for each owner.
- Notice the Net Income account listed in the **Equity** section of the report. This is the same amount of Net Income shown on the Profit & Loss Report.

7

Your Name Mountain Sports
Balance Sheet
As of January 31, 2015

	Jan 31, 15
ASSETS	
Current Assets	72,462.65
Fixed Assets	9,340.00
TOTAL ASSETS	81,802.65
LIABILITIES & EQUITY	
Liabilities	14,876.46
Equity	
3100 · Your Last Name & Muir, Capital	
3110 · First and Last Name, Capital	
3111 · First and Last Name, Investment	20,000.00
3112 · First and Last Name, Drawing	-1,000.00
Total 3110 · First and Last Name, Capital	19,000.00
3120 · Larry Muir, Capital	
3121 · Larry Muir, Investment	20,000.00
3122 · Larry Muir, Drawing	-1,000.00
Total 3120 · Larry Muir, Capital	19,000.00
3100 · Your Last Name & Muir, Capital - Other	26,159.44
Total 3100 · Your Last Name & Muir, Capital	64,159.44
Net Income	2,766.75
Total Equity	66,926.19
TOTAL LIABILITIES & EQUITY	81,802.65

Partial Report

Do not close the report

QUICKZOOM TO VIEW CAPITAL – OTHER ACCOUNT

As you learned earlier, QuickZoom is a QuickBooks feature that allows you to make a closer observation of transactions, amounts, etc. With QuickZoom, you may zoom in on an item when the mouse pointer turns into a magnifying glass with a Z inside. If you point to an item and you do not get a magnifying glass with a Z inside, you cannot zoom in on the item.

As you view the Balance Sheet, you will notice that the balance for 3100 - Your Last Name & Muir, Capital - Other is $26,159.44. To determine why there is an amount in Capital-Other, use QuickZoom to see the Transactions by Account report. You will see that the amounts for the beginning balances of the assets, liabilities, and the owners' equity have been entered in this account. Thus, the value of the Other Capital account proves the fundamental accounting equation of Assets = Liabilities + Owner's Equity.

Use QuickZoom to view the Your Last Name & Muir, Capital – Other account

Point to the amount 26,159.44, and double-click the primary mouse button
Change the report dates **From** is **12/31/14** and **To** is **01/31/15**, press Tab to generate the report

Your Name Mountain Sports
Transactions by Account
As of January 31, 2015

Type	Date	Num	Adj	Name	Memo	Clr	Split	Debit	Credit	Balance
Inventory Adjust	12/31/2014				Boots Opening balance	✓	1120 · Inventory Asset		600.00	12,775.00
Inventory Adjust	12/31/2014				Boots-Ski Opening balance	✓	1120 · Inventory Asset		1,125.00	13,900.00
Inventory Adjust	12/31/2014				Boots-Snowbrd Opening balance	✓	1120 · Inventory Asset		900.00	14,800.00
Inventory Adjust	12/31/2014				Gloves Opening balance	✓	1120 · Inventory Asset		330.00	15,130.00
Inventory Adjust	12/31/2014				Hats Opening balance	✓	1120 · Inventory Asset		240.00	15,370.00
Inventory Adjust	12/31/2014				Pants-Ski Opening balance	✓	1120 · Inventory Asset		2,850.00	18,220.00
Inventory Adjust	12/31/2014				Parkas Opening balance	✓	1120 · Inventory Asset		4,375.00	22,595.00
Inventory Adjust	12/31/2014				Poles-Ski Opening balance	✓	1120 · Inventory Asset		540.00	23,135.00
Inventory Adjust	12/31/2014				Skis Opening balance	✓	1120 · Inventory Asset		5,000.00	28,135.00
Inventory Adjust	12/31/2014				Snowboard Opening balance	✓	1120 · Inventory Asset		3,000.00	31,135.00
Inventory Adjust	12/31/2014				Socks Opening balance	✓	1120 · Inventory Asset		225.00	31,360.00
Inventory Adjust	12/31/2014				Sweaters Opening balance	✓	1120 · Inventory Asset		1,875.00	33,235.00
Inventory Adjust	12/31/2014				Underwear Opening balance	✓	1120 · Inventory Asset		264.00	33,499.00
Credit Card Charge	12/31/2014				Account Opening Balance		2100 · Visa	150.00		33,349.00
General Journal	12/31/2014				Account Opening Balance		2510 · Office Equipment Loan	3,000.00		30,349.00
General Journal	12/31/2014				Account Opening Balance		2520 · Store Fixtures Loan	2,500.00		27,849.00
Deposit	12/31/2014				Account Opening Balance		1100 · Checking		25,943.00	53,792.00
Deposit	12/31/2014				Account Opening Balance		1311 · Office Supplies		850.00	54,642.00
General Journal	12/31/2014				Account Opening Balance		1511 · Original Cost		5,000.00	59,642.00
General Journal	12/31/2014				Account Opening Balance		1521 · Original Cost		4,500.00	64,142.00
Deposit	12/31/2014				Account Opening Balance		1340 · Prepaid Insurance		250.00	64,392.00
General Journal	12/31/2014				Account Opening Balance		3111 · First and Last Name, Investment	20,000.00		44,392.00
General Journal	12/31/2014				Account Opening Balance		3121 · Larry Muir, Investment	20,000.00		24,392.00
Deposit	12/31/2014				Account Opening Balance		1312 · Sales Supplies		575.00	24,967.00
General Journal	12/31/2014						4999 · Uncategorized Income		6,942.44	31,909.44
General Journal	12/31/2014						6999 · Uncategorized Expenses	8,500.00		23,409.44
Inventory Adjust	01/08/2015				Sleds Opening balance	✓	1120 · Inventory Asset		675.00	24,084.44
Inventory Adjust	01/08/2015				Toboggans Opening balance	✓	1120 · Inventory Asset		1,375.00	25,459.44
Inventory Adjust	01/08/2015				Helmets Opening balance	✓	1120 · Inventory Asset		700.00	26,159.44
Total 3100 · Your Last Name & Muir, Capital								54,150.00	80,309.44	26,159.44
TOTAL								**54,150.00**	**80,309.44**	**26,159.44**

7

- Notice that the amounts shown include the amounts for the opening balances of all the assets including each inventory item, all the liabilities, the original investment amounts (equity), and uncategorized income and expenses.
- Uncategorized Income and Expenses reflect the income earned and expenses incurred prior to the current period. This prevents previous income/expenses being included in the calculation for the net income or loss for the current period.

Close the Transactions by Account report without printing
Do not close the Balance Sheet

DISTRIBUTE CAPITAL TO EACH OWNER

The Balance Sheet does not indicate how much of the Capital-Other should be distributed to each partner because 3100 - Your Last Name & Muir, Capital, is a combined Capital account. In order to clarify this section of the report, the capital should be distributed between the two owners. Since each owner has contributed an equal amount as an investment in the business, Capital-Other should be divided equally.

Make an adjusting entry to distribute Capital-Other between the two owners
Access the **Make General Journal Entries** screen as previously instructed
The **Date** is **01/31/15**
This is not an adjusting entry, so remove the check mark
Transfer the amount in the account **3100 - Your Last Name & Muir, Capital –Other** to the owners' individual capital accounts by debiting Account **3100** for **26159.44**
Memo for all entries in the transaction is **Transfer Capital to Partners**
Transfer one-half of the amount entered in the DEBIT column to **3110 – First and Last Name, Capital**, by crediting this account

- To determine one-half of the amount use QuickMath as follows: Click after the credit amount, press **/**, enter **2**, and press **Enter**.

Credit **3120 - Larry Muir, Capital**, for the other half of the amount

DATE 01/31/2015 ENTRY NO. ADJUSTING ENTRY

ACCOUNT	DEBIT	CREDIT	MEMO	NAME	BILLABLE?
3100 · Your Last Name & Muir, Capital	26,159.44		Transfer Capital to Partners		
3110 · First and Last Name, Capital		13,079.72	Transfer Capital to Partners		
3120 · Larry Muir, Capital		13,079.72	Transfer Capital to Partners		
Totals	26,159.44	26,159.44			

Click **Save & Close** to record and return to the Balance Sheet

- If the report does not automatically refresh, click **Refresh**.
- Notice the change in the Equity section of the Balance Sheet.
- The total of 3100 - Your Last Name & Muir, Capital, is still $64,159.44. There is no longer a 3100 - Your Last Name & Muir, Capital – Other account. Now, each owner has a Capital-Other account that shows 13,079.72.
- Look closely at the following balance sheet's equity section. Verify that your account setup matches the one shown in the text. Keep in mind that 3100 – Your Last Name & Muir, Capital, will show your actual last name. For example, the author's account would be Horne & Muir, Capital.
- Accounts 3110, 3111, 3112, and 3110 – Other should all have your actual <u>first</u> and <u>last</u> name rather than the words First and Last Name. For the author, Accounts 3110, 3111, 3112, and 3110 – Other would all have Janet Horne rather than First and Last Name.

Your Name Mountain Sports
Balance Sheet
As of January 31, 2015

	Jan 31, 15
▶ ASSETS	81,802.65
▼ LIABILITIES & EQUITY	
▶ Liabilities	14,876.46
▼ Equity	
▼ 3100 · Your Last Name & Muir, Capital	
▼ 3110 · First and Last Name, Capital	
3111 · First and Last Name, Investment	20,000.00
3112 · First and Last Name, Drawing	-1,000.00
3110 · First and Last Name, Capital - Other	13,079.72
Total 3110 · First and Last Name, Capital	32,079.72
▼ 3120 · Larry Muir, Capital	
3121 · Larry Muir, Investment	20,000.00
3122 · Larry Muir, Drawing	-1,000.00
3120 · Larry Muir, Capital - Other	13,079.72
Total 3120 · Larry Muir, Capital	32,079.72
Total 3100 · Your Last Name & Muir, Capital	64,159.44
Net Income	2,766.75
Total Equity	66,926.19
TOTAL LIABILITIES & EQUITY	81,802.65

Partial Report

Do not close the report

CLOSING ENTRIES

In traditional accrual-basis accounting, there are four entries that need to be made at the end of a fiscal year. These entries close income, expenses, and the drawing accounts and transfer the net income (or loss) into owners' equity.

Income and Expense accounts are closed when QuickBooks is given a closing date. This will occur later in this chapter. Once the closing date has been entered, reports prepared during the next fiscal year will not show any amounts in the income and expense accounts for the previous year.

However, QuickBooks does not close the owners' drawing accounts, nor does it transfer the net income into the owners' Capital accounts. If you prefer to use the power of the program and omit the last two closing entries, QuickBooks will keep a running account of the owner withdrawals, and it will put net income into an Owners' Equity account. However, transferring the net income and drawing into the owners' Capital accounts provides a clearer picture of the value of the owners' equity.

ADJUSTMENT TO TRANSFER NET INCOME

Because Your Name Mountain Sports is a partnership, the amount of net income should appear as part of each owner's capital account rather than appear as Owners' Equity. In many instances, this is the type of adjustment the CPA makes on the Accountant's Copy of the QuickBooks company files. The adjustment may be made before the closing date for the fiscal year, or it may be made after the closing has been performed. Because QuickBooks automatically transfers Net Income into Owner's Equity, which is categorized as a Retained Earnings Account type, the closing entry will transfer the net income into Owners' Equity and into each owner's capital account. This transfer is made by debiting Owners' Equity and crediting the owners' individual capital accounts. When you view a report before the end of the year, you will see an amount in Net Income and the same amount as a negative in Owners' Equity. If you view a report after the end of the year, you will not see any information regarding Owners' Equity or Net Income because the entry correctly transferred the amount to the owners' capital accounts.

On the Balance Sheet, Owners' Equity and/or Net Income appear as part of the equity section. The owners' Drawing and Investment accounts are kept separate from Owners' Equity at all times.

Evenly divide and transfer the net income into the 3110 - First and Last Name, Capital and 3120 - Larry Muir, Capital accounts

Open the **General Journal** as previously instructed
- Leave Adjusting Entry unmarked.

The **Date** is **01/31/15**
The first account used is **3000 Owners' Equity**
Debit **3000 Owners' Equity**, the amount of Net Income **2,766.75**
- Remember, Owner's Equity is a Retained Earnings type of account and contains all of the net income earned by the business.

For the Memo record **Transfer Net Income into Capital**
Click the drop-down list arrow on the second line and select **3110 - First and Last Name, Capital** as the account
Use QuickMath to divide the 2,766.75 in half
Click after the 2,766.75 in the credit column, type /, type **2**, press **Enter**
- A credit amount of **1,383.38** should be entered for **3110 - First and Last Name, Capital**.

Click the drop-down list arrow and select **3120 Larry Muir, Capital** as the account, press Tab
- QuickBooks enters **1,383.37** as the credit amount for the next line.
- Because QuickBooks accepts only two numbers after a decimal point, the cents must be rounded. Thus, there is a 1¢ difference in the distribution between the two owners. If there is an uneven amount in the future, Larry will receive the extra amount.

The Memo should be the same for all three lines

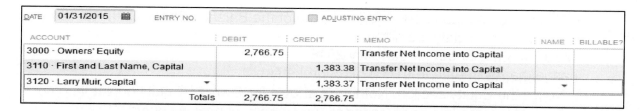

DATE 01/31/2015 ENTRY NO. ADJUSTING ENTRY

ACCOUNT	DEBIT	CREDIT	MEMO	NAME	BILLABLE?
3000 - Owners' Equity	2,766.75		Transfer Net Income into Capital		
3110 - First and Last Name, Capital		1,383.38	Transfer Net Income into Capital		
3120 - Larry Muir, Capital		1,383.37	Transfer Net Income into Capital		
Totals	2,766.75	2,766.75			

- Not all companies have a profit each month. If your business has a negative amount for net income, in other words, a loss, the appropriate adjustment would be to debit each owner's individual capital account and to credit Owners' Equity. For example, if Net Income (Loss) was -500.00, you would record the following: 3110 - First and Last Name, Capital—debit 250; 3120 - Larry Muir, Capital—debit 250; and 3000 Owners' Equity—credit 500.

Click **Save & Close** to record and close the **General Journal**

- If you get a Retained Earnings dialog box regarding posting a transaction to the Retained Earnings account "Owners' Equity," click **OK**.

VIEW BALANCE SHEET

Once the adjustment for Net Income/Owners' Equity has been performed, viewing or printing the Balance Sheet will show you the status of the Owners' Equity. If you keep the year as 2015, both Owners' Equity and Net Income are shown in the report. However, a Balance Sheet prepared for 2016 will show nothing for Owners' Equity or Net Income.

Observe the effect of the adjustment to the owners' equity

Since you did not close the report, the Balance Sheet should still be on the screen

Your Name Mountain Sports
Balance Sheet
As of January 31, 2015

	Jan 31, 15
ASSETS	81,802.65
LIABILITIES & EQUITY	
Liabilities	14,876.46
Equity	
3000 · Owners' Equity	-2,766.75
3100 · Your Last Name & Muir, Capital	
3110 · First and Last Name, Capital	
3111 · First and Last Name, Investment	20,000.00
3112 · First and Last Name, Drawing	-1,000.00
3110 · First and Last Name, Capital - Other	14,463.10
Total 3110 · First and Last Name, Capital	33,463.10
3120 · Larry Muir, Capital	
3121 · Larry Muir, Investment	20,000.00
3122 · Larry Muir, Drawing	-1,000.00
3120 · Larry Muir, Capital - Other	14,463.09
Total 3120 · Larry Muir, Capital	33,463.09
Total 3100 · Your Last Name & Muir, Capital	66,926.19
Net Income	2,766.75
Total Equity	66,926.19
TOTAL LIABILITIES & EQUITY	81,802.65

Partial Report

7

- Notice the change in the **Equity** section of the Balance Sheet. Both Net Income and Owners' Equity are shown.

View a **Balance Sheet** for **January 2016**

Change the **As of** date to **01/31/2016**, press **Tab**

- Notice the Equity section. Nothing is shown for Owners' Equity or Net Income.
- The net income has been added to the owners' capital accounts.

Your Name Mountain Sports
Balance Sheet
As of January 31, 2016

	Jan 31, 16
ASSETS	81,802.65
LIABILITIES & EQUITY	
Liabilities	14,876.46
Equity	
3100 · Your Last Name & Muir, Capital	
3110 · First and Last Name, Capital	
3111 · First and Last Name, Investment	20,000.00
3112 · First and Last Name, Drawing	-1,000.00
3110 · First and Last Name, Capital - Other	14,463.10
Total 3110 · First and Last Name, Capital	33,463.10
3120 · Larry Muir, Capital	
3121 · Larry Muir, Investment	20,000.00
3122 · Larry Muir, Drawing	-1,000.00
3120 · Larry Muir, Capital - Other	14,463.09
Total 3120 · Larry Muir, Capital	33,463.09
Total 3100 · Your Last Name & Muir, Capital	66,926.19
Total Equity	66,926.19
TOTAL LIABILITIES & EQUITY	81,802.65

Partial Report

Change the **As of** date for the Balance Sheet to **01/31/15**

- The Equity section once again shows both Owners' Equity and Net Income.

Do not close the report

CLOSE DRAWING

The entry transferring the net income into each owner's capital account has already been made. While this is not the actual end of the fiscal year for Your Name Mountain Sports, the closing entry for the Drawing accounts will be entered at this time so that you will have experience in recording this entry.

MEMO
DATE: January 31, 2015

Record the closing entry to close 3112 – First and Last Name, Drawing, and 3122 - Larry Muir, Drawing, into each owner's capital account.

Closing Drawing for each owner

Access **Make General Journal Entries** as previously instructed

The DATE is **01/31/2015**

- Leave Adjusting Entry unmarked.

Debit **3110 – First and Last Name, Capital**, for the amount of the drawing account **1,000**

The Memo for the transaction is **Close Drawing**

Credit **3112 – First and Last Name, Drawing**, for **1,000**

DATE 01/31/2015 ENTRY NO. ADJUSTING ENTRY

ACCOUNT	DEBIT	CREDIT	MEMO	NAME	BILLABLE?
3110 · First and Last Name, Capital	1,000.00		Close Drawing		
3112 · First and Last Name, Drawing		1,000.00	Close Drawing		
Totals	1,000.00	1,000.00			

Click the **New** icon on the Make General Journal Entries Main Icon bar

Repeat the above steps to close **3122 - Larry Muir, Drawing** to his Capital account

DATE 01/31/2015 ENTRY NO. ADJUSTING ENTRY

ACCOUNT	DEBIT	CREDIT	MEMO	NAME	BILLABLE?
3120 · Larry Muir, Capital	1,000.00		Close Drawing		
3122 · Larry Muir, Drawing		1,000.00	Close Drawing		
Totals	1,000.00	1,000.00			

Click **Save & Close** and return to the Balance Sheet

- Notice the change in the **Equity** section of the Balance Sheet.

Your Name Mountain Sports
Balance Sheet
As of January 31, 2015

	Jan 31, 15
ASSETS	81,802.65
LIABILITIES & EQUITY	
Liabilities	14,876.46
Equity	
3000 · Owners' Equity	-2,766.75
3100 · Your Last Name & Muir, Capital	
3110 · First and Last Name, Capital	
3111 · First and Last Name, Investment	20,000.00
3110 · First and Last Name, Capital - Other	13,463.10
Total 3110 · First and Last Name, Capital	33,463.10
3120 · Larry Muir, Capital	
3121 · Larry Muir, Investment	20,000.00
3120 · Larry Muir, Capital - Other	13,463.09
Total 3120 · Larry Muir, Capital	33,463.09
Total 3100 · Your Last Name & Muir, Capital	66,926.19
Net Income	2,766.75
Total Equity	66,926.19
TOTAL LIABILITIES & EQUITY	81,802.65

Partial Report

Close the report and the Report Center

JOURNAL ENTRIES ENTERED/MODIFIED TODAY REPORT

When you record several entries into the General Journal during a given day, it can be helpful to see what has been recorded. The report is prepared in the Accountant Center.

Prepare Journal Entries Entered/Modified Today report in the Accountant Center

Point to **Accountant** on the Menu bar; click **Accountant Center**
In the **Memorized Reports** section, click **Journal Entries Entered/Modified Today**

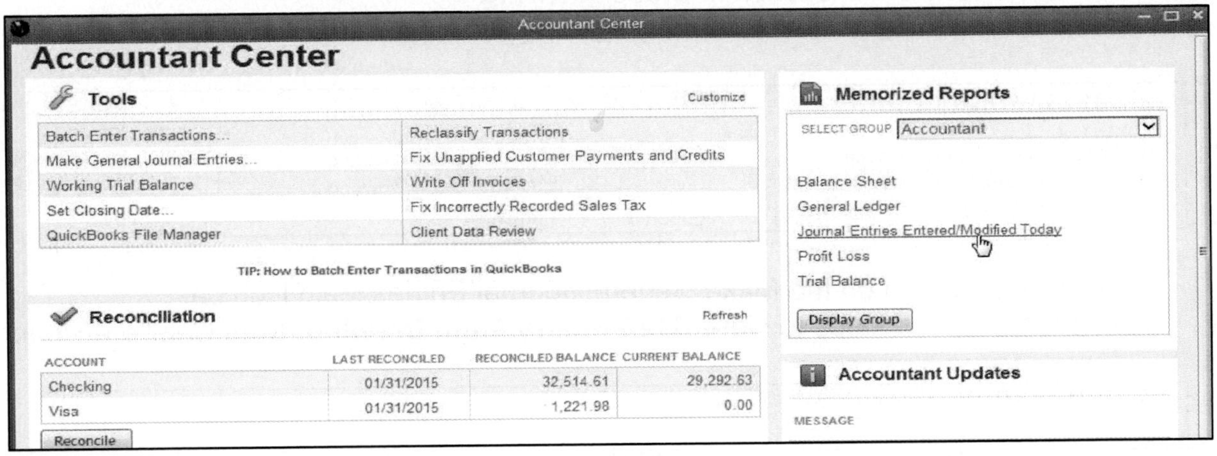

Since the date of your computer will not be 01/31/2015, enter the dates **From 01/31/15** and **To 01/31/15**, press Tab

Remove the Date Prepared and Time Prepared from the header

- This is a Memorized Report so does not use our header preferences.

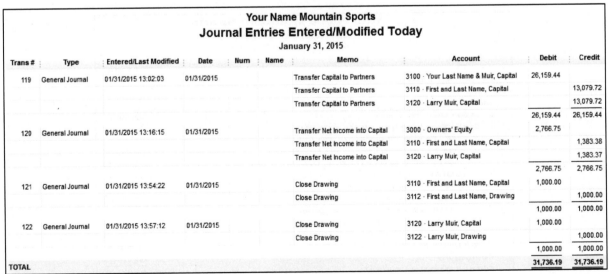

Your Name Mountain Sports
Journal Entries Entered/Modified Today
January 31, 2015

Trans #	Type	Entered/Last Modified	Date	Num	Name	Memo	Account	Debit	Credit
119	General Journal	01/31/2015 13:02:03	01/31/2015			Transfer Capital to Partners	3100 · Your Last Name & Muir, Capital	26,159.44	
						Transfer Capital to Partners	3110 · First and Last Name, Capital		13,079.72
						Transfer Capital to Partners	3120 · Larry Muir, Capital		13,079.72
								26,159.44	26,159.44
120	General Journal	01/31/2015 13:16:15	01/31/2015			Transfer Net Income into Capital	3000 · Owners' Equity	2,766.75	
						Transfer Net Income into Capital	3110 · First and Last Name, Capital		1,383.38
						Transfer Net Income into Capital	3120 · Larry Muir, Capital		1,383.37
								2,766.75	2,766.75
121	General Journal	01/31/2015 13:54:22	01/31/2015			Close Drawing	3110 · First and Last Name, Capital	1,000.00	
						Close Drawing	3112 · First and Last Name, Drawing		1,000.00
								1,000.00	1,000.00
122	General Journal	01/31/2015 13:57:12	01/31/2015			Close Drawing	3120 · Larry Muir, Capital	1,000.00	
						Close Drawing	3122 · Larry Muir, Drawing		1,000.00
								1,000.00	1,000.00
TOTAL								31,736.19	31,736.19

Partial Report

Do not print the report; close the report unless you are completing the following exercise

EXPORTING REPORTS TO EXCEL (OPTIONAL)

Many of the reports prepared in QuickBooks can be exported to Microsoft Excel. This allows you to take advantage of extensive filtering options available in Excel, hide detail for some but not all groups of data, combine information from two different reports, change titles of columns, add comments, change the order of columns, and experiment with "what if" scenarios. In order to use this feature of QuickBooks you must also have Microsoft Excel available for use on your computer.

Optional Exercise: Export a report from QuickBooks to Excel

With the **Journal Entries Entered/Modified Today** report showing on the screen, click the **Excel** button, click **Create New Worksheet**

On the Send Report to Excel message, make sure **Create New Worksheet** and **in a new workbook** are selected or click to select

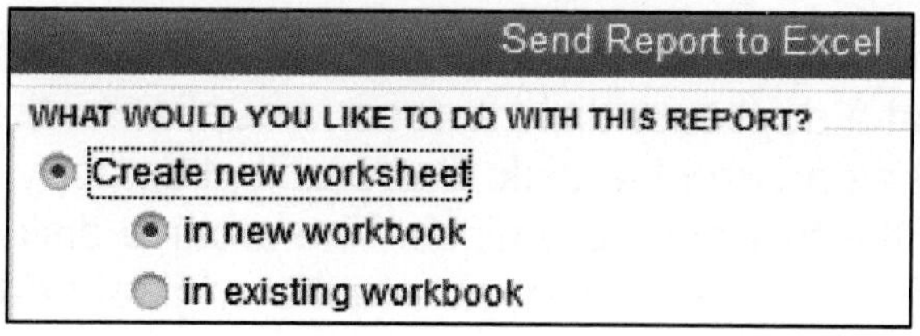

Click **Export**

- The report will be displayed in Excel.

Scroll through the report and click in Cell A31

Type **JOURNAL ENTRIES ENTERED/MODIFIED TODAY EXPORTED TO EXCEL**

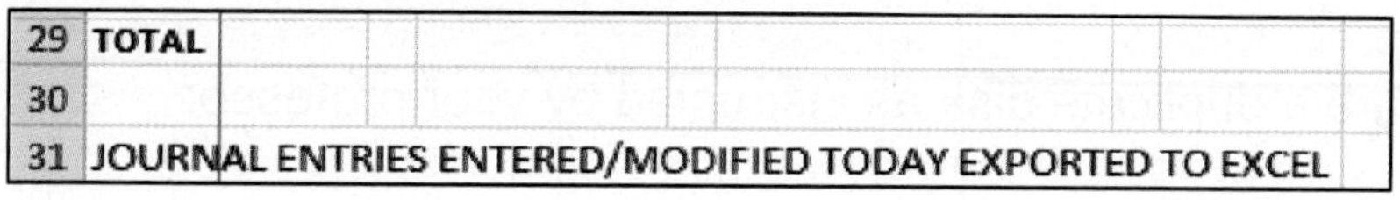

Click the **Close** button in the upper right corner of the Excel title bar to close **Excel**

Click **Don't Save** to close without saving

- You will see a Book number on the screen. The Book number changes depending on how many times you export reports to Excel.

Return to QuickBooks and close the report and the Accountant Center

IMPORTING DATA FROM EXCEL

There are several ways to import data into QuickBooks: You may use Intuit Interchange Format (.IIF) files to import lists, transactions, and data. You may also import an existing Excel or CSV file; you can enter data into a specially formatted spreadsheet and then add it to QuickBooks; or you can copy and paste data from Excel into QuickBooks by using the Add/Edit Multiple List Entries. An import file must conform to a specific structure for QuickBooks to interpret the data in the file correctly. QuickBooks has a built in Reference Guide for Importing Files that may be accessed and printed through Help. (Refer to Appendix B for more detailed information.)

JOURNAL FOR JANUARY

It is always wise to have a printed or hard copy of the data on disk. After all entries and adjustments for the month have been made, the Journal for January should be printed. This copy should be kept on file as an additional backup to the data stored on your disk. If something happens to your disk to damage it, you will still have the paper copy of your transactions available for re-entry into the system. Normally, the Journal would be printed before closing the period; however, we will print the Journal at the end of the chapter so that all entries are included.

END-OF-PERIOD BACKUP

Once all end-of-period procedures have been completed, in addition to a regular backup copy of company data and a duplicate disk, a second duplicate disk of the company data should be made and filed as an archive disk. Preferably, this copy will be located someplace other than on the business premises. The archive disk or file copy is set aside in case of emergency or in case damage occurs to the original and current backup copies of the company data.

Back up company data and prepare an archive copy of the company data

Prepare a Back Up as previously instructed

- In the **File Name** text box enter **Sports (Archive 1-31-15)** as the name for the backup.

Also prepare a duplicate disk as instructed by your professor

PASSWORDS

Not every employee of a business should have access to all the financial records. In some companies, only the owner(s) will have complete access. In others, one or two key employees will have full access while other employees are provided limited access based on the jobs they perform. Passwords are secret words used to control access to data. QuickBooks has several options available to assign passwords.

In order to assign any passwords at all, you must have an administrator. The administrator has unrestricted access to all QuickBooks functions and sets up users, user passwords, and assigns areas of transaction access for each user. Areas of access can be limited to transaction entry for certain types of transactions or a user may have unrestricted access into all areas of QuickBooks and company data. To obtain more information regarding QuickBooks' passwords, refer to Help.

A password should be kept secret at all times. In QuickBooks passwords are case sensitive. It is wise to use a complex password. The requirements for a password to be accepted as complex are: a minimum of seven characters including at least one number and one uppercase letter. Use of special characters is also helpful. Complex passwords should be changed every 90 days. Make sure your password is something you won't forget. Otherwise, you will not be able to access your Company file. Since the focus of the text is in training in all aspects of QuickBooks, no passwords will be assigned.

CLOSE THE PERIOD

A closing date assigned to transactions for a period helps to prevent changing data from the closed period. To change a transaction after closing, you must acknowledge the entry in a dialog box before the change will be recorded. This is helpful to discourage casual changes or transaction deletions to a previous period. Setting the closing date is done by accessing Accounting Preferences in QuickBooks. Setting a closing date also closes the income and expenses for the period.

MEMO

DATE: January 31, 2015

Now that the closing entries for drawing and net income have been made, you want to protect the data and close income and expenses for the period. Set a closing date of 1/31/15.

Assign the closing date of **01/31/15** to the transactions for the period ending 1/31/15

Click **Edit** on the menu bar, click **Preferences**
Click **Accounting**, click **Company Preferences** tab
Click the **Set Date/Password** button
Enter **01/31/15** as the closing date in the Closing Date section of the Company Preferences for Accounting
Do not set any passwords at this time

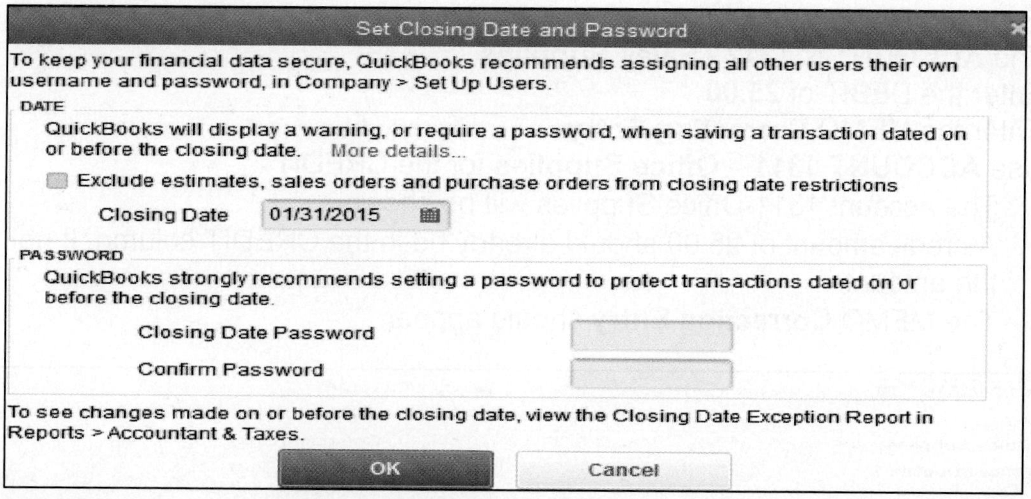

Set Closing Date and Password
To keep your financial data secure, QuickBooks recommends assigning all other users their own username and password, in Company > Set Up Users.
DATE
QuickBooks will display a warning, or require a password, when saving a transaction dated on or before the closing date. More details...
Exclude estimates, sales orders and purchase orders from closing date restrictions
Closing Date
01/31/2015
PASSWORD
QuickBooks strongly recommends setting a password to protect transactions dated on or before the closing date.
Closing Date Password
Confirm Password
To see changes made on or before the closing date, view the Closing Date Exception Report in Reports > Accountant & Taxes.
OK
Cancel

Click **OK**

Click **No** on the No Password Entered dialog box

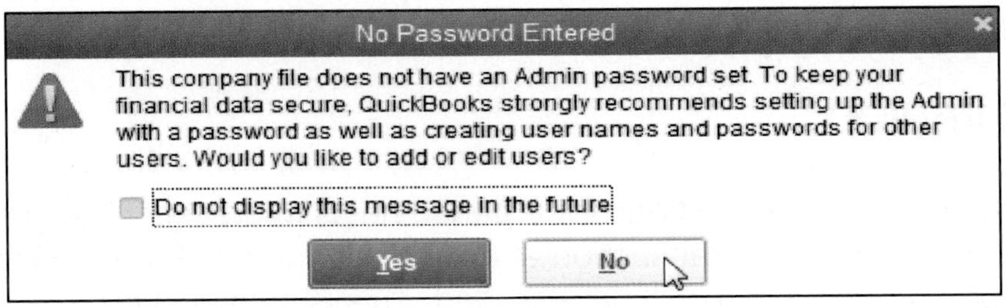

Click **OK** to close Preferences

ENTER CORRECTION TO CLOSED PERIOD

If it is determined that an error was made in a previous period, a correction is allowed. Before it will record any changes for previous periods, QuickBooks requires answering Yes on a dialog box warning of a change to a transaction that is prior to the closing date.

MEMO
DATE: January 31, 2015

After entering the closing date, Ruth reviews the Journal and reports printed at the end of January. She finds that $25 of the amount of Office Supplies should have been recorded as Sales Supplies. Transfer $25 from Office Supplies to Sales Supplies.

Transfer $25 from Office Supplies to Sales Supplies

Access the **General Journal** as previously instructed
ADJUSTING ENTRY should be marked
Enter the DATE of **01/31/15**
The **ACCOUNT** is **1312 - Sales Supplies**
Enter the DEBIT of **25.00**
Enter the MEMO **Correcting Entry**
Use **ACCOUNT 1311 – Office Supplies** for the CREDIT

- The account 1311-Office Supplies will be shown.
- A credit amount of 25.00 should already be in the CREDIT column. If not, enter the amount.
- The MEMO **Correcting Entry** should appear.

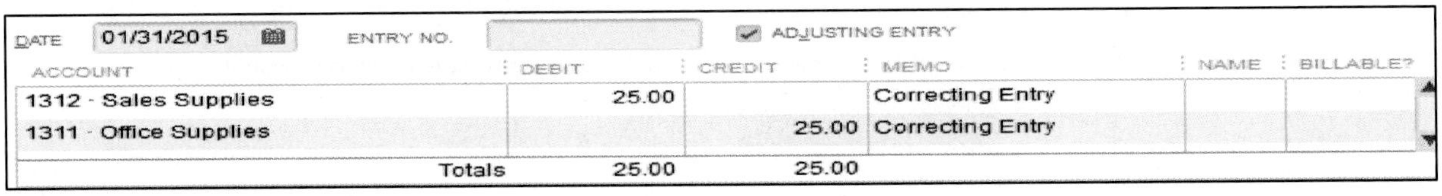

DATE 01/31/2015
ENTRY NO.
ADJUSTING ENTRY
ACCOUNT
DEBIT
CREDIT
MEMO
NAME
BILLABLE?
1312 · Sales Supplies
25.00
Correcting Entry
1311 · Office Supplies
25.00
Correcting Entry
Totals
25.00
25.00

Click **Save & Close**

Click **Yes** on the **QuickBooks** dialog box

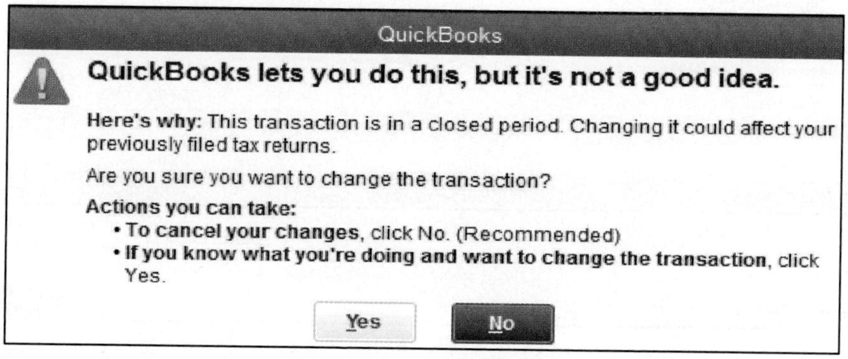

VERIFY CORRECTION TO OFFICE AND SALES SUPPLIES

Once the correction has been made, it is important to view the change in the accounts. The transfer of an amount of one asset into another will have no direct effect on the total assets in your reports. The account balances for Office Supplies and Sales Supplies will be changed. To view the change in the account, open the Chart of Accounts and look at the balance of each account. You may also use the account register to view the correcting entry as it was recorded in each account.

MEMO
DATE: January 31, 2015

Access the Chart of Accounts and view the change in the account balances and the correcting entry in each account's register.

View the correcting entry in each account

Open the **Chart of Accounts** as previously instructed

- The balance for Office Supplies has been changed from 521.98 to 496.98.
- The balance for Sales Supplies has been changed from 400.00 to 425.00.

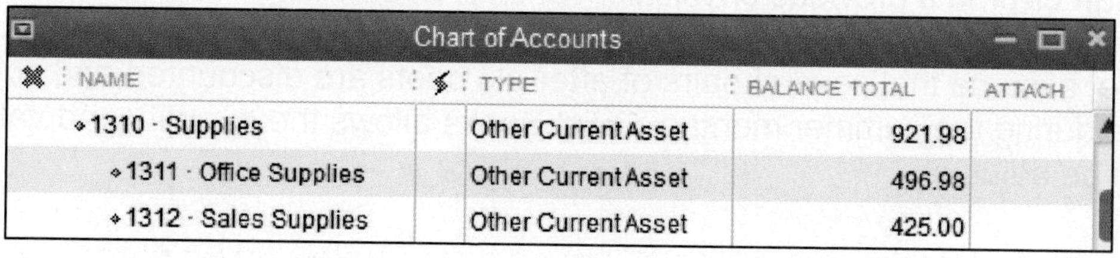
Chart of Accounts

NAME	TYPE	BALANCE TOTAL	ATTACH
◆1310 · Supplies	Other Current Asset	921.98	
◆1311 · Office Supplies	Other Current Asset	496.98	
◆1312 · Sales Supplies	Other Current Asset	425.00	

Double-click **Office Supplies** to open the account register

- Verify that the correcting entry was recorded for Office Supplies.

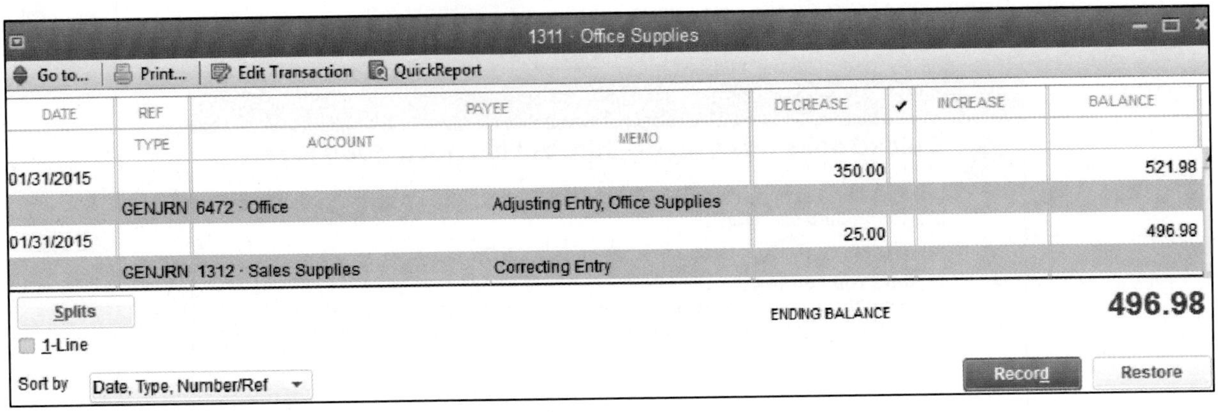

Close the **Office Supplies Register**
Repeat the steps to view the correcting entry in Sales Supplies

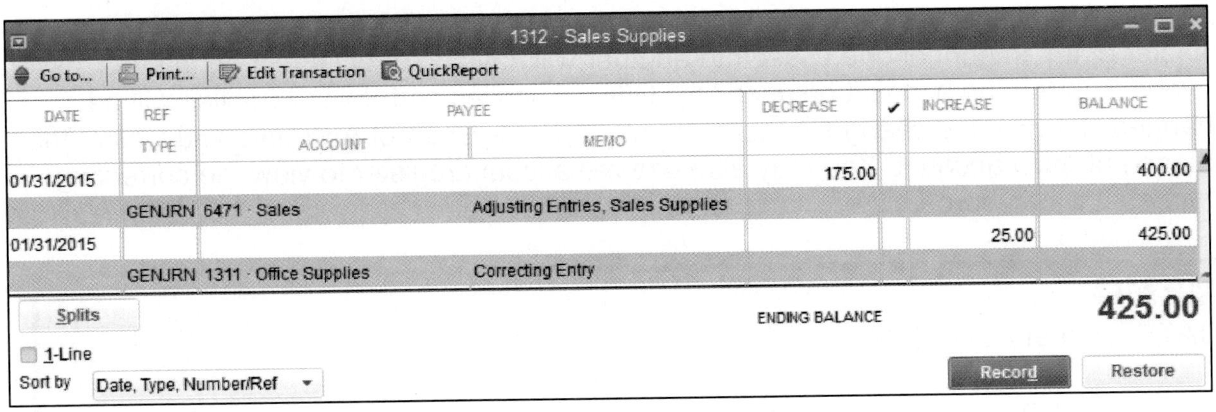

Close the **Sales Supplies Register** and the **Chart of Accounts**

INVENTORY ADJUSTMENTS

In a business that has inventory, it is possible that after a physical inventory is taken the number of items on hand is different from the quantity shown in QuickBooks. This can be caused by a variety of items: loss due to theft, fire, or flood; damage to an item in the stockroom; an error in a previous physical inventory. Even though QuickBooks uses the average cost method of inventory valuation, the value of an item can be changed as well. For example, assume that several pairs of after-ski boots are discounted and sold for a lesser value during the summer months. QuickBooks allows the quantity and value of inventory to be adjusted.

MEMO

DATE: January 31, 2015

After taking a physical inventory, you discover two hats were placed next to the cleaning supplies and are discolored because bleach was spilled on them. These hats must be discarded. Record this as an adjustment to the quantity of inventory. Use the Expense account 6190 Merchandise Adjustments to record this adjustment.

Adjust the quantity of hats

QuickBooks values inventory using the Average Cost Method

Open the Item List as previously instructed, double-click **Hats**

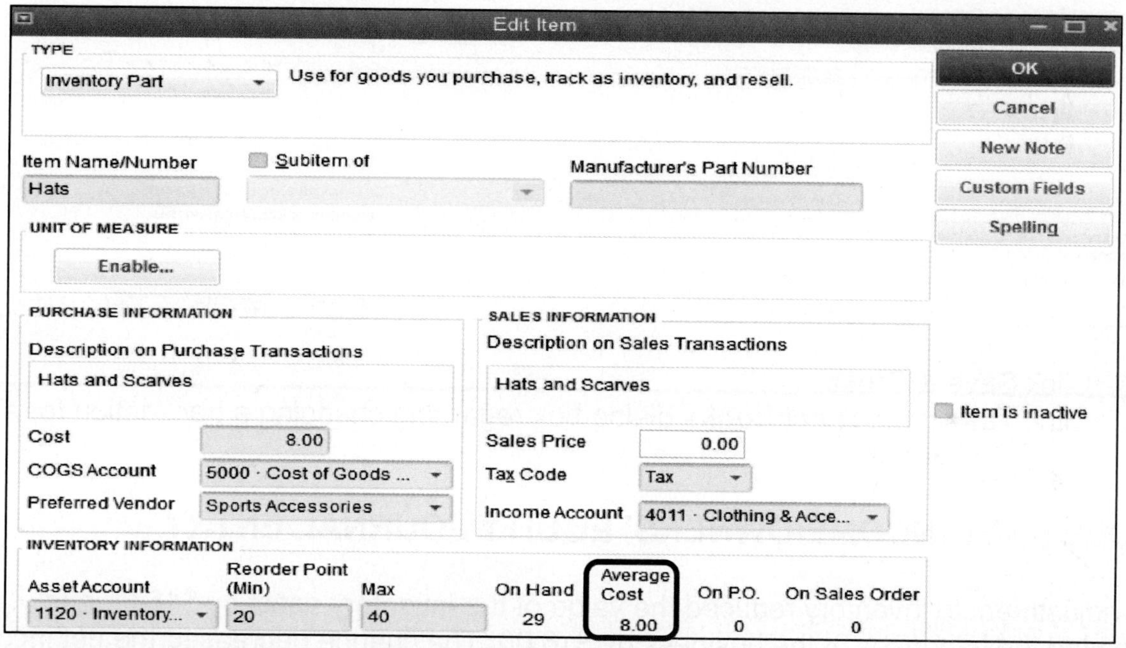

- Note the Avg. Cost of 8.00 for Hats.

Close the Edit Item screen and the Item List

Click the drop-down arrow on the **Inventory Activities** icon in the Company section of the QuickBooks Home Page

Click **Adjust Quantity/Value On Hand...** in the list shown

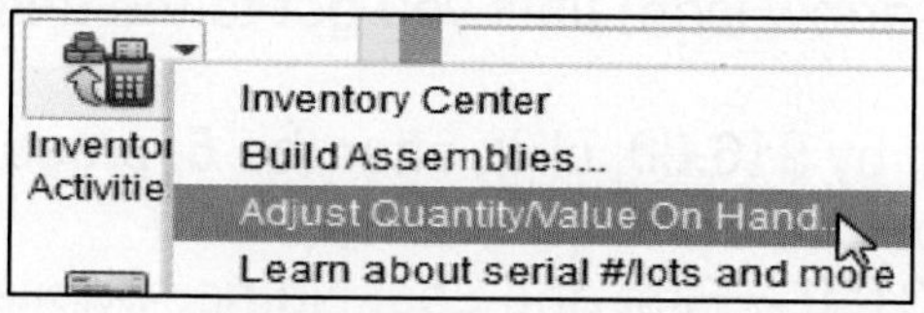

Enter the adjustment date of **013115**

Click the drop-down list arrow next to **Adjustment Account**

Click **<Add New>**

Enter the new account information:

Type is **Expense**; Number is **6190**; Name is **Merchandise Adjustments**

Click **Save & Close** to add the account

Click in the **ITEM** column, click the drop-down list arrow, and click **Hats**

Click in the **NEW QUANTITY** column for Hats

Enter **27**

Press **Tab** to enter the change

- Notice that the Total Value of the Adjustment is -16.00, which is -8.00 for each hat. The number of Item Adjustments is one. The Quantity on Hand is 27, Avg. Cost per Item is 8.00, and the Value is 216.00.

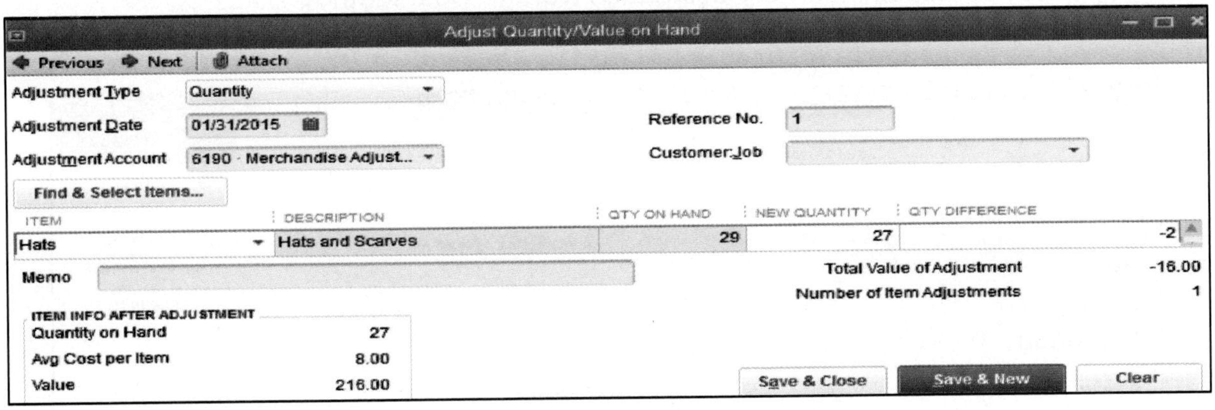

Click **Save & Close**

Click **Yes** on the **QuickBooks** dialog box regarding changing a transaction for a closed period

ADJUST NET INCOME/OWNERS' EQUITY JOURNAL ENTRY

The adjustment to inventory reduced the value of the inventory asset by $16.00 and increased the expenses of the business by $16.00. The change decreased the net income by $16.00; thus, the entry for Net Income/Owners' Equity made previously needs to be changed.

Adjust the net income

Access **Make General Journal Entries**

Click **Previous** (back arrow icon) until you get to the entry debiting Owners' Equity for 2,766.75

To reduce the amount by $16.00, click after the **5**, press **–**, key in **16**, press **Enter** to change the debit to Owners' Equity to **2,750.75**

Change the credit to 3110 – First and Last Name, Capital by half of the amount of the adjustment (16 / 2 = 8) thus, 1383.38 – 8 = **1,375.38**

Change the credit to 3120 - Larry Muir, Capital by half the amount to **1,375.37**

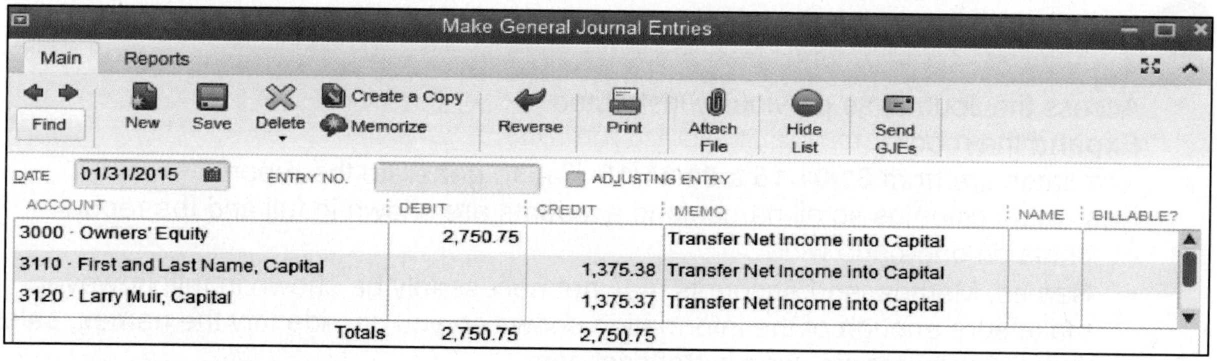

Click **Save & Close**

Click **Yes** or **OK** on all the dialog boxes for saving a changed transaction, recording a transaction for a closed period, and posting a transaction to Retained Earnings/Owners' Equity

REDO ARCHIVE COPY OF COMPANY FILE

Since we have made changes to transactions for the closed period, the archive copy of the company file should be redone.

Create an archive copy of the company data

Replace the previous file **Sports (Backup Archive 1-31-15)**

Follow the procedures given previously to make your backup files

REPORTS

After closing entries have been entered, it is important to print post-closing reports. Normally, those reports are dated as of the last day of or for the period. The only exception to the reports is the Profit & Loss Statement. In order to see that the income and expenses have been closed, the report has to be prepared as of the first day of the next period.

MEMO

DATE: January 31, 2015

Prepare and print the following reports for Your Name Mountain Sports as of or for 01/31/15: Journal, Trial Balance, Profit & Loss Report, and Balance Sheet.

JOURNAL

Since the Journal was not printed before closing the period, it should be printed at this time. This will give a printed copy of all the transactions made in Chapters 5, 6, and 7.

Print the **Journal** for January

Access the Journal as previously instructed
Expand the report
The dates are from **01/01/15** to**01/31/15**; Tab to generate the report
Resize the columns so all names and accounts are shown in full and the report prints on one-page wide

- Names, Memos, and Accounts may not necessarily be shown in full; however, make sure enough of the information shows so you can identify the names, sales items, and accounts used in transactions.

Your Name Mountain Sports
Journal
January 2015

Trans #	Type	Date	Num	Adj	Name	Memo	Account	Debit	Credit
119	General Journal	01/31/2015				Transfer Capital to Partners	3100 · Your Last Name & Muir, Capital	26,159.44	
						Transfer Capital to Partners	3110 · First and Last Name, Capital		13,079.72
						Transfer Capital to Partners	3120 · Larry Muir, Capital		13,079.72
								26,159.44	26,159.44
120	General Journal	01/31/2015				Transfer Net Income into Capital	3000 · Owners' Equity	2,750.75	
						Transfer Net Income into Capital	3110 · First and Last Name, Capital		1,375.38
						Transfer Net Income into Capital	3120 · Larry Muir, Capital		1,375.37
								2,750.75	2,750.75
121	General Journal	01/31/2015				Close Drawing	3110 · First and Last Name, Capital	1,000.00	
						Close Drawing	3112 · First and Last Name, Drawing		1,000.00
								1,000.00	1,000.00
122	General Journal	01/31/2015				Close Drawing	3120 · Larry Muir, Capital	1,000.00	
						Close Drawing	3122 · Larry Muir, Drawing		1,000.00
								1,000.00	1,000.00
123	General Journal	01/31/2015		✓		Correcting Entry	1312 · Sales Supplies	25.00	
				✓		Correcting Entry	1311 · Office Supplies		25.00
								25.00	25.00
124	Inventory Adjust	01/31/2015	1				6190 · Merchandise Adjustments	16.00	
						Hats Inventory Adjustment	1120 · Inventory Asset		16.00
								16.00	16.00
TOTAL								81,285.13	81,285.13

Partial Report

Print the report in **Landscape** orientation
Close the **Journal**

PREPARE MULTIPLE REPORTS

When you are preparing a lot of reports at the same time, you have the option of telling QuickBooks to prepare multiple reports. While not every available report may be selected, there are a number of frequently prepared reports available. If you have customized report preferences, they will not be applied to multiple reports.

Prepare and print the Trial Balance, the Profit & Loss Report, and the Balance Sheet using Multiple Reports

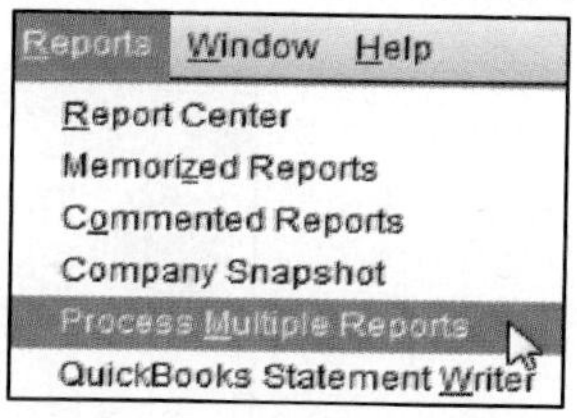

Click **Reports** on the Menu Bar
Click **Process Multiple Reports**
On the Process Multiple Reports screen, select <All Reports>
Click **Accountant: Balance Sheet**, enter the report dates
From **01/01/15** To **01/31/15**
Repeat for Accountant: Profit & Loss, and Accountant: Trial Balance

- You can print reports directly from this screen or you can display the reports and then print from the actual reports.

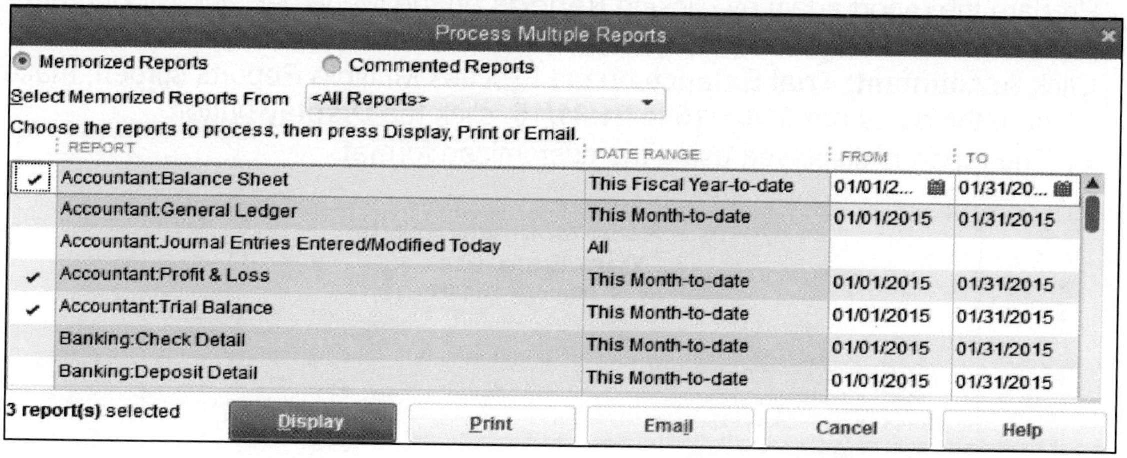

Click the **Display** button
With the reports on the screen, complete the following sections

TRIAL BALANCE

After closing the period has been completed, it is helpful to print a Trial Balance. This proves that debits still equal credits.

Print a **Trial Balance** to prove debits still equal credits

7

Scroll through the report and study the amounts shown

- Notice that the final totals of debits and credits are equal.
- In Chapter 5, the header information for the report was customized so that it did not show the Date Prepared, Time Prepared, or Report Basis. That would apply to reports prepared from the Report Center or Reports menu not to Multiple Reports.

Customize the Report so the Date Prepared, Time Prepared, and Report Basis are not displayed
Make sure the columns are displayed in full
To save this format in the Multiple Report list, click the **Memorize** button

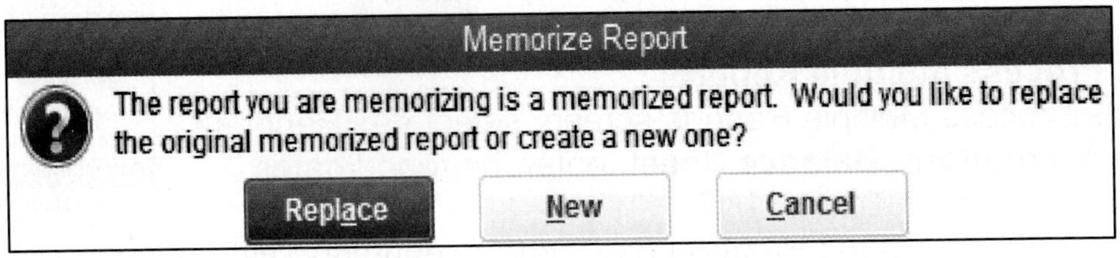

Click **Replace** on the Memorize Report message box

Close the Trial Balance

Prepare the report again by clicking **Reports** on the Menu bar, and clicking **Multiple Reports**

Click **Accountant: Trial Balance** on the Process Multiple Reports screen, make sure the dates are **01/01/15** to **01/31/15**, click the **Display** button

- The report is displayed using the customized format.

Your Name Mountain Sports
Trial Balance
As of January 31, 2015

	Jan 31, 15	
	Debit	Credit
6120 · Bank Service Charges	18.00	
6140 · Advertising Expense	95.00	
6150 · Depreciation Expense	160.00	
6181 · Liability Insurance	125.00	
6190 · Merchandise Adjustments	16.00	
6212 · Loan Interest	97.93	
6300 · Rent	950.00	
6340 · Telephone	156.40	
6391 · Gas and Electric	359.00	
6392 · Water	85.00	
6471 · Sales	175.00	
6472 · Office	350.00	
7010 · Interest Income		54.05
TOTAL	91,271.55	91,271.55

Partial Report

Print in **Portrait** orientation, then close the report

PROFIT & LOSS REPORT

Since the closing was done as of January 31, 2015, the Profit & Loss Report for January 31, 2015 will give the same data as a Profit & Loss Report prepared manually on January 31, 2015. To verify the closing of income and expense accounts for January, you would prepare a Profit & Loss Report for February 1. Since no income had been earned or expenses incurred in the new period, February, the Net Income will show $0.00.

Print a Profit & Loss report for January and view the report for February

The report should be showing on the screen, remove the Date Prepared, Time Prepared, and Report Basis as previously instructed

Your Name Mountain Sports
Profit & Loss
January 2015

	Jan 15
Ordinary Income/Expense	
Income	
4010 · Sales	9,195.95
4050 · Sales Discounts	-494.36
4090 · Returned Check Charges	25.00
Total Income	8,726.59
Cost of Goods Sold	
5000 · Cost of Goods Sold	3,442.56
Total COGS	3,442.56
Gross Profit	5,284.03
Expense	2,587.33
Net Ordinary Income	2,696.70
Other Income/Expense	
Other Income	54.05
Net Other Income	54.05
Net Income	2,750.75

Partial Report

- Note the Net Income of $2,750.75.

Print the January report in **Portrait** orientation
To view the effect of closing the period, prepare a Profit & Loss for February
Change the dates From **02/01/15** to **02/01/15**, tab to generate the report

Your Name Mountain Sports
Profit & Loss
February 1, 2015

	Feb 1, 15
Net Income	0.00

- Note the Net Income of **0.00**.

Close the **February Profit & Loss Report** without printing

BALANCE SHEET

The proof that assets equal liabilities and owners' equity after the closing entries have been made needs to be displayed in a Balance Sheet. Because this report is for a month, the adjustment to Owners' Equity and Net Income will result in both of the accounts being included on the Balance Sheet. If, however, this report were prepared for the year, neither account would appear.

Print a Balance Sheet report for January 31, 2015

The report should be showing on the screen, customize the header to remove the Date Prepared, Time Prepared, and Report Basis
Scroll through the report to view the assets, liabilities, and equities listed

- Because this report is for a one-month period, both Owners' Equity and Net Income are included on this report.

Your Name Mountain Sports
Balance Sheet
As of January 31, 2015

	Jan 31, 15
▶ ASSETS	81,786.65
▼ LIABILITIES & EQUITY	
▶ Liabilities ▶	14,876.46 ◀
▼ Equity	
3000 · Owners' Equity	-2,750.75
▼ 3100 · Your Last Name & Muir, Capital	
▼ 3110 · First and Last Name, Capital	
3111 · First and Last Name, Investment	20,000.00
3110 · First and Last Name, Capital - Other	13,455.10
Total 3110 · First and Last Name, Capital	33,455.10
▼ 3120 · Larry Muir, Capital	
3121 · Larry Muir, Investment	20,000.00
3120 · Larry Muir, Capital - Other	13,455.09
Total 3120 · Larry Muir, Capital	33,455.09
Total 3100 · Your Last Name & Muir, Capital	66,910.19
Net Income	2,750.75
Total Equity	66,910.19
TOTAL LIABILITIES & EQUITY	81,786.65

Partial Report

Print the report, orientation is **Portrait**, then close the **Balance Sheet**

BACKUP COMPANY

As in previous chapters, you should back up your company and then close the company.

Follow instructions previously provided to back up company files, name the backup **Sports (Backup Ch. 7)**, close the company, and make a duplicate disk

SUMMARY

In this chapter, end-of-period adjustments were made, a bank reconciliation and a credit card reconciliation were performed, backup (duplicate) and archive disks were prepared, and adjusting entries were made. A credit card reconciliation was "undone" and then completed correctly. The use of Drawing, Net Income, and Owners' Equity accounts were explored and interpreted for a partnership. The closing date for a period was assigned. Account names were changed, and new accounts were created. Even though QuickBooks focuses on entering transactions on business forms, a Journal recording each transaction is kept by QuickBooks. This chapter presented transaction entry directly into the General Journal. The difference between accrual-basis and cash-basis accounting was discussed. Owner withdrawals and distribution of capital to partners were examined. Many of the different report options and preparation procedures available in QuickBooks were explored, and a report was exported to Microsoft Excel. A variety of reports were printed after closing the period. Correction of errors was analyzed, and corrections were made after the period was closed and adjustments were made to inventory. The fact that QuickBooks does not require an actual closing entry at the end of the period was addressed.

END-OF-CHAPTER QUESTIONS

TRUE/FALSE

ANSWER THE FOLLOWING QUESTIONS IN THE SPACE PROVIDED BEFORE THE QUESTION NUMBER.

F 1. The owner's drawing account should be transferred to capital each week.

T 2. Frequent transactions may be memorized.

F 3. You must access the General Journal in order to close a period.

F 4. If Show All is selected, inactive accounts will not appear in the Chart of Accounts.

T 5. When you reconcile a bank statement, anything entered as a service charge will automatically be entered as a transaction when the reconciliation is complete.

F 6. Once an account has been used, the name cannot be changed.

F 7. Once the reconciliation of an account is completed, it may not be undone.

F 8. At the end of the year, QuickBooks transfers the net income into Owners' Equity.

T 9. A withdrawal by an owner in a partnership reduces the owner's capital.

F 10. Reports prepared using the Report Center may not be customized and memorized.

7

MULTIPLE CHOICE

WRITE THE LETTER OF THE CORRECT ANSWER IN THE SPACE PROVIDED BEFORE THE QUESTION NUMBER.

B 1. To print a Reconciliation Report that lists only totals, select ___.
A. none
B. summary
C. detail
D. complete

D 2. The report that proves debits equal credits is the ___.
A. Sales Graph
B. Balance Sheet
C. Profit & Loss Statement
D. Trial Balance

A 3. If reports are prepared for the month of January in the current year, net income will appear in the ___ .
A. Profit & Loss Statement
B. Balance Sheet
C. both A and B
D. neither A nor B

B 4. In QuickBooks, you export reports to Microsoft Excel in order to ___.
A. print the report
B. explore "what if" scenarios with data from QuickBooks
C. prepare checks
D. all of the above

B 5. QuickBooks uses the ___ method of inventory valuation.
A. LIFO
B. Average Cost
C. FIFO
D. Actual Cost

D 6. If a transaction is recorded in the General Journal, it may be viewed ___.
A. in the Journal
B. in the register for each balance sheet account used in the transaction
C. by preparing an analysis graph
D. in both A and B

C 7. Entries for bank collections of automatic payments ___.
A. are automatically recorded at the completion of the bank reconciliation
B. must be recorded after the bank reconciliation is complete
C. should be recorded when reconciling the bank statement
D. should be recorded on the first of the month

A 8. The account(s) that may be reconciled is (are) ___.
A. Balance Sheet accounts
B. Profit & Loss accounts
C. the Customer list account
D. Trial Balance accounts

C 9. The closing entry for a drawing account transfers the balance of an owner's drawing account into the ___ account.
A. Retained Earnings
B. Net Income
C. Owner's Capital
D. Investment

D 10. When you prepared a Commented Report, it may not be ___.
A. Printed
B. Saved
C. Emailed
D. Exported to Excel

FILL-IN

IN THE SPACE PROVIDED, WRITE THE ANSWER THAT MOST APPROPRIATELY COMPLETES THE SENTENCE.

1. Accrual -basis accounting matches income and expenses against a period, and Cash -basis accounting records income when the money is received and expenses when the purchase is made or the bill is paid.

2. The Balance Sheet proves that Assets = Liabilities + Owners' Equity.

3. In a partnership, each owner has a share of all the assets and liabilities based on the percentage of his or her investment in the business or according to any partnership agreements.

4. In order to close a period, a closing date must be provided.

5. No matter where transactions are recorded, they all appear in the Journal.

SHORT ESSAY

Describe the entry that is made to transfer net income into the owner's capital account. Include the reason this entry should be made and how income will be listed if transfer is not recorded.

____

____

____

____

____

____

NAME___________________________

CHAPTER 7: TRANSMITTAL

YOUR NAME MOUNTAIN SPORTS

Check the items below as you print them; then attach the documents and reports in the order listed when you submit them to your instructor.

___ Account Listing
___ Check 6: Your First and Last Name
___ Check 7: Larry Muir
___ Bank Reconciliation Detail Report, January 31, 2015
___ Visa Reconciliation Detail Report, January 31, 2015
___ Check 8: Old Mammoth Bank
___ Journal, January, 2015
___ Trial Balance, January 31, 2015
___ Profit & Loss, January, 2015
___ Balance Sheet, January 31, 2015

END-OF-CHAPTER PROBLEM

YOUR NAME RESORT CLOTHING

Chapter 7 continues with the end-of-period adjustments, bank and credit card reconciliations, archive disks, and closing the period for Your Name Resort Clothing. The company does use a certified public accountant for guidance and assistance with appropriate accounting procedures. The CPA has provided information for Karen to use for adjusting entries, etc.

INSTRUCTIONS

Continue to use the copy of Your Name Resort Clothing you used in the previous chapters. Open the company—the file used is **Clothing.qbw**. Record the adjustments and other transactions as you were instructed in the chapter. Always read the transaction carefully and review the Chart of Accounts when selecting transaction accounts. Print the reports and journals as indicated and resize columns for a full display of information.

RECORD TRANSACTIONS

<u>January 31, 2015</u>—Enter the following:

- Change the names and/or the account numbers and delete the descriptions of the following accounts.
  - **6260 - Printing and Reproduction** to **6260 Printing and Duplication**
  - **6350 - Travel & Ent** to **6350 - Travel Expenses**
  - **3010 - Your Name & Olsen, Capital** to **3100 - Your Last Name & Olsen, Capital**
    - Remember to use your actual <u>last</u> name.
- Add the following accounts:
  - Equity account **3110 - First and Last Name, Capital** (subaccount of **3100**)
    - Remember to use both your real first and last name.
  - Equity account **3120 - Karen Olsen, Capital** (subaccount of **3100**)
- Change the following accounts:
  - **3011 – Student's Name, Investment** to **3111 - First and Last Name, Investment** (subaccount of **3110**)
    - Remember to use both your real first and last name.
  - **3013 – Student's Name, Drawing** to **3112 - First and Last Name, Drawing** (subaccount of **3110**)
    - Remember to use both your real first and last name.
  - **3012 - Karen Olsen, Investment** to **3121 - Karen Olsen, Investment** (subaccount of **3120**)
  - **3014 - Karen Olsen, Drawing** to **3122 Karen Olsen, - Drawing** (subaccount of **3120**)
  - **6422 – Office** to **6422 – Office Supplies** (subaccount of 6420 - Supplies Expense)

7

- Make the following accounts inactive:
  - **6291 - Building Repairs**
  - **6351 - Entertainment**
- Delete the following accounts:
  - **6182 - Disability Insurance**
  - **6213 - Mortgage**
  - **6823 - Property**
- Print an Account Listing in Landscape orientation
  - Do *not* show inactive accounts (If necessary, click Include inactive to remove the check mark)
  - Click the Reports button at the bottom of the Chart of Accounts, and click Account Listing to display the report
  - Resize the columns to display the Account Names in full and to hide the columns for Description, Accnt. #, and Tax Line
  - Change the Header/Footer so the report date is January 31, 2015
  - Print the report
- Create a Fixed Asset Item List for:
  - Asset Name/Number: **Office Equipment**, Item is: **New**, Purchase and Asset Description: **Office Equipment**, Date: **12/31/14**, Cost: **$8,000**, Asset Account: **1510**
  - Asset Name/Number: **Store Fixtures**, Item is: **New**, Purchase and Asset Description: **Store Fixtures**, Date: **12/31/14**, Cost: **$9,500**, Asset Account: **1520**
- Enter adjusting entries in the General Journal and use the memo Adjusting Entry for the following:
  - Office Supplies Used, the amount used is $35
  - Sales Supplies Used, account balance (on hand) at the end of the month is $1,400
  - Record a compound entry for depreciation for the month: Office Equipment, $66.67 and Store Fixtures, $79.17
  - The amount of insurance remaining in the Prepaid Insurance account is for six months of liability insurance. Record the liability insurance expense for the month
- Prepare a Working Trial Balance. For each account, use the amount in the Beginning Balance column, add or subtract the amounts in Transactions column and/or Adjustments column to verify the totals in the Ending Balance column. Do not print the report.
- Each owner withdrew $500. (Memo: January Withdrawal) Print Check Nos. 7 and 8 for the owners' withdrawals.
- Prepare Bank Reconciliation and Enter Adjustments for the Reconciliation. (Refer to the chapter for appropriate Memo notations).

CENTRAL COAST BANK
1234 Coast Highway
San Luis Obispo, CA 93407
805-555-9300

Your Name Resort Clothing
784 Marsh Street
San Luis Obispo, CA 93407

Acct. 987-352-9152 January 31, 2015

Beginning Balance, 1/1/15			32,589.00
1/15/15, Deposit	3,023.30		35,612.30
1/15/15, Deposit	2,450.05		38,062.35
1/15/15, NSF Returned Check Kristie Carson		325.00	37,737.35
1/15/15, NSF Charges, Kristie Carson		15.00	37,722.35
1/15/15, Check 1		59.39	37,662.96
1/18/15, Check 2		343.00	37,319.96
1/18/15, Check 3		156.80	37,163.16
1/25/15, Check 4		1,150.00	36,013.16
1/25/15, Check 5		79.85	35,933.31
1/31/15, Service Charge 10.00		10.00	35,923.31
1/31/15, Office Equipment Loan Pmt.: $44.51 Interest, $8.61 Principal		53.12	35,870.19
1/31/15, Store Fixtures Loan Pmt.: $53.42 Interest, $10.33 Principal		63.75	35,806.44
1/31/15, Interest	73.30		35,879.74
Ending Balance			$35,879.74

- Print a Detailed Reconciliation Report in Portrait. Adjust column widths so the report fits on one page.
- Reconcile the Visa account using the following statement

CENTRAL COAST BANK
1234 Coast Highway
San Luis Obispo, CA 93407
805-555-9300

Your Name Resort Clothing
784 Marsh Street
San Luis Obispo, CA 93407

VISA Acct. #4187-5234-9153-235 January 31, 2015

Beginning Balance, 1/1/15			0.00
1/9/15 Contempo Clothing		196.00	196.00
1/18/15, Office Masters		250.00	446.00
Minimum Payment Due: $50.00		Payment Due Date: February 5, 2015	

7

- Print a Detailed Reconciliation Report in Portrait. Pay Central Coast Bank for the Visa bill using Check 9. Print Check 9.
- Prepare an Adjusted Trial Balance for 01/01/15 to 01/31/15. Verify the Adjusted Balance by adding or subtracting the Adjustments from the Unadjusted Balance. Size the columns to display information in full. Print the report. (Is your adjusted balance $76,553.07?)
- Distribute capital to each owner: divide the balance of 3100 - Your Last Name & Olsen, Capital - Other equally between the two partners. (View a Balance Sheet (Standard) to see the balance of the Capital – Other account.) Record an entry to transfer each owner's portion of the Capital Other to the individual capital accounts. (Memo: Transfer Capital to Partners) Remember, this is not an adjusting entry.
- Divide in half and transfer Net Income/Owners' Equity into owners' individual Capital accounts. Remember, this is not an adjusting entry.
- Close Drawing accounts into owner's individual Capital accounts.
- Prepare an archive copy of the company file.
- Close the period as of January 31, 2015 (Do not assign passwords).
- After closing the period on 01/31/15, discovered an error in the amount of Office Supplies and Sales Supplies: Transfer $40 from Office Supplies to Sales Supplies.
- After closing the period on 01/31/15, found one damaged tie. Adjust the quantity of ties on 01/31/15 using the Expense account 6190 Merchandise Adjustments.
- Change the net income/Owners' Equity adjustment to reflect the merchandise adjustment for the ties.
- Backup the company and redo the archive copy of the company file as well.
- Print the Journal for January, 2015 (Landscape orientation, Fit to one page wide).
- Print the following reports:
  - Trial Balance, January 1-31, 2015
  - Profit & Loss Report, January 31, 2015
  - Balance Sheet, January 31, 2015

NAME______________________

CHAPTER 7: TRANSMITTAL

YOUR NAME RESORT CLOTHING

Check the items below as you print them; then attach the documents and reports in the order listed when you submit them to your instructor.

___ Account Listing
___ Check 7: Your First and Last Name
___ Check 8: Karen Olsen
___ Bank Reconciliation Detail Report, January 31, 2015
___ Visa Reconciliation Detail Report, January 31, 2015
___ Check 9: Central Coast Bank
___ Adjusted Trial Balance, January, 2015
___ Journal, January 1-31, 2015
___ Trial Balance, January 31, 2015
___ Profit & Loss, January, 2015
___ Balance Sheet, January 31, 2015

SECTION 2 PRACTICE SET, MERCHANDISING BUSINESS:

YOUR NAME'S ULTIMATE GOLF

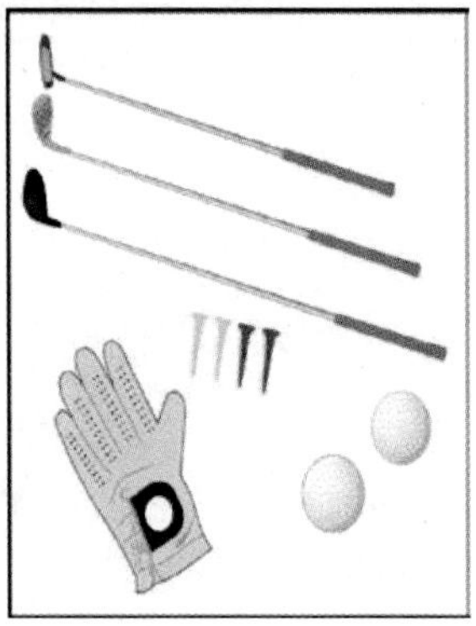

The following is a comprehensive practice set combining all the elements of QuickBooks studied in Chapters 5-7 of the text. Since the version of QuickBooks is 2015, the text shows the year as 2015. In this practice set, you will record transactions for the month of January, 2015. Check with your instructor to find out what year you should use when recording transactions. Entries will be made to record invoices, sales orders, receipt of payments on invoices, cash sales, credit card sales, debit card sales, receipt and payment of bills, orders and receipts of merchandise, credit memos for invoices and bills, sales tax payments, and credit card payments. Account names will be added, changed, deleted, and made inactive. Customers, vendors, owners, and fixed assets will be added to the appropriate lists. Reports will be prepared, customized, memorized, and commented on to analyze sales, bills, receipts, and items ordered. Formal reports including the Trial Balance, Profit and Loss Statement, and Balance Sheet will be prepared. Adjusting entries for depreciation, supplies used, insurance expense, and automatic payments will be recorded. Both bank and credit card reconciliations will be prepared. Entries to display partnership equity for each partner will be made. The end of period closing will be completed.

STUDENT'S NAME'S ULTIMATE GOLF

Located in La Quinta, California, Student's Name's Ultimate Golf is a full-service golf shop that sells golf equipment and clothing. Even though Valerie's name is not part of the company name, Student's Name's Ultimate Golf is a partnership owned and operated by Valerie Childers and you. Each partner contributed an equal amount to the partnership. You buy the equipment and manage the store. Valerie buys the clothing and accessory items and keeps the books for the company. There are several part-time employees working for the company selling merchandise.

INSTRUCTIONS

Use the file **Golf.qbw**.

When entering transactions, you are responsible for entering any memos. Unless otherwise specified, the terms for each sale or bill will be the terms specified on the Customer List or Vendor List. Customer Message is usually *Thank you for your business*. However, any other appropriate message may be used. If a customer's order exceeds the established credit limit, accept the order and process it.

If the terms allow a discount for a customer, make sure to apply the discount if payment is made within the discount period. Use the Income account 4050 Sales Discounts as the discount account. On occasion, a payment may be made within the discount period but not received or recorded within it. Information within the transaction will indicate whether or not the payment is equivalent to a full payment. For example, if you received $98 for an invoice for $100 shortly after the discount period and the transaction indicated payment in full, apply the discount. If a customer has a credit and has a balance on the account, apply the credit to the appropriate invoice for the customer. If a customer pays a bill within the discount period and has a credit, make sure to calculate the discount on the payment amount after subtracting the credit. If there is no balance for a customer and a return is made, issue a credit memo and a refund check.

Always pay bills in time to take advantage of purchase discounts. Use the Cost of Goods Sold Account 5200 Merchandise Discounts for the discount account. Remember that the discount due date will be ten days from the date of the bill.

Invoices, sales orders, purchase orders, and other business forms should be printed as they are entered. To save time, printing Payment Receipts or Bills is optional. Check with your professor for printing assigned. (All required and optional printouts are listed on the transmittal sheet.)

You may memorize transactions and reports at your discretion. If you wish to use the Prepare Multiple Reports feature, make sure to remove the Date Prepared, Time Prepared, and Report Basis from the heading.

Print business forms with lines around each field. Determine the orientation of the document for printing. Whenever possible, adjust the column widths so that account names, amounts, and item names are displayed in full and so that reports fit on one page wide. If necessary, select Fit report to one page wide.

Back up your work at the end of each week.

The following lists are used for all vendors, customers, and sales items. You will be adding additional customers and vendors as the company is in operation.

Vendors:

Vendors | Transactions

Active Vendors

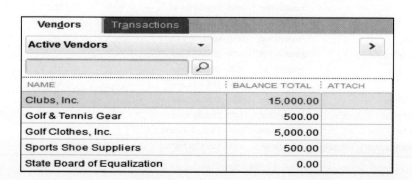

NAME	BALANCE TOTAL	ATTACH
Clubs, Inc.	15,000.00	
Golf & Tennis Gear	500.00	
Golf Clothes, Inc.	5,000.00	
Sports Shoe Suppliers	500.00	
State Board of Equalization	0.00	

Customers:

Customers & Jobs | Transactions

Active Customers

NAME	BALANCE TOTAL	ATTACH
Anderson, Oscar	0.00	
Bridges, Drew	0.00	
Carter, Marion	1,850.00	
Chiang, Charlene	0.00	
Donlon, Mark	850.00	
Hammar, Azar	0.00	
Hiji, Momo	375.00	
Kincaid, Charles	950.00	
Miller, Joan	550.00	
Nakama, Tsugio	450.00	
O'Neil, Doris	850.00	
Potter, Gene	1,200.00	
Rosen, Robert	750.00	
Schaub, Wade	150.00	
Sweeney, Lori	1,775.00	
Thomas, Jean	350.00	
Tokumoto, Russ	2,775.00	
Yanov, Tamara	0.00	

Sales Items:

Item List

Look for [ ] in All fields | Search | Reset | Search within results

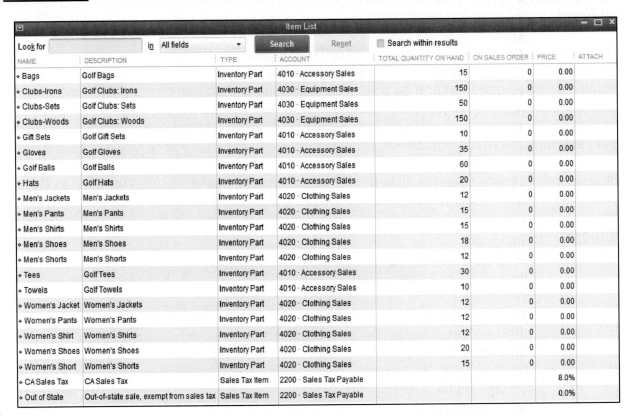

NAME	DESCRIPTION	TYPE	ACCOUNT	TOTAL QUANTITY ON HAND	ON SALES ORDER	PRICE	ATTACH
Bags	Golf Bags	Inventory Part	4010 · Accessory Sales	15	0	0.00	
Clubs-Irons	Golf Clubs: Irons	Inventory Part	4030 · Equipment Sales	150	0	0.00	
Clubs-Sets	Golf Clubs: Sets	Inventory Part	4030 · Equipment Sales	50	0	0.00	
Clubs-Woods	Golf Clubs: Woods	Inventory Part	4030 · Equipment Sales	150	0	0.00	
Gift Sets	Golf Gift Sets	Inventory Part	4010 · Accessory Sales	10	0	0.00	
Gloves	Golf Gloves	Inventory Part	4010 · Accessory Sales	35	0	0.00	
Golf Balls	Golf Balls	Inventory Part	4010 · Accessory Sales	60	0	0.00	
Hats	Golf Hats	Inventory Part	4010 · Accessory Sales	20	0	0.00	
Men's Jackets	Men's Jackets	Inventory Part	4020 · Clothing Sales	12	0	0.00	
Men's Pants	Men's Pants	Inventory Part	4020 · Clothing Sales	15	0	0.00	
Men's Shirts	Men's Shirts	Inventory Part	4020 · Clothing Sales	15	0	0.00	
Men's Shoes	Men's Shoes	Inventory Part	4020 · Clothing Sales	18	0	0.00	
Men's Shorts	Men's Shorts	Inventory Part	4020 · Clothing Sales	12	0	0.00	
Tees	Golf Tees	Inventory Part	4010 · Accessory Sales	30	0	0.00	
Towels	Golf Towels	Inventory Part	4010 · Accessory Sales	10	0	0.00	
Women's Jacket	Women's Jackets	Inventory Part	4020 · Clothing Sales	12	0	0.00	
Women's Pants	Women's Pants	Inventory Part	4020 · Clothing Sales	12	0	0.00	
Women's Shirt	Women's Shirts	Inventory Part	4020 · Clothing Sales	12	0	0.00	
Women's Shoes	Women's Shoes	Inventory Part	4020 · Clothing Sales	20	0	0.00	
Women's Short	Women's Shorts	Inventory Part	4020 · Clothing Sales	15	0	0.00	
CA Sales Tax	CA Sales Tax	Sales Tax Item	2200 · Sales Tax Payable			8.0%	
Out of State	Out-of-state sale, exempt from sales tax	Sales Tax Item	2200 · Sales Tax Payable			0.0%	

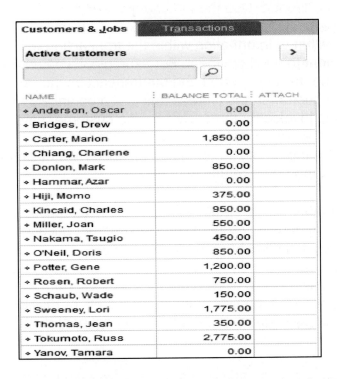

Note: Individual golf clubs are categorized as irons or woods. A complete set of clubs would be categorized as a set. The type of material used in a golf club makes no difference in a sales item. For example, graphite is a material used in the shaft of a golf club. A set of graphite clubs would refer to a set of golf clubs. Titanium is a type of metal used in the head of a golf club. A titanium wood would be sold as a wood. Golf balls are sold in packages called sleeves; thus, a quantity of one would represent one package of golf balls.

RECORD TRANSACTIONS:

Enter the transactions for Student's Name Ultimate Golf and print as indicated. If you get messages you do not want, click the selection that will not display this in the future.

Week 1—January 2-8, 2015:

- ▶ Add your First and Last name to both the company name and legal name for Student's Name Ultimate Golf. Even though this is a partnership, the company name will be **Your Name's Ultimate Golf**. (Remember to use your actual name *not* the words Your Name. Don't forget the apostrophe s after your last name. For example, Sue Smith would be Sue Smith's Ultimate Golf.)
- ▶ Customize the Payment Methods list to add MasterCard and Debit Card. Remove Discover Card.
- ▶ Change Report Preferences: The Report Header/Footer should *not* include the Date Prepared, Time Prepared, or Report Basis.
- ▶ Change the names and delete the descriptions of the following accounts:
  - o **3100** change the words Your Name to your actual last name to make the Account Name **Last Name & Childers, Capital**
  - o **4200 Sales Discounts** to **4200 Purchases Discounts**
  - o **4050 Reimbursed Expenses** to **Sales Discounts**
  - o **6350 Travel & Ent** to **6350 Travel Expenses**
  - o **6381 Marketing** to **6381 Sales** (this is a subaccount of 6380 Supplies Expense)
- ▶ Delete the following accounts:
  - o **4070 Resale Discounts**
  - o **4090 Resale Income**
  - o **4100 Freight Income**
  - o **6130 Cash Discounts**
  - o **6213 Mortgage**
  - o **6265 Filing Fees**
  - o **6285 Franchise Fees**
  - o **6351 Entertainment**
- ▶ Make the following accounts inactive:
  - o **6182 Disability Insurance**
  - o **6311 Building Repairs**
  - o **6413 Property**
- ▶ Add the following accounts:
  - o Equity account: **3110 First and Last Name, Capital** (subaccount of **3100**) Use your real first and last name.
  - o Equity account: **3120 Valerie Childers, Capital** (subaccount of **3100**)

  - Cost of Goods Sold account: **5200 Merchandise Discounts** (subaccount of **5000**)
- Change the following accounts:
  - **3500 Student's Name, Investment** to **3111 First and Last Name, Investment** (subaccount of **3110**). Use your real first and last name.
  - **3400 Student's Name, Drawing** to **3112 First and Last Name, Drawing** (subaccount of **3110**). Use your real first and last name.
  - **3300 Valerie Childers, Investment** to **3121** (subaccount of **3120**)
  - **3200 Valerie Childers, Drawing** to **3122** (subaccount of **3120**)
- Use the Reports Menu to access the List reports. Print the **Account Listing** in portrait orientation. Resize the columns so the Account Names, Type, and Balance Total show in full. Do *not* show the Description, Accnt. #, or Tax Line columns. Click the Customize Report button; on the Header/Footer tab change the report date to January 2, 2015.
- Create Fixed Asset Item List:
  - Asset Name: **Office Equipment**, Item is: **New**, Purchase and Asset Description: **Office Equipment**, Date: **12/31/**(use the end of previous year), Cost: **5,000.00**, Asset Account: **1510 Office Equipment**.
  - Asset Name: **Store Fixtures**, Item is: **New**, Purchase and Asset Description: **Store Fixtures**, Date: **12/31/**(use the end of previous year), Cost: **6,000.00**, Asset Account: **1520 Store Fixtures**.
- Customize **Sales Receipts**, **Purchase Orders**, **Sales Orders**, **Credit Memos**, and **Intuit Product Invoices** so that the Default Title is in all capital letters and your name will print in full on the same line as the company name.
- Add the Vendor: **Palm Springs Rentals**; Main Phone: **760-555-8368**; Fax **760-555-8638**; Address: **11-2951 Palm Canyon Drive, Palm Springs, CA 92262**; Payment Terms: **Net 30**. Account Settings: **6280 Rent**.
- Prepare a bill for Palm Springs Rentals enter the amount $2800; then Memorize the Transaction. Select **Add to my Reminders List**, How Often **Monthly**, Next Date **01/25/15**, click **OK** to memorize. Do not save the bill, click the **Clear** button and then close Enter Bills
- Add the credit card information to Russ Tokumoto's account. Preferred Payment Method: **Visa**. Credit Card Number **4684 4568 9872 123**, Expiration **03/16**. Remember to tab to fill in the name, address, and zip code.
- Once you complete adding Russ Tokumoto's Visa to his account, go to the Company menu, select, Customer Credit Card Protection. Click **Disable Protection**, click **Yes** to Disable Sensitive Data Protection. If you do not complete this now, when you close and then reopen QuickBooks and Golf you will need to do this.
- Print invoices, checks, sales orders, and other items as they are entered in the transactions. Check with your instructor to see if you should print Bills and Payment Receipts. They are listed on the Transmittal just in case you print them.

1/2/2015

- Sold 2 pairs of women's shorts @ $64.99 each, 2 women's shirts @ $59.99 each, 1 women's jacket @ $129.99, and 1 pair of women's shoes @ $179.99 to Tamara Yanov on account. (Remember: Use Copy of: Intuit Product Invoice.) Print Invoice 1.
- Having achieved her goal of a handicap under 30, Marion Carter treated herself to the new clubs she had been wanting. Sold on account 1 set of graphite clubs for $750, 1

golf bag for $129.95, and 5 sleeves (packages) of golf balls @ $6.95 each. (Remember to accept sales that are over the credit limit.)

- Change the terms for Drew Bridges to Net 10 (Add a new Payment Term for Net 10.)
- Change Marion Carter's credit limit to $3,000.00.
- Change Azar Hammar's credit limit to $2,500.00.
- Azar heard that titanium would give him extra yardage with each shot. Sold 4 titanium woods (Clubs-Woods) on account to Azar Hammar @ $459.00 each.
- Sold 5 golf bags @ $59.99 each and 5 sets of starter clubs @ $159.99 each to Palm Springs Schools on account for the high school golf team. Palm Springs Schools, Main Phone: 760-555-4455, Main Email: PSSchools@ps.edu, Address: 99-4058 South Palm Canyon Drive, Palm Springs, CA 92262 is a nonprofit organization, Payment Terms: Net 30, Preferred Delivery Method: Mail, Credit Limit: $1,500. Even though this is a nonprofit organization, it does pay California Sales Tax on all purchases. Include a subtotal for the sale and apply a 10% sales discount for a nonprofit organization. (Create any new sales items necessary.)
- Received a telephone sales order from Wade Schaub for 2 pairs of men's shorts @ $49.95 each, 2 men's shirts @ $59.99 each, 1 pair of men's golf shoes @ $119.99, a starter set of golf clubs for his son @ $250.00, and a new titanium driver for himself @ $549.95 (a driver is a Golf Club: Woods). Prepare Sales Order 1.
- Correct and reprint Invoice 2 to Marion Carter. The golf bag price should be $179.95.
- Received from Russ Tokumoto, $2,175, in partial payment of his account. He made his payment using the Visa Credit Card on file. (Did you leave this as an underpayment?)

1/3/2015

- Sold 3 gift sets @ $14.99 each and 3 sleeves (packages) of golf balls @ $8.95 each, and 5 Golf Hats @ $25.99 to Dr. Lori Sweeney on account to be given away as door prizes at an upcoming ladies' club tournament.
- Wade Schaub came into the store to pick up the merchandise on Sales Order 1. Create an invoice for all items from the sales order. (Use the date January 3, 2015.) Since a Sales Order Invoice is different from a regular Product Invoice, customize the Sales Order Invoice so the Default Title is INVOICE and resize the title INVOICE and Your Name's Ultimate Golf so there is room for your name on the same line. Print the invoice. (Go to Sales Order 1 and verify that each item is CLSD and that it is marked "Invoiced in Full.")
- Received Check 102-33 for payment in full from Mark Donlon for $850.
- Sold a golf bag @ $99.95 and 2 golf towels @ $9.95 each to a cash customer using Visa Card Number 4682 4852 6394 782, Expiration 07/17. (Remember to print Sales Receipt 1.) Did you use QuickAdd to add the Cash Customer?
- Took a telephone sales order from a new customer Laura Hansen for 1 pair of women's golf shoes @ $149.95 and a set of golf clubs @ $895.00. New Customer info: Laura Hansen (Remember, last name first in the Customer List), Main Phone: 760-555-3322, Address: 45-2215 PGA Drive, Rancho Mirage, CA 92270, Copy the Address to Ship To 1, Payment Terms: 1% 10 Net 30, Preferred Delivery Method: Mail, Credit Limit $1,500, taxable customer for California Sales Tax.
- Received Debit Card Number 7651 1589 7652 134, Expiration 06/16 for $950 from Gene Potter in partial payment of his account.

1/5/2015

- Laura Hansen came into the store to pick up merchandise ordered on Sales Order 2. Create the invoice from the sales order. Use the sales order date (January 3, 2015).
- In the Item List, change the Item Name/Number from Hats to Men's Hats. The purchase and sales descriptions should be Men's Golf Hats. Change the Reorder Point (Min) from 15 to 12 and Max from 25 to 20.
- Prepare and print an Inventory Stock Status by Item Report for January 1-5, 2015. Resize the columns, use Landscape orientation, and select Fit Report to 1 page wide.
- Prepare Purchase Orders for all items marked Order on the Inventory Stock Status by Item Report. Place all orders with the preferred vendors. Prepare only one purchase order per vendor. For all items, order the number shown in the Reorder Quantity column of the Inventory Stock Status by Item report. The cost of golf bags are $40 each, gift sets are $3 each, men's shorts are $20 each, towels are $2 each, and women's shirts are $20 each. (Remember to print the purchase orders. If you get a message to change the cost for the item, click No.)
- Add a new inventory sales item: Women's Hats. The purchase and sales description is Women's Golf Hats. Leave the cost and sales price at 0.00. The COGS account is 5000. Head Gear, Inc. is the preferred vendor (Add the new vendor: Head Gear, Inc., Main Phone: 310-555-8787, Main Email: HeadGear@la.com, Fax: 310-555-7878, Address: 45980 West Los Angeles Street, Los Angeles, CA 90025, Credit Limit $500, Payment Terms: 2% 10 Net 30). The hats are taxable. The Income account is 4010-Accessory Sales. The Asset account is 1120-Inventory Asset. The Reorder Point (Min) is 10 and the Max is 20. Quantity on Hand is 0 as of 01/05/2015.
- Order 5 women's hats @ $10.00 each from Head Gear, Inc. Print the Purchase Order
- Print a Purchase Order QuickReport in Landscape orientation for January 1-5, 2015.

1/8/2015

- Received Check 1822 for a cash sale of 2 men's golf hats @ $49.95 each.
- Deposit all receipts (cash, checks, debit cards, and credit cards) for the week. Print the Deposit Summary.
- Backup your work for Week 1. Name your backup file **Golf (Backup Week 1)**

Week 2—January 9-15:

1/10/2015

- Received the order from Head Gear, Inc. without the bill.
- Use 01/10/2015 for the bill date for both of the following transactions. Received the merchandise ordered and the bill from Golf & Tennis Gear. All items were received in full except the golf bags. Of the 12 bags ordered, only 8 were received. The remaining golf bags are on backorder. Also received all of the merchandise ordered and the bill from Golf Clothes, Inc.
- Dr. Lori Sweeney returned 1 of the gift sets purchased on January 3. Issue a credit memo and apply to Invoice 5. Create a new customer message to use on credit memos: **Your return has been processed.**
- Mark Donlon returned 1 pair of men's golf shorts that had been purchased for $59.95. (The shorts had been purchased previously and were part of his $850 opening

balance.) Since his balance was paid in full, issue and print a refund check. Did you use the new credit memo message?

- ▶ Received a telephone order for 1 complete set of golf clubs from Russ Tokumoto for $1,600.00.
- ▶ Sold two irons—a graphite sand wedge and a graphite gap wedge--@ $119.95 each to a cash customer using Debit Card Number 7213 4568 5987 444, Expiration Date 02/2016. (Both clubs are classified as irons.)

<u>**1/12/2015**</u>

- ▶ Russ Tokumoto came to the store and picked up the merchandise from Sales Order 3. Create the invoice from the sales order and use the sales order date for the invoice.
- ▶ Received the telephone bill for the month, $85.15 from Desert Telephone Co., Main Phone: 760-555-9285, Address: 11-092 Highway 111, Palm Springs, CA 92262, Payment Terms: Net 30, Account Settings: 6340 Telephone.
- ▶ Use the company Visa card to purchase $175 of <u>office supplies</u> to have on hand from Indio Office Supply, Main Phone: 760-555-1535, Fax 760-555-5351, Address: 3950 46th Avenue, Indio, CA 92201. (Credit card charges may not be printed.)

<u>**1/14/2015**</u>

- ▶ The bill for the items received from Head Gear, Inc. on 1/10 arrived. Use 01/14/2015 for the bill date.
- ▶ Received Check 3801 for $1,963.05 from Azar Hammar in full payment of his bill. (The transaction date is 01/14/15. The payment appropriately includes the discount since the check was dated 01/10/15.)
- ▶ Received Check 783 for $598.69 from Tamara Yanov in full payment of her bill. (The payment includes the discount since the check was dated 01/11/15.)
- ▶ Deposit all receipts (checks, debit and credit cards, and/or cash) for the week. Print the Deposit Summary.
- ▶ Back up your work for Week 2. Name the file **Golf (Backup Week 2)**.

<u>**Week 3—January 16-22**</u>**:**

<u>**1/17/2015**</u>

- ▶ Dr. Charles Kincaid purchased 1 set of golf clubs, $1,200.00, 1 golf bag, $250.00, 1 pair of men's shoes, $195.00, and 1 putter (iron), $195.00 on account.
- ▶ Received Check 67-08 for $1,976.72 from Dr. Lori Sweeney in full payment of her account. (Note: The Payment amount for Invoice 5 includes the credit for the gift set.)
- ▶ Received the remaining 4 golf bags and the bill from Golf & Tennis Gear on earlier purchase order. The date of the bill is 01/16/2015.

<u>**1/18/2015**</u>

- ▶ Prepare an Unpaid Bills Detail report. Add a column for Terms. Memorize the Report and name it Unpaid Bills with Terms Detail. Using the date of the bill and the 10 day discount period, calculate which bills are eligible to receive a discount if paid between <u>January 18 and 22</u>. Write the comment <u>Pay this Bill</u> on each bill to be paid. (If you can take a discount for a bill paid after January 22, do <u>not</u> include it on this report.) Print the commented report. (Remember, if you have been instructed to export reports to Excel, you cannot export a comment report.)

- Pay all bills marked in the Commented Unpaid Bills Report. Use Account 5200 Merchandise Discounts as the Discount Account. (Print the checks: you may use Print Forms or you may print them individually.) Did you pay two bills?
- Sold 1 golf bag @ $199.95, 1 set of graphite golf clubs @ $1,200.00, 1 putter @ $129.95 (record the putter as Golf Clubs: Irons), and 3 sleeves of golf balls @ $9.95 each on account to Dr. Lori Sweeney.
- Returned 2 men's shirts that had poorly stitched seams at a cost of $20 each to Golf Clothes, Inc. Received Credit Memo 1045 from the company.

1/20/2015

- Dr. Charles Kincaid returned the putter (iron) he purchased on January 17. Issue a Credit Memo and apply to Invoice 11. Did you use the credit memo customer message?
- Sold 1 men's golf hat @ $49.95, 1 men's jacket @ $89.95, 1 towel @ $9.95, 2 packages of golf tees @ $1.95 each, and 16 sleeves of golf balls at $5.95 to a customer using Master Card Number 5189 4687 2372 598, Expiration 04/18.
- A businessman in town with his wife bought them each a set of golf clubs @ $1,495.00 per set and a new golf bag for each of them @ $249.95 per bag. He purchased 1 men's jacket for $179.95. His wife purchased 1 pair of golf shoes for $189.99 and 1 women's jacket for $149.99. Paid for the purchases using his Visa Card Number 4198 5682 3894 561, Expiration 05/16.
- Prepare and print an Inventory Stock Status by Item Report for January 1-20.
- Edit the Item Golf Balls insert a space in the Purchase Description between Golf and Balls.
- Prepare Purchase Orders to order any inventory items indicated on the report. As with earlier orders, use the preferred vendor and issue only one purchase order per vendor. For all items except Men's Hats, order the number shown in the Reorder Quantity column of the Inventory Stock Status by Item report. For Men's Hats, we get a better price if we order at least 10 hats, so order a quantity of 10. (Golf balls cost $3.50 per sleeve, men's and women's jackets cost $20 each, and men's and women's hats cost $10 each.)
- Deposit all receipts (checks, credit cards, and/or cash) for the week. Print the Deposit Summary.
- Back up your work for Week 3. Name the file **Golf (Backup Week 3)**.

Week 4 and End of Period—January 23-31:

1/23/2015

- Prepare the memorized report Unpaid Bills with Terms Detail. Using the date of the bill and the 10 day discount period, calculate which bills are eligible to receive a discount if paid between January 23 and 30. Write the comment Pay this Bill on each bill to be paid. Print the commented report. (Remember, if you have been instructed to export reports to Excel, you cannot export a comment report.)
- Pay all bills indicated in the Commented Unpaid Bills with Terms Detail report. Did you pay two bills?

- Dr. Lori Sweeney was declared Club Champion and won a prize of $500. She brought in the $500 cash as a partial payment to be applied to the amount she owes on her account.

1/24/2015

- Received the bill and all the items ordered from Golf Clothes, Inc. and Golf & Tennis Gear. The bills are dated 01/23/2015.
- Received Check 1205 from Marion Carter as payment in full on her account. (No discounts applicable.)

1/25/2015

- Received Check 305 for $1,741.07 as payment in full for Invoice 11 from Dr. Charles Kincaid. Since a Credit Memo was issued for Invoice 11, recalculate the discount to determine the appropriate amount. Since he is not paying his opening balance of $950.00, include a memo of Partial Payment.
- Received the bill and all the hats ordered from Head Gear, Inc. The date of the bill is 01/23/2015.
- Purchased <u>sales supplies</u> to have on hand for $150 from Indio Office Supply. Used the company Visa for the purchase.
- Prepare an Unpaid Bills with Terms Detail Report for January 25, 2015. Add comments to indicate payment and amounts for bills dated 12/31/14. Golf Clothes, Inc. pay $1000 (Your comment should say <u>Pay $1,000</u>. Also, add a comment for the Credit <u>Use this Credit</u>.), Clubs, Inc. pay $5000, Golf & Tennis Gear pay $500, and Sports Shoe Suppliers pay $500. Print the commented report. (Remember, if you have been instructed to export reports to Excel, you cannot export a comment report.)
- Pay the following bills for the amounts indicated in the Commented Report and print checks. Due Date for all bills will show as 01/10/2015.
  - $1,000 to Golf Clothes, Inc., for the amount owed on 12/31/2014. (NOTE: Select the bill you want to pay. Apply the credit you have from Golf Clothes, Inc., because of returned merchandise. You want to pay $1,000 plus use the $40 credit and reduce the amount owed by $1,040, *not* $960. Once the credit is applied, you will see the Amount To Pay as $4,960. Since you are not paying the full amount owed, click in Amt. To Pay column and enter the amount you are paying. In this case, enter 1,000 as the amount you are paying. When the payment is processed, $1,000 will be deducted from cash to pay for this bill and the $40 credit will be applied.)
  - Pay $5,000 to Clubs, Inc. toward the amount owed on 12/31/2014. (Again, change the payment amount in the Amt. To Pay column.)
  - Pay $500 to Golf & Tennis Gear to pay the amount owed on 12/31/2014.
  - Pay $500 to Sports Shoe Suppliers to pay the amount owed on 12/31/2014.
- After reviewing each of the checks in Write Checks, you notice that the check for Clubs, Inc. says PRINT AS: Golf Clubs, Inc. Go to the Vendor Center, Edit Clubs, Inc. and change the PRINT NAME ON CHECK AS on the Payment Settings Tab to Clubs, Inc. Reprint Check 6.
- Received the bill dated 01/25/15 for $2,800 rent from Palm Springs Rentals. Use Memorized Transaction List to Enter Transaction and record the bill.

1/26/2015

- Use the Reports menu, Vendors & Payables section to prepare an Unpaid Bills Detail Report for January 26, 2015. (*Note:* check Golf Clothes, Inc., the total amount owed should be $4,360. If your report does not show this, check to see how you applied the credit when you paid bills. If necessary, QuickBooks does allow you to delete the previous bill payment and redo it. If this is the case, be sure to apply the credit, and record $1,000 as the payment amount.) Print the Report.
- Russ Tokumoto used his Visa card on file to pay $1,600 as a partial payment. (The opening balance has $600 applied and Invoice 10 has $1,000 applied automatically by QuickBooks. Accept these amounts.)

1/29/2015

- Deposit all receipts for the week.

1/30/2015

- Use Pay Bills and pay the Rent. Print Check 10.
- Received the NSF (Bounced) Check 1205 Check from Marion Carter back from the bank. This check was for $2,891.88. Charge her the bank charge of $15 plus Your Name's Ultimate Golf's own NSF charge of $30. In the Chart of Accounts, change the Account Number for Returned Check Charges to 4090. Change the Terms to "Due on Receipt" for the Opening Balance Invoice, for Invoice 2 and Invoice 14 for the Bounced Check Charge. For Invoice 14, make sure the date is 01/30/15 and use the Copy of: Intuit Product Invoice. Print all three invoices. (The Opening Balance Invoice was prepared before customizing invoices. Use it as is.)
- Prepare Sales Tax Liability Report from January 1-30, 2015. Adjust the column widths and print the report in Landscape orientation. The report should fit on one page.
- Pay sales tax due as of January 30, 2015 and print Check 11.
- Print a Sales by Item Summary Report for January 1-30. Use Landscape orientation and, if necessary, adjust column widths so the report fits on one page wide.
- Enter the following adjusting entries:
  - Office Supplies Used for the month is $125.
  - The balance of the Sales Supplies is $600 on January 30.
  - The amount of Prepaid Insurance represents the liability insurance for 12 months. Record the adjusting entry for the month of January.
  - Depreciation for the month is: Office Equipment, $83.33, Store Fixtures, $100.
- Record the transactions for owner's equity:
  - Each owner's withdrawal for the month of January is $2,000.
  - Divide the amount in account 3100-Your Last Name & Childers, Capital - Other, and transfer one-half the amount into each owner's individual Capital account. (You may view a Standard Balance Sheet for January 30 to determine the amount to divide.)
- Prepare and print an Adjusted Trial Balance for January.
- Back up your work for Week 4. Name the file **Golf (Backup Week 4)**.

01/31/2015

▶ Use the following bank statement to prepare a bank reconciliation. Enter adjustments.

DESERT BANK
1234-110 Highway 111
Palm Springs, CA 92270
(760) 555-3300

Your Name's Ultimate Golf
55-100 PGA Boulevard
Palm Springs, CA 92270
Acct. # 9857-32-922
January 2015

Beginning Balance, January 1, 2015			$35, 275.14
1/8/2015, Deposit	4,212.33		39,487.47
1/10/2015, Check 1		64.75	39,422.72
1/14/2015, Deposit	2,820.83		42,243.55
1/18/2015, Check 2		365.54	41,878.01
1/25/2015, Check 3		392.00	41,486.01
1/23/2015, Check 4		156.80	41,329.21
1/23/2015, Check 5		49.00	41,280.21
1/25/2015, Deposit	6,576.21		47,856.42
1/25/2015, Check 6		5,000.00	42,856.42
1/25/2015, Check 7		500.00	42,356.42
1/25/2015, Check 8		1,000.00	41,356.42
1/25/2015, Check 9		500.00	40,856.42
1/25/2015, Check 10		2,800.00	38,056.42
1/30/2015, NSF Returned Check Marion Crostini		2,891.88	35,164.54
1/30/2015, NSF Bank Charge		15.00	35,149.54
1/31/2015, Service Charge, $15		15.00	35,134.54
1/31/2015, Store Fixtures Loan Pmt.: Interest, $89.03; Principal, $17.21		106.24	35,028.30
1/31/2015, Office Equipment Loan Pmt: Interest, $53.42; Principal, $10.33		63.75	34,964.55
1/31/2015, Interest	76.73		35,041.28
Ending Balance, 1/31/2015			**35,041.28**

▶ Print a Detailed Reconciliation Report.

▶ Received the Visa bill. Prepare a Credit Card Reconciliation.

DESERT BANK
VISA DEPARTMENT
1234-110 Highway 111
Palm Springs, CA 92270 (760) 555-3300

Your Name's Ultimate Golf
55-100 PGA Boulevard
Palm Springs, CA 92270
VISA Acct. # 9287-52-952 January 2015

Beginning Balance, January 1, 2015			0.00
1/12/2015, Indio Office Supply		175.00	175.00
1/25/2015, Indio Office Supply		150.00	325.00
Ending Balance, 1/25/2015			325.00

Minimum Payment Due, $50.00 **Payment Due Date: February 7, 2015**

▶ Print Check 14 for the payment to Desert Bank and print a Reconciliation Summary Report.
▶ View a Profit & Loss (Standard) report for 01/01/15 to 01/31/15 to get the information needed to divide the net income in half. Close the report without printing.
▶ Divide the Net Income/Owners' Equity in half and transfer one-half into each owner's individual capital account. (This is not an adjusting entry.)
▶ Close the drawing account for each owner into the owner's individual capital account. (This is not an adjusting entry.)
▶ Close the period using the closing date of 01/31/2015. Do not use a password.
▶ Edit a transaction from the closed period: Discovered an error in the Supplies accounts. Transfer $50 from 1320-Sales Supplies to 1310-Office Supplies.
▶ Adjust the number of tees on hand to 24. Use the expense account 6190 for Merchandise Adjustments. Be sure to correct the adjustment for net income/ retained earnings.
▶ Prepare an Archive Backup named **Golf (Archive 01-31-15)**.

Print Reports and Back Up

▶ Print the following:
- Journal (Landscape orientation, Fit on one page wide) for January , 2015.
- Trial Balance, January 31, 2015 (Portrait orientation).
- Standard Profit and Loss Statement, January 1-31, 2015.
- Standard Balance Sheet, January 31, 2015.

▶ Back up your work to **Golf (Backup Complete)**.

NAME______________________

SECTION 2 PRACTICE SET: TRANSMITTAL

YOUR NAME'S ULTIMATE GOLF

Check the items below as you complete and/or print them; then attach the documents and reports in the order listed when you submit them to your instructor. Printing is optional for Payment Receipts and Bills (unless your instructor requires them to be printed); however, they are included on the transmittal sheet so they can be checked as they are completed.

(Note: When paying bills and printing a batch of checks, your checks may be in a different order than shown below. As long as you print the checks to the correct vendors and have the correct amounts, do not be concerned if your check numbers are not an exact match.)

Week 1

__ Account Listing
__ Invoice 1: Tamara Yanov
__ Invoice 2: Marion Carter
__ Invoice 3: Azar Hammar
__ Invoice 4: Palm Springs Schools
__ Sales Order 1: Wade Schaub
__ Invoice 2 (Corrected): Marion Carter
__ Payment Receipt: Russ Tokumoto
__ Invoice 5: Dr. Lori Sweeney
__ Invoice 6: Wade Schaub
__ Payment Receipt: Mark Donlon
__ Sales Receipt 1: Cash Customer
__ Sales Order 2: Laura Hansen
__ Payment Receipt: Gene Potter
__ Invoice 7: Laura Hansen
__ Inventory Stock Status by Item Report, January 1-5, 2015
__ Purchase Order 1: Golf & Tennis Gear
__ Purchase Order 2: Golf Clothes, Inc.
__ Purchase Order 3: Head Gear, Inc.
__ Purchase Order QuickReport, January 5, 2015
__ Sales Receipt 2: Cash Customer
__ Deposit Summary, January 8, 2015

Week 2

__ Item Receipt: Head Gear, Inc. (Optional)
__ Bill: Golf & Tennis Gear (Optional)
__ Bill: Golf Clothes, Inc. (Optional)
__ Credit Memo 8: Dr. Lori Sweeney
__ Credit Memo 9: Mark Donlon
__ Check 1: Mark Donlon
__ Sales Order 3: Russ Tokumoto
__ Sales Receipt 3: Cash Customer
__ Invoice 10: Russ Tokumoto
__ Bill: Desert Telephone Co. (Optional)
__ Bill: Head Gear, Inc. (Optional)
__ Payment Receipt: Azar Hammar
__ Payment Receipt: Tamara Yanov
__ Deposit Summary, January 14, 2015

Week 3

__ Invoice 11: Dr. Charles Kincaid
__ Payment Receipt: Dr. Lori Sweeney
__ Bill: Golf & Tennis Gear (Optional)
__ Commented Unpaid Bills with Terms Detail, January 18, 2015
__ Check 2: Golf & Tennis Gear
__ Check 3: Golf Clothes, Inc.
__ Invoice 12: Dr. Lori Sweeney
__ Bill Credit: Golf Clothes, Inc. (Optional)
__ Credit Memo 13: Dr. Charles Kincaid
__ Sales Receipt 4: Cash Customer
__ Sales Receipt 5: Cash Customer
__ Inventory Stock Status by Item, January 1-20, 2015
__ Purchase Order 4: Golf & Tennis Gear
__ Purchase Order 5: Golf Clothes, Inc.
__ Purchase Order 6: Head Gear, Inc.
__ Deposit Summary, January 20, 2015

Week 4 and End of Period

__Commented Unpaid Bills with Terms Detail, January 23, 2015
__Check 4: Golf & Tennis Gear
__ Check 5: Head Gear, Inc.
__ Payment Receipt: Dr. Lori Sweeney
__ Bill: Golf Clothes, Inc. (Optional)
__ Bill: Golf & Tennis Gear (Optional)
__ Payment Receipt: Marion Carter
__ Payment Receipt: Dr. Charles Kincaid
__ Bill: Head Gear, Inc. (Optional)
__ Commented Unpaid Bills with Terms Detail, January 25, 2015
__ Check 6: Golf Clubs, Inc.
__ Check 7: Golf & Tennis Gear
__ Check 8: Golf Clothes, Inc.
__ Check 9: Sports Shoe Suppliers
__ Check 6 (Corrected): Clubs, Inc.
__ Bill: Palm Springs Rentals (Optional)
__ Unpaid Bills Detail, January 26, 2015
__ Payment Receipt: Russ Tokumoto
__ Deposit Summary, January 29, 2015
__ Check 10: Palm Springs Rentals
__ Payment Receipt (Revised) Marion Carter
__ Invoice 2 (Revised): Marion Carter
__ Invoice 14: Marion Carter
__ Sales Tax Liability Report, January 1-30, 2015
__ Check 11: State Board of Equalization
__ Sales by Item Summary, January 1-30, 2015
__ Check 12: Your First and Last Name
__ Check 13: Valerie Childers
__ Adjusted Trial Balance, January 30, 2015
__ Bank Reconciliation, January 31, 2015
__ Credit Card Reconciliation, January 31, 2015
__ Check 14: Desert Bank
__ Journal, January 2015
__ Trial Balance, January 31, 2015
__ Standard Profit and Loss Statement, January 1-31, 2015
__ Standard Balance Sheet, January 31, 2015

8

PAYROLL

LEARNING OBJECTIVES

At the completion of this chapter, you will be able to:

1. Create, preview, and print payroll checks.
2. Adjust pay stub information.
3. Correct, void, and delete paychecks.
4. Change employee information and add a new employee.
5. Print a Payroll Summary by Employee Report.
6. View an Employee Earnings Summary Report.
7. Print a Payroll Liabilities Report.
8. Pay Taxes and Other Liabilities.
9. Print a Journal

PAYROLL

Many times, a company begins the process of computerizing its accounting system simply to be able to do the payroll using the computer. It is much faster and easier to let QuickBooks look at the tax tables and determine how much withholding should be deducted for each employee than to have an individual perform this task. Because tax tables change frequently, QuickBooks requires its users to enroll in a payroll service plan in order to obtain updates. In order to enroll in a payroll service plan, you must have a company tax identification number. Intuit has a variety of payroll service plans that are available for an additional charge. If you do not subscribe to a payroll plan, you must calculate and enter the payroll taxes manually.

Intuit's payroll plans are changed and updated frequently; however, at the time of writing, Intuit has the following Payroll Plans available on a subscription basis:

Online Payroll: Different levels available: Basic, and Enhanced. (Basic is available for $20.00 per month, Enhanced is $31.20 per month. Both versions charge an additional $2.00 per month for each employee). Subscribing to either of these plans enables you to pay your employees. You may even use your iPhone or Android. Basic is used to pay employees. Enhanced is used to pay employees and 1099 contractors. Enhanced calculates, files, and pays federal and state taxes; and processes W-2s. Free direct deposit is included. Intuit Online Payroll is a standalone program that is integrated with QuickBooks software.

Payroll Basic: Essentially, this version only processes paychecks (From $14.58 to $20.00 per month plus $2.00 per month per employee). Subscribing to this plan enables you to download up-to-date tax tables into QuickBooks. If you use this, you enter your employee information once. Then, each pay period you will enter the hours and QuickBooks will use this information to automatically calculate deductions and prepare paychecks for your employees. Direct deposit is available for no additional fee. Since no tax forms are included, you will work with your accountant; or use QuickBooks reports to generate the data you need in order to fill in state and federal tax forms by hand.

Payroll Enhanced: Primarily used to prepare paychecks and pay taxes (From $22.75 to $31.20 per month plus $2.00 per employee). This is a more comprehensive do-it-yourself payroll solution used to calculate deductions, earnings, and payroll taxes. Enter hours and get instant paychecks. Enhanced payroll includes federal and most state tax forms, tools for tracking payroll expenses and workers compensation. Direct deposit is available for no additional fee. Enhanced payroll automatically fills in your data on quarterly federal and state tax forms. Just print, sign & mail your tax filings or use E-File to file and pay payroll taxes electronically. Year-end W-2s are included. The program is integrated with QuickBooks.

Full Service Payroll: Setup, paychecks, taxes, filings, and reports are done for you ($79 per month plus $2 per employee). Complete setup done for you. Receive guidance when submitting employee hours online. Unlimited payrolls each month may be prepared, free direct deposit, free new hire reporting, free W-2 and 1099 printing and processing. Alerts for discrepancies are generated and each payroll you submit is reviewed for accuracy by Intuit's experts. Payroll taxes are filed and tax payments are made for you. Service is guaranteed to be accurate and on-time. The service is completely integrated with QuickBooks.

Payroll for Accounting Professionals: Intuit offers two payroll plans for accountants:

QuickBooks Online Essentials with Payroll: online version of QuickBooks that includes payroll. Clients enter hours, then payroll taxes and deductions are automatically calculated. Paychecks may then be approved and printed. Direct deposit is free. Accountants review the clients' payroll taxes. Quarterly and year-end payroll taxes are calculated within QuickBooks. Guaranteed to be accurate on tax calculations. (Priced from $29.49 to $43.99 per month at the time of writing.) Direct deposit, electronic payments and filings, and the ability to share data with clients are included.

QuickBooks Online Plus with Payroll: Contains everything that Essentials has plus provides more QuickBooks features. In addition to running payroll as in Essentials, you may prepare and print 1099s from this package. (Priced from $34.49 to $51.49 per month.)

MANUAL PAYROLL

The ability to process the payroll manually is part of the QuickBooks program and does not require a subscription or cost additional fees. However, if you use manual payroll for your business, it is your responsibility to obtain up-to-date payroll tax tables and tax forms.

Since all of our businesses in this text are fictitious and we do not have a FEIN, (Federal Employer's Identification Number), we will not be subscribing to any of the QuickBooks Payroll Services. As a result, we will be entering all tax information for paychecks manually based on data provided in the text. Calculations will be made for vacation pay, sick pay, medical and dental insurance deductions, and so on. Paychecks will be created, printed, corrected, and voided. Tax reports, tax payments, and tax forms will be explored.

Payroll is an area of accounting that has frequent changes; for example, tax tables are frequently updated, changes in withholding or tax limits are made, etc. As a result, QuickBooks is modified via updates to implement changes to payroll. As a word of caution, the materials presented in this chapter are current at the time of writing. It may be that as Intuit updates QuickBooks some of the things displayed in the chapter may change. If this happens, please read the information and ask your professor how to proceed.

TRAINING TUTORIAL AND PROCEDURES

The tutorial will work with the sole proprietorship, Student's Name Fitness Solutions, which has a gym with memberships, personal training, exercise classes, and a small boutique with fitness clothing, accessories, and equipment. Use the company file **Fitness**. Once you open your copy of the company file, transactions will be recorded for the fictitious company. To maximize training benefits, you should follow the procedures previously provided.

You have four employees Mark Adams, who provides the management and supervision of the gym; Steven Morales, who is a personal trainer; Scarlette Sharp, who manages the boutique shop and is the bookkeeper; and Laura Waters, the Pilates instructor.

Mark Adams and Scarlette Sharp are salaried employees. Steven Morales and Laura Waters are paid on an hourly basis, and any hours in excess of 160 for the pay period will be paid as overtime. Paychecks for all employees are issued on a monthly basis.

DATES AND REPORT PREFERENCES

Throughout the text, the year used for the screen shots is 2015, which is the same year as the version of the program. You may want to check with your instructor to see if you should use 2015 as the year. As in earlier chapters, verify the printing assignment with your instructor. The text will continue to include all printable items on the transmittal.

➲ In Reports & Graphs Company Preferences, turn off the Date Prepared, Time Prepared, and Report Basis in the Header/Footer.

ADD YOUR NAME TO THE COMPANY NAME

As with previous companies, each student in the course will be working with the same company and printing the same documents. Personalizing the company name to include your name will help identify many of the documents you print during your training.

Add your first and last name to the Company Name and Legal Name as previously instructed; make sure to add **'s** at the end of your last name

- Example: Sue Smith's Fitness Solutions

CHANGE NAME OF CAPITAL ACCOUNTS

Since the owner's equity accounts have the words Student's Name as part of the account name, replace *Student's Name* with your actual name.

Change the owner equity account names as previously instructed. Change the following:

- Remember to use your real name. If you run out of room for your name and the rest of the title, use your first initial and your last name.

Student's Name, Capital to **First and Last Name, Capital**
Student's Name, Investment to **First and Last Name, Investment**
Student's Name, Withdrawals to **First and Last Name, Withdrawal**

SELECT PAYROLL OPTION

Before entering any payroll transactions, QuickBooks must be informed of the type of payroll service you are selecting. Once QuickBooks knows what type of payroll process has been selected for the company, you will be able to create paychecks. In order to create paychecks manually, you must go through the Help menu to designate this choice.

Select a **Manual** payroll option

Press **F1** to access Help
Type **Manual Payroll** on the Have a Question? screen; click the **Search** button
On the Have a Question? screen, which shows the Answers in Help, click **Process payroll manually (without a subscription to QuickBooks Payroll)**

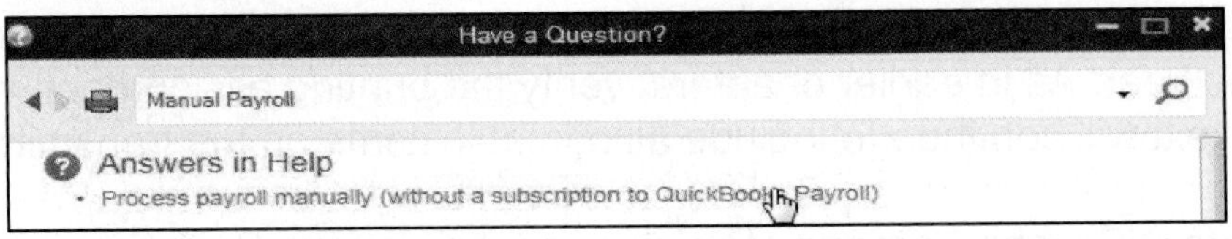

On the next Have a Question? screen, click the words <u>**manual payroll calculations**</u>

- If you get your information in a Help Article, click the same words.

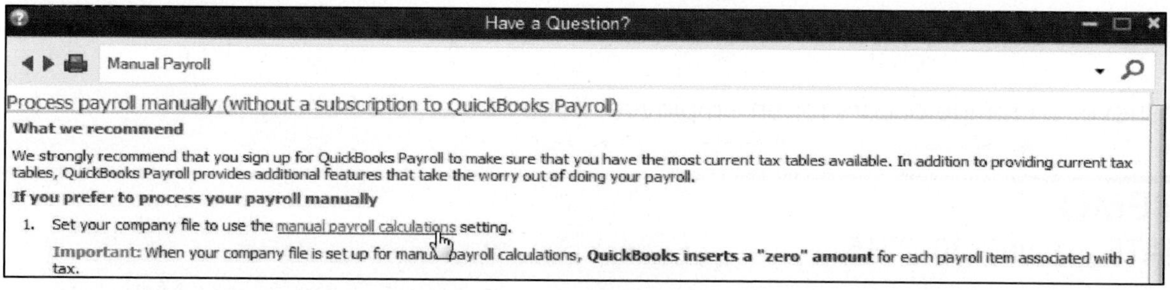

Read the information for "Are you sure you want to set your company file to use manual calculations", and then click **Set my company file to use manual calculations**

The manual calculations setting is applied immediately and you will get a QuickBooks Information screen

- The message may hide behind the Help screen. If so, close Help.

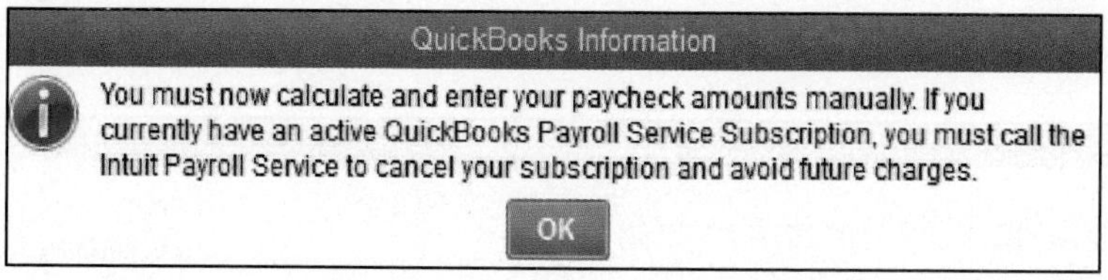

Read the message, click **OK**, close **Help** (if still open)

PAYROLL SCHEDULES

If you subscribe to a payroll plan, you will have the option to set up Payroll schedules for processing the payroll. To set up a new payroll schedule, you will give the schedule a name, indicate how often you pay your employees on the schedule, provide the pay period end date, the date that should appear on paychecks for this pay period, and what day should appear on paychecks for this pay period.

8

Once a payroll schedule is created, employees are assigned to it based on the frequency of payment. For example, you assign the employees paid monthly to one schedule and the employees paid weekly to a different schedule. When it is time to process the payroll, you access the Payroll Center (not available without a subscription), click the Pay Employees tab, select the payroll schedule you want to run, and then click Start Scheduled Payroll. After that, you verify the hours worked and the amounts for each employee listed on the schedule, review the paycheck summary, and, finally, create paychecks.

Since we are processing payroll manually, we cannot use Payroll Schedules in the text.

CHANGE EMPLOYEE INFORMATION

Whenever a change occurs for an employee, it may be entered at any time.

> **MEMO**
> **DATE:** January 30, 2015
>
> Effective today, Mark Adams will receive a pay raise to $30,000 annually. In addition, all employees will be paid on a monthly basis.

Change the salary and pay period for Mark Adams

Click the **Employees** icon to open the Employee Center
Double-click **Mark Adams** in the Employee list
On the Edit Employee screen, click the **Payroll Info** Tab
On the **Payroll Info** tab, click the drop-down list arrow for PAY FREQUENCY, click **Monthly**
Click in the text box for the **HOURLY/ANNUAL RATE** and change the amount to **30,000**

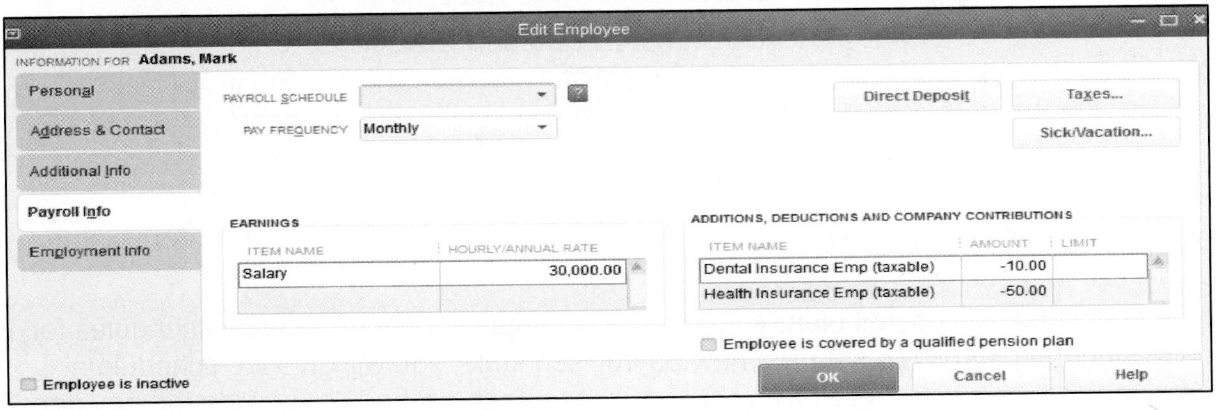

Click **OK**
Do <u>not</u> close the **Employee Center**

Change the other three employees to a monthly Pay Frequency following the steps listed above

ADD NEW EMPLOYEE

As new employees are hired, they should be added.

MEMO

DATE: January 30, 2015

Effective 01/30/15 hired a part-time employee to teach yoga classes. Ms. Lindsey King, Social Security. No.: 100-55-6936, Female, Birth date: 02/14/80, Marital Status: Single, U.S. Citizen: Yes, Ethnicity: White, Disability: No, Address: 2379 Bayshore Drive, Venice, CA 90405, Main Phone 310-555-6611. Pay frequency is monthly. Paid an hourly rate of $15.00 and an overtime rate of $22.50. Federal and state withholding: Single, 0 Allowances. No local taxes, dental insurance, medical insurance, sick time, or vacation time.

Add the new employee, Lindsey King

Click the **New Employee** button at the top of the Employee Center

On the **Personal** tab, click in the text box for **LEGAL NAME**, enter **Ms.**

Using the information provided in the memo, tab to or click in each field and enter the information for the **Personal** tab

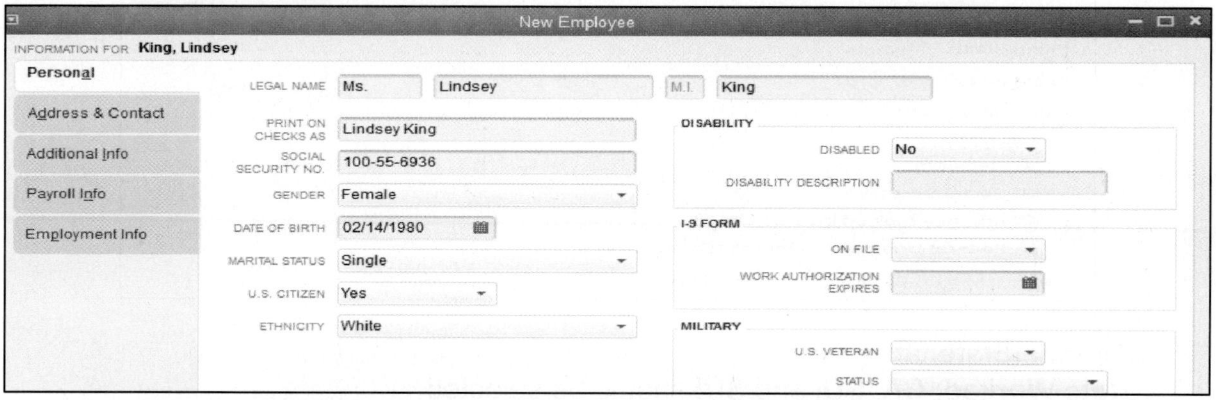

Click the **Address & Contact** tab; enter the information provided in the memo

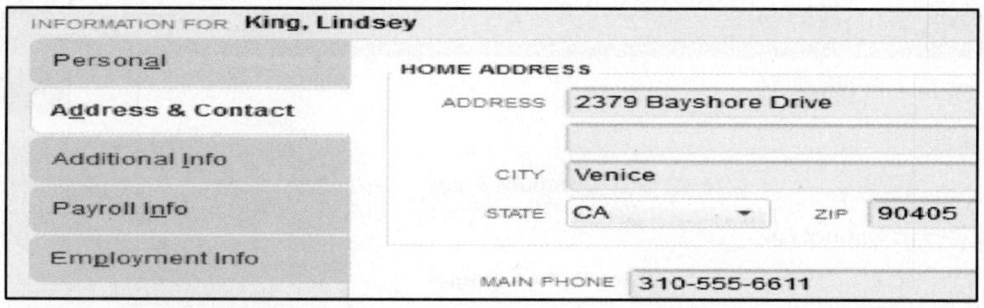

Click the **Payroll Info** tab

Select a **Monthly** pay frequency

Click in the **ITEM NAME** column under **EARNINGS**, click the drop-down list arrow that appears, and click **Hourly Rate**

Tab to or click in the text box for **HOURLY/ANNUAL RATE**, enter the **15.00** hourly rate she will be paid

Click in the **ITEM NAME** column under **Hourly Rate**, click the drop-down list arrow that appears, click **Overtime Rate**

- QuickBooks enters the rate of 22.50.

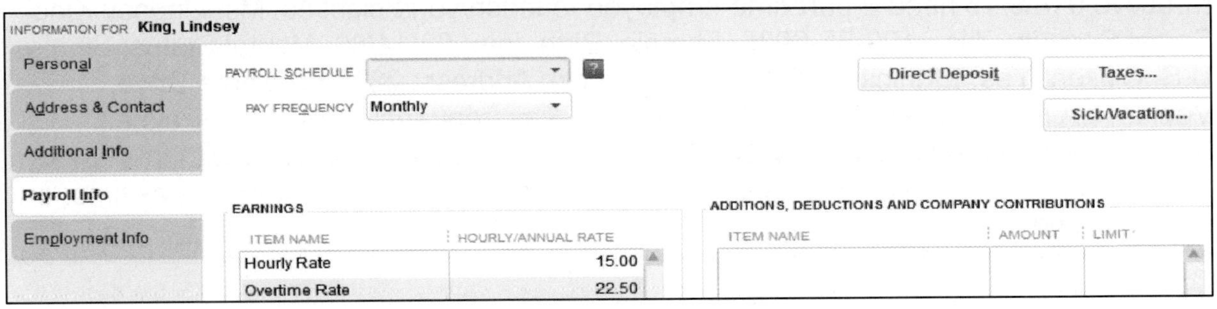

Click the **Taxes** button and complete the tax information:
Federal should show Filing Status: **Single,** Allowances: **0,** Extra Withholding: **0.00**
Subject to **Medicare**, **Social Security**, and **Federal Unemployment Tax (Company Paid)** should have a check mark

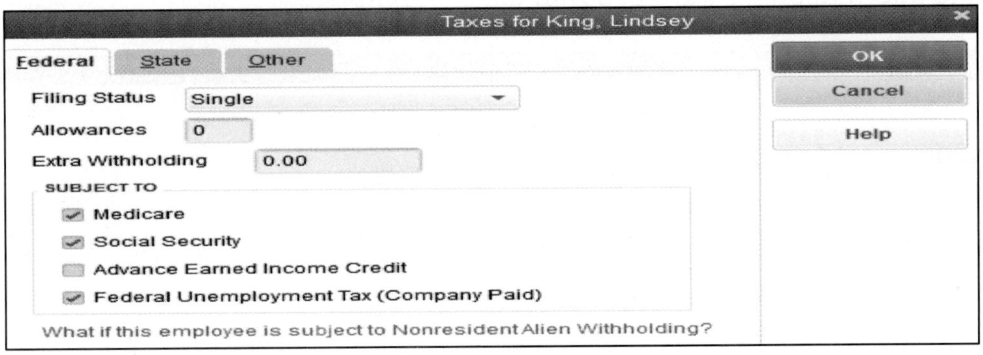

Click the **State** tab:
State Worked: **CA**, **SUI** and **SDI** should be selected
State Subject to Withholding: State: **CA**, Filing Status: **Single**, Allowances: **0**, Extra Withholding: **0.00**; Estimated Deductions: **0**

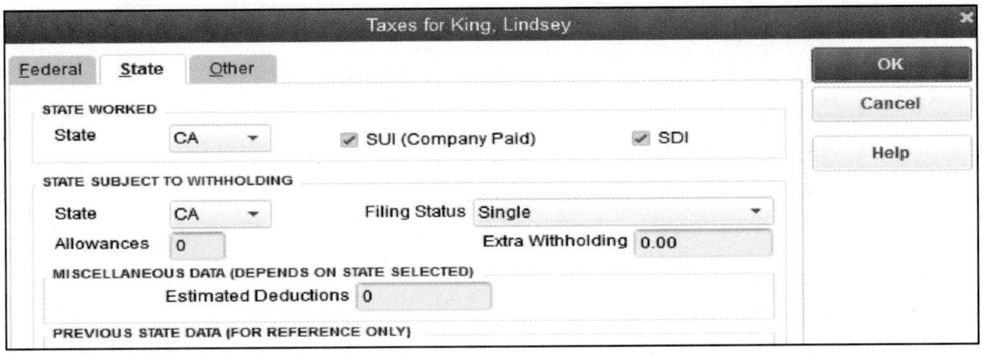

Click the **Other** tab
CA – Employment Training Tax and Medicare Employee Addl Tax should be shown

- If not, click the drop-down list arrow for **ITEM NAME**, and click **CA-Employment Training Tax**. Repeat if Medicare Employee Addl Tax is not shown.

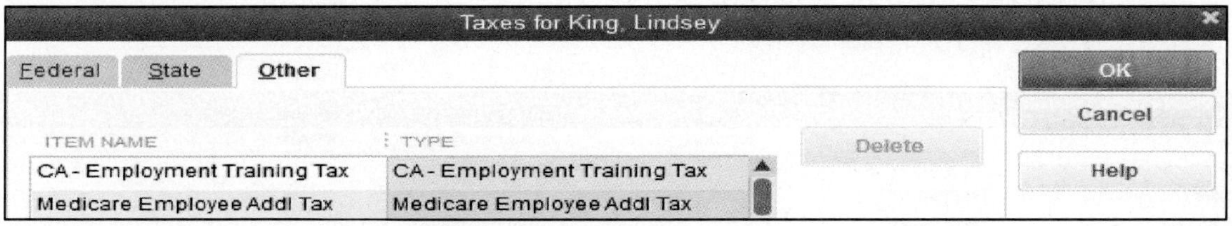

Click **OK** to complete the tax information
Click **Employment Info**
The **HIRE DATE** is **01/30/15** and in the **EMPLOYMENT DETAILS** section the **EMPLOYMENT TYPE** is **Regular**

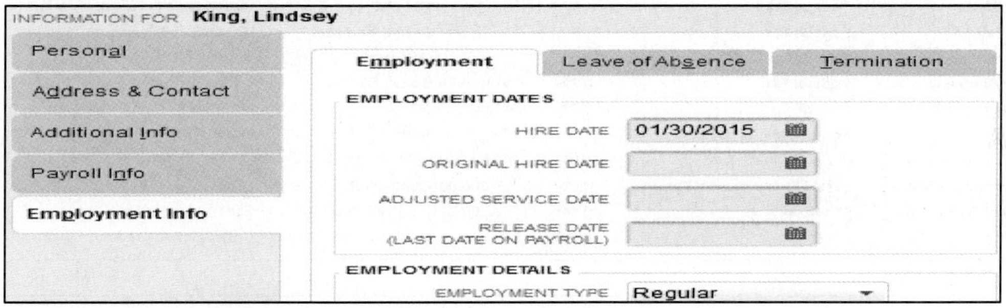

Click **OK** to complete the addition of the new employee

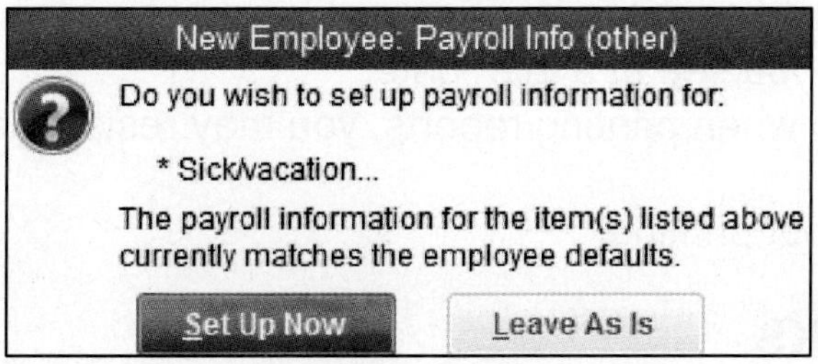

Since Lindsey does not have any sick/vacation hours, click **Leave As Is** on the New Employee: Payroll Info (other), close the Employee Center

VIEW PAYROLL ITEM LIST

The Payroll Item list contains a listing of all payroll items, and information regarding the item type, amount of deduction, annual limit for deductions (if applicable), tax tracking, vendor for payment, and the account ID.

View the Payroll Item List

Click **Employees** on the Menu bar

Click **Manage Payroll Items**, click **View/Edit Payroll Item List**

- If you get a message box regarding subscribing to a payroll service, click No anytime you see the message.

The Payroll Item List is displayed

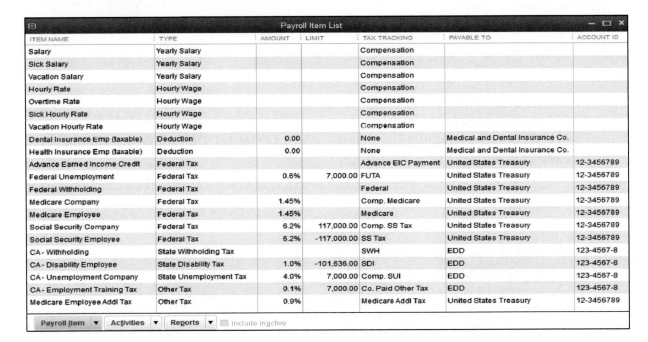

Payroll Item List

ITEM NAME	TYPE	AMOUNT	LIMIT	TAX TRACKING	PAYABLE TO	ACCOUNT ID
Salary	Yearly Salary			Compensation		
Sick Salary	Yearly Salary			Compensation		
Vacation Salary	Yearly Salary			Compensation		
Hourly Rate	Hourly Wage			Compensation		
Overtime Rate	Hourly Wage			Compensation		
Sick Hourly Rate	Hourly Wage			Compensation		
Vacation Hourly Rate	Hourly Wage			Compensation		
Dental Insurance Emp (taxable)	Deduction	0.00		None	Medical and Dental Insurance Co.	
Health Insurance Emp (taxable)	Deduction	0.00		None	Medical and Dental Insurance Co.	
Advance Earned Income Credit	Federal Tax			Advance EIC Payment	United States Treasury	12-3456789
Federal Unemployment	Federal Tax	0.6%	7,000.00	FUTA	United States Treasury	12-3456789
Federal Withholding	Federal Tax			Federal	United States Treasury	12-3456789
Medicare Company	Federal Tax	1.45%		Comp. Medicare	United States Treasury	12-3456789
Medicare Employee	Federal Tax	1.45%		Medicare	United States Treasury	12-3456789
Social Security Company	Federal Tax	6.2%	117,000.00	Comp. SS Tax	United States Treasury	12-3456789
Social Security Employee	Federal Tax	6.2%	-117,000.00	SS Tax	United States Treasury	12-3456789
CA - Withholding	State Withholding Tax			SWH	EDD	123-4567-8
CA - Disability Employee	State Disability Tax	1.0%	-101,636.00	SDI	EDD	123-4567-8
CA - Unemployment Company	State Unemployment Tax	4.0%	7,000.00	Comp. SUI	EDD	123-4567-8
CA - Employment Training Tax	Other Tax	0.1%	7,000.00	Co. Paid Other Tax	EDD	123-4567-8
Medicare Employee Addl Tax	Other Tax	0.9%		Medicare Addl Tax	United States Treasury	12-3456789

Payroll Item ▼ Activities ▼ Reports ▼ Include inactive

View the Payroll Item List to see the ITEM NAME, TYPE, AMOUNT, LIMIT, TAX TRACKING, PAYABLE TO, and ACCOUNT ID

- Remember, Limits and Amounts are subject to change so this chart may not match the one you see at a later date.
- As you learned when printing reports, you may resize the columns in the Payroll Item List.

Close the list without printing

CREATE PAYCHECKS

Once the manual payroll option has been selected, paychecks may be created. You may enter hours and preview the checks before creating them, or, if using a payroll service, you may create the checks without previewing. Once the payroll has been processed, checks may be printed.

Since you process the payroll manually, you must enter the payroll data for withholdings and deductions. QuickBooks will enter other payroll items such as medical and dental insurance deductions, and it will calculate the total amount of the checks.

MEMO
DATE: January 31, 2015

Create and print paychecks for January 31, 2015. Use this date as the pay period ending date and the check date.

Pay all employees using the hours and deductions listed in the following table:

PAYROLL TABLE: JANUARY 31, 2015					
	Mark Adams	**Lindsey King**	**Steven Morales**	**Scarlette Sharp**	**Laura Waters**
HOURS					
REGULAR	160	8	72	140	160
OVERTIME					8
SICK			8		
VACATION				20	
DEDUCTIONS OTHER PAYROLL ITEMS: EMPLOYEE					
DENTAL INS.	10.00			10.00	
MEDICAL INS.	50.00			50.00	
DEDUCTIONS: COMPANY					
CA-EMPLOYMENT TRAINING TAX	2.50	0.00	2.00	1.67	2.58
SOCIAL SECURITY	155.00	7.44	124.00	103.33	159.96
MEDICARE	36.25	1.74	29.00	24.17	37.41
FEDERAL UNEMPLOYMENT	15.00	0.00	12.00	10.00	15.48
CA-UNEMPLOYMENT	100.00	4.80	80.00	66.67	103.20
DEDUCTIONS: EMPLOYEE					
MEDICARE EMPLOYEE ADDL TAX	0.00	0.00	0.00	0.00	0.00
FEDERAL WITHHOLDING	312.00	0.00	132.50	124.60	276.34
SOCIAL SECURITY	155.00	7.44	124.00	103.33	159.96
MEDICARE	36.25	1.74	29.00	24.17	37.41
CA-WITHHOLDING	75.00	0.00	30.31	34.06	42.48
CA-DISABILITY	25.00	1.20	20.00	16.67	25.80

Click **Pay Employees** icon in the **Employees** section of the **Home Page**
The **Enter Payroll Information** screen appears

8

Enter the **PAY PERIOD ENDS** date of **01/31/15**
Enter the **CHECK DATE** of **01/31/15**
The **BANK ACCOUNT** is **Checking** with a **BANK ACCOUNT BALANCE** of **35,840.00**
CHECK OPTIONS should be **Print Paychecks on check stock**
Click the **Check All** button to select all of the employees

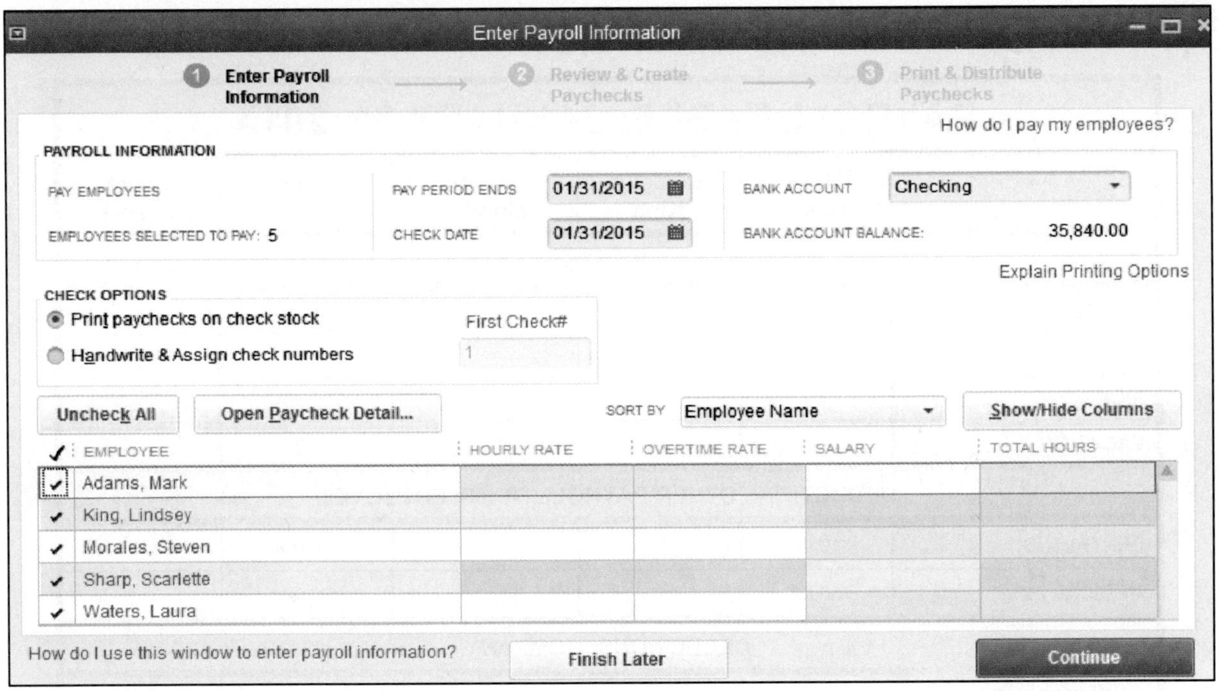

- Notice the check mark in front of each employee name.

Click the **Continue** button

- Notice the amounts given for each employee. There is nothing listed for taxes, employer taxes, contributions, or total hours. This information needs to be entered when preparing payroll manually.
- Remember, if you do subscribe to a QuickBooks payroll service, you will not enter the taxes manually. QuickBooks will calculate them and enter them for you. Since tax tables change frequently, the taxes calculated by QuickBooks may not be the same as the amounts listed on the Payroll Table in the text.
- As you record the information for each employee, refer to the payroll chart listed earlier in the chapter.

Click the **Open Paycheck Detail...** button on the Review and Create Paychecks screen

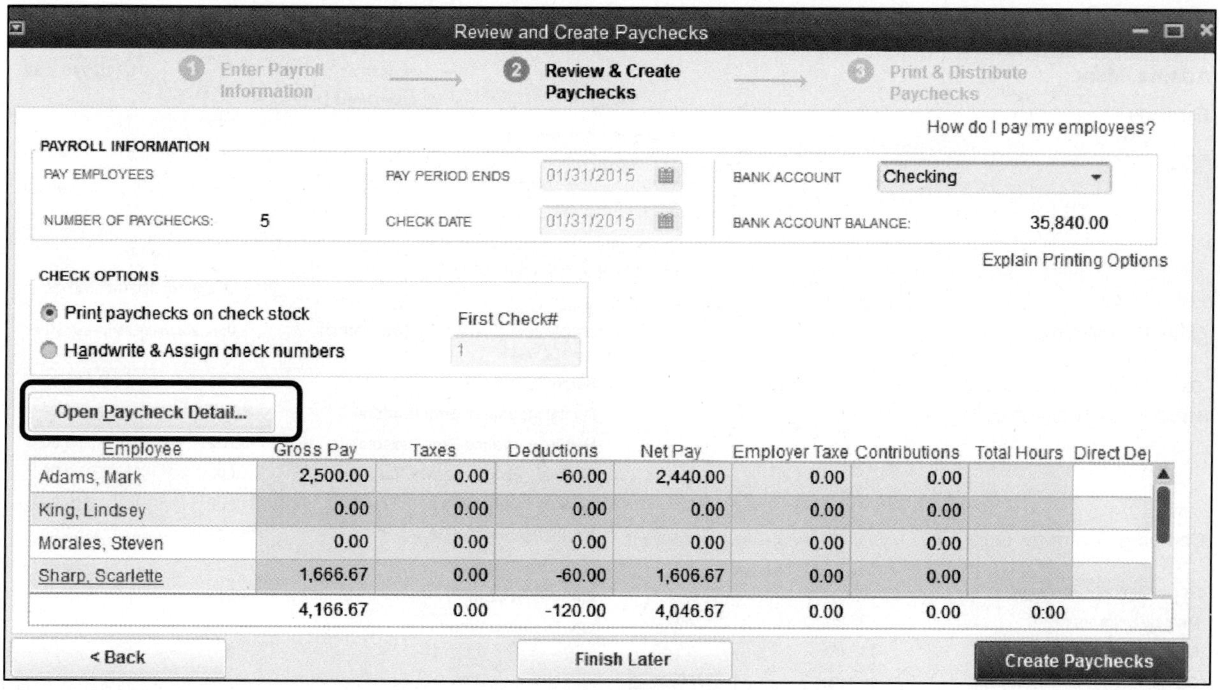

The **Preview Paycheck** screen for Mark Adams appears.

- Notice that QuickBooks calculated the monthly salary based on the annual salary.

Tab to or click in the **HOURS** column, enter **160**

The section for Other Payroll Items is automatically completed by QuickBooks

- Because these deductions were set up previously for Mark, the amounts deducted for Dental and Health Insurance paid by the employee shows.

Complete the **Company Summary (adjusted)** information:

Click in the **AMOUNT** column for **CA-Employment Training Tax,** enter **2.50**
Tab to or click in the **AMOUNT** column for **Social Security Company**, enter **155.00**
Tab to or click in the **Medicare Company** line, enter **36.25**
Tab to or click in the **Federal Unemployment** line, enter **15.00**
Tab to or click in the **CA-Unemployment Company** line, enter **100.00**

- You may need to scroll down the list to see this item.

Complete the **Employee Summary (adjusted)** information:

- You will be leaving Medicare Employee Addl Tax at 0.00 for all employees. The additional 0.9% tax is levied on people and/or couples with higher levels of income. Currently, income more $125,000 married filing separately, $200,000 single, and $250,000 married will be taxed.
- QuickBooks will automatically insert the – in front of the amount.

Click in the **AMOUNT** column for **Federal Withholding**, enter **312.00**
Tab to or click in the **Social Security Employee** line, enter **155.00**
Tab to or click in the **Medicare Employee** line, enter **36.25**
Tab to or click in the **CA-Withholding** line, enter **75.00**
Tab to or click in the **CA-Disability Employee** line, enter **25.00**, press **Tab**

8

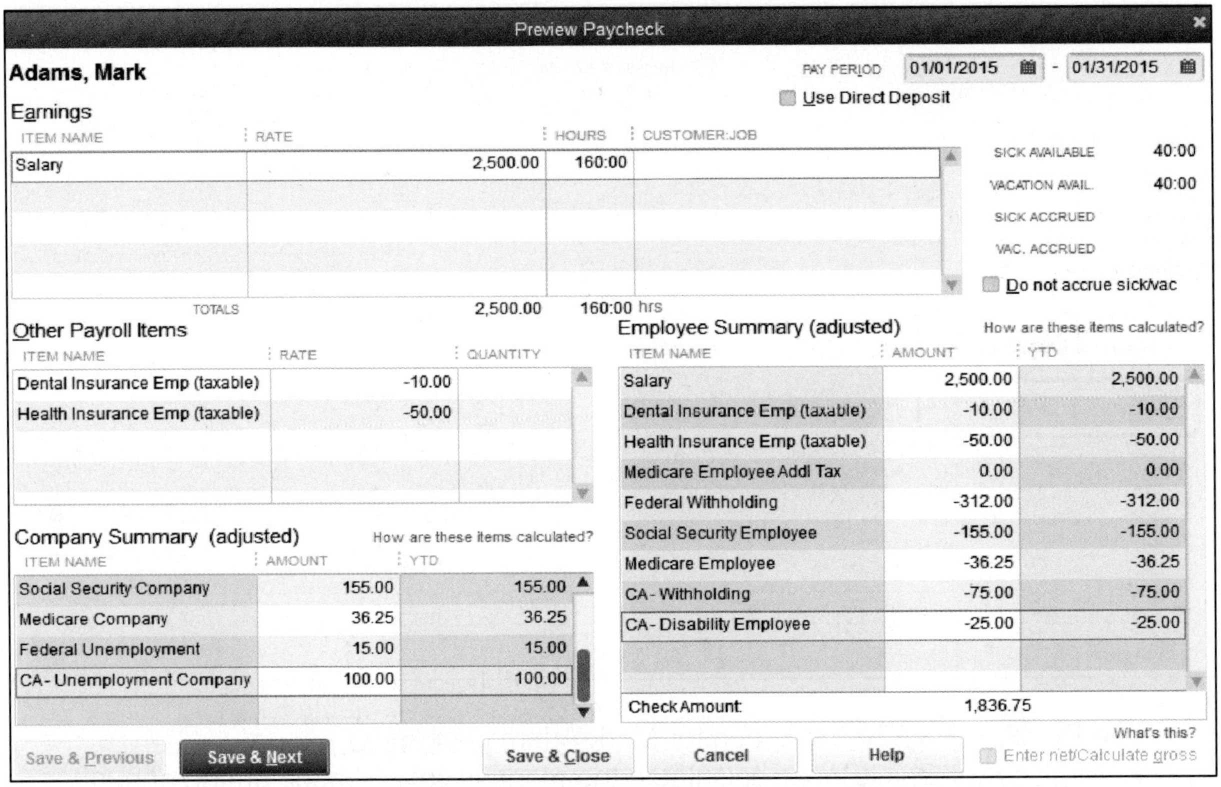

- In the Company Summary for all of the paychecks, the line for CA – Employment Training Tax is not shown in the screen shot.

After verifying that everything was entered correctly, click **Save & Next**

The next Preview Paycheck screen should be for **Lindsey King**

Tab to or click the **Hours** column next to **Hourly Rate** for **Lindsey King**, enter **8**

Refer to the Payroll Table for January 31, 2015, and enter the information

- You may need to use the scroll bar in the Company Summary section in order to complete the information for CA – Employment Training Tax.

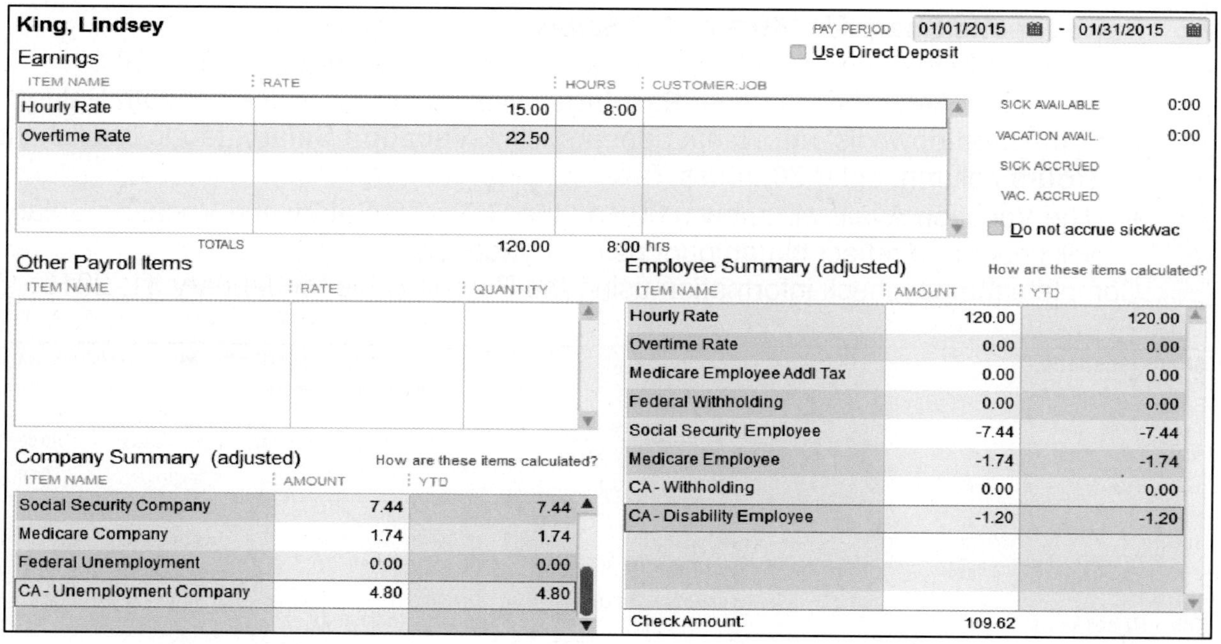

Click **Save & Next**

Pay **Steven Morales** for **72** hours of **Hourly Regular Rate**

In the **ITEM NAME** column for **Earnings**, click the line below Overtime Rate

Click the drop-down list arrow, click **Sick Hourly Rate**

Enter **8** for the number of hours Steven was out sick

Enter the company and employee deductions from the Payroll Table for January 31, 2015

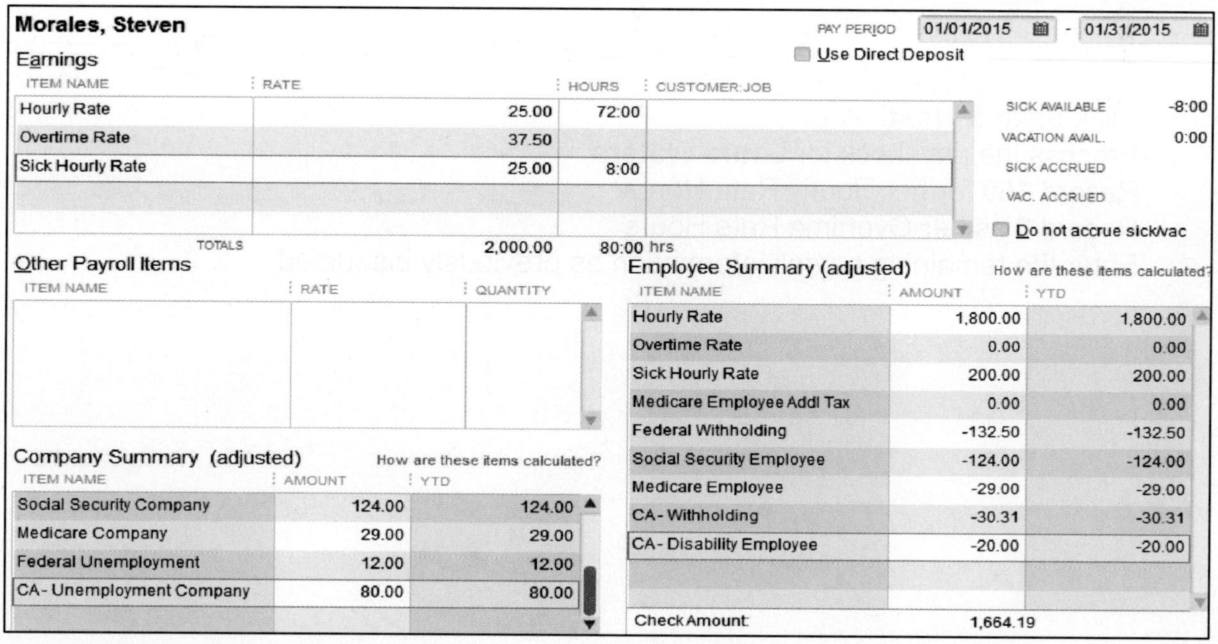

Click **Save & Next**

8

Pay **Scarlette Sharp** for **140** hours of **Salary**

- Notice that the number of Vacation Hours listed in **Vacation Avail. is 20.00**.

In the **ITEM NAME** column under **Earnings**, click on the blank line beneath Salary

Click the drop-down list arrow that appears, click **Vacation Salary**, tab to or click the **Hours** column, enter **20**, press **Tab**

- The Vacation Avail. will show 0.00 and the Rates for Salary and Vacation Salary will change to reflect the amount paid for vacation.

Complete the paycheck information using the Payroll Table for January 31, 2015

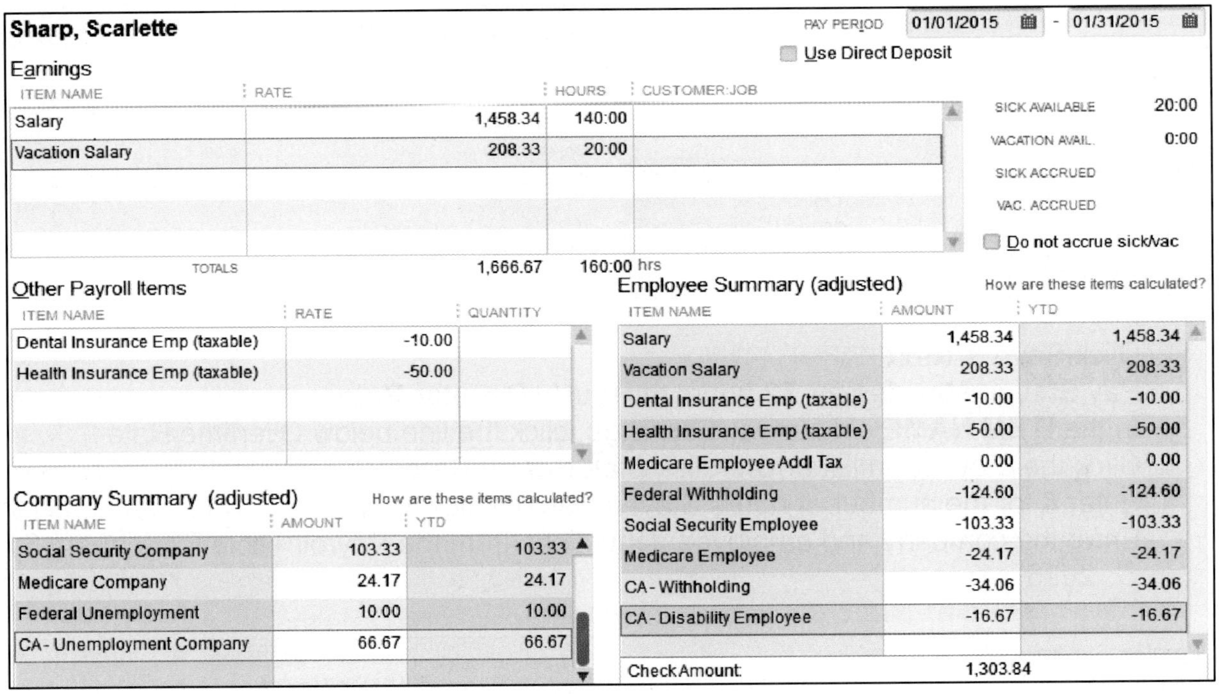

Sharp, Scarlette

PAY PERIOD 01/01/2015 - 01/31/2015

Use Direct Deposit

Earnings

ITEM NAME	RATE	HOURS	CUSTOMER:JOB
Salary	1,458.34	140:00	
Vacation Salary	208.33	20:00	
TOTALS	1,666.67	160:00 hrs	

SICK AVAILABLE	20:00
VACATION AVAIL.	0:00
SICK ACCRUED	
VAC. ACCRUED	

Do not accrue sick/vac

Other Payroll Items

ITEM NAME	RATE	QUANTITY
Dental Insurance Emp (taxable)	-10.00	
Health Insurance Emp (taxable)	-50.00	

Employee Summary (adjusted) How are these items calculated?

ITEM NAME	AMOUNT	YTD
Salary	1,458.34	1,458.34
Vacation Salary	208.33	208.33
Dental Insurance Emp (taxable)	-10.00	-10.00
Health Insurance Emp (taxable)	-50.00	-50.00
Medicare Employee Addl Tax	0.00	0.00
Federal Withholding	-124.60	-124.60
Social Security Employee	-103.33	-103.33
Medicare Employee	-24.17	-24.17
CA - Withholding	-34.06	-34.06
CA - Disability Employee	-16.67	-16.67
Check Amount	1,303.84	

Company Summary (adjusted) How are these items calculated?

ITEM NAME	AMOUNT	YTD
Social Security Company	103.33	103.33
Medicare Company	24.17	24.17
Federal Unemployment	10.00	10.00
CA - Unemployment Company	66.67	66.67

Click **Save & Next**

Process the paycheck for **Laura Waters**

Record **160** for her Hourly Rate Hours

Record **8** as her Overtime Rate Hours

Enter the remaining payroll information as previously instructed

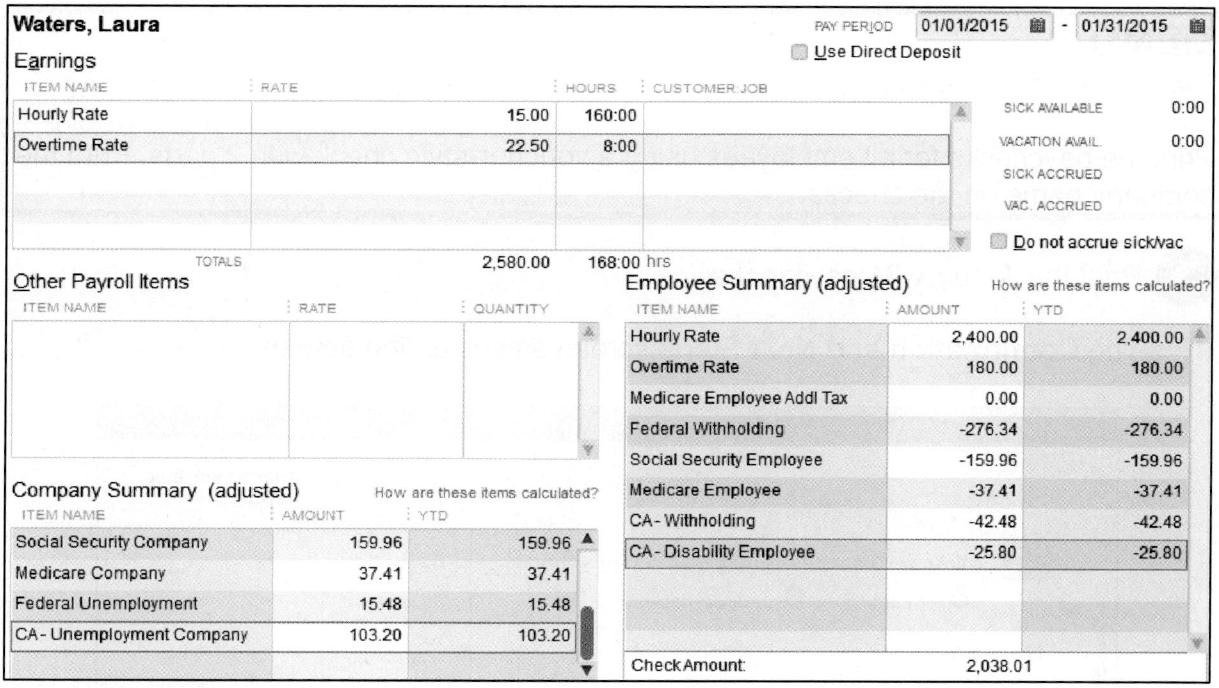

Click **Save & Close**

The Review and Create Paychecks screen appears with the information for Taxes and Deductions completed

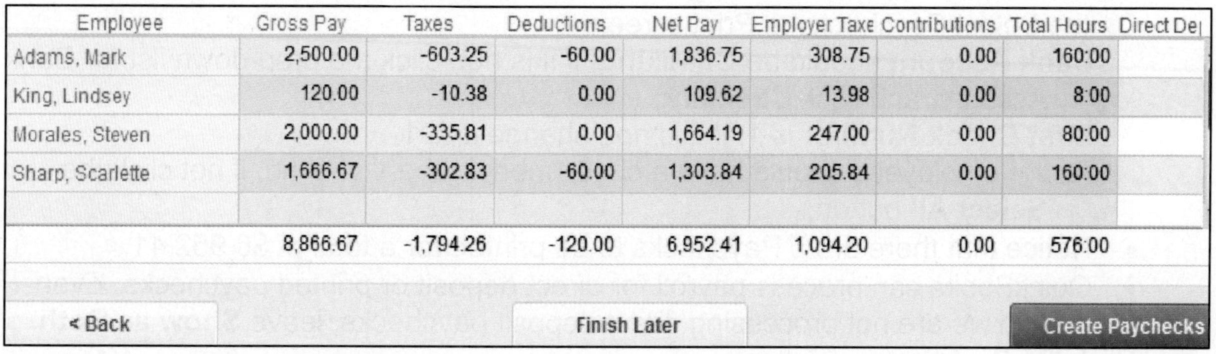
Employee Gross Pay Taxes Deductions Net Pay Employer Taxe Contributions Total Hours Direct De
Adams, Mark 2,500.00 -603.25 -60.00 1,836.75 308.75 0.00 160:00
King, Lindsey 120.00 -10.38 0.00 109.62 13.98 0.00 8:00
Morales, Steven 2,000.00 -335.81 0.00 1,664.19 247.00 0.00 80:00
Sharp, Scarlette 1,666.67 -302.83 -60.00 1,303.84 205.84 0.00 160:00
8,866.67 -1,794.26 -120.00 6,952.41 1,094.20 0.00 576:00
< Back
Finish Later
Create Paychecks

Click **Create Paychecks**

8

PRINT PAYCHECKS

Paychecks may be printed one at a time or all at once. You may use the same printer setup as your other checks in QuickBooks or you may print using a different printer setup. If you use a voucher check, the pay stub is printed as part of the check. If you do not use a voucher check, you may print the pay stub separately. The pay stub information includes the employee's name, address, Social Security number, the pay period start and end dates, pay rate, the hours, the amount of pay, all deductions, sick and vacation time used and available, net pay, and year-to-date amounts.

MEMO
DATE: January 31, 2015

Print the paychecks for all employees using a voucher-style check with 2 parts. Print the company name on the checks.

Print the January 31 paychecks

The **Confirmation and Next Steps** screen shows on the screen

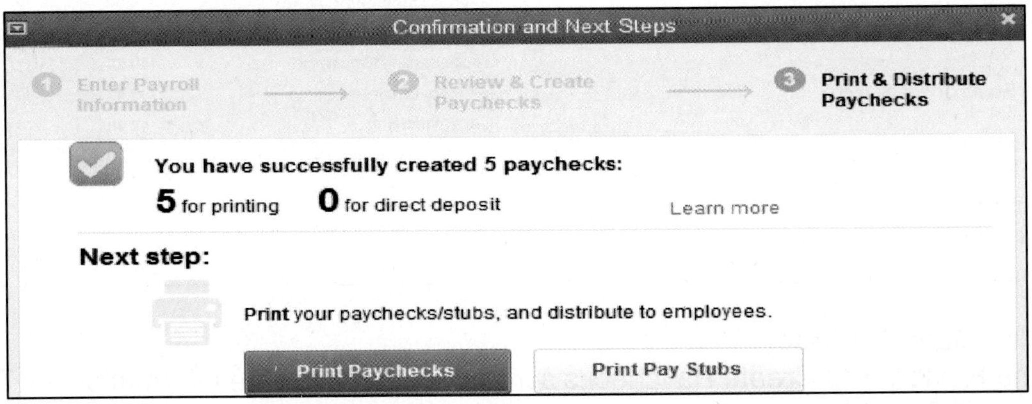

Click the **Print Paychecks** button
On the Select Paychecks to Print screen:
- **Bank Account** should be **Checking**; if it is not, click the drop-down list for Bank Account, and click **Checking**
- **First Check Number** is **1**; if it is not, change it to 1
- All the employees should have a check mark in the √ column, if not click the **Select All** button,

- Notice that there are 5 Paychecks to be printed for a total of $6,952.41.
- QuickBooks can process payroll for direct deposit or printed paychecks. Even though we are not processing direct deposit paychecks, leave **Show** as **Both**.

Click the **Preferences** button

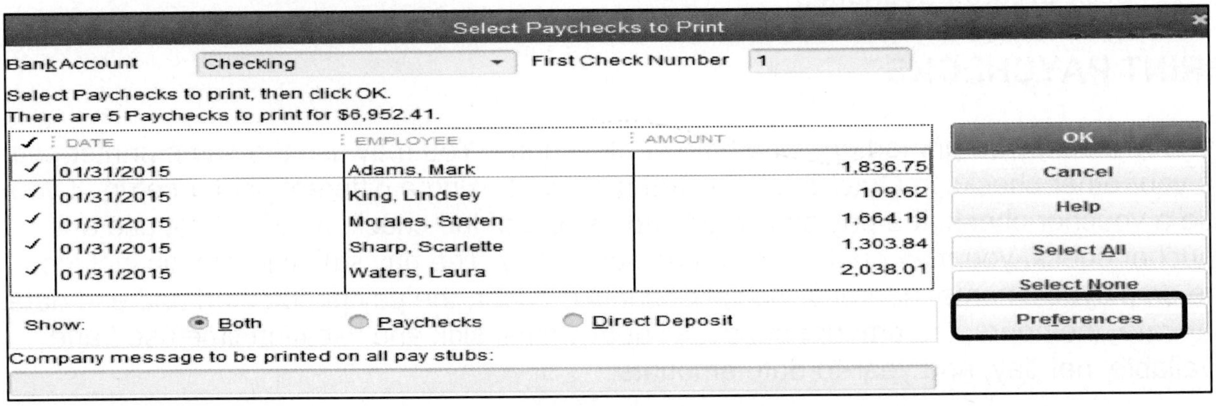

Verify that all items for Payroll Printing Preferences for Paycheck Vouchers and Pay stubs have been selected

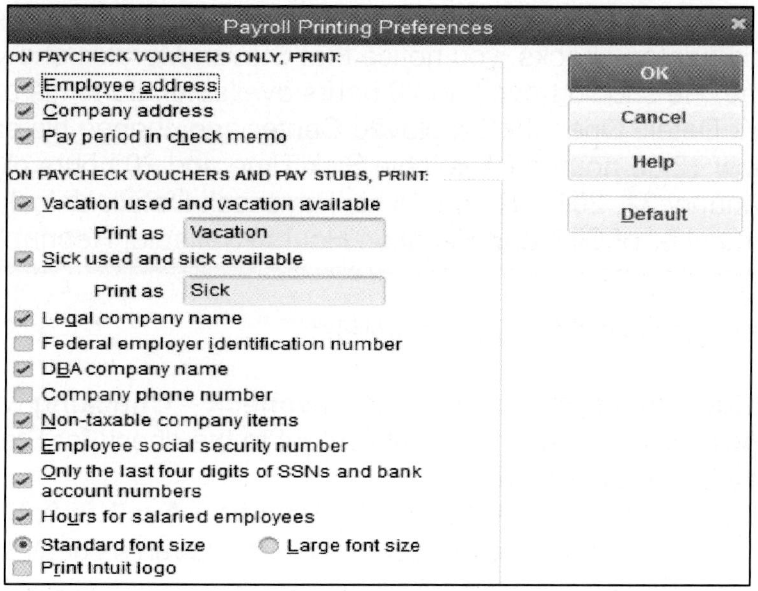

Click **OK**
Click **OK** on the Select Paychecks to Print screen

- Printer Name and Printer Type will be the same as in the earlier chapters.

Click **Voucher Checks** to select as the check style

- If necessary, click **Print company name and address** to select. There should not be a check mark in Use logo. **Number of copies** should be **1**.

Click **Print**

- *Note*: The pay stub information may be printed on the check two times. This is acceptable.

If the checks print correctly, click **OK** on the **Print Checks Confirmation** screen
Click **Close** on the **Confirmation and Next Steps** screen

PREVIEW PAYCHECK DETAIL AND EDIT EMPLOYEE

As in earlier chapters, checks may be viewed individually and printed one at a time. A paycheck differs from a regular check. Rather than list accounts and amounts, it provides a Payroll Summary and an option to view Paycheck Detail at the bottom of the screen. When you are viewing the paycheck detail, corrections may be made. If the corrections do not affect the net pay, they may be made without unlocking the check. If the corrections affect the net pay, the check must be unlocked before you will be allowed to enter the appropriate corrections.

MEMO
DATE: January 31, 2015

After reviewing the printed checks, you notice that Steven Morales shows -8.00 for Available Sick time. He should have had 20 hours available. Go to his paycheck and view his Paycheck Detail. Open the Employee Center and change his employee information to show 12.00 hours of Available Sick Time and 20 hours of vacation time available as of January 31, 2015. Return to his Paycheck Detail, Unlock the Net Pay, and re-enter the number of Sick and Vacation Hours Available. Reprint his check.

View the paycheck detail for Steven Morales

Click the **Write Checks** icon to open the **Paycheck – Checking** window
Click **Previous** (Back Arrow icon) until you get to the check for Steven Morales
Click the **Paycheck Detail** button
Notice the **Sick Available** is **-8:00** and the **Vacation Avail.** is **0:00**
Click **OK** to close the **Paycheck Detail** but leave Steven's check showing on the screen
Click the **Employees** icon to open the **Employee Center**
Double-click **Steven Morales** to **Edit Employee**
Click the **Payroll Info** tab
Click the **Sick/Vacation** button
Enter **12:00** for the Sick Hours available as of **01/31/15**

- Since Steven should have had 20 hours available, you would subtract the 8 hours of sick time he used. This leaves 12 hours available.

If necessary, enter the date of **12/31/14** for **Begin accruing sick time on**
Enter **20:00** for the Vacation Hours available as of **01/31/15**
If necessary, enter the date of **12/31/14** for **Begin accruing vacation time on**

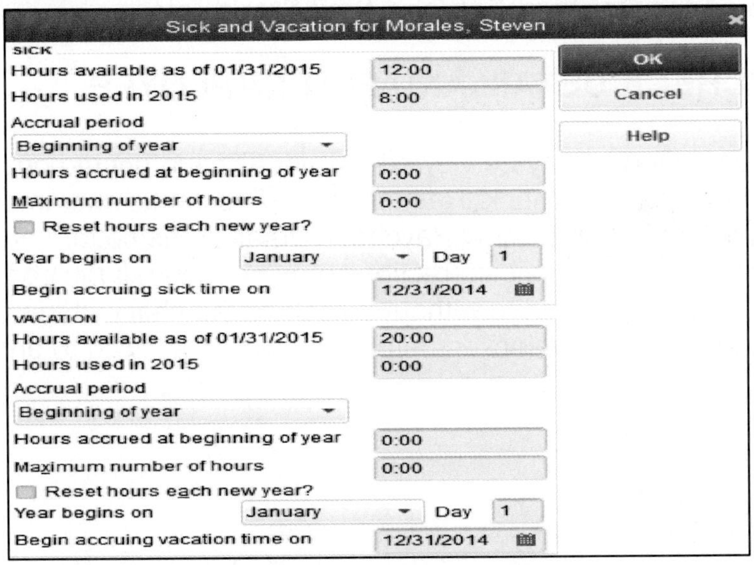

Click **OK** for Sick/Vacation, and click **OK** on the Edit Employee Screen

- If you get a Save message box, click **Yes**.

Close the **Employee Center** and return to Steven Morales's check

- The change in sick and vacation hours entered in the Employee Center will be effective for automatic calculation on the next paycheck but will not be updated on the paycheck prepared January 31, 2015.

On the check for **Steven Morales** for **01/31/15**, click the **Paycheck Detail**

- Notice that the Sick Available shows 12:00 and Vacation Avail. shows 20:00.
- Even though the correct hours appear, the check will need to be unlocked and the information changed before the corrected hours will appear on the paycheck voucher stub.

Even though the correct hours show, delete the hours and re-enter them: Sick Available is **12:00** and Vacation Avail. is **20:00**

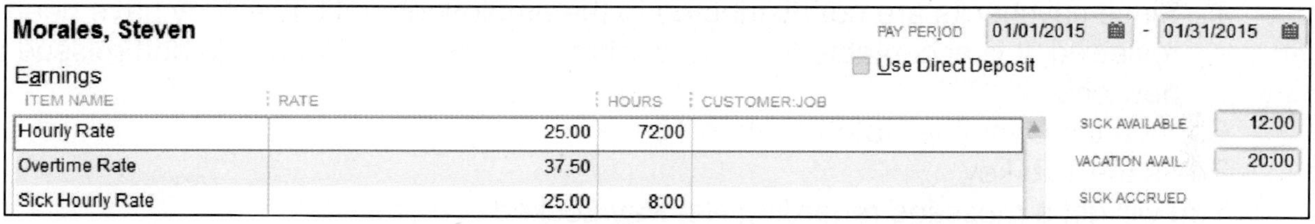

Click **OK**

- Even though the amount of the check is not changed by this adjustment, the check should be reprinted so the correct sick leave information is shown.

To reprint Check **3**, click **Print**

- Click **Yes** on the Recording Transaction dialog box to record the changes.

If 3 is not shown as the check number, enter **3** as the Printed Check Number, and click **OK**

Verify the information on the Print Checks screen including the selection of Voucher checks, click **Print**

When the check has printed successfully, click **OK** on the **Print Checks Confirmation** screen

Do not close the Paycheck – Checking window

MAKE CORRECTIONS TO PAYCHECK DETAIL

When you need to make changes to Paycheck Detail that effect the amount of pay, you may do so by unlocking the Net Pay, entering the required changes, and reprinting the check.

MEMO
DATE: January 31, 2015

Laura Waters should have been paid for 10 hours overtime. Change her overtime hours and change her deductions as follows: CA-Employment Training Tax 2.63, Social Security (Company and Employee) 162.75, Medicare (Company and Employee) 38.06, Federal Unemployment 15.75, CA-Unemployment 105.00, Federal Withholding 330.65, CA Withholding 45.45, and CA Disability 26.25. Reprint the check

Correct and reprint the paycheck for Laura Waters

Click **Next** (Forward Arrow icon) until you get to **Laura Waters'** paycheck
Click **Paycheck Detail**

- Since paychecks are not distributed to the employees until after they have been reviewed, it is acceptable to change this paycheck rather than void and reissue a new one.

Change the Overtime Rate Hours to **10**
Press the **Tab** key
You will get a message regarding Net Pay Locked

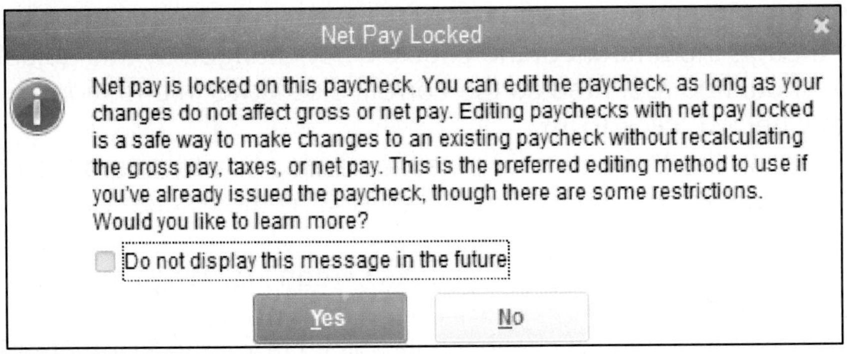

Click **No**
At the bottom of the paycheck, click **Unlock Net Pay**

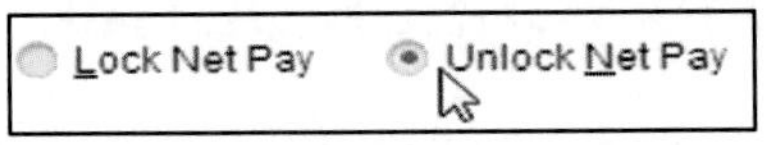

You will get a **Special Paycheck Situation** screen to allow the paycheck to be changed

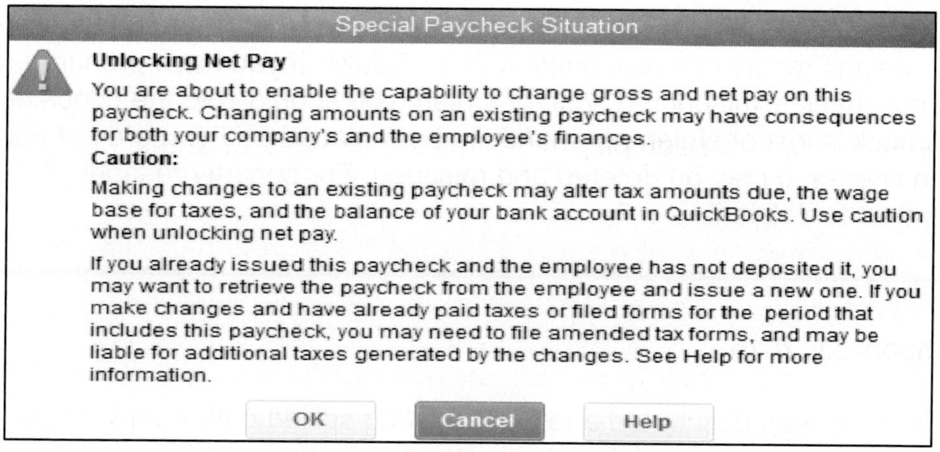

Click **OK** on the **Special Paycheck Situation** screen

Enter the changes to the tax amounts as indicated in the Memo

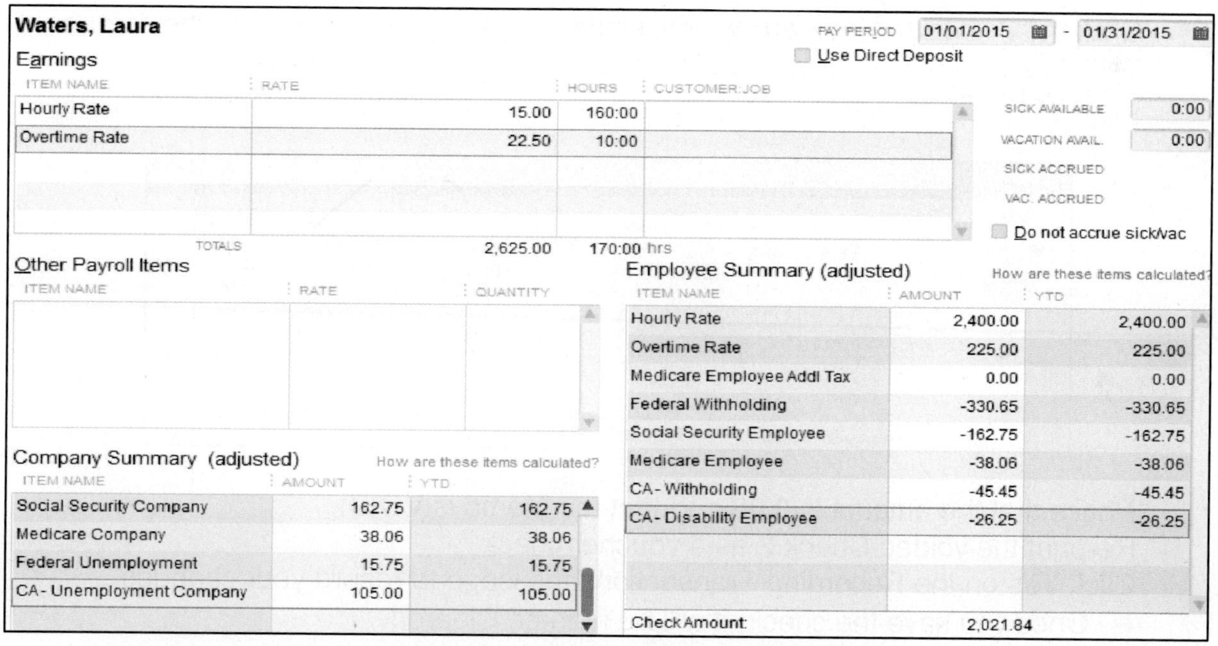
Waters, Laura
PAY PERIOD 01/01/2015 - 01/31/2015
Use Direct Deposit
Earnings
ITEM NAME RATE HOURS CUSTOMER:JOB
Hourly Rate 15.00 160:00
Overtime Rate 22.50 10:00
TOTALS 2,625.00 170:00 hrs
SICK AVAILABLE 0:00
VACATION AVAIL. 0:00
SICK ACCRUED
VAC. ACCRUED
Do not accrue sick/vac
Other Payroll Items
ITEM NAME RATE QUANTITY
Company Summary (adjusted)
How are these items calculated?
ITEM NAME AMOUNT YTD
Social Security Company 162.75 162.75
Medicare Company 38.06 38.06
Federal Unemployment 15.75 15.75
CA - Unemployment Company 105.00 105.00
Employee Summary (adjusted)
How are these items calculated?
ITEM NAME AMOUNT YTD
Hourly Rate 2,400.00 2,400.00
Overtime Rate 225.00 225.00
Medicare Employee Addl Tax 0.00 0.00
Federal Withholding -330.65 -330.65
Social Security Employee -162.75 -162.75
Medicare Employee -38.06 -38.06
CA - Withholding -45.45 -45.45
CA - Disability Employee -26.25 -26.25
Check Amount: 2,021.84

Click **OK**, click **Yes** on the Recording Transactions message

- If you return to the Paycheck Detail, you will find that Lock Net Pay is once again selected.

Reprint Check 5,

Do not close the Paycheck-Checking window

VOIDING AND DELETING PAYCHECKS

As with regular checks, paychecks may be voided or deleted. A voided check still remains as a check, but it has an amount of 0.00 and a Memo that says VOID. If a check is deleted, it is completely removed from the company records. The only way to have a record of the deleted check is in the Voided/Deleted Transactions reports and the audit trail, which keeps a behind the scenes record of every entry in QuickBooks. If you have prenumbered checks and the original check is misprinted, lost, or stolen, you should void the check. If an employee's check is lost or stolen and needs to be replaced and you are not using prenumbered checks, it may be deleted and reissued. For security reasons, it is better to void a check than to delete it.

MEMO
DATE: January 31, 2015

The checks have been distributed and Lindsey King spilled coffee on her paycheck for the January 31 pay period. Void the check, issue and print a new one.

Void Lindsey's January 31 paycheck and issue a new one

Click the **Previous/Back** arrow until Lindsey's paycheck appears on the screen
Click the drop-down arrow under **Delete** on the Paycheck Icon bar
Click **Void**

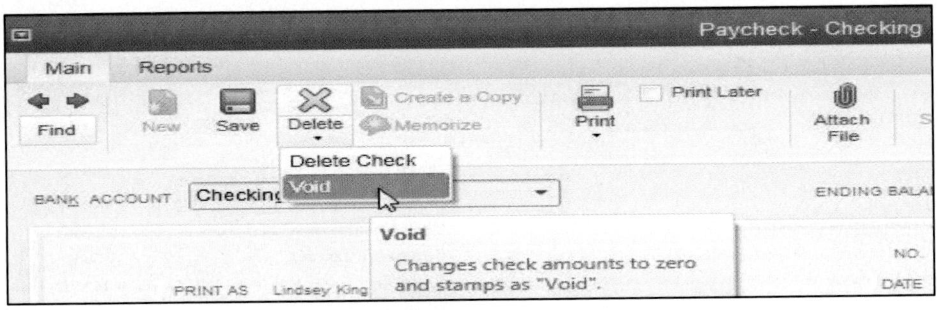

Notice that the amount is **0.00** and that the Memo is **VOID:**.
Re-print the voided Check **2** as a voucher check
Click **Yes** on the Recording Transactions message to record your changes

- Once you save the check, it will be marked Cleared.

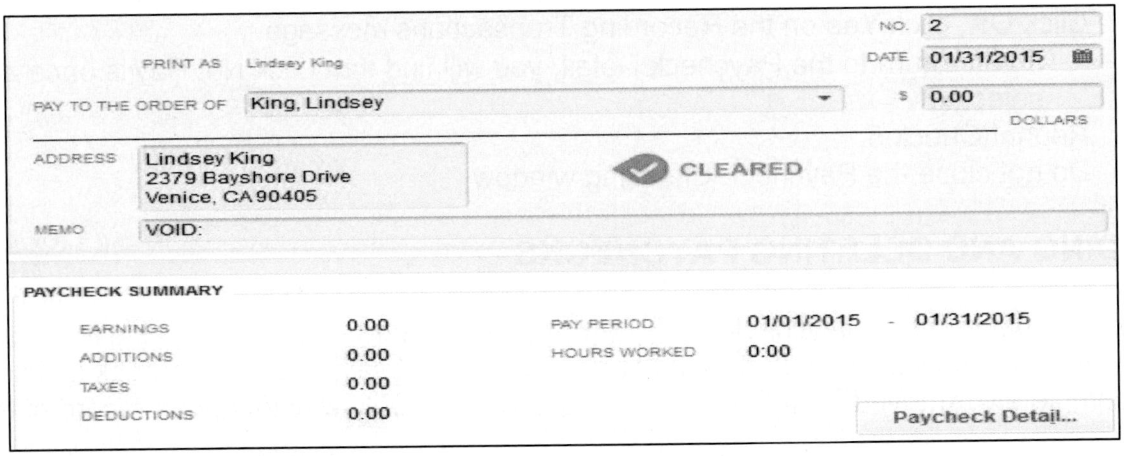

Click **Save & Close** on **Paycheck-Checking** screen
To issue Lindsey's replacement check, click **Pay Employees** in the Employees section of the Home Page
The **Pay Period Ends 01/31/15** and the **Check Date** is **01/31/15**
The Bank Account is **Checking**
Click in the check column for **Lindsey King** to select her
Click **Continue**, then click the **Open Paycheck Detail** button
Pay Period is **01/01/15 - 01/31/15**
Lindsey worked **8** hours at the **Hourly Regular Rate**
Enter the deductions listed on the Payroll Table for January 31, 2015
Click **Save & Close**
Click the **Create Paychecks** button
Click **Print Paychecks**
Print the replacement check as Check **6**
Click **OK** on the **Confirmation and Next Steps** screen
Print the Voucher-style check
After the check has been printed successfully, click **OK**
Close the Confirmation and Next Steps screen

MISSING CHECK REPORT

Since the same account is used for paychecks and regular checks, the Missing Check report will provide data regarding all the checks issued by Your Name's Fitness Solutions After entering a number of checks, it is wise to review this report.

View the Missing Check report

Open the **Report Center**, click **Banking** for the type of report, double-click **Missing Checks**
Specify Account is **Checking**

1:04 PM
01/31/15

Your Name's Fitness Solutions
Missing Checks
All Transactions

Type	Date	Num	Name	Memo	Account	Split	Amount
Paycheck	01/31/2015	1	Adams, Mark		Checking	-SPLIT-	-1,836.75
Paycheck	01/31/2015	2	King, Lindsey	VOID:	Checking	-SPLIT-	0.00
Paycheck	01/31/2015	3	Morales, Steven		Checking	-SPLIT-	-1,664.19
Paycheck	01/31/2015	4	Sharp, Scarlette		Checking	-SPLIT-	-1,303.84
Paycheck	01/31/2015	5	Waters, Laura		Checking	-SPLIT-	-2,021.84
Paycheck	01/31/2015	6	King, Lindsey		Checking	-SPLIT-	-109.62

- Note: The Date and Time Prepared are in the header. Fitness does not have Report Preferences customized.

Review the report and close without printing, do not close the Report Center

8

PAYROLL SUMMARY REPORT

The Payroll Summary Report shows gross pay; the amounts and hours for salary, hourly, overtime, sick, and vacation; adjusted gross pay; taxes withheld; deductions from net pay; net pay; and employer-paid taxes and contributions for each employee individually and for the company.

Print the Payroll Summary Report for January

Since the Report Center is on the screen, click **Employees & Payroll**
Double-click **Payroll Summary**
Enter the report dates from **01/01/15** to **01/31/15**
- View the information listed for each employee and for the company.

Remove the Date Prepared and Time Prepared from the Header
Print the report in Landscape orientation, and close the report

PREPARE EMPLOYEE EARNINGS SUMMARY REPORT

The Employee Earnings Summary Report lists the same information as the Payroll Summary Report above. The information for each employee is categorized by payroll items.

Prepare the Employee Earnings Summary report

Double-click **Employee Earnings Summary** as the report
Use the dates from **01/01/15** to **01/31/15**
Scroll through the report
- Notice the way in which payroll amounts are grouped by item rather than employee.

Close the report without printing

PAYROLL LIABILITY BALANCES REPORT

Another payroll report is the Payroll Liability Balances Report. This report lists the company's payroll liabilities that are unpaid as of the report date. This report should be prepared prior to paying any payroll taxes.

Prepare and print the Payroll Liability Balances report

Double-click **Payroll Liability Balances** in the Employees & Payroll section of the Report Center
The report dates should be **01/01/15** to **01/31/15**

Your Name's Fitness Solutions
Payroll Liability Balances
January 2015

	BALANCE
Payroll Liabilities	
Federal Withholding	899.75
Medicare Employee	129.22
Social Security Employee	552.52
Federal Unemployment	52.75
Medicare Company	129.22
Social Security Company	552.52
CA - Withholding	184.82
CA - Disability Employee	89.12
CA - Unemployment Company	356.47
Medicare Employee Addl Tax	0.00
CA - Employment Training Tax	8.80
Dental Insurance Emp (taxable)	20.00
Health Insurance Emp (taxable)	100.00
Total Payroll Liabilities	**3,075.19**

Remove the Date Prepared and Time Prepared from the Header
Print the report in Portrait orientation; close the report and the Report Center

PAY PAYROLL TAXES AND LIABILITIES

QuickBooks keeps track of the payroll taxes and payroll liabilities that you owe. When it is time to make your payments, QuickBooks allows you to choose to pay all liabilities or to select individual liabilities for payment. When the liabilities have been selected, QuickBooks will consolidate all the amounts by vendor and prepare one check for a vendor.

> **MEMO**
> **DATE:** January 31, 2015
>
> Based on the information in the Payroll Liabilities Report, pay all the payroll liabilities.

Pay all the payroll liabilities

Click the **Pay Liabilities** icon in Employees section of the Home Page
Enter the dates From **01/01/15** Through **01/31/15** on the **Select Date Range For Liabilities** screen

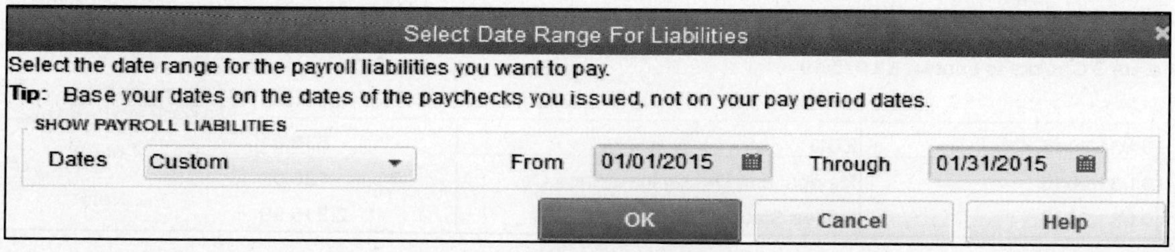

Click **OK**

On the Pay Liabilities screen, select **To be printed** if necessary

Bank Account should be **Checking**; if it is not, select it from the drop-down list.

Check Date is **01/31/15**

Sort by is **Payable To**

Select **Create liability check without reviewing**

Show payroll liabilities from **01/01/15** to **01/31/15**

Click in the check column to place a check mark next to each liability listed; be sure to scroll through the list to view and mark each liability

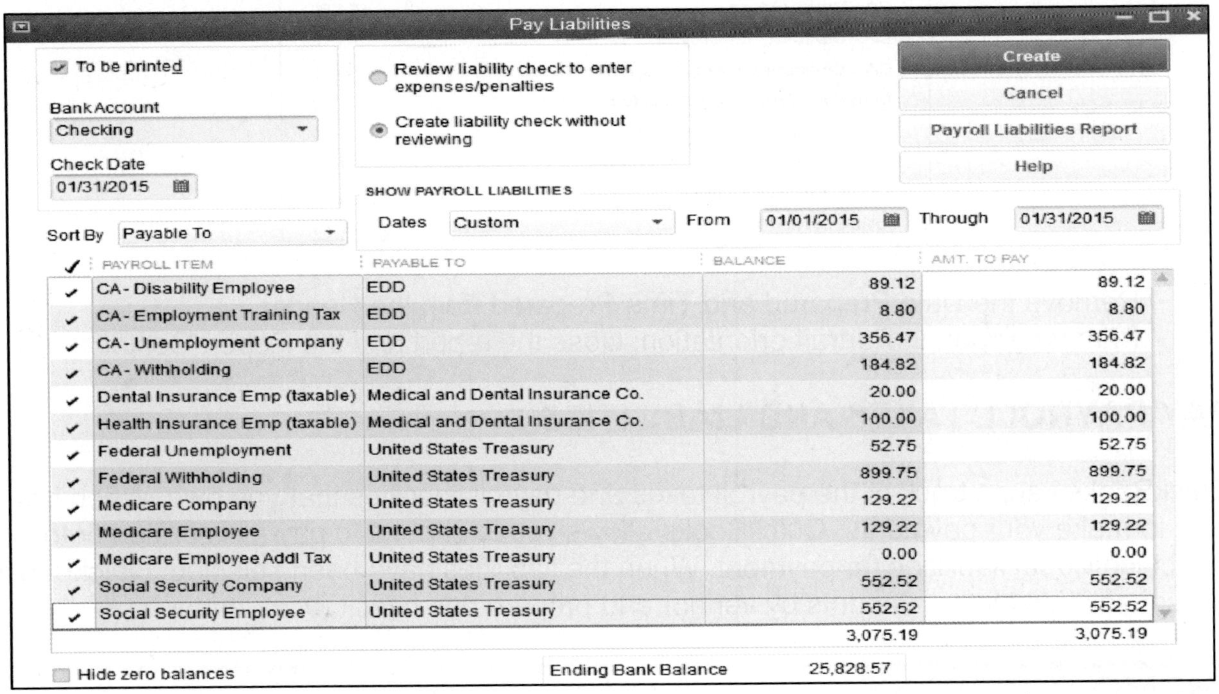

Click **Create**

To print the checks, access **Write Checks** as previously instructed

Click the drop-down list arrow below the **Print** icon at the top of the window

Click **Batch**

On the **Select Checks to Print** screen, the first check number should be **7**

- The names of the agencies receiving the checks and the check amounts should be listed and marked with a check. If not, click the **Select All** button.

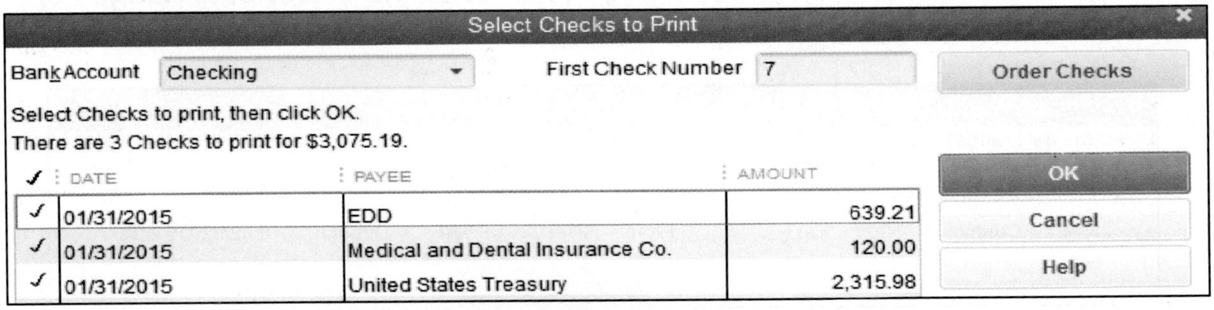

Click **OK**
Change the style of checks to **Standard**, click **Print**
When the checks have printed successfully, click **OK** on the confirmation screen

- Standard style checks print three to a page so all three checks will print on one page.
- If you wish to have each check printed separately, you would go to each check and print individually as previously instructed.

Close the Liability Check - Checking window

PAYROLL TAX FORMS

Depending on the type of payroll service to which you subscribe, QuickBooks will prepare, print, and sometimes submit your tax forms for Quarterly Form 941, Annual Form 944, Annual Form 940, Annual Form 943, Annual W-2/W-3, and State SUI Wage Listing.

Since we do not subscribe to a payroll service, QuickBooks will not complete any of these forms. However, at the time of writing, QuickBooks includes several reports that enable you to link payroll data from QuickBooks to Excel workbooks. The workbooks provided contain worksheets designed to summarize payroll data collected and to organize data needed to prepare the state and federal tax forms listed above. Many of the worksheets are preset with an Excel Pivot Table. The worksheets may be used as designed or they may be modified to suit your reporting needs. You may only prepare these Excel reports if you have entered payroll data; i.e., paychecks and withholding, in QuickBooks and have Microsoft Excel 2000 or later installed on your computer with Macros enabled.

To access the various tax forms, click Employees on the menu bar, point to Payroll Tax Forms & W-2s; and then, click Tax Form Worksheets in Excel.

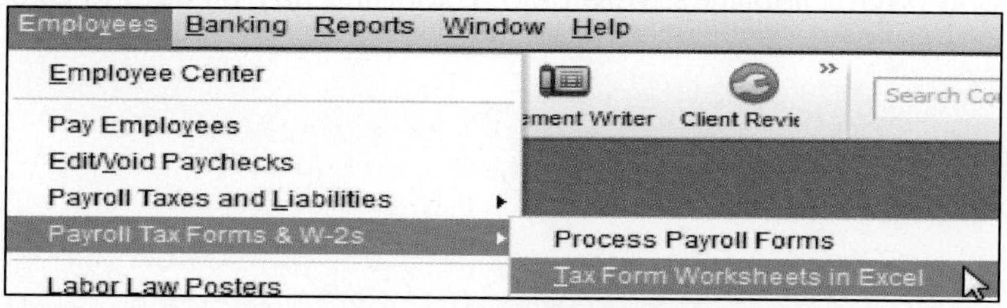

At this point you are taken to Excel where you need to turn on Macros. Once Macros have been enabled, you may select the form being prepared. Data from QuickBooks will be inserted into the Excel spreadsheet and may be used to manually complete the tax forms. We will not use this feature at this time.

8

PRINT JOURNAL

As in the previous chapters, it is always a good idea to print the Journal to see all of the transactions that have been made. If, however, you only want to see the transactions for a particular date or period of time, you can control the amount of data in the report by restricting the dates.

Print the Journal for January 31 in landscape orientation

Prepare the report as previously instructed
Use the dates from **01/01/15** to **01/31/15**
Expand the report
Remove the Date Prepared and Time Prepared from the Header
Adjust column widths so the information in each column is displayed in full and print

BACK UP

Follow the instructions provided in previous chapters to make a backup file. If you get a message in QuickBooks about rebuilding your company file, follow the prompts to rebuild.

SUMMARY

In this chapter, paychecks were generated for employees who worked their Standard number of hours, worked overtime hours, took vacation time, took sick time, and were just hired. Rather than have QuickBooks calculate the amount of payroll deductions, a table was provided and deductions to paychecks were recorded manually. Changes to employee information were made, and a new employee was added. Payroll reports were printed and/or viewed, and payroll liabilities were paid. Exporting payroll data to Excel workbooks was explored.

END-OF-CHAPTER QUESTIONS

TRUE/FALSE

ANSWER THE FOLLOWING QUESTIONS IN THE SPACE PROVIDED BEFORE THE QUESTION NUMBER.

F 1. When you process payroll manually, QuickBooks automatically prepares your paychecks and files all of your payroll tax reports.

T 2. Once a paycheck has been prepared, you must unlock the paycheck detail before editing amounts that will affect net pay.

F 3. Paychecks may be printed only as a batch.

_____ 4. While a payroll check may be voided, it may never be deleted.

F 5. Once an employee is hired, you may not change the pay period from semi-monthly to monthly.

T 6. An employee may be added at any time.

_____ 7. If several taxes are owed to a single agency, QuickBooks generates a separate check to the agency for each tax liability item.

T 8. If a salaried employee uses vacation pay, QuickBooks will automatically distribute the correct amount of earnings to Vacation Salary once the number of vacation hours has been entered.

F 9. Processing the Payroll Liabilities Balances Report also generates the checks for payment of the liabilities.

F 10. All payroll reports must be printed before payroll liabilities may be paid.

MULTIPLE CHOICE

WRITE THE LETTER OF THE CORRECT ANSWER IN THE SPACE PROVIDED BEFORE THE QUESTION NUMBER.

D 1. When completing paychecks manually, you ___.
A. provide the information about hours worked
B. provide the amounts for deductions
C. provide the number of sick and/or vacation hours used
D. all of the above

C 2. To change the amount of a deduction entered on an employee's check that has been created but not distributed, you ___.
A. must void the check and issue a new one
B. adjust the next check to include the change
C. unlock and change the Paycheck Detail for the check and reprint it
D. must delete the check

D 3. When paying tax liabilities, you may ___.
A. pay all liabilities at one time
B. select individual tax liabilities and pay them one at a time
C. pay all the tax liabilities owed to a vendor
D. all of the above

A 4. A new employee may be added ___.
A. at any time
B. only at the end of the week
C. only at the end of the pay period
D. only when current paychecks have been printed

D 5. Pay stub information may be printed ___.
A. as part of a voucher check
B. separate from the paycheck
C. only as an individual employee report
D. both A and B

C 6. The Employee Earnings Summary Report lists payroll information for each employee categorized by ___.
A. employee
B. department
C. payroll item
D. date paid

D 7. A voided check ___.
A. shows an amount of 0.00
B. has a Memo of VOID
C. remains as part of the company records
D. all of the above

B 8. When the payroll liabilities to be paid have been selected, QuickBooks will ___.
A. create a separate check for each liability
B. consolidate the liabilities paid and create one check for each vendor
C. automatically process a Payroll Liability Balances Report
D. all of the above

C 9. You may void or delete checks by ___.
A. clicking Void Checks or Delete Checks in the Banking Menu
B. clicking either the Void icon or the Delete icon in the Write Checks window
C. clicking the drop-down arrow under the Delete icon in the Write Checks window; then clicking either Void or Delete
D. all of the above

A 10. Changes made to an employee's pay rate will become effective ___.
A. immediately
B. at the end of the next payroll period
C. at the end of the quarter
D. after a W-2 has been prepared for the employee

FILL-IN

IN THE SPACE PROVIDED, WRITE THE ANSWER THAT MOST APPROPRIATELY COMPLETES THE SENTENCE.

1. In the Employee Center, the individual employee's name, address, and telephone number is displayed in the Employee Information area.

2. The Journal is the report that lists transactions in debit/credit format.

3. The reports that show an employee's gross pay, sick and vacation hours and pay, deductions, taxes, and other details are the Payroll Summary Report and the Employee Earnings Summary Report.

4. When the Employee Center is on the screen, the New Employee button is used to add a new employee.

5. The report listing the company's unpaid payroll liabilities as of the report date is the ____________ Report. Payroll Liability Balances.

SHORT ESSAY

What is the difference between voiding a paycheck and deleting a paycheck? Why should a business prefer to void paychecks rather than delete them?

8

NAME ____________________

CHAPTER 8: TRANSMITTAL

YOUR NAME'S FITNESS SOLUTIONS

Check the items below as you print them; then attach the documents and reports in the order listed when you submit them to your instructor.

___ Check 1: Mark Adams
___ Check 2: Lindsey King
___ Check 3: Steven Morales
___ Check 4: Scarlette Sharp
___ Check 5: Laura Waters
___ Check 3: Steven Morales After Editing Sick Time
___ Check 5: Laura Waters After Editing Overtime
___ Check 2: Lindsey King Voided Check
___ Check 6: Lindsey King Replacement Check
___ Payroll Summary, January, 2015
___ Payroll Liability Balances, January, 2015
___ Check 7: EDD
___ Check 8: Medical and Dental Insurance Co.
___ Check 9: United States Treasury
___ Journal, January 31, 2015

END-OF-CHAPTER PROBLEM

YOUR NAME'S POOL & SPA

You will be working with a company called Your Name's Pool & Spa. Transactions for employees, payroll, and payroll liabilities will be completed.

INSTRUCTIONS

For Chapter 8 use the company file, **Pool.qbw**. Open the company as previously instructed. If you get a message to update your company file, click Yes. You will select a manual payroll option; record the addition of and changes to employees; create, edit, and void paychecks; pay payroll liabilities; and prepare payroll reports.

RECORD TRANSACTIONS:

January 30, 2015

- ▶ Add your first and last name to the company name and the legal name. (Add **'s** to your last name.)
- ▶ Change the owner equity account names to: First and Last Name, Capital; First and Last Name, Withdrawal; and First and Last Name, Investment.
- ▶ Turn off the Date Prepared, Time Prepared, and Report Basis in the Header/Footer. For instructions, refer to Chapter 5.
- ▶ Select Manual processing for payroll.
- ▶ Add a new employee, Nalani Grant to help with pool supply sales. Social Security No.: 100-55-2145; Gender: Female, Date of Birth: 04/23/1977, Marital Status: Single, U.S. Citizen: Yes, Ethnicity: Hawaiian/Pacific Islander, Disability: No. Address: 2325 Summerland Road, Summerland, CA 93014, Main Phone: 805-555-9845. Nalani has a pay frequency of Monthly, is an hourly employee with a Regular Rate of $7.00 per hour and an Overtime Hourly Rate 1 of $10.50. She is not eligible for medical or dental insurance. She is single, claims no exemptions or allowances, and is subject to Federal Taxes: Medicare, Social Security, and Federal Unemployment Tax (Company Paid), State Taxes for CA: SUI (Company Paid), and SDI; Other Taxes: CA-Employment Training Tax. Nalani does not accrue vacation or sick leave. Hire Date: January 30, 2015, Employment Type: Regular.
- ▶ Dori Stevens changed her Main Phone number to 805-555-5111. Edit the employee on the employee list and record the change.

January 31, 2015

- ▶ Use the following Payroll Table to prepare and print checks for the monthly payroll. The pay period ends **January 31, 2015** and the check date is also **January 31, 2015**: Checking is the appropriate account to use. (Remember, if you get a screen regarding signing up for QuickBooks Payroll service, click **No**.)

8

PAYROLL TABLE: JANUARY 31, 2015				
	Nalani Grant	Joe Masterson	Manuel Nunez	Dori Stevens
HOURS				
Regular	8	152	160	120
Overtime			20	
Sick		8		
Vacation				40
DEDUCTIONS OTHER PAYROLL ITEMS: EMPLOYEE				
Dental Ins.		25.00	25.00	25.00
Medical Ins.		25.00	25.00	25.00
DEDUCTIONS: COMPANY				
CA-Employment Training Tax	0.00	2.42	1.71	2.60
Social Security	3.47	149.83	106.00	161.20
Medicare	.81	35.04	24.80	37.70
Federal Unemployment	0.00	14.50	10.26	15.60
CA-Unemployment	2.24	96.67	68.40	104.00
DEDUCTIONS: EMPLOYEE				
Medicare Employee Addl Tax	0.00	0.00	0.00	0.00
Federal Withholding	0.00	188.75	145.90	168.75
Social Security	3.47	149.83	106.00	161.20
Medicare	.81	35.04	24.80	37.70
CA-Withholding	0.00	39.48	35.96	43.51
CA-Disability	0.00	24.17	17.10	26.00

▶ Print the checks.
- Verify the Payroll Printing Preferences: make sure the Intuit logo is not printed.
- Print the company name and address on the voucher checks.
- Checks begin with number 1.

- ▶ Change Manuel Nunez's check to correct the overtime hours. (Remember to Unlock Net Pay before recording the changes.) He worked 12 hours overtime. Because of the reduction in overtime pay, his deductions change as follows: CA-Employment Training Tax: 1.60; Social Security Company and Employee: 99.32; Medicare Company and Employee: 23.23; Federal Unemployment: 9.61; CA-Unemployment: 64.08; Federal Withholding: 129.70; CA-Withholding: 31.21; and CA-Disability: 16.02. Reprint Check 3.
- ▶ Nalani spilled coffee on her check. Void her Check 1 for January 31, print the voided check.
- ▶ Reissue Nalani's paycheck, and print it using Check 5. Remember to use 01/31/15 as the check and pay period ending date. The pay period is 01/01/15 to 01/31/15. Refer to the payroll table for information on hours and deductions.
- ▶ Prepare and print the Payroll Summary Report for January 1-31, 2015 in Landscape orientation.
- ▶ Prepare and print the Payroll Liability Balances Report for January 1-31, 2015 in Portrait orientation.
- ▶ Pay <u>all</u> the taxes and other liabilities for January 1-31, 2015. The Check Date is 01/31/15. Print the checks using a Standard check style with the company name and address.
- ▶ Prepare, expand, and print the Journal for January 31, 2015 in Landscape orientation.
- ▶ Backup your work.

NAME ______________________________

CHAPTER 8: TRANSMITTAL

YOUR NAME'S POOL & SPA

Check the items below as you print them; then attach the documents and reports in the order listed when you submit them to your instructor.

__ Check 1: Nalani Grant
__ Check 2: Joe Masterson
__ Check 3: Manuel Nunez
__ Check 4: Dori Stevens
__ Check 3: Manuel Nunez (Corrected)
__ Check 1: Nalani Grant (Voided)
__ Check 5: Nalani Grant
__ Payroll Summary, January, 2015
__ Payroll Liability Balances, January, 2015
__ Check 6: Dental and Medical Ins.
__ Check 7: Employment Development Department
__ Check 8: United States Treasury
__ Journal, January, 2015

CREATING A COMPANY IN QUICKBOOKS

9

LEARNING OBJECTIVES

At the completion of this chapter, you will be able to:

1. Set up a company using the QuickBooks Setup and the EasyStep Interview.
2. Establish a Chart of Accounts for a company.
3. Set up Company Info and start dates.
4. Create lists for items, customers, vendors, employees, and others.
5. Complete the Payroll setup and create payroll items and employee defaults.
6. Customize reports and company preferences.
7. Add a company logo.

COMPUTERIZING A MANUAL SYSTEM

In previous chapters, QuickBooks was used to record transactions for businesses that were already set up for use in the program. In this chapter, you will actually set up a business, create a chart of accounts, create various lists, add names to lists, add opening balances, and delete unnecessary accounts. QuickBooks makes setting up a business user-friendly by going through the process using the EasyStep Interview. Once the EasyStep Interview is completed, you will make refinements to accounts and opening balances, add customers, vendors, and sales items. Reports and preferences will be customized, and a company logo will be added. The Payroll Setup will be completed and employees will be added. Uncategorized Income and Expenses will be transferred to the owner's equity account.

TRAINING TUTORIAL AND PROCEDURES

The following tutorial is a step-by-step guide to setting up the fictitious company Your Name's Dog Dayz. Company information, accounts, items, lists, and other items must be provided before transactions may be recorded in QuickBooks. The EasyStep Interview will be used to set up company information. After that, the Chart of Accounts will need to be completed and some beginning balances will be added. Then, Customers, Vendors, and Sales Items, will be added. Preferences will be changed and a company logo will be added. The Payroll Setup will be completed and employees will be added. As in earlier chapters, information for the company setup will be provided in memos. Information may also be shown in lists or within the step-by-step instructions provided.

Please note that QuickBooks is updated on a regular basis. If your screens are not always an exact match to the text, check with your instructor to see if you should select something that is similar to the text. For example, QuickBooks has been known to change the type of businesses or industries that it uses in the EasyStep Interview. If that happens, your instructor may suggest that you select the company type closest to Your Name's Dog Dayz. A different company type may result in a different chart of accounts. This would mean adjusting the chart of accounts to match the one given in the text.

DATES

Throughout the text, the year used for the screen shots is 2015. Check with your instructor to see what year to use for the transactions. Sometimes, the difference in the computer and text dates will cause a slight variation in the way QuickBooks' screens are displayed and they may not match the text exactly. If you cannot change a date that is provided by QuickBooks, accept it and continue with your training. Instructions are given where this occurs. The main criterion is to be consistent with the year you use throughout the chapter.

COMPANY PROFILE: YOUR NAME'S DOG DAYZ

Your Name's Dog Dayz is a fictitious company that provides boarding in the Doggie Digs Hotel, playtime at Doggie Dayz camp, and grooming in the Dog Salon. In addition, Your Name's Dog Dayz has a Dog Dayz boutique that carries collars, leashes, sweaters, treats, and toys for dogs. Your Name's Dog Dayz is located in San Diego, California, and is a sole proprietorship owned by you. You are involved in all aspects of the business. Your Name's Dog Dayz has one full-time employee who is paid a salary: Angela Aguilar, whose duties include running the Doggie Digs Hotel, ordering and managing the boutique, and completing all paperwork and forms for dog services. There is one full-time hourly employee: Drake Childs, who does the grooming in the Doggie Salon, supervises Doggie Dayz Camp, and cares for the dogs staying at the Doggie Digs Hotel.

CREATE A NEW COMPANY

Since "Your Name's Dog Dayz" is a new company, it does not appear as a company file. You may create a new company by clicking New Company on the File menu or the "Create a new company" button on the No Company Open screen.

There are four ways in which to setup a company. You may create a company using Express Start where you give QuickBooks a company name, the type of industry, type of ownership, tax ID#, legal name, address, telephone, email, and Web site. You may use the Detailed Start to complete the QuickBooks Setup using the EasyStep Interview, which provides more detailed company information than Express Start. You may use Create to make a new company file based on an existing company. Finally, you may use Other Options to convert a file from another program.

MEMO
DATE: January 1, 2015

Because this is the beginning of the fiscal year for Your Name's Dog Dayz, it is an appropriate time to set up the company information in QuickBooks. Use the QuickBooks Setup and EasyStep Interview to create a new company.

Open QuickBooks as previously instructed

Insert a USB drive as previously instructed or use the storage location you have been using throughout the text

Click **File** menu, click **New Company** or click the **Create a new Company** icon on the **No Company Open** dialog box

- The QuickBooks Setup will appear with the screen "Let's get your business set up quickly!"

QUICKBOOKS SETUP AND EASYSTEP INTERVIEW

The QuickBooks Setup uses the EasyStep Interview as a step-by-step guide to entering your company information as of a single date called a start date. The EasyStep Interview provides screens with questions that, when answered, enables QuickBooks to set up the company file, create a Chart of Accounts designed for your specific type of business or industry, and establish the beginning of a company's fiscal year and income tax year.

Once a screen has been read and any required items have been filled in or questions answered, the Next button is clicked to tell QuickBooks to advance to the next screen. If you need to return to a previous screen, click the Back button. If you need to stop the Setup before completing everything, you may exit by clicking the Leave button in the bottom-left corner of the screen or by clicking the close button at the top-right corner of the EasyStep Interview screen. Depending on where you are in the interview, you data may or may not be saved.

Begin the EasyStep Interview

Click **Detailed Start**

9

MEMO

DATE: January 1, 2015

Use the following information to complete the QuickBooks Setup and EasyStep Interview for Your Name's Dog Dayz:

Company and Legal Name: Your Name's Dog Dayz (*Key in your actual first and last name*)
Federal Tax ID: 15-9828654
Address: 8795 Mission Bay Drive, San Diego, CA 92109
Phone: 760-555-7979; Fax: 760-555-9797
E-mail: YourName@DogDayz.com (use *your actual nameDogDayz*@info.com)
Web: www.DogDayz.com
Type of Business: Retail Shop or Online Commerce
Company Organization: Sole Proprietorship
Fiscal year starts in January
Do not use Passwords
File Name: Your Name's Dog Dayz
File Type: .qbw
Sell Both services and products
Record each sale individually, do charge sales tax
Do not use estimates, statements, progress invoicing, or track time
Do track customer orders (sales orders) and inventory
Do manage bills
Employees: Yes, W-2 Employees
Date to start tracking finances: 01/01/2015
Use QuickBooks to set up the Income and Expense Accounts. Add Service Sales and remove Merchant Account Fees

Use the information in the Memo above to create Your Name's Dog Days by completing the EasyStep Interview in QuickBooks Setup

Enter the Company Name **Your Name's Dog Dayz**, press the Tab key

- To identify your work, type your own name, not the words "Your Name's" as part of the company name. For example, Selma Anderson would have **Selma Anderson's Dog Dayz**.
- Your Name's Dog Dayz is entered as the Legal name when the Tab key is pressed.

Tab to **Tax ID number**, enter **15-9828654**

Enter the Company Address information in the spaces provided, tab to or click in the blanks to move from item to item

For the state, California, type **C** and QuickBooks will fill in the rest or click the drop-down list arrow for State and click CA

- The country is automatically filled in as US.

Enter the telephone number, fax number, e-mail address, and Web address as given in the Memo

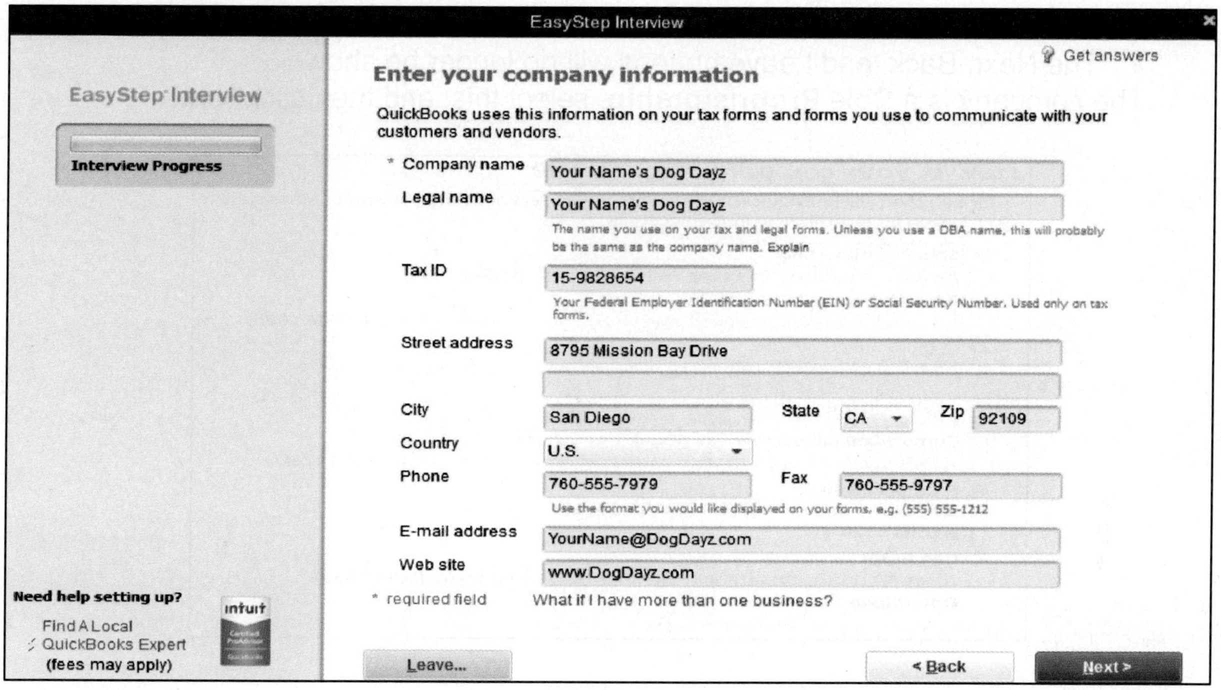

Click **Next**
Scroll through the list of industries
Click **Retail Shop or Online Commerce**, click **Next**

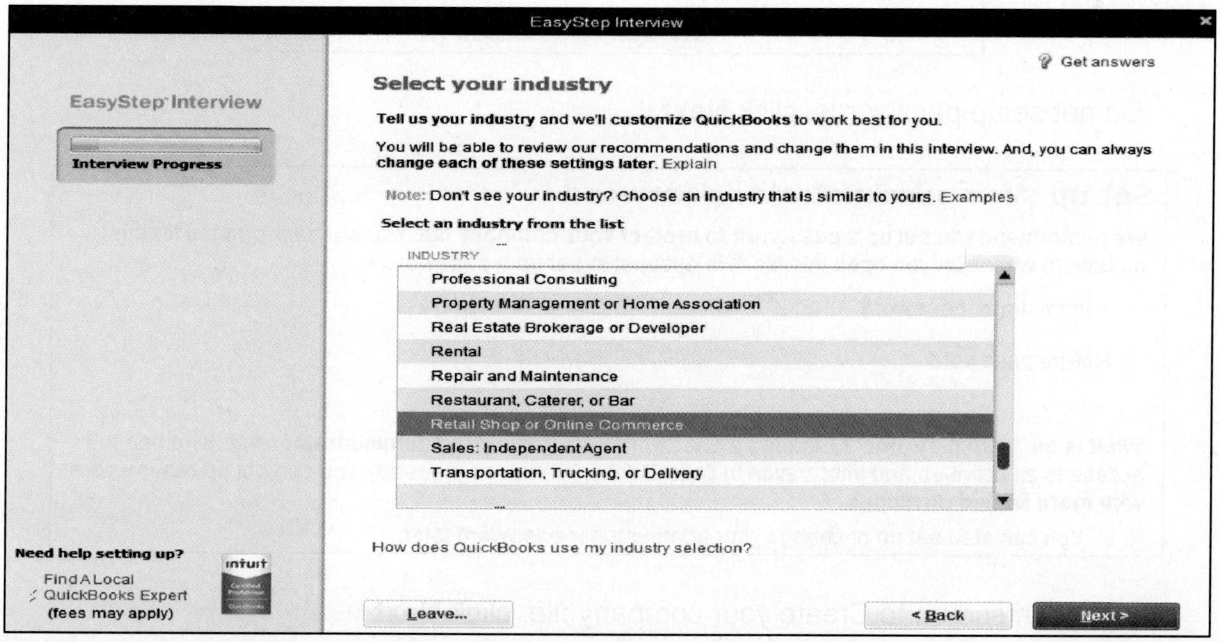

9

- Notice the Interview Progress in the upper-left side of the EasyStep Interview. This shows how much of the Interview has been completed.
- This Interview Progress portion of the screen will no longer be shown in every screen shot in the text but it will be shown on your QuickBooks screen.
- The Next, Back, and Leave buttons will no longer be shown.

The company is a **Sole Proprietorship**, select this, and then click **Next**

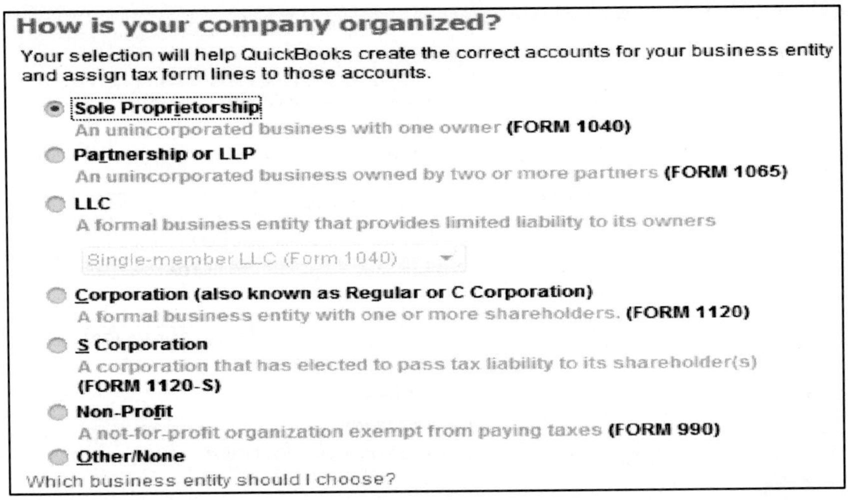

The fiscal year starts in **January**, click **Next**

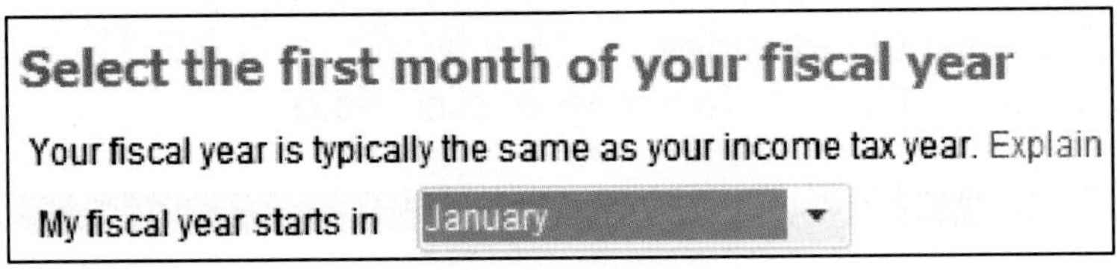

Do not setup passwords, click **Next**

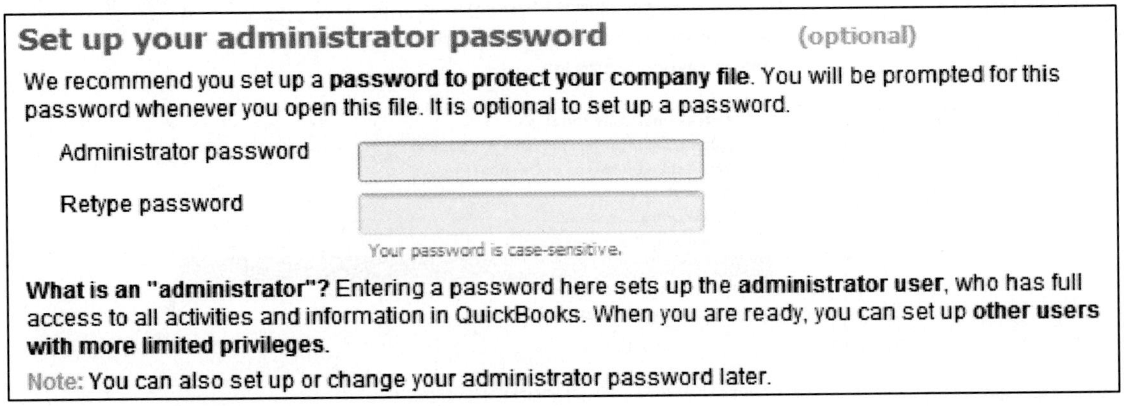
Set up your administrator password
(optional)
We recommend you set up a password to protect your company file. You will be prompted for this password whenever you open this file. It is optional to set up a password.
Administrator password
Retype password
Your password is case-sensitive.
What is an "administrator"? Entering a password here sets up the administrator user, who has full access to all activities and information in QuickBooks. When you are ready, you can set up other users with more limited privileges.
Note: You can also set up or change your administrator password later.

Read the screen to Create your company file, click **Next**

Click the drop-down list for **Save in:** and click the storage location you have been instructed to use (The example provided shows a USB drive in G: as the storage location.)

The File name is **Your Name's Dog Dayz**

Save as type: should show **QuickBooks Files (*.QBW, *.QBA)**

- Think: QuickBooks Working file = QBW

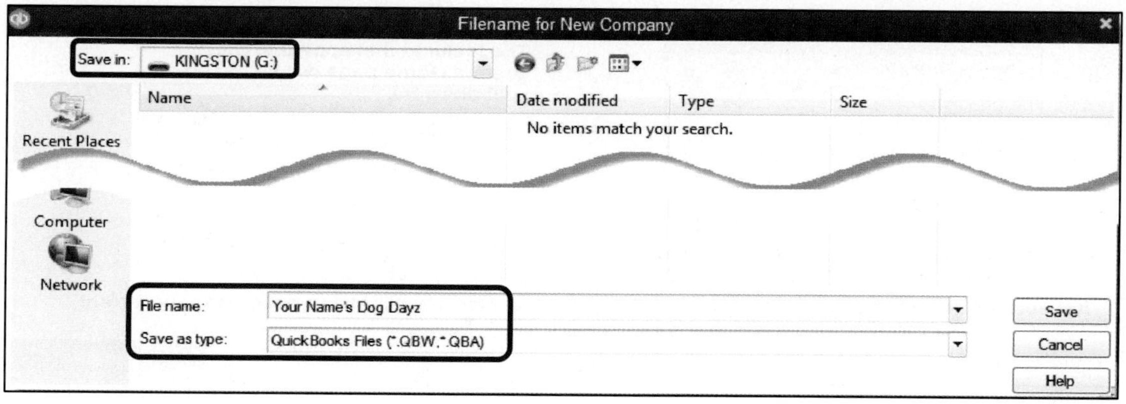

Click **Save**

- You may or may not see the other company files that you used throughout the text.
- Once the company file has been saved, you may click **Leave** and then click **OK** to exit the setup without losing the information entered during the EasyStep Interview. Close QuickBooks as previously instructed.

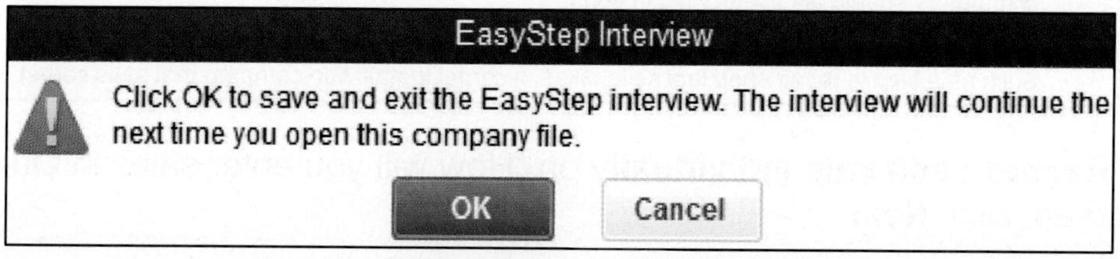

- When you resume, you will open QuickBooks. You must then open the company Your Name's Dog Dayz. When you do, QuickBooks will give you a Welcome Back screen. Simply click **OK** and resume the company setup.

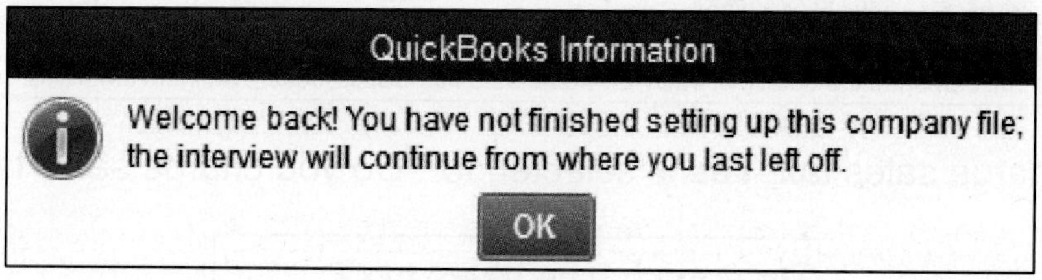

Read the screen regarding Customizing QuickBooks for your business; then click **Next**

- Some screens will require that you click a selection; on others the selection will already be marked.

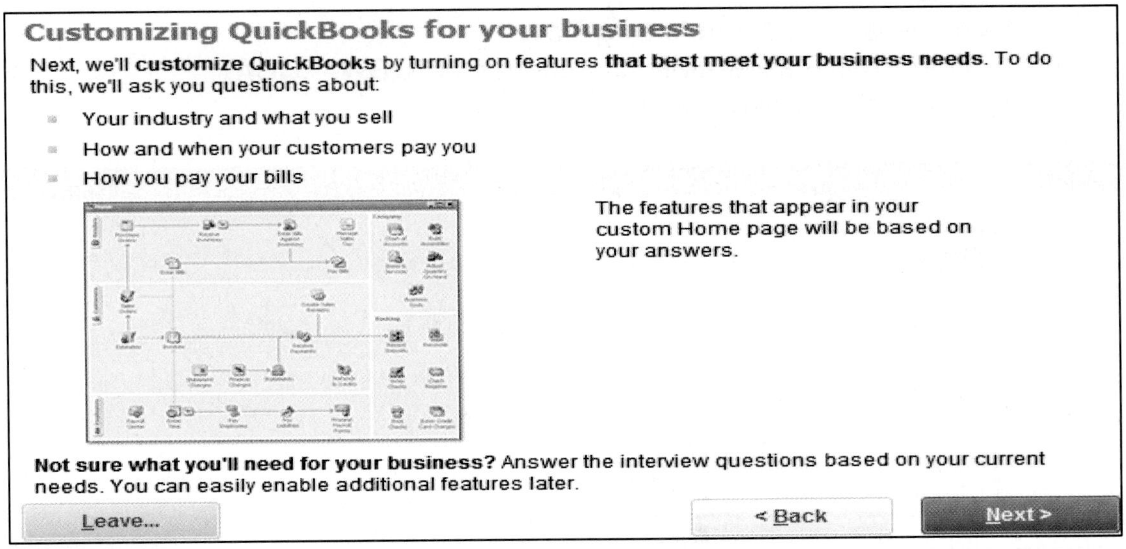

Click **Both services and products** on "What do you sell?" screen; click **Next**

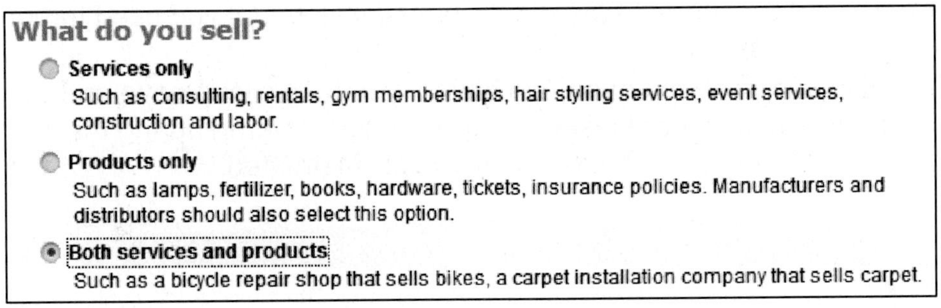

Click **Record each sale individually** on "How will you enter sales in QuickBooks" screen; click **Next**

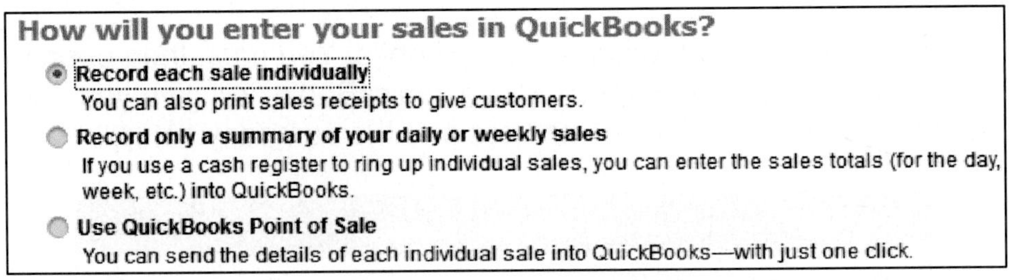

You do charge sales tax, **Yes** is selected for "Do you charge sales tax?"; click **Next**

No is selected on "Do you want to create estimates in QuickBooks?," click **Next**

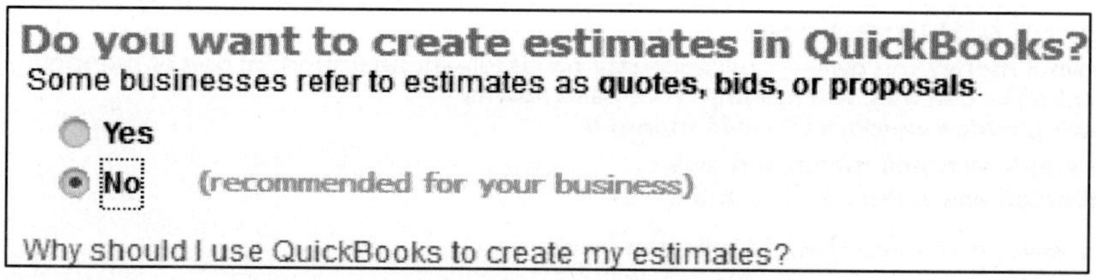
Do you want to create estimates in QuickBooks?
Some businesses refer to estimates as quotes, bids, or proposals.
Yes
No (recommended for your business)
Why should I use QuickBooks to create my estimates?

Yes is selected on "Tracking customer orders in QuickBooks," click **Next**

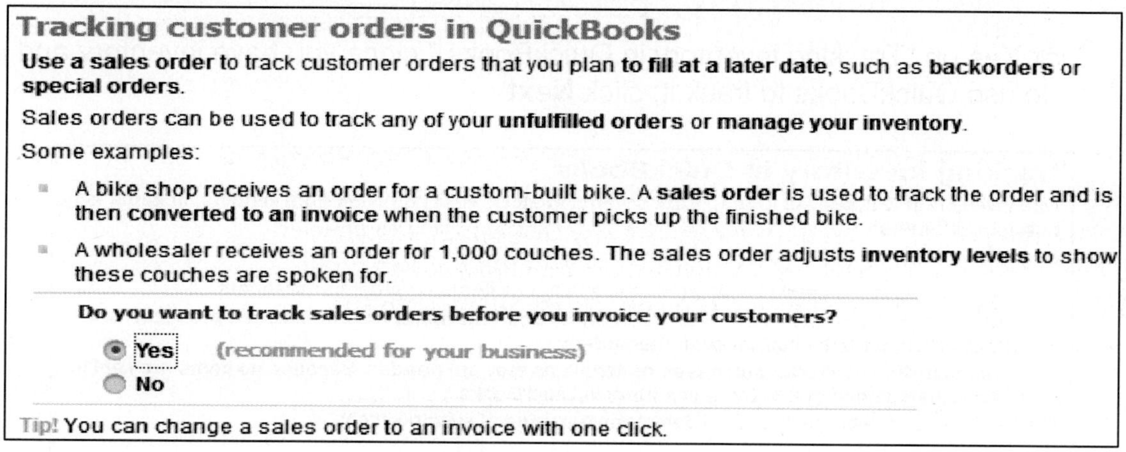
Tracking customer orders in QuickBooks
Use a sales order to track customer orders that you plan to fill at a later date, such as backorders or special orders.
Sales orders can be used to track any of your unfulfilled orders or manage your inventory.
Some examples:
A bike shop receives an order for a custom-built bike. A sales order is used to track the order and is then converted to an invoice when the customer picks up the finished bike.
A wholesaler receives an order for 1,000 couches. The sales order adjusts inventory levels to show these couches are spoken for.
Do you want to track sales orders before you invoice your customers?
Yes (recommended for your business)
No
Tip! You can change a sales order to an invoice with one click.

No is selected on "Using statements in QuickBooks," click **Next**

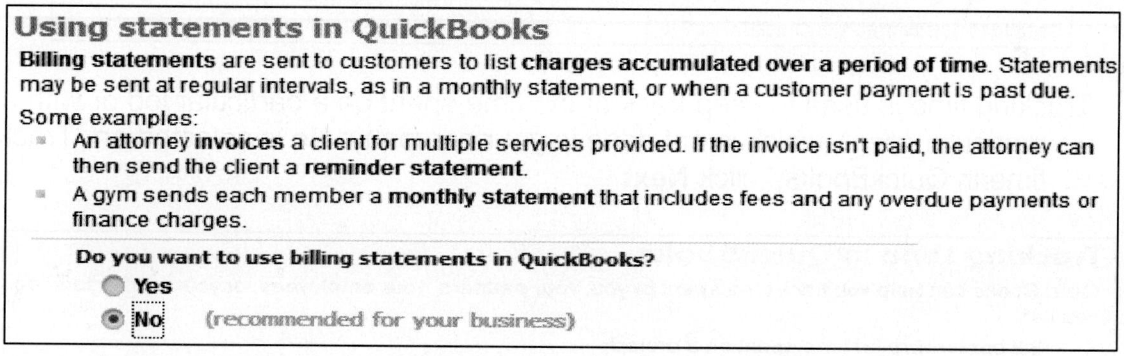
Using statements in QuickBooks
Billing statements are sent to customers to list charges accumulated over a period of time. Statements may be sent at regular intervals, as in a monthly statement, or when a customer payment is past due.
Some examples:
An attorney invoices a client for multiple services provided. If the invoice isn't paid, the attorney can then send the client a reminder statement.
A gym sends each member a monthly statement that includes fees and any overdue payments or finance charges.
Do you want to use billing statements in QuickBooks?
Yes
No (recommended for your business)

No is selected for "Using progress invoicing," click **Next**

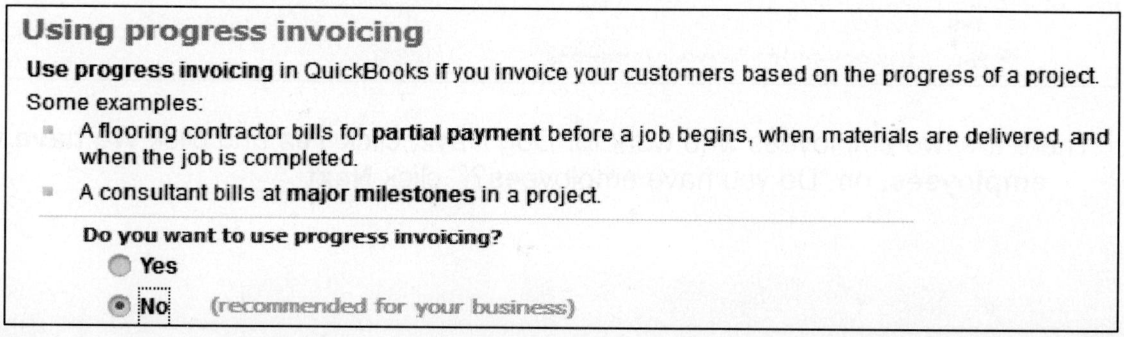
Using progress invoicing
Use progress invoicing in QuickBooks if you invoice your customers based on the progress of a project.
Some examples:
A flooring contractor bills for partial payment before a job begins, when materials are delivered, and when the job is completed.
A consultant bills at major milestones in a project.
Do you want to use progress invoicing?
Yes
No (recommended for your business)

Yes is selected on "Managing bills you owe," click **Next**

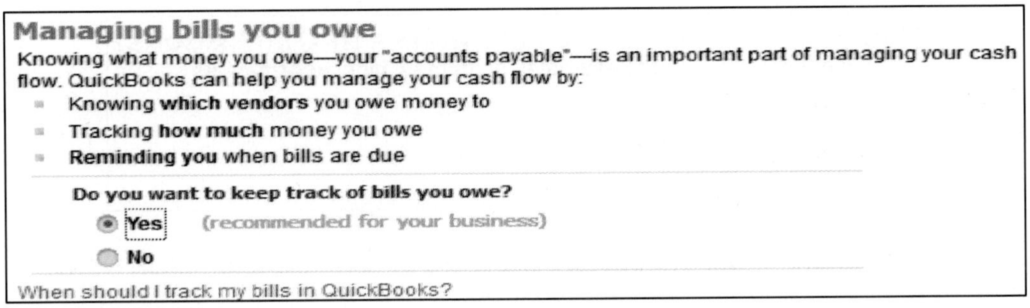
Managing bills you owe
Knowing what money you owe—your "accounts payable"—is an important part of managing your cash flow. QuickBooks can help you manage your cash flow by:
Knowing which vendors you owe money to
Tracking how much money you owe
Reminding you when bills are due
Do you want to keep track of bills you owe?
Yes (recommended for your business)
No
When should I track my bills in QuickBooks?

Click **Yes** on "Tracking inventory in QuickBooks," since you have inventory and plan to use QuickBooks to track it; click **Next**

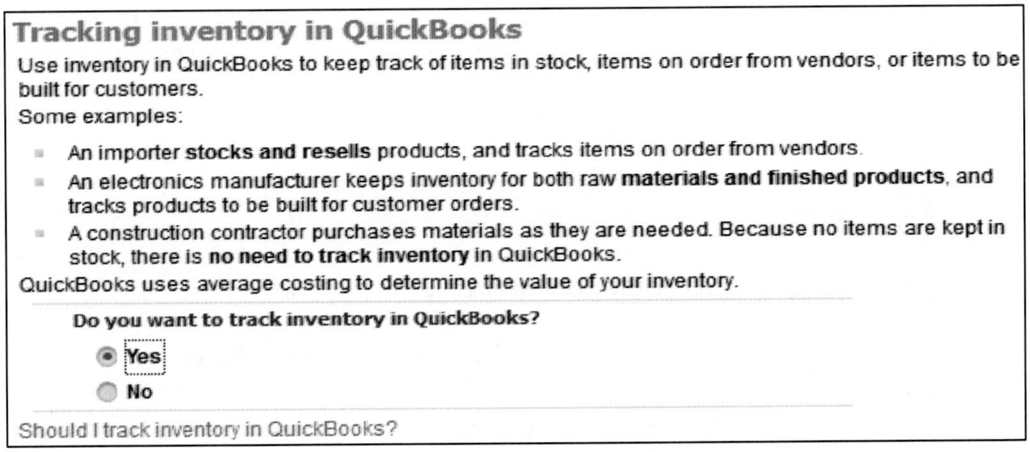
Tracking inventory in QuickBooks
Use inventory in QuickBooks to keep track of items in stock, items on order from vendors, or items to be built for customers.
Some examples:
An importer stocks and resells products, and tracks items on order from vendors.
An electronics manufacturer keeps inventory for both raw materials and finished products, and tracks products to be built for customer orders.
A construction contractor purchases materials as they are needed. Because no items are kept in stock, there is no need to track inventory in QuickBooks.
QuickBooks uses average costing to determine the value of your inventory.
Do you want to track inventory in QuickBooks?
Yes
No
Should I track inventory in QuickBooks?

Tracking time is used to keep track of the time spent on a particular job or with a particular client, which is not done in your company; **No** is selected on "Tracking time in QuickBooks," click **Next**

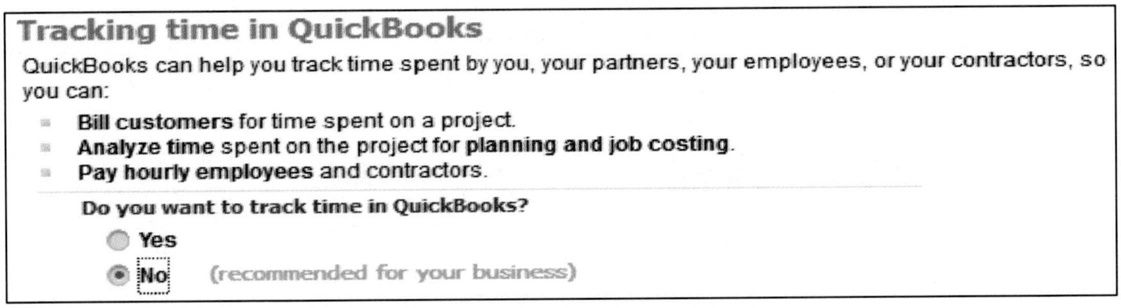
Tracking time in QuickBooks
QuickBooks can help you track time spent by you, your partners, your employees, or your contractors, so you can:
Bill customers for time spent on a project.
Analyze time spent on the project for planning and job costing.
Pay hourly employees and contractors.
Do you want to track time in QuickBooks?
Yes
No (recommended for your business)

There are two employees who work for Dog Dayz, click **Yes** and click **We have W-2 employees.** on "Do you have employees?," click **Next**

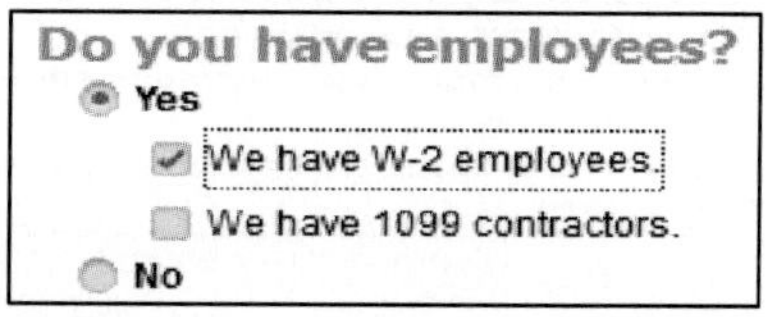

Do you have employees?
- (•) Yes
  - [x] We have W-2 employees.
  - [ ] We have 1099 contractors.
- ( ) No

You want to use QuickBooks to set up the Chart of Accounts; read the screen for Using accounts in QuickBooks; click **Next**

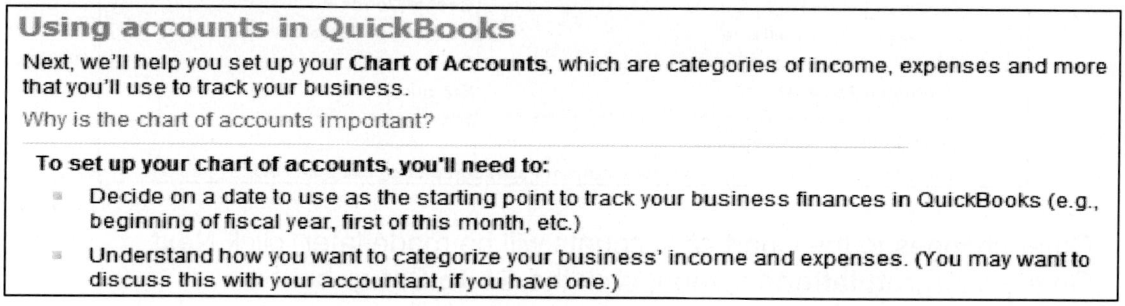

Using accounts in QuickBooks

Next, we'll help you set up your **Chart of Accounts**, which are categories of income, expenses and more that you'll use to track your business.

Why is the chart of accounts important?

To set up your chart of accounts, you'll need to:

- Decide on a date to use as the starting point to track your business finances in QuickBooks (e.g., beginning of fiscal year, first of this month, etc.)
- Understand how you want to categorize your business' income and expenses. (You may want to discuss this with your accountant, if you have one.)

Click **Use today's date or the first day of the quarter or month.**
Enter the date **01/01/2015**; click **Next**

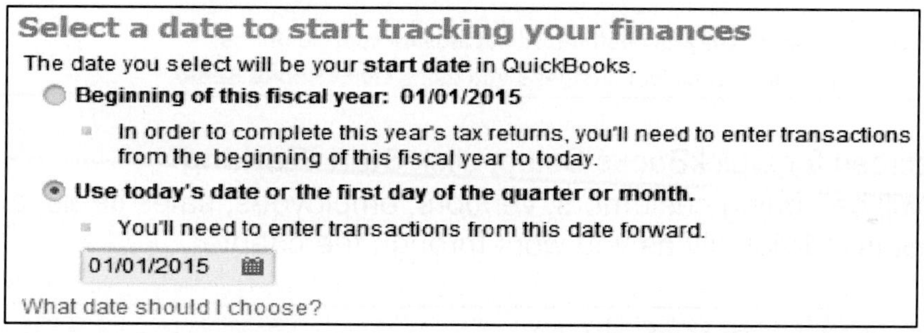

Select a date to start tracking your finances

The date you select will be your **start date** in QuickBooks.

( ) **Beginning of this fiscal year: 01/01/2015**
- In order to complete this year's tax returns, you'll need to enter transactions from the beginning of this fiscal year to today.

(•) **Use today's date or the first day of the quarter or month.**
- You'll need to enter transactions from this date forward.

01/01/2015

What date should I choose?

Scroll through the list of Income and Expense accounts created by QuickBooks

- The accounts recommended by QuickBooks are marked with a check. These accounts may or may not match your chart of accounts. You may make changes at this time to add and delete accounts from this list, or you may customize your chart of accounts later.
- To customize the income and expense section of the chart of accounts now, you add an account by clicking the unmarked account name.
- To remove an account that has been marked, click the account name to deselect.

Service Sales is not checked; click **Service Sales** to add the Income account to the Chart of Accounts

Merchant Account Fees has a check mark, click **Merchant Account Fees** to remove the check mark so it is no longer shown as a selected account

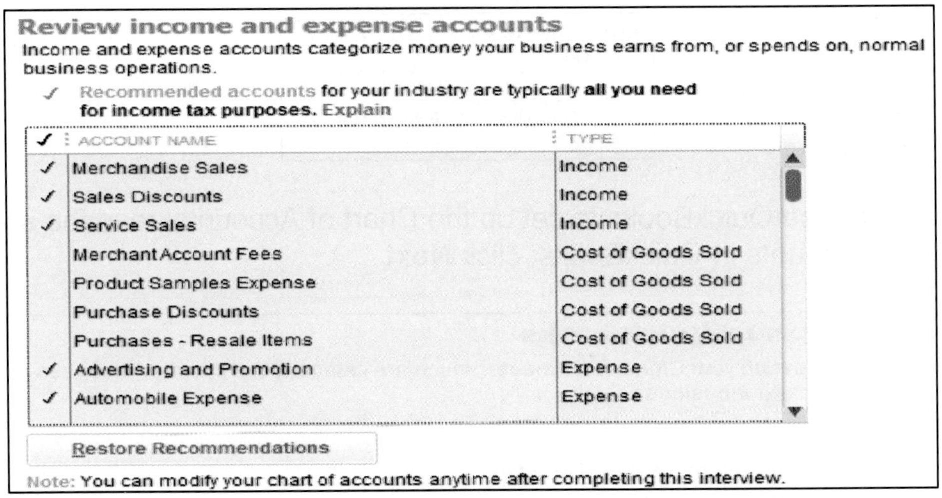

Other changes to the Chart of Accounts will be made later, click **Next**
On the **Congratulations** screen, click the **Go to Setup** button

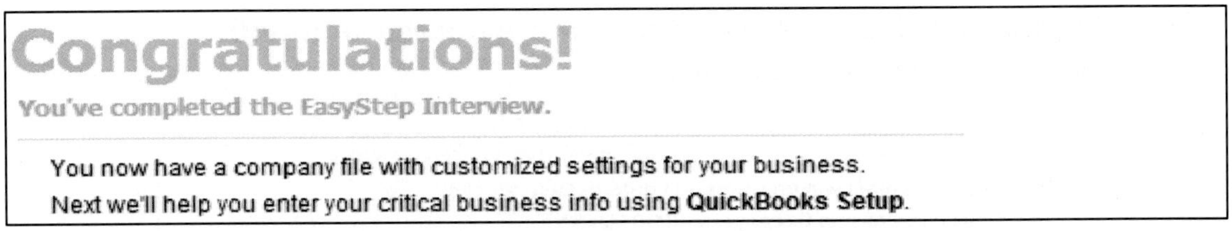

On the screen for QuickBooks Setup, click **Start Working**

- You will be adding customers, vendors, employees, sales items, and bank accounts individually as you work through the chapter.

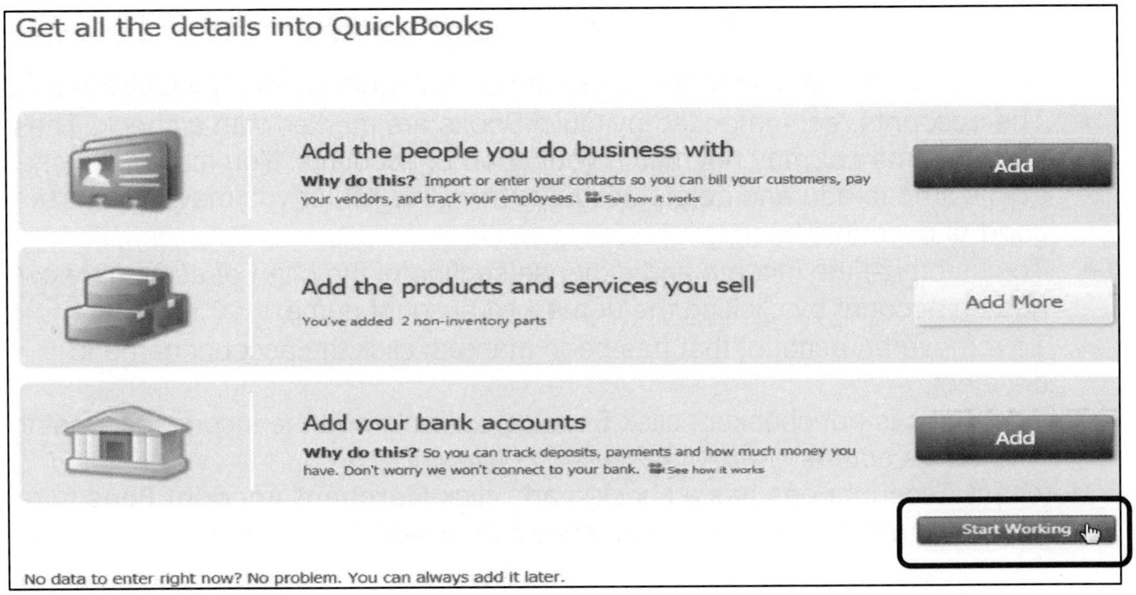

If you get a screen showing Quick Start Center, close it

SELECT A TOP ICON BAR

Throughout the textbook, the Top Icon Bar has been used. The Left Icon Bar is the default icon and shows when the company setup is complete. QuickBooks allows you to use either of the icon bars. Since the Left Icon Bar takes up a lot of room on the screen, we will continue to use the Top Icon Bar.

Select a Top Icon Bar

Click **View** on the Menu Bar
Click **Top Icon Bar**

- The Top Icon Bar is now shown in grayscale. We will change to color in Preferences later in the chapter.

CHART OF ACCOUNTS

Using the QuickBooks Setup to set up a company is a user-friendly way to establish the basic structure of the company. However, the Chart of Accounts created by QuickBooks may not be the exact Chart of Accounts you wish to use in your business. In order to customize your chart of accounts, additional accounts need to be created, balances need to be entered for balance sheet accounts, some account names need to be changed, and some accounts need to be deleted or made inactive.

The Chart of Accounts is not only a listing of the account names and balances but also the General Ledger used by the business. As in textbook accounting, the General Ledger/Chart of Accounts is the book of final entry.

At the completion of the QuickBooks EasyStep Interview and Setup, you will have the following Chart of Accounts, which is not complete. Please be aware that the Chart of Accounts created in the QuickBooks EasyStep Interview may be different from the one shown.

9

Chart of Accounts

NAME	⚡	TYPE	BALANCE TOTAL
Inventory Asset		Other Current Asset	0.00
Accumulated Depreciation		Fixed Asset	0.00
Furniture and Equipment		Fixed Asset	0.00
Security Deposits Asset		Other Asset	0.00
Payroll Liabilities		Other Current Liability	0.00
Sales Tax Payable		Other Current Liability	0.00
Opening Balance Equity		Equity	0.00
Owners Draw		Equity	0.00
Owners Equity		Equity	
Merchandise Sales		Income	
Sales Discounts		Income	
Service Sales		Income	
Cost of Goods Sold		Cost of Goods Sold	
Advertising and Promotion		Expense	
Automobile Expense		Expense	
Bank Service Charges		Expense	
Computer and Internet Expens...		Expense	
Depreciation Expense		Expense	
Insurance Expense		Expense	
Interest Expense		Expense	
Janitorial Expense		Expense	
Meals and Entertainment		Expense	
Office Supplies		Expense	
Payroll Expenses		Expense	
Professional Fees		Expense	
Rent Expense		Expense	
Repairs and Maintenance		Expense	
Telephone Expense		Expense	
Uniforms		Expense	
Utilities		Expense	
Ask My Accountant		Other Expense	

Use the following Chart of Accounts table and balances as a reference while you customize Your Name's Dog Dayz Chart of Accounts. Information regarding changes, additions, etc. is provided in the Memo that follows the Chart of Accounts. As usual, the steps used in making changes to the Chart of Accounts are detailed after the memo.

As you review the Chart of Accounts, look at the descriptions provided by QuickBooks. In many instances, the descriptions provided are explanatory and quite lengthy; and, frequently, they are unnecessary for clarification. In these instances, the descriptions should be deleted.

In addition to the changes you will be making in the Chart of Accounts, the Customer List, Vendor List, and Sales Items will also have information entered before your Chart of Accounts will match the following:

YOUR NAME'S DOG DAYZ
CHART OF ACCOUNTS

ACCOUNT	TYPE	BALANCE	ACCOUNT	TYPE
Checking	Bank	29,385.00	Sales	Inc.
Accounts Receivable (QB)	Accts. Rec.	***2,950.00	Boarding	Inc.
Inventory Asset	Other C.A.	***33,750.00	Day Camp	Inc.
Office Supplies	Other C.A.	350.00	Grooming	Inc.
Prepaid Insurance	Other C.A.	1,200.00	Merchandise	Inc.
Sales Supplies	Other C.A.	500.00	Sales Discounts	Inc.
Equipment	Fixed Asset	***	Cost of Goods Sold (QB)	COGS
Original Cost	Fixed Asset	8,000.00	Advertising and Promotion	Exp.
Depreciation	Fixed Asset	-800.00	Automobile Expense	Exp.
Fixtures	Fixed Asset	***	Bank Service Charges	Exp.
Original Cost	Fixed Asset	15,000.00	Computer and Internet Expenses	Exp
Depreciation	Fixed Asset	-1,500.00	Depreciation Expense	
Accounts Payable (QB)	Other C.L.	***5,000.00	Insurance Expense	Exp.
Payroll Liabilities	Other C.L.	0.00	Interest Expense	Exp.
Sales Tax Payable	Other C.L.	0.00	Janitorial Expense	Exp.
Equipment Loan	Long Term L.	2,000.00	Office Supplies Expense	Exp.
Fixtures Loan	Long Term L.	2,500.00	Payroll Expenses	Exp.
First & Last Name, Capital	Equity	***	Professional Fees	Exp.
First & Last Name, Investment	Equity	25,000.00	Rent Expense	Exp.
First & Last Name, Withdrawals	Equity	0.00	Repairs and Maintenance	Exp.
Owner's Equity (QB*)	Equity	***	Sales Supplies Expense	Exp.
			Telephone Expense	Exp.
			Utilities	Exp.
			Other Income	Other Inc
			Other Expenses	Other Exp

<u>Chart Abbreviations:</u>
(QB)=Account Created by QuickBooks
(QB*)=Account Created by QuickBooks. Name change required.
Indented Account Names indicate that the account is a subaccount
*** means that QuickBooks will enter the account balance
C.A.=Current Asset, F.A.=Fixed Asset; C.L.=Current Liability; Long Term L.=Long Term Liability; COGS=Cost of Goods Sold, Inc.=Income, Exp.=Expense.

9

MEMO

DATE: January 1, 2015

Since Your Name's Dog Dayz' Chart of Accounts/General Ledger needs to be customized, make the following changes to the accounts:

Add: **Checking**, Type: **Bank**; Bank Acct. No. 456114865, Routing Number: 122235894, Statement Ending Balance: **$29,385**, Statement Ending Date: **12/31/14**
Delete: Accumulated Depreciation, Furniture and Equipment, Security Deposits Asset, Uniforms, and Ask My Accountant
Make inactive: Meals and Entertainment
Edit Equity Accounts: Change the name of Opening Balance Equity to **First & Last Name, Capital**; change Owners Equity to **Owner's Equity**, change Owners Draw to **First & Last Name, Withdrawals**; Subaccount of First & Last Name, Capital
Add Equity Accounts: **First & Last Name, Investment**; Subaccount of First & Last Name, Capital; Opening Balance **$25,000** as of **01/01/15**
Add Income Accounts: Add **Sales**; add **Boarding**, a subaccount of Sales; add **Grooming**, a Subaccount of Sales; add **Other Income**
Edit Income Accounts: rename Merchandise Sales to **Merchandise** and make it a subaccount of Sales, rename Service Sales to **Day Camp** and make it a subaccount of Sales
Add Expense Accounts: **Sales Supplies Expense**, and **Other Expenses**
Edit Expense Accounts: Rename Office Supplies to **Office Supplies Expense**
Delete Account Descriptions: Check each account and delete the descriptions entered by QuickBooks.
Change Tax-Line Mapping: Select Unassigned for all Tax-Line Mapping

Make the changes indicated above and delete the descriptions in all of the accounts

Click **Chart of Accounts** in the Company section of the Home Page
Use the keyboard shortcut **Ctrl+N** to add a new account
Account Type click **Bank**, click **Continue**
Enter Account Name **Checking**, enter Bank Acct. No **456114865**, Routing Number **122235894**
Click **Enter Opening Balance**, enter the Statement Ending Balance: **29,385**
Enter the date of the last bank statement received prior to setting up the company in QuickBooks for the Statement Ending Date: **12/31/2014**

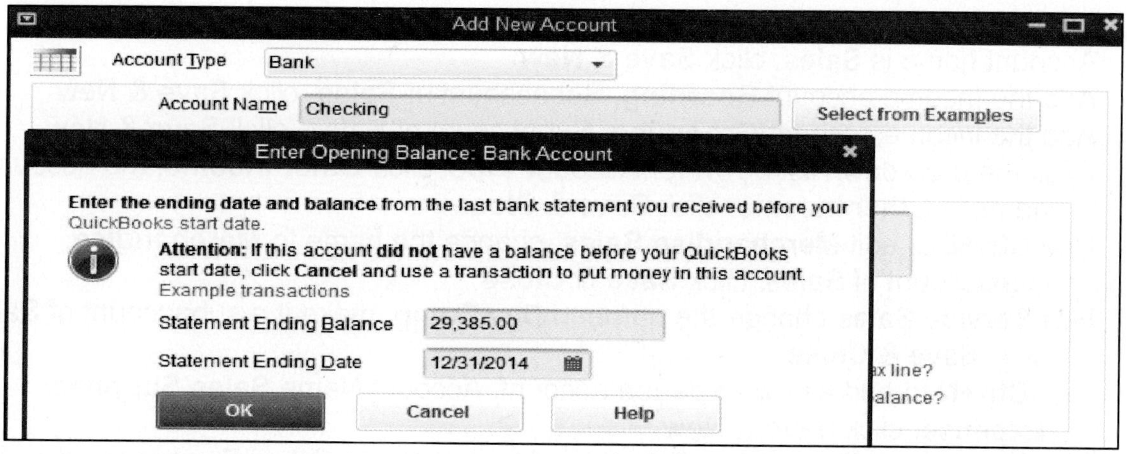

Click **OK** on Enter Opening Balance: Bank Account; then click **Save & Close**
If you get a Set Up Bank Feed message, click **No**
Click the account **Accumulated Depreciation** to highlight, use the keyboard **Ctrl+D** to delete the account, click **OK** to delete
Repeat to delete the other accounts listed in the memo
Position the cursor on the expense account, **Meals and Entertainment**, click the **Account** button, and click **Make Account Inactive**
Position the cursor on **Opening Balance Equity**, click the **Account** button, click **Edit Account**, enter **First & Last Name, Capital** as the account name (use your actual first and last name), click **Save & Close**
Edit **Owners Equity** and change the name to **Owner's Equity**, click **Save & Close**
Edit **Owners Draw** and rename it **First & Last Name, Withdrawals** (use your actual first and last name), click **Subaccount of**, click **First & Last Name, Capital**, click **Save & Close**
Click the **Account** button, click **New**, account type is **Equity**, click **Continue**
Enter the account name **First & Last Name, Investment** (use your first and last name), click **Subaccount**, click **First & Last Name, Capital**
Click the **Enter Opening Balance** button, enter **25,000** as of **12/31/14**

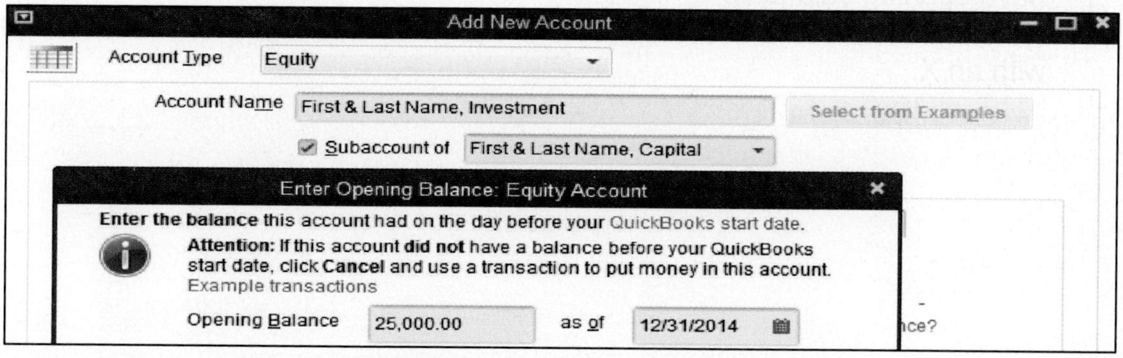

Click **OK**; and then, click **Save & Close**

- If you get a screen warning about a transaction being 30 days in the future or 90 days in the past, click **Yes**.

Click the **Account** button, click **New**, account type is **Income**, click **Continue**
Account name is **Sales**, click **Save & New**
Add the Income account **Boarding**, Subaccount of **Sales**, click **Save & New**
Add the income account **Grooming**, Subaccount of **Sales**, click **Save & New**
Click the drop-down list arrow for Account Type, click **Other Income**, the account name is **Other Income**, click **Save & Close**
Use **Ctrl+E** to edit **Merchandise Sales**, change the name to **Merchandise**, Subaccount of **Sales**; click **Save & Close**
Edit **Service Sales** change the name to **Day Camp**, make it a subaccount of **Sales**; click **Save & Close**
Use **Ctrl+N** to add a new **Expense** account, Account Name **Sales Supplies Expense**, click **Save & New**
Change Account Type **Other Expense**, Account Name **Other Expenses**, click **Save & Close**
Edit the Expense Account **Office Supplies** change the Account Name to **Office Supplies Expense**, click **Save & Close**
In order to remove unwanted and lengthy account descriptions and a variety of tax-line mappings, use **Ctrl + E** to edit each account individually, delete descriptions added by QuickBooks, and change tax-line mapping to **<Unassigned>**, when finished, click **Save & Close**
Begin with Checking and repeat for all of the accounts

- Lengthy account descriptions are provided by QuickBooks when it establishes the Chart of Accounts. These descriptions are designed to help those with limited accounting. They will print on reports so removing them helps to streamline QuickBooks reports.
- QuickBooks will include appropriate tax-line mapping for some accounts but not others. Since our focus is not on tax-line mapping, making all of the tax lines <Unassigned> is appropriate.

At this point, the Chart of Accounts appears as follows on the next page:

- As you can see, income and expense accounts do not have opening balances. Only some balance sheet accounts—assets, liabilities, and equity accounts—have opening balances.
- Note that the inactive account Meals and Entertainment is shown and is marked with an X.

Chart of Accounts

NAME		TYPE	BALANCE TOTAL
Checking		Bank	29,385.00
Inventory Asset		Other Current Asset	0.00
Payroll Liabilities		Other Current Liability	0.00
Sales Tax Payable		Other Current Liability	0.00
First & Last Name, Capital		Equity	4,385.00
First & Last Name, Investment		Equity	25,000.00
First & Last Name, Withdrawals		Equity	0.00
Owners Equity		Equity	
Sales		Income	
Boarding		Income	
Day Camp		Income	
Grooming		Income	
Merchandise		Income	
Sales Discounts		Income	
Advertising and Promotion		Expense	
Automobile Expense		Expense	
Bank Service Charges		Expense	
Computer and Internet Expenses		Expense	
Depreciation Expense		Expense	
Insurance Expense		Expense	
Interest Expense		Expense	
Janitorial Expense		Expense	
Meals and Entertainment		Expense	
Office Supplies Expense		Expense	
Payroll Expenses		Expense	
Professional Fees		Expense	
Rent Expense		Expense	
Repairs and Maintenance		Expense	
Telephone Expense		Expense	
Utilities		Expense	
Other Income		Other Income	
Other Expenses		Other Expense	

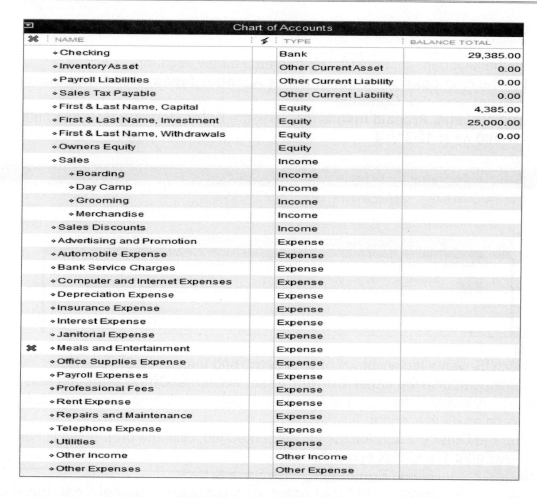

Do not close the Chart of Accounts, continue with the following:

MEMO

DATE: January 1, 2015

Set up the following Balance Sheet accounts and balances. The as of dates for opening balances is 12/31/14, the day before the start date.

Other Current Asset: Prepaid Insurance, Opening Balance $1,200
Other Current Asset: Office Supplies, Opening Balance $350
Other Current Asset: Sales Supplies, Opening Balance $500
Fixed Asset: Equipment
Fixed Asset: Original Cost, Subaccount of Equipment, Opening Balance $8,000
Fixed Asset: Depreciation, Subaccount of Equipment, Opening Balance -$800
Fixed Asset: Fixtures
Fixed Asset: Original Cost, Subaccount of Fixtures, Opening Balance $15,000
Fixed Asset: Depreciation, Subaccount of Fixtures, Opening Balance -$1,500
Long-term liability: Equipment Loan, Opening Balance $2,000
Long-term liability: Fixtures Loan, Opening Balance $2,500

Add the additional Balance Sheet accounts and their balances

Use the keyboard shortcut **Ctrl+N** to create a new account
Click the drop-down list arrow for **Other Account Types**, click **Other Current Asset**, and click **Continue**.
Account Name: **Prepaid Insurance**, click the **Enter Opening Balance** button, enter **1,200** as of **12/31/14**

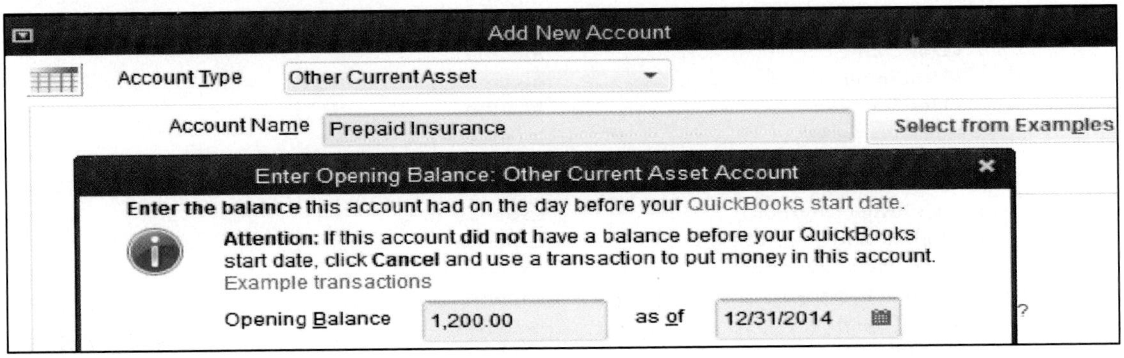

Click **OK**, verify the accuracy of your entry, and then, click **Save & New**
Continue adding the **Other Current Asset** accounts: **Office Supplies** and **Sales Supplies** and the Opening Balances listed in the Memo, click **Save & New** after adding each account
After the Other Current Assets have been added, click the drop-down list arrow for Account Type, click **Fixed Asset**
Enter Account Name **Equipment**, click **Save & New**
The type of account is still Fixed Asset, Account Name **Original Cost**, Subaccount of **Equipment**
Click the **Enter Opening Balance** button, enter **8,000** as of **12/31/14**, click **OK**

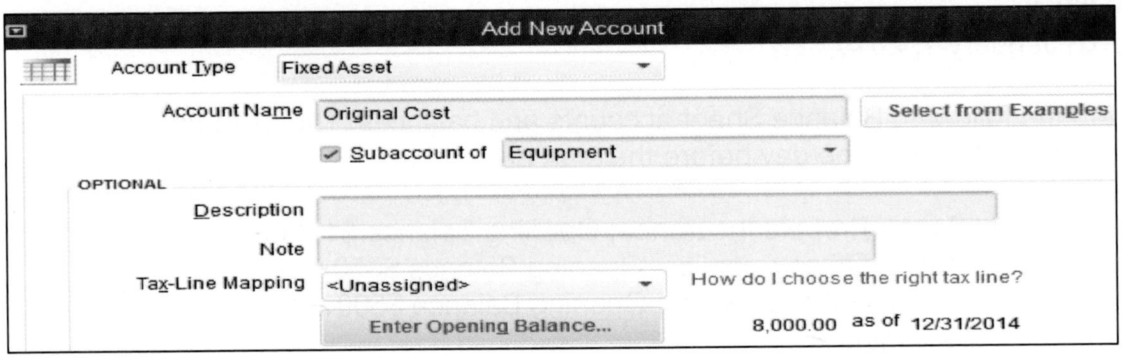

Click **Save & New** and add Account Name **Depreciation**, Subaccount of **Equipment** with an Opening Balance of **-800** as of **12/31/14**

- Be sure to use a minus (-) sign in front of the 800. Remember, depreciation reduces the value of the asset.

Click **OK** on the Opening Balance screen

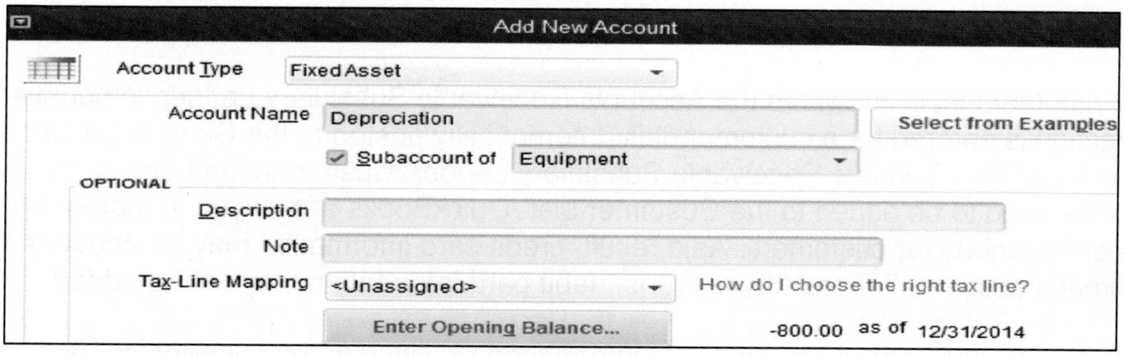

Click **Save & New**

Add the other fixed asset, **Fixtures**

Use the information in the Memo to add the Subaccounts of Fixtures **Original Cost** and **Depreciation** and the Opening Balances listed in the Memo, click **Save & New** after adding each account

Change the account Type to **Long Term Liability**, Account Name **Equipment Loan**

Click the **Enter Opening Balance** button; enter **2,000** as of **12/31/14**, click **OK**

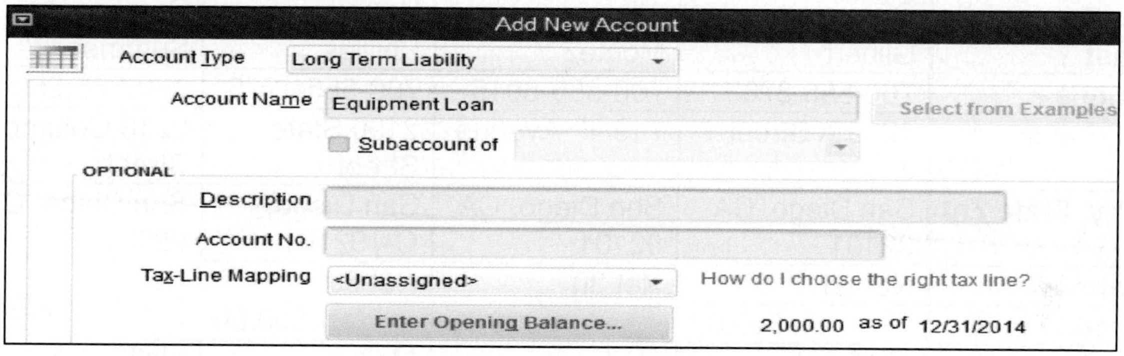

Click **Save & New**

Add the Long-Term Liability account **Fixtures Loan** and its Opening Balance, click **Save & Close**

Review the Chart of Accounts; then close it

- Note the value of Store Equipment, Store Fixtures, and the two loans.
- You will notice that Accounts Receivable and Accounts Payable are not in the account listing. QuickBooks will add these accounts when the customers and vendors and their opening balances are added.
- In addition, Inventory Asset has a 0.00 balance. QuickBooks will calculate the balance once all inventory items and total values are added.
- The Chart of Accounts will be printed once we have added customers, vendors, and sales items.

ADD CUSTOMERS

The Customer List is known as the Accounts Receivable Subsidiary Ledger. Whenever a transaction is entered for a customer, it is automatically posted to the General Ledger account and the Accounts Receivable Subsidiary Ledger. Customers and any opening balances need to be added to the Customer List. QuickBooks allows you to store preferred payment methods for customers. As a result, credit card information may be added to the customer's account. For security reasons, debit card information may not be added.

As you add customers, enter the information provided in the following chart:

CUSTOMERS				
Customer Name	Gilbert, Oliver	Montez, Alice	Phillips, Henry	Summer, Carol
Opening Balance	500.00	800.00	1,500.00	150.00
As of	12/31/14	12/31/14	12/31/14	12/31/14
First	Oliver	Alice	Henry	Carol
Last	Gilbert	Montez	Phillips	Summer
Phone	760-555-8763	760-555-8015	760-555-1275	760-555-2594
Address	1839 A Street	719 4th Avenue	2190 State Street	2210 Columbia Street
City, State Zip	San Diego, CA 92101	San Diego, CA 92101	San Diego, CA 92101	San Diego, CA 92101
Terms	Net 30	Net 30	Net 30	Net 30
Credit Limit	500.00	1,000.00	1,500.00	500.00
Preferred Delivery Method	Mail	Mail	Mail	Mail
Preferred Payment Method	Visa	Check	Check	Debit Card
Credit Card Information	4123 4907 8901 237			
Exp. Date	02/2018			
Tax Code	Tax	Tax	Tax	Tax
Tax Item	State Tax	State Tax	State Tax	State Tax

Use **Ctrl+J** to open the **Customer Center**, click the **New Customer & Job** button; and then click **New Customer**

Enter **Gilbert, Oliver**

- Since you want your Customer List to be sorted according to the customer's last name, type the last name first.

Tab to or click in OPENING BALANCE, enter **500**, AS OF enter **12/31/14**
Complete the Address Info tab:

For the FULL NAME, click in **First**, enter **Oliver**, tab to **Last**, enter **Gilbert**
Click in or tab to **Main Phone**, enter **760-555-8763**
Click at the end of the name in the ADDRESS DETAILS section for INVOICE/BILL TO, press the Enter key
Enter the address **1839 A Street**, press Enter, type **San Diego, CA 92101**

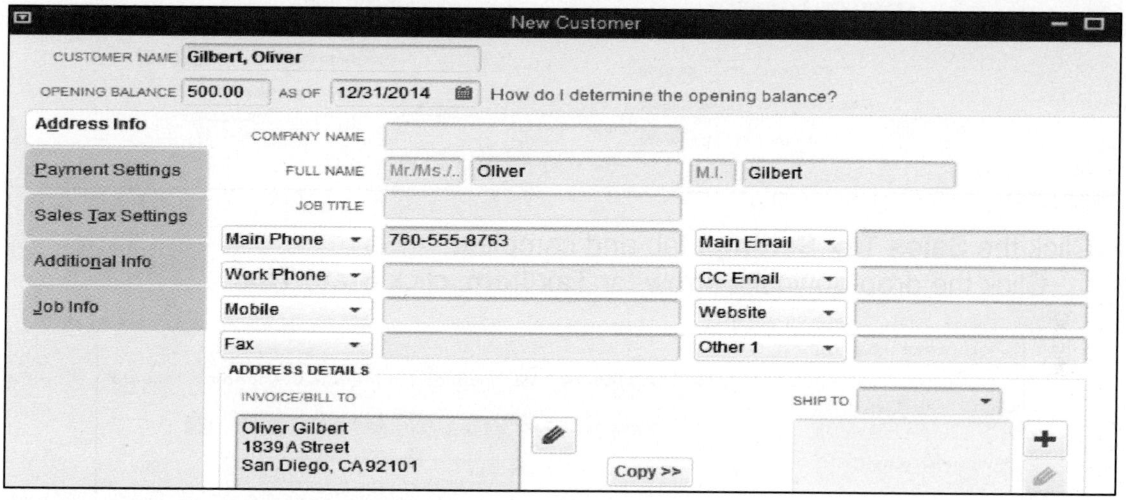

Click the **Payment Settings** tab and complete:

Click the drop-down list arrow for **PAYMENT TERMS**, click **Net 30**
Click in the text box for **CREDIT LIMIT**, enter **500**
Select the PREFERRED DELIVERY METHOD: **Mail**
Select the PREFERRED PAYMENT METHOD: **Visa**
Since Visa is the preferred payment method, enter the CREDIT CARD INFORMATION
CREDIT CARD NO. **4123-4907-8901-237**, EXP. DATE **02/2018**
Tab through NAME ON CARD, ADDRESS, and ZIP/POSTAL CODE (QuickBooks enters the information)

- Once a credit card number is entered into QuickBooks, when you close the program, you will get a Customer Credit Card Protection screen the next time you open QuickBooks. As you did in earlier chapters, click **Disable Protection**; and then click **Yes** on the Disable Sensitive Data Protection.

9

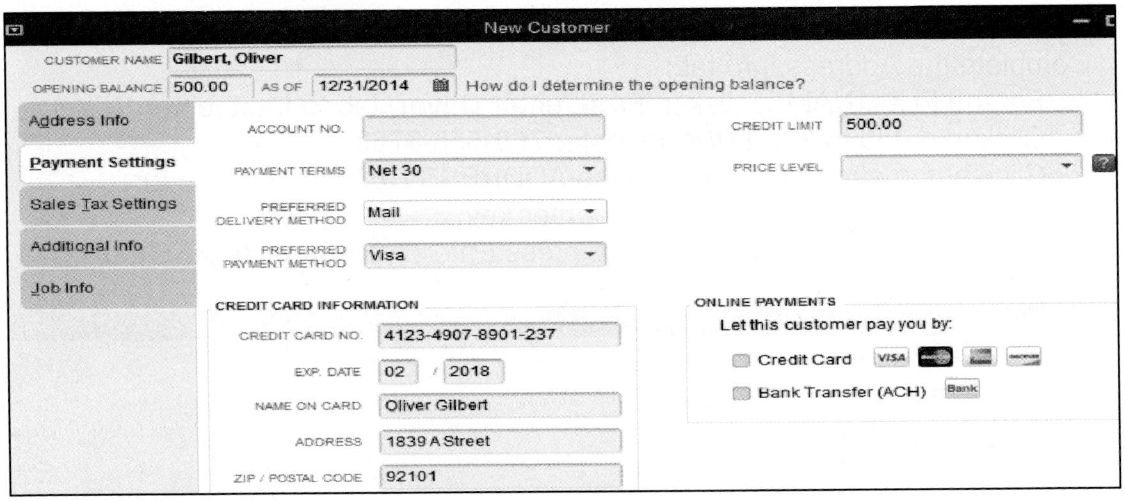

Click the **Sales Tax Settings** tab and complete:

Click the drop-down list arrow for **Tax Item**, click **State Tax**

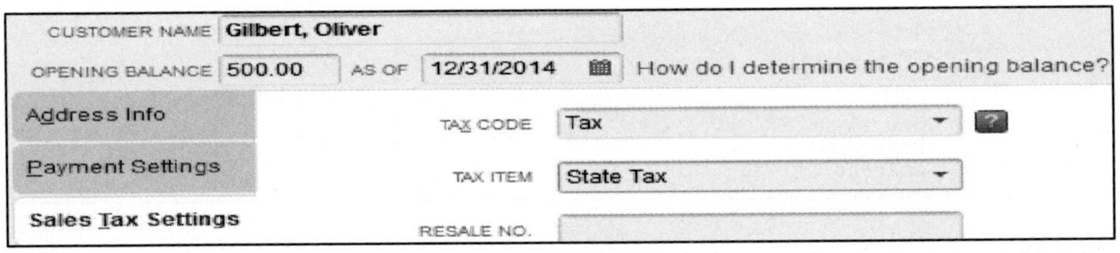

Click **OK**

Use the Customer Chart above and enter the information for the remaining customers

- When you enter the information for Carol Summer, remember that you cannot save Debit card information in QuickBooks.

Click the **Print** icon in the Customer Center, click **Customer & Job List**, print in Portrait orientation

If you get a message for List Reports, click **Do not display this message in the future**, then click **OK**

- The date of your computer will show as the report date and the Date Prepared and Time Prepared will be shown.

Your Name's Dog Dayz
Customer & Job List
January 1, 2015

Customer	Balance Total	Attach
Gilbert, Oliver	500.00	No
Montez, Alice	800.00	No
Phillips, Henry	1,500.00	No
Summer, Carol	150.00	No

Close the Customer Center

ADD VENDORS

The Vendor List is known as the Accounts Payable Subsidiary Ledger. Whenever a transaction is entered for a vendor, it is automatically posted to the General Ledger account and the Accounts Payable Subsidiary Ledger.

For ease of entry, vendors are divided into two tables. Use these tables as you add Vendors.

VENDORS			
Vendor and Company Name	Canine Grooming Supplies	Bow-Wow Supplies	Dog Toys & Treats
Opening Balance	3,000.00	2,000.00	0.00
As of	12/31/14	12/31/14	12/31/14
Main Phone	310-555-6971	760-555-2951	310-555-6464
Fax	310-555-1796	760-555-1592	310-555-4646
Address	10855 Western Avenue	5787 Broadway Avenue	1970 College Boulevard
City, State, Zip	Los Angeles, CA 90012	San Diego, CA 92101	Hollywood, CA 90028
Payment Terms	2% 10, Net 30	Net 30	2% 10, Net 30
Credit Limit	10,000	5,000	8,500

VENDORS				
Vendor and Company Name	Employment Development Department	San Diego Bank	Health Insurance, Inc.	State Board of Equalization
Main Phone	310-555-8877	760-555-9889	310-555-7412	916-555-0000
Fax	310-555-7788	760-555-9988	310-555-2147	916-555-1111
Address	11033 Wilshire Boulevard	350 Second Street	2085 Wilshire Boulevard	7800 State Street
City, State, Zip	Los Angeles, CA 90007	San Diego, CA 92114	Los Angeles, CA 90017	Sacramento, CA 94265

Add the vendors and their information from the tables provided

Open the **Vendor Center**, click the **New Vendor** button, then click the selection **New Vendor**

Enter VENDOR NAME: **Canine Grooming Supplies**

Enter the OPENING BALANCE: **3,000.00**, AS OF **12/31/14**

Complete the **Address Info** tab

Tab to COMPANY NAME, enter **Canine Grooming Supplies**

9

Click in text box for **Main Phone**, enter **310-555-6971**
Click in text box for **Fax**, enter **310-555-1796**
Click at the end of the name in the ADDRESS DETAILS section for BILLED FROM, press the Enter key
Enter the address **10855 Western Avenue**, press Enter, type **Los Angeles, CA 90012**

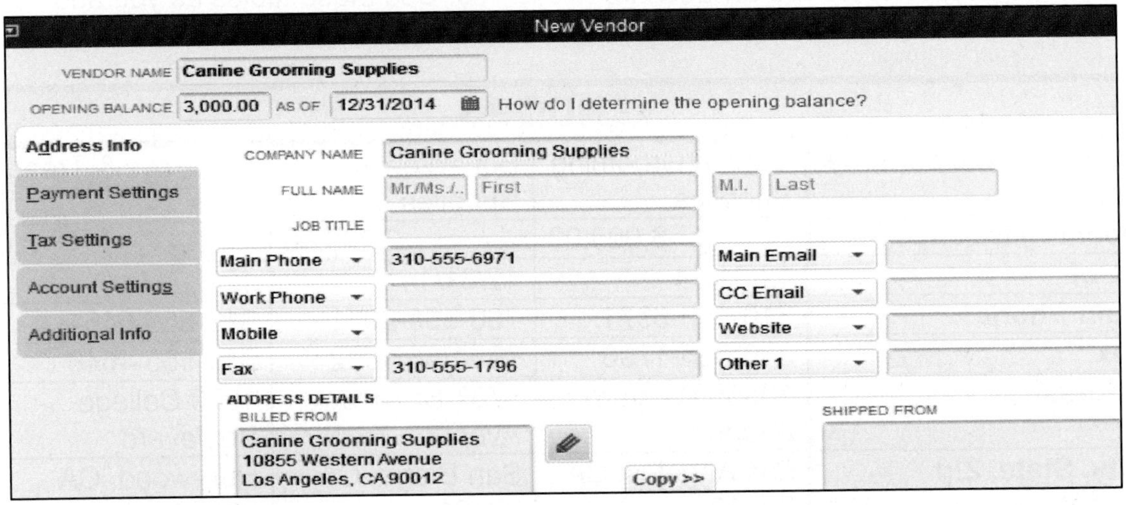

Click the **Payment Settings** tab and complete:

Click the drop-down list arrow for **PAYMENT TERMS**, click **2% 10, Net 30**
Click in the text box for **CREDIT LIMIT**, enter **10,000**, and click **OK**

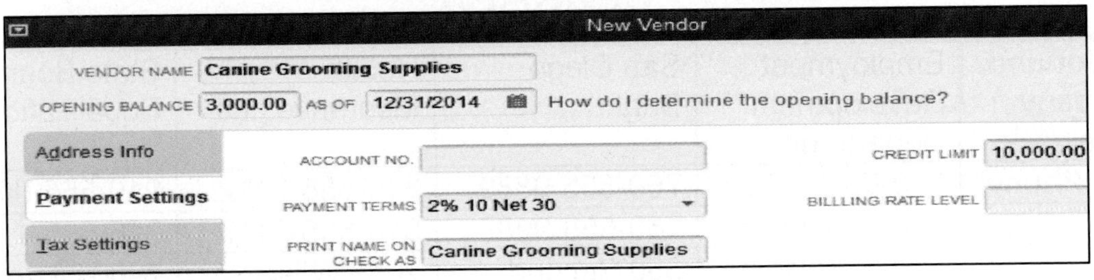

Repeat the steps above to enter all of the vendors in both charts
Print the **Vendor List** in Portrait as previously instructed

- Remember, the date of your computer will show as the report date and the Date Prepared and Time Prepared will be shown.

Your Name's Dog Dayz
Vendor List
January 1, 2015

Vendor	Balance Total	Attach
Bow-Wow Supplies	2,000.00	No
Canine Grooming Supplies	3,000.00	No
Dog Toys & Treats	0.00	No
Employment Development Department	0.00	No
Health Insurance, Inc.	0.00	No
San Diego Bank	0.00	No
State Board of Equalization	0.00	No

ADD SALES ITEMS

The Items list contains information about all of the items sold or services performed by the business. During the EasyStep Interview, QuickBooks added additional tax, consignment, and non-inventory items. Some of these will need to be edited and/or deleted.

> **MEMO**
> **DATE:** January 1, 2015
>
> Use the information in the tables provided to add Service Items and Inventory Items. Delete the items: Consignment Item and Non-Inventory Item.

Use the information in the following chart to add each service item

SERVICE ITEMS

Item Name	Doggie Digs Hotel	Doggie Dayz Camp	Doggie Salon
Description	Boarding	Day Camp	Grooming
Rate	55.00	30.00	0.00
Tax Code	Non	Non	Non
Income Account	Boarding	Day Camp	Grooming

Open the **Item List**, click the **Item** button; click **New** to begin entering Service items
Click the drop-down list arrow for Type, click **Service**
Enter the Item Name/Number **Doggie Digs Hotel**, enter the Description **Boarding**
Enter the Rate **55**, the Tax Code is **Non**
The **Account** is **Boarding**, a subaccount of Sales

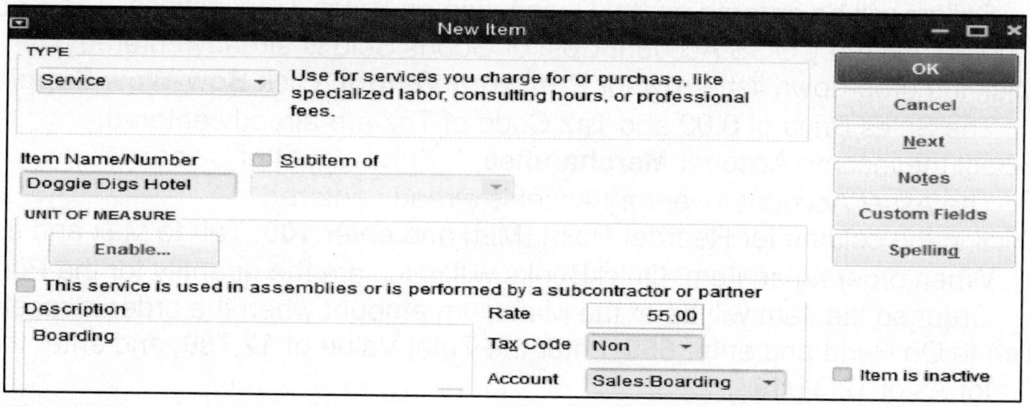

Click **Next** and add the remaining Service Items using the information in the chart
When finished adding service items, click **Next**

Use the following chart and add the Inventory Items

INVENTORY PART ITEMS				
Item Name	Collars	Leashes	Sweaters	Toys & Treats
Purchase and Sales Description	Collars	Leashes	Sweaters	Toys & Treats
Cost	0.00	0.00	0.00	0.00
COGS Account	Cost of Goods Sold	Cost of Goods Sold	Cost of Goods Sold	Cost of Goods Sold
Preferred Vendor	Bow-Wow Supplies	Bow-Wow Supplies	Bow-Wow Supplies	Dog Toys & Treats
Sales Price	0.00	0.00	0.00	0.00
Tax Code	Tax	Tax	Tax	Tax
Income Account	Merchandise	Merchandise	Merchandise	Merchandise
Inventory Asset Account	Inventory Asset	Inventory Asset	Inventory Asset	Inventory Asset
Reorder Point (Min)	100	100	100	100
Max	700	500	375	3500
On-Hand	650	450	325	3,450
Total Value	12,750	6,250	7,500	7,250
As Of	12/31/14	12/31/14	12/31/14	12/31/14

Click the drop-down list arrow for Type, click **Inventory Part**
Enter the Item Name/Number **Collars**
Enter **Collars** as the Description on Purchase Transactions, press **Tab**

- Collars will be entered as the Description on Sales Transactions. The Cost of 0.00 and the COGS Account Cost of Goods Sold is already entered.

Click the drop-down list arrow for **Preferred Vendor**, click **Bow-Wow Supplies**

- The Sales Price of 0.00 and Tax Code of Tax are already entered.

Select the Income Account **Merchandise**, a Subaccount of Sales

- The Asset Account Inventory Asset is already entered

Click in the column for Reorder Point (Min) and enter **100**, Tab to Max and enter **700**

- When ordering an item, QuickBooks will calculate the quantity for the Purchase Order so the item will be at the Maximum amount when the order is received.

Tab to On Hand and enter **650**, enter the Total Value of **12,750**, and enter the date for As of **12/31/14**

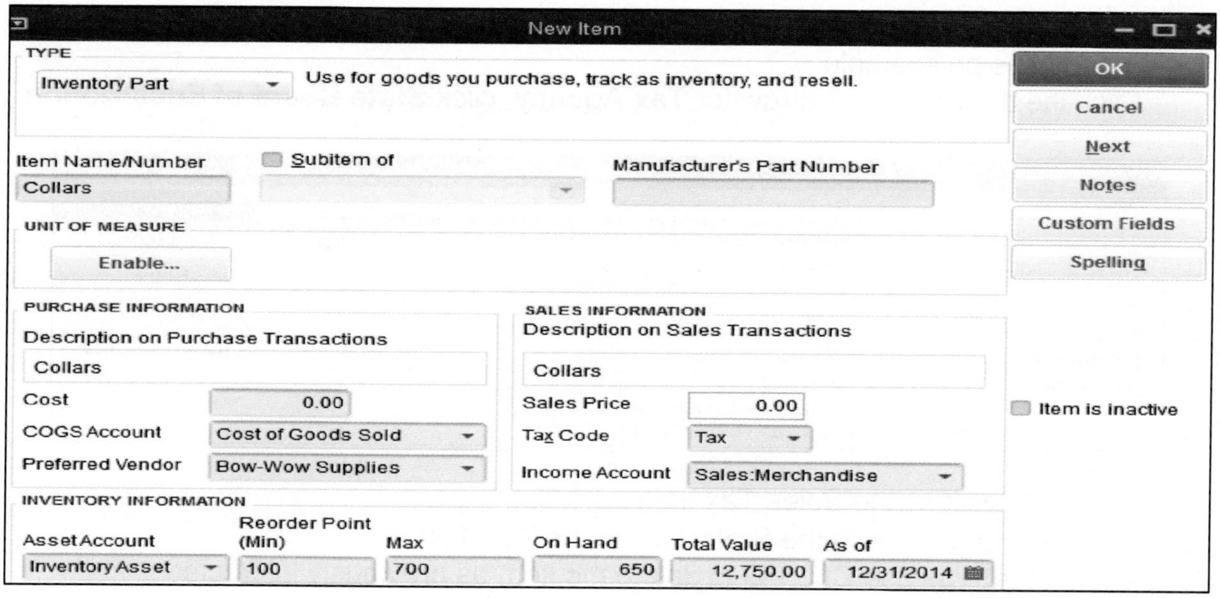

Click **Next**

Repeat for each inventory item, click **OK** after all Inventory Part Items have been entered

- Don't forget to enter the max and the reorder point for inventory items.

After the service and inventory items have been added, click **Consignment Item** in the Item list, use **Ctrl+D** to delete the item, click **OK** on Delete Item dialog box

Repeat the procedures to delete the Non-inventory Item; and continue to the next section without closing the Item List

ENTER SALES TAX INFORMATION

As you view the Item List, you will notice that the State Tax shows 0.0%. This should be changed to show the appropriate amount of sales tax deducted for the state. If you also collect local sales tax, this amount needs to be provided as well. In addition to the amount of tax collected, the Tax Agency needs to be identified. The Tax Agency was already added to the company's vendor list.

MEMO

DATE: January 1, 2015

Complete the CA Sales Tax: Tax rate of 8% paid to State Board of Equalization, delete the item for Local taxes.

Enter the amount of sales tax information for CA Sales Tax

Click **State Tax** in the Item List; use **Ctrl+E** to edit the Item

Change the Sales Tax Name and Description to **CA Sales Tax**

Enter **8%** as the tax rate

- Since sales tax rates vary and may change at any given time, the rate of 8% is used as an example.

Click the drop-down list arrow for **Tax Agency**, click **State Board of Equalization**

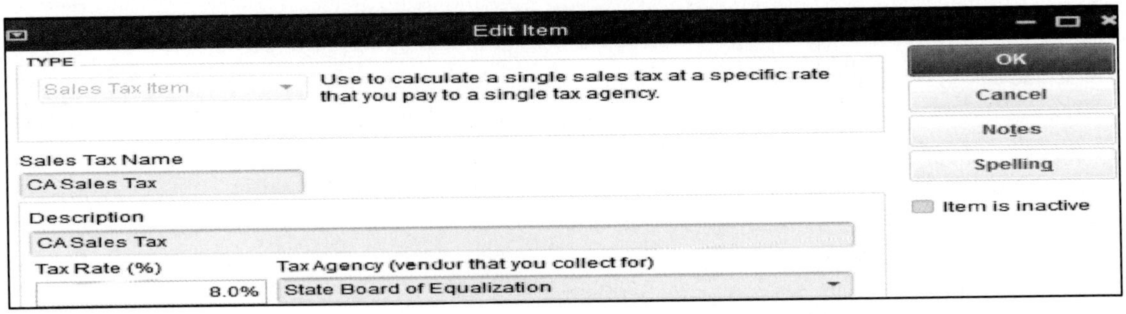

Click **OK** to close the Sales Tax Item

- Note the change to the State Tax on the Item List.

Click **Local Tax** use **Ctrl + D** to delete the item as previously instructed

The Item List appears as follows:

NAME	DESCRIPTION	TYPE	ACCOUNT	TOTAL QUANTITY ON HAND	ON SALES ORDER	PRICE	ATTACH
Doggie Dayz Camp	Day Camp	Service	Sales:Day Camp			30.00	
Doggie Digs Hotel	Boarding	Service	Sales:Boarding			55.00	
Doggie Salon	Grooming	Service	Sales:Grooming			0.00	
Collars	Collars	Inventory Part	Sales:Merchandise	650	0	0.00	
Leashes	Leashes	Inventory Part	Sales:Merchandise	450	0	0.00	
Sweaters	Sweaters	Inventory Part	Sales:Merchandise	325	0	0.00	
Toys & Treats	Toys & Treats	Inventory Part	Sales:Merchandise	3,450	0	0.00	
CA Sales Tax	CA Sales Tax	Sales Tax Item	Sales Tax Payable			8.0%	
Out of State	Out-of-state sale, exempt from sales tax	Sales Tax Item	Sales Tax Payable			0.0%	

To print the List, click the **Reports** button at the bottom of the Item List

Click **Item Listing**

Click the **Customize Report** button, click the **Header/Footer** tab, change the **Subtitle** to show the report date of **January 1, 2015**, deselect **Date Prepared** and **Time Prepared**, click **OK**

Adjust the column widths to remove extra space and to allow the information to display in full. Since all amounts are zero in the columns for Quantity on Sales Order and Quantity on Purchase Order hide the columns

Click **Print**, click **Landscape**, and click the **Print** button

Close the report and close the Item List

PRINT ACCOUNT LISTING

When customers, vendors, and sales items have been entered, the Chart of Accounts will contain all of the beginning balances and should match the complete Chart of Accounts shown earlier in the chapter.

Print the **Account Listing** in Landscape orientation

Click the **Reports** menu, point to **List**; click **Account Listing**

- Notice the descriptions entered for Accounts Receivable, Accounts Payable, and Uncategorized Income and Uncategorized Expenses. A Tax Line for Uncategorized Income has also been selected by QuickBooks.

With the Account Listing on the screen, use **Ctrl+A** to open the Chart of Accounts and delete the Descriptions for Accounts Receivable, Accounts Payable, and Uncategorized Expenses. For Uncategorized Income, delete the account description and change the Tax Line to <Unassigned>

Close the Chart of Accounts and return to the Account Listing

Resize columns to eliminate extra space, display columns in full, and remove Description and Tax Line from the report

- The Account column shows both the master and the subaccount in the report.

Click the **Customize Report** button, click the **Header/Footer** button, change the report date to **January 1, 2015**, click **Date Prepared** and **Time Prepared** to remove from the heading, click **OK**

Click the **Print** button, select **Portrait** orientation

- The report is shown on the next page

Your Name's Dog Dayz
Account Listing
January 1, 2015

Account	Type	Balance Total
Checking	Bank	29,385.00
Accounts Receivable	Accounts Receivable	2,950.00
Inventory Asset	Other Current Asset	33,750.00
Office Supplies	Other Current Asset	350.00
Prepaid Insurance	Other Current Asset	1,200.00
Sales Supplies	Other Current Asset	500.00
Equipment	Fixed Asset	7,200.00
Equipment:Depreciation	Fixed Asset	-800.00
Equipment:Original Cost	Fixed Asset	8,000.00
Fixtures	Fixed Asset	13,500.00
Fixtures:Depreciation	Fixed Asset	-1,500.00
Fixtures:Original Cost	Fixed Asset	15,000.00
Accounts Payable	Accounts Payable	5,000.00
Payroll Liabilities	Other Current Liability	0.00
Sales Tax Payable	Other Current Liability	0.00
Equipment Loan	Long Term Liability	2,000.00
Fixtures Loan	Long Term Liability	2,500.00
First & Last Name, Capital	Equity	81,385.00
First & Last Name, Capital:First & Last Name, Investment	Equity	25,000.00
First & Last Name, Capital:First & Last Name, Withdrawals	Equity	0.00
Owner's Equity	Equity	
Sales	Income	
Sales:Boarding	Income	
Sales:Day Camp	Income	
Sales:Grooming	Income	
Sales:Merchandise	Income	
Sales Discounts	Income	
Uncategorized Income	Income	
Cost of Goods Sold	Cost of Goods Sold	
Advertising and Promotion	Expense	
Automobile Expense	Expense	
Bank Service Charges	Expense	
Computer and Internet Expenses	Expense	
Depreciation Expense	Expense	
Insurance Expense	Expense	
Interest Expense	Expense	
Janitorial Expense	Expense	
Office Supplies Expense	Expense	
Payroll Expenses	Expense	
Professional Fees	Expense	
Rent Expense	Expense	
Repairs and Maintenance	Expense	
Sales Supplies Expense	Expense	
Telephone Expense	Expense	
Uncategorized Expenses	Expense	
Utilities	Expense	
Other Income	Other Income	
Other Expenses	Other Expense	

Close the Report

PREPARE A DAILY BACKUP

A backup file is prepared as a safeguard in case you make an error. After the company has been created and customers, vendors, and items have been entered, it is wise to prepare a backup file. In addition, a backup should be made at the end of every work session.

Prepare the Your Name's Dog Dayz (Daily Backup).qbb file

Follow the steps presented in Chapter 1 for creating a backup file
Name the file **Your Name's Dog Dayz (Daily Backup)**
The file type is **QBW Backup (* .QBB)**

PREFERENCES

Many preferences used by QuickBooks are selected during the QuickBooks Setup. However, there may be some preferences you would like to select, change, or delete. The Preferences section has two tabs where you may indicate My Preferences or Company Preferences. The Preferences that may be customized are: Accounting, Bills, Calendar, Checking, Desktop View, Finance Charge, General, Integrated Applications, Items & Inventory, Jobs & Estimates, Multiple Currencies, Payments, Payroll & Employees, Reminders, Reports & Graphs, Sales & Customers, Sales Tax, Search, Send Forms, Service Connection, Spelling, Tax: 1099, and Time & Expenses.
In previous chapters, some of the Preferences were changed. In this chapter, all the Preferences available will be explored and some changes will be made.

MEMO
DATE: January 1, 2015

Open the Preferences screen and explore the choices available for each of the areas. When you get to the following preferences, make the changes indicated below:

Accounting: Delete the Date Warnings for past and future transactions
Checking: My Preferences—Select Default Accounts to Checking for Open the Write Checks, Open the Pay Bills, Open the Pay Sales Tax, and Open the Make Deposits; Company Preferences— Select Default Accounts to use should be Checking for Open the Create Paychecks and Open the Pay Payroll Liabilities
Desktop View: My Preferences—Select Switch to colored icons/light background on the Top Icon Bar, use Purple-Blue for the Company Color
General: My Preferences—Turn off pop-up messages for products and services
Payroll & Employees: Company Preferences—Deselect Job Costing for paycheck expenses and Display Employee List by Last Name
Reports & Graphs: My Preferences—Refresh reports automatically, Company Preferences—Display Report Items by Name only and modify the report Format for the Header/Footer to remove the Date Prepared, Time Prepared, and Report Basis from reports
Sales & Customers: Company Preferences—select No Custom Pricing
Sales Tax: Company Preferences—Most common sales tax is State Tax

Access Preferences from the Edit menu

- In the following sections the Preferences are shown in the exact order listed on the Preferences screen.

Click the icons for each category and explore the choices available on both the My Preferences tab and the Company tab
When you get to a Preference that needs to be changed, make the changes indicated in the Memo above

ACCOUNTING PREFERENCES

Company Preferences tab is accessed to select the use of account numbers. Class tracking may be selected. This screen instructs QuickBooks to automatically assign general journal entry numbers and to warn when posting a transaction to Retained Earnings. There are two check boxes for warning when transactions are 90 days within the past or 30 days within the future. The closing date for a period is entered after clicking the Set Date/Password button on this screen.

Remove the Date Warnings

Click **Accounting**, and then, if necessary, click the **Company Preferences** tab
Click the check boxes for **Date Warnings** to deselect the two warnings

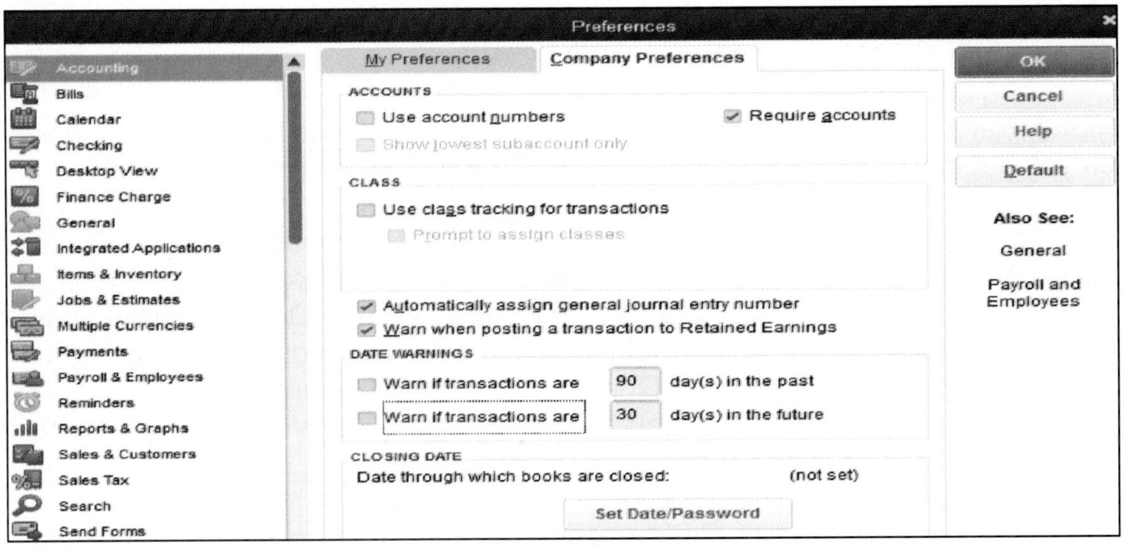

Click **Bills** in the list of **Preferences**
Each time you change a Preference and click on another Preference you get a dialog box to Save Changes to the Preference, always click **Yes**

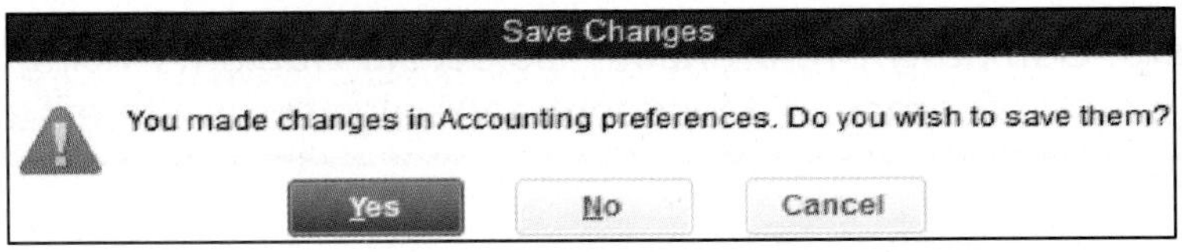

BILLS PREFERENCES

Company Preferences has selections for Entering Bills and Paying Bills. You may tell QuickBooks the number of days after the receipt of bills that they are due. You may select "Warn about duplicate bill numbers from the same vendor." When paying bills, you may tell QuickBooks to use discounts and credits automatically.

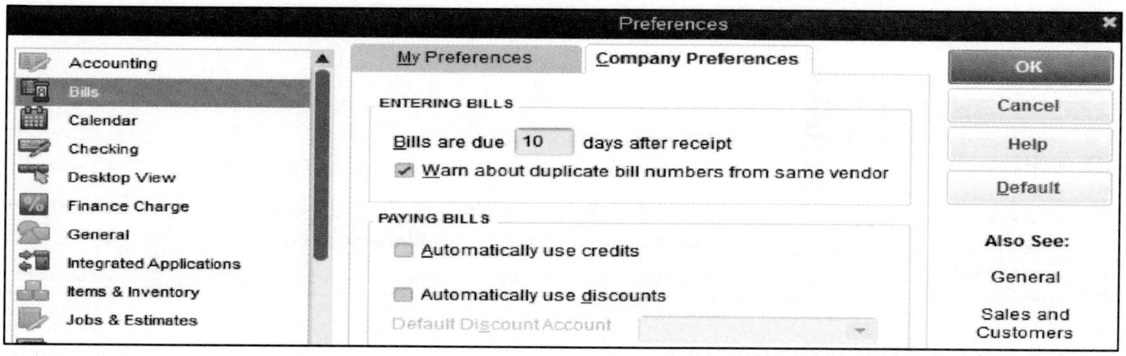

CALENDAR PREFERENCES

QuickBooks has a calendar that may be used to view transactions entered, transactions that are due, and to do's for a selected day. My Preferences is used to indicate the calendar view, the weekly view, and the types of transactions you wish to appear. You may also select settings for the number of days to display upcoming and past due data.

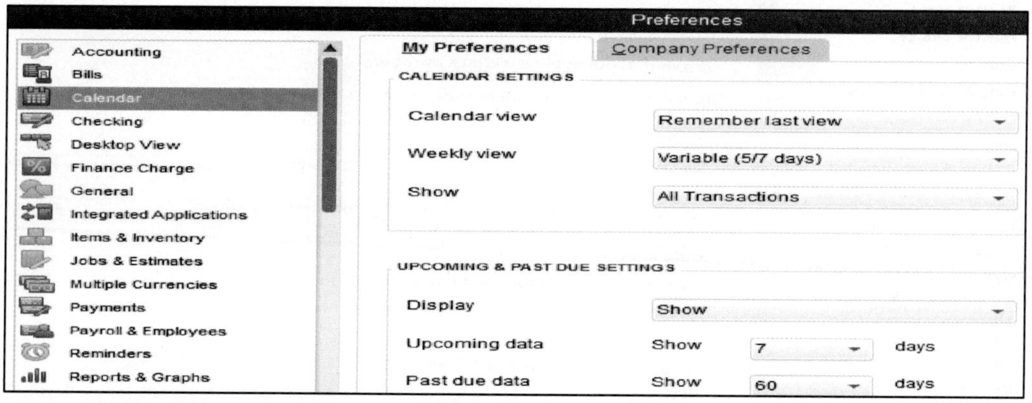

CHECKING PREFERENCES

The preferences listed for checking allows QuickBooks to print account names on check vouchers, change the check date when a non-cleared check is printed, start with the payee field on a check, warn of duplicate check numbers, autofill payee account number in check memo, set default accounts to use for checks, and to view and enter downloaded transactions in Bank Feeds in either the Express Mode or the Classic (Register) Mode.

Select Default Accounts to use Checking

Click **Checking** in the **Preferences** list; and, if necessary, click **My Preferences** tab
Click the Check box for **Open the Write Checks** to select
Click the drop-down list arrow for Account
Click **Checking**
Repeat for **Open the Pay Bills**, **Open the Pay Sales Tax**, and **Open the Make Deposits**

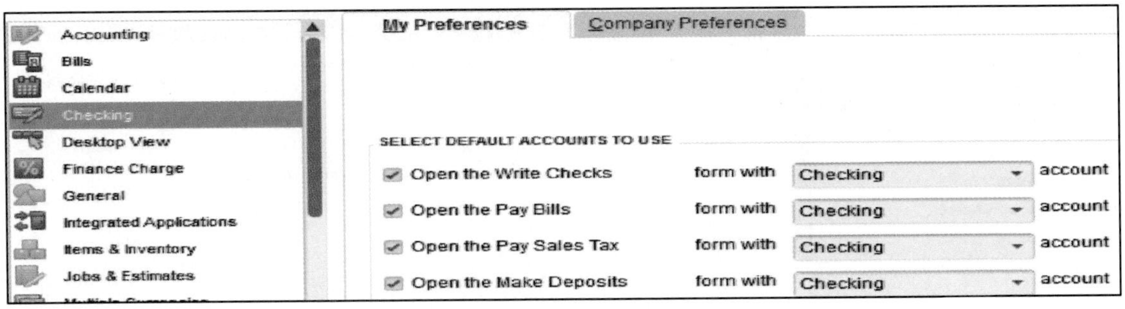

Click the **Company Preferences** tab
Click the check box for **Open the Create Paychecks**
Click **Checking** on the drop-down list for account
Repeat for **Open the Pay Payroll Liabilities**

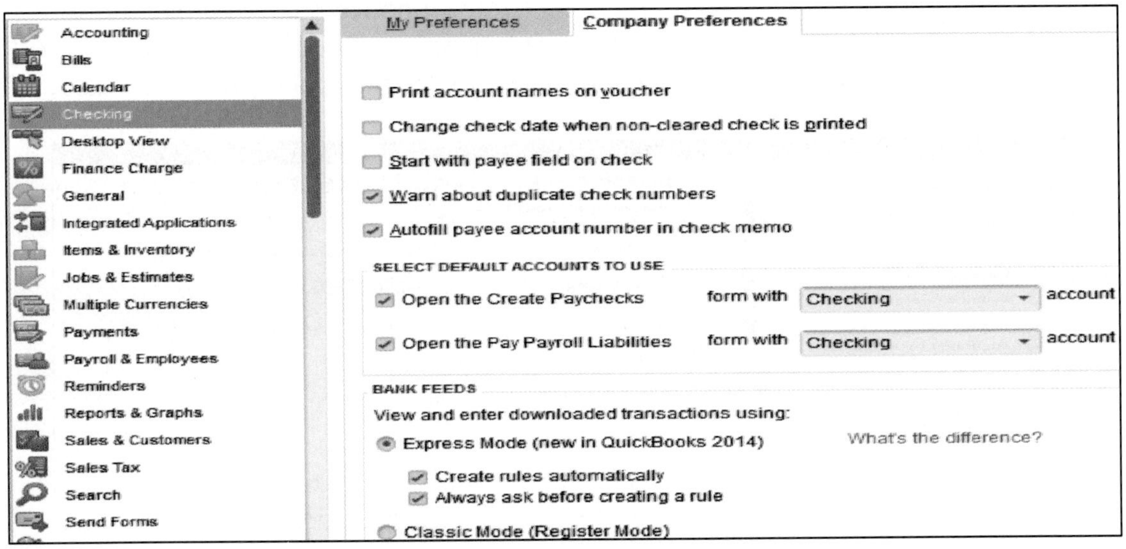

Click the **Desktop View Preference**, and then click **Yes** on **Save Changes**

DESKTOP VIEW PREFERENCES

My Preferences has selections to customize your QuickBooks screens to view one or multiple windows, to display the Home Page, to save the desktop, to switch to colored icons on the Top Icon Bar, to select color schemes and sounds, and to add a Company File Color Scheme. Company Preferences allows you to select features that you want to show on the Home Page and to explore Related Preferences.

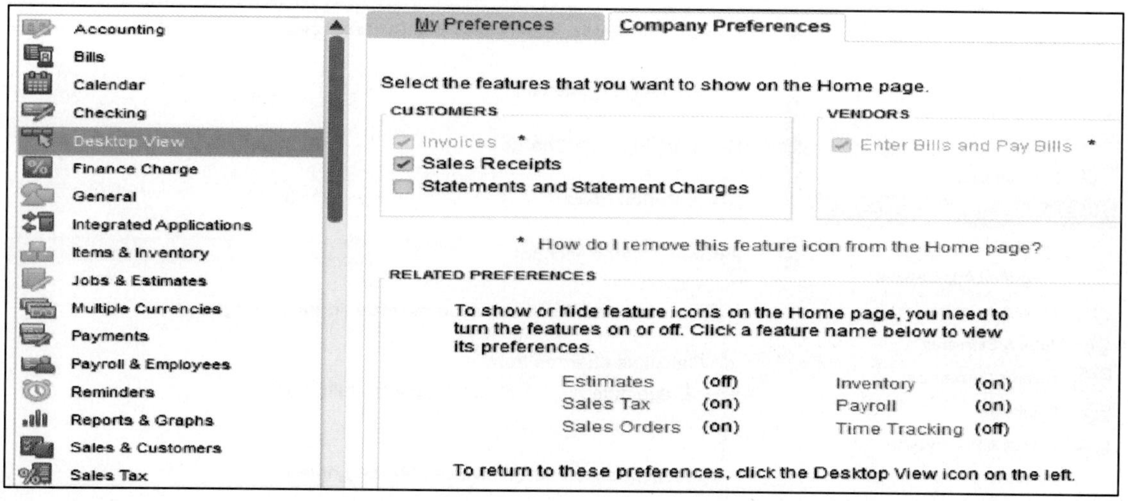

Select colored icons with light backgrounds for the Top Icon Bar and add a Company File Color Scheme

On the **Desktop View Preference**, click **My Preferences Tab**
Click **Switch to colored icons/light background on the Top Icon Bar** to select
Click the drop-down list arrow for **Company File Color Scheme**, click **Purple-Blue**

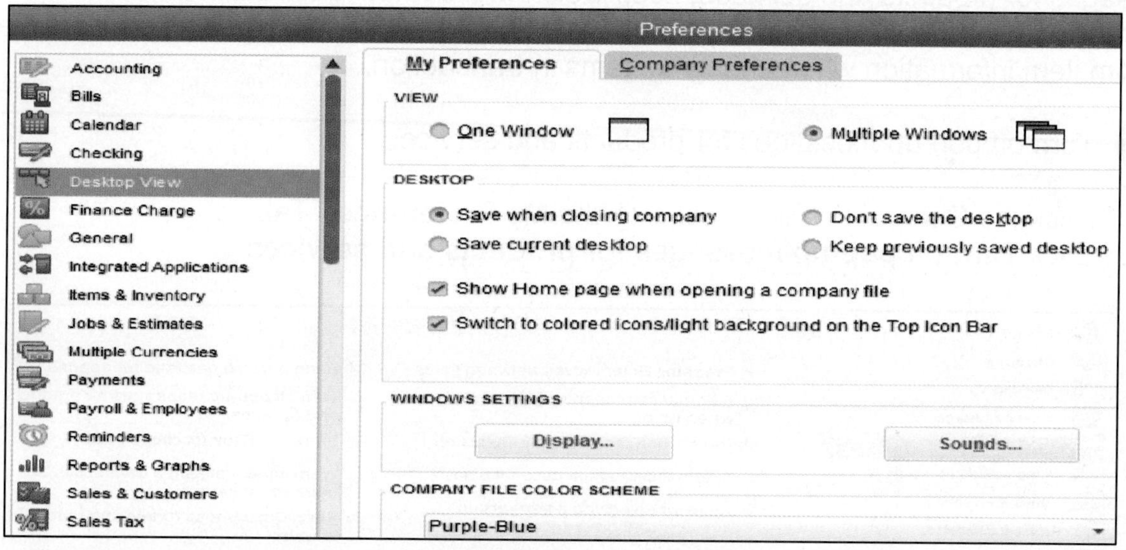

Click **Finance Charge** in the Preferences list, and then click **Yes** on **Save Changes**

FINANCE CHARGE PREFERENCES

This preference allows you to tell QuickBooks if you want to collect finance charges and to provide information about finance charges. The information you may provide includes the annual interest rate, the minimum finance charge, the grace period, the finance charge account, whether to calculate finance charges from the due date or from the invoice/billed date, and to mark finance charge invoices "To be printed".

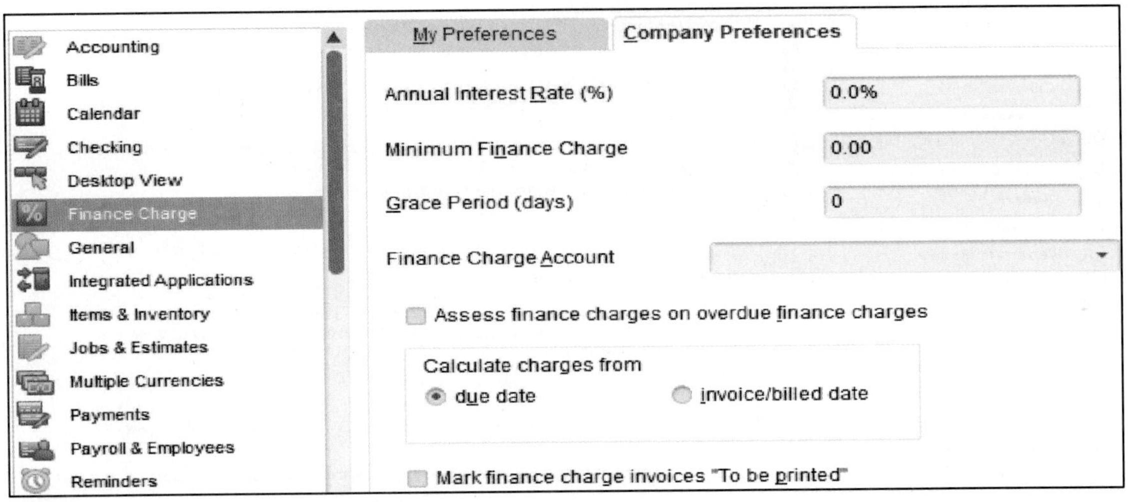

GENERAL PREFERENCES

Use the Company Preferences tab to set the time format, to display the year as four digits, select whether to update name information when saving transactions, and to save transactions before printing. My Preferences tab is used to indicate decimal point placement, set warning screens and beeps, bring back messages, turn off pop-up messages for products and services, keep QuickBooks running for quick startups, automatically recall information, indicate default date to use in new transactions, and keep custom item information when changing items in transaction.

➔ Turn off pop-up messages for products and services

Click the General Preferences, click the **My Preferences Tab**
Click **Turn off pop-up messages for products and services**

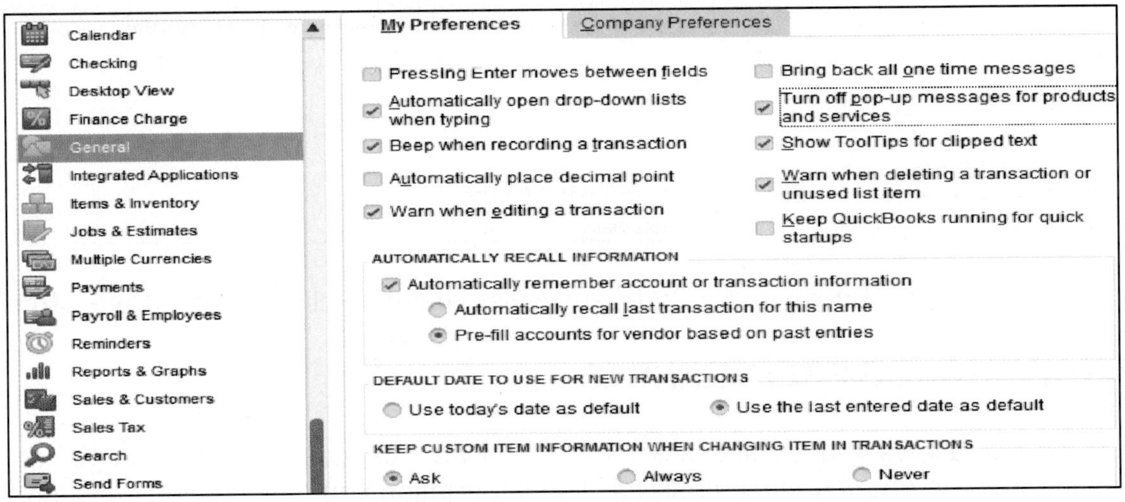

Click the **Integrated Applications** Preferences; click **Yes** on Save Changes

INTEGRATED APPLICATIONS PREFERENCES

Integrated preferences are used to manage all applications that interact with the current QuickBooks company file.

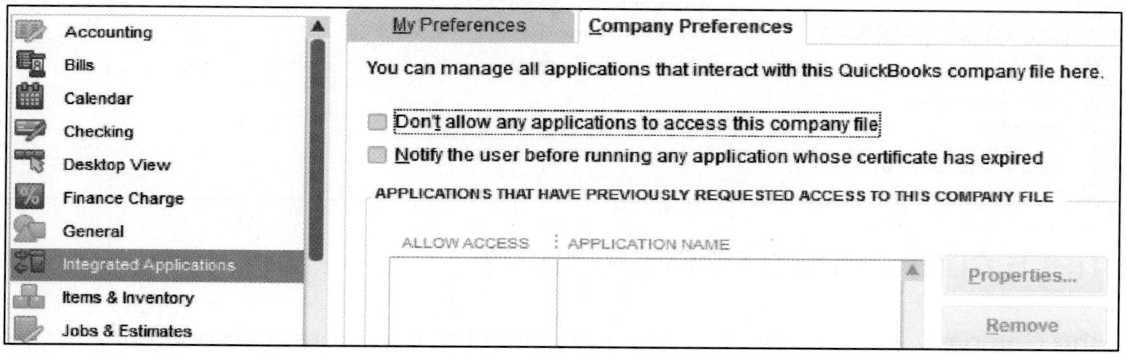

ITEMS & INVENTORY PREFERENCES

This section is used to activate the inventory and purchase orders features of the program, enable units of measure, provide warnings if there is not enough inventory to sell or there are duplicate purchase order numbers.

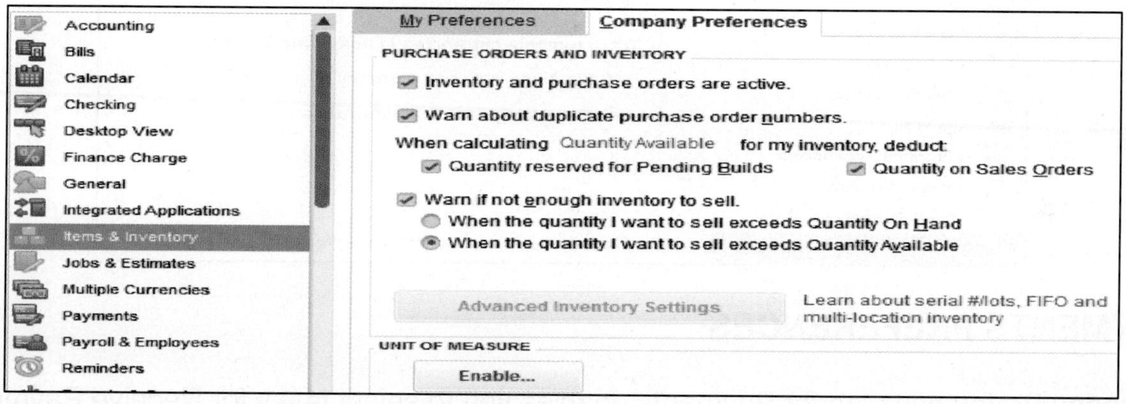

JOBS & ESTIMATES PREFERENCES

This preference allows you to indicate the status of jobs and to choose whether or not to use estimates.

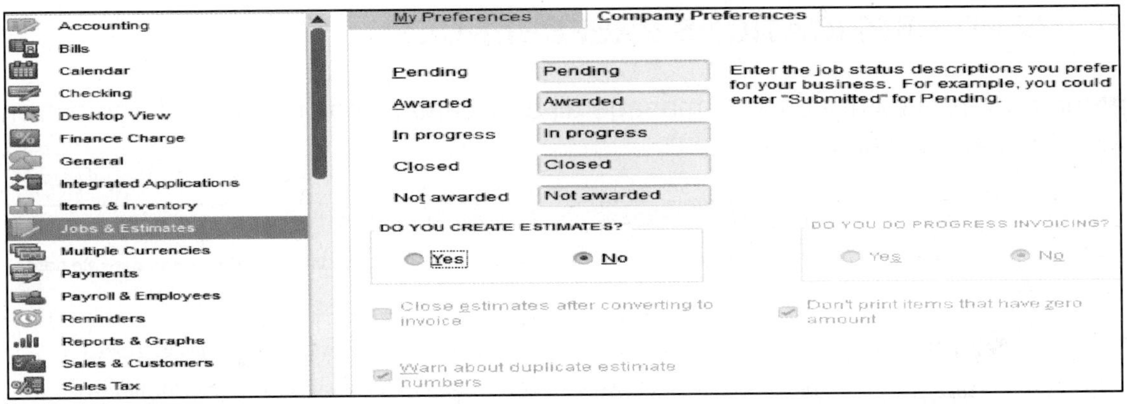

MULTIPLE CURRENCIES PREFERENCES

Using the Company Preferences tab, you may select to use more than one currency. If you use multiple currencies, a currency may be assigned to customers, vendors, price levels, bank and credit card accounts as well as accounts receivable and accounts payable accounts. You must designate a home currency that will be used for income and expense accounts. Once you choose to use multiple currencies, you may not change the preference to discontinue the use of multiple currencies.

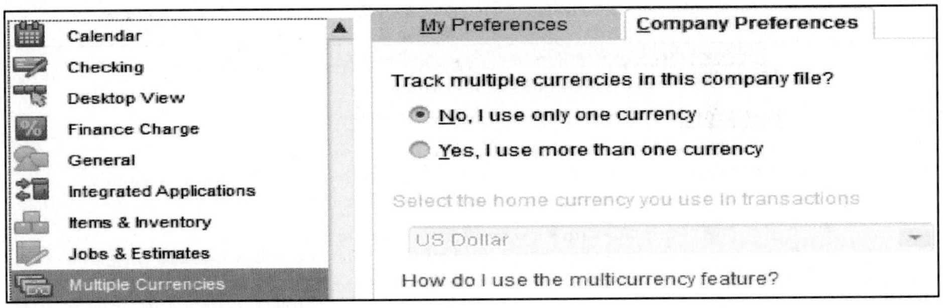

PAYMENTS PREFERENCES

Company Preferences tab for Payments enables you to select tasks for Receive Payments that will automatically apply payments, automatically calculate payments, and use Undeposited Funds as a default deposit to account. If you accept Online Payments, you may select Credit Card and Bank Transfer (ACH) payments.

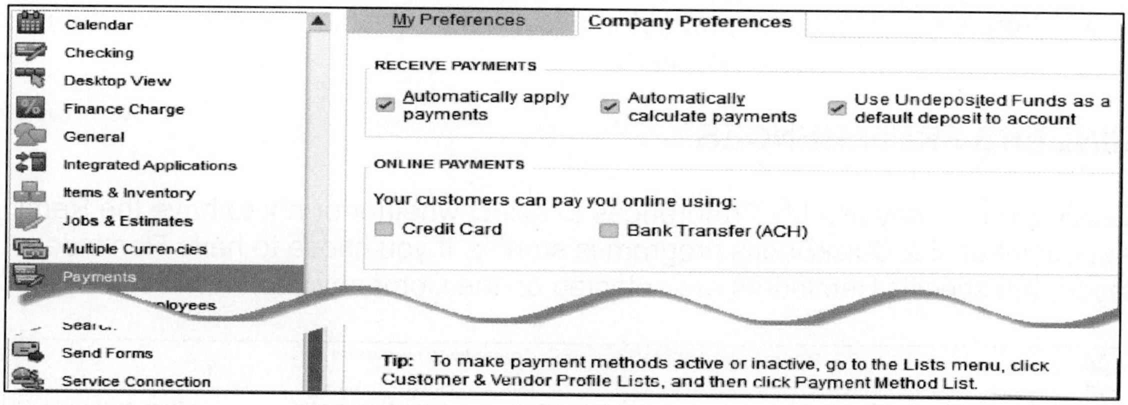

PAYROLL & EMPLOYEES PREFERENCES

Company Preferences include selecting the payroll features, if any, you wish to use. Set Preferences for pay stub and voucher printing, workers compensation, and sick and vacation may be selected. Copying earnings details, recalling quantities and/or hours, and job costing for paycheck expenses may be marked or unmarked. You may choose the method by which employees are sorted. Employee Defaults may be accessed from this screen. Once accessed, the Employee Defaults may be changed and/or modified.

Change the Display Employee List to Last Name

Click **Payroll & Employees** Preference; click the **Company Preferences** tab
Click **Job Costing for paycheck expenses** to deselect
Click **Last Name** in the section for Display Employee List by

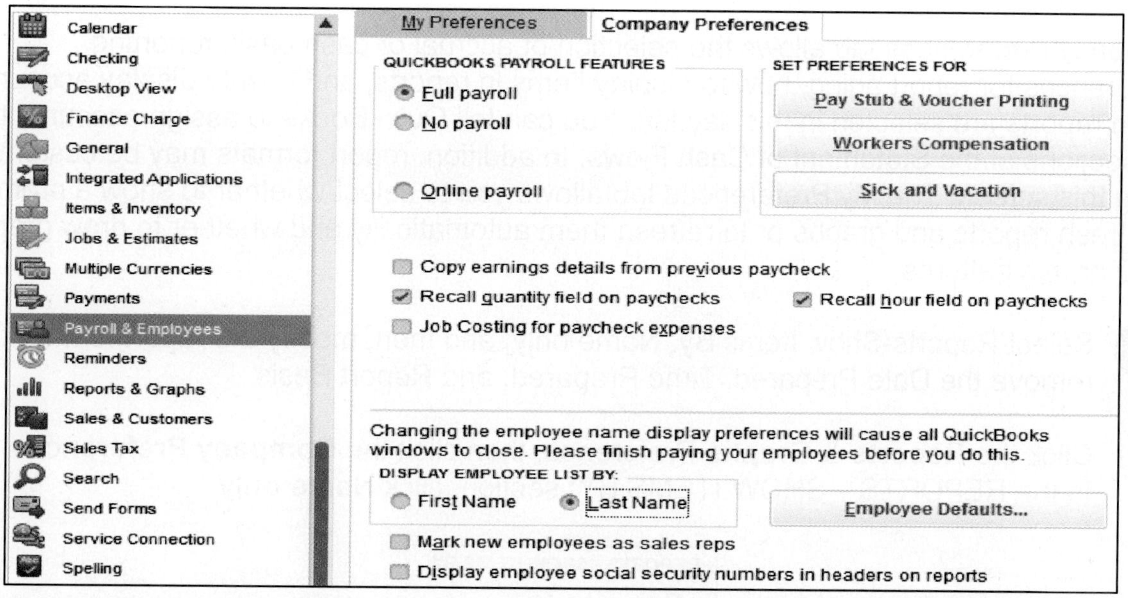

Click **Reminders** Preference; click **Yes** on the Save Changes dialog box
Click **OK** on the Warning screen

- Preferences should reopen automatically. If it does not, click the Edit menu, click Preferences, and click Reminders.

REMINDERS PREFERENCES

In this section you may use My Preferences to select whether or not to have the Reminders List appear when the QuickBooks program is started. If you chose to have Reminders displayed, the specific Reminders are selected on the Company Preferences tab.

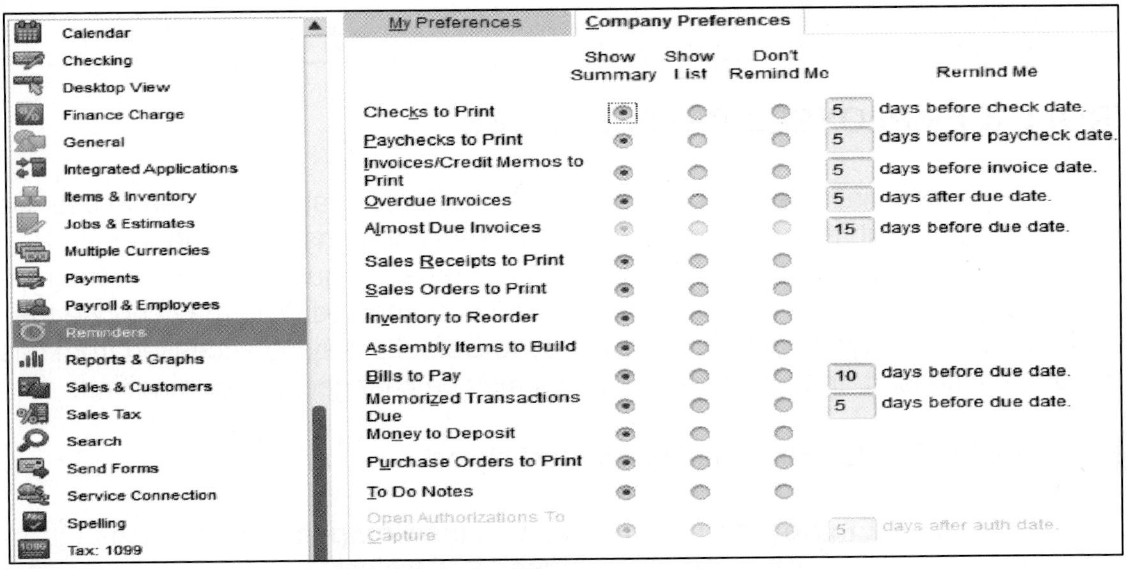

REPORTS & GRAPHS PREFERENCES

Company Preferences tab allows the selection of accrual or cash basis reporting. Preferences for report aging, how to display items in reports, and how to display accounts within reports are selected in this section. You can tell QuickBooks to assign accounts to the sections of the Statement of Cash Flows. In addition, report formats may be customized using this screen. The My Preferences tab allows you to select whether to show a prompt to refresh reports and graphs or to refresh them automatically and whether to draw graphs in 2D or use patterns.

Select Reports-Show Items By: Name only; and then, modify the report format to remove the Date Prepared, Time Prepared, and Report Basis

Click the **Reports & Graphs** Preference, then click the **Company Preferences** tab
In the REPORTS – SHOW ITEMS BY: section, click **Name only**

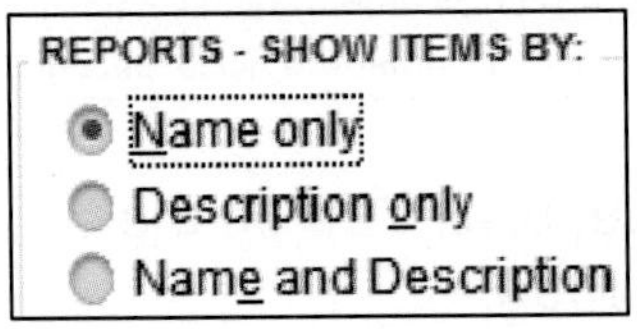

Click the check box for **Default formatting for reports** to deselect
Click the **Format** button
On the Header/Footer tab, click **Date Prepared**, **Time Prepared**, and **Report Basis** to remove the check marks

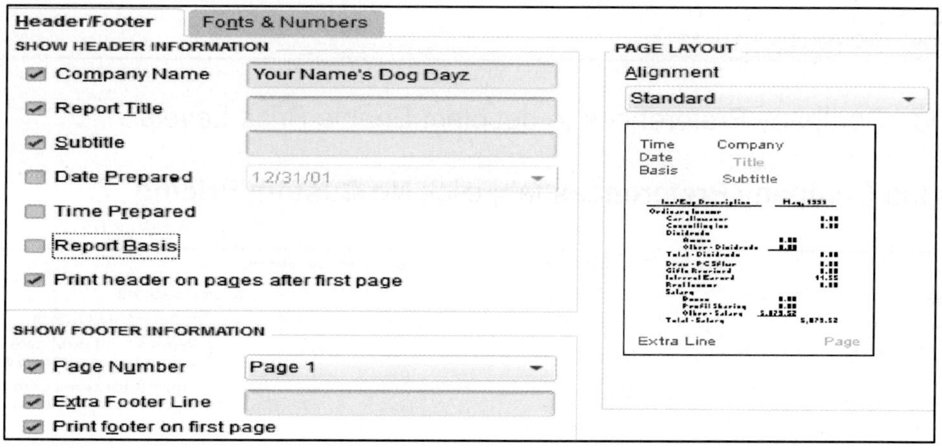

Click **OK**

Change My Preferences to have the reports refresh automatically

Click **My Preferences** tab
Click **Refresh Automatically**

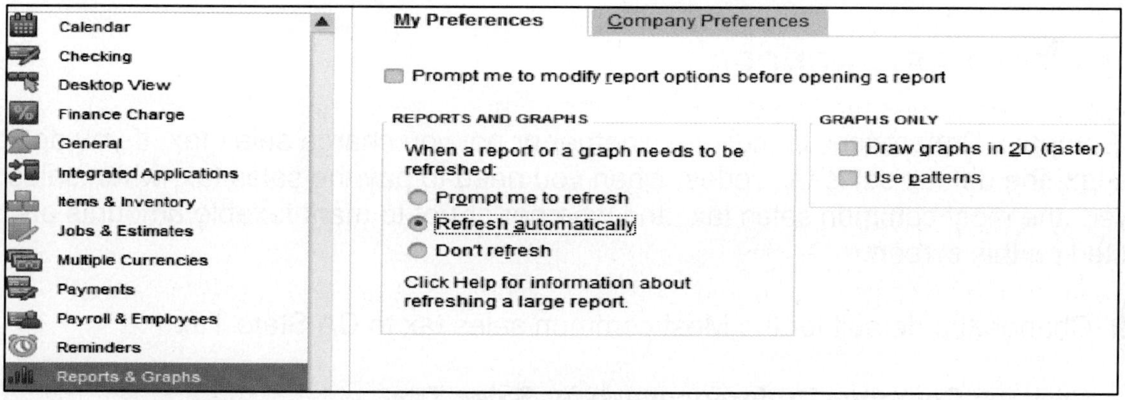

Click the **Sales & Customers Preference**, click **Yes** to save the changes

SALES & CUSTOMERS PREFERENCES

9

Company Preferences is used to select usual shipping methods, usual FOB (free on board) preferences, the use of Price Levels, enable Sales Orders, and the templates for packing slips used for invoices and for sales orders, as well as the sales order pick list. The My Preferences tab allows you to add Available Time/Costs to Invoices for Selected Jobs.

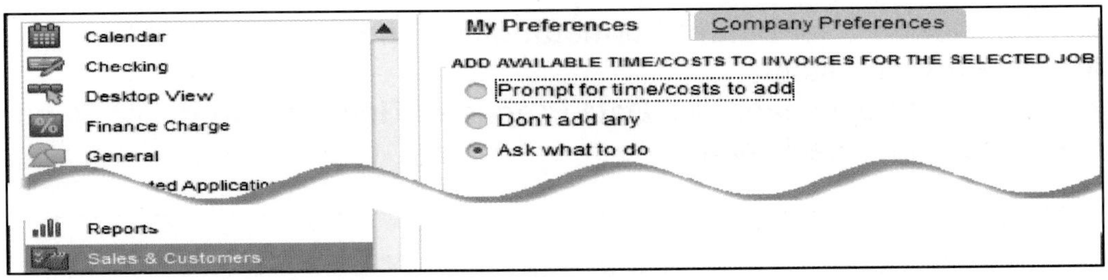

Change Company Preferences to deselect Enable Price Levels

Click the **Company Preferences** tab; click **No Custom Pricing**

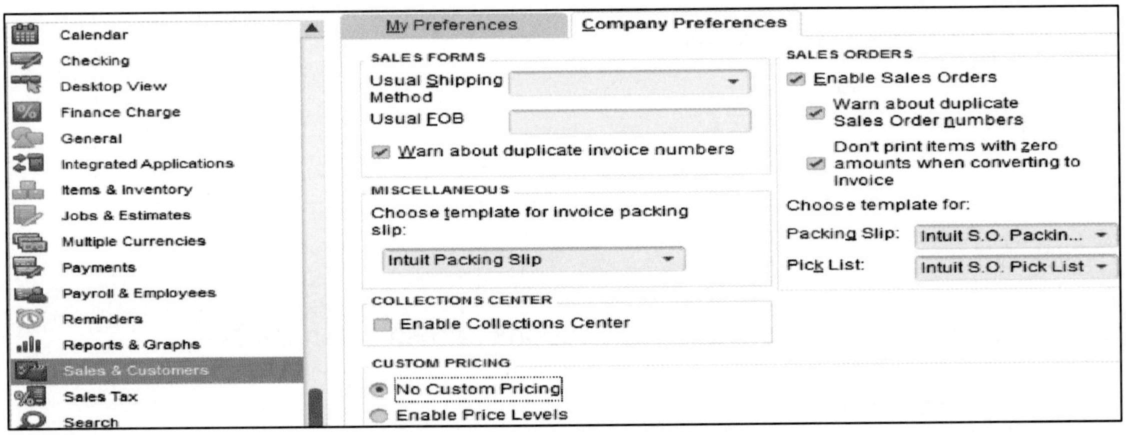

Click **Sales Tax Preferences**, and click **Yes to** Save the changes

SALES TAX PREFERENCES

Use Company Preferences to indicate whether or not you charge sales tax. If you do collect sales tax, the default sales tax codes, when you need to pay the sales tax, when sales tax is owed, the most common sales tax, and whether or not to mark taxable amounts are selected on this screen.

Change the default for the Most common sales tax to CA State Tax

Click the **Company Preferences** tab for **Sales Tax**
Click the drop-down list arrow for **Your most common sales tax item**
Click **CA State Tax**

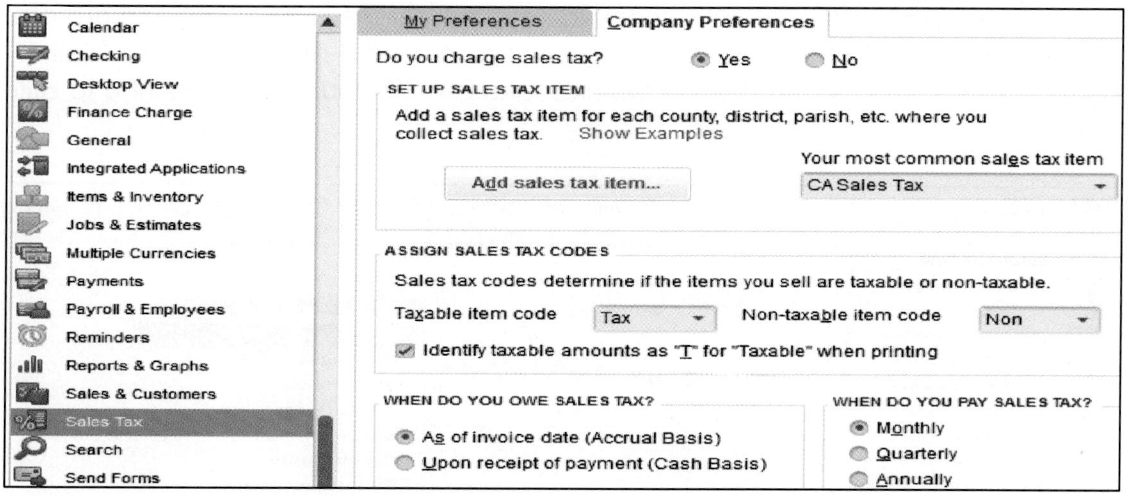

Click **Search** in the Preferences List; then click **Yes** to Save Changes

SEARCH PREFERENCES

Company Preferences include how often to update search information and to use Update Now. My Preferences allows the selection of "Show Search field in the Icon Bar" and of "Choose where to search by default."

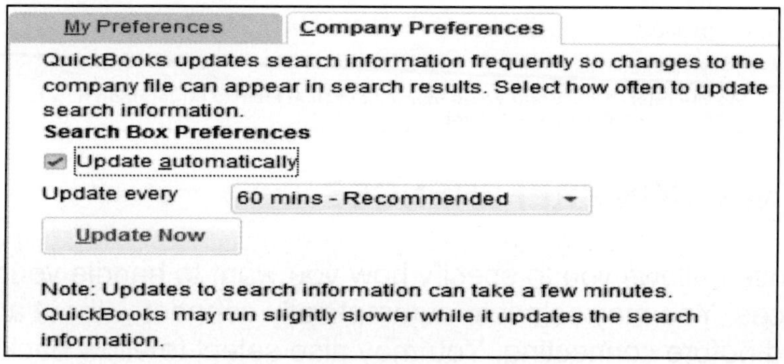

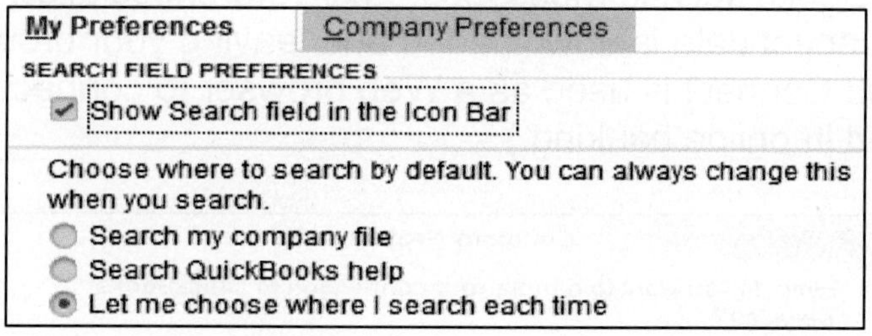

SEND FORMS PREFERENCES

Default text is provided for business documents that are sent by email. The text may be changed for invoices, estimates, statements, sales orders, sales receipts, credit memos, purchase orders, reports, pay stubs, overdue invoices, almost due invoices, and payment receipts. My Preferences allows auto-check to determine if the customer's and preferred send method is e-mail. You may also select whether to send e-mail using Web Mail, Outlook, or QuickBooks E-mail. To use QuickBooks E-mail, you must subscribe to Billing Solutions.

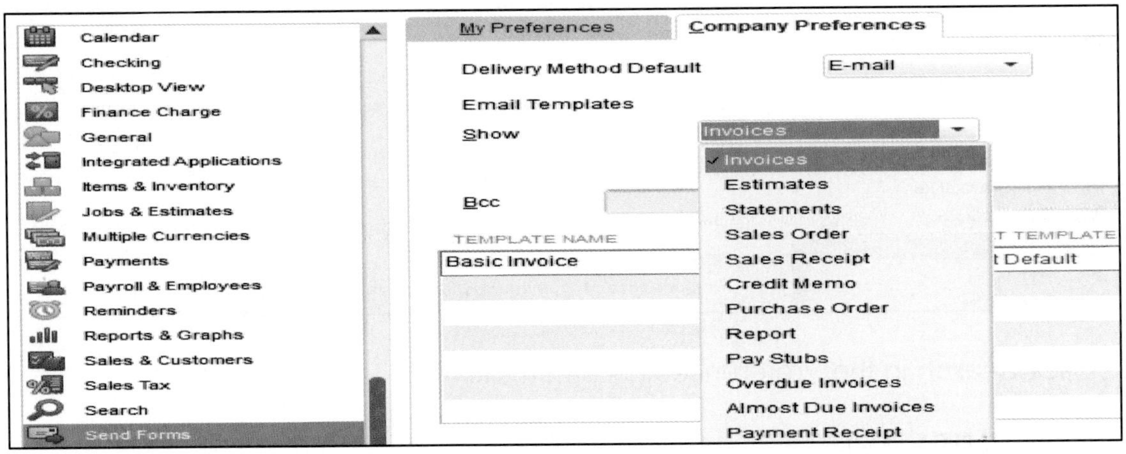

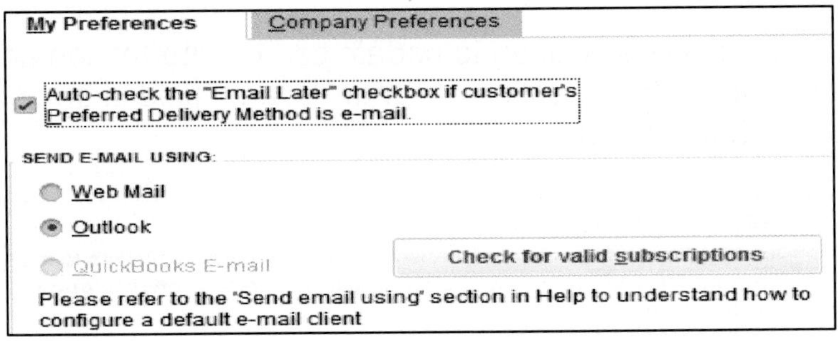

SERVICE CONNECTION PREFERENCES

Company Preferences allows you to specify how you want to handle your connections to QuickBooks Services. You may select to automatically connect without a password or to require a password before connecting. You may also select to allow background downloading of QuickBooks service messages. My Preferences allows settings for saving a file whenever Web Connect data is downloaded and leaving your browser open after Web Connect is done. (Web Connect is used as a Web browser to connect to financial institutions and is used in online banking.)

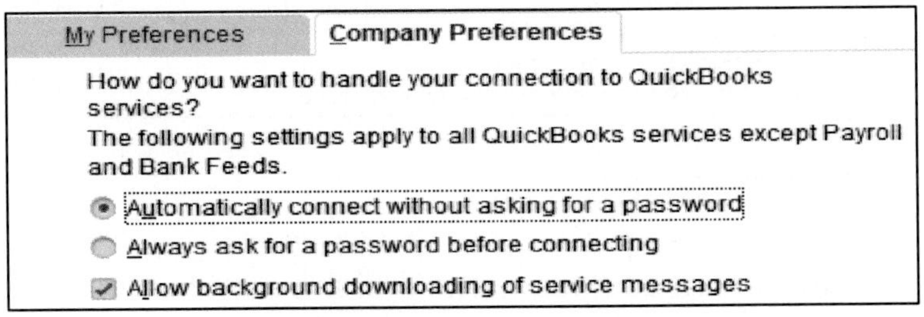

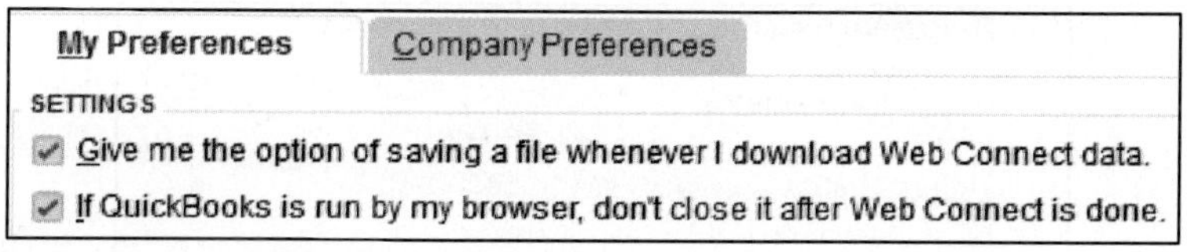

SPELLING PREFERENCES

You can check the spelling in the fields of most sales forms including invoices, estimates, sales receipts, credit memos, purchase orders, and lists. You can run Spell Checker automatically or change the preference and run the Spell Checker manually. There is also a selection for words to ignore. A list of words added to the dictionary is also shown. These words may be deleted if you do not want them.

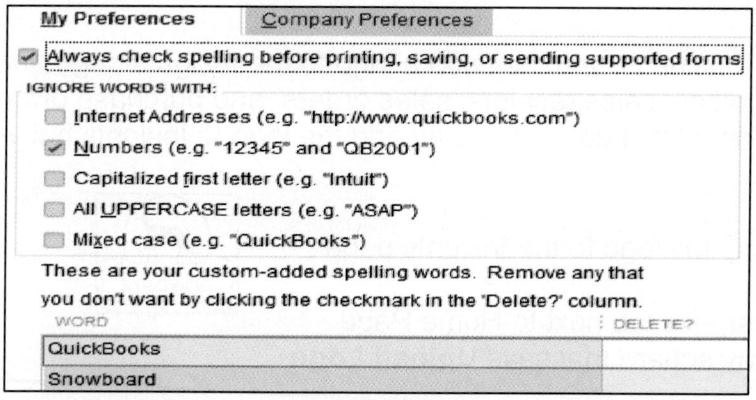

TAX: 1099 PREFERENCES

The only selection is on the Company Preferences screen. This is where you indicate whether or not you file 1099-MISC forms.

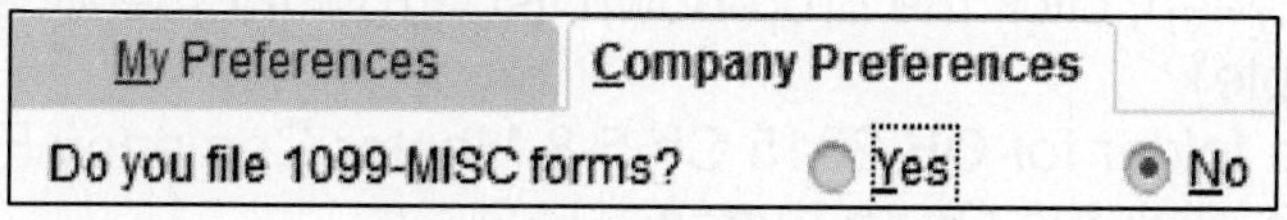

TIME & EXPENSES PREFERENCES

Company Preferences is used to indicate whether you track time, which is useful if you bill by the hour. There are also some Invoicing Options associated with tracking time available.

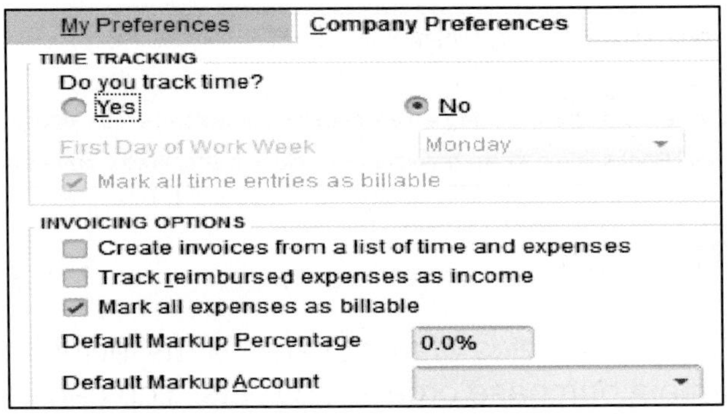

Click **OK** to close Preferences

ADD COMPANY LOGO

To customize your business, you may add a logo to the Insights page and to business forms; such as, invoices, sales receipts, sales orders, and purchase orders. If you store your company file on a USB drive, you may add the logo to Insights but you may not add it to business forms.

Add the company logo to the Insights page

Click the **Insights** tab next to Home Page
Click the gray square that says **Upload Logo**

On the **Open** screen, click the drop-down list arrow for the location of your USB (G: in the example)
Double-click the folder for QB 2015 Ch 5-8 Master Company Files
Click **Dog Dayz**, click the **Open** button

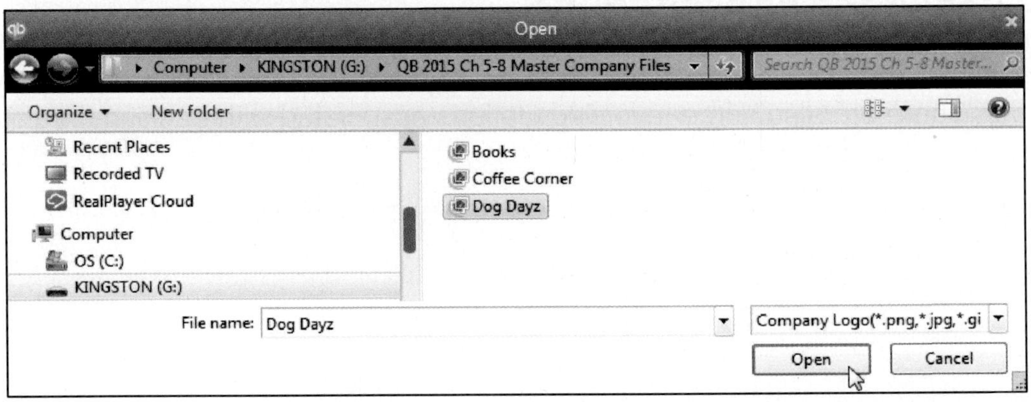

You will see the company logo inserted on Insights

READ ONLY: Since you store your company file on your USB drive, you cannot add the Company Logo to invoices, sales receipts, sales orders, credit memos, and purchase orders. As a result, the steps to add a logo to a business form when your company is stored on your hard drive will be illustrated below.

Click **Home Page**, click the **Create Invoices** icon, click the **Formatting** tab on the Create Invoice icon bar

- The steps to add logos to business forms are the same except that you must use a copy of an invoice, which is illustrated below.

Click **Customize Data Layout**, click **Make a Copy** on the Locked Template message
Click **Basic Customization...** button on the Additional Customization screen
Click **Use logo** to select
Click the drop-down list arrow on the **Select Image** screen; click the location of your USB drive (G: in the example)
Double-click the folder **QB 2015 Ch 5-8 Master Company Files**
Click **Dog Dayz** to highlight, click the **Open** button

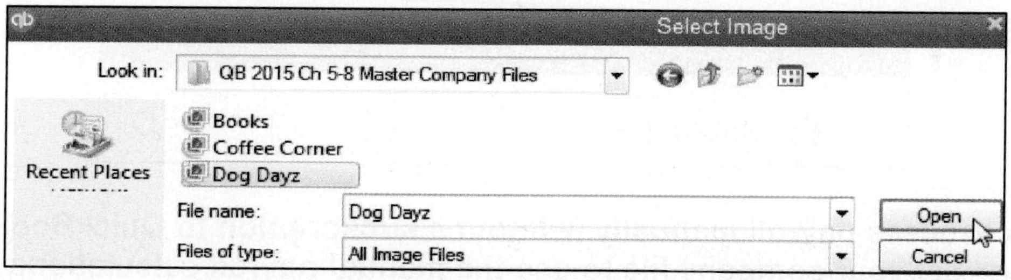

You will get a Warning screen for QuickBooks to copy your image into Your Name's Dog Dayz – Images, click **OK**

- The next business form you customize will use the logo from the Images folder.
- You will not see the logo unless your preview a business document or print it.

Click **OK** on the Basic Customization screen, then click **OK** on the Additional Customization screen
The heading area of the invoice appears as follows:

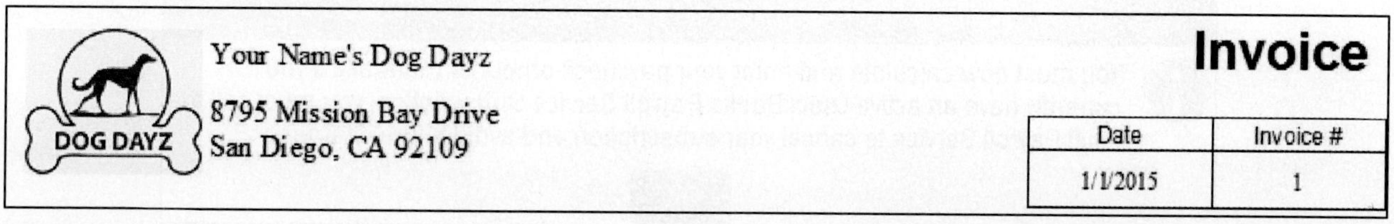

PREPARE A DAILY BACKUP

Use Create Local Backup and Your Name's Dog Dayz (Daily Backup).qbb file to update the backup

PAYROLL

When you completed the tutorial in Chapter 8, you paid the employees who worked for the company. In order to use QuickBooks to process payroll, you need to complete the Payroll Set up and provide individual information regarding your employees.

SELECT A PAYROLL OPTION

Before entering any payroll transactions, QuickBooks must be informed of the type of payroll service you are selecting. Once QuickBooks knows what type of payroll process has been selected for the company, you will be able to create paychecks. As in you did in Chapter 8, you must go through the Help menu to designate the selection of the Manual payroll option.

Select a **Manual** payroll option

Press **F1** to access Help
Type **Manual Payroll** and click the **Start Search** icon

Click **Process payroll manually (without a subscription to QuickBooks Payroll)**
In the **"Set your company file to use the manual payroll calculations setting"** section, click the words **manual payroll calculations**
In the section **"If you are sure you want to manually calculate your payroll taxes in QuickBooks,"** click **Set my company file to use manual calculations**
Once QuickBooks processes the selection, you will get a QuickBooks Information message, which may be hidden behind the Help screen
Close Help
Click **OK** on the QuickBooks Information screen

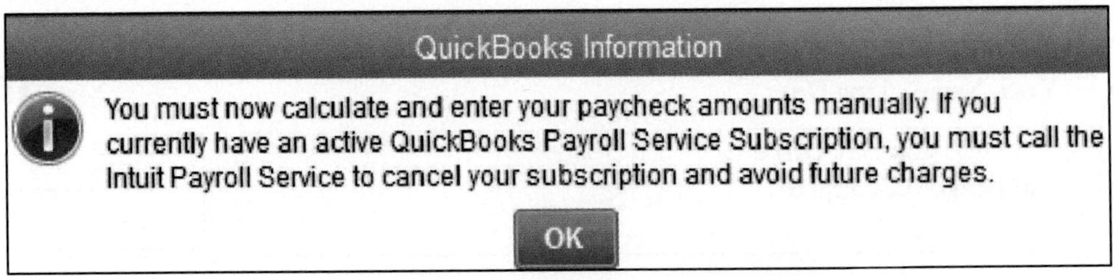

GENERAL NOTES ON QUICKBOOKS PAYROLL SETUP

Once the payroll processing method is selected, you must complete the QuickBooks Payroll Setup. QuickBooks is setup with Automatic Update turned on. Periodically, Intuit will send out program updates via the Internet that will be downloaded to your computer. It is important to note that sometimes information in the program changes. If your screens differ from the ones shown, do not be alarmed, you will enter the same information; but, perhaps, in a slightly different format or order.

You may find that some of your screens are different from the ones shown in the text. This is due to the fact that the computer date used when writing the text is January 1, 2015 and your computer will use the current date. If you see a different year on your screen, and you are not able to change it, just continue with the training and leave the date as it appears.

THE QUICKBOOKS PAYROLL SETUP

There are six sections in the QuickBooks Payroll Setup to guide you through the process of setting up the payroll in QuickBooks.

The first section is an introductory screen. The second section is the Company Setup for payroll. This section helps you identify and setup your methods of compensation, benefits your company offers, and additions and deductions your employees might have.

The third section leads you through adding employee information or setting up individual employees. When establishing the Employee Defaults, you will specify which payroll items apply to all or most of the employees of the company. Payroll items are used to identify and/or track the various amounts that affect a paycheck. These items include salaries and wages, taxes, types of other deductions, commissions, and company-paid benefits.

The fourth section, Taxes, automatically sets up the payroll items for federal, state, and local taxes. Payroll tax liabilities and payroll withholding items need to be associated with a vendor in order to have payments processed appropriately.

The fifth section, Year-to-Date Payrolls, enter earnings and withholdings for employees and payroll liability payments for the current year. This is important if you are installing QuickBooks and have already made payroll payments during the calendar year.

The final section, Finishing Up, takes companies with a subscription to QuickBooks Payroll to the Payroll Center. If you are using manual payroll, you are taken to the Home Page.

CAUTION: If you exit the payroll setup before everything is complete, be sure to click the **Finish Later** button. If you exit the payroll setup by any other method, you may lose all of the information you have entered and will need to re-enter it. Sometimes, QuickBooks will retain the information and will re-enter it for you as you click through each of the sections in the QuickBooks Payroll Setup.

BEGIN QUICKBOOKS PAYROLL SETUP

Click the **Employees** menu, click **Payroll Setup**

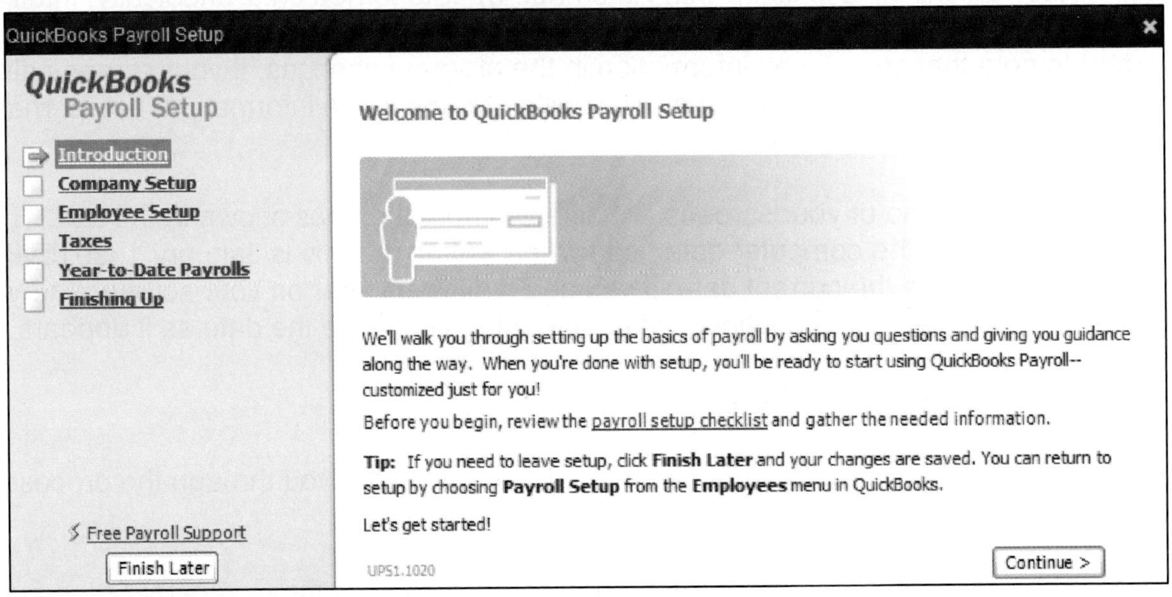

Read the Introduction screen

- If you click payroll setup checklist you will go to an Adobe pdf file that contains information about the data needed in order to setup your payroll.

Click **Continue**

COMPANY SETUP

In this section of the QuickBooks Payroll Setup, information about the methods of paying employees, deductions, and benefits is entered.

MEMO
DATE: January 1, 2015

Complete the Company portion of the QuickBooks Payroll Setup:

Methods used to compensate employees: Salary, Hourly wage and overtime
Insurance Benefits: Health Insurance, Dental Insurance both are fully paid by the employee after taxes have been deducted
Retirement Benefits: None
Paid Time Off: Sick Time and Vacation Time
Other Payments and Deductions: None

Complete the Company Setup portion of the QuickBooks Payroll Setup
Read the first screen regarding Company Setup: Compensation and Benefits

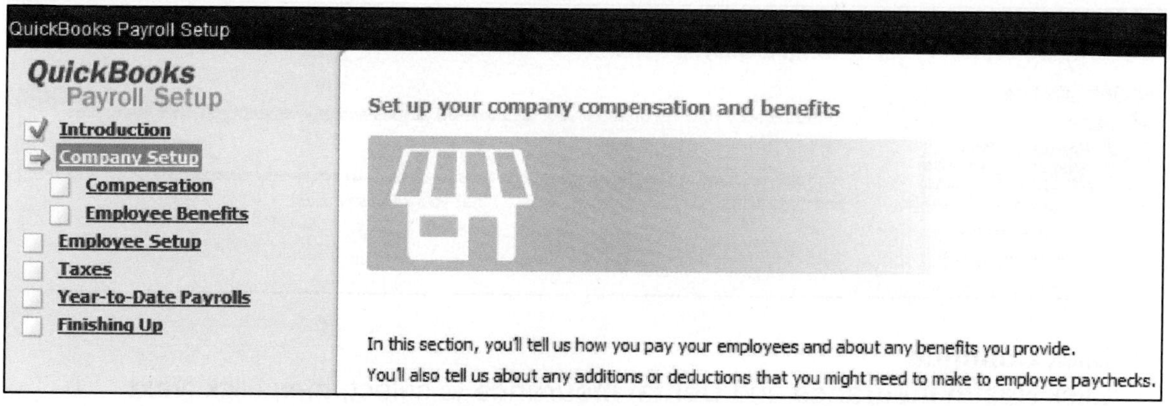

Click the **Continue** button (located in the lower-right corner of the screen)
Click **Bonus, award, or one-time compensation** to unmark

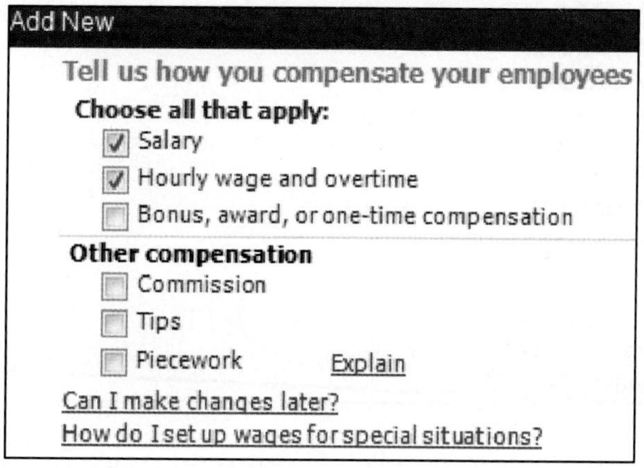

Click **Finish** (located in the lower-right corner of the screen)
Review the Compensation List

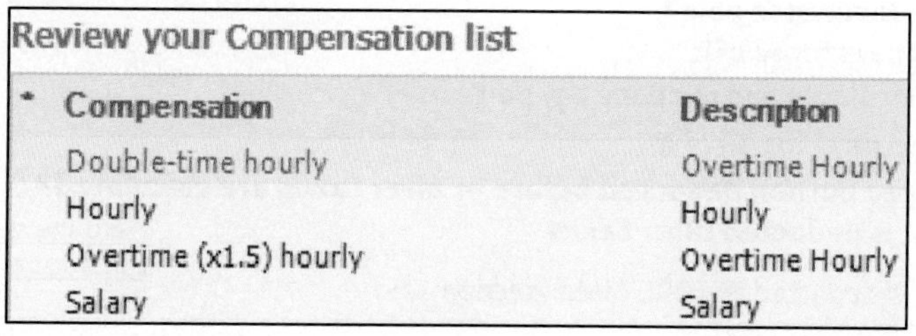
Review your Compensation list
Compensation
Description
Double-time hourly
Overtime Hourly
Hourly
Hourly
Overtime (x1.5) hourly
Overtime Hourly
Salary
Salary

Click **Continue**
Read the screen regarding **Set up employee benefits**

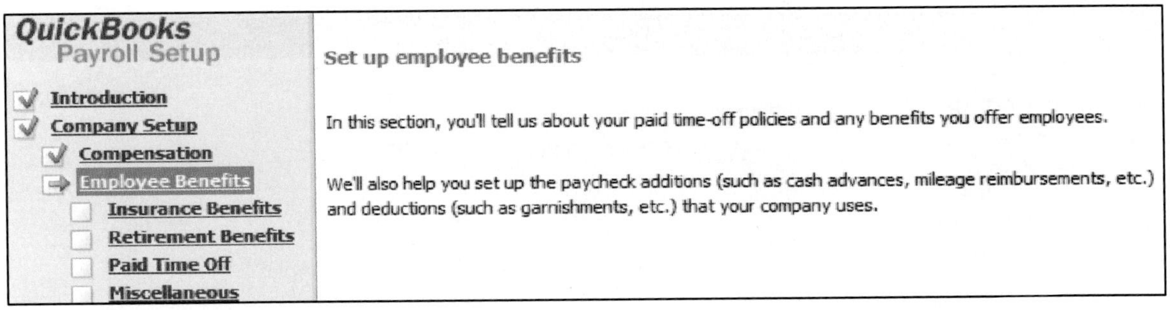

Click **Continue**
Click **Health insurance** and **Dental insurance** to select; then click **Next**

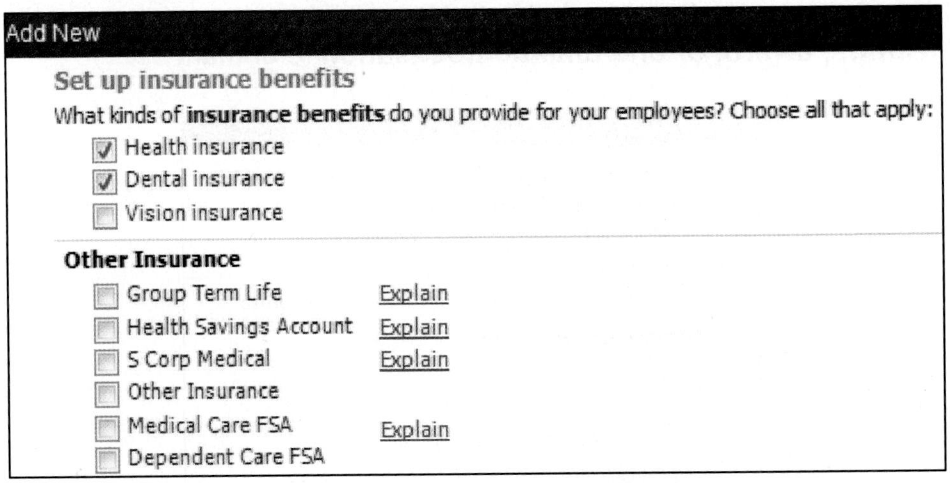

On the Health Insurance screen, click **Employee pays for all of it**
Payment is deducted after taxes should appear and be selected; then click **Next**

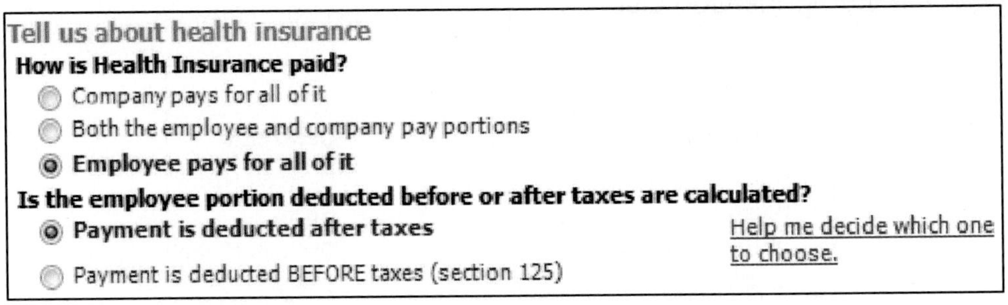

Click the drop-down list arrow for **Payee (Vendor)**, click **Health Insurance, Inc.** to select the Vendor that receives payment for health insurance premiums
Make sure **I don't need a regular payment schedule for this item** is selected

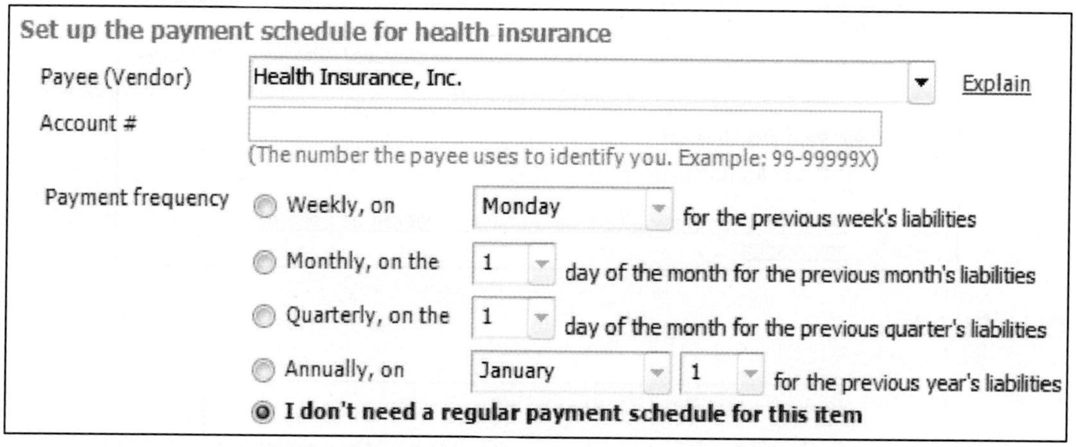

Click **Next**

On The Dental Insurance screen, click **Employee pays for all of it** and verify that **Payment is deducted after taxes** is checked; click **Next**

The Payee for Dental Insurance is **Health Insurance, Inc.**

Make sure **I don't need a regular payment schedule for this item** is selected

Click **Finish**

Review your Insurance Benefits list

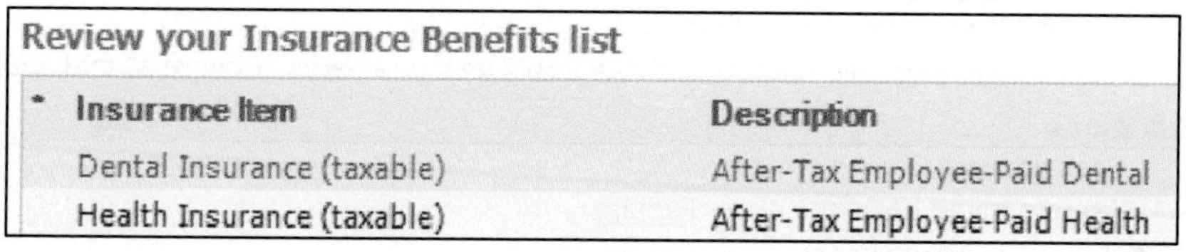

Review your Insurance Benefits list
Insurance Item
Description
Dental Insurance (taxable)
After-Tax Employee-Paid Dental
Health Insurance (taxable)
After-Tax Employee-Paid Health

Click **Continue**

The next screen allows you to select retirement benefits

We do not provide any retirement benefits for our employees

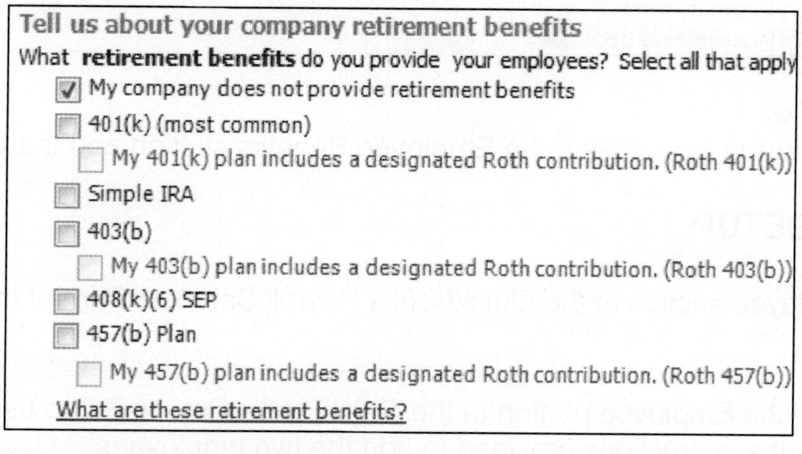

Tell us about your company retirement benefits
What retirement benefits do you provide your employees? Select all that apply
My company does not provide retirement benefits
401(k) (most common)
My 401(k) plan includes a designated Roth contribution. (Roth 401(k))
Simple IRA
403(b)
My 403(b) plan includes a designated Roth contribution. (Roth 403(b))
408(k)(6) SEP
457(b) Plan
My 457(b) plan includes a designated Roth contribution. (Roth 457(b))
What are these retirement benefits?

Click **Finish**, and then click **Continue**

For Paid Time Off, we do provide paid time off for Sick Leave and Vacation Leave, click **Paid sick time off** and **Paid vacation time off** to select

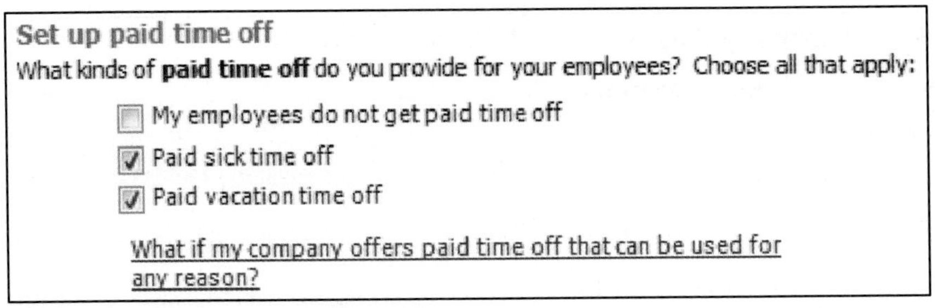

Set up paid time off
What kinds of **paid time off** do you provide for your employees? Choose all that apply:
My employees do not get paid time off
Paid sick time off
Paid vacation time off
What if my company offers paid time off that can be used for any reason?

Click **Finish**

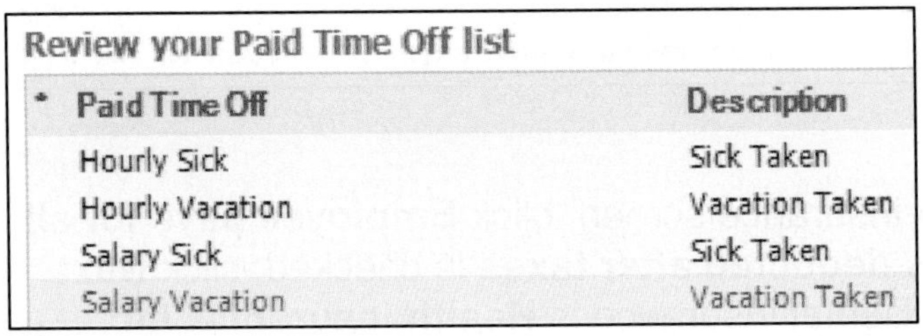

Review your Paid Time Off list
Paid Time Off
Description
Hourly Sick
Sick Taken
Hourly Vacation
Vacation Taken
Salary Sick
Sick Taken
Salary Vacation
Vacation Taken

Review the Paid Time Off list, click **Continue**
We do not have any other Additions or Deductions

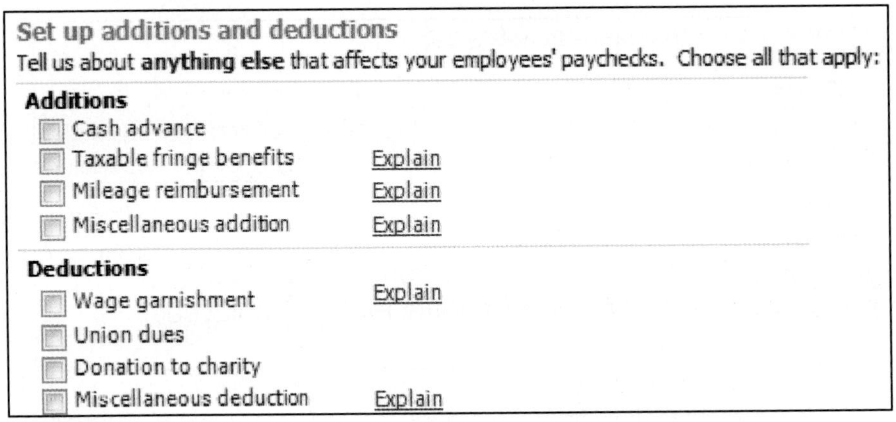

Click **Finish**
Click **Continue** to complete the Employee Benefits section and the Company Setup

EMPLOYEE SETUP

During the Employee section of the QuickBooks Payroll Setup, individual employees are added.

Complete the Employee portion of the QuickBooks Payroll Setup using the following chart and the instructions provided to add the two employees

EMPLOYEES Angela Aguilar and Drake Childs		
Legal Name	Angela Aguilar	Drake Childs
Employee Status	Active	Active
Home Address	2062 Columbia Street	2985 A Street
City	San Diego	San Diego
State	CA	CA
Zip Code	92101	92101
Employee Type	Regular	Regular
Social Security No.	100-55-2525	100-55-9661
Hire Date	04/23/2001	06/30/2004
Birth Date	12/07/1979	09/27/1977
Gender	Female	Male
Pay Period	Monthly	Monthly
Compensation	Salary: $26,000 per year	Hourly: Hourly wage: $15.50 Double-time hourly: $31.00 Overtime (x1.5) hourly: $23.25
Dental Insurance	$10 per month, annual limit $120	$10 per month, annual limit $120
Health Insurance	$50 per month, annual limit $600	$25 per month, annual limit $300
Sick Time Earns	40:00 at beginning of year	40:00 at beginning of year
Unused Sick Hours	Have an accrual limit	Have an accrual limit
Maximum Hours	120:00	120:00
Earns	Time off currently	Time off currently
Hours Available as of 01/01/15 (Your computer date will show)	20:00	50:00
Vacation Time Earns	40:00 at beginning of year	40:00 at beginning of year
Unused Vacation Hours	Have an accrual limit	Have an accrual limit
Maximum Hours	120:00	120:00
Earns	Time off currently	Time off currently
Hours Available as of 01/01/15 (Your computer date will show)	20:00	40:00
Payment Method	Check (no Direct Deposit)	Check (no Direct Deposit)

EMPLOYEES Angela Aguilar and Drake Childs		
State Subject to Withholding	CA	CA
State Subject to Unemployment Tax	CA	CA
Live or Work in Another State in 2015	No	No
Federal Filing Status	Single	Married
Allowances (Federal)	0	2
Extra Withholding	0.00	0.00
Nonresident Alien Withholding	Does not apply	Does not apply
HIRE Act Exemption	Not a qualified employee	Not a qualified employee
Subject to (Federal)	Medicare Social Security Federal Unemployment	Medicare Social Security Federal Unemployment
State Filing Status	Single	Married (two incomes)
Regular Withholding Allowances (State)	0	2
Subject to (State)	CA-Unemployment CA-Employment Training Tax CA-Disability	CA-Unemployment CA-Employment Training Tax CA-Disability
Local Taxes	No	No
Wage Plan Code	S	S

Read the screen about the Employee Setup

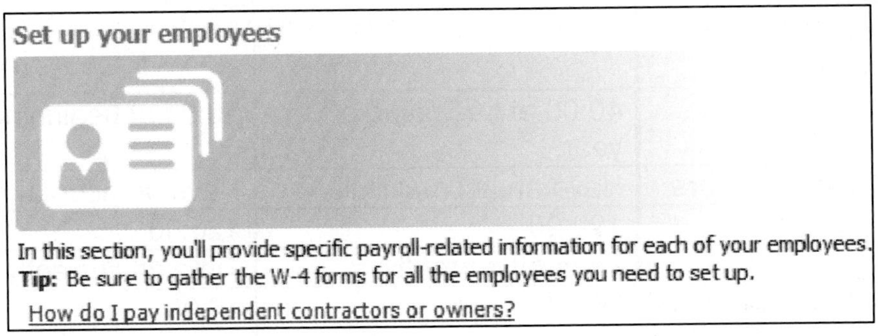

Click **Continue**

Use the Employees table and complete New Employee screens for Angela Aguilar:

First name: **Angela**; Last name: **Aguilar**; Employee status: **Active**

Home Address: **2062 Columbia Street**; City: **San Diego**; State: **CA**; Zip Code **92101**

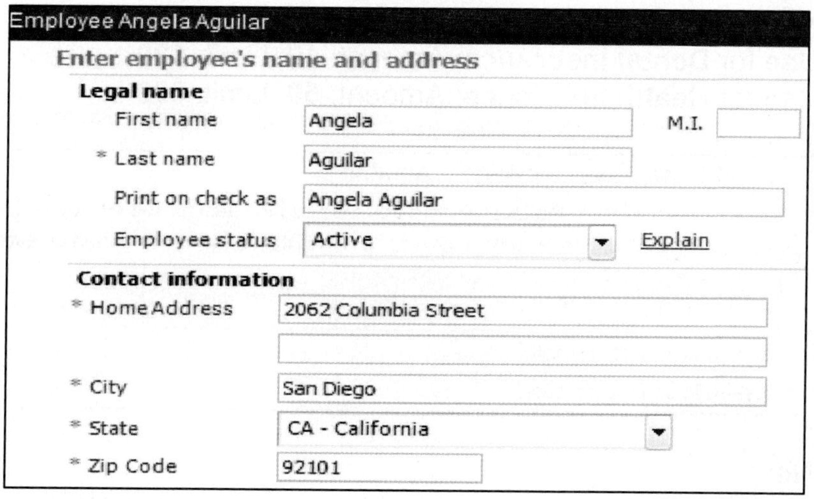

Click **Next**

Social Security # **100-55-2525**; Hire date: **04/23/01**; Birth Date: **12/07/79**; Gender: **Female**

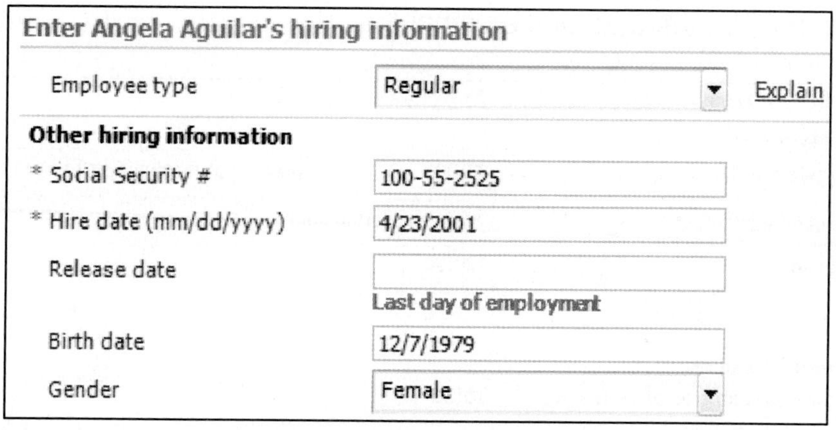

Click **Next**

How often?: **Monthly**; click the radio dial for **Salary**; Salary amount: **26,000**; Per: **Year**

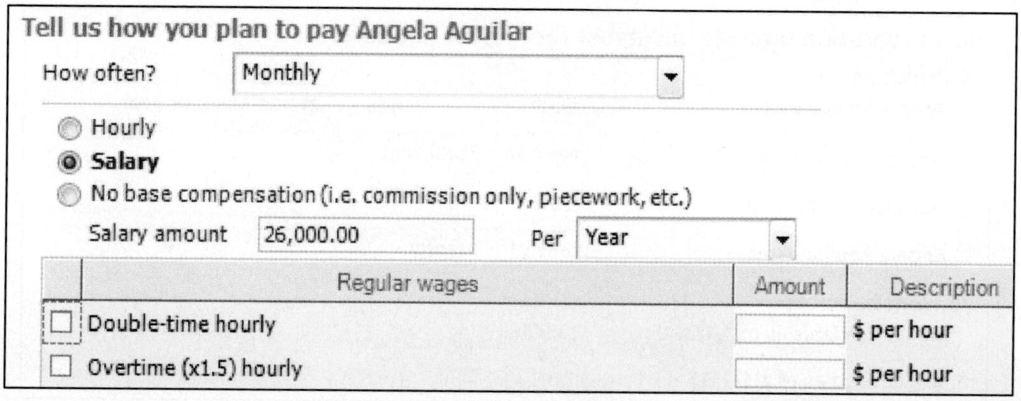

Click **Next**
Click **Use** for **Dental Insurance**; Amount: **10**; Limit: **120**
Click **Use** for **Health Insurance**; Amount: **50**; Limit: **600**

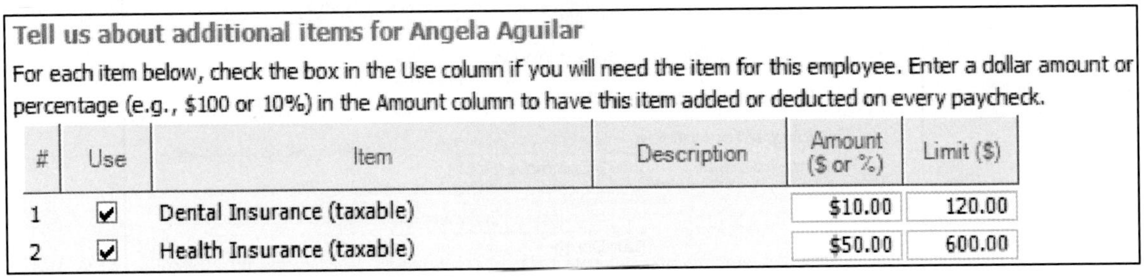
Tell us about additional items for Angela Aguilar

For each item below, check the box in the Use column if you will need the item for this employee. Enter a dollar amount or percentage (e.g., $100 or 10%) in the Amount column to have this item added or deducted on every paycheck.

#	Use	Item	Description	Amount ($ or %)	Limit ($)
1	☑	Dental Insurance (taxable)		$10.00	120.00
2	☑	Health Insurance (taxable)		$50.00	600.00

Click **Next**

Using the data provided in the Employees table, enter the information about Angela's sick time

- Be sure to select hours "at beginning of year."
- In the **Current balances** section of the screen you may not see the dates of 1/1/2015. Use whatever date is automatically inserted by QuickBooks. The date shown may be the date of the computer.

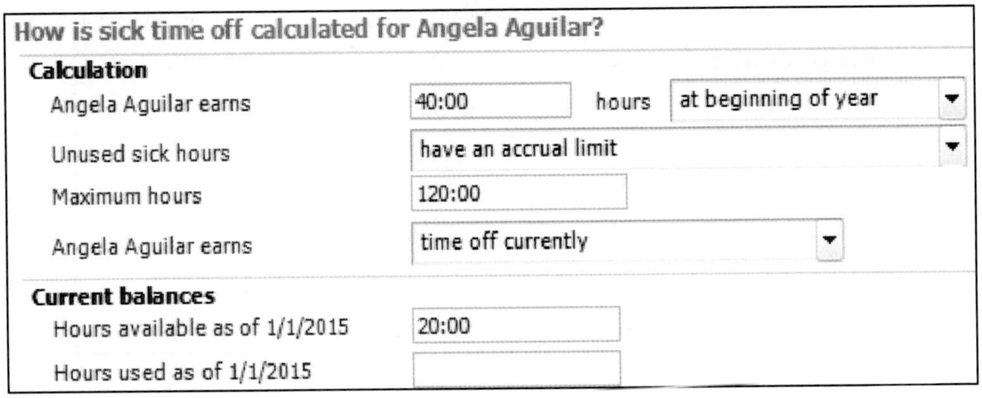
How is sick time off calculated for Angela Aguilar?

Calculation

Angela Aguilar earns	40:00 hours at beginning of year
Unused sick hours	have an accrual limit
Maximum hours	120:00
Angela Aguilar earns	time off currently

Current balances

Hours available as of 1/1/2015	20:00
Hours used as of 1/1/2015	

Click **Next**

Using the Employees table, enter the information for Angela's vacation time

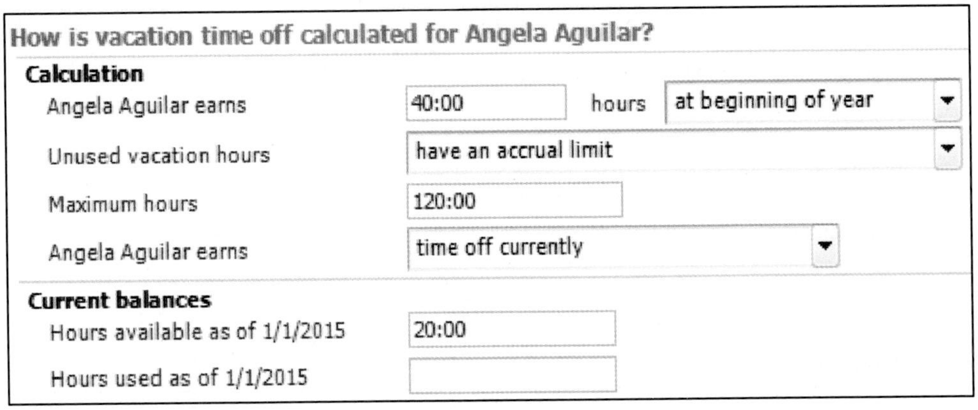
How is vacation time off calculated for Angela Aguilar?

Calculation

Angela Aguilar earns	40:00 hours at beginning of year
Unused vacation hours	have an accrual limit
Maximum hours	120:00
Angela Aguilar earns	time off currently

Current balances

Hours available as of 1/1/2015	20:00
Hours used as of 1/1/2015	

Click **Next**

We do not pay using Direct Deposit, click **Next** on the direct deposit screen

Enter **CA** as the state where Angela is subject to withholding and unemployment tax. She has not lived or worked in another state in 2015

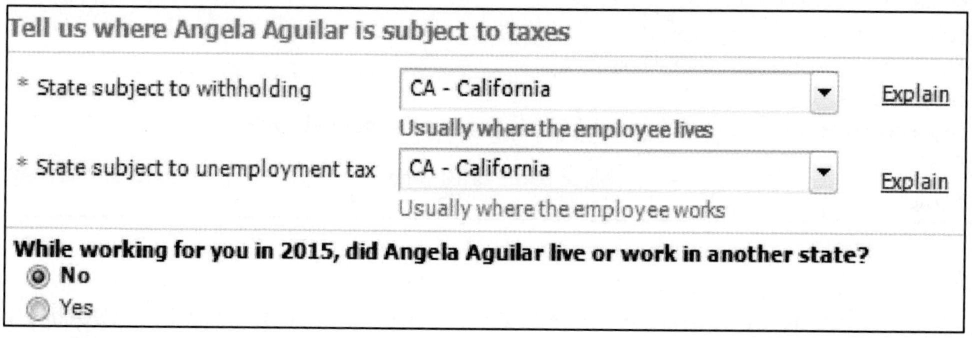

Click **Next**

Use the Employees table and enter the federal tax information for Angela

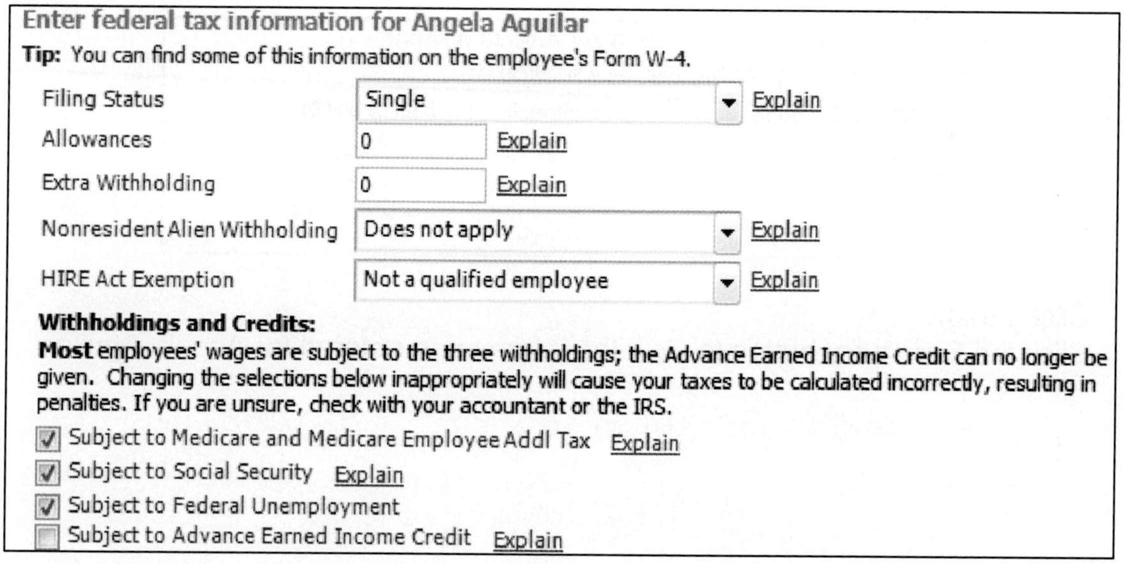

Click **Next**

Use the Employees table and enter the state tax information for Angela

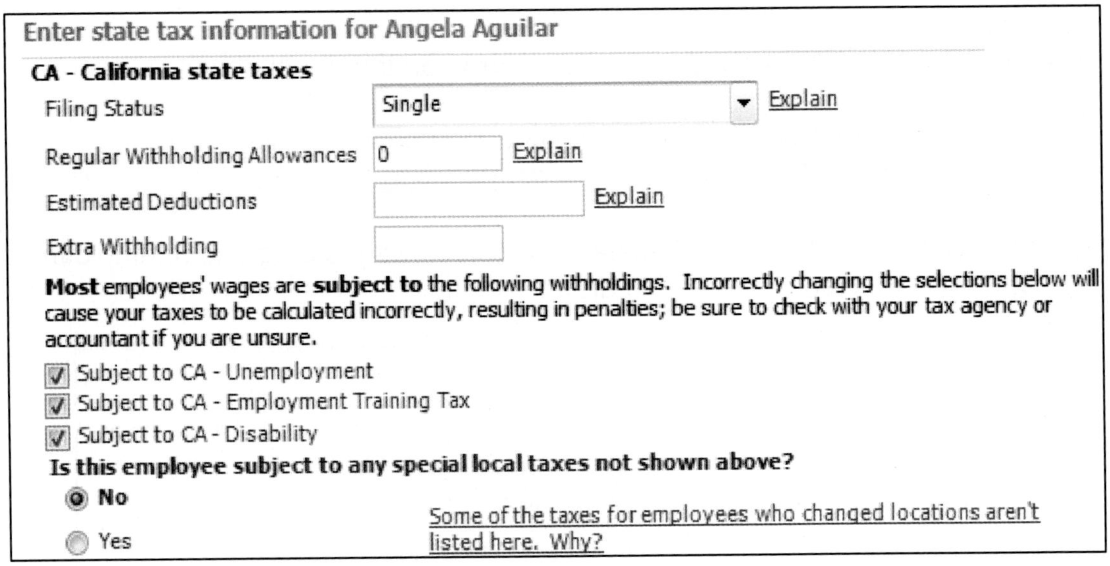

Click **Next**

- The California Employment Development Department agency requires employers who file electronically to select a Wage Plan Code.

Since you do participate in the state unemployment and disability insurance programs, select **S** as the code

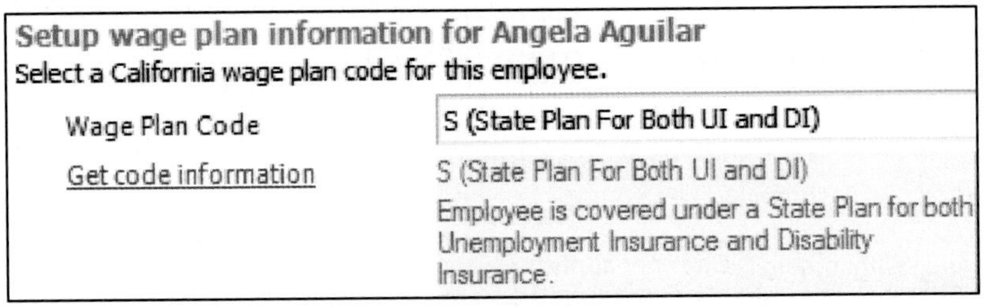

Click **Finish**

Click the **Summary** button to view the information entered for Angela Aguilar

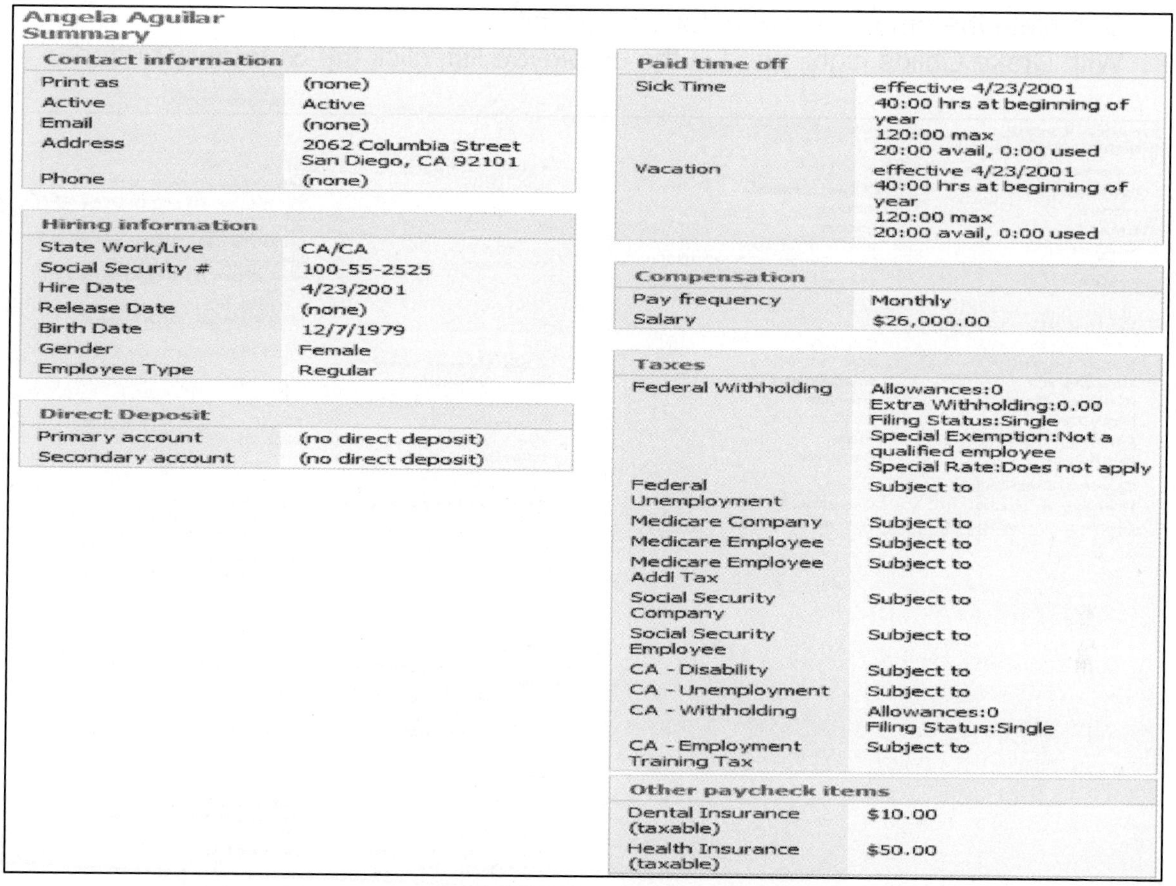

Angela Aguilar Summary

Contact information	
Print as	(none)
Active	Active
Email	(none)
Address	2062 Columbia Street San Diego, CA 92101
Phone	(none)

Hiring information	
State Work/Live	CA/CA
Social Security #	100-55-2525
Hire Date	4/23/2001
Release Date	(none)
Birth Date	12/7/1979
Gender	Female
Employee Type	Regular

Direct Deposit	
Primary account	(no direct deposit)
Secondary account	(no direct deposit)

Paid time off	
Sick Time	effective 4/23/2001 40:00 hrs at beginning of year 120:00 max 20:00 avail, 0:00 used
Vacation	effective 4/23/2001 40:00 hrs at beginning of year 120:00 max 20:00 avail, 0:00 used

Compensation	
Pay frequency	Monthly
Salary	$26,000.00

Taxes	
Federal Withholding	Allowances:0 Extra Withholding:0.00 Filing Status:Single Special Exemption:Not a qualified employee Special Rate:Does not apply
Federal Unemployment	Subject to
Medicare Company	Subject to
Medicare Employee	Subject to
Medicare Employee Addl Tax	Subject to
Social Security Company	Subject to
Social Security Employee	Subject to
CA - Disability	Subject to
CA - Unemployment	Subject to
CA - Withholding	Allowances:0 Filing Status:Single
CA - Employment Training Tax	Subject to

Other paycheck items	
Dental Insurance (taxable)	$10.00
Health Insurance (taxable)	$50.00

- If you selected 40:00 hours per year rather than 40:00 at the beginning of the year, your summary will show 3:20 per paycheck.

Click **Print** on the Summary screen and print Angela's information

Close the **Employee Summary** window for Angela

Click **Add New**, use the Employees table and add the information for **Drake Childs** following the steps provided for Angela Aguilar

When you complete the wages and compensation section for Drake, after selecting **Monthly** as How often?, click **Hourly**, enter **15.50** for Hourly wage

Click, **Double-time hourly** to select, enter **31.00;** click **Overtime (x1.5) hourly** to select, enter the amount **23.25**

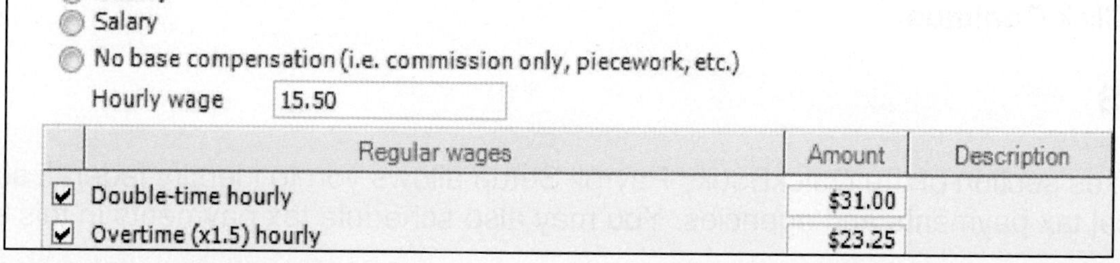

9

Complete the employee setup for Drake Childs
With Drake Childs highlighted in the employee list, click the **Summary** button

Drake Childs
Summary

Contact information	
Print as	Drake Childs
Active	Active
Email	(none)
Address	2985 A Street San Diego, CA 92101
Phone	(none)

Hiring information	
State Work/Live	CA/CA
Social Security #	100-55-9661
Hire Date	6/30/2004
Release Date	(none)
Birth Date	9/27/1977
Gender	Male
Employee Type	Regular

Direct Deposit	
Primary account	(no direct deposit)
Secondary account	(no direct deposit)

Paid time off	
Sick Time	effective 4/23/2001 40:00 hrs at beginning of year 120:00 max 50:00 avail, 0:00 used
Vacation	effective 4/23/2001 40:00 hrs at beginning of year 120:00 max 40:00 avail, 0:00 used

Compensation	
Pay frequency	Monthly
Double-time hourly	$31.00
Hourly	15.50
Overtime (x1.5) hourly	$23.25

Taxes	
Federal Withholding	Allowances:2 Extra Withholding:0.00 Filing Status:Married Special Exemption:Not a qualified employee Special Rate:Does not apply
Federal Unemployment	Subject to
Medicare Company	Subject to
Medicare Employee	Subject to
Medicare Employee Addl Tax	Subject to
Social Security Company	Subject to
Social Security Employee	Subject to
CA - Disability	Subject to
CA - Unemployment	Subject to
CA - Withholding	Allowances:2 Filing Status:Married (two incomes)
CA - Employment Training Tax	Subject to

Other paycheck items	
Dental Insurance (taxable)	$10.00
Health Insurance (taxable)	$25.00

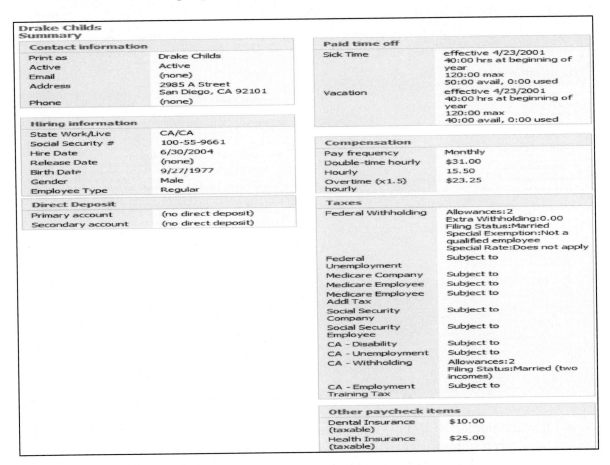

- Sometimes QuickBooks will use the effective date for sick time and vacation time that was used for the last employee. If this happens, disregard the date. Angela's effective date of 4/23/2001 was also used for Drake.

Print **Drake Childs'** Summary, close the Summary
Review the Employee List

Review your Employee list

Employee	Social Security	Summary
Aguilar, Angela	100-55-2525	
Childs, Drake	100-55-9661	

Click **Continue**

TAXES

The Taxes section of the QuickBooks Payroll Setup allows you to identify federal, state, and local tax payments and agencies. You may also schedule tax payments in this section.

Complete the Taxes section of the QuickBooks Payroll Setup

Read the screen for "Set up your payroll taxes"

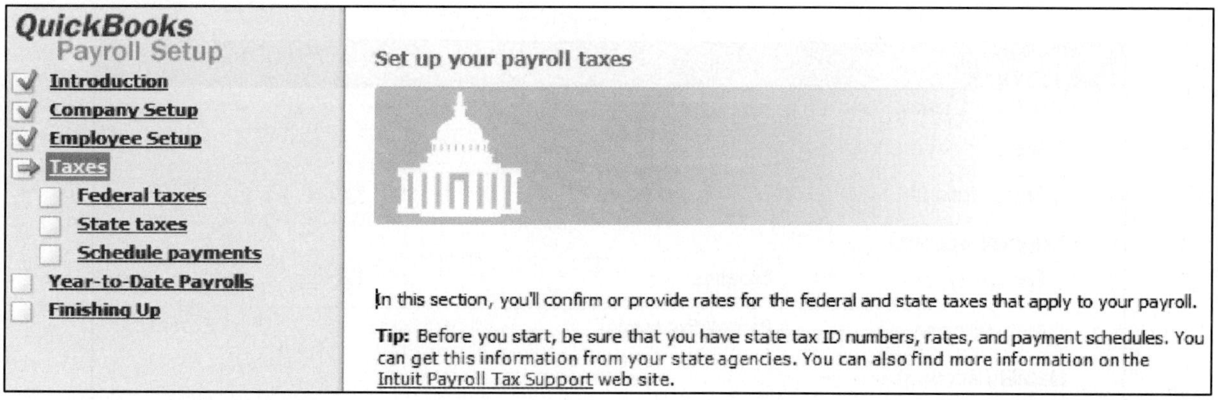

Click **Continue**
Review the list of Federal taxes

Here are the federal taxes we set up for you
Click **Edit** if you need to review or make changes to any of these taxes.

*	Federal Tax	Description
	Federal Withholding	Also known as Federal Withholding Tax
	Advance Earned Income Credit	Also known as AEIC
	Federal Unemployment	Also known as FUTA
	Medicare Company	Medicare Tax
	Medicare Employee	Medicare Tax
	Medicare Employee Addl Tax	Medicare Additional Tax
	Social Security Company	Also known as FICA
	Social Security Employee	Also known as FICA

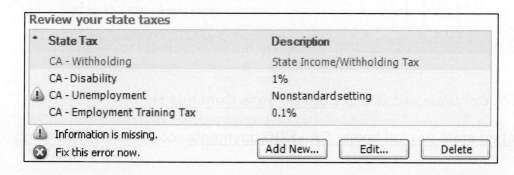

Click **Continue**
You will see one of two screens: either "Review your state taxes" **or** "Set up state payroll taxes" for CA – EDD Payments

- Depending on which screen you see, complete the steps provided for the screen.

Review your state taxes: complete the following:

Review your state taxes

*	State Tax	Description
	CA - Withholding	State Income/Withholding Tax
	CA - Disability	1%
⚠	CA - Unemployment	Nonstandard setting
	CA - Employment Training Tax	0.1%

⚠ Information is missing.
Fix this error now. [Add New...] [Edit...] [Delete]

9

- Notice that CA-Unemployment is marked "Information is missing."

Click **CA-Unemployment**, click **Edit**

Make sure your Edit CA-Unemployment screen matches the following; when it does, click **Next**

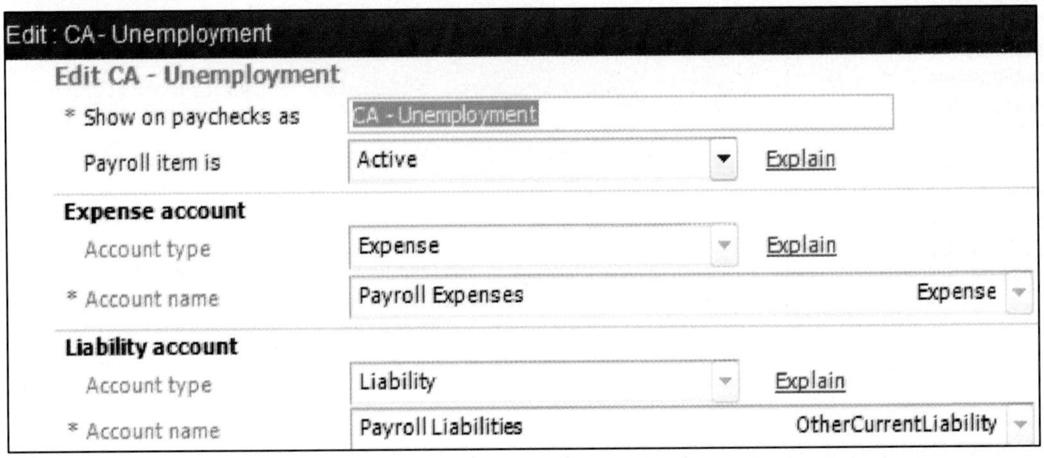

Enter the California-Unemployment Company Rate of **3.4%**; click **Finish**

- California has a variable rate schedule for Unemployment Insurance for companies. A new company will pay 3.4% for the first three years. After that, the rate is determined by a variety of factors and can range from 1.5 to 6.2%.

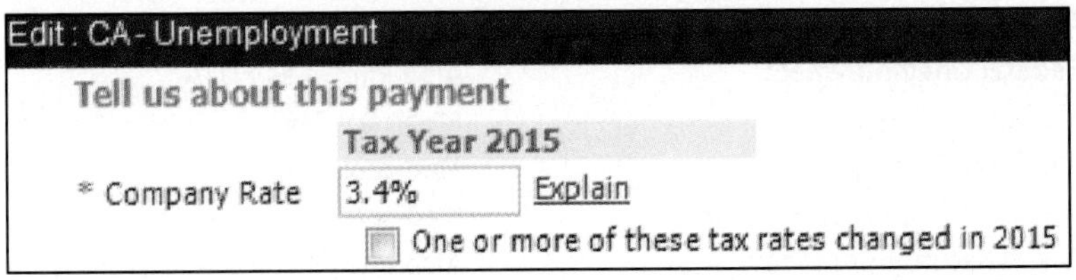

Review your state taxes

- If your State Tax listing appears in a different order, that is not a concern. The important thing is whether or not the correct rates are shown. If the rates are not correct, edit the tax as demonstrated for CA – Unemployment.

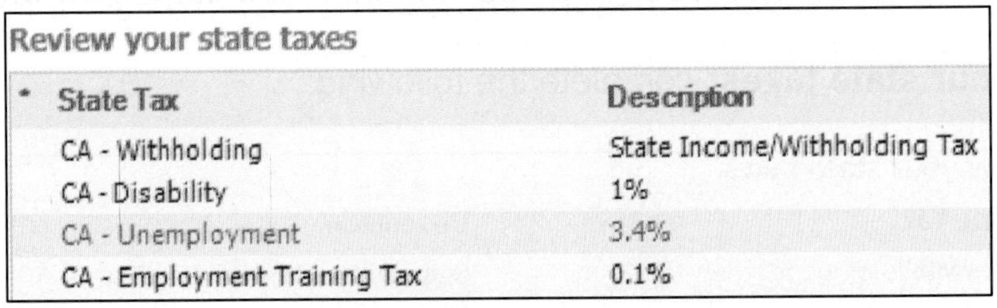

Click **Continue** and skip to **Both Screens Continue Here:**

Set up state payroll taxes: CA - EDD payments: complete the following:

If you are taken directly to the Set up state payroll taxes screen showing **CA – EDD payments**, complete the following:

CA – Disability Employee Rate should show 1%; if not change it

CA – Employment Training Tax Company Rate should be 0.1%; if not change it

CA – Unemployment Company Rate enter **3.4%**

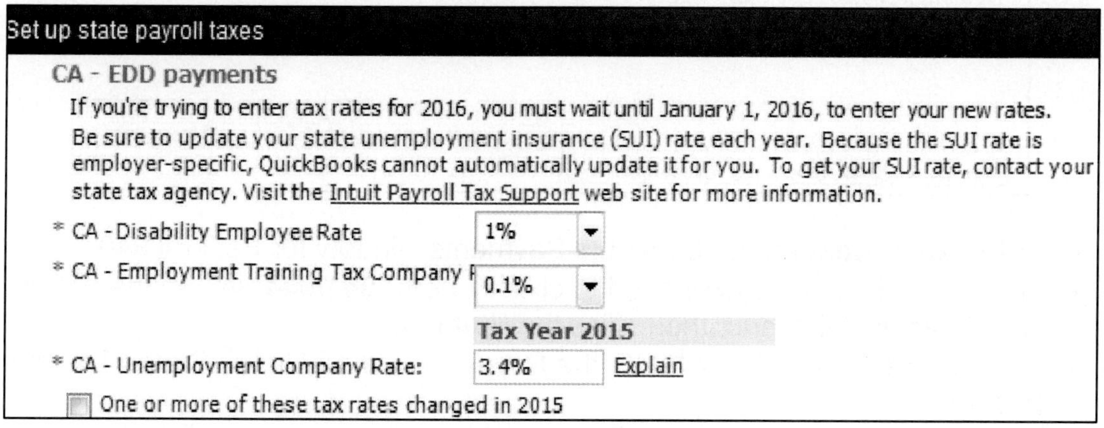
Set up state payroll taxes
CA - EDD payments
If you're trying to enter tax rates for 2016, you must wait until January 1, 2016, to enter your new rates.
Be sure to update your state unemployment insurance (SUI) rate each year. Because the SUI rate is employer-specific, QuickBooks cannot automatically update it for you. To get your SUI rate, contact your state tax agency. Visit the Intuit Payroll Tax Support web site for more information.
* CA - Disability Employee Rate
1%
* CA - Employment Training Tax Company R
0.1%
Tax Year 2015
* CA - Unemployment Company Rate:
3.4%
Explain
One or more of these tax rates changed in 2015

Click **Finish**; your screen should show the following:

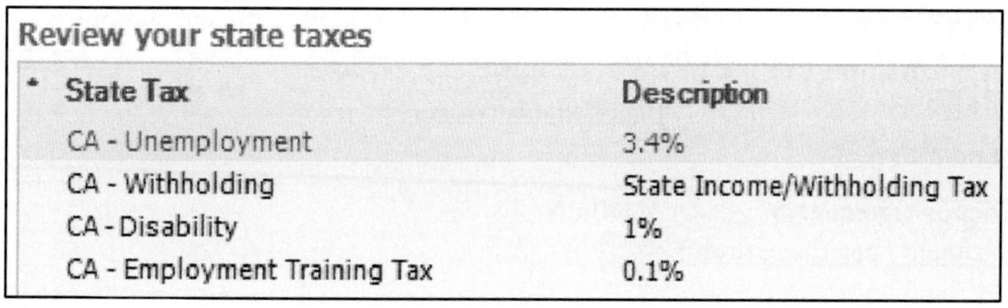
Review your state taxes
State Tax
Description
CA - Unemployment
3.4%
CA - Withholding
State Income/Withholding Tax
CA - Disability
1%
CA - Employment Training Tax
0.1%

Click **Continue**

<u>Both Screens Continue Here</u>:

The Schedule Payments window for Federal 940 should appear

- If you get a screen to Review your Scheduled Tax Payments list, click Federal 940; and then, click the **Edit** button.
- For Federal Form 940, the Payee should be United States Treasury, the deposit frequency is Quarterly. Enter these if necessary.

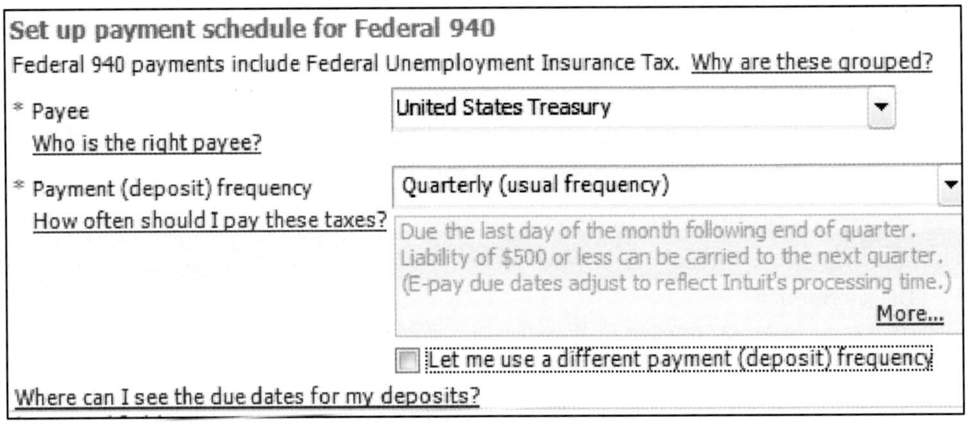
Set up payment schedule for Federal 940
Federal 940 payments include Federal Unemployment Insurance Tax. Why are these grouped?
* Payee
Who is the right payee?
United States Treasury
* Payment (deposit) frequency
How often should I pay these taxes?
Quarterly (usual frequency)
Due the last day of the month following end of quarter. Liability of $500 or less can be carried to the next quarter. (E-pay due dates adjust to reflect Intuit's processing time.)
More...
Let me use a different payment (deposit) frequency
Where can I see the due dates for my deposits?

Click **Finish** or **Next** on the Schedule Payments window for Federal 940

- If you click Finish, you will need to click **Federal 941/944/943** on the Scheduled Tax Payments list; and, then, click the **Edit** button.
- For Federal Form 941/944/943, the Payee should be United States Treasury, enter this if necessary.

Click the drop-down list arrow for Payment (deposit) frequency, click **Quarterly**

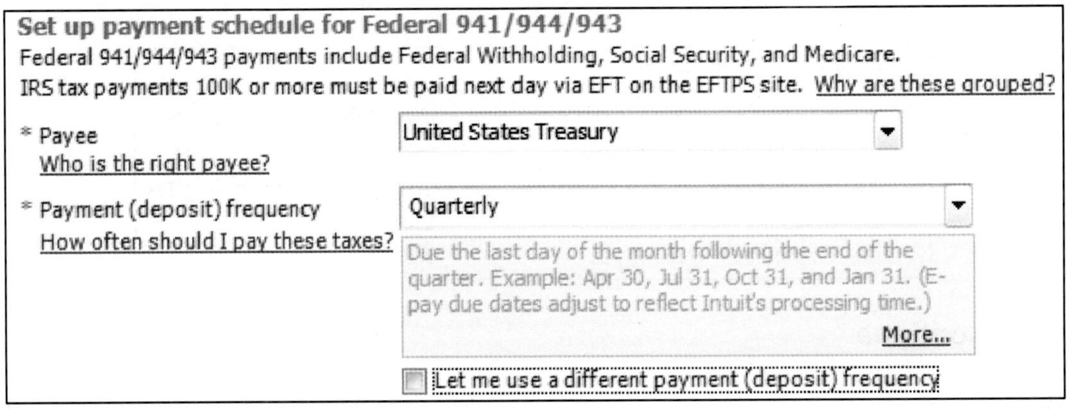
Set up payment schedule for Federal 941/944/943
Federal 941/944/943 payments include Federal Withholding, Social Security, and Medicare.
IRS tax payments 100K or more must be paid next day via EFT on the EFTPS site. Why are these grouped?
* Payee
Who is the right payee?
United States Treasury
* Payment (deposit) frequency
How often should I pay these taxes?
Quarterly
Due the last day of the month following the end of the quarter. Example: Apr 30, Jul 31, Oct 31, and Jan 31. (E-pay due dates adjust to reflect Intuit's processing time.)
More...
Let me use a different payment (deposit) frequency

Click **Finish** or **Next**

- If you click Finish, you will need to click **CA UI and Employment Training Tax** on the Scheduled Tax Payments list; and, then, click the **Edit** button.
- If the screens advance by clicking Next, they may be displayed in a different order than shown. If that occurs, enter the information pertinent to the screen and continue until all payment schedule information is complete.

Complete the information for CA UI and Employment Training Tax

Click the drop-down list arrow for Payee, and then click **Employment Development Department**

Employer Acct No. is **999-9999-9**

Deposit Frequency is **Quarterly**

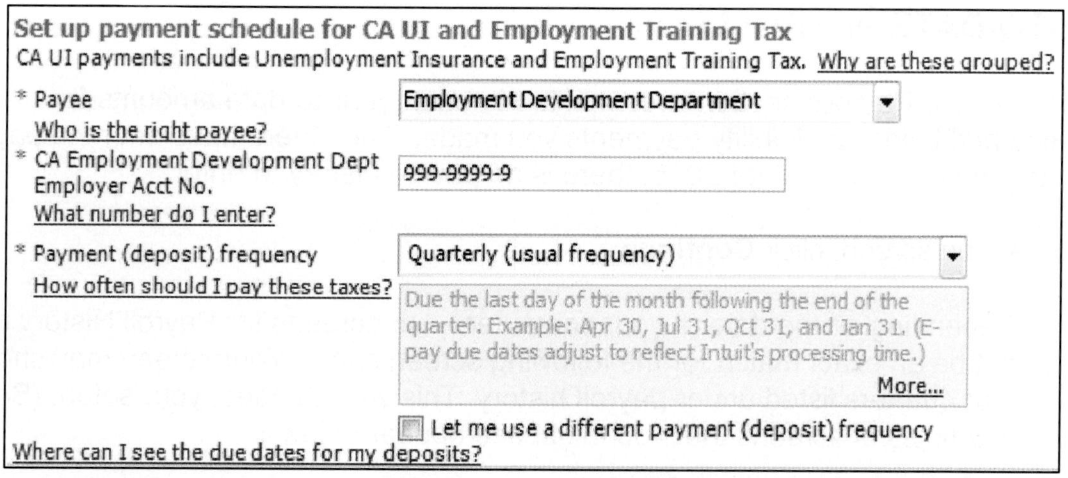

Click **Finish** or **Next**

Repeat the steps to enter the information for **CA Withholding and Disability Insurance**, selecting **Employment Development Department** as the Payee, an Employer Acct No. of **999-9999-9**, and a Deposit Frequency of **Quarterly**

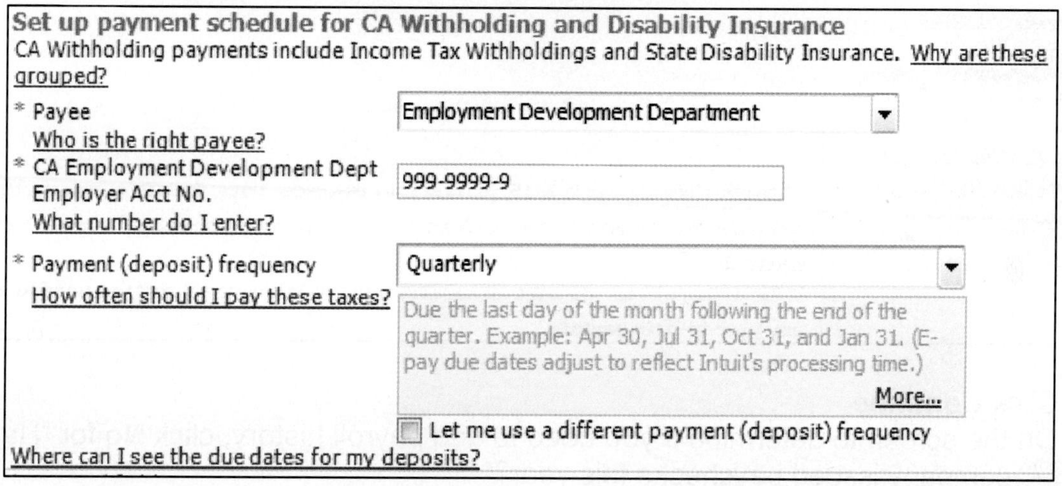

Click **Finish**, view the finalized **Scheduled Tax Payment List**

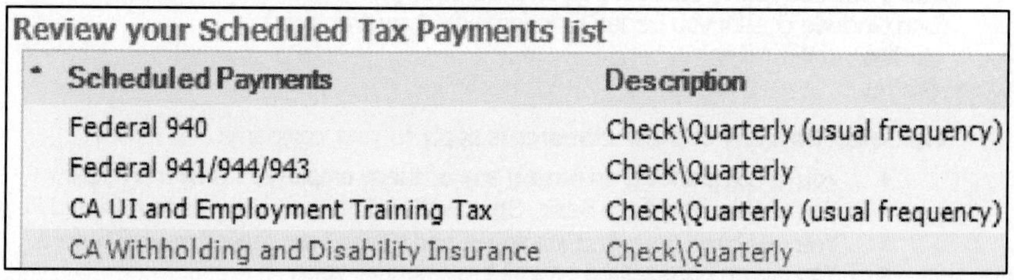

Review your Scheduled Tax Payments list
Scheduled Payments
Description
Federal 940
Check\Quarterly (usual frequency)
Federal 941/944/943
Check\Quarterly
CA UI and Employment Training Tax
Check\Quarterly (usual frequency)
CA Withholding and Disability Insurance
Check\Quarterly

- As with previous screen, the Scheduled Tax Payments list may show the Scheduled Payments in a different order than in the text. As long as the information on the screen is complete, the order displayed is of no concern.

Click **Continue**

YEAR-TO-DATE PAYROLLS

The Year-to-Date Payrolls section is completed to enter year-to-date amounts for employees and to identify liability payments you made. Since there have been no payroll payments processed or paid for 2015, there is no payroll history to enter.

Read the screen, click **Continue**

- Depending on the date of your computer, your screens for Payroll History may not be an exact match for the following screen shots. Your screen may show all four quarters listed under payroll history. This will not affect your setup. (Some examples of screens that you might see appear below.)

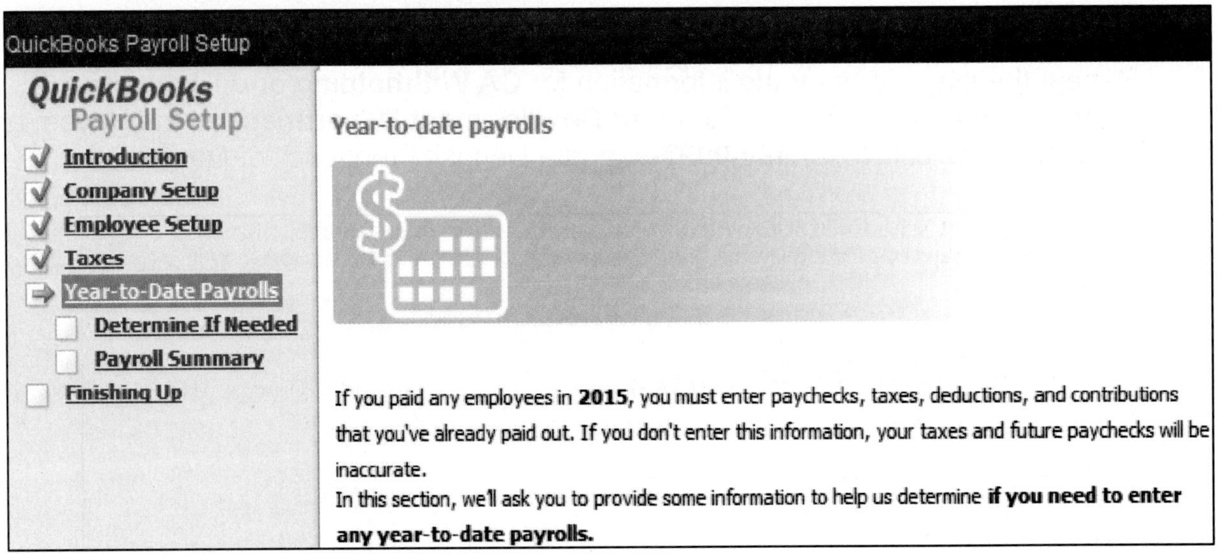

Click **Continue**

On the screen to determine if you need to add payroll history, click **No** for "Has your company issued paychecks this year?"

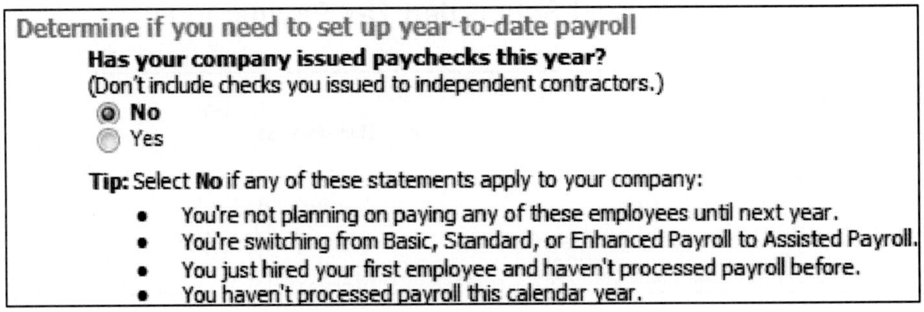

Click **Continue**

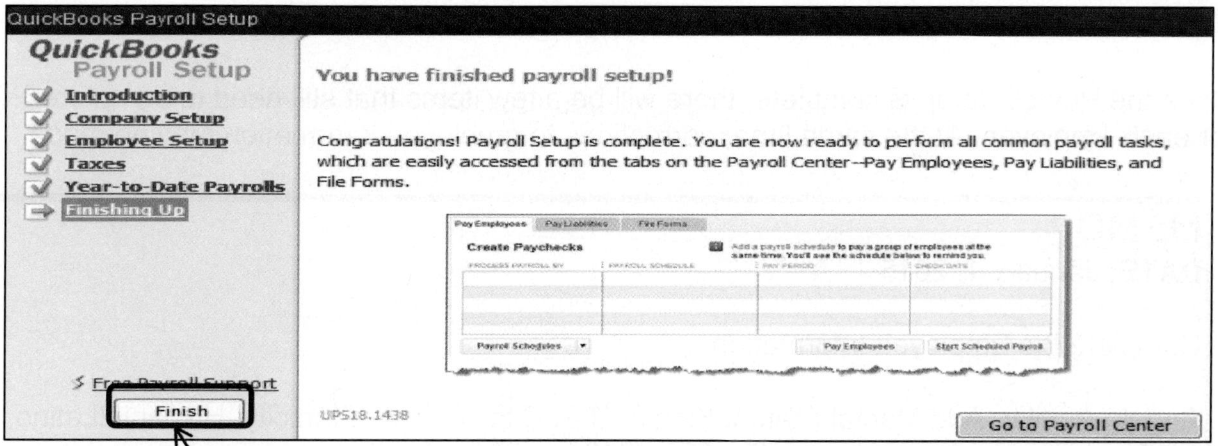

Click the **Finish** button, click **Home** on the Icon Bar to display the Home Page

- If you click Go to Payroll Center, you will be taken to the Employee Center, which you will need to close.

PRINT PAYROLL ITEM LISTING

To verify the payroll items used, it is wise to print a listing of the Payroll Items.

Print the **Payroll Item Listing** for January 1, 2015

Click the **Reports** menu; point to **List** as the report type, click **Payroll Item Listing**
Adjust the column widths and print the report in **Landscape** orientation

Your Name's Dog Dayz
Payroll Item Listing

Payroll Item	Type	Amount	Limit	Expense Account	Liability Account	Tax Tracking
Salary	Yearly Salary			Payroll Expenses		Compensation
Salary Sick	Yearly Salary			Payroll Expenses		Compensation
Salary Vacation	Yearly Salary			Payroll Expenses		Compensation
Double-time hourly	Hourly Wage			Payroll Expenses		Compensation
Hourly	Hourly Wage			Payroll Expenses		Compensation
Hourly Sick	Hourly Wage			Payroll Expenses		Compensation
Hourly Vacation	Hourly Wage			Payroll Expenses		Compensation
Overtime (x1.5) hourly	Hourly Wage			Payroll Expenses		Compensation
Dental Insurance (taxable)	Deduction	0.00			Payroll Liabilities	None
Health Insurance (taxable)	Deduction	0.00			Payroll Liabilities	None
Advance Earned Income Credit	Federal Tax				Payroll Liabilities	Advance EIC Payment
Federal Unemployment	Federal Tax	0.6%	7,000.00	Payroll Expenses	Payroll Liabilities	FUTA
Federal Withholding	Federal Tax				Payroll Liabilities	Federal
Medicare Company	Federal Tax	1.45%		Payroll Expenses	Payroll Liabilities	Comp. Medicare
Medicare Employee	Federal Tax	1.45%			Payroll Liabilities	Medicare
Social Security Company	Federal Tax	6.2%	117,000.00	Payroll Expenses	Payroll Liabilities	Comp. SS Tax
Social Security Employee	Federal Tax	6.2%	117,000.00		Payroll Liabilities	SS Tax
CA - Withholding	State Withholding Tax				Payroll Liabilities	SWH
CA - Disability	State Disability Tax	1.0%	101,636.00		Payroll Liabilities	SDI
CA - Unemployment	State Unemployment Tax	3.4%	7,000.00	Payroll Expenses	Payroll Liabilities	Comp. SUI
CA - Employment Training Tax	Other Tax	0.1%	7,000.00	Payroll Expenses	Payroll Liabilities	Co. Paid Other Tax
Medicare Employee Addl Tax	Other Tax	0.9%			Payroll Liabilities	Medicare Addl Tax

Close the report

9

COMPLETE EMPLOYEE INFORMATION

Once the Payroll Setup is complete, there will be a few items that still need to be entered for each employee. At the same time, corrections to employee information may be made.

MEMO
DATE: January 1, 2015

Complete the Employee Information

Angela Aguilar: Add Marital Status: Single, U.S. Citizen: Yes, Ethnicity: Hispanic/Latino, Disability: No. Main Phone: 760-555-8348.
Drake Childs: Add Marital Status: Married, U.S. Citizen: Yes, Ethnicity: White, Disability: No. Main Phone: 760-555-1386. Correct the accrual dates for sick and vacation time to 06/30/2004

Open the Employee Center and enter the required information and changes

Open the **Employee Center** as previously instructed
Double-click **Aguilar, Angela** in the Employee List
On the Personal tab, enter her MARITAL STATUS: **Single**; U.S. CITIZEN: **Yes**; ETHNICITY: **Hispanic/Latino**; DISABILITY: **No**

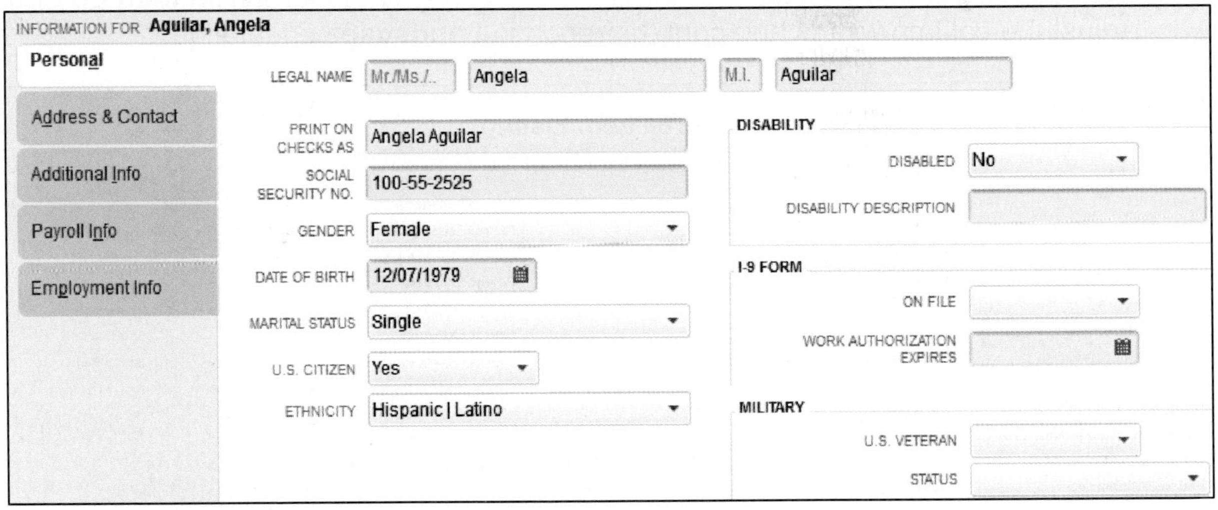

Click the **Address & Contact** tab, enter MAIN PHONE: **760-555-8348**
Click **OK** to save her new information
For Drake Childs, complete the information on the Personal and Address & Contact tabs using the information in the memo
When that is complete, click the **Payroll Info** tab; click the **Sick/Vacation** button
Change the Begin accruing dates for sick time and vacation time to his employment date of **06/30/2004**

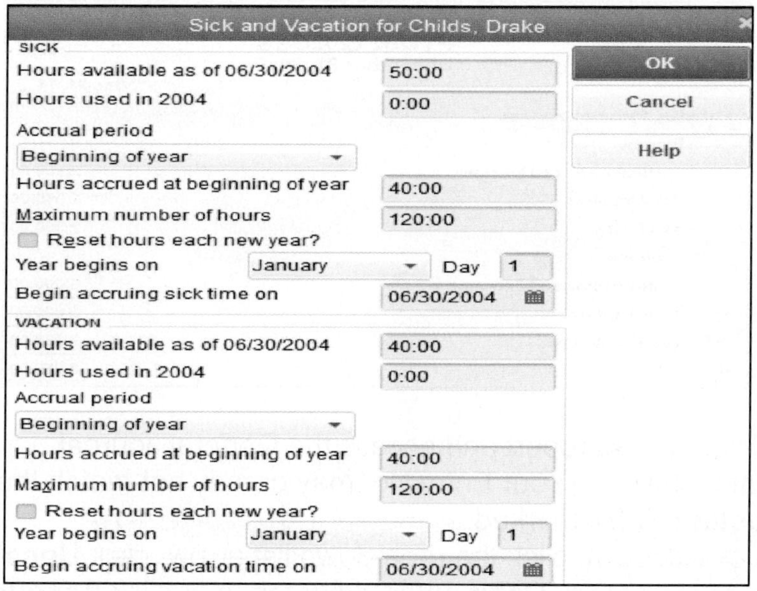

Click **OK** on the Sick and Vacation screen for Childs, Drake; click **OK** on the Edit Employee screen; close the Employee Center

ADJUSTING ENTRIES

When the company setup is completed, the amounts for money due (Income) and money owed (Expenses) are placed in Uncategorized Income and Uncategorized Expenses accounts. That way the amounts listed will not be interpreted as income or expenses for the current period. An adjustment need to be entered in the General Journal to close Uncategorized Income and Uncategorized Expenses.

MEMO
DATE: January 1, 2015

Use the date 12/31/14 and make the adjusting entry to transfer Uncategorized Income and Uncategorized Expenses to First & Last Name, Capital

Transfer the Uncategorized Income and Expenses to the owner's capital account

Prepare a Profit & Loss Statement for **12/31/14**
Note the amount for Uncategorized Income of $2,950.00 and the amount for Uncategorized Expenses of $5,000.00
- A General Journal entry needs to be made to transfer the two amounts into First & Last Name, Capital.

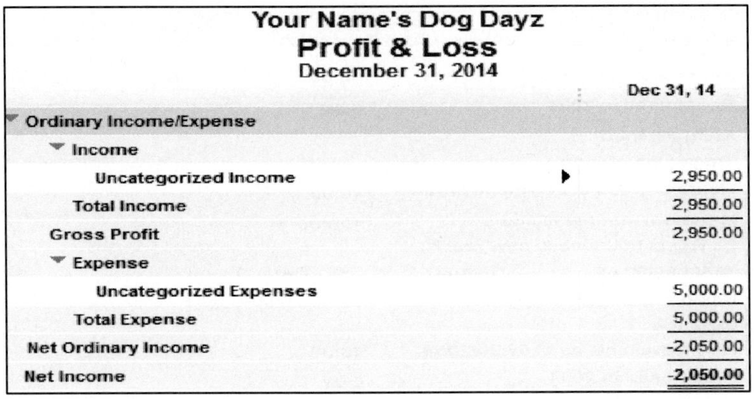
Your Name's Dog Dayz
Profit & Loss
December 31, 2014

	Dec 31, 14
Ordinary Income/Expense	
Income	
Uncategorized Income	2,950.00
Total Income	2,950.00
Gross Profit	2,950.00
Expense	
Uncategorized Expenses	5,000.00
Total Expense	5,000.00
Net Ordinary Income	-2,050.00
Net Income	-2,050.00

Close the Profit & Loss report and access the General Journal
Enter the date **12/31/14** (Your Entry No. may or may not match the illustration.)
Leave **Adjusting Entry** marked
Tab to or click **Account**, click the drop-down list arrow, click **Uncategorized Income**, tab to or click **Debit** enter **2950**, tab to or click **Account**, click the drop-down list arrow, click **First & Last Name, Capital**

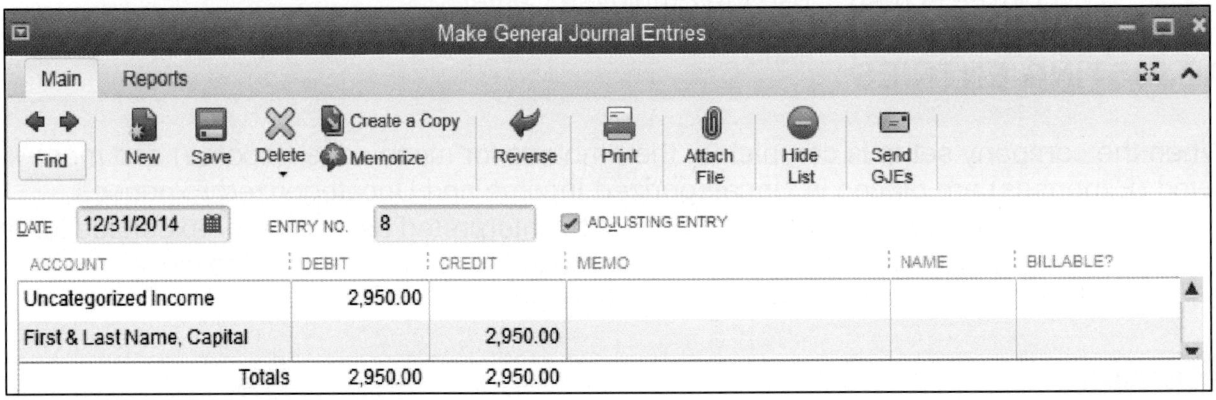

Click **Save & New**
Enter the adjustment to transfer the amount of **Uncategorized Expenses** to **First & Last Name, Capital**

- Remember, you will debit the Capital account and credit the Uncategorized Expenses account.

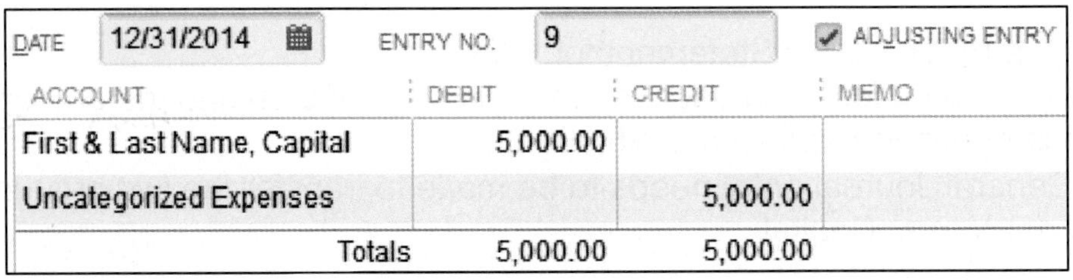

DATE 12/31/2014
ENTRY NO. 9
ADJUSTING ENTRY
ACCOUNT
DEBIT
CREDIT
MEMO
First & Last Name, Capital 5,000.00
Uncategorized Expenses 5,000.00
Totals 5,000.00 5,000.00

Click **Save & Close**

PRINT BALANCE SHEET

At the completion of the company setup, it is helpful to print a Balance Sheet to confirm that Assets = Liabilities + Owner's Equity

Prepare a **Standard Balance Sheet** for **January 1, 2015**

Total Assets of **$88,835.00** should equal the Total Liabilities + Owners Equities of **$88,835.00**

Your Name's Dog Dayz
Balance Sheet
As of January 1, 2015

	Jan 1, 15
ASSETS	
Current Assets	68,135.00
Fixed Assets	20,700.00
TOTAL ASSETS	88,835.00
LIABILITIES & EQUITY	
Liabilities	9,500.00
Equity	
First & Last Name, Capital	
First & Last Name, Investment	25,000.00
First & Last Name, Capital - Other	54,335.00
Total First & Last Name, Capital	79,335.00
Total Equity	79,335.00
TOTAL LIABILITIES & EQUITY	88,835.00

Print the report in Portrait orientation; then close the report

BACKUP

As in previous chapters, a backup of the data file for Your Name's Dog Dayz should be made.

Back up the company file to **Dog Dayz (Backup Ch. 9)** as instructed in earlier chapters and make a duplicate disk as instructed by your professor

SUMMARY

In this chapter a company was created using the QuickBooks Setup and the Easy Step Interview. Once the Setup and Interview were complete, the Chart of Accounts/General Ledger was customized. Sales items, customers and vendors were added. Preferences were customized. A company logo was added. The Payroll Setup was completed and employees were added. Adjusting entries were made

END-OF-CHAPTER QUESTIONS

TRUE/FALSE

ANSWER THE FOLLOWING QUESTIONS IN THE SPACE PROVIDED BEFORE THE QUESTION NUMBER.

F 1. You must use the Quick Setup to add customers and vendors.

F 2. The QuickBooks Setup is used to add year-to-date earnings for employees.

T 3. If you setup a company using the EasyStep Interview, you will enter the company name, address, and Tax ID number as part of the Interview.

F 4. Permanently removing the date prepared and time prepared from a balance sheet heading is done the first time you complete a balance sheet.

T 5. The start date is the date you select to begin tracking financial information for your company in QuickBooks.

T 6. The EasyStep Interview allows you to have QuickBooks generate a chart of accounts.

F 7. When the QuickBooks Setup is complete, the Uncategorized Expenses account contains a balance that reflects the total amount of all receivables accounts.

F 8. When using the EasyStep Interview to set up income and expenses, you must type in the name of every income and expense account you use.

F 9. The Item List is automatically generated in the QuickBooks Payroll Setup.

T 10. Customer credit terms and credit limits are entered into customer accounts in the Customer Center.

MULTIPLE CHOICE

WRITE THE LETTER OF THE CORRECT ANSWER IN THE SPACE PROVIDED BEFORE THE QUESTION NUMBER.

__B__ 1. Send Forms preferences contain default text for business documents sent by ___.
A. Fax
B. E-mail
C. Fed-Ex
D. All of the above

__C__ 2. Adjusting entries that must be made after the company setup are ___.
A. Close Uncategorized Income to Capital
B. Close Uncategorized Expenses to Capital
C. Both of the above
D. None of the above

__D__ 3. Colored icons and Company File Color Schemes are selected in the ___ Preference.
A. General
B. Customize
C. Other
D. Desktop View

__C__ 4. The Payroll Setup is accessed on the ___.
A. File menu
B. Payroll & Employees Preferences
C. Employees menu
D. All of the above

__B__ 5. In order to process payroll manually, you must go through the ___ to designate this choice.
A. Payroll menu
B. Help menu
C. QuickBooks Setup
D. Company Configuration

__D__ 6. The Company File has a _____ extension.
A. .qbb
B. .qbi
C. .qbp
D. .qbw

C 7. When a(n) ___ account is created, you must provide an opening balance.
A. Income
B. Expense
C. Asset
D. Posting

A 8. Select to display employee names by last name on the ___.
A. Payroll & Employees Preferences
B. Employee List
C. Employee Center
D. All of the above

B 9. Employee deductions for medical and dental insurance may be created ___.
A. during the QuickBooks EasyStep Interview
B. during the QuickBooks Payroll Setup
C. by clicking the Reports button at the bottom of the employee list
D. on the Employee Menu

D 10. Sales tax is listed on the ___.
A. Vendor List
B. Company List
C. Banking List
D. Item List

FILL-IN

IN THE SPACE PROVIDED, WRITE THE ANSWER THAT MOST APPROPRIATELY COMPLETES THE SENTENCE.

1. The asset account used for Inventory sales items is Inventory Asset.
2. In the Chart of Accounts, only Balance Sheet accounts have opening balances.
3. Accounts that are listed individually but are grouped together under a main account are called Sub accounts.
4. Checking Preferences warns you of duplicate check numbers.
5. The Year-to-Date Payrolls section of the QuickBooks Payroll Setup allows information for earnings, withholding, and payroll liabilities to be entered for the year-to-date.

SHORT ESSAY

List the six sections in the Payroll Setup and describe the purpose of each section.

____
____
____
____
____

NAME______________________

CHAPTER 9: TRANSMITTAL

YOUR NAME'S DOG DAYZ

Check the items below as you print them; then attach the documents and reports in the order listed when you submit them to your instructor.

___ Customer & Job List
___ Vendor List
___ Item Listing
___ Account Listing
___ Angela Aguilar Employee Summary
___ Drake Childs Employee Summary
___ Payroll Item Listing
___ Balance Sheet, January 1, 2015

END-OF-CHAPTER PROBLEM

YOUR NAME'S COFFEE CORNER

Your Name's Coffee Corner is a fictitious company located in San Francisco, California, and is a sole proprietorship owned by you. You sell coffee and pastries and provide catering service for meetings and lunches. You are involved in all aspects of the business. There is one full-time employee, Carole Chen, who is paid a salary. She manages the store, is responsible for the all the employees, and keeps the books. There is one full-time hourly employee, Colleen Stevens, who works in the shop and provides catering service.

CREATE A NEW COMPANY

➤ Use the following information to complete the QuickBooks Setup and EasyStep Interview for Your Name's Coffee Corner.

- **Your Name's Coffee Corner** *(Use your actual name)* is the Company Name and the Legal Name
- Federal Tax ID 45-6221346
- Address: 550 Powell Street, San Francisco, CA 94102
- Phone: 415-555-4646; Fax: 415-555-6464
- E-mail: YourName@CoffeeCorner.com (*Use your actual name*)
- Web: www.CoffeeCorner.com
- Type of Business: Retail Shop or Online Commerce
- Company Organization: Sole Proprietorship
- Fiscal year starts in January
- Do not use Passwords
- File Name: Your Name's Coffee Corner
- File Type: qbw
- Sell: Both services and products
- Record each sale individually, do charge sales tax
- Do not use estimates, statements, progress invoicing, or track time
- Do track customer orders (sales orders) and inventory
- Do manage bills
- Employees: Yes, W-2 Employees
- Date to start tracking finances is: 01/01/2015 (If your date is not 01/01/15, select "Use today's date or the first day of the quarter" and enter 01/01/15.)
- Scroll through the list of the income and expense accounts created by QuickBooks, remove the check marks for Merchant Account Fees, Uniforms, and Ask My Accountant (New Accounts will be added later.)

➤ Click Start Working on the QuickBooks Setup screen.

9

SELECT A TOP ICON BAR

➤ Rather than use the Left Icon Bar, use the View menu to select a Top Icon Bar.

CHART OF ACCOUNTS

After QuickBooks Setup using the EasyStep Interview has been completed, you have created a partial Chart of Accounts. The Chart of Accounts must be customized to reflect the actual accounts used by Your Name's Coffee Corner.

▶ Customize the Chart of Accounts provided by QuickBooks:

- Add Bank Account: **Checking**, Bank Acct. No.: **5147965513**, Routing Number: **121000273**, Statement Ending Balance: **35,871**, Statement Ending Date **12/31/14**
- Delete: Accumulated Depreciation, Furniture and Equipment, and Security Deposits Asset
- Make Inactive: Meals and Entertainment
- Edit Equity Accounts:
  - Change the name of Opening Balance Equity to **First & Last Name, Capital** (use your real name) and delete the description
  - Change Owners Equity to **Owner's Equity**, delete the description
  - Change Owners Draw to **First & Last Name, Withdrawals** (use your real name); Subaccount of First & Last Name, Capital, delete the description
- Add Equity Accounts:
  - **First & Last Name, Investment** (use your real name); Subaccount of First & Last Name, Capital; Opening Balance **$35,000** as of **12/31/14**
- Edit Income Accounts:
  - Rename Merchandise Sales to **Sales**, delete the description, Tax-Line **<Unassigned>**
- Add Income Accounts:
  - Add **Catering Sales**, subaccount of Sales
  - Add **Coffee Sales**, subaccount of Sales
  - Add **Pastry Sales**, subaccount of Sales
- Add Other Income Account: **Other Income**
- Add Expense Account: **Store Supplies Expense**
- Add Other Expense Account: **Other Expenses**
- Edit Expense Accounts: Rename Office Supplies to **Office Supplies Expense**, Tax-Line **<Unassigned>**
- Delete: Descriptions for each account
- Change: Tax-Line Mapping to **Unassigned** for each account

▶ Set up the following Balance Sheet accounts and balances. The Opening Balance date is **12/31/14**.

CHART OF ACCOUNTS			
Account Type	**Account Name**	**Sub-Account of**	**Opening Balance 12/31/14**
Other Current Asset	Prepaid Insurance		$1,200.00
Other Current Asset	Office Supplies		$950.00
Other Current Asset	Store Supplies		$1,800.00
Fixed Asset	Store Fixtures		
Fixed Asset	Original Cost	Store Fixtures	$18,000.00
Fixed Asset	Depreciation	Store Fixtures	$-1,800.00
Long-Term Liability	Store Fixtures Loan		$2,000.00

▶ Close the Chart of Accounts without printing.

ADD CUSTOMERS

▶ Access the Customer Center and enter the information provided in the following chart.

CUSTOMERS		
Customer Name	Melissa Johnson, Inc.	Training, Inc.
Opening Balance	1,500.00	5,245.00
As of	12/31/14	12/31/14
Company Name	Melissa Johnson, Inc.	Training, Inc.
Main Phone	415-555-1248	415-555-8762
Address	583 Mason Street	490 Harvard Street
City, State Zip	San Francisco, CA 94102	San Francisco, CA 94102
Payment Terms	Net 30	Net 30
Credit Limit	2,000.00	8,000.00
Preferred Delivery Method	Mail	Mail
Preferred Payment Method	Check	Visa
Credit Card Information		4178 2671 6492 357
Exp. Date		02/19
Name on Card		Training, Inc.
Address		490 Harvard Street
Zip		94102
Tax Code	Tax	Tax
Tax Item	State Tax	State Tax

▶ Print the Customer & Job List in Portrait orientation.

- Remember, once a credit card number is entered into QuickBooks, when you close the program, you will get a Customer Credit Card Protection screen the next time you open QuickBooks. Click **Disable Protection**; and then click **Yes** on the Disable Sensitive Data Protection.

ADD VENDORS

▶ Access the Vendor Center and enter the information provided in the following two charts.

VENDORS		
Vendor and Company Name	Coffee Royale	Elegant Pastries
Opening Balance	1,000.00	500.00
As of	12/31/14	12/31/14
Main Phone	415-555-3614	415-555-8712
Fax	415-555-4163	415-555-2178
Address	195 N. Market Street	671 7th Street
City, State, Zip	San Francisco, CA 94103	San Francisco, CA 94102
Payment Terms	2% 10, Net 30	2% 10, Net 30
Credit Limit	3,000.00	2,500.00

VENDORS				
Vendor and Company Name	Employment Development Department	SF Bank	Insurance Organization of California	State Board of Equalization
Main Phone	415-555-5248	415-555-9781	415-555-2347	916-555-0000
Fax	415-555-8425	415-555-1879	415-555-7432	916-555-1111
Address	10327 Hyde Street	205 Hill Street	20951 Oakmont Avenue	7800 State Street
City, State, Zip	San Francisco, CA 94107	San Francisco, CA 94104	San Francisco, CA 94103	Sacramento, CA 94265

→ Print the Vendor List in Portrait orientation.

ADD SALES ITEMS

▶ Use the information in the following chart to add the Service Item.

SERVICE ITEM	
Item Name	Catering
Description	Catering
Rate	50.00
Tax Code	Non
Income Account	Catering Sales

► Use the information in the following chart to add the Inventory Items.

INVENTORY ITEMS		
Item Name	Coffee	Pastry
Purchase and Sales Description	Coffee	Pastry
Cost	0.00	0.00
COGS Account	Cost of Goods Sold	Cost of Goods Sold
Preferred Vendor	Coffee Royale	Elegant Pastries
Sales Price	0.00	0.00
Tax Code	Tax	Tax
Income Account	Coffee Sales	Pastry Sales
Inventory Asset Account	Inventory Asset	Inventory Asset
Reorder Point (Min)	500	600
Max	1,550	1,800
On-Hand	1,500	1,750
Total Value	12,000	1,750
As Of	12/31/14	12/31/14

► Delete the following sales items: Consignment Item, Non-Inventory Item, and Local Tax.
► Edit the State Tax item. The name and description should be CA Sales Tax The rate is 8.75% and is paid to the State Board of Equalization.
► Print the Item Listing in Landscape orientation. Resize the columns; do not display columns for Quantity on Sales Order and Quantity on Purchase Order. Customize the report to use the date of **January 1, 2015** as the Subtitle and to remove Date and Time Prepared.

PRINT AN ACCOUNT LISTING

9

► Prepare the Account Listing; then open the Chart of Accounts to the accounts in that have descriptions and Tax Lines that are not <Unassigned>. Delete the descriptions and change the tax line.

► Print an Account Listing in Portrait orientation. Customize the report to use the date of **January 1, 2015** as the Subtitle and to remove Date and Time Prepared. Resize columns and do not include the Description or Tax Line columns in your report.

Your Name's Coffee Corner
Account Listing
January 1, 2015

Account	Type	Balance Total
Checking	Bank	35,871.00
Accounts Receivable	Accounts Receivable	6,745.00
Inventory Asset	Other Current Asset	13,750.00
Office Supplies	Other Current Asset	950.00
Prepaid Insurance	Other Current Asset	1,200.00
Store Supplies	Other Current Asset	1,800.00
Store Fixtures	Fixed Asset	16,200.00
Store Fixtures:Depreciation	Fixed Asset	-1,800.00
Store Fixtures:Original Cost	Fixed Asset	18,000.00
Accounts Payable	Accounts Payable	1,500.00
Payroll Liabilities	Other Current Liability	0.00
Sales Tax Payable	Other Current Liability	0.00
Store Fixtures Loan	Long Term Liability	2,000.00
First & Last Name, Capital	Equity	67,771.00
First & Last Name, Capital:First & Last Name, Investment	Equity	35,000.00
First & Last Name, Capital:First & Last Name, Withdrawals	Equity	0.00
Owner's Equity	Equity	
Sales	Income	
Sales:Catering Sales	Income	
Sales:Coffee Sales	Income	
Sales:Pastry Sales	Income	
Sales Discounts	Income	
Uncategorized Income	Income	
Cost of Goods Sold	Cost of Goods Sold	
Advertising and Promotion	Expense	
Automobile Expense	Expense	
Bank Service Charges	Expense	
Computer and Internet Expenses	Expense	
Depreciation Expense	Expense	
Insurance Expense	Expense	
Interest Expense	Expense	
Janitorial Expense	Expense	
Office Supplies Expense	Expense	
Payroll Expenses	Expense	
Professional Fees	Expense	
Rent Expense	Expense	
Repairs and Maintenance	Expense	
Store Supplies Expense	Expense	
Telephone Expense	Expense	
Uncategorized Expenses	Expense	
Utilities	Expense	
Other Income	Other Income	
Other Expenses	Other Expense	

CUSTOMIZE PREFERENCES

► Make the following changes to Preferences:
- Accounting: Company Preferences—Deselect the Date Warnings for past and future transactions

- Checking: Company Preferences—Select Default Accounts for Open the Create Paychecks and Open the Pay Payroll Liabilities to Checking
- Checking: My Preferences—Select Default Accounts to Checking for Open the Write Checks, Open the Pay Bills, Open the Pay Sales Tax, and Open the Make Deposits
- Desktop View: My Preferences—Switch to colored icons/light background on the Top Icon Bar and select a Company File Color Scheme of Brown
- Payroll & Employees: Company Preferences—Deselect Job Costing for paycheck expenses and select Display Employee List by Last Name
- Reports & Graphs: Company Preferences— For Reports-Show Items By: Select Name only, remove the checkmark from "Default formatting for reports" and then modify the report Format for the Header/Footer to remove the Date Prepared, Time Prepared, and Report Basis from reports
- Reports & Graphs: My Preferences—Refresh reports automatically
- Sales & Customers: Company Preferences—select No Custom Pricing
- Sales Tax: Company Preferences—Most common sales tax is CA Sales Tax

ADD COMPANY LOGO

▶ Add the company logo for Coffee Corner to the Insights page (Remember to look in your QB 2015 Ch 5-8 Master Company Files folder for the logo.)

SELECT MANUAL PAYROLL

▶ Prior to completing the QuickBooks Payroll Setup, select **Manual Payroll**.

▶ Begin the QuickBooks Payroll Setup.

QUICKBOOKS PAYROLL SETUP

▶ Complete the **Company** portion of the QuickBooks Payroll Setup:

- Compensation List: Salary, Hourly wage and overtime; deselect Bonus, award, or one-time compensation
- Insurance Benefits: Health Insurance, Dental Insurance (both are fully paid by the employee after taxes have been deducted) (The vendor for Health and Dental insurance is Insurance Organization of California.) Make sure **I don't need a regular payment schedule for this item** is selected
- Retirement Benefits: None
- Paid Time Off: Sick Time and Vacation Time
- Additions and Deductions: None

▶ Use the following information to add the two employees. Print a Summary Report for each employee.

EMPLOYEES Carole Chen and Colleen Stevens		
Legal Name	Carole Chen	Colleen Stevens
Employee Status	Active	Active
Home Address	9077 Harvard Avenue	1088 17th Street
City	San Francisco	San Francisco
State	CA	CA
Zip Code	94101	94103
Employee Type	Regular	Regular
Social Security No.	100-55-9107	100-55-5201
Hire Date	02/19/2001	06/30/2007
Birth Date	09/29/1975	07/17/1980
Gender	Female	Female
Pay Period	Monthly	Monthly
Compensation	Salary: $21,000 per year	Hourly wage: $9.50 Double-time hourly: $19.00 Overtime (x1.5) hourly: $14.25
Dental Insurance	$10 per month, annual limit $120	$10 per month, annual limit $120
Health Insurance	$35 per month, annual limit $420	$25 per month, annual limit $300
Sick Time Earns	40:00 at beginning of year	40:00 at beginning of year
Unused Sick Hours	Have an accrual limit	Have an accrual limit
Maximum Hours	120:00	120:00
Earns	Time off currently	Time off currently
Hours Available as of 01/01/2015 (your computer date will show)	30:00	20:00
Vacation Time Earns	40:00 at beginning of year	40:00 at beginning of year
Unused Vacation Hours	Have an accrual limit	Have an accrual limit
Maximum Hours	120:00	120:00
Earns	Time off currently	Time off currently
Hours Available as of 01/01/15 (Your computer date will show)	40:00	20:00
Payment Method	Check (no Direct Deposit)	Check (no Direct Deposit)

EMPLOYEES Carole Chen and Colleen Stevens		
State Subject to Withholding	CA	CA
State Subject to Unemployment Tax	CA	CA
Live or Work in Another State in 2015	No	No
Federal Filing Status	Single	Married
Allowances (Federal)	0	2
Extra Withholding	0.00	0.00
Nonresident Alien Withholding	Does not apply	Does not apply
HIRE Act Exemption	Not a qualified employee	Not a qualified employee
Subject to	Medicare Social Security Federal Unemployment	Medicare Social Security Federal Unemployment
State Filing Status	Single	Married (two incomes)
Regular Withholding Allowances	0	2
Subject to	CA-Unemployment CA-Employment Training Tax CA-Disability	CA-Unemployment CA-Employment Training Tax CA-Disability
Special Local Taxes	No	No
Wage Plan Code	S	S

- Print the Summary for each employee.
- Complete the **Taxes** section of the QuickBooks Payroll Setup:
  - State Payroll Tax Rates— CA-Disability Employee Rate: 1%; CA-Employment Training Tax Company: 0.1%; California-Unemployment Company Rate: 3.4%
  - Federal Payroll Taxes— Schedules 940 and 941/944/943: Payee: United States Treasury, Frequency: Quarterly
  - State Payroll Taxes—Payee: Employee Development Department; Employer Account No.: 999-9999-9, Payment frequency: Quarterly
- Complete the **Year-to-Date Payrolls** section of the QuickBooks Payroll Setup. No paychecks have been issued this year.
- After completing the Payroll Setup, print the Payroll Item Listing in Landscape orientation using the Report menu or Report Center.

COMPLETE EMPLOYEE INFORMATION

- Open the Employee Center; enter additional employee information in the table below:

EMPLOYEES		
Employee Name	Chen, Carole	Stevens, Colleen
Marital Status	Single	Married
U.S. Citizen	Yes	Yes
Ethnicity	Asian	Black/African American
Disability	No	No
Main Phone	415-555-7801	415-555-7364

- ▶ Check the accrual dates for sick and vacation for Colleen Stevens; if the date is 02/19/01 change it to her hire date of 06/30/07.

ADJUSTMENTS, BALANCE SHEET, AND BACKUP

- ▶ Record the adjusting entry to transfer Uncategorized Income and Uncategorized Expenses to Your Name's, Capital. Date the entry 12/31/14.
- ▶ Print the Balance Sheet for January 1, 2015 in Portrait orientation.
- ▶ Backup your company file to **Your Name's Coffee Corner (Backup Ch. 9)**.

NAME________________________

CHAPTER 9: TRANSMITTAL

YOUR NAME'S COFFEE CORNER

Check the items below as you print them; then attach the documents and reports in the order listed when you submit them to your instructor.

___ Customer & Job List
___ Vendor List
___ Item Listing
___ Account Listing
___ Carole Chen Employee Summary
___ Colleen Stevens Employee Summary
___ Payroll Item Listing
___ Balance Sheet, January 1, 2015

COMPREHENSIVE PRACTICE SET:

YOUR NAME'S CAPITOL BOOKS

The following is a comprehensive practice set that includes all the elements of QuickBooks studied throughout the text. In this practice set you will set up a company and keep the books for January 2015 (or the year that your instructor specifies). You will use the QuickBooks Setup/EasyStep Interview to create Your Name's Capitol Books. Once the company has been created, you will add customers, vendors, and sales items, finalize the Chart of Accounts, and select Preferences. The QuickBooks Payroll Setup will be completed and employees added. Adjustments will be made to accounts and various items, transactions will be recorded, and reports will be prepared.

YOUR NAME'S CAPITOL BOOKS

Your Name's Capitol Books is a fictitious company that provides keyboarding services and sells books and educational supplies. Your Name's Capitol Books is located in Sacramento, California, and is a sole proprietorship owned by you. You do all the purchasing and are involved in all aspects of the business. Your Name's Capitol Books has one full-time employee who is paid a salary, Ms. Andrea Nahid, who manages the store, is responsible for the all the employees, and keeps the books. Tom Parker is a full-time hourly employee who works in the shop. The store is currently advertising for a part-time employee who will provide keyboarding services.

CREATE A NEW COMPANY

▶ Use the following information to complete the QuickBooks Setup:
- Company and Legal Name: **Your Name's Capitol Books** (*Key in your actual name*)
- Federal Tax ID: **46-6521446**
- Address: **1055 Front Street, Sacramento, CA 95814**
- Phone: **916-555-9876**; Fax: **916-555-6789**
- E-mail: **YourName@CapitolBooks.com** (don't forget to use your real name)
- Web: **www.CapitolBooks.com**
- Type of Business: **Retail Shop or Online Commerce**
- Company Organization: **Sole Proprietorship**
- Fiscal Year Starts: **January**
- Passwords: **No**
- File Name: **Your Name's Capitol Books.qbw (**don't forget to use your real name)
- Sell **Both Services and Products**, record each sale **individually**
- Charge Sales tax: **Yes**

- Estimates, statements, progress invoicing, or track time: **No**
- Track customer orders (sales orders), track inventory: **Yes**
- Manage bills: **Yes**
- Employees**: Yes, W-2 Employees**
- Date to start tracking finances: **01/01/15** (If your date is not 01/01/15, select "Use today's date or the first day of the quarter" and enter 01/01/15.)
- Use QuickBooks to set up the **Income and Expense Accounts**
- Review Income and Expense Accounts: Refer to the Chart of Accounts on Page 672
  - Remove: Merchant Account Fees, Merchandise Sales, Advertising and Promotion, Automobile Expense, Meals and Entertainment, Professional Fees, Uniforms, and Ask My Accountant by clicking the √ column to remove the checkmark
  - Add: Purchase Discounts, Equipment Rental, Miscellaneous Expense, Postage and Delivery, Printing and Reproduction, and Interest Income

► Start Working

SELECT A TOP ICON BAR (OPTIONAL)

► If you wish to use a Top Icon Bar, use the View Menu to change from the Left Icon Bar.

DATES

► The year used in the text is 2015. As usual, check with your instructor to determine the year you should use. When creating a new company, all As of dates and dates for Opening Balances is **12/31/14**.

CHART OF ACCOUNTS

► Use the following chart of accounts and balances to customize the chart of accounts for Your Name's Capitol Books:
- To save space when printing, delete account descriptions for all accounts
- Use <Unassigned> for tax line mapping for all accounts
- Add Bank Account: Name: **Checking**; Bank Acct. No.:**123-456-10987**; Routing Number: **123025987**; Statement Ending Balance: **130,870.25**; Statement Ending Date: **12/31/14**
- Delete: Security Deposits Asset
  - If you did not delete the listed income and expense accounts during the company setup, do so now
- Edit Equity Accounts:
  - Change Opening Balance Equity to **First & Last Name, Capital** (use your real name)
  - Change Owners Equity to **Owner's Equity**
  - Change Owners Draw to **First & Last Name, Withdrawals**, subaccount of First & Last Name, Capital

- Add Equity Accounts: **First & Last Name, Investment**; Subaccount of First & Last Name, Capital; Opening Balance **75,000** as of **12/31/14**
- Add Income Accounts:
  - **Sales and Services Income**
  - **Keyboarding Services**; Subaccount of Sales and Services Income
  - **Book Sales**; Subaccount of Sales and Services Income
  - **Supplies Sales**; Subaccount of Sales and Services Income
- Add Master Card: Type: Credit Card, Account Name: **Master Card**, Opening Balance/Statement Ending Balance: **500.00**, Statement Ending Date: **12/31/14**
- Add Other Current Assets:
  - **Prepaid Insurance**, Opening Balance **1,200** as of **12/31/14**
  - **Supplies**, Opening Balance **1,950** as of **12/31/14**
- Edit Fixed Assets:
  - Change Furniture and Equipment to **Store Equipment & Fixtures**
  - Change Accumulated Depreciation to **Depreciation**, Subaccount of Store Equipment & Fixtures, Opening Balance **0.00** as of **12/31/14**
- Add Fixed Assets: Type: Fixed Asset, Account Name: **Original Cost**, Subaccount of: Store Equipment & Fixtures, Opening Balance: **18,000** as of **12/31/14**
- Add Long-Term Liability: **Store Equipment & Fixtures Loan**, Opening Balance **8,000** as of **12/31/14**
- Add Expense Accounts:
  - **Fire Insurance**, Subaccount of Insurance Expense
  - **Liability Insurance**, Subaccount of Insurance Expense
- Edit Expense Accounts: Change Office Supplies to **Supplies Expense**
- Make any other changes necessary to match your Chart of Accounts with the one on the next page
- Remember, once all the customers, vendors, and sales items are added, QuickBooks will add accounts and balances for Accounts Receivable, Accounts Payable, Cost of Goods Sold, Uncategorized Income, Uncategorized Expenses. Several other accounts will have balances inserted by QuickBooks; example, Inventory Asset.
- Not all changes to the Chart of Accounts have been made. They will be completed later in the practice set.
- Chart Abbreviations:
  - (QB)=Account Created by QuickBooks—Do not do anything for these
  - *** means that QuickBooks will enter the account balance
  - Indented Account Names indicate that the account is a subaccount
  - C.A.=Current Asset, F.A.=Fixed Asset, C.L.=Current Liability, Long Term L.=Long Term Liability, COGS=Cost of Goods Sold

YOUR NAME'S CAPITOL BOOKS CHART OF ACCOUNTS				
ACCOUNT	**TYPE**	**BALANCE**	**ACCOUNT**	**TYPE**
Checking (Statement Date: 12/31/14	Bank	130,870.25	Cost of Goods Sold (QB)	COGS
Accounts Receivable(QB)	Accts. Rec.	***2,850.00	Merchandise Discounts	COGS
Inventory Asset	Other C.A	***101,655.00	Bank Service Charges	Expense
Prepaid Insurance	Other C.A.	1,200.00	Computer and Internet Expenses	Expense
Supplies	Other C.A.	1,950.00	Depreciation Expense	Expense
Undeposited Funds (QB)	Other C.A.	***	Equipment Rental	Expense
Store Equipment & Fixtures	F.A.	***	Insurance Expense	Expense
Depreciation	F.A.	0.00	Fire Insurance	Expense
Original Cost	F.A.	18,000.00	Liability Insurance	Expense
Accounts Payable (QB)	Acct. Pay.	***2,300.00	Interest Expense	Expense
MasterCard (Statement Date: 12/31/14)	Credit Card	500.00	Janitorial Expense	Expense
Payroll Liabilities	Other C.L.	0.00	Miscellaneous Expense	Expense
Sales Tax Payable	Other C.L.	0.00	Payroll Expenses	Expense
Store Equipment & Fixtures Loan	Long Term L.	8,000.00	Postage and Delivery	Expense
First & Last Name, Capital	Equity	***	Printing and Reproduction	Expense
First & Last Name, Investment	Equity	75,000.00	Rent Expense	Expense
First & Last Name, Withdrawals	Equity	0.00	Repairs and Maintenance	Expense
Owner's Equity (QB)	Equity	***	Supplies Expense	Expense
Sales and Services Income	Income		Telephone Expense	Expense
Book Sales	Income		Uncategorized Expenses (QB)	Expense
Keyboarding Services	Income		Utilities	Expense
Supplies Sales	Income		Interest Income	Other Income
Sales Discounts	Income			
Uncategorized Income (QB)	Income			

► Close the Chart of Accounts without printing.

ADD CUSTOMERS

► Access the Customer Center and enter the information provided in the following chart:

CUSTOMERS				
Customer Name	**Total Training, Inc.**	**Johnson, Pamela**	**Sacramento Schools**	**Yu, Charlie**
Opening Balance	1,400.00	100.00	1,000.00	350.00
As of	12/31/14	12/31/14	12/31/14	12/31/14
Company Name	Total Training, Inc.		Sacramento Schools	
First Name		Pamela		Charlie
Last Name		Johnson		Yu
Main Phone	916-555-8762	916-555-8961	916-555-1235	916-555-2264
Address	212 Harvard Street	8025 Richmond Street	1085 2nd Street	253 Mason Street
City, State, Zip	Sacramento, CA 95814	Sacramento, CA 95814	Sacramento, CA 95814	Sacramento, CA 95814
Payment Terms	Net 30	2% 10, Net 30	2% 10, Net 30	Net 30
Credit Limit	1,500.00	500.00	5,000.00	350.00
Preferred Delivery Method	Mail	Mail	Mail	Mail
Preferred Payment Method		Check	Visa	Check
Credit Card Information			4388 3548 9987 358	
Exp. Date			06/2018	
Name on Card			Sacramento Schools	
Address			1085 2nd Street	
Zip			95814	
Tax Code	Tax	Tax	Tax	Tax
Tax Item	State Tax	State Tax	State Tax	State Tax

- Remember, once a credit card number is entered into QuickBooks, when you close the program, you will get a Customer Credit Card Protection screen the next time you open QuickBooks. Click **Disable Protection**; and then click **Yes** on the Disable Sensitive Data Protection.

ADD VENDORS

► Access the Vendor Center and enter the information provided in the following two charts:

VENDORS			
Vendor and Company Name	**Textbook Co.**	**Pens Galore**	**Supplies Co.**
Opening Balance	1,000.00	500.00	800.00
As of	12/31/14	12/31/14	12/31/14
Main Phone	916-555-2788	415-555-3224	916-555-5759
Fax	916-555-8872	415-555-4223	916-555-9575
Address	559 4th Street	8572 Market Street	95 8th Street
City, State, Zip	Sacramento, CA 95814	San Francisco, CA 94103	Sacramento, CA 95814
Payment Terms	2% 10, Net 30	2% 10, Net 30	2% 10, Net 30
Credit Limit	25,000.00	5,000.00	15,000.00

VENDORS				
Vendor and Company Name	**State Board of Equalization**	**Employment Development Department**	**Sacramento State Bank**	**Medical Ins., Inc.**
Main Phone	916-555-0000	916-555-8877	916-555-6446	415-555-2369
Fax	916-555-1111	916-555-7788	916-555-6464	415-555-9632
Address	7800 State Street	1037 California Street	102 8th Street	20865 Oak Street
City, State, Zip	Sacramento, CA 95814	Sacramento, CA 95814	Sacramento, CA 95814	San Francisco, CA 94101

ADD SALES ITEMS

► Use the following chart to add the Service Item.

SERVICE ITEM	
Name	Keyboarding
Description	Keyboarding Services
Rate	0.00
Tax Code	Non
Income Account	Keyboarding Services

► Use the information in the following chart to add the Inventory Part Items.

INVENTORY ITEMS					
Item Name	Paper	Paperback Books	Pen's, etc.	Stationery	Textbooks
Purchase and Sales Description	Paper Supplies	Paperback Books	Pen's, etc.	Stationery	Textbooks
Cost	4.00	5.00	3.00	7.50	50.00
COGS Account	Cost of Goods Sold	Cost of Goods Sold	Cost of Goods Sold	Cost of Goods Sold	Cost of Goods Sold
Preferred Vendor	Supplies Co.	Textbook Co.	Pens Galore	Supplies Co.	Textbook Co.
Sales Price	0.00	0.00	0.00	0.00	0.00
Tax Code	Tax	Tax	Tax	Tax	Tax
Income Account	Supplies Sales	Book Sales	Supplies Sales	Supplies Sales	Book Sales
Subaccount of	Sales and Services Income	Sales and Services Income	Sales and Services Income	Sales and Services Income	Sales and Services Income
Asset Account	Inventory Asset	Inventory Asset	Inventory Asset	Inventory Asset	Inventory Asset
Reorder Point (Min)	150	30	50	25	2,000
Max	200	40	60	35	2,010
On-Hand	200	45	50	30	2,000
Total Value	1,000.00	180.00	250.00	225.00	100,000.00
As of Date	12/31/14	12/31/14	12/31/14	12/31/14	12/31/14

- Delete: Local Tax (If Consignment or Non-inventory Part Item appear, delete them as well)
- Edit: the State Sales Tax Item, change the name and description to CA Sales Tax, tax rate of 8.0%, paid to State Board of Equalization

FINALIZE CHART OF ACCOUNTS

- Edit a Cost of Goods Sold Account: Purchase Discounts to Merchandise Discounts, Subaccount of Cost of Goods Sold

CUSTOMIZE PREFERENCES

▶ Change the following preferences:
- **Accounting**: Deselect the **Date Warnings** for past and future transactions
- **Checking**: My Preferences—Default Accounts to use is **Checking** for Open the Write Checks, Open the Pay Bills, Open the Pay Sales Tax, and Open the Make Deposits; Company Preferences— Select Default Accounts to use is **Checking** for Open the Create Paychecks and Open the Pay Payroll Liabilities

- **Desktop View**: My Preferences—Switch to **colored icons/light background** on the Top Icon Bar (if using). The Company File Color Scheme should be **Blue-Gray**
- **Payroll & Employees**: Company Preferences—Display Employee List by **Last Name**; deselect "Job Costing for paycheck expenses"
- **Reports & Graphs**: My Preferences—**Refresh** reports automatically, Company Preferences—Reports – Show Items By: **Name only**; Reports – Show Accounts By: **Name only**; modify the report Format for the Header/Footer to remove the **Date Prepared, Time Prepared, and Report Basis** from reports
- **Sales & Customers**: Company Preferences—select **No Custom Pricing**
- **Sales Tax**: Company Preferences—Most common sales tax is **CA Sales Tax**

ADD COMPANY LOGO

► Add the company logo for Books to the Insights page (Remember to look in your QB 2015 Ch 5-8 Master Company Files folder for the logo.)

PAYROLL

► Select Manual as the payroll option.

► Complete the Payroll Setup. (Remember that on some screens QuickBooks will show you the current computer date or current year. This should not make a difference as long as, whenever you enter a date, you use the same year as the one you used in the QuickBooks Setup.)

- Complete the Company portion of the setup:
  - Compensation List: **Salary** and **Hourly Wage and Overtime**
  - Insurance Benefits: **Health Insurance** and **Dental Insurance**. Both are fully **paid by the employee after taxes** have been deducted. The Payee/Vendor is **Medical Ins., Inc.**, you do not need a payment schedule
  - Retirement Benefits: **None**
  - Paid Time Off**: Sick Time** and **Vacation Time**
  - Additions and Deductions: **None**
- Use the Employee List below to add Employees
  - Print the Summary for each employee

EMPLOYEES Tom Parker and Andrea Nahid		
Legal Name	**Parker, Tom**	**Nahid, Andrea**
Employee Status	Active	Active
Home Address	383 Oak Avenue	1777 Watt Avenue
City	Sacramento	Sacramento
State	CA	CA
Zip Code	95814	95814

EMPLOYEES Tom Parker and Andrea Nahid		
Employee Type	Regular	Regular
Social Security No.	100-55-6886	100-55-5244
Hire Date	04/03/96	02/17/10
Birth Date	12/07/75	11/28/85
Gender	Male	Female
Pay Period	Monthly	Monthly
Compensation	$10.00 per hour $20.00 Double-time hourly $15.00 Overtime (x1.5) hourly	$26,000.00 per year
Dental Insurance	$20 per month, annual limit $240	$30 per month, annual limit $360
Health Insurance	$20 per month, annual limit $240	$30 per month, annual limit $360
Sick Time Earns	40:00 at beginning of year	40:00 at beginning of year
Unused Sick Hours	Have an accrual limit	Have an accrual limit
Maximum Hours	120:00	120:00
Earns	Time off currently	Time off currently
Hours Available as of 01/01/15	40:00	40:00
Vacation Time Earns	40:00 at beginning of year	40:00 at beginning of year
Unused Vacation Hours	Have an accrual limit	Have an accrual limit
Maximum Hours	120:00	120:00
Earns	Time off currently	Time off currently
Hours Available as of 01/01/15	40:00	40:00
Payment Method	Check (no Direct Deposit)	Check (no Direct Deposit)
State Subject to Withholding	CA	CA
State Subject to Unemployment Tax	CA	CA
Live or Work in Another State in 2015	No	No
Federal Filing Status	Married	Single
Allowances (Federal)	1	0
Extra Withholding	0.00	0.00
Nonresident Alien Withholding	Does not apply	Does not apply
HIRE Act Exemption	Not a qualified employee	Not a qualified employee
Subject to	Medicare Social Security Federal Unemployment	Medicare Social Security Federal Unemployment
State Filing Status	Married (one income)	Single
Regular Withholding Allowances	1	0
Subject to	CA-Unemployment CA-Employment Training Tax CA-Disability	CA-Unemployment CA-Employment Training Tax CA-Disability
Special Local Taxes	No	No
Wage Plan	S	S

- (Did you print each employee's summary?)

- Enter Payroll Tax information:
  - State Payroll Tax Rates: CA-Disability Employee Rate: 1%; CA-Employment Training Tax Company: 0.1%; California-Unemployment Company Rate: **3.4%**
  - Federal Payroll Taxes: Schedules 940 and 941/944/943: Payee **United States Treasury**, Frequency: **Quarterly**
  - State Payroll Taxes: Payee: **Employment Development Department**, Employer Account No. **999-9999-9**, Payment frequency: **Quarterly**

▶ Complete the **Year-to-Date Payrolls** section of the QuickBooks Payroll Setup.
- No paychecks have been issued this year.

COMPLETE EMPLOYEE INFORMATION

▶ Open the Employee Center; enter additional employee information in the table below:

EMPLOYEES		
Employee Name	Tom Parker	Andrea Nahid
Marital Status	Married	Single
U.S. Citizen	Yes	Yes
Ethnicity	White	Two or More Races
Disability	No	No
Main Phone	916-555-7862	916-555-1222

▶ Check the accrual dates for sick and vacation for Andrea Nahid; if the date is 04/03/96 change it to her hire date of 02/17/10.

MAKE ADJUSTMENTS

▶ Transfer the Uncategorized Income and Uncategorized Expenses to Your First & Last Name, Capital account. Date the General Journal entry **12/31/14**.

PRINT

▶ Compare your Chart of Accounts with the one shown on Page 673. When everything matches, prepare the Account Listing; then open the Chart of Accounts to the accounts in that have descriptions and Tax Lines that are not <Unassigned>. Delete the descriptions and change the tax line. Print an Account Listing in Portrait orientation. Customize the report to use the date of **January 1, 2015** as the Subtitle Resize the columns to display the names in full and remove the Description and Tax Line columns.

▶ Delete the Out of State Sales Tax Item. Print an Item Listing in Landscape orientation after resizing the columns to display all information in full and removing the columns for Quantity on Sales Order and Quantity on Purchase Order.

▶ Use the Report menu or Reports Center to print a Transaction List by Customer From December 31, 2014 To January 1, 2015 in Landscape orientation after resizing the columns to display all information in full.

- Use the Report menu or Reports Center to print a Transaction List by Vendor From December 31, 2014 To January 1, 2015 in Landscape orientation after resizing the columns to display all information in full.
- Print a Balance Sheet as of January 1, 2015.

CUSTOMIZE

- Customize business forms: Make the default title all capital letters, and use Layout Designer to make the area for the company name wide enough for your name. Use a duplicate of a Product Invoice. Then, customize Sales Receipts, Credit Memos, Sales Orders, and Purchase Orders so they have the same format as the invoice.

ENTER TRANSACTIONS

- During the month, add new customers, vendors, employees, items, and accounts as necessary.
- Create a Customer message for Credit Memos: **Your return has been processed.**
- You determine which memos to include in transactions.
- Unless otherwise specified, the terms for each sale or bill will be the one specified in the Customer or Vendor List.
- The transaction date will be the date the entry is made unless instructed otherwise.
- If a customer's order exceeds the established credit limit, accept the order.
- If the terms allow a discount for a customer, make sure to apply the discount if payment is received in time for the customer to take it. Remember, the discount period starts with the date of the invoice. If an invoice or bill date is not provided, use the transaction date to begin the discount period.
- Use Sales Discounts as the discount account.
- If a bill or customer payment is eligible for a discount and a return has been made, subtract the amount of the credit from the amount due and recalculate the discount based on the actual amount owed.
- If a customer has a credit and has a balance on the account, apply the credit to the invoice used for the sale. If there is no balance for a customer and a return is made, issue a credit memo and a refund check.
- Always pay bills in time to take advantage of purchase discounts.
- Most reports will be printed in Portrait orientation; however, if the report (such as the Journal) will fit across the page using Landscape orientation, use Landscape
- Whenever possible, adjust the column widths so that reports fit on one-page wide without selecting Fit report to one page wide.
- If a report format is changed and you prepare the report frequently, memorize the report.
- Print invoices, sales receipts, purchase orders, checks, and other items as they are entered in the transactions. Check with your instructor to see what should be printed.
- It is your choice whether or not to print lines around each field.

- Use the customized product invoice for all invoices (except those prepared from sales orders), and the customized credit memo for customer returns, voucher checks for payroll, and standard checks for all other checks.
- Prepare an Inventory Stock Status by Item Report every five days as the last transaction of the day to see if anything needs to be ordered. Print the report and hide the For Assemblies column. (This would be a good report to memorize.) Unless instructed otherwise, if anything is less than the Reorder Point (Min), order enough of the item so you will have the Max on hand. (For example, if you needed to order an item and the Reorder Point (Min) is 100, and the Max is 110, you would order enough to have 110 available. If sales orders have been recorded, the number of items available may be less than the number of items on hand so base your order on the number available. If you have 100 items on hand and 75 items available, you would order 35 items to reach the 110 Max Reorder Point.) For each item, use the Cost in the Item List.
- Full-time employees usually work 160 hours during a payroll period. Hourly employees working in excess of 160 hours in a pay period are paid overtime.
- Create a new report called Unpaid Bills with Terms Detail. Prepare an Unpaid Bills Detail report; then customize it by adding a column for Terms. When the report is memorized, use it every five days to determine which bills are eligible for discounts if they are paid within the discount period given in the transaction. If any bills qualify for payment, make comments on the report; such as, "Pay this bill." If there is a credit that should be applied, make a comment "Use this credit." Print the commented report. Remember, an opening balance is not eligible for a discount.
- In addition to preparing the Unpaid Bills with Terms report to determine bill payment, there will be some bills where payment instructions will be given in the transactions.
- Backup the company file every five days. Create your first backup file before recording transactions. Name the file **Your Name's Capitol Books (Backup Company)**, name subsequent files with the date. For example, your first backup that includes transactions would be named **Your Name's Capitol Books (Backup 01-05-15**). The final backup should be made at the end of the practice set. Name it **Your Name's Capitol Books (Backup Complete)**.

January 1

- Create a backup file and name it **Your Name's Capitol Books (Backup Company)**
- Add a new part-time hourly employee:
  - Personal Info:
    - Katie Gonzalez
    - Social Security No.: 100-55-3699
    - Gender: Female
    - Birthday: 1/3/90
    - Marital Status: Single
    - U.S. Citizen: Yes
    - Ethnicity: Hispanic/Latino
    - Disability: No

- Address & Contact
  - Address: 1177 Florin Road
  - City: Sacramento
  - State: CA
  - Zip: 95814
  - Main Phone: 916-555-7766
- Payroll Info:
  - Pay Frequency: Monthly
  - Hourly: $8.00, Overtime (x1.5) hourly: $12.00, Double-time hourly: $16.00
  - Dental and Health Insurance: None
  - Federal Taxes:
    - Filing Status and Allowance: Single, 0
    - Subject to: Medicare, Social Security, Federal Unemployment
  - State Taxes:
    - State Worked and State Subject to Withholding: California
    - Subject to, CA Unemployment (SUI), CA Disability taxes (SDI)
    - Filing Status and Allowance: Single, 0
  - Other Taxes:
    - CA Employment Training Tax
    - Medicare Employee Addl Tax
- Employment Info:
  - Hire Date: 01/01/15
  - Type: Regular
- On the Exit Message regarding Sick and Vacation Hours, click Leave as is

January 2:

- Katie typed a five-page paper at the rate of $5 per page, sold one $80 textbook, and three paperback books at $6.99 each to a Cash Customer. Received Check 2951 for the full payment. (QuickBooks may give you a variety of messages, mark so they do not display in the future.)
- Total Training, Inc. purchased 30 copies of a textbook on account for $95 each. (Accept transactions that are over the established credit limit.) (Did you use your customized invoice?)
- Received Check 1096 from Pamela Johnson for $100 as payment in full on her account. (An opening balance is not eligible for a discount.)
- Received a telephone call for a Sales Order from Sacramento Schools for 25 pens on account at $8.99 each and five reams of paper at $6.99 per ream.
- Sold one textbook at $79.99, one textbook for $95.99, one textbook for $125.00, one textbook for $139.95, and one textbook for $145.00 for the new quarter to a student using Visa # 4981 1292 7639 688, Expiration 02/2016.
- Prepare an Inventory Stock Status by Item report for January 1-2, 2015 to see if anything needs to be ordered. After resizing the columns and removing the column "For Assemblies," memorize the report, fit on 1-page wide, then print in Landscape. (Are pens and textbooks marked to order?)
- Prepare and print Purchase Orders for any merchandise that needs to be ordered. Check the number available and refer to the Reorder Qty column in the Inventory Stock

Status by Item report. Use this information to calculate the number of items to order. (Hint: Pens have a Max of 60 and because there are 25 pens on sales order, 25 are available. You will need to order more than the number shown in Reorder Qty column.)

- Check bills for discount eligibility. Pay any bills that qualify for a discount between January 1-4. If a bill is eligible for a discount but can be paid in five days and still get the discount, pay it later. (Remember opening balances do not qualify for a discount.) If any bills qualify, print the commented report Unpaid Bills with Terms.

January 3:

- Memorize a transaction for the bill. Add it to my Reminders List, How Often: Monthly, Next Date: 01/15/15. The bill will be recorded on the 15th and will be paid on January 30. The amount is $1,200 and is paid to Sacramento Rental, Main Phone: 916-555-1234, Fax: 916-555-4321, 1234 Front Street, Sacramento, CA 95814, Payment Terms Net 15, Account Setting: Rent Expense.
- Sacramento Schools picked up the merchandise from Sales Order 1. Create the invoice dated January 2, 2015 from the Sales Order. (Even though the "Product Invoice" was customized earlier in the practice set, the Sales Order Invoice was not. Once you create the invoice from the sales order, you should customize the Sales Order Invoice so that the default title, INVOICE, is all capital letters; and then, use Layout Designer to make room for your full name to print.
- Received Check 915 for $350 from Charlie Yu for the full amount due on his account.
- Sold two pens on account at $12.99 each and five boxes of stationery at $10.99 per box to Pamela Johnson.
- Received payment of $1,400 as payment in full for the opening balance from Total Training, Inc., Debit Card # 7681 8971 2685 556, Expiration 06/2016.

January 5:

- Sold two textbooks on account at $125 each to a new customer: Hector Gomez, Main Phone: 916-555-6841, Main E-mail: HGomez@email.com, 478 Front Street, Sacramento, CA 95814, Payment Terms: Net 10 (Do you need to add a new Standard Term for Net 10?), Credit Limit $500, Taxable, CA Sales Tax.
- Received the pens ordered from Pens Galore with the bill. (Did you date the transaction 01/05/15?)
- Received the textbooks ordered from Textbook Co. without the bill.
- Prepare and print Inventory Stock Status by Item Report for January 1-5, 2015. (Did you use your memorized report?)
- Order any items indicated. (Stationery) on the Inventory Stock Status by Item Report.
- Prepare an Unpaid Bills with Terms Detail report.
    - If the Terms column shows a discount percentage, calculate the discount date for the bill.
    - If a bill is eligible for a discount but can be paid on or after January 10 and still get the discount, do not pay it now.
    - If a bill qualifies for a discount between January 5-9, add the comment "Pay this bill" to the report.
    - If a bill qualifying for a discount has a credit, add the comment "Use this credit" to the report.

   - If you make comments on the report, print it. Otherwise, close without printing. Do not save the commented report.
- Pay any bills and credits marked in the commented report. Remember, if a credit is shown, apply it; and then, recalculate the discount. (Amount Due – Credit * Discount % = Discount) Remember, no discounts are available for opening balances.
- Deposit all cash, checks, debit card, and credit card payments received.
- Backup the company file.

January 7:

- Pamela Johnson returned two pens purchased on January 3. She did not like the color. Apply the credit to the invoice and print after you apply the credit to the invoice. (Did you use your Customer Message for Credit Memos?)
- Received the bill for the textbooks ordered from Textbook Co. Use the transaction date January 5, 2015.
- The nonprofit organization, State Schools, bought a classroom set of 30 computer training textbooks on account for $110.00 each and 15 reams of paper at $4.99 each. Add the new customer: State Schools, Main Phone: 916-555-8787, Fax: 916-555-7878, 451 State Street, Sacramento, CA 95814, Payment Terms: Net 30, Credit Limit: $5,000, Preferred Delivery Method: Mail, Preferred Payment Method: Check, Taxable, CA Sales Tax. Include a subtotal for the sale and apply a 10% sales discount for a nonprofit organization. (Create any new sales items necessary. Use Sales Discounts as the account for the nonprofit discount.)
- Add a new inventory part sales item for Gift Ware, Purchase Description: Gift Ware, Cost: 5.00, COGS Account: Cost of Goods Sold, Preferred Vendor: Abundant Gifts (Main Phone: 916-555-5384, Main E-mail: gifts@abc.com, Fax: 916-555-4835, 125 Oak Street, Sacramento, CA 95814, Payment Terms: Net 30, Credit Limit: $1,500), Sales Description: Gift Ware, Sales Price: 0.00, Tax Code: Tax, Income Account: Supplies Sales, Asset Account: Inventory Asset, Reorder Point (Min): 15; Max: 25, Quantity on Hand: 0, Value: 0.00, as of 01/07/2015.
- Order 15 gift ware items from Abundant Gifts.

January 8:

- Katie typed a 15-page report at $5.00 per page and sold ten reams of paper at $5.99 per ream on account to Pamela Johnson.
- Use Pay Bills to pay Textbook Co. the full amount owed on the opening balance of $1,000. Print Check 1 using Standard Checks. (Remember, no discounts are available for opening balances.)
- Received a telephone order for eight additional computer textbooks on account to Sacramento Schools at $110 each.

January 10:

- Sold three pens at $14.95 each, two sets of stationery at $14.99 each, and three paperback books at $6.99 each to a cash customer using cash as the payment method.
- Sacramento Schools picked up the merchandise on sales order. (Use January 10, 2015 for the invoice date.)

- Received Visa payment (card on file) from Sacramento Schools for the 01/02/15 Invoice for $274.87, the full amount due, less discount. (Did you use Sales Discounts as the Discount Account?)
- Received $1,000 as partial payment on account from Total Training, Inc., MasterCard # 5813 9878 3769 565, Expiration 03/2016.
- Deposit all cash, checks, debit card, and credit card receipts.
- Prepare Inventory Stock Status by Item Report for January 1-10, 2015. Order any items indicated. (If an item is marked to order but a purchase order has already been prepared, do not order any more of the item. Since Gift Ware was ordered on 01/07/15, it does not need to be ordered.)
- Prepare an Unpaid Bills with Terms Detail report.
  - If the Terms column shows a discount percentage, calculate the discount date for the bill.
  - If a bill is eligible for a discount but can be paid on or after January 15 and still get the discount, do not pay it now.
  - If a bill qualifies for a discount between January 10-4, add the comment "Pay this bill" to the report.
  - If a bill qualifying for a discount has a credit, add the comment "Use this credit" to the report.
  - If you make comments on the report, print it. Otherwise, close without printing. Do not save the commented report.
- Pay any bills and credits marked in the commented report. Remember, if a credit is shown, apply it; and then, recalculate the discount. (Amount Due – Credit * Discount % = Discount) Remember, no discounts are available for opening balances.
- Backup the company file.

January 11:

- Sold fifteen paperback books at $8.99 each and two pens at $35.99 each to a customer using MasterCard # 5928 7138 9129 741, Expiration 02/2017.
- Sold ten reams of paper $5.99 each, one pen $8.99, and one box of stationery $12.99 to a cash customer. Received Debit Card # 7134 2445 6123 789, Expiration 04/2018.

January 12:

- Katie typed a one-page letter with an envelope on account for Charlie Yu, $8.00. (Qty 1)
- Received gift ware ordered from Abundant Gifts. A bill was not included with the order.

January 13:

- Received Check 1265 from Pamela Johnson in payment for full amount due for Invoice 3 after discounts, $58.15. (Since the invoice has a return, subtract the amount of the Credit from the Amount Due; and, then, recalculate the discount.) Payment date is 01/13/2015.
- Received the textbooks and the bill from Textbook Co. for Purchase Order 5. Date the bill January 13, 2015.
- Received a notice from the bank that Check 915 for $350.00 from Charlie Yu was marked NSF and returned. Record the NSF check, the bank's $25 fee for the bad check, and Your Name's Capitol Books' fee of $40. Use the items created by

QuickBooks for the bounced check charges. Use the Copy of the Intuit Product Invoice, Terms: Due on Receipt, and the Customer Message: Please Remit to above address for Invoice 10 for the Bounced Check Charges and the Opening Balance Invoice. Print both invoices.

January 14:

- Received Check 10-283 for $270.00 from Hector Gomez in payment of Invoice 4.
- Received Charlie Yu's Debit Card # 7982 5698 7632 453, Expiration 03/2016 for payment in full payment of $398.00 for his account. (Record this just like you would record a regular payment on account.)
- Received seven boxes of stationery ordered from Supplies Co. The bill was included with the stationery and the three missing boxes are on back order. (Was your Purchase Order 3 to Supplies Co. for 10 boxes of stationery?)

January 15:

- Use your memorized transaction to record the bill for rent.
- Received Check 1278 from Pamela Johnson in payment for full amount due for Invoice 7 after discounts $136.90.
- Deposit all cash, checks, debit card, and credit card receipts.
- Prepare an Unpaid Bills with Terms Detail report.
  - If the Terms column shows a discount percentage, calculate the discount date for the bill.
  - If a bill is eligible for a discount but can be paid on or after January 20 and still get the discount, do not pay it now.
  - If a bill qualifies for a discount between January 15-19, add the comment "Pay this bill" to the report.
  - If a bill qualifying for a discount has a credit, add the comment "Use this credit" to the report.
  - If you make comments on the report, print it. Otherwise, close without printing. Do not save the commented report.
- Pay any bills and credits marked in the commented report. Remember, if a credit is shown, apply it; and then, recalculate the discount. (Amount Due – Credit * Discount % = Discount) Remember, no discounts are available for opening balances. (Did you use Merchandise Discounts for the Discount Account?)
- Received the bill from Abundant Gifts for the gift ware ordered January 7 and received January 12. Date the bill January 15.
- Prepare and print an Inventory Stock Status by Item Report for January 1-15 in Landscape orientation. Prepare Purchase Orders for all items marked Order on the Inventory Stock Status by Item Report. Use the Reorder Qty column to determine the number of items to order. Place all orders with preferred vendors.
- Backup the company file.

January 17:

- Sold eight textbooks on account at $125 each to State Schools, a nonprofit organization.

- Hector Gomez returned one textbook he had purchased for $125. Prepare a refund, then print the credit memo. Finally, print the check.
- Received Credit Memo 721 from Supplies Co. for the return of five boxes of stationery at 7.50 each. (Apply the credit to the bill dated 01/14/15 when you pay the bill.)

January 20:

- A cash customer purchased four textbooks at $109.99 each, one textbook for $89.95, and one gift ware item at $15.90 using Debit Card # 7289 1773 9631 753, Expiration 04/2016.
- Received Visa payment (card on file) from Sacramento Schools for $931.39 for payment in full of Invoice 8—not the beginning balance.
- Change the Reorder Point (Min) for Textbooks to 1,500 and Pens to 45.
- Prepare Inventory Stock Status by Item Report for January 1-20, 2015. Prepare Purchase Orders for marked items. (If nothing is marked, do not print the report.)
- Prepare an Unpaid Bills with Terms Detail report.
    - If the Terms column shows a discount percentage, calculate the discount date for the bill.
    - If a bill is eligible for a discount but can be paid on or after January 25 and still get the discount, do not pay it now.
    - If a bill qualifies for a discount between January 20-24, add the comment "Pay this bill" to the report.
    - If a bill qualifying for a discount has a credit, add the comment "Use this credit" to the report.
    - If you make comments on the report, print it. Otherwise, close without printing. Do not save the commented report.
- Pay any bills and credits marked in the commented report. Remember, if a credit is shown, apply it; and then, recalculate the discount. (Amount Due – Credit * Discount % = Discount) Remember, no discounts are available for opening balances.
- Record the bank deposit on January 20. Deposit all cash, checks, debit card, and credit card receipts.
- Backup the company file.

January 21:

- Katie typed an eight-page exam for at $5 per page for Hector Gomez on account. Hector also purchased 2 pens at 12.99 each and one box of stationery for $14.99.

January 22:

- Sold five gift ware items at $19.99 each, three paperback books at $8.99 each, and three pens at $8.99 each to Pamela Johnson on account.

January 25:

- Received Check 127 for $162.88 as payment in full from Pamela Johnson.
- Increase the Credit Limit for Total Training, Inc. to $20,000.00.
- Received a telephone order for 60 textbooks for $99.95 each and 45 textbooks for 119.95 each on account to Total Training, Inc.

- Prepare Inventory Stock Status by Item Report. Print only if an item needs to be ordered.
- Prepare an Unpaid Bills with Terms Detail report.
  - If the Terms column shows a discount percentage, calculate the discount date for the bill.
  - If a bill is eligible for a discount but can be paid on or after January 30 and still get the discount, do <u>not</u> pay it now.
  - If a bill qualifies for a discount between January 25-29, add the comment “Pay this bill” to the report.
  - If a bill qualifying for a discount has a credit, add the comment “Use this credit” to the report.
  - If you make comments on the report, print it. Otherwise, close without printing. Do not save the commented report.
- Pay any bills and credits marked in the commented report. Remember, if a credit is shown, apply it; and then, recalculate the discount. (Amount Due – Credit * Discount % = Discount) Remember, no discounts are available for opening balances.
- Deposit all cash, checks, debit card, and credit card receipts.
- Backup the company file.

<u>January 29</u>:

- Received Check 4325 for $84.25 from Hector Gomez as payment on his account.
- Received $2,078.00 from Total Training as payment on account using Debit Card # 7681 8971 2685 556, Expiration 06/2016.
- Received the back order of three boxes of stationery and the bill from Supplies Co. Date the bill January 29, 2015.
- Received bills and the paperback books ordered from Textbook Co. and the gift ware ordered from Abundant Gifts. Date the bills January 29, 2015.
- Total Training, Inc. picked up the merchandise ordered by telephone. (Did you prepare an invoice from the sales order?)

<u>January 30</u>:

- Prepare Inventory Stock Status by Item Report. If nothing is marked to order, do not print.
- Deposit all checks, cash, debit card, and credit card receipts.
- Use Pay Bills to pay:
  - Both bills due to Supplies Co. (Be sure to take discounts if eligible.)
  - Rent
- Prepare an Unpaid Bills with Terms Detail report.
  - If the Terms column shows a discount percentage, calculate the discount date for the bill.
  - If a bill is eligible for a discount but can be paid on or after February 5 and still get the discount, do <u>not</u> pay it now.
  - If a bill qualifies for a discount between January 30 and February 4, add the comment “Pay this bill” to the report.
  - If a bill qualifying for a discount has a credit, add the comment “Use this credit” to the report.

  - If you make comments on the report, print it. Otherwise, close without printing. Do not save the commented report.
- Pay any bills and credits marked in the commented report. Remember, if a credit is shown, apply it; and then, recalculate the discount. (Amount Due – Credit * Discount % = Discount) Remember, no discounts are available for opening balances.
- Use Write Checks to pay the utility bill of $257 and the telephone bill of $189 to the vendor State Utilities & Telephone, Main Phone: 916-555-8523, 8905 Richmond, Sacramento, CA 95814, Payment Terms Net 30. (Did you write just one check?)
- Backup the company file.

<u>January 31:</u>

- Pay the payroll: The pay period is 01/01/15 through 01/31/15. The check date is 01/31/15. Use the information in the following table to prepare the checks.

PAYROLL TABLE: JANUARY 31, 2015			
	Katie Gonzalez	**Andrea Nahid**	**Tom Parker**
HOURS			
Regular	80	158	144
Overtime (x1.5)			3
Sick			16
Vacation		2	
DEDUCTIONS OTHER PAYROLL ITEMS: EMPLOYEE			
Dental Ins.		30.00	20.00
Medical Ins.		30.00	20.00
DEDUCTIONS: COMPANY			
CA Employment Training Tax	.64	1.27	1.65
Social Security	39.68	78.53	101.99
Medicare	9.28	31.42	23.85
Federal Unemployment	3.84	7.60	9.87
CA-Unemployment	21.76	43.07	55.93
DEDUCTIONS: EMPLOYEE			
Medicare Employee Addl Tax	0.00	0.00	0.00
Federal Withholding	46.10	126.90	65.53
Social Security	26.88	53.20	69.09
Medicare	9.28	31.42	23.85
CA-Withholding	7.39	56.06	22.50
CA-Disability	6.40	12.67	16.45

- Print the paychecks using a <u>voucher</u>-style check. (If the voucher prints two times, it is fine.) Be sure to remove the Intuit logo from the Payroll Printing Preferences.

- Before distributing paychecks, you realize that the Social Security Employee Deductions for each employee are incorrect. Go to the checks, unlock them and change the amount of Social Security Employee Deductions for Katie to 39.68, for Andrea to 78.53, and for Tom to 101.99. Reprint the checks using Voucher style.
- Prepare and print the Payroll Summary Report for January in Landscape orientation. (Adjust column widths and fit the report to print on one page.)
- Prepare and print the Payroll Liabilities Balances Report for January in Portrait orientation.
- Pay all the payroll liabilities for January 1-31, 2015. Print the standard checks. You may print the checks individually or as a batch.
- Prepare Sales Tax Liability Report for January 1-31, 2015. Print in Landscape orientation. Adjust column widths so the report fits on one page, maintains the same font, and has column headings shown in full.
- Pay Sales Tax for January 31, 2015 and print the check.
- Print a Sales by Item Summary Report for January 1-31 in Landscape orientation. Adjust column widths so report fits on one-page wide.
- Print a Trial Balance for January 1-31 in Portrait orientation.
- Enter adjusting entries: Depreciation—Store Equipment & Fixtures $266.66. Supplies used—$400.00. Insurance used a total of $100—$50 fire Insurance, $50 Liability Insurance. (Use a compound entry to record insurance adjustment.)
- Record the owner withdrawal for the month $2,000.00. (Did you use QuickAdd to add your name to the Other Names list?)
- Prepare a bank reconciliation and record any adjustments. Be sure to use the date of 01/31/15 for the bank statement date, service charges, and interest earned.
- When the reconciliation is complete, print the Detail Reconciliation Report.

SACRAMENTO STATE BANK
102 8TH Street
Sacramento, CA 95814
(916) 555-9889

Your Name's Capitol Books
1055 Front Street
Sacramento, CA 95814 Acct. # 91-1132-7022 January, 2015

Beginning Balance, January 1, 2015			$130,870.25
1/5/2015, Deposit	2,616.85		133,487.10
1/10/2015, Check 1		1,000.00	132,487.10
1/10/15, Deposit	1,378.33		133,865.43
1/13/15, Check 6 NSF Charlie Yu		350.00	133,515.43
1/13/15, NSF Bank Charge Charlie Yu		25.00	133,490.43
1/15/15, Deposit	1,174.86		134,665.29
1/15/15, Check 2		102.90	134,562.39
1/15/15, Check 3		2,254.00	132,308.39
1/18/15, Check 4		135.00	132,173.39
1/20/15, Deposit	1,520.86		133,694.25
1/20/15, Check 5		14.70	133,679.55
1/20/15, Check 6		1,960.00	131,719.55
1/25/15, Deposit	162.88		131,882.43
1/31/15, Service Charge		15.00	131,867.43
1/31/15, Store Equipment & Fixtures Loan Pmt.: Interest $124.71, Principal $22.65		147.36	131,720.07
1/31/15, Interest	1,976.10		133,696.17
1/31/15, Ending Balance			$133,696.17

- After printing the Reconciliation Detail Report, close the Drawing account.
- Transfer the Net Income/Owner's Equity into the capital account
- Adjust the Merchandise Item of Gift Ware for 1 Gift Set that was damaged. (Use the expense account Merchandise Adjustments.)
- Correct the Amount of Net Income to reflect the merchandise adjustment.
- Print a Standard Profit & Loss Statement for January 1-31, 2015.
- Print a Standard Balance Sheet As of January 31, 2015.
- Make an Archive Copy backup of the company. Name it **Your Name's Capitol Books (Archive 01-31-15)**
- Close the period with a closing date of **01/31/15**. (Do not use passwords.)
- Print the Journal, expand the columns, use the dates from **12/31/2014** to **01/31/2015**, adjust columns, and print in Landscape orientation. (If need be, select Fit report to 1 page(s) wide.)The order in which your transactions appear may be different from any answer keys provided. As long as all of the transactions have been entered, the order of entry does not matter.
- Backup the company file. Name it **Your Name's Capitol Books (Backup Complete)**.

NAME____________________

COMPREHENSIVE PRACTICE SET: TRANSMITTAL

YOUR NAME'S CAPITOL BOOKS

Check the items below as you complete and/or print them; then attach the documents and reports in the order listed when you submit them to your instructor. Printing is optional for Payment Receipts and Bills (unless your instructor requires them to be printed); however, they are included on the transmittal sheet so they can be checked as they are completed.

(Note: When paying bills and printing a batch of checks, your checks may be in a different order than shown below. As long as you print the checks to the correct vendors and have the correct amounts, do not be concerned if your check numbers are not an exact match.)

___ Employee Summary for Tom Parker
___ Employee Summary for Andrea Nahid
___ Account Listing
___ Item Listing
___ Transaction List by Customer
___ Transaction List by Vendor
___ Standard Balance Sheet, January 1, 2015
___ Sales Receipt 1: Cash Customer
___ Invoice 1: Total Training, Inc.
___ Payment Receipt: Pamela Johnson
___ Sales Order 1: Sacramento Schools
___ Sales Receipt 2: Cash Customer
___ Inventory Stock Status by Item, January 2, 2015
___ Purchase Order 1: Pens Galore
___ Purchase Order 2: Textbook Co.
___ Invoice 2: Sacramento Schools
___ Payment Receipt: Charlie Yu
___ Invoice 3: Pamela Johnson
___ Payment Receipt, Total Training, Inc.
___ Invoice 4: Hector Gomez
___ Bill: Pens Galore
___ Item Receipt: Textbook Co.
___ Inventory Stock Status by Item, January 1-5, 2015
___ Purchase Order 3: Supplies Co.
___ Deposit Summary, January 5, 2015
___ Credit Memo 5: Pamela Johnson
___ Bill: Textbook Co.
___ Invoice 6: State Schools
___ Purchase Order 4: Abundant Gifts
___ Invoice 7: Pamela Johnson
___ Check 1: Textbook Co.
___ Sales Order 2: Sacramento Schools
___ Sales Receipt 3: Cash Customer
___ Invoice 8: Sacramento Schools
___ Payment Receipt: Sacramento Schools
___ Payment Receipt: Total Training, Inc.
___ Deposit Summary, January 10, 2015
___ Inventory Stock Status by Item, January 1-10, 2015
___ Purchase Order 5: Textbook Co.
___ Sales Receipt 4: Cash Customer
___ Sales Receipt 5: Cash Customer
___ Invoice 9: Charlie Yu
___ Item Receipt: Abundant Gifts
___ Payment Receipt: Pamela Johnson
___ Bill: Textbook Co.
___ Invoice 10: Charlie Yu
___ Opening Balance Invoice: Charlie Yu
___ Payment Receipt: Hector Gomez
___ Payment Receipt: Charlie Yu
___ Bill: Supplies Co.
___ Bill: Sacramento Rental

___ Payment Receipt: Pamela Johnson
___ Deposit Summary, January 15, 2015
___ Commented Unpaid Bills with Terms Detail
___ Check 2: Pens Galore
___ Check 3: Textbook Co.
___ Bill: Abundant Gifts
___ Inventory Stock Status by Item, January 1-15, 2015
___ Purchase Order 6: Abundant Gifts
___ Purchase Order 7: Textbook Co.
___ Invoice 11: State Schools
___ Credit Memo 12: Hector Gomez
___ Check 4: Hector Gomez
___ Bill Credit: Supplies Co.
___ Sales Receipt 6: Cash Customer
___ Payment Receipt: Sacramento Schools
___ Commented Unpaid Bills with Terms Detail
___ Check 5: Supplies Co.
___ Check 6: Textbook Co.
___ Deposit Summary, January 20, 2015
___ Invoice 13: Hector Gomez
___ Invoice 14: Pamela Johnson
___ Payment Receipt: Pamela Johnson
___ Sales Order 3: Total Training, Inc.
___ Deposit Summary, January 25, 2015
___ Payment Receipt: Hector Gomez
___ Payment Receipt: Total Training, Inc.
___ Bill: Supplies Co.
___ Bill: Textbook Co.
___ Bill: Abundant Gifts
___ Invoice 15: Total Training, Inc.
___ Deposit Summary, January 30, 2015
___ Check 7: Supplies Co.
___ Check 8: Sacramento Rental
___ Check 9: State Utilities & Telephone
___ Check 10: Katie Gonzalez (Note: Checks may print in a different order)
___ Check 11: Andrea Nahid
___ Check 12: Tom Parker
___ Check 10: Katie Gonzalez (Corrected)
___ Check 11: Andrea Nahid (Corrected)
___ Check 12: Tom Parker (Corrected)
___ Payroll Summary, January 2015
___ Payroll Liability Balances, January 2015
___ Check 13: Employment Development Department
___ Check 14: Medical Ins., Inc.
___ Check 15: United States Treasury
___ Sales Tax Liability Report, January 2015
___ Check 16: State Board of Equalization
___ Sales by Item Summary, January 2015
___ Trial Balance, January 31, 2015
___ Check 17: Your First & Last Name
___ Bank Reconciliation Detail Report
___ Standard Profit and Loss, January 2015
___ Balance Sheet, January 31, 2015
___ Journal, December 31, 2014 – January 31, 2015

A

QUICKBOOKS PROGRAM INTEGRATION

QuickBooks is integrated to work in conjunction with Microsoft Word and Excel to prepare many different types of letters or send QuickBooks reports directly to an Excel workbook. In order to use the integration features of the program, you must have Microsoft© Word 2007 (or higher) and Microsoft© Excel 2007 (or higher) installed on your computer.

This appendix will use the sample company, Larry's Landscaping & Garden Supply, to provide information regarding program integration with QuickBooks. Since saving the demonstration transactions will make permanent changes to the sample company, you will not need to do the demonstration transactions unless they are assigned by your instructor. Because the material presented in the appendix is for illustration purposes only, memo text boxes and detailed data for entry are not included.

QUICKBOOKS LETTERS

There are many times in business when you need to write a letter of one type or another to your customers. This is an important feature because QuickBooks will insert information, from your customer files directly into a letter.

To prepare a letter to Active Customers, Click **Open a sample file**, and the click the type of sample company you wish to explore—**Sample service-based business**

- If you get an Update Company File message, click **Yes**.

A notification regarding QuickBooks Information appears

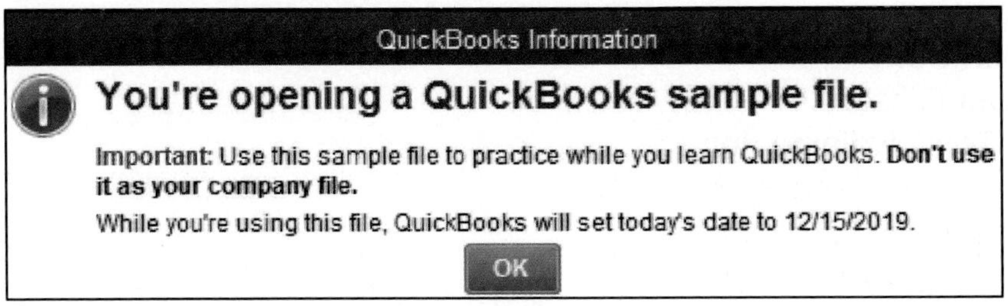

Click **OK** on the QuickBooks Information screen
Open the Customer Center
Click the **Word** button
Click **Prepare Customer Letters**

- If you get a screen regarding the lack of available templates, click **Copy**.

For "Include names that are:" click **Active**
For "Create a letter for each:" click **Customer**

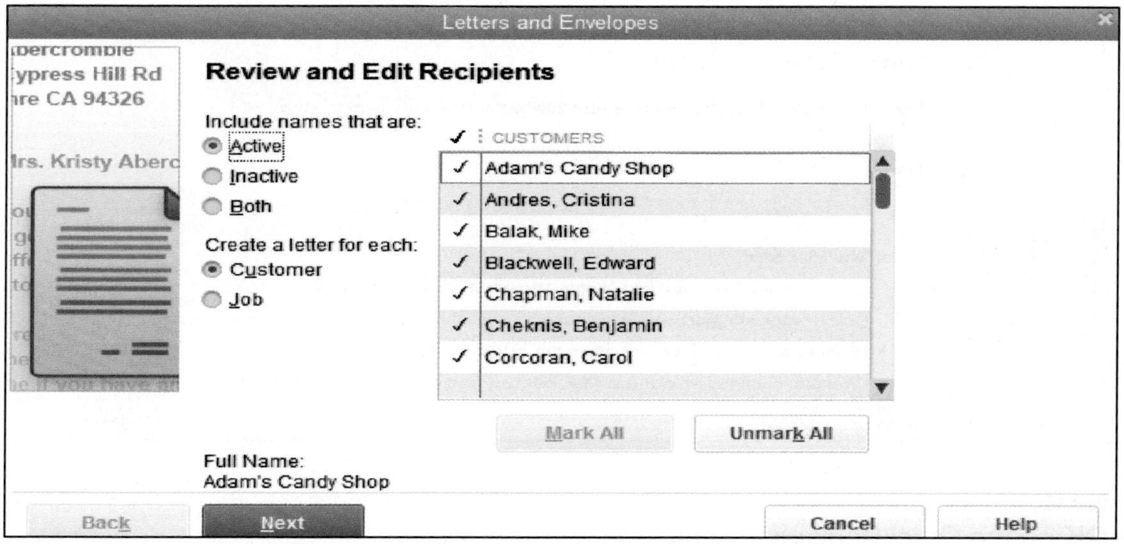

Click **Next**
Scroll through the list of Letter Templates
Click **Thanks for business (service)**

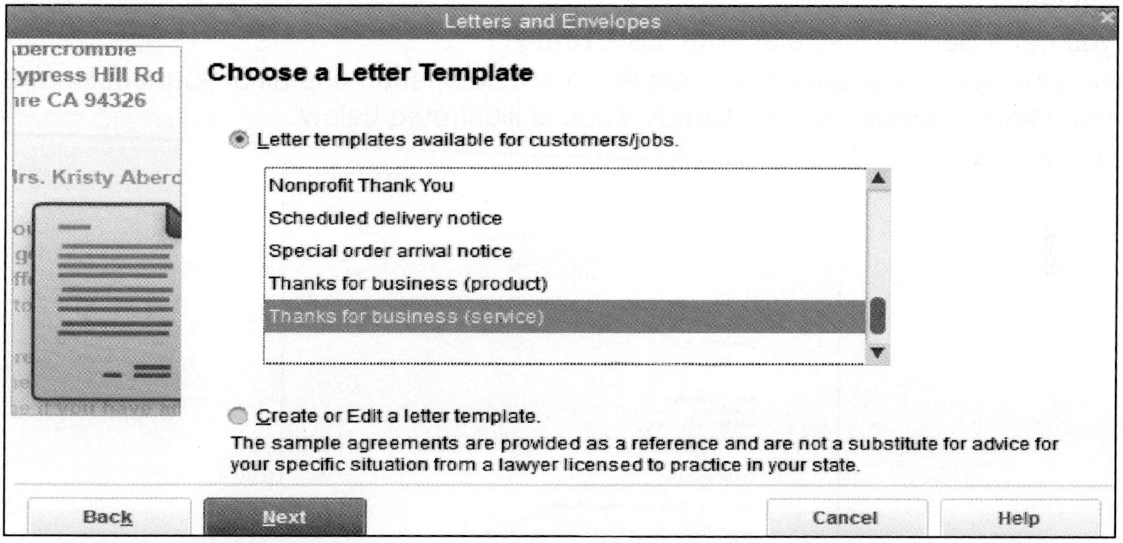

- If you do not find a template that is appropriate or you wish to make permanent changes to one of the existing letter templates, you may do so by clicking Create or Edit a letter template.

Click **Next**
Enter **Your First and Last Name** (your actual name not the words your name) for the name at the end of the letter
Enter your title as **President**

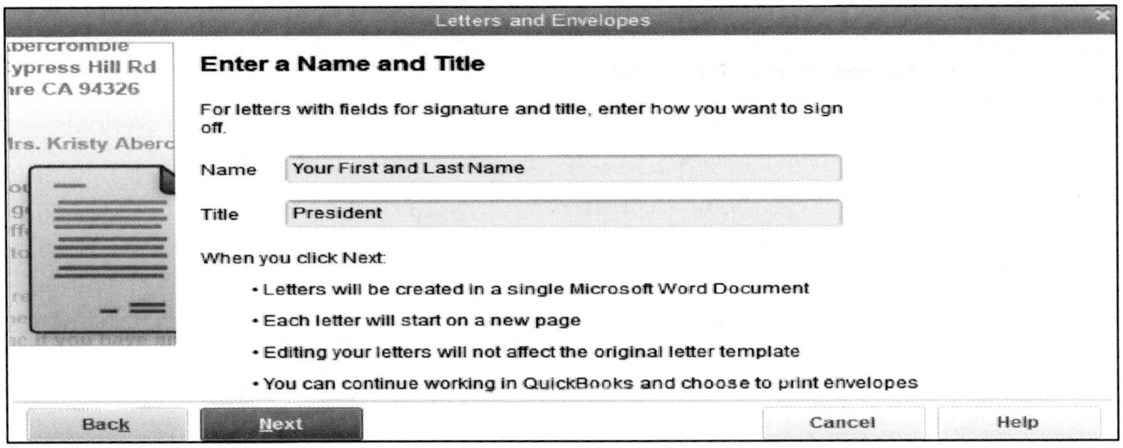

Click **Next**

Click **OK** on the QuickBooks Information Is Missing screen

- Since many of your customers do not have titles or some other information stored in the Customer Center, you may get a "QuickBooks Information Is Missing" screen indicating that information to complete this letter was missing from the QuickBooks Data File. Once the letters are shown in Word, you will need to enter the missing information for each letter.
- If you get a Server Busy message, click **Retry**
- When the letter is created, Microsoft Word will be opened and all of your customers will have a letter created. Adam's Candy Shop is illustrated below:

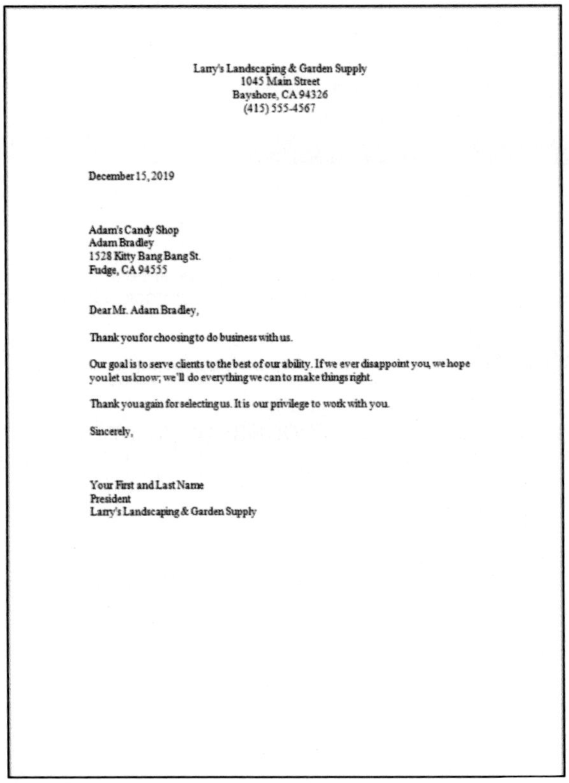

Larry's Landscaping & Garden Supply
1045 Main Street
Bayshore, CA 94326
(415) 555-4567

December 15, 2019

Adam's Candy Shop
Adam Bradley
1528 Kitty Bang Bang St.
Fudge, CA 94555

Dear Mr. Adam Bradley,

Thank you for choosing to do business with us.

Our goal is to serve clients to the best of our ability. If we ever disappoint you, we hope you let us know; we'll do everything we can to make things right.

Thank you again for selecting us. It is our privilege to work with you.

Sincerely,

Your First and Last Name
President
Larry's Landscaping & Garden Supply

- The letters are not technically correct with formats and spacing so may need some adjustment on your part. However, it is much easier to edit letters prepared for you than it is to create a letter for each customer.

To make the short letter appear more balanced:
Press **Ctrl+A** to select the entire document
Click the **Page Layout** tab, click **Margins**, and click the words **Custom Margins**
Change the Top and Bottom margins to **1"**
Change the Left and Right margins to **2"**

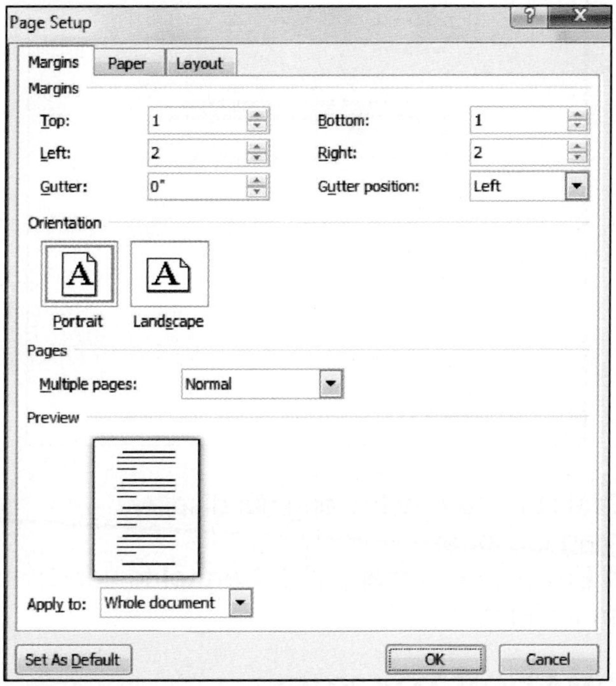

Click **OK**
Position the cursor between the date and the letter address
Press the **Enter** until there are 8 blank lines between the date and the letter address
Delete one of the blank lines between the letter address and the salutation (Dear Mr. Adam Bradley,)
Since the appropriate salutation is: Dear Mr. Bradley:, you should delete his first name.
Click the **View** tab; and then, click **Print Layout**

- Your letter should look like the following. Notice how much more balanced the letter appears.
- Notice that Adam's Candy Shop address information was automatically inserted in the letter.

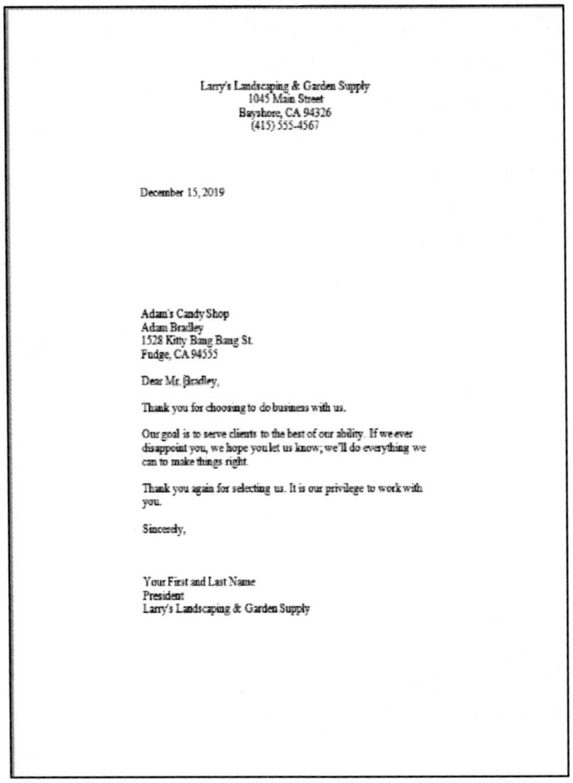

Larry's Landscaping & Garden Supply
1045 Main Street
Bayshore, CA 94326
(415) 555-4567

December 15, 2019

Adam's Candy Shop
Adam Bradley
1528 Kitty Bang Bang St.
Fudge, CA 94555

Dear Mr. Bradley,

Thank you for choosing to do business with us.

Our goal is to serve clients to the best of our ability. If we ever disappoint you, we hope you let us know; we'll do everything we can to make things right.

Thank you again for selecting us. It is our privilege to work with you.

Sincerely,

Your First and Last Name
President
Larry's Landscaping & Garden Supply

On the View tab, click **Draft** to return to the original display
Close **Word** without saving the letter
On the Print Letters and Envelopes screen, click **Cancel** to cancel the Letters to Customers
Do <u>not</u> close the Customer Center

EXPORTING INFORMATION TO EXCEL

Many of the reports prepared in QuickBooks can be exported to Microsoft Excel. This allows you to take advantage of extensive filtering options available in Excel, hide detail for some but not all groups of data, combine information from two different reports, change titles of columns, add comments, change the order of columns, and experiment with *what if* scenarios. Exporting reports to Excel from within a report was demonstrated within the chapters. Information may also be exported from the Customer, Vendor, and Employee Centers.

To export a Customer List to Excel, click the **Excel** button in the **Customer Center**, and click **Export Customer List**
On the Export dialog box click **Create new worksheet** and **in new workbook**
Click the **Export** button

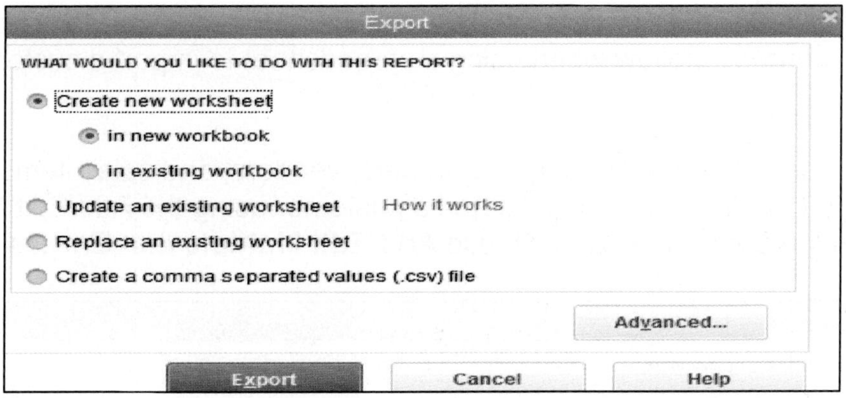

- A detailed Customer List will be displayed in Excel.

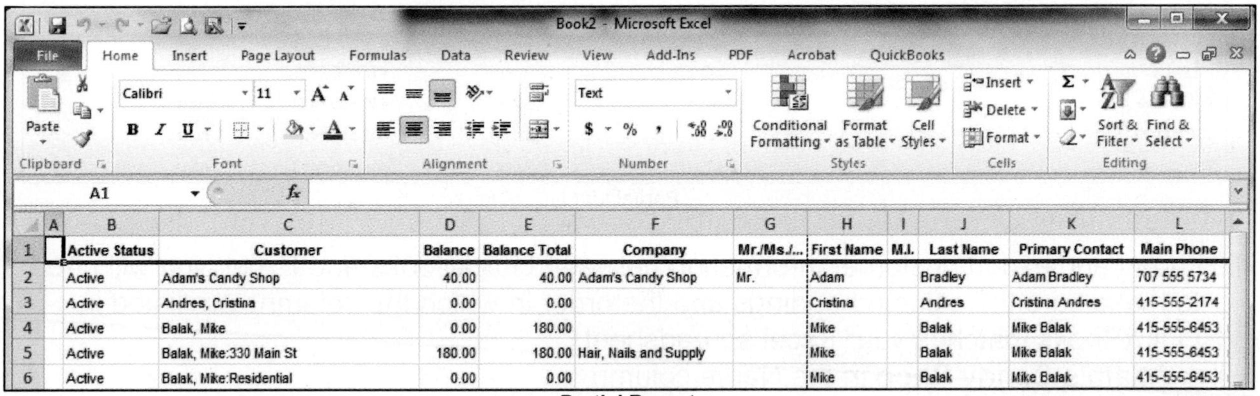
Book2 - Microsoft Excel
Active Status
Customer
Balance
Balance Total
Company
Mr./Ms./...
First Name
M.I.
Last Name
Primary Contact
Main Phone
Active Adam's Candy Shop 40.00 40.00 Adam's Candy Shop Mr. Adam Bradley Adam Bradley 707 555 5734
Active Andres, Cristina 0.00 0.00 Cristina Andres Cristina Andres 415-555-2174
Active Balak, Mike 0.00 180.00 Mike Balak Mike Balak 415-555-6453
Active Balak, Mike:330 Main St 180.00 180.00 Hair, Nails and Supply Mike Balak Mike Balak 415-555-6453
Active Balak, Mike:Residential 0.00 0.00 Mike Balak Mike Balak 415-555-6453
Partial Report

Click the **Close** button in the upper right corner of the Excel title bar to close **Excel**
Click **Don't Save** to close **Book2** without saving
Close the **Customer Center**

IMPORTING DATA FROM EXCEL

Another feature of QuickBooks is the ability to import data from Excel into QuickBooks. You may have Excel or .csv (comma separated value) files that contain important business information about customers, vendors, sales items, and other lists that are not contained in your QuickBooks Company File. That information can be imported directly into QuickBooks and customized as desired. An import file must conform to a specific structure in order for QuickBooks to interpret the data in the file correctly.

You may import your data from Excel in three ways. First, you may use an advanced import method to modify and use an existing Excel or CVS file, use a specially formatted spreadsheet and then add it to QuickBooks, or you may copy and paste your data from Excel directly into QuickBooks using the Add/Edit Multiple List Entries window.

Since importing data is not reversible, a backup should be made prior to importing data. An example of procedures to follow when using a spreadsheet to import a customer is shown below:

QuickBooks makes it possible to import customers, vendors, and sales items by using the Add/Edit Multiple List Entries feature. To add a customer using the Add/Edit Multiple List Entries, click on the **Lists** menu and choose **Add/Edit Multiple List Entries**

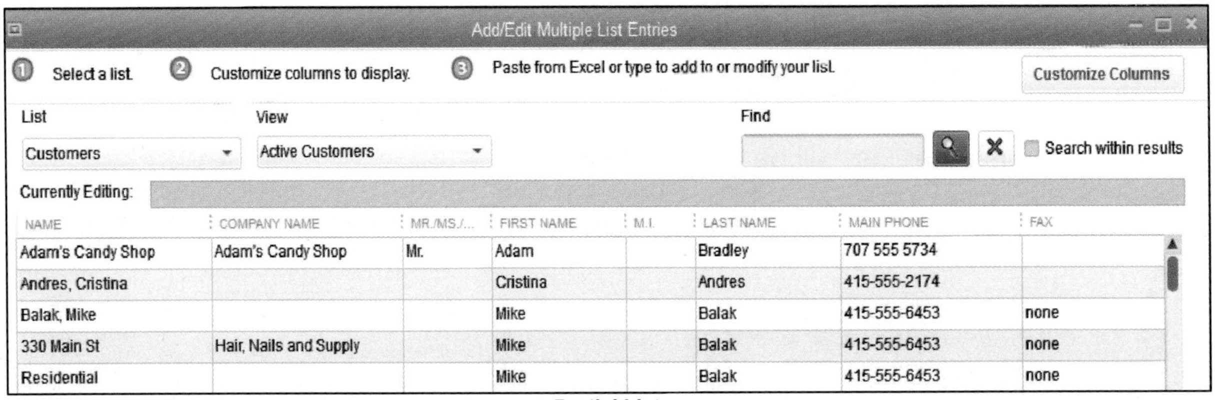

Partial List

To import and export customer information between QuickBooks and Excel, you will need to make sure the column headings and the order in which the columns are listed in QuickBooks matches your Excel spreadsheet

Click **Adam's Candy Shop** in the Name column

- If you get a Time Saving Tip regarding Copy Down, click **OK**.

Right-click **Adam's Candy Shop**, and then click **Insert line**

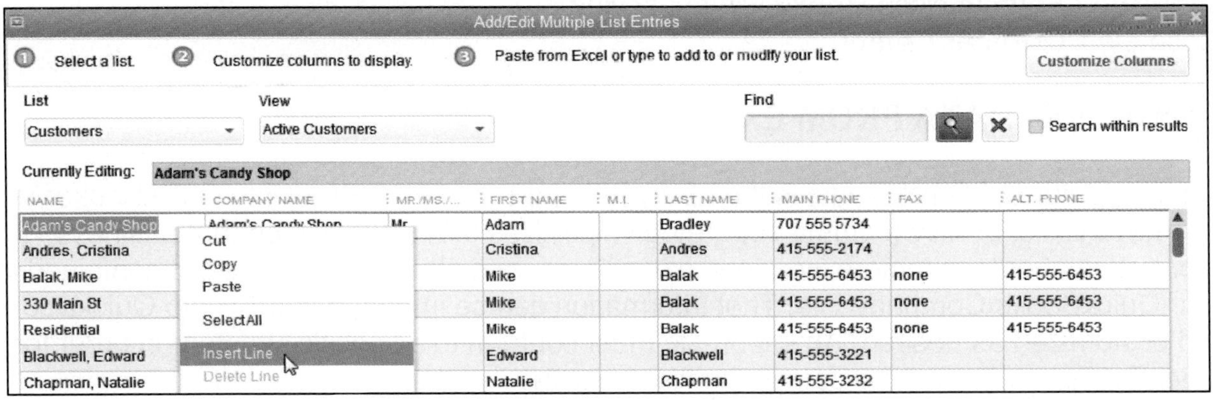

Enter the customer information for **Acme Rentals** on the blank line (or copy and paste from an existing Excel spreadsheet)

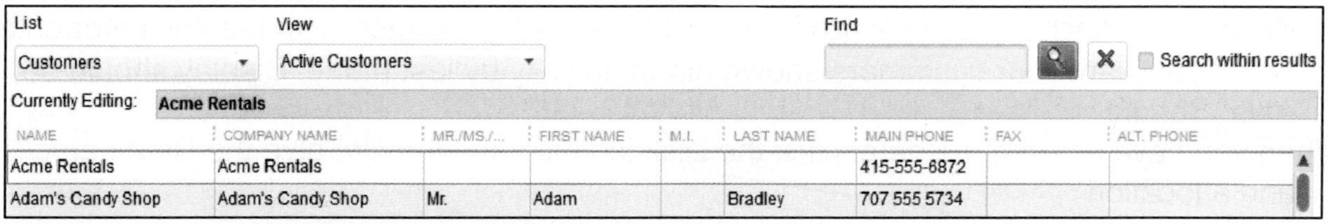

Click the **Save Changes** button

Click **OK** on the Record(s) Saved screen; and then, click **Close** on the Add/Edit Multiple List Entries Screen

An alternate method of adding customers is shown below:

In the Customer Center, click the drop-down list arrow for the Excel menu, and click **Import from Excel**.
Click **No** on the Add/Edit Multiple List Entries
Complete the **Wizard**

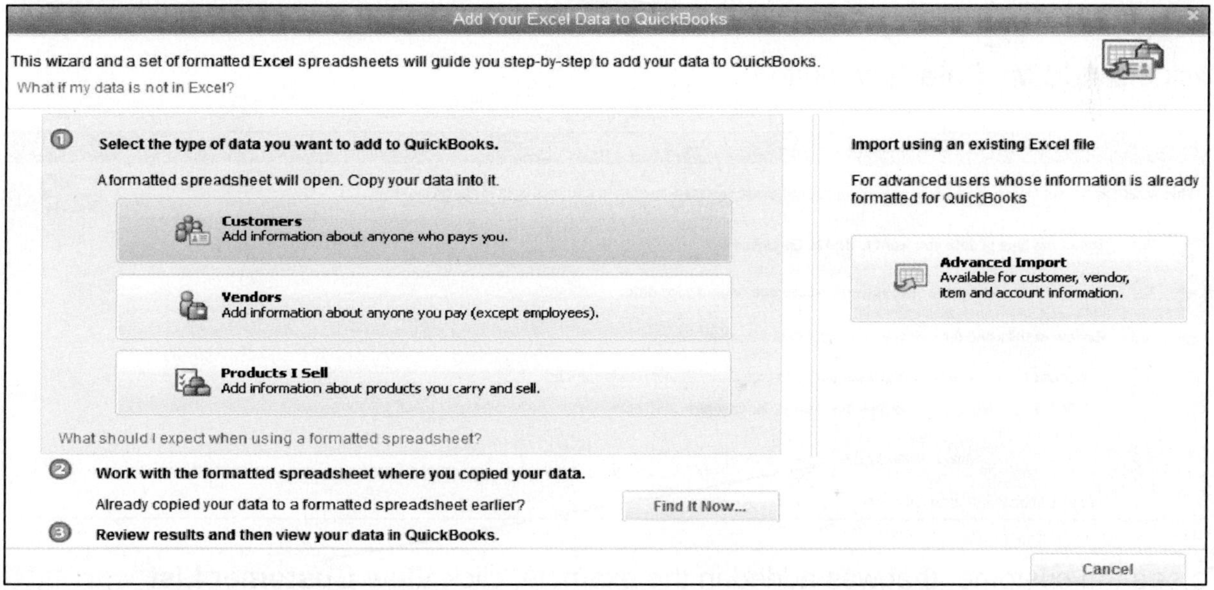

Click **Customers**
Click **Yes** on the Import textbox.
You are taken to a pre-formatted spreadsheet that is ready for data entry.
Click in the Company Name column in Row 8 on the QuickBooks screen
Enter the customer data for **Able, Sandra** (or copy it from an existing Excel document)

- Notice the Coach Tips as you go from field to field as you enter all of the customer data.
- Since you want your customers shown alphabetically by last name, Display should be Able, Sandra.

When you have entered the data, click the Disk icon to save the file, give the file a name and a location

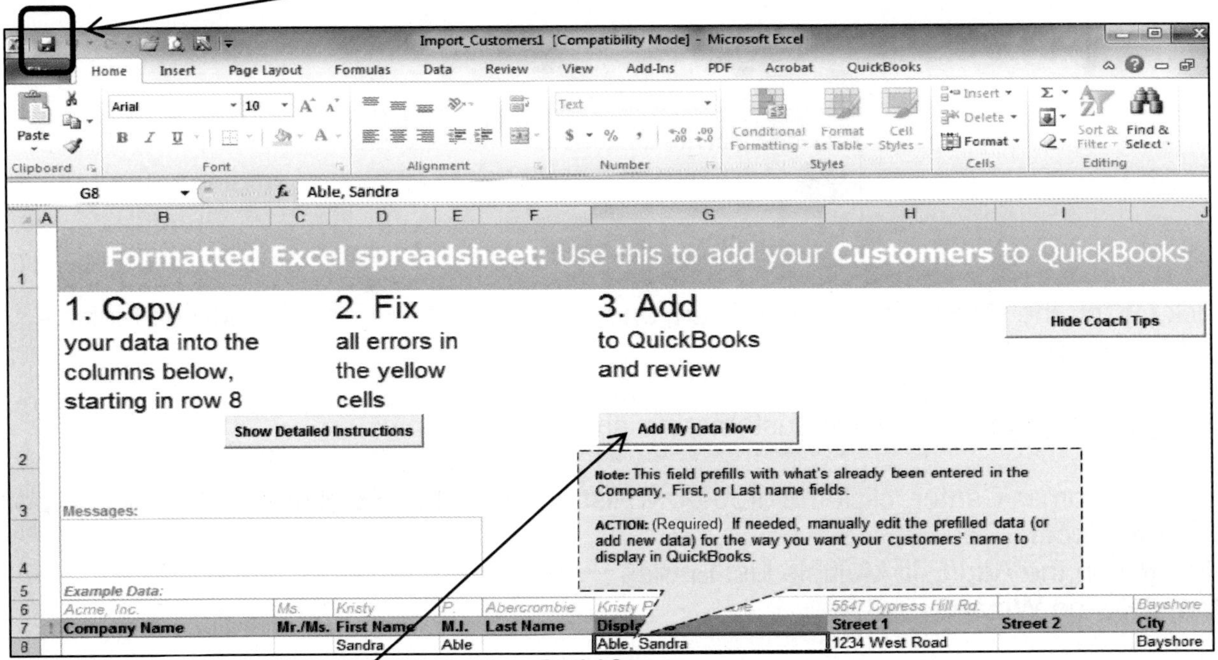

Partial Screen

Click the **Add My Data Now** button

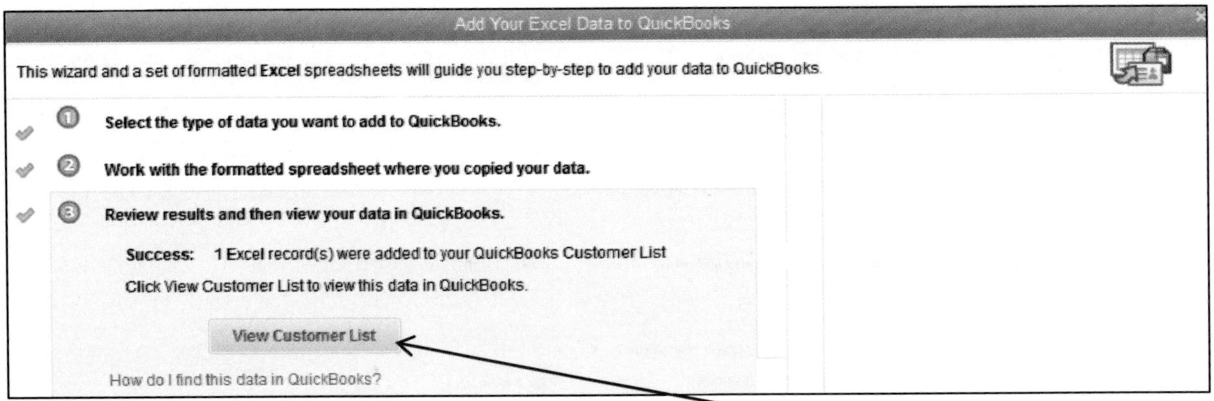

To see the customer that was added in the example, click **View Customer List**

- You will go to the Customer Center in QuickBooks.

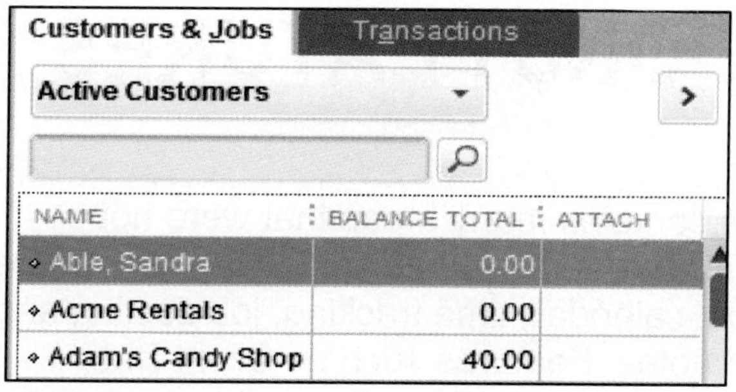

Close the **Customer Center**

MICROSOFT OUTLOOK (Information Only)

If you have Microsoft Outlook 2007 or later, you may use Send Preferences to setup Outlook for use in QuickBooks. In order to synchronize your contacts with QuickBooks, you download and install QuickBooks Contact Sync for Outlook (available for no charge). Once you have Contact Sync for Outlook installed, synchronization simultaneously updates data in both your contact manager and QuickBooks. For example, a customer's telephone number changes and you enter the new number in your contact manager but not in QuickBooks or you enter an address change for a vendor in QuickBooks but not your contact manager; when you synchronize, the telephone number gets updated in QuickBooks and the address gets updated in your contact manager. This brings QuickBooks and your contact manager up to date with each other.

APPS (Information Only)

There are Apps available that connect directly with QuickBooks. Some of these Apps are free while others are available for a fee. When you open the App Center, you will see several Apps displayed. You will also see key categories; such as, Just Added, Mobile, Billing/Invoicing, Customer Management, Expense Management, and eCommerce. You may click on any of these categories to see the available Apps displayed. You may also click Intuit's App Center to see all of the Apps available. At the time of writing, there is a button for All Apps and categories for New, Top Rated, and Featured. There are also App Categories for Sales and Marketing, Productivity, Operations, Finance & Accounting. Finally, there are selections for apps that work with QuickBooks Desktop and for apps developers.

If you opened the Sample Company to view the information presented in this appendix, close it.

B

QUICKBOOKS FEATURES

The QuickBooks Program contains many areas that were not explored during the training chapters of the text. Some of these areas are portable company files, calendar, time tracking, job costing and tracking, price levels, and notes. Features such as Client Data Review, batch invoicing, the Document Center, attaching documents, and customizing the icon bar are also addressed in this appendix.

When possible, the Sample Product-Based Business, Rock Castle Construction, will be used to explore these features. As was done in the chapters, the Top Icon bar will be used.

Since saving the demonstration transactions will make permanent changes to the sample company, you will not need to do the demonstration transactions unless they are assigned by your instructor. Since the material presented in the appendix is for illustration purposes only, memo text boxes and detailed data for entry are not included.

PORTABLE COMPANY FILES

During training in the text, you used Company (.QBW) files, made Backup (.QBB) files, and restored a Backup file to a Company file. In addition to these types of files, QuickBooks also has a Portable Company (.QBM) file, which is a compact version of your company file that contains only financial data. A portable file is small enough to be emailed and saved to portable media. It cannot be used to record transactions and, just like a Backup file, must be restored to a Company (.QBW) file before use. Data entered and then saved to a portable file cannot be merged into an existing company file because a portable file that is restored overwrites data just like restoring a backup file. In order to restore a portable file, you must have an Administrator password.

NEW BUSINESS CHECKLIST

Many businesses use QuickBooks from the time they begin operations. There is a **New Business Checklist** provided in QuickBooks. It is accessed from the Help menu when no company is open. This checklist helps a new business work through all the details involved in starting a business. Even existing businesses may profit from working through the checklist to make sure nothing was forgotten during the business setup. Of course, a business may have special items that are very specific in nature that are not on the checklist. When you complete the **Steps to Startup Success** on the New Business Checklist, there are categories for

1. Conceive your business
2. Structure your business
3. Prepare all necessary forms, permits, and licenses

4. Fund your business
5. Taxes and insurance

Within each category, there will be topics with check boxes that may be marked when the topic is completed. Help opens with an explanation for each topic provided when you click the topic.

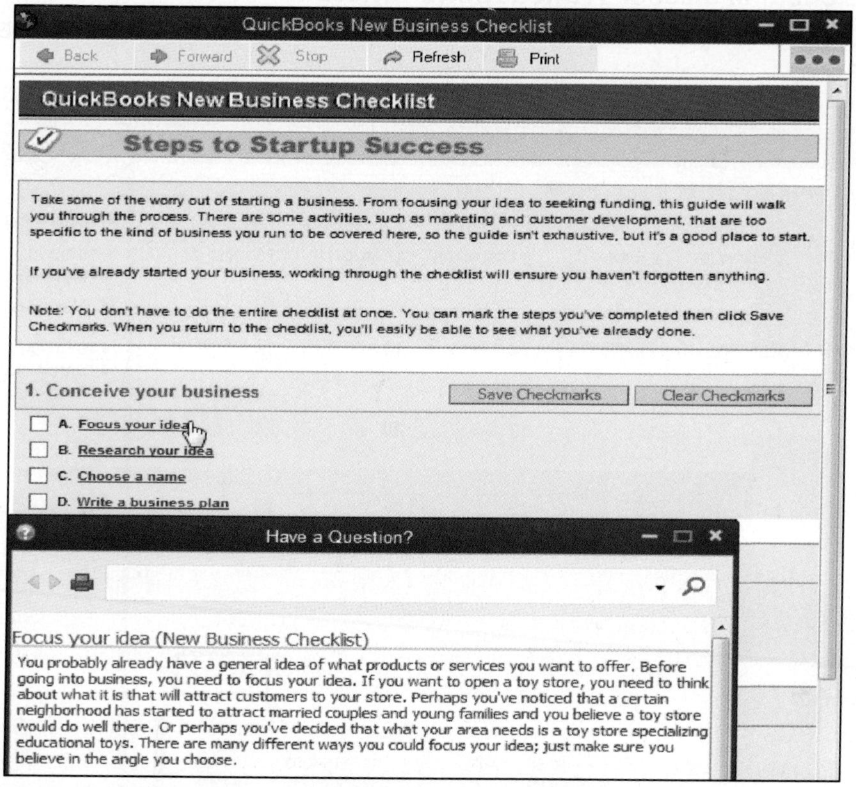

The checklist does not have to be completed all at once. After you finish a topic, click it to mark it. When leaving the QuickBooks New Business Checklist, click Save Checkmarks. When you return to the checklist, you will see where you left off.

QUICKBOOKS CALENDAR

QuickBooks Calendar is an easy way to view transactions that have been entered, transactions that are due, and tasks shown on the To Do list. You may view the calendar for an entire month, a week, or a day. You may choose which types of transactions appear on the calendar. You may decide whether to show or hide detail and may double-click a transaction to view or edit it.

<u>Open the Calendar</u>

Click the **Calendar** icon in the Company Section of the Home Page to open the Calendar or click Calendar on the drop-down menu for Company

The Monthly Calendar for December, 2019 is shown

The "current" date of **15** is highlighted with the note of **Entered (40)**

- This tells you the number of transactions entered that day.

On the right-side of the Calendar is a list of **Upcoming: Next 7 days** and **Due: Past 60 days**

- This lets you know about transactions that need to be completed.

Beneath the Calendar is a list of **Transactions Entered**

- This shows you exactly what transactions were entered on the selected date of December 15.

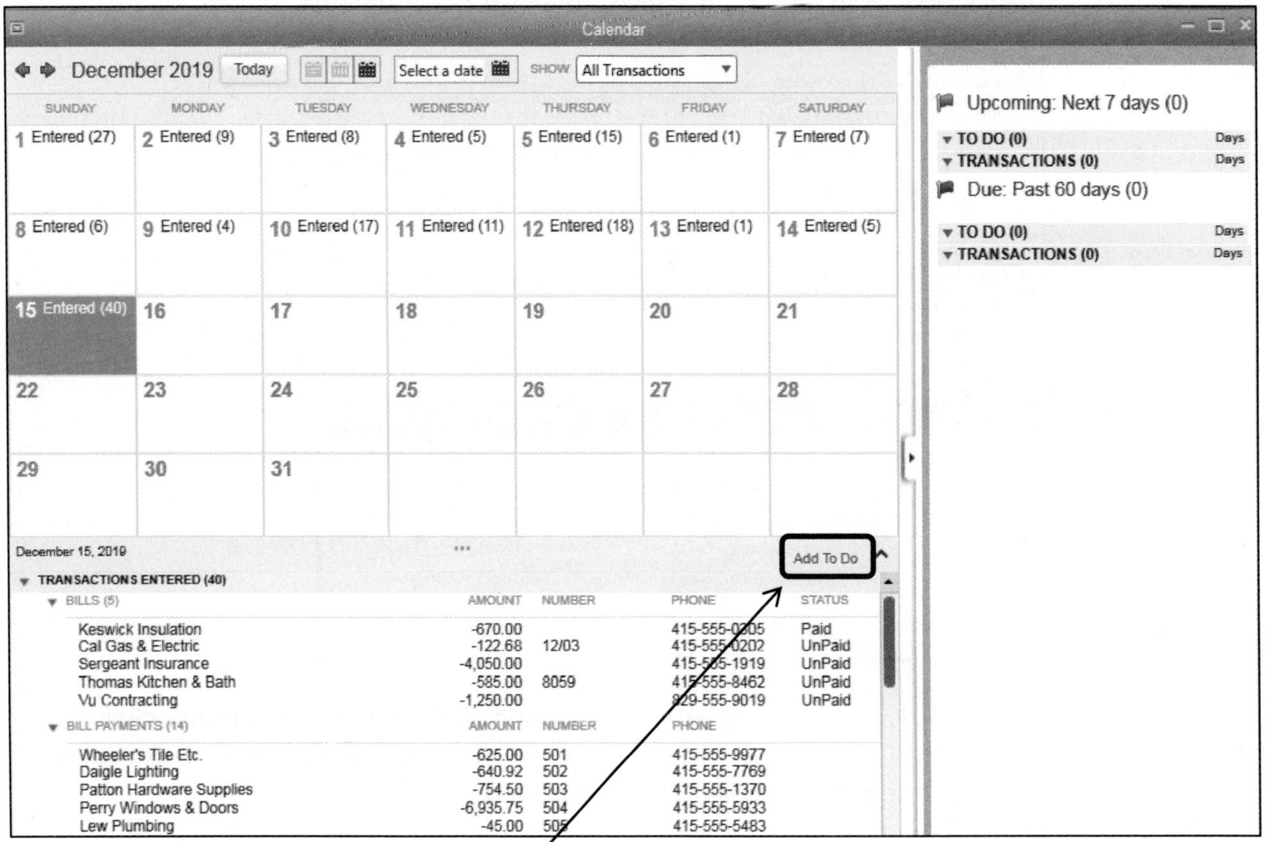

Add a To Do Note:

Add a To Do by clicking **Add To Do** beneath the calendar

Create a To Do Note by selecting the **Type** and **Priority**; if appropriate, **With** and the **Customer Name**; **Due**, and click the checkbox for **Time** to enter different times.

Once the information is selected, type the note in the **Details** section

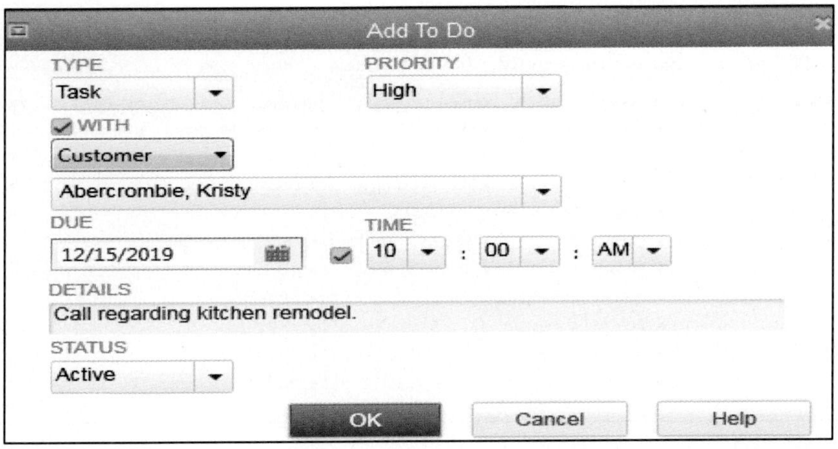

Click **OK** and the To Do is added to the Calendar, in the listing for Upcoming Next 7 days, and below the calendar

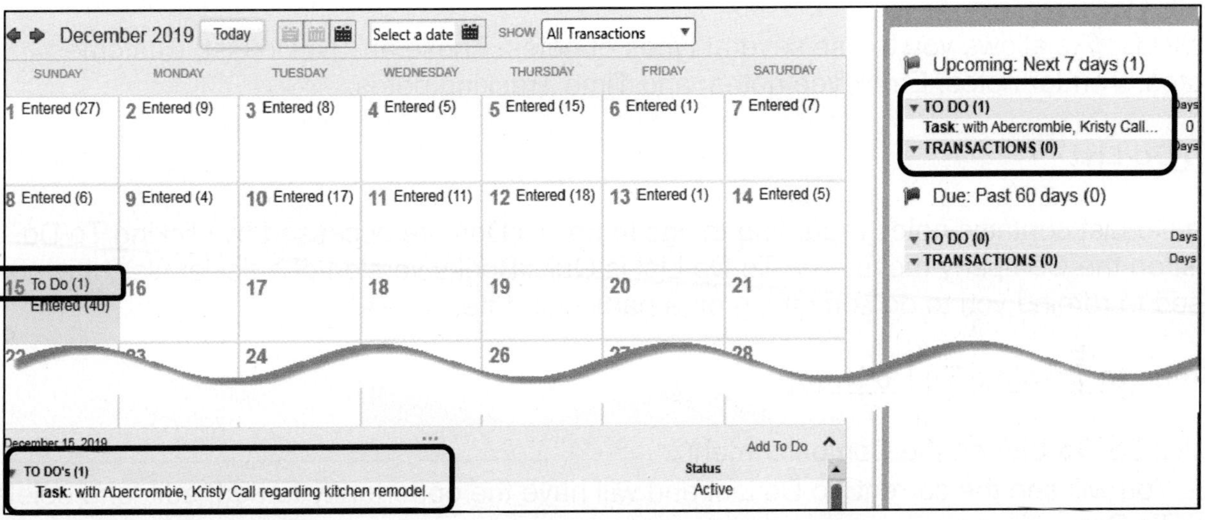

Change Calendar Views

To change the view click one of the icons at the top of the calendar 

The first icon will show a daily view, which contains the same information that was shown below the monthly calendar

The middle icon will show you the five-day weekly view (shown on the next page)

- In the screen shot for the week of December 8-14, the Upcoming, Past Due, and Transactions Entered information is not shown.

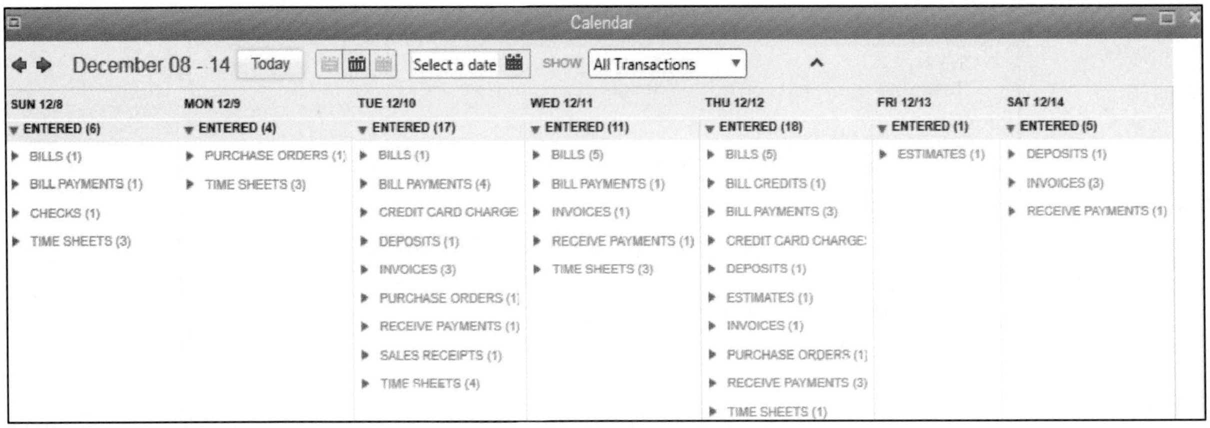

Close the Calendar

QUICKBOOKS NOTES

QuickBooks allows you to use several types of notes. These are To Do List, Customer notes, Vendor notes, Employee notes, and Time Tracking notes.

To Do List

To Do List contains notes regarding things to do. To Dos are accessed by clicking To Do List on the Company menu. The To Do List is QuickBooks version of a tickler file, which is used to remind you to do something on a particular date.

Steps to Create a To Do Note:

Click **To Do List** on the Company menu

- You will see the current To Do List and will have the opportunity to add, edit, and delete To Dos.

Click the drop-down list arrow for **To Do** and click **New To Do**

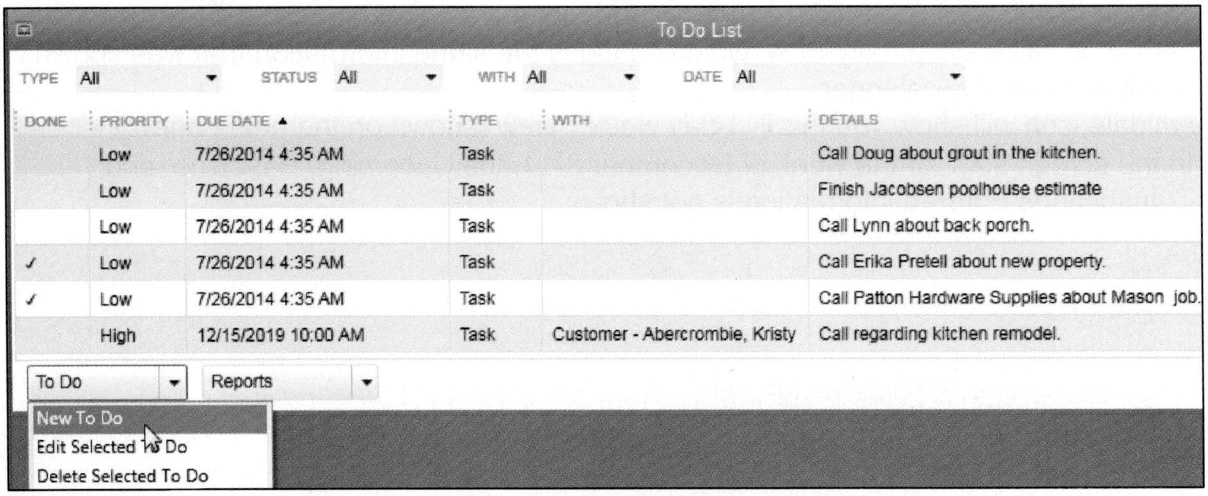

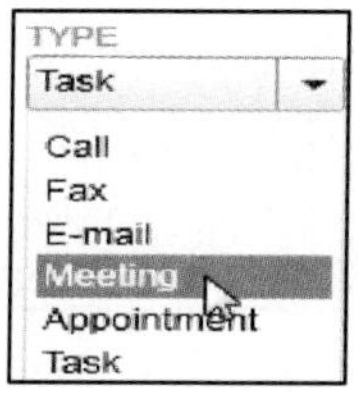

B

Click the **drop**-down arrow for **Type**, click the appropriate selection (in the example, Meeting is selected)
Click the drop-down arrow for **Priority**, click High, Medium, or Low (in the example, Medium is selected)
Click the drop-down list arrow for **With**, then click Lead, Customer, or Vendor
Click the drop-down list arrow and select the appropriate name

- In the screen shot, **Customer** and **Babcock's Music Shop** are selected

Enter the information for **Due**, **Time**, and the **text** of the note

- For this To Do, Due is **12/19/2019** and Time is **09:00 AM**

Click **OK**

- The note will be added to the list of To Do notes and will appear in the Calendar.

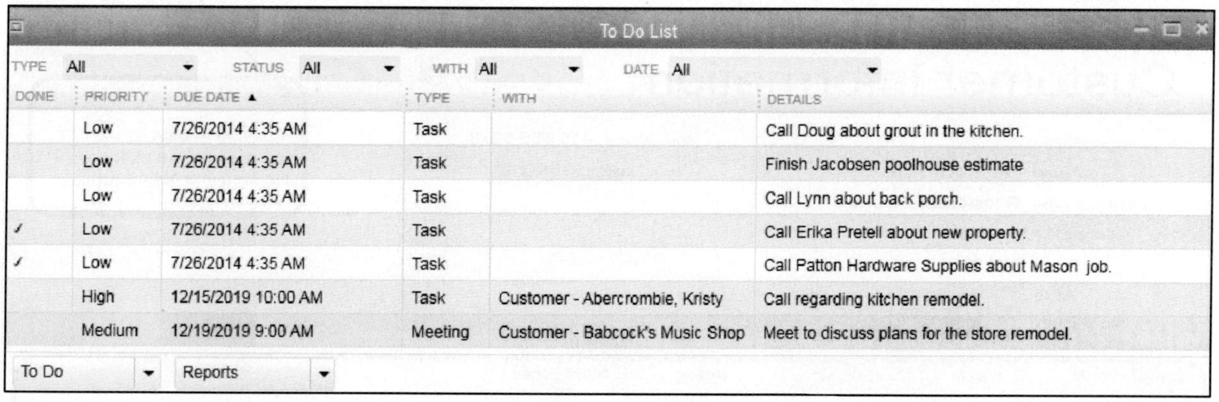

Close the **To Do List**

Customer Notes

In the Customer Center, QuickBooks provides a notepad for recording notes about each customer or job. Approximately ten windows worth of text can be displayed on each customer's notepad. You can also write on the customer notepad when viewing a customer's record or when entering a transaction. When using the customer notepad, an entry may be date stamped, To Do notes may be accessed, and the note may be printed.

Steps to Create Customer or Job Notes

Open the **Customer Center**
Click on the Customer you wish to view or add notes (Kristy Abercrombie)
To access the Customer Notepad, click the **Notes** tab

- In the section below Customer Information, there are tabs for Transactions, Contacts, To Do's, Notes, and Sent Email.

Click the **Manage Notes** button at the bottom of the list of notes, click **Add New**
Click the **Date/Time Stamp** button and QuickBooks will enter the date and time of the note (the current date and time of your computer), then type the note

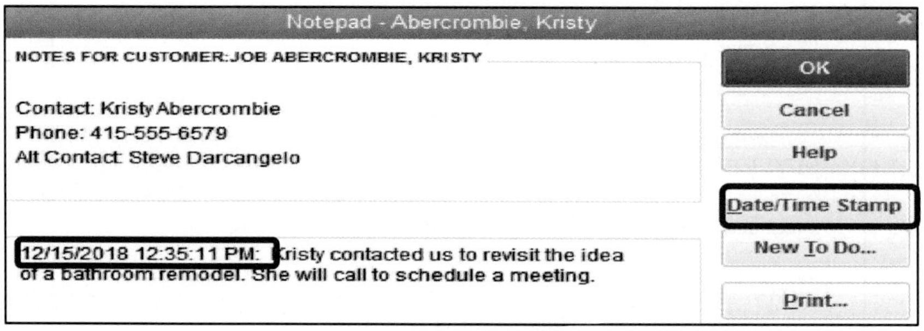

Click **OK** to save
The note is added to her list of notes and displayed in full on the right side of the notes tab
If you want to add the note to her Customer Information dashboard, click the icon and the note will be shown there as well

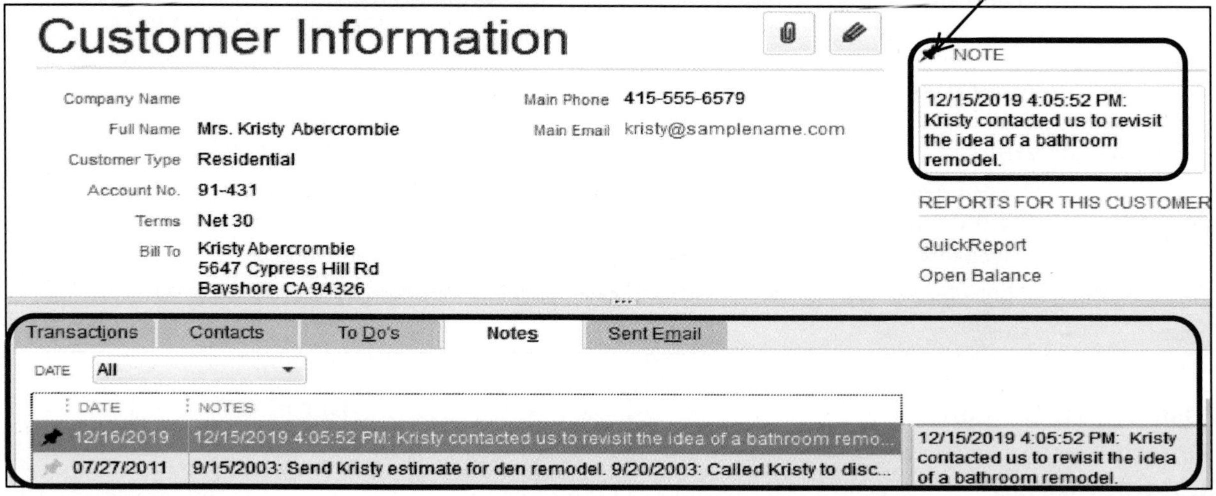

Exit the notepad, close the **Customer Center**

B

Vendor, Employee, and Other Names Notes

Vendor notes are recorded on the notepad for individual vendors in the Vendor Center. As with customer notes, this is where important conversations and product information would be recorded. The vendor notepad can be accessed from the Vendor Center. When using the vendor notepad, an entry may be date stamped, To Do notes may be accessed, and the note may be printed. Each entry on your Vendor, Employee, and Other Names lists has its own notepad where you can keep miscellaneous notes to yourself about that vendor, employee, or name. The procedures followed for vendors, employees, or other names are the same as those illustrated for customers.

Notes for Time Tracking

The Timer is a separate program that is installed and works in conjunction with QuickBooks. Notes regarding the time spent working on a task are entered when using the stopwatch. Time Tracking in QuickBooks will be demonstrated later in this appendix.

Steps to Create Notes for Time Tracking

Click the **Employees** menu and click **Enter Time**
Click **Time/Enter Single Activity**
Click the drop-down list arrow for **Name** and select the employee (Elizabeth N. Mason)
Click the drop-down list arrow for **Customer:Job** and select the customer (Abercrombie, Kristy: Kitchen)
Click the drop-down list arrow for **Service Item**, click the item (Blueprint Changes)
Click in the **Notes** section of the window
Enter the note: **Revise plan for kitchen remodel.**

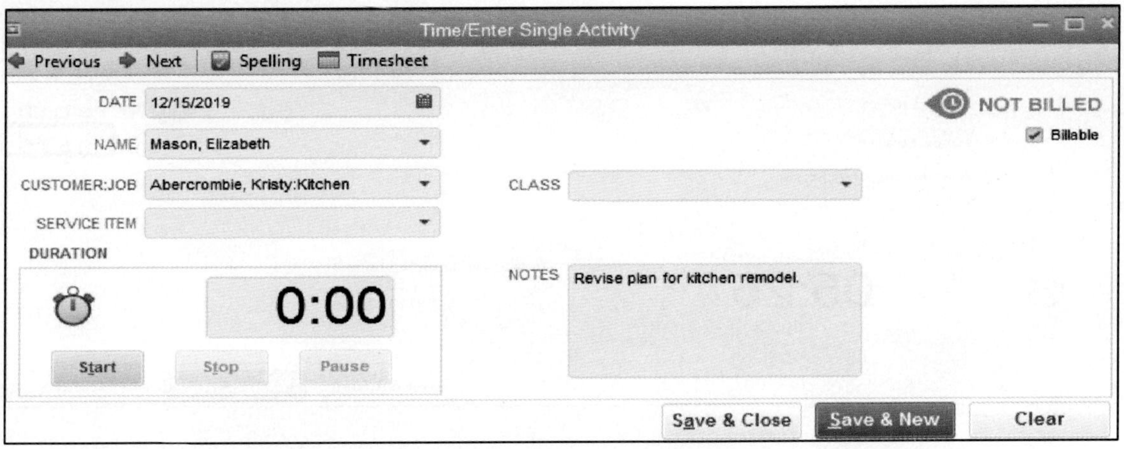

Do <u>not</u> close the Time/Enter Single Activity screen

TRACKING TIME

Many businesses bill their customers or clients for the actual amount of time they spend working for them. In this case you would be tracking billable time. When you complete the invoice to the customer, you can add the billable time to the invoice with a few clicks. In other situations, you may not want to bill for the time; but you may want to track it. For example, you may want to find out how much time you spend working on a job that was negotiated at a fixed price. This will help you determine whether or not you estimated the hours for the job correctly. Also, you may want to track the amount of time employees spend on various jobs, whether or not you bill for the time.

QuickBooks comes with a separate Timer program. You have a choice between tracking time via the Timer and then importing the time data to QuickBooks, using the Stopwatch on the Time/Enter Single Activity window to time an activity while you are performing it, or entering time directly into QuickBooks manually on the Weekly Timesheet window or the Time/Enter Single Activity window.

Steps to Track Time as a Single Activity

With the **Time/Enter Single Activity** screen showing the time for Elizabeth N. Mason and the blueprint changes for Kristy Abercrombie, indicate whether or not the time recorded is billable

- A check in the billable box means that this is recorded as billable time. No check means that the time is being tracked but not billed.

Click **Start** on the timer, and when finished with the work, click **Stop** on the timer

- If work is stopped at any time, you may click Pause when stopping and click Start when resuming work.

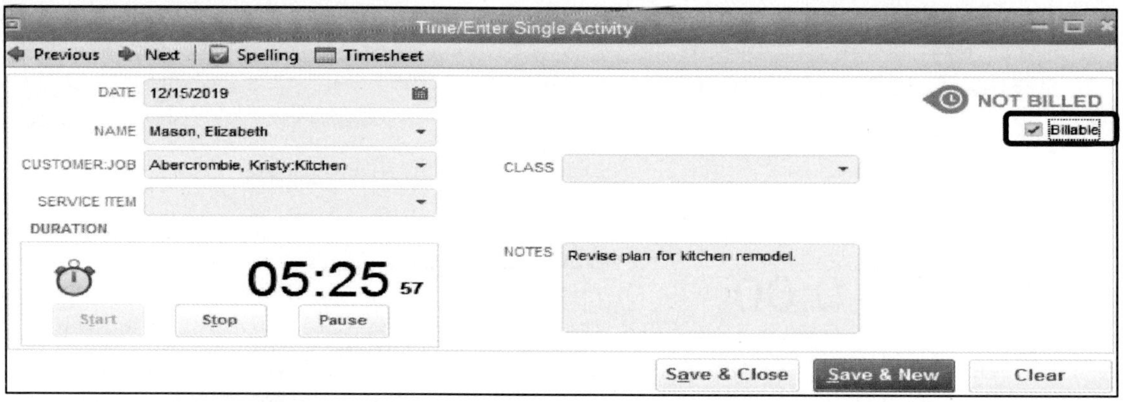

When finished, click **Stop** and **Save & Close**

Steps to Track Time on a Timesheet

Click **Employees** menu, point to **Enter Time**, and click **Use Weekly Timesheet**

Click the drop-down list arrow for **Name**, and click the name of the employee doing the work: **Elizabeth N. Mason**

- Accept the date the computer provides.
  - If you want to change the date of the time sheet, click the calendar button, and click the date for the time sheet.
- Any work completed as a Single Activity will appear on the time sheet. Notice the time and note entered for Abercrombie, Kristy.

To enter information for a time period directly on the time sheet, click the next available blank line, then click the drop-down list arrow for **Customer:Job** in the Customer:Job column

Click the name of the customer for whom work is being performed: **Babcock's Music Shop: Remodel**

Click the drop-down list arrow for **Service Item**, click the name of the service item: **Blueprint Changes**

Enter any notes regarding the work: **Correct Blueprints**

Click in the appropriate columns for the days of the week: **TH 12** enter the number of hours worked **2:15** and **F 13** enter **8:00**

- If the information is the same as the previous timesheet, click Copy Last Sheet.
  - The information for the previous timesheet will be entered for this time period.

Indicate whether or not the hours are billable

- QuickBooks Timer records all hours as billable unless otherwise indicated.

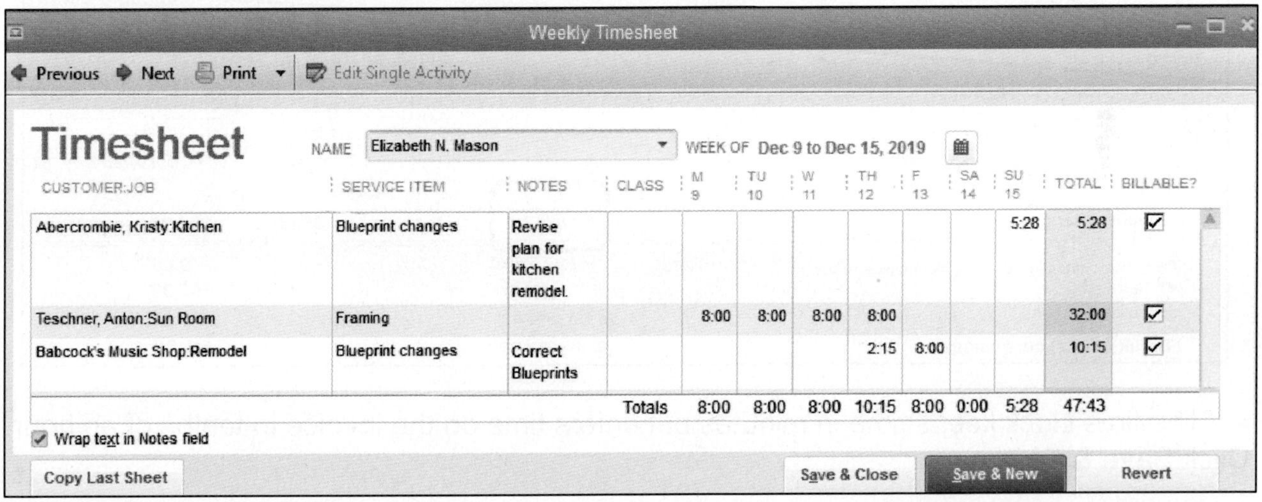

- Notice the Blueprint changes for Abercrombie Kristy:Kitchen were recorded when using the Timer and the information for Babcock's Music Shop:Remodel were added manually. The information for Teschner, Anton: Sun Room was previously added.

When the timesheet is complete, click **Save & Close**

Prepare an Invoice Using Billable Hours

Click the **Create Invoices** icon on the Home Page

Enter the name of the **Customer:Job: (Abercrombie, Kristy: Kitchen)**

The Billable Time/Costs screen appears

"**Select the outstanding billable time and costs to add to this invoice?"** should be selected, click **OK**.

- If the Billable Time/Costs screen does not appear, click the Add Time/Costs button on the Invoice Icon Bar.

Scroll through the list of Time and Costs for the customer

Click the time you wish to bill

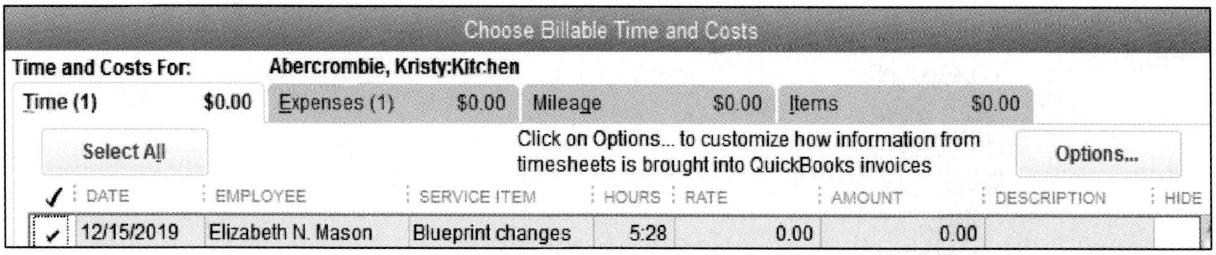

Click **OK**

- The time will be entered on the invoice.

The invoice would be completed as previously instructed

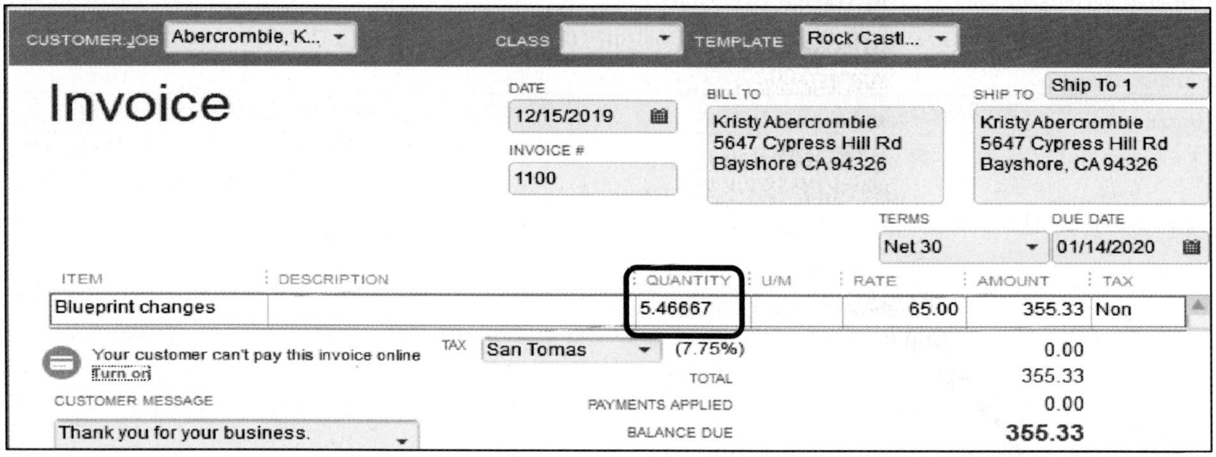

- The time clock keeps time in minutes but enters time on the invoice in tenths of an hour.

Click **Save & Close**

REMINDERS

Reminders is a list that gives you alerts and reminds you of tasks that need to be completed. It is accessed by clicking the clock on the Menu bar or from the Company menu. The dashboard for Reminders shows several categories in collapsed mode. On the left side of the Reminders list are alerts and today's tasks. When you click a category, it is expanded and the individual tasks/alerts are shown. If a task is overdue, it appears in red. If you click the Plus icon you may add a To Do. If you click the Gear

B

icon [gear icon] you may choose reminders for tasks, when, and how. If you double-click an alert, transaction, or To Do, you will open it.

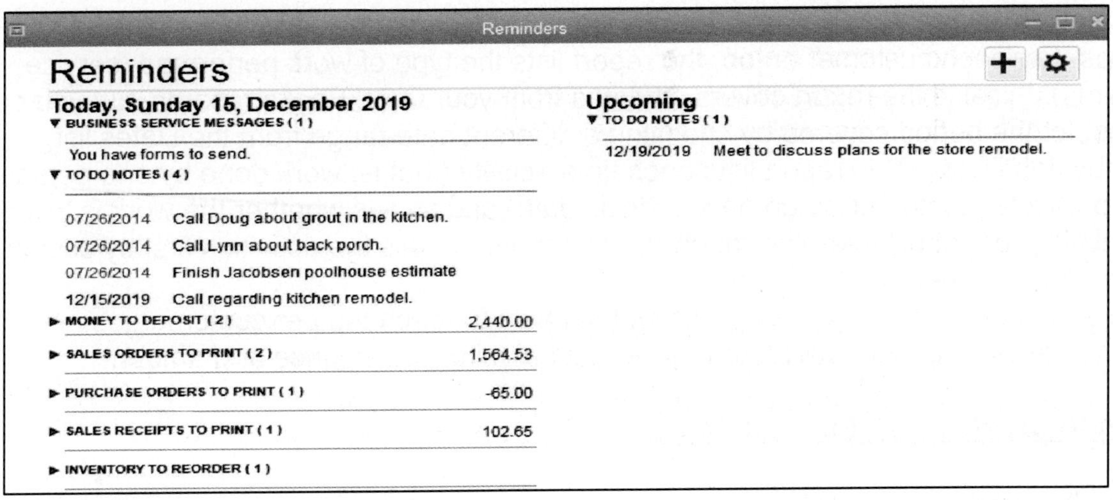

JOB COSTING AND TRACKING

Many companies complete work based on a job for a customer rather than just the customer. In QuickBooks, a job is a project done for a particular customer; for example, a kitchen remodel. You must always associate a job with a customer. However, if you are only doing one job for the customer, you do not have to add a new job to the Customer:Job list. Instead, you can use the Job Info tab to track the status of the job. When you have not set up any jobs for the customer, the Job Info tab is available in the New Customer (or Edit Customer) window. You may also track several jobs for one customer.

When tracking jobs, there are several reports that may be prepared. These are listed in the Jobs, Time & Mileage section of the Report Center. These reports use the information provided when tracking the jobs to display data that may help you answer questions about how well you estimate jobs, how much time you spend on jobs, how profitable jobs are, and mileage costs for the jobs. Some, but not all, of the reports available are:

Job Profitability Summary: This report summarizes how much money your company has made or lost on each job.

Job Profitability Detail: This report shows how much money your company has made to date on the customer or job whose name you entered. The report lists costs and revenues for each item you billed to the customer so you can see which parts of the job were profitable and which parts were not.

Profit & Loss by Job: Shows how much money you are making or losing on each job.

Job Estimates vs. Actuals Summary: This report summarizes how accurately your company estimated the job-related costs and revenues. The report compares estimated cost to actual cost and estimated revenue to actual revenue for all customers.

Job Estimates vs. Actuals Detail: This report shows how accurately your company estimated costs and revenues for the customer or job whose name you entered. The report compares estimated and actual costs and estimated and actual revenues for each item that you billed. That way, you can see which parts of the job you estimated accurately and which parts you did not.

Time by Job Summary: This report shows how much time your company spent on various jobs. For each customer or job, the report lists the type of work performed (service items). Initially, the report covers all dates from your QuickBooks records, but you can restrict the period covered by choosing a different date range from the Dates list.

Time by Job Detail: This report lists each time activity (that is, work done by one person for a particular customer or job on a specific date) and shows whether the work is billed, unbilled, or not billable. The report groups and subtotals the activities first by customer and job and then by service item.

Mileage by Job Detail: This report shows the miles for each trip per customer:job and includes the trip date, billing status, item, total miles, sales price and amount.

Steps to Create a Job for a Customer

Open the **Customer Center**

Select the customer for whom you want to add a job

- In this example, it is **Abercrombie, Kristy**.

Click the **New Customer & Job** button, click **Add Job**

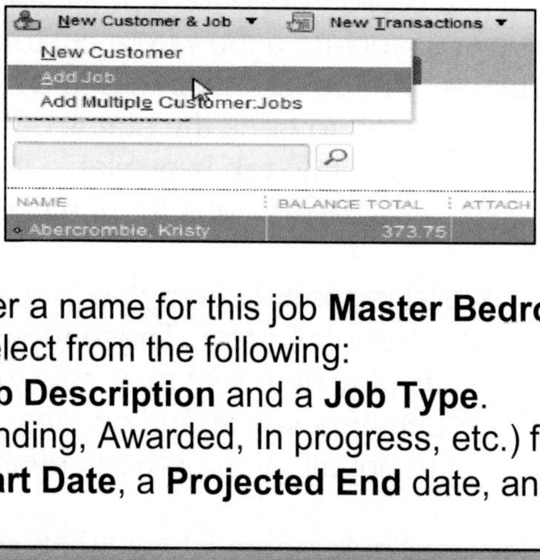

In the New Job window, enter a name for this job **Master Bedroom Remodel**

Click the Job Info tab and select from the following:

- (Optional) Enter a **Job Description** and a **Job Type**.

Select a **Job Status** (Pending, Awarded, In progress, etc.) from the drop-down list

- (Optional) Enter a **Start Date**, a **Projected End** date, and/or an **End Date** for the job

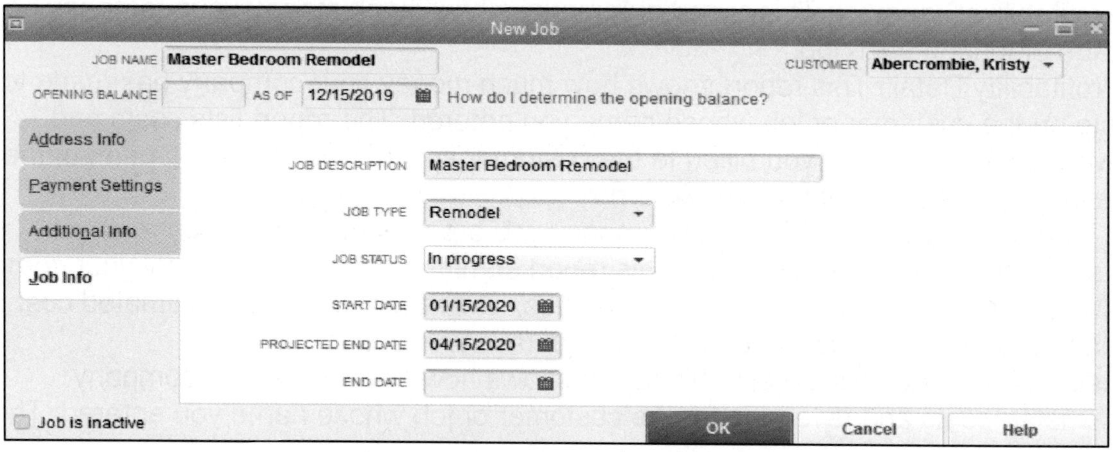

Click **OK** to record the new job

- The job is added to the customer or the Customer List

NAME	BALANCE TOTAL	ATTACH
◆ Abercrombie, Kristy	355.33	
◆ Master Bedroom Remodel	0.00	
◆ Family Room	0.00	
◆ Kitchen	355.33	
◆ Remodel Bathroom	0.00	

Close the **Customer Center**

Steps to Create a Bill Received for Job Expenses and Purchases

Enter the bill information as instructed in Chapter 6
Enter the date and amount of the bill
Enter the expense on the Expenses tab

- In example, the expense account **54520: Freight & Delivery** is used.

Click the drop-down list arrow for Customer:Job in the Customer:Job column on the Expenses tab
Click the appropriate Customer:Job

- In the example, the Customer:Job is **Babcock's Music Shop: Remodel**.

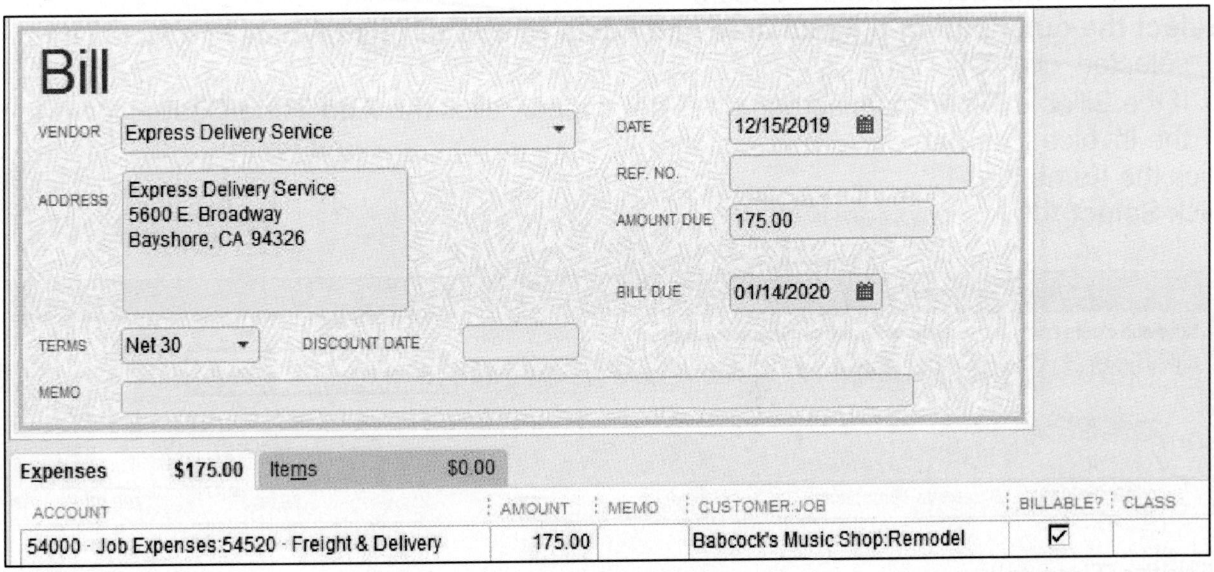

If a bill was for both expenses and items and expenses have been entered, you would then click the Items tab and enter the appropriate information for the Items including the Customer:Job

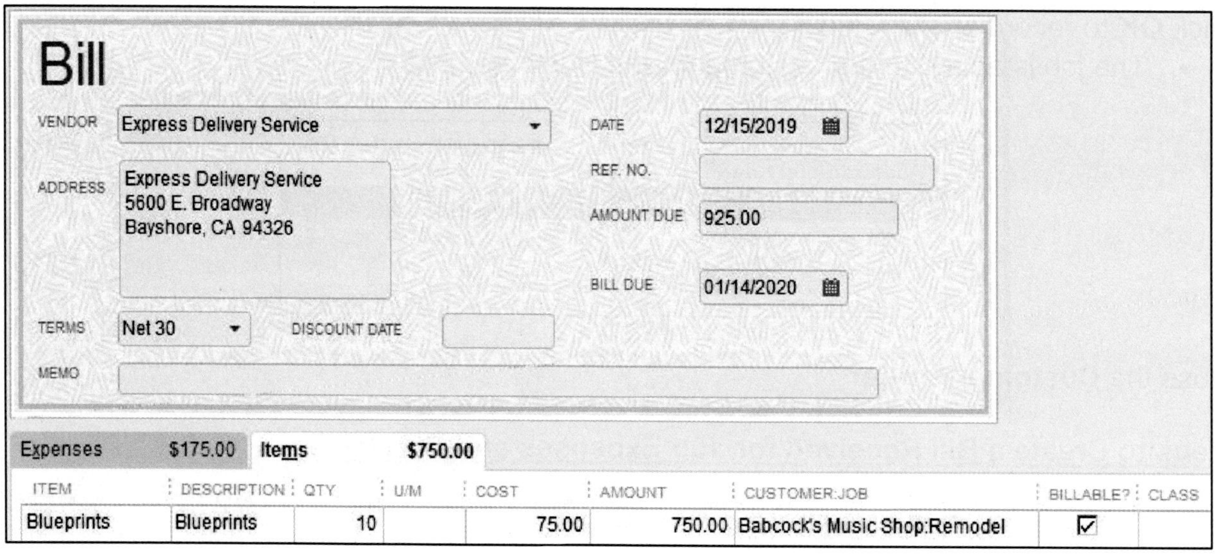

Click **Save & Close**

Steps to Create an Invoice for Items and Time Billed for a Job

Open an Invoice, select the Customer:Job

- In the example, the Customer:Job is **Babcock's Music Shop: Remodel**.

The Billable Time/Costs screen appears

"**Select the outstanding billable time and costs to add to this invoice?"** should be selected, click **OK**

- If the Billable Time/Costs screen does not appear, click the **Add Time/Costs** icon on the Invoice Icon Bar.

Click the **Items** tab

Click **Select All**

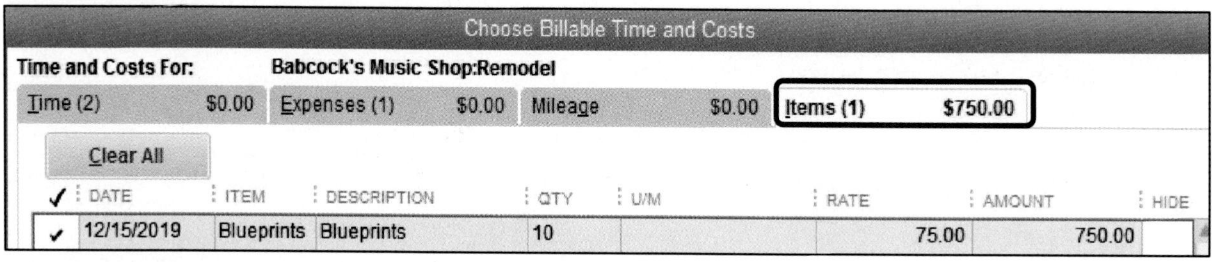

Click the **Time** tab

Click **Select All** to select

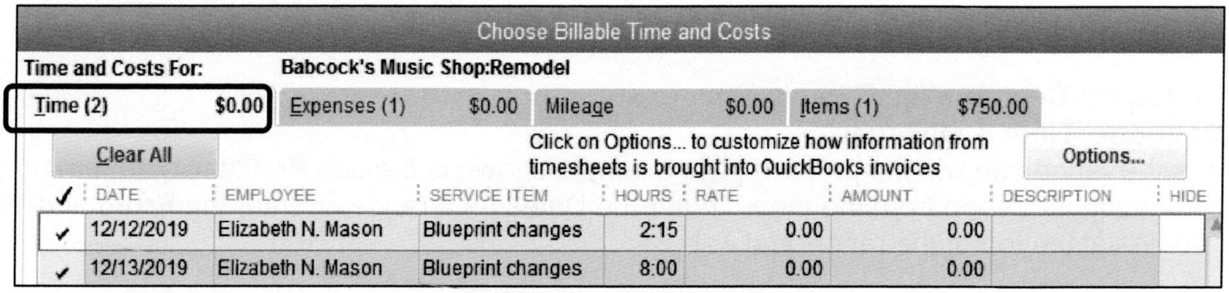

Click the **Expenses** tab to add the cost of the Delivery to the invoice
Either click **Select All** or click the individual expense

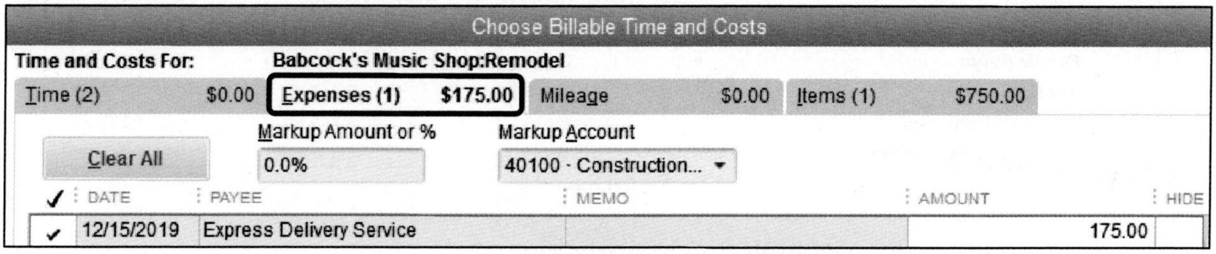

Click **OK** on the Choose Billable Time and Costs
To complete the invoice, enter the Rate of **85.00** for the Blueprint Changes

- Note this is the rate Rock Castle Construction charges customers for the time spent preparing the changes to blueprints. Since the amount did not appear on the Choose Billable Time and Costs screen, it must be entered manually.
- The $750 was the cost of the changed Blueprints from Express Delivery (in the earlier example) and was entered by QuickBooks after choosing billable time and costs.

Add the Description **Delivery** to the $175 charge for Express Delivery Service

- The amount was entered by QuickBooks after choosing billable time and costs.

Complete the Invoice

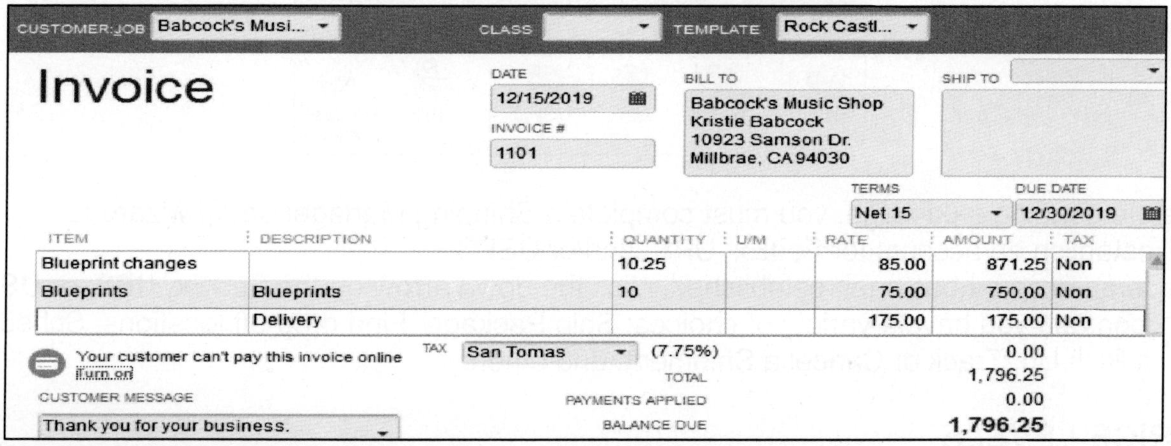

Notice that the Balance Due includes the amount for the delivery, the blueprints, and time billed for blueprints
Click **Save & Close**

Creating Reports Using Jobs and Time

Use **Report Center** or the Reports Menu
Click **Jobs, Time & Mileage**
Click the report you wish to prepare (The example shown is the Job Profitability Summary.)
If preparing the report from the menu, enter the Dates as a range or enter the **From** and **To** dates at the top of the report and Tab

Rock Castle Construction
Job Profitability Summary
All Transactions

	Act. Cost	Act. Revenue	($) Diff.
Abercrombie, Kristy			
Family Room	2,150.00	2,961.05	811.05
Kitchen	2,645.00	5,147.33	2,502.33
Remodel Bathroom	5,416.23	6,749.50	1,333.27
Total Abercrombie, Kristy	10,211.23	14,857.88	4,646.65

Partial Report

Scroll through the report to evaluate the information
Close the report

SENDING MERCHANDISE USING QUICKBOOKS SHIPPING MANAGER

QuickBooks has a shipping manager that works in conjunction with FedEx, UPS, or USPS. In order to send merchandise to a customer, you must set up the shipping manager and have an account with FedEx. Since we are working for a fictitious company we are unable to do this.

To set up the Shipping Manager, you would click the **Send/Ship** tab at the top of an invoice

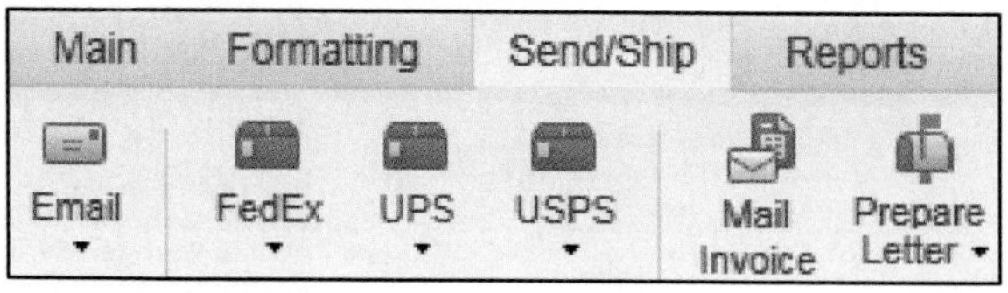

Before sending a package, you must complete a Shipping Manager setup wizard to establish an account for FedEx, UPS, and/or USPS
Once an account has been established, click the down arrow on the **FedEx**, **UPS**, or **USPS** icon and you have a variety of choices: Ship Package, Find drop off locations, Schedule a Pick Up, Track or Cancel a Shipment, and others

PRICE LEVELS

Price levels are created to increase or decrease inventory, non-inventory, and service item prices. For each price level you create, you assign a name and percentage of increase or decrease. You can use price levels on invoices, sales receipts, or credit memos. When you apply a price level to an item on a sales form, the adjusted price appears in the Rate column. You can assign price levels to customers and jobs. Then, whenever you use that customer and job on a sales form, the associated price level is automatically used to calculate the item price.

Create a Price Level List

From the Lists menu, choose **Price Level List**
Click the **Price Level** button, choose **New**
In the New Price Level window, enter the name of the new price level (Valued Customer in the example below)
In the area for **This price level will**, select either **increase** or **decrease** for **item prices by**
In the Percentage % field, enter the number and the % sign for the percentage by which the item price will be increased or reduced
Indicate whether QuickBooks should round numbers

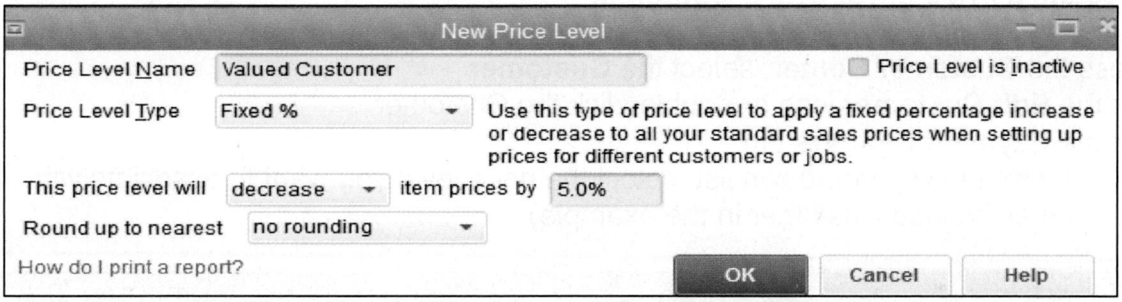

Click **OK** to go back to the Price Levels list, and close the **Price Level List**

Apply a Price Level on an Invoice

Fill out the invoice as previously instructed (shown on the next page)
Click the drop-down list arrow for **Rate**, and click a price level to apply to the item (Valued Customer in this example)

- The amount shown next to each price level is the adjusted rate for the item.

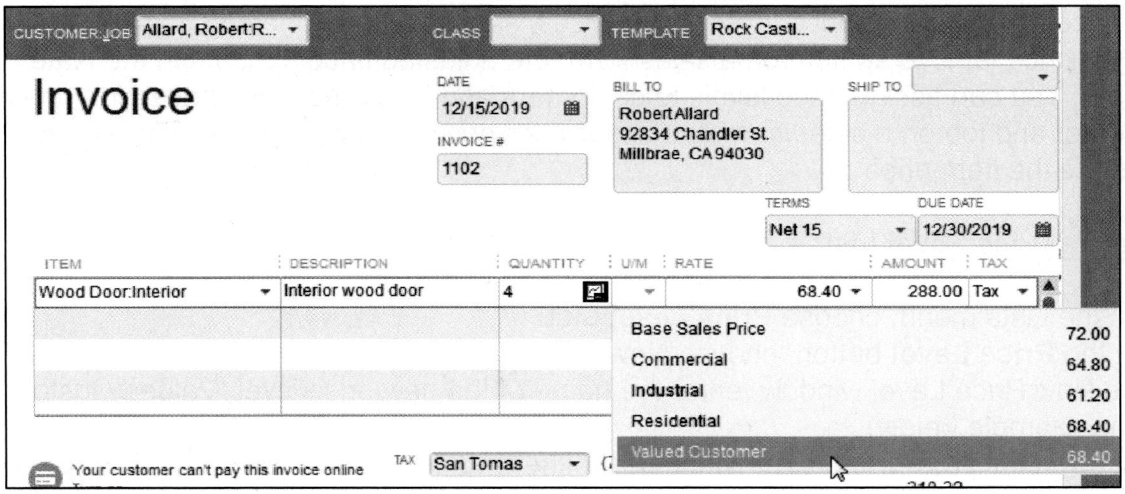

Save & Close the invoice

Associate a Price Level with a Customer

Access the **Customer Center**, select the **Customer**
Click the **Edit Customer** icon or double-click the Customer
Click the **Payment Settings** tab
From the Price Level drop-down list, select the price level you want to associate with the customer (Valued Customer in the example)

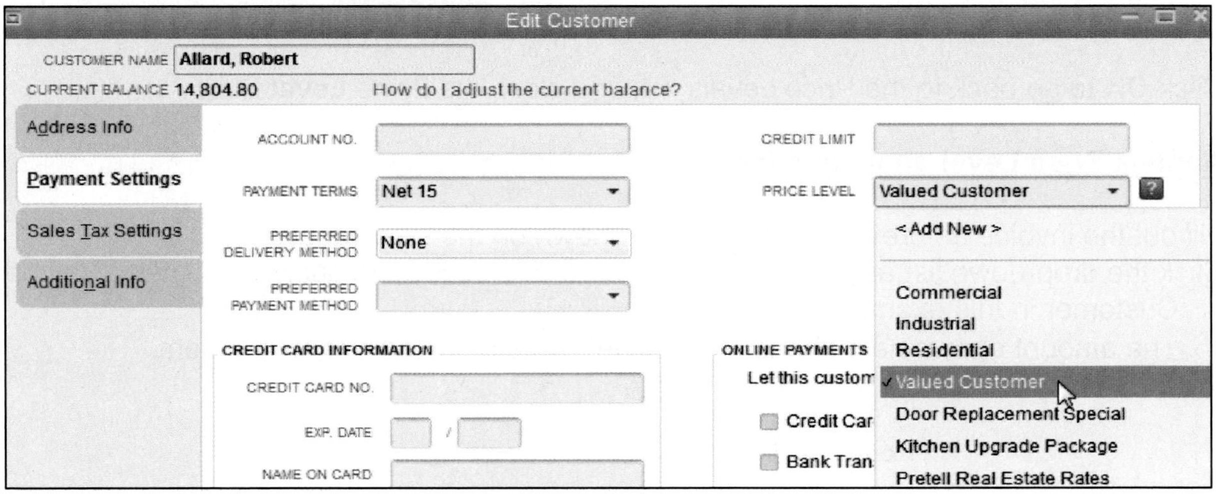

Click **OK**

Associate a Price Level with a Job

To apply a Price Level to a Job, click the **Job** listed beneath the customer in the Customer Center
Click the **Edit Job** icon or double-click the Job

Click the appropriate **price level** on the **Payment Settings** tab
In this example, **Valued Customer** is selected as the Price Level, click **OK**

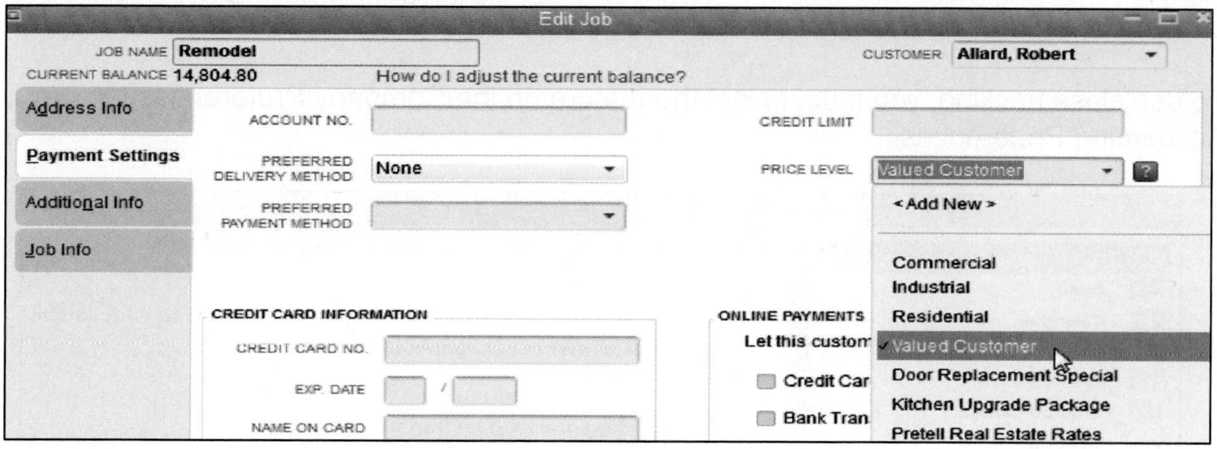

Prepare an Invoice Using Selected Price Levels

When preparing an invoice, items will automatically appear at the price level selected for the customer or job
To verify this, create a new invoice, and then click the drop-down list arrow for Rate

- Notice that Robert Allard is identified as a Valued Customer and that the price for the Standard Doorknobs in the example below has been entered at the price level selected for the customer (Valued Customer).

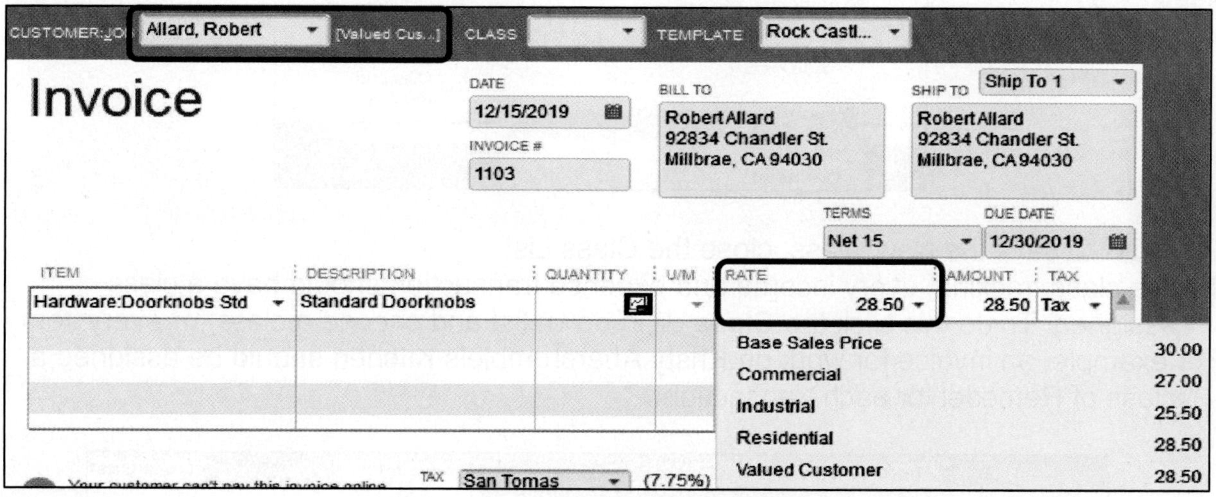

CLASSES

QuickBooks allows you to create classes that you assign to transactions. This lets you track account balances in various segments of your business. Reports may be prepared for the different classes you track. For example, in a construction company like Rock Castle Construction, you may want reports that itemize account balances for each construction division on your jobs. This lets you know how well you managed income and expenses. You may want to track your subcontractors by setting up a subset of the construction divisions; i.e. Rough Electrical and Finish Electrical to distinguish one segment of construction from the other.

To use class tracking, you must select the feature on the Company Preferences tab for Accounting Preferences.

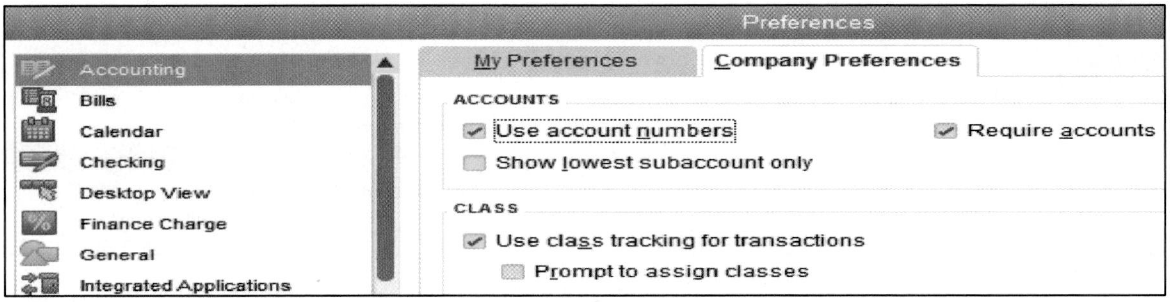

To use or create a Class, click **Class List** on the Lists menu
Click the **Class** button, and then click **New**; or use the Ctrl + N shortcut
To complete the following example, enter **Advertising** as the Class Name
Click **Subclass of**, and then click **New Construction**

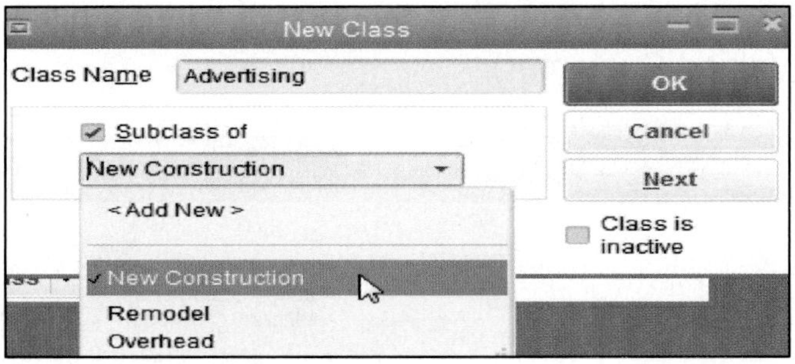

Click **OK** to save the New Class, close the Class List
To use class tracking, every income and expense transaction should have a class assigned. To do this click the **Class** drop-down list and choose a class for every item.
For example, an invoice for work on Kristy Abercrombie's Kitchen should be assigned a class of Remodel for each transaction.

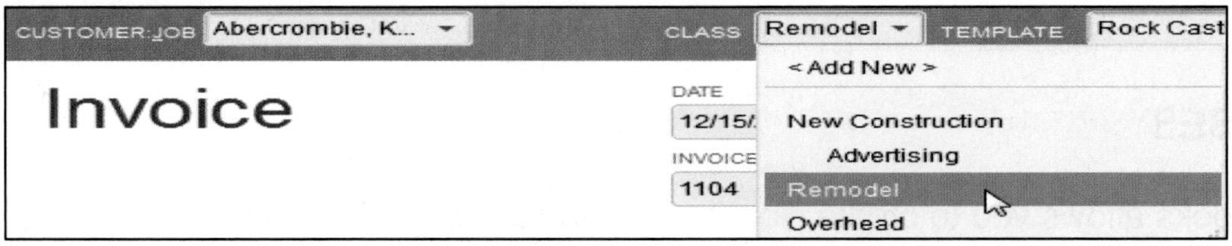

Several reports, such as, a Balance Sheet by Class and a Profit & Loss by Class, etc. are available when working with classes. The example below shows the Construction income section of Rock Castle Construction's Profit & Loss by Class report. This report shows the income earned, the cost of goods sold, and expenses incurred for each account categorized by class; i.e. New Construction, Remodel, Overhead, and Unclassified. The report includes a Totals column so you can see the total amounts for each account and each section of the report.

11:13 AM
12/15/19
Accrual Basis

Rock Castle Construction
Profit & Loss by Class
January 1 through December 15, 2019

	New Construction	Remodel	Overhead	Unclassified	TOTAL
Ordinary Income/Expense					
Income					
40100 · Construction Income					
40110 · Design Income	3,152.74	33,576.51	0.00	1,226.58	37,955.83
40130 · Labor Income	52,696.44	155,528.98	0.00	0.00	208,225.42
40140 · Materials Income	68,401.16	51,519.51	0.00	302.10	120,222.77
40150 · Subcontracted Labor Income	58,492.30	24,218.05	0.00	0.00	82,710.35
40199 · Less Discounts given	0.00	-48.35	0.00	0.00	-48.35
40100 · Construction Income - Other	0.00	0.00	0.00	0.00	0.00
Total 40100 · Construction Income	182,742.64	264,794.70	0.00	1,528.68	449,066.02

Partial Report

BATCH INVOICING

If you have an invoice that you want to send to multiple customers, you may create a single batch of invoices rather than an invoice for each individual customer.

Click the **Customers** menu and click **Create Batch Invoices**
Click **OK** on the "Is your customer info set up correctly?" message box
You may add customers to the batch individually or by billing group.

- If you were adding a group, you would click the drop-down list arrow for **Billing Group**, and click the group name. (Not shown.)

To add customers to the batch, click the customer you want to include, then click the **Add** button; repeat for each customer you want to add

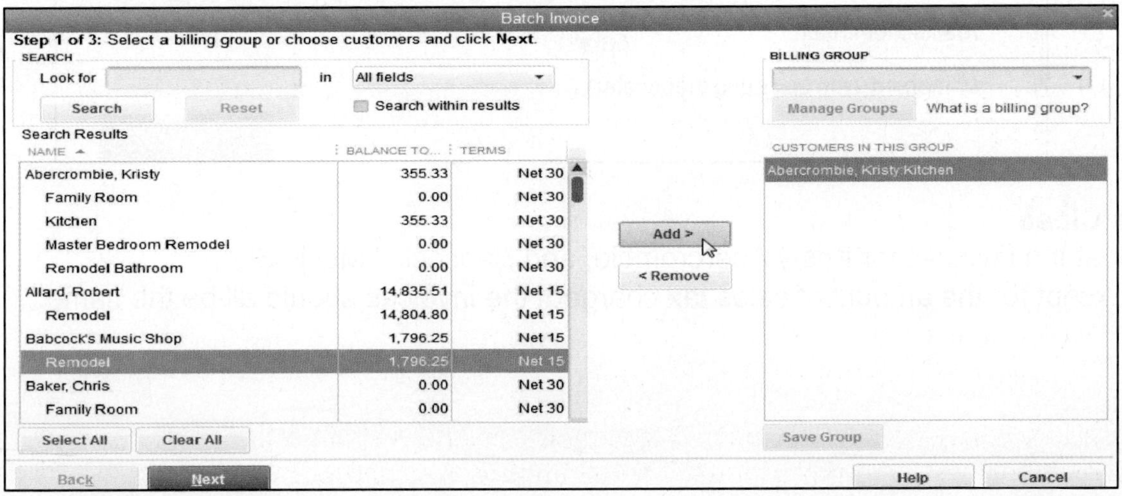

Click **Next**, select the Items used in the invoices, enter the quantity, select the message

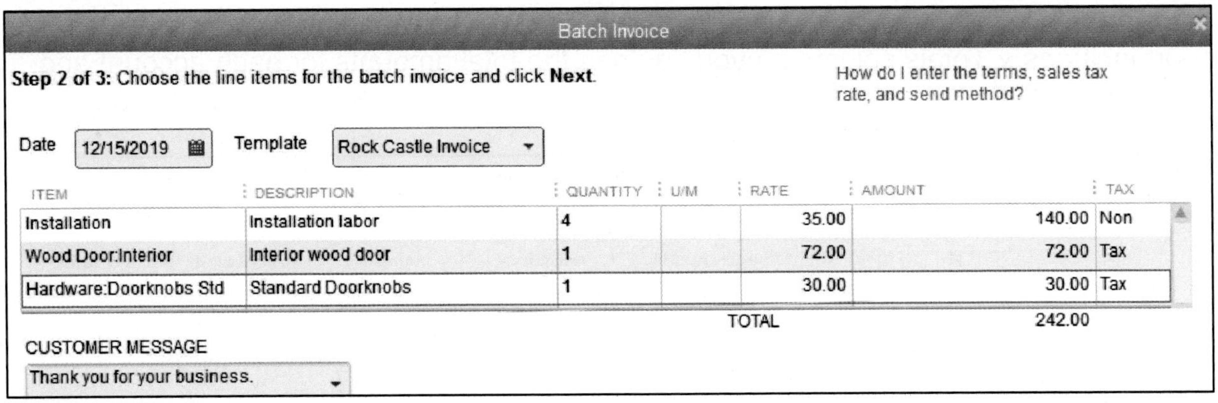

Click **Next** , review the list

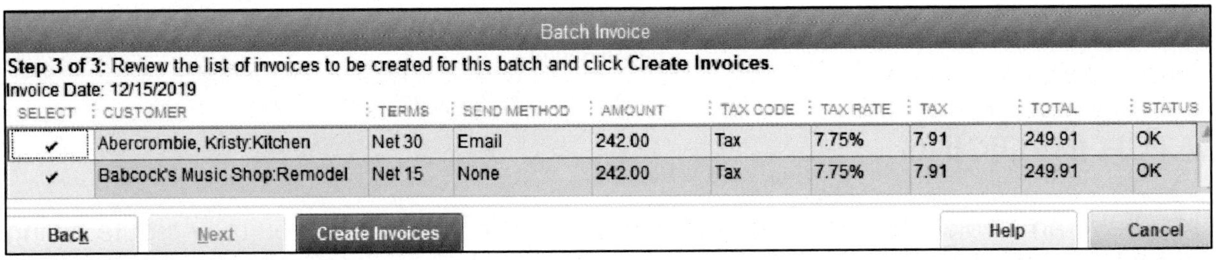

Click **Create Invoices**

On the Batch Invoices Summary you will see how many invoices are being emailed, printed, or need to be sent later

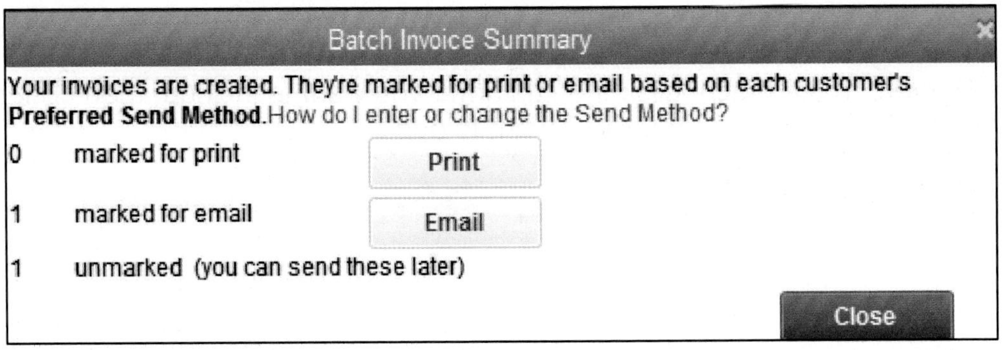

Click **Close**

Look at the invoices for Kristy Abercrombie, and Babcock's Music Shop

- Except for the amount of sales tax charged, the invoices should all be the same.

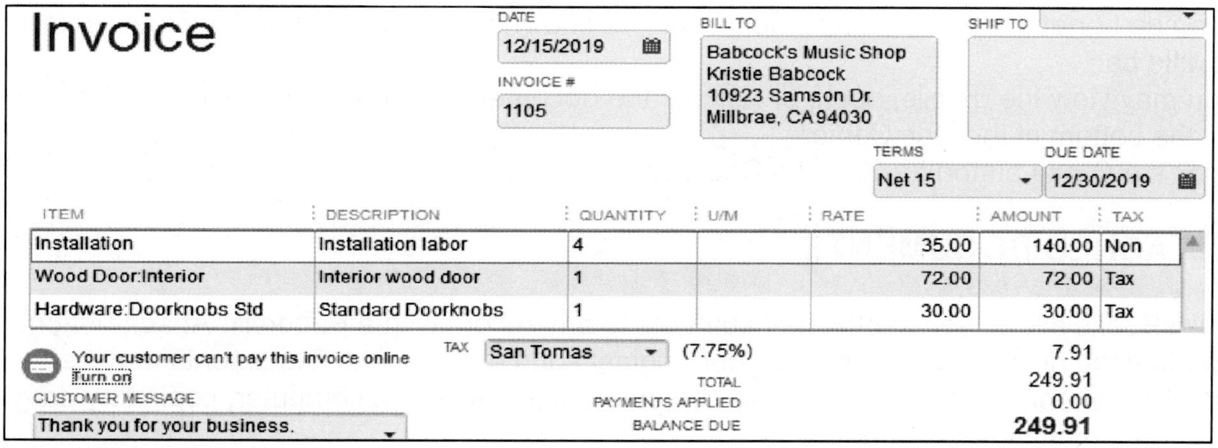

DOCUMENT CENTER

The Doc Center keeps track of documents you use with QuickBooks. You may add a document from your computer, scan a document, or drag and drop a document from Outlook or Explorer to the Doc Center. The documents may then be attached to QuickBooks records such as invoices, customers, etc.

Click the **Docs** icon on the Top Icon bar to open the Doc Center

To add a document from your computer, click the **Add a Document Folder** icon, find the document, click it to select, click **Open**

The document is added to the Doc Center

To scan a document, click the **Scanner** icon; place the document on your scanner; click **Scan**; on the "What do you want to scan?" screen; select the option for the type of picture or document; click **Scan**; when finished, click **Done Scanning**; give the document a name; click **OK**

To drag and drop a document on the desktop, point to the document icon, hold down the primary mouse button, drag the document to the section that says Drop documents from Outlook, your desktop, or folders here, release the mouse button

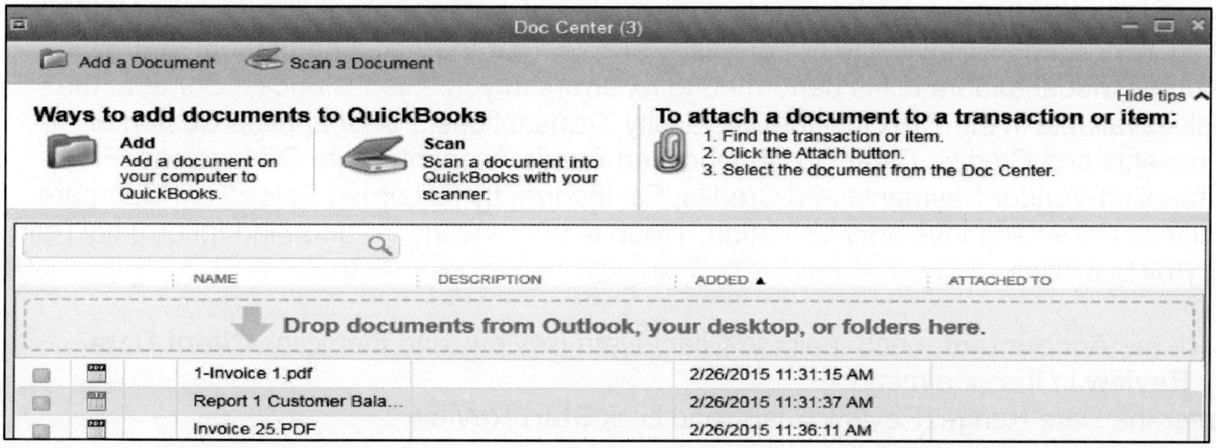

The number of documents in the Doc Center is shown in parentheses on the Doc Center title bar
You may view the details, open, or remove the document by clicking one of the buttons at the bottom of the Doc Center
Click the **Close** button to close the Doc Center

ATTACHED DOCUMENTS

QuickBooks allows you to attach documents to any record with a Paperclip Attach button. An attached document is a copy of your original source document. Documents may be attached when they are stored on the computer, scanned to the computer, copied by drag and drop, or in the Doc Center.

To attach a document from the Doc Center to a transaction, open and complete the business form

- In the example, a Bill from Thomas Kitchen & Bath was selected.

Click the icon for Attach File on the Enter Bills Main icon bar

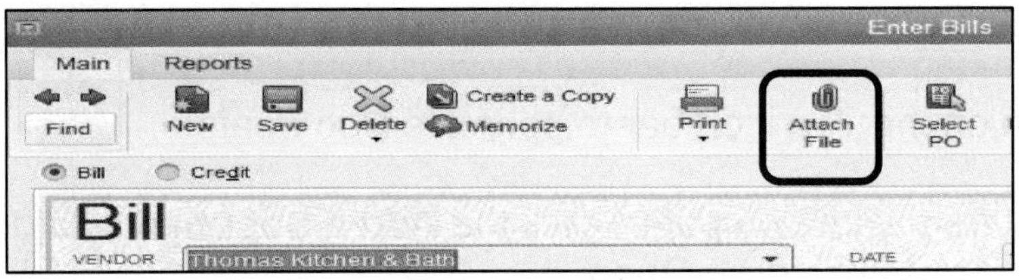

Select the **Doc Center** for the document location
Click the document to select, click the **Attach** button
The document is attached to the business document
To view the attached document, simply click on the attachment and click the **Open** button
When finished attaching documents from the Doc Center, click **Done**
You will see the number of attached documents on the Attach File icon on the bill

CLIENT DATA REVIEW

The Client Data Review (CDR) Center is available from the Accountant menu and has features that automate tasks performed to fix errors in your client's books. Some of the tasks available in the CDR include Reclassify Transactions, Fix Unapplied Customer Payments and Credits, Clear Up Undeposited Funds Account, Write Off Invoices, Fix Unapplied Vendor Payments and Credits, Fix Incorrectly Recorded Sales Tax, Compare Balance Sheet and Inventory Valuation, Troubleshoot Inventory, and Find Incorrectly Paid Payroll Liabilities.

Click the **Accountant** menu, point to Client Data Review, and then click **Client Data Review** in the side menu
Enter the Date Range, Review Basis, and click **Start Review**

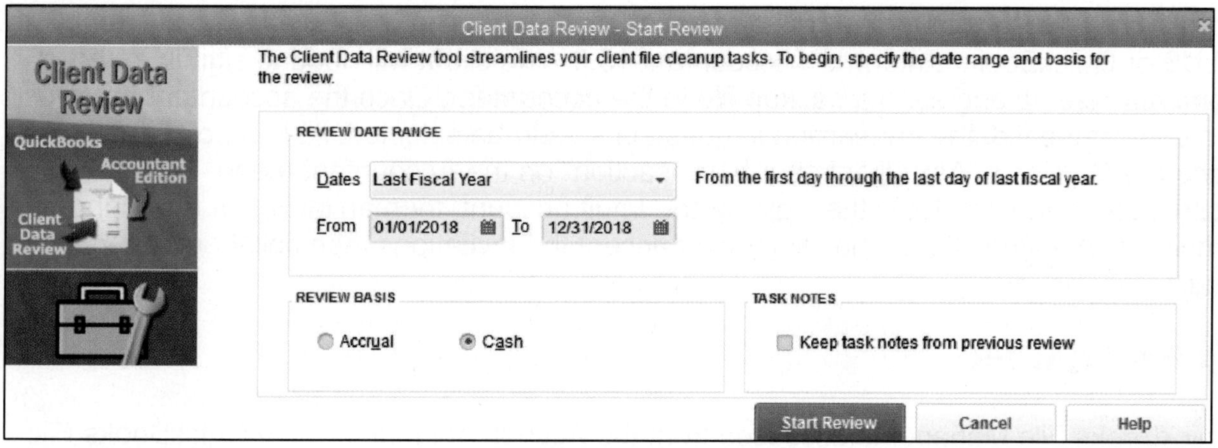

The Client Data chart appears with the tasks listed. As you work on the different review areas, you can indicate the Status of the review, add Task Notes, and add Review Notes

Task areas include: Account Balances, Review List Changes, Accounts Receivable, Accounts Payable, Sales Tax, Inventory, Payroll, Bank Reconciliation, and Miscellaneous

The Review may be printed or saved as a PDF file. You may get an Audit Trail of Review, and when finished, mark the review as complete

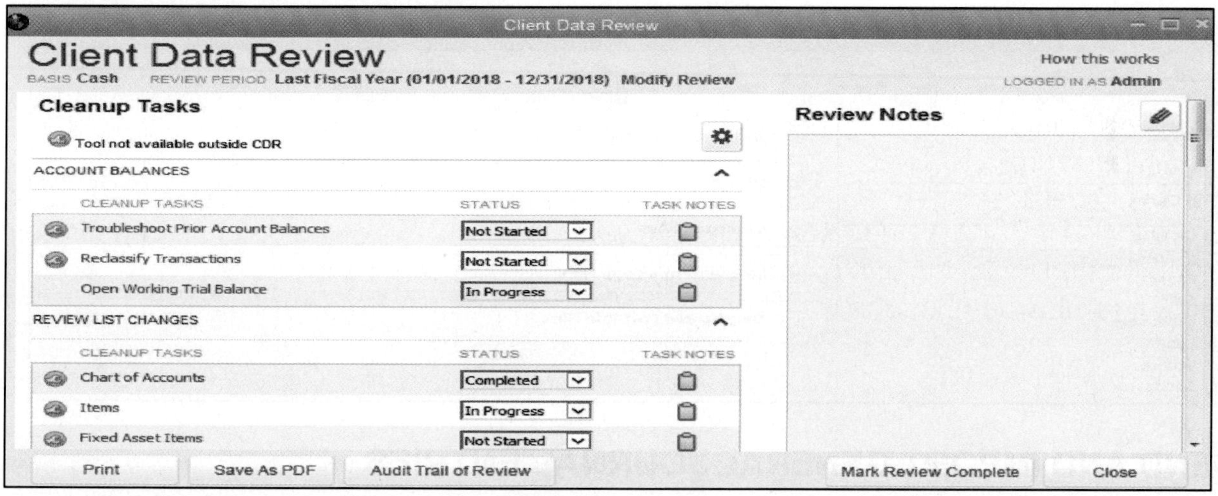

Close the Client Data Review when finished

CLIENT COLLABORATOR

Frequently, accountants will need to get clarification from clients regarding transactions or data entered into the company file. Using Client Collaborator allows the client and accountant to communicate directly through the client's QuickBooks file. The conversations are tracked, associated with specific transactions, and stored in the cloud so the accountant always has a point of reference.

To use the Client Collaborator, the accountant must be using QuickBooks Accountant 2015 PLUS or QuickBooks Enterprise Accountant 15.0. The client will need to sign in to the company, create and send a backup file to the accountant. Once the accountant receives the copy of the file, the transaction in question should be selected. At that point, the accountant selects "Ask Client about Transaction" on the Accountant menu. The accountant now completes the login for the Intuit account; then an invitation to collaborate email is sent to the client. The client must accept the invitations then collaboration may begin.

FILE MANAGER

QuickBooks File Manager is accessed from the Accountant menu or the QuickBooks File Manager icon. File Manager enables you to open and manage clients' QuickBooks files. This is a very helpful component of QuickBooks Accountant and QuickBooks Enterprise Accountant; especially if you manage company files from multiple years.

When using QuickBooks File Manager, you may build a client list that organizes QuickBooks files by client, create clients groups that will display files for specific types of clients, upgrade clients' QuickBooks files in batches, store client passwords in the Password Vault, and automatically open your client's files with the correct version of QuickBooks.

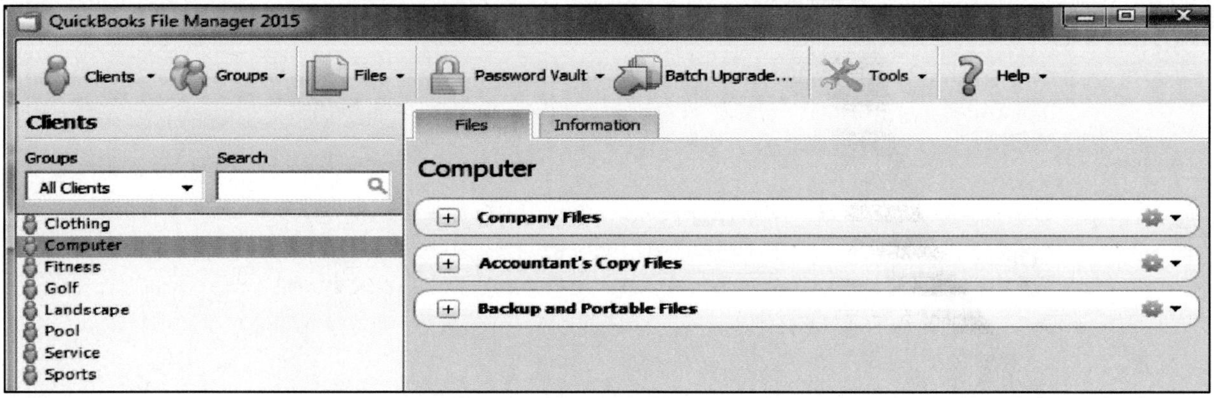

SEND AND IMPORT GENERAL JOURNAL ENTRIES

Using the Accountant menu, you may use the Make General Journal Entries to enter General Journal entries and then click the icon **Send GJEs** to add them to a list of entries to be sent from the accountant to the client. Once the entries have been selected, click Send General Journal Entries on the Accountant menu to select which entries to send. You will send the entries as either an email attachment to send the entries now or as a saved .QBJ file, which you can attach to an email or store on a USB drive.

After the accountant has sent the General Journal entries, the client opens the .QBJ file from email or Windows Explorer and the Add General Journal Entries to Your File window opens in QuickBooks. At this point, the client clicks Add GJEs to import the transactions into your company file. You then get a GJEs Import Summary window, which lists the imported journal entries.

STATEMENT WRITER

The QuickBooks Statement Writer (QSW) allows you to create customized financial reports from a QuickBooks company file. The QuickBooks Statement Writer contains a library of templates that may be used for statements and supporting documents; in addition, a template may be created. The QSW uses data directly from the QuickBooks company file. You can set preferences, formats, and styles for all of your reports. You may combine accounts and subaccounts automatically or by specification. Supporting documents may also be prepared using the same look as the one used in statements.

To use this feature, click **Statement Writer** on the icon bar 

or select QuickBooks Statement Writer on the Accountant menu

- There may be a fairly lengthy and detailed install update required in order to use the Statement Writer.

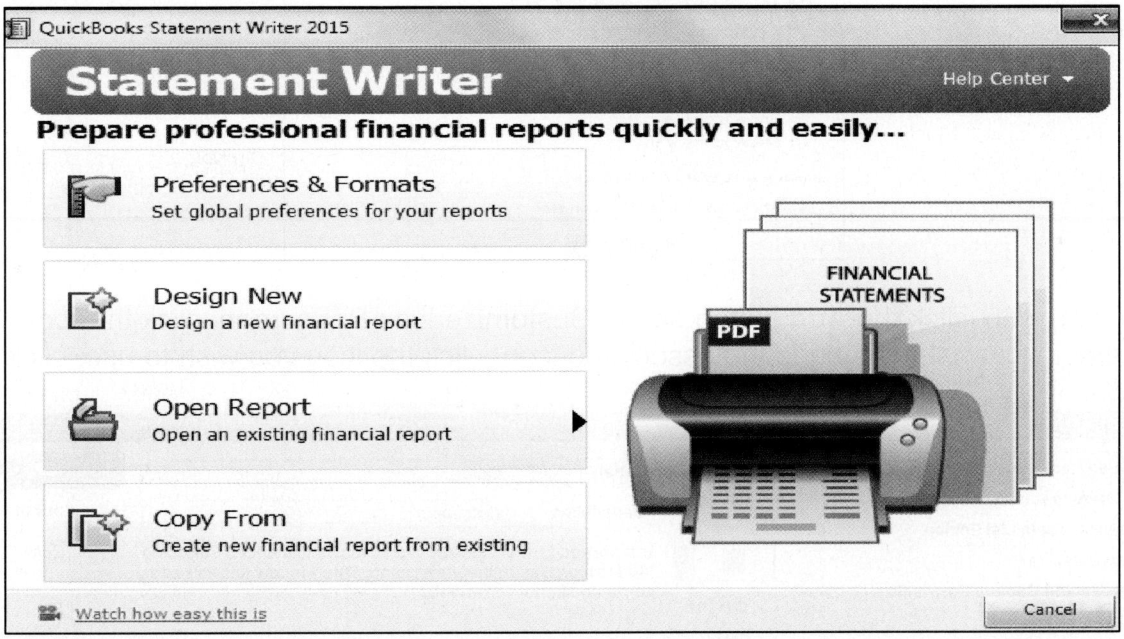

When QuickBooks Statement Writer is on the screen, there are buttons available that allow you to select General Preferences for Reports and Templates, Design New financial reports, Open Reports to select existing reports, and Copy From to create new financial report from existing reports reports.

CUSTOMIZE THE ICON BAR(S)

As previously demonstrated within the text, you may use the default Left Icon Bar or the Top Icon bar. Both the Left and Top Icon Bars may be customized to display Centers and frequently used Commands. If you do not use an icon or shortcut shown on the Icon Bar, you may delete it.

If you are using the Left Icon Bar, right-click anywhere on it to get Customize Shortcuts; and then click **Customize Shortcuts**
If you are using the Top Icon Bar, right-click anywhere on it to get Customize Icon Bar; and then, click the **Customize Icon Bar** button
Either method takes you to the Customize Icon Bar screen, where you may Add, Edit, Delete, or Add Separator to the Icon Bar Content. You may also choose to display icons and text or icons only. The final selection is whether to Show Search Box in Icon Bar
To delete an icon, you would click the icon and then click the Delete button

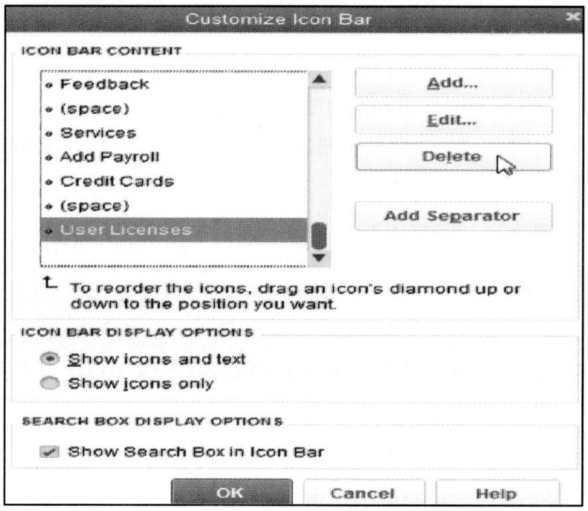

To add an icon, click the **Add** button on the Customize Icon Bar screen, click the **Icon Bar Item**; if you wish to change the associated icon, click the icon you wish to use, click **OK**

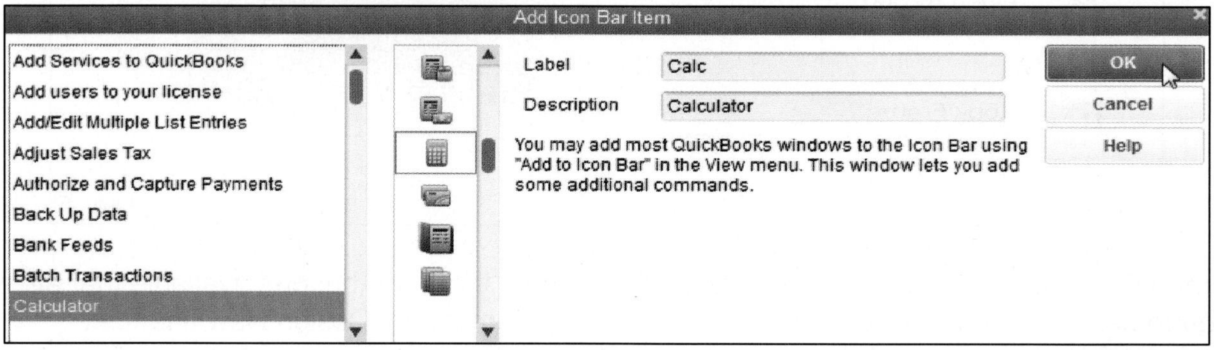

To position an added icon, drag the icon's diamond up or down within the icon bar content on the Customize icon Bar screen
Click **OK** to close Customize Icon Bar
In this example, the Icon Bar no longer shows an icon for **User Licenses** but it does show an icon for **Calc**

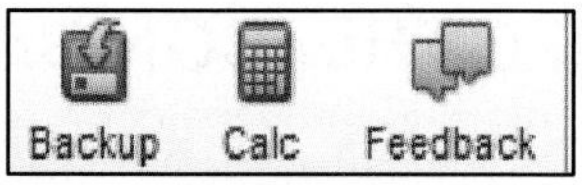

Top Icon Bar

Left Icon Bar

C

QUICKBOOKS ONLINE FEATURES

QuickBooks uses the Internet as an integral part of the program. Subscribers to the Payroll Services can receive online updates to tax tables and forms. Online banking and vendor payments can be performed within the program. You can order supplies, obtain product support, access training resources, find a QuickBooks expert in your area, get suggestions for resources for your business, and access Live Community (where you may post questions, give advice, and participate in Webinars).

In addition to the included online items, there are several online subscription programs that may be used in conjunction with QuickBooks. These include Payroll Services; QuickBooks Bill Pay; QuickBooks Payments (Merchant Service), Billing Solutions, Direct Deposit, Intuit Data Connect, QuickBooks Point of Sale, and many others.

Use QuickBooks' App Center to access free and for fee Apps that work with QuickBooks and bring together both mobile and web-based applications that companies have created to integrate their software products with QuickBooks Premier and QuickBooks Enterprise Solutions.

Intuit makes frequent changes to the applications, programs, and services that are available to work with or through QuickBooks. This appendix explores some of those features that were available at the time of writing.

Since many of the features listed above, may not be completed unless you have an active Intuit Account and subscribe to the services, they cannot be illustrated. Thus, this Appendix will explore only some of the online options available. And, as with the other appendices, you should just read the information presented and not try to complete what is illustrated.

INTUIT AND THE INTERNET

At Intuit's Web site you may get up-to-date information about QuickBooks and other products by Intuit. You can access the Intuit Web site at www.Intuit.com.

CONNECTING TO INTUIT IN QUICKBOOKS

Before connecting to Intuit's Web Site using QuickBooks, you must have the QuickBooks program and a company open. In addition, you must have a modem for your computer, and the modem must be connected to a telephone line or cable. Once the modem is connected and QuickBooks and a company are open, you may establish your Internet connection.

QuickBooks has a step-by-step tutorial that will help you do this. Clicking Internet Connection Setup on the Help menu allows you to identify an internet connection and complete the setup. The first screen you see informs QuickBooks of your choice for your Internet connection. You may select one of three connection options: you have an Internet connection that you identify; you plan to use your computer's Internet connection; or you want to sign up for an Internet account with limited access.

The three choices and their accompanying screens are shown in the following:

To Use Other Internet Connection

Click the **Help** menu, click **Internet Connection Setup**
Click **Use the following connection**, click **Other Internet connection**, and click the **Next** button at the bottom of the screen

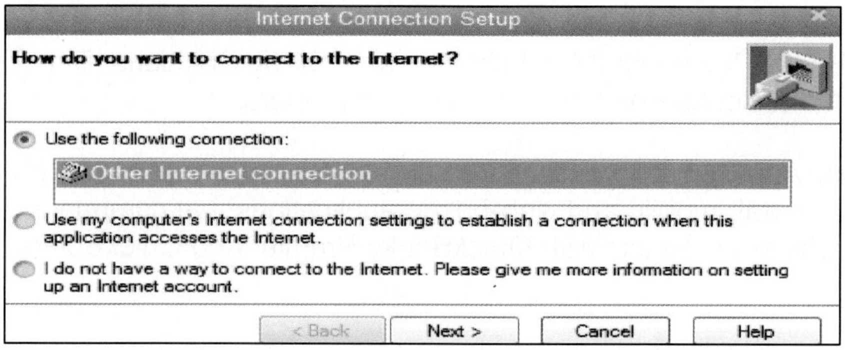

Verify the information provided, click the **Done** button at the bottom of the screen

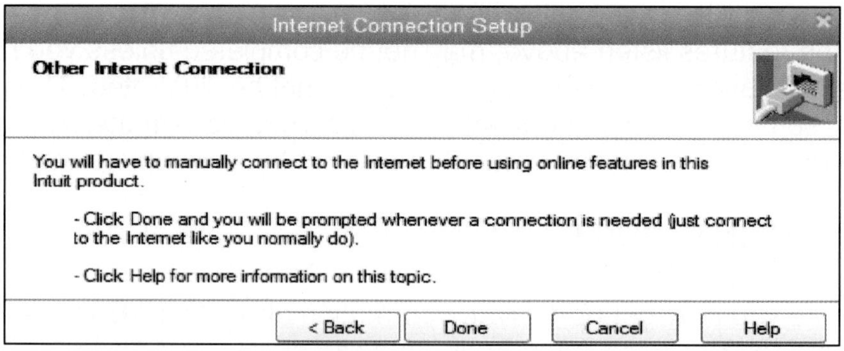

To Use a Computer's Internet Connection

If you have a direct Internet connection, select **Use my computer's Internet connection settings to establish a connection when this application accesses the Internet**, click the **Next** button at the bottom of the screen

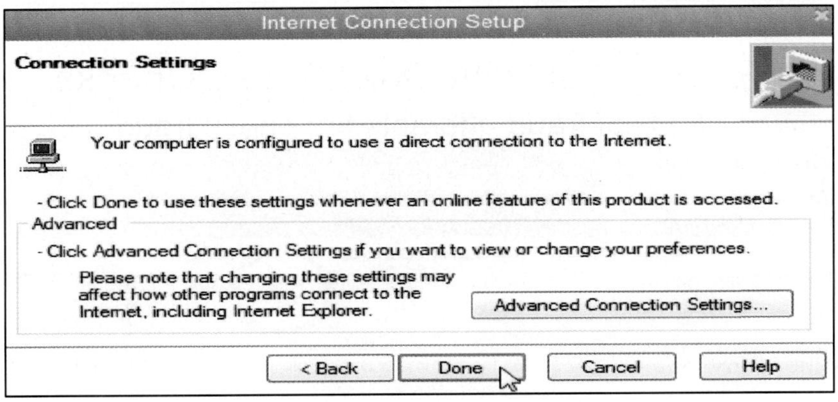

Verify the information; click the **Done** button at the bottom of the screen

To Establish an Internet Provider and Connection

If you do not have an Internet provider, click **I do not have a way to connect to the Internet. Please give me more information on setting up an Internet account**
Click **Next**

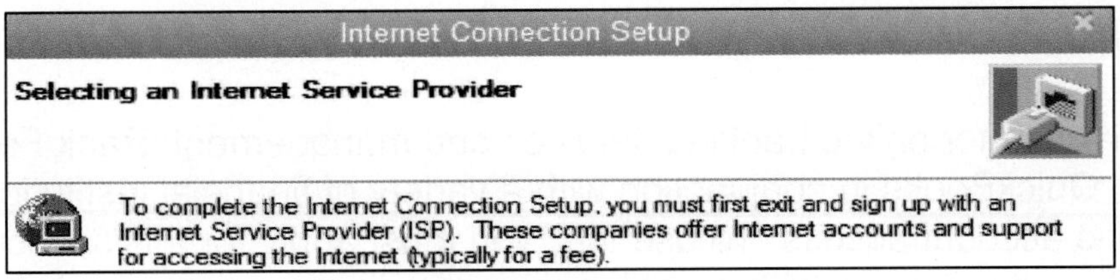

The screen will tell you that you must sign up with an Internet Service Provider.
Click **Done**

ACCESS QUICKBOOKS' ONLINE FEATURES

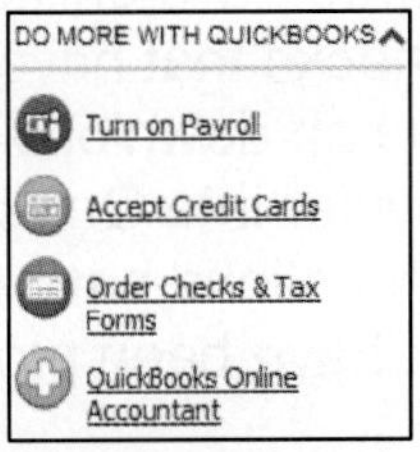

When you see a section on the Home Page or the Left Icon Bar that says "Do More with QuickBooks," clicking one of the items will take you to the areas requested if you have a direct Internet connection.

For example, Order Checks & Tax Forms in the Do More with QuickBooks section of the Home Page was clicked. QuickBooks connected to the Web and brought up a screen describing QuickBooks Checks and Supplies that are designed to work with QuickBooks and that may be ordered.

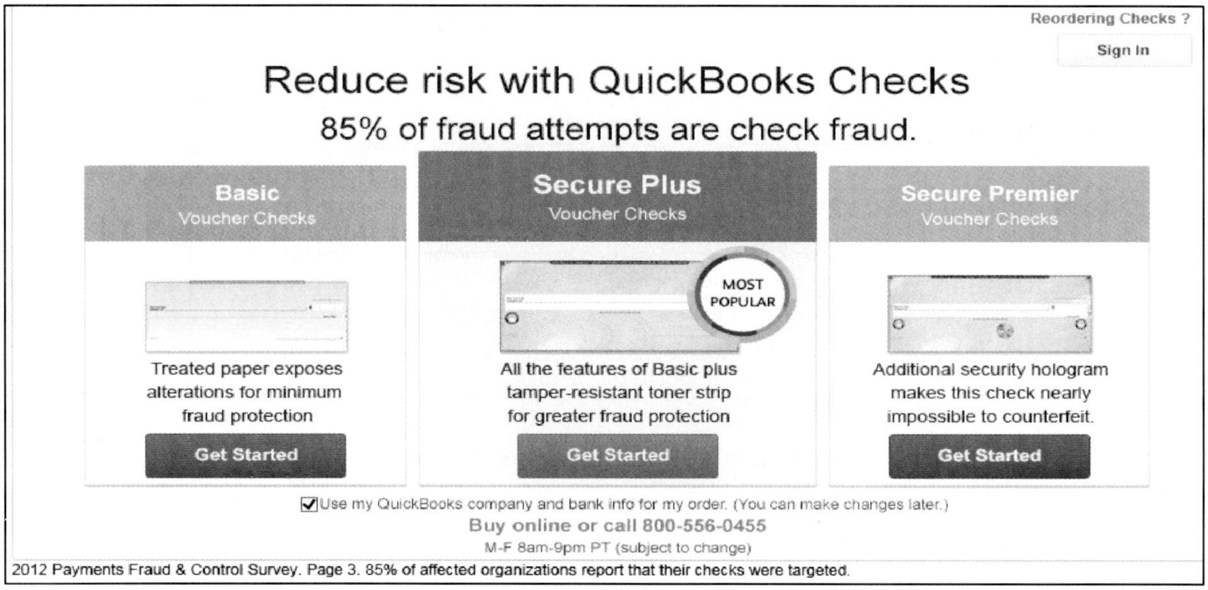

Apps are another example of online access through QuickBooks and were previously discussed.

BANK FEEDS AND ONLINE BILL PAYMENTS

Bank Feeds are used for online banking services and management. Bank Feeds are offered through QuickBooks in conjunction with a variety of financial institutions. This is also called online account access. To use this, you must apply for this service through your financial institution. If you bank with or make payments to more than one institution, you must sign up with each institution separately. Most banks will charge a fee for online services and may not offer both online banking and online payment services. Some institutions provide enhanced services, such as allowing QuickBooks to transfer money between two online accounts, accepting online customer payments, and accepting eChecks that have been processed by telephone or scanned. With the Bank Feeds service, you can download electronic statements from your financial institution or credit card provider into QuickBooks. Once statements have been downloaded, you can see what transactions have cleared your account, find out your current balance, and add transactions that have been processed but have not been entered in QuickBooks.

Some financial institutions allow you to pay bills from your vendor electronically. Once you set up the service with your bank, you use QuickBooks to send payment instructions to your financial institution. If your bank does not use electronic payments, QuickBooks has an online bill payment service that you may access on a subscription basis. For a monthly fee, you may write checks or pay bills as you would normally; then select Online Bank Payment and the date on which you would like the payment delivered. You then send the payments from the Online Banking Center within QuickBooks and they will be made by the delivery date. It is suggested that you allow up to four business days for processing.

Bank Feeds

Bank Feeds allow you to download transactions from your financial institution or credit card provider into QuickBooks.

To use the Bank Feeds services for account access or payment, you need access to the Internet and an account at a participating financial institution. You must also apply for the service through QuickBooks or through a participating financial service.

To see a list of participating financial institutions, click the **Banking** menu, point to **Bank Feeds**, and click **Participating Financial Institutions**

QuickBooks connects to the Internet and a list of banks appears

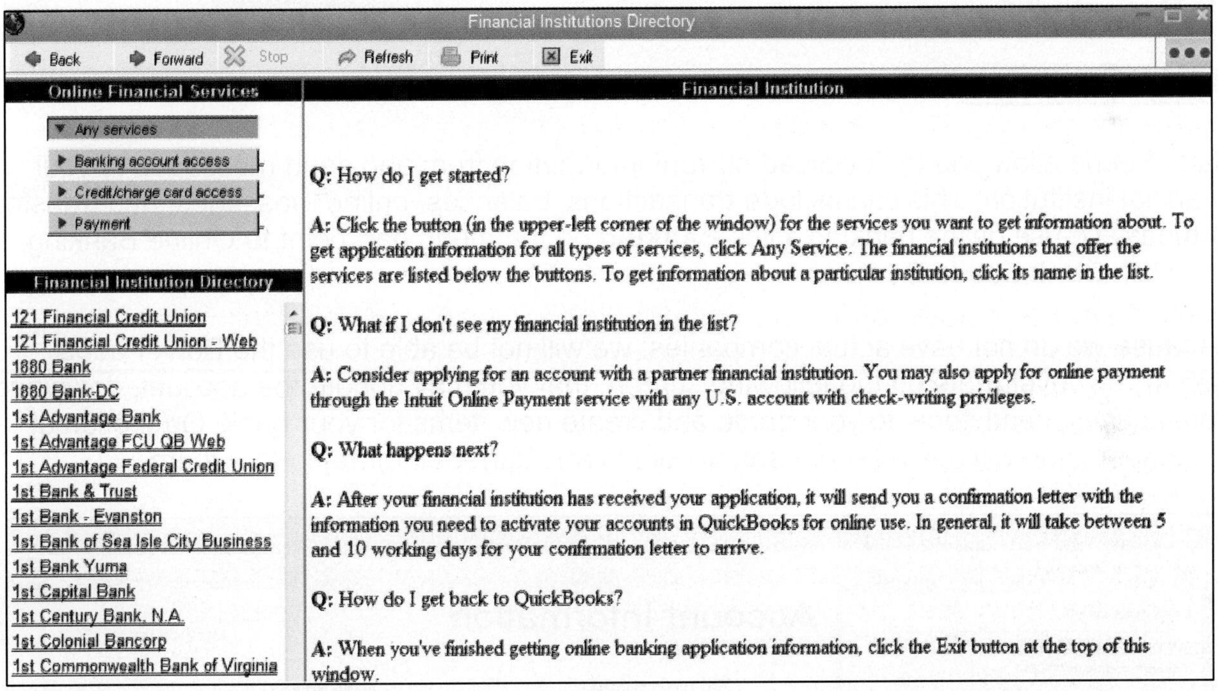

In order to provide security and confidentiality in online services, QuickBooks uses state-of-the-art encryption and authentication security features. All of your online communications with your financial institution require a Personal Identification Number (PIN) or password, which only you possess. You may also use passwords within QuickBooks.

Set Up Bank Feeds

Since we do not have an actual company, we are unable to setup an online banking account. However, to create an online banking account for your own business, click the **Banking** menu, point to **Bank Feeds**, and click **Set Up Bank Feeds for an Account**. Complete the Online Setup Interview. Once you have setup online banking, the Checking account and any other bank accounts that are setup for online banking will have a second screen for Bank Feed Settings that is accessible when you edit the account.

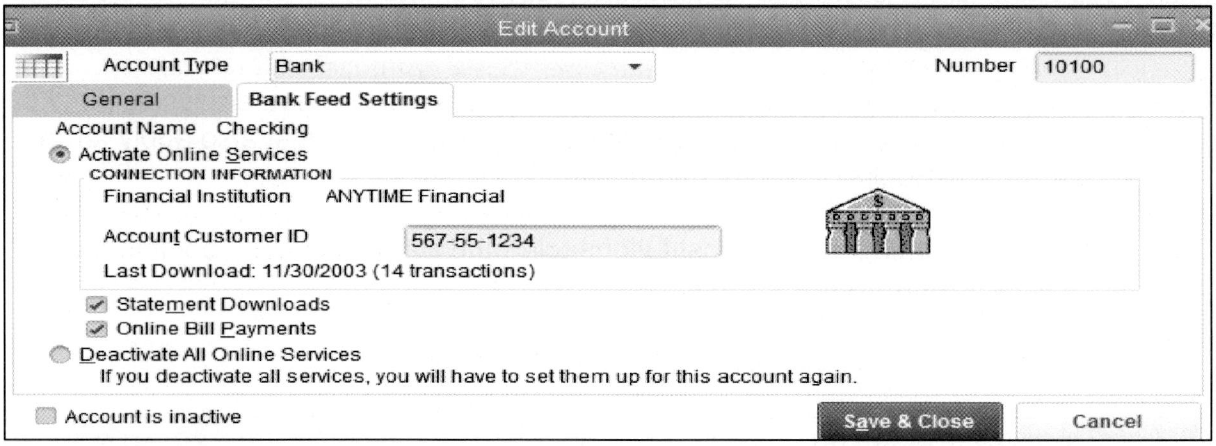

Using Bank Feeds

Bank Feeds allow you to download current information from and send messages to your financial institution. This can include transactions, balances, online messages, and transfer of funds. To use online banking, click **Banking** on the menu bar, point to Online Banking, and click **Bank Feeds Center**.

Because we do not have actual companies, we will not be able to use the Bank Feeds Center; however, note on the following screen, that you may update the account, download transactions, send items to your bank, and create new items for your bank. On the left of the screen, you will see a list of bank accounts and current information for them.

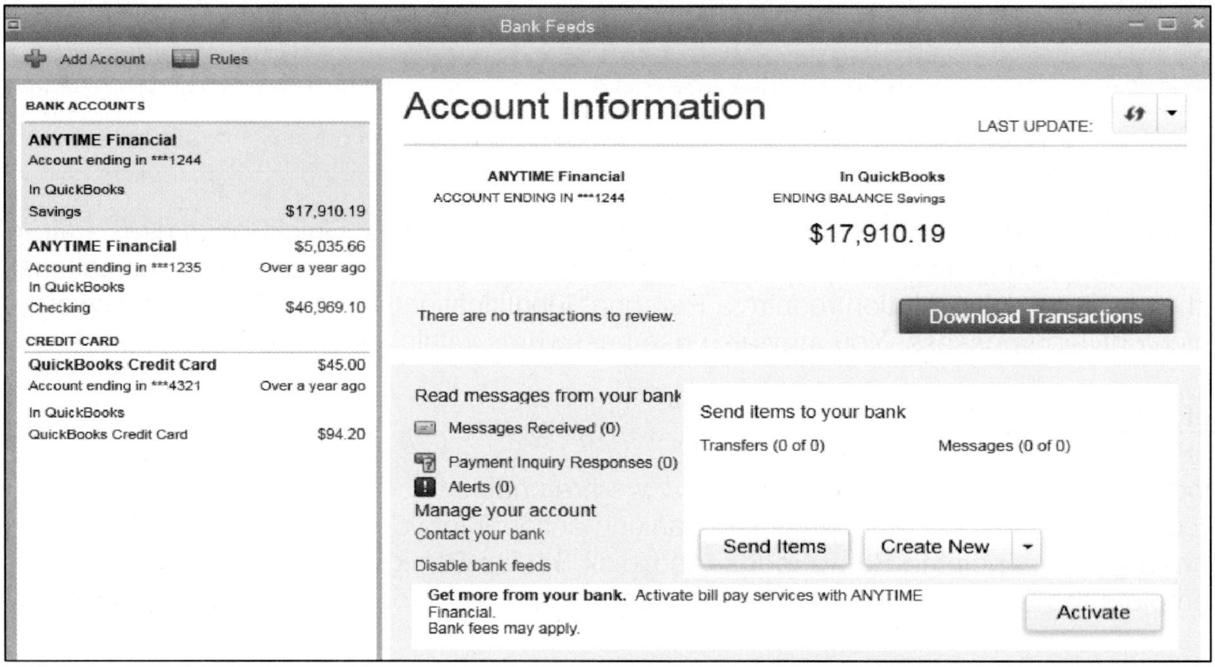

Online Payments

If your financial institution provides online bill payment services, you may subscribe to QuickBooks Bill Pay. This enables your company to make payments to any business or individual in the United States, establish internal business controls for payments, create online payment instructions for one or more payments, schedule payments in advance, and make payments from up to ten different accounts. You may schedule a payment to arrive on a certain date, inquire about online payments, and cancel them if need be. You can record and pay your bills at the same time, all from within QuickBooks. Online banking through QuickBooks uses state-of-the-art encryption technology and requires a PIN to send transactions. You can use online payments with any U.S. bank account with check-writing privileges.

To use online payments, you need to set up a payee. Once the payee is set up, you may either send an electronic funds transfer (EFT) to the payee's institution or have your financial institution print a check and send it to the payee. An electronic funds transfer deducts money from your account and transfers it into the payee's account electronically. This usually takes one or two business days; however, payments should be scheduled four days before they are due. This is called lead time and must be considered when sending online payments.

You may prepare an online payment by:

- Writing a check in Write Checks.
- Paying a bill in Pay Bills.
- Or clicking Write Checks or Pay Bills in the Bank Feeds (Online Banking) Center.
- Prepare the check or bill using these methods the same way you always do, except that you designate the transaction as an online transaction and send the payment instructions to your financial institution.

For a check, record the check in QuickBooks, click **Online Payment**, and then select the date you want the check delivered.

When using Pay Bills to pay your bill, click the drop-down list arrow for **Method**, click **Online Bank Pmt**, and then select the date you want your payment delivered.

After the Check or the Bill Payment has been prepared, you send the payments from the Online Banking Center within QuickBooks and the payment will be made by the delivery date selected. You need to allow up to four business days for processing.

The Bank Feeds Preference was changed to Classic Mode in order to show the online payments recorded.

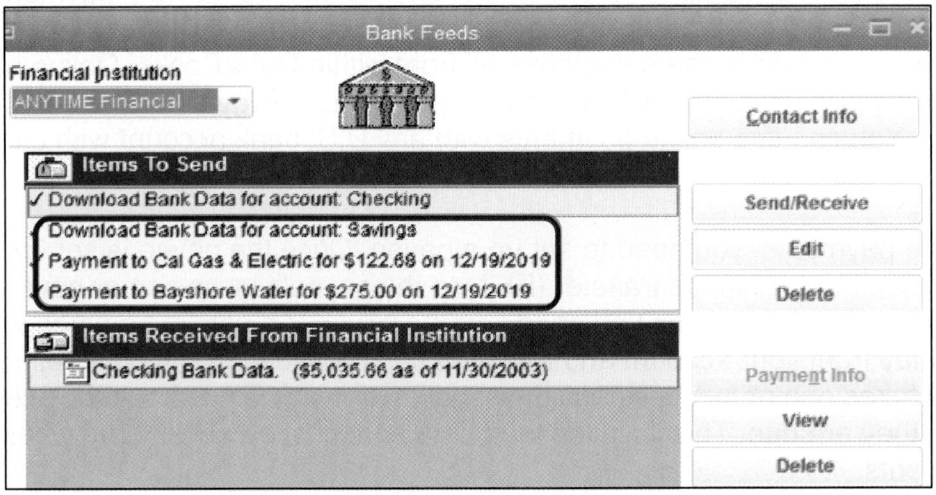

QUICKBOOKS PAYMENTS (MERCHANT SERVICES)

QuickBooks offers a variety of services to help with processing Customer Payments. With QuickBooks Payments (Merchant Service), you may accept online credit card payments, scan and/or accept telephone eChecks, swipe credit cards, and use Merchant Service Deposits to make bank deposits.

To accept online credit card payments from customers, a subscription to "Billing Solution for QuickBooks" and "QuickBooks Payments (Merchant Service)" are required. Then, invoices may be enabled for online payment by clicking the "Allow online payment" checkbox on the Create Invoices window. Customers may pay for invoices and statements online by entering their credit card information in the Customer Account Center, which is a secure Web site hosted by Intuit. Charges to your company for this service are processed through QuickBooks Merchant Service. Because we do not use actual companies within the text and are unable to sign up for a Merchant Services account, these features cannot be demonstrated.

ACH/eCheck payment options allow you to accept electronic checks by telephone or by scanning paper checks into QuickBooks. QuickBooks Payments (Merchant Service) was designed to support check scanning but also allows you to accept checks by telephone. Whether you scan checks or accept checks by phone, you are required to follow certain procedures. A phone check must have your customer's verbal authorization for processing the check and a scanned check must be stamped "for Deposit Only" and retained for 60 days before shredding.

To process customer credit card payments by swiping a credit card, you will need to purchase a card reader from Intuit. The card reader attaches to your computer so your transactions can be recorded in QuickBooks automatically. In addition, you may join the Intuit Payment Network and have customer payments processed and deposited directly into your bank account. Each of these options will incur charges from Intuit.

A faster way to match credit card deposits and fees to your bank statement is to use the Merchant Service Deposit feature. Clicking the Merchant Service Deposits icon enables you to access tabs for Deposits and Fees, Pending Payments, and Problems to be resolved.

DIRECT DEPOSIT

Rather than mail or give paychecks to your employees, you may sign up for Direct Deposit if you have a subscription to QuickBooks Payroll. You will go to the Employees menu and click My Payroll Service and Activate Direct Deposit. In order to activate direct deposit, you will need your federal employer identification number, the company's legal name and address, your financial institution routing and account numbers, and your QuickBooks registration number.

You also need to set up those employees who wish to receive their checks by direct deposit. To do this, access the Employee Center, double-click the employee you want to set up for direct deposit, click the Payroll Info tab in the Edit Employee window, click the Direct Deposit button and complete the required information.

INTUIT DATA PROTECT

In addition to having a backup stored in the office, having an offsite backup copy of your company data files is extremely important. This is necessary in case something happens to your computer or your office. For a fee, you may subscribe to Intuit Data Protect. Files are automatically backed up once a day on a predetermined schedule. Bank-level security encryptions and safeguards are used. During the Intuit Data Protect backup, your computer must be on and connected to the Internet. Since the backup runs in the background, you may continue to use QuickBooks while the backup is being made. In addition to data, everything you need to re-create your company file and QuickBooks environment is backed up. Each backup is stored for 45 days.

Index

B

C

F

G

H

I

J

K

L

M

N

O

P

Q

R

S

T

U

V

W

Y